ACRONYM	FULL NAME
GFA	General Fixed Assets
GFAAG	General Fixed Assets Account Group
GFOA	Government Finance Officers Association
GLTD	General Long-Term Debt
GLTDAG	General Long-Term Debt Account Group
GPFS	General Purpose Financial Statements
HFMA	Healthcare Financial Management Association
IIA	Institute of Internal Auditors
ISF	Internal Service Fund(s)
JAG	Joint Accounting Group (Colleges and Universities, NACUBO & NCHEMS)
JFMIP	Joint Financial Management Improvement Program
MFAP	Major Federal Assistance Program
MF/BA	Measurement Focus and Basis of Accounting
MFOA	Municipal Finance Officers Association (now GFOA)
NACUBO	National Association of College & University Business Officers
NCGA	National Council on Governmental Accounting (succeeded by GASB)
NCHEMS	National Center for Higher Education Management Systems
NETF	Nonexpendable Trust Fund(s)
NPO	Nonprofit Organization(s)
OMB	Office of Management and Budget (U.S.)
ONPO	Other Nonprofit Organization(s)
PERISA	Public Employee Retirement Income Security Act
PERS	Public Employee Retirement System
PG	Primary Government
PPB	Planning-Programming-Budgeting
PPBS	Planning-Programming-Budgeting System
PREF	Plant Replacement and Expansion Fund
PTF	Pension Trust Fund(s)
RAN	Revenue Anticipation Note
RET	Residual Equity Transfer
SA	Special Assessment
SAS	Statements on Auditing Standards (AICPA)
SEC	Securities and Exchange Commission (U.S.)
SGL	Standard General Ledger (Federal)
SLG	State and Local Government
SOP	Statement of Position (AICPA)
SRF	Special Revenue Fund(s)
T&A	Trust & Agency
TAN	Tax Anticipation Note
VHWO	Voluntary Health & Welfare Organization
ZBB	Zero Base Budget

PRENTICE HALL SERIES IN ACCOUNTING
CHARLES T. HORNGREN, CONSULTING EDITOR

AUDITING: AN INTEGRATED APPROACH, 5/E
Arens/Loebbecke

KOHLER'S DICTIONARY FOR ACCOUNTANTS, 6/E
Cooper/Ijiri

FINANCIAL STATEMENT ANALYSIS, 2/E
Foster

FINANCIAL ACCOUNTING: PRINCIPLES AND ISSUES, 4/E
Granof/Bell

FINANCIAL ACCOUNTING
Harrison/Horngren

COST ACCOUNTING: A MANAGERIAL EMPHASIS, 7/E
Horngren/Foster

ACCOUNTING, 2/E
Horngren/Harrison

INTRODUCTION TO FINANCIAL ACCOUNTING, 5/E
Horngren/Sundem/Elliott

INTRODUCTION TO MANAGEMENT ACCOUNTING, 9/E
Horngren/Sundem

ADVANCED MANAGEMENT ACCOUNTING, 2/E
Kaplan/Atkinson

GOVERNMENTAL AND NONPROFIT ACCOUNTING: THEORY & PRACTICE, 4/E
Freeman/Shoulders

INTRODUCTORY FINANCIAL ACCOUNTING, 3/E
Mueller/Kelly

AUDITING PRINCIPLES, 5/E
Stettler

BUDGETING, 5/E
Welsch/Hilton/Gordon

4th GOVERNMENTAL AND NONPROFIT ACCOUNTING Theory and Practice

EDITION

ROBERT J. FREEMAN
Texas Tech University

CRAIG D. SHOULDERS
*Virginia Polytechnic Institute
and State University*

PRENTICE HALL, Englewood Cliffs, New Jersey 07632

Library of Congress Cataloging-in-Publication Data

Freeman, Robert J.
    Governmental and nonprofit accounting : theory and practice / Robert
J. Freeman, Craig D. Shoulders. — 4th ed.
      p.   cm.
    Includes index.
    ISBN 0-13-362344-0
    1. Municipal finance—United States—Accounting. 2. Local
finance—United States—Accounting. 3. Finance, Public—United
States—Accounting. 4. Fund accounting—United States.
5. Nonprofit organizations—United States—Accounting.
    I. Shoulders, Craig D. II. Title.
HJ9777.A3L95 1993
657′.835′00973—dc20   92-39401
                                         CIP

Acquisitions editor: *Don Hull*
Editorial/production supervision
  and interior design: *Robert C. Walters*
Cover design: *Bruce Kenselaar*
Cover photos: (*top*) Colorado State Capital Building
            by *John Sohm/The Stock Market* © 1988
      (*bottom*) Michigan State University, Linton Hall
          by *Gordon R. Gainer/The Stock Market* © 1991
Prepress buyer: *Trudy Pisciotti*
Manufacturing buyer: *Patrice Fraccio*

 © 1993, 1988, 1983, 1974 by Prentice-Hall, Inc.
A Simon & Schuster Company
Englewood Cliffs, New Jersey 07632

Printed in the United States of America

10 9 8 7 6 5 4 3 2 1

ISBN 0-13-362344-0

Prentice-Hall International (UK) Limited, *London*
Prentice-Hall of Australia Pty. Limited, *Sydney*
Prentice-Hall Canada Inc., *Toronto*
Prentice-Hall Hispanoamericana, S.A. *Mexico*
Prentice-Hall of India Private Limited, *New Delhi*
Prentice-Hall of Japan, Inc., *Tokyo*
Simon & Schuster Asia Pte. Ltd., *Singapore*
Editora Prentice-Hall do Brasil, Ltda., *Rio de Janeiro*

**Dedicated in Loving Honor
of Our Wives**

Beverly Freeman and Nancy Shoulders

Who embody for us
the declaration of the Holy Scriptures
about a
Virtuous Wife

. . . For her worth is far above rubies.
The heart of her husband safely trusts her;
So he will have no lack of gain.
She does him good and not evil all the days of her life. . . .
Proverbs 31:10-31

BRIEF CONTENTS

CONTENTS

PREFACE

Governmental and nonprofit accounting, reporting, and auditing continue to evolve rapidly. Moreover, their concepts, standards, and practices probably will continue to evolve rapidly because of the increased attention being focused on them by Congress, practitioners, investors and creditors, standards setters, and academicians. One result of this increased attention is that it soon will be virtually impossible to pass the Uniform CPA Examination without an understanding of governmental and nonprofit accounting.

We have **updated** this edition of our text to incorporate the relevant portions of all authoritative pronouncements issued through early 1993—**including GASB Statements 11, 14, and 16** on measurement focus and basis of accounting for governmental fund operating statements, the financial reporting entity, and compensated absences. Too, other key GASB projects—including those on service efforts and accomplishments reporting and on the financial reporting model—are discussed. In addition, while retaining the successful approach, comprehensiveness, and other strengths of previous editions, we have enhanced the emphasis on the foundational aspects of governmental accounting and financial reporting—such as the nature and purposes of the various accounting entities—and have **incorporated a "new" approach for teaching** the state and local government accounting and reporting **model.** Even as we made these improvements, we **shortened** the **text significantly.**

"KEY" IMPROVEMENT

Students will be able to understand and apply the state and local government accounting and reporting model better and more quickly using our new approach to introducing them to the model in Chapter 2. We combine a strong emphasis on the underlying nature of the various fund types and account groups with transaction analysis, using the accounting equations of the various fund types and account groups to break students out of the "business accounting mindset," and help them understand how the "pieces" of the government model complement one another. Over the past five years, this approach has been tried and proven both in the college classroom and in continuing professional education courses. This pedagogy

enables students to grasp concepts and principles at this **early** stage that most would not understand until well into the course without it. Indeed, for many this approach provides the "key" to unlock the door to understanding state and local government accounting and financial reporting.

COVERAGE OF MFBA AND THE MFBA IMPLEMENTATION PROJECT

The coverage of the GASB's ongoing measurement focus and basis of accounting project has been updated from the last edition. **Chapter 10 explains** and illustrates the **key requirements of GASB Statement 11,** "Measurement Focus and Basis of Accounting—Governmental Fund Operating Statements." We cover this important statement at this point in the text, rather than earlier, for several reasons:

1. *Application* of Statement 11 is *prohibited until* its *effective date*—which the GASB has recently moved to delay. The originally scheduled effective date for Statement 11 was for fiscal years ending after June 15, 1995. In December 1992 the **GASB** issued an exposure draft of a **Statement** that, if adopted, **would delay the effective date of Statement 11 indefinitely.**

2. Thus, the currently effective measurement focus and basis of accounting must be emphasized at this time. It would be *detrimental to the learning process to* attempt to *teach both* of these different *measurement focuses at the same time.* Students trying to understand this unique accounting and reporting model can reasonably be expected to be confused if the Statement 11 measurement focus is taught before they have a reasonable mastery of the basic model currently required to be used.

3. Too, it is *conceivable that* GASB conclusions on the reporting project and on related issues will necessitate *some Statement 11 provisions* being modified and therefore *never* being *applicable in practice.*

To **further** enhance student understanding of the implications and importance of GASB Statement 11, **Chapter 15 includes** a discussion of **the two primary approaches** being considered **for implementing Statement 11.** The fundamental differences between these two approaches are explained in understandable terms, as are the primary advantages and disadvantages of each implementation method. Together, the first parts of Chapters 10 and 15 provide the only up-to-date, manageable, and comprehensive coverage of this important topic available for the college classroom.

OTHER CHANGES

Several other aspects of this revision are noteworthy as well. Among these are:

- **Chapters 5, 7, 8, and 9** incorporate the appropriate general government, special assessment accounting guidance—**eliminating** the need for a separate **Special Assessments chapter.**
- **Chapters 12 and 13, Internal Service Funds and Enterprise Funds,** include a clear and thorough discussion of the **unique cash flow reporting requirements** established in GASB Statement 9, "Reporting Cash Flows of Proprietary and Nonexpendable Trust Funds and Governmental Entities That Use Proprietary Fund Accounting."

- **Chapter 14, Financial Reporting, incorporates** the requirements of **GASB Statement 14, "The Financial Reporting Entity,"** and illustrates financial reporting for entities with "simple entity structures" as well as for those with "complex entity structures."

- **Chapter 15, "Contemporary Issues"** provides a basis for discussing GASB's key agenda projects and other unresolved state and local government accounting and reporting issues. In addition to the **MFBA implementation project,** this chapter covers the GASB project on **service efforts and accomplishments reporting.**

- **Chapter 16, "Federal Government Accounting,"** has been updated for recent changes in federal financial management and in accounting and reporting for federal agencies. Bruce K. Michelson of the U.S. General Accounting Office provided invaluable assistance in determining the appropriate depth of coverage for this important chapter and in updating for changes since the last addition. J. Thomas Luter of the U.S. Department of the Treasury also was extremely helpful.

- **Chapter 17, "Accounting for Health Care Organizations,"** incorporates the requirements of the new health care audit guide of the AICPA and illustrates some of the reporting differences between government and nongovernment health care organizations.

- **Chapter 19, "Accounting for Voluntary Health and Welfare and Other Nonprofit Organizations,"** has been reordered, condensed, and better illustrated. VHWOs and ONPOs are discussed in distinct sections of the chapter, eliminating the simultaneous discussion approach of the last edition.

- **Chapter 20, "Auditing,"** is **updated for** the single audit requirements for nonprofit entities **(OMB Circular A-133) and** for **Statement on Auditing Standards 68** on compliance auditing. Key concepts and requirements are better illustrated than in the previous edition.

DOING MORE WITH LESS

In this age that emphasizes increasing efficiency, we are pleased to have both updated and significantly improved the text—and to have added even more illustrations, "live" financial statement examples, and problem materials—while **shortening** this edition **by more than 100 pages** compared to the prior edition. We were extremely careful, of course, not to eliminate any material essential to understanding the uniquenesses of governmental and nonprofit accounting and reporting.

ACKNOWLEDGMENTS

We appreciate the many excellent suggestions made by these persons who reviewed the 1988 edition in preparation for this edition:

L. Charles Bokemeier, University of Michigan-Flint
Marilynn Collins, John Carroll University
Michele D. Cox, Lincoln Memorial University
Carol A. Hilton, Ohio University
Joan Pritchard, University of Central Arkansas
Robert B. Yahr, Marquette University

Likewise, we appreciate the detailed reviews of the drafts of several specific chapters and related assistance by:

David R. Bean, Director of Research, Governmental Accounting Standards Board

Amber G. Best, Frederick B. Hill and Co.

Robert Bramlett, Federal Accounting Standards Advisory Board

Patrick S. Callahan, Frederick B. Hill and Co.

Stanley Y. Chang, Arizona State University-West

Herbert K. Folpe, KPMG Peat Marwick

Norwood J. Jackson, Jr., U.S. Office of Management and Budget

Robin E. Jenkins, National Association of College and University Business Officers

Randall L. Kinnersley, Texas Tech University

Ronald R. Kovener, Healthcare Financial Management Association

Ray L. Krause, McGladrey Hendrickson & Pullen

James A. Lampe, Texas Tech University

J. Thomas Luter, U.S. Department of the Treasury

Brian W. Marshall, Ernst & Young

T. Douglas McQuade, KPMG Peat Marwick

Bruce K. Michelson, U.S. General Accounting Office

G. Robert Smith, Jr., Texas Tech University

John E. Svoboda, Caldwell County (KY) Hospital

Penelope S. Wardlow, Governmental Accounting Standards Board

J. Michael Williams, Carilion Health System

Robert Smith, Jr. and Randy Kinnersley assisted us throughout the revision process and also searched hundreds of comprehensive annual financial reports to identify government financial statement examples for the text.

Finally, we can never adequately express our appreciation to our wives, Beverly Freeman and Nancy Shoulders, for the essential roles they play in all that we do—including the revision of this text. They encouraged, supported, and advised us as we labored over this revision and took care of many responsibilities that were rightfully ours in order to enable us to have the time and the energy to complete this task. Clearly, they multiply what we are able to accomplish by their help and support. Indeed, Beverly and Nancy are full partners in all that we do.

Robert J. Freeman
Craig D. Shoulders

GOVERNMENTAL AND NONPROFIT ACCOUNTING: Environment and Characteristics

Financial reporting for governments and for nonprofit organizations involves concepts, standards, and procedures designed to accommodate the uniquenesses of the environment in which they operate and the unique needs of the financial report users. This book deals with financial accounting and reporting concepts, standards, and procedures applicable to (1) state and local governments—including counties, cities, and school districts, as well as townships, villages, other special districts, and public authorities; (2) the federal government; and (3) nonprofit and governmental universities, hospitals, voluntary health and welfare organizations, and other nonprofit (or not-for-profit) organizations. Financial management and accountability considerations peculiar to government and nonprofit (G&NP) organizations are emphasized throughout the book, and the distinctive aspects of auditing G&NP organizations are discussed in the last chapter.

CHARACTERISTICS AND TYPES OF G&NP ORGANIZATIONS

Governments and other nonprofit organizations are unique in that:

- The profit motive is not inherent in their inception or operation.
- They are usually owned collectively by their constituents: ownership is not normally evidenced by individually owned equity shares which may be sold or exchanged.
- Those contributing financial resources to the organization do not necessarily receive a direct or proportionate share of its goods or services; for example, the welfare recipient most likely did not pay the taxes from which his or her benefits are paid.
- Their major policy decisions, and perhaps some operating decisions, typically are made by consensus vote of an elected or appointed governing body—for example, a state legislature, a city council, or a hospital board of directors—whose members serve part time and have diverse backgrounds, philosophies, capabilities, and interests.

A G&NP organization exists because a community or society decides to provide certain goods or services to its group as a whole. *Often the goods or services are provided regardless of whether costs incurred will be recovered through charges for the goods or services or whether those paying for the goods or services are those benefiting from them.* Most G&NP goods or services are not commercially feasible to produce through private enterprise. Too, these goods or services frequently are deemed so vital to the public well-being that it is felt that their provision should be supervised by elected or appointed representatives of the populace.

The major types of government and nonprofit organizations may be classified as follows:

1. *Governmental:* federal, state, county, municipal, township, village, and other local governmental authorities, including special districts
2. *Educational:* kindergartens, elementary and secondary schools, vocational and technical schools, and colleges and universities
3. *Health and welfare:* hospitals, nursing homes, child protection agencies, the American Red Cross, and the USO, for example
4. *Religious:* YMCA, Salvation Army, and other church-related organizations
5. *Charitable:* United Way, Community Chest, and similar fund-raising agencies, related charitable agencies, and other charitable organizations
6. *Foundations:* private trusts and corporations organized for educational, religious, or charitable purposes

This list is a general classification scheme, and much overlap occurs. Many charitable organizations are church-related, for example, and governments are deeply involved in education, health, and welfare activities.

Growth and Importance of the G&NP Sector

Governments and other nonprofit organizations have experienced dramatic growth in recent years and have emerged—individually and collectively—as major economic, political, and social forces in our society. Indeed, the G&NP sector now accounts for more than *one-third* of all expenditures within the U.S. economy and includes many "growth industries." The total value of resources devoted to this sector is gigantic, both absolutely and relatively.

Governments have experienced particularly dynamic growth both in the scope and in the magnitude of their activities. More than 18 million people work in government positions—about 20% of the employed civilian labor force—and total and per capita expenditures and debt of governments have increased dramatically in recent years. Indeed, if the *Fortune* 500 ranking of the largest business organizations (by sales) included the state governments (by general revenues), it would be the *Fortune* 550. That is, as shown in Figure 1–1, all 50 states would qualify in the top 343, 26 states would be in the top 100, and 2 states would be in the top 10.

Sound financial management—including thoughtful budgeting, appropriate accounting, meaningful financial reporting, and timely audits by qualified auditors—**is at least as important in the G&NP sector as in the private business sector.** Furthermore, because of the scope and diversity of its activities, proper management of the financial affairs of a city or town, for example, may be far more complex than that of a private business with comparable assets or annual expenditures.

Figure 1–1

THE *FORTUNE* 500 + THE 50 STATES (THE *FORTUNE* 550?)

Combined Rank	Industrial Corporation or State	Sales or General Revenues (in millions)
1	General Motors	$126,017
2	Exxon	105,885
3	Ford Motor Company	98,275
4	**CALIFORNIA**	**69,251**
5	IBM	69,018
6	Mobil	58,770
7	General Electric	58,414
8	**NEW YORK**	**52,441**
9	Philip Morris	44,323
10	Texaco	41,235

In addition, 26 states are in the Combined Top 100 and all 50 states are in the Combined Top 343.
The smallest state, South Dakota (#343), has $1.3 billion in general revenues.

Source: Robert D. Behn, *The Fortune 500 and the 50 States: A Combined Ranking* (Durham, NC: The Governors Center, Duke University), February 1992. The data were adapted from the *Fortune* 500 data for 1990 released in April 1991 and Census Bureau data for 1990 released in August 1991.

The increased size and complexity of governments and nonprofit organizations have increased the number of career employment opportunities in this sector for college graduates majoring in accounting (and other disciplines) in recent years. Moreover, it has led to a significantly increased (and increasing) number of government and nonprofit organization auditing and consulting engagements with independent public accounting firms. Accordingly, approximately 10% of the theory and practice sections of the Uniform CPA examination is on governmental and nonprofit organization accounting concepts, principles, and procedures. Further, G&NP topics soon will be a larger and even more important part of the CPA exam.

The G&NP Environment

G&NP organizations are ***similar*** in many ways to profit-seeking enterprises. For example:

1. They are integral parts of the same economic system and use similar resources in accomplishing their purposes.
2. Both must acquire and convert scarce resources into their respective goods or services.
3. Financial management processes are essentially similar in both. And both must have viable information systems—of which the accounting system is an integral component—in order for managers, governing bodies, and others to receive relevant and timely data for planning, directing, controlling, and evaluating the use of the scarce resources.
4. Inasmuch as their resources are relatively scarce, cost analysis and other control and evaluation techniques are essential to ensure that resources are utilized economically, effectively, and efficiently.
5. In some cases, both produce similar products; for example, both governments and private enterprises may own and operate transportation systems, sanitation services, and electric or gas utilities.

There are also significant ***differences*** between profit-seeking and G&NP organizations. Although broad generalizations about such a diversified group as

G&NP organizations are difficult, the major differences arise from differing (1) organizational objectives, (2) sources of financial resources, and (3) regulation and control.

Organizational Objectives

Expectation of income or gain is the principal factor motivating investors to provide resources to profit-seeking enterprises. On the other hand, G&NP organizations provide certain goods or services to a community or society as a whole, often without reference to whether costs incurred are recouped through charges levied on those receiving them and without regard to whether those receiving the goods or services are those paying for them. There is no profit motive; there are no individual shareholders to whom dividends are paid; and the success or failure of G&NP organizations usually cannot be evaluated in terms of net income or earnings per share.

The objective of most government and nonprofit organizations is to provide as many goods or as much service each year as their financial and other resources permit. G&NP organizations typically operate on a year-to-year basis, raising as much financial resources as possible and expending them in serving their constituency. They may seek to increase the amount of resources made available to them each year—and most do—but this is to enable the organization to provide more or better goods and services—not to increase its wealth. In sum, private businesses seek to increase their wealth for the benefit of their owners; G&NP organizations seek to expend their available financial resources for the benefit of their constituency. *Financial management in the G&NP environment thus typically focuses on acquiring and using financial resources—upon sources and uses of working capital, budget status, and cash flow—rather than on net income or earnings per share.*

Sources of Financial Resources

The sources of financial resources differ between business and G&NP organizations, as well as among G&NP organizations. And, **in the absence of a net income determination emphasis, no distinction is generally made between invested capital and revenue of G&NP organizations. A dollar is a financial resource whether acquired through donations, user charges, sales of assets, loans, or in some other manner.**

The typical nondebt sources of financial resources for business enterprises are investments by owners and sales of goods or services to customers. These sources of financing usually are not the primary sources of G&NP organization financial resources.

Governments have the unique power to force involuntary financial resource contributions through **taxation**—of property, sales, and income—and all levels rely heavily on this power. **Grants and shared revenues** from other governments also are important state and local government revenue sources, as are charges levied for goods or services provided, such as those of utilities.

Other nonprofit and governmental organizations also derive financial resources from a variety of sources. Religious groups and charitable organizations usually rely heavily on **donations,** although they may have other revenue sources. Some colleges and universities rely heavily on donations and **income from trust funds;** others depend primarily on **state appropriations** and/or tuition charges for support. Finally, hospitals generally charge their clientele, although few admit their patients solely on the basis of ability to pay. Indeed, many G&NP hospitals serve numerous charity patients and/or have large amounts of uncollectible accounts; and some rely heavily on gifts and bequests.

There are other, more subtle, differences in sources of G&NP organization financial resources as compared with profit-seeking businesses. For example:

- **Many services or goods** provided by these organizations are **monopolistic** in nature, and there is **no open market** in which their value may be objectively appraised or evaluated.
- **User charges,** where levied, usually are based on the **cost** of the goods or services rendered **rather than** on **supply and demand-related** pricing policies common to private enterprise.
- **Charges levied** for goods or services **often cover only part of the costs incurred** to provide them; for example, tuition generally covers only a fraction of the cost of operating state colleges or universities, and token charges (or no charges) may be made to a hospital's indigent patients.

Regulation and Control

The goods or services offered the consuming public by unregulated profit-seeking enterprises will be modified or withdrawn if they are not profitable. The direct relationship between the financial resources each consumer provides profit-seeking enterprises and the goods or services that consumer receives from each enterprise essentially dictates the type and quality of goods and services each profit-seeking enterprise will provide. Firms with inept or unresponsive management will be unprofitable and ultimately will be forced out of business. Therefore, the profit motive and profit measurement constitute an *automatic allocation and regulating device* in the free enterprise segment of our economy.

This profit test/regulator device is *not* present in the usual G&NP situation, and most G&NP organizations must strive to attain their objectives without its benefits. In addition, as noted earlier, many G&NP organizations provide goods or services having no open market value measurement by which to test consumer satisfaction. This problem exists because the goods and services (1) are unique or (2) are provided to some or all consumers without charge, or at a token charge. Thus, these consumers have no "dollar vote" to cast.

Evaluating the performance and "operating results" of most G&NP organizations is extremely difficult for several reasons.

1. There is no open market supply and demand test of the value of the goods and services they provide.
2. The relationship, if any, between the resource contributors and the recipients of the goods and services is remote and indirect.
3. Such organizations are not profit-oriented in the usual sense and are not expected to operate profitability.
4. *The profit test is thus neither a valid performance indicator nor an automatic regulating device.*
5. Governments can force resource contributions through taxation.

Accordingly, *other "operating results" measures and controls must be employed* to ensure that G&NP organization resources are used appropriately and to prevent uneconomical or ineffective G&NP organizations from continuing to operate in that manner indefinitely. **Governmental and nonprofit organizations, particularly governments, are therefore subject to more stringent legal, regulatory, and other controls than are private businesses.**

All facets of a G&NP organization's operations **may be affected by legal or quasi-legal requirements** (1) **imposed externally,** such as by federal or state statute, grant regulations, or judicial decrees, or (2) **imposed internally** by charter, bylaw, ordinance, trust agreement, donor stipulation, or contract. Further-more, *the need to ensure compliance with such extensive legal and contractual requirements often results in more stringent operational and administrative controls than in private enterprise.* Aspects of G&NP organization operations that may be regulated or otherwise controlled include:

1. *Organization structure:* form; composition of its governing board or similar body; the number and duties of its personnel; lines of authority and responsibility; which officials or employees are to be elected, appointed, or hired from among applicants.

2. *Personnel policies and procedures:* who will appoint or hire personnel; tenure of personnel; policies and procedures upon termination; extent of minority group representation on the staff; compensation levels; promotion policies; and permissible types and amounts of compensation increments.

3. *Sources of financial resources:* the types and maximum amounts of taxes, licenses, fines, or fees a government may levy; the procedure for setting user charges; tuition rates; debt limits; the purposes for which debt may be incurred; the allowable methods for soliciting charitable contributions.

4. *Use of financial resources:* the purpose for which resources may be used, including earmarking of certain resources for use only for specific purposes; purchasing procedures to be followed; budgeting methods, forms, or procedures to be used.

5. *Accounting:* any or all phases of the accounting system; for example, chart of accounts, bases of accounting, forms, procedures.

6. *Financial Reporting:* type and frequency of financial reports; report format and content; report recipients.

7. *Auditing:* frequency of audit; who is to perform the audit; the scope and type of audit; the time and place for filing the audit report; who is to receive or have access to the audit report; the wording of the auditor's report.

Thus, managers of G&NP organizations may have limited discretion compared with managers of business enterprises. **The role and emphasis of G&NP financial accounting and reporting are correspondingly altered, therefore, as compared with the profit-seeking enterprise environment.**

OBJECTIVES OF G&NP ACCOUNTING AND FINANCIAL REPORTING

A major committee of the American Accounting Association stated that the objectives of *accounting* for any type of organization are to provide information for:

1. Making decisions concerning the use of limited resources, including the identification of crucial decision areas and determination of objectives and goals.
2. Effectively directing and controlling an organization's human and material resources.
3. Maintaining and reporting on the custodianship of resources.
4. Contributing to the effectiveness of all organizations, whether profit-oriented or not, in fulfilling the desires and demands of all society for social control of their functions.[1]

---

[1] American Accounting Association, Committee to Prepare a Statement of Basic Accounting Theory, *A Statement of Basic Accounting Theory* (Evanston, Ill.: AAA, 1966), p. 4.

Financial Accounting Standards Board (FASB) *Statement of Financial Accounting Concepts No. 4* (SFAC 4), "Objectives of Financial Reporting by Nonbusiness Organizations," addresses the objectives of general purpose **external** financial **reporting** by nonbusiness (nonprofit) organizations. SFAC 4 notes that:

- The objectives stem primarily from the needs of external users who generally cannot prescribe the information they want from an organization.
- In addition to information provided by general purpose external financial reporting, managers and, to some extent, governing bodies need a great deal of internal accounting information to carry out their responsibilities in planning and controlling activities. That information and information directed at meeting the specialized needs of users having the power to obtain the information they need are beyond the scope of this Statement.[2]

The financial reporting objectives set forth in SFAC 4 state that **financial reporting** by **nonbusiness** organizations **should provide information** that is **useful** to present and potential resource providers and other users **in:**

- Making rational decisions about the allocation of resources to those organizations.
- Assessing the services that a nonbusiness organization provides and its ability to continue to provide those services.
- Assessing how managers of a nonbusiness organization have discharged their stewardship responsibilities and other aspects of their performance.

Accordingly, nonbusiness organization **financial reporting should provide information about:**

- The economic resources, obligations, and net resources of an organization and the effects of transactions, events, and circumstances that change resources and interests in those resources.
- The performance of an organization during a period. Periodic measurement of the changes in the amount and nature of the net resources of a nonbusiness organization and information about its service efforts and accomplishments provide the information most useful in assessing its performance.
- How an organization obtains and spends cash or other liquid resources, its borrowing and repayment of debt, and other factors that may affect an organization's liquidity.

In addition, nonbusiness organization **financial reporting should include explanations and interpretations** to help users understand financial information provided.[3]

CHARACTERISTICS AND G&NP ACCOUNTING AND FINANCIAL REPORTING

Some G&NP organization activities (such as utilities and public transportation), parallel those of some profit-seeking enterprises. **In such cases the accounting typically parallels that of their privately owned counterparts.** In most of their operations, however, governments and nonprofit organizations are **not** concerned with profit measurement. (Even those G&NP entities that account for revenues, expenses, and net income may not seek to maximize profits, but only to ensure continuity and/or improvement of service.)

---

[2] Financial Accounting Standards Board, *Statement of Financial Accounting Concepts No. 4,* "Objectives of Financial Reporting by Nonbusiness Organizations" (Stamford, Conn.: FASB, December 1980), p. xii.
[3] Ibid., pp. xiii–xiv.

Accounting is a service function and must meet the information demands in a given environment. In the **G&NP environment,** decisions concerning financial resource acquisition and allocation, managerial direction and control of financial resource utilization, and custodianship of financial and other resources have traditionally been framed in terms of *social and political objectives and constraints rather than profitability.* Legal and administrative constraints have been used as society's methods of directing its G&NP institutions in achieving those objectives. Thus, **G&NP organization accounting and reporting usually emphasize control of and accountability for expendable financial resources.** The two most important types of legal and administrative control provisions affecting accounting in this environment are (1) the use of *funds* and (2) the distinctive role of the *budget.*

Funds and Fund Accounting

Recall that the financial resources provided to a G&NP organization may be *restricted;* that is, their **use** may be **limited to specified purposes or activities.** For example, a church may receive donations for a building addition; a hospital may receive a grant for adding an intensive care facility; a city may borrow money to construct a sewage treatment plant; a university may receive a federal grant for research purposes. Such *external* restrictions carry significant *accountability* obligations. Management also may *"designate"* specific purposes for which certain resources must be used. For example, management may wish to accumulate resources for equipment replacement or facility enlargement. Since management designations are *internal* restrictions and may be changed by management, they carry **only internal accountability** requirements. In any event, using the resources in accordance with stipulations inherent in their receipt and reporting on this compliance to others are essential custodianship obligations.

G&NP organizations establish **funds** in order **to control restricted and designated resources and to both ensure and demonstrate compliance with legal and administrative requirements.** "Funds" are separate fiscal and accounting entities, and include both cash and noncash resources—segregated according to the purpose(s) or activities for which they are to be used—as well as related liabilities. A **fund** is:

> a fiscal and accounting entity with a self-balancing set of accounts recording cash and other financial resources, together with all related liabilities, and residual equities or balances, and changes therein, which are segregated for the purpose of carrying on specific activities or attaining certain objectives in accordance with special regulations, restrictions, or limitations.[4]

Two basic types of fund accounting entities are used by most G&NP organizations:

1. *Expendable (governmental) funds:* to account for the current assets, related liabilities, changes in net assets, and balances that may be expended in its "nonbusiness-type" activities (e.g., for fire and police protection).
2. *Nonexpendable (proprietary) funds:* to account for the revenues, expenses, assets, liabilities, and equity of its "business-type" activities (e.g. utilities, cafeterias, or transportation systems) and some trust funds.

---

[4] Governmental Accounting Standards Board, *Codification of Governmental Accounting and Financial Reporting Standards* (Stamford, Conn.: GASB, 1992), sec. 1100.102 and 1300.

The fund concept involves an **accounting segregation,** not necessarily the physical separation of resources; however, resources are often also physically segregated—for example, through use of separate checking accounts for cash resources of various funds.

Use of the term "fund" in G&NP situations should be sharply distinguished from its use in private enterprise. A fund of a commercial enterprise is simply a portion of its assets that has been restricted to specific uses, not a separate and distinct accounting entity. Revenues and expenses related to such funds are part of enterprise operations; that is, fund revenue and expense accounts appear side by side in the general ledger with other enterprise revenue and expense accounts. On the other hand, *a fund in the G&NP accounting sense is a self-contained accounting entity with its own asset, liability, revenue, expenditure or expense, and fund balance or other equity accounts*—and with its own ledger(s) (see Figure 1-2). Indeed, *a complete set of financial statements* may be prepared for *each fund* of a G&NP organization *as well as for the organization as a whole.*

Although experts agree that the fund device is essential to sound financial management of most G&NP organizations, its use has an unfortunate *fragmenting* effect on their accounting and reporting. The statements of a profit-seeking enterprise present in one place the information regarding the enterprise. It is possible, by looking at its balance sheet, to determine the nature and valuation of its assets, liabilities, and owners' equity. The nature and amounts of the components of change in owners' equity occasioned by enterprise operations are presented in its periodic operating statements.

Most G&NP organization financial reports, however, consist of a *series* of independent or combined (columnar) fund entity balance sheets and operating statements. Consolidated statements are **not** in widespread use in G&NP financial reporting.

Figure 1-2 **SINGLE ACCOUNTING ENTITY VS. MULTIPLE ACCOUNTING ENTITIES**

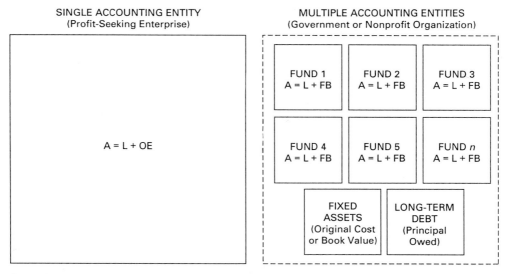

Legend:

A = Assets
L = Liabilities
OE = Owner's Equity (of the enterprise)
FB = Fund Balance (of the individual fund)
‒‒‒ = The government or nonprofit organization as a whole

Budgets and Appropriations

The creation of an *expendable (governmental) fund* ordinarily does *not* carry with it the authority to expend its resources. In most G&NP organizations, especially governments, expenditures may be made only within the authority of *appropriations*—which are *authorizations to make expenditures for specified purposes*—or similar authorizations by the governing body.

A *fixed-dollar budget* is commonly prepared for *each expendable fund.* That is, the organization's chief executive (or perhaps each department head) asks the governing body for permission to incur a set ("fixed") amount of expenditures—for salaries, equipment, supplies, and so on—during the budget period to carry out the department's mission. This budget is the vehicle normally used to make and communicate resource allocation decisions establishing the types and quantities of goods and services to be provided during the budget period.

When approved by the governing body, the budgetary expenditure estimates become binding *appropriations—that both authorize expenditures for various specified purposes and limit the amounts that can be expended for each specified purpose.* Appropriations must indicate the *fund* from which the expenditure may be made and specify the *purposes,* the *maximum amount,* and the *period* of time for which the expenditure authority is granted. A *department or activity* may be financed from *several* funds. In such cases at least one appropriation must be made from each supporting fund in order to provide the requisite expenditure authority.

In order to control and demonstrate budgetary compliance, it is common—for governments, in particular—to establish **budgetary accounts** within *expendable* fund ledgers. This technique (explained later) permits managers to determine their remaining expenditure authority at any time during the period. Integrating budgetary accounts into the accounting system is particularly important where budget "overruns" subject officials to fine, dismissal, or other disciplinary action.

Nonexpendable (proprietary) funds, on the other hand, may be controlled by **flexible budgets**—such as those used in businesses—rather than by fixed-dollar budgets. Budgetary accounts are *not* used in these instances. But budgetary accounts *are* used by most G&NP organizations that control their nonexpendable funds by *fixed-dollar* budgets.

Fixed-dollar budgeting of expendable and/or nonexpendable funds often gives rise to a unique *"dual basis" of accounting and reporting* for G&NP organizations. This is because (1) **generally accepted accounting principles (GAAP)** prescribe *specific standards* for the measurement of revenues, expenditures, expenses, and other amounts reported in financial statements that "present fairly in conformity with GAAP"; yet (2) **for budgetary purposes,** G&NP governing boards may estimate revenues and authorize expenditures on a *variety of non-GAAP bases*—on the cash receipts and disbursements basis, for example.

Where the budgetary basis differs from the GAAP basis:

1. *The accounts are maintained on the budgetary basis during the year* to effect budgetary control through the accounts, so that interim and annual budgetary statements may be prepared on the budgetary basis;

2. *Adjustments are made at year end*—to convert the budgetary basis data in the accounts to the GAAP basis—so that GAAP basis annual statements may be prepared; and

3. *The differences* between the budgetary basis and the GAAP basis statements *are explained and reconciled* in the annual financial report of the government or nonprofit organization.

Budgetary accounting and reporting are distinctive characteristics of G&NP organizations, particularly governments, and are discussed and illustrated at numerous points throughout this text.

Some Other Distinguishing Characteristics

The emphasis on fund and budgetary controls causes the accounting for most G&NP organizations to resemble *working capital change analysis*—or even cash flow analysis—rather than commercial accounting, in which net income determination is a paramount consideration. **The focal point of most G&NP accounting and reporting is expendable financial resources, accounted for in expendable fund entities and allocated by the budget and appropriation process.**

The **"cost"** measurement focus of *nonexpendable (proprietary)* fund accounting of G&NP organizations, like that of business accounting, is **"expenses"** —the cost of *assets consumed* during the period. In contrast, the "cost" measurement focus of *expendable (governmental)* fund accounting is **"expenditures"**—the amount of *financial resources expended* during the period for:

- *current operations* (e.g., salaries, utilities),
- *capital outlay* (acquiring fixed assets), and
- *long-term debt principal retirement and interest.*

More specifically, *expenditures* has been defined as "the cost of goods delivered or services rendered, whether paid or unpaid, including current operating costs, provision for debt retirement not reported as a liability of the fund from which retired, and capital outlays."[5] Thus, the term **"expenditures"—the term that is significant in expendable fund accounting—should not be confused with "expenses"** as defined for accounting for profit-seeking enterprises.

Fixed assets normally are not appropriable financial resources and are commonly listed and accounted for separately from the expendable fund accounting entities. Similarly, **unmatured long-term debt** that is not a liability of a particular fund (but of the government as a whole) may be listed in a separate nonfund accounting entity. Accordingly, *the cost of acquiring a fixed asset is considered an "expenditure" (use of financial resources) in the period in which it occurs, as is the retirement of maturing long-term debt, since both reduce the net financial assets of an expendable fund.* Furthermore, since net income determination is not a consideration in most G&NP organizations, in *expendable funds* (1) *inventory* valuation may receive only passing attention, and (2) *depreciation* of fixed assets usually is not accounted for because it does not require the use of appropriable financial resources (expenditure) during the current period.

Summary Comparison with Commercial Accounting

Though commercial-type accounting is employed where G&NP organizations are engaged in commercial-type activities (e.g., electric utilities), accounting and reporting for other G&NP endeavors have evolved largely in view of these key differences from profit-seeking enterprises:

1. **Objectives:** acquiring resources and expending them in a legal and appropriate manner, as opposed to seeking to increase, or even maintain, capital.
2. **Control:** substitution of statutory, fund, and budgetary controls in the absence

---

[5] Adapted from National Committee on Governmental Accounting, *Governmental Accounting, Auditing, and Financial Reporting* (Chicago: Municipal Finance Officers Association of the United States and Canada, 1968), p. 160.

of the supply and demand and profit regulator/control devices inherent in profit-seeking endeavors.

These factors—**objectives and control**—underlie the major differences between commercial and G&NP accounting. The primary consideration in the G&NP environment is on **compliance and accountability**—and *G&NP accounting, reporting, and auditing have developed principally as tools of compliance control and demonstration.*

The student should constantly note the similarities and differences between commercial and G&NP accounting in concept, approach, and terminology. Be particularly observant in those cases where the same concepts and terms are used in both, but with different connotations. In G&NP accounting, for example:

1. The *accounting entity* concept relates to the separate fund or fund-type entities, not the organization as a whole; generally, there is no unified *accounting entity* for the organization in its entirety, which is referred to as the *"reporting entity."*

2. The *periodicity* concept relates to the flow of financial resources during the year or other period and to budgetary comparisons, rather than to income determination, in *expendable funds;* it relates to income determination only in *nonexpendable funds.*

3. The *matching* concept as understood in commercial accounting is used similarly for *commercial-type activities* of G&NP organizations that are accounted for in *nonexpendable* funds. *In all other cases* reference is to matching revenues and *expenditures*—current operating, capital outlay, and debt retirement—and to matching *estimated (budgeted) and actual* revenues and expenditures. *Expendable fund accounting emphasizes the inflows, outflows, and balances of expendable financial resources rather than the determination of revenue, expense, and net income.*

4. The *going-concern* concept usually is considered relevant only when commercial-type or self-supporting activities are involved in G&NP organizations. *Expendable financial resource funds exist on a year-by-year or project-by-project basis and may be intentionally exhausted and "go out of business."*

AUTHORITATIVE SOURCES OF G&NP ACCOUNTING PRINCIPLES AND REPORTING STANDARDS

Governmental and nonprofit accounting and reporting principles and standards have evolved *separately* from those for business enterprises. Furthermore, unique principles and standards have evolved separately for *each* of the several major types of G&NP organizations.

The National Council on Governmental Accounting and several similar predecessor committees led the formulation of accounting principles and standards for state and local governments until the Governmental Accounting Standards Board was created in 1984. The American Hospital Association and the Healthcare Financial Management Association have fostered the development of accounting principles and standards for hospitals and other health care institutions; and the American Council on Education and the National Association of College and University Business Officials have led the development of those for colleges and universities. Similarly, committees of the American Institute of Certified Public Accountants (AICPA) set forth accounting principles and standards for nonprofit organizations in AICPA audit and accounting guides; and the Comptroller General of the United States led the federal government accounting standards effort until the Federal Accounting Standards Advisory Board (FASAB) was established in 1990. In addition, each field has its own journals, newsletters, and professional societies.

Evolution of Separate Principles

The separation of business and G&NP accounting principles was formalized in the 1930s when the first accounting standards-setting bodies were established in the United States. The Securities Acts of 1933 and 1934 created the Securities and Exchange Commission (SEC), charged it with overseeing the financial reporting of business enterprises under its jurisdiction, and empowered the SEC to establish accounting and reporting standards for those business enterprises. The American Institute of Accountants (now the American Institute of Certified Public Accountants) then established a senior Committee on Accounting Procedure (CAP), the predecessor to the AICPA's Accounting Principles Board and the Financial Accounting Standards Board. The CAP made recommendations on business accounting and reporting issues, particularly those of concern to the SEC. Indeed, the SEC relied heavily on the CAP in determining what constituted generally accepted accounting principles (GAAP) for business enterprises. In view of its focus on business enterprise financial accounting and reporting, CAP pronouncements were accompanied by the following statement:

> The committee has not directed its attention to accounting problems or procedures of religious, charitable, scientific, educational, and similar non-profit institutions, municipalities, professional firms, and the like. Accordingly . . . its opinions and recommendations are directed primarily to business enterprises organized for profit.[6]

Although the Institute directed the CAP to concentrate on business accounting and reporting, AICPA leaders also recognized the need for nonbusiness accounting and reporting principles to be codified and further developed. Accordingly, the AICPA encouraged the appropriate college and university, hospital, and municipal professional organizations to sponsor committees similar to the CAP to focus on accounting and reporting concerns of those types of G&NP organizations. Thus, several separate G&NP accounting standards-setting bodies were established, each charged with responsibility for a specific subset of the G&NP sector. These committees and their successors have provided leadership in the development of G&NP accounting and reporting principles since the 1930s—and have developed distinctly different subsets of GAAP applicable to hospitals, colleges and universities, and state and local governments.

The AICPA's Accounting Principles Board (APB), which succeeded the CAP in 1959, likewise focused its attention on business enterprises. Only one of its pronouncements (*Opinion 20,* "Disclosure of Accounting Policies") was specifically directed to G&NP organizations as well as for-profit organizations.

AICPA Audit and Accounting Guides

Several AICPA auditing committees studied the pronouncements of the various G&NP accounting standards bodies in depth in the course of preparing a series of audit guides during the late 1960s and early 1970s. Each of these audit guides—for state and local government, college and university, hospital, and voluntary health

---

[6] American Institute of Certified Public Accountants, *Accounting Research and Terminology Bulletins,* final ed. (New York: AICPA, 1961), p. 8.

and welfare organization audits—recognized the principles set by the several G&NP standards-setting bodies as "authoritative," although the AICPA audit guides took exception to certain G&NP principles or permitted alternative methods. All substantive differences between the AICPA committees and the various G&NP standards-setting bodies were resolved by the late 1970s.

The AICPA audit guides were of immense significance to the G&NP standards-setting process. Whereas the several G&NP standards bodies had functioned independently of the AICPA for 40 years, now G&NP accounting standards were in essence being established jointly by concurrence of the respective G&NP standards bodies and their counterpart AICPA committees. Further, the AICPA issued a Statement of Position in 1978 (SOP 78-10) setting forth its views with respect to what constituted generally accepted accounting principles and reporting practices for those other types of nonprofit organizations that did not have separate standards-setting bodies and audit guides. These are commonly referred to as *other* nonprofit organizations (*ONP* organizations, or *ONPOs*).

The FASB

The Financial Accounting Standards Board (FASB), which succeeded the APB in 1973, is financed and overseen by a multisponsored Financial Accounting Foundation rather than by the AICPA; and the seven FASB members serve full time, whereas APB and CAP members served only part time, as did members of the various G&NP accounting standards committees. The FASB was not limited by its *original* charter or rules of procedure to setting business accounting standards. Indeed, the AICPA recognized the FASB as *the* body authorized to establish accounting standards—elevating the FASB's authority above that of the several G&NP standards committees. Rule 203 of the AICPA Code of Professional Conduct thus required compliance with FASB pronouncements in virtually all circumstances.

The FASB devoted its efforts almost exclusively to business accounting concepts and standards during its first several years in operation, and deferred the decision on what role, if any, it would play in the G&NP standards area. By 1979, the FASB had decided to issue one or more statements of financial accounting concepts (such as SFAC 4 discussed earlier) but continued to defer the assumption of responsibility for G&NP accounting and reporting standards.

Later in 1979, the FASB agreed to exercise responsibility for all specialized accounting and reporting principles and practices set forth in AICPA statements of position, accounting guides, and audit guides *except those dealing with state and local governments (FASB Statement No. 32).* The FASB designated the principles and practices described in the AICPA pronouncements—related to colleges and universities, hospitals, voluntary health and welfare organizations, and other nonprofit organizations—as *"preferable."* Further, the FASB noted that it planned to extract them and issue them as FASB statements. Thereafter, the Board would assume responsibility for amending and interpreting such standards in the future. The FASB's **"specialized industry"** action changed the roles of the AICPA and the various bodies that previously had set standards for nonprofit organizations (other than state and local governments) from setting standards to serving in an advisory capacity to the FASB standards-setting process.

The FASB deferred action with respect to state and local government standards in view of discussions then under way among representatives of interested organizations, including the National Council on Governmental Accounting and the AICPA, regarding the appropriate structure for setting governmental accounting standards. At issue was whether state and local government accounting

Figure 1-3

FINANCIAL ACCOUNTING AND REPORTING
STANDARDS-SETTING STRUCTURE

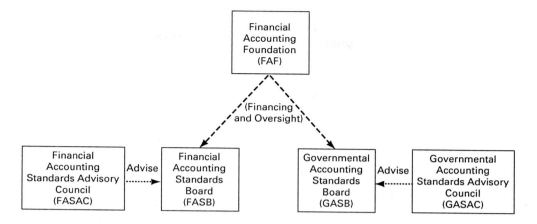

standards should continue to be established by the National Council on Governmental Accounting or should be set by the FASB, or perhaps a new standards-setting body. These discussions led to formation of the Governmental Accounting Standards Board in 1984 to succeed the National Council on Governmental Accounting as the authoritative standards-setting body for state and local government accounting and financial reporting.

The GASB

The five-member Governmental Accounting Standards Board (GASB) was established under the auspices of the Financial Accounting Foundation (FAF), which also finances and oversees the FASB. However, the GASB and FASB are separate, independent standards-setting bodies (Figure 1-3).

The FASB-GASB jurisdiction policy states that (1) the **GASB** will establish standards for activities and transactions of ***state and local governmental entities,*** and (2) the **FASB** will establish standards for activities and transactions of ***all other entities.*** The AICPA affirmed this policy, recognized the GASB-FASB jurisdiction under Rule 203 of the AICPA Code of Professional Conduct, and revised its "hierarchy of GAAP" guidelines accordingly.

GAAP "Hierarchy"

The AICPA **GAAP "hierarchy"** indicates the ***relative authoritativeness*** of the various standards pronouncements and other literature on financial accounting and reporting principles and procedures. The **GAAP hierarchy** that was ***recognized during 1984–1991*** for **state and local government entities**—including government hospitals, colleges and universities, and nonprofit organizations—is presented in Figure 1-4. Many current practices are based on this 1984–1991 SLG GAAP hierarchy.

Both the GASB and the FASB have been *designated by* the *AICPA Council* to establish standards—pursuant to *Rule 203* of the AICPA *Code of Professional Conduct*—and this 1984–1991 GAAP hierarchy was last recognized and explained in AICPA *Statement on Auditing Standards 52* (1988) under the heading "The Meaning of 'Present Fairly in Conformity with Generally Accepted Accounting Principles' in the Independent Auditor's Report."

Figure 1-4

GAAP "HIERARCHY": 1984–1991

State and Local Government
Accounting and Financial Reporting

1. **Pronouncements of the Governmental Accounting Standards Board** [includes, to the extent that they have not been superseded, National Council on Governmental Accounting Statements and Interpretations and excerpts from certain AICPA pronouncements that were recognized as authoritative in GASB Statement No. 1]
2. **Pronouncements of the Financial Accounting Standards Board** [includes, to the extent that they have not been superseded, Accounting Principles Board Opinions and Accounting Research Bulletins]
3. **Pronouncements of [other] bodies** composed of expert accountants that follow a due process procedure, including broad distribution of proposed accounting principles for public comment, for the *intended purpose* of establishing accounting principles or describing existing practices that are generally accepted [includes AICPA audit and accounting guides and Statements of Position, as well as pronouncements of hospital, college and university, and nonprofit organization association committees]
4. **Practices or [other] pronouncements** that are *widely recognized* as being *generally accepted* because they represent *prevalent practice* in a particular industry *or* the *knowledgeable application to specific circumstances* of pronouncements that are generally accepted [includes AICPA "Trends and Techniques" and other studies of current accounting and reporting practices]
5. **Other accounting literature** [includes textbooks, journal articles, speeches, and the like]

Source: Adapted from AICPA, "The Auditor's Consideration of Accounting Principles Promulgated by the Governmental Accounting Standards Board: An Interpretation of SAS No. 5 . . . , "*Journal of Accountancy* (December 1984), p. 198.

The *essence* of the *1984–1991 GAAP hierarchy for state and local governments* (Figure 1-4) was that:

1. GASB Statements and Interpretations were recognized as the *most authoritative* source of GAAP applicable to state and local government entities—and *superseded* any guidance at levels 2–5.

2. If the GASB had *not* issued a Statement or Interpretation that addressed the issue, FASB Statements and Interpretations were to be researched next for guidance. (But FASB guidance was to be implemented within the context of state and local government accounting principles.)

3. If *neither* the GASB nor the FASB had addressed the matter in a Statement or Interpretation, the level 3 pronouncements—which included GASB and FASB Technical Bulletins, AICPA audit and accounting guides and Statements of Position, and pronouncements of the hospital and college and university accounting standards committees—were to be followed.

4. *If no guidance* was found at *levels 1–3,* then *what had become accepted in practice*—preferably evidenced by "trends and techniques" and similar studies of contemporary accounting and reporting practices—was to be researched for guidance.

5. Finally, *if guidance was not available at levels 1–4,* refer to *other accounting literature,* such as textbooks, professional organization position papers and other publications, journal articles, and speeches.

Neither the GASB nor the FASB has issued a comprehensive statement of GAAP applicable to hospitals, colleges and universities, or other nonprofit organizations. Accordingly, accountants and auditors rely heavily on relevant AICPA audit and accounting guides and industry committee publications, as well as on

GASB and FASB pronouncements, in determining GAAP applicable to such non-profit organizations.

A *significant difficulty* was encountered during the first five years (1984–89) of experience with the **1984–1991** *SLG GAAP hierarchy: What if the FASB should issue a new standard on a topic on which the GASB had not issued a pronouncement?* A literal interpretation of the GAAP hierarchy would indicate that SLGs must follow the new FASB standard—even if the FASB had neither considered the SLG environment nor intended the new standard to apply to SLGs. This aspect of the SLG hierarchy caused much confusion in practice and led the GASB to issue several "negative" standards whose primary purpose was to instruct SLGs *not* to follow a new FASB standard.

As a result of its five-year review of the activities of the GASB and the FASB under the 1984 GASB-FASB jurisdiction and hierarchy agreement, the Board of Trustees of the Financial Accounting Foundation (FAF) adopted an *objective* for a new GAAP hierarchy applicable to SLGs. The *basic idea* of the *new GAAP hierarchy* approach is that:

- Both the GASB and the FASB should have **primary** authority and responsibility for those organizations **within** their respective **jurisdictions.**
- Accordingly, *all* SLGs are subject to GASB standards—and must change their practices to conform to GASB guidance. But SLGs would **not** be required to change their practices because of new FASB pronouncements **unless** instructed to do so by the GASB.

The Chairmen of the GASB and FASB drafted a suggested revised GAAP hierarchy agreement, which was approved by the FAF and forwarded to the AICPA Auditing Standards Board (ASB). The ASB issued revised GAAP hierarchies for both SLGs and non-SLG entities in AICPA Statement on Auditing Standards (SAS) 69 issued in January, 1992.

The *1992 SLG GAAP hierarchy—effective* for audits of financial statements for *periods ending after March 15, 1992*—is summarized in **Figure 1-5.**

Figure 1-5

GAAP "HIERARCHY": 1992–

State and Local Government
Accounting and Financial Reporting

a. 1. GASB Statements and Interpretations, *and*
   2. AICPA and FASB pronouncements that have been *made applicable to SLGs by GASB* Statements and Interpretations
b. 1. GASB Technical Bulletins, *and*
   2. AICPA Industry Audit and Accounting Guides and AICPA Statements of Position that are
      —specifically *made applicable* to SLGs by the AICPA *and*
      —*cleared* by the GASB
c. 1. Consensus positions of any GASB Emerging Issues Task Force (EITF) that may be established [*no GASB EITF has been established*], *and*
   2. AICPA Accounting Standards Executive Committee (AcSEC) Practice Bulletins *if*
      a. specifically *made applicable* to SLGs by AcSEC, *and*
      b. *cleared* by the GASB
d. 1. GASB staff Implementation Guides (Qs & As), *and*
   2. Practices that are *widely recognized and prevalent* in SLGs.
e. Other accounting literature relevant in the circumstances—giving consideration to (1) its relevance to the particular circumstances, (2) the specificity of the guidance, and (3) the general recognition of the issuer or author as an authority.

Source: Adapted from AICPA, Statement on Auditing Standards No. 69, "The Meaning of 'Fairly Presents' in the Auditor's Report," January 1992.

The "new" and "old" SLG GAAP hierarchies are summarized and compared in Figure 1-6. ***Note*** that:

- the pronouncements included in category (a) of the new (1992) hierarchy are essentially the same as those in category "1" of the old (1984–1991) hierarchy.
- FASB (and effective APB and CAP) standards pronouncements formerly in category "2" are now either in category (a) (if GASB has endorsed them) or in category (e).
- SAS 69 states that an entity following an accounting treatment in category (c) or (d) as of March 15, 1992 *need not* change to an accounting treatment in a category (b) or category (c) pronouncement *if* its effective date is *before* March 15, 1992.

Figure 1-6

SOURCES OF GOVERNMENT GAAP
"NEW" vs. "OLD" GAAP HIERARCHY

"New" (1992–) *Hierarchy*	*"Old"* (1984–1991) *Hierarchy*	*Changes Per "New" Hierarchy*
a. GASB Statements and Interpretations	1. GASB Statements and Interpretations	
AICPA and FASB pronouncements "adopted" by GASB in GASB Statements and Interpretations	—	GASB can make AICPA and FASB pronouncements highest level by "adopting" them in GASB Statements and Interpretations
b. GASB Technical Bulletins	2. FASB Statements and Interpretations (includes predecessor APB and CAP pronouncements still in effect)	FASB Statements and Interpretations are *not* presumed to apply to SLGs *unless adopted by GASB* Statements or Interpretations (level "**a**"); otherwise FASB pronouncements are level "**e**"
AICPA Audit Guides and Accounting Guides and SOPs *if* (1) made applicable to SLGs by AICPA *and* (2) cleared by GASB		
c. GASB Emerging Issues Task Force (EITF) consensus positions (if and when GASB establishes an EITF)	3. Pronouncements of other "expert bodies" that follow due process, including exposure drafts, that attempt to establish or describe accounting principles (includes AICPA, NACUBO, and so on)	AICPA guides and SOPs applicable to SLGs and cleared by GASB now level "**b**," as are GASB staff Technical Bulletins; pronouncements of other "expert bodies" now level "**e**"
AcSEC Practice Bulletins	—	AcSEC Practice Bulletins new to SLG hierarchy
d. GASB staff Implementation Guides (Qs and As)	—	GASB staff Implementation Guides (Qs and As) are a new type of publication
Widely recognized and prevalent SLG accounting practices	4. Widely recognized practices or pronouncements that represent prevalent practice or knowledgeable application of other GAAP pronouncements to specific circumstances.	Only "practices" are level "**d**"; "other pronouncements" are level "**e**"; and "knowledgeable application of other GAAP pronouncements" *deleted.*
e. All not in levels "**a**"–"**d**" is level "**e**"	5. All not in levels "**1**"–"**4**" is level "**5**"	Same concept—but changes in levels "**a**"–"**d**" change level "**e**" content

CONCLUDING COMMENTS

In sum, there continue to be **several sources of authoritative pronouncements** concerning G&NP accounting and financial reporting **and several distinct subsets of GAAP** applicable to the various types of G&NP organizations. This text is based on the most authoritative pronouncements relevant to each of the several types of G&NP organizations discussed. Sources of authoritative support are cited as appropriate throughout the text.

Accounting is often referred to as the "language" of business. It is also the "language" of government and nonprofit organizations. While most terms and their meanings are the same in both, each has some of its own terms and occasionally uses the same term with a different connotation than the other. Accordingly, **new terms and the occasional use of a familiar term in an unfamiliar way should be noted carefully in reviewing this and later chapters.**

State and local government budgeting, accounting, and financial reporting concepts, principles and standards, and procedures are discussed and illustrated in the next several chapters. Federal government accounting and reporting and that for public sector and nonprofit hospitals, colleges and universities, and other nonprofit organizations are discussed in later chapters, as is auditing in the G&NP organization environment.

QUESTIONS

1-1 What characteristics differentiate government and nonprofit organizations from profit-seeking organizations?

1-2 List four factors that cause society to subject G&NP organizations to more stringent legal, regulatory, and other controls than it imposes on private businesses.

1-3 Discuss (a) the similarities in accounting for profit-seeking and G&NP organizations, and (b) the unique aspects of accounting for G&NP organizations designed to help ensure compliance with budgeted spending limits.

1-4 (a) Define "fund" as used in not-for-profit organizations. (b) Contrast that definition with the same term as used in a profit-seeking organization. (c) Does the creation of a fund constitute authority to spend or obligate its resources? Explain.

1-5 Distinguish between "expendable" funds and "nonexpendable" funds.

1-6 Discuss the funds-flow concept as it applies to the operations of G&NP organizations.

1-7 Contrast the terms "expense" and "expenditure."

1-8 Contrast the following concepts as they are used in commercial and G&NP accounting; (a) accounting entity; (b) periodicity; (c) matching; (d) going concern.

1-9 It was noted in this chapter that most of the differences between commercial accounting and that for G&NP organizations result from differences in (a) organizational objectives and (b) methods of fiscal control employed. Explain.

1-10 Discuss the roles of the GASB, the FASB, and the AICPA in standards setting for G&NP organizations.

1-11 Legal and administrative constraints are society's tools for directing G&NP institutions in achieving their objectives. This results in a control of and accountability for expendable financial resources emphasis in G&NP organization accounting and reporting rather than an income determination emphasis. Explain why the profitability measure cannot provide this direction and identify various legal and administrative control provisions unique to G&NP organizations and their impact on accounting and reporting for such organizations.

1-12 The revenues of profit-seeking organizations are based on user charges. Users may be charged for various services provided by G&NP organizations as well. However, differences often exist in the nature and purpose of user charges of G&NP organizations and those of profit-seeking organizations. Explain.

1-13 Different sets of accounting and reporting concepts, principles, and procedures have evolved for state and local governments, hospitals, colleges and universities, nonprofit organizations, and business enterprises. Given the differences between and among them, how can they all be considered "generally accepted accounting principles"?

1-14 (a) What is the purpose of the AICPA GAAP "hierarchy" guidelines? (b) How would the hierarchy be used by an accountant or auditor who found conflicting guidance in a GASB Statement and an AICPA audit and accounting guide while researching the proper accounting treatment of a state government transaction or event?

PROBLEMS

P 1-1 Indicate the best answer for each of the following:

1. The body with primary accounting standards-setting authority for state and local governments is the
   a. American Institute of Certified Public Accountants.
   b. Financial Accounting Standards Board.
   c. Government Finance Officers Association.
   d. Governmental Accounting Standards Board.
   e. U.S. General Accounting Office.

2. The body with primary accounting standards-setting authority for colleges and universities is the
   a. National Association of College and University Business Officers.
   b. Financial Accounting Standards Board.
   c. Governmental Accounting Standards Board.
   d. Governmental Accounting Standards Board for governmental colleges and universities and the Financial Accounting Standards Board for all other colleges and universities.
   e. U.S. Department of Education.

3. An expendable fund accounting entity
   a. is optional (expendable), but is often useful in accounting for general government activities.
   b. includes only current financial resources and related liabilities and depreciable (expendable) fixed assets. Nondepreciable fixed assets are not reported in expendable funds.
   c. includes only financial resources and liabilities to be repaid from those resources.
   d. has its operating activities measured and reported in terms of revenues and expenses, but the timing of expense recognition differs from that in similar business organizations.

4. In which of the following situations would the amount of expense and expenditure for the period differ?
   a. An entity uses and is billed for utilities, but has paid only half of the amount billed at year end.
   b. An entity purchases equipment by issuing a 90-day note that matures in the next period. The purchase occurred on the last day of the fiscal year.
   c. Interest accrued, but was not paid, on a nine-month note payable.
   d. Salaries and wages incurred and paid during the period were $100,000. Additional salaries and wages accrued at year end were $4,000.
   e. The amount of expense and expenditure to be recognized differs in more than one of the preceding situations.

5. Legally adopted budgets of expendable funds of governments are
   a. Fixed-dollar budgets which establish expenditure limits that are not to be exceeded.
   b. Fixed budgets that cannot be modified during the budget year.
   c. Flexible budgets in which the expenditure limits are automatically modified to reflect larger than budgeted levels of various services.
   d. Always adopted using the same basis of accounting required by GAAP.

6. Which of the following statements is false? A fund:

   a. Is an entity for which financial statements can be prepared.

   b. Has a self-encompassing, self-balancing accounting equation.

   c. Is used to account for a subset of an organization's resources that are to be used for a specific purpose or to achieve a particular objective.

   d. Is an accounting entity that is used for one year only. Each year a new set of funds must be established.

   e. None of the above is false.

7. Under SAS 69, with respect to financial reporting for state and local governments, FASB Statements of Financial Accounting Standards are:

   a. More authoritative than Statements of the GASB.

   b. More authoritative than Statements of Positions of the AICPA that have not been "cleared" by the GASB—but which the AICPA developed for the purpose of providing guidance for governments.

   c. More authoritative than GASB Technical Bulletins.

   d. More authoritative than the AICPA state and local government audit guide.

   e. None of the above is true.

   f. None of the above is true unless the GASB has "adopted" the FASB Statement.

8. One unique characteristic of most government and nonprofit organizations is that

   a. A primary source of financing is sales of services and goods to customers.

   b. Their constituency automatically dictates what the government or nonprofit organization's resources are used to accomplish.

   c. There is no direct relationship between the amount of goods or services that most individual resource providers receive and the amount of resources provided by that individual.

   d. These entities sometimes have restrictions placed on what their resources may be used for, while such restrictions cannot be placed on business resources.

9. Organizations that are considered to be nonprofit organizations include such organizations as:

   a. Churches

   b. The Boy Scouts and Girl Scouts

   c. Church-supported hospitals

   d. State CPA societies

   e. All of the above

10. A key underlying difference between government or nonprofit organizations and business entities is

   a. Businesses have scarce resources that must be allocated to different uses; governments and nonprofits are able to command sufficient resources to avoid the need for such allocations.

   b. The absence of the profit motive in most government and nonprofit organizations.

   c. The amount of restricted resources held by governments and nonprofits.

   d. The use of fund accounting by governments and nonprofits.

P 1-2 (Expenditures vs. Expenses) Family Services, a small social service nonprofit agency, began operations on January 1, 19X1 with $40,000 cash and $150,000 of equipment, on which $60,000 was owed on a note to City Bank. The equipment was expected to have a remaining useful life of 15 years with no salvage value. During its first year of operations ending December 31, 19X1, Family Services paid or accrued the following:

1. Salaries and other personnel costs, $100,000

2. Rent, utilities, and so on, $24,000

3. Debt service—interest, $5,500, and payment on note principal, $10,000

4. Capital outlay—additional equipment purchased January 3, $30,000, expected to last 6 years and have a $6,000 salvage value

5. Other, $10,500

There were no prepayals or unrecorded accruals at December 31, 19X1, and no additional debt was incurred during the year.

Required Compute for the Family Services agency, for the year ended December 31, 19X1, its total (a) expenses and (b) expenditures.

P 1-3 (Statement of Revenues and Expenditures—Worksheet) Hatcher Township prepares its annual General Fund budget on the cash basis and maintains its accounting records on the cash basis during the year. At the end of Hatcher Township's 19X9 calendar year you determine the following:

General Fund	Budget (Cash) Basis		Accruals	
	Budget	Actual	1/1/X9	12/31/X9
Revenues:				
Taxes	$600,000	$595,000	$ —	$6,000
Licenses	200,000	206,000	—	—
Intergovernmental	100,000	110,000	9,000	1,000
Other	50,000	45,000	5,000	—
	950,000	956,000	14,000	7,000
Expenditures:				
Salaries	700,000	704,000	17,000	11,000
Utilities	80,000	85,000	—	—
Supplies	70,000	64,000	—	7,000
Equipment	60,000	58,000	2,000	12,000
Other	30,000	31,000	—	—
	940,000	942,000	19,000	30,000
Excess of Revenues Over (Under) Expenditures	$ 10,000	$ 14,000		

Required (1) Prepare a worksheet to derive a GAAP basis (including accruals) statement of revenues and expenditures for the Hatcher Township General Fund for the 19X9 fiscal year.

(2) Might the readers of the budgetary basis and GAAP basis statements get different impressions of the 19X9 "operating results" of the Hatcher Township General Fund? Explain.

STATE AND LOCAL GOVERNMENT ACCOUNTING:
Environment, Objectives, and Principles

State and local government is truly "big business." The 50 states and 85,000 local governments within these United States employ more than 15 million persons—over four times as many as are employed by the federal government—and spend about $1 trillion annually. Although the federal government accounts for over half of all government expenditures, state and local governments spend more for nondefense purposes than the federal government. Furthermore, state and local government revenues, expenditures, debt, and employment—both in total and per capita—have been increasing at higher rates than those of the federal complex in recent years. Today it is common to find that the state government is the largest industry within a state or that city hall houses the biggest business in a town.

The types and numbers of local governments are shown in Figure 2-1. However, the extent of local government jurisdictional overlap is not obvious from that figure. It is common for a given geographic area to be served by a municipality, a school district, a county, and one or more special districts. In fact, many metropolitan areas have 100 or more separate and distinct local government units.

Figure 2-1

TYPES OF LOCAL GOVERNMENTS

Counties	3,044
Municipalities	19,265
Townships	16,652
School districts	14,613
Special districts	31,800
Total	85,374

Source: U.S. Department of Commerce, number of active governments as of 7/1/90.

State and local governments have increased both the types and levels of goods and services provided their citizens in recent years, and many governments have become among the most complex and diversified organizations in existence. No doubt their scope and complexity as well as their relative importance in our economy and society will continue to grow as our society becomes increasingly urban and governments at all levels attempt to meet the demands of their constituencies for more and better goods and services.

Three major topics are covered in this introductory chapter to state and local government (SLG) accounting and reporting:

- The **evolution** of SLG accounting principles
- The SLG **environment** and the **objectives** of SLG financial reporting
- The GASB **principles** (standards) of SLG accounting and financial reporting

While each of these topics is important, the "principles" section is particularly important to understanding SLG accounting and financial reporting.

EVOLUTION OF ACCOUNTING PRINCIPLES

Although the origin of the profession of accountancy is sometimes traced to ancient governments, modern municipal accounting developed in the twentieth century—its beginning inseparably woven within the municipal reform movement near the turn of the century. About that time, attention was focused on scandalous practices in the financial administration of many cities; the National Municipal League suggested uniform municipal reporting formats, and the Census Bureau encouraged more uniformity in city accounts and reports.

Initial Evolution (1900–1933)

A flurry of change in municipal accounting and reporting practices occurred during the first decade. In 1901, the firm of Haskins and Sells, Certified Public Accountants, investigated the affairs of the City of Chicago at the request of the Merchants' Club. Subsequently, the firm installed a completely new system of accounting for that city. The cities of Newton, Massachusetts, and Baltimore, Maryland, published annual reports during 1901 and 1902 along lines suggested by the National Municipal League, and the states of New York and Massachusetts passed legislation in the areas of uniform accounting and reporting in 1904 and 1906, respectively. There were many other examples of progress during this period as other cities and states followed suit.

During this era Herman A. Metz was elected Comptroller of the City of New York on a "business man for the head of the city's business office" slogan. At that time an estimated one-fourth of New York's $80 million personal services budget was being lost through collusion, idleness, or inefficiency. Too, city departments commonly issued bonds to finance current operating expenditures.

Although Metz was said to have been an outstanding comptroller, his most important contribution was the formation of the Bureau of Municipal Research. One of its purposes was "to promote the adoption of scientific methods of accounting [for] and of reporting the details of municipal business...."[1]

The *Handbook of Municipal Accounting,* commonly referred to as "The Metz Fund Handbook," was called "the most significant contribution of the 1910 decade ... [because] it brought together for the first time many of the basic characteristics and requirements of municipal accounting and outlined methods of appropriate treatment."[2] Similarly, the Bureau's publications were the "first organized materials that could be called a treatise in Municipal Accounting."[3]

Pamphlets, articles, and a few textbooks appeared, as others became more

---

[1] Bureau of Municipal Research, *Making a Municipal Budget: Functional Accounts and Operative Statistics for the Department of Greater New York* (New York: BMR, 1907), p. 5.

[2] Lloyd Morey, "Trends in Governmental Accounting," *Accounting Review,* 23 (July 1948), p. 224.

[3] W. K. Newton, "New Developments and Simplified Approaches to Municipal Accounting," *Accounting Review,* 29 (October 1954), p. 656.

interested in the subject. Municipal leagues were formed in various states and, as Newton expressed it, "we soon began a very serious development of the specialized field of Municipal Accounting."[4]

Interest waned during the 1920s and early 1930s. In a study of Illinois cities during 1931 and 1932, W. E. Karrenbrock found that few had accounting systems adequate to segregate transactions of different activities, and none had budgetary accounts coordinated within the regular accounting system.[5]

Writing in 1933, R. P. Hackett observed:

> The first fact that we are confronted with when searching for recent developments, or any developments, in governmental accounting, particularly that of municipal governments, is the marked absence of any general improvement. . . . it must be admitted that there is very little development in the actual practice of governmental and institutional accounting.[6]

National Committees on Municipal and Governmental Accounting (1934–1974)

The National Committee on Municipal Accounting was organized in 1934, under the auspices of the Municipal Finance Officers Association, to bring together representatives of various groups concerned with municipal accounting and to put into effect sound principles of accounting, budgeting, and reporting. (Its membership included representatives of the American Association of University Instructors in Accounting, the American Institute of Accountants, the American Municipal Association, the American Society of Certified Public Accountants, the International City Managers' Association, the Municipal Finance Officers Association, the National Association of Cost Accountants, the National Association of State Auditors, Controllers, and Treasurers, the National Municipal League, and the Bureau of the Census.[7]) Each group represented also had a subcommittee on municipal accounting within its own ranks.

At its organizational meeting, the Committee tentatively adopted certain "principles" of municipal accounting and reporting and began an extensive municipal accounting research program. The Committee's formation was hailed as "the first effort on a national scale to establish principles and standards for municipal accounting and actively promote their use."[8] It was the major event in municipal accounting until that time. Indeed, the Committee's principles were officially recognized by the American Institute of Accountants, predecessor of the American Institute of Certified Public Accountants (AICPA).[9]

Numerous publications defining proper or improved municipal accounting and financial administration practices were issued by the Committee and the Municipal Finance Officers Association (MFOA) in the 1930s and 1940s. In 1948, Morey stated:

> There is no longer any doubt as to what constitutes good accounting, reporting, and auditing for public bodies. The work of the National Committee on Municipal Accounting in particular, in establishing standards and models in these subjects,

---

[4] Ibid.

[5] R. P. Hackett, "Recent Developments in Governmental and Institutional Accounting," *Accounting Review,* 8 (June 1933), p. 122.

[6] Ibid., pp. 122, 127.

[7] Carl H. Chatters, "Municipal Accounting Progresses," *Certified Public Accountant,* 14 (February, 1934), p. 101.

[8] Ibid.

[9] American Institute of Accountants, *Audits of Governmental Bodies and Accounts of Governmental Bodies* (New York: AIA, 1934 and 1935).

provides an authority to which officials, accountants, and public may turn with confidence.[10]

In 1951, the Committee, by then known as the National Committee on Governmental Accounting, issued *Municipal Accounting and Auditing*.[11] This book combined and revised the major publications of the Committee and became the basis for the major textbooks in the area as well as for many state laws and guides relating to municipal accounting, auditing, and reporting. This "Bible of municipal accounting," as it came to be called, was succeeded in 1968 by *Governmental Accounting, Auditing, and Financial Reporting* (GAAFR),[12] often referred to as the "blue book."

In 1974, the AICPA issued an audit guide, *Audits of State and Local Governmental Units* (ASLGU),[13] to assist its members in the conduct of governmental audits. ASLGU recognized GAAFR as authoritative and stated that, except as modified in ASLGU, the principles in GAAFR constituted generally accepted accounting principles.

The National Committee on Governmental Accounting was not a staff-supported, permanent body that met regularly. Rather, a new committee was formed of appointees of various government agencies, public administration groups, and accounting organizations whenever deemed necessary—historically about every ten years—and served in an advisory and review capacity with respect to revisions proposed by its members and consultants.

National Council on Governmental Accounting (1974–1984)

The National **Council** on Governmental Accounting (NCGA) was established in 1974 to succeed its predecessor, the National **Committee** on Governmental Accounting. The MFOA—now the Government Finance Officers Association (GFOA)—established the NCGA as an ongoing body to reconcile the differences between GAAFR and ASLGU and continually evaluate and develop state and local government accounting principles.

The Council consisted of 21 members who served four-year terms on a part-time voluntary basis and met for about two days, two to four times each year. The NCGA maintained close liaison with the Financial Accounting Standards Board (FASB), AICPA, and other organizations concerned with state and local government accounting and financial reporting standards.

The NCGA's major agenda project, termed the GAAFR Restatement Project, was to develop a statement described as "a modest revision to update, clarify, amplify, and reorder GAAFR." An important related objective was to incorporate pertinent aspects of ASLGU and reconcile any significant differences between GAAFR and ASLGU.

NCGA *Statement 1,* "Governmental Accounting and Financial Reporting Principles," commonly known as the GAAFR Restatement Principles, was issued in 1979. The GAAFR-ASLGU differences had been reconciled during the principles restatement. Accordingly, the AICPA issued a statement of position in 1980 (SOP 80-2)[14] amending ASLGU to incorporate NCGA *Statement 1* by reference and pro-

[10] Morey, "Trends in Governmental Accounting," p. 231.
[11] Published by the Municipal Finance Officers Association (Chicago, 1951).
[12] Published by the Municipal Finance Officers Association (Chicago, 1968). Hereafter cited as GAAFR (68).
[13] Committee on Governmental Accounting and Auditing, American Institute of Certified Public Accountants, *Audits of State and Local Governmental Units* (New York: AICPA, 1974).
[14] Audit Standards Division, American Institute of Certified Public Accountants, Inc., *Statement of Position 80-2,* "Accounting and Financial Reporting by Governmental Units" (New York: AICPA, June 30, 1980).

vide additional guidance to auditors of state and local government financial statements.

The NCGA issued seven Statements, eleven Interpretations, and one Concepts Statement during its 1974–1984 tenure. Its early years coincided with a turbulent period marked by the "fiscal emergency" of the City of New York and by similar financial problems, including debt defaults, in several other major cities and school districts. These crisis situations led to demands that the NCGA issue additional accounting standards. But the NCGA's efforts to provide timely guidance were hampered by the fact that its members served part time, at no pay, and had limited staff support. Thus, leaders of the accounting profession—including members of the NCGA—sought to devise an improved approach to setting accounting standards applicable to state and local governments.

Governmental Accounting Standards Board (1984–   )

The Governmental Accounting Standards Board (GASB) was established in 1984 to succeed the NCGA as the body authorized to establish accounting standards for state and local governments. As noted in Chapter 1, the GASB is financed and overseen by the Financial Accounting Foundation (FAF), as is the Financial Accounting Standards Board (FASB); and the GASB, FASB, and FAF offices are in the same building in Norwalk, Connecticut. *The GASB is responsible for establishing accounting standards for activities and transactions of state and local governments;* the *FASB* sets accounting standards for *all other* organizations.

The GASB has five members. The chairperson and vice chairperson serve full time, while the three other members serve part time. The Board is assisted by a full-time professional staff of about 12 persons, led by the Director of Research, and meets in open session for approximately two days each month. The GASB "mission statement" is presented in Figure 2-2.

GASB activities center around its agenda topics and projects. While it is researching and analyzing topics it may issue *nonauthoritative* invitations to comment, discussion memorandums, preliminary views, and exposure drafts—to obtain viewpoints of practitioners and others—before issuing an authoritative pronouncement. Its *authoritative* pronouncements are issued as *Statements, Interpretations, Technical Bulletins,* and *Implementation Guides.* The GASB issues an *Action Report* newsletter each month to inform interested persons of its activities, and also issues Concepts Statements, research studies, and other nonauthoritative publications from time to time.

GASB *Statement No. 1,* "Authoritative Status of NCGA Pronouncements and AICPA Industry Audit Guide," issued in 1984 provided a transition from the old standards-setting arrangement to the current one. *Statement 1* recognized the then effective NCGA pronouncements and certain accounting and reporting guidance in the then effective AICPA state and local government audit guide (ASLGU, 1974) as authoritative—stating that they are "continued in force until altered, amended, supplemented, revoked, or superseded by a subsequent GASB pronouncement."[15] These NCGA and AICPA pronouncements—now recognized as GASB pronouncements—were integrated into one authoritative publication, *Codification of Governmental Accounting and Financial Reporting Standards,*[16] in 1985.

The **GASB Codification** is revised annually to incorporate subsequent

---

[15] Governmental Accounting Standards Board, *Statement No. 1,* "Authoritative Status of NCGA Pronouncements and AICPA Industry Audit Guide" (GASB, July 1984).
[16] Governmental Accounting Standards Board and Governmental Accounting Research Foundation of the Government Finance Officers Association, *Codification of Governmental Accounting and Financial Reporting Standards as of November 1, 1984* (GASB, 1985).

Figure 2-2 THE MISSION OF THE GOVERNMENTAL ACCOUNTING STANDARDS BOARD

The Mission of the Governmental Accounting Standards Board

Mission Statement

The mission of the Governmental Accounting Standards Board is to establish and improve standards of state and local governmental accounting and financial reporting that will:

- Result in useful information for users of financial reports and
- Guide and educate the public, including issuers, auditors, and users of those financial reports.

Uses and Users of Governmental Accounting and Financial Reporting

Accounting and financial reporting standards are essential to the efficient and effective functioning of our democratic system of government:

a. Financial reporting plays a major role in fulfilling government's duty to be publicly accountable.
b. Financial reporting by state and local governments is used to assess that accountability and to make economic, social, and political decisions.

The primary users of state and local government financial reports are those:

a. To whom government is primarily accountable—its citizens,
b. Who directly represent the citizens—legislative and oversight bodies, and
c. Who finance government or who participate in the financing process—taxpayers, other governments, investors, creditors, underwriters, and analysts.

Government administrators are also users of financial reports; whether they are considered primary users depends on whether they have ready access to internal information.

How the Mission Is Accomplished

To accomplish its mission, the GASB acts to:

a. Issue standards that improve the usefulness of financial reports based on the needs of financial report users; on the primary characteristics of understandability, relevance, and reliability; and on the qualities of comparability and consistency.
b. Keep standards current to reflect changes in the governmental environment.
c. Provide guidance on implementation of standards.
d. Consider significant areas of accounting and financial reporting that can be improved through the standards-setting process.
e. Improve the common understanding of the nature and purposes of information contained in financial reports.

The GASB develops and uses concepts to guide its work of establishing standards. Those concepts provide a frame of reference, or conceptual framework, for resolving accounting and financial reporting issues. This framework helps to establish reasonable bounds for judgment in preparing and using financial reports; it also helps the public understand the nature and limitations of financial reporting.

The GASB's work on both concepts and standards is based on research conducted by the GASB staff and others. The GASB actively solicits and considers the views of its various constituencies on all accounting and financial reporting issues. The GASB's activities are open to public participation and observation under the "due process" mandated by its Rules of Procedure.

Guiding Principles

In establishing concepts and standards, the GASB exercises its judgment after research, due process, and careful deliberation. It is guided by these principles:

- *To be objective and neutral in its decision making* and to ensure, as much as possible, that the information resulting from its standards is a faithful representation of the effects of state and local government activities. Objective and neutral mean freedom from bias, precluding the GASB from placing any particular interest above the interests of the many who rely on the information contained in financial reports.
- *To weigh carefully the views of its constituents* in developing concepts and standards so that they will:

  a. Meet the accountability and decision-making needs of the users of government financial reports, and
  b. Gain general acceptance among state and local government preparers and auditors of financial reports.

- *To establish standards only when the expected benefits exceed the perceived costs.* The GASB strives to determine that proposed standards (including disclosure requirements) fill a significant need and that the costs they impose, compared with possible alternatives, are justified when compared to the overall public benefit.
- *To consider the applicability of its standards* to the separately issued general purpose financial statements of governmentally owned special entities. The GASB specifically evaluates similarities of special entities and of their activities and transactions in both the public and private sectors, and the need, in certain instances, for comparability with the private sector.
- *To bring about needed changes in ways that minimize disruption of the accounting and financial reporting processes.* Reasonable effective dates and transition provisions are established when new standards are introduced. The GASB considers it desirable that change should be evolutionary to the extent that can be accommodated by the need for understandability, relevance, reliability, comparability, and consistency.
- *To review the effects of past decisions* and interpret, amend, or replace standards when appropriate.

Due Process

The GASB is committed to following an open, orderly process for standard setting. The GASB will endeavor at all times to keep the public informed of important developments in its operations and activities.

The due process procedures followed by the GASB are designed to permit timely, thorough, and open study of accounting and financial reporting issues. These procedures encourage broad public participation in the accounting standards-setting process and communication of all points of view and expressions of opinion at all stages of the process. The GASB recognizes that general acceptance of its conclusions is enhanced by demonstrating that the comments received in due process are considered carefully.

Source: GASB, *Facts About GASB: 1991–92,* p. 4.

GASB pronouncements, as is its companion **Original Pronouncements** volume that contains the complete text of all GASB and NCGA pronouncements. All of the GASB and predecessor literature is available also on readily accessible computer disk through the GASB Governmental Accounting Research System (GARS).

ENVIRONMENT AND OBJECTIVES

The discussions of the government and nonprofit (G&NP) organization environment, objectives of G&NP accounting and financial reporting, and characteristics of G&NP accounting in Chapter 1 deal with G&NP organizations generally. This section builds on those discussions and considers similar factors from the state and local government *(SLG)* perspective, as set forth in GASB *Concepts Statement No. 1*, "Objectives of Financial Reporting." The **primary purposes of this section** are to

■ help the reader understand the most significant unique features of the SLG environment and how they have influenced the development of SLG accounting and financial reporting objectives, concepts, and principles—particularly those that differ from those of business enterprises; and

■ provide background necessary for the reader to understand and apply the GASB's basic principles, which are discussed in the next section of this chapter.

This section is drawn, with permission, primarily from GASB *Concepts Statement No. 1*, "Objectives of Financial Reporting."[17] The *environment* of SLG accounting and reporting is considered first, followed by a discussion of the *users and uses* of SLG financial reports. A summary of the *objectives* of SLG external financial reporting in GASB *Concepts Statement 1* concludes this section.

One unique aspect of the SLG environment is that governments may be involved in **both** governmental-type and business-type activities. **Governmental-type activities** include fire and police protection, the courts, and other "general governmental" activities, whereas **business-type activities** include public utilities (e.g., electricity, water) and other activities for which user fees are charged and that are operated similarly to private businesses. The environments of governmental-type and business-type activities may differ, even within one government, as may financial statement user information needs. Thus, the SLG environment, financial statement users, and user information needs are discussed first for governmental-type activities, then are compared with those of business-type activities.

Environment—Governmental-Type Activities

The *governmental-type* activity *environment* is *unique* in several respects. These include *unique SLG:*

1. purpose
2. sources of resources
3. mechanisms for allocating financial resources for various uses
4. accountabilities
5. reporting complexities

---

[17] Governmental Accounting Standards Board, *Codification of Governmental Accounting and Financial Reporting Standards as of June 30, 1992* (GASB, 1992), sec. 100. Hereafter cited GASB *Codification.*

Unique Purpose

A government's **primary reason** for **existence**—particularly for its "government-type" activities—is **uniquely different** from that of business enterprises. The key objective and rationale for the existence of businesses is to earn a profit. But the primary goal for **governmental-type activities** is to **provide** goods or **services** that its constituency has agreed should be available to all who need them—often **without regard to** the *individual* service **recipient's ability to pay** for the goods or services.

  Absence of the **profit motive** in "governmental-type activities" underlies several other differences between governments and businesses. For instance, **the basic performance evaluation measure in business—net income—does *not* apply to governmental-type activities.** Consequently, governments do **not** attract significant resources for "governmental-type activities" from

 a. **investors in equity securities** who expect an equity-type return on their investment, or

 b. **service charges** to **individual users of SLG services** in proportion to the services used.

Since proportionate service charges are not a key source of "general government" financial resources, the uses of government resources are not "automatically" allocated to the services for which individual users are willing and able to pay. That is, **the "market supply and demand allocation mechanism does not function as it does for business.** (In government, financial resources provided by one person or group may be used to finance services for another person or group.)

Unique Sources of Financial Resources

Since the primary nonloan sources of financial resources of businesses are not available to governments for governmental-type activities, governments must raise financial resources from sources different than those of business enterprises. Two primary examples of these unique revenue sources are taxes and intergovernmental grants and subsidies.

Taxation. The **power to tax is unique to governments**—and most "governmental type" SLG services are financed by taxes. **Most "general government" services**—e.g., police and fire protection, elementary and secondary education, and streets and highways—usually are **financed** almost exclusively **by tax revenues.** Indeed, even when SLGs charge **fees** for "general government" services they often must be subsidized with tax revenues (e.g., many public health clinics).

  The power to tax causes **taxpayers** to be **involuntary resource providers.** Individual taxpayers **cannot refuse to pay taxes** if they think the government is using the resources improperly, or pay a lesser amount if they do not use as many of the government's services as do others. Rather, the amount of **taxes** a taxpayer must pay is **based on** the **value of** the taxpayer's real and/or personal **property** (property taxes), the amount of his or her income (**income** taxes), **or retail purchases** (sales taxes), and so forth—**not** on the amount or value of **services received.**

  Thus, **taxation eliminates any direct association between**

 1. the amount and quality of the services a constituent **receives** from the government, **and**

 2. the amount the constituent **pays** to the government.

This absence of the "market" resource allocation mechanism makes it **difficult to measure** the **"success"** of a governmental unit **in financial terms.**

Many governments **also have powers—similar to taxation—to levy license and permit fees, fines,** and **other charges.** This ability of governments to **exact resources** from individuals, businesses, and others by taxation and similar levies—**without** an **"arm's-length" exchange transaction**—means that the types, levels, and quality of services that a government provides are **not** automatically dictated or regulated by what its constituents are willing to pay for the services.

Intergovernmental Revenues. Grants and subsidies from higher-level governments are another significant source of SLG revenues. The federal government provides several hundred billions of dollars of revenues to SLGs every year and states provide still more resources for local governments. These **intergovernmental revenues** are not provided as a direct result of services received by the resource provider, but to help finance certain services for the recipient's constituency.

Unique Resource Allocation Mechanisms

General government resource allocations are derived from processes uniquely different from business enterprises. Absence of a direct relationship between the resources provided by an individual taxpayer and the services provided to that individual taxpayer makes it impossible for the resource allocations to be made in the same manner as for businss enterprises. Rather, for the most part, the nature of the U.S. system of governance determines how the allocations are made.

The primary mechanism used for allocating general government resources to various uses is for *"restrictions"* to be placed on financial resource use by the resource providers or their representatives. One level of restriction is a broad restriction requiring that certain resources be used for a particular purpose(s) or program(s). Such restrictions arise as a result of:

- Intergovernmental grantors requiring that the resources provided be used for a particular purpose.
- Taxes and similar resources being levied for a specific purpose, such as for roads, education, or debt service.
- Borrowings being restricted to a specific purpose(s).

These numerous broad restrictions are the primary reason for the use of funds and account groups—to account for resources segregated according to the purpose(s) for which they may or must be used. The GASB recognizes the importance of the governmental *fund structure and* the fund accounting *control mechanism* in the SLG environment, observing that *funds and fund accounting* controls:

- *complement* the *budgetary process* and annual budget in *assuring* that a government's *financial resources* are *used in manners that comply* with both external restrictions and the annual budget, and
- *facilitate fulfilling* the SLG's *accountability* to its constituency, grantors, and so on.

Taxes and other revenues are allocated to various uses by placing more detailed restrictions on their use as well. Theoretically, this could be accomplished by taxpayers meeting and deciding as a group how the various resources are to be used. However, in our *representative form of government* citizens have *delegated* that *power to public officials* through the *election* process. Too, a system of "checks and balances" over the potential abuse of power is provided by the **separation of powers among the executive, legislative, and judicial branches of government.**

These more detailed restrictions thus are placed on the use of resources by elected officials through the **budget** process. The **budget** is adopted into law and essentially becomes a **"contract"** between the executive branch, the legislative branch, and the citizenry. In most jurisdictions, significant changes in this budget "contract" should be made only through a process similar to the budget process itself. In the *budget process:*

- The **executive branch** typically prepares a budget and submits appropriation requests to the legislative branch.
- The **legislative branch** has the power to approve those requests, thus authorizing the executive branch to make expenditures within the limits of the appropriations and any laws that may effect programs covered by those appropriations.
- The **executive branch is accountable to the legislative branch** for operating within those appropriations and laws, **and both branches are accountable to the citizenry.**

The **annual budgetary process** and budget are **extremely important** in the SLG "governmental-type" activities environment. The **budget** is an expression of *public policy* and intent. It also is a **financial plan** that indicates the proposed expenditures for the year and the means of financing them.

Morever, an **adopted** budget has the force of **law.** It **both:**

- **authorizes** amounts to be expended for various specified purposes, **and**
- **limits** (or restricts) the amount that may be expended for each of those purposes. (Budgetary limitations generally cannot be exceeded without due process.)

Thus, the **budget is both** a form of **control and** a **basis for evaluating performance** in a budgetary context. Accordingly, a **government must demonstrate** its **"budgetary accountability."** Budgetary accountability entails reporting whether revenues were obtained and expended as anticipated, and whether authorized expenditure limitations (appropriations) were exceeded.

Further, **establishing the budget**—determining the types and amounts of taxes and other revenues to be exacted from the citizenry and how those resources will be used—is **one of the most important functions** that **elected representatives perform.** Indeed, the citizenry's perception of a representative's budgetary process *"performance"* is a significant factor in voting decisions. Hence, **the budget process is a vital part of the political process.**

Unique Accountabilities

The numerous environmental uniquenesses discussed earlier result in unique SLG "accountabilities." "SLG accountabilities" are unique both in terms of (1) **to whom** SLGs and their officials are **accountable and** (2) the **focuses of** their **accountability.**

To Whom Accountable. The need for accountability exists between (1) SLGs and their constituencies, (2) SLGs and other governments, and (3) the SLG's own legislative and executive bodies.

SLGs are accountable to their constituencies for various reasons. Elected officials are in essence empowered by citizens to act on their behalf. Elected officials are evaluated by voters in part on their "fiscal and budgetary performance" as well as on the perceived efficiency and effectiveness with which the SLG is operated. SLG officials must demonstrate to citizens that revenues or bond proceeds approved for specific purposes were in fact used for those purposes.

An SLG's accountability to other governments arises in part because senior levels of government often have some oversight authority over lower levels of government. It also results when other governments provide grants or other intergovernmental subsidies to the SLG.

Finally, one need for accountability between each SLG's legislative and executive bodies focuses on demonstrating that the budget contract has been complied with and that resources have been used efficiently and effectively.

Accountability Focuses. SLG accountabilities have ***various focuses*** such as ***accountability for:***

- The ***use of financial resources*** from various revenue sources or bond issues ***in accordance with*** any ***restrictions*** on their use.
- ***Compliance*** with the budget.
- ***Efficient and effective use*** of SLG ***resources.***
- ***Maintaining*** their "general government" ***capital assets.***

Unique Reporting Problems

These unique aspects of the SLG general government environment also create ***unique problems*** that must be dealt with ***in SLG financial reporting and/or auditing,*** including:

1. The ***need to demonstrate compliance*** with restrictions on the use of financial resources.
2. The ***need for*** appropriate ***budgetary reporting.***
3. The ***impact of restrictions*** on the use of financial resources (such as from intergovernmenal grants) on revenue recognition.
4. The **difficulty of measuring and reporting** the **efficiency and effectiveness** of SLGs in providing services.
5. The ***opportunity to "hide" or "disguise" the use or availability of resources*** for various purposes by (a) improper reporting of transactions between the various SLG accounting entities—funds and account groups—and (b) the misuse of funds by developing an inappropriate fund structure.
6. The ***lack of comparability*** that can result between financial reports of two similarly designated governments that perform different functions (which is common in SLGs).
7. Existence of ***taxation and debt limits.***
8. The ***impact on materiality and reporting judgments*** caused by (a) overexpenditure of appropriations being a violation of law and (b) failure to follow technical conditions related to intergovernmental revenues, possibly requiring forfeiture of such revenues or loss of future revenues.

Further, financial reporting for governments must be responsive to the temptations that result because the budget process is a vital part of the political process. ***Elected representatives serve*** for relatively ***short terms*** and officials may be tempted to employ practices that permit a budget to be ***technically*** "in balance" under many budgetary bases of accounting—including the commonly used cash basis—***even when*** there may ***not*** be ***true*** budgetary ***equilibrium.***

Accordingly, to appropriately reflect the degree of budgetary equilibrium, the GASB notes that **financial reporting should indicate the extent to which:**

- ***current operations*** were ***financed by nonrecurring revenues or*** by ***incurring long-term liabilities,*** and

■ certain essential *costs,* such as normal maintenance of government fixed assets, have been *deferred to future periods.*

This final unique reporting problem is particularly significant because, as the GASB notes:

> Governmental entities invest large amounts of resources in non-revenue-producing capital assets such as government office buildings, highways, bridges, and sidewalks. Most governmental capital assets have relatively long lives, and an adequate program of maintenance and rehabilitation is needed to ensure that those estimated useful lives will be realized. That is, **governments,** in essence, **have an implicit commitment to maintain their capital assets,** whether or not they are used directly to produce revenues.[18]

Revenue-producing fixed assets must be maintained in order to continue generating that revenue. But failure to maintain nonrevenue-producing capital assets does not affect a government's revenues currently. Indeed, deferring maintenance of its fixed assets can make more financial resources available currently for expenditure for other purposes. However, this practice also causes higher maintenance costs in later years, reduces the useful lives of the fixed assets, or both. Those consequences usually are not apparent until later years, however, and, even then, the resultant additional costs and taxes are not always blamed on the inappropriate maintenance in earlier years.

Governments have an implicit commitment to maintain their capital assets, even if they are not used directly to produce revenues. Thus, maintenance programs should not be neglected because of the competition for limited resources.

Users of Financial Reports—Governmental-Type Activities

The GASB originally identified three groups of **primary users** of external financial reports of SLGs;[19] and added a fourth group in its "mission statement" (Figure 2-2).

1. **The citizenry:** those to whom the government is primarily accountable—including citizens (taxpayers, voters, service recipients), the media, advocate groups, and public finance researchers
2. **Legislative and oversight bodies:** those who directly represent the citizens—including members of state legislatures, county commissions, city councils, boards of trustees and school boards, and executive branch officials with oversight responsibility over other levels of government
3. **Investors and creditors:** those who lend or participate in the lending process—including individual and institutional investors and creditors, municipal security underwriters, bond rating agencies, bond insurers, and financial institutions

The needs of intergovernmental grantors and other users are considered by the GASB to be encompassed within those of these three primary user groups. Further, *internal executive branch managers* usually have ready access to a SLG's financial information through internal reports—and are *not* considered primary

---

[18] Ibid., sec. 100.126, emphasis added.
[19] Ibid., sec. 100.130–.131.

users of external financial reports. However, if this is **not** the case, a fourth primary user group is:

4. **Government administrators:** internal executive branch managers—**if** they do **not** have ready access to the government's internal information.

Uses of Financial Reports—Governmental-Type Activities

The GASB notes that *financial reporting should provide information useful in making economic and political decisions and in assessing accountability* by:[20]

1. Comparing *actual* financial results *with* the legally adopted *budget.*
2. Assessing *financial condition and results of operations.*
3. Assisting in determining *compliance* with finance-related laws, rules, and regulations.
4. Assisting in evaluating *efficiency and effectiveness.*

Environment, Users, and Uses—Business-Type Activities

In contrast to SLG governmental-type activities, a government's *business-type activities:*

- Provide the **same types of services as private sector** businesses.
- **Involve exchange relationships**—that is, the consumer is charged a fee for services received, and there is a direct relationship between the services provided and the fee charged the consumer.
- **Are often separate, legally constituted, self-sufficient organizations**—though some resemble governmental-type activities because they are regularly subsidized by the SLG or are operated as departments of the SLG.

Environment

The GASB contrasts the "general government" environment factors discussed earlier with those for a SLG's *business-type* activities as follows.[21]

The Relationship between Services Received and Resources Provided by the Consumer. The financial resources raised by **general government** activities usually are **not** derived from the specific services rendered. (For example, there is no specific charge for public safety services; they are financed along with many other services from general property or income taxes.) However, **business-type activities** often involve a **direct relationship between the charge and the service.** In that relationship—termed an **"exchange relationship"**—a user fee is charged for a specific service provided, for example, a toll for use of a road, a charge for water, or a fare to ride the bus.

This **exchange relationship causes users** of financial reports **to focus on measuring the costs (or financial resource outflows, or both) of providing the service, the revenues obtained** from the service, **and the difference** between the two. The difference is particularly important since it may affect future user charges.

---

[20] Ibid., sec. 100.132, emphasis added.
[21] Ibid., sec 100.144–.150.

Measurement of **both** the cost of services and financial resource outflows is useful. **Whether one is more important** than the other **depends** on various factors, including the way in which user charges are calculated and whether or not subsidies are provided by the general government.

Cost of services information is useful for public policy decisions. For example, the amount a business-type activity charges for its services may be based on recovery of all costs. In other cases, capital assets may be provided by direct subsidies (general governmental or intergovernmental grants) and therefore not included in calculating user charges. However, in both cases, **financial statement users need to know the full cost of operating the business-type activity;** the financial implications of the subsidies or grants need to be understood. At the same time, **information about financial resource flows is also useful.** For example, user charges may be based on resource flows rather than costs; subsidies from the general government may be based on net cash outflows rather than the net operating deficit after depreciation.

Revenue-Producing Capital Assets. **Most capital assets of business-type activities are revenue producing.** Therefore, **the incentive for business-type activities to defer needed maintenance may not be as great as that for governmental-type activities.** However, when business-type activities receive general government **subsidies,** they need to compete for financial resources with governmental-type activities and are subject to the same constraints.

Similarly Designated Activities and Potential for Comparison. Governmental **business-type activities** often perform only a **single function.** If the function is supplying water, for example, the problems, procedures, and cost elements of obtaining, treating, and delivering it are similar, regardless of whether the function is performed by a private sector business, a public authority, an Enterprise Fund, or as an activity financed by the government's General Fund. As a result, **there is normally a greater potential for comparability among business-type activities performing similar functions than among governmental-type activities,** which vary from government to government.

The Nature of the Political Process. Some governmental business-type activities are designed to be insulated from the political process—they are not part of the general governmental budgetary process, they have a direct relationship between fees and services rendered, and they are separate, legally constituted agencies. In some instances, however, this **insulation from the political process has less substance than appearances suggest.** Indeed, especially in **subsidized** activities, **rate setting**—even by independent boards—is **political** in nature. For example, charging mass transit users sufficient fares to pay all costs of the system may be politically or economically undesirable—so subsidies are provided from general tax revenues or grants from other jurisdictions. If operating or capital **subsidies are provided,** the **influences of the political process** often **are as significant as in governmental-type activities.**

Budgets and Fund Accounting. The use **of fixed budgets** and multiple-fund accounting is **less common for business-type activities** than for governmental-type activities. Unless the business-type activity is operated as a governmental department, budgetary processes and budgets often are internal management processes and tools that lack the force of law. Similarly, because business-type organizations often perform a single function, multiple-fund accounting is not as common as it is in governmental-type activities.

Users and Uses of Financial Reports

Several similarities and differences between the users and uses of financial reports on a SLG's business-type activities, as compared with its governmental-type activities, are noted in GASB *Concepts Statement No. 1.*[22]

- The **users and uses** of governmental financial reports typically are **essentially the same** regardless of **whether** the activity is **business-type or governmental-type. However, the users and uses of financial reports for business-type** activities **may differ depending on whether the activity reports separately or as part of a broader general government.**

- The **uses** of financial reports of business-type activities generally **differ only in emphasis** from the uses of financial reports of governmental-type activities. Users of separate financial reports of **business-type** activities are concerned **primarily** with the **financial condition and results of operations** for that activity; they are **often not concerned with comparing actual results with budgeted amounts.**

- **Investors and creditors** are concerned **primarily** with **whether** the business-type activity is **generating, and will continue to generate, sufficient cash to meet debt service requirements.** And many investors and creditors are as concerned with **compliance with bond provisions** by business-type activities as they are about compliance by governmental-type activities.

- **Citizen groups and consumers** may use results of operations information primarily to **assess the reasonableness of user charges. Legislative and oversight** officials and executive branch officials review financial reports of business-type activities from **both cash flow and user charge reasonableness** perspectives. Legislative and oversight officials also use financial reports to **assess** the potential **need to subsidize the activity** with general governmental revenues, **or** the potential **to subsidize the general government** with business-type activity resources.

- Both citizen groups and legislative and oversight officials need information about **effectiveness, economy, and efficiency,** particularly because that information has an effect on user charges.

- Finally, all user groups may be concerned with the **relationship between the financial position and operating results of the business-type activity and** that of the **government as a whole—particularly if the business-type activity is subsidized by, or subsidizes, the general government.**

Objectives of Financial Reporting

Financial reporting **objectives** set forth what SLG financial statements ***should*** accomplish. GASB *Concepts Statement No. 1,* "Objectives of Financial Reporting," does ***not*** establish GAAP standards, however, but ***describes concepts to be used by the GASB as a framework*** for evaluating present standards and practices and for establishing financial reporting standards in the future.

The GASB notes that its financial reporting objectives are intended to describe broadly the nature of information needed to meet the needs of users of SLG external financial reports, giving consideration to the SLG environment. Further, the GASB concluded that there are ***no major differences in the financial reporting objectives of governmental-type and business-type activities, though the objectives may apply in differing degrees and with differing emphases*** to

---

[22] Ibid., sec. 100.151 and 100.153–.155, adapted.

governmental-type and business-type activities of SLGs. For example, budgetary comparisons may be less important in business-type activities, but cost of services information may be more important.

Briefly stated, the GASB concluded in its "Objectives" Concepts Statement that **accountability** is the "cornerstone"—the **paramount objective**—of government financial reporting and that **interperiod equity** is a significant part of accountability. Moreover, the GASB concluded that governmental financial reporting should provide information to assist users in (1) **assessing accountability** and in (2) **making economic, social, and political decisions.** Accordingly, **SLG financial reporting should provide:**

1. **A means of demonstrating the SLG's accountability that enables users to assess that accountability.** Specifically, the information provided should:
    a. Permit users to determine *whether* current-year *revenues were sufficient* to pay for the current year's services *and/or* whether *future-years' citizens must assume burdens for services previously provided.*
    b. *Demonstrate* the SLG's *budgetary accountability and compliance with other finance-related legal and contractual requirements.*
    c. *Assist users in assessing* the SLG's *service efforts, costs, and accomplishments.*
2. **Information necessary to evaluate the SLG's operating results for the period,** including information:
    a. About the *sources and uses of financial resources.*
    b. *On how* the SLG *financed* its *activities and met* its *cash requirements.*
    c. Necessary to determine **whether** the SLG's *financial condition improved or deteriorated* during the year.
3. *Information necessary to assess the level of SLG services and its ability to continue to finance its activities and meet its obligations,* including:
    a. Information about the SLG's *financial position and condition.*
    b. Information about the SLG's **physical and other nonfinancial resources having useful lives that extend beyond the current year**—including information that can be used to assess their *service potential.*
    c. **Disclosure** of (1) **legal and contractual restrictions** on the use of resources and (2) **risks of potential loss** of resources.[23]

THE GASB PRINCIPLES

As the GASB indicates in introducing its **Codification of Governmental Accounting and Financial Reporting Standards,** governmental accounting entails many of the same basic concepts, conventions, and characteristics as business accounting. However, the basic **objectives of business and government differ.** Not surprisingly then, the manner in which we report on each type of entity's progress toward its objectives also differs.

Consequently, the basic accounting and financial reporting principles for government entail many notable differences from those principles that apply to business activities. As noted earlier, those principles applicable to SLGs are established by the GASB. Many of the uniquenesses of governmental accounting and most of the GASB's guidance relate to the use of multiple **fund accounting entities and account groups** to account for and report upon a state or local gov-

---

[23] Ibid., sec. 100.176–.179.

ernment. Most other uniquenesses and GASB authoritative guidance are associated with the **"general government"** activities and transactions.

The **GASB** has to date *focused its attention primarily on "general government" activities and transactions* that are *accounted for in governmental (expendable) funds and in nonfund account groups* for "general government" fixed assets and long-term debt. The public enterprise and other business-type activities of state and local governments are accounted for in proprietary (nonexpendable) funds using business accounting methods. Indeed, FASB standards are applied in accounting for the business-type activities where relevant unless the GASB has issued a pronouncement applicable to the activity or transaction.

The twelve basic GASB principles are divided into the following seven groups for ease of discussion: (1) GAAP and Legal Compliance, (2) Fund Accounting, (3) Fixed Assets and Long-Term Liabilities, (4) Basis of Accounting, (5) The Budget and Budgetary Accounting, (6) Classification and Terminology, and (7) Financial Reporting.

GAAP and Legal Compliance

Governments must comply with the many varied legal and contractual requirements, regulations, restrictions, and agreements that affect their financial management and accounting; and such compliance must be demonstrable and reported upon regularly. Compliance is necessary even though legal requirements may be archaic, useless, or even detrimental to sound financial management. Governments should also prepare financial statements in conformity with generally accepted accounting principles (GAAP), which provide uniform minimum national standards of and guidelines to financial reporting.

Whereas business accounting systems must provide data both for GAAP reporting and for income tax reporting, the first GASB principle recognizes that *governmental accounting systems must provide data both for reporting in conformity with GAAP and for controlling and reporting on finance-related legal compliance matters.*

> **Principle 1**
> **Accounting and Reporting Capabilities**
>
> A governmental accounting system must make it possible both (a) to present fairly and with full disclosure the financial position and results of financial operations of the funds and account groups of the governmental unit in conformity with generally accepted accounting principles and (b) to determine and demonstrate compliance with finance-related legal and contractual provisions.

In some instances the only finance-related legal compliance provision is that the government prepare both its annual operating budget and its financial statements in conformity with GAAP. In such cases, legal compliance provisions and GAAP do not conflict, and the accounting system should be established on a GAAP basis.

In other instances certain finance-related legal provisions conflict with GAAP. *The most common GAAP-legal provision conflict* occurs where a government's *annual operating budget* is prepared on a *basis significantly different from GAAP.* For example:

- A school district may budget on the *cash basis,* under which revenues are not recorded until cash is received and expenditures are not recognized until cash is disbursed; or

- A city may budget on a cash basis but also consider *"encumbrances"*—the estimated cost of goods or services ordered but not yet received—to be expenditures for budgetary purposes, even though encumbrances do not represent expenditures or liabilities under GAAP.

Another common conflict occurs where federal or state **grantor agencies require** a local government to keep its grant accounting records on a **non-GAAP basis.**

The requirement that the accounting system must provide data for **both** legal compliance and GAAP reports does **not** necessitate two accounting systems. Rather, the accounts will be kept on one basis, and the system will also provide the additional data needed to convert the accounts to the other basis. Since GAAP statements typically are prepared only at year end, the accounts are usually kept on the budgetary (or other legal compliance basis) on which control is exercised daily and on which interim reports must be prepared.

GAAP statements are necessary to ensure proper reporting and a reasonable degree of comparability among the statements of governments across the nation. GAAP reporting also assures that the financial reports of all state and local governments, regardless of their legal provisions and customs, contain the same types of financial statements and disclosures for the same categories and types of funds and account groups, and are based on the same measurement and classification criteria.

Fund Accounting

The significance the GASB attributes to fund accounting—the most distinctive feature of governmental accounting—is indicated by the fact that three of its twelve principles directly concern this topic. These three principles deal with the need for fund accounting, definition of the term "fund," and the fund and account group categories (Principle 2); the types of funds recommended for state and local governments (Principle 3); and the need to use an appropriate number of fund entities (Principle 4). Understanding the fund structure, model, and interrelationships described in these principles is essential to mastering the subject matter in this text.

"Fund"; Fund and Account Group Categories

The second GASB principle is

> **Principle 2**
> **Fund Accounting Systems**
>
> [1] Governmental accounting systems should be organized and operated on a fund basis. [2] A fund is defined as a fiscal and accounting entity with a self-balancing set of accounts recording cash and other financial resources, together with all related liabilities and residual equities or balances, and changes therein, which are segregated for the purpose of carrying on specific activities or attaining certain objectives in accordance with special regulations, restrictions, or limitations.

In discussing this principle the GASB notes that the diverse nature of government operations and the necessity of ensuring legal compliance preclude recording and summarizing all governmental financial transactions and balances in a single accounting entity. Thus, from an accounting and financial management viewpoint, a governmental unit is a combination of several distinctly different fiscal and accounting entities, each having a separate set of accounts and functioning independently of the other funds and account groups (see Figure 2-3).

In broad terms a single fund accounting entity is somewhat like a business accounting entity. Each **business accounting entity** has a self-balancing set of accounts—sufficient to capture all the reported attributes for the whole business

Figure 2-3   **ACCOUNTING ENTITIES OF STATE AND LOCAL GOVERNMENTS**

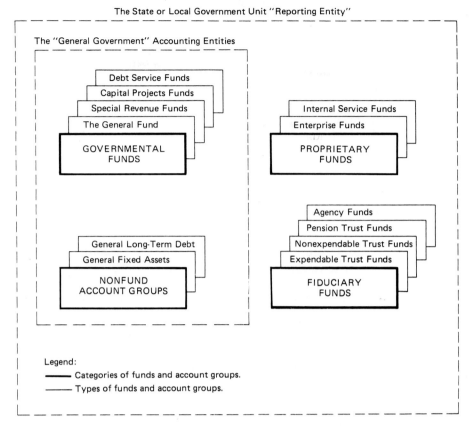

The State or Local Government Unit "Reporting Entity"

The "General Government" Accounting Entities

Debt Service Funds
Capital Projects Funds
Special Revenue Funds
The General Fund
GOVERNMENTAL FUNDS

Internal Service Funds
Enterprise Funds
PROPRIETARY FUNDS

General Long-Term Debt
General Fixed Assets
NONFUND ACCOUNT GROUPS

Agency Funds
Pension Trust Funds
Nonexpendable Trust Funds
Expendable Trust Funds
FIDUCIARY FUNDS

Legend:
——— Categories of funds and account groups.
——— Types of funds and account groups.

Notes:
1. Each fund and account group is an independent accounting entity with a separate self-balancing set of accounts. (There is no single central accounting entity for the state or local government.)
2. As discussed later at "Financial Reporting," financial statements are prepared for each fund (individual fund statements), for all funds of each type (combining statements), and for the government reporting entity (combined statements).

and all its transactions. Likewise, *each fund* of a government has a self-balancing set of accounts sufficient to capture all the attributes—that are reported for a government fund of this type—of the portion of a government's activities and resources that are accounted for in each particular fund. A **key difference** is that one accounting entity is used to account for all the activities and resources of a business, whereas **each fund accounting entity is used to account for only a certain subset of a government's activities and resources.**

Likewise, *each business* accounting entity has its own journals, its own ledger, its own trial balance, and its own financial statements. Similarly, for *each fund* of a government there are separate journals, a separate ledger(s) and trial balance, and separate financial statements are prepared and presented.

Four distinct categories of accounting entities—three categories of funds and the nonfund account groups—are employed in governmental accounting. A few points discussed regarding the state and local government environment should help explain the categories of funds and account groups that are used and the nature of those accounting entities.

First, recall that a general-purpose unit of government has a "dual nature." Some of its activities are "general government" in nature; others are "business-type" activities. Next, recall that the "general government" activities typically have unique sources of financing such as taxes and grants. The allocation of these resources to various purposes and the control of general government activities focuses heavily upon sources and uses of financial resources. The business-type activities function and may be controlled much like their business counterparts. The information needs of financial report users with respect to these activities are similar to those for similar business activities.

Consistent with these key points, two broad **categories** of funds are used to account for state and local government activities and resources (other than those held in a fiduciary capacity).

1. *Governmental funds* are used to account for the sources, uses, and balances of a government's expendable "general government" financial resources (and the related current liabilities). In their simplest form governmental funds are in essence segregations of general government working capital according to the purpose(s) for which it is to be used.

    The *accounting equation* for a simple governmental fund is essentially the *working capital* equation. *Expendable assets are assigned to the several governmental funds according to the purposes for which they may (or must) be expended. Current liabilities are accounted for in the fund from which the expenditures giving rise to the liabilities were made, and thus from which they are to be paid. The difference between governmental fund assets and liabilities, the fund equity, is known as the "Fund Balance."* In sum, the accounting equation of a simple **governmental fund** is:

    Current Assets − Current Liabilities = Fund Balance

    Governmental fund accounting *measures fund financial position and changes in fund financial position—sources, uses, and balances of fund financial resources* (working capital)—*rather than net income.* The statement of revenues, expenditures, and changes in fund balance is the primary governmental fund operating statement. Indeed, it is more similar to a statement of cash flows than to an income statement.

2. *Proprietary funds* are used to account for a government's continuing business-type organizations and activities. *All assets, liabilities, equities, revenues, expenses, and transfers pertaining to these business (and quasi-business) organizations and activities are accounted for through proprietary funds.* In other words, the **proprietary fund** accounting equation is:

    Current Assets + Noncurrent (including fixed) Assets =
    Current Liabilities + Long-Term Liabilities + Contributed Capital +
    Retained Earnings.

    Proprietary fund accounting therefore *measures net income, financial position, and cash flows.* Most of the generally accepted accounting *principles* here *are those applicable to similar private businesses.*

3. *Fiduciary funds* are used to *account for assets held by a government in a trustee or agency capacity,* whether for individuals, private organizations, other governmental units, or other funds of the government. Expendable Trust Fund accounting parallels that for governmental funds; Nonexpendable Trust Fund and Pension Trust Fund accounting is similar to that for proprietary funds. Agency Funds are purely custodial (assets equal liabilities), and Agency Fund accounting is concerned only with recording the changes in fund assets held for others.

Note that **the governmental (and expendable trust) funds accounting equations do not provide for fixed assets used in "general government" activities or long-term debt incurred for those activities.** Only proprietary fund fixed assets and long-term debt are accounted for in the proprietary funds. However, significant amounts of fixed assets typically are used in general government activities and significant amounts of long-term debt are related to those activities.

Accountability for these "general government" fixed assets and long-term liabilities is maintained in two separate nonfund accounting entities called account groups.

4. **Account groups** are essentially lists of a government's **"general government" fixed assets,** called "general fixed assets" **(General Fixed Assets Account Group)** and its **"general government" long-term liabilities,** known as "general long-term debt **(General Long-Term Debt Account Group).** Offsetting accounts, counterbalancing the list of general fixed assets or of general long-term debt, complete the accounting equation of each account group. Consequently, the accounting equation for the **General Fixed Assets Account Group** is:

Fixed Assets = Investment in General Fixed Assets

The accounting equation for the **General Long-Term Debt Account Group** is:

Amount Available in Debt Service Funds to Retire General Long-Term Debt	+	Amount to be Provided in the Future to Retire General Long-Term Debt	=	Long-Term Debt Payable

The government's "general fixed assets"—all fixed assets not related to (and hence not accounted for in) proprietary funds or Trust Funds—are *not financial resources available to finance governmental fund expenditures.* Similarly, the unmatured principal of a government's "general obligation long-term debt"—long-term liabilities not related to (and hence not accounted for in) proprietary funds or Trust Funds—does not require a governmental fund expenditure (use of financial resources) until the liabilities mature and must be paid, perhaps many years in the future. Thus, neither general fixed assets nor general long-term debt are accounted for in the governmental funds, but in nonfund account groups. These account groups are not funds since they do not contain or account for expendable financial resources and related liabilities. Rather, they are self-balancing sets of accounting records of the "general government" fixed assets and long-term debt, respectively.

The *governmental funds and* the *nonfund account groups* are the **"general government"** accounting entities—the most unique feature of governmental accounting—whereas the proprietary funds and fiduciary funds are used to account for government organizations and relationships that are similar to those in the private sector. Only those assets, liabilities, transactions, and events that clearly relate specifically to the proprietary funds and fiduciary funds are recorded in those fund categories. *All other* assets, liabilities, transactions, and events are recorded in the "general government" accounting entities—the governmental funds and account groups.

Further, given the governmental fund accounting equation, *the "operating results" of governmental funds*—and of the "general government"—are necessarily **measured in terms of sources, uses, and balances of net expendable**

financial resources rather than net income. Recognize that in most situations this means net working capital increases, decreases, and balances, rather than net income. Since the nonfund account groups do not account for sources, uses, and balances of net expendable financial resources—but for "general government" fixed assets and unmatured long-term debt—changes in their accounts do *not* directly affect the "operating results" of the "general government."

Types of Funds

The third GASB principle recognizes seven specific types of funds within the three broad fund categories. As you study Principle 3, note that the governmental funds are distinguished from one another by the purpose or purposes for which the financial resources accounted for in each fund may or must be used. These distinctions are highlighted in Figure 2-4. Note also that the primary distinction between the two types of proprietary funds is who the "customers" are—i.e., the general public for Enterprise Funds and other departments or agencies of the government (or other governments) for Internal Service Funds.

Principle 3
Types of Funds

The following types of funds should be used by state and local governments:

Governmental Funds

1. *The General Fund*—to account for all financial resources except those required to be accounted for in another fund.
2. *Special Revenue Funds*—to account for the proceeds of specific revenue sources (other than expendable trusts or for major capital projects) that are legally restricted to expenditure for specified purposes.
3. *Capital Projects Funds*—to account for financial resources to be used for the acquisition or construction of major capital facilities (other than those financed by proprietary funds and Trust Funds).
4. *Debt Service Funds*—to account for the accumulation of resources for, and the payment of, general long-term debt principal and interest.

Proprietary Funds

5. *Enterprise Funds*—to account for operations (a) that are financed and operated in a manner similar to private business enterprises—where the intent of the governing body is that the costs (expenses, including depreciation) of providing goods or services to the general public on a continuing basis be financed or recovered primarily through user charges; or (b) where the governing body has decided that periodic determination of revenues earned, expenses incurred, and/or net income is appropriate for capital maintenance, public policy, management control, accountability, or other purposes.
6. *Internal Service Funds*—to account for the financing of goods or services provided by one department or agency to other departments or agencies of the governmental unit, or to other governmental units, on a cost-reimbursement basis.

Fiduciary Funds

7. *Trust and Agency Funds*—to account for assets held by a governmental unit in a trustee capacity or as an agent for individuals, private organizations, other governmental units, and/or other funds. These include (a) *Expendable Trust Funds,* (b) *Nonexpendable Trust Funds,* (c) *Pension Trust Funds, and* (d) *Agency Funds.*

As noted earlier, fund accounting evolved because portions of a government's resources may be restricted as to use. Restrictions may stem from grantor

Figure 2-4

**GOVERNMENTAL FUND TYPES: CLASSIFICATION AND
TYPICAL TYPES OF EXPENDITURES**

I. Classification

Purposes for Which General Government Financial Resources May or Must be Used	Governmental Fund Type to be Used
Available for general SLG uses	General Fund (GF)
For specific operating purposes or activities	Special Revenue Fund (SRF)
Acquiring major general government capital facilities	Capital Projects Fund (CPF)
Payment of general long-term debt principal and interest	Debt Service Fund (DSF)

II. Typical Types of Expenditures

	GF	SRFs	CPFs	DSFs
Operating (e.g., salaries, rent, utilities)	XXX	XXX		
Capital outlay	X	X	XXX	
Debt service	X	X	X	XXX

Legend

XXX = Most expenditures of this type
  X = May have some of this type, usually minor

---

or donor stipulations, laws, contractual agreements, actions by the legislature or council, or other sources. The several fund types recommended by the GASB vary primarily in accordance with (1) whether the resources of the fund may be expended (governmental funds) or are to be maintained on a self-sustaining basis (proprietary funds) and (2) the extent of budgetary control normally employed. Furthermore, the various types of governmental and similar fiduciary funds differ principally according to the uses to which the resources accounted for therein may be put: (1) general operating (unrestricted); (2) special purpose or project, such as for certain services or for capital outlay or debt service; or (3) merely managed for and remitted to those for whom the government is acting as a trustee or agent.

The types of fund and nonfund accounting entities recommended by the GASB are summarized in Figure 2-5; typical governmental and similar fiduciary fund resource flow patterns are indicated in Figure 2-6. Note the purposes of each fund type and account group, and that a state or local government will have **only one** General Fund, General Fixed Assets Account Group, and General Long-Term Debt Account Group. It may have **one, none, several, or many** of the **other** types of funds. Note also that at least one chapter of this text is devoted to each fund type and to the nonfund account groups.

Number of Funds

Finally, the GASB recognizes the need both to maintain those funds necessary to appropriately manage and demonstrate accountability for government resources and to avoid excessive fragmentation of the financial report by establishing unnecessary funds. Accordingly, the GASB **cautions against using too few or too many funds** in its fourth principle:

Figure 2-5

**STATE AND LOCAL GOVERNMENT (SLG) FUNDS,
ACCOUNT GROUPS, ACCOUNTING EQUATIONS, AND STATEMENTS**

The "General Government" Funds and Account Groups		The Proprietary Funds

The Governmental Funds		The Proprietary Funds
General Special Revenue Capital Projects Debt Service	$CA - CL = FB$	Enterprise Internal Service $CA + FA = CL + LTD + CC + RE$
<u>Statements</u> Balance Sheet Statement of Revenues, Expenditures, and Changes in Fund Balances—GAAP Basis If budgeted annually, a budgetary comparison statement: Statement of Revenues, Expenditures, and Changes in Fund Balances—Budget and Actual—Budgetary Basis		<u>Statements</u> Balance Sheet Statement of Revenues, Expenses, and Changes in Retained Earnings/Equity Statement of Cash Flows

The Account Groups		The Fiduciary Funds	
<u>General Fixed Assets</u> GFA = Investment in GFA	<u>General Long-Term Debt</u> Amount Available in DSF + Amount to be Provided in Future Years = GLTD	Agency Nonexpendable Trust Expendable Trust Pension Trust	Assets = Liabilities Proprietary Governmental Proprietary
<u>Statement</u> Balance Sheet (Changes Disclosed in Notes)			

Adapted with permission from Robert J. Freeman and Craig D. Shoulders, *Governmental Accounting and Financial Reporting Principles* (New York: AICPA, 1993) pp. 3–10.

**Principle 4
Number of Funds**

[1] Governmental units should establish and maintain those funds required by [a] law and [b] sound financial administration. [2] Only the minimum number of funds consistent with legal and operating requirements should be established, however, since unnecessary funds result in inflexibility, undue complexity, and inefficient financial administration.

In sum, the government

- must establish and maintain those funds required by law or contractual agreement, just as it must observe other finance-related legal and contractual provisions.
- should maintain other funds that assist in ensuring effective control over and accountability for its finances.

However, maintaining too many funds is almost as detrimental as maintaining too few funds.

Selecting the specific funds a government needs requires professional judgment, and the funds in use should be reviewed from time to time to ensure that all funds needed are in use and that no unneeded funds are in use. In amplify-

Figure 2-6

TYPICAL RESOURCE FLOW PATTERN
GOVERNMENTAL AND SIMILAR FIDUCIARY FUNDS*

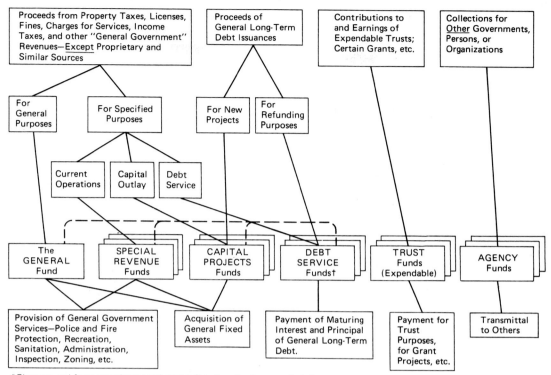

*Flows to and from proprietary and similar fiduciary funds are excluded.

†As indicated by − − −, resources may be transferred to the Debt Service Funds from other funds; also, General Long-Term Debt may be serviced directly from other governmental funds.

ing the fourth principle the GASB offers the following guidance to the exercise of professional judgment in determining the fund structure of a state or local government:

> Some governmental units often need several funds of a single type, such as Special Revenue or Capital Projects Funds. On the other hand, many governmental units do not need funds of all types at any given time. Some find it necessary to use only a few of the specified types. For example, many small governmental units do not require Internal Service Funds. Moreover, [1] resources restricted to expenditure for purposes normally financed from the General Fund may be accounted for through the General Fund provided that applicable legal requirements can be appropriately satisfied; and [2] use of Special Revenue Funds is not required unless they are legally mandated. [3] Debt Service Funds are required if they are legally mandated and/or if financial resources are being accumulated for principal and interest payments maturing in future years.

> The general rule is to establish the minimum number of separate funds consistent with legal specifications, operational requirements, and the principles of fund classification discussed above. Using too many funds causes inflexibility and undue complexity in budgeting, accounting, and other phases of financial management, and is best avoided in the interests of efficient and economical financial administration.[24]

[24] Ibid., sec. 1300.107 and 1300.108.

Caution must be exercised in opting to account for resources restricted for current operating or debt service purposes in the General Fund. These resources typically are accounted for in Special Revenue and Debt Service Funds, respectively, to ensure that applicable legal requirements are met. Inadequate accountability may result when these resources are accounted for in the General Fund in governments with less than excellent accounting systems. Accordingly, it is assumed hereafter that these options are **not** exercised and that restricted resources are accounted for in Special Revenue Funds and Debt Service Funds, for example, rather than in the General Fund.

Transaction Analysis and Fund Accounting

Understanding the nature and interrelationships of the funds and account groups is critical to understanding the remainder of the principles and, indeed, to understanding governmental accounting. Thus, it is useful at this point to examine fund accounting at a practical level to assure that the way the fund accounting model works is understood. To do this, review the analyses of the transactions described in Figure 2-7. Pay particular attention to the first eight transactions, which relate to "general government" activities. We discuss the first three transactions to help assure that you understand the transaction analysis. Review the others on your own to solidify your understanding of the model.

In **Transaction 1:**

1. $8,000 of General Fund cash is used (hence the decrease in General Fund current assets).
2. The fixed asset acquired does not "fit" in the General Fund accounting equation because fixed assets are **not** current assets and thus are **not** part of fund working capital.
3. Since General Fund current assets decreased and its current liabilities did not change, the transaction decreased the General Fund Fund Balance by $8,000.
4. This decrease in General Fund Fund Balance will be reported as an expenditure in the General Fund operating statement. (Recall that this statement is somewhat similar in function to a cash flow statement. Similar transactions are reported as decreases in a cash flow statement as well.)
5. The fixed asset is added to the General Fixed Asset Account Group (list of fixed assets) and the offsetting account is increased by a corresponding amount.

Two general government accounting entities also are affected by **Transaction 2:**

1. The cash received from issuing the bonds is to be used to finance construction of a major general government capital facility (fire station). Therefore, this cash increases the amount of current assets in the Capital Projects Fund.
2. The bonds payable are long-term debt and thus do not "fit" in the accounting equations of any of the governmental funds because long-term debt is not part of working capital.
3. Since Capital Projects Fund assets increased $1,000,000 and its liabilities did not change, this transaction increases the Capital Projects Fund Fund Balance by $1,000,000. The increase in Fund Balance from issuing the bonds must be reported in the Capital Projects Fund operating statement.
4. Bond proceeds are not revenues. Accordingly, the increase will be reported in a separate "Other Financing Sources" category of Fund Balance increases.

ANALYSIS OF TRANSACTIONS

Figure 2-7

	General Fund			Capital Projects Fund			Debt Service Fund			General Fixed Asset Account Group		General Long-Term Debt Account Group		
	CA −	CL =	FB	CA −	CL =	FB	CA −	CL =	FB	FA =	Investment in GFA	Amount to be Provided +	Amount Available =	Long-Term Liabilities
1	($8,000)		($8,000)							$8,000	$8,000			
2	$1,000,000		$1,000,000	$1,000,000		$1,000,000						$1,000,000		$1,000,000
3	$1,000,000	$1,000,000												
4					$300,000	($300,000)				$300,000	$300,000			
5	$8,000		$8,000							($20,000)	($20,000)			
6	($100,000)		($100,000)				$100,000		$100,000			($100,000)	$100,000	
7							($80,000)		($80,000)			$30,000	($80,000)	($50,000)
8	($1,030,000)	($1,000,000)	($30,000)											

Enterprise Fund

	CA +	NCA −	CL −	LTL =	CC +	RE
9	($8,000)	$8,000				
10	$1,000,000			$1,000,000		

Transactions

1 Purchased a general government fixed asset with General Fund cash, $8,000.

2 Issued $1,000,000 of bonds to finance construction of a fire station.

3 Issued a $1,000,000 six-month note to provide temporary financing for the General Fund.

4 Received a bill from the contractor for $300,000 of construction costs on the fire station.

5 Sold a general fixed asset for $8,000; its original cost was $20,000.

6 Transferred $100,000 of General Fund cash to the fund from which the fire station bonds will be repaid.

7 $50,000 of the fire station bonds and $30,000 of interest matured and were paid.

8 The six-month General Fund note matured and was paid along with $30,000 of interest.

9 Purchased a fixed asset for an Enterprise Fund with Enterprise Fund cash, $8,000.

10 Issued $1,000,000 of Enterprise Fund revenue bonds to finance plant expansion.

Legend

CA	Current Assets
CC	Contributed Capital
CL	Current Liabilities
FA	Fixed Assets
FB	Fund Balance
GFA	General Fixed Assets
LTL	Long-Term Liabilities
NCA	Noncurrent Assets (including fixed assets)
RE	Retained Earnings

49

(Again, note the similarity of the operating statement to a cash flow statement —in which such transactions are reported as cash flows from financing activities.)

5. The bonds payable are added to the General Long-Term Debt Account Group (list of general long-term debt). An offsetting balance is recorded in the "Amount to be Provided in Future Years to Retire Debt Principal" account.

Finally, in **Transaction 3,** note the differences in the effects of issuing long-term debt and issuing short-term general government debt. In this particular case, the borrowing was for General Fund purposes and affects the General Fund as follows:

1. Current assets are increased by $1,000,000.
2. Current liabilities are increased by $1,000,000.
3. Fund Balance is unaffected because the changes in Current Assets and Current Liabilities of the fund were equal, i.e., working capital did not change.
4. Consequently, this transaction has no affect on the General Fund operating statement.

Note that no other funds or account groups are affected by Transaction 3.

Observe the effects of the remaining transactions (4–10) in Figure 2-7. Understanding the transaction analyses presented in Figure 2-7 indicates that you are getting a firm grip on the basics of the governmental accounting model. Indeed, if you understand the model, much of the guidance set forth in Principles 5–7, for example, will be intuitively obvious. Moreover, you will be well on your way to understanding the "general government" accounting methods discussed in Chapters 3–9.

Fixed Assets and Long-Term Liabilities

The GASB sets forth three principles of accounting for government fixed assets and long-term liabilities within the fund and account group structure specified in principles 2 and 3. These three principles relate to (1) distinguishing and accounting differently for "specific fund" and "general" fixed assets and long-term liabilities, (2) valuation of fixed assets, and (3) depreciation of fixed assets.

"Specific Fund" vs. "General" Fixed Assets and Long-Term Liabilities

As noted earlier, in a fund accounting environment, **specific fund** fixed assets and long-term debt, which are accounted for in the appropriate funds, must be distinguished from those related to the government in its entirety, the **"general government,"** which are accounted for in the **account groups.** The fifth GASB principle emphasizes this important distinction:

> **Principle 5**
> **Accounting for Fixed Assets and Long-Term Liabilities**
>
> A clear distinction should be made between (a) fund fixed assets and general fixed assets and (b) fund long-term liabilities and general long-term debt.
>
> a. Fixed assets related to specific proprietary funds or Trust Funds should be accounted for through those funds. All other fixed assets of a governmental unit should be accounted for through the General Fixed Assets Account Group.
> b. Long-term liabilities of proprietary funds and Trust Funds should be accounted for through those funds. All other unmatured general long-term liabilities of the

governmental unit, including special assessment debt for which the government is obligated in some manner, should be accounted for through the General Long-Term Debt Account Group.

Thus, the term *"General Fixed Assets"* means **"general government fixed assets,"** and *"General Long-Term Debt"* means **unmatured "general government long-term liabilities."**

In discussing the reasons underlying the need to distinguish fund and nonfund fixed assets and long-term debt the GASB notes:

> **General fixed assets** do **not** represent **financial resources available for expenditure,** but are items for which financial resources have been used and for which accountability should be maintained. They are not assets of any fund but of the governmental unit as an instrumentality. Their inclusion in the financial statements of a governmental fund would increase the fund balance, which could mislead users of the fund balance sheet. *The primary purposes for governmental fund accounting are to reflect its revenues and expenditures—the sources and uses of its financial resources—and its assets, the related liabilities, and the net financial resources available for subsequent appropriation and expenditure.* These objectives can most readily be achieved by excluding general fixed assets from the governmental fund accounts and recording them in a separate GFAAG.
>
> The **general long-term debt** of a state or local government is secured by the general credit and revenue-raising powers of the government rather than by the assets acquired or specific fund resources. Further, just as general fixed assets do not represent financial resources available for appropriation and expenditure, the **unmatured principal of general long-term debt does not require current appropriation and expenditure of governmental fund financial resources.** To include it as a governmental fund liability would be misleading and dysfunctional to the current period management control (for example, budgeting) and accountability functions.[25]

Further, the GASB principles give governments the **option** to record (or not record) *"infrastructure"* or "public domain" *general* fixed assets (but **not** specific fund fixed assets) in the *General Fixed Assets Account Group:*

> **Reporting** public domain or *"infrastructure"* fixed assets—roads, bridges, curbs and gutters, streets and sidewalks, drainage systems, lighting systems, and similar items that are *immovable and of value only to the governmental unit*—is *optional.*[26]

The theoretical and practical rationale for the infrastructure fixed asset capitalization option is discussed further in Chapter 9.

Valuation of Fixed Assets

The sixth principle specifies that *cost* is the basic valuation method for both fund fixed assets and general fixed assets:

> **Principle 6**
> **Valuation of Fixed Assets**
>
> Fixed assets should be accounted for at cost or, if the cost is not practicably determinable, at estimated cost. Donated fixed assets should be recorded at their estimated fair value at the time received.

---

[25] Ibid., sec. 1400.107 and 1500.104, emphasis added.
[26] Ibid., sec. 1400.109, emphasis added.

Estimated cost (at the time of acquisition) is allowed because some governments have not maintained adequate fixed asset records before beginning to report in conformity with generally accepted accounting principles. This principle (1) allows a government to estimate the original cost of ***both*** general fixed assets ***and*** specific fund assets for which costs cannot reasonably be determined but (2) requires that its other fixed assets and all fixed assets acquired subsequently be recorded at cost (or estimated value, if donated).

Depreciation

Accounting for depreciation of a government's fixed assets is the subject of the seventh principle:

> **Principle 7**
> **Depreciation of Fixed Assets**
>
> a. Depreciation of general fixed assets should not be recorded in the accounts of governmental funds. Depreciation of general fixed assets may be recorded in cost accounting systems or calculated for cost finding analyses; and accumulated depreciation may be recorded in the General Fixed Assets Account Group.
> b. Depreciation of fixed assets accounted for in a proprietary fund should be recorded in the accounts of that fund. Depreciation is also recognized in those Trust Funds where expenses, net income, and/or capital maintenance are measured.

Thus, Principle 7 is consistent with the governmental fund and proprietary fund accounting models discussed earlier. The essence of this principle is that (1) depreciation expense ***should*** be recorded in those funds where expenses are accounted for—the proprietary funds and similar trust funds—but (2) depreciation expense should ***not*** be recorded in those funds where expenditures (not expenses) are accounted for—the governmental funds and similar trust funds—since depreciation expense is not an expenditure.

The GASB rationale for this principle is as follows:

> **Depreciation** accounting is an important element of the income-determination process. Accordingly, it **is recognized in the proprietary funds and in those trust funds where expenses, net income, and/or capital maintenance are measured.**
>
> **Expenditures, not expense, are measured in governmental fund accounting.** To record depreciation expense in governmental funds would inappropriately mix two fundamentally different measurements, expenses, and expenditures. General fixed asset acquisitions ***require*** the use of governmental fund financial resources and are recorded as expenditures. General fixed asset sale proceeds ***provide*** governmental fund financial resources. Depreciation expense is neither a source nor a use of governmental fund financial resources, and thus is not properly recorded in the accounts of such funds.[27]

Basis of Accounting

Consistent with its distinction between governmental fund accounting methods and those for proprietary funds, the GASB specifies different methods of applying the accrual concept in accounting for governmental funds and proprietary funds.

---

[27] Ibid., sec. 1400.115–116, emphasis added.

Principle 8
Accrual Basis in Governmental Accounting

The modified accrual or accrual basis of accounting, as appropriate, should be utilized in measuring financial position and operating results.

a. ***Governmental fund*** revenues and expenditures should be recognized on the modified accrual basis. Revenues should be recognized in the accounting period in which they become available and measurable. Expenditures should be recognized in the accounting period in which the fund liability is incurred, if measurable, except for unmatured interest on [and principal of] general long-term debt, which should be recognized when due.[28]

b. ***Proprietary fund*** revenues and expenses should be recognized on the accrual basis. Revenues should be recognized in the accounting period in which they are earned and become measurable; expenses should be recognized in the period incurred, if measurable.

c. ***Fiduciary fund*** revenues and expenses or expenditures (as appropriate) should be recognized on the basis consistent with the fund's accounting measurement objective. Nonexpendable Trust and Pension Trust Funds should be accounted for on the accrual basis; Expendable Trust Funds should be accounted for on the modified accrual basis. Agency Fund assets and liabilities should be accounted for on the modified accrual basis.

d. ***Transfers*** should be recognized in the accounting period in which the interfund receivable and payable arise.

The essence of this principle is that, ***in governmental accounting:***

- The ***"accrual"*** basis refers to recognition of revenues and expenses of ***proprietary*** funds and similar (***proprietary-type***) trust funds ***as in business accounting.***

- The ***"modified accrual"*** basis refers to recognition of revenues and expenditures using the ***"flows of financial resources"*** measurement focus of ***governmental*** funds and similar (***governmental-type***) trust funds:

  1. ***Revenues*** must be ***"available"***—collectible within the period or soon enough thereafter to pay liabilities incurred for expenditures of the period, ***as well as levied for the period or earned and measurable***—or must be deferred (recorded as "deferred revenues") and recognized as revenues when "available." (Thus, revenues may be recognized later in governmental-type funds than in proprietary-type funds.)

  2. ***Expenditures*** (not expenses)—for operations, capital outlay, and debt service—are recognized (1) ***when*** operating or capital outlay ***liabilities to be paid from governmental-type funds are incurred and (2) when "general government" debt service*** (principal and interest) ***payments on long-term debt are due.***

- ***"Transfers"*** of resources among funds (***"interfund transfers"***) should be recorded ***when they occur***—when the interfund payable and receivable arise—even though cash (or noncash assets) has not been remitted from one fund to another fund.

---

[28] The basis of accounting for governmental fund operating statements will be changed upon implementation of GASB Statement 11, "Measurement Focus and Basis of Accounting—Governmental Fund Operating Statements" (GASB, May 1990). However, these changes **must *not be applied*** by a government ***until the* statement becomes effective.** Statement 11 was originally scheduled to become effective for fiscal years ending after June 15, 1995. However, in late 1992 the **GASB voted to defer** the **effective date indefinitely** to permit the GASB to complete related projects that are to be implemented concurrently with Statement 11. The key aspects of Statement 11 are discussed in Chapter 10.

Figure 2-8

"EXPENSES" vs. "EXPENDITURES"

Expenses *(Costs Expired)*	**Expenditures** *(Financial Resources Expended)*
Operating: Salaries Utilities Etc. **Capital:** Depreciation **Debt Service:** Interest	**Operating:** Salaries Utilities Etc. **Capital:** Capital Outlay **Debt Service:** Interest Long-term debt retirement

Observations

1. **Operating.** Operating expenses and expenditures often are identical, but may differ somewhat because of accrual or allocation differences in expense and expenditure measurement standards.
2. **Capital.** The entire cost of fixed assets acquired during the period is accounted for as a capital outlay expenditure, whereas a portion of all exhaustible fixed asset costs incurred to date is allocated to each period as depreciation expense.
3. **Debt Service.** Interest is both an expenditure and an expense, whereas long-term debt retirement is an expenditure but not an expense.

The distinction between "expenditures" and "expenses" is extremely important in governmental accounting. ***Expenses—the measurement focus of proprietary fund accounting***—are ***"costs expired"*** during a period, including depreciation and other allocations, as in business accounting. ***Expenditures— the measurement focus of governmental fund accounting***—are ***"financial resources expended"*** during a period for operations, capital outlay, and long-term debt principal retirement and interest. With the exception of long-term debt principal retirement expenditures, expenditures reflect the cost incurred to ***acquire*** goods or services, whereas expenses reflect the cost of goods or services ***used***. This important distinction is illustrated in Figure 2-8.

In sum, the **"modified accrual"** method is, in essence, the accrual method of accounting for the ***flows and balances of financial resources*** of governmental funds and similar trust funds, as contrasted with the cash basis of accounting. The term **"accrual"** basis refers to accounting for ***revenues earned and expenses incurred,*** as for business enterprises, in proprietary funds and similar trust funds. The application of the modified accrual and accrual bases is discussed and illustrated throughout this text.

The Budget and Budgetary Accounting

The importance of budgeting, budgetary control, and budgetary accountability in the governmental-type activities environment is recognized in the ninth GASB principle:

> **Principle 9**
> **Budgeting, Budgetary Control, and Budgetary Reporting**
>
> a. An annual budget(s) should be adopted by every governmental unit.
> b. The accounting system should provide the basis for appropriate budgetary control.
> c. Budgetary comparisons should be included in the appropriate financial statements and schedules for governmental funds for which an annual budget has been adopted.

Principle 9 is essentially a ***"bridge"*** between

- ***Principle 1***—which requires that governmental accounting systems make it possible to determine and demonstrate compliance with finance-related legal and contractual provisions—such as the annual operating budget(s)—as well as report in conformity with GAAP; and

- *Principle 12*—discussed later, which requires presentation of financial statements on both the budgetary basis and the GAAP basis, as well as an explanation and reconciliation of the differences between the budgetary and GAAP bases.

As noted earlier, the annual operating budget of a government—which typically includes the General, Special Revenue, and Debt Service Funds—is a legally enacted plan of fund financial operations. Indeed, as discussed earlier, it is a key allocation mechanism in the general government environment. Its revenue estimates provide legal authority for the levy of taxes, charges for services, fines, and so on for the year. Its appropriations both legally authorize and legally limit the expenditures to be incurred during the year. Thus, *budgetary accounting control and accountability are essential aspects of governmental accounting and financial reporting.*

Furthermore, governments often budget on a *non-GAAP* basis. Some governments budget revenues and expenditures on a cash receipts and cash disbursements basis, for example, and some consider "encumbrances"—the estimated costs of goods and services ordered but not yet received—to be expenditures for budgetary purposes, even though encumbrances are not considered expenditures under GAAP. Since many governments budget on a non-GAAP basis, *it is important to identify a government's "budgetary basis." If the budgetary basis differs significantly from the GAAP basis,* a government must (1) clearly distinguish its budgetary basis from the GAAP basis; (2) maintain budgetary accounting control during the year on the budgetary basis and also accumulate the additional data needed for GAAP reporting; and (3) prepare financial statements on both bases, and explain and reconcile the differences between the budgetary and GAAP bases. Budgeting, budgetary accounting control, and budgetary reporting are considered in depth in Chapter 3 and in the chapters that deal with funds for which budgeting, budgetary control, and budgetary accountability are particularly important.

Classification and Terminology

The needs (1) to classify accounting data in different ways to meet different information needs, (2) to distinguish internal shifts of resources and long-term borrowings from revenues, expenditures, and expenses, and (3) for consistent classification and terminology are the subjects of the tenth and eleventh GASB principles.

Transfer, Revenue, Expenditure, and Expense Classification

The tenth GASB principle establishes the broad categories of increases and decreases to be reported in SLG operating statements. It also establishes the revenue and expenditure or expense classifications that may be used. Principle 10 states:

> **Principle 10**
> **Transfer, Revenue, Expenditure, and Expense Account Classification**
>   a. Interfund transfers and proceeds of general long-term debt issues should be classified separately from fund revenues and expenditures or expenses.
>   b. Governmental fund revenues should be classified by fund and source. Expenditures should be classified by fund, function (or program), organization unit, activity, character, and principal classes of objects.

c. Proprietary fund revenues and expenses should be classified in essentially the same manner as those of similar business organizations, functions, or activities.

Interfund Transactions

Four types of interfund transactions commonly encountered in state and local government are defined as follows:

1. **Quasi-External Transactions.** Transactions that would be treated as revenues, expenditures, or expenses if they involved organizations **external** to the governmental unit—e.g., payments in lieu of taxes from an Enterprise Fund to the General Fund; Internal Service Fund billings to departments; routine employer contributions from the General Fund to a Pension Trust Fund; and routine service charges for inspection, engineering, utilities, or similar services provided by a department financed from one fund to a department financed from another fund—should be **accounted for as revenues, expenditures, or expenses in the funds involved.**

2. **Reimbursements.** Transactions which constitute reimbursements of a fund for expenditures or expenses initially made from it which are properly applicable to another fund—e.g., an expenditure properly chargeable to a Special Revenue Fund was initially made from the General Fund, which is subsequently reimbursed—should be recorded as **expenditures or expenses (as appropriate) in the reimbursing fund and as reductions of the expenditure or expense in the fund that it reimbursed.**

3. **Residual Equity Transfers. Nonrecurring or nonroutine transfers of equity between funds**—e.g., contribution of Enterprise Fund or Internal Service Fund capital by the General Fund, subsequent return of all or part of such contribution to the General Fund, and transfers of residual balances of discontinued funds to the General Fund or a Debt Service Fund.

4. **Operating Transfers. All other interfund transfers**—e.g., legally authorized transfers from a fund receiving revenue to the fund through which the resources are to be expended, transfers of tax revenues from a Special Revenue Fund to a Debt Service Fund, transfers from the General Fund to a Special Revenue or Capital Projects Fund, operating subsidy transfers from the General or a Special Revenue Fund to an Enterprise Fund, and transfers from an Enterprise Fund other than payments in lieu of taxes to finance General Fund expenditures.[29]

Proper accounting and reporting for these types of interfund transactions are summarized in Figure 2-9.

Quasi-external interfund transactions are the only interfund transactions for which it is proper to recognize fund revenues, expenditures, or expenses that are not revenues, expenditures, or expenses of the governmental unit. The GASB views accounting for quasi-external transactions as fund revenues, expenditures, and expenses as essential **both** (1) to proper determination of **proprietary fund operating results** and (2) to reporting accurately the **revenues and expenditures of programs or activities** financed through **governmental funds.**

Reimbursements are necessary when an expenditure attributable to one fund initially was made from another fund. Accounting for interfund reimbursements as specified ensures that such transactions are reflected only once—and in the proper fund—as expenditures or expenses, as appropriate.

All interfund transactions except loans or advances, quasi-external transactions, and reimbursements are *transfers:*

■ *Residual equity transfers* are reported separately after the results of operations—usually immediately before the ending fund balance—in the statement of revenues, expenditures, and changes in fund balances of *governmental*

---

[29] Ibid., sec. 1800.103 and 1800.106.

Figure 2-9

SUMMARY OF INTERFUND TRANSACTIONS REPORTING

	Reporting Treatment	
Category of Interfund Transaction	*Payee (Recipient) Fund*	*Payer Fund*
Quasi-external transactions	Revenue	Expenditure or expense, as appropriate.
Reimbursements	Reduce expenditures or expenses, as appropriate	Expenditure or expense, as appropriate.
Residual equity transfers (RETs)	Residual Equity Transfers In (1) In governmental and trust funds—reported after operations (separate from revenues, bond issue proceeds, and operating transfers in) immediately before ending fund balance. (2) In proprietary funds—increase in contributed capital.	Residual Equity Transfer Out (1) In governmental and trust funds—reported after operations (separate from expenditures or expenses and operating transfers out) immediately before ending fund balance. (2) In proprietary funds—reported as a decrease in retained earnings or contributed capital, depending on circumstances.
Operating transfers	Operating Transfers In reported (1) as "Other Financing Sources" in the governmental funds operating statement and (2) separately as "Operating Transfers In" in the proprietary funds operating statement.	Operating Transfers Out reported (1) in "Other Financing Uses" section of the governmental funds operating statement and (2) separately as "Operating Transfers Out" in the proprietary funds operating statement.

funds. Residual equity transfers *to proprietary funds* are reported as additions to contributed capital of the proprietary fund; *those from proprietary funds* are reported as reductions of retained earnings or contributed capital, as appropriate.

■ *Operating transfers* are reported in the *"Other Financing Sources (Uses)"* section in the statement of revenues, expenditures, and changes in fund balance *(governmental funds)* and in the *"Operating Transfers"* section in the statement of revenues, expenses, and changes in retained earnings or equity *(proprietary funds).*

GLTD Proceeds

The GASB also states that *proceeds of general long-term debt issues* not recorded as fund liabilities—for example, proceeds of general obligation bonds or notes expended through Capital Projects or Debt Service Funds—should be reported as "Bond Issue Proceeds" or "Proceeds of Long-term Notes" in the *"Other Financing Sources"* section of the operating statement of the recipient *governmental fund.* (Note that this applies only to GLTD, not to proprietary and similar fiduciary fund long-term debt.)

Reporting Interfund Transactions and GLTD Proceeds

The GASB classification principles—on quasi-external transactions, reimbursements, residual equity transfers, operating transfers, and general long-term debt issue proceeds—are extremely important in government accounting and financial reporting. Accordingly, they are discussed further and illustrated at numerous points in this text.

The reporting effects of the GASB classification principles are illustrated in Figure 2-10, using comparative, side by side, operating statement format illustrations for governmental and proprietary funds. Essentially, this principle creates three classifications of increases in fund balance—revenues, other financing sources, and residual equity transfers in—to be presented in governmental fund operating statements. Likewise, it requires three categories of fund balance decreases to be presented in those statements—expenditures, other financing uses, and residual equity transfers out. The principle also dictates the major categories in which changes in proprietary fund equity will be reported. In studying Figure 2-10, *note* (1) *the distinct "operating statement" formats* for governmental funds and for proprietary funds *and the differences* between these formats, (2) the *reporting* of *operating transfers* and *residual equity transfers* in both operating statements and of *GLTD issue proceeds* in the governmental fund operating statement, and (3) that *neither quasi-external transactions nor reimbursements are separately reported* in the operating statements.

Governmental Fund Expenditure Classification

The GASB recommends classifying governmental fund expenditures by fund, function or program, activity, organization unit, character, and major object classes. These classifications are recommended to facilitate (1) assembling data for internal analysis purposes in manners that cross fund and departmental lines and (2) ready availability of data required for various intergovernmental comparisons and analyses. Classification of governmental fund revenues and expenditures is discussed in detail in Chapters 5 and 6.

Consistent Classification and Terminology

Consistent classification and terminology among the budget, the accounts, and the budgetary reports is a prerequisite to valid comparisons. In addition, effective budgetary control and accountability require that the accounts and budgetary reports—particularly those related to appropriations and expenditures—be in at least as much detail as appropriation control points. The GASB recognizes the necessity of such *consistency and comparability* in its eleventh principle:

> **Principle 11**
> **Common Terminology and Classification**
>
> A common terminology and classification should be used consistently throughout the budget, the accounts, and the financial reports of each fund.

Financial Reporting

The final GASB principle emphasizes the importance of both interim internal financial reporting and annual external financial reporting.

> **Principle 12**
> **Interim and Annual Financial Reports**
>
> a. Appropriate *interim* financial statements and reports of financial position, operating results, and other pertinent information should be prepared to facilitate management control of financial operations, legislative oversight, and, where necessary or desired, for external reporting purposes.

Figure 2-10

"OPERATING STATEMENT" FORMATS

Governmental Funds and Proprietary Funds
Reporting Interfund Transfers and
General Long-term Debt Issue Proceeds

Governmental Fund	Proprietary Fund
Statement of Revenues, Expenditures, and Changes in Fund Balance *For Year Ended (Date)*	**Statement of Revenues, Expenses, and Changes in Fund Equity** *For Year Ended (Date)*

Governmental Fund			Proprietary Fund	
Revenues:			**Operating Revenues:**	
Taxes		X	Sales of goods	X
Licenses and permits		X	Billings for services	X
Intergovernmental		X	Other	X
Charges for services		X		XX
Miscellaneous		X		
		X	**Operating Expenses:**	
			Operations	X
Other Financing Sources:			Depreciation	X
Operating transfers *from* other funds		X	Other	X
Bond issue proceeds		X		XX
		X		
Total Revenues and Other			Operating Income	X
Financing Sources		XX	**Nonoperating Revenues (Expenses)**	
Expenditures:			Interest revenue	X
Operations		X	Interest expense	(X)
Capital Outlay		X	Other	X
Debt Service				X
Bond principal	X			
Interest	X	X	Income before Operating Transfers	X
		XX	**Operating Transfers:**	
Other Financing Uses:			*From* other funds	X
Operating transfers *to* other funds		X	*To* other funds	(X)
Other		X		X
		X	**Net Income (Loss)**	X
Total Expenditures and Other				
Financing Uses		XX	Fund Equity—Beginning of Period	XX
Excess of Revenues and Other			**Residual Equity Transfers:**	
Financing Sources over (under)			*From* other funds	X
Expenditures and Other			*To* other funds	(X)
Financing Uses		X	Fund Equity—End of Period	XX
Fund Balance—Beginning of Period		XX		
Residual Equity Transfers:				
From other funds		X		
To other funds		(X)		
Fund Balance—End of Period		XX		

Notes:

1. Quasi-external transactions and reimbursements are not reported separately since (a) quasi-external transactions are included in the revenues of the payee (recipient) fund and in the expenditures or expenses, as appropriate, of the payer fund; and (b) reimbursements reduce the expenditures or expenses of the payee (recipient) fund and increase the expenditures or expenses of the payer fund.

2. Other acceptable formats for the governmental fund "operating statement" are discussed later, as are other examples of "other financing sources (uses)" and reporting restatements of beginning fund balance for prior period error corrections and changes in accounting principles.

3. Governmental fund expenditures are classified by "character" in this example; classification of expenditures by function or program and other classifications are discussed and illustrated in Chapters 5 and 6.

b. A ***comprehensive annual financial report*** [CAFR] covering all funds and account groups of the ***reporting entity***—including introductory section; appropriate combined, combining, and individual fund statements; notes to the financial statements; required supplementary information; schedules; narrative explanations; and statistical tables—should be prepared and published.

c. ***General purpose financial statements*** [GPFS] of the ***reporting entity*** may be issued separately from the comprehensive annual financial report. Such statements should include the basic financial statements and notes to the financial statements that are essential to fair presentation of financial position and results of operations (and cash flows of proprietary fund types and nonexpendable trust funds). These statements may also be required to be accompanied by required supplementary information. . . .

d. A ***component unit financial report*** [CUFR] covering all funds and account groups of a component unit—including introductory section; appropriate combined, combining, and individual fund statements; notes to the financial statements; required supplementary information; schedules; narrative explanations; and statistical tables—may be prepared and published as necessary.

e. ***Component unit financial statements*** [CUFS] of a component unit may be issued separately from the component unit financial report. Such statements should include the basic financial statements and notes to the financial statements that are essential to the fair presentation of financial position and results of operations (and cash flows of proprietary fund types and nonexpendable trust funds). These statements may also be required to be accompanied by required supplementary information. . . .

Annual Reporting Emphasis

No generally accepted accounting principles have been promulgated for monthly, quarterly, or other interim financial reporting, the topic of Principle 12a. Interim reporting is discussed and illustrated at various points throughout the text, although annual financial reporting in conformity with generally accepted accounting principles, the topic of Principles 12b through 12e, is emphasized. Financial reporting is covered comprehensively in the Financial Reporting Chapter.

Individual, Combining, and Combined Statements

A unique feature of state and local government financial reporting is that three categories of financial statements—of balance sheets, operating statements, and other statements—are used: (1) individual fund and account group statements, (2) combining statements, and (3) combined statements:

1. ***Individual fund and account group statements,*** as the name implies, present status or operating data for a single fund or account group, often in detail and/or with budget-to-actual or current year-to-prior year comparative data.

2. ***Combining fund statements*** present, in adjacent columns, ***data for all funds of a type*** (e.g., Special Revenue Funds), an "all funds" total, and perhaps a current year-to-prior year comparative total. Combining statements typically are in less detail than individual fund statements.

3. ***Combined fund and account group statements,*** known as the ***General Purpose Financial Statements (GPFS),*** present in adjacent columns ***data by fund type and account group,*** perhaps with "memorandum only" total and comparative columns. ***Combined*** statements have only one column for each ***fund type and account group.*** Where there is more than one fund of a type ***the total data from the combining statement*** for that fund type ***appears in the combined statement.*** Combined statements typically are more summarized than combining or individual fund and account group statements.

The distinctions between combined, combining, and individual fund statements are important, and are illustrated in Figure 2-11. Notice that the individual fund financial statements in Figure 2-11 do not contain any information that is not provided in the combining statements. Hence, individual fund financial statements need be presented only if more detail is provided than in the combining statements, or if individual fund prior year comparative data or budgetary comparisons are presented. Combining statements do provide information that is not reported in the combined statements, however, since individual fund information is presented in the combining statements but not in the combined statements. All three types of statements are illustrated in the following chapters.

Annual Financial Reports and Statements

State and local government units are required to issue an annual Comprehensive Annual Financial Report (CAFR), which includes the combined General Purpose Financial Statements (GPFS) as well as combining and (usually) individual fund and account group statements for the reporting entity. The **CAFR** is viewed as **the "official" annual financial report** of the government and includes introductory materials and statistical data as well as financial statements and schedules. The GPFS can be separately issued for readers not requiring the detail in the CAFR, as long as the reader is made aware of the CAFR.

The **combined** statements required in the **GPFS** are:

1. **Combined Balance Sheet:** All Fund types and Account Groups
2. **Combined Statement of Revenues, Expenditures, and Changes in Fund Balances:** All Governmental (and Expendable Trust) Fund types
3. **Combined Statement of Revenues, Expenditures, and Changes in Fund Balances—Budget and Actual:** General and Special Revenue Fund Types (and similar fund types for which annual budgets have been legally adopted)
4. **Combined Statement of Revenues, Expenses, and Changes in Retained Earnings (or Equity):** All Proprietary (and Nonexpendable and Pension Trust) Fund Types
5. **Combined Statement of Cash Flows:** All Proprietary (and Nonexpendable Trust) Fund types

Each of these statements is explained and illustrated in Chapter 14, "Financial Reporting." However, the authors recommend that they be previewed briefly as this "principles" section is concluded.

"Reporting Entity" and "Component Units"

A government's **"reporting entity" may include several separate legal entities**—for example, the city per se, a city water and sewer utility, and the city airport. Although the financial statements of all of these **component units** are included in the city CAFR and GPFS, **it may be necessary to prepare separate, more detailed, financial statements for some or all of the component units of the city reporting entity.** This is often the case where component unit revenue bonds are outstanding—for example, water and sewer revenue bonds—and creditors want detailed financial statements for the component unit. **To avoid possible confusion between reporting entity financial statements and those for component units, the GASB requires that component unit financial reports and statements be identified as the Component Unit Financial Report (CUFR) and Component Unit Financial Statements (CUFS), respectively, rather than as the CAFR and GPFS of a component unit.** The Component Unit Financial Report (CUFR) and

Figure 2-11

INDIVIDUAL FUND vs. COMBINING vs. COMBINED FINANCIAL STATEMENTS

Condensed and Simplified Illustrative Governmental Fund Statements of
Revenues, Expenditures, and Changes in Fund Balance

Individual Fund Statements

Special Revenue Fund A	
Revenues	$500
Other financing sources	80
Total revenues and other financing sources	580
Expenditures	400
Other financing uses	150
Total expenditures and other financing uses	550
Excess of revenues and other financing sources over(under) expenditures and other financing uses	30
Fund balance, beginning	120
Residual equity transfer in(out)	(90)
Fund balance, ending	$ 60

Special Revenue Fund B	
Revenues	$300
Other financing sources	30
Total revenues and other financing sources	330
Expenditures	300
Other financing uses	50
Total expenditures and other financing uses	350
Excess of revenues and other financing sources over(under) expenditures and other financing uses	(20)
Fund balance, beginning	200
Residual equity transfer in(out)	
Fund balance, ending	$180

Combining Statements All Special Revenue Funds

Special Revenue Funds	Fund A	Fund B	Total
Revenues	$500	$300	$800
Other financing sources	80	30	110
Total revenues and other financing sources	580	330	910
Expenditures	400	300	700
Other financing uses	150	50	200
Total expenditures and other financing uses	550	350	900
Excess of revenues and other financing sources over(under) expenditures and other financing uses	30	(20)	10
Fund balance, beginning	120	200	320
Residual equity transfer in(out)	(90)		(90)
Fund balance, ending	$ 60	$180	$240

Combined Statements All Governmental Funds

	General	Special Revenue	Capital Projects	Debt Service	Total (Memorandum only)
Revenues	$5,000	$800			$5,800
Other financing sources	1,200	110	4,000	300	5,610
Total revenues and other financing sources	6,200	910	4,000	300	11,410
Expenditures	4,500	700	1,500	500	7,200
Other financing uses	1,000	200			1,200
Total expenditures and other financing uses	5,500	900	1,500	500	8,400
Excess of revenues and other financing sources over(under) expenditures and other financing uses	700	10	2,500	(200)	3,010
Fund balance, beginning	2,000	320		400	2,720
Residual equity transfer in(out)		(90)			(90)
Fund balance, ending	$2,700	$240	$2,500	$200	$5,640

Note: *The statements presented here are condensed and otherwise simplified for illustrative purposes—and are not appropriately headed or detailed for GAAP reporting purposes.*

Component Unit Financial Statements (CUFS) for state and local governments are discussed and illustrated in Chapter 14, as are the comprehensive annual financial report (CAFR) and the general purpose financial statements (GPFS).

CONCLUDING COMMENTS

Orienting oneself to state and local government accounting and reporting requires that particular attention be given to the *GASB principles, fund types, measurement focuses, budgetary control and accountability, and terminology. New and unique terms should be noted carefully. Familiar terminology also deserves analysis, as it may be used with either usual or unique connotations.* Definitions of pertinent terms may be found in most chapters.

Adapting to a situation in which there are many accounting entities requires both concentration and practice. The nature, role, and distinguishing characteristics of each of the seven types of funds and the two nonfund account groups recommended by the GASB must be understood thoroughly. Each is discussed in depth in later chapters.

A peculiarity of the multiple-entity approach of fund accounting is that *a single transaction may require entries in more than one accounting entity;* for example, the purchase of a *general* fixed asset necessitates entries to record both the expenditure in a governmental fund and the asset in the General Fixed Assets Account Group. Further, one must both accept and adapt to virtual personification of the fund accounting entities and the definitions of "revenues" and "expenditures" in a fund accounting context.

Organizational units financed from different funds may buy from and sell to one another *(interfund transactions)* and resources of one fund may be owed to another *(interfund relationships).* Therefore, a fund may have revenues or incur expenditures that are not revenues or expenditures of the government as a whole **(quasi-external transactions).** For example, payment from the General Fund to the fund through which the government's central repair shop is financed (a quasi-external transaction) constitutes a General Fund expenditure and an Internal Service Fund revenue, even though the transaction does not result in an expenditure or revenue of the government as a whole.

Finally, the budget is of such importance in governments that governmental accounting is often referred to as *"budgetary" accounting.* It is appropriate, therefore, to examine the role of the budget and major budgetary approaches, in the next chapter, before delving into the details of fund accounting technique.

QUESTIONS

2-1 The terms "fund" and "funds" are used with varying connotations. For example, a college student may consider his cash and checking account balance to be his "funds" and his savings account his "fund." Indicate (a) the various meanings associated with these terms in business and (b) the principal manner in which these terms are used in state and local government accounting.

2-2 A state or local government may employ only one of certain fund or nonfund account group entities but one, none, or many of other types. Of which would you expect a government to have only one? One, none, or many?

2-3 The following are names of funds encountered in governmental reports and the purposes for which these funds have been established. Indicate the corresponding fund type recommended by the Governmental Accounting Standards Board.

a. School Fund (to account for special taxes levied by a county to finance the operation of schools)

b. Bond Redemption Fund (to account for taxes and other revenues to be used in retiring bonds)

c. Bridge Construction Fund (to account for the proceeds from the sale of bonds)

d. Park Fund (to account for special taxes levied to finance the operation of parks)

e. Interdepartmental Printing Shop Fund (to account for revenues received from departments for printing done for them by the interdepartmental printing shop)

f. City Bus Line Fund (to account for revenues received from the public for transportation services)

    g. Money Collected for the State Fund (to account for money collected as agent for the state)

    h. Operating Fund (to account for unrestricted revenues not related to any other fund)

    i. Electric Fund (to account for revenues received from the sale of electricity to the public)

    j. Federal Fund (to account for federal construction grant proceeds)

    k. Bond Redemption Fund (to account for proceeds of bond refunding issue)

    l. Federal Fund (to account for shared revenue grants which may be used for any of several broad purpose categories)

    m. Bond Proceeds Fund (to account for proceeds of bonds issued to finance street construction)

    n. Employees' Pension and Relief Fund (to provide retirement and disability benefits to employees)

2-4 Why are a municipality's general fixed assets and general long-term debt accounted for through nonfund account groups rather than within one of its funds, such as the General Fund?

2-5 What differences would you expect to find between the accounting principles for the General Fund and for Special Revenue Funds?

2-6 Revenues or expenditures of a specific fund may not represent increases or decreases in the net assets of the government as a whole. Why is this true?

2-7 It has been asserted that terms such as "sources" and "uses" should be substituted for "revenues" and "expenditures," respectively, in accounting and reporting for governmental (expendable) funds. Do you agree? Why or why not?

2-8 The GASB principles classify all of the funds and account groups used in state and local government accounting and financial reporting into four categories: (1) Governmental Funds, (2) Proprietary Funds, (3) Fiduciary Funds, and (4) Account Groups. What are the major accounting and other *commonalities* shared by specific funds and account groups in these categories?

2-9 It is not uncommon to find the terms "expenditures" and "expenses" erroneously used as synonyms. How do "expenditures" differ from "expenses"?

2-10 What is the difference, if any, between a revenue and expenditure statement prepared on a cash basis and a statement of cash receipts and disbursements?

2-11 Governmental fund and proprietary fund "operating results" are determined differently under GASB standards. Explain.

2-12 GASB Principle 11 states that "A common terminology and classification should be used consistently throughout the budget, the accounts, and the financial reports." Why is this important?

2-13 The principal financial statements of business enterprises are the Balance Sheet, Income Statement, and Statement of Cash Flows. What *similarities* are there, if any, among these statements and the operating and position statements of a proprietary (nonexpendable) fund? A governmental (expendable) fund?

2-14 Fund accounting and budgetary control are deemed of such importance by the GASB that four of its twelve principles deal directly with these topics and most of the others relate to them at least indirectly. Why?

2-15 In what funds and account groups are (a) fixed assets and (b) long-term debt accounted for? Why are they not accounted for in the other funds and account groups?

2-16 Discuss the current roles of the GASB, FASB, AICPA, and NCGA in setting standards for governmental accounting and financial reporting.

2-17 Harvey Township budgets its resources on the cash basis in accordance with state laws. State law also requires financial statements prepared on the cash basis. To comply with this requirement, Harvey Township prepares the financial statements in its Comprehensive Annual Financial Report on the cash basis rather than on the GAAP basis.

    a. Discuss the appropriateness of the statements in Harvey Township's CAFR.

    b. Explain what, if anything, Harvey Township should change in its CAFR.

2-18 Define the following interfund transaction terms and explain how each is accounted for and reported by a municipality: (a) Reimbursement, (b) Quasi-External Transaction, (c) Residual Equity Transfer, and (d) Operating Transfer.

2-19 The City of Horner's Corner publishes general purpose financial statements (GPFS), but considers it unnecessary to publish a comprehensive annual financial report (CAFR). The city's only funds are a General Fund, three Special Revenue Funds, two Capital Projects Funds, an Internal Service Fund, and two Enterprise Funds. A citizen has asked you if this practice is appropriate according to GASB principles. Discuss.

2-20 Distinguish between (a) the comprehensive annual financial report and the general purpose financial statements of a government; and (b) combining and combined financial statements of a government.

PROBLEMS

P 2-1 (Multiple Choice) Select the lettered response that best completes the numbered statements.

1. The operations of a public library receiving the majority of its support from property taxes levied for that purpose should be accounted for in
   a. the General Fund
   b. a Special Revenue Fund
   c. an Enterprise Fund
   d. an Internal Service Fund
   e. none of the above

2. The proceeds of a federal grant made to assist in financing the future construction of an adult training center should be recorded in
   a. the General Fund
   b. a Special Revenue Fund
   c. a Capital Projects Fund
   d. a Special Assessment Fund
   e. none of the above

3. The receipts from a special tax levy to retire and pay interest on general obligation bonds issued to finance the construction of a new city hall should be recorded in a
   a. Debt Service Fund
   b. Capital Projects Fund
   c. Revolving Interest Fund
   d. Special Revenue Fund
   e. none of the above

4. The operations of a municipal swimming pool receiving the majority of its support from charges to users should be accounted for in
   a. a Special Revenue Fund
   b. the General Fund
   c. an Internal Service Fund
   d. an Enterprise Fund
   e. none of the above

5. The monthly remittance to an insurance company of the lump sum of hospital-surgical insurance premiums collected as payroll deductions from employees should be recorded in
   a. the General Fund
   b. an Agency Fund
   c. a Special Revenue Fund
   d. an Internal Service Fund
   e. none of the above

6. A transaction in which a municipality issued general obligation serial bonds to finance the construction of a fire station requires accounting recognition in the
   a. General Fund
   b. Capital Projects and General Funds
   c. Capital Projects Fund and the General Long-Term Debt Account Group
   d. General Fund and the General Long-Term Debt Account Group
   e. none of the above

7. Expenditures of $200,000 were made during the year on the fire station in item 6. This transaction requires accounting recognition in the
   a. General Fund
   b. Capital Projects Fund and the General Fixed Assets Account Group
   c. Capital Projects Fund and the General Long-Term Debt Account Group
   d. General Fund and the General Fixed Assets Account Group
   e. none of the above

8. The activities of a central motor pool that provides and services vehicles for the use of municipal employees on official business should be accounted for in
   a. an Agency Fund
   b. the General Fund
   c. an Internal Service Fund
   d. a Special Revenue Fund
   e. none of the above

9. A transaction in which a municipal electric utility paid $150,000 out of its earnings for new equipment requires accounting recognition in
   a. an Enterprise Fund
   b. the General Fund
   c. the General Fund and the General Fixed Assets Account Group
   d. an Enterprise Fund and the General Fixed Assets Account Group
   e. none of the above

10. The activities of a municipal employee retirement plan that is financed by equal employer and employee contributions should be accounted for in
    a. an Agency Fund
    b. an Internal Service Fund
    c. a Special Revenue Fund
    d. a Trust Fund
    e. none of the above

11 A city collects property taxes for the benefit of the local sanitary, park, and school districts and periodically remits collections to these units. This activity should be accounted for in
   a. an Agency Fund
   b. the General Fund
   c. an Internal Service Fund
   d. a Special Revenue Fund
   e. none of the above

12. A transaction in which a municipal electric utility issues bonds (to be repaid from its own operations) requires accounting recognition in
    a. the General Fund
    b. a Debt Service Fund
    c. Enterprise and Debt Service Funds
    d. an Enterprise Fund, a Debt Service Fund, and the General Long-Term Debt Account Group
    e. none of the above
    (AICPA, adapted)

P 2-2 (Fund Identification) Using the appropriate fund abbreviations, indicate which governmental fund(s) might be used to account for the following items and give the reasons for your answer(s).

1. Revenues not restricted as to use
2. Revenues restricted for specified current operating purposes
3. Purchase of equipment, furniture, and fixtures
4. Depreciation of equipment used in general government functions
5. Payment of short-term debt interest and principal
6. Payment of maturing long-term debt interest and principal
7. Construction of a major capital facility or improvement
8. Charges for services
9. Revenues restricted to payment of general obligation long-term debt interest and principal
10. Proceeds of long-term debt issuances

Solution Format				*Fund Abbreviations*	
No.	*Fund(s) to Be Used*	*Reason(s)*		GF	General Fund
				SRF	Special Revenue Fund
				CPF	Capital Projects Fund
				DSF	Debt Service Fund

P 2-3   (Transaction Analysis)

a. Analyze the effects of each of the following transactions on each of the funds and account groups of the City of Nancy, Virginia.

b. Indicate how each transaction would be reported in the operating statement for each fund affected.

EXAMPLE: Cash received for licenses during 1991, $8,000.

ANSWER:

GENERAL FUND (GF)
>   Increases Current Assets (CA) $8,000
>   Increases Fund Balance (FB) $8,000
>   Revenues of $8,000 reported

1. Salaries and wages for firemen and policemen incurred but not paid, $75,000.
2. Borrowed $9,000,000 to finance construction of a new city executive office building by issuing bonds at par.
3. The city paid $5,000,000 to the office building contractor for work performed during the fiscal year.
4. The city purchased a computer by issuing a $5,000, 8%, six-month note to the vendor. The note is due March 1 of the next fiscal year—which is the calendar year.
5. General Fund resources of $5,000,000 were paid to a newly established Airport Enterprise Fund to provide initial start-up capital.
6. A $3,000,000 personal injury lawsuit has been filed against the city. The controller determines that it is probable that a judgment in that amount will be made in the future but does not expect to have to pay the judgment for another three years. The incident relates to general government activities.
7. The city repaid $10,000,000 of general obligation bonds that had been issued several years before to finance construction of a school building. Interest of $1,000,000 was also paid. All amounts were paid from resources accumulated previously for this purpose.
8. The city sold general fixed assets with an original cost of $50,000 at the end of their useful life for $1,500. There are no restrictions on the use of the money.

P 2-4   (Revenue and Expense vs. Revenue and Expenditure Statements) The following revenue and expense statement was prepared by a municipality's bookkeeper.

City of B
Internal Service Fund
Revenue and Expense Statement
For the Fiscal Year Ended December 31, 19XX

Sales to departments	$145,000	
Borrowed from other funds	17,500	
Borrowed from bank (5-year note)	40,000	$202,500
Less: Costs of operating:		
Materials	$ 58,000	
Labor	45,000	
Heat	2,000	
Light and power	4,000	
Superintendent's salary	23,000	
Purchase of machinery	51,000	
Payment of liabilities to other funds	15,000	
Payment of principal on bank note	4,000	
Payment of interest on bank note	1,600	203,600
Net income (loss)		($ 1,100)

Additional information:

1. The cost of materials shown in the statement is the total amount paid for materials during the year. An inventory of $10,000 was carried over from last year; $5,000 was paid for materials purchased during the preceding year; materials costing $15,000 were purchased during the year but have not yet been paid for; the closing inventory is $24,000.

2. The amounts shown for labor, heat, light and power, and superintendent's salary represent actual payments. Charges incurred last year but not paid until this year include the following: labor $450; heat, $100; light and power, $225; superintendent's salary, $190. Charges incurred but not yet paid include the following: labor, $750; heat, $150; light and power, $300; superintendent's salary, $150.

3. The amount shown for sales represents actual receipts of cash from other funds; only $135,000 of the total collections is applicable to sales made this year; $20,000 is still due from other funds on account of sales made this year.

4. No interest is charged on the interfund loans, but six-months' interest on the bank note, $1,200, is due two months after year end.

5. The equipment purchased (on January 3) is the only depreciable fixed asset in the fund. The equipment is expected to last five years and have a $1,000 salvage value. The city depreciates its proprietary fund assets on the straight line method.

Required

(a) Prepare a correct statement of revenues and expenses for the Internal Service Fund on the accrual basis.

(b) Prepare a statement of revenues and expenditures for this service activity assuming it is accounted for through a governmental fund (modified accrual basis) rather than a proprietary fund.

P 2-5 (Modified Accrual vs. Accrual Bases) In order to ensure continuous and dependable bus service to its citizens "from now on," Mobiline County acquired the following assets of Mobiline Transit, Inc., a privately owned bus line in financial difficulty:

Assets	Amount Paid by County
Land	$ 10,000
Garage and office building	30,000
Inventory of tires and parts	15,000
Shop equipment	5,000
Buses	140,000
Total paid—February 1, 19X3	$200,000

Additional information:

1. The purchase was financed through the issue of 6% general obligation notes payable, scheduled to mature in amounts of $20,000 each February 1, for ten years. Interest is payable annually each February 1.

2. Bus line revenues and expenditures are accounted for through the General Fund. The fixed assets acquired were recorded in the General Fixed Assets Account Group and the notes payable were recorded in the General Long-Term Debt Account Group.

3. In November 19X3, following the close of the county's fiscal year on October 31, the Mobiline *Daily Banner* published a feature story about the county-owned bus line under the heading "Bus Line Prospers under County Management." The following Operating Statement, prepared by the county clerk from the General Fund records, appeared within the newspaper article:

Mobiline County Bus Line
Operating Statement
For the Nine-Month Period Ending October 31, 19X3

Revenues:
Passenger fares—routine route service.	$77,000	
Special charter fees	3,000	$80,000

Expenditures:
Salaries (superintendent, drivers, mechanics)	52,000	
Fuel and lubrication	12,000	
Tires and parts	1,000	
Contracted repairs and maintenance	8,000	
Miscellaneous.	1,000	74,000
Net profit.		$ 6,000

The story quoted a county commissioner as saying:

> We are extremely pleased with our bus line operating results to date. Through sound management, we have turned a losing operation into a profitable one—and we expect an even greater profit next year. When we got into the bus line business we determined that the buses would last five years and the building and shop equipment would suffice for ten years—so we do not anticipate any capital outlay expense for some time. In addition, we have $3,000 worth of tires and parts on hand that do not appear in the Operating Statement but will help us hold down our expenses during the next few months, and we should collect another $500 fee for an October charter this week.

Required (a) Prepare an accrual basis Statement of Revenues and Expenses (Income Statement) for Mobiline County Bus Line for the nine-month period ending October 31, 19X3.

(b) Evaluate the propriety of the information contained within the *Daily Banner* feature story.

P 2-6 (Entries Using Different Bases of Accounting) (a) Record each of the following transactions on (1) the cash basis, (2) the modified accrual basis, and (3) the accrual basis.

January   1 Billed customers $400 for services rendered
             3 Purchased $50 of supplies on account
             5 Purchased a truck costing $5,000 (to be paid for on February 3)
           11 Collected $200 from customers on account
           15 Recorded accrued wages to date, $1,000
           17 Paid for supplies
           21 Paid wages
February 3 Paid for the truck
            5 $20 of supplies have been used
           6 Depreciation on the truck for the month was $100

Solution Format

		Cash Basis		Modified Accrual Basis		Accrual Basis	
Date	Accounts	Dr.	Cr.	Dr.	Cr.	Dr.	Cr.

(b) Explain the similarities and differences between the modified accrual and accrual bases of accounting.

P 2-7 (Interfund Transactions) (a) Identify the type of each following interfund transaction or indicate that it is not an interfund transaction. Indicate why you classified the transaction as you did.

1. $50,000 of General Fund cash was contributed to establish an Internal Service Fund.

2. A truck—acquired two years ago with General Fund revenues for $8,000—with a fair market value of $4,000 was contributed to a department financed by an Enterprise Fund.

3. The Sanitation Department, accounted for in the General Fund, billed the Municipal Airport, accounted for in an Enterprise Fund, $400 for garbage collection.

4. General Fund cash amounting to $40,000—to be repaid in 90 days—was provided to enable construction to begin on a new courthouse before a bond issue was sold.

5. A $1,000,000 bond issue to finance construction of an addition to the civic center was sold at par.

6. General Fund disbursements during May included a nonloan payment of $30,000 to a Capital Projects Fund to help finance a major capital project.

7. After retirement of the related debt, the remaining net assets of a Debt Service Fund, $1,500, were transferred to the General Fund.

8. General Fund cash amounting to $10,000 was contributed to a Capital Projects Fund as the city's portion of the cost of the project.

9. An Internal Service Fund department paid $5,000 to the General Fund for Internal Service Fund supplies paid for by, and recorded as expenditures in, the General Fund during the year.

10. $50,000 was allocated and paid from the General Fund to the Enterprise Fund to finance its budgeted operating deficit.

Solution Format

No.	Classification	Reason(s)

b. Discuss how each type of interfund transaction should be reported in the Statement of Revenues, Expenditures, and Changes in Fund Balance.

c. Why is it important to distinguish interfund transfers and bond issue proceeds from fund revenues, expenditures, and expenses?

	Fund or Account	
Service, Asset, or Liability	Group to Be Used	Reason(s)

P 2-8 (Financial Reporting Purposes and Depreciation—Government vs. Business) William Bates is executive vice president of Mavis Industries, Inc., a publicly held industrial corporation. Bates has just been elected to the city council of Gotham City. Prior to assuming office as a city councilman, he asks you to explain the major differences in accounting and financial reporting for a large city as compared to a large industrial corporation.

Required (a) Describe the major differences in the purpose of accounting and financial reporting and in the types of financial reports of a large city as compared to a large industrial corporation.

(b) Under what circumstances should depreciation be recognized in accounting for local governmental units? Explain. (AICPA, adapted)

P 2-9 (Transaction Analysis)

Required (a) Analyze the effects of the following transactions on the accounting equations of the various funds and account groups of a state or local government.

(b) Indicate how each transaction would be reported in the operating statement for each fund affected.

1. The government-owned and -operated electric utility billed users $2,000,000 for electricity usage. This included $100,000 billed to general government departments for electricity usage.

2. $50,000 of General Fund money was loaned to a Capital Projects Fund to allow construction on the project to begin before the related bonds were to be issued. The loan is to be repaid in 6 months.

3. $1,000,000 of property taxes were levied during the year to provide financing for the budget of the year of levy. $800,000 was collected by year end. Another $85,000 was collected during the first 60 days of the next fiscal year. An additional $100,000 is expected

to be collected during the remainder of the second fiscal year, and $15,000 is estimated to be uncollectible.

4. The government issued a $1,000,000, 6%, 5-year note halfway through the fiscal year to provide partial financing for construction of a bridge.

5. The government issued a $1,000,000, 6%, 1-year note halfway through the fiscal year to provide temporary financing for a special program which will be financed ultimately by reimbursements from a restricted grant awarded to the government for the specific purpose of financing that program. However, no cash has been received from the grantor to date.

6. Purchased a truck for a general government department for $40,000 cash.

7. Repaid outstanding bonds at maturity, $2,100,000 (including $100,000 interest).

8. The government paid $1,000,000 in vacation pay during the year. Employees who do not use their vacation time are paid for unused vacation time upon termination. The government's liability for accumulated unused vacation pay (measured per FASB 43 and GASB 16) increased by $250,000 during the year—all of which is considered long-term in nature.) Half of the the vacation-related costs are for General Fund employees, half are for Enterprise Fund employees.

9. The 1-year note from transaction 5 matured and was paid along with the interest of $60,000.

10. A utility department truck was sold halfway through its useful life for $17,000. The truck, which originally cost $45,000, had an estimated residual value of $5,000.

BUDGETING, BUDGETARY ACCOUNTING, AND BUDGETARY REPORTING

Budgeting is the process of allocating scarce resources to unlimited demands, and a ***budget*** is a ***dollars and cents plan of operation for a specific period of time.*** At a minimum, such a plan should contain information about the types and amounts of proposed expenditures, the purposes for which they are to be made, and the proposed means of financing them.

Although practices are by no means uniform, ***budgeting and budgets typically play a far greater role in the planning, control, and evaluation of governmental operations than in those of privately owned businesses.*** The GASB recognizes the importance of the budget process in the following principle:

9. a. An annual budget(s) should be adopted by every governmental unit.
   b. The accounting system should provide the basis for appropriate budgetary control.
   c. Budgetary comparisons should be included in the appropriate financial statements and schedules for governmental funds for which an annual budget has been adopted.[1]

The adoption of a budget implies that decisions have been made—on the basis of a ***planning*** process—as to how the unit is to reach its objectives. The accounting system then assists the administrators to ***control*** the activities authorized to carry out the plans and to prepare the statements that permit comparison of actual operations with the budget and ***evaluation*** of variances. These three budgetary phases and functions—***planning, control,*** and ***evaluation***—are crucial aspects of all budgetary approaches and processes.

Budgeting, budgetary accounting, and budgetary reporting are uniquely important and distinctive features of governmental fund accounting and financial reporting. Indeed, governmental fund accounting is often referred to as "budgetary accounting"; and, as noted in Chapter 2, governmental fund operating statements are prepared on both the GAAP basis and the SLG's budgetary basis. Further, many questions and problems on the Uniform CPA Examination require knowledge of governmental fund budgeting, budgetary accounting, and budgetary reporting.

[1] GASB Codification, sec. 1100.109.

Accordingly, the first part of this chapter considers the role of the annual budget in governmental fund planning, control, and evaluation; basic budgetary terminology; the major alternative budgeting approaches and emphases found in practice (and on the CPA Exam); and the usual procedures in the preparation and enactment of a SLG annual operating budget. The latter part of the chapter is devoted to introductory "overview" discussions and illustrations of budgetary accounting techniques and budgetary reporting methods. These discussions and illustrations are also designed to provide a "bridge" to the budgetary accounting entries and budgetary statement examples in the following several chapters.

BUDGETARY PLANNING, CONTROL, AND EVALUATION

Planning

The prominence of the budgetary process in government is a natural outgrowth of its environment. *Planning* is a special concern here since, as noted previously, (1) the type, quantity, and quality of governmental goods and services provided are not normally evaluated and adjusted through the open market mechanism; (2) these goods and services (e.g., education, police and fire protection, and sanitation) are often among the most critical to the public interest; (3) the immense scope and diversity of modern government activities make comprehensive, thoughtful, and systematic planning a prerequisite to orderly decision making; and (4) government planning and decision making is generally a joint process involving its citizens (or "owners"), either individually or in groups, their elected representatives within the legislative branch, and the members of the executive branch.

The *legislative-executive division of powers,* the so-called *"checks-and-balances"* device, is operative in all states and in most local governments. In these and in most manager-council forms of organization, "the executive proposes, the legislature disposes"; that is, the executive is responsible for drafting tentative plans, but final plans are made by the legislative body—often after public hearings in which interested citizens or groups are able to participate. Written budget proposals are essential to communication, discussion, revision, and documentation of plans by those concerned with and responsible for planning.

Control

Budgets are also widely used *control* devices in governments, *both* in regard to (1) *legislative* branch control *over* the *executive* branch *and* (2) *chief* executive control *over subordinate* executive agencies or departments. As observed earlier, when a budget is enacted by the legislative branch, the expenditure estimates become **appropriations**— both *authorizations* to expend *and* expenditure *limitations* upon the executive branch.

Appropriations may be enacted in very broad categorical terms or in minute detail. When appropriations are enacted in broad categorical terms, the legislature exercises general or policy-level control only—and the executive is given much managerial discretion in the conduct of governmental business. But when appropriations are enacted in minute detail, the chief executive has almost no discretion, and is restricted to carrying out various specific, detailed orders from the legislature. Similarly, the chief executive may restrict subordinates by granting agency or departmental expenditure authority in more detailed or specific categories (*"allocations"*) than those approved by the legislature. Likewise the chief executive may ration expenditure authority to subordinate agencies or departments in terms of monthly or quarterly expenditure ceilings, referred to as *"allotments."* Thus, *the accounting system must provide information that enables (1) agencies or departments to keep their expenditures within limitations imposed by the chief executive and demonstrate compliance with those limitations, and (2) the chief executive to keep the expenditures of the government as a whole within limitations imposed by the legislative branch and demonstrate such compliance.*

Evaluation

The budgetary authority extended one branch or level of government by another therefore becomes a **standard** for measurement of legal and administrative compliance or noncompliance. Appropriate *financial reports*—that compare the budgeted and actual revenue and expenditure amounts for the period—serve as a **basis for evaluating the extent of compliance** with standards established by the various *"dollar stewardship" accountability* relationships in this environment.

BASIC BUDGETARY TERMINOLOGY

Although the operating budget of each year stands alone from a legal standpoint, **budgeting is a continuous process.** Budget officials will be engaged during any given year in ensuring that the prior year's budgetary reports are properly audited and appropriately distributed, in administering the budget of the current year, and in preparing the budget for the upcoming year(s). The budget for any year (see Figure 3-1) goes through five phases: (1) preparation, (2) legislative enactment, (3) administration, (4) reporting, and (5) postaudit.

State and local governments typically prepare and utilize several types of financial plans referred to as "budgets." It is important, therefore, to distinguish among various types of budgets, to understand the phases through which each may pass, and to be familiar with commonly used budgetary terminology. For purposes of this discussion, budgets may be classified as:

1. capital or current
2. tentative or enacted
3. general or special
4. fixed or flexible
5. executive or legislative

Capital vs. Current Budgets

Sound governmental fiscal management requires continual planning for several periods into the future. Most governments are involved in programs to provide certain goods or services continuously (or at least for several years); in acquisitions of buildings, land, or other major items of capital outlay that must be scheduled and financed; and in long-term debt service commitments. Although some prepare comprehensive multiyear plans that include all of these, such multiyear plans most frequently include only the capital outlay plans for the organization. Such a plan generally covers a period of two to six years and is referred to as a **"capital program."**

Each year the current segment of the capital program is considered for inclusion as the **"capital budget,"** in the **"current budget."** The current budget also includes the proposed expenditures for current operations and debt service, as

Figure 3-1

THE BUDGET CYCLE

A Governmental Unit

well as estimates of all financial resources expected to be available during the current period.

The typical *interrelationships* of a *capital program, capital budget, and current budget* are illustrated in Figure 3-2. The *remainder of this chapter is concerned primarily* with *current or operating budgets.*

Tentative vs. Enacted Budgets

One key distinction among budgets is their *legal status.* Various documents may be called "budgets" prior to approval by the legislative body. Such documents have varying degrees of finality, but none is a final, legally enacted budget. For example, capital programs represent plans but not requests by the executive branch and are subject to change from year to year. Similarly, while a departmental budget request may be called a budget, it may be changed several times by the department head or higher authority before being included in the chief executive's final budget presented to the legislature. *Enactment of an appropriation bill by the legislative branch is the legal basis of its control over the executive branch.* Only the legislature may revise the terms or conditions of this final *"legally en-*

Figure 3-2

**INTERRELATIONSHIPS OF
CAPITAL PROGRAM—CAPITAL BUDGET—OPERATING BUDGET**

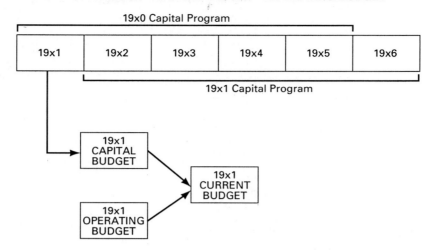

acted" budget, which *is the basis for executive branch accountability to the legislature.*

General vs. Special Budgets

The budgets of *"general governmental"* activities—commonly financed through the General, Special Revenue, and Debt Service Funds—are referred to as *"general"* budgets. A budget prepared for any *other* fund is referred to as a *"special"* budget. Special budgets are commonly limited to those for Capital Projects Funds, though Internal Service and Enterprise Funds are sometimes formally budgeted. Appropriations are normally required for Trust and Agency Funds since the government usually is acting merely as a fiduciary in such situations; consequently, formal budgets are rarely prepared for these types of funds.

Fixed vs. Flexible Budgets

Fixed budgets are those in which appropriations are for *specific (fixed) dollar amounts* of expenditures or expenses. These appropriated amounts may not be exceeded because of changes in demand for governmental goods or services. On the other hand, expenditures or expenses authorized by **flexible budgets** are *fixed per unit* of goods or services, *but* are *variable in total* according to demand for either production or delivery of the goods or services.

    Fixed budgets are relatively simple to prepare and administer and are more easily understood than flexible budgets. Additionally, fixed budgets lend themselves to the desire of "strong" legislatures to limit (control) the discretion of the executive (and his or her subordinates). Finally, fixed budgets are readily adaptable to integrating budgetary control techniques into accounting systems and are consistent with the intent of allocating a fixed amount of financial resources among various departments or programs. *Governmental fund* budgets are almost invariably *fixed expenditure budgets.*

    Flexible budgets are more realistic when changes in the quantities of goods or services provided directly affect resource availability and expenditure or expense requirements, and when formal budgetary control (in the account structure) is not deemed essential. Flexible budgets—on the expense or expenditure basis—are most appropriate for Enterprise and Internal Service Funds.

Executive vs. Legislative Budgets

Budgets are also sometimes categorized **by preparer.** As noted earlier, budget preparation is usually considered an executive function, though the legislature may revise the budget prior to approval. In some instances, however, the legislative branch prepares the budget, possibly subject to executive veto; in other instances, the budget may originate with a joint legislative-executive committee (possibly with citizen representatives) or with a committee composed solely of citizens or constituents. Such budgets are frequently referred to by terms such as "executive budget," "legislative budget," "joint budget," and "committee budget" respectively.

BUDGETARY APPROACHES AND EMPHASES

Rarely does one find two governments with identical budgetary approaches and procedures. A government's budgetary system should be designed to fit its environmental factors—some of which may be unique—and should provide a budgetary planning, control, and evaluation balance that is appropriate to its circumstances.

The Budget as Information

Both in practice and in budgetary theory **the budget is designed to provide information to decision makers and to indicate the decisions that have been made.** Top officials in the executive branch develop policy guidelines for departmental supervisors to use in support of departmental budget requests. The chief executive, with the assistance of the budgetary staff, decides what information and budget requests will go to the legislative body. The ultimate example of the use of the budget to indicate the decisions that have been made is the enacted appropriations bill, a law.

Typically, the **expenditure budget** proposed by the executive branch includes:

1. Descriptions of programs, functions, and activities carried on by organizational units of the government
2. Objectives of programs, functions, and activities
3. Quantitative data regarding the service efforts (inputs) and accomplishments (outputs) of the programs, functions, and activities
4. Benefits provided at increased (maximum?) and/or decreased (minimum?) levels of service
5. Methods now in use for delivering services; alternative methods for delivering services; and systems analyses and cost-benefit analyses of methods for delivering services
6. Expenditure and/or cost data:
   a. By organization units
   b. By programs, functions, and activities
   c. By object of expenditure
   d. Per unit of service effort (input) or accomplishment (output) at
      - present levels
      - reduced levels
      - expanded levels

Although no budget provides all these kinds of information, every budget provides some of them. The budget approach selected tends to determine the kinds of planning analyses that will be used and the data that will be provided.

The several general approaches to governmental budgeting have marked differences in their emphases on planning, control, and evaluation. As we discuss these approaches we shall point out their suitability for planning, control, and evaluation. The principal groups that exercise control are executive branch officials and the legislature. But citizens, creditors, officials of higher governments, and other groups often have control powers that indirectly affect the budgetary planning, control, and evaluation processes.

Alternative Expenditure Budgeting Approaches

The most common approaches to *operating expenditure budgeting* may be characterized as follows:

1. Object-of-expenditure
2. Performance
3. Program and planning-programming-budgeting (PPB)
4. Zero-base budgeting (ZBB)

A complete discussion of each approach—or possible combinations of approaches—is beyond the scope of this text. Moreover, bear in mind that *budgetary nomenclature is not standardized,* that *each approach may be implemented to varying degrees,* that *these approaches overlap significantly,* and that *elements of all four approaches are often found in a single budget system.* Furthermore, always look to the *substance* of a system rather than to the terminology used in reference to it; for example, an object-of-expenditure budget may be referred to publicly as a performance, program, or zero-base budget, since these have been considered the more modern approaches in recent years.

The Object-of-Expenditure Approach

The object-of-expenditure approach to budgeting, often referred to as the *"traditional"* approach, has an expenditure *control* orientation. The object-of-expenditure approach became popular as the basis for legislative control over the executive branch; and it continues to be the *most widely used,* though elements of newer approaches are often added.

Simply described, the *object-of-expenditure* method involves three facets. First, subordinate agencies submit budget requests to the chief executive in terms of the type of expenditures to be made, that is, the number of people to be hired in each specified position and salary level and the specific goods or services to be purchased during the upcoming period. Next, the chief executive compiles and modifies the agency budget requests and submits an overall request for the organization to the legislature in the same object-of-expenditure terms. Finally, the legislature usually makes *"line-item" appropriations,* possibly after revising the requests, along object-of-expenditure "input" lines. Performance or program data may be included in the budget document, but only to supplement or support the object-of-expenditure requests. The basic elements of this approach are illustrated in Figure 3-3.

Figure 3-3

SIMPLIFIED OBJECT-OF-EXPENDITURE BUDGET

(Classified by Organizational Unit and Object-of-Expenditure)

Mayor's Office

~~~~~~

Police Department

Salaries and Wages:

	Rate		
1—Chief	$ 37,000	$ 37,000	
2—Captains	29,500	59,000	
3—Sergeants.	24,000	72,000	
22—Patrolmen	18,000	396,000	
3—Radio operators.	15,000	45,000	
10—School guards (part time)	2,800	28,000	$ 637,000

Supplies:

Stationery and other office supplies	12,200	
Janitorial supplies	1,100	
Gasoline and oil	33,000	
Uniforms	2,200	
Other	500	49,000

Other Services and Charges:

Telephone	11,400	
Out-of-town travel.	11,800	
Parking tickets	1,600	
Utilities	13,000	
Other	9,200	47,000

Capital Outlay:

1—Motorcycle (net)	6,600	
1—Patrol car (net)	14,400	21,000
Total Police Department.		754,000

Fire Department

Salaries and Wages:

~~~~~~

Total Budget.	$3,801,720

Control Points

Various degrees of appropriation control that a legislature might exercise through object-of-expenditure budgets may be illustrated by identifying the possible **"control points"** in the example in Figure 3-3. A great degree of legislative control will be typified if appropriations are stated in terms of the most detailed level. For example, the police department appropriation might be in terms of one chief, $37,000; two captains, $59,000; and so on. Alternatively, a lesser amount of control would result if appropriations are stated in terms of object classes, that is, Salaries and Wages, $637,000; Supplies, $49,000; Other Services and Charges, $47,000; and Capital Outlay, $21,000. In this case the detailed objects listed would be indicative of the types of goods and services to be secured, but the executive branch would have discretion as to an appropriate "input mix" so long as these expenditure category subtotals were not exceeded. Next, an even greater degree of executive discretion would be granted if appropriations are stated in "lump sum" at the departmental level, for example, Police Department, $754,000. Even though all of the supporting details would have been developed during the budget process and likely would have been presented to the legislature, only departmental totals would be legally binding on the executive in such a situation.

In any event, *the accounting system must capture data in sufficient detail to permit budgetary control and accountability at the legislative-to-executive budgetary control points.*

Further, recall that the chief executive *may* refine the level of legislative control—and make departmental allotments and/or allocations—in order to achieve the desired degree of fiscal control over subordinates. In such cases, the *budgetary accounting system must accumulate data* in sufficient detail to permit budgetary control and accountability *at the chief executive-department head budgetary control points.*

Advantages

Advocates of the object-of-expenditure approach note its longstanding use, its simplicity, and its ease of preparation and understanding by all concerned. Too, they note that budgeting by organizational units and object-of-expenditure closely fits patterns of responsibility accounting, that this method facilitates accounting control in the budget execution process, and that comparable data may be accumulated for a series of years in order to facilitate trend comparison. In addition, they contend that (1) most programs are of an ongoing nature; (2) most expenditures are relatively unavoidable; (3) decisions must, in the real world, be based on *changes* in programs, and attention can most readily be given to changes proposed, compared with prior year data, on this approach; and (4) the object-of-expenditure approach does not preclude supplementing object-of-expenditure data with planning and evaluation information commonly associated with other budgetary approaches. Finally, they observe that where activities are the basis for organizational units, costs of activities are accumulated as costs of the related organizational units. Identification of activity costs permits summations of program and function costs.

Criticisms

Despite its long-term and widespread use, the object-of-expenditure budget has been severely criticized. In its simplest form it provides no genuine information base for decision makers. Figure 3-3 provides only a list of the proposed personnel to be hired and objects or services to be acquired. Only decision makers familiar with the function and activities of a police department will understand the justifications for such expenditures.

Some critics of the object-of-expenditure approach feel that it is overly control-centered, to the detriment of the planning and evaluation processes. They assert that in practice a disproportionate amount of attention is focused on short-term dollar inputs of specific departments (personnel, supplies, and so on); and, consequently, that both long-run considerations and those relevant to the programs of the organization as a whole usually receive inadequate attention. Too, they argue that crucial planning decisions tend to originate at the lowest levels of the organization and flow upward; whereas broad goals, objectives, and policies should originate in the upper echelon and flow downward to be implemented by subordinates. As a result, governmental goals tend to be stated in terms of uncoordinated aggregations of goals of the various department heads.

Critics also assert that planning may be neglected, budgets being based on requests based merely on present expenditure levels and patterns. This "budgeting by default" leads to perpetuation of past activities, whether or not appropriate, failure to set definite goals and objectives, and failure to consider all possible alternatives available to the organization in striving to accomplish its purposes.

Further, some assert that the legislative branch is given more object-of-expenditure detail than it can possibly assimilate, yet is not given data pertaining to the functions, programs, activities, and outputs of executive branch agencies. Consequently, the legislative branch tends to exercise control over such items as the number of telephones to be permitted or the salary of a particular individual, rather than focusing its attention on broad programs and policies of the organization.

This approach is also criticized as being out of date. Line-item appropriations are encouraged by the approach. But critics assert that in today's complex environment the executive branch must have reasonable discretion and flexibility to manage diverse and complex programs.

Finally, critics contend that this method encourages spending rather than economizing, and that department heads feel compelled to expend their full appropriations—whether needed or not. This philosophy arises because (1) performance evaluation tends to be focused on spending, and the manager who keeps spending within budgetary limitations is assumed to be "good," and (2) a manager's subsequent budgets may be reduced as a result of spending less than was appropriated for a given year, since legislators often base appropriations on prior expenditures and also may consider underexpenditure of appropriations to be indicative of budget request "padding."

Comment

Most of these advantages and criticisms of the object-of-expenditure approach are substantive. However, since budgetary control and accountability are paramount considerations in government—both between the legislative and executive branches and within the executive branch— the **control orientation** of the object-of-expenditure approach is apt to ensure its continuing predominance. But because of the validity of the criticisms of the object-of-expenditure approach, it is increasingly being **supplemented** by certain features of the **performance, program, and zero-base budgeting approaches**—which are discussed in the **Appendix** to this chapter.

Because of its widespread use and adaptability to budgetary accounting, *illustrations in the remainder of this text generally assume that an appropriations bill based on organization units and objects of expenditure is in use.* The concepts and procedures illustrated apply generally to all budgetary systems, though expenditure account classifications may need to be changed and additional data gathered to achieve program or performance accountability and reporting.

BUDGET PREPARATION

A substantial part of most government budgeting textbooks is devoted to designing, planning, and implementing appropriate budget preparation procedures. In addition, many SLGs have developed extensive and detailed budget preparation procedures manuals. Our "Budget Preparation" discussions are *not* comparably exhaustive and detailed but summarize the usual budget preparation process from the perspective of the governmental accountant and auditor.

Overview

Sound financial planning requires that budget preparation begin in time for its adoption before the beginning of the budget period. To ensure that adequate time will be allowed, a *budget calendar* listing each step in the budgetary process and the time allowed for its completion should be prepared. The budget preparation then proceeds in a manner similar to that shown in Figure 3-4.

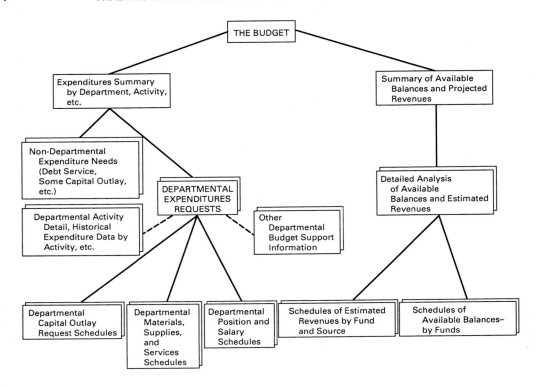

Preliminary Steps

The budget officer and chief executive typically begin preliminary work on the budget for the upcoming year before the steps indicated in the budget cycle (Figure 3-1) are begun in order to:

- Make preliminary estimates of the overall budgetary outlook and parameters—such as the overall levels of expected revenues and appropriations that might be made, including the probable ranges of overall appropriations increases and decreases.

- Inform department heads and others involved in the budgeting process of the plausible ranges of appropriation requests, the chief executive's priorities for the upcoming year, and related matters.

    The preliminary estimates of the *ideal* levels of appropriations and expenditures during the upcoming year almost always *exceed* the *financial resources to be available.* Thus, budgeting has been described "as the process of allocating scarce resources to unlimited demands."

    The *basic formula* for *budget decision makers* is:

Estimated fund balance, beginning of budget year	$	X
Add: Estimated revenues and other financing sources (e.g., transfers from other funds), budget year		Y
Total appropriable resources, budget year	$	X + Y
Deduct: Estimated expenditures (appropriations) and other uses of financial resources (e.g., transfers to other funds), budget year		Z
Estimated fund balance, end of year		$X + Y − Z

After estimating the fund balance to be available at the beginning of the upcoming budget year, the budget officer must obtain estimates of (1) the revenues that will be produced by all revenue sources at current rates of taxes, fees, and other charges; (2) any other sources of appropriable resources (e.g., transfers from other funds); and (3) the fund balance needed at the end of the upcoming budget year for carryover to the next year. Having produced such estimates, the budget officer and the chief executive can compare them with revenues, expenditures, and interfund transfers of prior years and with their knowledge of changes in demands on the government and its programs. Such comparisons should provide an impression of the adequacy of estimated revenues to meet the needs for expenditures.

Preparing the Budget

Preparation of the annual budget for the upcoming year now proceeds along lines indicated in the **budget cycle** (Figure 3-1). The chief executive and department heads typically interact frequently during the budget preparation process. For example:

- The chief executive indicates the overall parameters and ranges of plausible departmental appropriation requests—for example, that appropriations will only be increased up to 3 percent—as well as budget priorities, and so forth.
- The department heads usually confer informally with the budget officer or chief executive during the budget preparation process—possibly seeking exceptions to the overall budget guidelines for certain activities or to persuade the chief executive to place special priority on certain programs.
- After reviewing the departmental appropriation requests, the budget officer or chief executive may confer with department heads to revise these requests in preparing the final executive budget.

Revenue Estimates

Each revenue source is analyzed in detail—in terms of past amounts, trends, factors apt to affect it next year, and expected level in the upcoming year—in preparing the budget. Since most revenues relate to the government as a whole—for example, property taxes, sales taxes, and interest—the budget officer makes most revenue estimates. However, the various departments often estimate the revenues that relate to specific departments—such as inspections, permits, and charges for services.

In order to simplify the illustrations here and in Chapter 4, we assume that the budget is presented, approved, controlled, accounted for, and reported in these broad revenue source categories:

- Taxes
- Licenses and Permits
- Intergovernmental
- Fines and Forfeits
- Other

Revenues typically are controlled, accounted for, and reported on in more detail in practice, of course.

Expenditure Estimates

Each departmental expenditure category is likewise analyzed in detail—in terms of past amounts, trends, factors apt to affect it next year, and its necessary level in the upcoming year—in preparing the budget. As noted earlier, much interaction may occur between and among the department heads, budget officer, and chief executive in determining the appropriation proposals for the upcoming year.

For purposes of illustration here and in Chapter 4, we assume that the appropriation requests are approved, controlled, accounted for, and reported in these broad functional expenditure categories:

- General Government
- Public Safety
- Highways and Streets
- Health and Sanitation
- Culture and Recreation
- Other

Appropriations usually would be made in more detail in practice, of course—typically by major category of expenditure (e.g., personal services, supplies, capital outlay) within each department.

Other Estimates

The budget officer and chief executive might also include other proposed sources and uses of financial resources in the executive budget. For example, interfund operating transfers or residual equity transfers might be proposed. For illustrative purposes here and in Chapter 4, it is assumed that interfund transfers are **not** included in the annual operating budget, but are **separately authorized nonbudgeted** sources and uses of financial resources.

The Budget Document

Given these simplifying assumptions, assume also that the executive budget proposed (and subsequently approved) for a governmental fund (e.g., the General Fund) of A Governmental Unit for the 19X2 fiscal year is that presented in Figure 3-5.

LEGISLATIVE CONSIDERATION AND ACTION

After receiving the executive budget document, the legislative body must adopt an official "budget." A legislature of a state or large city usually turns the proposed budget over to a committee or committees to make investigations, to call on department heads and the chief executive for justifications of their requests, and to conduct public hearings. The committee then makes its recommendations to the legislature. In smaller municipalities the council or board of supervisors may act as a committee of the whole in its consideration of the budget.

After completing the budget hearings and investigations, the legislative body adopts the budget, as revised, by passing an **appropriation act or ordinance.** The amount of detail in which the act is expressed determines the flexibility granted to the executive branch by the legislative body. Lump-sum appropriations may be made for functions or activities, or, more likely, for organization units. If proper internal control, accounting, reporting, and postaudit procedures are used, the legislative body can retain control of operations without recourse to detailed appropriations. However, most legislative bodies insist on fairly detailed

Figure 3-5

ANNUAL OPERATING BUDGET

Governmental Fund
A Governmental Unit
19X2 Fiscal Year

Estimated Revenues:	
Taxes	$ 900,000
Licenses and permits	400,000
Intergovernmental	350,000
Charges for services	50,000
Fines and forfeits	100,000
Other	200,000
	2,000,000
Appropriations:	
General government	250,000
Public safety	575,000
Highways and streets	500,000
Health and sanitation	375,000
Culture and recreation	200,000
Other	50,000
	1,950,000
Excess of Estimated Revenues over Appropriations	50,000
Estimated Fund Balance—Beginning of 19X2	450,000
Estimated Fund Balance—End of 19X2	$ 500,000

Note: *In practice, the estimated revenue and revenue accounts would be established in more detailed source categories, and the appropriation and expenditure accounts would be established by department and object-of-expenditure category.*

object-of-expenditure data in the executive budget, and they may be appropriated in comparable detail.

The appropriation act or ordinance merely authorizes expenditures. It is also necessary to provide the means of financing them. Some revenues (for example, interest on investments) will accrue to the governmental unit without any legal action on its part. Other revenues will come as a result of legal action taken in the past. Examples of these are licenses and fees, income taxes, and sales taxes, the rates for which continue until they are changed by the legislative body. A third type of revenue—for example, the general property tax—usually requires new legal action each year. Accordingly, as soon as the legislative body has passed the appropriation ordinance or act, it proceeds to levy general property taxes.

BUDGET EXECUTION

Just as the budget approved by the legislative body expresses in financial terms the government's planned activities, the process of budget execution includes every operating decision and transaction made during the budget period. For this reason Figure 3-1, "The Budget Cycle," lists the many activities of administration as aspects of budget execution. *Accounting keeps a record of the results of the transactions and permits their summarization, reporting, and comparison with plans (the budget).* Therefore, the following chapters that describe the accounting and reporting for the governmental funds are all related to budget execution.

The legally adopted revenue estimates and appropriations are such a controlling influence in government that, contrary to business practice, **the budget is**

recorded as an integral part of the accounting system. In the general ledger, as well as in the subsidiary ledgers for revenues and expenditures, budgeted amounts are recorded and can be directly compared with their actual counterparts. **Similarly, accountability for budget compliance is reported in the financial statements** together with the information accountants expect from the financial statements of the profit-seeking sector of the economy. Accordingly, the remainder of this chapter is devoted to brief illustrative overviews of governmental fund budgetary accounting and budgetary reporting.

BUDGETARY ACCOUNTING OVERVIEW

Effecting budgetary control in the accounting system requires that **budgetary accounts**—for total estimated revenues, appropriations, and encumbrances—be included in the *general ledger* of a governmental fund, and *subsidiary ledgers* be established to account for *each* revenue source and *each* expenditure category in at least as much detail as in the legally adopted budget. The manner in which this is accomplished is illustrated in Figure 3-6, "Budgetary Accounting Overview." Alternatively, only the detailed accounts may be maintained and the totals derived through summation.

General Ledger

The integration of **budgetary accounts** into the **general ledger** does not affect the asset and liability accounts, which record only actual assets and liabilities. Rather, it involves the use of both:

1. Estimated Revenues and Revenues (actual) control accounts to record the *total* estimated and actual revenues at any time during the year; and
2. Accounts for *total* Appropriations (authorized estimated expenditures), actual Expenditures, and Encumbrances—the estimated cost of goods and services ordered but not received—to indicate the *total* appropriations, expenditures, and encumbrances outstanding at any point during the year.

In addition to providing data on *total budgeted and actual* revenues and expenditures to date and on encumbrances (expenditures in process), these general ledger accounts serve as **control accounts** over the more detailed revenues and expenditures subsidiary ledgers.

Revenues and Expenditures Subsidiary Ledgers

Revenues and expenditures **subsidiary ledgers** are established to effect *detailed* budgetary control over *each* revenue source and *each* appropriation category. *Note* the *relationships between* these *subsidiary ledgers and* the *general ledger,* as illustrated in Figure 3-6, as well as the *column heading* of the *accounts* of *each* subsidiary ledger. Note also that *a separate account is established for each revenue source and appropriation category in the legally adopted budget.*

Revenues Subsidiary Ledger

Responsible persons or departments can monitor individual revenue sources using the data accumulated in the Revenue Subsidiary Ledger. These data include *both estimated and actual revenues* for each significant revenue source. Further,

Figure 3-6

BUDGETARY ACCOUNTING OVERVIEW

(Governmental Fund)
General Ledger and Subsidiary Ledgers

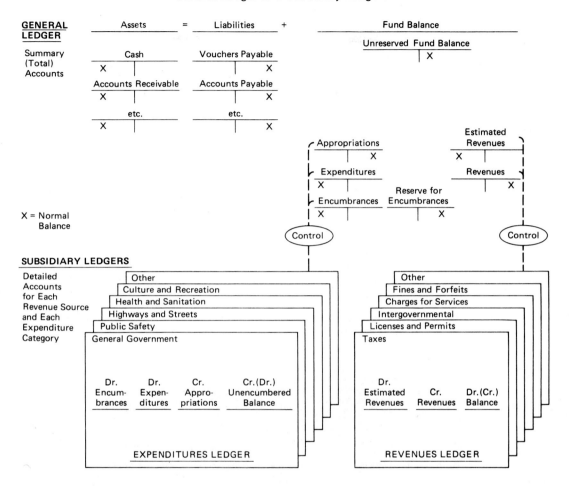

such data help the finance officer monitor the revenue management process, and may signal a need to revise the budget during the year. For example, significant shortfalls in budgeted revenue sources may necessitate both lowering revenue estimates for the year and reducing appropriations.

The relationship of the Estimated Revenues and Revenues *general ledger control accounts* and the more detailed **Revenues Subsidiary Ledger accounts** is illustrated in Figure 3-7. Note the following in studying Figure 3-7:

1. **When the Budget Is Adopted.**
   a. The *total* of the *estimated* revenues for the year is **debited** to the Estimated Revenues *general ledger* **control account** when the annual budget is adopted.
   b. *Each* revenue source component estimate is posted to the "Estimated Revenues" column of its *Revenues Subsidiary Ledger account.*
   c. At this point the balances of the Revenues Subsidiary Ledger accounts represent the amounts of revenues *expected* to be recognized during the year.

Figure 3-7

**RELATIONSHIP OF GENERAL LEDGER ESTIMATED REVENUES
AND REVENUES CONTROL ACCOUNTS
AND THE REVENUES SUBSIDIARY LEDGER ACCOUNTS**

(Governmental Fund)

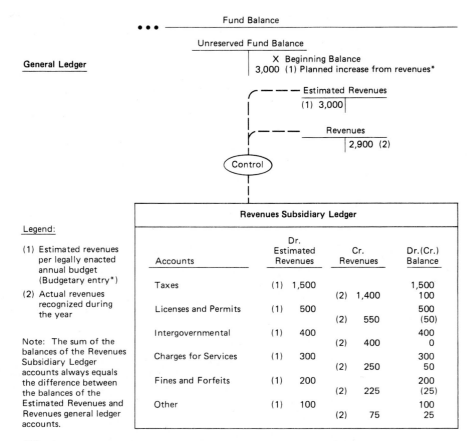

The general ledger budgetary entry is explained and illustrated further in Chapter 4.
Note: *Only one estimated revenue entry and one actual revenue entry are illustrated. In practice, several estimated revenue entries and many actual revenue entries are made each year.*

2. **When Revenues are Recognized.**
   a. The **total** of the **actual** revenues is **credited** to the Revenues **general ledger control account** as revenues are recognized.
   b. **Each** actual revenue source component amount is posted to the "Revenues" (actual) column of its **Revenues Subsidiary Ledger account.**
   c. The balances of the Revenues Subsidiary Ledger accounts now represent the **differences** between budgeted and actual revenues to date.

3. **"Control" Relationship.** At any time during the year the **sum** of the **balances** of the **Revenues Subsidiary Ledger accounts** should equal the **difference** between the balances of the Estimated Revenues and Revenues **general ledger** accounts.

Only six revenue accounts are included in the Revenues Subsidiary Ledger illustrated in Figure 3-7. In practice, 50–100 or more Revenues Subsidiary Ledger accounts may be necessary to properly control and monitor the various revenue sources. For example, instead of a single Taxes revenue account it may be appropriate to establish separate revenue accounts for

Real Property Taxes—Residential	Sales Taxes
Real Property Taxes—Commercial	Income Taxes—Individuals
Personal Property Taxes—Residential	Income Taxes—Corporations
Personal Property Taxes—Commercial	

Further, while only one estimated revenue entry and one actual revenue entry are illustrated in Figure 3-7, many entries are apt to be made during the year in practice. Estimated revenue entries are made only upon the adoption or revision of the official revenue estimates—so only a few estimated revenue entries may be made annually. But one or more actual revenue entries may be made daily.

Expenditures Subsidiary Ledger

The Expenditures Subsidiary Ledger accumulates data during the year on **each appropriation,** including the related (1) expenditures to date, (2) encumbrances outstanding, and (3) unencumbered balance. The Expenditures Subsidiary Ledger thus facilitates the monitoring and control of each appropriation by the department head responsible and by the finance officer. For example, proposed purchase orders for public safety purposes are compared with the unencumbered balance of the public safety appropriation (against which the related expenditures will be charged) before approval. Approved purchase orders are charged as encumbrances against the appropriation. This (1) ensures that sufficient appropriations will be available as authority for the subsequent expenditure for the goods or services ordered and, correspondingly, (2) reduces the "unencumbered balance" of the related Expenditures Subsidiary Ledger account.

The **relationship** of the Appropriations, Expenditures, and Encumbrances *general ledger* **control accounts** and the more detailed *Expenditures Subsidiary Ledger accounts* is illustrated in Figure 3-8. Note the following in studying Figure 3-8:

1. **When the Budget Is Adopted.**
    a. The **total** of the **appropriations**—the total authorized and estimated expenditures for the year—is credited to the Appropriations *general ledger* control account when the annual budget is adopted.
    b. **Each** appropriation component is posted to the "Appropriations" column of its *Expenditures Subsidiary Ledger account.*
    c. At this point, the balances of the Expenditures Subsidiary Ledger accounts represent the amounts of expenditures **authorized** to be incurred during the year.

2. **When Encumbrances Are Incurred.**
    a. The **total** amounts of **encumbrances**—expenditures **expected** to be incurred for goods or services ordered or contracted for—are recorded in **offsetting general ledger** Encumbrances and Reserve for Encumbrances accounts.
    b. **Each** encumbrance is posted to the "Encumbrances" column of the **Expenditures Subsidiary Ledger account** against which the resulting expenditures will be charged, thus reducing its **"Unencumbered Balance"** available for expenditure.
    c. This effectively "reserves" a sufficient balance of each appropriation for the expenditures expected to result from the encumbrances; hence, the term "reserve for encumbrances."

Figure 3-8   RELATIONSHIP OF GENERAL LEDGER APPROPRIATIONS, EXPENDITURES, AND ENCUMBRANCES ACCOUNTS AND THE EXPENDITURES SUBSIDIARY LEDGER ACCOUNTS

(Governmental Fund)

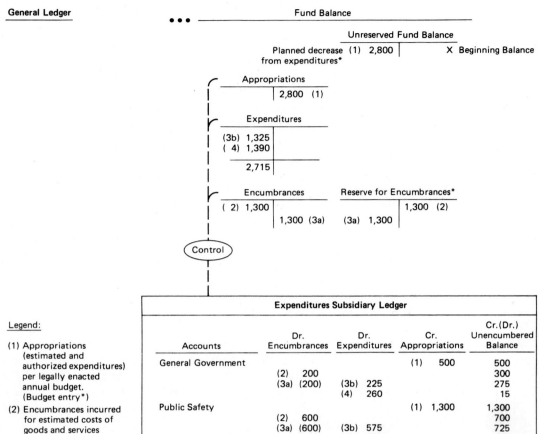

Legend:

(1) Appropriations (estimated and authorized expenditures) per legally enacted annual budget. (Budget entry*)

(2) Encumbrances incurred for estimated costs of goods and services ordered (purchase orders) or contracted for (contracts).

(3) Goods and services ordered were received; actual costs sometimes more or less than estimated. (Entry 3a reverses the encumbrance entry (2); Entry 3b records the actual expenditures.)

(4) Expenditures incurred that were not previously encumbered (e.g., salaries, utilities)

Accounts	Dr. Encumbrances	Dr. Expenditures	Cr. Appropriations	Cr.(Dr.) Unencumbered Balance
General Government			(1) 500	500
	(2) 200			300
	(3a) (200)	(3b) 225		275
		(4) 260		15
Public Safety			(1) 1,300	1,300
	(2) 600			700
	(3a) (600)	(3b) 575		725
		(4) 700		25
Highways and Streets			(1) 400	400
	(2) 300			100
	(3a) (300)	(3b) 300		100
		(4) 100		0
Health and Sanitation			(1) 300	300
	(2) 100			200
	(3a) (100)	(3b) 125		175
		(4) 160		15
Culture and Recreation			(1) 200	200
	(2) 75			125
	(3a) (75)	(3b) 75		125
		(4) 100		25
Other			(1) 100	100
	(2) 25			75
	(3a) (25)	(3b) 25		75
		(4) 70		5

*The general ledger budgetary entry and the Reserve for Encumbrances account are explained and illustrated in Chapter 4.

Notes:

1. The sum of the unencumbered balances of the Expenditures Subsidiary Ledger accounts always equals the difference between the balance of the Appropriations general ledger account and the sum of the Expenditures and Encumbrances general ledger accounts.

2. Only a few appropriation, encumbrance, and expenditure entries are illustrated here. In practice, several appropriation entries and many encumbrance and expenditure entries are made each year.

3. **When Encumbrances Result in Expenditures.** When goods or services ordered are received, the government no longer has an encumbrance, but an expenditure. Accordingly,

   a. the *encumbrances are "reversed"* (removed from the accounts).

   b. the *expenditures are recorded* in the accounts.

   c. the "Unencumbered Balance" of the Expenditures Subsidiary Ledger accounts is adjusted for any difference between the estimated expenditures (encumbrances) and actual expenditures.

4. **When Unencumbered Expenditures Are Incurred.**

   a. Expenditures not resulting from purchase orders or other contracts—for example, salaries and utilities—are recorded when incurred.

   b. No encumbrance reversal entry is needed.

   c. All expenditures, whether or not previously encumbered, reduce the "Unencumbered Balance" of the related Expenditures Subsidiary Ledger accounts.

5. **"Control" Relationship.**

   a. At any time during the year, the *sum* of the *"Unencumbered Balance" column amounts* of the Expenditures Subsidiary Ledger accounts should equal the **difference** between the balance of the Appropriations *general ledger* account and the sum of the Expenditures and Encumbrances *general ledger* accounts.

   b. Further, to ensure proper budgetary control and avoid appropriation overruns, most computerized accounting systems are programmed to reject (not process) any encumbrance or expenditure transaction that would cause the "Unencumbered Balance" column of an Expenditures Subsidiary Ledger account to have a debit balance.

Only six expenditures accounts are included in the Expenditures Subsidiary Ledger illustrated in Figure 3-8. In practice several hundred Expenditures Subsidiary Ledger accounts may be necessary to monitor and control the numerous appropriations properly. For example, instead of a single General Government expenditures account it usually is necessary to establish more detailed accounts, such as:

General Government—Legislative Branch
General Government—Executive Branch
General Government—Judicial Branch
General Government—Elections
General Government—Financial Administration
General Government—Other

Further, depending on the level of detail at which the appropriations are enacted, it is often necessary to establish even more detailed object-of-expenditure accounts for each departmental and other appropriation, such as:

General Government—Legislative Branch—Personal Services
General Government—Legislative Branch—Supplies
General Government—Legislative Branch—Other Services and Charges
General Government—Legislative Branch—Capital Outlay

Finally, while only a few appropriations, encumbrances, and expenditures entries are illustrated in Figure 3-8, many entries are likely to be made each year in practice. Appropriations entries are made only upon adoption or revision of the budget—so only a few appropriations entries may be made annually. But several encumbrances and expenditures entries may be made daily.

BUDGETARY REPORTING OVERVIEW

Because of the unique importance of budgeting, budgetary control, and budgetary accountability in the state and local government environment, ***both interim (e.g., monthly) and annual budgetary statements are prepared.*** Further, the GASB requires extensive budgetary reporting in the comprehensive annual financial report (CAFR), which includes the general purpose financial statements (GPFS). These requirements include:

1. a ***summary budgetary comparison statement*** by function or program—***prepared on the unit's budgetary basis***—for its ***annually budgeted governmental funds;***
2. a similar budgetary basis ***schedule(s)*** at the ***legislative-to-executive branch "budgetary control points" level of detail;*** and
3. an **explanation** of the unit's budgetary basis ***and*** a ***reconciliation*** of the budgetary basis data and the GAAP basis data.

The Budgetary Basis

Another unique feature of governmental budgeting, budgetary control, and budgetary accountability is that ***the governing body can choose the basis on which its annual budget will be prepared and adopted, controlled, and reported upon.*** Accordingly, whereas some governments budget their governmental funds on the modified accrual (GAAP) basis, others budget revenues and expenditures on the cash basis. That is, for budgetary accounting and reporting purposes they do not recognize revenues and expenditures until the related cash is received or disbursed, respectively. In either event, most governments maintain their ***accounts*** on the ***budgetary*** basis ***during*** the year—for budgetary control and for interim and annual ***budgetary reporting*** purposes—then ***adjust*** the accounts to the ***GAAP*** basis at ***year end*** for annual ***GAAP basis reporting*** purposes.

Further, ***some*** governments consider **encumbrances outstanding** to be the ***equivalent of expenditures*** for **budgetary reporting** purposes—and compare the sum of expenditures and encumbrances with appropriations. This is known as the **"encumbrances method."** But ***other*** governments consider encumbrance accounting to be only an internal budgetary control technique to avoid incurring expenditures in excess of appropriations. Since these governments do ***not*** consider encumbrances to be equivalent to expenditures for budgetary reporting purposes, they (1) compare budgetary basis expenditures (only) with appropriations and report the "unexpended" (not "unencumbered") appropriation balances, and (2) disclose encumbrances outstanding in the notes to the financial statements or in a fund balance "reserve" (discussed later).

Because of the variation of budgetary bases in practice, the need for effective budgetary control, and GAAP requirements related to budgetary reporting, the ***governmental accountant and auditor must:***

- Carefully ***identify the budgetary basis*** used by each state or local government, particularly for its annually budgeted governmental funds, and
- ***Ensure*** that the ***budgetary basis is appropriately used*** in budgetary accounting and reporting, ***and*** that the ***differences*** between the budgetary basis and

the GAAP basis are adequately *explained and reconciled* in the CAFR and GPFS.

Interim Budgetary Statements

Monthly or quarterly interim budgetary statements typically are *prepared directly from the revenues and expenditures subsidiary ledger accounts* illustrated in Figures 3-7 and 3-8. Since GAAP require only that interim statements be "appropriate" for their management control, legislative oversight, or other purposes—i.e., the GASB has *not* established interim financial statement formats, contents, and so on—interim budgetary reports may contain whatever statements, schedules, and other information management deems appropriate.

Interim Revenues Statements

Interim revenues statements typically include, as a minimum, data from the Revenues Subsidiary Ledger accounts (Figure 3-7) on

1. the revenues recognized to date and
2. the estimated revenues for the year. Too, interim statements often include the difference between the two.

Further, percentage data are frequently presented—such as the percent of the estimated annual revenues realized to date, by revenue category and in total, and the percent of each revenue source and total revenues that had been realized at this time last year. For example, a monthly budgetary revenues statement might present—for each revenue source and in total:

		Percent Realized to Date	
Revenues Year to Date	*Estimated Revenues for the Year*	*Current Year*	*Prior Year*

In addition, management commentary accompanying the interim revenue statement should describe any significant factors affecting revenues to date or apt to affect the revenues in the upcoming months and for the year. Indeed, evaluations of budgetary reports are often the basis on which the governing body revises the estimated revenues budget during the year.

Interim Expenditures Statements

Interim expenditures statements typically include, as a minimum, data drawn from the Expenditures Subsidiary Ledger accounts (Figure 3-8) at the interim statement date on

1. appropriations for the year,
2. expenditures to date,
3. encumbrances outstanding at the interim date, and
4. the unencumbered balance of each appropriation.

For example, a monthly budgetary expenditures statement might present—for each appropriation and in total:

Year to Date				
Expenditures	*Encumbrances*	*Total*	*Annual Appropriations*	*Unencumbered Balance*

Governments using monthly allotments controls would also include data for the allotment period; and those budgeting on the encumbrances method may present only the expenditures and encumbrances total. Further, as in interim revenues budgetary reporting, interim expenditure budgetary statements (1) may contain year-to-date and/or prior year comparative percentage data, (2) should contain management commentary on any significant factors affecting expenditures and encumbrances to date or apt to affect total expenditures for the year or encumbrances outstanding at year end, and (3) often serve as the basis for governing body revisions of appropriations during the year.

Interim Revenues and Expenditures Statements

Although interim budgetary statements for revenues and expenditures may be presented separately, they often are presented in the same statement. This type of interim budgetary comparison statement is illustrated in Figure 3-9. Further, the budgetary comparison data may be summarized in the budgetary comparison statement, which may be supported by separate, more detailed revenues and expenditures budgetary schedules.

Figure 3-9

INTERIM BUDGETARY COMPARISON STATEMENT

(Budgetary Basis)
A Governmental Unit
Governmental Fund
At End of (Month), 19X2

	Actual (To Date)	Annual Budget	Unrealized/ Unencumbered	Percent (%) Actual to Date to Total 19X2	19X1
Revenues:					
Taxes	$ 550,000	$ 900,000	$ 350,000	61.1	66.0
Licenses and permits	150,000	400,000	250,000	37.5	31.0
Intergovernmental	200,000	350,000	150,000	57.1	60.7
Charges for services	25,000	50,000	25,000	50.0	45.4
Fines and forfeits	40,000	100,000	60,000	40.0	35.6
Other	70,000	200,000	130,000	35.0	33.3
	1,035,000	2,000,000	$ 965,000	51.8	49.7
Expenditures and Encumbrances:					
General government	120,000	250,000	130,000	48.0	51.3
Public safety	300,000	575,000	275,000	52.2	48.0
Highways and streets	175,000	500,000	325,000	35.0	55.0
Health and sanitation	225,000	375,000	150,000	60.0	51.4
Culture and recreation	70,000	200,000	130,000	35.0	41.6
Other	60,000	50,000	(10,000)	120.0	55.4
	950,000	1,950,000	$1,000,000	48.7	46.0
Excess of Revenues over (under) Expenditures and Encumbrances	$ 85,000	$ 50,000			

Notes:
1. *This statement may also contain beginning fund balance and anticipated ending fund balance amounts.*
2. *Expenditures and encumbrances may be presented separately as well as in total.*
3. *If encumbrances are not viewed as equivalent to expenditures for budgetary purposes, only expenditures (not encumbrances) are presented in this statement.*

Annual Budgetary Statements

As noted earlier, GASB standards require extensive budgetary reporting presentations in the governmental unit's CAFR (which includes the GPFS). The CAFR budgetary reporting requirements include:

1. A summary budgetary comparison statement—**prepared on the unit's budgetary basis**—for its annually budgeted governmental funds (Figure 3-10);
2. A similar budgetary basis schedule(s) at the legislative-to-executive branch "budgetary control points" level of detail;
3. An explanation of the unit's budgetary basis; and
4. A reconciliation of the unit's budgetary basis and GAAP basis operating data.

Figure 3-10

STATEMENT OF REVENUES, EXPENDITURES AND ENCUMBRANCES, AND CHANGES IN FUND BALANCE—BUDGET AND ACTUAL

(Budgetary Basis)

A Governmental Unit
Governmental Fund
For Fiscal Year Ended (Date)

	Budget (As Revised)	Actual	Variance— Favorable (Unfavorable)
Revenues:			
Taxes	$ 900,000	$ 918,000	$ 18,000
Licenses and permits	400,000	395,000	(5,000)
Intergovernmental	350,000	364,000	14,000
Charges for services	50,000	49,000	(1,000)
Fines and forfeits	100,000	102,000	2,000
Other	200,000	197,000	(3,000)
	2,000,000	2,025,000	25,000
Expenditures and Encumbrances:			
General government	250,000	249,000	1,000
Public safety	575,000	570,000	5,000
Highways and streets	500,000	490,000	10,000
Health and sanitation	375,000	371,000	4,000
Culture and recreation	200,000	194,000	6,000
Other	50,000	65,000	(15,000)
	1,950,000	1,939,000	11,000
Excess of Revenues over Expenditures and Encumbrances	50,000	86,000	36,000
Fund Balance—Beginning of Period	450,000	450,000	—
Fund Balance—End of Period	$ 500,000	$ 536,000	$ 36,000

Notes:

1. Data on the original budget, before revisions, may be presented in a "Budget (Original)" column preceding the "Budget (As Revised)" column of this statement. (For illustrative simplicity, the examples in this chapter assume that no budget revisions were enacted.)
2. This statement assumes that the budgetary basis in use considers encumbrances outstanding equivalent to expenditures for budgetary control, accountability, and evaluation purposes. Thus, "expenditures and encumbrances" are reported rather than only "expenditures."
3. The GASB requires that published financial statements include an explanation of the unit's budgetary basis and a reconciliation of the differences between its budgetary basis and GAAP basis operating data.

Further, the GASB Codification includes illustrative examples of a summary budgetary comparison statement—the Statement of Revenues, Expenditures, and Changes in Fund Balances—**Budget and Actual**—as well as guidance to (1) preparing and presenting the more detailed "budgetary control points" schedules(s) and (2) explaining the budgetary basis and reconciling the budgetary basis and GAAP basis operating data.

An example of a summary annual budgetary comparison statement—in this case, the Statement of Revenues, Expenditures and Encumbrances, and Changes in Fund Balance—Budget and Actual—is presented in Figure 3-10. This statement is prepared on the *budgetary basis—here assumed to consider encumbrances the budgetary equivalent of expenditures*—and would be accompanied by a budgetary-GAAP basis explanation and reconciliation. Variations of this format, other approaches to preparing the summary budgetary comparison statement (e.g., for a GAAP basis budget and for budgets on other budgetary bases), preparing detailed budgetary schedules, and presenting budgetary-GAAP basis explanations and reconciliations are discussed and illustrated in later chapters of this text.

CONCLUDING COMMENTS

Budgeting, budgetary accounting, and budgetary reporting are uniquely important features of the governmental fund accounting and financial reporting environment. Indeed, governmental fund accounting is sometimes referred to as "budgetary accounting"; and budgeting, budgetary accounting, and budgetary reporting are recurring topics on the Uniform CPA Examination.

Accordingly, much of this chapter is devoted to discussions of budgetary terminology, the major budgetary approaches and emphases, and preparation of the annual operating budget. The budgetary accounting and reporting "overview" discussions and illustrations that conclude this chapter, both introduce these important topics and provide a bridge to the budgetary accounting entries and budgetary statement examples in the next several chapters. Thus, these overview discussions and illustrations should be reviewed before proceeding to Chapter 4, "General and Special Revenue Funds," and reviewed again while studying that chapter.

Appendix 3–1
ALTERNATIVE EXPENDITURE BUDGETING APPROACHES

As noted in Chapter 3, the most common approaches to *operating expenditure budgeting* may be characterized as:

1. Object-of-expenditure
2. Performance
3. Program and planning-programming-budgeting (PPB)
4. Zero-base budgeting (ZBB)

The object-of-expenditure or "line-item" approach is discussed and illustrated in Chapter 3. This appendix focuses on the remaining three alternative expenditure budgeting approaches.

THE PERFORMANCE APPROACH

Although the **performance** approach originated near the turn of the century, it received its biggest impetus from the report of the first Hoover Commission in 1949 and came into popular usage in the 1950s. The Hoover Commission report included the statement:

> We recommend that the whole budgetary concept of the federal government should be refashioned by the adoption of a budget based on functions, activities, and projects: this we designate a "performance budget."[1]

Confusion accompanied the report of the Commission's Task Force, however, because it used the terms "performance" and "program" synonymously:

> A program or performance budget should be substituted for the present budget, thus presenting a document . . . in terms of services, activities, and work projects rather than in terms of the things bought.[2]

Although these terms have been used synonymously by many eminent authorities, the term "program budgeting" has taken on different connotations from that of "performance budgeting" and these terms will be distinguished here.[3] A **performance budget** is

> A budget wherein expenditures are based primarily upon measurable performance of activities and work programs. A performance budget may also incorporate other bases of expenditure classification, such as character and object class, but these are given a subordinate status to activity performance.[4]

This approach ***shifts budgeting emphasis from objects of expenditure to "measurable performance of activities and work programs."*** The ***primary focus*** is on ***evaluation*** of the efficiency with which existing activities are being carried out; its primary tools are cost accounting and work measurement. The gist of this method may be summarized as (1) classifying budgetary accounts by function and activity, as well as by organization unit and object of expenditure, (2) investigating and measuring existing activities in order to obtain maximum efficiency and to establish cost standards, and (3) basing the budget of the succeeding period on unit cost standards multiplied by the expected number of units of the activity estimated to be required in that period. The total budget for an agency would be the sum of the products of its unit cost standards multiplied by the expected units of activity in the upcoming period. The ***enacted budget*** is viewed somewhat as a ***performance contract*** between the legislative branch and the chief executive.

---

[1] Commission on Organization of the Executive Branch of the Government, *Budgeting and Accounting* (Washington, D.C.: U.S. Government Printing Office, 1949), p. 8.

[2] Task Force Report, *Fiscal, Budgeting, and Accounting Activities* (Washington, DC.: U.S. Government Printing Office, 1949), p. 43.

[3] The confusion has arisen primarily over differing uses of the term "program." In performance budgeting the term has been applied generally to specific activities within a single department (street sweeping, police patrol, and so on), whereas in program or planning-programming-budgeting (PPB) the term usually has a broader connotation (preservation of life and property, alleviation of pain and suffering, and so on) which may include activities of many departments of a government.

[4] GAAFR (88), p. 173.

Advantages

Probably the most important contributions of the performance approach have been (1) its emphasis on including a narrative description of each proposed activity within the proposed budget, (2) organization of the budget by activities, with requests supported by estimates of costs and accomplishments in quantitative terms, and (3) its emphasis on the need to measure output as well as input. The performance budget thus emphasizes the activities for which appropriations are requested rather than merely how much will be spent, and requires answers to questions such as these:

1. What are the agency's objectives; for what reason does the agency ask for appropriations; what services does the agency render to justify its existence?
2. What programs or activities does the agency use to achieve its objectives?
3. What volume of work is required in each of the activities?
4. What levels of services have past appropriations provided?
5. What level of activity or service may legislators and the taxpayers expect if the requested amounts are appropriated?

To provide the legislative body with a reasonable justification for its budget request, each department must do some clear thinking about what it is trying to do and how it can do it best. In addition, when the legislators fully understand the department's work, its objectives, and its problems, the appropriation ordinance achieves its full meaning as a contract between the executive and legislative branches.

Performance data also provide legislators additional freedom to reduce or expand the amounts requested for particular functions or activities. Where information is available as to particular functions and activities, these may be readily expanded or contracted at the will of legislature. On the other hand, where only object-of-expenditure data are available, the legislature must deal with minute details and may be tempted to make arbitrary changes such as slashing all requests a given percentage. When final appropriations under the performance approach differ from the requested amounts for certain functions or activities, the executive branch must, of course, revise its plans in order to make the most effective use of amounts appropriated.

The performance approach also provides the chief executive with an additional avenue of control over his or her subordinates. Rather than being restricted merely to how much subordinates spend, he or she may evaluate the performance of activities in terms of both dollar and activity unit standards.

Limitations

Although much has been written about the performance approach, it does not appear to have often been adopted in its "pure" state. The approach is fundamentally sound, but (1) few state and local governments have sufficient budgetary or accounting staffs to identify units of measurement, perform cost analyses, and so on; (2) many government services and activities do not appear readily measurable in meaningful output units or unit cost terms; and (3) accounts of governments have typically been maintained on a budgetary expenditure basis, rather than on a full cost basis, making data gathering difficult if not impossible. In practice, expenditure data often have been substituted indiscriminately for cost (expense) data; and input measures have been used in place of output measures. In addition, activities sometimes have been costed and measured in great detail without sufficient consideration being given to the necessity or desirability of the activities them-selves—that is, without concern for whether the activity was the best means (or even contributed) to achieving the government's goals. For these and other rea-sons, most attempts to install comprehensive performance budgeting systems were disappointing and no doubt discouraged others from experimenting with the approach. Advocates of the performance approach feel that it has helped instill an attitude of cost consciousness in government, however, and note the many gov-ernmental activities now being measured objectively.

Comment

Although the performance budgeting approach never achieved widespread use in its entirety, the approach has proved extremely helpful—especially when its ap-plication has been limited to discrete, tangible, routine types of activities such as street sweeping, police patrol, and garbage collection. Further, performance data are frequently used to **supplement** or support **object-of-expenditure** budget re-quests and are **essential** to **program budgeting.**

THE PROGRAM AND PLANNING-PROGRAMMING-BUDGETING (PPB) APPROACHES

Another reason for the apparent demise of the performance budget (as such) was the shift in emphasis in the late 1950s and early 1960s to the program approach and then, in the mid-1960s, to what has come to be known as the Planning-Programming-Budgeting System, often referred to as PPB or PPBS. Here again, ter-minology is a problem. The term "program budget" is sometimes used to refer to PPB systems or approaches and at other times is used in distinctly different ways. The GFOA, for example, defines a **program budget** as:

> A budget wherein expenditures are based primarily on programs of work and sec-ondarily on character and object . . . a transitional type of budget between the tra-ditional character and object class budget, on the one hand, and the performance budget, on the other.[5]

Others distinguish between "full program" and "modified program" budgetary ap-proaches, the latter being essentially a performance approach in which unit cost measurement is attempted only selectively. The following definition is preferred by the authors:

> Program budgets deal principally with broad planning and the costs of functions or activities. A **full** program approach to budgeting would require that the full cost of a function, e.g., juvenile delinquency control, would be set forth under the *program* regardless of the organizational units that may be involved in carrying such pro-grams into execution. Thus, in the juvenile delinquency "program," certain activi-ties of the welfare agency, the police department, the juvenile courts, the law department, and the district attorney would be included . . . .
> **A modified** program budget approach would be organized solely within major or-ganizational units, e.g., departments.[6]

As the term is used here, *"program budgeting"* refers to a *planning-oriented* approach which emphasizes *programs, functions, and activities*—with much

[5] Ibid., p. 174
[6] L. Moak and K. Killian, *Operating Budget Manual* (Chicago: Municipal Finance Officers Association, 1963), pp. 11–12. (Emphasis added.)

less emphasis on evaluation or control. Also, the program approach is ***communication-oriented,*** with budgetary requests and reports summarized in terms of a few broad programs rather than in myriad object-of-expenditure or departmental activity detail—though such details may be provided in the executive budget and the final appropriation may be on a line-item basis.

The most elaborate version of program budgeting has come to be known as the Planning-Programming-Budgeting System (PPB or PPBS). As with performance budgeting, PPB emphasis originated with the federal government when concepts developed in the early part of this century were refined by the Rand Corporation in the late 1950s and experimented with in the Department of Defense in the early 1960s. The movement to PPB received its greatest impetus in 1965 when President Johnson instructed most federal departments and agencies to apply this approach to their program planning and budgeting.

PPB or PPBS is not so much a new system or approach as a reordered synthesis of time-honored budgetary concepts and techniques, with additional emphasis on long-run considerations, systems analyses, and cost-benefit analyses of alternative courses of action. As Hatry observed:

> Its essence is development and presentation of information as to the full implications, the costs and benefits, of the major alternative courses of action relevant to major resource allocation decisions.
>
> The main contribution of PPBS lies in the *planning* process, i.e., the process of making program policy decisions that lead to a specific budget and specific multi-year plans. The *budget* is a detailed short term resource plan for implementing the program decisions. PPBS does not replace the need for careful budget analysis to assure that approved programs will be carried out in an efficient and cost-conscious manner, nor does it remove the need for the preparation of the detailed, line-item type of information to *support* budget submission.[7]

The major distinctive characteristics of PPB, as described by Hatry, are:

1. It focuses on identifying the fundamental objectives of the government and then relating all activities to these (regardless of organizational placement).
2. Future year implications are explicitly identified.
3. All pertinent costs are considered.
4. Systematic analysis of alternatives is performed [e.g., cost-benefit analysis and systems analysis and operations research.][8]

Advantages

Those closely associated with PPB do not claim it to be a panacea. But this approach is designed to overcome criticisms that have been made of object-of-expenditure and performance budgeting. Both of these other approaches are based principally on historical data and focus on a single period. On the other hand, PPB emphasizes long-range planning in which (1) ultimate goals and intermediate objectives must be explicitly stated, and (2) the costs and benefits of major alternative courses to achieve these goals and objectives are to be explicitly evaluated—in quantitative terms where practicable and narratively in all cases.

PPB theory assumes that all programs are to be evaluated annually, so that poor ones may be weeded out and new ones added. Changes in existing programs

---

[7] Harry P. Hatry and John F. Cotton, *Program Planning for State, County, City* (Washington, D.C.: George Washington University, 1967), pp. 14–15. (Emphasis added.)
[8] Ibid., p. 15.

are evaluated in terms of discounted marginal costs (and benefits), whereas object-of-expenditure budgets focus on total expenditures, and performance budgets are based on an average cost or average expenditure concept.

Program decisions are to be formulated at upper management levels under PPB, and department or agency heads are expected to gear their activities to fulfilling those agreed-upon objectives and goals. Finally, though PPB can be adapted to any level of appropriation specificity, many of its advocates hope to encourage (1) decision making and appropriations by legislatures in broader policy terms, and (2) increased executive powers by use of "lump-sum" appropriations.

Limitations

Although the logic of PPB is convincing, many barriers impede implementation of a complete PPB system. For example:

1. It is quite difficult to formulate a meaningful, explicit statement of a government's goals and objectives that can be agreed upon by all concerned—regardless of how worthwhile such a statement may be.
2. Not only do goals change, but elected officials, in particular, often prefer not to commit themselves to more than very general statements lest they be precluded from changing their positions when politics dictates.
3. The time period considered relevant by an elected official may be limited to that remaining prior to the expiration of his or her current term of office—resulting perhaps, at least subconsciously, in a greater interest in short-run costs and results than in long-run costs or results.
4. PPB, like performance budgeting, assumes both an adequate data base and a high level of analytical ability to be readily available to the government. Relatively few state or local governments have sophisticated program data or the luxury of sophisticated staff analysts. Thus, there has been little or no accounting follow-up for comparisons of PPBS plans with results. Governmental accounting systems are geared first to typical departmental object-of-expenditure budgetary accounting and only secondarily to supplemental data.
5. Objective measurement is even more of a problem here than in the performance approach, since both costs and benefits, over a period of several years, must be estimated. Both are often quite difficult to measure and the ratio or relationship between two such estimates is apt to imply far more precision than actually exists.
6. Despite its planning strengths, the PPBS focus on programs differs from the departmental object-of-expenditure control orientations of most legislatures and chief executives. Indeed, many of these officials view PPBS as a threat to their "power of the purse strings."

Comments

The full PPBS approach requires the consideration of government-wide programs and their evaluation without regard to departmental assignments. That requirement—together with the habits of years of object-of-expenditure budgeting and a jealously guarded legislative power of the purse strings—has required that PPBS budgets contain explanations of the relationships between programs, program plans, and program budget requests, on the one hand, and units of government (agencies) and objects of expenditure, on the other. Such **"crosswalks"** are illus-

Figure 3-11

PPBS "CROSSWALK"

19X1 Budget, All Departments

Programs

Department or Agency and/or Object of Expenditure	Total	Public Safety	Health	Education	Transportation	Recreation and Culture	Social Services	Legal, Fiscal Management	Community Welfare	Non-program Items
Mayor/Council										
City Clerk										
City Attorney										
Personnel										
City Planning										
Retirement Administration										
Office of Finance										
Office of Budget										
Police Department										
Fire Department										

Note: Totals of each column indicate program sums; totals for each organization unit indicate the amounts requested for each. If necessary or desired, the amounts requested for each unit may be listed by classes of objects in varying degrees of detail.

trated in Figure 3-11. *Appropriations typically continue to be made on the basis of organization units and objects of expenditure rather than in "lump sum" by program.*

PPBS thus is generally viewed as more useful for **planning** than for operation and control. Accordingly, PPBS information appears to be used in practice more to **supplement and support** traditional budget information than vice versa.

ZERO-BASE BUDGETING

The newest approach to budgetary planning is **zero-base budgeting (ZBB)**. It came on the scene about 1970 from the profit-seeking sector of the economy, was adopted by a few governments, and was popularized when President Carter required its use for the federal government.

The *essential idea of ZBB* is that the continued existence of programs or activities is not taken for granted; *each service must be justified in its entirety every year.* The *basic processes* of ZBB are as follows:

1. Divide all the operations of the government into *"decision units."* These are programs, activities, or relatively low level organization units. In general, ZBB does not attempt to go outside major organizational units in its definition of programs, though it can be combined with PPBS in this respect.
2. Divide the operations of each decision unit into *"decision packages."* The bases for these may be specific activities, specific services rendered, organizational subunits of the decision unit, or alternative activities to be carried out to achieve, say, program goals.
3. Select the best option for providing service based on cost-benefit or other analysis (or on a political basis).
4. Divide the selected option into **levels of service** to be provided, such as last year's level, minimal, reduced, increased, or maximum. The levels of service should be costed and the costs compared with the services to be provided.
5. Rank the decision packages. As the budget requests move upward through the executive branch, managers at each level rank the decision packages in terms of governmental priorities. These priorities may have been developed through PPB; if not, priorities set at the highest levels should be used as assumptions in ranking decision packages. The chief executive, having the priorities assigned by those below him or her in the administrative hierarchy, makes the ultimate decisions required to produce the executive budget.

ZBB is designed to force an annual review of all programs, activities, and expenditures; to save money by identifying outdated programs and unnecessarily high levels of service; to concentrate the attention of officials on the costs and benefits of services; to cause a search for new ways of providing services and achieving objectives; to improve the abilities of management to plan and evaluate; to provide better justification for the budget; and, finally, to improve the decisions made by the executive and legislative branches of the government. But it requires a great deal of paperwork, staff time, and effort to identify and rank decision units and decision packages. Further, it is difficult to obtain the data to compute costs of alternative methods of achieving objectives and of alternative levels of service. Accordingly, ZBB usage appears to lead to reductions in the rigor of the theory. For instance, some have determined that full justification need be required of specific activities *only once every few years* rather than for every budget (periodic **"sun-**

set reviews" of agencies fit nicely with this adaptation). Further, a government may decide that **some** or all of the **services** provided by agencies **must be provided at some minimum level** and that crucial judgments need be applied only to the levels of service to be provided. Indeed, the **primary use** of ZBB appears to be to **supplement** the **object-of-expenditure approach**—particularly where the overall level of spending must be reduced by a specified percentage, and in periodic "sunset reviews" of agencies and programs.

IN SUM

The budgetary approaches outlined here represent, **in theory,** a record of changes from devices (object-of-expenditure budget and line-item appropriations) designed primarily to authorize and fiscally control expenditures. These changes have sought to bring program planning, analysis (systems, cost-benefit), and performance measurement into the process. The primarily incremental approach has given way to the consideration of complete programs and activities (program budgets, PPBS, ZBB). Techniques encouraging executive branch managerial control have been developed. Legislative involvement has, in many instances, moved from minute control of details to broad control of functions, programs, and activities. Emphasis has shifted from input to output.

     In practice the changes have not been as dramatic. Few budgets, no matter what their planning bases may have been, have avoided specification of objects of expenditures. Program planning on a government-wide basis, as in PPBS, must be related to agencies responsible for elements of the programs. The relationship may be stated in the executive budget or in the appropriation bill, but **few legislative bodies are willing to appropriate without identifying agencies and objects of expenditure.** PPBS has proved useful for planning, but not for execution, and has not been considered successful. Performance budgeting has led to gradual increases in the number of activities having defined units of output. Nonetheless, it has proved feasible in a relatively small number of such activities. ZBB, concentrating at the decision package level, may prove to be more easily convertible into appropriation bills and legislative control on program or activity bases within specific agencies. But the **organization unit and objects of expenditure continue to be the primary basis for budgetary reporting and accountability.**

     The typical **"good"** budget for a municipality at this time, then, probably consists of program or activity descriptions *within organization units,* quantitative descriptions of levels of program activity where units of service effort (input) or accomplishment (output) have been defined, and object-of-expenditure units of input in dollars and numbers of employees.

SELECTING AN APPROPRIATE APPROACH

Designing an appropriate approach to expenditure budgeting for a specific government requires (1) knowledge of the various general approaches that have been developed, (2) insight into the history and activities of the organization in question and the attitudes and capabilities of its personnel, in order to assess the proper planning-control-evaluation balance to be sought, (3) originality in combining the strengths of the object-of-expenditure, performance, program, and ZBB approaches, while avoiding their weaknesses, and (4) patience in system design and implementation and the ability to adapt the system to changed circumstances. Experimentation with PPBS and ZBB analyses is highly desirable in the hope that they will be suited or adaptable to state and local government needs.

QUESTIONS

3-1 Governmental budgeting and budgetary control are deemed so important by the GASB that it devotes an entire "principle" to the subject. Why?

3-2 Distinguish between the following types of budgets: (a) capital and current; (b) tentative and enacted; (c) general and special; (d) fixed and flexible; and (e) executive and legislative.

3-3 Budgeting is a continuous process. Explain.

3-4 What are budgetary "control points"? How do they affect budgetary accounting and reporting?

3-5 A municipality's budget is prepared on a cash basis. What basis of accounting would you recommend? Explain.

3-6 Why are General, Special Revenue, and other governmental (expendable) funds typically controlled by fixed budgets integrated within the account structure, while Enterprise and other proprietary (nonexpendable) funds are subject to less formal control through flexible budgets not integrated within the account structure?

3-7 Some persons contend that an inherent limitation of the line-item department or object-of-expenditure budget is that it is based on a "backwards" or "reverse" decision-making process. Explain and evaluate this assertion.

3-8 A General Fund balanced budget has been amended to increase the total appropriations. From what sources may the increase be financed?

3-9 Discuss the meaning and implications of the following statements pertaining to budgeting:

a. "A budget is just a means of getting money."

b. "*Never* underexpend an appropriation—the more you spend, the more you get next year."

c. "Budgeting is easy! You just take last year's budget and add 10%—or twice what you think you might need. The council will cut your request in half and you'll wind up getting what you wanted in the first place."

d. "The traditional line-item budget only appears to provide an orderly and seemingly objective approach to financial planning and control. In too many instances, all it really provides is a uniform framework for establishing and maintaining a set of orderly records which comply with legal requirements, but which provide very little in the way of useful management information."

3-10 Revenue estimates and appropriations enacted are "standards" against which performance is subsequently measured. What implications can be drawn at year end if there are variances from these standards? If there are no variances?

3-11 In business accounting a single general ledger account—such as Cash, Accounts Receivable, Investments, or Accounts Payable—typically "controls" the related subsidiary ledger accounts. Referring to Figure 3-6, explain how in governmental fund accounting the general ledger accounts control (a) the Revenues Subsidiary Ledger accounts, and (b) the Expenditures Subsidiary Ledger accounts.

3-12 Figures 3-6 through 3-8 illustrate Revenues Subsidiary Ledger accounts classified by major revenue source category and Expenditures Subsidiary Ledger accounts classified by function. Might more detailed subsidiary ledger accounts be necessary in practice? Explain.

3-13 An interim budgetary comparison statement for a governmental fund is illustrated in Figure 3-9. (a) Should this statement be prepared on the unit's budgetary basis or on the GAAP basis? Why? (b) Why are interim budgetary comparison statements important to effective management control and legislative oversight?

3-14 An annual budgetary comparison statement for a governmental fund is illustrated in Figure 3-10. (a) Should this statement be prepared on the unit's budgetary basis or on the GAAP basis? (b) Why does the GASB require that a state or local government's CAFR and GPFS include budgetary comparison statements and schedules for governmental funds that are budgeted annually? (c) Some governments include both "original" and "as revised" budget data in budgetary comparison statements. Why?

3-15 **(Appendix)** Behavioral scientists tell us that "the measurement employed affects the performance of the person or group measured." What implications for performance and program budgeting are contained in this statement?

3-16 (Appendix) What major strengths and weaknesses are generally associated with the (a) line-item or object-of-expenditure, (b) performance, and (c) program approaches to budgeting?

3-17 (Appendix) (a) What are the major distinctive characteristics of the PPB approach to budgeting? (b) What is a budgetary "crosswalk"?

3-18 (Appendix) (a) What is the essential idea of ZBB? (b) What benefits is ZBB designed to produce?

3-19 (Appendix) (a) What are the processes required to produce a ZBB? (b) What are the difficulties that may prevent ZBB from achieving success and continuing application?

3-20 (Appendix) Most "performance measures" (number of arrests made, tons of garbage collected, miles of street cleaned, and so on) do not adequately measure the quantity or quality of performance but are only "indicators" of certain aspects of performance. Discuss (a) the validity of this statement and (b) how "performance measures" or "indicators" may be properly and beneficially employed in evaluating performance.

3-21 (Appendix) Proponents of zero-based budgeting contend that a government's budgetary process should begin each year with the assumption that no program or department has a vested interest—that each should comprehensively justify its existence, its activities, and its appropriation requests annually as if it were a proposed program or department not in existence previously. Evaluate the merits of this approach.

PROBLEMS

P 3-1 (Operating Budget Preparation) The finance director of the Bethandy Independent School District is making preliminary estimates of the budget outlook for the 19X8 fiscal year so that the superintendent can properly advise the department heads when budget instructions and forms are distributed. She has assembled the following information:

1. Revenues	Estimated 19X7	Expected Change—19X8
Property taxes	$2,000,000	+6%
State aid	1,000,000	+3%
Federal grants	500,000	−$40,000
Other	300,000	+$10,000
	$3,800,000	

2. Expenditures		
Salaries and wages	$2,700,000	?
Utilities	400,000	+4%
Maintenance	300,000	+$24,000
Capital outlay	200,000	−$15,000
Debt service	100,000	+$20,000
Other	50,000	+5,000
	$3,750,000	

3. Fund balance at the end of 19X7 is expected to be $1,600,000; at least $1,500,000 must be available at the end of 19X8 for carryover to help finance 19X9 operations.

Required (a) Prepare a draft operating budget for the Bethandy Independent School District for the 19X8 fiscal year—including 19X7 comparative data and expected change computations —assuming the budget is to be "balanced" in the sense that19X8 appropriations are to equal 19X8 estimated revenues.

(b) What total salaries and wages amount and average percentage increase or decrease is implied in the draft operating budget prepared in part (a)? What is the maximum salary and wage amount and percentage increase that seems to be feasible in 19X8?

P 3-2   (Expenditures Subsidiary Ledger) Refer to Figure 3-3, "Simplified Object-of-Expenditure Budget."

Required   (1) What would be the *minimum* number of Expenditures Subsidiary Ledger accounts required for the Police Department if:

(a) The council enacted the appropriations ordinance by department?

(b) The council enacted the appropriations by department and broad object-of-expenditure category (e.g., supplies)?

(c) Same as (a) except the mayor apportioned the appropriations by broad object-of-expenditure category.

(d) The council enacted appropriations by department and specific object class (e.g., gasoline and oil).

(e) Same as (b) except the controller wants to accumulate accounting data by specific object-of-expenditure classes.

(2) Refer also to Figure 3-8. "Relationship of General Ledger Appropriations, Expenditures, and Encumbrances Accounts and the Expenditures Subsidiary Ledger Accounts," and set up the Police Department Expenditures Subsidiary Ledger accounts. Then record directly in the subsidiary ledger accounts:

(a) The Police Department appropriations, assuming they were made at the broad object-of-expenditure level.

(b) Issuance of purchase orders for office supplies (estimated cost, $800) and a motorcycle (estimated cost, $6,400).

(c) Payment of monthly salaries ($48,000) and utilities ($1,000).

(d) Delivery of the office supplies (cost, $790) and motorcycle (cost, $6,500, including freight, and so on).

(e) Council approval of the police chief's request to use $2,800 appropriated for telephone costs to employ another school guard.

P 3-3   (Budgetary and Other Entries—General and Subsidiary Ledgers) The Murphy County Commissioners adopted the following General Fund budget for the 19X3 fiscal year:

General Fund
Murphy County
Budget—19X3

Estimated Revenues:	
Taxes	$8,000,000
Licenses and Permits	800,000
Intergovernmental	2,000,000
Charges for Services	200,000
Fines and Forfeits	400,000
Other	600,000
	12,000,000
Appropriations:	
General Government	1,000,000
Public Safety	4,000,000
Highways and Streets	5,000,000
Health and Sanitation	900,000
Culture and Recreation	400,000
Other	600,000
	11,900,000
Excess of Estimated Revenues over Appropriations	100,000
Fund Balance—Beginning	1,400,000
Fund Balance—Ending (Anticipated)	$ 1,500,000

The following events occurred during 19X3:

1. Purchase orders issued and contracts let were expected to cost:

General Government.	$ 300,000
Public Safety	1,200,000
Highway and Streets.	2,500,000
Health and Sanitation	500,000
Culture and Recreation	300,000
Other.	200,000
	$ 5,000,000

2. The commissioners reviewed the budget during the year and (a) revised the estimate of Intergovernmental Revenues to $1,500,000 and reduced the Public Safety and Highways and Streets appropriations by $225,000 each to partially compensate for the anticipated decline in intergovernmental revenues; and (b) increased the Health and Sanitation appropriation by $70,000 because of costs incurred in connection with an unusual outbreak of Tasmanian flu.

3. Revenues (actual) for 19X3 were:

Taxes	$ 8,150,000
Licenses and Permits	785,000
Intergovernmental	1,520,000
Charges for Services.	210,000
Fines and Forfeits	395,000
Other.	500,000
	$11,560,000

4. Goods and services under purchase orders and contracts were received:

	Estimated Cost	Actual Cost
General Government	$ 280,000	$ 278,000
Public Safety	900,000	910,000
Highways and Streets	2,500,000	2,500,000
Health and Sanitation	440,000	440,000
Culture and Recreation	300,000	295,000
Other	180,000	181,000
	$ 4,600,000	$ 4,604,000

The remaining orders are still outstanding.

5. Other expenditures incurred were:

General Government.	$ 700,000
Public Safety	2,560,000
Highways and Streets	2,271,000
Health and Sanitation	485,000
Culture and Recreation	45,000
Other.	391,000
	$ 6,452,000

Required

(1) Set up general ledger "t" accounts like those in Figure 3-6 and revenues and expenditures subsidiary ledgers like those in Figures 3-7 and 3-8.

(2) Record the Murphy County 19X3 General Fund budget in the general ledger and subsidiary ledger accounts, keying these entries "B" (for budget). Then record the numbered transactions and events, keying these entries by those numbers.

P 3-4 (Budgetary Comparison Statement) This problem is based on the information about the Murphy County General Fund budgeted and actual transactions and events described in Problem 3-3.

(1) Prepare a budgetary comparison statement for the General Fund of Murphy County for the 19X3 fiscal year. The statement should present revenues (by source category), expenditures and encumbrances (by function), and the excess of revenues over (under) expenditures and encumbrances. Use these column headings:

> Budget (Revised)
>
> Actual
>
> Variance—Favorable (Unfavorable)

and assume that no encumbrances were outstanding at the beginning of 19X3.

(2) Since encumbrances do not constitute expenditures, some governmental fund budgetary comparison statements omit data on encumbrances. (a) Assuming no encumbrances were outstanding at the beginning of 19X3, what effects would omission of encumbrances data have on the Murphy County General Fund budgetary comparison statement for the 19X3 fiscal year? (b) In what circumstances would including or excluding encumbrances data mislead users of a governmental fund budgetary comparison statement?

(3) What may have caused the variations between the appropriations and the actual expenditures and encumbrances reported in the 19X3 Murphy County General Fund budgetary comparison statement for (a) Health and Sanitation? (b) Culture and Recreation?

P 3-5 (Property Tax Levy Computation) The comptroller of the City of Helmaville recently resigned. In his absence, the deputy comptroller attempted to calculate the amount of money required to be raised from property taxes for the General Fund for the fiscal year ending June 30, 19X7. The calculation is to be made as of January 1, 19X6, to serve as a basis for setting the property tax rate for the following fiscal year. The mayor has requested you to review the deputy comptroller's calculations and obtain other necessary information to prepare a formal statement for the General Fund which will disclose the amount of money required to be raised from property taxes for the fiscal year ending June 30, 19X7. Following are the calculations prepared by the deputy comptroller:

City resources other than proposed tax levy:	
Estimated General Fund working balance, January 1, 19X6.	$ 352,000
Estimated receipts from property taxes (January 1, 19X6–June 30, 19X6) . .	2,222,000
Estimated revenue from investments (January 1, 19X6–June 30, 19X7). . . .	442,000
Estimated proceeds from sale of general obligation bonds in August 19X6 .	3,000,000
	$6,016,000
General Fund requirements:	
Estimated expenditures (January 1, 19X6–June 30, 19X6)	$1,900,000
Proposed appropriations (July 1, 19X6–June 30, 19X7)	4,300,000
	$6,200,000

Additional information:

1. The General Fund working balance required by the city council for July 1, 19X6, is $175,000.

2. Property tax collections are due in March and September of each year. Your review indicates that during the month of February 19X6 estimated expenditures will exceed available funds by $200,000. Pending collection of property taxes in March 19X6, this deficiency will have to be met by the issuance of 30-day tax anticipation notes of $200,000 at an estimated interest rate of 9 percent per annum.

3. The proposed general obligation bonds will be issued by the City Water Enterprise Fund and will be used for the construction of a new water pumping station.

Required Prepare a statement as of January 1, 19X6, calculating the property tax levy required for the City of Helmaville General Fund for the fiscal year ending June 30, 19X7. (*Hint:* Requirements — Resources other than property tax levy = Amount of the required levy.)

(AICPA, adapted)

P 3-6 (Appendix: Program to Object-of-Expenditure Crosswalk) The following is a portion of a draft of the 19X5 budget for the City of Woodbridge which is being compiled by its administrator. The major programs and subprograms are indicated by notations in brackets; the departmental responsibility for program elements is indicated in parentheses.

City of Woodbridge

19X5 Budget (Draft)

Public Safety [Program]:
  Prevent and Prosecute Crime [Subprogram]:
    Community Police Surveillance (Police Department):

Salaries and Wages	$399,796
Materials and Supplies	34,023
Contractual Services	41,905
Permanent Property	1,734
	$477,458

    Investigate and Prosecute Adult Crime (Police Department):

Salaries and Wages	$258,944
Materials and Supplies	7,760
Contractual Services	7,750
	$274,454

    Investigate and Prosecute Juvenile Crimes (Police Department):

Salaries and Wages	$207,450
Materials and Supplies	1,100
Contractual Services	2,150
	$210,700

    Detain Accused Law Violators (Police Department):

Materials and Supplies	$ 50
Contractual Supplies	750
	$ 800

    Cooperate with Regional Law Enforcement Agencies (Police Department):

Materials and Supplies	$ 50	
Total		$963,462

  Adjudication of Crimes [Subprogram]:
    Litigate Civil Cases (Municipal Court):

Salaries and Wages	$ 6,468
Materials and Supplies	200
Contractual Services	494
	$ 7,162

    Penalize Criminal Violators (Municipal Court):

Salaries and Wages	$ 14,325	
Materials and Supplies	575	
Contractual Services	644	
Permanent Property	400	
	$ 15,944	
Total		$23,106

Community Development and Environmental Control [Program]:
  Community Development [Subprogram]:
    Planning Land Use (Director of Planning):

Salaries and Wages	$ 54,439
Materials and Supplies	2,422
Contractual Services	7,825
	$ 64,686

Grand Total—Public Safety [Program] $7,261,500

The grand total budgeted (all programs) for the object-of-expenditure classifications included above was:

Salaries and Wages	$5,126,197
Materials and Supplies	1,817,923
Contractual Services	291,060
Permanent Property.	2,140,781
	$9,375,961

Required   Using the data given, prepare a budget presentation in a program to object-of-expenditure crosswalk format, with subprogram and program element detail.

P 3-7   (Appendix: Program to Department Crosswalk) Using the information contained in Problem 3-6, prepare a crosswalk budgetary presentation relating programs, subprograms, and program elements to departments. (You need not include object-of-expenditure detail.) The grand total budgeted for the departments with which this problem deals are as follows:

Police	$1,717,476
Municipal Court	81,050
Director of Planning...	124,292

GENERAL AND SPECIAL REVENUE FUNDS

The General Fund and Special Revenue Funds typically are used to finance and account for most "general government" activities of state and local governments. "General government" activities include police protection, fire protection, central administration, street maintenance, and similar "general operating" activities of independent school districts and nonproprietary special districts. They are discussed together because accounting and reporting for General and Special Revenue Funds are **identical.**

Special Revenue Funds are established to account for "general government" financial resources that are **restricted** by law or by contractual agreement to specific purposes. The **General Fund** is used to account for all financial resources **not** restricted to specific purposes or otherwise required to be accounted for in another fund. The General Fund is established at the inception of a government and exists throughout the government's life. Special Revenue Funds exist as long as the government has resources dedicated to specific purposes. In the typical case, most of the resources of both types of funds are expended each year and are replenished on an annual basis.

The financial resources of the General Fund and Special Revenue Funds typically are expended primarily for current operating purposes (e.g., salaries, supplies) rather than for capital outlay or debt service. Significant amounts to be expended for capital outlay or debt service from these funds usually are transferred to Capital Projects and Debt Service Funds, respectively, and expended through those funds. But routine capital outlay expenditures (e.g., for vehicles and equipment), and debt service expenditures (e.g., for capital leases and equipment notes payable), generally are made directly from the General and Special Revenue Funds.

Further, recall from the discussion of the GASB principles in Chapter 2 that:

1. Resources restricted to expenditure for purposes normally financed from the General Fund may be accounted for through the General Fund as long as applicable legal requirements are met, and
2. Use of Special Revenue Funds is not required unless they are legally mandated.

Thus, some restricted resources may be accounted for through the General Fund rather than through Special Revenue Funds. This option is **not** assumed in Chapter 4, but is discussed and illustrated later.

Measurement Focus

Because of the recurring nature of their revenues and commitments, and the necessity of meeting current commitments from the currently expendable (appropriable) financial resources, the accounting principles for General and Special Revenue Funds are based on the **"flows and balances of financial resources"** concept rather than on the income determination concept of business accounting. Consistent with this measurement focus, recall that General and Special Revenue Funds are "working capital" entities. The basic accounting equation for each is "Current Assets − Current Liabilities = Fund Balance." Accordingly, purchases of fixed assets with the financial resources of these funds decrease their fund balance. Expenditures for fixed assets thus have the same effect in these funds as expenditures for wages and salaries, since fixed assets are not capitalized in the General or Special Revenue Funds but in the General Fixed Assets Account Group. Similarly, if maturing general obligation bonds of the government—which are carried as liabilities in the General Long-Term Debt Account Group prior to maturity —are paid from the resources of these funds, the expenditure decreases their fund balance in the same manner as expenditures for salaries and wages.

As a result of the flows and balances of financial resources concept, the General or Special Revenue Fund year-end **balance sheet** *presents the financial resources on hand, any related current liabilities, and the "fund balance"— the net financial resources of the fund.* Further, if some of the fund's net assets are **not** available for expenditure—as when a three-year interfund loan has been made from the General Fund to another fund—this is indicated by **"reserving"** a portion of the total fund balance, **thus segregating total fund balance as between its "reserved fund balance" and "unreserved fund balance" components.** Accordingly, the **unreserved** fund balance at year end is expected to be available, together with the revenues and transfers in of the following year, to meet the needs of that year. Additional references to this concept—and to the **"unreserved"** and **"reserved"** components of total fund balance—will be made as transactions and statements of these funds are discussed.

Purposes and Assumptions of This Chapter

This chapter discusses and illustrates the **basic** accounting procedures and financial statements for the General Fund and Special Revenue Funds. Accordingly, except where stated otherwise, the **discussions and illustrations in this chapter assume that:**

1. The annual operating budget is prepared and adopted on a GAAP basis, and
2. The accounts are maintained on a GAAP basis during the year.

Most Uniform CPA Examination problems are based on these assumptions, which may also be found in practice.

The discussions and illustrations in this chapter focus on demonstrating **one way a transaction or event may properly be accounted for and reported—** typically the manner in which it might appear in unofficial solutions to CPA exams —even though there may be acceptable alternatives. Some of these alternatives are discussed and illustrated in later chapters.

Further, to enhance illustrative clarity, small numerical dollar amounts are used in the illustrative journal entries, trial balances, and financial statements. Likewise, **only a few Revenues Subsidiary Ledger accounts** (by broad revenue source category) **and a few Expenditures Subsidiary Ledger accounts** (by function) are used. Hundreds of subsidiary ledger accounts may be needed in practice —at least one account for each significant revenue source and appropriation line item in the adopted budget (as discussed in Chapter 3).

Since accounting and reporting for the General Fund and Special Revenue Funds are identical, this chapter deals primarily with General Fund accounting and reporting, with only occasional reference to Special Revenue Funds. The principles, procedures, and illustrations are equally applicable to Special Revenue Funds, however.

GENERAL FUND ACCOUNTING ILLUSTRATIVE EXAMPLE

To illustrate the essential aspects of General and Special Revenue Fund accounting, assume that a **new** local governmental unit, a city which we shall call "A Governmental Unit," was founded late in 19X0. A Governmental Unit uses revenues and expenditures subsidiary ledgers like those illustrated in Figures 3-6, 3-7, and 3-8, and the trial balance of the General Fund of A Governmental Unit at January 1, 19X1, appears in Figure 4-1.

Note that the "Unreserved Fund Balance" in Figure 4-1 is also the total fund balance, and might be called simply "Fund Balance." However, since total fund balance may have both "reserved" and "unreserved" components, as illustrated later in this chapter, the "Unreserved Fund Balance" title is preferable.

The **annual operating budget** adopted for the General Fund of A Governmental Unit for the fiscal year beginning January 1, 19X1—the government's first full year of operation—is summarized in Figure 4-2.

Note that the General Fund budget illustrated in Figure 4-2 **assumes that:**

1. The **annual budget** is **adopted on the modified accrual GAAP basis,** as indicated earlier, and thus there should be no budgetary-GAAP basis differences.
2. Appropriations are made for **"operating expenditures"** by function and for **"capital outlay"** and **"debt service"** expenditures to be made directly from the General Fund.

Figure 4-1

**GENERAL LEDGER TRIAL BALANCE—
BEGINNING OF 19X1**

A Governmental Unit
General Fund

General Ledger Trial Balance

January 1, 19X1

	Debit	Credit
Cash	14,000	
Accounts Receivable	12,000	
Vouchers Payable		15,000
Unreserved Fund Balance		11,000
	26,000	26,000

Figure 4-2

ANNUAL OPERATING BUDGET FOR 19X1

A Governmental Unit
General Fund
Annual Operating Budget
For 19X1 Fiscal Year
(Budgetary Basis Is the Modified Accrual GAAP Basis)

Estimated Revenues:

Taxes	$250,000
Licenses and permits	70,000
Intergovernmental	50,000
Charges for services	40,000
Fines and forfeits	20,000
Other	1,000
	431,000

Appropriations:

Current operating

General government	40,000
Public safety	150,000
Highways and streets	120,000
Health and sanitation	60,000
Other	25,000
	395,000
Capital outlay	30,000
Debt service	1,000
	426,000

Excess of Estimated Revenues over Appropriations	$ 5,000

Notes:

1. *The enacted budget appropriates "operating" expenditures by function but includes separate appropriations for the "capital outlay" and "debt service" expenditures of this fund. (Major capital outlay and debt service expenditures typically are financed by interfund transfers to Capital Projects and Debt Service Funds.)*
2. *The governmental unit may (and will) **separately authorize interfund transfers** during the year **and,** if appropriate, **revise** this original budget.*
3. Since the **budgetary basis is the modified accrual (GAAP) basis,** there will be no differences between the budgetary basis and the GAAP basis in this example.

3. The budget does **not** include appropriations for **interfund transfers**—though it might—but assumes that any interfund transfers will be *separately* authorized by the governing body.

The ***accounting implications*** of this budget are that (1) the accounts should be maintained during the year on the modified accrual (GAAP) basis, (2) accounts should be established in the Revenues Subsidiary Ledger and Expenditures Subsidiary Ledger at the level of detail (at least) of the official budget, and (3) any **interfund transfers or other fund balance changes** will be recorded in appropriately titled **General Ledger** accounts, but will *not* be recorded in **subsidiary ledger** accounts, *since only revenues and expenditures are subject to formal budgetary accounting control procedures.*

Entries During 19X1

Budgetary Entry

The operation of the General Fund of A Governmental Unit begins with the adoption of the budget. The appropriations it contains, together with the revenue estimates on which the appropriations are based, provide the basis for the following **budgetary entry** on the first day of the new year:

(1)	**Estimated Revenues**	431,000	
	Appropriations		426,000
	Unreserved Fund Balance		5,000

To record appropriations and revenue estimates.

Revenues Ledger (Estimated Revenues):

Taxes	250,000
Licenses and Permits	70,000
Intergovernmental	50,000
Charges for Services	40,000
Fines and Forfeits	20,000
Other	1,000
	431,000

Expenditures Ledger (Appropriations):

General Government	40,000
Public Safety	150,000
Highways and Streets	120,000
Health and Sanitation	60,000
Other	25,000
Capital Outlay	30,000
Debt Service	1,000
	426,000

Note the format of this entry:

■ The General Ledger entry appears first, followed by the subsidiary ledger entries.

■ *The subsidiary ledger entries do not "balance,"* but sum to the related Estimated Revenues and Appropriations control account entry amounts in the General Ledger.

Note also that the General Ledger budgetary entry causes the **Unreserved Fund Balance** account to be stated at its $16,000 ($11,000 beginning balance plus $5,000 planned increase) *planned end-of-year balance.* This is the manner by which the Estimated Revenues and Appropriations **budgetary accounts** traditionally have been incorporated into the General Ledger and subsidiary ledgers in order to effect budgetary control during the period.

The budgetary accounts do **not** affect the "actual" asset, liability, revenue, or expenditure General Ledger accounts. Further, carrying the Unreserved Fund Balance account at its planned end-of-year balance focuses attention during the year on the *"target"* ending fund balance ("where we want to be") rather than on the beginning-of-period fund balance ("where we used to be"). In any event, **neither the Estimated Revenues and Appropriations accounts nor the budgetary entry permanently affects the Unreserved Fund Balance account.** At year end—having effected budgetary control during the year—**the budgetary entry is reversed in the closing entries.**

Entry 1 *compounds* two possible separate General Ledger budgetary entries:

(1a) Estimated Revenues 431,000
       Unreserved Fund Balance 431,000

    To record estimated revenues and the expected fund
    balance increase to result during the period.

(1b) Unreserved Fund Balance 426,000
       Appropriations 426,000

    To record appropriations and the expected fund balance
    decrease to result during the period.

Should the revenue estimate be revised upward during the period, the increase would be debited to Estimated Revenues and credited to Unreserved Fund Balance. A decrease in estimated revenues would be recorded by debiting the expected decrease to Unreserved Fund Balance and crediting Estimated Revenues. Similarly, if additional appropriations are made during the year, Unreserved Fund Balance would be debited and Appropriations credited for the increase: the opposite would be true should appropriations be decreased.

    Therefore, if during the year the governing body had increased the official estimate of tax revenues by $1,000 and also increased the public safety appropriations by $3,000, thus reducing the year-end Unreserved Fund Balance estimate by $2,000, the entry would be:

Estimated Revenues 1,000
Unreserved Fund Balance 2,000
    Appropriations 3,000
To record budget revisions.
Revenues Ledger (Estimated Revenues):
Taxes 1,000
Expenditures Ledger (Appropriations):
Public Safety 3,000

    The illustrative example in this chapter assumes that no budget revisions were made during the year. Budget revisions are discussed further in Chapters 5 and 6.

Property Tax Levy

Property taxes usually are a major revenue source of local governments. They accrue when they are formally levied by the legislative body of the city. (The assessment date is the date on which the value and ownership of property are determined for purposes of assigning tax liability and usually precedes the date of levy by a substantial period.) On the date that A Governmental Unit's current-year taxes are levied, assuming the taxes are considered "available"—that is, are collectible during the year or soon thereafter—the following entry is made:

(2) **Taxes Receivable—Current** 200,000
    Allowance for Uncollectible Current Taxes 3,000
    Revenues 197,000
    To record accrual of property taxes.
    Revenues Ledger (Revenues):
    Taxes 197,000

    The Allowance for Uncollectible Current Taxes amount is the portion of the tax levy not expected to be collected. At this time the city does not know which specific tax bills will not be collected. As specific amounts are determined to be uncollectible they are written off by charging the Allowance for Uncollectible Current Taxes account and crediting Taxes Receivable. Since such taxes are a primary lien on the property, no loss is incurred until the city has gone through foreclosure proceedings that result in the sale of the property for taxes. The accounting for tax liens and for such disposition of property is discussed in Chapter 5.

Observe in entry 2 that only the net expected tax collections are credited to Revenues. This **net revenue** approach differs from business accounting, where the gross receivable is credited to revenues and the estimated uncollectible amounts are debited to expense. But governmental funds account for expenditures, not expenses; and the amount of taxes levied that is uncollectible does not constitute an expenditure—and is not "available" revenue—so is considered a deduction from revenue.

Other Revenues Billed or Accrued

As other revenues are billed or accrue, the following entries are made:

(3) Accounts Receivable.	36,000	
Allowance for Uncollectible Accounts Receivable		1,000
Revenues		35,000
To record accrual of revenues and related allowance for estimated losses.		
Revenues Ledger (Revenues):		
Charges for Services		<u>35,000</u>

The foregoing charges for services revenues might represent charges for court costs and fees, inspection fees, or parking fees, for example. Those revenues that do **not** accrue, or are **not** deemed sufficiently measurable to be accrued in the accounts prior to collection, are debited to Cash and credited to Revenues at the time of collection.

Encumbrances and Related Expenditures

A primary objective of governmental accounting is to assist the administration in controlling the expenditures, including the control of overexpenditure of appropriations. Thus, accounts must be kept both for total expenditures (General Ledger) and for expenditures chargeable to each appropriation (Expenditures Subsidiary Ledger). Usually a record of the estimated **expenditures "in process"** is maintained—in total in the General Ledger and by each appropriation in the Expenditures Subsidiary Ledger—through the use of an **Encumbrances** account. Encumbrances are recorded when purchase orders are issued for goods and services. Thus, if we assume that orders are placed for materials and equipment estimated to cost $30,000 for the functions indicated, the entry at the time the **orders are placed** would be:

(4) **Encumbrances**	30,000	
Reserve for Encumbrances		30,000
To record encumbering appropriations.		
Expenditures Ledger (Encumbrances):		
General Government.	2,000	
Public Safety	8,000	
Highways and Streets	10,000	
Other	4,000	
Capital Outlay	<u>6,000</u>	
	<u>30,000</u>	

Comparison of appropriations with expenditures and encumbrances shows the amount of uncommitted **(unencumbered)** appropriations available for expenditure. **When the actual expenditure is determined, the entry setting up the encumbrances is reversed and the actual expenditure is recorded.**

If the materials and equipment subsequently *received* cost only $29,900, the entries will be:

(5a) **Reserve for Encumbrances** 30,000
        Encumbrances 30,000
    To reverse the entry encumbering the Appropriations
      account.
    Expenditures Ledger (Encumbrances):
    General Government 2,000
    Public Safety. 8,000
    Highways and Streets. 10,000
    Other. 4,000
    Capital Outlay. 6,000
                             30,000

(5b) **Expenditures** 29,900
        Vouchers Payable 29,900
    To record expenditures.
    Expenditures Ledger (Expenditures):
    General Government 1,700
    Public Safety. 8,000
    Highways and Streets. 10,100
    Other. 4,000
    Capital Outlay. 6,100
                             29,900

These entries accomplish two things. The **"unencumbered balance"** of the Appropriations, Expenditures, and Encumbrances accounts in the General Ledger, and of the individual accounts in the Expenditures Subsidiary Ledger, against which the expenditures for materials and equipment are chargeable was *temporarily reduced*—while the order was outstanding—*by the estimated amount of the expenditures,* the **encumbrance.** Now, however, the exact amount of the expenditures is known; accordingly, *the entry setting up the encumbrances is reversed and the actual expenditures are recorded.* The General Ledger *effects of these entries* are as follows:

	After Entry 1	After Entry 4	After Entries 5a and 5b
Appropriations	$426,000	$426,000	$426,000
Less: Expenditures	-0-	-0-	29,900
Unexpended Balance	$426,000	$426,000	$396,100
Less: Encumbrances	-0-	30,000	-0-
Unencumbered Balance	$426,000	$396,000	$396,100

Note again, as discussed in Chapter 3, that the sum of the "Unencumbered Balance" column amounts of the several Expenditures Subsidiary Ledger accounts should always equal the total "unencumbered balance" computed from the General Ledger accounts.

Note also from entries 5a and 5b that encumbrances are **estimates** of subsequent expenditures—and that the resulting **actual** expenditures may be more than, less than, or equal to the encumbrances. In this case the Public Safety and

Other expenditures were exactly as planned—perhaps the result of an exact price quotation or bid on a firm price purchase order. But the General Government order cost less than anticipated—perhaps because of a price decline but also possibly because part of the order was not filled or was cancelled. On the other hand, the Highways and Streets and Capital Outlay expenditures were more than originally estimated—possibly because of freight, delivery, or similar costs that were not anticipated or because of an approved change in specifications after the purchase order was issued. In any case, the accounting upon receipt of encumbered goods or services is simply: **"reverse the encumbrance entry and record the actual expenditure."**

Finally, recall from Chapter 2 that the purchase of equipment also impacts the General Fixed Assets Account Group. The equipment would be accounted for in the GFAAG, resulting in the following changes in the GFAAG accounting equation:

$$\text{Equipment} = \text{Investment in GFA}$$
$$+\$6,100 \qquad +\$6,100$$

Unencumbered Expenditures

If an expenditure is controlled by devices other than encumbrances, the appropriation is not encumbered. Rather, the amount of the available appropriation is reduced only at the time of the expenditure. This is usually true with payrolls, for example, which are controlled by specified employment procedures and payroll system controls. Thus, if the payroll at the end of a pay period was $40,000, the entry at the time the payroll was approved for payment would be:

(6) Expenditures..	40,000	
Vouchers Payable.............................		40,000
To record approval of payroll.		
Expenditures Ledger (Expenditures):		
General Government............................	5,000	
Public Safety.....................................	16,000	
Highways and Streets........................	13,000	
Health and Sanitation........................	4,000	
Other..	2,000	
	40,000	

Other Transactions and Events

Additional entries illustrating the operation of the General Fund of A Governmental Unit follow. Note that entries are made in the Revenues Subsidiary Ledger or Expenditures Subsidiary Ledger **only** when the General Ledger entries affect the Revenues or Expenditures accounts or the related Estimated Revenues, Appropriations, or Encumbrances budgetary accounts. (All amounts are assumed.)

(7) Cash...	175,000	
Taxes Receivable—Current		160,000
Accounts Receivable...........................		15,000
To record collection of taxes receivable and accounts receivable.		
(8) Taxes Receivable—Delinquent....................	40,000	
Taxes Receivable—Current		40,000
(9) Allowance for Uncollectible **Current** Taxes	3,000	
Allowance for Uncollectible **Delinquent** Taxes		3,000
To record reclassification of allowance for estimated losses on taxes (to correspond with the reclassification of the taxes receivable in entry 8).		

(10) Cash. 205,000
     Revenues 205,000
To record receipt of revenues not previously accrued.
Revenues Ledger (Revenues):

Taxes	58,000
Licenses and Permits	68,000
Intergovernmental	52,500
Charges for Services.	6,000
Fines and Forfeits.	19,000
Other	1,500
	205,000

(11) Vouchers Payable. 40,000
     Cash. 40,000
To record payment of payroll voucher.

(12) Encumbrances. 20,000
     Reserve for Encumbrances 20,000
To record reduction of appropriation available for future
   expenditure by amount of estimated cost of purchase
   orders issued.
Expenditures Ledger (Encumbrances):

Public Safety	7,000
Health and Sanitation	13,000
	20,000

(13) Cash. 20,200
     Taxes Receivable—Delinquent 20,000
     Revenues 200
To record collection of delinquent taxes, together with
   interest and penalties thereon that had not been accrued.
Revenues Ledger (Revenues):

Other	200

(14) Investments. 10,000
     Cash. 10,000
To record temporary investment of excess cash.

(15) **Expenditures** 30,000
     Due to Stores Fund 30,000
To record supplies provided by an Internal Service Fund.
Expenditures Ledger (Expenditures):

General Government.	4,000
Public Safety	6,000
Highways and Streets	10,000
Health and Sanitation	7,000
Other	3,000
	30,000

This *quasi-external transaction* would have the following
   impact on the Stores Internal Service Fund:

Assets − Liabilities = Contributed Capital + Retained Earnings
  + $30,000   + $30,000 (Revenues)

(16) **Due from Special Revenue Fund**. 1,500
     Expenditures 1,500
To record **reimbursement** due from Special Revenue Fund
   for expenditure made initially from the General Fund.
Expenditures Ledger (Expenditures):

General Government.	1,500

This **reimbursement** transaction would have the following
   effect on the specific Special Revenue Fund accounting
   equation:

Current Assets − Current Liabilities = Fund Balance
  + $1,500   − $1,500 (Expenditures)

(17) **Operating Transfer to Debt Service Fund**   5,000

    Due to Debt Service Fund.   5,000

To record annual transfer to Debt Service Fund to meet
debt service and fiscal charges.

Note that *interfund operating transfers* must be reported
separately from Revenues and Expenditures, and that
this transfer effects the Debt Service Fund as follows:

Current Assets − Current Liabilities = Fund Balance
+ $5,000   = + $5,000 (Other Financing Sources)

(18) Due from Special Revenue Fund.   10,000

    Operating Transfer from Special Revenue Fund   10,000

To record interfund transfer from Special Revenue Fund
ordered by governing board.

The impact of this transfer on the Special Revenue Fund
accounting equation is:

Current Assets − Current Liabilities = Fund Balance
           + $10,000   − $10,000 (Other Financing Uses)

(19) **Residual Equity Transfer to Enterprise Fund**.   6,000

    Cash   6,000

To record residual equity transfer to provide contributed
capital to a new Enterprise Fund.

Note that *interfund residual equity transfers* must be
reported separately from Revenues, Expenditures, and
Operating Transfers, and that this residual equity transfer
impacts the Enterprise Fund accounting equation as
follows:

Assets − Liabilities = Contributed Capital + Retained Earnings
+ $6,000   + $6,000 (Residual
                        Equity Transfer)

(20) Expenditures.   300,000

    Vouchers Payable   300,000

To record **unencumbered** expenditures.

Expenditures Ledger (Expenditures):

General Government.	30,000
Public Safety	112,000
Highways and Streets	90,000
Health and Sanitation	35,400
Other	9,600
Capital Outlay	23,000
	300,000

The capital outlay expenditures ($23,000) increase the
fixed asset accounts and the Investment in General Fixed
Assets balance in the General Fixed Assets Account
Group.

(21) Vouchers Payable.   320,000

    Cash   320,000

To record payment of vouchers.

(22) Cash.   20,000

    Notes Payable   20,000

To record borrowing on *short-term* note at bank to maintain
an adequate cash balance.

(23) Due to Stores Fund.   22,500

    Cash   22,500

To record partial payment of amount due the Stores Fund.
This transaction also results in a corresponding increase in
"Cash" and decrease in "Due from General Fund" in the
Stores Internal Service Fund.

(24)	Cash...	13,000	
	Accounts Receivable		13,000
	To record collections of accounts receivable.		
(25)	Allowance for Uncollectible Accounts Receivable........	400	
	Accounts Receivable		400
	To record write-off of accounts receivable determined to be uncollectible.		
(26)	**Notes Payable**.................................	5,000	
	Expenditures	600	
	Cash		5,600
	To record payment of part of the **short-term** note principal and interest to date.		
	Expenditures Ledger (Expenditures):		
	Debt Service (Interest)...........................	600	
(27)	**Correction of Prior Year Error**	300	
	Vouchers Payable		300
	To record **correction of prior period (19X0) error** (failure to record 19X0 expenditure and liability at December 31, 19X0).		

In reviewing the illustrative general journal entries above, note particularly entries 15 through 19. Entry 15 records an interfund **quasi-external transaction,** while entry 16 reflects an **interfund reimbursement;** entries 17 and 18 are for **interfund operating transfers** and entry 19 records an **interfund residual equity transfer.** Also note entries 22 and 26, which record issuance of a **short-term note payable** as a current liability of the General Fund and the payment of part of the note principal and interest, respectively, and entry 27, which records the **correction of a prior year error.**

Alternative Account Structure and Entries

As noted in Chapter 3, many governments no longer use the traditional General Ledger—subsidiary ledger account structure and entry approach illustrated in this chapter. Modern computerized systems facilitate the use of detailed General Ledger accounts in lieu of the General Ledger control accounts supported by detailed subsidiary ledgers. To familiarize readers with this approach—which is preferred by some practitioners and professors and is sometimes useful on the CPA Examination—entries using the **detailed General Ledger accounts approach** are presented below for transactions 1, 5, and 10. This approach also is used in selected subsequent chapters.

(1)	Estimated Revenues—Taxes........................	250,000	
	Estimated Revenues—Licenses and Permits...........	70,000	
	Estimated Revenues—Intergovernmental.............	50,000	
	Estimated Revenues—Charges for Services	40,000	
	Estimated Revenues—Fines and Forfeits	20,000	
	Estimated Revenues—Other	1,000	
	Appropriations—General Government..............		40,000
	Appropriations—Public Safety		150,000
	Appropriations—Highways and Streets		120,000
	Appropriations—Health and Sanitation		60,000
	Appropriations—Other		25,000
	Appropriations—Capital Outlay		30,000
	Appropriations—Debt Service		1,000
	Unreserved Fund Balance		5,000
	To record appropriations and revenue estimates.		

(5a)	Reserve for Encumbrances	30,000	
	Encumbrances—General Government		2,000
	Encumbrances—Public Safety		8,000
	Encumbrances—Highways and Streets		10,000
	Encumbrances—Other		4,000
	Encumbrances—Capital Outlay		6,000

To reverse the entry encumbering the Appropriations
account.

(5b)	Expenditures—General Government	1,700	
	Expenditures—Public Safety	8,000	
	Expenditures—Highways and Streets	10,100	
	Expenditures—Other	4,000	
	Expenditures—Capital Outlay	6,100	
	Vouchers Payable		29,900

To record expenditures.

(10)	Cash	205,000	
	Revenues—Taxes		58,000
	Revenues—Licenses and Permits		68,000
	Revenues—Intergovernmental		52,500
	Revenues—Charges for Services		6,000
	Revenues—Fines and Forfeits		19,000
	Revenues—Other		1,500

To record receipt of revenues not previously accrued.

Some instructors prefer this approach and require its use in solving problems requiring both General Ledger and subsidiary ledger entries. It may also be required or preferred on some CPA examination problems.

Adjusting Entries at Year End

Regardless of the account structure and entry approach used, the accounts should be reviewed at year end to determine whether any **adjusting entries** are needed to properly reflect fund operating results and financial position. Among the types of **revenues** that might be accrued in adjusting entries are interest on investments and delinquent taxes, unbilled charges for services, and unrestricted intergovernmental grants that are due but have not been received by year end. **Expenditures** that might need to be accrued in adjusting entries include interest on short-term debt, accrued payroll, and amounts recorded as encumbrances that have become expenditures by year end.

To illustrate year-end adjusting entries, assume that A Governmental Unit had no significant payroll or other expenditure accruals, but that two revenue accruals and one expenditure accrual are in order:

(A1)	**Interest and Penalties**		
	Receivable—Delinquent Taxes	550	
	Allowance for Uncollectible Interest and Penalties		50
	Revenues		500

To record interest and penalties accrued on delinquent taxes
outstanding and to provide for estimated losses.

Revenues Ledger (Revenues):

Other		500

(A2)	**Accrued Interest Receivable**	400	
	Revenues		400

To record interest accrued on investments.

Revenues Ledger (Revenues):

Other		400

(A3) Expenditures 250

     Accrued Interest Payable 250

    To record interest accrued on short-term notes payable.

    Expenditures Ledger (Expenditures):

Debt Service (Interest). 250

Preclosing Trial Balance—End of 19X1

Figure 4-3 presents the **preclosing trial balance** of the **General Ledger** accounts after the preceding illustrative journal entries are posted. Figure 4-4 presents the **preclosing trial balances** of the **Revenues Subsidiary Ledger and Expenditures Subsidiary Ledger.** These trial balances are the basis for the closing entries discussed in the following section and for the statements later in the chapter. Appendix 4-1 includes for the General Fund of A Governmental Unit for the year ended December 31, 19X1:

1. Figure 4-13—**General Ledger Worksheet**
2. Figure 4-14—**Revenues Subsidiary Ledger** (Preclosing)
3. Figure 4-15—**Expenditures Subsidiary Ledger** (Preclosing)

Figure 4-3   **PRECLOSING TRIAL BALANCE—GENERAL LEDGER—END OF 19X1**

A Governmental Unit
General Fund
Preclosing Trial Balance
General Ledger
December 31, 19X1

	Debit	*Credit*
Cash	43,100	
Investments	10,000	
Accrued Interest Receivable	400	
Taxes Receivable—Delinquent.	20,000	
Allowance for Uncollectible Delinquent Taxes		3,000
Interest and Penalties Receivable—Delinquent Taxes	550	
Allowance for Uncollectible Interest and Penalties		50
Accounts Receivable	19,600	
Allowance for Uncollectible Accounts Receivable.		600
Due from Special Revenue Fund	11,500	
Vouchers Payable.		25,200
Notes Payable		15,000
Accrued Interest Payable		250
Due to Stores Fund		7,500
Due to Debt Service Fund		5,000
Reserve for Encumbrances		20,000
Unreserved Fund Balance (11,000 + 5,000)		16,000
Estimated Revenues.	431,000	
Revenues		438,100
Appropriations		426,000
Expenditures.	399,250	
Encumbrances.	20,000	
Operating Transfer to Debt Service Fund	5,000	
Operating Transfer from Special Revenue Fund		10,000
Residual Equity Transfer to Enterprise Fund	6,000	
Correction of Prior Year Error	300	
	966,700	966,700

Figure 4-4

**PRECLOSING TRIAL BALANCES
REVENUES AND EXPENDITURES SUBSIDIARY LEDGERS
END OF 19X1**

A Governmental Unit
General Fund
**Preclosing Trial Balances
Revenues and Expenditures Subsidiary Ledgers**
December 31, 19X1

Revenues Subsidiary Ledger

Taxes		5,000
Licenses and Permits	2,000	
Intergovernmental		2,500
Charges for Services		1,000
Fines and Forfeits	1,000	
Other		1,600
	3,000	10,100

Proof: $10,100 − $3,000 = $7,100

Compare to General
Ledger control accounts:

Revenues	$438,100
Estimated Revenues .	431,000
Difference	$ 7,100

Expenditures Subsidiary Ledger

General Government		800
Public Safety		1,000
Highways and Streets	3,100	
Health and Sanitation		600
Other		6,400
Capital Outlay		900
Debt Service		150
	3,100	9,850

Proof: $ 9,850 − $3,100 = $ 6,750

Compare to General
Ledger control accounts:

Appropriations		$426,000
Expenditures	$399,250	
Encumbrances	20,000	419,250
Difference		$ 6,750

CLOSING ENTRIES—END OF 19X1

At the end of the fiscal year, entries are made closing the accounts. The closing process summarizes the results of operations in the Unreserved Fund Balance account. More specifically, the **purposes** of **closing entries** are to:

1. *Close the budgetary* (e.g., Estimated Revenues and Appropriations) *and related actual* (e.g., Revenues and Expenditures) *operating accounts* in the *General Ledger* so they will begin the next year with zero balances—ready to record that year's budgetary and actual operations.

2. *Close the other General Ledger operating accounts*—e.g., the transfer and restatement (correction of prior year error) accounts—to "zero out" these ac-

counts and have them ready to record the next year's transfers and restatements.

3. *Update the Unreserved Fund Balance account to its actual end-of-year balance*—which is accomplished simultaneously with (1) and (2).

4. Usually, as assumed here, *convert the Reserve for Encumbrances account from a memorandum offset General Ledger account to a true "reserve" of fund balance* by closing the Encumbrances account to Unreserved Fund Balance—thus reducing the Unreserved Fund Balance account and, since the Reserve for Encumbrances is no longer offset by the Encumbrances account, making it a true fund balance "reserve."

5. *Close the Revenues Subsidiary Ledger and Expenditures Subsidiary Ledger accounts* so they are ready to record the next year's detailed budgetary and actual operating data.

These purposes may be accomplished in differing sequences of entries—depending on personal preferences of accountants or on how the computer software is designed—but any proper closing entry sequence must accomplish *all* of these purposes.

Closing the Encumbrances Account

Whether the Encumbrances account is closed at year end, the appropriate procedures for closing the Encumbrances account, are determined by the government's legal and policy provisions pertaining to the lapsing of appropriations and to the treatment of encumbrances outstanding at year end. An appropriation is said to lapse when it terminates, that is, when it no longer is an authorization to make an expenditure.

The illustration of A Governmental Unit is completed on the assumption that the law and policy state that:

1. All **unexpended** appropriations **lapse** at the end of the year, **even if encumbered;**

2. The Unit is **committed** to accepting the goods or services on order at year end;

3. Expenditures resulting from encumbrances outstanding at the end of the year must be charged against appropriations of the **next** year; and

4. The closing entry should leave on the books a **Reserve for Encumbrances** account to indicate the commitment of the resources of the fund.

This assumption is the most common in practice with respect to annually budgeted governmental funds, and is the usual assumption in Uniform CPA Examination questions and problems. We shall call this **Assumption A1;** other types of laws and policies relating to appropriations and encumbrances are discussed in Chapter 6.

Closing Entry Approaches

Three closing entry sequences—referred to as the "reverse the budget—close the actual," "variance," and "compound entry" approaches—are commonly encountered on the Uniform CPA Examination and in practice. **All achieve the same end result.** The "reverse the budget—close the actual" and "compound" approaches are discussed and illustrated in this chapter. All three approaches, including the "variance" approach, are illustrated in later chapters.

Reverse the Budget—Close the Actual Approach

The **reverse the budget—close the actual** closing entry sequence approach focuses first on closing the General Ledger accounts, then closes the subsidiary ledger accounts in a separate entry or entries. The **rationale** of this approach—with respect to the *General Ledger* accounts—is that:

- The budgetary entry (and any budget revision entries) caused the Unreserved Fund Balance account to be carried at its *planned* end-of-year balance during the year.
- Since the budgetary control purposes of the budgetary entry (or entries) have been served by year end—and the revenue estimates and appropriations in the annual operating budget typically expire at year end—the first closing entry should **reverse the budgetary entry** (including any revisions), which **changes the amount in the Unreserved Fund Balance account from its planned end-of-year balance to its actual preclosing balance.**
- Next, **closing** the **actual** revenues, expenditures, transfers, and restatement accounts **updates the Unreserved Fund Balance account from its actual preclosing amount to its actual year-end balance.**
- Finally, a portion of the Unreserved Fund Balance may be **"reserved"** for encumbrances (or other reasons).

General Ledger Closing Entries

The **general ledger closing entries** using the **"reverse the budget—close the actual"** closing entry sequence (see Figure 4-13) are:

Reverse the Budgetary Entry:

(C1)	Appropriations.	426,000	
	Unreserved Fund Balance	5,000	
	Estimated Revenues		431,000

To close the budgetary accounts and bring the Unreserved Fund Balance account to its actual preclosing balance.

Close the Revenue and Expenditure Accounts:

(C2)	Revenues	438,100	
	Unreserved Fund Balance		38,850
	Expenditures.		399,250

To close the Revenues and Expenditures accounts to Unreserved Fund Balance.

Close the Transfer and Restatement Accounts:

(C3)	Operating Transfer from Special Revenue Fund	10,000	
	Unreserved Fund Balance	1,300	
	Operating Transfer to Debt Service Fund.		5,000
	Residual Equity Transfer to Enterprise Fund		6,000
	Correction of Prior Year Error		300

To close the transfer and restatement accounts.

Close the Encumbrances Account to "Reserve" Fund Balance:

(C4)	Unreserved Fund Balance[1]	20,000	
	Encumbrances		20,000

To close the Encumbrances account and establish the Reserve for Encumbrances account as a reservation of fund balance.

Note that since closing entry C1 reverses the budgetary entry, closing entries C2 and C3 summarize the *actual change* in **total** fund balance during the year, $37,550 ($38,850 − $1,300). Further, entries C2, C3, and C4 summarize the *actual change* in **unreserved** fund balance during the year, $17,550 ($37,550 − $20,000). These amounts are not so readily apparent in the other closing entry approaches, though all yield the same end result.

This illustration assumes that only revenues and expenditures are subject to formal budgetary accounting control procedures. This is often the case since the governing board directly controls interfund transfers. Alternatively, budgetary accounts such as Estimated Operating Transfers In, Estimated Operating Transfers Out, and Estimated Residual Equity Transfers Out could have been used and would be closed at this time. Accounting procedures where interfund transfers and debt issue proceeds are subject to formal budgetary accounting control are considered in later chapters.

Subsidiary Ledger Closing Entries

Under the "reverse the budget—close the actual" approach, the accounts in the **Revenues Subsidiary Ledger and the Expenditures Subsidiary Ledger are closed by simply debiting the credit balances and crediting the debit balances** —thus bringing all accounts to a zero balance. This may be done automatically in computerized systems or manually by observing the preclosing account balances (see Figures 4-4, 4-14, and 4-15):

(C)	**Revenues Ledger (Balance):**		
	Taxes	5,000	
	Licenses and Permits.		2,000
	Intergovernmental	2,500	
	Charges for Services	1,000	
	Fines and Forfeits.		1,000
	Other	1,600	
		10,100	3,000

Proof: $10,100 − $3,000 =   7,100

Compare to General Ledger control accounts:

Revenues	$438,100
Estimated Revenues.	431,000
Difference.	$ 7,100

---

[1] Entry C4 is in essence a compounding of the following two General Ledger entries:

(C4a)	Reserve for Encumbrances	20,000	
	Encumbrances.		20,000

To close the offsetting encumbrances and reserve for encumbrances memorandum accounts.

(C4b)	Unreserved Fund Balance	20,000	
	Reserve for Encumbrances		20,000

To reduce unreserved fund balance and increase reserved fund balance (for encumbrances).

(C) **Expenditures Ledger (Balance):**

General Government	800	
Public Safety	1,000	
Highways and Streets		3,100
Health and Sanitation	600	
Other	6,400	
Capital Outlay	900	
Debt Service	150	
	9,850	3,100

Proof: $9,850 − $3,100 = $6,750

Compare to General Ledger control
  accounts:

Appropriations		$426,000
Expenditures	$399,250	
Encumbrances	20,000	419,250
Difference		$6,750

Compound Entry Approach

Although the reverse the budget—close the actual and other closing entry approaches are based on different rationales and involve different closing entry sequences, all have precisely the same result. That is, the accounts that should be closed are closed, the Unreserved Fund Balance account is updated to its actual year-end balance, and the accounts that should be left open are left open. **_The postclosing trial balance account balances are the same in either event._** Thus, some accountants prefer to prepare a single **compound** closing entry.

  A **compound** General Fund general ledger closing entry for A Governmental Unit at December 31, 19X1, under the assumptions illustrated so far, would appear as follows:

(C) Revenues	438,100	
Appropriations	426,000	
Operating Transfer from Special Revenue Fund	10,000	
Unreserved Fund Balance		12,550
Estimated Revenues		431,000
Expenditures		399,250
Encumbrances		20,000
Operating Transfer to Debt Service Fund		5,000
Residual Equity Transfer to Enterprise Fund		6,000
Correction of Prior Year Error		300

To close the general ledger accounts.

The **subsidiary ledger** closing entries under the **compound** closing entry approach would be identical to those illustrated for the "reverse the budget—close the actual" approach.

Reserve for Encumbrances

At this point a review of the nature of the Reserve for Encumbrances account is appropriate. It started life as an **offset** to the Encumbrances account in the General Ledger. Throughout 19X1 both accounts contained a balance representing the amount (with Expenditures) to be deducted from the Appropriations account, to arrive at the estimated spendable balance of appropriations. In other words, the Encumbrances and Reserve for Encumbrances accounts were offsetting **memorandum budgetary** accounts in the General Ledger. The closing entry for expenditure accounts closed the Encumbrances account but not the Reserve for Encumbrances: the Reserve for Encumbrances was **converted** into a *reservation of fund* *balance.* Thus, the Reserve for Encumbrances, any other reserve accounts, and the Unreserved Fund Balance account should be added to obtain the total fund balance at year end.

Reserves usually indicate that a portion of the total fund balance is not available for appropriation, that only the **unreserved** fund balance may be appropriated. *Under Assumption A1, however, the Reserve for Encumbrances indicates the amount of total fund balance that must be appropriated next year (19X2) to authorize completion of transactions in process at year end (19X1).* Thus, **under Assumption A1** the amount in the Reserve for Encumbrances is **available** for 19X2 appropriation, but **only** to provide for **past** commitments, while the **unreserved** fund balance is available to finance **new** 19X2 expenditure commitments.

Since the amount represented by the Reserve for Encumbrances is available for appropriation under Assumption A1, many accountants prefer to **disclose** encumbrances outstanding at year end in the notes to the financial statements rather than in a Reserve for Encumbrances account in the balance sheet. Assumption A2, discussed in Chapter 6, provides for disclosure of encumbrances outstanding at year end in the notes to the financial statements rather than by reporting a Reserve for Encumbrances in the balance sheet.

Postclosing Trial Balance—End of 19X1

Following the posting of the 19X1 closing entries (see Figure 4-13), the trial balance of the General Fund appears as in Figure 4-5.

Figure 4-5

**POSTCLOSING TRIAL BALANCE—GENERAL LEDGER—
END OF 19X1**

A Governmental Unit
General Fund
**Postclosing Trial Balance
General Ledger**
December 31, 19X1

	Debit	Credit
Cash	43,100	
Investments.	10,000	
Accrued Interest Receivable	400	
Taxes Receivable—Delinquent	20,000	
Allowance for Uncollectible Delinquent Taxes .		3,000
Interest and Penalties Receivable—		
Delinquent Taxes	550	
Allowance for Uncollectible Interest and		
Penalties		50
Accounts Receivable	19,600	
Allowance for Uncollectible Accounts		
Receivable		600
Due from Special Revenue Fund.	11,500	
Vouchers Payable		25,200
Notes Payable		15,000
Accrued Interest Payable		250
Due to Stores Fund		7,500
Due to Debt Service Fund		5,000
Reserve for Encumbrances.		20,000
Unreserved Fund Balance		28,550
	105,150	105,150

The essential character of the General Fund should be kept constantly in mind as balance sheets and balance sheet accounts are discussed. ***Though the General Fund presumably will exist as long as the governmental unit exists, the operation of the Fund is on a year-to-year basis.*** Each year the problem of financing a new year's operations with financial resources on hand and the new year's revenues and other financial resource inflows (e.g., transfers) is the central concern of those managing the finances of the Fund. The balance sheet is prepared to provide information that assists in the solution of this problem.

The Interim Balance Sheet

Interim balance sheets may be prepared monthly, quarterly, or when needed for bond issue or other purposes. SLGs rarely issue audited interim balance sheets. Accordingly, the GASB Codification provides balance sheet standards and guidance only for year-end balance sheets.

The Year-End Balance Sheet

The Balance Sheet of the General Fund of A Governmental Unit at December 31, 19X1 (Figure 4-6) is based on the postclosing trial balance at that date after the closing entries illustrated. The statement is largely self-explanatory, but comments on some of the accounts should help clarify its characteristics. The comments deal with (1) the significance of the Unreserved Fund Balance account, (2) the nature of several fund balance reserve accounts, and (3) the exclusion of fixed assets and long-term (noncurrent) liabilities from the General Fund accounts and its Balance Sheet.

Unreserved Fund Balance

As previously indicated, the General Fund is a current fund. Its fiscal operations are concerned with the current-year revenues and other financing sources and the current-year expenditures and other uses of financial resources. As a general rule the Fund is intended to show **neither** a surplus nor a deficit. *A credit balance in the Unreserved Fund Balance account after closing entries* does **not** in any sense represent retained earnings. Rather, it *indicates an excess of the assets of the fund over its liabilities and fund balance reservations,* if any, and would more properly be titled **"Unreserved, Unappropriated Fund Balance."** Accordingly, the legislative body is likely to use the available assets, as indicated by the credit balance, in financing the budget for the succeeding year. But, as noted earlier, under Assumption A1 the budget officials and the legislative body should realize that the Reserve for Encumbrances also is available for 19X2 appropriation for the 19X1 commitments.

    During a fiscal year the balance of the Unreserved Fund Balance account may be of a nature *substantially different from that of the year-end balance.* Suppose that the year-end Unreserved Fund Balance (postclosing) is $5,000, and that in the following year budgeted revenues are $100,000 and appropriations total $97,000. The Unreserved Fund Balance account will be carried at the ***planned*** end-of-year balance of $8,000 after the recording of the budget. The exact ***nature of the balance during the year*** can be determined only by examining all the facts. Its balance ***is neither exclusively budgetary nor exclusively proprietary.***

    If the General Fund has a **deficit,** the amount of the deficit should be exhibited on the balance sheet in the same position as the Unreserved Fund Balance

Figure 4-6

BALANCE SHEET—END OF 19X1

A Governmental Unit
General Fund
Balance Sheet
December 31, 19X1

Assets

Cash.		$ 43,100
Investments		10,000
Accrued interest receivable		400
Taxes receivable—delinquent.	$20,000	
Less: Allowance for uncollectible		
delinquent taxes	3,000	17,000
Interest and penalties receivable on taxes.	550	
Less: Allowance for uncollectible		
interest and penalties	50	500
Accounts receivable.	19,600	
Less: Allowance for uncollectible accounts	600	19,000
Due from Special Revenue Fund.		11,500
Total Assets		$101,500

Liabilities and Fund Balance

Liabilities:		
Vouchers payable	$25,200	
Notes payable	15,000	
Accrued interest payable	250	
Due to Stores Fund	7,500	
Due to Debt Service Fund	5,000	$52,950
Fund Balance:		
Reserved for encumbrances	20,000	
Unreserved	28,550	48,550
Total Liabilities and Fund Balance		$101,500

and called a "Deficit." Typical municipal financial administration policy requires that the deficit be eliminated in the following fiscal year and that the necessary revenues for this purpose be provided in the budget.

Fund Balance Reserves

Assets in an amount equal to the Unreserved Fund Balance account are assumed to be available to finance appropriations for expenditures of the current year and/or succeeding year. Thus, it is desirable to ***remove from that account any portions that are not available for that purpose.*** Fund balance reserves are essentially ***"tags"*** attached to part of total fund balance to indicate that ***some portion(s) of the fund net assets are not available for discretionary appropriation and expenditure.***

The Reserve for Encumbrances left in the accounts by the closing entries made has already been discussed as a fund balance reserve at the end of the year. This reserve indicates that some of the General Fund assets are not available to finance ***new*** purchase commitments in 19X2 because they will be needed to pay for the 19X2 expenditures that result from the outstanding 19X1 purchase commitments. It also serves to remind those preparing the 19X2 budget to make sufficient appropriations to provide for the expenditures to result in 19X2 from the 19X1 purchase commitments.

Frequently, some of the General Fund assets need to be maintained at a certain level rather than expended. For example, such assets as petty cash and inventories of materials and supplies may not be available for financing expenditures of a subsequent period because they must be maintained at or near the required level. The entries to account for materials and supplies and the related Reserve for Inventories are discussed in Chapter 6. Entries for **petty cash** are as follows:

Petty Cash	2,000	
Cash		2,000
To record the creation of a petty cash fund out of general cash.		
Unreserved Fund Balance	2,000	
Reserve for Petty Cash Fund		2,000
To record a reservation of fund balance in the amount of the petty cash fund.		

As another example, suppose that a $5,000 **loan to be repaid in 19X3** had been made from the General Fund to a Special Revenue Fund at the **end of 19X1.** The General Fund entries at the end of 19X1 would be:

Advance to Special Revenue Fund	5,000	
Cash		5,000
To record interfund loan to be repaid in 19X3.		
Unreserved Fund Balance	5,000	
Reserve for Advance to Special Revenue Fund.		5,000
To record a reservation of fund balance in the amount of the interfund advance.		

The Reserve for Advance to Special Revenue Fund indicates that the General Fund asset represented by the Advance to Special Revenue Fund is **not** available to finance 19X2 expenditures. The Reserve for Advance to Special Revenue Fund will be canceled at the end of 19X2 since the loan will be repaid in 19X3.

     Similar reservations may be made for other assets that are not expected to be available to finance current operations. Examples of such assets are long-term accounts and claims receivable. *Fund balance reserves are reported in the "Fund Balance" section of the balance sheet* as shown in Figure 4-6. **Alternatively, separate "Reserved Fund Balance" and "Unreserved Fund Balance" categories may be used,** especially when there are several reserves. But a *"Total Fund Balance" amount should be reported* and reserves should **not** be reported with liabilities or between the liabilities and fund balance sections of the balance sheet.

Unreserved Fund Balance Designations

Governments **may** also "tag" a portion of the **unreserved** fund balance of a governmental fund to indicate **tentative management plans** to use specified amounts of fund financial resources for certain specified purposes.

     The general journal entry to record a designation would be:

Unreserved Fund Balance	8,000	
Designed for Equipment Replacement		8,000
To record a designation of unreserved fund balance for equipment replacement.		

The entry would be reversed to remove the designation.

     The use of such designations is **optional.** But if designations are used, they should be:

- clearly **distinguished from reserves,** and
- reported as part of the **unreserved** fund balance **"designated"** for the speci-

fied purpose <u>or</u> disclosed parenthetically or in the notes to the financial statements.

Due To/From and Advance To/From

The illustration of the interfund "advance" in the discussion of fund balance reserves points out a significant terminology distinction that warrants further discussion. The illustrative example entries earlier in the chapter recorded interfund receivables and payables in "Due from (Fund)" and "Due to (Fund)" accounts. Yet, in the case of a two-year interfund loan, the term "Advance to (Fund)" was used and a corresponding fund balance reserve was established.

The distinction is that the terms **"Due to (Fund)" and "Due from (Fund)"** should be used **only** to describe **currently receivable and currently payable interfund balances.** During the year, "currently" means collectible or payable within the year or soon thereafter, though at year end, amounts to be received or paid in the next year may properly be classified as "current" and thus recorded as "due from" and "due to" other funds.

Any **"noncurrent" interfund receivable or payable** should be recorded as **Advance to (Fund)"** or **"Advance from (Fund)."** Further, any governmental fund **advance** to another fund **requires** that a **corresponding reserve** be established to indicate that the fund financial resources that are loaned on a *"noncurrent"* basis are *not* currently available for expenditure and thus should not be appropriated. An interfund advance for which repayment is expected in the next fiscal year is not reclassified as a "Due from (Fund)" or "Due to (Fund)" account. But any corresponding governmental fund fund balance reserve for advances should be eliminated, however, since the advance is now "available."

Exclusion of Fixed Assets and Long-Term Debt

Although some General Fund expenditures represent outlays that should be capitalized, fixed assets are **not** included in the balance sheet of the General Fund. For example, $6,100 of the total expenditures of $29,900 shown in entry 5b on page 119 was for equipment. In commercial accounting this $6,100 would be shown in the general balance sheet as part of the assets. *In governmental fund accounting the fixed assets are capitalized in a separate nonfund account group rather than as assets of the General Fund (see Chapter 9).*

Similarly, even if general obligation long-term debt (such as bonds) is ultimately payable out of the General Fund, and even if it has been issued to eliminate a deficit in the General Fund, *unmatured general obligation long-term debt is not recorded as a liability of the General Fund but in a separate nonfund account group (see Chapter 9). The only long-term debt included in the General Fund is that which has matured and is payable from the current resources of the General Fund* (an unusual occurrence, except for capital leases, since matured bonds and other long-term debts are ordinarily repaid from a Debt Service Fund[2]).

Fixed assets are excluded from the General Fund balance sheet because they do not represent financial resources with which the government intends to fi-

---

[2] Taxes designated for debt service usually are treated as revenues of a Debt Service Fund and do not affect the General Fund. In specific cases, however, the taxes may be collected through the General Fund and used to service debt directly from the General Fund. Alternatively, such taxes may be transferred to the Debt Service Fund. In the latter case they would be accounted for as General Fund revenues and as an operating transfer to the Debt Service Fund. It is also permissible to report the transfer to the Debt Service Fund as a deduction from General Fund gross revenues and report the revenues in the Debt Service Fund.

nance its current activities or pay its liabilities. These assets are not acquired for resale, but for the purpose of rendering service over a relatively long period of time.

Bonds and other long-term general obligation debts payable are not included as part of the liabilities of the General Fund because the existing resources of the Fund are not expected to be used for their payment. The governmental unit's future taxing power will ultimately provide resources to pay them.

STATEMENT OF REVENUES, EXPENDITURES, AND CHANGES IN FUND BALANCE

The second major General and Special Revenue Fund financial statement is the **Statement of Revenues, Expenditures, and Changes in Fund Balance.** As its title indicates, this *"operating"* statement presents the revenues, expenditures, and other increases and decreases in fund balance during a year (or other time period), and reconciles the beginning and ending fund balances. (Recall from Chapter 2 that increases and decreases in fund balance are essentially changes in working capital.) It is prepared on the **GAAP basis,** regardless of the basis of the budget, and is the **"GAAP basis operating statement."**

The Statement of Revenues, Expenditures, and Changes in Fund Balance may present data pertaining to *either* the Unreserved Fund Balance account—or the *total* fund balance, including reserves. *The unreserved fund balance approach* reconciles the beginning and ending Unreserved Fund Balance *account* balances, and thus has a "changes in reserves" section. The more widely used **total fund balance** approach, illustrated here (Figure 4-7), presents only the items that changed **total** fund balance, and reconciles beginning and ending **total** fund balances. Significant changes in reserves are disclosed in the notes to the financial statements.

Total Fund Balance Approach

A Statement of Revenues, Expenditures, and Changes in Fund Balance for the General Fund of A Governmental Unit for the 19X1 fiscal year is presented in Figure 4-7. Although the Statement of Revenues, Expenditures, and Changes in Fund Balances is largely self-explanatory, it should be studied carefully. *Observe the major components of this statement and the order in which they appear:*

	Revenues
−	Expenditures
	Excess of Revenues over (under) expenditures
±	Other financing sources (uses)
	Excess of revenues and other sources over (under) expenditures and other uses
+	Fund balance, beginning of period
±	Residual equity transfers
	Fund balance, end of period

Observe also in Figure 4-7 that (1) the **beginning** fund balance is reported **as previously reported, followed by the error correction and the restated amount;** (2) **operating transfers** are reported separately from revenues and expenditures—as "Other Financing Sources (Uses)"; (3) **residual equity transfers** are reported separately from operating transfers; and (4) the statement explains the changes in **total** fund balance during the period.

The Statement of Revenues, Expenditures, and Changes in Fund Balance may acceptably be presented in at least three alternate formats. **The format outlined above and illustrated in Figure 4-7—known as "Format A" and as "Pres-**

Figure 4-7

**STATEMENT OF REVENUES, EXPENDITURES, AND CHANGES
IN FUND BALANCE—FOR 19X1
(GAAP OPERATING STATEMENT)**

A Governmental Unit
General Fund
**Statement of Revenues, Expenditures,
and Changes in [Total] Fund Balance**
For the 19X1 Fiscal Year

Revenues		
Taxes	$255,000	
Licenses and permits	68,000	
Intergovernmental	52,500	
Charges for services	41,000	
Fines and forfeits	19,000	
Other	2,600	
Total Revenues		$438,100
Expenditures		
Current Operating:		
General government	39,200	
Public safety	142,000	
Highways and streets	123,100	
Health and sanitation	46,400	
Other	18,600	
Total Current Operating Expenditures	369,300	
Capital Outlay	29,100	
Debt Service (interest)	850	
Total Expenditures		399,250
Excess of Revenues over Expenditures . .		38,850
Other Financing Sources (Uses)		
Operating transfer from Special Revenue Fund	10,000	
Operating transfer to Debt Service Fund	(5,000)	5,000
Excess of Revenues and Other Financing Sources Over Expenditures and Other Uses		43,850
Fund Balance—Beginning of 19X1—As Restated		
As previously reported	11,000	
Correction of prior year error	(300)	10,700
Residual equity transfer to Enterprise Fund		(6,000)
Fund Balance—End of 19X1		$ 48,550

entation 1"—is the most common in practice. The other major alternative statement arrangement—known as *"Format B"* and as *"Presentation 2"—is equally acceptable.* Format B (Presentation 2), which is preferred by many practitioners and instructors, is illustrated in Figure 4-11.

Residual Equity Transfers

The GASB Codification says at one point that "residual equity transfers should be reported as additions to or deductions from the beginning fund balance of governmental funds."[3] At another point it says that "residual equity transfers should be

[3] GASB Codification, sec. 1800.107.

reported after the results of operations"[4] and illustrates presentation of residual equity transfers after "Excess of revenues and other sources over (under) expenditures and other uses" and immediately before ending Fund Balance. *Either presentation approach is acceptable:* (1) as the *last item* in the Statement of Revenues, Expenditures, and Changes in Fund Balance *before* the *Fund Balance section, or* (2) as the *last item before* the *ending Fund Balance.* We have chosen to illustrate the latter approach because it seems preferable in the GASB Codification and is most in keeping with current practice.

Restatements

Occasionally, a governmental fund Statement of Revenues, Expenditures, and Changes in Fund Balance for an accounting period must report a *restatement* of the *beginning* fund balance because of an *error correction* or the *change to a preferable accounting principle.* The restatement may be reported in either of two ways. The beginning fund balance in the statement can be *noted as being "as previously reported,"* as in Figure 4-7, and *followed by the restatement amount and a restated beginning fund balance,* presented as follows:

Fund balance, beginning of period, as previously reported
± Restatements (e.g., correction of prior period errors)
Fund balance, beginning of period, as restated

Or only the restated beginning fund balance may be presented in the statement, noted as being *"as restated," with reference* made *to* the *explanation* of the restatement contained *in the notes* to the financial statements:

Fund balance, beginning of period, as restated (Note X)

Note X would contain the information presented on the face of the statement in the first method and in Figure 4-7.

In comparative statements covering two or more periods (1) the *cumulative* restatement effect on periods *prior to* the *earliest* period being reported on should be reported as a *restatement* of the *beginning* fund balance *of that period,* and (2) the data reported for *later periods* should be *restated* to reflect the changed accounting principle or error correction.

STATEMENT OF REVENUES, EXPENDITURES, AND CHANGES IN FUND BALANCE— BUDGET AND ACTUAL

A third statement required for General and Special Revenue Funds (and for similar governmental funds that are budgeted annually) *compares budgeted and actual operating results.* This Statement of Revenues, Expenditures, and Changes in Fund Balance—*Budget and Actual* is prepared on the *budgetary basis*—which often differs from GAAP—and thus is the *"budgetary operating statement."*

Whereas the GAAP basis operating statement must comply with GAAP standards and guidelines, *the budgetary basis operating statement must demonstrate budgetary accountability in terms of the government's own methods of budgeting, including its budgetary basis and format.* Thus, the budgetary operating statement may be presented in any of the alternative formats for the State-

---

[4] Ibid., sec. 2200.117.

ment of Revenues, Expenditures, and Changes in Fund Balance, or in the format in which the budget is adopted. However, regardless of basis or format, it usually *has columns headed:*

		Variance— Favorable
Budget	Actual	(Unfavorable)

The "Budget" column should contain the *revised* budget data; and terms other than "Variance—Favorable (Unfavorable)" may be used to describe the "Variance" column. Indeed, some governments omit the "Variance" column to conserve space in combining statements or because the variance is deemed obvious from the data in the "Budget" and "Actual" columns.

　　If the legally adopted budget is prepared on a basis consistent with GAAP, the *"actual" data* in this statement *will correspond* with the data presented in the Statement of Revenues, Expenditures, and Changes in Fund Balance (Figure 4-7). *However, if the budget is prepared on a basis other than GAAP—* for example on the cash receipts and disbursements basis or an "encumbrances" basis—*both the "budget" data and the "actual" data* should be *presented on* the *budgetary basis,* so that the statement will display an accurate budgetary comparison and the "variance—favorable (unfavorable)" comparison will be meaningful.

　　If the budget is prepared on a *basis other than GAAP,* and thus the Statement of Revenues, Expenditures, and Changes in Fund Balance—Budget and Actual is prepared on a non-GAAP basis, the "actual" data in the budgetary comparison statement will *not* correspond with the data presented in the GAAP-basis operating statement. In such cases, the *notes* to the financial statements should contain an *explanation* of the budgetary basis employed *and* a *reconciliation* of the budgetary data with the GAAP data.

　　Alternatively, the budgetary basis may be explained in the notes and the reconciliation of the budgetary-basis and GAAP-basis data included in the Statement of Revenues, Expenditures, and Changes in Fund Balance—Budget and Actual. *Preparing the budgetary statement where the budget is not prepared on the GAAP basis and reconciling the budgetary basis-GAAP basis differences are discussed in Chapters 10 and 14.*

　　A Statement of Revenues, Expenditures, and Changes in Fund Balance—Budget and Actual for the General Fund of A Governmental Unit for the 19X1 fiscal year is presented in Figure 4-8. **Since the illustrative example in this chapter assumes that the budget is prepared on the GAAP basis, this budgetary operating statement is prepared on the GAAP basis—which in this case is also the budgetary basis.** Note in studying Figure 4-8 that:

- The **title** of the statement **includes** the term **"Budget and Actual"** and indicates **the budgetary basis** on which the statement is prepared.
- Had there been **budget revisions** during the year the **revised** budgetary data would be presented, although **both** the original and revised budgets may be presented (in adjacent columns) in the budgetary comparison statement.
- **Encumbrances** are **not** reported (only expenditures), since encumbrances are not considered equivalent to expenditures for budgetary or other purposes on the modified accrual basis.
- Since the **interfund transfers** were not included in the fiscal budget, but **were separately authorized,** no "budget" amounts are presented for interfund transfers.

Figure 4-8

**STATEMENT OF REVENUES, EXPENDITURES, AND CHANGES IN
FUND BALANCE—BUDGET AND ACTUAL—FOR 19X1
(BUDGETARY COMPARISON STATEMENT)**

A Governmental Unit
General Fund

**Statement of Revenues, Expenditures, and Changes in Fund Balance—
Budget and Actual (Budgetary Basis is Modified Accrual Basis)**

For the 19X1 Fiscal Year

	Revised Budget (Note 1)	Actual	Variance— Favorable (Unfavorable)
Revenues			
Taxes	$250,000	$255,000	$ 5,000
Licenses and permits	70,000	68,000	(2,000)
Intergovernmental	50,000	52,500	2,500
Charges for services	40,000	41,000	1,000
Fines and forfeits	20,000	19,000	(1,000)
Other	1,000	2,600	1,600
Total Revenues	431,000	438,100	7,100
Expenditures (Note 2)			
Current Operating			
General government	40,000	39,200	800
Public safety	150,000	142,000	8,000
Highways and streets	120,000	123,100	(3,100)
Health and sanitation	60,000	46,400	13,600
Other	25,000	18,600	6,400
Total Current Operating Expenditures	395,000	369,300	25,700
Capital outlay	30,000	29,100	900
Debt service	1,000	850	150
Total Expenditures	426,000	399,250	26,750
Excess of Revenues over Expenditures	5,000	38,850	33,850
Other Financing Sources (Uses)			
Operating transfer from Special Revenue Fund	—	10,000	10,000
Operating transfer to Debt Service Fund	—	(5,000)	(5,000)
	—	5,000	(5,000)
Excess of Revenues and Other Financing Sources over Expenditures and Other Uses	5,000	43,850	38,850
Fund Balance—Beginning of 19X1—As Restated (Note X)	11,000	10,700	(300)
Residual equity transfer to Enterprise Fund	—	(6,000)	(6,000)
Fund Balance—End of 19X1	$ 16,000	$ 48,550	$32,550

Notes: 1. *This column should reflect the revised budget amounts, if there are budget revisions. In this example the governing body authorized interfund transfers that were not included in the original budget.*
2. *Since this illustrative example assumes that the budget is prepared and adopted on the modified
accrual (GAAP) basis, only expenditures are reported (encumbrances are excluded).*

The exclusion of encumbrances from the modified accrual basis budgetary statement is debatable, although acceptable under present GAAP, and many consider it
misleading. This contentious issue is discussed further in Chapter 9.

ENTRIES DURING 19X2

The only new subject that must be covered in order to account for the General
Fund in 19X2 is the treatment of the Reserve for Encumbrances account and the
related expenditures made in 19X2. At the first of 19X2 the entry that closed En-

cumbrances to Fund Balance to establish the Reserve for Encumbrances as a true fund balance reserve is **reversed:**

Encumbrances	20,000	
Unreserved Fund Balance		20,000

To return the Encumbrances account to its usual offset relationship with the Reserve for Encumbrances and increase Unreserved Fund Balance accordingly.

Expenditures Ledger (Encumbrances):

Public Safety	7,000	
Health and Sanitation	13,000	
	20,000	

(Note that this is the reverse of entry C4.)

This entry **reestablishes** the Encumbrances and Reserve for Encumbrances accounts in their **usual offset relationship,** causing the Reserve for Encumbrances to no longer be a true fund balance reserve, **and increases** the **Unreserved** Fund Balance account to the **total appropriable** fund balance **amount** so that 19X2 appropriations for encumbrances outstanding at the end of 19X1 can be recorded.

When the goods or services are received in 19X2 the usual "reverse the encumbrances, record the actual expenditures" entries are made and the expenditures are charged against the 19X2 appropriations. Assuming that the goods or services actually cost $21,000, the entry to record their receipt would be:

Reserve for Encumbrances	20,000	
Expenditures	21,000	
Encumbrances		20,000
Vouchers Payable		21,000

To record expenditures for goods and services and reverse the related encumbrance entry.

Expenditures Ledger (Encumbrances):

Public Safety		7,000
Health and Sanitation		13,000
		20,000

Expenditures Ledger (Expenditures):

Public Safety	7,400	
Health and Sanitation	13,600	
	21,000	

If the government wanted to account separately for the goods or services received during 19X2 that were ordered in 19X1, it could use separate General Ledger and/or Expenditures Subsidiary Ledger accounts classified by the year in which the appropriations were made. Further, some or all of the year end 19X1 adjusting entries may be **reversed** at the beginning of 19X2—to facilitate the 19X2 accounting process and routine.

COMBINING SRF STATEMENTS

Recall from the "principles" discussions in Chapter 2 that **combining** financial statements should be prepared whenever a government has two or more funds of a type, such as Special Revenue Funds. Excerpts from a recent City of Memphis comprehensive annual financial report (CAFR) are presented in the final four fig-

ures of this chapter to illustrate the presentation of **combining** Special Revenue
Fund financial statements:

- Figure 4-9: **Narrative Explanations—Special Revenue Funds**—which are
  concise descriptions of each Special Revenue Fund used by the City of Memphis.

Figure 4-9   **NARRATIVE EXPLANATIONS**

City of Memphis
TENNESSEE

SPECIAL REVENUE FUNDS

Special Revenue Funds are used to account for the proceeds of specific revenue sources (other than expendable trusts or major capital projects) that are legally restricted to expenditures for specific purposes. Included in the Special Revenue Funds are:

Municipal State Aid – This fund is used to account for the funds received from the local share of the tax on motor fuel. Funds are restricted to use only on street and road construction and maintenance.

Federal Revenue Sharing – This fund is used to account for the funds received under the Federal Revenue Sharing Program.

Community Development – This fund is used to account for the Community Development Block Grant and other related grants. Funds are restricted to uses approved under Federal guidelines.

Job Training Partnership Act – This fund is used to account for the funds received from the Federal Department of Labor for use in the training of qualified individuals.

Board of Education – This fund is used to account for the receipts and disbursements of the Board's General Fund and Special Revenue Funds. The General Fund includes all financial resources except those required to be accounted for in another fund. The Special Revenue Funds include resources obtained and used under certain federal and state programs and from other sources upon which legal restrictions are imposed. The Special Revenue Funds are the Categorically Aided Fund and the Food Service Fund.

- Figure 4-10: **All Special Revenue Funds—Combining Balance Sheet**—which is like individual fund financial statements presented side by side, as are all combining financial statements.

Figure 4-10

ALL SPECIAL REVENUE FUNDS
COMBINING BALANCE SHEET
June 30, 19x1

CITY OF MEMPHIS, TENNESSEE
Exhibit C-1

	Municipal State Aid	Federal Revenue Sharing	Community Development	Job Training Partnership Act	Board of Education	TOTALS 19x1	TOTALS 19x0
ASSETS							
Cash and cash equivalents	$ –	–	107,354	–	47,554,708	47,662,062	49,826,532
Equity in cash and investment pool	–	–	–	–	–	–	1,247,502
Receivables:							
Federal grants and entitlements	–	–	1,490,664	887,218	539,661	2,917,543	2,305,039
State grants and entitlements	2,893,932	–	471,627	–	8,260,024	11,625,583	5,994,589
Interest on investments	–	–	3,347	–	–	3,347	74,626
Housing and other rehabilitation loans	–	–	38,957,549	–	–	38,957,549	35,606,297
Other	–	–	5,112	9,774	460,487	475,373	284,617
Due from other funds	–	–	3,548	–	279,430	282,978	288,919
Due from other agencies and governments	–	–	–	–	5,146,739	5,146,739	6,265,286
Inventory	–	–	–	–	4,659,256	4,659,256	6,652,070
Total assets	$2,893,932	–	41,039,201	896,992	66,900,305	111,730,430	108,545,477
LIABILITIES AND FUND BALANCES							
Liabilities:							
Accounts payable	$ –	–	–	668,161	843,242	1,511,403	1,147,837
Accrued liabilities	–	–	–	1,144	18,188,366	18,189,510	15,867,326
Due to other funds	2,893,932	–	2,012,371	200,505	120,237	5,227,045	5,424,406
Due to other agencies and governments	–	–	–	27,182	–	27,182	269,338
Deferred revenue	–	–	39,026,830	–	5,047,583	44,074,413	38,315,036
Vacation, sick and other leave benefits	–	–	–	–	1,302,842	1,302,842	1,298,012
Total liabilities	2,893,932	–	41,039,201	896,992	25,502,270	70,332,395	62,321,955
Fund balances:							
Reserved for:							
Encumbrances	–	–	–	–	5,441,550	5,441,550	4,342,958
Inventory	–	–	–	–	4,659,256	4,659,256	6,652,070
Unreserved:							
Designated for:							
Legal claims and transportation liability	–	–	–	–	700,000	700,000	700,000
Subsequent years expenditures	–	–	–	–	15,205,348	15,205,348	14,352,030
Fire losses	–	–	–	–	2,500,000	2,500,000	2,500,000
Undesignated	–	–	–	–	12,891,881	12,891,881	17,676,464
Total fund balances	–	–	–	–	41,398,035	41,398,035	46,223,522
Total liabilities and fund balances	$2,893,932	–	41,039,201	896,992	66,900,305	111,730,430	108,545,477

See accompanying notes to financial statements.

- Figure 4-11: **All Special Revenue Funds—Combining Statement of Revenues, Expenditures, and Changes in Fund Balances**—which is presented in **format B,** or presentation 2. (Note that it reports the termination of the Federal Revenue Sharing Fund.)

Figure 4-11

ALL SPECIAL REVENUE FUNDS
COMBINING STATEMENT OF REVENUES, EXPENDITURES
AND CHANGES IN FUND BALANCES
For the fiscal year ended June 30, 19x1

CITY OF MEMPHIS, TENNESSEE
Exhibit C-2

	Municipal State Aid	Federal Revenue Sharing	Community Development	Job Training Partnership Act	Board of Education	TOTALS	
						19x1	19x0
REVENUES							
Property and other taxes (City and County)	$ –	–	–	–	95,520,972	95,520,972	97,543,089
State taxes (local share)	16,493,183	–	–	–	60,228,009	76,721,192	76,986,979
Use of money and property	–	23,560	–	–	–	23,560	85,249
Federal grants and entitlements	–	–	13,564,826	8,092,750	53,385,943	75,043,519	60,495,979
State grants	–	–	970,576	–	147,791,953	148,762,529	141,918,530
Other	–	–	2,211,207	–	16,889,996	19,101,203	19,107,933
Total revenues	16,493,183	23,560	16,746,609	8,092,750	373,816,873	415,172,975	396,137,759
Other sources:							
Operating transfers in	29,021	9,239	–	–	–	38,260	2,000,000
Total operating transfers in	29,021	9,239	–	–	–	38,260	2,000,000
Proceeds from capital lease obligations	–	–	–	–	–	–	7,541,324
Total other sources	29,021	9,239	–	–	–	38,260	9,541,324
Total revenues and other sources	16,522,204	32,799	16,746,609	8,092,750	373,816,873	415,211,235	405,679,083
EXPENDITURES AND OTHER USE							
Expenditures:							
General government	–	–	15,919,418	–	–	15,919,418	11,231,758
Instruction and administration	–	–	–	–	286,361,161	286,361,161	269,020,893
Plant operations and maintenance	–	–	–	–	47,579,553	47,579,553	45,859,570
Community service	–	–	–	8,092,750	96,623	8,189,373	9,145,689
Transportation	–	–	–	–	7,371,485	7,371,485	5,925,425
Food service	–	–	–	–	23,533,799	23,533,799	24,308,926
Capital outlay	–	–	–	–	1,701,510	1,701,510	821,123
Capital leases-transportation	–	–	–	–	–	–	7,541,324
Debt service:							
Redemption of serial bonds and notes	–	–	–	–	238,693	238,693	1,194,381
Interest	–	–	–	–	49,495	49,495	403,662
Total expenditures	–	–	15,919,418	8,092,750	366,932,319	390,944,487	375,452,751
Other use - operating transfers out:							
General fund	8,170,000	–	–	–	–	8,170,000	7,099,055
Debt service fund	8,352,204	1,280,301	–	–	9,954,337	19,586,842	20,986,565
Capital projects fund	–	–	–	–	–	–	338,401
Community services fund	–	–	827,191	–	–	827,191	1,421,769
Total other use	16,522,204	1,280,301	827,191	–	9,954,337	28,584,033	29,845,790
Total expenditures and other use	16,522,204	1,280,301	16,746,609	8,092,750	376,886,656	419,528,520	405,298,541
Revenues and other sources over(under) expenditures and other use	–	(1,247,502)	–	–	(3,069,783)	(4,317,285)	380,542
Fund balances - July 1	–	1,247,502	–	–	44,976,020	46,223,522	44,944,168
Increase (decrease) in reserve for textbook inventory	–	–	–	–	(953,402)	(953,402)	411,612
Residual equity transfer	–	–	–	–	445,200	445,200	487,200
Fund balances - June 30	$ –	–	–	–	41,398,035	41,398,035	46,223,522

See accompanying notes to financial statements.

- Figure 4-12: **All Special Revenue Funds—Combining Schedule of Revenues and Expenditures—Budget and Actual on Budgetary Basis**—which is presented vertically in a "pancake" format. Note that some Special Revenue Funds are budgeted on a non-GAAP basis under which encumbrances are considered essentially expenditures, and how the "Adjustment for encumbrances" explains the difference between the budgetary and GAAP bases in this example.

Figure 4-12   **ALL SPECIAL REVENUE FUNDS (WITH ANNUAL BUDGETS)**   CITY OF MEMPHIS, TENNESSEE
COMBINING SCHEDULE OF REVENUES AND EXPENDITURES –   **Exhibit C-3**
BUDGET AND ACTUAL ON BUDGETARY BASIS (Non-GAAP)
For the fiscal year ended June 30, 19x1

	19x1			19x0
	Actual on Budgetary Basis	Budget	Variance Favorable (Unfavorable)	Actual on Budgetary Basis
MUNICIPAL STATE AID FUND				
Revenues:				
State gasoline tax (local share)	$16,493,183	17,200,978	(707,795)	16,895,645
Use of money and property	–	–	–	–
Total revenues	16,493,183	17,200,978	(707,795)	16,895,645
Other source:				
Operating transfer in–capital projects	29,021	–	29,021	–
Total revenues and other source	16,522,204	17,200,978	(678,774)	16,895,645
Use – operating transfers out:				
General fund	8,170,000	8,170,000	–	7,099,055
Debt service fund	8,352,204	9,030,978	678,774	9,596,590
Capital projects fund	–	–	–	200,000
Total use	16,522,204	17,200,978	678,774	16,895,645
Revenues and other source over (under) use (Budgetary and GAAP Basis)	$ –	–	–	–

〰〰〰〰〰〰〰〰〰〰〰〰〰〰〰〰〰〰〰〰〰〰〰〰〰〰〰〰〰〰〰

BOARD OF EDUCATION				
Revenues:				
Property and other taxes (City and County)	$ 95,520,972	100,502,581	(4,981,609)	97,543,089
State taxes (local share)	60,228,009	60,228,009	–	60,091,334
Federal grants	53,385,943	48,531,108	4,854,835	43,515,435
State grants	147,791,953	147,279,998	511,955	141,259,188
Other	16,889,996	13,938,764	2,951,232	16,742,427
Total revenues	373,816,873	370,480,460	3,336,413	359,151,473
Other source:				
Operating transfers in–general fund	–	–	–	2,000,000
Total revenues and other source	373,816,873	370,480,460	3,336,413	361,151,473
Expenditures and other use:				
Expenditures:				

〰〰〰〰〰〰〰〰〰〰〰〰〰〰〰〰〰〰〰〰〰〰〰〰〰〰〰〰〰〰〰

Total expenditures	367,771,975	367,524,809	(247,166)	349,370,244
Other use–operating transfer out - Debt service fund	9,954,337	9,955,651	1,314	10,289,975
Total expenditures and other use	377,726,312	377,480,460	(245,852)	359,660,219
Revenues and other source over (under) expenditures other use (budgetary basis)	(3,909,439)	(7,000,000)	3,090,561	1,491,254
Adjustment for encumbrances	839,656			42,440
Revenues and other source over (under) expenditures other use (GAAP basis)	$ (3,069,783)			1,533,694

〰〰〰〰〰〰〰〰〰〰〰〰〰〰〰〰〰〰〰〰〰〰〰〰〰〰〰〰〰〰〰

TOTAL SPECIAL REVENUE FUNDS (WITH ANNUAL BUDGETS)				
Revenues:				
Property and other taxes (city and county)	$ 95,520,972	100,502,581	(4,981,609)	97,543,089
State taxes (local share)	76,721,192	77,428,987	(707,795)	76,986,979

〰〰〰〰〰〰〰〰〰〰〰〰〰〰〰〰〰〰〰〰〰〰〰〰〰〰〰〰〰〰〰

Revenues and other source over (under) expenditures and other use (budgetary basis)	(5,156,941)	(7,000,000)	1,843,059	338,102
Adjustment for encumbrances	839,656			42,440
Revenues and other source over (under) expenditures and other use (GAAP basis)	$ (4,317,285)			380,542

CONCLUDING COMMENTS

The General and Special Revenue Funds typically account for significant portions of the financial resources of state and local government units. Thus, a thorough understanding of General and Special Revenue Fund accounting is important to governmental accountants, auditors, and systems specialists.

Moreover, accounting and reporting for the other governmental funds (Capital Projects, Debt Service, and Expendable Trust Funds) closely parallel that for the General and Special Revenue Funds and can be understood largely by analogy. Thus, a firm **foundation** in General and Special Revenue Fund accounting and reporting is **essential** for both students and practitioners.

This chapter discusses and illustrates the basic accounting and reporting procedures for the General Fund and Special Revenue Funds—which apply also to other governmental funds—and necessarily includes several simplifying assumptions. For example, we assumed that:

- The annual budget was prepared and legally enacted on the modified accrual (GAAP) basis.
- The accounts were accordingly maintained on a GAAP basis during the year and there were no budgetary basis-GAAP basis differences in the accounts or in the financial statements.
- Where alternative methods of accounting for certain transactions and events are acceptable, only one acceptable method should be discussed and illustrated in this "basics" chapter.

The chapters that follow build on this chapter. The next two chapters refine and expand the basic discussions in this chapter on revenue accounting and expenditure accounting, respectively. Then the other governmental funds are considered.

Appendix 4:1
GENERAL LEDGER WORKSHEET AND SUBSIDIARY LEDGERS

As noted in Chapter 4, this appendix presents, for the General Fund of A Governmental Unit, for the year ended December 31, 19X1:

- Figure 4-13—General Ledger Worksheet
- Figure 4-14—Revenues Subsidiary Ledger (Preclosing)
- Figure 4-15—Expenditures Subsidiary Ledger (Preclosing)

Figure 4-13

GENERAL LEDGER WORKSHEET
GENERAL FUND
A GOVERNMENTAL UNIT
FOR THE YEAR ENDED DECEMBER 31, 19X1

Accounts	Transactions Debit	#	Transactions Credit	#	Preclosing Trial Balance Debit	Preclosing Trial Balance Credit	Closing Entries Debit	#	Closing Entries Credit	#	Postclosing Trial Balance Debit	Postclosing Trial Balance Credit
Cash	14,000	(BB)	40,000	(11)								
	175,000	(7)	10,000	(14)								
	205,000	(10)	6,000	(19)								
	20,200	(13)	320,000	(21)								
	20,000	(22)	22,500	(23)								
	13,000	(24)	5,600	(26)	43,100						43,100	
Investments	10,000	(14)			10,000						10,000	
Accrued Interest Receivable	400	(A2)			400						400	
Taxes Receivable—Current	200,000	(2)	160,000	(7)								
			40,000	(8)								
Allowance for Uncollectible Current Taxes	3,000	(9)	3,000	(2)								
Taxes Receivable—Delinquent	40,000	(8)	20,000	(13)	20,000						20,000	
Allowance for Uncollectible Delinquent Taxes			3,000	(9)		3,000						3,000
Interest and Penalties Receivable —Delinquent Taxes	550	(A1)			550						550	
Allowance for Uncollectible Interest and Penalties			50	(A1)		50						50
Accounts Receivable	12,000	(BB)	15,000	(7)	19,600						19,600	
	36,000	(3)	13,000	(24)								
			400	(25)								
Allowance for Uncollectible Accounts Receivable	400	(25)	1,000	(3)		600						600
Due from Special Revenue Fund	1,500	(16)			11,500						11,500	
	10,000	(18)										
Vouchers Payable	40,000	(11)	15,900	(BB)								
	320,000	(21)	29,900	(5b)								
			40,000	(6)								
			300,000	(20)								
			300	(27)		25,200						25,200
Notes Payable	5,000	(26)	20,000	(22)		15,000						15,000
Accrued Interest Payable			250	(A3)		250						250
Due to Stores Fund	22,500	(23)	30,000	(15)		7,500						7,500
Due to Debt Service Fund			5,000	(17)		5,000						5,000
Reserve for Encumbrances	30,000	(5a)	30,000	(4)								
			20,000	(12)		20,000						20,000
Unreserved Fund Balance			11,000	(BB)								
	5,000	(1)				16,000	5,000	(C1)	38,850	(C2)		
							1,300	(C3)				
							20,000	(C4)				28,550
Estimated Revenues	431,000	(1)			431,000				431,000	(C1)		
Revenues			197,000	(2)								
			35,000	(3)								
			205,000	(10)								
			200	(13)								
			500	(A1)								
			400	(A2)		438,100	438,100	(C2)				
Appropriations			426,000	(1)		426,000	426,000	(C1)				
Expenditures	29,900	(5b)	1,500	(16)								
	40,000	(6)										
	30,000	(15)										
	300,000	(20)										
	600	(26)										
	250	(A3)			399,250				399,250	(C2)		
Encumbrances	30,000	(4)	30,000	(5a)								
	20,000	(12)			20,000				20,000	(C4)		
Operating Transfer to Debt Service Fund	5,000	(17)			5,000				5,000	(C3)		
Operating Transfer from Special Revenue Fund			10,000	(18)		10,000	10,000	(C3)				
Residual Equity Transfer to Enterprise Fund	6,000	(19)			6,000				6,000	(C3)		
Correction of Prior Year Error	300	(27)			300				300	(C3)		
	2,071,600		2,071,600		966,700	966,700	900,400		900,400		105,150	105,150

147

Figure 4-14

REVENUES SUBSIDIARY LEDGER
GENERAL FUND
A GOVERNMENTAL UNIT
FOR THE YEAR ENDED DECEMBER 31, 19X1: PRECLOSING

Revenues Ledger

	Dr. Estimated Revenues	Cr. Revenues	Dr. (Cr.) Balance
Taxes	250,000 (1)		250,000
		197,000 (2)	53,000
		58,000 (10)	(5,000)
Totals/Balance	250,000	255,000	(5,000)
Licenses and Permits	70,000 (1)		70,000
		68,000 (10)	2,000
Totals/Balance	70,000	68,000	2,000
Intergovernmental	50,000 (1)		50,000
		52,500 (10)	(2,500)
Totals/Balance	50,000	52,500	(2,500)
Charges for Services	40,000 (1)		40,000
		35,000 (3)	5,000
		6,000 (10)	(1,000)
Totals/Balance	40,000	41,000	(1,000)
Fines and Forfeits	20,000 (1)		20,000
		19,000 (10)	1,000
Totals/Balance	20,000	19,000	1,000
Other	1,000 (1)		1,000
		1,500 (10)	(500)
		200 (13)	(700)
		500 (A1)	(1,200)
		400 (A2)	(1,600)
Totals/Balance	1,000	2,600	(1,600)

Figure 4-15

EXPENDITURES SUBSIDIARY LEDGER
GENERAL FUND
A GOVERNMENTAL UNIT
FOR THE YEAR ENDED DECEMBER 31, 19X1: PRECLOSING

Expenditures Ledger

	Dr. Encumbrances	Dr. Expenditures	Cr. Appropriations	Cr. (Dr.) Unencumbered Balance
General Government			40,000 (1)	40,000
	2,000 (4)			38,000
	(2,000)(5a)	1,700 (5b)		38,300
		5,000 (6)		33,300
		4,000 (15)		29,300
		(1,500)(16)		30,800
		30,000 (20)		800
Totals/Balance	0	39,200	40,000	800
Public Safety			150,000 (1)	150,000
	8,000 (4)			142,000
	(8,000)(5a)	8,000 (5b)		142,000
		16,000 (6)		126,000
	7,000 (12)			119,000
		6,000 (15)		113,000
		112,000 (20)		1,000
Totals/Balance	7,000	142,000	150,000	1,000
Highways and Streets			120,000 (1)	120,000
	10,000 (4)			110,000
	(10,000)(5a)	10,100 (5b)		109,900
		13,000 (6)		96,900
		10,000 (15)		86,900
		90,000 (20)		(3,100)
Totals/Balance	0	123,100	120,000	(3,100)
Health and Sanitation			60,000 (1)	60,000
		4,000 (6)		56,000
	13,000 (12)			43,000
		7,000 (15)		36,000
		35,400 (20)		600
Totals/Balance	13,000	46,400	60,000	600
Other			25,000 (1)	25,000
	4,000 (4)			21,000
	(4,000)(5a)	4,000 (5b)		21,000
		2,000 (6)		19,000
		3,000 (15)		16,000
		9,600 (20)		6,400
Totals/Balance	0	18,600	25,000	6,400
Capital Outlay			30,000 (1)	30,000
	6,000 (4)			24,000
	(6,000)(5a)	6,100 (5b)		23,900
		23,000 (20)		900
Totals/Balance	0	29,100	30,000	900
Debt Service			1,000 (1)	1,000
		600 (26)		400
		250 (A3)		150
Totals/Balance	0	850	1,000	150

QUESTIONS

4-1 Why is there no chapter in this text devoted to describing operations and accounting procedures of Special Revenue Funds?

4-2 What are the characteristics of "expenditures" that distinguish them from "expenses" in the financial accounting sense?

4-3 What is the nature of the Unreserved Fund Balance account as it appears (a) in the interim balance sheet? (b) in a postclosing trial balance?

4-4 Why are encumbrances not considered expenditures under the modified accrual (GAAP) basis of governmental fund accounting?

4-5 Although the illustrative examples in this chapter use only a few Revenues Subsidiary Ledger and Expenditures Subsidiary Ledger accounts, a state or local government probably will use hundreds or even thousands of such accounts in practice. Why?

4-6 Why might a local government not prepare and adopt its General Fund annual operating budget on the modified accrual (GAAP) basis?

4-7 Explain what is meant by General Ledger "control" over the Revenues Subsidiary Ledger and the Expenditures Subsidiary Ledger.

4-8 The illustrative example in this chapter uses the term "Unreserved Fund Balance" to describe the unreserved fund balance account. Yet in practice one often sees that account titled simply "Fund Balance," even though it is accompanied by a Reserve for Encumbrances, Reserve for Interfund Advances, and perhaps other "reserve" accounts. Is this acceptable?

4-9 Explain the "net revenue" approach to revenue recognition employed in General and Special Revenue Fund (and other governmental fund) accounting and reporting, including why it is used.

4-10 Why might a General Fund "reserve" be established?

4-11 Why are nonrevenue financing sources and nonexpenditure uses of financial resources distinguished from governmental fund revenues and expenditures?

4-12 Explain the nature and purpose of the Reserve for Encumbrances account (a) during the year, and (b) at year end.

4-13 The terms "Advance To (From) Other Funds" and "Due From (To) Other Funds" have distinct meanings in governmental fund accounting and financial reporting. Explain.

4-14 Explain the purpose, nature, and effect of the entry reestablishing Encumbrances in the accounts at the beginning of a new year.

4-15 The budget was assumed to be enacted on the GAAP basis in this chapter. What differences in the General Fund financial statements and disclosures would you expect if the budget were adopted on the cash basis or another non-GAAP basis?

4-16 (a) Distinguish between "unreserved" fund balance and "total" fund balance. (b) How does a governmental fund statement of revenues, expenditures, and changes in fund balance prepared on the usual "total fund balance" approach differ from such a statement prepared on the "unreserved fund balance" approach?

PROBLEMS

P 4-1 (Multiple Choice) Indicate the best answer to each question.

1. A city levies property taxes of $500,000 for its General Fund for a year and expects to collect all except the estimated uncollectible amount of $5,500 by year end. To reflect this information, the city should record General Fund revenues of

   a. $500,000 and General Fund expenses of $5,500.

   b. $500,000 and General Fund expenditures of $5,500.

   c. $500,000 and no General Fund expenses or expenditures.

   d. $494,500 and no General Fund expenses or expenditures.

   e. None of the above. The correct answer is _____.

2. At year end, a school district purchases instructional equipment costing $10,000 by issuing a six-month note to be repaid from General Fund resources. This transaction should be reflected in the General Fund as

   a. Expenditures of $10,000 and a $10,000 liability.

   b. Expenditures of $10,000 and a $10,000 other financing source from the issuance of the note.

   c. A fixed asset of $10,000 and a liability of $10,000.

   d. Expenditures of $10,000 and revenues of $10,000 from issuance of the note.

3. Which of the following statements is true?

   a. Encumbrances are equivalent to expenditures, and encumbrances outstanding at the end of a year should be reported as liabilities.

   b. No expenditure can be reported without first being encumbered.

   c. Encumbrances are recorded at the estimated cost of goods ordered or services contracted for. The subsequent amount recognized as expenditures upon receipt of the goods or services must be equal to the encumbered amount.

   d. Encumbrances are recorded at the estimated cost of goods ordered or services contracted for. The subsequent amount recognized as expenditures upon receipt of the goods or services may differ from the encumbered amount.

4. A state borrowed $10,000,000 on a nine-month, 9% note payable to provide temporary financing for the General Fund. At year end, the note has been outstanding for six months. The state should report General Fund interest expenditures and interest payable on the note in its financial statements in the amount of

   a. $0, the interest will be recognized when it matures.

   b. $450,000.

   c. $450,000 unless the state does not expect to be able to pay the interest when it matures—in which case no interest expenditures should be reported for the current year.

   d. $675,000.

5. Charges for services rendered by a county's General Fund departments totaled $500,000 —of which $5,500 is expected to be uncollectible. The county expects to collect $494,500 by year end. To reflect this information, the county should record General Fund revenues of

   a. $500,000 and General Fund expenses of $5,500.

   b. $500,000 and General Fund expenditures of $5,500.

   c. $500,000 and no General Fund expenses or expenditures.

   d. $494,500 and no General Fund expenses or expenditures.

   e. None of the above. The correct answer is _____.

6. Which of the following transactions requires entries in an Expenditures Subsidiary Ledger?

   a. Legal adoption of the General Fund budget.

   b. Purchase of equipment on account.

   c. Accrual of salaries and wages.

   d. Order of supplies.

   e. All of the above.

7. If a county Special Revenue Fund has a long-term receivable from another county fund, the receivable will be reported as a(n)

   a. Advance from Other Funds with an equivalent amount of fund balance reserved for advances from other funds.

   b. Advance from Other Funds with no fund balance reserve needed.

   c. Advance to Other Funds with an equivalent amount of fund balance reserved for advances to other funds.

    d. Advance to Other Funds with no fund balance reserve needed.

    e. Due from Other Funds.

    f. Due to Other Funds.

8. Which of the following items is reported differently in a statement of revenues, expenditures, and changes in unreserved fund balance than it is in a statement of revenues, expenditures, and changes in total fund balance?

    a. Personal services expenditures

    b. Encumbrances outstanding

    c. Changes in fund balance reserves

    d. Proceeds of general long-term debt issuances

    e. Residual equity transfers

9. The budget data presented in a school district General Fund statement of revenues, expenditures, and changes in fund balance—budget and actual is to be

    a. The original, legally adopted budget.

    b. The original, legally adopted budget, as amended.

    c. Presented on the modified accrual basis of accounting even if the budget is adopted on the cash basis.

    d. Adjusted to equal the actual in the expenditure portion of the statement to avoid any overexpenditures of budget being presented.

10. In the statement of revenues, expenditures, and changes in fund balance, operating transfers in must be reported

    a. In a separate section immediately following revenues.

    b. In a section immediately following the excess of revenues over(under) expenditures.

    c. Either a or b is permissible.

    d. Immediately following beginning fund balance.

P 4-2   (General Ledger Entries) (a) Prepare general journal entries to record the following transactions in the General Ledger of the General Fund or a Special Revenue Fund, as appropriate. (b) Explain how these transactions and events are reported in the General or Special Revenue Fund statement of revenues, expenditures, and changes in fund balance.

1. $100,000 of General Fund cash was contributed to establish a new Internal Service Fund.

2. A truck—acquired two years ago with General Fund revenues for $9,000—with a fair market value of $4,000 was contributed to a department financed by an Enterprise Fund. Record the contribution of the asset to the Enterprise Fund—not the purchase.

3. The Sanitation Department, accounted for in the General Fund, billed the Municipal Airport, accounted for in an Enterprise Fund, $800 for garbage collection.

4. General Fund cash of $50,000—to be repaid in 90 days—was provided to enable construction to begin on a new courthouse before a bond issue was sold.

5. A $9,000,000 bond issue to finance construction of a major addition to the civic center was sold at par. The civic center will be accounted for in the governmental funds and account groups.

6. General Fund disbursements during May included a contribution of $35,000 to a Capital Projects Fund to help finance a major capital project.

7. After retirement of the related debt, the balance of the net assets of a Debt Service Fund, $8,500, was transferred to the General Fund.

8. General Fund cash of $70,000 was loaned to an Enterprise Fund, to be repaid in three years.

9. An accounting error made during the prior accounting period caused the Cash balance at the beginning of the current year to be understated by $6,500.

10. Another accounting error was discovered: expenditures of $4,000, properly chargeable to a Capital Projects Fund, were inadvertently charged to a Special Revenue Fund during the current year.

P 4-3 (Closing Entries) The preclosing trial balance of a Special Revenue Fund of Mesa County at the end of its 19X3 fiscal year is:

Cash	25,000	
Taxes Receivable—Delinquent	70,000	
Allowance for Uncollectible Delinquent Taxes		10,000
Due from General Fund	16,000	
Advance to Enterprise Fund	45,000	
Accrued Receivables	9,000	
Vouchers Payable		21,000
Due to Internal Service Fund		4,000
Accrued Payables		6,000
Reserve for Interfund Advance		45,000
Reserve for Encumbrances		20,000
Unreserved Fund Balance		52,000
Estimated Revenues	800,000	
Appropriations		810,000
Revenues		798,000
Expenditures	789,000	
Encumbrances	20,000	
Operating Transfer to Debt Service Fund	15,000	
Residual Equity Transfer from Capital Projects Fund		35,000
Correction of Prior Year Error	12,000	
	1,801,000	1,801,000

Revenues Ledger:

Taxes	3,000	
Intergovernmental		4,000
Charges for Services	1,000	
Other	2,000	
	6,000	4,000

Expenditures Ledger:

General Government		1,500
Parks and Recreation		2,500
Social Services	3,500	
Other		500
	3,500	4,500

Required
(a) Prepare the entry or entries to close the General Ledger and subsidiary ledger accounts at the end of the 19X3 fiscal year.

(b) Prepare any related entry(ies) needed at the beginning of the 19X4 fiscal year.

P 4-4 (GL & SL Entries) Prepare the journal entries to record the following transactions and events in the General Ledger, Revenues Ledger, and Expenditures Ledger of a local government General Fund.

1. The annual budget was adopted as follows:

Estimated Revenues:	
Property taxes	$400,000
Sales taxes	200,000
Charges for services	100,000
Other	50,000
	$750,000

Appropriations:	
General administration	$ 80,000
Police	310,000
Fire	320,000
Other	30,000
	$740,000

2. Property taxes of $408,000 were levied, of which $7,000 is expected to be uncollectible.

3. Purchase orders and contracts were approved for goods and services expected to cost:

Police.	$ 50,000
Fire	90,000
	$140,000

4. Most of the goods and services ordered were received.

	Encumbered For	Actual Cost
Police.	$ 40,000	$ 41,000
Fire	70,000	68,500
	$110,000	$109,500

5. The budget was revised during the year to decrease the sales tax revenue estimate by $5,000 and increase the Police appropriation by $7,000.

6. Interfund transfers were ordered as follows:

From the General Fund	
To provide for principal and interest payments on GLTD	$30,000
To establish a new data processing Internal Service Fund	50,000
	$80,000
To the General Fund	
Balance of Capital Projects Fund terminated upon project completion	$60,000
Routine annual transfer from a Special Revenue Fund	25,000
	$85,000

All of the transfers were paid or received except that from the Special Revenue Fund, which will be paid soon.

7. It was discovered that $2,000 of supplies charged to Police in transaction 4 should be charged to Parks, which is financed through a Special Revenue Fund.

P 4-5 (GL & SL Entries) Prepare the journal entries to record the following transactions and events in the General Ledger, Revenues Ledger, and Expenditures Ledger of a Special Revenue Fund of a local independent school district.

1. The annual operating budget provides for:

Estimated Revenues:	
State appropriation	$500,000
Property taxes.	300,000
Other	100,000
	$900,000
Appropriations:	
Administration.	$100,000
Instruction	750,000
Other	40,000
	$890,000

2. Purchase orders and contracts for goods and services were approved at estimated costs of:

Administration.	$ 15,000
Instruction	60,000
Other	20,000
	$ 95,000

3. Property taxes were levied, $320,000, of which $15,000 is estimated to be uncollectible.

4. Most of the goods and services ordered at 2 arrived and the invoices were approved and vouchered for payment:

	Encumbered At	Actual Cost
Administration.	$ 15,000	$ 14,800
Instruction	40,000	40,000
Other	20,000	20,300
	$ 75,000	$ 75,100

5. Cash receipts and year-end revenue accruals were:

	Cash Receipts	Year End Accrued Receivable
State appropriation	$460,000	$ 38,000
Current property taxes	290,000	—
Delinquent property taxes	15,000	—
Accrued revenue receivable (beginning). .	30,000	—
Other	41,000	2,000
	$836,000	$ 40,000

6. Cash disbursements, including payment of payroll and other unencumbered expenditures, and year-end expenditure accruals were:

	Cash Disbursements	Year End Accrued Payable
Administration.	$ 84,000	$ 1,000
Instruction	700,000	8,000
Other	20,000	—
Accrued expenditures payable (beginning)	30,000	—
	$834,000	$ 9,000

7. Interfund transfers were ordered (not yet paid) as follows: (a) $25,000 to the Debt Service Fund to be used to pay general long-term debt principal and interest, and (b) $40,000 from an Internal Service Fund that is being discontinued.

8. It was discovered that $1,500 charged to Instruction (in 6) should be charged to Transportation, which is financed through the General Fund.

P 4-6 (General Ledger Entries) The following information was abstracted from the accounts of the General Fund of the City of Ragus after the books had been closed for the fiscal year ended June 30, 19X2:

	Postclosing Trial Balance June 30, 19X1	Transactions July 1, 19X1 to June 30, 19X2		Postclosing Trial Balance June 30, 19X2
		Debit	Credit	
Cash	$700,000	$1,820,000	$1,852,000	$668,000
Taxes receivable	40,000	1,870,000	1,828,000	82,000
	$740,000			$750,000
Allowance for uncollectible taxes	$ 8,000	8,000	10,000	$ 10,000
Vouchers payable	132,000	1,852,000	1,840,000	120,000
Fund balance:				
Reserved for encumbrances. . .	—	1,000,000	1,070,000	70,000
Unreserved	600,000	140,000	60,000	550,000
			30,000	
	$740,000			$750,000

Additional information:

The budget for the fiscal year ended June 30, 19X2 provided for estimated revenues of $2,000,000 and appropriations of $1,940,000.

Required Prepare general journal entries to record the budgeted and actual transactions in the General Ledger of the General Fund of the City of Ragus for the fiscal year ended June 30, 19X2.
(AICPA, adapted)

P 4-7 (General Ledger Entries) The trial balance of the General Fund of the City of Claire on January 1, 19X0, was as follows:

Cash	$15,000	
Taxes Receivable—Delinquent.	20,000	
Allowance for Uncollectible Taxes—Delinquent		$ 3,000
Interest and Penalties Receivable on Taxes	1,000	
Allowance for Uncollectible Interest and Penalties		75
Accounts Receivable.	10,000	
Allowance for Uncollectible Accounts.		1,000
Vouchers Payable		20,500
Reserve for Encumbrances (Assumption A1).		10,000
Unreserved Fund Balance.		11,425
	$46,000	$46,000

The following transactions and events took place during 19X0:

1. Revenues were estimated at $110,000; appropriations of $108,000 were made.
2. An order placed at the end of the preceding year and estimated to cost $10,000 was received; the invoice indicated an actual cost of $9,500.
3. Taxes of $110,000 accrued; an allowance of 5% was made for possible losses.
4. Collections were made as follows:

Current Taxes	$90,000
Delinquent Taxes	10,000
Interest and Penalties Receivable on Taxes. .	300
Accounts Receivable	5,000

5. Taxes amounting to $20,000 have become delinquent: the balance of Allowance for Uncollectible Taxes—Current was transferred to Allowance for Uncollectible Taxes—Delinquent.

6. Delinquent Taxes amounting to $2,000 were written off: Interest and Penalties Receivable on Taxes of $20 were also written off.

7. Orders were placed for (a) materials estimated to cost $20,000 and (b) a truck estimated to cost $8,000.

8. Delinquent Taxes amounting to $200, which were written off in preceding years, were collected with interest and penalties of $35 ($25 of which had been previously accrued and written off).

9. Payments were made as follows:

Vouchers Payable.	$15,500
Payrolls	45,000

10. The materials and truck ordered (in 7) were received; bills for $21,000 and $8,000, respectively, were also received.

11. Operating lease payments of $15,000 were paid.

12. Interest of $600 accrued on Delinquent Taxes, and an allowance for uncollectible losses thereon of 10% was provided.

13. An order was placed for materials estimated to cost $19,000.

Required (a) Complete a worksheet headed as follows:

Columns	Heading
1–2	Trial Balance, 1/1/19X0
3–4	19X0 Transactions
5–6	Preclosing Trial Balance, 12/31/19X0
7–8	19X0 Closing Entries
9–10	Postclosing Trial Balance, 12/31/19X0

In lieu of requirement (a) you may:

1. Post the opening trial balance to "T" accounts.
2. Prepare journal entries.
3. Post to "T" accounts.
4. Prepare closing entries.
5. Post to "T" accounts.
6. Prepare a postclosing trial balance at December 31, 19X0.

(b) Prepare a balance sheet at December 31, 19X0.

P 4-8 (General Ledger Entries) The following is a trial balance of the General Fund of the City of Lynnville as of December 31, 19X0, after closing entries:

Cash.	$33,600	
Taxes Receivable—Delinquent	25,400	
Allowance for Uncollectible Delinquent Taxes		$ 5,900
Accounts Receivable	15,500	
Allowance for Uncollectible Accounts		2,500
Vouchers Payable		42,000
Reserve for Encumbrances.		16,000
Unreserved Fund Balance		8,100
	$74,500	$74,500

(Interest and penalties on taxes are not material, so are not accrued.)

The following transactions took place during 19X1:

1. The budget for the year was adopted. Revenues were estimated at $216,000; appropriations of $229,000 were made, including an appropriation of $16,000 for materials ordered in 19X0, covered by the Reserve for Encumbrances.

2. Delinquent Taxes of $2,800 were declared uncollectible and written off.

3. Property taxes of $210,000 were levied; a 3% allowance for estimated losses was provided.

4. Uniforms estimated to cost $15,000 were ordered, as was a snowplow estimated to cost $3,500.

5. The materials ordered in 19X0 and set up as an encumbrance of that year for $16,000 were received; the actual cost, $15,000, was vouchered for later payment.

6. Collections were made as follows:

Current Taxes	$182,000
Delinquent Taxes	8,500
Interest and Penalties on Taxes	200
Accounts Receivable	7,300

7. Received a bill for $3,000 from the city central printing shop.

8. Payroll vouchers for $100,000 were approved and paid, as was a transfer of $38,000 to a Debt Service Fund to cover serial bond debt service.

9. The uniforms and snowplow (ordered in 4) were received; the invoices were for $16,000 and $3,800, respectively.

10. Delinquent taxes of $350, written off in preceding years, were collected.

11. Current taxes receivable became delinquent.

12. Paid $200 to the Special Revenue Fund for supplies acquired for General Fund purposes, but originally paid for from (and recorded as expenditures in) the Special Revenue Fund; and paid $60,000 of vouchers payable.

13. An order was placed for civil defense equipment estimated to cost $24,000.

14. Miscellaneous revenues of $5,000 were collected and $5,000 was received from a discontinued Capital Projects Fund.

Required   (a) Complete a worksheet headed as follows:

Columns	Heading
1–2	Trial Balance, 1/1/19X1
3–4	19X1 Transactions
5–6	Preclosing Trial Balance, 12/31/19X1
7–8	Closing Entries 12/31/19X1
9–10	Postclosing Trial Balance, 12/31/19X1

In lieu of requirement (a) you may:

1. Post the opening trial balance to "T" accounts.
2. Prepare journal entries.
3. Post to "T" accounts.
4. Prepare preclosing trial balance at December 31, 19X1.
5. Prepare closing entries.
6. Post to "T" accounts.
7. Prepare a postclosing trial balance at December 31, 19X1.

(b) Prepare a balance sheet at December 31, 19X1.

P 4-9 (GL & SL Entries) Marcus County adopted the following budget for one of its Special Revenue Funds for the 19X9 fiscal year, its first year in operation:

Revenues:

Property taxes	$ 500,000
Sales taxes	200,000
Federal grants	100,000
Service charges	80,000
Fines	50,000
Other	20,000
	950,000

Expenditures:

Manager	110,000
Commission	90,000
Roads and bridges	400,000
Courts	60,000
Sheriff	180,000
Jail	70,000
Other	30,000
	940,000
Budgeted Excess of Revenues over Expenditures	$ 10,000

The following transactions and events occurred during 19X9.

1. The property taxes were levied, $530,000, of which $25,000 is expected to be uncollectible.

2. Purchase orders and contracts were approved at the following estimated costs:

Manager	$ 20,000
Roads and bridges	200,000
Sheriff	40,000
Jail	10,000
	$270,000

3. The goods and services ordered on these purchase orders and contracts were delivered at the following actual costs which were approved as vouchers payable:

Manager	$ 19,500
Roads and bridges	200,000
Sheriff	40,300
Jail	9,900
	$269,700

4. Property taxes collected during 19X9 totaled $503,000, and the balance of the uncollected taxes became delinquent.

5. Other cash receipts during 19X9 were:

Sales taxes	$180,000
Federal grants	106,000
Service charges	74,000
Fines	52,000
Other	18,000
	$430,000

6. Cash was disbursed for payroll and other unencumbered expenditures as follows:

Manager	$ 88,700
Commission	84,300
Roads and bridges	197,000
Courts	56,000
Sheriff	133,000
Jail	61,500
Other	29,500
	$650,000

Vouchers payable of $260,000 also were paid.

7. Additional purchase orders and contracts were issued at these estimated costs:

Commission	$ 4,000
Roads and bridges	2,000
Courts	3,700
Sheriff	5,800
	$ 15,500

8. Accrued receivables and payables at year end were:

a. Revenues receivable:

Sales taxes	$19,000
Service charges	4,000
Other	1,000
	$24,000

b. Expenditures payable:

Manager	$ 500
Commission	1,200
Other	300
	$ 2,000

Required   Prepare the journal entries required to record the adoption of the budget and the numbered transactions and events in the General Ledger and in the Revenues and Expenditures Subsidiary Ledgers of the Marcus County Special Revenue Fund for the 19X9 fiscal year. Key the budgetary entry "B" and key the numbered transactions and events by number.

P 4-10, Part I   (GL Worksheet & SL Accounts)

Instructor Note   This problem may be assigned either as a continuation of or instead of Problem 4-9.

Required   Based on the information about the Marcus County Special Revenue Fund in Problem 4-9:

(a) Record the effects of the 19X9 budget adoption and the numbered transactions and events in an appropriate General Ledger worksheet and in Revenues Subsidiary Ledger and Expenditures Subsidiary Ledger accounts.

(b) Prepare the entries to close the accounts at the end of 19X9 and record them on the General Ledger worksheet and in the subsidiary ledger accounts.

P 4-10, Part II   (Financial Statements; Encumbrances)

Required   Based on the solution to Part I of this problem:

(a) Prepare the year end 19X9 Balance Sheet and the Statement of Revenues, Expenditures, and Changes in Fund Balance—Budget and Actual for the 19X9 fiscal year for the Marcus County Special Revenue Fund.

(b) Briefly explain why the actual excess of revenues over expenditures differed from that budgeted.

(c) How would the budgetary comparison statement prepared in part (a) differ if the Marcus County Commissioners considered encumbrances equivalent to expenditures for budgetary compliance evaluation purposes?

(d) Prepare the entry necessary to reestablish the encumbrances in the accounts at the beginning of the next year, 19Y0.

P 4-11 (GL & SL Entries) The trial balance of the General Fund of Mann Independent School District at the beginning of its 19X5 fiscal year was:

	Dr.	Cr.
Cash	20,000	
Taxes Receivable—Delinquent	15,000	
Allowance for Uncollectible Delinquent Taxes		8,000
Accrued Receivables	43,000	
Vouchers Payable		12,000
Accrued Payables		10,000
Unreserved Fund Balance		48,000
	78,000	78,000

The following transactions and events affected the Mann Independent School District General Fund during 19X5:

1. The annual budget (GAAP basis) adopted provided for:

Estimated Revenues:	
Property taxes	$400,000
State assistance	300,000
Federal grants	200,000
Other	50,000
	$950,000

Appropriations:	
Administration	$100,000
Instruction	700,000
Maintenance	90,000
Other	55,000
	$945,000

Planned Increase in Fund Balance	$ 5,000

2. Property taxes totaling $420,000 were levied: some $15,000 were expected to prove uncollectible.

3. Cash receipts during 19X5 and additional accrued receivables at the end of 19X5 were as follows:

	Cash Receipts	Accrued at End of 19X5
Property taxes—current	$391,000	$ —
Property taxes—delinquent	6,000	—
State assistance	260,000	38,000
Federal grants	190,000	14,000
Other	47,000	—
Accrued receivables (beginning)	43,000	—
	$937,000	$52,000

4. The uncollected current property taxes became delinquent at year end, and $16,000 of delinquent property taxes were written off during 19X5 by action of the school board.

5. Purchase orders and contracts were issued and related goods and services were delivered and vouchered as payable as follows:

	Orders and Contracts	Goods and Services Received	
	Encumbered For	Encumbered For	Actual Cost
Administration	$ 20,000	$ 15,000	$ 14,800
Instruction.	80,000	80,000	79,200
Maintenance.	50,000	50,000	50,000
Other.	25,000	21,000	21,500
	$175,000	$166,000	$165,500

6. Cash disbursements—for payroll, other unencumbered expenditures, and vouchers payable—during 19X5 and additional accrued expenditures at the end of 19X5 were as follows:

	Cash Disbursements	Accrued at End of 19X5
Administration	$ 79,000	—
Instruction.	617,000	2,800
Maintenance.	38,000	2,700
Other	27,000	2,000
Vouchers Payable.	163,000	—
Accrued Payables (beginning)	10,000	—
	$934,000	$7,500

Required   Prepare the journal entries to record the numbered transactions and events in the General Ledger, Revenues Subsidiary Ledger, and Expenditures Subsidiary Ledger.

P 4-12, Part I   (GL Worksheet and SL Accounts)

Instructor Note   This problem may be assigned either as a continuation of or instead of Problem 4-11.

Required   Based on the information about the General Fund of the Mann Independent School District in Problem 4-11:

(a) Record the beginning trial balance and the numbered transactions and events in an appropriate General Ledger worksheet and in Revenues Subsidiary Ledger and Expenditures Subsidiary Ledger accounts.

(b) Prepare the entry or entries to close the accounts at the end of 19X5 and record it (them) on the General Ledger worksheet and in the subsidiary ledger accounts. (The Reserve for Encumbrances should become a true reservation of fund balance.)

P 4-12, Part II   (Financial Statements; Encumbrances)

Required   (a) Prepare a Statement of Revenues, Expenditures, and Changes in Fund Balance for the General Fund of Mann Independent School District for the 19X5 fiscal year and a Balance Sheet as of the end of 19X5.

(b) How would the Statement of Revenues, Expenditures, and Changes in Fund Balance—Budget and Actual differ from (a) if the Mann Independent School District budgetary basis considered both encumbrances and expenditures to be uses of appropriation authority?

(c) Prepare the entry to reestablish encumbrances in the accounts at the beginning of 19X6.

P 4-13 (GL & SL Entries; Statements) The following financial activities affecting Judbury City's General Fund took place during the year ended June 30, 19X1:

1. The following budget was adopted:

Estimated revenues:	
Property taxes	$4,500,000
Licenses and permits	300,000
Fines	200,000
Total	$5,000,000

Appropriations:	
General government	$1,500,000
Police services	1,200,000
Fire department services	900,000
Public works services	800,000
Acquisition of fire engines	400,000
Total	$4,800,000

2. Property tax bills totaling $4,650,000 were mailed. It was estimated that $300,000 of this amount will be delinquent, and $150,000 will be uncollectible.

3. Property taxes totaling $3,900,000 were collected. The $150,000 previously estimated to be uncollectible remained unchanged, but $750,000 was reclassified as delinquent. It is estimated that delinquent taxes will be collected soon enough after June 30, 19X1, to make these taxes available to finance obligations incurred during the year ended June 30, 19X1. There was no balance of uncollected taxes at July 1, 19X0.

4. Tax anticipation notes in the face amount of $300,000 were issued.

5. Other cash collections were as follows:

Licenses and permits	$270,000
Fines	200,000
Sale of public works equipment (original cost, $75,000)	15,000
Total	$485,000

6. The following purchase orders were executed:

	Total	Outstanding at 6/30/X1
General government	$1,050,000	$ 60,000
Police services	300,000	30,000
Fire department services	150,000	15,000
Public works services	250,000	10,000
Fire engines	400,000	—
Totals	$2,150,000	$115,000

No encumbrances were outstanding at June 30, 19X0.

7. The following vouchers were approved:

General government	$1,440,000
Police services	1,155,000
Fire department services	870,000
Public works services	700,000
Fire engines	400,000
Total	$4,565,000

8. Vouchers totaling $4,600,000 were paid.

Required (a) Prepare journal entries to record the foregoing financial activities in the General Fund General Ledger and in the Revenues and Expenditures Subsidiary Ledgers. Omit explanations. Ignore interest accruals.

(b) Prepare a Statement of Revenues, Expenditures, and Changes in Fund Balance for the General Fund of Judbury City for the fiscal year ended June 30, 19X1. Assume that the beginning total fund balance was $80,000. (AICPA, adapted)

P 4-14 (Statement of Revenues, Expenditures, and Changes in Fund Balance) Using the following information, prepare the Statement of Revenues, Expenditures, and Changes in (Total) Fund Balance for the City of Nancy General Fund for the fiscal year ended December 31, 19X1.

1. Unreserved Fund Balance, January 1, 19X1, was $150,000.

2. Fund balance reserves, January 1, 19X1, were for:

Encumbrances	$ 25,000
Advances	50,000

The advance is due in 19X2.

3. Revenues for 19X1 totaled $2,500,000, including:

Property taxes	$1,800,000
Licenses and permits	190,000
Intergovernmental revenues	310,000
Proceeds from short-term note	50,000
Other	150,000

Other revenues include $40,000 received from a Capital Projects Fund upon completion of the project and termination of the fund and a $65,000 routine annual transfer from the City's Water Enterprise Fund.

4. Expenditures for 19X1 totaled $2,600,000, including:

General government	$ 800,000
Public safety	1,000,000
Highways and streets	600,000
Health and sanitation	150,000
Other	50,000

Included in the public safety expenditures is $85,000 for the estimated cost of a fire truck that has been ordered but not received. A second truck costing $55,000 was received during 19X1.

Also, the highways and streets expenditures includes $42,000 for work contracted out to independent contractors but not performed as of year end.

REVENUE ACCOUNTING—
GOVERNMENTAL FUNDS

Revenue accounting in government parallels that for business enterprises in many respects. In both, revenues must be distinguished from nonrevenue resource inflows, and accounting guidelines have been established regarding the timing of revenue recognition. Proprietary fund revenue recognition is virtually identical to that in business accounting.

Significant differences and unique considerations are also involved, however, particularly in revenue accounting for governmental (expendable) funds. These differences and special considerations provide the principal focus of this chapter. Specifically, this chapter addresses

1. The definition of revenue in the governmental environment and the revenue recognition criteria used;
2. Classification of revenue accounts;
3. Accounting for revenue sources that are unique to governments, such as taxes and intergovernmental grants; and
4. Other revenue-related accounting topics, including budget revisions, changes in accounting principles, and restatements.

The discussions and illustrations in this chapter focus primarily on *GAAP basis* revenue accounting and reporting. Thus, as in Chapter 4, we assume that the SLG governmental fund budgetary basis is the GAAP basis, except where noted otherwise, and that the governmental fund revenue accounts are maintained on (or near) the GAAP basis during the year. *Non*-GAAP budgetary basis accounting and reporting, including adjustment of non-GAAP revenue account data to the GAAP basis, are discussed and illustrated in Chapter 10.

REVENUE DEFINITION AND RECOGNITION

Governmental fund **revenues** are increases in the net assets of a governmental fund that either

a. result in a corresponding increase in the net assets of the governmental unit as a whole, *or*
b. result from quasi-external interfund transactions.

Revenues may be *operationally defined* in a governmental fund accounting context as *all increases in fund net assets except those arising from interfund reimbursements, interfund operating and residual equity transfers, or long-term debt issues.*

Governments have a wide variety of revenue sources. Some revenues, such as property taxes, are levied in known amounts prior to collection and uncollectible amounts usually can be estimated with reasonable accuracy. Such revenues are recorded on the accrual basis, as are other revenues billed by the government. On the other hand, it often is not practicable to accrue other types of government revenues. For example, sales taxes theoretically accrue to the government as retail merchants sell goods and collect sales taxes on behalf of the government. The government does not know the amount of the sales taxes until merchants file sales tax returns. Thus, sales tax revenues usually cannot be accrued prior to receipt of the sales tax returns, which normally coincides with payment of the taxes due. Hence, sales taxes normally are recorded essentially on the cash basis. Similarly, the amounts of self-assessed income taxes and business licenses are not known prior to receipt of the tax return or license application by the government, and typically are not accrued until then.

The **modified accrual basis of governmental fund revenue recognition** takes into account the diverse government revenue sources and the varying degrees to which government revenues can be recorded on the accrual basis. Under the modified accrual basis, only those revenues that are "susceptible to accrual" are recognized on the accrual basis; others are recognized on the cash basis or are recorded initially as "deferred revenues."

Revenues are considered **"susceptible to accrual"** *if* they are *both* (1) objectively **measurable** and (2) **available** to finance current period expenditures. An item is "available" only if it

a. is *legally usable* to finance current period expenditures *and*
b. is *to be collected* in the current period or soon enough thereafter to be used to pay liabilities of the current period. (This cut-off period for revenue recognition is limited to a 60-day maximum.)

Further, taxes collected before the year for which they are levied or that will not be collected until a later year are recorded initially as **"deferred revenues."** "Unearned" revenues such as restricted grants that are received before qualifying expenditures are made also are recorded as deferred revenues. Thus, *governmental fund revenues are recognized conservatively on a "cash or near cash" approach under the modified accrual basis.*

The GASB notes that *application* of the "susceptibility to accrual" criteria requires (1) *judgment,* (2) consideration of the *materiality* of the item in question, (3) due regard for the *practicality* of accrual, and (4) *consistency* in application.[1] In commenting further on revenue accrual the GASB observes that:

> ... *some revenues are assessed and collected in such a manner that they can appropriately be accrued, whereas others cannot.* Revenues and other increases in governmental fund financial resources (which usually can and should be recorded on the accrual [modified accrual] basis) include property taxes, regularly billed charges for inspection or other routinely provided services, most grants from other governments, interfund transfers, and sales and income taxes where taxpayer liability has been established and collectibility is assured or losses can be reasonably estimated.[2]

---

[1] GASB Codification, sec. 1600.106.
[2] Ibid., sec. 1600.107. (Emphasis added.)

167

Chapter 5
REVENUE
ACCOUNTING—
GOVERNMENTAL
FUNDS

The GASB also states:

> The susceptibility to accrual of the various revenue sources of a governmental unit may differ significantly. Likewise, the susceptibility to accrual of similar revenue sources (for example, property taxes) differs among governmental units. Thus, *each governmental unit should [1] adopt revenue accounting policies that appropriately implement the susceptibility to accrual criteria, [2] apply them consistently, and [3] disclose them in the Summary of Significant Accounting Policies.*[3]

Applying the susceptibility to accrual criteria—particularly the "availability" criterion—often proves difficult in practice. Application of the criteria is discussed further at several points in this chapter and in later chapters dealing with specific governmental fund types.

CLASSIFICATION OF REVENUE ACCOUNTS

A chart of accounts is designed to provide a vehicle for summarizing information in a useful form. Revenues are classified by *source* in the accounts in order to produce information that management may use to (1) prepare and control the budget, (2) control the collection of revenues, (3) prepare financial statements and schedules for reporting to the public, and (4) prepare financial statistics. The revenue accounts provide the basic data for revenue statements used for all these purposes.

General Fund Revenues

The following are the *main revenue source classes* for the General Fund:

- **Taxes** (including property, sales, income, and other taxes; penalties and interest on delinquent taxes)
- **Licenses and Permits**
- **Intergovernmental Revenues** (including grants, shared revenues, and payments by other governments in lieu of taxes)
- **Charges for Services** (excluding revenues of public enterprises)
- **Fines and Forfeits**
- **Miscellaneous Revenues** (including interest earnings, rents and royalties, sales of and compensation for loss of fixed assets, contributions in lieu of taxes from the government's own public enterprises, escheats, and contributions and donations from private sources)

The preceding *classes* are *not account titles.* Rather, they are *broad* revenue source *categories* that are useful for reporting purposes just as Current Assets and Fixed Assets are category groupings on the balance sheet of a private enterprise. For example, though we do so for illustrative purposes, no account would be set up for fines and forfeits. Instead, individual accounts would be provided for each type of revenue falling in that class, including Court Fines, Library Fines, and Forfeits. The total revenues accrued or received from fines and forfeits would be the sum of the balances of these accounts.

---

[3] Ibid., sec. 1600.108. (Emphasis added.)

Revenues of Other Funds

The revenue classes described for the General Fund also are suitable for the other governmental funds of a governmental unit. For example, taxes may be a revenue source of Special Revenue Funds and Debt Service Funds, and interest earnings are likely to be a revenue source of all governmental funds. Clearly, no other fund is likely to have as many different revenue sources as the General Fund. Enterprise and Internal Service Funds use revenue accounts and revenue recognition principles similar to those of business enterprises.

Revenues of a Fund vs. Revenues of the Governmental Unit

A distinction must be made between the revenues of a fund and the revenues of the governmental unit as a whole. As noted earlier, interfund *transfers and reimbursements* are *not* reported as *revenues. However quasi-external transaction receipts or accruals are reported as fund revenues even though they are not revenues of the governmental unit.* To illustrate, charges for services rendered to departments financed out of the General Fund are revenues of the Internal Service Fund but not of the governmental unit as a whole, since these charges must be paid from the General Fund. *Quasi-external transactions are the only instance where fund revenues (and related expenditures or expenses, as appropriate) should be recognized when they are not revenues of the government as a whole.*

In classifying revenues for the purpose of statewide or national financial statistics, only those revenues of the governmental unit as a whole should be included. Ideally, any material amounts arising from quasi-external transactions would be eliminated. Further, some accountants prefer to supplement the fund statements with consolidated or consolidating statements for these funds, the unit as a whole, or its major subdivisions, where interfund revenues are significant in amount.

This chapter is concerned with accounting for the principal revenue sources of the General Fund, Special Revenue Funds, and other governmental funds. Those types of revenues that are peculiar to another fund type are discussed in the chapter on that fund type.

TAXES

As noted earlier, taxes are forced contributions made to a government to meet public needs. Typically, the amount of a tax bears no direct relationship to any benefit received by the taxpayer.

The amount of any tax is computed by applying a rate or rates set by the governmental unit to a defined base, such as value of property, amount of income, or number of units. From the standpoint of administration, taxes may be divided into two groups—those that are **self-assessed** and those that are **levied.** For the levied group the governmental unit establishes the amount of the tax base to which the rate or rates will be applied. The general property tax on real and personal property is the chief representative of this group. Taxes on income, inheritance, severance of natural resources, gasoline, general sales, tobacco, alcoholic beverages, and chain stores are self-assessed. For these taxes, the taxpayer is expected to determine the amount of the tax base, apply the proper rate or rates thereto, and submit the payment with the return that shows the computation.

169

Chapter 5
REVENUE
ACCOUNTING—
GOVERNMENTAL
FUNDS

Self-Assessed Taxes

When the taxpayer assesses his or her own tax, verifying the amount of tax requires (1) determining that the tax **base** has been properly reported by the taxpayer and (2) determining that the proper **rates** have been applied accurately to the tax base to arrive at the total amount of the tax. The first is the most difficult problem, of course. For example, in the case of the income tax it is necessary to ascertain that all income that should have been reported has been disclosed. Furthermore, investigations should *not* be limited to those taxpayers who file returns. The governmental unit must also make certain that all taxpayers who should pay taxes have filed returns.

Self-assessed taxes are usually accounted for on a cash basis because the return and the remittance are ordinarily received at the same time. Further, there may be no objectively measurable basis upon which to set up accruals because the amount of tax is not known before the return is filed.

The GASB notes with regard to taxpayer-assessed taxes that:

> It is **neither necessary nor practical to attempt to accrue taxpayer-assessed** income and gross receipts [including sales] **taxes unless taxpayer liability and collectibility have been established**—as when tax returns have been filed but collection, while assured, is delayed beyond the normal time of receipt. **Such items are best recognized as cash is received.**[4]

Further, the Board states with respect to **sales** taxes that:

> Sales taxes collected by merchants but **not** yet required to be remitted to the taxing authority at the end of the fiscal year should **not** be accrued. However, **taxes collected and held by one government agency for another** at year-end **should** be accrued **if** they are to be **remitted in time** to be used as a resource for payment of obligations incurred during the preceding fiscal year.[5]

Being remitted "in time" to be used to pay liabilities for current operations is not defined by the GASB, but is generally considered to mean collected during the year or within about 60 days after year end.

Finally, the GASB indicates that year-to-year comparability should be considered in determining whether to recognize sales taxes and other self-assessed revenues:

> . . . material revenues otherwise not recorded until received should be accrued if receipt is delayed beyond the normal time of receipt. For example, if material sales tax revenues should have been received prior to the financial statement date but are delayed until after the statement date, the amount should be accrued. Material revenues received prior to the normal time of receipt should be recorded as deferred revenue.[6]

Many cities, counties, and states with **income taxes** have continually improved their ability to reasonably estimate income tax revenues for the year and the related income tax receivables and refund liabilities. This is often an extremely difficult task since estimated income tax payments may have been re-

---

[4] Ibid., sec. 1600.110. (Emphasis added.)
[5] Ibid., sec. S10.103. (Emphasis added.)
[6] Ibid., sec. S10.104.

ceived during the year but income tax returns for the year will not be filed until the next year. The AICPA audit guide notes with respect to income taxes:

> No matter what the fiscal year-end . . . there is generally an estimated payable to, or receivable from, taxpayers as a group. States generally estimate the amounts based on historical experience.[7]

In some jurisdictions income tax returns are filed at a specified time and the tax is paid in installments. In such a case, since the amount of the tax is known, the revenues are accrued as soon as the return is filed.

Some taxes require the attachment of stamps to an article to indicate that the tax has been paid. For example, liquor taxes and tobacco taxes are frequently paid through the purchase of stamps to be affixed to bottles or packages. In such cases the taxes are considered to be revenue as soon as the stamps are sold to the manufacturer, dealer, or other business, even though the articles to which the stamps are affixed may not be sold for an indefinite period following the purchase of the tax stamps.

Property Taxes

Property taxes are ***ad valorem taxes in proportion to the assessed valuation of real or personal property.*** The procedure for administering general property taxes is as follows: (1) The assessed valuation of each piece of real property and of the taxable personal property of each taxpayer is determined by the local tax assessor; (2) a local board of review hears complaints regarding assessments; (3) county and state boards of equalization assign equalized values to taxing districts; (4) the legislative body levies the total amount of taxes which it needs, but not in excess of the amount permitted by law; (5) the tax levy is distributed among taxpayers on the basis of the assessed value of property owned by them; (6) taxpayers are billed; (7) tax collections are credited to taxpayers' accounts; and (8) tax collections are enforced by the imposition of penalties and the sale of property for taxes. Each of these steps in general property tax administration is discussed briefly in the following sections.

Assessment of Property

Valuing property for purposes of taxation is called ***assessment.*** Assessment of property for local taxes usually is performed by an elected or appointed official known as an ***assessor.*** The ***assessed value*** of each piece of real property or of the personal property of every taxpayer is recorded on an ***assessment roll.*** The ***tax roll*** of ***real property*** typically contains columns entitled:

Taxpayer's Name and General Description of Property

Block and Lot Number

Value of Land

Value of Improvements

Total Assessed Valuation

Each such sheet contains the assessed value of several pieces of property or the assessed values of the personal property of several owners. In the case of real property, a separate continuing record for each piece of property is maintained containing the assessed valuation for that piece and its full description.

Not all real and personal property in the jurisdiction of a government will be subject to real or personal property assessment and taxation. ***Properties***

[7] AICPA, *Audits of State and Local Governmental Units*, 1993, para. 8.12.

171

Chapter 5
REVENUE
ACCOUNTING—
GOVERNMENTAL
FUNDS

owned by governments and religious organizations usually are exempt from such taxes and are referred to as *"exempt properties."*

The *total assessed value* of real estate in the governmental unit is the *sum* of the assessed values of the individual pieces of property within its jurisdiction; the total assessed value of personal property is the sum of the assessed values of the personal property of the individual owners residing within the limits of the governmental unit. Thus *several governmental units,* such as a state, county, city, and school district, *may tax each piece of property.* Ordinarily only one of these jurisdictions will have the assessment responsibility, and separate assessment rolls are prepared for each of the governmental units for the property within its jurisdiction.

Review of Assessment

Each property owner is notified of the assessment of his or her property and is permitted to *protest* the assessment to a local *reviewing board.* This board may be composed of officials of the government or of nonofficial residents of the governmental unit. The board hears objections to assessments, weighs the evidence, and changes the assessment if deemed appropriate. Taxpayers may appeal the board action to the courts.

Equalization of Assessments

In most states the assessment of property is made by a local government. The taxes of the state and perhaps even the county are, therefore, levied on the basis of assessments made by a number of different assessors, each of whom may have different ideas as to the valuations that should be assigned to property. The law usually requires that the assessment be the equivalent of "fair market value" in the accountant's terminology, but in practice the actual valuations in a state or even a county will cover a wide range of percentages of market value. Lack of equalization or poor equalization leads to "competitive underassessment" in the several assessing districts and to widespread dissatisfaction with the property tax as a revenue source. Thus, both state and county *equalization boards* may attempt to ensure that assessments are made equitably—that is, at fair market value or at the same percentage of fair market value—among and within the counties.

Levying the Tax

Taxes are *levied* through the passage of a *tax levy act or ordinance,* usually passed at the time the appropriation act or ordinance is passed. The levy is ordinarily applicable to only one year.

Tax levies vary in detail and restrictiveness. Some governments levy taxes in one or two lump sums for *unrestricted "general government" purposes* or perhaps also for one or two *broad specified purposes* (e.g., schools). Other tax levies are very *detailed and restricted.* A statute or even a charter may require that certain taxes are to be levied for *specific identified purposes.* In that event the legislative body must indicate specifically the amount levied for each purpose. *Another effect of detailed tax levies is to require the creation of Special Revenue Funds.* For example, if a special levy is made for parks, a Special Revenue Fund for parks normally must be established to ensure that the taxes collected are used only for parks.[8]

---

[8] Recall that the GASB Codification (sec. 1300.107) states that "use of Special Revenue Funds is not required unless they are legally mandated." Property tax authorization legislation typically specifies that a separate fund be maintained, however, and many accountants feel that Special Revenue Funds are needed to assure sound financial administration of restricted property taxes even if not legally mandated.

Determining the Tax Rate. The tax rate is determined by dividing the amount of taxes levied by the assessed valuation. Thus, if a government has an assessed valuation of $10,000,000 and its total tax levy is $250,000, the tax rate is 2.5 percent of, or 25 mills per dollar of, assessed value ($250,000 ÷ $10,000,000). The total tax rate consists of the tax rate for general purposes and special tax rates, if any, for particular purposes. For example, if we assume that the total levy of $250,000 consisted of $150,000 for general purposes, $10,000 for parks, $50,000 for schools, and $40,000 for debt service, the tax rates would be as follows.

Purpose	*Rate* (mills per dollar of assessed value)
General	15
Parks	1
Schools	5
Debt Service	4
	25

Maximum tax rates are frequently prescribed for governmental units by the constitution, statutes, or charters. The legislative body must recognize such limitations as it plans the total levy. If the amount the legislative body would like to produce from the tax will require a rate higher than the maximum permitted by law, the amount of the levy must be reduced. When a government finds itself thus limited in the amount of taxes it can levy, it would ordinarily review the assessment process in the hope that the total assessed valuation, the tax base, could be increased.

Determining the Amount Due from Each Taxpayer. The amount of tax due from each taxpayer is arrived at by ***multiplying*** the ***assessed value*** of his or her property ***by the tax rate.*** For example, a taxpayer who owns real estate with an assessed value of $8,000 during a year when the city tax rate is 25 mills per dollar of assessed value will owe taxes of $200 ($8,000 × 0.025).

Setting Up Taxes Receivable and Billing Taxpayers

As soon as the amount due from each taxpayer is determined, it is entered on the tax roll.

The Tax Roll. A ***tax roll*** is a record showing the amount of taxes levied against each piece of real property and against each owner of personal property.

The assessment roll previously described may be used for this purpose by adding several columns, or tax rolls may be prepared separately. The tax roll provides a record of each parcel of real or personal property—including its assessed *value, taxes levied against the property, and property tax collections and balances owed with respect to the property.* **The tax roll *also serves as a subsidiary ledger supporting the Taxes Receivable control accounts in the General Ledger.*** If interest and penalties on delinquent taxes are accrued at the end of each year, provision is made for showing the accruals.

Recording Taxes on the Books. Some of the entries to record taxes on the books have already been introduced in Chapter 4. For example, when taxes are levied, the usual entry in each fund is a debit to Taxes Receivable—Current and credits to

173

Chapter 5
REVENUE
ACCOUNTING—
GOVERNMENTAL
FUNDS

Allowance for Uncollectible Current Taxes and to Revenues. (If the tax is levied prior to the year to which it applies, a Deferred Revenues account is credited initially). Later, if the taxes become delinquent, a reclassification entry is made debiting Taxes Receivable—Delinquent and Allowance for Uncollectible Current Taxes and crediting Taxes Receivable—Current and Allowance for Uncollectible Delinquent Taxes.

Separate Taxes Receivable accounts should be set up for each kind of taxes, such as real property taxes, personal property taxes, and income taxes that may have been accrued. Further, all these taxes should be recorded in a way that allows the amount applicable to each year to be readily determined. One way to accomplish this objective is to set up control accounts for each kind of taxes receivable by years.

Because the proportion of the total tax levy made for each purpose may vary from year to year, each year's levy must be identified so that the proper Taxes Receivable accounts may be credited and the cash collected may be allocated to the proper fund(s). For example, suppose that the property tax levy is $100,000 both for this year and for last year but that the levies are divided as follows:

Fund	This Year		Last Year	
	Amount Levied	Percentage of Total	Amount Levied	Percentage of Total
General Fund.	$ 46,700	46.7	$ 40,000	40.0
Parks Fund	13,300	13.3	13,300	13.3
School Fund	26,700	26.7	33,400	33.4
Debt Service Fund.	13,300	13.3	13,300	13.3
	$100,000	100.0	$100,000	100.0

The General Fund portion of the proceeds of this year's tax levy is found by multiplying the amount collected from the levy by 46.7%. Thus, if $90,000 is collected, $42,030 is placed to the credit of the General Fund ($90,000 × 46.7%). On the other hand, the amount of collections from last year's levy that is for General Fund purposes is obtained by multiplying the collections from that levy by 40%. For example, if collections total $10,000, $4,000 ($10,000 × 40%) is for the General Fund. Collections from other years' levies are allocated to the proper funds in the same manner. Clearly, ***tax collections cannot be applied to the proper funds unless the amount collected from each year's levy is known.***

Recording Tax Collections

Assume that the preceding $100,000 property tax levy was for 19Y0 and that the delinquent receivables and related allowance are as follows:

Property Taxes Receivable—Delinquent:

Levy of 19X9	$30,000
19X8	20,000
19X7	10,000
19X6	5,000
19X5 and prior	3,000
	68,000
Less: Allowance for Uncollectible Delinquent Taxes	10,000
	$58,000

As taxes are collected, the entry in the recipient fund is as follows:

Cash	100,000	
Taxes Receivable—Current		80,000
Taxes Receivable—Delinquent		20,000

To record collection of current and delinquent taxes, as follows:

Year of Levy	Amount
19Y0	$ 80,000
19X9	10,000
19X8	5,000
19X7	3,000
19X6	1,000
19X5	500
19X4	500
	$100,000

Collection of a Government's Taxes by Another Unit. Frequently, one governmental unit acts as collecting agent for other units. In that case, each governmental unit certifies its tax levy to the collecting unit, which in turn bills the taxpayers. These taxes are accounted for by the collecting unit in an **Agency Fund,** for which the accounting procedures are discussed in Chapter 11.

    The accounting procedures outlined thus far for governmental units that collect their own taxes also apply to those that do not. In the latter case the collecting unit transmits a report indicating the amount collected for each year's levy of real property taxes and of personal property taxes. The receiving unit, on the basis of this report, distributes the proceeds among the various funds and credits the proper General Ledger accounts. However, a governmental unit that does not collect its own taxes does not prepare a tax roll and probably does not keep a record of the amounts paid or owed by the individual taxpayers. The latter records are kept for it by the collecting governmental unit.

Discounts on Taxes. Some governmental units allow discounts on taxes paid before a certain date. These **discounts** should be considered as **revenue deductions.** An Allowance for Discounts on Taxes account should be provided and the tax revenues recognized should equal only the **net** amount of the tax. For example, if the tax levy was $300,000, including $9,000 expected to be uncollectible and $2,000 of discounts expected to be taken, the **entry to record the levy of the tax and the estimated discounts and uncollectible taxes is:**

Taxes Receivable—Current	300,000	
Allowance for Uncollectible Current Taxes		9,000
Allowance for Discounts on Taxes		2,000
Revenues		289,000
To record levy of taxes, estimated losses, and estimated		
discounts to be taken.		
Revenues Ledger (Revenues):		
Taxes		289,000

    As taxes are collected and discounts are taken, the discounts are charged against the Allowance account. For example, if tax collections amounted

175

Chapter 5
REVENUE
ACCOUNTING—
GOVERNMENTAL
FUNDS

to $150,000 and discounts of $1,500 had been taken, the entry to record the transaction would be:

Cash	150,000	
Allowance for Discounts on Taxes	1,500	
Taxes Receivable—Current		151,500

To record collection of taxes net of discounts.

As the discount period expires, the following entry is made:

Allowance for Discounts on Taxes	500	
Revenues		500

To record increase in revenues by amount of estimated discounts
  which were not taken.

Revenues Ledger (Revenues):

Taxes	500

Had discounts taken **exceeded** the balance of the Allowance for Discounts on Taxes account, the **excess** would be **debited to Revenues.**

Taxes Levied But Not Available. In some governments taxes are **levied** in one year **but** are **not available,** and *hence **not revenue,*** in that year. Revenue recognition is **deferred** when either (1) the taxes were **levied to finance the next year's operations,** and thus are not legally available in the year of levy, or (2) the taxes **will not be collected until well into the next period** and thus are not available to finance current year expenditures.[9] The entry upon **levy** of taxes in either case would be:

Taxes Receivable—Current	100,000	
Allowance for Uncollectible Current Taxes		3,000
Deferred Revenues		97,000

To record levy of taxes not available to finance current period
  expenditures.

At the **beginning** of the **next** period the Deferred Revenues would be reclassified as revenues by the following entry:

Deferred Revenues	97,000	
Revenues		97,000

To record the taxes levied last period becoming available.

Revenues Ledger (Revenues):

Taxes	97,000

Deferred Revenues for property taxes may also need to be established in the **year-end adjusting entry process.** Whenever a government records the property tax levy under the assumption that the revenues are "available"—as in the illustrative example in Chapter 4—the related amounts in the preclosing trial balance (Figure 4-3) should be examined to determine whether significant amounts are indeed "available" at year end. **The amount of the current property tax levy that has been recorded as Revenues during the period but is not ex-**

---

[9] The GASB Codification (sec. P70.103) states that property taxes collected within approximately 60 days after year end would be considered "available" at year end and thus recognized as revenue in the year preceding collection.

pected to be collected within about 60 days after year end should be reclassified as Deferred Revenues as follows:

Revenues	12,000	
Deferred Revenues		12,000

To adjust the accounts for property taxes that are not available
  at year end.

<u>Revenues Ledger (Revenues):</u>

Taxes	<u>12,000</u>	

This adjusting entry is *reversed* at the beginning of the next year.

Governments that recognize property tax revenues on the cash basis *during the year* use a similar deferred revenue accounting technique. They record the property tax levy as deferred revenue, as described previously, then recognize revenue (and reduce deferred revenue) as property taxes are collected. This approach is illustrated later.

Taxes Collected in Advance. Sometimes a taxpayer will pay his or her *subsequent year's* taxes *before the tax has been levied or billed.* Such tax collections are subsequent period revenue, not revenue of the period in which they are collected, and may be recorded initially in a Trust or Agency Fund. *If* they are *recorded in* the General Fund or another *governmental fund,* the entry is:

Cash	2,500	
Taxes Collected in Advance		2,500

To record collection of taxes on next year's roll.

These tax collections represent a *deferred credit to revenues,* and the Taxes Collected in Advance account is therefore reported as *deferred revenues* in the balance sheet.

The *deferred revenues* are recognized as *revenues* of the *next (or subsequent) year.* After the taxes have been officially *levied and* the usual *tax levy entry* has been made recording the Taxes Receivable—Current, the related allowance(s), and Revenues—which *includes* those collected and *deferred previously* —the entry in the General Fund or other governmental fund is:

Taxes Collected in Advance	2,500	
Taxes Receivable—Current		2,500

To record application of taxes collected in advance to reduce
  General Fund taxes receivable.

If the amount of taxes collected in advance exceeds the amount levied, the excess is either refunded or continues as deferred revenues until the next levy is made. If, on the other hand, the amount collected is less than the amount levied, the taxpayer is billed for the difference.

Enforcing the Collection of Taxes

The laws for most jurisdictions prescribe a date after which unpaid taxes become *delinquent* and are *subject to specified penalties and accrual of interest.* Taxes, interest, and penalties in most states become a *lien* against property without any action by the governmental unit. After a specified period of time the governmental unit can *sell* the property to satisfy its lien.[10] Sale proceeds in excess of the lien for taxes, interest, penalties, and the cost of holding the sale are paid to the property owner. If the sale proceeds are less than the amount due, the property owner may

---

[10] In some states the state government pays the delinquent taxes and related amounts to the local governments, obtains their liens on the properties, and disposes of the properties at tax sales.

177

Chapter 5
REVENUE
ACCOUNTING—
GOVERNMENTAL
FUNDS

or may not be legally liable for the difference. Further, the SLG may **"bid in"** (retain) the property at the tax sale rather than sell it.

The property owner usually is given the privilege of **redeeming** the property within a certain period of time. **If** the property was **purchased** by an individual it can be redeemed by payment to the buyer of the purchase price plus interest. **If** it was **bid in** by the governmental unit, the property can be redeemed by payment of the taxes, interest, penalties, and other charges. If the property is not redeemed by the specified date, the acquirer secures title.

Typically, **more than one** governmental unit has liens against property that is being sold for delinquent taxes. If each government were left to enforce its own lien and sell the property for taxes, not only would the cost of sale greatly increase but considerable confusion would result. Accordingly, the **statutes ordinarily provide for transferring delinquent tax rolls to a single governmental unit.** This unit attempts to collect the delinquent taxes and performs all the steps necessary to enforce the lien. In the absence of statutory provisions, each unit receives from the collecting unit its proportionate share of tax collections, net of collection costs.

Recording Interest and Penalties on Taxes.   Some governmental units accrue interest and penalties on delinquent taxes, while others do not record them until they are collected. They should be accrued if material, of course, and added to the tax roll or other subsidiary record. The entry to record the **accrual of interest and penalties** is:

Interest and Penalties Receivable—Delinquent Taxes	15,000	
Allowance for Uncollectible Interest and Penalties		1,000
Revenues		14,000
To record interest and penalties revenues on delinquent taxes		
net of the estimated uncollectible.		

Revenues Ledger (Revenues):

Interest and Penalties	14,000

If the "available" criterion is not met when interest and penalties receivable are accrued, **Deferred Revenues** would be credited (rather than Revenues) and revenue would be recognized when the receivable becomes "available," usually upon collection.

In any event, it is **essential to identify the revenues from interest and penalties with the particular tax levy to which they apply.** The reasons for this distinction are the same as those given for recording taxes receivable by year of levy.

Accounting for Tax Sales.   After the legally specified period has passed without payment of taxes, penalties, and interest, the assets are converted into **tax liens:**

Tax Liens Receivable	28,000	
Taxes Receivable—Delinquent		25,000
Interest and Penalties Receivable—Delinquent Taxes		3,000
To record conversion of delinquent taxes and of interest and		
penalties thereon to tax liens as follows:		

Levy of	Taxes	Interest and Penalties	Total
19X8	$10,000	$1,000	$11,000
19X7	15,000	2,000	17,000
	$25,000	$3,000	$28,000

Subsidiary taxes receivable records (including penalties and interest) for each piece of property are credited at this time, and subsidiary records of the individual tax liens are established.

Court and other costs are ordinarily incurred in the process of converting property into tax liens and in selling the properties. In some jurisdictions the law provides that the **costs of holding a tax sale** are covered by interest and penalties levied against the property. Such costs are charged to expenditures in those jurisdictions. In most cases, however, the costs are recoverable from the taxpayer and should be **added to** the amount of the **tax lien:**

Tax Liens Receivable	1,000	
Cash		1,000

To record court costs and other costs incurred in the conversion of
delinquent taxes and interest and penalties thereon into tax liens.

When the assets are converted into tax liens, appropriate amounts of the related allowance for uncollectible accounts are converted into an Allowance for Uncollectible **Tax Liens.** The amount to be reclassified is determined by comparing the tax liens receivable and the estimated salable value of each property, individually and in total. Only some (perhaps none) of the allowance may need to be reclassified.

Allowance for Uncollectible Delinquent Taxes	2,000	
Allowance for Uncollectible Interest and Penalties	100	
Allowance for Uncollectible Tax Liens		2,100

To reclassify the allowances for estimated uncollectible taxes,
interest, and penalties to the allowance for uncollectible tax liens.

If the proceeds from the sale of the property equals the amount of the tax liens, there is simply a debit to Cash and a credit to Tax Liens Receivable. If the property is sold for **more** than the amount of the liens, the excess is paid to the property owner. On the other hand, if the cash received from the sale of the property is **not sufficient** to cover the tax liens, and if taxes are a lien only against the property, **the difference is charged to Allowance for Uncollectible Tax Liens.**

If the governmental unit **bids in** (retains) properties at the time of the sale, it becomes, as is any other purchaser, subject to the redemption privilege by the property owners. As properties are redeemed, an entry is made debiting Cash and crediting Tax Liens Receivable.

If some of the properties are not redeemed and the governmental unit **decides to use them for its own purposes**—for example, for playgrounds—the Tax Liens Receivable accounts are removed from the funds in which they are carried through the following entry:

Expenditures	4,000	
Allowance for Uncollectible Tax Liens	2,000	
Tax Liens Receivable		6,000

To record the expenditure for tax sale property retained.

Expenditures Ledger (Expenditures):

Capital Outlay	4,000

The debit to **Expenditures** is for the **estimated salable value** of the property, while the debit to Allowance for Uncollectible Tax Liens is the **difference** between the salable value of the property and the liens receivable against it. **If** the property's **salable value** is **more than** the **receivable,** only the amount of the receivable—the government's **"cost"**—is charged to Expenditures. Thus the amount

179

Chapter 5
REVENUE
ACCOUNTING—
GOVERNMENTAL
FUNDS

charged to Expenditures when a government retains "bid in" property is the *lesser* of its salable value and the Tax Liens Receivable.

The "bid in" property retained becomes a general fixed asset and must be recorded in the *General Fixed Assets Account Group.* Such fixed assets are capitalized at the *lower* of cost or market value of the property (in this case, $4,000). The joint cost incurred should be *allocated* between the land and building *in proportion to their relative fair values.*

As noted earlier, several governmental units may have liens on the same piece of property. The accounting procedure for the sale of the property is the same as that for property sold to satisfy the lien of only one governmental unit. The proceeds from the sale of the property are distributed among the various units to satisfy their liens, and any remaining cash is turned over to the property owner. If the proceeds are not sufficient to cover all the liens, each governmental unit receives a proportionate share of the money realized, unless statutes specify another basis of distribution.

Property Tax Statements

Several types of property tax statements and schedules usually are prepared to provide adequate disclosure of the details of property taxes. These statements and schedules may be divided into two classes: (1) those related to the financial statements of the *current period* and (2) those showing data for *other periods* as well as for this period.

Some property tax statements and schedules are prepared primarily for internal use. Others are included in either the financial section or the statistical section of the comprehensive annual financial report (CAFR) of a state or local government (see Chapter 14). The general property tax statements and schedules that are directly related to the financial statements of the current period belong in the *financial section* of the annual report, while those that show data for a number of periods are known as *statistical statements* and appear in the *statistical section.*

LICENSES AND PERMITS

Governments have the right to permit, control, or forbid many activities of individuals or corporations. Governments issue licenses or permits to grant *the privilege of performing acts that would otherwise be illegal.* Licenses and permits revenues may be divided into business and nonbusiness categories. In the *business* category are alcoholic beverages, health, corporations, public utilities, professional and occupational, and amusements licenses, among others. In the *nonbusiness* category may be found building permits and motor vehicle, motor vehicle operator, hunting and fishing, marriage, burial, and animal licenses.

The rates for licenses and permits are established by the passage of an ordinance or statute. In contrast to property taxes, however, new rates need not be established each year. Instead, the legislative body usually adjusts the rates of particular licenses from time to time.

Revenues from most licenses and permits are not recognized until received in cash. This is because the amount is not known until the licenses and permits are issued, and cash is collected upon their issuance.

Proper control over these revenues must ensure not only that the revenues actually collected are properly handled but also that all the revenues that should be collected are collected. In other words, the governmental unit must see that all those who should secure licenses or permits do so. For example, if a license is required to operate a motor vehicle, no vehicle should be operated without one. Of course, the governmental unit must also institute controls to ensure that the revenues actually collected are recorded. This is accomplished in part by using sequentially numbered licenses, permits, and similar documents.

INTERGOVERNMENTAL REVENUES

Intergovernmental revenues consist of grants (grants-in-aid), entitlements, shared revenues, and payments received from other governmental units in lieu of taxes. The GASB Codification (sec. G60.501–.505) *defines* grants, entitlements, and shared revenues as follows:

- **Grants.** A grant is a contribution or gift of cash or other assets from another government to be used or expended for a specified purpose, activity, or facility. *Capital grants* are restricted by the grantor for the acquisition and/or construction of fixed (capital) assets. All other grants are *operating grants.*
- **Entitlements and Shared Revenues.** An *entitlement* is the amount of payment to which a state or local government is entitled as determined by the federal government. . . . pursuant to an allocation formula contained in applicable statutes. A *shared revenue* is a revenue levied by one government but shared on a predetermined basis, often in proportion to the amount collected at the local level, with another government or class of government.[11]

Federal or state grants for buses, subway systems, and wastewater treatment systems are examples of *capital* grants. All other grants, such as for the operation of social welfare programs, are *operating* grants.

The primary distinction between entitlements and shared revenues lies in the difference between the nature of the amounts being allocated by formula. **Entitlements** are portions of a *fixed,* appropriated amount of money—for example, a federal or state "revenue-sharing" appropriation—that are allocated among eligible state or local governments by some formula, such as according to their relative populations. **Shared revenues,** on the other hand, are portions of a federal or state revenue source that *varies* in amount each month, quarter, or year—for example, gasoline, sales, liquor, and tobacco taxes. Shared revenues also are allocated among eligible state or local governments according to some formula, such as by relative number of vehicles registered or by relative sales of the products or services taxed at the federal or state level. This distinction is often confused in practice and in political rhetoric. For example, federal and state "revenue-sharing" programs usually are actually "entitlements," and state tax-sharing programs are often referred to as "entitlements."

Payments in lieu of taxes—a significant intergovernmental revenue source of some local government public school systems—are amounts paid to one government by another to reimburse the payee for revenues lost because the payer government does not pay taxes. The maximum amount usually would be computed by determining the amount that the receiving government would have collected had the property of the paying government been subject to taxation.

Payments in lieu of taxes are particularly significant where the federal government makes payments in lieu of taxes to local governments and school districts near its major military bases. Presumably, the receiving government would record payments in lieu of taxes in the same fund(s) and manner as it records its tax revenues. State-collected, locally shared taxes should be identified in the Revenues Subsidiary Ledger according to the kind of tax being received.

---

[11] Adapted from GASB Codification, sec. G60.501–.505. (Emphasis added.)

181

Chapter 5
REVENUE
ACCOUNTING—
GOVERNMENTAL
FUNDS

Intergovernmental Revenue Account Classifications

A total of twelve possible classifications of intergovernmental revenues may be prepared for a municipality by listing the four kinds of intergovernmental revenue under federal, state, and local unit categories. For example, there would be federal grants, state grants, local grants, federal entitlements, and so on.

As already indicated, grants ordinarily are made for a specified purpose(s). Entitlements and shared revenues may also be restricted as to use, but frequently are not. Accordingly, **restricted** grants, entitlements, and shared revenues—whether from federal, state, or local government sources—should be recorded in the appropriate fund and classified both by source and according to the function for which the grants are to be spent (e.g., general government, public safety, highways and streets, sanitation, and health). On the other hand, **unrestricted** entitlements and shared revenues should be classified into accounts according to the source of the revenues since they may be used for a variety of purposes. Similarly, **payments in lieu of taxes** are classified only by governmental source—federal, state, or local unit—since they ordinarily are not restricted as to use.

Accounting for Intergovernmental Revenues

The section of the GASB Codification on "Grants, Entitlements, and Shared Revenues" emphasizes that

> The purpose of this section is to clarify the application of GAAP to grants, entitlements, and shared revenues received by state and local governments. This section does **not** apply [1] to **interfund transactions,** [2] to **unrestricted** resources received from other governments, nor [3] to resources received from **private contributors** such as individuals, commercial enterprises, or foundations.[12]

This section of this text has the same **intergovernmental restricted resource** focus, and likewise the guidance here should **not** be applied to any other resources.

Fund Identification

The purpose and requirements of each grant, entitlement, or shared revenue must be analyzed to identify the proper fund(s) to be utilized. Existing funds should be used where possible; it is **not** always necessary to establish a separate fund for each grant, entitlement, or shared revenue. Indeed, the GASB Codification provides that:

> Grants, entitlements, or shared revenues received **for purposes normally financed through the general fund may be accounted for within that fund provided that applicable legal requirements can be appropriately satisfied; use of special revenue funds is not required unless they are legally mandated.** Such resources received for the payment of principal and/or interest on general long-term debt should be accounted for in a **debt service fund.** Capital grants or shared revenues restricted for capital acquisitions or construction, other than those associated with Enterprise and Internal Service Funds, should be accounted for in a **capital projects fund.**
>
> Grants, entitlements, or shared revenues received or utilized for **enterprise or internal service fund** operations and/or capital assets should be accounted for in

---

[12] GASB Codification, sec. G60.102. (Emphasis added.)

these fund types. A ***trust fund*** should be used for such resources that establish a continuing trustee relationship. Such resources received by one governmental unit on behalf of a secondary recipient ***("pass through"),*** governmental or other, should be accounted for in an ***agency fund.***[13]

Further, the GASB Codification observes that:

> ***Some*** grants, entitlements, and shared revenues ***may be used in more than one fund at the discretion of the recipient.*** Pending determination of the fund(s) to be financed, such resources should be accounted for in an ***agency fund.*** When the decision is made about the fund(s) to be financed, the asset(s) and revenues should be recognized in the fund(s) financed and removed from the agency fund. Revenues and expenditures or expenses are not recognized in agency funds. Assets being held in agency funds pending a determination of the fund(s) to be financed should be disclosed in the notes to the financial statements.[14]

"Pass-Through" Grants

The distinction between "pass-through" and other types of grants is important. A **"pass-through"** grant is one where:

- The **primary recipient,** such as a state government, receives the grant—say, from the federal government—as an ***agent*** of the grantor.
- The primary recipient cannot spend the resources for its own purposes, but merely ***"passes through"*** the resources to a **secondary recipient**—say, a local government or public school district—which is referred to as the **subrecipient.**
- The **subrecipient** then ***spends*** the grant resources for the specified purposes —perhaps under both federal and state regulations and oversight—*or may "pass through"* some or all of the resources, if permitted, *to its subrecipients, or sub-subrecipients.*

State governments, in particular, are primary recipients of significant pass-through grants for public education and other purposes.

Pass-through grants are not recognized as revenues by the primary recipient. Likewise the primary recipient does not report the payments and accruals of pass-through grants to the secondary recipients (subrecipients) as expenditures. Rather, as noted by the GASB:

> ***Pass-through resources*** are received by a government to transfer to or spend on behalf of another entity in accordance with legal or contractual provisions. The ***receipt or disbursement*** of such resources ***does not affect the operations of the agent government except for the imposed accounting and reporting requirements.*** Pass-through resources ***should be reported*** as ***revenues or contributed capital and as expenditures or expenses, as appropriate,*** by the ***secondary*** recipient.[15]

Revenue Recognition

Regarding governmental fund revenue recognition for grants, entitlements, and shared revenues, the GASB Codification states that:

> [1] Grants, entitlements, or shared revenues recorded in ***governmental funds*** should be recognized as revenue in the accounting period when they become susceptible to accrual, that is, both measurable and available (modified accrual

---

[13] Ibid., sec. G60.105–.106. (Emphasis added.)
[14] Ibid., sec. G60.108. (Emphasis added.)
[15] Ibid. sec. G60.106. (Emphasis added.)

183

Chapter 5
REVENUE
ACCOUNTING—
GOVERNMENTAL
FUNDS

basis). [2] In applying this definition, *legal and contractual requirements should be carefully reviewed* for guidance. [3] *Some such resources,* usually entitlements or shared revenues, are *restricted more in form than in substance.* Only a failure on the part of the recipient to comply with prescribed regulations will cause a forfeiture of the resources. *Such resources* should be *recorded as revenue at the time of receipt or earlier if the susceptible-to-accrual criteria are met.* [4] For *other* such resources, usually grants, *expenditure is the prime factor for determining eligibility,* and *revenue should be recognized when the expenditure is made.* Similarly, *if cost sharing or matching requirements exist, revenue recognition depends upon compliance* with these requirements.[16]

Whereas *unrestricted* grants, entitlements, and shared revenues are recognized immediately as revenues of governmental funds, if "available," *restricted* grants are not recognized as revenue until they are "earned." In the usual case a restricted grant must be expended for the specific purposes to be considered "earned." Thus, such grants are often referred to as **"expenditure driven" grants since deferred grant revenue is recorded initially and the grant revenue is recognized only when qualifying expenditures are incurred.** That is, grant revenue recognition is "driven" by grant-related expenditures being incurred. Further, if a restricted grant has been awarded to a governmental unit but (1) has not been received and (2) has not been earned by the SLG making qualifying expenditures, the grant awarded is not recorded in the accounts or reported in the financial statements, though it may be disclosed in the notes to the financial statements.

Grant Received Before Earned. Where revenues should *not* be recognized at the time the grant, entitlement, or shared revenue is received, the following entry is appropriate:

Cash 100,000
    Deferred Revenues 100,000
To record receipt or accrual of grant, entitlement, or shared
   revenue prior to revenue recognition.

This entry also would be appropriate where an entitlement or shared revenue applicable to the next year is received currently, as well as when a cash grant has been received but is not yet earned.

When the conditions of the grant, entitlement, or shared revenue restrictions have been met, the deferred revenue is recognized as revenue. For example, assuming that any local matching requirements have been met and the remaining requirement is that the resources be expended for a specified purpose(s), the following entries are made *upon incurring a qualifying expenditure:*

(1) Expenditures 40,000
      Vouchers Payable 40,000
    To record expenditures qualifying under restricted grant
      program.
    Expenditures Ledger (Expenditures):
    Grant (Specify type) 40,000

(2) Deferred Revenues 40,000
      Revenues 40,000
    To record recognition of revenues concurrent with
      expenditures meeting grant restrictions.
    Revenues Ledger (Revenues):
    Intergovernmental 40,000

---

[16] Ibid. sec. G60.109. (Emphasis added.)

A more detailed subsidiary ledger account title—such as Federal Grants or even by grant name and number—would be used in practice. Broad account titles such as Intergovernmental are used only for illustrative purposes.

Grant Earned Before Received. A state or local government *may make qualifying expenditures* under a grant *before* the grant *cash is received.* Although this may occur in many grant programs, some grants—known as **"reimbursement grants"**—specify that the government must first incur qualifying expenditures, then file for reimbursement under the grant program.

A government that makes an expenditure that qualifies for reimbursement under an approved grant should record both (1) the expenditure and (2) the corresponding grant revenue accrual:

(1)	Expenditures	75,000	
	Vouchers Payable		75,000
	To record expenditure that qualifies for reimbursement under approved grant.		
	Expenditures Ledger (Expenditures):		
	Grant X	75,000	
(2)	Due from Grantor	75,000	
	Revenues		75,000
	To record grant revenues earned and receivable under reimbursement grant.		
	Revenues Ledger (Revenues):		
	Intergovernmental—Grant X		75,000

This entry assumes both that the grant is a *"pure"* reimbursement grant—that is, only the actual expenditures are reimbursed under the grant—*and* that collection of the receivable is expected soon enough for the revenue to be considered *"available."*

- *If* the reimbursement grant *pays more or less than the expenditures* incurred, that amount is, of course, recorded as the grant receivable and revenue.
- *If* the grant receivable is *not expected to be collected soon enough* for the related revenue to be considered "available," *Deferred Revenues* (not Revenues) is credited initially, and revenue is recognized when the grant receivable becomes "available."

The qualifying expenditure entry and the entry to accrue the related grant revenue are not always made simultaneously in practice. For example, the total qualifying expenditures for a month or quarter may be filed for reimbursement after being incurred. Thus, controls should be established to ensure that all qualifying expenditures are properly filed for reimbursement and are indeed reimbursed. Further, qualifying expenditure entries should be reviewed at year end to ensure that revenues have been properly accrued or are accrued in the year-end adjusting entries.

Revenue recognition for grants, entitlements, and shared revenues restricted for proprietary fund purposes is discussed in Chapters 12 and 13.

Compliance Accounting

Grant, entitlement, and shared revenue provisions often require that *special accounting procedures* be followed and certain *special reports* that are *not in conformity with generally accepted accounting principles* be made to grantors. Also, they may specify that reports be prepared for a *fiscal year different* from

185

Chapter 5
REVENUE
ACCOUNTING—
GOVERNMENTAL
FUNDS

that of the recipient government *or* for a *period other than a fiscal year,* for example, the duration of the grant. In this regard, the GASB Codification states that:

> *In some instances,* it may be *necessary or desirable* to record grant, entitlement, or shared revenue *transactions in* an *agency fund* in order *to provide an audit trail and/or to facilitate the preparation of special purpose financial statements.* The transactions are recorded as they occur in the agency fund utilizing *"memoranda"* revenue and expenditure accounts coded in accordance with specialized needs. The *same transactions* are *subsequently recorded* as revenues or contributed capital and expenditures or expenses, as appropriate, *in conformity with GAAP in the fund(s) financed.* The agency fund memoranda accounts are *not* reported as operating accounts. *The "dual" recording approach* may be *especially helpful where* a *grant* is received *for multiple purposes and/or* where the *grant accounting period* is *different from that of the fund(s) financed,* i.e., multiyear or different operating year awards. This "dual" recording approach is suggested only when a beneficial purpose is served. When an *agency fund* is utilized for this purpose, *fund assets and liabilities should be combined with those of the fund(s) financed* for *financial statement presentation.*[17]

Accounting for grants, entitlements, and shared revenues initially through an Agency Fund in this manner is discussed further and illustrated in Chapter 11.

CHARGES FOR SERVICES

Revenues from Charges for Services consist of *charges made by various general government departments for goods or services rendered by them to the public, other departments of the government, or other governments.* The revenues of Enterprise Funds are also derived from the sale of goods or services, but because of their proprietary nature and importance they are treated separately. Similarly, special assessments for capital improvements can in a sense be considered revenues of the department that constructs the improvements; but, because of their special nature, they are treated differently. However, special assessments for current services are considered departmental charges for services revenues.

It is important to distinguish between revenues derived from departmental earnings and those from licenses and permits. *Only those charges that result directly from the activity of the department and that are made for the purpose of recovering part of the costs of the department are considered charges for current services.* Some of these charges may involve the issuance of permits, but the revenues should not be classed as coming from permits but rather as charges for services.

Distinguishing Quasi-External Transactions and Reimbursements

It is also *important to distinguish* charges for services rendered by one department to other departments, which constitute *quasi-external transactions, from reimbursements.*

- *Quasi-external* transactions result in (1) **revenues** being recognized in the fund financing the provider department and (2) expenditures or expenses being recognized in the fund financing the department receiving the goods or services.

---

[17] Ibid., sec. G60.108. (Emphasis added.)

- **Reimbursements** result in expenditures or expenses being recognized in the fund from which the department receiving the goods or services is financed but a **reduction (recovery) of expenditures or expenses** being recorded in the fund through which the provider department is financed.

A quasi-external transaction should be deemed to occur only when interdepartmental services (or goods) of the type routinely rendered to external parties are provided in the equivalent of an interdepartmental "arm's-length" transaction and charged for at established rates. Such instances are uncommon except between departments financed from governmental funds and those financed through Internal Service and Enterprise Funds. Therefore, most interdepartmental charges for goods and services should be accounted for as reimbursements.

Accounting for Charges for Services

Some charges for services are collected when the services are rendered and are recorded as revenues at that time. If not collected at the time services are rendered or immediately thereafter, revenues should be recorded as the persons or governments served are billed or, if not yet billed at year end, in adjusting entries. *The following entries illustrate some transactions that result in revenues being recorded as soon as they are earned:*

Due from Other Governmental Units	25,000	
Revenues		25,000

To record earnings resulting from charges to other governmental units for patients in mental hospitals and for board of prisoners.

Revenues Ledger (Revenues):

Hospital Fees	10,000
Prison Fees	15,000
	25,000

Accounts Receivable	20,000	
Revenues		20,000

To record street lighting, street sprinkling, and garbage collection charges made to property owners.

Revenues Ledger (Revenues):

Street Light Charges	5,000
Street Sanitation Charges	8,000
Refuse Collection Fees	7,000
	20,000

The following entry, on the other hand, *illustrates some of the transactions in which revenues typically are recorded only as cash is collected, that is, are not billed or accrued:*

Cash	38,200	
Revenues		38,200

To record receipt of cash representing charges for services.

Revenues Ledger (Revenues):

Sale of Maps and Publications	4,200
Building Inspection Fees	9,000
Plumbing Inspection Fees	5,000
Swimming Pool Inspection Fees	2,000
Golf Fees	7,000
Fees for Recording Legal Instruments	6,000
Animal Control and Shelter Fees	5,000
	38,200

187

Chapter 5
REVENUE
ACCOUNTING—
GOVERNMENTAL
FUNDS

Finally, some government services may be provided in one period, billed to service recipients, and collected in a later period. Thus, **expenditures may be recognized before the related revenues are recognized.** A common example is street maintenance or improvement programs financed by special assessments against benefitted properties or citizens. Some assessments are essentially taxes; others are charges for services. **The following entries illustrate transactions in which governments render services and bill service recipients in one period but collect the charges (say, special assessments) and recognize revenues during one or more future periods.** (Subsidiary ledger entries are omitted.)

Mid-19X1: Services rendered; service recipients billed—charges payable in five annual installments, with 6% interest, beginning in mid-19X2:

Expenditures	100,000	
Vouchers Payable		100,000

To record expenditures incurred.

Assessments Receivable—Deferred	100,000	
Deferred Revenues		100,000

To record levy of special assessments.

Mid-19X2: One-fifth of the deferred receivables became due and reminder notices were mailed.

Assessments Receivable—Current	20,000	
Assessments Receivable—Deferred		20,000

To record currently maturing special assessment receivables.

Deferred Revenue	20,000	
Revenues—Special Assessments		20,000

To recognize special assessment revenues.

Interest Receivable on Special Assessments (6%)	6,000	
Revenues—Interest on Special Assessments		6,000

To record current interest billed on special assessments.

The special assessments would mature and be collected during 19X2–19X6, with interest on the unpaid balances. This example is highly simplified, of course; more complex special assessment situations are addressed in Chapters 7 and 8.

As implied by the foregoing discussions and illustrations, the chart of accounts for charges for services should be based on the activity for which the charge is made. These activities can be classified according to the function of the government in which the activity is carried on. For example, under the *general government function* we would expect to find *accounts* for the following:

- Court costs, fees, and charges
- Recording of legal instruments
- Zoning and subdivision fees
- Plan checking fees
- Sale of maps and publications
- Building inspection fees

FINES AND FORFEITS

Revenues from fines and forfeits are not usually an important source of a governmental unit's income, often are not susceptible to accrual prior to collection, and usually are accounted for on a cash basis. *Fines are penalties imposed for the commission of statutory offenses or for violation of lawful administrative rules.* Penalties for the delinquent payment of taxes are not included in this category of revenue since they are considered part of tax revenues. Similarly, penalties for late payment of utility bills are considered utility operating revenues. *Fines and other penalties included in this section are primarily those imposed by the courts.*

Where courts accept cash bonds or fine payments, adequate cash receipt and related controls are essential. In any event, all activities of the court should be documented so that there is an appropriate record of all cases brought before the court, the cash or property bond or bail related to each case, and the disposition of each case, including any bond or bail forfeitures ordered and fines levied.

Similar types of controls are essential when any police department, sheriff's office, or other law enforcement agency accepts cash for any reason. Effective cash and related controls, such as over traffic and parking tickets, are essential. Even small improprieties within courts and law enforcement agencies damage their credibility, public image, and effectiveness.

The money from forfeits of cash bonds and bail is often first accounted for in a Trust or Agency Fund (Chapter 11). Unless the law provides otherwise, forfeited bail money is paid from the Trust or Agency Fund to the General Fund, where it is recorded:

Cash	5,000	
Revenues		5,000

To record receipt of money representing forfeited bail.

Revenues Ledger (Revenues):

Fines and Forfeits	<u>5,000</u>

MISCELLANEOUS REVENUES

Included in the **miscellaneous** category are such sources of revenues as **interest earnings, rents and royalties, sales and compensation for loss of fixed assets, certain nontransfer payments from the government's public enterprises, escheats, and contributions and donations from private sources.** All of the revenues discussed in this chapter may be found in General and Special Revenue Funds; some of them may also appear in other funds. In addition, other funds may have sources of revenues that have not been described here but will be treated in subsequent chapters. Most of the revenues in the miscellaneous category are self-explanatory, but a discussion of some of them may prove useful.

Interest Earnings

Short-term investment of cash available in excess of current needs is authorized by legislative bodies throughout the country. Indeed, many state and local governments have highly sophisticated cash management systems. Thus, in addition to interest on long-term investments of Debt Service and Trust Funds, for example, interest earned on short-term investments of idle cash is a substantial general revenue source in many municipalities. **Interest should be accrued as it is earned by the governmental unit.**

Government finance officers, accountants, and auditors should ensure that any state or local regulations relating to short-term investments are observed, as well as those of the federal government with respect to **"arbitrage"** in the Internal Revenue Code (IRC) and related regulations. Briefly, the IRC provides that a state or local government **investing tax-exempt debt issue proceeds** (interest exempt from federal income taxes) at rates higher than that being paid on the debt may have to **rebate** the **excess interest** earned to the U.S. Treasury. SLGs that do not comply may be assessed a 50% penalty. Or they may have the tax-exempt status of their debt issues revoked. While the immediate and direct impact of such revocation would adversely affect the investors in those debt securities rather than the government, its future debt issues would probably be difficult to sell and carry much higher interest rates than formerly. Further, GASB Statement No. 3 re-

189

Chapter 5
REVENUE
ACCOUNTING—
GOVERNMENTAL
FUNDS

quires numerous ***disclosures*** about each government's investment activities in the notes to its financial statements.[18]

Sales and Compensation for Loss of Fixed Assets

Although fixed assets financed from General and Special Revenue Funds are not carried as part of the assets of such funds, the ***net proceeds from the sale and compensation for loss of these fixed assets are reported as either revenues or other financing sources of these funds.*** Net general fixed asset sales proceeds and loss compensation traditionally have been reported as revenues, which parallels the reporting of general fixed asset acquisitions as expenditures. It has also become acceptable recently to report such sale and loss compensation proceeds as nonrevenue other financing sources since they may be viewed as resulting from the conversion of general fixed assets to financial resources rather than as revenue transactions.

As a general rule, such proceeds should be recorded in the fund that financed the acquisition of the asset that has been sold or destroyed. Since identifying the source from which assets were financed may be difficult—and since in many instances the funds that financed the purchase of assets are abolished before the assets are disposed of—the net proceeds from the sale and compensation for loss of general fixed assets usually flow into the General Fund, and thus are reported as revenues or other financing sources of that fund. As we shall see, proceeds from the sale and compensation for loss of assets carried in Internal Service Funds, Enterprise Funds, and Trust Funds are ordinarily accounted for in those funds rather than in the General Fund.

Nontransfer Payments from Public Enterprises

Payments made to the government by a publicly owned enterprise ***in lieu of property or other taxes*** from which they are legally exempt may be ***reported either as miscellaneous revenues or as tax revenues.*** Other contributions made by its Enterprise Funds should be classified as operating transfers or residual equity transfers, as appropriate in the circumstances.

Escheats

The laws of most states specify that the net assets of deceased persons who died intestate (without having a valid will) and with no known relatives revert to the state. Similarly, most state laws specify that amounts in inactive checking accounts (and perhaps other accounts) in banks revert to the state after a period of time, often seven years. Such laws result in what are referred to as ***escheats*** to the state. The cash or equivalent values of financial resources (e.g., cash, stocks, and bonds) received by escheat are recognized as revenues by the recipient state; fixed assets received by escheat are recorded in the General Fixed Assets Account Group at fair market value at time of receipt by the state.

Private Contributions

Occasionally, a government will receive contributions or donations from private sources. Where these are ***unrestricted*** as to use, which is rare, they would be recognized as General Fund revenues. ***Restricted*** donations (except those in trust) usually would be recognized as Special Revenue or Capital Projects Fund revenue, as appropriate to the operating or capital purpose; those in trust would be accounted for initially in a Trust Fund as discussed in Chapter 11.

---

[18] Ibid., sec. C20.

REVENUE BUDGET REVISIONS

Budgets usually are prepared several months before the beginning of the year to which they apply based on the best information available at that time. While preliminary estimates often are revised prior to formal adoption of the budget, revisions may also be appropriate after the budget has been adopted. For example, the government may find it is not going to receive a sizable grant it had expected to receive during the budget year, or it may be granted a significantly different amount than planned. Such an event may well signal a need to revise appropriations also, as discussed in Chapter 6.

The entry to record formal approval of a revenue estimate *increase* would parallel the original budgetary entry for estimated revenues:

Estimated Revenues	75,000	
Unreserved Fund Balance		75,000
To record an increase in estimated revenues.		
Revenues Ledger (Estimated Revenues):		
Intergovernmental	75,000	

The entry to record a formally authorized *decrease* in estimated revenues would be *the reverse:*

Unreserved Fund Balance	50,000	
Estimated Revenues		50,000
To record a decrease in estimated revenues.		
Revenues Ledger (Estimated Revenues):		
Intergovernmental		50,000

In the event two or more revenue estimate revisions net to zero—for example, the estimate of general property tax revenues is reduced $30,000 but those for income taxes and for sales taxes are increased $20,000 and $10,000, respectively—the following entry is required:

Estimated Revenues	30,000	
Estimated Revenues		30,000
To record offsetting revenue estimate revisions.		
Revenues Ledger (Estimated Revenues):		
Income Taxes	20,000	
Sales Taxes	10,000	
Property Taxes		30,000
	30,000	30,000

The only effect of this entry, of course, is to change the estimated revenue amounts in the several Revenues Subsidiary Ledger accounts affected. The offsetting Estimated Revenues entries in the General Ledger are needed since the subsidiary ledger is normally accessed, in both manual and automated systems, through the General Ledger.

CHANGES IN ACCOUNTING PRINCIPLES

Restatement of the beginning fund balance of a governmental fund to correct a prior year error was illustrated briefly in Chapter 4. Restatements may also be necessary to report the *cumulative effect* of *changes in accounting principles.*

191

Chapter 5
REVENUE
ACCOUNTING—
GOVERNMENTAL
FUNDS

Three types of events that might cause a government to change its governmental fund revenue recognition principles are:

- Management decides to **change from one acceptable revenue recognition principle to another** acceptable alternative revenue recognition policy. (This is *not* common in governmental fund accounting.)
- Changed circumstances require a **change in the method of applying the acceptable principle in use.** For example, a revenue source not previously deemed objectively measurable and/or available is now considered to be both objectively measurable and available at year end. (This type of change *is* common in governmental fund accounting.)
- The GASB or another recognized **standards-setting body issues a new revenue recognition standard** that requires a different revenue accounting policy than that presently used.

In any event, (1) *changes* in accounting principles are made *effective* at the *beginning* of the year in which the change occurs, the "current year"; (2) the *cumulative effect of the change*—computed by *comparing* the revenues recognized and effects on fund balance of the governmental fund under the *"old"* accounting policy *with* the *effects "as if"* the *new* accounting policy *had been in effect*—are *reported as a restatement of the beginning fund balance of the earliest year presented;* (3) *revenues* are reported under the *new* accounting policy for each year presented; and (4) the change in accounting principle is *disclosed and explained in the notes* to the current year financial statements.

Changed GASB Standards

Most changes in governmental fund accounting principles occur because the GASB—or another recognized standards-setting body discussed in Chapter 2—issues a new revenue recognition standard or revises an existing standard. *If the new or revised revenue recognition standard requires a different revenue recognition policy* than that presently being used in its governmental fund accounting, a state or local government *must change its accounting policy to comply with the new or revised standard.*

GASB Statements and Interpretations include an *"Effective Date and Transition" section that specifies when and how the new standards are to be implemented,* as do FASB and AICPA pronouncements. Further, such standards typically encourage (but do not require) "early application," that is, implementation prior to the effective date specified.

"Prospective" Application

Occasionally the transition instructions are that a new accounting policy is to be applied *"prospectively"*—that is, *applied only to transactions occurring on or after the effective date* or, if implemented earlier, the implementation date. For example, a revised standard might require that a type of transaction previously recognized as "revenues" be reported as "other financing sources" in the future; or a new standard might specify that transactions previously reported as giving rise to gains and losses by some governments (e.g., advance refundings of GLTD) be reported as "other financing sources (uses)" in the future, with no gain or loss recognized. *Since changed standards that are implemented "prospectively" apply only to transactions and events occurring on or after the implementation date—that is, they do not require retroactive application as if the new standard had been in effect earlier—*they do not require restatement of governmental fund assets, liabilities, and fund balance.* Thus, new standards that are applied "prospectively" do ***not*** give rise to "cumulative effect of changes in accounting principles" restatements.

"Retroactive" Application

Most new and revised GASB and other standards are required to be implemented ***"retroactively"***—that is, ***as if the new standard had been in effect earlier.*** Thus, they require that (1) assets, liabilities, and fund balance at the **beginning** of the year in which the new standard is implemented be **restated** as if the new standard had been applied earlier, and (2) the **cumulative effect** of applying the changed accounting principle retroactively be reported as a **restatement** of the **beginning** fund balance of that year. *The logic and approach involved in implementing a new accounting principle are identical to those for correcting errors that require retroactive restatement.*

CONCLUDING COMMENTS

Proper revenue administration, including revenue accounting and reporting, has never been more important to state and local governments. During periods of rapid economic growth, some governments become lax on revenue administration, assuming that growth in revenues would compensate for any administrative shortcoming. Well-managed governments, however, place equal emphasis on excellent revenue administration and expenditure administration.

Several important revenue sources were discussed in this chapter, and additional types of revenue accounting entries were illustrated. Current rules for revenue recognition require that revenue(s) be both measurable and available before being recognized. Applying these criteria in practice requires judgment, consistency in application, and disclosure of the major judgments made in the notes to the financial statements. Too, intergovernmental grant revenues are subject to special revenue recognition criteria. Further, it is important to distinguish revenues from reimbursements, bond issue proceeds, operating transfers in, and residual equity transfers in.

Finally, Revenues Subsidiary Ledger accounting, revenue budgetary revision entries, and entries to effect changes in revenue accounting principles were discussed and illustrated. These procedures and the concepts and procedures discussed above are essential in practice and will be applied throughout subsequent chapters.

QUESTIONS

5-1 What is the meaning of the term "available" as used in governmental fund revenue recognition?

5-2 A revenue item must be "objectively measurable" as well as "available" to be accrued as governmental fund revenue. (a) What is meant by the term "objectively measurable" in this context? (b) Might revenue items be "available" but not "objectively measurable" prior to collection? Explain.

5-3 The controller of a school district had recorded the entire property tax levy, $20,000,000, as revenues when levied during the first month of the year. At year end the auditor states that $3,000,000 must be reclassified as deferred revenues since that amount of the property tax levy will not be collected until more than 60 days into the next year or later. The controller objects, noting that the property tax receivables are as "available" as cash since the school district regularly uses them as the basis for borrowing on tax anticipation notes at local banks. Further, the penalties and interest charged on delinquent taxes exceed the interest charges on the tax anticipation notes. With whom do you agree? Why?

193

Chapter 5
REVENUE
ACCOUNTING—
GOVERNMENTAL
FUNDS

5-4 The term "deferred revenues" seems out of place in governmental fund accounting. It would seem that a government either has or does not have expendable financial resources as a result of a property tax, grant, or other revenue transaction. Further, "deferred working capital" is not reported in business accounting. Explain the use of the term "deferred revenues" in governmental fund accounting.

5-5 (a) Should estimated uncollectible amounts of taxes be accounted for as direct deductions from revenues or as expenditures? Why? (b) Should discounts on taxes be accounted for as direct deductions from revenues or as expenditures? Why?

5-6 (a) What are "expenditure driven" intergovernmental grants? (b) When and how are revenues from such grants recognized?

5-7 Why are pass-through grants not reported as revenues or expenditures of the primary grantee recipient?

5-8 The taxes of City A are collected by County C, while City B collects its own taxes. In what respects will the tax accounting procedures for the two cities differ?

5-9 For which of the following would you set up accounts in the Revenues Subsidiary Ledger?

Case 1: Taxes	Case 2: Intergovernmental Revenue
General Property Taxes	State-Shared Revenues
Real Property	Property Taxes
Personal Property	Individual Income Taxes
Tangible Personal	Corporate Income Taxes
Intangible Personal	

5-10 The controller of the City of F, who is independent of the chief executive, purposely underestimates revenues and publishes revenue statements that show actual revenues only. (a) How can one discover the controller's practice? (b) The controller, when discovered in the practice, points with pride to the city's solvency and states that his underestimates have kept the city from overspending. Comment.

5-11 What purposes do revenue statements serve in the administration of the General Fund?

5-12 A recently elected city council member of the City of Lynne has returned from a two-day course on governmental accounting that she attended to assist her in understanding the city financial statements and budgeting process. She is perplexed by a point the instructor emphasized during the course, however, and asks the city finance officer about it. "Why did the instructor keep harping about the need to distinguish between fund revenues and the revenues of the governmental unit? It seems to me that if the governmental unit as a whole has a net increase in resources, one or more of the funds has to recognize net increases totaling the same amount. So, what's the big problem?" Respond.

5-13 A county decided to keep land it "bid in" at its property tax sale to use for parks and recreation purposes. The redemption period has passed and the county has a valid deed to the land. Taxes, interest, penalties, and sheriff's sale costs applicable to the land total $15,000, and the land could have been sold for $12,000. The Tax Liens Receivable account in the General Fund has been charged to the Allowance for Uncollectible Tax Liens Receivable account and the land has been capitalized (recorded) at $15,000 in the General Fixed Assets Account Group. (a) Do you agree with the recording of this transaction? (b) Would your answer differ if the land could be sold for $18,000?

5-14 During the course of your audit of a city, you noted an $800,000 payment to the General Fund from an Enterprise Fund. The payment was recorded in both funds as a payment in lieu of property taxes, as similar payments had been in past years. Your inquiries at the local tax appraisal and assessment offices indicate that, if taxed, the Enterprise Fund property taxes would be $450,000 annually. What should you do?

5-15 Some state laws prohibit revisions of a government's annual operating budget, perhaps because it is an official, legally enacted document. (a) What is wrong with such a law? (b) What might you do in view of such a law if you were the chief finance officer of a county in one of these states?

5-16 What is "arbitrage"? Why is an awareness of arbitrage important to a government finance officer?

PROBLEMS

P 5-1 (Multiple Choice) Indicate the best answer to each question.

1. Which of the following is not to be reported as governmental fund revenue?
   a. Taxes
   b. Fines and forfeitures
   c. Special assessments
   d. Proceeds from the sale of general fixed assets
   e. Payments in lieu of taxes
   f. All of the above are properly reported as governmental fund revenues

2. Generally, sales tax revenues should be recognized by a local government in the period
   a. In which the local government receives the cash.
   b. That the underlying sale occurs, whether or not the local government receives the cash in that period.
   c. In which the state—which collects all sales taxes in the state—receives the cash from the collecting merchants.
   d. In which the state—which collects all sales taxes in the state—receives the cash from the collecting merchants if the local government collects the taxes from the state in that period or soon enough in the next period to be used as a resource for payment of liabilities incurred in the first period.

3. On June 1, 19X4 a school district levies the property taxes for its fiscal year that will end on June 30, 19X5. The total amount of the levy is $1,000,000 and it is expected that 1% will prove uncollectible. Of the levy, $250,000 is collected in June 19X4 and another $500,000 is collected in July and August 19X4. What amount of property tax revenue associated with the June 1, 19X4 levy should be reported as revenue in the fiscal year ending June 30, 19X4?
   a. $0   c. $760,000
   b. $750,000   d. $990,000

4. A city levied $2,000,000 of property taxes for its current fiscal year. The city collected $1,700,000 cash on its taxes receivable during the year and granted $72,000 in discounts to taxpayers who paid within the legally established discount period. It is expected that the city will collect another $88,000 on these taxes receivable during the first two months of the next fiscal year. One percent of the tax levy is expected to be uncollectible. What amount of property tax revenues should the city report for the current fiscal year?
   a. $1,788,000   c. $1,980,000
   b. $1,860,000   d. $2,000,000

5. What would the answer to 4 be if the city also collected $100,000 of prior year taxes during the first two months of the current fiscal year and another $53,000 of prior year taxes during the remainder of the current year?
   a. $1,788,000   c. $1,941,000
   b. $1,860,000   d. $1,980,000
   e. None of the above. The correct answer is $ _____.

6. A county received $3,000,000 from the state. Under an entitlement program, $1,500,000 was received and was not restricted as to use. The remainder was received under a grant agreement which requires the funds to be used for specific health and welfare programs. The county accounts for the resources from both of these programs in a Special Revenue Fund. Expenditures of that fund that qualified under the grant agreement totaled $900,000 in the year that the grant and entitlement were received. What amount of revenues should the county recognize with respect to the entitlement and the grant?
   a. $0   d. $1,800,000
   b. $900,000   e. $2,400,000
   c. $1,500,000

195

Chapter 5
REVENUE
ACCOUNTING—
GOVERNMENTAL
FUNDS

7. A Special Revenue Fund expenditure of $40,000 was initially paid for and recorded in the General Fund. The General Fund is now being reimbursed. The General Fund should report

   a. Revenues of $40,000

   b. Other financing sources of $40,000

   c. A $40,000 reduction in expenditures

   d. Other changes in fund balance of $40,000

   e. Residual equity transfers in of $40,000

8. A state acquired $80,000 of equipment through the enforcement of escheat laws. The General Fund statement of revenues, expenditures, and changes in fund balance

   a. Should report revenues from escheat of $80,000

   b. Another financing source of $80,000

   c. Both capital outlay expenditures and revenues from escheat of $80,000

   d. Is not affected if the state plans to retain the equipment for its use since no financial resources were involved.

9. A city has formalized tax liens of $50,000 against properties on which there are delinquent taxes receivable. The estimated salable value of the property is $39,000. The remaining balances in Property Taxes Receivable—Delinquent and the related allowance are $113,000 and $28,000, respectively. What amount should be reclassified from Allowance for Uncollectible Delinquent Taxes to Allowance for Uncollectible Tax Liens?

   a. $0

   b. $11,000

   c. $28,000

   d. $8,589

10. If the city in 9 decides to keep the property for its own use, what amount of expenditures should be recognized?

   a. $0

   b. $39,000

   c. $50,000

   d. None of the above

P 5-2 (GL & SL Entries; SL Trial Balance) The City of Ladner had the following transactions, among others, in 19X7:

1. The Council estimated that revenues of $210,000 would be generated for the General Fund in 19X7. The sources and amounts of expected revenues are as follows:

Property taxes	$150,000
Parking meters	5,000
Business licenses	30,000
Amusement licenses	10,000
Charges for services	8,000
Other revenues	7,000
	$210,000

2. Property taxes of $152,000 were levied by the Council; $2,000 of these taxes are expected to be uncollectible.

3. The Council adopted a budget revision increasing the estimate of amusement licenses revenues by $2,000 and decreasing the estimate for business licenses revenues by $2,000.

4. The following collections were made by the city:

Property taxes	$140,000
Parking meters	5,500
Business licenses	28,000
Amusement licenses	9,500
Charges for services (not previously accrued)	9,000
Other revenues	10,000
	$202,000

5. The resources of a Capital Projects Fund being discontinued were transferred to the General Fund, $4,800.

6. Enterprise Fund cash of $5,000 was paid to the General Fund to subsidize its operations.

Required   (a) Prepare general journal entries to record the transactions in the General Ledger and Revenues Subsidiary Ledger accounts.

(b) Prepare a trial balance of the Revenues Ledger after posting the general journal entries prepared in item 1. Show agreement with the control accounts.

(c) Prepare the general journal entry(ies) to close the revenue accounts in the General and Revenues Ledgers.

P 5-3   (GL & SL Entries; Statement) The following are the estimated revenues for a Special Revenue Fund of the City of Marcelle at January 1, 19X0:

Taxes	$175,000
Interest and Penalties	2,000
Fines and Fees	700
Permits	300
Animal Licenses	900
Rents	500
Other Licenses	3,500
Interest	1,000
	$183,900

The city records its transactions on a cash basis during the year and adjusts to the modified accrual basis at year end. At the end of January, the following SRF collections had been made.

Taxes	$90,000
Interest and Penalties	1,000
Fines and Fees	50
Permits	140
Animal Licenses	800
Rents	45
Other Licenses	2,000
	$94,035

An unanticipated grant-in-aid of $5,000 was received from the state on February 1. SRF collections for the remaining 11 months were as follows:

Taxes	$70,000
Interest and Penalties	800
Fines and Fees	400
Permits	30
Animal Licenses	70
Rents	455
Other Licenses	300
Interest	900
	$72,955

Accrued SRF revenues at year end were as follows:

Taxes	$20,000
Interest and Penalties	300
Rents	10
Interest	50
	$20,360

Required   (a) Prepare the general and subsidiary ledger entries necessary to record the SRF estimated revenues, revenue collections, and revenue accruals.

(b) Post to SRF General Ledger worksheet (or T-accounts) and to subsidiary revenue accounts.

197

Chapter 5
REVENUE
ACCOUNTING—
GOVERNMENTAL
FUNDS

(c) Prepare SRF closing entries for both the General and Revenues Subsidiary Ledgers.

(d) Post to the SRF General Ledger worksheet (or T-accounts) and to the subsidiary revenue accounts.

(e) Prepare a SRF statement of estimated revenues compared with actual revenues for 19X0.

P 5-4 (GL & SL Entries; Trial Balance) The City of Corky's Corner had the following transactions, among others, in 19X3:

1. The city council estimated that revenues of $212,000 would be generated for the General Fund in 19X3, as follows:

Property tax	120,000
City sales tax	40,000
Parking meters	8,000
Business licenses	20,000
Amusement licenses	10,000
Fines and forfeitures	12,000
Interest earnings	2,000
	$212,000

2. Property taxes of $124,000 were levied by the council; $2,500 of these taxes are expected to be uncollectible and discounts of $1,500 are expected to be taken.

3. The following General Fund collections were made by the city:

Property taxes—current.	$105,000
City sales tax	41,000
Parking meters	7,900
Business licenses	29,000
Amusement licenses	7,000
Fines and forfeitures	12,200
Interest earnings	1,100
Proceeds of five-year note.	25,000
Annual transfer from Special Revenue Fund	12,000
	$240,200

4. Discounts of $1,400 were taken on property taxes before the discount period lapsed. Of the remaining balance of 19X3 taxes, $12,000 is expected to be collected by mid-19X4; the remainder is expected to be collected in 19X5 or later, or not collected.

5. A 30-day $3,000 note dated September 30, 19X3, was issued to provide cash needed temporarily in the General Fund.

Required (a) Prepare general journal entries to record the 19X3 transactions in the General Ledger and in the Revenues Ledger accounts.

(b) Prepare a trial balance of the Revenues Ledger after posting the entries in (a). Prove its agreement with the control accounts.

(c) Prepare general journal entries to close the revenue accounts in the General Ledger and in the Revenues Ledger at the end of 19X3.

P 5-5 (Revenue Recognition) In auditing the City of Pippa Passes General Fund a staff member asks whether the following items should be reported as calendar year 19X4 revenues:

1. Property Taxes—which are levied in December and due the following April 30
   a. Levied in 19X3 and collected in April 19X4, $800,000
   b. Levied in 19X4 and collected in May 19X5, $850,000
   c. Levied in 19X2 and collected in January 19X4, $8,000
   d. Levied in 19X3 and collected in January 19X5, $137,000
   e. Collected in 19X4 on taxes levied for 19X5, $22,000

f. Levied in 19X3, not expected to be collected until late 19X5 or 19X6, $12,000

2. Proceeds of 6%, ten-year general obligation bond issued December 28, 19X4, $540,000

3. Income Taxes

   a. 19X3 returns filed during 19X4 and taxes collected in mid-19X4, $150,000

   b. 19X4 returns filed in 19X4 and taxes collected in 19X4, $18,000

   c. 19X4 returns filed in 19X4 and taxes not collected until mid-19X5, $4,000

4. Payment from the Capital Projects Fund of net assets after completion of the project, $3,000

5. Sales Taxes

   a. Returns filed and taxes collected in 19X4, $42,000

   b. Returns filed in 19X3 and taxes collected in June 19X4, $7,400

   c. Returns filed in 19X4 and taxes collected in the first week of 19X5, $6,200

6. Proceeds of 10 percent note payable, dated November 1, 19X4, and due March 1, 19X5, $15,000

7. Grant awarded in 19X4—received in full in mid-19X4 (Portion not used for designated purposes by 19X7 must be refunded.)

   a. Total amount of award, $250,000

   b. Qualifying expenditures made in 19X4, $172,000

8. Repayment in 19X4 of an advance made to the Internal Service Fund in 19X0, $72,300

9. 19X4 payment from Enterprise Fund in lieu of taxes, $2,500

10. 19X4 payment from a Special Revenue Fund to finance street improvements, $12,000

11. Interest and Penalties

    a. Accruing and collected during 19X4, $2,200

    b. Accruing, but not recorded in the accounts, during 19X0-X3 and collected in mid-19X4, $7,800

    c. Accruing during 19X4 and expected to be collected in early 19X5, $3,400

    d. Accruing during 19X4 and expected to be collected in 19X6 and later, $1,200

Required (a) What is your recommendation for each of the items above? (Indicate how each item not reported as 19X4 revenue should be reported.) Explain your recommendation using this format:

Item	Recommendation(s)	Reason(s)

(b) What total revenue amount should Pippa Passes report for 19X4?

P 5-6 (Property Tax Allocation) (a) The 19X7, 19X6, and 19X5 tax rates for the City of Coker are:

	Rate per $100 of Assessed Value		
	19X7	19X6	19X5
General Fund	$1.00	$1.10	$1.20
Library Fund	.09	.09	.09
Municipal Bonds—Redemptions.	.20	.18	.16
	$1.29	$1.37	$1.45

The total assessed value for 19X7 was $88,400,000.

Required Compute the amount of taxes levied for each fund for 19X7.

199

Chapter 5
REVENUE
ACCOUNTING—
GOVERNMENTAL
FUNDS

(b) Collections were made in 19X7 as follows:

19X7 levy	$1,000,000
19X6 levy	100,000
19X5 levy	50,000
	$1,150,000

Compute the amount of collections applicable to each fund for each year.

P 5-7　(Property Tax Entries) Prepare the general journal entries to record the following transactions in the general ledger accounts of a General or Special Revenue Fund of a city:

1. The city levied current year property taxes of $1,000,000, of which 5% is estimated to be uncollectible. Also, 70% of the taxes collected are normally collected within the 2% discount period; and all collectible taxes are expected to be collected during the year.

2. Current property taxes billed at $600,000 (gross) were collected within the recently expired discount period.

3. Assume current property taxes billed at $700,000 (instead of $600,000 in item 2) were collected before the discount period expired.

4. After item 3, $100,000 of current taxes (not collected in item 3) were collected after the discount period and the balance of current property taxes became delinquent. Interest and penalties of $5,000—one-quarter of which is estimated to be uncollectible—were assessed on delinquent taxes.

5. $110,000 of delinquent taxes and $1,400 of previously accrued interest and penalties were collected and $30,000 was collected on taxes not to be levied or due until the next fiscal year.

6. A taxpayer is protesting a delinquent property tax billing of $2,000, on which $50 of interest and penalties were assessed in item 4. While the city expects to collect the taxes, interest, and penalties, the protest process will probably delay the collection until late in the following year.

P 5-8　(Tax Liens & Tax Sales) On February 4, 19X6, selected accounts for the City of Robinson General Fund had the following balances:

	Debit	Credit
Taxes Receivable—Delinquent.	$83,000	
Allowance for Uncollectible Delinquent Taxes		$26,500
Interest and Penalties Receivable	4,000	
Allowance for Uncollectible Interest and Penalties		1,500

Required　Prepare general journal entries to record the following transactions in the General Ledger of the City of Robinson General Fund:

(1) Robinson formalized tax liens against properties with delinquent taxes of $9,000 and related interest and penalties of $1,000. The estimated salable value of the properties was $11,500.

(2) Robinson sold the properties at a tax sale for $11,000. Costs of selling the property totaled $400.

(3) How would your answers to items 1 and 2 differ if the estimated fair value of the properties was $9,000 and the property sold for $9,400?

(4) How would your answers to items 1 and 2 differ if the estimated fair value of the property was $9,000 and the City of Robinson decided to use it for a playground development?

P 5-9 (GL & SL Entries) The following Special Revenue Fund transactions and events occurred in Annette County during 19X1. They are not related unless indicated otherwise.

1. The annual budget adopted included these estimated revenues:

Property taxes	$ 500,000
Payment in lieu of taxes	200,000
Federal grants	150,000
State grants	50,000
Interest	10,000
Other	90,000
	$1,000,000

2. Property taxes of $520,000 were levied for 19X1. It was estimated that 3% discounts for early payment would total $8,000, and that $12,000 of the taxes would never be collected; but the balance is expected to be available to finance 19X1 expenditures.

3. Property taxes billed at $280,000 in transaction 2 were collected within the 3% discount period.

4. Cash was received (drawn down) on a restricted federal grant for which no expenditures had been made, $50,000.

5. A state grant of $60,000 was awarded, but no related expenditures have been made; nor has any grant cash been received.

6. Qualifying expenditures incurred were vouchered: (a) $45,000 for the federal grant program (transaction 4) and (b) $30,000 for the state grant program. The federal grant program reimburses 80% of qualifying costs, while the state grant pays cost plus a 20% of cost overhead allowance.

7. An annual payment in lieu of property taxes from the water, sewer, and electricity utility fund was received, $300,000. The property taxes that would be paid if these properties were taxable would be $225,000.

8. The revenue estimates in the original budget adopted (transaction 1) were revised. The estimate for federal grants was reduced by $5,000, and that for interest earnings was increased by $2,000.

9. It was discovered that the 19X1 beginning Accounts Receivable balance was overstated by $15,000, and that $4,000 of 19X1 revenues had improperly been credited to the Federal Grants revenue account rather than to the State Grants revenue account.

10. At the end of 19X1, the following information was learned in the adjusting entry process:

    a. Some $30,000 of collectible 19X1 property tax receivables will not be collected until mid-19X2.

    b. Additional qualifying expenditures of $10,000 on the state grant program (transactions 5 and 6) have been incurred and recorded, but no related revenues have been recognized.

    c. Unrecorded interest earnings accrued at year end were $1,000.

Required Prepare the general journal entries to record these 19X1 transactions and events in the General Ledger, Revenues Subsidiary Ledger, and Expenditures Subsidiary Ledger of the Special Revenue Fund of Annette County.

P 5-10 (Error Correction, Change in Principle, and Adjusting Entries) The following transactions and events affected a Special Revenue Fund of Stem Independent School District during 19X4.

1. The chief accountant discovered that (a) the $20,000 proceeds of a sale of used educational equipment in 19X3 had been recorded as 19X4 Revenues when received in early 19X4, and (b) $150,000 of property taxes receivable were not "available" at the end of 19X3 but were reported as Revenues in 19X3.

2. Because of a change in the timing of the payments of the state minimum education program assistance grants to school districts, the related revenue recognition policy was

201

Chapter 5
REVENUE
ACCOUNTING—
GOVERNMENTAL
FUNDS

changed. Substantial amounts of the state payments for the prior fiscal year previously were accrued as deferred revenue at year end under the old policy, but most will now be considered "available" revenue. The comparative Deferred State Assistance account balances at the end of the current year and prior year under the old and new policies were determined to be:

Deferred State Assistance	Old Policy	New Policy
End of 19X4.	400,000	100,000
End of 19X3.	300,000	75,000

3. The auditor discovered the following errors:

   a. Special instruction fees of $8,000 paid for the hearing-impaired education program, properly charged to the 19X4 Education—Hearing-Impaired account in the General Fund, were charged to that account in this Special Revenue Fund.

   b. Some $130,000 of federal grant revenues were earned by incurring qualifying expenditures during 19X3, but no grant cash had been received and no revenues were recorded in 19X3. Further, the federal grantor agency has not been billed for this payment.

   c. An operating transfer from the General Fund during 19X4, $85,000, was credited to the Revenues—Other account in this Special Revenue Fund.

   d. Interest revenue earned and received during 19X4, $15,000, was improperly recorded as "other" revenues, whereas a separate Revenues—Interest account is maintained.

   e. A 19X4 payment in lieu of taxes by the federal government was erroneously credited to the Education—General and Administrative expenditures account, $50,000.

4. The following adjusting entries were determined to be necessary at the end of 19X4:

   a. State special education grants received during 19X4 and recorded as 19X4 revenues, $800,000, were only 75% earned by incurring qualifying expenditures during 19X4.

   b. The Stem Independent School District was notified that the state had collected $300,000 of sales taxes for its benefit and would remit them early in 19X5.

Required Prepare the journal entries to record these error corrections, changes in accounting principle, and adjustments in the general ledger and subsidiary ledger accounts of the Special Revenue Fund of Stem Independent School District.

EXPENDITURE ACCOUNTING— GOVERNMENTAL FUNDS

The annual operating budget prepared by the executive branch contains the activity and expenditure plans the chief executive wants to carry out during a fiscal year. The legislative branch reviews the plans, and by providing appropriations it enters into a *contract* with the executive branch for putting into effect those plans —or as much of the plans as it endorses. The executive branch is then charged with the responsibility of carrying out the contract in a legal and efficient manner.

Since the primary measurement focus of governmental funds is on financial position and changes in financial position, activities financed through such funds are usually planned, authorized, controlled, and evaluated in terms of expenditures. Therefore, *expenditures* is the *primary "outflow" measurement in governmental fund accounting.* Expenditures is a different measurement concept than expenses in that *expenditures* is a measure of fund liabilities incurred (or fund financial resources used) during a period for operations, capital outlay, and debt service. *Expenses* is a measure of costs expired or consumed during a period.

This chapter focuses on *expenditure accounting* for *governmental funds.* Specifically, it addresses

1. the definition of expenditures in the governmental fund accounting environment and the expenditure recognition criteria used
2. expenditure accounting controls and procedures,
3. classification of expenditure accounts, and
4. several important expenditure accounting topics—including claims and judgments, compensated absences, unfunded and underfunded pension contributions, appropriations revisions, and changes in expenditure accounting principles.

Three appendices to this chapter discuss and illustrate multiple classifications of expenditure accounts, accounting for annual appropriations under differing encumbrance-lapsing provisions, and accounting for multiyear or continuing appropriations.

203

Chapter 6
EXPENDITURE
ACCOUNTING—
GOVERNMENTAL
FUNDS

The discussions and illustrations in this chapter, like those in Chapters 4 and 5, assume that there are no significant differences between the SLG's budgetary basis and the GAAP basis and, except where noted otherwise, that the accounts are maintained on (or near) the GAAP basis during the year. Non-GAAP basis budgetary accounting and reporting, adjustment of non-GAAP basis accounting data to the GAAP basis, and related topics are discussed and illustrated in Chapter 10.

EXPENDITURE DEFINITION AND RECOGNITION

Expenditures may be *defined* in a governmental fund accounting context as **all decreases in fund net assets**—for current operations, capital outlay, or debt service—*except* those arising from operating and residual equity *transfers* to other funds. Only quasi-external transactions result in the recognition of fund expenditures that are not expenditures of the government as a whole.

The GASB Codification states that:

> The **measurement focus** of governmental fund accounting is upon **expenditures**—decreases in net financial resources—rather than expenses.[1]

The Codification observes that *most* expenditures and transfers out are objectively measurable and should be recorded when the related fund liability is incurred. Specifically, it provides that:

> Expenditures should be recognized in the accounting period in which the *fund liability* is *incurred,* if measurable, *except* for *unmatured* interest [and principal] on general long-term debt, which should be recognized *when due.*[2]

The reasons why principal and interest expenditures on general long-term debt usually are *not* accrued at year end, and when they should be accrued, are explained as follows:

> The *major exception* to the general rule of *expenditure accrual* relates to *unmatured principal and interest* on *general obligation long-term debt.* . . . Financial resources usually are appropriated in other funds for transfer to a debt service fund in the period in which maturing debt principal and interest must be paid. Such amounts thus are *not current liabilities* of the debt service fund as their settlement *will not require expenditure of existing fund assets.*[3]

Thus, both GLTD principal and related interest expenditures usually are recorded when they are *due* to be paid rather than being accrued at year end. But the Codification also states that:

> On the other hand, *if* debt service fund *resources have been provided* during the current year for payment of principal and interest *due early in the following year,* the expenditure and related liability *may* be recognized in the debt service fund and the debt principal amount removed from the GLTDAG.[4]

---

[1] GASB Codification, sec. 1600.117. (Emphasis added.)
[2] Ibid., sec. 1100.108. (Emphasis added.)
[3] Ibid., sec. 1600.121. (Emphasis added.)
[4] Ibid. (Emphasis added.)

Further, the Codification provides two *other expenditure recognition alternatives:*

1. *Inventory* items (for example, *materials and supplies*) may be considered expenditures *either* when purchased (*purchases method*) or when used (*consumption method*), but significant amounts of inventory should be reported in the balance sheet.
2. Expenditures for *insurance and similar services* extending over more than one accounting period [*prepayments*] *need not be allocated* between or among accounting periods, but may be accounted for as expenditures of the period of acquisition.[5]

Capital Outlay Expenditures

Accounting for **capital outlay expenditures** typically financed from the General Fund and Special Revenue Funds—such as for equipment, machinery, and vehicles—was discussed and illustrated in Chapter 4. One additional type of capital outlay transaction that may be accounted for in the General Fund and Special Revenue Funds—the acquisition of fixed assets by capital lease—is discussed and illustrated in this chapter. Most major general government capital outlay expenditures usually are accounted for through Capital Projects Funds, however, though many are at least partially financed by transfers from the General or Special Revenue Funds. Accordingly, accounting for major capital expenditures is discussed and illustrated further in Chapter 7, "Capital Projects Funds."

Debt Service Expenditures

The main reason for the usual "when due" recognition of **GLTD principal and interest expenditures** is that most governments *budget* on a *"when due" basis.* Thus, the *appropriations* for GLTD principal and interest expenditures *equal* the *payments* to be made during the year, irrespective of any accruals at year end. Permitting governments to account and report for GAAP purposes on the basis on which the budget is prepared avoids a significant GAAP-budgetary difference that would have to be explained and reconciled in almost every governmental fund financial statement. There also are other practical and theoretical reasons for this "when due" approach.

Most GLTD debt service is accounted for through Debt Service Funds, though (1) capital lease debt service may be accounted for in the General Fund and in Special Revenue Funds, and (2) financial resources may be transferred from the General Fund and Special Revenue Funds to finance debt service payments accounted for in Debt Service Funds. Accordingly, accounting for capital lease debt service is discussed and illustrated in this chapter; and both "when due" recognition of GLTD principal and interest expenditures and the alternative "before due" recognition for payments "due early in the following year" are discussed and illustrated further in Chapter 8, "Debt Service Funds."

Intergovernmental Expenditures

State governments, in particular, often incur **intergovernmental expenditures** under state revenue-sharing, grant, and other financial aid programs to counties, cities, school districts, and other local governments. State gasoline taxes may be "shared" with cities and counties, for example, and program grants and other aid may be provided to school districts within the state. The *"intergovernmental"* ex-

---

[5] Ibid., sec. 1600.122. (Emphasis added.)

205

Chapter 6
EXPENDITURE
ACCOUNTING—
GOVERNMENTAL
FUNDS

penditure classification signals that these state-level expenditures were not for goods and services at that level, but were payments to local governments for local-level expenditure.

Current Operating Expenditures

All governmental fund expenditures *other than* those *for capital outlay, GLTD debt service, or intergovernmental* purposes are referred to as *"current operating"* expenditures or simply *"operating"* expenditures.

Payroll and related personnel costs are the largest current operating expenditures of most state and local governments. Indeed, *payroll and related costs often compose 65–75% of the General and Special Revenue Fund expenditures of cities, counties, and other local governments and 75–85% of public school system expenditures of these fund types.* Accordingly, accounting procedures for personal services expenditures are discussed in this chapter, as are those for inventories and prepayments.

Inventories and Prepayments

The GASB *permits* inventories and prepayments to be charged as expenditures immediately because—from a "cash or convertible to cash" perspective—such items are not financial resources available for financing future expenditures. In essence, this alternative permits those governments that wish to do so to follow a "quick assets" concept of working capital in accounting for fund balance and changes in fund financial position. Also, many governments make *appropriations* in terms of the *inventory to be acquired or insurance to be purchased* during a fiscal year. Permitting them to report such items on the budgetary basis in the governmental fund Statement of Revenues, Expenditures, and Changes in Fund Balance avoids a potential conflict between budgetary accounting procedures and generally accepted accounting principles that would have to be explained and reconciled in the notes to the financial statements. Governmental fund inventory accounting procedures are discussed and illustrated further later in this chapter.

EXPENDITURE ACCOUNTING CONTROLS

The accounting system is a powerful tool for control of both the legality and efficiency of expenditures. Though its obvious role is financial, it may also be used to record and report quantitative data of all kinds. Indeed, the statistical data that must be estimated and accumulated to plan and control virtually all the operations of a government are best used in conjunction with financial data, and frequently the two kinds of data can be accumulated simultaneously. The accounting system also plays important managerial roles with respect to the following problems and controls:

- Misapplication of assets
- Illegal expenditures
  —Overspending of appropriations
  —Spending for illegal purposes
- Use of improper methods and procedures
- Unwise or inappropriate expenditures
- Allocation and allotment of appropriations

In general the expenditure control principles are those of internal control, and an exhaustive discussion of that topic is not presented here.[6]

EXPENDITURE ACCOUNTING PROCEDURES

Expenditures are classified and coded during the preaudit step of the expenditure control process. *Preaudit* consists of approving transactions before they occur, as in the case of purchase order encumbrances, or before they are recorded, as in the case of expenditures. The chief accounting officer is usually responsible for this function, although large departments may have accountants who perform some or all of the preaudit functions. The preaudit of expenditures is directed to the control of methods and procedures involved in the expenditure process as well as to the prevention of illegal expenditures.

Most governmental units use some form of the **voucher system,** which requires that all disbursements be authorized by an approved voucher. The voucher itself constitutes an outline of the steps that must be performed in making sure that appropriate procedures have been followed in the process of requisitioning, purchasing, receiving, and approving invoices for payment.

Vouchers usually provide a space by each step in the approval and preaudit process where the persons responsible for each step sign or initial to indicate that the step has been completed. These *"signature blocks"* also are an important part of the postaudit "trail" of transactions that is evaluated both in the study of internal controls and as transactions are tested in the postaudit process.

All governmental fund expenditures—whether current operating, capital outlay, debt service, or intergovernmental—*should be properly controlled through the voucher and preaudit processes and included in the scope of the postaudit.* Since most accounting procedures for capital outlay and debt service expenditures are discussed in the Capital Projects Funds and Debt Service Funds chapters, the discussions in this chapter focus primarily on accounting for *current operating expenditures.*

Personal Services

The steps in accounting for personal services are (1) ensuring that the person is a bona fide employee, (2) determining rates of pay, (3) ascertaining the amounts earned by employees, (4) recording payments made to employees, and (5) charging the resultant expenditures to the proper accounts.

The *personal services expenditures* charged against the departmental appropriations *properly include employee fringe benefit costs*—such as employer payroll taxes, insurance costs, pension and other retirement benefit costs, and the costs of compensated absences such as vacation and sick leave time—as well as employee salaries and wages. However, many governments make separate appropriations for such fringe benefit costs, rather than departmental appropriations, and thus charge the expenditures against such separate appropriations rather than as departmental expenditures. Although such expenditures are preferably appropriated and recorded as department or activity costs, the use of sepa-

---

[6] See Auditing Standards Board, American Institute of Certified Public Accountants, *Codification of Statements on Auditing Standards,* sec. 319, and related interpretations.

207

Chapter 6
EXPENDITURE
ACCOUNTING—
GOVERNMENTAL
FUNDS

rate fringe benefit appropriations and expenditure accounts is an accepted alternative in practice.

Pension Cost Expenditure Recognition

Most state and local governments contribute to a pension or retirement plan for the benefit of their employees. Some participate in state-wide or other group plans, but others manage their own plans. *Transactions between a government and its self-managed pension plans are considered quasi-external transactions.* Therefore, properly determined pension contributions are recognized as expenditures, not transfers, in the employer governmental funds (and as revenues in the Pension Trust Fund). A few smaller governments have no pension plans or have informal arrangements where certain employees receive retirement benefits that are charged as expenditures on a "pay-as-you-go" cash basis. But most governments have or participate in either **"defined contribution"** or **"defined benefit"** pension plans.

Defined Contribution Plans

The government employer's *obligation* under a **defined contribution** pension plan *is limited to making appropriate contributions* to the plan. Retiree benefits are determined by the total contributions to the defined contribution plan on the retiree's behalf and by the plan's investment performance over time. Benefits are *not* guaranteed by the employer government. Governments with defined contribution plans **should** *charge the appropriate* **contribution amount—including accruals at year end—to expenditures** in the year it was earned by the employees. Most state and local governments comply with this expenditure recognition requirement. Once the appropriate contribution is paid, these governments have no further liability under the defined contribution pension plan.

Defined Benefit Plans

Most state and local government pension and retirement plans are defined benefit plans. Under a **defined benefit** plan the government *guarantees* the employee-retiree a *determinable pension benefit,* which is usually based on a *formula* such as:

1. number of years service ×
2. average compensation during the highest 3–5 years ×
3. a percentage, such as 1 1/2–2% =
4. annual pension or retirement benefit.

The annual benefit is divided by 12 to determine the monthly benefit.

Defined benefit pension plan contributions must of necessity be based on *actuarial estimates* of such matters as the number of years an employee will serve; levels of inflation and pay rates over time; employee turnover; retiree life spans and mortality rates; and plan funding, investment returns, and administrative costs. Further, plan provisions may be changed in the future, or other events may occur that necessitate major revisions of actuarial estimates of the government employer's ultimate liabilities under the defined benefit pension plan. Thus, the amount that should properly be recognized as governmental fund expenditures and liabilities (current and noncurrent) each year under defined benefit pension plans is difficult to estimate—and has been a contentious issue for several years.

The *preferred* accounting approach, in the view of the authors, is that in NCGA Statement 6—which is included in the GASB Codification as one of the several alternatives—which states that:

> . . . employers shall *report* as an *expenditure/expense* the *employer contribution amount developed by an acceptable actuarial cost method regardless of whether* such amount has actually been *contributed.*[7]

However, NCGA Statement 6 also specifies that:

> *To the extent* that such amount has not been or *will not be funded with expendable available financial resources,* such *unfunded amount* shall be *reported in the General Long-Term Debt Account Group* (governmental funds) or as a fund liability (proprietary and nonexpendable trust funds.)[8]

This results in only part of the actuarially determined pension cost being recognized as governmental fund expenditures currently, with the balance being reported as a long-term liability in the GLTD accounts.

Accounting for pension plan contributions—including the notion of "expendable available financial resources" and dividing the pension cost and liability recognition between the governmental funds and the GLTD Account Group—is discussed and illustrated later in the Adjusting Entries section of this chapter. Pension Trust Fund accounting and reporting are discussed and illustrated in Chapter 11.

Materials and Supplies

The accounting procedures for materials and supplies may be divided into two parts: (1) accounting for **purchases** and (2) accounting for the **use of** materials and supplies.

Accounting for Purchases

The details of purchasing procedures vary according to whether

1. the materials and supplies are purchased directly by individual departments or through a central purchasing agency, and
2. the materials and supplies are purchased for a central storeroom or directly for departments.

Nearly all city, county, and state governments, as well as the federal government, use varying degrees of central purchasing. Throughout this chapter purchases are assumed to be made through a central agency. If a central storeroom is not used, all materials and supplies are delivered directly to the departments; and, even if a storeroom is used, many deliveries will be made directly to departments.

The purchasing procedure and the related accounting procedures consist of the following steps:

1. preparing purchase requisitions and placing them with the purchasing agent,
2. securing prices or bids,
3. placing orders,
4. receiving the materials and supplies,

[7] GASB Codification, sec. P20.110. (Emphasis added.)
[8] Ibid. (Emphasis added.)

209

Chapter 6
EXPENDITURE
ACCOUNTING—
GOVERNMENTAL
FUNDS

5. receiving the invoice and approving the liability, and
6. paying the liability.

Accounting for Materials and Supplies Used

As in all governmental activities, the law may to some degree determine the practices a government uses to provide and account for materials and supplies used by its departments, but the law and policy may allow substantial latitude. Two legal assumptions are dealt with in the following paragraphs:

1. the Expenditures account is to be charged with the amount of materials and supplies *consumed* (**consumption basis**) and
2. the Expenditures account is to be charged with the amount of materials and supplies *purchased* (**purchases basis**).

Both are recognized as *acceptable alternatives* in the GASB Codification, and a state or local *government typically selects the alternative that corresponds with the basis of the inventory appropriations in its annual operating budget in order to avoid a budget-GAAP basis difference.*

Consumption Basis

When stores accounting is on the *consumption* basis, the inventory-related *appropriations* are provided on the basis of *estimated usage* and the Expenditures accunt is charged with *actual usage.* The inventory may be kept on either the periodic or the perpetual basis.

Periodic Method. When the **periodic** inventory method is used with the **consumption** basis, typical entries (encumbrances and subsidiary ledger entries omitted) are as follows:

When Purchased:

Expenditures	850,000	
Vouchers Payable		850,000

To record inventory purchases during the year.

When Issued:
No entry

End of Year:

Inventory of Supplies	72,500	
Expenditures		72,500

To record the **increase** in inventory during the fiscal period, **or** to record the inventory at the **end of the first year** of the fund's existence, and reduce expenditures accordingly.

These entries *may* be accompanied by an entry to adjust the *reserve* account—even though the supplies **are** available to finance subsequent period expenditures since (1) having the inventory obviates the need to buy the items later, and (2) inventory costs are not charged to Expenditures until the items are used—because inventory is **not** an expendable financial resource. The entry to adjust the Reserve for Inventory of Supplies to "fully reserve" fund balance for the inventory on hand—as is usually assumed in Uniform CPA Examination Unofficial Solutions—would be:

Unreserved Fund Balance	72,500	
Reserve for Inventory of Supplies		72,500

To adjust the reserve to equal the valuation of the supplies on hand.

The debits and credits in the last two entries are reversed if the inventory has de-creased.

Other accountants would **not** routinely "fully reserve" fund balance for inventory under the **consumption** basis. Rather, they believe that under the consumption basis inventory is in substance as available to finance future expenditures as is cash—since inventory on hand is an asset that is not charged to Expenditures until issued and obviates future cash disbursements. Thus, they do **not** reserve fund balance unless some of the inventory is **not** available. For example, if a minimum "base stock" of $15,000 of inventory must be maintained at all times, they would reserve $15,000 of fund balance since that amount of the inventory is not "available" for issuance to finance expenditures or avoid future cash disbursements.

Practice varies with regard to reserving fund balance under the consumption method. Indeed, fully reserving, not reserving, and partially reserving inventory all are common in practice. The authors believe that the "partial reserving" approach is most in keeping with the theory underlying the **consumption basis** of inventory accounting.

Perpetual Method. When a **perpetual** inventory system is used with the **consumption** basis, typical entries to be made are as follows (encumbrances and subsidiary ledger entries again omitted):

When Purchased:

Inventory of Supplies	850,000	
Vouchers Payable		850,000

To record the purchases of supplies.

When Issued:

Expenditures	774,000	
Inventory of Supplies		774,000

To charge Expenditures for the amount of stores issued.

End of Year:

Expenditures	3,500	
Inventory of Supplies		3,500

To record inventory **shortage,** per physical inventory. (If there is an overage, the accounts debited and credited in this entry are reversed.)

If Inventory "Fully Reserved":

Unreserved Fund Balance	72,500	
Reserve for Inventory of Supplies		72,500

To adjust the reserve for the increase in inventory during the period. (If there has been a decrease in inventory during the period, the entry is reversed.)

Note that the preceding entry affecting the Reserve for Inventory of Supplies is based on the assumption that the Reserve for Inventory of Supplies is to be maintained at an amount equal to the inventory. Again, while this "fully reserving" is common in practice, theoretically only the normal minimum (base stock) amount of inventory should be reserved—because under the **consumption** method of inventory accounting inventory is not charged to Expenditures until consumed and hence may be viewed as a financial resource available to finance future expenditures.

The primary **advantage** of the **perpetual** method is that the government knows **both** (1) the inventory that **should** have been on hand at year end and (2) by comparison with what actually **is** on hand, the amount of the inventory **overage or shortage** at year end. Under the **periodic** method, the government knows **only** what **is** on hand at year end and **cannot distinguish what was used from what**

211

Chapter 6
EXPENDITURE
ACCOUNTING—
COVERNMENTAL
FUNDS

was stolen, damaged, or improperly accounted for. Thus, as in business accounting, under the **periodic** inventory system what is termed "cost of goods sold" is in fact "cost of goods sold, stolen, or otherwise mysteriously disappeared or not accounted for properly."

Ideally, then, all governments (and other organizations) would use the *perpetual* inventory method. But, whereas perpetual inventory systems have the benefit of providing better accounting control and information, they also add accounting system implementation and operating costs. Thus, accounting method decisions, like other decisions, must be evaluated from a *cost-benefit* perspective. The usual result is that (1) the **perpetual** inventory method is used to account for large amounts of supplies and other inventories that justify the accounting control costs involved from an asset management and/or expenditure accounting perspective; but (2) lesser amounts of inventory, inventories that do not lend themselves to perpetual methods (e.g., sand and gravel), and inventories that may be controlled otherwise (e.g., by department personnel) are accounted for on the **periodic** method—*on either the consumption basis or the purchases basis.*

Purchases Basis

The **purchases** basis is used when the inventory-related *appropriations* are based on *estimated purchases.* Its use is *limited to* the **periodic** method since it is *not compatible with the perpetual inventory method.* Under the **purchases** basis the Expenditures account is charged with inventory *purchases* during the year.

Assuming the same dollar amounts used in the preceding consumption basis illustration (and again omitting encumbrance and subsidiary ledger entries), the entries under the **purchases** basis would be:

When Purchased:

Expenditures	850,000	
Vouchers Payable		850,000

To record the purchase of supplies.

During the Year:
No entry.

End of Year:

(a) Inventory of Supplies	72,500	
Other Financing Sources—Inventory Increase		
(or Unreserved Fund Balance)		72,500

To record the increase in inventory during the year, or to record the inventory at the end of the first year of the fund's existence.

(b) Unreserved Fund Balance	72,500	
Reserve for Inventory of Supplies.		72,500

To "fully reserve" the inventory of supplies.

Note that under the purchases basis all inventory purchases are charged to Expenditures and no inventory-related entries are made during the year. In these ways it is like the consumption basis using the **periodic** inventory method. However, *at year end,* the increase in the inventory is debited to Inventory of Supplies in both cases but is:

- Credited to **Expenditures** under the **consumption** basis, adjusting that account to the cost of goods used (assuming no shortage or overage because of theft, accounting errors, and so on).

- Credited to **Other Financing Sources—Inventory Increase** (or Unreserved Fund Balance), rather than to Expenditures, under the **purchases** basis, *leaving the total cost of inventory purchased charged to* Expenditures.

The credit to Other Financing Sources—Inventory Increase (or Unreserved Fund Balance) in entry (a) at year end results from the fact that GAAP permits use of the purchases method **only** for **expenditure** accounting. Any significant amounts of inventory **must** be reported in the governmental fund **balance sheet.** Since, as compared with the consumption method, the purchases method "overstates" Expenditures—in this case, by $72,500—the Unreserved Fund Balance account will be understated $72,500 after the Expenditures account is closed. Thus, the $72,500 credit to Other Financing Sources—Inventory Increase—which is closed at year end to Unreserved Fund Balance—or directly to Unreserved Fund Balance may be viewed as correcting for its understatement caused by the Expenditures overstatement.

The inventory must be "fully reserved" under the purchases basis. This is because **it has already been charged to Expenditures,** even though reported as an asset on the balance sheet, and thus is not available to finance subsequent expenditures. Accordingly, inventory is **not** considered a financial resource under the purchases method, and **is always fully reserved.**

The **change** in the inventory and reserve must be reported as an **"Other Financing Source (Use)"** or as a **Fund Balance Increase (Decrease)** in the governmental fund Statement of Revenues, Expenditures, and Changes in Fund Balance when the **purchases** basis is used. This is because the Expenditures and Unreserved Fund Balance "misstatements" noted above were "corrected" not only by debiting the Inventory of Supplies account but by crediting either the Other Financing Sources—Inventory Increase or the Unreserved Fund Balance account, thus increasing **total** fund balance. Thus, the increase in the Unreserved Fund Balance because of the inventory increase must be reported as an "other financing source," and a decrease in inventory would be reported as an "other financing use"—**under the purchases method (only)**—in the Statement of Revenues, Expenditures, and Changes in Fund Balance. Furthermore, the beginning and ending fund balance amounts will not reconcile otherwise.

Finally, note that end-of-year entries (a) and (b) above are often **compounded:**

Inventory of Supplies	72,500	
Reserve for Inventory of Supplies		72,500
To record the increase in, and "fully reserve," the inventory of supplies.		

This may be one reason that some governmental accountants view the purchases method end-of-year inventory adjustment as a "balance sheet plug" and do not realize that it must be reported as an other financing source (use). Indeed, the purchases basis will no longer be acceptable under GAAP when GASB Statement 11, "Measurement Focus and Basis of Accounting—Governmental Fund Operating Statements," becomes effective.

Other Services and Charges

When services are being acquired under contract, an entry is made **encumbering** appropriations for the amount of the estimated ultimate contractual liability at the time the contract is awarded. As services and the related invoices are received, the encumbering entries are reversed and the actual expenditures are recorded.

Whereas the accounting for most other services and charges is apparent from the discussions in this text, several specific types of other services and charges expenditures warrant at least brief mention in this chapter. Two types are

213

Chapter 6
EXPENDITURE
ACCOUNTING—
GOVERNMENTAL
FUNDS

discussed here: (1) prepayments and (2) capital leases. Related topics—including (a) interest on short-term governmental fund debt, (b) claims and judgments, (c) compensated absences, and (d) pension contribution underfunding—are discussed in the Adjusting Entries section later in this chapter.

Prepayments. Governments may ***prepay*** costs that benefit two or more accounting periods. For example, a two-year insurance policy may be purchased or rental on a building may be paid for a year in advance at midyear. As in the case of inventories, governments are permitted to use **either the consumption basis or the purchases basis** in accounting for prepayments (prepayals).[9] Moreover, those using the ***purchases*** basis need not report prepayments on the balance sheet. Thus, if a two-year insurance policy were purchased at the beginning of 19X1, the entries (omitting subsidiary ledger entries) would be:

When Purchased:

Expenditures	88,000	
Vouchers Payable		88,000

To record payment for two-year insurance policy at beginning of 19X1.

End of 19X1:
(a) **Purchases Basis**—No entry.
(b) **Consumption Basis**—

Prepaid Insurance	44,000	
Expenditures		44,000

To record prepaid insurance.

Beginning of 19X2:
(a) **Purchases Basis**—No entry.
(b) **Consumption Basis**—

Expenditures	44,000	
Prepaid Insurance		44,000

To reverse the 19X1 adjusting entry and charge the applicable insurance cost to 19X2 expenditures.

The purchases method of prepayment accounting will no longer be acceptable under GAAP once GASB Statement 11 becomes effective.

Capital Lease Payments. Many governments lease assets—such as vehicles, computers, photocopy machines, other equipment, and buildings—rather than buying them. ***When such leases are ordinary rentals***—such as monthly rentals that may be cancelled with little notice—the amounts paid the lessors usually are recorded as ***rental expenditures.*** (Advance rental payments might be initially recorded as prepayments, as discussed above.) ***However, if the government is in substance buying the assets or is leasing them for most or all of their useful lives,*** GAAP requires that the accounting for such **"capital leases"** reflect their ***substance*** instead of their legal form.

Accordingly, NCGA Statement 5 adapted the FASB Statement 13[10] capital lease accounting requirements, as amended and interpreted, for governmental accounting. The GASB Codification includes NCGAS 5, of course, and requires that:

- ***General fixed assets acquired*** in ***capital*** lease agreements should be ***capitalized*** in the ***GFAAG*** at the ***inception*** of the lease at the ***present value*** of the ***future lease payments,*** as determined under FASB Statement 13; ***and*** a ***general***

---

[9] Ibid., sec. 1600.122.
[10] These requirements are discussed in intermediate accounting textbooks.

long-term debt liability in the same amount should be *recorded concurrently* in the *GLTDAG.*

■ When a general fixed asset is acquired by capital lease, its *acquisition* should be *reported* in an appropriate *governmental fund* as *both* (1) a capital outlay *expenditure* for a fixed asset *and* (2) an *"other financing source,"* as if long-term debt had been issued to finance the fixed asset acquisition.[11]

■ Capital lease proceeds need *not* be accounted for through a Capital Projects Fund, *nor does* capital lease debt service have to be accounted for through a Debt Service Fund, *unless* use of such funds is *legally or contractually required.*

The General Fixed Assets Account Group (GFAAG) and General Long-Term Debt Account Group (GLTDAG) entries are illustrated in Chapter 9. *The key points here are that* (1) a governmental fund expenditure and other financing source must be recognized at the inception of the lease; (2) neither use of a Capital Projects Fund at the inception of the capital lease nor use of a Debt Service Fund to service the capital lease debt is required unless legally or contractually required, which is rare; and thus (3) both the governmental fund expenditure and other financing source and the related debt service on the capital lease may be accounted for in the General Fund or perhaps a Special Revenue Fund.

Regardless of the governmental fund in which the capital lease transaction and debt service are recorded, the entries are:

Inception of Capital Lease:

Expenditures	900,000	
Other Financing Sources—Capital Lease		900,000

To record capital lease expenditure and related other financing source.

Expenditures Ledger (Expenditures):

Capital Outlay	900,000

First Debt Service Payment:

Expenditures	17,821	
Vouchers Payable		17,821

To record capital lease debt service payment due.

Expenditures Ledger (Expenditures):

Debt Service—Interest (Capital Lease)	5,250
Debt Service—Principal (Capital lease)	12,571
	17,821

Note that the entry at the inception of the lease has no effect on the fund balance of the governmental fund—which is increased by the $900,000 other financing source and decreased by the $900,000 expenditure, both the amount of the fair market value of the fixed asset acquired, which is also the present value of the capital lease. *Note also that the capital lease debt service payment must be allocated between interest expenditures and debt principal reduction based on the effective interest rate* of the capital lease agreement. The amounts in the debt service entry above assume that (1) the fair market value of the fixed asset acquired is $900,000, (2) the capital lease is a five-year lease, (3) lease payments are made monthly, (4) the interest rate implied in the capital lease is 7% per year, and (5) the monthly lease payments are $17,821. The effective interest *amount* for the first payment thus is computed by multiplying the effective interest rate, 7%, by the carrying amount (book value) of the lease, initially $900,000, and dividing by 12. The next month's effective interest amount would be computed based on

[11] GASB Codification, sec. L20.116.

the new book value of the liability—$900,000 − $12,571 = $887,429—and so on throughout the term of the capital lease.

CLASSIFICATION OF EXPENDITURES

A governmental unit's expenditures are classified in several ways to serve several managerial and financial reporting purposes. As observed in the GASB Codification:

> Multiple classification of governmental fund expenditure data is important from both internal and external management control and accountability standpoints. It facilitates the aggregation and analysis of data in different ways for different purposes and in manners that cross fund and organizational lines, for internal evaluation, external reporting, and intergovernmental comparison purposes. **The major accounting classifications of expenditures are by fund, function (or program), organization unit, activity, character, and object class.**[12]

Since appropriations are made in terms of specified funds, the basic classification of expenditures is by fund. To produce all the required information, the expenditures of a fund are also classified by function or program, activity, organization unit, character, and object class.

The GASB Codification does not contain a detailed chart of expenditure accounts for state and local governments. However, the National Committee on Governmental Accounting, the predecessor of the National Council on Governmental Accounting and the GASB, prepared a standard classification of accounts, including expenditure accounts.[13] Although no longer required to be used, that classification of accounts has been updated by the GFOA staff, is contained in *Governmental Accounting, Auditing and Financial Reporting,* issued by the GFOA in 1988,[14] and is widely used (and adapted) in practice.

The budgeting, accounting, and reporting systems of a governmental unit should be based on the same structure of accounts. *Some* state and local governments have accounting systems and charts of accounts that classify every expenditure transaction by fund, function or program, organization unit, activity, character, and object class. On the other hand, *others* use systems and charts of accounts that record expenditure data only in certain essential classifications—such as by fund, organization unit, and object class—and compile these data at year end to derive data for the other expenditure classifications.

Classification of expenditures by fund has been discussed at length earlier in this text, and is discussed further in later chapters. **Appendix 6-1** discusses and illustrates governmental fund expenditure classification by (1) function or program, (2) activity, (3) organization unit, (4) character, and (5) object classes.

ACCOUNTING FOR ALLOCATIONS AND ALLOTMENTS

Allocations, further executive branch subdivisions of legislative appropriations, do *not* cause any unique accounting procedures. Rather, they *are accommodated in the Expenditures Ledger by establishing subsidiary accounts in at least as much detail as the allocations.* To illustrate, assume that the legislative body made a lump-sum appropriation for the Police Department, but the executive

---

[12] Ibid., sec. 1800.115. (Emphasis added.)
[13] GAAFR (68), "Appendix B: Use of Account Classifications," pp. 175–201.
[14] GAAFR (88), Appendix C, pp. 183–216.

branch then allocated specific maximum amounts by object of expenditure class. Only one subsidiary account (Police Department) would be needed to satisfy legislative budgetary control and accountability requirements in this instance, but a series of more detailed accounts (Police Department—Personal Services, etc.) would be needed to meet the more stringent executive branch budgetary control and accountability requirements. Hence, *the subsidiary accounts must provide at least as much detail as is required to meet the more stringent requirements.*

The chief executive may not allocate all the appropriations to the agencies immediately, but may hold back some expenditure authority for contingencies that might arise during the year. In such cases an account such as **Unallocated Appropriations** should be established in either the General Ledger or the Expenditures Ledger.

Allotments—divisions of appropriations authority by *time period,* usually months or quarters—require modification of the General Ledger accounts and accounting procedures discussed so far. To illustrate, assume that the annual General Fund appropriations of A Governmental Unit—now made by organization unit and object class rather than by function—are allotted on a monthly basis, that $35,000 was allotted for the month of January 19X1, and that $350 of the total allotment was allotted to the Fire Department for supplies expenditures during January 19X1. *Since only allotted appropriations constitute valid expenditure authority at the department or agency level,* separate **Unallotted Appropriations** and **Allotted Appropriations** (or **Allotments**) *control accounts* are established in the *General Ledger* and the *budgetary entry* to record appropriations for the year and the allotments for January 19X1 would appear:

Unreserved Fund Balance	426,000	
Unallotted Appropriations		391,000
Allotments (or **Allotted Appropriations**)		35,000

To record the 19X1 appropriations and January 19X1 allotments.

Expenditures Ledger (**Allotments**):

Fire Department—Firefighting Supplies	350
Fire Department—Other	XX
Other Departments	XX
	35,000

Note that the *Allotments* (or Allotted Appropriations), Expenditures, and Encumbrances accounts in the General Ledger *control* the Expenditures Ledger accounts where formal allotments are used. Thus, as noted earlier, the **"Appropriations"** column of the subsidiary ledger account is *retitled* "Allotments" (or Allotted Appropriations) and the *"Unencumbered Balance"* column—which previously contained the unencumbered balance of the annual appropriation—is *retitled* **"Unencumbered Allotments."**

At the beginning of each month or quarter (1) an appropriate amount will be reclassified from the Unallotted Appropriations account to the Allotments (or Allotted Appropriations) account in the General Ledger and, correspondingly, (2) appropriate amounts will be credited to the "Allotments" columns of the various Expenditures Ledger accounts. Assuming that all appropriations have been allotted by the end of 19X1, the Unallotted Appropriations account will have a zero balance and will require no closing entry at the end of 19X1. Some governments do not allot all of the appropriations so that they have a "cushion" in the event that contingencies occur. If some appropriations have not been allotted, the balance of the Unallotted Appropriations account is closed at year end unless unexpended or unencumbered appropriations do not lapse (discussed in the Continuing Appropriations Appendix to this chapter).

APPROPRIATIONS REVISIONS

Appropriations may be revised during the year for a variety of reasons. Increases in revenues over those estimated—whether from regular sources or because of unanticipated special grants—may either permit or require additional expenditures that must be appropriated. Or, conversely, declines in revenues as compared with the original expectations may necessitate that appropriations be reduced to avoid a fund balance deficit.

Appropriations revisions may also arise because of utility cost increases, damage to streets caused by unusually cold or wet weather, unanticipated costs of patrolling and cleaning up the town after the hometown university won the national football championship, or for an infinite variety of other reasons. Appropriations increases are not necessarily "bad," of course, nor are appropriations decreases necessarily "good."

The continuing process of reviewing budgeted and actual revenues and comparing appropriations, expenditures, and encumbrances—and revising the budget as needed in view of changed and changing circumstances—is considered good financial management. Thus, as noted earlier, an annual budget that may have been enacted well before the beginning of the current year should not be considered unchangeable, but should be continually reviewed and appropriately revised throughout the year.

The accounting for appropriations revisions during the year parallels that discussed and illustrated in Chapter 5 for revenue budget revisions. Thus, it seems sufficient at this point to illustrate three common types of appropriations revisions and entries:

Appropriations Increased:

Unreserved Fund Balance	10,000	
Appropriations.		10,000
To record increase in appropriations.		
Expenditures Ledger (Appropriations):		
Police Department—Salaries		10,000
(The entry would be reversed if the appropriations were decreased.)		

Both Estimated Revenues and Appropriations Decreased:

Appropriations.	10,000	
Estimated Revenues		10,000
To record reduction in appropriations because of reduction in estimated revenues.		
Expenditures Ledger (Appropriations):		
Parks and Recreation—Supplies	4,000	
Mayor's Office—Equipment	6,000	
	10,000	
Revenues Ledger (Estimated Revenues):		
Sales Taxes		10,000

Appropriation Shift between Departments:

Appropriations.	10,000	
Appropriations.		10,000
To record shift of appropriations from police department to fire department.		
Expenditures Ledger (Appropriations):		
Police Department—Equipment	10,000	
Fire Department—Supplies		10,000

Most of the expenditure-related adjusting entries that may be required in a governmental fund at year end are similar to those covered in intermediate accounting courses. That is, the accountant must ensure that there is a proper year end "cutoff" of expenditures for payrolls, utilities, and similar costs.

The "available" revenue recognition criterion is *not* applicable in governmental fund expenditure accounting, and an expenditure payable beyond 60 days into the next year may be considered a current liability that should be recorded as a governmental fund expenditure and liability. However, the governmental fund expenditure recognition criteria are *not* as clearly defined as the "available" revenue recognition criterion. The general rule is that *any* expenditure and related liability applicable to a fund *are* recorded as a fund expenditure and liability *unless* the *liability* is a *"noncurrent"* liability that is properly classified as *general long-term debt,* and thus is recorded in the GLTDAG. In this regard the GASB Codification states that:

> . . . general long-term debt is *not* limited to liabilities arising from debt issuances *per se,* but it *may also include noncurrent liabilities for other commitments* that are *not current liabilities properly recorded in governmental funds.*[15]

This paragraph of the Codification concludes with the statement that:

> . . . in *governmental* funds, liabilities usually are *not* considered *current* [and thus fund expenditures] *until* they are *normally expected to be liquidated with expendable available financial resources.*[16]

This expenditure recognition criterion does not define the term "expendable available financial resources." The term seems to refer to the ending fund balance of the governmental fund, and has proven to be difficult to implement in practice. Further, differing interpretations of the criterion and varying levels of governmental fund "expendable available financial resources" have resulted in expenditure recognition inconsistencies among governments.

The notion of "to be liquidated with expendable available financial resources" is not an issue in most routine adjusting entries made at year end. Such accrued expenditure liabilities as payroll, utilities, and similar costs usually are presumed to be payable from existing fund resources and are accrued. Rather, **the "to be liquidated with expendable available financial resources" notion relates primarily to accruing expenditures for (1) debt service, (2) claims and judgments, (3) accrued vacation and sick leave, referred to as "compensated absences," and (4) pension plan contributions.** These are the main topics of this section, and are considered after a brief discussion of encumbrances as they relate to the year end adjusting entries.

Encumbrances

The encumbrances outstanding at year end should be reviewed because, as noted in the GASB Codification:

> If performance on an executory contract is complete, or virtually complete, an expenditure and liability should be recognized rather than an encumbrance.[17]

---

[15] GASB Codification, sec. C50.104. (Emphasis added.)
[16] Ibid. (Emphasis added.)
[17] Ibid., sec. 1700.129(c).

219

Chapter 6
EXPENDITURE
ACCOUNTING—
GOVERNMENTAL
FUNDS

The failure to record completed contracts as governmental fund expenditures and liabilities (rather than encumbrances) may be unintentional. Often the goods or the invoice for the goods or services will not have arrived at the government's offices by year end, for example, and they are inadvertently recorded as expenditures in the next year. On the other hand, it may be intentional—as when recording expenditures for an encumbered order would cause departmental expenditures to exceed appropriations. This might occur where the budgetary basis is the modified accrual basis—on which encumbrances are not considered equivalent to expenditures and thus are not charged against appropriations—or where the budgetary basis includes encumbrances but the encumbrance recorded is significantly less than the actual expenditure incurred.

In any event, the encumbrances outstanding against a governmental fund at year end should be analyzed. And **if any are found to be expenditures misclassified as encumbrances,** the adjusting entry (omitting subsidiary ledger entries) would be:

Reserve for Encumbrances	19,000	
Expenditures	20,000	
Encumbrances		19,000
Accounts Payable (or Accrued Liabilities)		20,000

To record reclassifying encumbrances as expenditures at year end.

Debt Service

As noted earlier, debt service on general long-term debt typically is *not* accrued at year end. This usually is consistent with the "to be liquidated with expendable available financial resources" criterion, since the property tax rates of many state and local governments are set to provide the financial resources required for the GLTD debt service payments due each year. Thus, the financial resources available at the end of a year ordinarily need not be used for the following year's debt service, since those resources will be provided by that year's tax levy. On the other hand, if resources have been provided currently to pay GLTD debt service payments due early in the next year, those debt service payments (principal and interest) *may* be accrued at year end as governmental fund expenditures and liabilities. Clearly, a SLG should adopt an appropriate debt service expenditure accounting policy and apply it consistently each year.

It was noted earlier that state and local governments may borrow on *short-term* notes such as tax anticipation notes (TANs), revenue anticipation notes (RANs), and similar debt instruments. The GASB Codification states that TANs, RANs, and similar short-term debt instruments should be accounted for as a **fund liability** of the governmental fund that receives the proceeds.[18] Also, the short-term note and interest usually would be paid from that fund. Thus, whereas interest on General Long-Term Debt is ordinarily recorded "when due" rather than accrued at year end, *interest on governmental fund (non-GLTD) short-term notes and other debts is accrued at year end:*

Expenditures	36,000	
Accrued Interest Payable		36,000

To record interest accrued at year end on **short-term** notes payable.

Expenditures Ledger (Expenditures):	
Interest	36,000

---

[18] Ibid., sec. B50.101.

Claims and Judgments

Lawsuits and other claims for personal injury, property damage, employee compensation, or other reasons have increasingly been filed against states and local governments in recent years. The GASB Codification observes that such claims *include*—but are by no means limited to—those arising from:

- *Employment*—such as worker compensation and unemployment claims;
- *Contractual Actions*—such as claims for delays or inadequate specifications;
- *Actions of Government Personnel*—such as claims for medical malpractice, damage to privately owned vehicles by government-owned vehicles, and improper police arrest; and
- *Government Properties*—such as claims relating to personal injuries and property damage.[19]

The GASB Codification also observes that many claims filed against state and local governments are characterized by conditions that make it *extremely difficult to reasonably estimate* the ultimate liability, if any, that will result:

- **Unreasonably High Claims.** Some claims may be filed in amounts far greater than those reasonably expected to be agreed to by the government and the claimant or awarded by a court.
- **Time Between Occurrence and Filing.** The time permitted (e.g., by law) between the occurrence of an event giving rise to a claim and the actual filing of the claim may be lengthy. (An event leading to a claim may occur during a year but the claim may not be filed by year end; thus, the government may not be aware of the claim at year end.)
- **Time Between Filing, Settlement, and Payment.** Likewise, many months or even years may elapse between (1) the filing of the claim and its ultimate settlement, perhaps after court appeals, and (2) the settlement of the claim and its ultimate payment, since adjudicated or agreed settlement amounts may be paid over a period of years after settlement.[20]

On the other hand, the outcome of some claims may be **readily estimable** (1) such as when a court has entered a judgment against the government that will not be appealed, or (2) because the government has appropriate estimates by its attorneys and/or sufficient data regarding past settlements of similar claims to reasonably estimate the ultimate liabilities to result from such claims, either individually or by type of claim.

GASB Standards

Claims outstanding against a government are **"contingencies"**—regardless of whether the claims have been filed, are being negotiated or arbitrated, or have resulted in judgments for or against the government that will be appealed by either the claimant or the government. Accordingly, the contingencies accounting standard of FASB Statement 5 have been adapted to state and local governments. The GASB Codification requires that the **liability** for *claims and judgments (CJ)* outstanding be recognized in the accounts *if* information available prior to issuance of the financial statements indicates that:

1. It is **probable** that an asset has been impaired or a *liability has been incurred—as of the date of the financial statements*—and
2. The **amount** of the loss *can be reasonably estimated.*

[19] Ibid., sec. C50.105.
[20] Ibid., sec. C50.106.

221

Chapter 6
EXPENDITURE
ACCOUNTING—
GOVERNMENTAL
FUNDS

If these contingencies recognition criteria are *not* met, the claims and judgments outstanding would be *disclosed* in the notes to the government's financial statements, but would *not* be recorded in the accounts or presented in the financial statements.

If the CJ recognition criteria *are* met, CJ expenditures and related liabilities are to be accounted for as follows:

> In governmental funds, the primary emphasis is on the flow of financial resources.... Accordingly, *if all conditions* of FASB Statement 5 *are met,* the amount of claims recorded as *expenditures* [and liabilities] in governmental funds shall be the *amount accrued during the year* that would *normally* be *liquidated with expendable available financial resources.* ...
>
> Because governmental fund balance sheets reflect current liabilities, **only** the **current portion** of the liability should be **reported** in the **fund.** The **current portion** is the **amount** left **unpaid** at the end of the reporting period **that normally would be liquidated with expendable available financial resources.** The **remainder** of the **liability** should be **reported** in the **GLTDAG.**[21]

Adjusting Entry(ies)—CJ

During the year a government typically will record the amounts paid or vouchered as payable for claims and judgments as expenditures. To illustrate CJ adjusting entries at year end, assume that CJ expenditures and current liabilities are recorded in the General Fund, that no CJ current liabilities were accrued at the end of the prior year (19X0), and that the following entry summarizes the CJ entries *during* 19X1:

During the Year (19X1)

Expenditures.	300,000	
Cash or Vouchers Payable.		300,000

To record CJ expenditures *paid or vouchered during 19X1.*
  (None accrued at end of 19X0.)

Expenditures Ledger (Expenditures):

Claims and Judgments	<u>300,000</u>

Assume also at *the end of 19X1* that:

1. claims and judgments totaling $900,000 are outstanding,
2. it is reasonably estimated that the ultimate CJ liabilities resulting—including legal fees and net of insurance recoveries—will be $200,000, and
3. $50,000 of the $200,000 total unrecorded CJ liability is reasonably expected to be paid from General Fund net assets available at the end of 19X1.

The $50,000 expected to be paid from existing available General Fund net assets typically represents amounts that must be paid in 19X2 on claims settled by the end of 19X1. (The government and its auditor often use information learned early in 19X2 to assist in estimating the liabilities at the end of 19X1 and when, and from which governmental fund, they will be paid.)

---

[21] Ibid., sec. C50.112–113. (Emphasis added.)

Given these facts, this **CJ adjusting entry** would be made in the General Fund accounts at the **end of 19X1:**

End of Year (19X1)

Expenditures	50,000	
Accrued Liabilities (CJ)		50,000

To record additional 19X1 *expenditures* for CJ *"current"* liabilities expected to be paid from existing fund assets.

Expenditures Ledger (Expenditures):

Claims and Judgments	50,000

The $150,000 **noncurrent** CJ liability would be recorded directly in the General Long-Term Debt Account Group (GLTDAG) accounts. Further, **all** of the outstanding claims and judgments ($900,000) would be **disclosed** in the notes to the 19X1 financial statements.

In sum, $350,000 of CJ **expenditures** would be reported in the General Fund during 19X1, and a $50,000 CJ **current liability** would be reported at the end of 19X1; a $150,000 CJ **noncurrent liability** would be added to the GLTDAG; and **all** CJ **contingencies,** including those not recorded in the accounts, would be **disclosed** in the notes to the 19X1 financial statements.

The 19X1 year-end adjusting entry usually would be **reversed** at the **beginning of 19X2:**

Beginning of Year (19X2)

Accrued Liabilities (CJ)	50,000	
Expenditures		50,000

To **reverse** CJ accrual adjusting entry made at end of 19X1.

Expenditures Ledger (Expenditures):

Claims and Judgments	50,000

To continue the illustration, assume that the following entry summarizes the General Fund CJ expenditures paid or accrued **during 19X2:**

During the Year (19X2)

Expenditures	450,000	
Cash or Vouchers Payable		450,000

To record CJ expenditures paid or vouchered during 19X2.

Expenditures Ledger (Expenditures):

Claims and Judgments	450,000

This summary entry presumably includes payment or vouchering of the 19X1 year-end CJ accruals of $50,000.

Assume at the **end of 19X2** that (1) claims and judgments totaling $1,200,000 are outstanding, (2) it is reasonably estimated that the ultimate CJ liabilities resulting—including legal and other related costs but net of insurance recoveries—will be $325,000, and (3) $75,000 of that $325,000 is reasonably expected to be paid from existing General Fund financial resources. The General Fund **19X2 year-end** CJ **adjusting entry** in this case would be:

End of Year (19X2)

Expenditures	75,000	
Accrued Liabilities (CJ)		75,000

To record *expenditures* for CJ *"current"* liabilities expected to be paid from existing fund assets.

Expenditures Ledger (Expenditures):

Claims and Judgments	75,000

223

Chapter 6
EXPENDITURE
ACCOUNTING—
GOVERNMENTAL
FUNDS

This adjusting entry increases the 19X2 CJ expenditures recognized to $475,000:

19X2 CJ Expenditures:

Paid or accrued during 19X2	$450,000
19X1 CJ expenditures—reversing entry	(50,000)
19X2 accrual at year end	75,000
	$475,000

Further, the GLTDAG **noncurrent** CJ liability account would be increased by $100,000—from the $150,000 year-end 19X1 balance to the $250,000 ($325,000 total less $75,000 recorded in the General Fund) balance at the end of 19X2. All outstanding CJ contingencies would be disclosed in the notes to the financial statements, including those not recorded in the General Fund and GLTDAG accounts.

To summarize, the CJ liabilities arising during a year that are paid or vouchered (as payable) during the year—plus any other CJ liabilities that are considered current liabilities at year end, and so are recorded in an adjusting entry— are accounted for and reported as governmental fund CJ expenditures of that year. Thus, CJ liabilities are **not** necessarily recorded as governmental fund expenditures of the year in which they arise. Rather, noncurrent CJ liabilities are recorded initially in the GLTDAG, and are recorded as governmental fund CJ expenditures in the year during which the CJ liabilities mature or become "current liabilities," as defined in a governmental fund context. All significant contingencies—whether or not recorded in the governmental fund or GLTD accounts—should be disclosed appropriately in the notes to the financial statements.

Insurance, Self-Insurance, and No Insurance

The discussions of CJ liability estimation noted that the final estimate of a CJ liability should include legal and other related costs, as well as the settled or adjudicated claim amount, but should be net of any insurance or similar recoveries. Thus, if a currently payable claim was settled in 19X1 for $250,000 but related insurance reimbursed the government for $200,000 of that amount, the governmental fund entry (omitting subsidiary ledger entries) would be:

During 19X1:

Expenditures	50,000	
Due from Insurance Company	200,000	
Due to Claimant		250,000

To record settlement of claim net of related insured recovery.

The insurance company and the insured government may occasionally disagree on the amount of a CJ expenditure to be reimbursed, however, and thus the insurance recovery might not be reasonably estimable or its receipt might be delayed until a subsequent year.

Suppose, for example, that the $200,000 insurance recovery in this example is reasonably estimable but will not be received until late in 19X2. Since the "available" criterion does not apply to expenditure recognition, the entry above would be made; further, no fund balance reserve is required at the end of 19X1 since the insurance recovery proceeds will be collected during 19X2. (But if the insurance recovery was not expected until 19X3, a fund balance reserve would be required during 19X2 to indicate that the receivable did not represent expendable financial resources during 19X2.)

On the other hand, suppose that (1) the insurance recovery amount was in dispute and was **not** reasonably estimable at the end of 19X1, but (2) was agreed to and received in 19X2, after the 19X1 financial statements were issued by the government. In this situation the entries would be:

During 19X1:

Expenditures	250,000	
Due to Claimant		250,000

To record settlement of claim. (Insurance recovery **not** reasonably estimable.)

During 19X2:

Due from Insurance Company	200,000	
Insurance Recovery Proceeds		200,000

To record insurance recovery on 19X1 claim expenditures.

The **Insurance Recovery Proceeds** account might be reported as a deduction from 19X2 CJ Expenditures, but—because the $250,000 (gross) related expenditures were reported in 19X1—is more often reported as an "Other Financing Source" in 19X2.

Liability insurance premiums have increased rapidly in recent years, and some governments have been unable to obtain adequate levels of insurance for what they consider reasonable or affordable premiums. Thus, many state and local governments have instituted self-insured plans—alone or in pools with other governments—or are uninsured. Self-insurance plans are discussed and illustrated in Chapter 12, "Internal Service Funds."

Governments that are uninsured assume more CJ risk than those that are insured or self-insured. Accordingly, some establish governmental fund "reserves" of fund balance to indicate that some net assets must be maintained in view of the uninsured CJ contingencies, and others obtain "umbrella" insurance policies—with large deductibles but covering large amounts above the deductibles—to insure partially against possible catastrophic CJ liabilities being incurred.

Compensated Absences

The accounting and reporting for **compensated absences (CA)**—such as accumulated vacation and sick leave—parallel that for claims and judgments. Indeed, both are covered in NCGA Statement 5—on claims, judgments, and compensated absences (CJCA)—and in adjoining sections of the GASB Codification.

The FASB Statement 43 standards were adapted by the NCGA for accounting for and reporting compensated absences of governments. Accordingly, the GASB standards require government employers to accrue a **liability** for future vacation, sick, and other leave benefits that meet **all** of these conditions:

    a. The employer's obligation relating to employees' rights to receive compensation for future absences is attributable to **employees' services** already **rendered.**

    b. The obligation relates to rights that **vest or accumulate.**

    c. **Payment** of the compensation **is probable.**

    d. The **amount** can be **reasonably estimated.**[22]

To determine whether an adjusting entry is required and (if so) the amount of the adjustment, the accumulated vacation, sick leave, and other CA liabilities at year end should be *"inventoried"* at *current salary levels.* Only the hours or days of each employee's accumulated CA time that carry over to the next year should be inventoried. For example, an employee may have accumulated 36

---

[22] Ibid., sec. C60.105. (Emphasis added.)

225

Chapter 6
EXPENDITURE
ACCOUNTING—
GOVERNMENTAL
FUNDS

days of vacation. But if only 24 days may be carried forward to the next year—that is, the other 12 days are "lost" if not taken currently—then only 24 days are inventoried.

Adjusting Entry(ies)—CA

To illustrate CA accounting, we use the 19X1 and 19X2 General Fund assumptions and amounts used in the Claims and Judgment (CJ) illustration earlier in this section. The General Fund CA entries—assuming reversing entries are *not* made and omitting subsidiary ledger entries—are as follows:

During the Year (19X1)

Expenditures	300,000	
Cash or Vouchers Payable.		300,000

To record CA expenditures *paid or vouchered during 19X1.*
(None accrued at the end of 19X0.)

End of Year (19X1)

Expenditures	50,000	
Accrued Vacation and Sick Leave Payable		50,000

To record additional 19X1 *expenditures* for *"current"* CA
liabilities expected to be paid from existing fund assets.

During the Year (19X2)

Expenditures	450,000	
Cash or Vouchers Payable.		450,000

To record CA expenditures *paid or vouchered during 19X2.*

(**Note:** This entry assumes that the Accrued Vacation and Sick
Leave Payable account is *not* changed during the year.)

End of Year (19X2)

Expenditures	25,000	
Accrued Vacation and Sick Leave Payable		25,000

To record additional 19X2 *expenditures* for the increase in
"current" CA liabilities expected to be paid from existing fund
assets.

Computation:	
CA current (fund) liability at end of 19X2	$75,000
CA current liability recorded at end of 19X1	50,000
Increase in current CA liability during 19X2	$25,000

The "no reversing entry" approach has the advantage of clearly emphasizing that it is the *change* in the *current* CA or CJ liability that is recorded as an additional governmental fund expenditure and liability in the year-end adjusting entry.

Rationale

The rationale of CA accounting and reporting is largely the same as that for CJ accounting and reporting. Only the measurement differs because of the differing natures of CJ and CA liabilities. Thus, the *noncurrent* CA liabilities recognized would be recorded in the *GLTDAG*—not in a governmental fund—and the *notes* to the financial statements would describe both the unit's vacation, sick leave, and other CA policies and the related CA accounting and reporting policies.

Measurement

Practice varies somewhat with respect to the measurement of both (1) the total CA liability at year end, and (2) the amount that is reasonably expected to be paid from existing available fund (usually General Fund) financial resources.

Total CA Liability. Some accountants consider the total CA time carried forward to the next year to be the proper number of hours or days to multiply times the current wage rate to derive the total CA liability. Others emphasize the third FASB Statement 43 criterion—**payment of the CA is probable**—and use an actuarial approach that considers the ***probability*** that some CA time will be "lost" in future years because of turnover, overaccumulation, or for other reasons. The actuarially calculated total liability is less under a probability approach, of course, than under the first approach. Still others interpret the FASB 43 "payment is probable" criteria to mean that only those CA amounts that are expected to be paid ***in addition to*** each employee's regular salary or wages should be included in the total CA liability. Thus, they include only CA time the employees could ***"cash in"*** (be paid for) upon retirement or other termination of employment with the government—and thus calculate an even smaller total CA liability than in the first two approaches.

The second and third approaches—based on the ***"payment is probable"*** criteria—appear to correspond with the intent of the NCGA when NCGA Statement 5 was issued. However, the NCGA did not clarify its intent with respect to calculating the total CA liability.

Amount to Be Paid from Existing Resources. Practice also varies with respect to computing the amount of the CA (and CJ) ***"current" liability*** to be recorded as a governmental fund expenditure and liability. Most accountants look for objective evidence that the CA liability is reasonably expected to be paid from the existing governmental fund financial resources. Thus, they would include CA amounts for employees that retired or otherwise terminated employment by year end but whose CA had not been paid or vouchered as payable by year end. They might also include those known to have retired or terminated early in the next year. But in either case, they would include only ***known*** amounts owed to retired or otherwise terminated employees that are ***due to be paid early in the next year.***

Other accountants, perhaps based on the practice in business accounting, would estimate the total CA payments expected to be made during the next year for CA earned by the end of the current year. The amount estimated by this ***"one year look out"*** approach would be recorded as the current CA liability and expenditure adjustment in the governmental fund.

The "one year look out" approach is used in business accounting and in proprietary fund accounting of governments, but is not presently accepted in governmental fund current liability determination generally. Accordingly, the authors consider the first approach to be preferable because it seems more in keeping with the intent of NCGA Statement 5.

GASB Statement 16

GASB Statement 16, "Accounting for Compensated Absences," essentially continues the FASB Statement 43 criteria and approach described earlier for accrued vacation and similar leave.[23] However, it does ***not*** require accrual of ***sick leave*** and similar compensated absence liabilities except to the extent that employees are expected to be paid for such accumulated benefits upon terminating their employment with the government. GASB Statement 16 is effective for years ending on or after June 15, 1994, with early application permitted.

---

[23] Governmental Accounting Standards Board, Statement No. 16 of the Governmental Accounting Standards Board, "Accounting for Compensated Absences" (Norwalk, CT: GASB, November 1992).

227

Chapter 6
EXPENDITURE
ACCOUNTING—
GOVERNMENTAL
FUNDS

Pension Plan Contributions

The GASB Codification (sec. Pe5.135–.136) requires, as noted earlier, that state and local government employers use acceptable actuarial methods in computing employer contribution liabilities under *defined benefit* pension plans, regardless of whether the actuarially required contribution has been made. Further, it requires that the *pension contribution expenditures and liabilities* be *recognized* in the *same* manner they are recognized for *CJCA.* Thus, if some of the actuarially required pension plan contributions for the year have not been paid or vouchered as payable at year end,

1. the amount that would normally be liquidated with expendable available financial resources of a governmental fund would be recorded as a fund expenditure and liability, and
2. the remaining amount would be recorded as a liability in the GLTDAG.

Most state-wide and other group plans require that participating employer governments make the actuarially required contributions promptly. However, some governments that manage their own single employer defined benefit pension plans do not make the actuarially required contributions. This may occur regularly, as when the legislative body routinely fails to appropriate the actuarially required amount, or only occasionally during financial crises. In any event, the amounts involved may be large—in the millions or even billions of dollars—both currently and cumulatively.

Since the **accounting and reporting for underfunded actuarially required pension contributions parallels that for CJCA,** a brief example should suffice here. Thus, if a government (1) that had no unfunded pension contribution liability at the beginning of the year, (2) had charged the pension contributions paid during the year to Expenditures, and (3) had an additional (unrecorded) unfunded actuarially required pension contribution of $800,000, of which $100,000 is considered a "current" liability of the General Fund, the adjusting entry (omitting subsidiary ledger entries) in the General Fund at year end would be:

Expenditures.	100,000	
Current Liability—Pension Contribution		100,000
To record additional *expenditures* for the *"current"* portion of		
the *unfunded actuarially required pension contribution* at		
year end.		

The remaining $700,000 would be recorded as a liability in the GLTDAG.

The main practical problem in recording unfunded actuarially required pension plan contributions, assuming acceptable actuarial information is available, lies in determining the "current" portion of the accrued liability. Whereas certain (sometimes different) rules of thumb have evolved for making this determination with respect to CJCA liabilities, no such guidelines appear to have evolved for unfunded pension plan liabilities. Thus, the amount considered to be that which "would normally be liquidated with expendable available financial resources"—a difficult standard to interpret and apply at best—appears to range from zero to the amount (if any) that is to be paid during the next year to alleviate the current year underfunding. The GASB is studying pension expenditure measurement and plans to issue new guidance on this area during the next two to three years.

Restatements may also be required to report the **cumulative effect** of **changes in accounting principles.** Four types of events that might cause, or result from, a change in the expenditure recognition accounting principles of a governmental fund are:

- A type of **expenditure not previously** deemed to be **objectively measurable** such as claims and judgments—may **now** be considered **reasonably estimable.**

- Where there are acceptable alternative expenditure recognition principles— such as the purchases and consumption bases of inventory and prepayment expenditure recognition—management might **change from one acceptable alternative principle to the other.**

- Where there are two or more acceptable methods of applying an accounting principle—such as the FIFO, LIFO, and average cost methods of inventory accounting on the consumption basis using a periodic method—management might **change the method of applying the principle.**

- The GASB or another recognized standards-setting body may issue a **new expenditure recognition standard** that requires a different expenditure accounting policy than that presently used.

Two of these types of events and changes in accounting principles and the methods of applying principles are discussed briefly in this section.

Changes between Alternative Principles

To illustrate the implementation of changes between acceptable alternative principles, assume that a government decides to change from the purchases to the consumption method of General Fund inventory accounting. The fully reserved purchases basis inventory at the end of the prior year was $100,000. The entry at the beginning of the current year to implement the change to the consumption method would be:

Reserve for Inventory.   100,000
    Cumulative Effect of Change in Accounting Principle   100,000
To effect change in inventory accounting from purchases to
    consumption basis.

The logic underlying this entry is that (1) under the purchases basis the inventory purchases had been charged to expenditures, resulting in an "understatement" of Unreserved Fund Balance, and (2) recording Inventory as required under the purchases method results in crediting Unreserved Fund Balance, correcting its "misstatement," but also requires that a Reserve for Inventory be established. Thus, assuming no reserve is needed under the consumption method, the consumption basis may be implemented by the above entry. If a reserve were desired, it could be established after this entry or compounded with it—for example, if a $30,000 reserve were desired the Reserve for Inventory account would be debited $70,000 and Unreserved Fund Balance would be debited $30,000.

Changed GASB Standards

Changes in accounting principles may also occur because the GASB (or another recognized standards-setting body, discussed in Chapter 2) issues a new expenditure recognition standard or revises an existing standard. If the new or revised ex-

229

Chapter 6
EXPENDITURE
ACCOUNTING—
GOVERNMENTAL
FUNDS

penditure recognition standard requires a different expenditure recognition principle than that presently being used in its governmental fund accounting, a state or local government must change its accounting policy to comply with the new or revised standard.

As noted in the discussion on revenue-related accounting changes in Chapter 5, GASB and other standards pronouncements specify when (at the latest) and how the new standards are to be implemented. If a new standard is to be applied ***"prospectively"***—that is, only to transactions and events occurring on or after the implementation date—the change will ***not*** have a "cumulative effect" on the beginning fund balance. For example, such a standard might specify that, from the implementation date forward, certain transactions that had previously been reported as expenditures be reported as "other financing uses."

Most new or revised standards require ***"retroactive"*** application, however. That is, the new expenditure recognition standard is to be implemented "as if" it had been applied in prior periods. Accordingly, the entry to implement new "retroactive application" expenditure recognition standards resembles a correction entry—as do those illustrated earlier in this section—except that the cumulative effect is reported as the "cumulative effect of change(s) in accounting principles."

CONCLUDING COMMENTS

Several significant conceptual, standards, and procedural considerations are important in governmental fund expenditure accounting and reporting. Most are discussed at least briefly in this chapter and some are discussed in detail and illustrated.

The concept and definition of expenditures in a governmental fund context were considered initially and at several points throughout the chapter, as were related GASB standards. Brief discussions of expenditure accounting controls and procedures—over personal services, purchases of materials and supplies, and other services and charges—included discussions and illustrations of related matters such as the purchases and consumption methods of inventory and prepayment accounting and accounting for capital leases. Other important expenditure accounting topics—including claims and judgments, compensated absences, unfunded pension contributions, debt service, and encumbrances—were discussed and illustrated in the section on adjusting entries. In addition, several other important expenditure accounting topics were discussed and illustrated—such as accounting for appropriations revisions, allocations and allotments, and changes in expenditure-related accounting principles—and expenditure account classification, varying annual appropriation encumbrance assumptions, and continuing appropriations are discussed and illustrated in Appendices 6-1, 6-2, and 6-3.

Some of the unresolved governmental fund expenditure-related issues also were noted. The most significant relate to the definitions of "fund liability" and "fund expenditure," particularly the definition of "current liability" in the CJCA context as the amount accrued during the year that would "normally be liquidated with expendable available financial resources" of a governmental fund. Significant changes in both revenue and expenditure recognition have been adopted by the GASB, but other major related issues are as yet unresolved. The GASB therefore prohibits implementation of its conclusions—set forth in GASB Statement 11, "Measurement Focus and Basis of Accounting—Governmental Fund

Operating Statements," until its effective date. Since **implementation is prohibited** until at least 1995, we discuss this guidance separately in Chapter 10. The GASB staff has these and several other such matters under study.

Appendix 6-1
CLASSIFICATION OF EXPENDITURES

The GASB Codification states that governmental fund expenditures should be classified by (1) function or program, (2) activity, (3) organization unit, (4) character, and (5) object classes, as well as by fund. Each of these expenditure classifications is discussed and illustrated here.

CLASSIFICATION BY FUNCTION OR PROGRAM

According to the GASB Codification:

> **Function or program** classification provides information on the **overall purposes** or **objectives** of expenditures. **Functions** group related activities that are aimed at accomplishing a major service or regulatory responsibility. **Programs** group activities, operations, or organizational units that are directed to the attainment of specific purposes or objectives.[24]

A government may choose between function and program classification, but should use one or the other. The reason for this is that some governments are organized and budgeted by functions, whereas others are organized and budgeted by programs (as noted in Chapter 3), so this *option* permits governments to use the corresponding functional or program classification in accounting and financial reporting.

A typical governmental unit provides a wide spectrum of services; many provide services that are also provided by other governmental units. For example, typical city, county, and state governments all provide for public safety. If they all select the accounts necessary to record their expenditures for public safety from a standard classification, a total figure may be accumulated for a state or for the nation as a whole. Further, it makes possible comparisons of expenditure data between and among cities and counties of comparable size that have similar problems. Thus, the functional classification provides the basic structure for the classification of expenditures in the general purpose financial statements (GPFS).

Figure 6-1 presents a condensed standard classification of expenditures by function. *Observe the relationship between the broad functional classifications and the more detailed functional classifications.* Both have been used for illustrative purposes in budgets and journal entries earlier in the text, with the caveat that more detailed department or other organization unit and object class accounts would be used in practice.

Note also that the more detailed functional classifications summarize the organizational structure of many governments. Many governments may have several departments within at least some of the functions, but many smaller

---

[24] GASB Codification, sec. 1800.116. (Emphasis added.)

Figure 6-1   EXPENDITURE CLASSIFICATION—BY FUNCTIONS

Broad Functions or Functional Classifications		Functions	
Code*	Title	Code*	Title
1000–1999	General Government	1000	Legislative Branch
		1100	Executive Branch
		1200	Judicial Branch
		1300	Elections
		1400	Financial Administration
		1500	Other
2000–2999	Public Safety	2000	Police Protection
		2100	Fire Protection
		2200	Correction
		2300	Protective Inspection
3000–4999	Public Works	3000	Highways and Streets
		4000	Sanitation
5000–6999	Health and Welfare	5000	Health
		6000	Welfare
7000–7999	Education (Schools)		
8000–9999	Culture-Recreation	8000	Libraries
		9000	Parks
10000–14999	Conservation of Natural Resources	10000	Water Resources
		11000	Agricultural Resources
		12000	Mineral Resources
		13000	Fish and Game Resources
		14000	Other Natural Resources
15000–15999	Urban Redevelopment and Housing		
16000–16999	Economic Development and Assistance		
17000–17999	Economic Opportunity		
18000–19999	Debt Service	18000	Interest
		19000	Principal
		19500	Paying Agent's Fees
20000–20999	Intergovernmental		
21000–21999	Miscellaneous		

*Code numbers are illustrative only.

governments have only one department, at most, in each function. For example, in many smaller governments the Police Department *is* the Police Protection function. ***Thus, many governmental budgets, accounting systems, and charts of accounts are classified by departments or other organization units, rather than by functions, and the function or functional data are derived by aggregating the expenditure data by organizational unit.***

CLASSIFICATION BY ORGANIZATION UNIT

The GASB Codification states that:

Classification of expenditures by **organization unit** is essential to responsibility accounting. This classification ***corresponds with the governmental unit's organization structure.*** A particular organization unit may be charged with carrying out one or several activities or programs. Moreover, the same activity or program is sometimes carried on by several organization units because of its inherent nature or because of faulty organization structure.[25]

Sound budgetary control requires that authority and responsibility for the activities of the government be assigned in a definite fashion to its officials and employees. *Assignment of appropriations and related expenditures to organization units is essential if department heads are to be held responsible* for planning their activities and for controlling those activities authorized by the legislative body through the appropriations process. *Classifying expenditures by organization unit is therefore important because it provides the means for controlling expenditures and for definitively allocating and evaluating expenditure responsibility.* Stated differently, classifying expenditures by organizational unit is a prerequisite to effective "responsibility accounting" and to ensuring and evaluating proper "stewardship" of public funds.

There is no **standard classification** of expenditure accounts by organization **unit.** Rather, this expenditure classification should correspond with however the government is organized into departments or other units and subunits. Thus, in a government where the police, fire, and jail are separate departments—organizationally and budgetarily—this department structure would be the basis for expenditure classification by organization unit. But, if in another government the jail is organized as an integral part of the Police Department, the jail would be budgeted and accounted for as a subunit of the Police Department.

Further, except in the smallest governments, departments may contain two or more subunits. For example, a Police Department may be organized by such subunits as street patrol, vehicle patrol, detectives, and vice and drug abuse control—each having separate appropriations line items or executive allocations. In all cases *the expenditure accounts should be set up in at least as much detail as is necessary for appropriations and allocations control and accountability.*

If the planning and execution of government functions, programs, and activities are to be properly controlled, activities must be properly allocated to departments. Ideally, a major department would be assigned responsibility for a function or program and its subunits would be assigned responsibility for the several activities necessary to carry out the function or program.

CLASSIFICATION BY ACTIVITY

An *activity* is a specific line of work performed by a governmental unit as part of one of its functions or programs. Ordinarily, several activities are required to fulfill a function or program.

A minimum requirement is that responsibility for an activity should be assigned to only one organization unit. Those units that cover more than one activity should have their budgeting, accounting, reporting, and administration arranged so that assignments or allocations of costs can be made by activity. Organization by activity is highly desirable because it facilitates precise assignment of authority and responsibility and because it simplifies accounting for and controlling activities.

---

[25] Ibid., sec. 1800.117. (Emphasis added.)

233

Chapter 6
EXPENDITURE
ACCOUNTING—
GOVERNMENTAL
FUNDS

The typical classifications of activities (and illustrative account codes) for the police protection function are:

2000 Police Protection Function
    2010 Police Administration
    2020 Crime Control and Investigation
        2021 Criminal Investigation
        2022 Vice Control
        2023 Patrol
        2024 Records and Identification
        2025 Youth Investigation and Control
        2026 Custody of Prisoners
        2027 Custody of Property
        2028 Crime Laboratory
    2030 Traffic Control
        2031 Motor Vehicle Inspection and Regulation
    2040 Police Training
    2050 Support Services
        2051 Communications Services
        2052 Automotive Services
        2053 Ambulance Services
        2054 Medical Services
        2055 Special Detail Services
        2056 Police Stations and Buildings

Expenditure data classified by activity are ***not*** required to be presented in ***published*** financial statements, but are intended primarily for ***managerial*** use. The GASB Codification observes that:

> **Activity** classification is particularly significant because it **facilitates evaluation of the economy and efficiency** of operations by providing data for calculating expenditures per unit of activity. That is, the expenditure requirements of performing a given unit of work can be determined by classifying expenditures by activities and providing for performance measurement where such techniques are practicable. These expenditure data, in turn, can be **used in preparing future budgets and in setting standards** against which future expenditure levels can be evaluated.[26]

In addition, it notes the usefulness of activity expenditure data when expense data need to be derived for managerial decision-making purposes:

> Further, activity expenditure data provide a convenient starting point for calculating total and/or unit expenses of activities where that is desired, for example, for "make or buy" or "do or contract out" decisions. Current operating expenditures (total expenditures less those for capital outlay and debt service) may be adjusted by depreciation and amortization data derived from the account group records to determine activity expense.[27]

---

[26] Ibid., sec. 1800.118. (Emphasis added.)
[27] Ibid.

Many services traditionally provided by state and local governments are being **"privatized"**—that is, contracted for from private firms or even relocated to the private sector, perhaps with regulation—or are being considered for partial or full privatization. Thus, while not required for external financial reporting, expenditure data classified by activity may be very important for internal uses.

Classifying expenditures by activity is essential to secure cost (expenditure basis) data for budget preparation and managerial control. Unit cost accounting (expenditure or expense basis) is possible only if (1) expenditures are classified by activities and (2) statistics concerning units of output are accumulated. Even if unit costs are not to be computed, the costs (expenditure and/or expense bases) of an activity should be compared with the benefits expected from it as a basis for deciding whether the scope of the activity should be increased, decreased, or left unchanged. Accumulating cost data by activities also permits comparing such costs between governmental units and accumulating cost data by function or program.

This discussion of activity classification also *illustrates the need to distinguish the expenditure and expense measurement concepts, both conceptually and in practice, and to use appropriate terminology.* Too often, the term "expense" is used (e.g., operating expense) when the measurement being described is "expenditures." Using these terms improperly, or interchangeably as if they were synonymous, causes confusion and should be avoided.

CLASSIFICATION BY CHARACTER

The **character** classification, which has been used in earlier illustrative examples, identifies expenditures by *the period benefited.* The three main character classifications are **current operating, capital outlay,** and **debt service.** A fourth category, *intergovernmental,* is needed where one government transfers resources to another, as when states transfer shared revenues to local governments. (As noted earlier, a state should account for *pass-through* grants to local governments in an Agency Fund. Only the amount to be retained by the state would be recognized as state revenues: amounts remitted to local governments would not be recognized as state revenues nor expenditures.)

Current operating expenditures are those expenditures expected to benefit primarily the current period, such as for salaries and utilities. **Capital outlays** are those expenditures expected to benefit not only the current period but also future periods. Purchases of desks, trucks, and buildings are examples of capital outlays. Maturing long-term debt principal, interest on debt, and related service charges are **debt service expenditures.** Payments made from the General Fund or Special Revenue Funds to Debt Service funds for these purposes are operating transfers that ultimately will finance Debt Service Fund expenditures, perhaps many years hence. Though debt service expenditures are sometimes said to be expenditures that are made for past benefits, where debt proceeds were used to acquire capital outlay items, the expenditures may "benefit" past, present, and future periods.

Just as expenditure data by function or program can be derived by summarizing departmental (organization unit) expenditure data, *data by character can be derived by aggregating data by object classes* (discussed later). Thus, some accounting systems and charts of accounts do not provide for expenditure classification by character, but obtain it by "rolling up" the expenditure data classified by object classes.

CLASSIFICATION BY OBJECT CLASSES

The **"object class" (object of expenditure)** classification groups expenditures according to the type of article purchased or service obtained. The following is a standard *classification of object classes related to the character classification* as indicated:

Character	Object Class
01–03* Current Operating	01 Personal Services
	02 Supplies
	03 Other Services and Charges
04–07 Capital Outlay	04 Land
	05 Buildings
	06 Improvements Other Than Buildings
	07 Machinery and Equipment
08–10 Debt Service	08 Debt Principal
	09 Interest
	10 Debt Service Charges
11 Intergovernmental	11 Intergovernmental

Code numbers are illustrative only.

The preceding object classes under Current Operating are *major* classifications. A small municipality, or a small organization unit in a larger municipality, might find that "personal service," "supplies," and "other services and charges" provide enough detail for administrative and reporting purposes. In most cases, however, each of these classifications would be subdivided into more detailed classifications. *Personal services* could be subdivided into salaries, wages, employer contributions to the retirement system, insurance, sick leave, terminal pay, and the like. The *supplies* category may be detailed in whatever way proves useful: at a minimum as among office supplies, operating supplies, and repair and maintenance supplies. *Other services and charges* include such costs as professional services, communications, transportation, advertising, printing, and binding. In certain circumstances it might be very useful to the administration to further subdivide some or all of the foregoing into even greater detail. For example, it might be useful to divide communications into such categories as telephone, telegraph, and postage.

The main object classes ordinarily provide sufficient detail for the GPFS and other summarized reports of the public, including the budgetary comparison statement of the GPFS. Classification by the main object classes also may provide sufficient detail to demonstrate budgetary compliance. This depends, of course, on the detail in which the appropriations by the legislative body are considered binding on the executive branch. *If budgetary compliance is at a more detailed level, then a budgetary compliance schedule must be presented at the more detailed level and the accounts must be classified at the more detailed level.* Thus, providing greater amounts of detail by object of expenditure in the accounts should be based on administrative need for such information for planning, controlling, and evaluating the operations of the governmental unit.

235

Appendix 6-2
ACCOUNTING FOR ANNUAL APPROPRIATIONS—
VARIOUS ENCUMBRANCES ASSUMPTIONS

The discussions and illustrations in Chapter 4 assumed that the annual appropriations lapse at the end of each year but that the Encumbrances account should be closed to Unreserved Fund Balance to establish the Reserve for Encumbrances account as a true reservation of fund balance. We referred to this assumption as "Assumption A1." This assumption is reviewed and several other assumptions that may be encountered in accounting for encumbrances of annually budgeted governmental funds in which appropriations lapse at year end are discussed and illustrated briefly in this appendix. Only General Ledger entries are presented since the Expenditures Subsidiary Ledger entries would be the same in all cases. These assumptions are summarized in Figure 6-2, along with other assumptions relating to continuing appropriations—which are discussed in the next appendix to this chapter.

ASSUMPTION A1

The General Fund closing entries illustrated in Chapter 4 (pages 128–129) were based on certain assumptions about the laws and policies of A Governmental Unit:

> **Assumption A1.** (1) All unexpended appropriations lapse at year end, even if encumbered; (2) the unit is committed to accept the goods or services on order at year end; (3) expenditures resulting from encumbrances outstanding at the end of a year must be charged against the next year's appropriations; and (4) the **Reserve for Encumbrances should be left open and be reported as a reservation of fund balance in the year-end balance sheet.**

Recall that the **"reserve"** entry at the **end of 19X1** was:

Unreserved Fund Balance	20,000	
Encumbrances		20,000

To close the Encumbrances account and cause the Reserve for
  Encumbrances to be a true reservation of fund balance.

Under Assumption A1, the Reserve for Encumbrances balance reported in the 19X1 year end balance sheet serves (1) as a reminder to those preparing the 19X2 budget to include $20,000 appropriations for 19X2 expenditures expected to result from encumbrances outstanding at the end of 19X1 as well as (2) to inform readers of the financial statements of the commitments outstanding at the end of 19X1 that are expected to result in expenditures in 19X2. The entry at the **start of 19X2** returns the Encumbrances and Reserve for Encumbrances accounts to their usual offsetting relationship in the General Ledger, causing the Reserve for Encumbrances to no longer be a true Fund Balance reserve, and increases the Unreserved Fund Balance account accordingly. In essence, this entry restores the affected accounts to the balances and relationships that would have existed if encumbrances had never been closed.

Encumbrances	20,000	
Unreserved Fund Balance		20,000

To reestablish Encumbrances in the accounts and return
  Encumbrances and Reserve for Encumbrances to offsetting
  memorandum accounts.

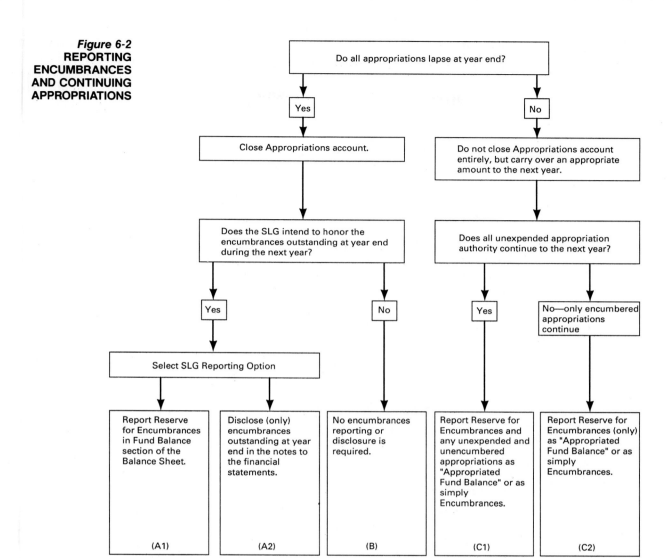

Figure 6-2
REPORTING ENCUMBRANCES AND CONTINUING APPROPRIATIONS

Do all appropriations lapse at year end?

Yes

Close Appropriations account.

Does the SLG intend to honor the encumbrances outstanding at year end during the next year?

Yes

No

Select SLG Reporting Option

Report Reserve for Encumbrances in Fund Balance section of the Balance Sheet.

(A1)

Disclose (only) encumbrances outstanding at year end in the notes to the financial statements.

(A2)

No encumbrances reporting or disclosure is required.

(B)

No

Do not close Appropriations account entirely, but carry over an appropriate amount to the next year.

Does all unexpended appropriation authority continue to the next year?

Yes

No—only encumbered appropriations continue

Report Reserve for Encumbrances and any unexpended and unencumbered appropriations as "Appropriated Fund Balance" or as simply Encumbrances.

(C1)

Report Reserve for Encumbrances (only) as "Appropriated Fund Balance" or as simply Encumbrances.

(C2)

ASSUMPTION A2

Another legal and policy situation that may be encountered is where all appropriations lapse, whether or not encumbered, as in Assumption A1—but there is **no statutory or policy requirement that the Reserve for Encumbrances be reported in the balance sheet.** This variation of Assumption A1, which we shall call Assumption **A2,** may be summarized:

> **Assumption A2.** (1) All unexpended appropriations lapse at year end, even if encumbered; (2) the unit is committed to accept the goods or services on order at year end; (3) expenditures resulting from encumbrances outstanding at the end of a year must be authorized by and charged against the next year's appropriations; and (4) **a Reserve for Encumbrances is *not* required to be reported in the year-end balance sheet.**

Under Assumption A2, management may choose to report the Reserve for Encumbrances in the balance sheet as required by Assumption A1. If so, the entries illustrated earlier for the end of 19X1 and the beginning of 19X2 are applicable.

Alternatively, management may choose to **report the encumbrances outstanding only in the notes to the financial statements and not by a Reserve for Encumbrances** in the 19X1 year-end balance sheet. In this case **both** the **Encumbrances and Reserve for Encumbrances** accounts usually are **closed.** Accordingly, the General Ledger closing entry for the General Fund appropriations, expenditures, and encumbrances would be:

Appropriations	426,000	
Reserve for Encumbrances	20,000	
Expenditures		398,400
Encumbrances		20,000
Unreserved Fund Balance		27,600

To close the accounts at year end.

Note that the Unreserved Fund Balance account would reflect total fund balance (except for any other reserves) in this case, and no Reserve for Encumbrances would be reported in the General Fund balance sheet. Note also that if both Encumbrances and Reserve for Encumbrances are closed at the end of 19X1 both must be reestablished in the accounts, by the reverse of the closing entry, at the start of 19X2:

Encumbrances	20,000	
Reserve for Encumbrances		20,000

To reestablish these accounts at the beginning of 19X2.

ASSUMPTION B

A third variation in the legal status of appropriations at year end, which we shall call Assumption **B,** may be summarized:

> Assumption B. (1) **All unexpended appropriations lapse,** even if encumbered; and (2) **all encumbrances are null and void after year end.**

The essence of this legal circumstance is that each year stands clearly apart. Vendors must perform by 19X1 year end or seek new 19X2 contracts, which may or may not be approved, to provide the goods or services in 19X2. Purchase orders typically carry a notice to this effect in boldface type in this situation. While the essence of Assumption B differs markedly from that of Assumptions A1 and A2, the General Fund accounting *entries at the end of 19X1* are the *same as* those for *Assumption A2,* illustrated previously. Under Assumption B both the Encumbrances and Reserve for Encumbrances accounts should be *closed* at the end of 19X1, and neither Encumbrances nor Reserve for Encumbrances is reported or disclosed in the General Fund statements at year end. There would be no Encumbrances and Reserve for Encumbrances entry in 19X2 until new 19X2 encumbrances were incurred.

Appendix 6-3
ACCOUNTING FOR CONTINUING APPROPRIATIONS

To this point we have assumed that annual appropriations of governmental funds are made for a year and that the appropriation authority lapses at year end. This is the usual case with appropriations of General, Special Revenue, and Debt Service

239

Chapter 6
EXPENDITURE
ACCOUNTING—
GOVERNMENTAL
FUNDS

Funds, and usually is the case with other annually budgeted governmental funds. However, the **appropriations** of Capital Projects Funds, in particular, are often made for the **project**—and thus **continue as valid appropriation authority until expended or the project has been completed**—and thus do not lapse at the end of each fiscal year. Continuing appropriations also may be made for all other governmental fund types—**for specified purposes and for two years or longer periods, or until expended**—particularly by state governments.

Two variations in the legal provisions and policies where some or all of the unexpended appropriations continue as expenditure authority until at least the following year are discussed and illustrated in this section. They are referred to as Assumption C1 and Assumption C2. While only one of these assumptions is commonly used in General Fund accounting, we illustrate them in the General Fund context of Chapter 4 so that the effects of all five assumptions may readily be compared.

ASSUMPTION C1

This assumption is commonly used with Capital Projects Fund and other appropriations made on a **project basis** rather than an annual basis. Appropriations made under Assumption **C1** thus **continue** as valid expenditure authority **until expended or the project is completed.** This assumption may be summarized succinctly:

> **Assumption C1. Unexpended appropriations continue** (do not lapse at year end) **to the next period(s);** that is, **only expended appropriations lapse** at year end.

In this situation—since **only** the **expended appropriations lapse at year end**—only the Expenditures, $398,400, should be closed against Appropriations. That is, the 19X1 year-end General Fund closing entry for A Governmental Unit under Assumption C1 should leave a $27,600 balance in the Appropriations account, and would be:

Appropriations [$27,600 left]	398,400	
Expenditures		398,400
To close the accounts at year end.		

Further, when appropriations continue the "Fund Balance" section of the governmental fund balance sheet must include a Reserve for Encumbrances for the encumbrances against the continuing appropriations. Accordingly, the Encumbrances account should be closed as in Assumption A1. But, **since it now relates to the continuing appropriation** (rather than to Unreserved Fund Balance), **the Encumbrances account is closed to the Appropriations account.**

Appropriations	20,000	
Encumbrances		20,000
To close encumbrances against continuing appropriations at year end.		

Note that the **postclosing** balance of the Appropriations account does not represent the total appropriation, but only the **unencumbered** appropriation, and that the fund balance section of the General Fund balance sheet (Figure 4-6) prepared under Assumption C1 at the end of 19X1 would appear as:

Fund Balance:
   Appropriated:
      Reserved for encumbrances (or Encumbered) $20,000
      Unencumbered 7,600 $27,600
   Unappropriated   21,800
                                       49,400

Alternatively, some practitioners prefer to present the fund balance section only as "reserved" and "unreserved":

Fund Balance:
   Reserved:
      For encumbrances $20,000
      For future years' expenditures 7,600 $27,600
   Unreserved   21,800
                                       49,400

       The encumbrances closing entry would be **reversed** at the **beginning of 19X2:**

Encumbrances 20,000
   Appropriations   20,000
To reverse the 19X1 entry closing the encumbrances account.

This reversing entry restores the Appropriations account to its full $27,600 **unexpended** balance, returns the Encumbrances and Reserve for Encumbrances accounts to their usual offsetting relationship, and records the encumbrances in the appropriate Expenditures Subsidiary Ledger accounts (omitted here).

ASSUMPTION C2

In order to avoid making new appropriations to authorize expenditures resulting from valid encumbrances incurred against the prior year's appropriations, the policy of some governments is that **encumbered** appropriations **continue** to the next period. In some cases the encumbered appropriations continue throughout the following year; but in other cases they continue for only a short period considered sufficient for the goods and services encumbered during the prior year to be delivered and billed—often 60–90 days—and then lapse. At that time the unexpended balance is restored to the Unreserved Fund Balance.

     The Assumption **C2** assumptions may be summarized succinctly:

> **Assumption C2. Encumbered appropriations continue** (do not lapse at year end) to the next period; that is, only **unencumbered appropriations lapse** at year end.

In this case—since **encumbered appropriations do not lapse**—the closing entry should leave on the books Appropriations, Encumbrances, and Reserve for Encumbrances in the $20,000 amount of the encumbrances outstanding. Thus, the

241

Chapter 6
EXPENDITURE
ACCOUNTING—
GOVERNMENTAL
FUNDS

General Ledger 19X1 closing entry for appropriations, expenditures, and encumbrances would appear as:

Appropriations [$20,000 left]	406,000	
Expenditures		398,400
Unreserved Fund Balance		7,600
To close the accounts at year end.		

Further, as in Assumption C1, the Encumbrances account would be closed against the Appropriations account to *"reserve" fund balance:*

Appropriations	20,000	
Encumbrances		20,000
To close encumbrances against continuing appropriations at year end.		

This leaves a zero balance in the postclosing Appropriations account—obviously the correct **unencumbered** balance under Assumption C2 since only encumbered appropriations continue (that is, unencumbered appropriations lapse). The fund balance section of the General Fund balance sheet at the end of 19X1 under assumption C2 would appear as:

Fund Balance:	
Appropriated:	
Reserved for Encumbrances	$20,000
Unappropriated	29,400
	49,400

Alternatively, under the "reserved-unreserved" approach the fund balance would appear:

Fund Balance	
Reserved for Encumbrances	$20,000
Unreserved	29,400
	49,400

Then, at the ***beginning of 19X2*** the encumbrance closing entry will be **reversed,** as in Assumption C1, returning the Appropriations account to its full $20,000 balance, restoring the Encumbrances–Reserve for Encumbrances offsetting relationship, and recording the encumbrances in the related Expenditures Subsidiary Ledger accounts (omitted here):

Encumbrances	20,000	
Appropriations		20,000
To reverse the 19X1 entry closing the encumbrances account.		

Finally, recall that a government's budgetary basis may be a **non**-GAAP basis that treats encumbrances as expenditures for budgetary purposes. If so, the substance of the budgetary and appropriations laws and policies must be recognized. Thus, if an SLG adopts an annual operating budget on a "modified accrual plus encumbrances" basis, it is ***in substance*** under Assumption C2 because (1) no new appropriation authority need be provided to complete the encumbered transactions and (2) some of the net assets on hand at year end are needed to complete these transactions and are therefore ***not*** available to finance expenditures arising from future year appropriations.

QUESTIONS

6-1 Distinguish between an expenditure in the governmental accounting sense and an expense in the commercial accounting sense.

6-2 When should General Fund expenditures be recognized? What are the major exceptions?

6-3 Distinguish between and among the four character-of-expenditures classifications.

6-4 What expenditures-related General Ledger control accounts might be used in the General Fund?

6-5 The appropriations of a certain government for current expenditures lapse at the end of the fiscal year for which made, while appropriations for capital outlay lapse two years later. Discuss the desirability of this dual arrangement.

6-6 On January 2, 19X1, materials costing $100 were issued from perpetual inventory to the Police Department. What General Ledger journal entry or entries should be made?

6-7 A governmental unit takes advantage of purchase discounts by paying its bills promptly. Should the full purchase price be recorded in the records with the discounts treated as revenues, or should the purchases be recorded at their net cost (i.e., after deduction of discounts)?

6-8 Some argue that General Fund payments to a pension fund for the city's share of pension fund contributions should be charged to the departments in which the covered employees work. Do you agree? Explain.

6-9 In one municipality vouchers must be approved not only by the finance officer but also by the finance committee of the city council. Is the approval of the finance committee desirable? Give reasons.

6-10 Explain how you would decide whether or not to encumber a planned expenditure.

6-11 The newly elected mayor of the Town of Dewey is a well-respected businessman. He is perplexed because the town's finance director has given him an interim financial statement that reports repayment of a ten-year note through the General Fund as an expenditure. The mayor is aware that several short-term notes were repaid during the interim period as well, and these are not reported. "Two things puzzle me," says the mayor. "First, why should repayment of a note be reported as an expenditure? We decreased our assets and liabilities by equal amounts; therefore, the city's equity did not change. Second, why is only part of the principal retirement reported as expenditures if such a practice is appropriate? Respond to the mayor.

6-12 Why would an executive branch make allocations and or allotments of appropriations authorized by the legislative branch? How do (a) allocations and (b) allotments of appropriations affect accounting for a governmental fund's expenditures?

6-13 An accountant for the Town of Don's Grove previously worked for the City of Victorville. Don's Grove records purchases of materials and supplies as expenditures and reports any change in the inventory of materials and supplies in its Statement of Revenues, Expenditures, and Changes in (Total) Fund Balance. The accountant recalls, however, that the City of Victorville recorded expenditures for materials and supplies when they were used, not when they were purchased. Also, Victorville did not report changes in inventory in its Statement of Revenues, Expenditures, and Changes in (Total) Fund Balance. The accountant asks his supervisors which way is correct. Respond.

6-14 When is "fully reserving" Fund Balance for inventory on hand appropriate? Explain.

6-15 Why do governmental fund accounting standards allow both the consumption basis and the purchases basis of inventory accounting?

6-16 Why might a school district change from using certain expenditure recognition principles to different expenditure recognition principles?

6-17 Why are adjusting entries often required in governmental funds at year end in accounting for claims and judgments?

6-18 (Appendix 6-1) Explain how an accounting system can be designed to produce information for all the bases of expenditure classification and still produce information useful for managerial purposes.

6-19 (Appendix 6-1) The clerk of the City of Wilmaton is revising the city accounting system so that she can report expenditures by function, organization unit, activity, character, and object class as well as by fund. Her assistant is perturbed because he

243

Chapter 6
EXPENDITURE
ACCOUNTING—
GOVERNMENTAL
FUNDS

considers all these classifications unnecessary and, he states: "It will take five extra sets of books to record expenditures this way. Every expenditure will have to be recorded six times!" Explain to the assistant (a) the purpose of each expenditure classification and (b) how to implement the multiple classification scheme without multiplying the work required to record expenditures.

6-20 (Appendices 6-2 and 6-3) Discuss the several common legal assumptions as to the lapsing of appropriations for the benefit of a committee to write the charter for a newly incorporated village.

6-21 (Appendices 6-2 and 6-3) The postclosing trial balance of the General Fund contains, in three different cases, balances for the following accounts, among others:

Case 1: Reserve for Encumbrances   Case 2: Unreserved Fund Balance
         Unreserved Fund Balance   Case 3: Reserve for Encumbrances
         Appropriations   Unreserved Fund Balance

On which legal assumption may the closing entries have been based in each case?

PROBLEMS

P 6-1 (Multiple Choice) Indicate the best answer to each question.

1. A county entered into a capital lease on June 30, 19X8 for equipment to be used by General Fund departments. The capitalizable cost of the leased asset was $200,000. An initial payment of $20,000 was made at the inception of the lease. The first annual lease payment of $35,000 is due on July 1, 19X9. Assuming a 10 percent implicit rate of interest on the lease, the county should report General Fund expenditures in the fiscal year ended December 31, 19X8 as follows:

    a. Capital outlay expenditures of $20,000

    b. Capital outlay expenditures of $200,000

    c. Capital outlay expenditures of $20,000 and interest expenditures of $9,000

    d. Capital outlay expenditures of $200,000 and interest expenditures of $9,000

    e. Rent expenditures of $20,000 and no capital outlay or debt service expenditures

2. The county in 1 paid its first $35,000 lease payment as scheduled on July 1, 19X9. The county should report General Fund expenditures for the fiscal year ended December 31, 19X9 as follows:

    a. Rent expenditures of $35,000

    b. Interest expenditures of $35,000

    c. Principal retirement expenditures

    d. Interest expenditures of $9,000 and principal retirement expenditures of $28,000

    e. Interest expenditures of $18,000 and principal retirement expenditures of $17,000

    f. Interest expenditures of $17,150 and principal retirement expenditures of $17,850

3. A city paid General Fund claims and judgments incurred during 19X1 of $20,000. Additional General Fund claims were incurred during 19X1 that are deemed probable to result in judgments against the city totaling $180,000. It is likely that these claims will not result in required payments for at least two years, however. The city General Fund expenditures reported for claims and judgments in 19X1 should be:

    a. $20,000

    b. $200,000

    c. $20,000 with $180,000 of other financing uses reported

    d. $200,000 with $180,000 of other financing sources reported

The following information pertains to questions 4 and 5.

A school district Special Revenue Fund's beginning materials inventory was $100,000; its ending materials inventory was $120,000. Materials costing $400,000 were purchased for the fund during the year. Accounts payable for the fund's materials were $17,000 at the beginning of the year and $7,000 at year end.

4. The school district should report expenditures for materials in its Special Revenue Fund of

If the School District Uses

	Purchases Method	Consumption Method
a.	$400,000	$400,000
b.	$400,000	$380,000
c.	$410,000	$380,000
d.	$400,000	$420,000
e.	$410,000	$420,000

5. If the school district presents its Special Revenue Fund statement of revenues, expenditures, and changes in fund balance in terms of changes in total fund balance, what amount(s) besides expenditures must be reported in that statement related to materials?

	Purchases Method	Consumption Method
a.	Nothing	Nothing
b.	Other financing source of $20,000	Other financing source of $20,000
c.	Nothing	Other financing source of $20,000
d.	Other financing source of $20,000	Nothing
e.	None of the above is correct.	

6. A state pays salaries and wages of $118 million to General Fund employees during a year. Unpaid, accrued salaries were $3 million at the beginning of the year and $6 million at year end. General Fund salary expenditures should be reported for the year in the amount of:

a. $115 million   c. $121 million

b. $118 million   d. $124 million

7. Equipment purchased for county General Fund departments on a line of credit with a supplier cost $800,000. $200,000 had been paid by year end, including $4,000 interest. The county expects to repay another $300,000, including $7,000 interest, during the first two months of the next fiscal year. The remaining balance is to be repaid by mid-year. Capital outlay expenditures should be reported for the county General Fund in the amount of:

a. $196,000   d. $493,000

b. $200,000   e. $800,000

c. $489,000

8. The minimum expenditure classifications required in the General Purpose Financial Statements for governmental funds are:

a. Fund and function or program

b. Fund, character, and function or program

c. Fund, character, and department

d. None of the above. The minimum required classifications are _____.

9. How should the purchase of land for General Fund purposes by issuing a three-year, $80,000, interest bearing note be reported in the General Fund statement of revenues, expenditures, and changes in fund balance?

a. No effect

b. Expenditures of $80,000

c. Expenditures of $80,000 and other financing sources of $80,000

d. Other financing uses of $80,000 and other financing sources of $80,000.

245

Chapter 6
EXPENDITURE
ACCOUNTING—
GOVERNMENTAL
FUNDS

10. Which of the following should be reported as expenditures in a county General Fund?

1. Reimbursement of a Special Revenue Fund for General Fund expenditures inadvertently paid for from and recorded in the Special Revenue Fund

2. Water services received from the town Water Enterprise Fund

3. Payment of the federal income tax withheld from employee paychecks to the federal government

4. Payment to a Debt Service Fund to provide resources for principal and interest payments that matured and were paid during the year

   a. 1 only

   b. 2 only

   c. 3 only

   d. 4 only

   e. 1 and 2 only

   f. None of the above. The correct answer is _____.

P 6-2 (GL & SL Budgetary Entries, Balances) The following General Fund appropriations were made for 19X4 by the City of Dulaney:

City Council	$ 15,000
Mayor.	15,000
Courts	30,000
City Clerk	15,000
Department of Finance.	30,000
Department of Police.	75,000
Department of Fire . . . . , ...	60,000
Department of Public Works	30,000
Interest.	15,000
Retirement of long-term notes	15,000
	$300,000

The following appropriations revisions and additional appropriations were subsequently authorized:

Reductions (from):	*Increases (to):*	*Amount*
City Council	City Clerk	$ 750
City Clerk	Mayor	1,500
Department of Finance	Department of Public Works	1,500
Department of Public Works	Courts	1,000

Additional Appropriations	*Appropriated for:*	*Amount*
	Department of Police	1,500
Reserve for Contingencies	Department of Fire	2,200
	City Council	750
	Department of Public Works	3,000

Estimated revenues are $350,000; the Council reserved $30,000 for contingencies.

Required (a) Prepare the GF journal entry necessary to record the adoption of the budget, showing both the General Ledger and the Expenditures Subsidiary Ledger accounts.

(b) Prepare the GF journal entry to record the revised and additional appropriations, showing both the General Ledger and the Subsidiary Ledger accounts involved.

(c) Prepare a statement showing the appropriation balances after the appropriations revisions and additional appropriations.

P 6-3 (Allotments) The following appropriations and first quarter allotments for 19X4 were made by Dogwood City's council and manager, respectively:

	19X4 Appropriations	First Quarter Allotments
City Council	$ 12,000	$ 3,000
Manager	40,000	11,000
Courts	30,000	7,000
City Clerk	20,000	5,000
Finance Department	35,000	10,000
Police Department	80,000	20,000
Fire Department	75,000	16,000
Public Works Department	45,000	12,000
Interest	15,000	—
Retirement of Notes	25,000	—
	$377,000	$84,000

Required Prepare the journal entry necessary to record the appropriations and first quarter allotments in both the General Ledger and the Expenditures Subsidiary Ledger accounts.

P 6-4 (Purchases vs. Consumption Basis) The City of Bettinger's Bend General Fund had a beginning inventory of materials and supplies of $6,000. The beginning balance of Fund Balance Reserved for Inventory was also $6,000.

1. Materials and supplies costing $74,000 were ordered during the year.
2. The materials and supplies ordered were received; actual cost, $72,800.
3. According to the physical inventory, $6,400 of materials and supplies were on hand at year end.

Required (a) Prepare general journal entries to record the information above using the **purchases** basis of accounting for inventories.

(b) Prepare general journal entries to record the information above using the **consumption** basis assuming (1) a periodic inventory system and (2) $6,000 is the base level of inventory.

P 6-5 (GL & SL Entries, Reconciliation) The City of Beverly Heights General Fund had the following transactions, among others, in 19X7:

1. Appropriations were made as follows:

Personal Services	$111,400
Contractual Services	8,700
Materials and Supplies	8,500
New Patrol Cars	21,000
Other	12,000
	$161,600

2. $2,000 of General Fund cash was paid to the Debt Service Fund to provide for debt service.
3. A long-term note of $8,300, including interest of $1,300, and a short-term note of $2,500 (including $150 interest) came due. The Beverly Heights Council had not made appropriations for these items. The necessary action was taken and the notes and interest were paid.
4. $100,000 of General Fund cash was paid to the Enterprise Fund to finance construction of a new auxiliary generator and $50,000 was contributed to establish a central motor pool facility. The Enterprise Fund will repay the General Fund in ten equal annual installments beginning January 1, 19X9.
5. The council increased the appropriation for personal services by $500.

247

Chapter 6
EXPENDITURE
ACCOUNTING—
GOVERNMENTAL
FUNDS

6. Materials and supplies are accounted for on the purchases basis. The beginning inventory was $200; $8,500 of materials and supplies were ordered during the year. New patrol cars costing $20,000 were also ordered.

7. The following expenditures were made by the city:

Personal Services.	$111,700	
Contractual Services	8,700	
Materials and Supplies.	7,500	(encumbered for $7,600)
New Patrol Cars	21,200	(encumbered for $20,000)
Other	11,800	
	$160,900	

The council passed the amendments to its appropriations necessary to make the foregoing expenditures legal.

8. Materials and supplies on hand at year end amounted to $1,000.

Required

(a) Prepare and post the general journal entries required to record the transactions in the General Ledger and in the Expenditures Ledger. Assume that there were no outstanding encumbrances at the beginning of 19X7.

(b) Prepare a trial balance of the Expenditures Ledger and prove its agreement with the control accounts.

(c) Prepare the general journal entries required to close the expenditure accounts in the General and Expenditures Ledgers. Assume that all appropriations lapse, but a reserve is reported for encumbrances outstanding at year end.

(d) Prepare the general journal entries required to close the expenditures accounts in the General and Expenditures Ledgers assuming that unexpended appropriations do not lapse.

P 6-6   (GL & SL Entries—Allotments) The Town of Dee's Junction General Fund was affected by the following transactions, among others, during its calendar 19X4 fiscal year:

1. Appropriations were made as follows:

Personal Services	$222,800
Contractual Services	17,400
Materials and Supplies	17,000
Firefighting Equipment	42,000
Other	24,000
	$323,200

The appropriation for materials and supplies covers a $1,800 order outstanding at the end of 19X3. An appropriate fund balance reserve is on the books (Assumption A1).

January transactions (2–8):

2. Allotments for the month of January were:

Personal Services	$20,800
Contractual Services	1,600
Materials and Supplies	3,000
Firefighting Equipment	35,000
Other	500
	$60,900

3. $15,000 of General Fund cash was paid to the Debt Service Fund to provide for debt service.

4. The Dee's Junction Council amended the budget, increasing the contractual services appropriation by $5,000 and decreasing the materials and supplies appropriation by $1,700. These budget amendments did not affect the January allotments.

5. Materials and supplies of $200 were acquired for cash and $1,200 of supplies were ordered during January. Materials ordered in 19X3 were received on January 8 at their estimated cost of $1,800. Materials and supplies are accounted for on the purchases basis.

6. The supplies ordered were received, with an invoice for $1,180.

7. Firefighting equipment costing $35,000 was ordered.

8. Other expenditures during January 19X4 were:

Personal Services	$20,800
Firefighting Equipment	
(included in January order–estimated cost	
$31,800)	32,000
Other	400
	$53,200

February through December transactions (9–11):

9. Allotments for the remainder of the year were:

Personal Services	$202,000
Contractual Services	15,800
Materials and Supplies	12,000
Firefighting Equipment	7,000
Other	11,500
	$248,300

10. Expenditures for the remainder of the year were:

Personal Services	$200,000
Contractual Services	12,000
Materials and Supplies	11,000
Firefighting Equipment	1,000
Other	11,500
	$235,500

11. In addition to the encumbrances for firefighting equipment, encumbrances of $1,000 for materials and supplies and $2,000 for contractual services were outstanding at year end. The inventory of materials and supplies decreased by $1,100 during the year.

Required   (a) Prepare the general journal entries to record the transactions in the General Ledger and in the Expenditures Ledger and post the Expenditures Ledger accounts.

(b) Prepare a trial balance of the January 31, 19X4, balances in the Expenditures Ledger. Show its agreement with the General Ledger control accounts.

(c) Prepare a preclosing trial balance of the year end balances in the Expenditures Ledger and show its agreement with the General Ledger control accounts.

(d) Prepare the general journal entries to close the expenditure accounts in the General and Expenditures Ledgers at year end.

P 6-7   (GL & SL Entries—Errors, Pensions, Changes, Leases, CJ, and so on) The following transactions and events relate to the General Fund of Antonio County for the 19X6 fiscal year.

1. Early in 19X6 it was discovered that at the end of 19X5 (a) the inventory of supplies was overstated $30,000, and (b) interest payable of $11,000 was not accrued.

249

Chapter 6
EXPENDITURE
ACCOUNTING—
GOVERNMENTAL
FUNDS

2. Appropriations were revised as follows:

Increased Appropriations:
Police Department—Supplies $10,000
Streets Department—Equipment 50,000
Decreased Appropriations:
Parks Department—Wages. 20,000

3. The county entered a capital lease for equipment that could have been purchased for $850,000 (which is also the net present value of the lease) for the Roads and Bridges Department.

4. An equipment capital lease payment, $80,000 (including $45,000 interest), was made.

5. Antonio County changed its method of inventory accounting from the purchases basis to the consumption basis (perpetual system) at the beginning of 19X6. The inventory of supplies at the end of 19X5 was $150,000; no inventory reserve is considered necessary under the consumption basis.

6. During the year it was found that (a) $12,000 charged to Fire Department—Contractual Services should have been charged to that account in the Police Department, and (b) $16,000 charged to salaries and wages in a Capital Projects Fund should have been charged to the Streets Department, which is financed from the General Fund.

7. At year end it was determined that the county had estimated liabilities (including legal fees and related costs and net of insurance reimbursements) for unsettled claims and judgments of $400,000, of which $100,000 is considered a current liability. The comparable estimated liability amounts (which had been properly recorded) at the end of 19X5 were $350,000 and $60,000, respectively.

8. The year-end physical count of the inventory of supplies revealed that $25,000 of supplies had been stolen; $20,000 will be recovered from the insurance company that bonds employees.

9. Although the actuarially required defined benefit pension plan contribution for 19X6 was $600,000, Antonio County made contributions of only $200,000. The County Commission voted to appropriate an additional $100,000 in the 19X7 budget—to be paid early in 19X7 and applied to the 19X6 contribution deficiency—but made no provision with respect to the remaining unfunded balance of the 19X6 contribution.

Required Prepare the journal entries to record these transactions and events in the General Ledger and Expenditures Subsidiary Ledger of the General Fund of Antonio County assuming that the county's accountant:

(a) Makes reversing entries at the beginning of the year for most prior year end adjusting entries.

(b) Does **not** make reversing entries at the beginning of each year for prior year end adjusting entries. (Make only those entries that differ from part a.)

P 6-8 (GL & SL Entries—Errors, Changes, Leases, Pensions, CJ, etc.) The following transactions and events relate to the General Fund of Harmer Township for the 19X8 fiscal year.

1. Early in 19X8 it was discovered that at the end of 19X7 (a) encumbrances recorded for equipment, $30,000, should have been recorded as an expenditure and liability, $31,000, and the liability was vouchered for payment; and (b) interest payable on tax anticipation notes, $16,000, was not accrued.

2. Appropriations were revised as follows:

Appropriations Decreased
Recreation Department—Salaries. $25,000
Parks Department—Equipment 30,000
Appropriations Increased
Fire Department—Equipment 70,000

3. The Township entered into a capital lease for computer equipment with a fair market value (and net present value) of $500,000.

4. A capital lease payment on the computer equipment, $60,000 (including $40,000 interest), was vouchered for payment.

5. Harmer Township changed its method of materials inventory accounting to the purchases basis from the consumption basis (no related reserve) at the beginning of 19X8. The beginning inventory of materials was $90,000.

6. During the year it was realized that (a) $44,000 of salaries and wages charged to the General Fund Parks Department appropriation should have been charged to a Special Revenue Fund, and (b) $19,000 charged to Police Department—Equipment should have been charged to the Fire Department.

7. At year end it was determined that the Township had estimated liabilities (including legal and related costs and net of insurance recoveries) for unsettled claims and judgments of $700,000, of which $160,000 is considered a current liability. This is the first year the school district has recorded such liabilities—they had not been considered reasonably estimable in prior years.

8. An internal audit during the year revealed that $30,000 had been embezzled and the Cash account was overstated by that amount. The insurance company that bonds employees has agreed to reimburse the Township $25,000 on this embezzlement.

9. Harmer Township paid only $150,000 to the trustee of its defined benefit pension plan during 19X8, even though the actuarially required contribution for 19X8 was $400,000. The governing board agreed to pay another $75,000 early in 19X9, but it is uncertain when the remaining pension plan underfunded contribution will be paid.

Required Prepare the journal entries to record these transactions and events in the General Ledger and Expenditures Ledger of the General Fund of Harmer Township for the 19X8 fiscal year.

P 6-9 **(Appendices 6-2 and 6-3)** (Various Appropriations & Encumbrances Assumptions) At December 31, 19X1, the City of X had in certain of its accounts the following balances: Appropriations, $200,000; Expenditures, $190,000; Encumbrances, $7,500; Reserve for Encumbrances, $7,500. On February 15, 19X2, the only item represented by the $7,500 encumbrance was billed to the city at $7,350. On the basis of the preceding information, prepare the closing entry, December 31, 19X1; entries required to be made January 1, 19X2, and February 15, 19X2; and the closing entry December 31, 19X2, for each of the five law and policy assumptions pertaining to the lapsing of appropriations and encumbrances outstanding at year end. Assume that continuing 19X1 appropriations lapse at the end of 19X2.

P 6-10 **(Appendices 6-2 and 6-3)** (Various Appropriations & Encumbrances Assumptions) Presented below are the balances of selected accounts of the Town of Bettinger's Haven General Fund at December 31, 19X5 before preparing year-end closing entries:

Unreserved Fund Balance	$ 85,000
Appropriations	1,000,000
Estimated Revenues	1,020,000
Expenditures	920,000
Encumbrances	50,000
Operating Transfers In	30,000
Revenues	980,000
Reserve for Advances	10,000
Reserve for Encumbrances	50,000

Required (a) Prepare the closing entry(ies) under each of the five law and policy assumptions pertaining to the lapsing of appropriations and encumbrances outstanding at year end.

(b) Prepare the fund balance section of the year-end balance sheet under each of the five assumptions.

(c) Indicate what footnote disclosures related to encumbrances are required under each assumption.

(d) Assuming the goods on order at year end were received January 15, 19X6 at an invoice price of $50,900, prepare any general journal entries required on January 1 and January 15, 19X6 under each of the five assumptions.

P 6-11 (Worksheets & Statements) The following information summarizes the operation of the Library Fund, a Special Revenue Fund of the City of Hillsdale:

1. The account balances at December 31, 19X0, were as follows:

Cash	$ 2,350
Reserve for Encumbrances.	1,000
Unreserved Fund Balance	1,350

2. Effective January 1, 19X1, the city council dedicated a portion of the property taxes of the city, together with all receipts from parking meters, to the Library Fund. The council's estimate of revenues from these sources follows:

Property Taxes	$ 50,000
Parking Meters	135,000
	$185,000

3. Planned expenditures for 19X1 were as follows:

General Administration	$ 50,000
Library-on-Wheels	40,000
Books.	90,000
	$180,000

The council's approval of expenditures included $1,000 for books ordered in 19X0.

4. Taxes of $52,500 were levied. It was expected that $2,000 would prove uncollectible.

5. Receipts during the year consisted of the following items:

Property Taxes	$ 51,500
Parking Meter Collections	136,000
Refund on Books Bought This Year	300
	$187,800

6. The following purchase orders were placed:

General Administration	$ 30,000
Library-on-Wheels	10,000
Books.	80,000
	$120,000

7. Certain of the orders placed in 19X0 and 19X1 were received. The vouchers together with the amount of the related purchase orders, are summarized as follows:

	Ordered	Vouchered
General Administration	$ 20,000	$ 21,500
Library-on-Wheels	10,000	10,000
Books	80,000	85,000
	$110,000	$116,500

8. Additional vouchers were prepared for the following purposes:

General Administration	$27,000
Library-on-Wheels	30,000
Books.	6,000
Refund of Overpayment of Taxes.	400
	$63,400

9. Vouchers were paid in the total amount of $178,000.

10. A physical inventory of $2,000 was taken on December 31, 19X1, and the city council directed that it be properly recorded. (Use the purchases method.) The $2,000 is applicable to General Administration.

11. Expenditures must be charged against appropriations of the year in which the expenditures are made. Any outstanding orders at year end must be honored, however, and are to be reported as fund balance reserves.

Required (a) Prepare a worksheet(s) that will show the Library Fund General Ledger and subsidiary ledger closing entries and balance sheet information at December 31, 19X1, and will summarize the information needed for the Statement of Revenues, Expenditures, and Changes in Fund Balance.

(b) Prepare the statements mentioned above.

P 6-12 (Worksheets, Closing Entries, Operating Statement) Waynesville had the following General Fund trial balance on January 1, 19X1, after the reversing entry for the 19X0 Encumbrances closing entry was made:

Cash	$ 7,000	
Taxes Receivable, Delinquent	48,000	
Allowance for Uncollectible Delinquent Taxes		$ 4,000
Due from Water Fund	500	
Vouchers Payable.		11,000
Due to Taxpayers.		1,000
Encumbrances.	3,000	
Reserve for Encumbrances		3,000
Appropriations (Police Department).		3,000
Unreserved Fund Balance.		36,500
	$58,500	$58,500

The following information summarizes the transactions of the General Fund during 19X1:

1. The city council approved the following budget for 19X1:

Expenditures:	
City Manager.	$20,000
Police Department	10,000
Fire Department.	10,000
Streets and Roads.	20,000
	$60,000

Revenues:	
Property Taxes	$75,000
Fines and Fees.	5,000
Miscellaneous	5,000
	$85,000

2. The council levied property taxes of $75,000. It was estimated that $2,000 of the amount would never be collected.

3. Cash collected during the year may be summarized as follows:

Prior years' levies.	$45,000
19X1 levy.	46,000
Fines and fees.	4,000
Taxes written off in prior years.	500
Interest.	500
Service charges	2,000
	$98,000

4. With council approval, $5,000 was borrowed on a 90-day note.

253

Chapter 6
EXPENDITURE
ACCOUNTING—
GOVERNMENTAL
FUNDS

5. Orders placed during the year were as follows:

City Manager	$ 4,000
Police Department	3,000
Fire Department.	3,000
Streets and Roads	5,000
	$15,000

6. Payrolls vouchered during the year were as follows:

City Manager	$15,000
Police Department	7,000
Fire Department.	6,500
Streets and Roads	14,000
	$42,500

7. Invoices vouchered during the year were as follows:

City Manager	$ 4,500
Police Department	6,100
Fire Department.	3,000
Streets and Roads	4,000
Repayment of note plus interest (see item 4)	5,200
	$22,800

The preceding invoices completed all orders except one dated June 1, 19X1, for an attachment for a Streets and Roads road grader for $950.

8. Payments to other funds:

Fund	Purpose	Amount
Debt Service Fund	Provide for payment of bond principal and interest	$ 8,000
Capital Projects	City contribution to construction of city park facilities	15,000
Water Fund	Water supply for Streets and Roads Department	1,500
		$24,500

9. Analysis of collections revealed that taxpayer A, to whom the city owed $1,000 on January 1, 19X1, for overpayment of taxes, had paid his tax for 19X1 less $1,000.

10. The Streets and Roads Department rendered services in the amount of $250 to the Water Fund.

11. The city council made an additional appropriation in the amount of $5,000 (including $600 interest) for a long-term note maturity which was overlooked in preparing the budget.

12. The note matured and was vouchered.

13. Vouchers of $70,000 were paid.

14. Delinquent Taxes in the amount of $500 were written off on the authority of the council.

15. Current taxes became delinquent.

Required (a) Prepare a worksheet or worksheets summarizing the year's operations in such a way that the General Ledger and subsidiary ledger closing entries and required statements may be easily prepared.

(b) Prepare the required closing entry(ies) for the General Ledger and subsidiary ledger accounts at year end.

(c) Prepare a Statement of Revenues, Expenditures, and Changes in Fund Balance for the General Fund of Waynesville for the year ended December 31, 19X1.

CAPITAL PROJECTS FUNDS

Capital Projects Funds are established to account for financial resources that are to be used to construct or otherwise acquire **major** long-lived **"general government" capital facilities**—such as buildings, highways, storm sewer systems, and bridges. Their principal purpose is to ensure the economical and legal expenditure of the resources, but they also serve as cost accounting mechanisms for controlling and accumulating the costs of major capital outlay projects. Further, Capital Projects Funds must be used whenever they are legally or contractually required for nonmajor capital asset acquisitions. Indeed, they may be used to account for any "general government" fixed asset acquisition.

Not all "general government" fixed asset acquisitions are financed through Capital Projects Funds. Routine fixed asset purchases—for example, school buses and photocopy equipment—may be acquired with resources of the General or Special Revenue Funds, unless prohibited by legal or contractual provisions. Likewise, capital leases usually do not involve "projects" and are reported in the General Fund or a Special Revenue Fund as discussed and illustrated in Chapter 6. And acquisitions of "specific fund" fixed assets are accounted for through proprietary funds and Trust Funds.

But major "general government" capital projects usually must be financed at least partly with bond issue proceeds or intergovernmental grants. And both bond covenants and grant agreements—as well as GAAP—often require that a Capital Projects Fund be used to account for the related projects. Further, many state and local government finance officers prefer to account for most "general government" capital projects through Capital Projects Funds—even when their use is not required—in order to better control and account for each project and its related resources. That is, since the accounting systems of Capital Projects Funds are designed to control the expenditure of resources for major capital assets, it may be desirable to transfer resources of General and Special Revenue Funds to Capital Projects Funds rather than to account for capital expenditures through systems oriented to current operations.

Similarly, not all long-term debt issue proceeds are accounted for in Capital Projects Funds. The GASB standards recommend accounting for the proceeds of bonds and other long-term debt issues in the following funds:

- Proceeds that are to be used to acquire capital assets should be accounted for in a Capital Projects Fund.
- Proceeds of refunding issues should be accounted for in a Debt Service Fund.
- Proceeds of issues of proprietary and Trust Funds should be accounted for in those funds because such liabilities are the primary responsibility of and will be serviced by the issuing funds.

The GASB standards are silent with respect to debt issued for other purposes. But it seems appropriate for proceeds of debt issued to finance a deficit to be accounted for in the fund that has the deficit. Further, it would seem that the proceeds of debt issued to provide disaster relief might properly be accounted for in Capital Projects or Special Revenue Funds, or even the General Fund.

The terms **"major"** and **"project"**—as used in determining when Capital Projects Funds must be used—are not defined in the GASB Codification and are subject to interpretation in practice. A $10,000,000 street improvement program would be a major capital project in a small town, for example, but might be considered a nonmajor, routine activity of a state highway department. Thus, assuming no legal or contractual requirements require a Capital Projects Fund, (1) the town would nonetheless use a Capital Projects Fund, whereas (2) the state might account for the capital expenditure through a Special Revenue Fund or the General Fund. Unless noted otherwise, we assume that the capital asset acquisitions discussed here **are** "major" capital "projects" that should be accounted for in Capital Projects Funds.

Further, some capital projects—such as neighborhood street construction or improvement projects—are financed by special assessments levied against the properties improved. Special assessments are essentially a special tax imposed only upon those properties or taxpayers benefitted by the capital improvement or service financed by the assessment. Special assessments for capital improvements normally are payable, along with related interest, over a period of five to ten years or longer. Therefore, long-term debt typically is issued to finance construction of the improvements. The special assessment collections are used to service the debt issued. The proceeds of long-term special assessment debt issued to finance general government capital improvement special assessment projects should be **reported** in the Capital Projects Fund financial statements. Any related debt service transactions and balances, including the special assessments receivable, normally should be reported in a Debt Service Fund.

This chapter begins with brief discussions of Capital Projects Fund operations and accounting standards. These discussions are followed by a comprehensive two-year CPF accounting and reporting illustrative case example, which comprises much of the chapter. Finally, several other CPF operations, accounting, and reporting matters are considered at the conclusion of the chapter.

CPF OPERATIONS AND ACCOUNTING STANDARDS

Capital Projects Fund operations and accounting standards are discussed briefly under these topic headings:

1. Sources of Resources
2. Number of Funds Required

Sources of Resources

Typical sources of Capital Projects Fund financial resources are bond or other long-term general obligation debt issues, special assessment indebtedness, grants or shared revenues from other governments, transfers from other funds, and interest earned on temporary investments of project resources. The classification of resource inflows is significant for reporting purposes because the government as a whole should be considered the entity for which financial statements are presented.

Capital Projects Fund inflows from intergovernmental grants and from financing interest on investments should be considered revenues when earned. But two typical financing sources do not represent revenues to the government as a whole: (1) interfund transfers should be classified as operating transfers (or as residual equity transfers if appropriate), and (2) proceeds of the issue of long-term debt should be labeled as other financing sources—since from the standpoint of the government as a whole they cannot be viewed as revenue. Operating transfers and bond issue proceeds are reported in the "Other Financing Sources" section of the Capital Projects Fund statement of revenues, expenditures, and changes in fund balance.

Number of Funds Required

Separate Capital Projects Funds are usually established for **each project or debt issue.** Separate funds are used because the nature of such projects varies widely, they typically involve significant amounts of resources, they are usually budgeted on an individual project or debt issue basis, and legal and contractual requirements differ significantly among projects. Where debt issues or grants are involved, a major purpose of the Capital Projects Funds is to show that the proceeds were used only for authorized purposes and that unexpended balances or deficits have been handled in accordance with applicable contractual agreements or legal provisions.

*A **single*** Capital Projects Fund will suffice, however, where a single debt issue is used to finance several projects or a series of closely related projects is financed through a single grant or by internal transfers from the General or Special Revenue Funds. Combining statements are used to present financial operation or position data where a government has more than one Capital Projects Fund in operation during a given year.

Some state or local governments properly use a single Capital Projects Fund accounting entity even when several restricted financing sources (e.g., bonds, grants) and several different capital projects are involved. This is done through what is known as a **"funds within a fund"** or **"subfund"** approach under which each capital project is accounted for as a separate subfund of the overall

Capital Projects Fund.[1] This "funds within a fund" or "subfund" approach should be used only where the substance of separate Capital Projects Fund accounting and control is achieved and the compliance reporting objectives of Capital Projects Funds are met.

Capital Projects Fund Life Cycle

A Capital Projects Fund is authorized by action of the legislative body on either the project or debt issue. The accrual and inflows, expenditures and encumbrances, and balances of project-related resources are then recorded in the Fund accounting records. The Fund is abolished at the conclusion of the project and the accounting records retained to evidence the fiscal stewardship of the government.

In extremely simple situations, such as where the project consists of purchasing existing facilities for a single payment, the life of the Capital Projects Fund may be brief and its entries uncomplicated: (1) receipts of all resources will occur and revenues or other financing sources will be credited, (2) expenditures will be recorded and paid, (3) the temporary fund balance accounts will be closed to Unreserved Fund Balance, and (4) any remaining resources and the balance of the Fund will be closed out when the assets are transferred to another fund (or disposed of in some other way as required by law or contract).

In other cases, however, a Capital Projects Fund is used to finance construction projects where the government acts as a general contractor, possibly using its own employees and equipment for part or all of the work. In this situation accounting procedures are more complicated and closely resemble those of the General Fund.

Laws or contracts will determine the disposition of any balance remaining unused in the Capital Projects Fund at completion of its mission. It may, for example, have to be refunded on a pro rata basis to the grantors who participated in financing the project. The city's portion is usually transferred to the fund that will service and pay off debt incurred to finance the project (usually a Debt Service Fund). If any bond premium is kept in the Capital Projects Fund in conformity with legal or debt indenture requirements, it will be transferred to a Debt Service Fund when the Capital Projects Fund is closed.

The Budget

The projects financed through Capital Projects Funds (1) usually are planned in the government's long-term **capital budget** and (2) are **appropriated** for on a **project basis;** that is, appropriations do **not** lapse at the end of each fiscal year (Assumption C1). If annual reappropriations are made of project appropriations, they are considered to be allotments.

In some cases adequate control is provided without the budgetary process, and appropriations are not made. In substance, the entire CPF is "appropriated" for the project in such cases. Reasons for not budgeting capital projects

---

[1] That is, the overall Capital Projects Fund is assigned a number in the governmental fund chart of accounts, say, 300, and each separate capital project is assigned a separate "300" number, such as 319 or 368. Thus, every subfund asset, liability, and fund balance—and every subfund revenue, expenditure, other financing source, and so on—is identified (coded) by **subfund within the overall Capital Projects Fund.**

include (1) only one project is financed from a single fund; and (2) control is provided by specifications, bids, inspections, and the like.

On the other hand, budgetary control is important where several projects are accounted for through a single CPF, where the government budgets the CPF in detail, where the government uses its own employees to construct a major capital asset, and where the CPF is budgeted annually. The case illustration in this chapter assumes that the capital project is appropriated on a project basis (Assumption C1) and full budgetary control is desirable.

Interim Financing

Cash may be borrowed short term, especially during the early stages of the CPF life cycle, to pay for project expenditures incurred before the bond issue proceeds or other CPF financial resources are received. Governments may use short-term financing to allow them to issue long-term debt close to the time that the bulk of the resources will be expended, to take advantage of anticipated improvements in bond market conditions, or to avoid delaying a project while technical details associated with a debt issuance are addressed. Such short-term borrowing may be from other funds of the governmental unit or by bond anticipation notes (BANs), revenue anticipation notes, or other notes issued to local banks or other creditors, and ordinarily is repaid when the bond issue proceeds or other CPF resources are received.

Most types of **interim borrowing** are considered **current liabilities of the CPF.** Accordingly, Cash is debited and Notes Payable or Due to General (or other) Fund is credited—**not** a debt proceeds "other financing source" account—to record the short-term loan. The entries are reversed when the loan is repaid and any interest (but not note principal) paid is recorded as Expenditures of the CPF. For example, if at mid-year a government issued a ten-month, $500,000, 6% bond anticipation note payable to provide temporary financing for a major general government capital project, and expended 90% of the proceeds on the project by year end, the following Capital Projects Fund entries would be required:

Cash	500,000	
Notes Payable		500,000
To record issuance of the notes at par.		
Expenditures—Capital Outlay	450,000	
Cash/Payables/And so on		450,000
To record expenditures incurred on the project.		
Expenditures—Debt Service	15,000	
Accrued Interest Payable		15,000
To record accrual of interest on the short-term, bond anticipation notes.		
Fund Balance	465,000	
Expenditures—Capital Outlay		450,000
Expenditures—Debt Service		15,000
To close the CPF accounts at year end.		

Note that this sequence of events results in a fund balance deficit in the Capital Projects Fund at year end.

An exception to this general rule of recording short-term loans as CPF fund liabilities is made in the GASB Codification with respect to **certain** bond anticipation notes **(BANs).** That is, a BAN Proceeds "other financing source" is reported in the Capital Projects Fund and the BAN liability is recorded in the GLTDAG—not the CPF—**if both:** (1) the BANs are issued in relation to a bond issue that is legally authorized and definitely issuable, **and** (2) the BANs legally must be paid from the bond issue proceeds. BANs not meeting both of these criteria are considered CPF liabilities. The logic underlying the treatment of qualifying BANs as general long-term debt is that they definitely will be repaid from the related bond issue proceeds, and thus their repayment will not require the use of existing CPF financial resources.

To illustrate, assume that the ten-month BANs in the previous example meet these criteria. The following entries would be made in the Capital Projects Fund to record the transactions described:

Cash	500,000	
Other Financing Sources—BAN Proceeds		500,000
To record issuance of the BANs.		
Expenditures—Capital Outlay	450,000	
Cash/Payables/And so on		450,000
To record expenditures incurred on the project.		
Other Financing Sources—BAN Proceeds	500,000	
Expenditures—Capital Outlay		450,000
Unreserved Fund Balance		50,000

Note that (1) the note payable is not recorded in the CPF—but in the General Long-Term Debt Account Group, (2) interest is not accrued at year end—since the BANs are viewed as if they are general long-term debt, and (3) the CPF fund balance at year end is positive.

The accounting for CPF interim financing described above is based on the "Bond, Tax, and Revenue Anticipation Notes" section of the GASB Codification. That guidance states that in accounting for governmental funds:

> . . . If [1] all legal steps have been taken to refinance the bond anticipation notes and [2] the intent is supported by an ability to consummate refinancing the short-term note on a long-term basis in accordance with the criteria set forth in FASB Statement No. 6, *Classification of Short-Term Obligations Expected to Be Refinanced,* they should be shown as part of the General Long-Term Debt Account Group.[2]

BANs that do not meet **both** criteria must be reported as a fund liability of the fund in which the proceeds are recorded, as are tax anticipation notes (TANs) and revenue anticipation notes (RANs).[3]

Costs Charged to Projects

All expenditures necessary to bring the capital facility to a state of readiness for its intended purpose are properly chargeable as Capital Projects Fund expenditures. In addition to the direct cost of items such as land, buildings, materials, and labor, total project cost would therefore include such **related items** as engineering and architect fees, transportation costs, damages occasioned by the project, and other costs associated with the endeavor.

Overhead

Although it may be contended that a share of **general government overhead** is a proper project cost, it is ***rarely charged*** to the project **unless** it is ***reimbursable,*** such as under terms of the grant through which the project is financed. Where

[2] GASB Codification, sec. B50.101.
[3] Ibid.

costs such as overhead are reimbursable, the reimbursable amount is frequently calculated in accordance with a predetermined formula rather than by being derived from cost accounting or similar records.

This is not to say that no overhead costs are charged to the project unless reimbursable. Overhead is charged to the project, for example, to the extent that such costs are included in charges for goods or services provided for the project through Internal Service Funds. And **additional overhead costs caused by** the **project** are properly *charged to the CPF.* Because of past manipulation abuses, however, and since intergovernmental grants are often intended only to supplement existing resources, charges for overhead may be specifically excluded from "project cost" as defined by statute, contractual agreement, or administrative determination.

Interest

Interest expenditures on interim **short-term** CPF notes are usually paid from the Fund and accounted for as project costs. But interest expenditures for bonds and other **long-term** debt issued to finance capital projects typically are financed and accounted for through a Debt Service Fund, and are not accounted for as project costs in the CPF. Interest earned by investing Capital Projects Fund cash is recognized as CPF revenue. However, interest earned by investing bond issue proceeds may be transferred to the appropriate Debt Service Fund to help finance the related bond interest expenditures.

Both interest revenues and interest expenditures related to capital projects must be carefully planned, controlled, and accounted for in the Capital Projects and Debt Service Funds. While this is true from sound financial management and accountability perspectives generally, both interest expenditures and interest revenues amounts are used in determining (1) whether the state or local government has complied with federal *"arbitrage"* provisions that require the interest earnings from investing tax-exempt bond issue proceeds that are in excess of the related interest costs to be remitted to the federal government; and (2) the *cost* of the project to be capitalized in the GFAAG.

Intergovernmental Revenues

Since grants, shared revenues, and contributions from other governments are revenues, they are subject to the modified accrual basis specified by the GASB for governmental funds. Thus, to be recognized as revenues, they must be both measurable and available. These two qualities are determined by the legal and contractual requirements of each case.

Both *unrestricted* grants received or receivable and those *restricted* to a specific program (but not to capital outlay) usually are recognized as assets and revenues of the General Fund or a Special Revenue Fund, as appropriate, then transferred to a Capital Projects Fund when authorized by the governing body. But some intergovernmental grants and other contributions are *restricted* to **capital** project use; and most such **"capital grants"** are *"expenditure-driven"*—that is, must be earned by the grantee's incurring of expenditures that qualify under the terms of the grant or other contribution agreement.

If upon receipt of *restricted* capital grant resources appropriate expenditures have *not* been made, both the assets and **deferred** revenue are recognized in the CPF. Thereafter, revenue is recognized as appropriate expenditures are made. But, if qualifying expenditures are made **before** the grant resources are received, the grant receivable and revenue should be accrued. Finally, if an expenditure-driven grant has been awarded but no cash has been received and no revenue has been earned by incurring qualifying expenditures, (1) neither the asset nor the deferred revenue are recorded, but (2) the grant award and the related potential resources may be disclosed in the notes to the financial statements.

Bond Premiums, Discounts, and Issuance Costs

Bond issue proceeds are recorded at the amount received, including any premium and net of any discount and issuance costs incurred.[4] Since interest on the bonds typically will be paid from a Debt Service Fund, the premium and any payment received for accrued interest usually are transferred to that fund. The project authorization must be reduced unless bond discounts and/or issuance costs are made up by acquiring additional resources from other funds, for example, or from interest earned on temporary investments of the Capital Projects Fund.

CPF CASE ILLUSTRATION BEGUN—19X1

To illustrate Capital Projects Fund accounting, assume that in 19X1 the governing body of A Governmental Unit decided to construct a bridge expected to cost $3,000,000. The bridge construction and related costs are to be financed as follows:

	Total	*Percent*
Federal grant	$1,200,000	40
State grant	600,000	20
Bond issue proceeds	900,000	30
Transfer from General Fund	300,000	10
	$3,000,000	100

The $600,000 **state** grant is a **fixed sum** irrevocably granted for the bridge project, and will revert to the state only if the bridge is not built. But the federal grant is for 40% of the qualifying project expenditures, with a maximum grant limit of $1,200,000; and any excess grant cash received would revert to the federal government. Thus, the **federal** grant is an **expenditure-driven** grant and federal grant revenues will be recognized accordingly.

The bridge is to be constructed by a private contracting firm, Defliese & Co., selected by sealed bids based on engineering specifications; the government's work force will do related earthmoving and landscape work. The estimated costs of the bridge project are:

Bridge Structure:		
Defliese & Co. contract		$2,400,000
Earthmoving and Landscaping (Government Roads Department):		
Labor	$300,000	
Machine time	200,000	
Fuel and materials	100,000	600,000
		$3,000,000

[4] GASB Statement 11, "Measurement Focus and Basis of Accounting—Governmental Fund Operating Statements," will change the accounting and reporting for bond premiums, discounts, and issuance costs when it becomes effective. However, governments are prohibited from applying GASB Statement 11 prior to its effective date.

Defliese & Co. is to post a performance bond guaranteeing the quality and timeliness of its work. In addition, 5% of the amounts payable to Defliese & Co. under the contract will be retained, as a further guarantee of the quality of the work. This retainage will be remitted upon final inspection of the bridge and its acceptance by the governing body of A Governmental Unit. The bridge construction will begin in 19X1 and should be completed in 19X2.

Budgetary Entry

When the governing body officially authorized the bridge capital project by ordinance—which included the estimated financing sources and appropriations as outlined earlier—the government's controller made the following **budgetary entry:**

(B)	Estimated Revenues—Federal Grant	1,200,000	
	Estimated Revenues—State Grant	600,000	
	Estimated Other Financing Sources—Bond Proceeds. . .	900,000	
	Estimated Other Financing Sources—Operating Transfer		
	from General Fund	300,000	
	Appropriations—Defliese & Co. Contract		2,400,000
	Appropriations—Labor		300,000
	Appropriations—Machine Time		200,000
	Appropriations—Fuel and Materials		100,000
	To record project budget.		

Note that budgetary control is to be achieved over **all** financing sources, not just revenues. The examples in earlier chapters assumed use of a Revenues Ledger—and that interfund transfers and long-term debt issues were separately authorized and thus were not included in the budget or budgetary accounts. This "pure" Revenues Ledger approach may also be used in Capital Projects Fund accounting. But the "detailed General Ledger account" approach better fits the typical Capital Projects Fund situation, so is used in this case example.

Note also that the controller established detailed General Ledger Expenditures accounts. Since all appropriations, expenditures, and encumbrances relate to the same bridge project and only one government department is involved—the accounts are set up to control and account for the appropriations for the most significant bridge costs: the (1) Defliese & Co. construction contract and (2) the government's labor, machine time, and fuel and materials related to the bridge. The Expenditures accounts would more appropriately be titled "Expenditures—Roads Department—Labor," and so on, but are shortened for illustrative purposes since only one department is involved. Were several contracts and/or departments involved, Appropriations, Expenditures, and Encumbrances accounts for each contract and for each government department participating in the project would be used.

19X1 Transactions and Events

The following entries summarize the several Capital Projects Fund transactions and events that occurred during 19X1.

(1) The contract with Defliese & Co. was signed and work began on the bridge.

Encumbrances—Defliese & Co. Contract	2,400,000	
Reserve for Encumbrances.		2,400,000

To record bridge contract let.

(2) The bonds were sold at a slight premium (101) for $909,000.

Cash	909,000	
Other Financing Sources—Bond Proceeds		909,000

To record sale of bonds at a premium.

(3) Fuel and materials ordered during the year totaled $55,000.

Encumbrances—Fuel and Materials.	55,000	
Reserve for Encumbrances.		55,000

To record encumbrances incurred.

(4) The state grant was received; but the governing body authorized only a $130,000 transfer from the General Fund during 19X1, which was received, and will authorize the remainder in 19X2.

Cash	730,000	
Revenues—State Grant		600,000
Other Financing Sources—Operating Transfer from		
General Fund		130,000

To record receipt of state grant and partial General Fund
   transfer.

(5) Invoices were received and vouchered for fuel and materials, $49,000 (encumbered at $48,000); machine time, $81,000; and the Defliese & Co. contract, $1,000,000 (as encumbered).

(a) Reserve for Encumbrances.	1,048,000	
Encumbrances—Fuel and Materials.		48,000
Encumbrances—Defliese & Co. Contract.		1,000,000
To reverse encumbrances.		
(b) Expenditures—Fuel and Materials.	49,000	
Expenditures—Machine Time.	81,000	
Expenditures—Defliese & Co. Contract.	1,000,000	
Contracts Payable—Retained Percentage.		50,000
Vouchers Payable		1,080,000

   To record vouchering expenditures for payment and 5%
     retainage on Defliese & Co. contract.

(6) Cash disbursements during 19X1 were:

Vouchers Payable	$ 970,000	
Investments.	400,000	
Payroll	140,000	
	$1,510,000	

Vouchers Payable	970,000	
Investments.	400,000	
Expenditures—Labor	140,000	
Cash		1,510,000

To record vouchers and payroll paid.

A Governmental Unit
Capital Project Fund
(Bridge Project)

Preclosing General Ledger Trial Balance, Closing Entries, and Postclosing Trial Balance Worksheet
End of 19X1
(Project Incomplete)

Accounts	Preclosing Trial Balance		Closing Entries (Actual or Worksheet Only)		Postclosing Trial Balance	
	Dr.	Cr.	Dr.	Cr.	Dr.	Cr.
Cash	129,000				129,000	
Investments	400,000				400,000	
Accrued Interest Receivable	18,000				18,000	
Due from Federal Government	508,000				508,000	
Vouchers Payable		110,000				110,000
Contracts Payable—Retained Percentage		50,000				50,000
Estimated Revenues—Federal Grant	1,200,000			1,200,000 (C1)		
Estimated Revenues—State Grant	600,000			600,000 (C1)		
Estimated Other Financing Sources—Bond Issue Proceeds	900,000			900,000 (C1)		
Estimated Other Financing Sources—Operating Transfer from General Fund	300,000			300,000 (C1)		
Appropriations—Defliese & Co. Contract		2,400,000	1,000,000 (C2) 1,400,000 (C3)			
Appropriations—Labor		300,000	140,000 (C2)			160,000
Appropriations—Machine Time		200,000	81,000 (C2)			119,000
Appropriations—Fuel and Materials		100,000	49,000 (C2) 7,000 (C3)			44,000
Revenues—Federal Grant		508,000	508,000 (C1)			
Revenues—State Grant		600,000	600,000 (C1)			
Revenues—Interest		18,000	18,000 (C1)			
Other Financing Sources—Bond Proceeds		909,000	909,000 (C1)			
Other Financing Sources—Operating Transfer from General Fund		130,000	130,000 (C1)			
Expenditures—Defliese & Co. Contract	1,000,000			1,000,000 (C2)		
Expenditures—Labor	140,000			140,000 (C2)		
Expenditures—Machine Time	81,000			81,000 (C2)		
Expenditures—Fuel and Materials	49,000			49,000 (C2)		
Encumbrances—Defliese & Co. Contract	1,400,000			1,400,000 (C3)		
Encumbrances—Fuel and Materials	7,000			7,000 (C3)		
Reserve for Encumbrances		1,407,000				1,407,000
	6,732,000	6,732,000				
Unreserved Fund Balance			835,000 (C1)		835,000	
					1,890,000	1,890,000

(7) Filed for federal grant reimbursement for 40% of the expenditures (transactions 5 and 6) incurred for the project during 19X1:

Due from Federal Government	508,000	
Revenues—Federal Grant		508,000

To record filing for federal grant reimbursement for qualifying expenditures.

Calculation: .4 ($1,130,000 + $140,000)

(8) Accrued interest receivable on investments at year end was $18,000.

Accrued Interest Receivable	18,000	
Revenues—Interest		18,000

To record accrued interest at year end.

Preclosing Trial Balance—End of 19X1—Project Incomplete

The preclosing trial balance of the bridge project Capital Projects Fund General Ledger accounts at the end of 19X1 appears in the first two columns of the worksheet illustrated in Figure 7-1. It differs from the preclosing trial balance for the General Fund example in Chapter 4 because detailed General Ledger control accounts are used instead of Revenues and Expenditures Subsidiary Ledgers.

Closing Entries—End of 19X1—Project Incomplete

The most relevant time frame in Capital Projects Fund accounting is that between its inception and its termination after the project is completed. Appropriations are made on a project life basis in this example, as is typical, and all budgetary compliance, project cost, and similar determinations are made when the project has been completed. Thus, whereas the Capital Projects Fund accounts must be closed at its termination, the end of a government's fiscal year within the Capital Projects Fund life cycle is an interim date that is not particularly significant from a CPF perspective.

Financial statements must be prepared for state and local governments at the end of each year, however. Accordingly, Capital Projects Fund financial statements must be prepared at the end of a government's fiscal year—even though they are **interim** statements from a Capital Projects Fund standpoint.

The Capital Projects Fund **accounts** need not be closed at the end of a government's fiscal year, however, and **may or may not be closed** in practice. Both closing the accounts and not closing them have advantages and disadvantages.

Accounts Not Closed

If the CPF accounts are **not** closed at fiscal year end, a worksheet giving effect to **pro forma** ("as if") **closing entries** is prepared. This type worksheet, illustrated in Figure 7-1, begins with the preclosing trial balance (columns 1 and 2), from which are derived the pro forma closing entries (columns 3 and 4) and the postclosing trial balance (columns 5 and 6).

The pro forma closing entries are *not* journalized and posted to the accounts under this approach. Rather, the information needed to prepare the Capital Projects Fund financial statements is obtained from the General Ledger closing entries (operating statement) and postclosing trial balance (balance sheet) **worksheet columns.**

The primary **advantage** of this "no closing entry" worksheet approach is that it saves time otherwise spent in journalizing Capital Projects Fund closing entries, posting them to the several CPF ledgers, and then reestablishing the appropriate amounts in those several CPF ledgers at the beginning of the next year. The primary **disadvantage** of the "no closing entry" approach is that it precludes the use of reversing entries to facilitate the accounting for accruals made at the end of one year during the next year. Thus, governmental accountants and auditors who use reversing entries will close the CPF accounts at year end. Further, some accountants and auditors prefer that worksheets not be used as a "bridge" between the ledger accounts and the financial statements. Accordingly, they prefer that the accounts be closed at year end so that the ledger account balances will correspond with the amounts reported in the financial statements.

Accounts Are Closed

If the accounts **are** closed, the **General Ledger** closing entries (see Figure 7-1)—using the "variance approach"—are:

(C1) Revenues—Federal Grant 508,000
Revenues—State Grant 600,000
Revenues—Interest 18,000
Other Financing Sources—Bond Proceeds 909,000
Other Financing Sources—Operating Transfer from
  General Fund 130,000
Unreserved Fund Balance 835,000
  Estimated Revenues—Federal Grant 1,200,000
  Estimated Revenues—State Grant 600,000
  Estimated Other Financing Sources—Bond
    Proceeds 900,000
  Estimated Other Financing Sources—Operating
    Transfer from General Fund 300,000
To close the estimated and actual revenues and other
financing sources accounts at year end.

(C2) Appropriations—Defliese & Co. Contract 1,000,000
Appropriations—Labor 140,000
Appropriations—Machine Time 81,000
Appropriations—Fuel and Materials 49,000
  Expenditures—Defliese & Co. Contract 1,000,000
  Expenditures—Labor 140,000
  Expenditures—Machine Time 81,000
  Expenditures—Fuel and Materials 49,000
To close the expenditures at year end and reduce the
continuing appropriations.

(C3) Appropriations—Defliese & Co. Contract 1,400,000
Appropriations—Fuel and Materials 7,000
  Encumbrances—Defliese & Co. Contract 1,400,000
  Encumbrances—Fuel and Materials 7,000
To close the encumbrances accounts and establish
corresponding reserves of appropriated fund
balance.

These **"variance approach"** closing entries **update** the **budgeted** (planned) Unreserved Fund Balance amount **to** its **actual** year-end balance by adding (or deducting) the differences ("variances") between the "budgeted" and "actual" amounts to date.

Note that entry C1 closes the entire balance of the Estimated Revenues and Estimated Other Financing Sources accounts—even though those amounts relate to the entire project rather than to only this fiscal year—which causes Unreserved Fund Balance to be debited $835,000. The reason is that the Estimated Revenues and Estimated Other Financing Sources accounts are budgetary "resource" accounts and their balances are not assets properly reported in the CPF balance sheet at year end. Thus, whereas the CPF statements are in substance interim statements, they must be reported on a basis consistent with the General Fund and other governmental funds in the government's year-end financial statements. This often gives rise to **"artificial deficits"** being reported in Capital Projects Fund financial statements (as is the case here), which is discussed further later in this section.

Entries C2 and C3 are consistent with the "unexpended appropriations continue" assumption of this case example, which are discussed and illustrated (Assumption C1) in Appendix 6-3. Entry C2 closes the various Expenditures accounts to the related Appropriations accounts so the remaining Appropriations balances represent the **unexpended** balances, while entry C3 closes the various Encumbrances accounts to the unexpended balance of the related Appropriations accounts, reducing them to their **unencumbered** balances. Entry C3 will be reversed, of course, at the beginning of 19X2.

Figure 7-2

BALANCE SHEET
END OF 19X1
(PROJECT INCOMPLETE)

A Governmental Unit
Capital Projects Fund
(Bridge Project)
Balance Sheet
End of 19X1
(Project Incomplete)

Assets

Cash	$ 129,000
Investments	400,000
Accrued interest receivable	18,000
Due from federal government	508,000
	$1,055,000

Liabilities and Fund Balance*

Liabilities		
Vouchers payable	$ 110,000	
Contracts payable—retained percentage	50,000	$ 160,000
Fund Balance:		
Appropriated—		
Reserved for encumbrances	1,407,000	
Unencumbered	323,000	
	1,730,000	
Unappropriated—Unreserved.	(835,000)	895,000
		$1,055,000

Alternatively, the Fund Balance section may be presented as follows:

Fund Balance:
Appropriated and encumbered (note X) 895,000
and the details explained in a note to the financial statements. This approach avoids reporting the potentially misleading "artificial" Unreserved Fund Balance deficit in the Balance Sheet in many situations.

Financial Statements—End of 19X1—Project Incomplete

Two annual financial statements are required for a Capital Projects Fund that is budgeted for the project, as in this case example: (1) a Balance Sheet (Figure 7-2) and (2) a Statement of Revenues, Expenditures, and Changes in Fund Balance (Figure 7-3). A budgetary comparison statement would also be required if the CPF were budgeted annually.

Balance Sheet

The Balance Sheet for the Capital Projects Fund at the end of 19X1 (Figure 7-2) is like that presented for the General Fund except for the "fund balance" section. The CPF appropriations are for the project, and thus the unexpended appropriations do not lapse at the end of 19X1, but continue as expenditure authority into 19X2. In this situation (1) the "fund balance" section should be classified as between its *"appropriated"* and *"unappropriated"* components, and (2) the Reserve for Encumbrances should be presented as a reservation of *appropriated* fund balance.

But whereas the appropriations are for the project, the unrealized estimated financial resources are not properly reported as assets in a GAAP basis year-end balance sheet. The net effect, as noted at closing entry C1, is that the

Figure 7-3

OPERATING STATEMENT FOR 19X1 FISCAL YEAR
(PROJECT INCOMPLETE)

Format A/Presentation 1
A Governmental Unit Capital Projects Fund
(Bridge Project)
Statement of Revenues, Expenditures, and Changes in Fund Balance
For 19X1 Fiscal Year
(Project Incomplete)

Revenues:		
Federal grant	$ 508,000	
State grant	600,000	
Interest	18,000	$1,126,000
Expenditures:*		
Defliese & Co. contract	1,000,000	
Labor	140,000	
Machine time	81,000	
Fuel and materials	49,000	1,270,000
Excess of Revenues Over (Under) Expenditures		(144,000)
Other Financing Sources (Uses):		
Bond proceeds	909,000	
Operating transfer from General Fund	130,000	1,039,000
Excess of Revenues and Other Financing Sources Over (Under) Expenditures and Other Uses		895,000
Fund Balance—Beginning of 19X1		—
Fund Balance—End of 19X1		$ 895,000

All are capital outlay expenditures and in practice may be reported in a single "Capital Outlay" total expenditures amount. The detailed expenditure amounts reported here would be for internal use, and are presented here for illustrative purposes.

unrealized estimated financial resources decrease the Unreserved Fund Balance reported in what is in substance an interim CPF Balance Sheet included in A Governmental Unit's financial statements prepared at the end of 19X1. In this example there was no Unreserved Fund Balance prior to the pro forma or actual closing entries. Thus, the difference between estimated financial resources for the project and those realized to date is reported as an Unreserved Fund Balance **deficit.**

This Unreserved Fund Balance deficit is an **"artificial deficit,"** however, since there is no indication that the Capital Projects Fund will indeed be in a deficit situation at the conclusion of the project. Again, it is the result of the fact that the year-end CPF Balance Sheet is an interim statement from a CPF perspective. The artificial deficit reported is unfortunate, however, because it may mislead users of the government's financial statements—who may understandably get the impression that the bridge Capital Projects Fund is $835,000 "in the red" even though the total fund balance is positive, $895,000 "in the black." At the least the Unreserved Fund Balance artificial deficit may confuse readers of the financial statements, and its origin and temporary nature should be explained in the notes to the financial statements. Indeed, many practitioners present the "Fund Balance" section of the CPF Balance Sheet as shown in the note to Figure 7-2. The authors prefer this alternative reporting approach.

Operating Statement

The GAAP basis operating statement for the Capital Projects Fund at the end of 19X1—the Statement of Revenues, Expenditures, and Changes in Fund Balance—

is presented in Figure 7-3. Its format is the same as that of the corresponding statement presented for the General Fund in Chapter 4.

Note that the CPF operating statement in Figure 7-3 presents an excess of expenditures over revenues of $144,000. Readers may interpret this negative excess—which may be many millions of dollars in practice—as being "bad," even though there is an excess of revenues and other financing sources over expenditures and other uses. Like the artificial deficit in the Unreserved Fund Balance account, this excess of expenditures over revenues is attributable (partly) to the fact that this CPF operating statement is indeed an interim statement.

However, the excess of expenditures over revenues also arises from the fact that Capital Projects Funds typically are financed differently than are General and Special Revenue Funds. Bond issue proceeds are usually major CPF financing sources, for example, whereas they would rarely be used to finance General Fund operations except in times of financial distress.

The format for the Statement of Revenues, Expenditures, and Changes in Fund Balance presented in Figure 7-3, like that presented in Chapter 4—known as "format A" or "presentation 1"—is by far the most widely used in practice. However, an acceptable alternate format—known as "format B" or "presentation 2"—is preferred by some state and local governments because it helps avoid **"artificial excesses"** of expenditures over revenues being reported in the operating statements of Capital Projects Funds, in particular, as well as in other governmental funds.

An alternate format Statement of Revenues, Expenditures, and Changes in Fund Balance for the Capital Projects Fund at the end of 19X1—in the **"format B"** or **"presentation 2"** arrangement—is presented in Figure 7-4. The difference between this format and that in Figure 7-3 is that (1) the "other (nonrevenue) financing sources" are presented immediately after the revenues and lead to a "Total Revenues and Other Financing Sources" subtotal; (2) any "other (nonexpenditure) financing uses" are presented after expenditures and lead to a "Total Expenditures and Other Uses" subtotal—though in the absence of "other uses," as in this example, the "Total Expenditures" amount is reported; and (3) the **optional** Excess of Revenues Over (Under) Expenditures amount is **not** presented—only the Excess of Revenues and Other Financing Sources Over (Under) Expenditures and Other Financing Uses, which is **required** by GAAP.

No Budgetary Comparison Statement Required

The **budgetary comparison statement**—the Statement of Revenues, Expenditures, and Changes in Fund Balance—***Budget and Actual***—is **not required** here since this **example assumes** that the Capital Projects Fund is **budgeted for the project life** span, **not annually.** (The budgetary comparison statement is required only for governmental funds that are budgeted annually.) Further, note that a budgetary comparison statement prepared at an interim point in the life of a Capital Projects Fund might be misleading because (1) the estimated financing sources and appropriations are for the entire project life cycle, but (2) the actual financing sources, expenditures, and encumbrances data are for a portion of the project life or at an interim point during the project life cycle. Thus, the ***GASB standards require budgetary comparison statements only for annually budgeted governmental funds.***

CPF Case Illustration Concluded—19X2

Whether any ***preliminary entries*** are required at the beginning of 19X2—before recording the 19X2 transactions and events—depends on whether closing entries

Figure 7-4

OPERATING STATEMENT FOR 19X1 FISCAL YEAR
(PROJECT INCOMPLETE)

Format B/Presentation 2
A Governmental Unit Capital Projects Fund
(Bridge Project)
Statement of Revenues, Expenditures, and Changes in Fund Balance
For 19X1 Fiscal Year
(Project Incomplete)

Revenues:		
Federal grant	$ 508,000	
State grant	600,000	
Interest	18,000	$1,126,000
Other Financing Sources:		
Bond proceeds	909,000	
Operating transfer from General Fund	130,000	1,039,000
Total Revenues and Other Financing Sources		2,165,000
Expenditures:*		
Defliese & Co. contract	1,000,000	
Labor	140,000	
Machine time	81,000	
Fuel and materials	49,000	1,270,000
Excess of Revenues and Other		
Financing Sources over Expenditures†		895,000
Fund Balance—Beginning of 19X1		—
Fund Balance—End of 19X1		$ 895,000

*All are capital outlay expenditures and in practice may be reported in a single "Capital Outlay"
total expenditures amount. The detailed expenditure amounts reported here would be for internal
use, and are presented here for illustrative purposes.
†If there had been "other (nonexpenditure) financing uses" during 19X1, they would have been
reported in an "Other Financing Uses" section immediately after the "Expenditures" section and
the "Excess of Revenues and Other Financing Sources Over (Under) Expenditures and Other Uses"
would have been reported.

were made at the end of 19X1. Further, if closing entries *were* made, the preliminary entries depend on whether reversing entries are used.

Accounts Closed in 19X1

If the **General Ledger** accounts **were** closed at the end of 19X1, three entries are needed at the beginning of 19X2:

(R1)	Estimated Revenues—Federal Grant.	692,000	
	Estimated Other Financing Sources—Operating		
	Transfer from General Fund	170,000	
	Unreserved Fund Balance.		862,000
	To record the budgeted revenues and other financing sources not received in 19X1.		
(R2)	Encumbrances—Defliese & Co. Contract.	1,400,000	
	Encumbrances—Fuel and Materials	7,000	
	Appropriations—Defliese & Co. Contract		1,400,000
	Appropriations—Fuel and Materials.		7,000
	To reverse the entry closing encumbrances made at the end of 19X1.		
(R3)	Revenues—Interest	18,000	
	Accrued Interest Receivable		18,000
	To reverse the interest accrual entry made at the end of 19X1.		

Entry R1 reestablishes the Estimated Revenues and Estimated Other Financing Sources budgetary accounts at the amount of project financial resources yet to be realized and removes the artificial deficit in the Unreserved Fund Balance account. Entry R2 restores the Appropriations account to its unexpended balance, while returning the various Encumbrances and Reserve for Encumbrances accounts to their usual offsetting status. Entry R3 records the 19X1 interest revenues as a debit (deduction) to the 19X2 Revenues—Interest account, thus permitting all interest received or accrued during 19X2 to be credited to the Revenues—Interest account.

Note that the entry recording the federal grant earned in 19X1 was not reversed. This is because that receivable was recorded as billed—and the Due from Federal Government account presumably is used to control the unpaid billings throughout the years the Capital Projects Fund exists. But had some unbilled federal grant revenue been accrued at the end of 19X1, that accrual entry would have been reversed at the beginning of 19X2.

Accounts Not Closed in 19X1

If the Capital Projects Fund *General Ledger* accounts were *not* closed at the end of 19X1, *no reversing entries* would be made at the beginning of 19X2. Again, many accountants consider the inability to use usual reversing entries a significant disadvantage of the "no closing entry" approach. However, not all SLG accountants use reversing entries. Further, some CPFs have only a relatively few (but large) transactions, and so reversing entries are not as useful as in governmental funds with numerous transactions.

Case Illustration Assumptions

The *General Ledger* accounting for 19X2 transactions is essentially the same (except reversing entries) regardless of whether the General Ledger accounts were closed at the end of 19X1. But the temporary accounts will accumulate (1) total project data if they were **not** closed at the end of 19X1, or (2) if they **were** closed at the end of 19X1, either total project data or 19X2 data, depending on whether gross balances or net remaining balances of budgetary accounts are reestablished at the beginning of 19X2. Our example assumes that only net remaining balances of the budgetary accounts are reestablished.

19X2 Transactions and Events

To conclude the bridge project Capital Projects Fund illustration, assume that the following entries summarize the transactions and events that occurred during 19X2.

(1) Invoices were received and vouchered for fuel and materials, $43,000 (partially encumbered at $7,000); machine time, $108,000; and the Defliese & Co. contract, $1,410,000 (encumbered at $1,400,000), including a $10,000 adjustment in the contract, approved by the governing body, for necessary work not anticipated in the contract specifications. No other encumbrances were incurred or outstanding.

(a)	Reserve for Encumbrances	1,407,000	
	Encumbrances—Defliese & Co. Contract		1,400,000
	Encumbrances—Fuel and Materials		7,000
	To reverse encumbrances outstanding.		

(b) Expenditures—Defliese & Co. Contract   1,410,000
    Expenditures—Fuel and Materials   43,000
    Expenditures—Machine Time   108,000
        Contracts Payable—Retained Percentage   70,500
        Vouchers Payable   1,490,500
    To record expenditures incurred.

(2) Cash receipts during 19X2 were from:

Federal grant	$1,198,000	
Investments (including interest)	430,000	
Operating Transfer from General		
Fund	170,000	
	$1,798,000	

Cash   1,798,000
    Due from Federal Government   508,000
    Investments   400,000
    Revenues—Federal Grant   690,000
    Revenues—Interest   30,000
    Other Financing Sources—Operating Transfer from
    General Fund   170,000
To record cash receipts.

(3) Cash disbursements made during 19X2 included:

Vouchers payable	$1,600,500	
Payroll	129,000	
	$1,729,500	

Vouchers Payable   1,600,500
Expenditures—Labor   129,000
    Cash   1,729,500
To record cash disbursements.

(4) Under terms of the federal grant: (a) the $10,000 additional payment to Defliese & Co. is not an allowable cost; (b) only the actual costs for earthmoving and landscaping are allowable; and (c) the otherwise allowable costs must be reduced by the interest earned by investing project monies. Accordingly, $30,000 was recorded as payable to the federal government, pending final inspection of the completed bridge.

Revenues—Federal Grant   30,000
    Due to Federal Government   30,000
To record liability for unallowable federal grant costs previously
    reimbursed.

Calculation:
Allowable costs and reimbursement—

Defliese & Co. Contract	$2,400,000
Labor	269,000
Machine Time	189,000
Fuel and Materials	92,000
	$2,950,000
Less: Interest earned	30,000
Allowable costs	$2,920,000
Federal grant share (40%)	.4
Reimbursement	$1,168,000
Federal grant revenue recognized to date	1,198,000
Due to federal government	$ 30,000

(5) The new bridge was approved by the inspectors and accepted by the governing body, which ordered that (a) the retained percentage be paid to the contractor, (b) the federal government be repaid (transaction 4), and (c) the remaining CPF fund balance be transferred to the related Debt Service Fund.

Contracts Payable—Retained Percentage	120,500	
Due to Federal Government	30,000	
Residual Equity Transfer to Debt Service Fund.	47,000	
Cash		197,500

To record payment of retained percentage, reimbursement to federal government, and transfer of remaining net assets.

(C) The accounts were closed and the bridge project Capital Projects Fund was terminated.

Revenues—Federal Grant.	660,000	
Revenues—Interest.	12,000	
Other Financing Sources—Operating Transfer from General Fund	170,000	
Appropriations—Defliese & Co. Contract	1,400,000	
Appropriations—Labor	160,000	
Appropriations—Machine Time	119,000	
Appropriations—Fuel and Materials	51,000	
Unreserved Fund Balance	27,000	
Estimated Revenues—Federal Grant		692,000
Estimated Other Financing Sources—Operating Transfer from General Fund.		170,000
Expenditures—Defliese & Co. Contract		1,410,000
Expenditures—Labor		129,000
Expenditures—Machine Time.		108,000
Expenditures—Fuel and Materials.		43,000
Residual Equity Transfer to Debt Service Fund		47,000

Note that the $47,000 **residual equity transfer** to the Debt Service Fund (transaction 5) is no doubt partially attributable to the $9,000 premium received upon sale of the bonds in 19X1. Had that bond premium been separately identified as a transfer to the Debt Service Fund, say, during 19X1, it would have been accounted for as an operating transfer. However, the transfer at the conclusion of a project is classified as a residual equity transfer because (1) the identity of the bond premium has been lost—since money is homogeneous, one cannot tell whether the bond premium dollars were spent on construction and the interest earned led to the transfer, for example, or vice versa; and (2) the GASB Codification requires that interfund transfers of residual balances of discontinued funds be classified as residual equity transfers.

Financial Statements—End of 19X2—Project Complete

Since the capital project is complete and the Capital Projects Fund has been terminated, no CPF balance sheet is prepared at the end of 19X2. The only statement required in this example, since the CPF was not budgeted annually, is a Statement of Revenues, Expenditures, and Changes in Fund Balance. Only the 19X2 operating statement need be presented in the government's annual financial report. But an operating statement *for the project* is prepared for internal use and may also be included in the annual financial report.

Figure 7-5

OPERATING STATEMENT FOR THE PROJECT—19X1 AND 19X2 FISCAL YEARS
(PROJECT COMPLETE)

Format B/Presentation 2

A Governmental Unit

Capital Projects Fund

(Bridge Project)

Statement of Revenues, Expenditures, and Changes in Fund Balance

For the Project—19X1 and 19X2 Fiscal Years

(Project Complete)

	19X2	19X1	Total
Revenues:			
Federal grant	$ 660,000	$ 508,000	$ 1,168,000
State grant	—	600,000	600,000
Interest	12,000	18,000	30,000
	672,000	1,126,000	1,798,000
Other Financing Sources:			
Bond proceeds.	—	909,000	909,000
Operating transfer from General Fund	170,000	130,000	300,000
	170,000	1,039,000	1,209,000
Total Revenues and Other Financing Sources . .	842,000	2,165,000	3,007,000
Expenditures:			
Defliese & Co. contract.	1,410,000	1,000,000	2,410,000
Labor	129,000	140,000	269,000
Machine time	108,000	81,000	189,000
Fuel and materials	43,000	49,000	92,000
	1,690,000	1,270,000	2,960,000
Excess of Revenues and Other Financing Sources Over (Under) Expenditures	(848,000)	895,000	47,000
Fund Balance—Beginning of Year	895,000	—	—
Residual equity transfer to Debt Service Fund	(47,000)	—	(47,000)
Fund Balance—End of Year.	$ —	$ 895,000	$ —

Project Operating Statement

A Statement of Revenues, Expenditures, and Changes in Fund Balances for the 19X1–19X2 project period is presented as Figure 7-5. Like the 19X1 operating statement in Figure 7-4, it is presented in Format B and thus does not include the excess of expenditures over revenues subtotal. While only the data in the 19X2 column needs to be presented in the government's annual financial statements, this operating statement for the project obviously is more useful than a single year statement and, accordingly, some governments include it in the annual financial report.

Project Budgetary Comparison Statement

Although not required for external reporting, government accountants usually prepare a budgetary comparison statement at the conclusion of a capital project. The CPF budgetary comparison statement is used primarily for internal purposes, but may also be required by project creditors and grantors.

A Statement of Revenues, Expenditures, and Changes in Fund Balance—Budget and Actual—for the bridge project Capital Projects Fund is illustrated in Figure 7-6. Clearly, this project budgetary comparison statement and the 19X1—X2

Figure 7-6

**BUDGETARY COMPARISON STATEMENT FOR THE PROJECT
19X1 AND 19X2 FISCAL YEARS
(PROJECT COMPLETE)**

Format B/Presentation

A Governmental Unit
Capital Projects Fund
(Bridge Project)

Statement of Revenues, Expenditures, and Changes in Fund Balance—Budget and Actual

For the Project—19X1 and 19X2 Fiscal Years
(Project Complete)

	Budget	Actual	Variance—Favorable (Unfavorable)
Revenues:			
Federal grant	$ 1,200,000	$ 1,168,000	$ (32,000)
State grant	600,000	600,000	—
Interest	—	30,000	30,000
	1,800,000	1,798,000	(2,000)
Other Financing Sources:			
Bond proceeds	900,000	909,000	9,000
Operating transfer from General Fund	300,000	300,000	—
	1,200,000	1,209,000	9,000
Total Revenues and Other Financing Sources	3,000,000	3,007,000	7,000
Expenditures:			
Defliese & Co. contract	2,400,000	2,410,000	(10,000)
Labor	300,000	269,000	31,000
Machine time	200,000	189,000	11,000
Fuel and materials	100,000	92,000	8,000
	3,000,000	2,960,000	40,000
Excess of Revenues and Other Financing Sources Over (Under) Expenditures	—	47,000	47,000
Fund Balance—Beginning of 19X1	—	—	—
Residual equity transfer to Debt Service Fund	—	(47,000)	(47,000)
Fund Balance—End of 19X2	$ —	$ —	$ —

operating statement for the project (such as that in Figure 7-5) provide the data managers and others need to evaluate the fiscal and budgetary management of the capital project, determine the cost of the fixed assets acquired, and understand the sources and uses of the Capital Projects Fund financial resources. Indeed, the data in Figures 7-5 and 7-6 are sometimes included in a single CPF summary operating and budgetary comparison statement with columns headed:

Actual		Total Project		Variance—Favorable (Unfavorable)
19X1	19X2	Actual	Budget	

OTHER CPF OPERATIONS, ACCOUNTING, AND REPORTING MATTERS

Several other CPF operations, accounting, and reporting matters warrant at least brief attention as we conclude this chapter. These include (1) Bond Anticipation Notes, (2) Investment of Idle Cash, (3) Disposing of Fund Balance or Deficit, (4)

Reporting Several Projects Financed through One Fund, and (5) Combining CPF Statements.

Bond Anticipation Notes (BANs)

We noted earlier in the chapter that bond anticipation notes (BANs) may be issued to provide **interim financing** for Capital Projects Funds prior to the issuance of authorized bonds. BANs may be issued for two main reasons: (1) Even though the bonds have been authorized, the bond issue process (including legal procedures, bond ratings, and so on) may take several weeks or months, yet CPF cash is required immediately; and (2) if long-term bond interest rates are expected to decline in the months ahead, the bond issue may be purposefully delayed to take advantage of the lower long-term interest rates. In any event, the **BANs should be repaid from the bond issue proceeds.**

To illustrate the issuance and repayment of BANs, suppose that A Governmental Unit has issued $500,000 of BANs in 19X1 prior to issuing the bonds (entry 2). As noted earlier, assuming the BANs met the GASB Codification **"noncurrent"** criteria, the entry to record the **BAN issue proceeds** in the **Capital Projects Fund** would be:

Cash	500,000	
Other Financing Sources—BAN Proceeds		500,000

To record issuance of **noncurrent** BANs.

Since these are **noncurrent** liability BANs, the related liability would be recorded in the General Long-Term Debt Account Group **(GLTDAG)** rather than in the CPF. Assume further that interest on the BANs was paid from a Debt Service Fund.

The **issuance** of the **bonds** would be recorded in the *Capital Projects Fund,* as illustrated in entry 2 earlier in the chapter:

Cash	909,000	
Other Financing Sources—Bond Proceeds		909,000

To record sale of bonds at a premium.

The liability for the bonds would be recorded in the GLTDAG. Then the **BAN retirement** would be recorded in the **Capital Projects Fund** as follows:

Other Financing Uses—BAN Principal Retirement	500,000	
Cash		500,000

To record retirement of BANs.

Also, the BAN liability would be removed from the GLTDAG. (Alternatively, the $500,000 might have been transferred to a Debt Service Fund through which the BANs were retired.)

As illustrated earlier, had the BANs **not** met the "noncurrent" criteria in the GASB Codification, a BAN Payable **liability** account—not the BAN Proceeds "other" financing source account—would be credited in the Capital Projects Fund upon BAN issuance. In that case, the BAN Payable liability account would be debited upon their retirement—not the BAN Principal Retirement "other" financing use account.

Investment of Idle Cash; Arbitrage

Significant sums of cash are commonly involved in capital project fiscal management. Cash receipt, investment, and disbursement therefore warrant careful planning, timing, and control.

Prudent financial management typically requires that loan transactions not be closed (and interest charges begun) until the cash is needed. There are exceptions to this rule, of course, as where statutes require that bonds be issued before the project begins, loan interest rates are expected to rise soon, or investments yield the government more than enough to cover the related interest costs. Similarly, significant sums should not be permitted to remain on demand deposit, but should be invested until such time as they are to be disbursed.

State and local governments that issue tax-exempt bonds or other debt issues must carefully observe the federal government's **"arbitrage"** regulations. Generally, the arbitrage regulations require state and local governments that issue *tax-exempt* debt securities (the interest on which is not subject to federal income tax) and invest the tax-exempt debt proceeds in *taxable* investments must *rebate* the arbitrage—the excess interest earned—to the federal government. The arbitrage rules and regulations are complex—much like the income tax code and regulations—and contain several exemptions and exceptions. In any event, investment revenues should be reduced and arbitrage rebate liabilities should be established when calculations indicate that arbitrage liabilities have been incurred during a period. Similarly, state and local governments that "draw down" federal grant money before it is expended for the grant project may owe interest to the federal government.

Both the authority to invest idle cash and the disposition of net investment earnings should be agreed upon and documented in the project authorization ordinance and in contractual agreements. Investment earnings might be used, for example, to reduce the government's share of the project cost or to increase the project expenditure authorization. Where monies have been borrowed and interest expenditures are being incurred, however, investment earnings should normally be transferred to the appropriate Debt Service Fund.

Disposing of Fund Balance or Deficit

Frequently, the governing body specifies what shall be done with any remaining CPF fund balance, as assumed in the case illustration. In the absence of legal or contractual restrictions, however, the balance is usually transferred to the Debt Service Fund from which the bonds or other related debt will be retired. The rationale for such action is that the balance arose because project expenditure requirements were overestimated, with the result that a larger amount than necessary was borrowed. Where resources were provided by intergovernmental grants or intragovernmental transfers, it may be either necessary or appropriate to refund a portion of these resources in disposing of the fund balance.

Government managers are well advised to provide in project authorizations, bond indentures, grant agreements, or otherwise for the possibility that costs have been overestimated and a fund balance might need to be disposed of at the conclusion of the project. In the absence of written authorization to rebate unneeded monies or transfer them to the related Debt Service Fund, officials may be precluded from doing so and forced to hold them, possibly indefinitely, until they are needed for the express purpose for which they were secured. (Such situations have arisen occasionally, for example, in cases in which money was borrowed "for the sole and exclusive purpose of extending existing waterlines and no other purposes.") Likewise, in the absence of such an agreement, grantors may insist that any remaining balance be returned to them—even though a project is only partially financed by grants.

A Capital Projects Fund deficit would ordinarily be disposed of in one of two ways. If small, it would probably be eliminated by transferring money from the General Fund; if large, it would probably be financed by additional "general government" borrowing.

Reporting Several Projects Financed Through One Fund

Earlier in this chapter it was noted that a single Capital Projects Fund may be used to finance several projects where only one debt issue or grant is involved or the projects are financed through internal transfers from other funds. For example, the capital project may consist of several "general improvements," possibly financed through a general obligation bond issue. It was also noted that several Capital Projects Funds may be accounted for on a "funds within a fund" or "subfund" approach within a single overall Capital Projects Fund accounting entity. Each project undertaken may be separately budgeted in such cases and, in any event, each must be separately controlled and accounted for within the CPF accounts.

Separate project control and accounting within a single CPF is best done by using distinctively titled (and coded) Estimated Revenues and Other Financing Sources, Revenues and Other Financing Sources, Appropriations, Expenditures, and Encumbrances control accounts and a set of appropriately named and coded subsidiary ledger accounts. Accounting for this type of fund corresponds with procedures discussed previously.

Financial statements for such **"composite"** CPFs, where the "subfunds" are in substance a series of separate Capital Projects Funds, often are presented as a series of separate fund statements—individually and/or in combining statements—as if each were accounted for separately. Financial statements for a multiproject fund thus would show data for each project. If assets, liabilities, and fund balance are identified by projects, the balance sheet may be presented in this columnar form, particularly for internal use:

A Governmental Unit
Capital Projects Fund
Balance Sheet
(Date)

Total	Completed Projects	Incomplete Projects	Projects Not Yet Determined
	Project A	Project B	

A supplemental schedule like that shown in Figure 7-7 may be prepared in "pancake" form—also primarily for internal use—to show operating data for individual projects. Information for this supplemental schedule is in the Expenditures Ledger.

Figure 7-7

MULTIPLE PROJECT BUDGETARY COMPARISON SCHEDULE
A Governmental Unit
Capital Projects Fund
Schedule of Appropriations, Expenditures, and Encumbrances
For the Fiscal Year Ended (Date)

	Appropriations	Expenditures	Encumbrances	Unencumbered Balance
Project A				
～～～	～～～	～～～	～～～	～～～
Total Project A	$ 500,000	$200,000	$ 10,000	$290,000
Project B				
～～～	～～～	～～～	～～～	～～～
Total Project B	$ 700,000	$600,000	$ 90,000	$ 10,000
Total—All Projects	$1,200,000	$800,000	$100,000	$300,000

Combining CPF Statements

In order to focus attention on capital projects activities as a whole and to reduce the number of separate statements required, statements of the several Capital Projects Funds of a government are usually presented in **combining** form. With adequate disclosure, such combining statements fulfill the requirement for separate statements for each fund. In general, combining totals should be shown with the details applicable to each fund either being presented in the statement itself or being incorporated by reference therein to a statement or schedule containing the separate fund details. (The totals are properly presented alone only in certain combined statements discussed and illustrated in Chapter 14.)

Combining CPF balance sheets and operating statements are presented in the formats illustrated earlier in this chapter, but the column headings might appear as:

Completed Projects		Incomplete Projects		Totals	
Bridge Fund	Sewer System Fund	Civic Center Fund	General Improvements Fund	This Period	Last Period

The distinction between completed and incomplete projects is made more often in combining statements prepared for internal use than in those published in the government's annual financial report. Likewise, the prior period comparative data are optional in combining statements. The combining Capital Projects Fund operating statement from a recent annual financial report of the City of Sioux City, Iowa is presented in Figure 7-8.

If a government has numerous Capital Projects Funds (i.e., more than six or seven), it may be desirable to prepare **combining schedules** for groups of funds and use such combining data, appropriately described and referenced to the schedules, in preparing the combining balance sheet for all Capital Projects

Figure 7-8

COMBINING CAPITAL PROJECTS FUNDS OPERATING STATEMENT

City of Sioux City, Iowa
Combining Statement of Revenues, Expenditures, and Changes in
Fund Balances—All Capital Project Funds
For the Year Ended June 30, 19X1

	Street Improvement	Storm Sewer Improvement	Special Improvement	Park Improvement	Miscellaneous Improvement	Totals
Revenues						
Special Assessments	$29,591					$29,591
Regulatory Fees					$150	150
Intergovernmental Revenue	1,071,137	$3,474	$50,000	$424,154	1,743,573	3,292,338
Revenue from Use of Property			324,424		579,753	904,177
Charges for Services					8,949	8,949
Interest	10,382		5,756	27,606	82,052	125,796
Contributions			1,000	33,437	47,893	82,330
Miscellaneous	16,891	8,144	332	3,382		28,749
Total Revenues	1,128,001	11,618	381,512	488,579	2,462,370	4,472,080
Expenditures						
Capital Outlay	4,507,769	567,592	1,178,754	3,508,438	3,311,889	13,074,442
Total Expenditures	4,507,769	567,592	1,178,754	3,508,438	3,311,889	13,074,442
(Deficiency) of Revenues Over Expenditures	(3,379,768)	(555,974)	(797,242)	(3,019,859)	(849,519)	(8,602,362)
Other Financing Sources (Uses)						
Proceeds from Issuance of Bonds	2,163,950	82,000	263,200	1,380,000	601,350	4,490,500
Operating Transfers In	1,732,860	652,000	15,986	366,655	1,265,727	4,033,228
Operating Transfers Out	(2,500)		(13,301)		(104,797)	(120,598)
Total Other Financing Sources (Uses)	3,894,310	734,000	265,885	1,746,655	1,762,280	8,403,130
Excess (Deficiency) of Revenues and Other Sources over Expenditures and Other Uses	514,542	178,026	(531,357)	(1,273,204)	912,761	(199,232)
Fund Balances—Beginning of Year	2,221,479	875,648	420,647	917,160	1,342,089	5,777,023
Equity Transfers In/(Out)	48,000				(111,960)	(63,960)
Fund Balances—End of Year	$2,784,021	$1,053,674	($110,710)	($356,044)	$2,142,890	$5,513,831

The notes to the financial statements are an integral part of this statement.

Source: Adapted from a recent annual financial report of the City of Sioux City, Iowa.

Funds. A similar technique often proves useful in connection with statements of multiproject funds.

CONCLUDING COMMENTS

Capital Projects Funds are used to account for a state or local government's major "general government" capital outlays for buildings, highways, storm sewer systems, bridges, and other fixed assets. Accordingly, they often involve millions of dollars (even hundreds of millions of dollars) of financial resources and expenditures.

The main aspects of Capital Projects Fund financing, financial management, and accounting discussed in this chapter include sources of CPF resources, number of funds required, CPF life cycle, interim financing, the CPF budget, costs charged to projects, investment of idle cash, and disposing of the CPF fund balance or deficit upon its termination. In addition, a Capital Projects Fund case illustration and illustrative financial statements were presented.

While this chapter illustrated the financing of Capital Projects Funds with general long-term bond proceeds, it did not address the repayment of that debt or the related interest and fiscal charges. Those topics are covered in Chapter 8 on "Debt Service Funds."

QUESTIONS

7-1 A Capital Projects Fund is, in essence, a special type of Special Revenue Fund. Explain.

7-2 Must all municipal capital outlays be financed and accounted for through Capital Projects Funds? Explain.

7-3 What is the "life cycle" of a Capital Projects Fund?

7-4 Why is each significant capital project usually financed and accounted for through a separate Capital Projects Fund?

7-5 In what situations might several capital projects properly be financed and accounted for through a single Capital Projects Fund?

7-6 The governing board of a city recently levied a gasoline tax "for the express purpose of financing the construction of a civic center, servicing debt issued to do so, or both" and instructed the comptroller to establish a Gasoline Tax Fund to account for the receipt, expenditure, and balances of the tax proceeds. What type fund should be established?

7-7 Why should a competent governmental accountant or auditor review proposed bond indentures, ordinances establishing Capital Projects Funds, and similar instruments or agreements before they are agreed to or enacted?

7-8 Why are statements for several Capital Projects Funds presented in combining form?

7-9 Neither the fixed assets acquired through a Capital Projects Fund nor the long-term debt issued to finance capital projects is normally accounted for therein. Why? Where are such fixed assets and long-term debt accounted for, and are there exceptions to this general rule?

7-10 Why might a grantor not permit general municipal overhead to be charged to a capital project financed by its grant, or insist that allowable (reimbursable) overhead be calculated by means of a predetermined formula related to direct project costs?

7-11 Proceeds of certain general obligation long-term debt issues are not accounted for through Capital Projects Funds. When is this the case? Through which funds or fund types are such debt proceeds accounted for?

7-12 How are the Unreserved Fund Balance, Appropriations, and Revenues accounts related?

7-13 What problems might one encounter in attempting to determine the proper disposition of a Capital Projects Fund balance remaining after the project has been completed and all Capital Projects Fund liabilities have been paid?

7-14 Some accountants prefer to close Capital Projects Fund Revenues, Expenditures, and Encumbrances accounts of incomplete projects at year end, whereas others prefer not to close them until the project is completed. Are both approaches acceptable? Why?

7-15 The Capital Projects Fund statements presented in a government's annual financial report are mostly interim statements for projects in process and may report "artificial" Unreserved Fund Balance deficits. (a) Why is this so? (b) What can be done about such "artificial deficit" situations?

7-16 A state finance director is concerned that the draft financial statements prepared for the state's Capital Projects Funds present large ($ millions) excesses of expenditures over revenues even though all of the funds are well within their appropriations and none is expected to have a deficit balance when the projects are completed. (a) Why are such excesses reported? (b) What do you suggest?

7-17 Bond anticipation notes (BANs) may properly be accounted for either as liabilities of the Capital Projects Fund or as general long-term debt—with the proceeds considered a nonrevenue financing source of the Capital Projects Fund—depending on the circumstances. Explain and illustrate with journal entries using amounts.

7-18 What is meant by "arbitrage" as the term is used in this chapter? Why should governmental accountants and auditors be concerned about arbitrage?

PROBLEMS

P 7-1 (Multiple Choice) Indicate the best answer to each question.

1. The City of Nancy is installing a lighting system in the Harvey Subdivision. The system is being financed by the issuance of $500,000 of five-year, 6%, special assessment notes payable. The notes and interest thereon are to be repaid from collections of special as-

sessments levied against the properties in the Harvey Subdivision. The construction and acquisition of the lighting system is deemed a major general government capital project for the city. The proceeds from the issuance of the notes would increase the fund balance of the city's Lighting System Capital Projects Fund by

a. $0. There should be no CPF for the lighting system. The proceeds are to be accounted for in a different fund type.

b. $0. The notes payable should be reported as liabilities of the Lighting System CPF because the debt is special assessment debt. Therefore, the fund's fund balance does not increase.

c. $500,000. The proceeds from the issuance of the note should be reported as Revenues—Special Assessment Note Proceeds.

d. $500,000. The proceeds from the issuance of the note should be reported as Other Financing Sources—Special Assessment Note Proceeds; essentially the same as any other general government long-term debt issuance for a general government capital project.

2. If the City of Nancy levies special assessments of $500,000—$100,000 of which is due and collected during the current year—what amount of special assessment revenues should be recognized in the Lighting System CPF in the current year?

a. $0. The special assessments should be reported in a debt service fund because collections of the assessments are to be used to pay principal and interest on the special assessment notes payable.

b. $100,000

c. $500,000

d. $0. Special assessments are reported as other financing sources, not as revenues.

3. Assume the City of Nancy is financing construction of the lighting system directly from its special assessment levy—i.e., no debt is being incurred. If, as in 2, the City of Nancy levies special assessments of $500,000—$100,000 of which is due and collected during the current year—what amount of special assessment revenues should be recognized in the Lighting System CPF in the current year?

a. $0. The special assessments should be reported in a special revenue fund.

b. $100,000

c. $500,000

d. $0. Special assessments are reported as other financing sources, not as revenues.

4. The City of Joni Fire Station Capital Project Fund has an excess of expenditures over revenues of $5 million reported in its statement of revenues, expenditures, and changes in fund balances. Which of the following explanations for that excess are plausible?

a. The city financed a substantial portion of the fire station project by issuing bonded indebtedness; therefore, its expenditures are likely to exceed its revenues.

b. The city financed a substantial portion of the fire station project with a federal capital grant which was recognized in the last year's revenues. Therefore, minimal revenues are being recognized this year, but a substantial fund balance exists as a result of the federal grant.

c. The city has incurred significant cost overruns on the project. This is the only reason that an excess of expenditures over revenues should be reported in a CPF operating statement.

d. None of the above is a plausible explanation.

5. Matthew County issued a six-month, 6%, $1,000,000 bond anticipation note to provide temporary financing for a major general government capital project. The bonds have not been authorized by the voters yet, but approval is anticipated by the county Board of Supervisors. In any event, the county has other financing sources that it can use to finance the project in the event that the voters reject the bond issue in the bond referendum election. What would be the fund balance of the Capital Projects Fund used to account for this project if the county incurred $800,000 of construction costs on the project by year end—which is three months before the bond anticipation note maturity date?

a. $185,000

b. $200,000

c. ($800,000)

d. ($815,000)

6. If Matthew County already had voter approval of the bond issue in 5 and intended to re-finance the bond anticipation note from the bond proceeds, what would the CPF fund balance be?

a. $185,000

b. $200,000

c. ($800,000)

d. ($815,000)

7. If Matthew County already had voter approval of the bond issue in 5 and intended to re-finance the bond anticipation note from the bond proceeds, what amount of expenditures would be reported for the CPF as a result of the repayment of the bond anticipation principal and interest in year 2?

a. $0

b. $1,000,000

c. $1,015,000

d. $1,030,000

8. Luke County issued $20,000,000 par of capital improvement bonds for a general government project. The bonds were issued at a premium of 2% of par. The bond indenture requires that any premium be set aside for debt service. This transaction should be reflected in Luke's CPF as:

a. Other financing sources—bond proceeds, $20,000,000

b. Other financing sources—bond proceeds, $20,400,000 and expenditures, $400,000

c. Other financing sources—bond proceeds, $20,400,000 and other financing uses—operating transfers out, $400,000

d. Other financing sources—bond proceeds, $20,000,000 and bond premium, $400,000

9. Upon completion of its new city office building, the City of Caleb had net assets of $880,000 remaining in its City Hall CPF. Council approves use of these net assets for future debt service on the City Hall Bonds. The reclassification of these assets as Debt Service Fund assets will be reflected in the CPF statement of revenues, expenditures, and changes in fund balances as:

a. Expenditures

b. Operating transfers out

c. Residual equity transfers out

d. Reductions of revenues for the final project period

10. A county's Courthouse CPF has the following balances in selected accounts at the end of its first year:

Revenues, $500,000

Bond proceeds, $5,000,000

Expenditures, $1,500,000

Encumbrances, $8,000,000

Appropriations, $9,500,000

The appropriation authority for the project continues from year to year. At the end of the first year of the project, what amount of Unreserved Fund Balance should be reported in the Courthouse CPF Balance Sheet?

a. $0

b. $4,000,000

c. ($4,000,000)

d. None of the above are correct.

P 7-2 (General Ledger Entries) The following transactions and events occurred in Lanesburg Township during 19X4:

1. The township assembly agreed that a new police and fire department building would be constructed at a cost not to exceed $150,000, on land owned by the township.

2. Cash with which to finance the project was received from the following sources:

Transfer from General Fund.	$ 10,000
State–Federal grant	50,000
Bank of Lanesburg (long-term note).	90,000
	$150,000

The state–federal grant is for one-third of the project cost, not to exceed $50,000, and any unearned balance must be returned to the state.

3. Cash was disbursed for building costs from the Capital Projects Fund as follows:

Construction contract	$140,000
Architect fees	5,000
Engineering charges	2,000
	$147,000

4. The unearned portion of the grant was refunded to the state, the remaining cash was transferred to the General Fund, and the Capital Projects Fund was terminated.

Required Prepare general journal entries to record the foregoing facts in the Capital Projects Fund General Ledger assuming that budgetary accounts and subsidiary ledgers are not used.

P 7-3 **Part I.** (General Ledger Entries; Statements) The following transactions took place in the Village of Burchette during 19A:

1. A bond issue of $120,000 was authorized for the construction of a library, and the estimated bond issue proceeds and related appropriations were recorded in the General Ledger accounts of a new Capital Projects Fund.
2. The bonds were sold at a premium of $900.
3. The cost of issuing the bonds, $800, was paid.
4. An order was placed for materials estimated to cost $65,000.
5. Salaries and wages amounting to $5,000 were paid.
6. The premium, net of bond issuance costs, was transferred to a Debt Service Fund.

Required (a) Prepare all entries, including closing entries, to record the Capital Projects Fund transactions for 19A.

(b) Post to T-accounts.

(c) Prepare a CPF balance sheet as of December 31, 19A.

(d) Prepare a CPF Statement of Revenues, Expenditures, and Changes in Fund Balance for the year ended December 31, 19A.

P 7-3 **Part II.** (General Ledger Entries; Project Operating Statement) The following transactions took place during 19B:

7. The materials were received; the actual cost was $65,850.
8. Salaries and wages amounting to $40,100 were paid.
9. All outstanding bills were paid.
10. The project was completed. The accounts were closed, and the remaining balance was to be transferred to a Debt Service Fund.

Required (a) Prepare all journal entries, including closing entries, to record the CPF transactions for 19B.

(b) Post to T-accounts.

(c) Prepare a CPF Statement of Revenues, Expenditures, and Changes in Fund Balance for the project, including (a) the years ended December 31, 19A and 19B, and (b) budgetary comparisons for the project.

P 7-4 (General Ledger Worksheet) From the data in Problem 7-3, Parts I and II, prepare a columnar worksheet for the two-year period ending December 31, 19B, using the following columnar headings:

1. 19A Transactions
2. Closing Entries, 12/31/19A
3. Postclosing Trial Balance, 12/31/19A
4. 19B Transactions
5. Closing Entries, 12/31/19B
6. Postclosing Trial Balance, 12/31/19B

P 7-5 **Part I.** (General Ledger Entries; Statements) The following transactions took place in Mills County during 19X4.

1. A bond issue of $500,000 was authorized for the construction of a bridge, and the estimated bond issue proceeds and appropriations were recorded in the General Ledger accounts of a new Bridge CPF.

2. One-half of the bonds were sold at par.

3. The cost of issuing the bonds, $700, was paid from the Capital Projects Fund.

4. A contract was entered into with White & Company for the construction of the bridge at a cost of $420,000.

5. A bill for $175,000 was received from White & Company for work done on the bridge to date.

6. Salaries of state engineers amounting to $5,350 were paid to the state.

Required (a) Prepare CPF General Ledger entries.

(b) Post to T-accounts.

(c) Prepare CPF financial statements as of December 31, 19X4.

P 7-5 **Part II.** (General Ledger Entries; Subfunds; Combining Statements) The following transactions took place during 19X5:

7. A bond issue of $400,000 was authorized at the beginning of 19X5 for the purpose of constructing a garage. As permitted by the bond indentures, both the bridge project (Bridge Fund) and the garage project (Garage Fund) are to be accounted for in the same Capital Projects Fund on a "funds within a fund" or "subfund" approach. Accordingly, "Bridge" was added to all existing Bridge Fund accounts and "Garage" is to be added to all Garage Fund accounts. The garage bond issue authorization was recorded in the accounts.

8. The bill due White & Company was paid.

9. Bonds (garage) of $200,000 were sold at a $4,000 premium.

10. The cost of issuing the garage bonds, $2,500, was paid.

11. Orders were placed for materials (garage project) estimated to cost $52,000.

12. A bill for $125,000 was received from White & Company for further work performed on the bridge contract.

13. Salaries and wages paid amounted to $51,100; of this total $4,000 applies to the bridge project and the remainder to the garage project.

14. The materials ordered (in 11) were received; the actual cost, $53,000, was vouchered for later payment.

15. An order was placed for materials (garage project) estimated to cost $100,000.

16. The net garage bond premium was transferred to the appropriate Debt Service Fund.

Required (a) Prepare CPF General Ledger journal entries.

(b) Post to T-accounts.

(c) Prepare a Combining Balance Sheet for the Capital Projects Funds as of December 31, 19X5.

(d) Prepare a CPF Combining Statement of Revenues, Expenditures, and Changes in Fund Balances for the year ended December 31, 19X5.

P 7-6 (General Ledger Worksheet) From the data in Problem 7-5, Parts I and II, prepare columnar worksheets for each fund for the two-year period ended December 31, 19X5. The worksheet for the Bridge (Capital Projects) Fund should have columnar headings as follows:

19X4 Transactions		Trial Balance, 12/31/19X4		19X5 Transactions		Trial Balance, 12/31/19X5	
Debit	*Credit*	*Debit*	*Credit*	*Debit*	*Credit*	*Debit*	*Credit*

The worksheet for the Garage (Capital Projects) Fund should contain similar headings relating to 19X5 transactions and balances. Entries should be keyed to the numbered items in Problem 7-5. (If statements were not prepared for Problem 7-5, they may be assigned here.)

P 7-7 (GL Entries; Bond Anticipation Notes) Rhea County issued $2,000,000 of nine-month, 9% notes in anticipation of bonds being issued to provide ultimate financing for construction of a county baseball stadium. This prevented undesirable delays in beginning the project, which had been approved at an estimated cost of $4,000,000. December 31 is the end of the county's fiscal year. The following transactions occurred during 19X8 and 19X9:

1. The bond anticipation notes were issued at par on July 1, 19X8.

2. The county signed a contract on July 1, 19X8 with the King of Swat Construction Company to build the stadium. The contract price was $4,000,000.

3. The King of Swat Construction Company billed the county $1,800,000 during 19X8 for work completed on the project. The county paid the amount billed less a 5% retainage to be remitted upon final inspection and approval of the stadium.

4. On February 20, 19X9 the county issued the baseball stadium bonds ($4,000,000 par) at a price of $4,180,000, net of bond issue costs.

5. The county repaid the bond anticipation notes and interest from the bond proceeds upon maturity.

6. The King of Swat Construction Company billed Rhea County $2,200,000 for work performed in 19X9 to complete the baseball stadium. The project was approved by the county and the King of Swat Construction Company was paid in full.

Required (a) Prepare the general journal entries to record the preceding transactions for Rhea County and prepare 19X8 and 19X9 financial statements for the county's Baseball Stadium CPF. Assume that the bond issue had not yet received voter approval in 19X8.

(b) Repeat the requirements in (a) under the assumption that the bond anticipation notes meet the criteria for being treated as general long-term debt.

P 7-8 (GL & SL Entries; Statement) Minars County undertook a major highway improvement project during 19X7 using both independent contractors and its own Highway Department. The following transactions and events affected the related Capital Projects Fund.

1. The county commission approved the following financial plan and appropriations:

Financing Plan

Bond issue proceeds	$ 4,000,000
Federal grant.	3,000,000
State grant	2,000,000
Transfer from General Fund	1,000,000
	$10,000,000

Appropriations

Contract #1	$ 3,500,000
Contract #2	2,700,000
Contract #3	1,300,000
Highway Department	2,500,000
	$10,000,000

The federal grant is for 30% of the actual allowable costs incurred, up to a maximum of $3,000,000, whereas the state grant is a fixed sum $2,000,000 grant.

2. The county commission let highway construction contracts as follows:

Contract #1	$ 3,300,000
Contract #2	2,800,000
Contract #3	1,300,000
	$ 7,400,000

The contract appropriations were revised accordingly. Also, the county Highway Department ordered materials estimated to cost $1,100,000.

3. Expenditures vouchered during 19X7 included:

Contract #1	$ 3,350,000
Contract #2	2,800,000
Contract #3	1,325,000
Highway Department	1,475,000
	$ 8,950,000

A billing for $50,000 of supplies for the Highway Department also was received from an Internal Service Fund. No encumbrances were outstanding at year end. The county retains 5% of contract billings pending final inspection and approval of contract projects, and revised the contract project appropriations to authorize the approved additional work reflected in the contractor billings.

4. Cash receipts during 19X7 included:

Bond issue proceeds	$4,100,000
Federal grant.	2,600,000
State grant	2,000,000
Transfer from General Fund	800,000
	$9,500,000

5. Cash disbursements during 19X7 included:

Vouchers payable	$8,576,250
Transfer of bond premium to Debt Service Fund	100,000
Highway Department payroll	730,750
Internal Service Fund	50,000
	$9,457,000

6. Expenditures of $85,250 recorded previously in the General Fund were found to relate to Highway Department CPF activities. The expenditures were not reimbursed, but were recorded as an in-substance operating transfer to the CPF from the General Fund.

7. The federal government was billed for its remaining share of the total project costs.

8. The final federal grant payment was received as billed, except for an $1,800 reimbursement disallowed because $6,000 of project costs incurred were unallowable under terms of the grant.

9. The highway improvement projects were inspected, approved, and accepted by the county commission. Accordingly, the retained percentages were paid to the contractors, and the remaining balance of the CPF was transferred to a Debt Service Fund.

10. The Capital Projects Fund accounts were closed, and the fund was terminated.

Required
(a) Prepare the journal entries to record the budgetary and actual transactions and events that affected the Minars County Highway Improvement Capital Projects Fund during 19X7 in the CPF General Ledger, Revenues Ledger, and Expenditures Ledger.

(b) Prepare a Statement of Revenues, Expenditures, and Changes in Fund Balance—Budget and Actual for the Minars County Highway Improvement Capital Projects Fund for 19X7.

P 7-9 (GL Worksheet and SLs) This problem requires an alternate solution approach to Problem 7-8 on the Minars County Highway Improvement Capital Projects Fund.

(a) Prepare a General Ledger worksheet and the Revenues Ledger and Expenditures Ledger accounts to record the budgetary and actual transactions and events that affected the Minars County Highway Improvement Capital Projects Fund during 19X7. The General Ledger worksheet should be headed

Columns	Heading
1–2	19X7 Budgetary and Transaction Entries
3–4	Closing Entries—End of 19X7

(b) Prepare a Statement of Revenues, Expenditures, and Changes in Fund Balance—Budget and Actual for the Minars County Highway Improvement Capital Projects Fund.

P 7-10 **Part I.** (GL & SL Entries; Trial Balances; Statements) The following transactions and events relate to the Harmer Independent School District high school building Capital Projects Fund during 19X3.

1. The school board appropriated $9,000,000 to construct and landscape a new regional high school building to be financed as follows:

Bond issue proceeds	$6,000,000
Federal grant (for 20% of cost)	1,800,000
State grant	700,000
Transfer from General Fund	500,000
	$9,000,000

The appropriations made for the high school building were:

Structure	$5,000,000
Plumbing and heating	1,800,000
Electrical	1,300,000
Landscaping	700,000
Other	200,000
	$9,000,000

2. Contracts were let to private contractors:

Structure	$4,700,000
Plumbing and heating	1,825,000
Electrical	1,300,000
	$7,825,000

Thus, the Plumbing and Heating appropriation was increased $25,000, and the Structure appropriation was decreased $300,000.

3. Cash receipts during 19X3 included:

Federal grant	$ 250,000
State grant	350,000
Bond issue proceeds (par $2,000,000) . . .	2,020,000
Transfer from General Fund	100,000
	$2,720,000

The federal grant is for 20% of actual qualifying costs incurred (expenditure-driven) up to its $1,800,000 maximum, but the state grant is an outright contribution to the project.

The remaining bonds authorized will be issued as needed, depending on market conditions; and the Board authorized only part of the General Fund transfer, but is expected to authorize the remainder during 19X4.

4. Invoices from contractors were received, approved, and vouchered for payment less a 5% retained percentage:

Structure	$2,000,000
Plumbing and heating	500,000
Electrical	700,000
Other (not encumbered)	50,000
	$3,250,000

5. Borrowed $150,000 on a short-term note from First State Bank of Harmer.

6. Cash disbursements during 19X3 included:

Vouchers Payable		$2,600,000
Payroll:		
Landscaping	$120,000	
Other	80,000	200,000
Machinery charges—Landscaping		50,000
		$2,850,000

7. Billed the federal government for the balance of its share of project costs incurred to date.

8. Accrued interest payable on the note at year end, $4,000. Interest expenditures on this note are considered a project cost (other), but are not reimbursable under terms of the federal grant.

Required

(a) Prepare the journal entries to record the preceding transactions and events in the General Ledger, Revenues Ledger, and Expenditures Ledger of the Harmer Independent School District high school building Capital Projects Fund during 19X3.

(b) Prepare a preclosing trial balance of the General, Revenues, and Expenditures Ledgers accounts at the end of 19X3.

(c) Prepare the journal entry(ies) to close the General Ledger accounts at the end of 19X3. (Do not close the subsidiary ledgers accounts.)

(d) Prepare a Balance Sheet for the Harmer Independent School District Capital Projects Fund at the end of 19X3 and a Statement of Revenues, Expenditures, and Changes in Fund Balance for the 19X3 fiscal year.

(e) Does it appear that the deficits reported are real or artificial? Explain.

P 7-10 **Part II.** (GL & SL Entries; Statement) The following transactions and events relate to the Harmer Independent School District high school building Capital Projects Fund during 19X4.

1. The Estimated Revenues and Estimated Other Financing Sources accounts were reestablished at their remaining balances, and the Encumbrances account was reestablished. (The interest expenditure accrual entry made at the end of 19X3 was not reversed.)

2. Cash receipts during 19X4 included:

Bond issue proceeds ($4,000,000 par) . . .	$3,985,000
Federal grant	1,440,000
State grant	350,000
Transfer from General Fund	375,000
	$6,150,000

3. Final invoices from contractors were received, approved, and vouchered for payment less a 5% retained percentage:

Structure	$2,750,000
Plumbing and heating	1,325,000
Electrical	600,000
Landscaping (not encumbered)	400,000
	$5,075,000

4. Cash disbursements during 19X4 included:

Vouchers Payable		$5,308,750
Short-term note payable (including interest)		160,000
Transfer of net bond issue premium to Debt Service Fund		5,000
Payroll:		
Landscaping	75,000	
Other	62,000	137,000
Machinery charges—Landscaping		60,000
		$5,670,750

5. Billed the federal government for the balance of its share of qualifying project costs (excluding interest expenditures).

6. Received final payment on the federal grant as billed, except for $400 disallowed because of a $2,000 unallowable cost included in the billing.

7. The high school building was inspected, approved, and accepted by the school board. Accordingly, the retained percentages were paid to the contractors.

8. The remaining cash was transferred to the Debt Service Fund.

9. The high school building Capital Projects Fund accounts were closed and the fund was terminated.

Required

(a) Prepare the journal entries to record the 19X4 transactions and events in the General Ledger, Revenues Ledger, and Expenditures Ledger of the Harmer Independent School District high school building Capital Projects Fund.

(b) Prepare a Statement of Revenues, Expenditures, and Changes in Fund Balance—Budget and Actual for the high school building Capital Projects Fund for the 19X3–19X4 period. The columns of the statement should be headed:

Actual				
19X4	19X3	Total	Budget (Revised)	Variance—Favorable (Unfavorable)

P 7-11 (GL Worksheet, Subsidiary Ledgers, and Statements) This problem requires an alternate solution approach to Problem 7-10, Parts I and II.

Required

(a) Prepare a General Ledger Worksheet, accompanied by Revenues and Expenditures Ledgers accounts, for the Harmer Independent School District Capital Projects Fund for the 19X3 and 19X4 fiscal years. Your General Ledger worksheet should be headed:

Columns	Heading
1–2	19X3 Budgetary and Transaction Entries
3–4	Preclosing Trial Balance—End of 19X3
5–6	Closing Entries—End of 19X3
7–8	Postclosing Trial Balance—End of 19X3
9–10	19X4 Budgetary and Transaction Entries
11–12	Closing Entries—End of 19X4

(b) Prepare a Balance Sheet for the Harmer Independent School District Capital Projects Fund at the end of 19X3 and a Statement of Revenues, Expenditures, and Changes in Fund Balance for the 19X3 fiscal year.

(c) Prepare a Statement of Revenues, Expenditures, and Changes in Fund Balance—Budget and Actual for the Harmer Independent School District Capital Projects Fund for the 19X3–19X4 period. The columns of the statement should be headed:

| Actual | | | Budget | Variance— |
| 19X4 | 19X3 | Total | (Revised) | Favorable (Unfavorable) |

DEBT SERVICE FUNDS

The purpose of Debt Service Funds is "to account for the accumulation of resources for, and the payment of, *general long-term debt* principal and interest."[1] Thus, only *"general government"* long-term debt that is recorded in the General Long-Term Debt Account Group (GLTDAG) is serviced through Debt Service Funds.

Further, not all general long-term debt must be serviced through Debt Service Funds. The GASB Codification provides that "Debt Service Funds are required [only] if they are legally mandated and/or if financial resources are being accumulated for principal and interest payments maturing in future years."[2]

Thus, capital lease and serial bond debt might properly be serviced directly from the General Fund or a Special Revenue Fund—rather than from a Debt Service Fund—if a Debt Service Fund is not required legally or contractually and debt service resources are **not** being accumulated beyond those needed currently. Of course, such debt **could** be serviced through a Debt Service Fund, and many government accountants prefer to account for all general long-term debt service through one or more Debt Service Funds (1) so that all general long-term debt is serviced through the same fund type, and (2) to enhance control over and accountability for debt service resources.

The responsibility of providing for the retirement of long-term general obligation debt is ordinarily indicated by the terms of the **debt indenture** or other contract. The term **"general obligation"** indicates that the **"full faith and credit"** of the governmental unit has been pledged to the repayment of the debt. The term **"revenue debt"** indicates that a *specific revenue source*—such as special assessments or tolls—is *dedicated* to repayment of the debt.

Liabilities of specific funds are not general long-term debt, even if "full faith and credit" debt; and they are normally serviced through those funds rather than the Debt Service Fund(s). For example, when general obligation bonds are issued for the benefit of a public enterprise, the enterprise frequently has primary responsibility for repayment of the bonds (Chapter 13). The same is true of Internal Service Fund debt (Chapter 12). Similarly, some Trust Funds (Chapter 11) may

---

[1] GASB Codification, sec. 1300.104. (Emphasis added.)

[2] Ibid., sec. 1300.107.

have long-term debt. In these situations the debt is *specific fund debt*—not general long-term debt—and is accounted for in and serviced through those funds.

This chapter includes discussions and illustrations of (1) the "general government" Debt Service Fund environment, including its unique terminology and debt service financing and expenditure recognition; (2) accounting and reporting for conventional serial bond DSFs and term bond DSFs (Appendix 7-1); (3) accounting for and reporting debt service on general government special assessment debt—debt that is issued to finance special capital improvements and is serviced by assessments levied against the owners of the property benefited; and (4) advance refundings and the accounting and reporting for DSFs for advance refundings. We begin with brief discussions of several important DSF environment, terminology, financing, and expenditure recognition matters.

DSF ENVIRONMENT, FINANCING, AND EXPENDITURE RECOGNITION

Several features of SLG long-term debt and debt service should be noted at this point. Some are similar to the business environment, but others are unique to the SLG environment.

Types of Long-term Debt

Four types of long-term debt are frequently incurred by state and local governments: bonds; notes; time warrants; and capital leases, lease-purchase agreements, and installment purchase contracts.

A *bond* is a written promise to pay a specified principal sum at a specified future date, usually with interest at a specified rate. Bond issues often are for many millions of dollars since bonds are a major source of long-term financing of capital improvements of most governments. Bonds usually are issued in $1,000 and $5,000 denominations with maturities scheduled over 15 to 25 years and interest paid semiannually or annually. *Term bonds* are those for which all of the principal is payable at a single specified maturity date. *Serial bonds,* by far the most widely used, provide for periodic maturities ranging up to the maximum period permitted by law in the respective states. Specific arrangements of maturities vary widely. Regular serial bonds are repayable in equal annual installments over the life of the issue. In some cases the beginning of the repayment series is deferred several years into the future, after which equal annual installments are to be paid. In some cases the indenture provides for increasing amounts of annual principal payments, computed so that the total annual payment of interest and principal is constant over the life of the issue. Other arrangements also may be provided in the bond indenture.

Notes are less formal documents than bonds that indicate an obligation to repay borrowed money at interest. Notes have a single maturity date, as do term bonds, but their maturity typically ranges from as soon as 30 to 90 days to as long as three to five years after issuance. Too, a single note usually evidences the borrowing transaction, whereas bonds are generally issued in $1,000 and $5,000 denominations. General obligation notes to be repaid within one year of the date of issue normally are carried as liabilities of the General Fund, whereas those to be repaid over a longer period are carried in the General Long-Term Debt Account Group and may be serviced through Debt Service Funds.

Warrants are orders by authorized legislative or executive officials directing the treasurer to pay a specific sum to order or bearer. If these warrants are to be paid more than one year after the date of issue, they also are recorded in the

General Long-Term Debt Account Group and may be serviced through a Debt Service Fund.

Capital leases, lease-purchase agreements, and installment purchase contracts have come into widespread use in government. A variation of lease agreements that has grown more common recently is the "carving up" of leases into shares, called "certificates of participation," that are sold to individual investors. Where the substance of these transactions indicates that a "general government" purchase (or capital lease) and liability exist, they should be recorded as General Fixed Assets and General Long-Term Debt, and may require a Debt Service Fund.

Arrangements of maturity dates of notes, warrants, leases, and similar debt may have substantial diversity. Indeed, some long-term debt issues have abnormally low (even zero) stated interest rates and are issued or sold at significant discounts from par. Such **"deep discount" debt** requires little or no interest payments during the life of the debt. But the entire par amount, which includes "balloon" payment of prior period interest, must be paid at maturity. Most "deep discount" debt is issued in conjunction with serial debt issues, rather than as "stand alone" issues. Indeed "stand alone" issuance of deep discount debt often is prohibited by state or local law. Debt Service Funds for notes, warrants, and other types of General Long-Term Debt are not discussed separately because the accounting for them is similar to that for bonds. However, deep discount debt security debt service is discussed later in this chapter.

Fixed vs. Variable Interest Rates

Municipal bonds issued by state and local governments traditionally have been **"fixed rate"** bonds. That is, the annual interest rate, say 6%, is determined upon issuance of the bonds and remains the same throughout the period the bonds are outstanding.

In recent years, some **"variable rate"** municipal bonds have been issued. In variable rate bond issues the interest rate is set initially, say at 6%. But the interest rate varies periodically while the bonds are outstanding—perhaps annually or semiannually—according to an agreed index such as a certain bank's prime rate or a specified federal security interest rate. Further, some variable rate bonds have interest "floor" (minimum) and "ceiling" (Maximum or "cap") rates—which establish a limited range within which the interest rate can vary.

Government interest expenditure planning, budgeting, and appropriating obviously is simpler and more precise where fixed rate bonds are issued. However, initial interest rates are often lower on variable rate bonds—since the SLG bears some or all of the interest rate change risk. Indeed, it is extremely difficult to predict whether an SLG will obtain lower interest costs over the life of a fixed rate or a variable rate issue, all other factors being equal. The examples in this chapter assume **fixed** interest rate bonds for the sake of illustrative simplicity.

Bond Registration and Fiscal Agents

Both serial bonds and term bonds may be either "registered" or "bearer" bonds. All municipal bonds issued since the mid-1980s are **registered bonds**—that is, the bonds are registered in the name of the investor-creditor, whose name appears on the bond, and bond principal and interest payments are made by checks issued to each investor-creditor. On the other hand, **bearer bonds**—which are no longer issued—are not registered, but are presumed to belong to whoever has possession of them (the "bearer"). Each bearer bond has dated ***interest coupons*** attached, which the bearer clips and deposits at a bank—which processes it like a check. (The bond is deposited and processed similarly upon its maturity.) Thus, bearer bonds are sometimes referred to as *"coupon bonds."*

A few state and local governments perform all bond-related registration and debt service payment functions internally. That is, they register and reregister their bonds, prepare individual interest and principal payment checks, and prepare required annual reports of their debt service activities and payments to the federal and state governments. However, most state and local governments retain a **registration agent** and/or a **paying agent (fiscal agent)** to perform such bond-related functions. A SLG that retains a bond registrar and paying agent—usually a large bank—sends its debt service checks (including a fiscal agent fee) to the fiscal agent. The fiscal agent prepares and processes the individual investor-creditor checks, registers and reregisters bonds as ownership changes, prepares and files the necessary federal and state reports on the SLG's debt service payments, and sends the SLG regular reports summarizing its activities on behalf of the SLG.

DSF Investments

The financial resources of Debt Service Funds are invested until such time as they are needed to pay maturing debt service. State laws and/or bond indenture requirements often specify the types of DSF investments that may be made, and such provisions must be complied with and audited for compliance.

The federal "arbitrage" regulations, discussed earlier, also may influence a SLG's Debt Service Fund investments. Recall that these federal *arbitrage regulations* generally **limit** the **yield** a SLG may earn **when investing** the **proceeds of tax-exempt debt issues**—and usually require that any excess be paid **"rebated"** to the U.S. Treasury. In turn, the U.S. Treasury makes available to SLGs a special type of investment security—known as *State and Local Governments (SLGs)*—which yield rates of return that are acceptable under federal arbitrage regulations.

Most SLG Debt Service Fund investments are in certificates of deposit, U.S. Treasury bills, SLGs, or other high-grade debt securities, though some may be in marketable equity securities. Investments are initially accounted for at cost, including any investment-related fees. Thereafter, debt securities are accounted for at amortized cost—unless a material and apparently permanent decline in the market value has occurred, in which case they are written down to market value—and marketable equity securities are accounted for at cost, with market disclosed, or at the lower of cost or market.

Planning Debt Service Payments

Interest expenditure is an annual cost and is directly proportional to the principal amount of debt outstanding. Since a common debt service planning objective is to keep the drain on each year's resources relatively constant, the pattern of debt service payments for long-term debt usually is designed so that total annual debt service requirements will not fluctuate materially.

Regular serial bonds meet the objective fairly well, and both serial bond issues and lease agreements may be structured to meet the objective extremely well, as do most term bonds. A term bond or deep discount debt security maturing 20 years in the future requires the governmental unit to accumulate the par amount due 20 years hence through annual contributions to a Debt Service Fund that, together with earnings on the invested contributions, will equal the par amount.

Required DSF "Reserves"

Many SLG bond indentures require the SLGs to maintain a specified level of Debt Service Fund **"reserves"** or **"funded reserves."** A common provision is that net assets in the amount of the highest year's principal and interest requirements of the bond issue be maintained in the DSF and be "fully reserved." A certain dollar amount, say, $2,000,000, may also be specified; and in some agreements the SLG can accumulate the "funded reserve" amounts over two to five years. Such "funded reserve" amounts typically may be expended only for (1) debt service payments in the event the SLG encounters financial difficulty during the time the bonds are outstanding, or (2) payment of the final year's debt service. Any amount remaining after the bonds are retired reverts to the SLG.

Such DSF "reserves" or "funded reserves" go by many names—such as Reserve for Contingencies, Reserve for Financial Exigencies, and Reserve for Debt Service Assurance—and the net assets may be held by the SLG or by the trustee for the bondholders, depending on the agreement. In any event, their **purpose is to provide bondholders additional assurance** that they will be paid promptly—even if the SLG encounters financial difficulty—and that the bonds will not be allowed to go into default. Such agreements are important contractual agreements that must be observed by SLG officials; and compliance with these agreements must be examined by the external auditor. Existence of such reserves also dictates that a Debt Service Fund—not the General or a Special Revenue Fund—be used to account for debt service for the debt issue. A DSF is required when "financial resources are being accumulated for principal and interest payments maturing in future years."[3]

Sources of Financing

The money for repaying long-term debt may come from numerous sources with varying legal restrictions. The typical source is property taxes. A special tax rate may be assessed for a single bond issue, or a total annual rate may be used with the proceeds prorated to several debt issues. Legislative bodies may earmark a tax for a specified purpose, with a proviso that the proceeds may be used for current operating expenditures, capital outlay, or to repay debt incurred to finance the specified purpose. In such cases the proceeds of the tax would be accounted for in a Special Revenue Fund; the portion of the proceeds allocated to debt service would be transferred to a Debt Service Fund. Also, general government special assessment debt service typically is financed from special assessments levied on benefited properties and interest charged on the unpaid assessments.

Still another method of providing for debt service is required by bond indentures or other contracts that specify that the debt shall be repaid out of "the first revenues accruing to the treasury." Such agreements require the government to contribute the necessary amounts to the Debt Service Fund from the General Fund; the obligation has first claim on the revenues of the General Fund.

When a term bond issue is to be repaid through a fund in which resources are being accumulated to retire the principal at maturity, the assets of the fund will be invested in income-producing securities. Similarly, some serial bond Debt Service Funds have investable resources. The income from these securities constitutes still another form of Debt Service Fund revenue.

Finally, maturing bonds may be refunded, that is, they may be retired by either (1) exchanging new bonds for old ones or (2) selling a new bond issue and

---

[3] Ibid.

using the proceeds to retire an old issue. The new bond issue constitutes the financing source in refunding transactions.

Debt Service Expenditure Recognition

Debt service payments are made routinely for three types of debt-related expenditures: (1) **interest** on long-term debt outstanding, (2) retirement of debt **principal** as it matures, and (3) **fiscal agent fees** charged by a bank or other institution for preparing and processing debt service checks, registering and reregistering bonds, and related services. Assuming a fiscal agent is used, a SLG typically issues only one annual or semiannual check—to its fiscal agent—for all debt service expenditures for each bond issue.

As discussed in detail early in Chapter 6 (pages 203–204), GLTD debt service expenditures usually are *not* accrued at year end, but are recorded as expenditures "when due," that is, when they mature and are due and payable. Several practical and conceptual reasons are the basis for the **"when due"** recording:

1. Most SLGs budget and appropriate on the basis of how much debt service must be paid during the year to bondholders, directly or through fiscal agents. Permitting SLGs to report debt service expenditures "when due" avoids a potential budgetary basis-GAAP basis difference that otherwise would have to be reported, explained, and reconciled in the financial statements and notes.

2. Few government budgets separate the bond interest—the main potentially accruable debt service component—from the bond principal payments and related fiscal agent fees. Rather, they view the total required payments as the debt service expenditures.

3. Many governments transfer resources from the General Fund or Special Revenue Funds to the Debt Service Fund(s) when debt service payments are due. Thus, to accrue interest expenditures and liabilities in the Debt Service Fund prior to the debt service due date would cause an "artificial" Fund Balance deficit to be reported in the Debt Service Fund.

4. Where financial resources are transferred from other funds to the Debt Service Fund, as in 3, payment of the unmatured debt service will not require the use of existing financial resources of the Debt Service Fund. Thus, such amounts are not current liabilities properly recorded as expenditures in the Debt Service Fund. Similarly, where governments levy property taxes sufficient to pay each year's debt service requirements, the debt service payments to be made in the following year will not require existing year end resources of any governmental fund, and thus are not current year expenditures and liabilities.

Although most SLGs recognize debt service expenditures on the "when due" approach, recall that the GASB Codification provides this **option:**

> . . . **if** debt service fund **resources have been provided** during the current year for payment of principal and interest **due early in the following year,** the [debt service] expenditure and related liability may be recognized [at year end] in the debt service fund and the debt principal amount removed from the general long-term debt account group.[4]

This option has arisen because some SLGs budget and appropriate in this manner. Note that under this option *the entire next debt service payment*—not just the in-

---

[4] Ibid., sec. 1600.121. (Emphasis added.)

terest expenditure accrued at year end—would be *recorded as a current year expenditure and liability.*

A SLG can combine the "when due" approach and "if due early next year" option by using the former for most issues and using the latter for those issues that meet its criteria. However, each SLG should adopt appropriate debt service expenditure recognition policies and apply them consistently so that 12 months' debt service is reported in each fiscal year.

DEBT SERVICE FUND FOR A SERIAL BOND ISSUE

To illustrate the operation of a Debt Service Fund for a serial issue assume that A Governmental Unit issued $1,000,000 of 5% Flores Park Serial Bonds on January 1, 19X1, to finance the purchase and development of a park. The bond indenture requires annual payments of $100,000 to retire the principal and annual payments of interest to date. The debt service requirements (principal and interest) are to be financed by a property tax levied for that purpose.

The bond indenture requires that a $150,000 "funded and invested" reserve for fiscal exigencies be accumulated—$80,000 in 19X1 and $70,000 in 19X2—to provide added assurance of timely payments to bondholders. The governing body of A Governmental Unit agreed to transfer such amounts from the General Fund to the Flores Park Serial Bonds Debt Service Fund.

The Third State Bank was retained as the bond registrar and paying agent (fiscal agent) for the Flores Park serial bond issue. The 19X1 fiscal agent fee will be $10,000.

The governing body of A Governmental Unit adopted the following budget for the Flores Park Serial Bonds Debt Service Fund for 19X1:

Estimated Revenues and Transfers In:	
Property taxes	$162,000
Interest on investments	6,000
Operating transfer from General Fund	80,000
	$248,000
Appropriations	
Bond principal retirement	$100,000
Interest on bonds	50,000
Fiscal agent fees	10,000
	$160,000
Budgeted increase in fund balance	$ 88,000

Furthermore, it ordered that the $80,000 transferred from the General Fund be invested and fully reserved.

Illustrative Entries

The following journal entries record the 19X1 transactions and events affecting the Flores Park Serial Bonds Debt Service Fund assuming subsidiary ledgers and budgetary accounts are used:

Entries during 19X1

(1)	Estimated Revenues	168,000	
	Estimated Operating Transfer from General Fund	80,000	
	Appropriations		160,000
	Unreserved Fund Balance		88,000
	To record 19X1 budget.		

Revenues Ledger (Estimated Revenues):

Property Taxes.	162,000	
Interest on Investments.	6,000	
	168,000	

Expenditures Ledger (Appropriations):

Bond Principal Retirement		100,000
Interest on Bonds.		50,000
Fiscal Agent Fees		10,000
		160,000

(2) Cash. 80,000

    Operating Transfer from General Fund 80,000

    To record transfer received.

(3) Investments. 80,000

    Unreserved Fund Balance 80,000

        Cash. 80,000

        Reserve for Fiscal Exigencies. 80,000

    To record establishing invested reserve as required by
        bond indenture.

(4) Taxes Receivable—Current 165,000

        Allowance for Uncollectible Current Taxes. 3,000

        Revenues 162,000

    To record property tax levy of $165,000 (estimated
        uncollectible taxes are $3,000).

Revenues Ledger (Revenues):

Property Taxes.		162,000

(5) Cash. 158,000

        Taxes Receivable—Current 158,000

    To record property tax collections.

(6) Cash. 4,000

        Revenues 4,000

    To record receipt of interest on investments.

Revenues Ledger (Revenues):

Interest on Investments.		4,000

(7) Expenditures. 160,000

    Matured Bonds Payable. 100,000

    Matured Interest Payable. 50,000

    Fiscal Agent Fees Payable 10,000

    To record liability for first annual serial bond maturity.

Expenditures Ledger (Expenditures):

Bond Principal Retirement	100,000	
Interest on Bonds.	50,000	
Fiscal Agent Fees	10,000	
	160,000	

(8) Matured Bonds Payable. 100,000

    Matured Interest Payable. 50,000

    Fiscal Agent Fees Payable 10,000

        Cash. 160,000

    To record payment of matured debt service liabilities.

Note: Entries 7 and 8 are often compounded into one expenditures and cash disbursement entry in practice since many governments pay the debt service to the paying agent several days before or upon its maturity.

(9a) Taxes Receivable—Delinquent. 7,000

     Allowance for Uncollectible Current Taxes. 3,000

        Taxes Receivable—Current 7,000

        Allowance for Uncollectible Delinquent Taxes 3,000

    To reclassify taxes receivable and related allowance
        accounts from current to delinquent.

| (9b) | Revenues . . . . | 2,000 | |
| | Deferred Property Tax Revenue . . . . | | 2,000 |

To record deferred revenue for the portion of the current
levy not considered "available."

Revenues Ledger (Revenues):

Property Taxes.   2,000

| (10) | Accrued Interest Receivable . . . . | 3,000 | |
| | Revenues . . . . | | 3,000 |

To accrue interest earned on investments at year end.

Revenues Ledger (Revenues):

Interest on Investments.   3,000

Closing Entries—End of 19X1

General Ledger

(C1)	Appropriations.	160,000	
	Unreserved Fund Balance	88,000	
	Estimated Revenues		168,000
	Estimated Operating Transfer from General Fund		80,000

To reverse budgetary entry.

(C2)	Revenues	167,000	
	Operating Transfer from General Fund	80,000	
	Expenditures.		160,000
	Unreserved Fund Balance		87,000

To close operating accounts.

Revenues Subsidiary Ledger

Property Taxes.   2,000

Interest on Investments.   1,000

Note that with so few operating accounts being needed, **this fund could readily have been accounted for entirely in the DSF General Ledger.** That is, **use of a series of detailed General Ledger accounts**—as illustrated in Chapter 7—would negate the need for the Revenues Subsidiary Ledger and Expenditures Subsidiary Ledger. Both approaches may be found in practice and on the Uniform CPA Examination.

Note also that there were few variances between budget and actual during 19X1. Indeed, the Expenditures Ledger accounts had zero preclosing balances, so no entry was required to close those accounts. Debt Service Fund expenditures usually can be budgeted precisely. Thus, especially where DSFs have little revenue—as when they are financed largely by interfund transfers—budgetary control accounts may not be used in practice in simple DSF situations.

Financial Statements

As for all governmental funds, the annual financial statements required for Debt Service Funds are:

- Balance Sheet
- Statement of Revenues, Expenditures, and Changes in Fund Balance (GAAP operating statement)
- Statement of Revenues, Expenditures, and Changes in Fund Balance—Budget and Actual (budgetary operating statement) **if** budgeted annually, as is usual with Debt Service Funds.

The Balance Sheet at the end of 19X1 for the Flores Park Serial Bonds Debt Service Fund is presented in Figure 8-1, and its Statement of Revenues, Expenditures, and Changes in Fund Balance—Budget and Actual (budgetary operating statement) is presented in Figure 8-2. Since the budget is prepared on the GAAP

Figure 8-1

SERIAL BONDS DEBT SERVICE FUND BALANCE SHEET

A Governmental Unit
Flores Park Serial Bonds Debt Service Fund
Balance Sheet
December 31, 19X1

Assets

Cash		$ 2,000
Taxes receivable—delinquent	$ 7,000	
Less: Allowance for		
uncollectible delinquent taxes	3,000	4,000
Investments		80,000
Accrued interest receivable		3,000
		$89,000

Liabilities and Fund Balance

Liabilities:		
Deferred property tax revenue		$ 2,000
Fund Balance:		
Reserved for exigencies	$80,000	
Unreserved	7,000	87,000
		$89,000

Figure 8-2

SERIAL BONDS DEBT SERVICE FUND BUDGETARY OPERATING STATEMENT

A Governmental Unit
Flores Park Serial Bonds Debt Service Fund
**Statement of Revenues, Expenditures, and
Changes in Fund Balance—Budget and Actual**
For Year Ended December 31, 19X1

	Budget	Actual	Variance— Favorable (Unfavorable)
Revenues:			
Property taxes	$162,000	$160,000	$(2,000)
Interest on investments	6,000	7,000	1,000
	168,000	167,000	(1,000)
Other Financing Sources:			
Operating transfer from General Fund	80,000	80,000	—
Total Revenues and Other Financing Sources	248,000	247,000	(1,000)
Expenditures:			
Bond principal retirement	100,000	100,000	—
Interest on bonds	50,000	50,000	—
Fiscal agent fees	10,000	10,000	—
	160,000	160,000	—
Excess of Revenues and Other Financing Sources			
Over Expenditures	88,000	87,000	(1,000)
Fund Balance—January 1	—	—	—
Fund Balance—December 31	$ 88,000	$ 87,000	$(1,000)

Note: *Under terms of the bond indenture, $80,000 of the total fund balance is invested and reserved for exigencies.*

basis in this example, the data in the GAAP operating statement are the same as the "actual" data in Figure 8-2.

SPECIAL ASSESSMENT DEBT SERVICE FUNDS

One unique type of Debt Service Fund, referred to as a **Special Assessment** Debt Service Fund, is used to account for servicing general long-term debt issued to finance special assessment capital improvement projects. As noted in previous chapters, a special assessment is, in substance, a special property tax that is levied only on properties or property owners benefited by a particular capital project—such as sidewalk construction in a new subdivision. The projects are referred to as "special assessment projects" because of the underlying financing source—the special assessments.

In the typical special assessment project, the benefited area is made a "special assessment district," and the local government serves as the general contractor and financing agent for the project. As the *general contractor,* the government oversees the project, arranges for the necessary engineering studies, prepares specifications for the project, and so on. As the *financing agent,* the government:

- Provides interim financing for construction either by issuing its own bonds or notes or by issuing special assessment bonds or notes, which the government typically guarantees.

- Upon completion, inspection, and approval of the project, levies assessments against the properties (property owners) benefited. Each property owner is billed for a full proportionate share of the project costs, but is allowed to pay in installments over a period of years. The government charges interest on the unpaid assessment receivable balances.

- Bills and collects the special assessments and related interest.

- Services the general long-term debt associated with the project out of the special assessment collections. If the government is responsible for part of the cost of the project, some "general government" cash may be transferred to the special assessment Debt Service Fund for this purpose as well.

The primary uniqueness of a special assessment Debt Service Fund is the noncurrent nature of the portion of the special assessment receivables that are not yet due and payable. Indeed, the key differences between special assessments and property taxes are that special assessments are (1) for amounts that are payable over several years and (2) levied only on a subset of properties in a government's jurisdiction. Given the similarities, revenue accounting for special assessments follows the same principles as that for property taxes. Revenue is recognized when it is measurable and available; therefore, the long-term special assessments receivable, called special assessments receivable—deferred, are offset by deferred revenues. Additionally, any portion of current or delinquent special assessments receivable that does *not* meet the revenue recognition criteria will result in additional deferred revenues being reported.

It should be noted that Debt Service Funds are not used to account for debt service of all special assessment indebtedness. Enterprise-related special assessment indebtedness may be accounted for entirely in the appropriate Enterprise Fund if the government chooses to do so, as discussed in Chapter 13. Also, if the government is *not* "obligated in some manner" on special assessment revenue debt:

- The debt is not viewed as debt of the government.

- No Debt Service Fund is required, since the debt is not an obligation of the government.

- An Agency Fund will be used to reflect the government's fiduciary responsibility as the "fiscal agent" for the special assessment district. This is illustrated in Chapter 11.

In the overwhelming majority of cases, governments *are* "obligated in some manner" for the debt issued to finance special assessment projects for their constituency. Indeed, the GASB, in describing the intended breadth of this criterion, notes that:

> Stated differently, the phrase **"obligated in some manner"** as used in this [Statement] is **intended to include all situations other than** those in which (a) the government is **prohibited** (by constitution, charter, statute, ordinance, or contract) from assuming the debt in the event of default by the property owner or (b) the government is **not legally liable** for assuming the debt **and makes no statement, or gives no indication, that it will, or may, honor the debt in the event of default.**[5]

Note that when a general government special assessment project is financed with special assessment debt for which the government is *not* obligated in *any* manner, the construction costs still will be reported in a Capital Projects Fund. This treatment is required because the fixed asset will become the property of the government when completed. The primary difference in reporting for the Capital Projects Fund under these circumstances is that the issuance of the special assessment indebtedness will be reported as "Other financing sources—contributions from property owners" rather than as "Other financing sources—general long-term debt issue proceeds."

Illustrative Entries

To illustrate the accounting and reporting for a Special Assessment Debt Service Fund, assume that A Governmental Unit financed a major, general government, special assessment capital project by issuing special assessment bonds backed by the full faith and credit of A Governmental Unit. General revenues are to be used for the first principal and interest payment on the special assessment bonds. This covers the portion of the project cost that the government agreed to contribute. The remaining costs are to be recovered through special assessments levied against benefited properties.

The par value of the five-year, 6%, special assessment bonds was $1,000,000 and the bonds were issued at par on July 1, 19X0. Interest and one-fifth of the principal are due each June 30, beginning June 30, 19X1. The project was completed during 19X0 at the budgeted cost of $1,000,000.

The bond proceeds and the construction phase of the project would be accounted for like any other major general government capital project—in a Capital Projects Fund. The fixed asset constructed would be reported in the General Fixed Assets Account Group (Chapter 9) and the bonds payable would be reported in the General Long-Term Debt Account Group (Chapter 9).

The following transactions, which assume that the government adopted a "project" budget for this fund, so need *not* present budgetary *statements* each year, are used to illustrate the accounting and reporting of the Special Assessment Debt Service Fund. Moreover, *budgetary entries* are *omitted* to focus on the entries for the *actual* transactions and events.

[5] Ibid., sec. S40.116. (Emphasis added.)

1. Special assessments of $800,000 were levied on benefited properties upon completion of the project on **December 31, 19X0.** One-fourth of the levy, along with 6% interest on the uncollected balance, is due each of the next four years beginning December 31, 19X1.

Assessments Receivable—Deferred	800,000	
Deferred Revenues—Assessments		800,000
To record levy of special assessments.		

      Note that the Special Assessment DSF financial statements at **December 31, 19X0** would consist only of a balance sheet reporting the accounts and amounts from the preceding entry. **The following transactions occurred in 19X1.**

2. $200,000 of special assessments became current in 19X1.

Assessments Receivable—Current	200,000	
Assessments Receivable—Deferred		200,000
To reclassify deferred assessments that are due in 19X1.		
Deferred Revenues—Assessments	200,000	
Revenues—Assessments		200,000
To recognize assessment revenues for current assessments.		

Note this entry assumes that the $200,000 will be collected by year end or within 60 days thereafter.

3. A $260,000 operating transfer is received from the General Fund.

Cash	260,000	
Operating Transfer from General Fund		260,000
To record receipt of General Fund transfer.		

4. The principal and interest on the special assessment bonds matured and were paid.

Expenditures—Principal Retirement	200,000	
Expenditures—Interest	60,000	
Cash		260,000
To record payment of debt service.		

5. Collections of special assessments included $185,000 principal and $55,000 interest.

Cash	240,000	
Assessments Receivable—Current		185,000
Revenues—Interest		55,000
To record collections during 19X1.		

6. The uncollected assessments receivable that were due in 19X1 were reclassified as delinquent and the uncollected interest ($5,000) was accrued. It is expected that all except $1,500 interest will be collected within the first 60 days of 19X2.

Assessments Receivable—Delinquent	15,000	
Accrued Interest Receivable	5,000	
Assessments Receivable—Current		15,000
Revenues—Interest		3,500
Deferred Revenues—Interest		1,500
To accrue interest receivable and reclassify assessment receivables.		

7. The accounts were closed.

Revenues—Assessments	200,000	
Revenues—Interest	58,500	
Operating Transfer from General Fund	260,000	
Expenditures—Principal Retirement		200,000
Expenditures—Interest		60,000
Unreserved Fund Balance		258,500

To close the accounts at the end of 19X1.

Financial Statements

The balance sheet for the Special Assessments Debt Service Fund of A Governmental Unit at the end of 19X1 is presented in Figure 8-3. The 19X1 Statement of Revenues, Expenditures, and Changes in Fund Balance is presented in Figure 8-4.

Figure 8-3

SPECIAL ASSESSMENT DEBT SERVICE FUND BALANCE SHEET

A Governmental Unit
Special Assessment Bonds Debt Service Fund
Balance Sheet
December 31, 19X1

Assets

Cash	$240,000
Special assessments receivable—deferred	600,000
Special assessments receivable—delinquent	15,000
Interest receivable on assessments	5,000
Total assets	$860,000

Liabilities and Fund Balance

Liabilities:	
Deferred assessment revenues	$600,000
Deferred interest revenues	1,500
Total liabilities	$601,500
Unreserved fund balance	258,500
Total liabilities and fund balance	$860,000

Figure 8-4

SPECIAL ASSESSMENT DEBT SERVICE FUND OPERATING STATEMENT

A Governmental Unit
Special Assessment Bonds Debt Service Fund
Statement of Revenues, Expenditures, and Changes in Fund Balance
For the Year Ended December 31, 19X1

Revenues		
Special assessments	$200,000	
Interest	58,500	$258,500
Other Financing Sources:		
Operating transfer from General Fund		260,000
Total Revenues and Other Financing Sources		518,500
Expenditures:		
Principal retirement	$200,000	
Interest	60,000	260,000
Excess of Revenues and Other Financing Sources over		
Expenditures		258,500
Fund Balance—January 1		—
Fund Balance—December 31		$258,500

The balance sheet continues to be quite simple as in the serial bond example, though it is complicated somewhat by the reporting of the special assessments receivable and deferred revenues. Note that only the assessments that meet the property tax revenue recognition criteria are reported in the operating statement.

OTHER CONVENTIONAL DSF CONSIDERATIONS

Several other accounting and reporting considerations should be noted or reviewed briefly at this point. These include (1) nonaccrual of interest payable, (2) the combining DSF balance sheet, (3) the combining DSF operating statement, (4) use of a single DSF for several bond issues, and (5) pooling of DSF investments.

Nonaccrual of Interest Payable

Recall that the GASB Codification **does not permit**—much less require—accrual of the year-end balances of interest payable on conventional bonds or other general long-term debt **unless** (1) the **resources** to pay the interest have been **accrued or received** in the Debt Service Fund **and** (2) the debt service **payment** is **due early** in the **next year.** If a fund is on a calendar year basis and the annual interest on its bonds was paid as scheduled on October 31, 19X1, the government clearly would be obligated, as of December 31, 19X1, for the interest for the last two months of 19X1. On the other hand, the 19X1 budget typically would provide for the payment of the interest expenditure falling due in the current year, and the following year's budget would provide for payment of interest due in 19X2. Since the resources that will be used to pay the interest for the months of November and December 19X1 cannot be accrued as of December 31, 19X1, accruing that interest expenditure and liability could result in (1) an unwarranted deficit being reported in serial bond Debt Service Funds and (2) an unwarranted fund balance deficiency being reported in term bond Debt Service Funds. Thus, interest payable at year end normally is **not** recorded in Debt Service Funds.

On the other hand, **if** Debt Service Fund taxes or other financial resources have been made available at the end of 19X1 to pay debt interest and/or principal maturing early in 19X2, the expenditure and related liability **may** be recorded in the Debt Service Fund in 19X1. In this case the amount of the debt principal that is recorded as a Debt Service Fund expenditure and liability should be removed from the General Long-Term Debt accounts.

Combining Balance Sheet

Separate balance sheets for each of the Debt Service Funds of A Governmental Unit are prepared, as in Figures 8-1 and 8-3, and may be sent to bond trustees. But if there are two or more funds, they are presented in a **combining** balance sheet, as shown in Figure 8-5, and the total data are presented in the SLG's combined balance sheet.

Debt Service Fund balance sheets might include such additional assets as Cash with Fiscal Agents, Taxes Receivable—Current, Tax Liens Receivable, and Interest and Penalties Receivable on Taxes. In addition, the unamortized premiums and discounts on investments may be presented in the combining balance sheet (as in Figure 8-9) rather than showing the investment figure at net amortized cost. Similarly, there may be such liability accounts as Matured Bonds Payable and Matured Interest Payable.

Figure 8-5

DEBT SERVICE FUNDS COMBINING BALANCE SHEET

A Governmental Unit
Debt Service Funds
Combining Balance Sheet
December 31, 19X1

	Flores Park Serial Bonds	Special Assessment Bonds	Total
Assets			
Cash.	$ 2,000	$240,000	$242,000
Special assessments receivable—deferred. . . .	—	600,000	600,000
Special assessments receivable—delinquent . .	—	15,000	15,000
Taxes receivable—delinquent (net of estimated uncollectible taxes)	4,000	—	4,000
Investments (net)	80,000	—	80,000
Interest receivable on investments	3,000	—	3,000
Interest receivable on assessments.	—	5,000	5,000
	$89,000	$860,000	$949,000
Liabilities and Fund Balances			
Liabilities:			
Deferred property tax revenues	$ 2,000	—	$ 2,000
Deferred assessment revenues.	—	600,000	600,000
Deferred interest revenues	—	1,500	1,500
	2,000	601,500	603,500
Fund Balances:			
Reserved for exigencies	80,000	—	80,000
Unreserved	7,000	258,500	265,500
	87,000	258,500	345,500
	$89,000	$860,000	$949,000

If a government has more than seven or eight Debt Service Funds, the format of Figure 8-5 becomes unwieldy. One option in such cases is to present a Combining Debt Service Funds Balance Sheet with a column for each major Debt Service Fund and an "Other Debt Service Funds" column presenting the combined data for the other Debt Service Funds. This should be accompanied by a Combining Balance Sheet (or schedule) for the "other" Debt Service Funds, the total of which agrees with the "Other Debt Service Funds" column of the main Combining Balance Sheet.

Combining Operating Statement

A Combining Statement of Revenues, Expenditures, and Changes in Fund Balances for the Debt Service Funds of A Government Unit is presented in Figure 8-6. Combining budgetary comparison statements also are presented by governments with two or more Debt Service Funds.

Additional revenue accounts that might appear in the statement include Interest and Penalties on Property Taxes; Revenue from Other Agencies, such as shared taxes from higher governments; and Gains or Losses on Disposition of Investments. Also, additional operating transfers and residual equity transfers may have increased the fund balance during the period.

Figure 8-6

DEBT SERVICE FUNDS COMBINING OPERATING STATEMENT

A Governmental Unit
Debt Service Funds
Combining Statement of Revenues, Expenditures, and Changes in Fund Balances
For the Year Ended December 31, 19X1

	Flores Park Serial Bonds	Special Assessment Bonds	Total
Revenues:			
Property taxes	$160,000	$ —	$160,000
Special assessments	—	200,000	200,000
Interest on investments	7,000	—	7,000
Interest on assessments	—	58,500	58,500
	167,000	258,500	425,500
Other Financing Sources:			
Operating transfer from General Fund	80,000	260,000	340,000
Total Revenues and Other Financing			
Sources	247,000	518,500	765,500
Expenditures:			
Bond principal retirement	100,000	200,000	300,000
Interest on bonds	50,000	60,000	110,000
Fiscal agent fees	10,000	—	10,000
	160,000	260,000	420,000
Excess of Revenues and Other Financing			
Sources Over Expenditures	87,000	258,500	345,500
Fund Balance—January 1	—	—	—
Fund Balance—December 31	$ 87,000	$258,500	$345,500

Single Debt Service Fund for Several Bond Issues

As a general rule, the number of Debt Service Funds should be held to a minimum. The law or contractual requirements may in some cases require a separate Debt Service Fund for each bond issue; in other cases they permit a single Debt Service Fund to service several or all issues.

A single Debt Service Fund is particularly desirable for all the issues to be financed from the general property tax. In such cases the budget for the single Debt Service Fund is prepared by analyzing the debt service requirements for each bond issue. That is, the Estimated Transfers In, Estimated Revenues, and Appropriations accounts are recorded in the **total** of those that would be recorded in individual Debt Service Funds for each issue. Revenues and transfers in are not allocated to specific issues in such cases, nor are assets and liabilities segregated by bond issue, though fund balances may be.

When a balance sheet is prepared for a single Debt Service Fund that is servicing several issues, two sections of the balance sheet may require specific identification of individual debt issues: (1) any matured debt issue in default is identified by name, and (2) the Fund Balance amount(s) should be supported by a schedule of the actuarial requirements, if any, for each debt issue.

Pooling of Investments

Even though the law, contractual agreements, or administrative judgment may require several Debt Service Funds, it may be feasible to pool the investments of the Debt Service Funds to achieve maximum efficiency and safety in the investment program. For example, a single investment counsel may be able to serve as easily for a major investment as for several minor ones. More important, the investments may be diversified when a substantial sum is involved and economies of purchase may result from investing large sums rather than small ones.

Also, higher yields may be earned and less of the total assets of all of the Funds may need to be kept in cash (nonearning) if the investable assets of the Debt Service Funds are pooled. In such cases well-defined rules for determining the equity of each Debt Service Fund in the assets and in the profits and losses from investments must be established and detailed records must be maintained.

Recall that the GASB Codification (sec. 1300.109) provides for practices such as pooling of investments—assuming they are permitted by a government's legal and contractual provisions—by stating that the GAAP requirement for a complete set of accounts for each fund refers to identification of accounts in the accounting records—and does not necessarily require physical segregation of assets. However, that Codification statement presumes that a sound accounting system is in place—which is a prerequisite both to "funds within a fund" accounting (discussed earlier) and pooling of investments.

DEBT SERVICE FUNDS FOR "DEEP DISCOUNT" ISSUES

Although most state and local government bond and note issues are conventional serial or term issues, some recent issues are nonconventional **"deep discount"** bonds and notes. The "pure" deep discount issue—the **"zero coupon"** bond—has a 0% *stated* interest rate and provides that **neither** interest **nor** principal will be paid during the term the bond issue is outstanding. Rather, **both** the principal and accumulated *effective* interest, compounded at the effective rate for the life of the bonds—typically ranging from 10–25 years—are paid in a lump sum payment of the par (face) amount upon maturity of the zero coupon bonds. Thus, zero coupon bonds are like term bonds, except that the total compound interest for the term of the bond—as well as the principal—is included in the single "balloon" payment of the par (face) amount upon maturity of the bonds 10–25 years or more after issuance.

A variation of the "pure" zero coupon deep discount bond, the **"low interest"** bond, may bear an interest rate of 1 to 2% when the market rate—the effective interest rate—is 6 to 8%.

Both zero coupon bonds and low interest bonds and notes are *discounted* from issuance *until maturity* at the *effective interest rate* by investors, of course, *so* their issue *proceeds* are *only* a *fraction* of their *par or face* value. The *discount from par (face) thus represents the interest (or additional interest) on the bonds that will not be paid until their maturity.*

"Deep discount" bonds and notes are generally **defined** as those issued with a stated (or face) interest rate less than 75% of the effective interest rate. Such deep discount debt issued as **general long-term debt** presents debt service accounting problems because either (1) current liabilities are not incurred until the maturity of the debt or (2) the current liabilities incurred on low interest debt are not a reasonable measure of the interest cost of such debt issues.

The GASB Codification does **not** contain guidance on accounting for and reporting these relatively new, nonconventional "deep discount" bond and note issues. Thus, most governments with deep discount debt appear to recognize debt service expenditures and liabilities on such debt—for both interest and principal retirement—on the "when due" or "due early next year" approaches discussed and illustrated earlier for conventional interest-bearing (at market rates) bonds and notes. The result is that most or all of the interest expenditures—as well as the principal retirement expenditures—are reported in the year the "deep discount" debt matures, perhaps 15–25 years after issuance of the debt instrument.

While such practices are consistent with the current GASB standards—and most governments with "deep discount" debt make extensive disclosures—the propriety of "lumping" all or most interest expenditures, in particular, in the year of debt maturity is questionable. Accordingly, the GASB plans to specify a method of accounting for deep discount general long-term debt. Debt service accounting for deep discount debt is discussed further in Chapter 15, "Contemporary Issues."

ADVANCE REFUNDINGS

The term and serial Debt Service Fund examples presented earlier in the chapter are based on the usual assumptions of conventional Debt Service Funds, that during the life of the debt issue (1) financial resources are accumulated in DSFs from **non-GLTD sources**—such as property taxes, special assessments, interest earned on investments, and interfund transfers; (2) DSF financial resources are expended to pay GLTD principal and interest **at their scheduled maturities;** and (3) the payments or accruals of GLTD principal and interest from non-GLTD financial resources as they mature are reported in accounts such as **Expenditures—Bond Principal Retirement,** to reflect the extinguishment of the GLTD principal, and **Expenditures—Interest on Bonds,** respectively.

But governments may issue **new** GLTD to pay (or service) **old** GLTD **prior to its maturity**—thus effectively *substituting the new GLTD issue for the old GLTD issue.* Accordingly, such transactions—known as **"advance refundings"**—are accounted for as *substitutions* of GLTD *rather than as extinguishments* of GLTD.

Reasons for Advance Refundings

State and local governments may issue new debt to advance refund old debt for a variety of reasons, including:

1. **Lower Effective Interest Rates.** A SLG may be able to issue new bonds or notes at interest rates sufficiently lower than those being paid on the old bonds or notes that—even after paying the related refunding costs—it obtains lower net effective interest rates (and costs) and thus has an economic gain as a result of the advance refunding.

2. **Extend Maturity Dates.** Where old debt principal matures soon, perhaps without an adequate sinking fund having been accumulated, a SLG may effectively extend the maturity date of the old debt by an advance refunding.

3. **Revise Payment Schedules.** If the total debt service requirements—including both interest and principal—of the old debt are not relatively stable for each future year, a SLG may effectively rearrange its debt service payment schedule by an advance refunding.

4. **Remove or Modify Restrictions.** Onerous restrictions of old debt indentures, covenants, or other agreements—such as those requiring large funded reserves or specifying that no (or limited) new debt may be incurred while the old debt is outstanding—may be removed or modified by issuing new advance refunding debt with changed indenture provisions.

In sum, certain advance refundings are undertaken to obtain an ***economic advantage***—such as lower net effective interest rates and interest costs—but other advance refundings are designed to obtain ***noneconomic advantages*** such as to extend maturity dates, revise debt service payment schedules, and remove or modify debt-related restrictions.

"Advance Refunding" Defined

The GASB states that:

> In an **advance refunding** transaction, new debt is issued [1] to provide monies to pay interest on old, outstanding debt as it becomes due, and [2] to pay the principal on the old debt either as it matures or at an earlier call date. An advance refunding occurs before the maturity or call date of the old debt, and the proceeds of the new debt are invested until the maturity or call date of the old debt.[6]

In some advance refundings, the SLG uses the proceeds of the new GLTD issue to retire the old GLTD issue directly within a few weeks or months. This may occur, for example, when the new GLTD is issued to refund an old term bond or deep discount note that matures soon but for which adequate resources have not been accumulated in a DSF sinking fund.

Most advance refundings do not result in immediate, direct retirement of the old GLTD issue, however. Rather, in most advance refunding transactions (1) the proceeds of the new GLTD issue are placed in escrow—in an irrevocable trust—with a bank or other financial institution trust department for the benefit of the old GLTD investors-creditors; (2) the proceeds are invested in appropriate securities—that are acceptable under any terms of the old GLTD issue indenture, covenant, or other agreement and in compliance with applicable federal arbitrage and other regulations; and (3) the invested proceeds and related earnings are used to pay interest and principal on the old debt—which remains outstanding—at the regularly scheduled maturities or, if the old debt is called for early redemption, until (and at) the call date.

"Defeasance" of Old Debt

The term **"defeased"** means "terminated" or "rendered null and void." Debt that has been defeased is thus considered to be ***extinguished***—and is ***removed from the GLTD accounts*** and is ***not*** reported in the SLG's balance sheet.

In ***conventional*** serial and term Debt Service Funds, the debt is defeased by being paid off directly at its scheduled maturity. An expenditure account such as Expenditures—Debt Principal Retirement is recorded in the DSF, the liability is removed from the GLTDAG accounts, the debt instrument is marked "paid" and canceled, and the debt is no longer reported in the balance sheet.

But in ***advance*** refundings it may not be possible or advantageous to actually pay off the old debt with the proceeds of the new substitute debt. Instead, the old debt may remain outstanding for much or all of its originally scheduled life and be serviced by the resources of an irrevocable trust financed (entirely or partly) by the proceeds of the new refunding debt issue. In such cases the old debt is considered to be ***extinguished***—and is removed from the GLTDAG accounts and the SLG's balance sheet—***if*** it is either **legally** defeased **or** is defeased **in substance.**

---

[6] Ibid., sec. D20.102. (Emphasis added.)

Legal Defeasance

In law, a debt may be considered **"defeased"**—terminated and rendered null and void—by being **"legally defeased"** when the debtor fulfills the defeasance provisions of the debt indenture or other agreement. **Defeasance provisions** of bond indentures may specify, for example, that if a sufficient sum is placed in an irrevocable trust for the benefit of the bondholders with a specified trustee, the debt will be considered to have been paid—that is, *legally defeased.*

In-Substance Defeasance

All bond and note agreements do not contain defeasance provisions, however. Indeed, many agreements are silent, that is, they do not contain provisions that either permit or prohibit defeasance. The FASB and GASB have established highly restrictive and specific standards for **in-substance defeasance.**[7] If the conditions of these in-substance defeasance standards are met in an advance refunding or otherwise, the old debt is considered to be defeased **in substance**—for accounting and financial reporting purposes—even though a legal defeasance has not occurred. Accordingly, the *old debt is removed from the GLTDAG accounts* and from the SLG's balance sheet *as in a legal defeasance.*

Nondefeasance

Most advance refundings are carefully planned and conducted to result in either legal defeasance or in-substance defeasance of the old debt. However, in the event the old debt is **not** defeased legally or in substance: (1) **both** the old debt and the new debt must be recorded in the GLTDAG and reported as liabilities in the SLG's balance sheet, and (2) amounts deposited in escrow (trust) are reported as **investments** in a Debt Service Fund.

DEBT SERVICE FUNDS FOR ADVANCE REFUNDINGS

Debt Service Funds for advance refundings that result in defeasance of the old debt are usually simple and short-lived. Indeed, they may involve only two transaction entries—one for the receipt of the refunding bond proceeds and another for the payment to the escrow trustee—and, after a closing entry, be terminated.

The accounting for advance refunding DSFs differs from that for conventional serial and term DSFs also in that the defeasance of the old debt is not considered an "extinguishment" but a **"substitution"** of the new debt for the old debt. Thus, whereas the payment of bond principal in a conventional serial or term DSF is recorded as Expenditures—Bond Principal Retirement, the **defeasance** of the old debt in an **advance refunding** is recorded as a **non**expenditure **Other Financing Use,** rather than as an expenditure, to the extent the defeasance is financed by issuance of new refunding debt. In other words, *debt principal retirement or defeasance is accounted for as an expenditure only if it is financed by non-GLTD financial resources; that financed by issuing new GLTD is accounted for as an Other Financing Use to signal that new debt has been substituted for old debt.*

Three types of advance refunding transactions are discussed and illustrated in this section. These transactions involve (1) retirement of the old issue, (2) legal or in-substance defeasance of the old issue, and (3) use of both existing financial resources and new debt proceeds to effect an advance refunding.

---

[7] Ibid., sec. D20. The FASB standards also are covered in most intermediate accounting textbooks.

Retirement of Old Debt

A government may not have accumulated sufficient sinking fund resources to retire a term bond upon its impending maturity. Thus, it may issue new bonds (or notes) to pay the maturing term bond principal—effectively refinancing the term bond to extend its debt service over the life of the new refunding issue.

To illustrate, assume that a $2,000,000 term bond will mature soon. The SLG has no sinking fund, but will pay the $55,000 interest due upon maturity of the term bonds directly from the General Fund or a Special Revenue Fund. However, it will advance refund the principal of the term bonds by issuing a $2,000,000 refunding bond. Assuming the new refunding bond is issued at 101, bond issue costs of $15,000 are withheld by the bond underwriter, and the old term bonds are retired at par before or upon maturity, the DSF General Ledger entries are:

Issuance of Refunding Bonds

Cash	2,005,000	
Other Financing Source—Proceeds of Refunding Bonds .		2,005,000

To record issuance of advance refunding bonds.

Calculations:

(1)	Gross refunding bond proceeds	
	$2,000,000 \times 1.01 =$	$2,020,000
(2)	Bond issue costs	15,000
(3)	Net refunding bond proceeds	$2,005,000

Retirement of Old Bonds:

Other Financing Use—Retirement of Refunded Term Bonds	2,000,000	
Cash		2,000,000

To record payment of term bond principal
  before or upon its maturity.

Note in this entry that the bond issue costs are not reported as an expenditure or other financing use, but are netted from the gross bond issue proceeds. This is the usual practice, though issue costs may be reported separately—but as an "other financing use." But only the *net* bond issue proceeds—whether more than, less than, or equal to the par (face) of the new advance refunding debt—typically are reported as an **Other Financing Source—Proceeds of Refunding Bonds.**

Note also that *no revenue, expenditure, gain, or loss is recorded* in accounting for this advance refunding. This is consistent both with the **"funds flow"** DSF accounting model **and** the **"substitution"** of the new debt for the old debt. The DSF Statement of Revenues, Expenditures, and Changes in Fund Balance reports these advance refunding transactions as affecting "other" financing sources and uses of DSF financial resources rather than as revenues, expenditures, gains, and/or losses from advance refunding.

The old term bond debt will be removed from the GLTDAG accounts, of course, and the new advance refunding debt will be recorded in the GLTDAG accounts. Then, when the $5,000 remaining fund balance has been disposed of—probably by transfer to the DSF for the new debt—the final closing entry will be made and the term bond principal refunding DSF will be terminated.

Legal and In-Substance Defeasance of Old Debt

To illustrate DSF accounting for the legal and in-substance defeasance of an old debt, assume the same facts as noted earlier except:

1. The new advance refunding bonds were issued at par, and $15,000 of bond issuance costs were withheld by the bond underwriter.

2. The old term bonds mature several years hence and the amount necessary to be invested at this time to service them, $1,900,000, was placed in an escrow trust that was properly invested in accordance with the bond indenture defeasance provisions of the GASB's in-substance defeasance standards.

The DSF entries to record this legal or in-substance defeasance are:

Issuance of Refunding Bonds:

Cash	1,985,000	
Other Financing Source—Proceeds of Refunding Bonds .		1,985,000

To record issuance of advance refunding bonds.

Calculations:

(1)	Gross refunding bond proceeds $2,000,000	
	at par (1.00)	$2,000,000
(2)	Bond issue costs	15,000
(3)	Net refunding bond proceeds	$1,985,000

Defeasance of Old Bonds:

Other Financing Use—Payment to Refunded Bond		
Escrow Agent	1,900,000	
Cash		1,900,000

To record payment to escrow agent to defease old bonds.

Note that the first entry is essentially the same in all cases. That is, the **_net_** proceeds—after bond issue and related costs—are reported as an Other Financing Source—Proceeds of Refunding Bonds.

      The second entry differs from that for a direct retirement, however, in that the amount expended to defease the debt is **_distinctly reported_** as an **Other Financing Use—Payment to Refunded Bond Escrow Agent.** The amount paid to the escrow trustee being less than the par (face) of the old bonds indicates that the amount paid can be invested at an interest rate higher than the rate the SLG is paying on the old defeased issue. However, U.S. government arbitrage regulations limit the amount of arbitrage permissible in advance refunding investment portfolios.

      The legal or in-substance defeasance of an old debt is considered to be a "settlement" that terminates the old debt. Thus, the old debt is removed from the GLTDAG accounts and the new refunding debt is recorded in the GLTDAG accounts. Further, neither the assets nor the operations of the escrow trustee's investment portfolio are reported in the SLG's financial statements. Accordingly, as soon as the DSF balance is disposed of—probably by transfer to another DSF—the defeasance DSF accounts will be closed and the fund will be terminated.

Use of Both Existing Resources and New Debt Proceeds

As a final example, assume the same facts as the legal or in-substance defeasance example except:

1. The SLG has $600,000 of net assets in an existing DSF for the old debt; and
2. The remaining $1,300,000 ($1,900,000 − $600,000) will be financed by (a) a $300,000 transfer to the DSF from the General Fund, and (b) a $1,000,000 advance refunding bond issue that is sold to net par (face) after issuance costs.

The advance refunding DSF entries in this situation are:

Transfer and Refunding Bond Issuance:

Cash	1,300,000	
Operating Transfer from General Fund.		300,000
Other Financing Source—Proceeds of Refunding Bonds. . .		1,000,000

To record interfund transfer and issuance of refunding bonds.

Defeasance of Old Bonds:

Expenditures—Payment to Refunded Bond Escrow Agent. .	900,000	
Other Financing Use—Payment to Refunded Bond		
Escrow Agent.	1,000,000	
Cash		1,900,000

To record payment to escrow agent to defease bonds.

The key point here is that **payments from existing financial resources**—to retire bonds directly or to an escrow agent—are accounted for as **expenditures,** whereas such **payments from advance refunding debt issue proceeds** are accounted for as **other financing uses** rather than as expenditures.

Like the DSFs illustrated earlier, this fund is short-lived. Since its function is accomplished and the fund has no remaining balance, the DSF accounts will now be closed and the fund terminated.

Financial Statement Presentation of Advance Refunding

The "substitution" aspect underlying the typical treatment of general government advance refunding transactions is reflected well in DSF operating statements. Note the equal amounts of advance refunding debt proceeds and other financing uses— bond retirement reported in the General Obligation Secondary Property Tax DSF in the City of Phoenix Combining Statement of Revenues, Expenditures, and Changes in Fund Balances for its DSFs (Figure 8-7). Also note the types of DSFs reported, the statement content and format, and the details presented in Figure 8-7.

Advance Refunding Disclosures

The GASB requires SLGs to make certain disclosures about their advance refundings in the notes to their financial statements. Most of these disclosures are made only in the year the advance refunding occurs, but one must be made each year as long as any old in-substance defeased debt remains outstanding.

The major GASB advance refunding **disclosure requirements** are:

I. **In the Year of the Advance Refunding**

   A. **General Description.** The advance refunding transaction(s) should be described generally—for example, which debt issues were advance refunded, what par (face) amounts were refunded, how the advance refundings were financed (e.g., refunding bonds, some existing resources), which defeasances were legal defeasances and which were in-substance defeasance transactions, and the name of the bank or other institution that serves as the escrow agent trustee.

   B. **Difference in Debt Service Requirements.** SLGs should disclose the **difference between** (1) the *total* of the remaining debt service requirements of the **old** defeased issue and (2) the *total* debt service requirements of the **new** issue, adjusted for any additional cash received or paid. These **totals and** the **difference** are computed using **scheduled**

Figure 8-7
Debt Service Funds
Combining Statement of Revenues, Expenditures and Changes in Fund Balances

For the Fiscal Year Ended June 30, 19x1
with comparative totals for the fiscal year ended June 30, 19x0
(in thousands)

	General Obligation/ Secondary Property Tax	Streets and Highways	Public Housing	City Improve- ment	Special Assess- ment	Totals 19x1	19x0
SOURCES OF FINANCIAL RESOURCES							
Revenues							
Secondary Property Taxes	$ 62,771	$ –	$ –	$ –	$ –	$ 62,771	$ 64,179
Special Assessments	–	–	–	–	1,309	1,309	1,308
Interest on Assessments	–	–	–	–	1,036	1,036	596
Interest on Investments	2,962	–	13	323	163	3,461	4,651
Other	558	254	–	–	13	825	236
Total Revenues	66,291	254	13	323	2,521	69,402	70,970
Other Sources							
Operating Transfers from Other Funds							
General Fund	380	–	–	1,878	–	2,258	1,574
Highway User Revenue	–	31,177	–	–	–	31,177	28,430
Excise Tax	–	–	–	8,567	–	8,567	7,926
Public Housing Special Revenue	–	–	1,299	–	–	1,299	1,312
Sports Facilities	–	–	–	4,099	–	4,099	3,935
Capital Projects Funds	–	–	–	274	–	274	1,613
Proceeds from Refunding Bonds	23,915	–	–	–	–	23,915	–
Total Other Sources	24,295	31,177	1,299	14,818	–	71,589	44,790
Total Sources of Financial Resources	90,586	31,431	1,312	15,141	2,521	140,991	115,760
USES OF FINANCIAL RESOURCES							
Expenditures							
Debt Service							
Principal	17,562	11,475	738	6,395	1,838	38,008	35,658
Interest	26,985	19,956	563	8,704	1,194	57,402	52,318
Total Expenditures	44,547	31,431	1,301	15,099	3,032	95,410	87,976
Other Uses							
Operating Transfers to Other Funds							
General Fund	–	–	–	–	454	454	837
Aviation	6,603	–	–	–	–	6,603	4,999
Refuse	1,057	–	–	–	–	1,057	5,014
Deposit to Refunding Escrow	23,915	–	–	–	–	23,915	–
Total Other Uses	31,575	–	–	–	454	32,029	10,850
Total Uses of Financial Resources	76,122	31,431	1,301	15,099	3,486	127,439	98,826
Net Increase (Decrease) in Fund Balances	14,464	–	11	42	(965)	13,552	16,934
FUND BALANCES, JULY 1	27,897	–	1,268	2,346	3,895	35,406	18,472
FUND BALANCES, JUNE 30	$ 42,361	$ –	$ 1,279	$ 2,388	$ 2,930	$ 48,958	$ 35,406

The accompanying notes are an integral part of these financial statements.

debt service amounts derived from the respective debt service requirement schedules—**not present values**—and indicate the overall **cash flow** consequences of the advance refundings without regard to the time value of money or present values.

C. **Economic Gain or Loss.** The **present value** of the net debt service savings or cost of the advance refunding transaction—referred to as the "**economic gain or loss**"—must also be disclosed. The economic gain or loss is the **difference between** (1) the **present value of the new** advance refunding debt issue debt service requirements, adjusted for any additional cash paid or received in the advance refunding transaction, and (2) the **present value** of the **old** defeased debt's debt service requirements. Both present values are calculated using the **net effective interest rate** (considering premiums, discounts, issuance costs, and so on) of the **new** refunding issue.

II. **As Long as In-Substance Defeased Debt Is Outstanding**

    D.   **Amount of In-Substance Defeased Debt Outstanding.** Any debt defeased **in substance** in an advance refunding—as opposed to being retired or legally defeased—must be disclosed as long as it is outstanding. This is because the SLG remains a guarantor of the debt, in effect, even though the possibility of its having to pay any of the debt is remote.

CONCLUDING COMMENTS

Most government bond issues in recent years have been serial issues; term bond issues have been less popular, though they still are encountered in practice. Likewise, most SLG bond issues have been traditional fixed rate issues, though some have been variable rate issues. Further, since many serial bonds have been serviced by annual transfers from the General or a Special Revenue Fund(s) to a Debt Service Fund(s)—and Debt Service Funds are not required legally or by GAAP in some cases—some governments now record such debt service directly in the General and Special Revenue Funds instead of making annual operating transfers to Debt Service Funds. On the other hand, the law or contractual agreements usually require Debt Service Funds for bonds and other long-term debt, and many finance officers prefer to control and account for all "general government" general obligation debt service through Debt Service Funds.

The use of various forms of lease arrangements has increased significantly in recent years. Those finance officers who prefer to centralize the control of and accounting for general long-term debt service in Debt Service Funds use them to service major capital leases, at least, and possibly other significant lease arrangements. Those finance officers who prefer to control and account for as much of the general operations of government as possible through the General and Special Revenue Funds do not use Debt Service Funds to service any lease arrangements unless required to do so by law or contractual agreement. Thus, the use of Debt Service Funds for leases varies widely among state and local governmental units.

Finally, the issuance of nonconventional "deep discount" bonds and notes by state and local governments has increased in recent years, as have SLG advance refundings of outstanding long-term debt. Accordingly, the GASB has proposed and/or issued new and revised standards to ensure that deep discount debt issues, advance refundings, and other debt- and debt service-related transactions of state and local governments are appropriately accounted for, reported, and disclosed in the notes to the financial statements.

Appendix 8-1
DEBT SERVICE FUND FOR A TERM BOND ISSUE

Although most recent bond issues have been serial issues, term issues may be found occasionally in practice. Term bond issues differ from serial issues in that, whereas some serial bond principal matures each year (or most years)—and thus some serial bond principal is paid each year, together with interest on the remaining outstanding principal balance—the **entire principal** of a **term** bond issue **matures** at the **end** of the bond issue term, say, 20 years. Thus, in **term** bond issues (1) interest is paid on the entire principal (par or face) balance throughout the life of the issue, and (2) all of the principal is paid at the end of the bond issue term.

To ensure timely payment of term bond interest and principal (at maturity), most term bond issue indentures require the issuing government to establish a Debt Service Fund that provides for:

1. Accumulation of any required "funded reserves,"
2. Payment of interest (and fiscal agent charges) during each year the term bonds are outstanding, and
3. Systematic accumulation of a **"sinking fund"** (savings subfund) within the Debt Service Fund that will be sufficient to retire the term bond **principal** upon its maturity at the end of the bond issue term.

Because of the "sinking" fund (subfund) provision, term Debt Service Funds are often referred to as **"sinking funds."**

The "sinking fund" assets and "funded reserves" may be held and invested by the issuing government or by a trustee for the bondholders, depending on terms of the bond issue indenture. In either event, the "sinking fund" requirements must be computed at the origination of the issue and the term Debt Service Fund must be maintained in compliance with the bond indenture provisions throughout the life of the issue.

SINKING FUND REQUIREMENTS

As noted earlier, term bonds ordinarily are repaid from a debt service "sinking" (savings) fund in which resources are accumulated over the life of the bonds by means of annual additions to the fund and by earnings of the fund assets. A **"Schedule of Sinking Fund Requirements"** (Figure 8-8) has been prepared for the City Hall bonds of A Governmental Unit. These are 9%, 20-year term bonds, $1,000,000 par, issued January 1, 19X0 to be repaid out of "the first revenues accruing to the treasury." Recall that the latter terminology indicates that the source of financing for the Debt Service Fund for these bonds is the General Fund of A Governmental Unit.

The first payment to the sinking fund is scheduled for the end of year 1 (19X0). A similar payment will be made at the end of each succeeding year until, when the twentieth payment has been made, fund resources should total $1,000,000—the amount required to pay the term bond principal upon its maturity.

An estimated earnings rate of 10% has been used in developing Figure 8-8. The amount of the required annual additions was determined by selecting from a table the amount of an ordinary annuity of $1 per period at 10% for 20 periods. As indicated in the schedule, the last addition is somewhat less than the preceding ones because of rounding errors. In any event, the final payment in 19Y9 will be in the amount that brings the sinking fund resources to the $1,000,000 required to retire the term bonds.

The schedule of sinking fund requirements provides the amounts of the budgetary requirements for the Debt Service Fund for the duration of the Fund, provided the accumulation process proceeds as planned or departs from the plan

Figure 8-8

SCHEDULE OF SINKING FUND REQUIREMENTS

$1 Million 20-Year Term Bond Issue
(Assuming an Annual Earnings Rate of 10 Percent)

Year	(1) Required Annual Additions	(2) Required Fund Earnings (4PY) × 10%	(3) Required Fund Increases (1) + (2)	(4) Required Fund Balances (3) + (4PY)
1 (19X0)	$ 17,460		$ 17,460	$ 17,460
2 (19X1)	17,460	$ 1,746	19,206	36,666
3 (19X2)	17,460	3,667	21,127	57,793
4 (19X3)	17,460	5,779	23,239	81,032
5 (19X4)	17,460	8,103	25,563	106,595
6 (19X5)	17,460	10,660	28,120	134,715
7 (19X6)	17,460	13,472	30,932	165,647
8 (19X7)	17,460	16,565	34,025	199,672
9 (19X8)	17,460	19,967	37,427	237,099
10 (19X9)	17,460	23,710	41,170	278,269
11 (19Y0)	17,460	27,827	45,287	323,556
12 (19Y1)	17,460	32,356	49,816	373,372
13 (19Y2)	17,460	37,337	54,797	428,169
14 (19Y3)	17,460	42,817	60,277	488,446
15 (19Y4)	17,460	48,845	66,305	554,751
16 (19Y5)	17,460	55,475	72,935	627,686
17 (19Y6)	17,460	62,769	80,229	707,915
18 (19Y7)	17,460	70,792	88,252	796,167
19 (19Y8)	17,460	79,617	97,077	893,244
20 (19Y9)	17,432*	89,324	106,756	1,000,000
	$349,172	$650,828	$1,000,000	

The last year's addition needs to be only $17,432 because of rounding errors.

PY = Prior year end Required Fund Balance.

by immaterial amounts. The **required fund balance at the end of each year** (Figure 8-8) provides a standard against which the actual accumulation may be compared—and may be a required minimum amount under terms of the bond indenture.

Further, failure to maintain the required fund balance may violate the bond issue covenants and—if not **"waived"** (permitted) by the bond trustee—could cause the bond issue to be in **"default"** and the entire principal balance to become due immediately. Thus, bond indenture provisions and compliance must be monitored closely by internal managers and auditors and examined by external auditors.

Several reasons may underlie differences between the actual and planned accumulation of a sinking fund. Contributions or revenues may fall short or exceed those planned, as may earnings on investments. Capital gains or losses on the disposition of investments are not contemplated in the accumulation schedule (except as they may be included in the expected earnings rate). Finally, a Debt Service Fund's resources may be used to purchase some of the bonds it is set up to service—which removes assets originally intended to be held to maturity of the debt issue and hence removes some of the Fund's earning capacity. If the actual accumulation falls short or exceeds the required fund balances by substantial amounts, a new schedule of sinking fund requirements should be computed by starting from the actual accumulation to date and computing the annual additions and fund earnings required to produce $1 million by the end of the twentieth year.

The calculation of the new schedule may be based on an altered expected annual earnings rate.

ILLUSTRATIVE ENTRIES

To illustrate the operation of a Debt Service Fund for a term issue we shall use the City Hall bonds described earlier and the schedule of sinking fund requirements presented in Figure 8-8. We assume that the only "funded reserve" required is that a "Reserve for Term Bond Principal" be established and adjusted at each year end to equal the "Required Fund Balances" indicated in Figure 8-8.

At the end of the first year of the Fund's operation, 19X0, there would have been a balance of $17,460 in both the Reserve for Term Bond Principal and Cash accounts of the Debt Service Fund. These would have resulted from the first payment to the sinking fund of the required annual additions and the initial entry creating the Reserve for Term Bond Principal.

The **budget** for 19X1 is calculated as follows:

Required transfers (from the General Fund).	$107,860	
Required interest earnings.	1,746	109,606
Appropriations:		
Annual interest charges.	90,000	
Fiscal agent's fee	400	90,400
Required fund balance increase		$ 19,206

The required transfer figure is computed as follows:

Required additions to sinking fund	$ 17,460
Annual interest charges ($9\% \times \$1,000,000$).	90,000
Fiscal agent's fee	400
	107,860

The following journal entries record the transactions of the City Hall Term Bonds Debt Service Fund for the second year of operation, 19X1, in the general ledger assuming that budgetary accounts are employed:

(1)	Required Operating Transfer In	107,860	
	Required Interest Revenues	1,746	
	Appropriations.		90,400
	Unreserved Fund Balance		19,206
	To record the budget for 19X1.		

Note that the credit to Unreserved Fund Balance is the amount of "Required Fund Increases" for year 2 (19X1) in Figure 8-8. This also is the amount of the required adjustment to the Reserve for Term Bond Principal.

The term **"required"**—as in Required Transfer In and Required Interest Revenues—is often used in term DSF budgetary accounts, since such amounts are both actuarially required and contractually required under provisions of term bond indentures. But the term **"estimated"**—for example, Estimated Transfer In and Estimated Interest Revenues—which is usually used in other governmental fund budgetary accounts, **is equally acceptable** in term DSFs. Likewise, terms such as Required Contributions and Required Additions often are used instead of the more specific Required (Estimated) Transfer In.

| (2) | Unreserved Fund Balance .... | 19,206 | |
| | **Reserve for Term Bond Principal** .... | | 19,206 |

To adjust the reserve for the required 19X1 increase to equal its actuarially required $36,666 balance at the end of 19X1.

The entry to adjust the Reserve for Term Bond Principal to the actuarially required amount may be made any time during the year, but must be made no later than year end.

(3)	Investments.................................	17,000	
	Unamortized Premiums on Investments..............	270	
	Interest Receivable on Investments.................	120	
	Unamortized Discounts on Investments............		80
	Cash.....................................		17,310

To record the purchase of investments, together with the related premiums, accrued interest, and discounts.

Alternatively, (1) the interest receivable on investments at the time of purchase may be debited to Interest Revenues rather than Interest Receivable on Investments; (2) entry 6 may be omitted except in the year-end adjustment process, after which it would be reversed; and (3) interest collections may be credited to Interest Revenues. In either event, note that premiums and discounts on investments in fixed rate investment securities (notes, bonds, and so on) must be recorded and should be amortized systematically and rationally in determining investment earnings.

| (4) | Due from General Fund .... | 107,860 | |
| | Operating Transfer from General Fund .... | | 107,860 |

To accrue the contribution from the General Fund.

| (5) | Cash... | 107,860 | |
| | Due from General Fund .... | | 107,860 |

To record the receipt of the contribution from the General Fund.

In practice, entries 4 and 5 are often compounded into one entry recording the cash receipt and operating transfer.

| (6) | Interest Receivable on Investments................. | 1,480 | |
| | Interest Revenues........................... | | 1,480 |

To record accrual of interest revenue on investments.

| (7) | Cash... | 1,600 | |
| | Interest Receivable on Investments.............. | | 1,600 |

To record collection of interest receivable.

As noted at entry 3, interest revenues may be recorded only as cash is received during the year and interest earned accrued only in the year end adjusting entries. Thus, entries 6 and 7 may be compounded into one entry recording cash receipts and interest revenues.

| (8) | Cash with Fiscal Agent .... | 90,400 | |
| | Cash..................................... | | 90,400 |

To record transfer of cash for payment of interest on the bonds and fiscal agent fees to the fiscal agent.

(9)	Expenditures—Interest	90,000	
	Expenditures—Fiscal Agent Fee	400	
	Cash with Fiscal Agent		90,400

To record payment of interest on the bonds by the fiscal
agent and the payment of agent's fees.

In practice, entries 8 and 9 may be **compounded** to one entry recording the expenditures and payment to the fiscal agent. Any cash remaining with the fiscal agent at year end—such as when all bearer bond interest coupons have not been submitted for payment—would be recorded during the year-end adjusting entry process, together with any related liability (e.g., for unpaid interest).

| (10) | Investments................................. | 18,000 | |
| | Cash..................................... | | 18,000 |

To record purchase of investments at face value, with no
accrued interest.

| (11) | Interest Receivable on Investments................. | 420 | |
| | Interest Revenues .... | | 420 |

To accrue interest receivable at year end.

(12)	Unamortized Discounts on Investments	20	
	Interest Revenues	10	
	Unamortized Premiums on Investments		30

To record amortization of premiums and discounts on
investments and the resultant correction of interest
earnings.

| (C1) | Operating Transfer from General Fund .... | 107,860 | |
| | Required Operating Transfer In .... | | 107,860 |

To close the estimated and actual transfer in accounts.

(C2)	Interest Revenues	1,890	
	Required Interest Revenues.....................		1,746
	Unreserved Fund Balance		144

To close the estimated and actual interest revenues
accounts to Unreserved Fund Balance.

When the budget was recorded in journal entry number 1, the credit to Unreserved Fund Balance was $19,206, the amount of the required fund increase for the second year according to Figure 8-8. That amount of fund balance was "reserved" in entry 2. The $144 difference between estimated and actual revenues for year 2 will result in a higher total fund balance at the end of year 2 than that required by the schedule of sinking fund requirements. Since the Reserve for Term Bond Principal is maintained at the actuarially required amount, the **excess or deficiency** of the **total** fund balance **compared with** that **required actuarially** (and contractually) is reported as **Unreserved** Fund Balance.

| (C3) | Appropriations................................. | 90,400 | |
| | Expenditures .... | | 90,400 |

To close the estimated and actual expenditures accounts.

Again, we have chosen to illustrate Debt Service Fund accounting with budgetary control accounts. Where formal budgetary control is not exercised, the budgetary entries are omitted.

Figure 8-9   **TERM BONDS DEBT SERVICE FUND BALANCE SHEET**

A Governmental Unit
City Hall Term Bonds Debt Service Fund
Balance Sheet
December 31, 19X1

Assets

Cash		$ 1,210
Investments, at par	$35,000	
Unamortized premiums on investments	240	
Unamortized discounts on investments	(60)	35,180
Interest receivable on investments		420
		$36,810

Liabilities and Fund Balance

Fund Balance:		
Reserved for term bond principal	$36,666	
Unreserved	144	$36,810

FINANCIAL STATEMENTS

The Balance Sheet for the City Hall Term Bonds Debt Service Fund of A Governmental Unit at the end of 19X1 is presented in Figure 8-9. The 19X1 budgetary comparison statement, the Statement of Revenues, Expenditures, and Changes in Fund Balance—Budget and Actual, is presented in Figure 8-10. Since the budget is prepared on the GAAP basis in this example, the actual data in the GAAP operating statement are identical to those in the budgetary operating statement (Figure 8-10). Thus, as in the serial bond DSF example, the GAAP operating statement is not illustrated here.

Note again the simplicity of the typical DSF Balance Sheet—as illustrated in Figures 8-1 and 8-9—since most Debt Service Funds are composed primarily of investments allowed under bond indenture and legal provisions. Note again also that the budget-actual variances of many simple DSFs are minor, especially those financed largely by interfund transfers rather than by independent tax or other revenue sources. However, the budgetary comparison operating statement is a particularly significant accountability report when bond identures contain actuarial requirements (see Figure 8-8) as in this illustrative example.

Term DSF Balance Sheet at Maturity

The *assumed* Balance Sheet of A Governmental Unit's City Hall Term Bonds Debt Service Fund at the date of maturity of the bonds, December 31, 19Y9, is presented in Figure 8-11. It assumes for illustrative purposes that the interest to date has been paid—in order to focus on the matured term bond principal retirement—and presents two problems. First, though the fund has assets in excess of the matured bonds payable, some of the assets have not yet been converted into cash. Therefore, the cash balance is not sufficient to pay the matured bonds. Second, the fund balance remaining after retiring the bonds must be disposed of.

The first problem is a minor one if the investments are readily marketable at or above cost. The Interest Receivable on Investments will also be liquidated upon sale of the investments. A more difficult problem is presented when the source of revenues for the Debt Service Fund is property taxes. Delinquent taxes

Figure 8-10

TERM BONDS DEBT SERVICE FUND BUDGETARY OPERATING STATEMENT

A Governmental Unit
City Hall Term Bonds Debt Service Fund
**Statement of Revenues, Expenditures, and
Changes in Fund Balance—Budget and Actual**
For the year ended December 31, 19X1

	Budget	Actual	Variance— Favorable (Unfavorable)
Revenues:			
Interest earnings	$ 1,746	$ 1,890	$144
Other Financing Sources:			
Operating transfer from General Fund	107,860	107,860	—
Total Revenues and Other Financing Sources	109,606	109,750	144
Expenditures:			
Interest	90,000	90,000	—
Fiscal agent fee	400	400	—
	90,400	90,400	—
Excess of Revenues and Other Financing			
Sources Over Expenditures	19,206	19,350	144
Fund Balance—January 1	17,460	17,460	—
Fund Balance—December 31	$ 36,666*	$ 36,810	$144

** This is the actuarially required amount under terms of the bond indenture, reported as Reserved for Term
Bond Principal in Figure 8-9. The $144 excess is reported as Unreserved Fund Balance.*
***Note** that although the variances reported in this statement are insignificant, it is a significant accountability
statement because it demonstrates A Governmental Unit's compliance with provisions of the related bond indenture.*

Figure 8-11

TERM BONDS DEBT SERVICE FUND BALANCE SHEET
AT MATURITY

A Governmental Unit
City Hall Term Bonds Debt Service Fund
Balance Sheet
December 31, 19Y9

Assets

Cash	$ 975,000
Investments	26,000
Interest receivable on investments	1,500
	$1,002,500

Liabilities and Fund Balance

Matured bonds payable	$1,000,000
Unreserved fund balance	2,500
	$1,002,500

receivable of a Debt Service Fund at maturity may ultimately be collected, but cash
is required immediately for the payment of the bonds. If the government has other
Debt Service Funds, and if the law permits, cash may be borrowed from other Debt
Service Funds. When delinquent taxes are collected, the interfund loan is repaid.
Alternatively, money may be loaned to the Debt Service Fund from the General
Fund, or the delinquent tax receivables may be transferred to the General Fund

when the necessary money is provided to the Debt Service Fund from the General Fund. If the law prohibits such interfund loans or interfund "sales" of delinquent receivables, short-term borrowing from nongovernment sources may be necessary.

The second problem is the disposition of the Fund Balance. If the law permits, the balance will be transferred (a residual equity transfer) to another Debt Service Fund, especially if the latter's contributions or earnings are short of requirements. Similarly, if the Fund had a deficit, it might be made up by transfers from the General Fund, by an additional tax levy, or by transfers of balances of other Debt Service Funds. Normally, the fund balance or deficit of a Debt Service Fund will be small because adjustments will have been made from time to time throughout the life of the Fund. Deficits are sometimes large, however, because of failure to make contributions at proper intervals, failure to compute actuarial requirements properly, or losses on investments. A special tax may have to be levied in such instances; or, if the deficit is quite large, the bonds may have to be refunded; and there may even be a default.

QUESTIONS

8-1 What is the nature of the Fund Balance account(s) in a Debt Service Fund at year end?

8-2 A sinking fund was established for the purpose of retiring Dorchester Street Bridge bonds, which have a 20-year maturity. In the fifth year $10,000 of Dorchester Street Bridge bonds were acquired by the Debt Service Fund. Should these bonds be retired, or should they be held "alive" until maturity? Why?

8-3 Why might A Governmental Unit want to refund an outstanding bond issue (a) at maturity? (b) prior to maturity?

8-4 Interest on its City Hall bonds is paid from City Z's Debt Service Fund on February 1 and August 1. Should interest payable be accrued at December 31, the end of the Fund's fiscal year? Why?

8-5 (a) General sinking fund investment securities have risen in value. Should the appreciation in value be recorded in the accounts of the Debt Service Fund? (b) Would your answer be different if the securities had declined in value?

8-6 Distinguish (a) between fixed and variable rate debt issues, and (b) between conventional serial and term bond issues and deep discount bond issues.

8-7 A certain municipality provides that its sinking fund is to be built up from various licenses and fines. The revenues from these sources have been as follows: 19X7, $5,000; 19X8, $3,000; 19X9, $8,000. What is the danger with such a provision?

8-8 What disposition should be made of the balance remaining in a Debt Service Fund after the bonds mature and are paid?

8-9 What is meant by defeasance? What conditions are necessary to achieve legal defeasance or in-substance defeasance?

8-10 What are the advantages of pooling the investments of a city's Debt Service Funds?

8-11 What are the main sources of assets for a Debt Service Fund?

8-12 Some accountants believe that budgetary control of Debt Service Fund operations such as those illustrated in this chapter is unnecessary unless required by law. Others disagree. What is your opinion?

8-13 When would bond interest or principal due soon in the next year be accrued as expenditures and current liabilities of a Debt Service Fund? When would they not be accrued?

8-14 Why might a government use a Debt Service Fund for a serial bond issue when it is not required to do so?

PROBLEMS

P 8-1 (Multiple Choice) Indicate the best answer to each of the following questions. Use the following information in responding to questions 1 through 3.

The City of Lora issued $5,000,000 of general government, general obligation, 8%, 20-year bonds at 103 on April 1, 19X1 to finance a major general government capital project. Interest is payable semiannually on each October 1 and April 1 during the term of the bonds. In addition, $250,000 of principal matures each April 1.

1. If Lora's fiscal year end is December 31, what amount of debt service expenditures should be reported for this DSF for the 19X1 fiscal year?
   a. $0
   b. $200,000
   c. $300,000
   d. $400,000

2. If Lora's fiscal year end is March 31 and Lora has a policy of accumulating resources in the DSF by fiscal year end sufficient to pay the principal and interest due on April 1 of the subsequent fiscal year, what amount of debt service expenditures must Lora report for the fiscal year ended March 31, 19X2?
   a. $200,000
   b. $400,000
   c. $650,000
   d. $200,000 or $650,000, depending on the city's policy

3. Assume the same information as in 1, except that Lora has not made the October 1, 19X1 interest payment as of the fiscal year end. What amount of debt service expenditures should be reported for this DSF for the 19X1 fiscal year?
   a. $0
   b. $200,000
   c. $300,000
   d. $400,000

4. A county had borrowed $18 million to finance construction of a general government capital project. The debt will be serviced from collections of a special assessment levy made for the project. The county levied the special assessments in 19X8. Ten percent of the assessments are due in 19X8 and, 19X8 and early 19X9 collections on the assessments total $1,500,000. The amount of special assessments revenue that should be recognized in the county's Special Assessments DSF for 19X8 is
   a. $0. Special assessments are reported as other financing sources.
   b. $1,500,000
   c. $1,800,000
   d. $18,000,000

Use the following information in questions 5 to 8.

The State of Exuberance issued $10,000,000 of 5%, 20-year, advance refunding bonds in 19X5 at par.

5. If the State used the proceeds to retire $10 million of general long-term debt upon its maturity, the State should report:
   a. Revenues of $10 million and Expenditures of $10 million.
   b. Other Financing Sources of $10 million and Expenditures of $10 million.
   c. Revenues of $10 million and Other Financing Uses of $10 million.
   d. Other Financing Sources of $10 million and Other Financing Uses of $10 million.

6. If the State placed the $10 million in an irrevocable trust that is to be used to service an outstanding $9 million general obligation bond issue and those bonds are deemed defeased in substance, the State should report:
   a. Expenditures of $9 million and Other Financing Uses of $1 million.
   b. Expenditures of $10 million.
   c. Expenditures of $1 million and Other Financing Uses of $9 million.
   d. Other Financing Uses of $10 million.
   e. No expenditures or other financing uses.

7. If the State placed the $10 million in an irrevocable trust as in 6, but the transaction did not meet the defeasance in-substance criteria, the State should report:
   a. Expenditures of $9 million and Other Financing Uses of $1 million.

    b. Expenditures of $10 million.

    c. Expenditures of $1 million and Other Financing Uses of $9 million.

    d. Other Financing Uses of $10 million.

    e. No expenditures or other financing uses.

8. If the State placed $12 million (the $10 million from the advance refunding plus $2 million from previously accumulated DSF resources) in the irrevocable trust in 6 and the debt were deemed defeased in substance, the State should report:

    a. Expenditures of $9 million and Other Financing Uses of $3 million.

    b. Expenditures of $3 million and Other Financing Uses of $9 million.

    c. Expenditures of $12 million.

    d. Other Financing Uses of $12 million.

    e. None of the above.

9. If the State of Exuberance defeased its $9 million debt in substance as in 8 except that there was no advance refunding debt issued, the State should report:

    a. Expenditures of $9 million and Other Financing Uses of $3 million.

    b. Expenditures of $3 million and Other Financing Uses of $9 million.

    c. Expenditures of $12 million.

    d. Other Financing Uses of $12 million.

    e. None of the above.

10. A government paid $3,500,000 to its fiscal agent on June 30, 19X6 to provide for principal ($2,000,000) and interest payments due on July 1, 19X6. The fiscal agent will make payments to bondholders on July 1. The payment to the fiscal agent does **not** constitute legal or in-substance defeasance of the principal and interest payments. If the government uses the option of accruing its principal and interest expenditures due early in the next year, which of the following assets and liabilities should be reported in the government's DSF balance sheet at June 30, 19X6?

    a. No assets or liabilities from the preceding information would be reported because the government has paid the fiscal agent.

    b. Cash with fiscal agent, $3,500,000

    c. Cash with fiscal agent, $3,500,000
       Matured bonds payable, $2,000,000
       Matured interest payable, $1,500,000

    d. Cash with fiscal agent, $3,500,000
       Accrued interest payable, $1,500,000

P 8-2 (General Ledger Entries) Gotham City issued $500,000 of 8% regular serial bonds at par (no accrued interest) on January 2, 19X0, to finance a capital improvement project. Interest is payable semiannually on January 2 and July 2 and $50,000 of the principal matures each January 2 beginning in 19X1. Resources for servicing the debt will be made available through a special tax levy for this purpose and transfers as needed from a Special Revenue Fund. The required transfer typically will be made on January 1 and July 1, respectively. The Debt Service Fund is not under formal budget control; the city's fiscal year begins October 1.

Required Prepare general journal entries to record the following transactions and events in the General Ledger of the Debt Service Fund.

(1) June 28, 19X0—The first installment of the special tax was received, $52,000.

(2) June 29, 19X0—A Special Revenue Fund transfer of $38,000 was received.

(3) July 2, 19X0—The semiannual interest payment on the bonds was made.

(4) July 3, 19X0—The remaining cash was invested.

(5) December 30, 19X0—The investments matured, and $73,000 cash was received.

(6) January 2, 19X1—The semiannual interest payment and the bond payment were made.

(7) January 2, 19Y0—At the beginning of 19Y0, the Debt Service Fund had accumulated $30,000 in investments (from transfers) and $25,000 in cash (from taxes). The investments were liquidated at face value, and the final interest and principal payment on the bonds was made.

(8) January 3, 19Y0—The Debt Service Fund's purpose having been served, the council ordered the residual assets transferred to the Special Revenue Fund and the Debt Service Fund terminated.

P 8-3 (GL Entries & Statements) Hatcher Village, which operates on the calendar year, issued a five-year, 8%, $100,000 note to the Bank of Hatcher on January 5, 19X4. The proceeds of the note were recorded in a Capital Projects Fund. Interest and one-tenth of the principal are due semiannually, on January 5 and July 5, beginning July 5, 19X4. A Debt Service Fund has been established to service this debt; financing will come from General Fund transfers and a small debt service tax levied several years ago.

Required (a) Prepare the general journal entries needed to record the following transactions and events, and (b) prepare a balance sheet at December 31, 19X4, and a statement of revenues, expenditures, and changes in fund balance for the year then ended for the Debt Service Fund.

(1) January 6—The Debt Service Fund budget for 19X4 was adopted. The General Fund contribution was estimated at $10,000; the tax levy was expected to yield $18,000. The appropriations included the January 5, 19X5 debt service payment.

(2) The tax levy was received, $20,000.

(3) The July 5, 19X4, payment of principal and interest was made.

(4) The General Fund contribution of $10,000 was received.

(5) The residual balance of a discontinued Capital Projects Fund, $6,000, was transferred to the Debt Service Fund.

(6) The January 5, 19X4, payment was accrued.

(7) Closing entries were prepared at December 31, 19X4.

P 8-4 (Special Assessment DSF; Entries, Statements) On September 30, 19X3 Duncan Township issued $100,000 of five-year, 6%, Zachary Addition Special Assessment Bonds to finance construction of storm sewers in the Zachary Addition. Duncan Township guarantees the bonds in the event that collections of the special assessments are inadequate to service the debt. Interest and $20,000 of principal are due and payable each September 30 beginning September 30, 19X4. The Duncan Township fiscal year ends on December 31. The following transactions related to servicing the Zachary Addition bonds occurred in 19X4 and 19X5.

1. On January 1, 19X4 Duncan Township levied special assessments totaling $100,000 on properties in the Zachary Addition Special Assessment District. Interest of 7% on the unpaid balance at the beginning of each year and $20,000 of principal are due each June 30.

2. Between January 1 and June 30, 19X4, Duncan Township collected $20,700 from the special assessments, including interest of $2,700.

3. Duncan Township transferred $2,400 to the Zachary Addition DSF on June 30, 19X4.

4. The bond principal and interest, along with $100 of fiscal agent fees, were paid to the township's fiscal agent on June 30, 19X4. Uncollected current assessments became delinquent.

5. The town collected one-half of the delinquent assessments and interest on September 30, 19X4.

6. In May and June 19X5 the town collected:

Current assessments	$19,000
Delinquent assessments	1,000
Interest on assessments	2,540
Total	$22,540

7. The bond principal and interest, along with $100 of fiscal agent fees, were paid to the township's fiscal agent on June 30, 19X5. Uncollected current assessments became delinquent.

Required (a) Prepare the journal entries to record the preceding transactions, assuming that the fiscal agent paid all principal and interest on the debt when it matured.

(b) Prepare the 19X4 financial statements for the Zachary Addition DSF.

P 8-5 **Part I.** (Advance Refunding) The State of Artexva advance refunded $8,000,000 par of 19X2 10% serial bonds by issuing $9,000,000 par of 19Y6 6% serial bonds.

Required Prepare the entries required to record the following advance refunding transactions, which occurred during 19Y6, in the Artexva Advance Refunding Debt Service Fund.

1. The new $9,000,000 6% 19Y6 serial bonds were issued at 101 (no accrued interest) less $290,000 issuance costs, and the net proceeds were accounted for in a new advance refunding Debt Service Fund.

2. The net proceeds of the 19Y6 serial bond issue were paid to the Second National Bank of Artexva as escrow agent of an irrevocable trust for the benefit of the holders of the 19X2 10% serial bonds. That amount is sufficient under terms of the defeasance provisions in the 19X2 10% serial bond covenant, as invested, to legally defease that issue.

3. The advance refunding Debt Service Fund accounts were closed, and, its purpose having been served, the fund was discontinued.

P 8-5 **Part II.** (Advance Refunding)

a. Assume that the State of Artexva advance refunding bonds yielded only $7,800,000, net of issuance costs; an additional $1,000,000 was transferred from the General Fund to the advance refunding DSF; and $8,800,000 was paid to the escrow agent. Prepare the entry necessary to record the payment to the escrow agent.

b. Assume the facts in part (a) except (1) the 19X2 10% serial bonds matured soon after the 19Y6 6% serial bonds were issued, and (2) the $8,800,000 payment was to retire the $8,000,000 of 19X2 serial bonds and to pay the $800,000 19Y6 interest on those bonds. Prepare the entry to record the bond principal and interest payment.

P 8-6 (Advance Refunding) The City of Andrew had outstanding $1,000,000 par of 12% Series A bonds issued several years ago when interest rates were high. The finance officer proposes to refinance the issue with a new 8% Series B issue and some cash to be transferred from the General Fund. Since the Series A bonds are now selling at a substantial premium and, in any event, it does not appear feasible to buy all of them back, the finance officer proposed to place sufficient monies in an irrevocable trust and meet all other conditions as set forth in the Internal Revenue Code and Regulations and in the GASB standards to achieve defeasance in substance. The council approved the plan and the following transactions occurred during 19X8:

1. A new 8% Series B serial bond issue was sold at par, $1,000,000.

2. A General Fund transfer of $145,000 was made to the Debt Service Fund.

3. It was determined that the amount that must be placed in the irrevocable trust to service the Series A issue until maturity and pay the principal at that time was $1,140,000. The payment to the trustee was made, as were payments of $5,000 of consultation fees and travel costs necessary to consummate the transaction.

Required (a) Prepare the general journal entries required in the Debt Service Fund to record the transactions and events described previously.

(b) Assume, instead, that the trust did not meet the conditions of the GASB defeasance in-substance standards.

(1) Prepare the general journal entries to record the preceding transactions and events under this assumption.

(2) Identify any differences in the accounting and reporting for the preceding transactions and events in the various governmental funds and account groups under these two differing assumptions.

P 8-7 (GL & SL Entries; Statements) The Leslie Independent School District services all of its long-term debt through a single Debt Service Fund. The LISD DSF balance sheet at December 31, 19X4 appeared as:

LESLIE INDEPENDENT SCHOOL DISTRICT

Debt Service Fund

Balance Sheet

December 31, 19X4

Assets

Cash		$220,000
Investments (net of $30,000 of unamortized		
premiums and $10,000 of unamortized discounts)		670,000
Accrued interest receivable		10,000
		$900,000

Liabilities and Fund Balance

Liabilities:

Matured interest payable.	$101,500	
Matured serial bonds payable	50,000	
Accrued fiscal agent fees payable.	1,005	$152,505
Fund Balance:		
Reserved for term bond principal.	$315,285	
Reserved for serial bond service assurance	350,000	
	665,285	
Unreserved.	82,210	747,495
		$900,000

1. The LISD adopted the following DSF budget for its 19X5 calendar fiscal year:

Appropriations:

(1) Serial bonds (8%, $2,500,000 unmatured at 1/1/X5):

(a)	7/5/X5—Principal	$ 50,000	
	Interest	100,000	
	Fiscal agent fees	1,000	$151,000
(b)	1/5/X6—Principal	$ 50,000	
	Interest	98,000	
	Fiscal agent fees	995	148,995
			$299,995

[The 1/5/X5 debt service payment was accrued at 12/31/X4 since resources were provided for that payment during 19X4.]

(2) Term bonds (6%, $1,000,000 unmatured at 1/1/X5):

(a)	4/15/X5—Interest.		$ 30,000
(b)	10/15/X5—Interest		30,000
			$ 60,000

[The board also approved a $21,019 addition to the sinking fund Reserve for Term Bond Principal as required by the term bond indenture.]

(3) Capital lease (7%, $400,000 book value at 1/1/X5):

Annual payment (including interest) due 3/25/X5		$ 38,986
Total Appropriations		$398,981

Required Financing:

Appropriations.	$398,981
Addition to term bond sinking fund	21,019
	$420,000

Authorized Financing Sources:

Estimated property tax revenues	$250,000
Estimated interest revenues.	52,000
Authorized operating transfer from General Fund	118,000
	$420,000

2. All debt service payment transactions occurred during 19X5 as they were budgeted and scheduled. Investments were liquidated—in $1,000 "blocks"—the day before cash was required; the cash balance was never permitted to be less than $5,000.

3. The General Fund transfer was made on 2/12/X5, was invested (at par); the sinking fund Reserve for Term Bond Principal was also adjusted on that date.

4. Investment earnings during 19X5 were $54,000 after amortization of $5,000 of premiums and $1,000 of discounts on investments and including $15,000 of accrued interest receivable at 12/31/X5. The ending cash balance at 12/31/X5 was $13,509. (Record all investment earnings transactions and events at 12/31/X5.)

5. Property taxes for the year, all received on 5/8/X5, totaled $256,000.

Required

(a) Prepare the summary journal entries necessary to record the above transactions and events in the General Ledger, Revenues Ledger, and Expenditures Ledger of the Leslie Independent School District during 19X5, including closing entries. Key the entries by date.

(b) Prepare a Balance Sheet at 12/31/19X5 and a Statement of Revenues, Expenditures, and Changes in Fund Balance—Budget and Actual for the year then ended for the LISD Debt Service Fund.

P 8-8 (GL Worksheet: SLs; Statements) This problem requires an alternate solution approach to Problem 8-7 on the Leslie Independent School District Debt Service Fund.

Required

(a) Based on the information in Problem 8-7, prepare a General Ledger worksheet and Revenues Ledger and Expenditures Ledger accounts for the LISD Debt Service Fund for the year 19X5. The General Ledger worksheet should be designed as follows:

Columns	Heading
1–2	Trial Balance, 1/1/X5
3–4	19X5 Reversing (optional), Transaction, and Adjusting Entries
5–6	Preclosing Trial Balance, 12/31/X5
7–8	Closing Entry(ies), 12/31/X5
9–10	Postclosing Trial Balance, 12/31/X5

(b) Prepare a Balance Sheet at 12/31/X5 and a Statement of Revenues, Expenditures, and Changes in Fund Balance—Budget and Actual for the year then ended for the LISD Debt Service Fund.

P 8-9 (GL & SL Entries, Statements) A serial Debt Service Fund of the State of Texona had the following postclosing trial balance at September 30, 19X7, the end of its fiscal year:

State of Texona

Serial Debt Service Fund No. 2

Postclosing Trial Balance

September 30, 19X7

Cash.	10,600,000	
Investments	7,600,000	
Matured Bonds Payable		5,000,000
Matured Notes Payable.		2,000,000
Matured Interest Payable.		3,500,000
Reserved for Bond Debt Service.		6,000,000
Unreserved Fund Balance		1,700,000
	18,200,000	18,200,000

The Debt Service Fund is financed by a share of state sales tax revenues, transfers from other funds, and interest earnings. Significant debt service payments fall due on October 1 each year and are provided for in the appropriations of the previous year. The following transactions and events affected the State of Texona Serial Debt Service Fund No. 2 during the 19X7–X8 fiscal year:

1. The matured bonds, notes, and interest payable were paid.
2. State sales taxes collected for the Debt Service Fund totaled $12,000,000.
3. All but $10,000 of the cash was invested.
4. The Reserve for Bond Debt Service was increased to $7,000,000 as required by the bond indenture.
5. Debt service maturities were:

Bonds	$5,000,000
Notes	2,000,000
Interest	3,000,000

6. Temporary investments of $9,200,000 were liquidated to pay the debt service due; the proceeds were $10,500,000. (Accrued interest receivable is debited to the Investments account at year end.)
7. The debt service payments due were made.
8. A $1,400,000 transfer was received upon termination of Debt Service Fund No. 6.
9. An $8,000,000 transfer was received from the General Fund.
10. A capital lease obligation, $1,500,000, was paid (includes $600,000 interest).
11. Debt service maturities at year end, on which payment is due October 1, 19X8, were:

Bonds	$5,000,000
Notes	2,000,000
Interest	2,500,000

12. Accrued interest receivable on investments at year end, $900,000.

Required (1) Prepare DSF general journal entries to record the preceding transactions and events in the General, Revenues, and Expenditures Ledgers.
(2) Prepare a preclosing trial balance for the Debt Service Fund at September 30, 19X8.
(3) Prepare DSF closing entries at September 30, 19X8.
(4) Prepare a balance sheet for the Debt Service Fund at September 30, 19X8.
(5) Prepare a statement of revenues, expenditures, and changes in fund balance for the Debt Service Fund for the 19X7–X8 fiscal year.

Alternatively, in lieu of requirements 1–4, prepare a worksheet headed as follows:

Columns	Heading
1–2	Postclosing Trial Balance, 9/30/19X7
3–4	19X7–X8 Transactions
5–6	Closing Entries, 9/30/19X8
7–8	Postclosing Trial Balance, 9/30/19X8

P 8-10 (Term DSF GL Entries, Statement) Burns County issued $5,000,000 par of 6% term bonds in 19X0 (year 1). The county has been paying interest and fiscal agent fees and accumulating financial resources to retire the bond principal upon its maturity in a term bond Debt Service Fund.

The balance sheet of the Burns County Term Bond Debt Service Fund at December 31, 19Y8, the end of year 19 of the term bond issue, appears as:

Burns County
Term Bond Debt Service Fund
Balance Sheet
December 31, 19Y8

Assets

Cash.	$ 19,000
Investment (net of $6,000 unamortized premiums and $8,000 unamortized	
discounts)	4,248,000
Accrued interest receivable.	240,000
	$4,507,000

Fund Balance

Reserved for term bond principal	$4,466,220
Unreserved.	40,780
	$4,507,000

The actuarial schedule of sinking fund requirements for 19Y8 and 19Y9, the last two years (19 and 20) of the term bond issue, was:

Year	Required Annual Additions	Required Fund Earnings	Required Fund Increases	Required Fund Balances
19Y8 (19)	$87,300	$398,085	$485,385	$4,466,220
19Y9 (20)	87,160*	446,620	533,780	5,000,000

Or whatever amount is required to increase the fund balance to $5,000,000 by the maturity date of the bonds.

The following transactions and events affected the Burns County Term Bond Debt Service Fund during 19Y9:

1. The annual budget was adopted:

Required transfer from General Fund:		
Required addition to sinking fund per		
actuarial table	$ 87,160	
Less: Unreserved fund balance.	40,780	
Net addition to sinking fund	$ 46,380	
Annual interest (6%) ($5,000,000)	300,000	
Fiscal agent fee.	2,000	$ 348,380
Required Earnings (per actuarial table)		446,620
		$ 795,000
Appropriations:		
Interest (payable annually on December 31) .		$ 300,000
Fiscal agent fee.		2,000
Term bond principal.		5,000,000
		$5,302,000

Also, the Reserve for Term Bond Principal was adjusted to its required $5,000,000 balance.

2. The General Fund transfer was made and invested (at par) in securities maturing (as do all other investments) three days prior to the maturity of the term bonds.

3. All investments matured and all unamortized premiums and discounts were amortized. Cash received for matured investments and interest (including accrued interest receivable at December 31, 19Y8) totaled $5,302,000.

4. The matured bonds, interest, and fiscal agent fees were paid and the Reserve for Term Bond Principal was restored to Unreserved Fund Balance.

5. The remaining cash was transferred to the Serial Bond Debt Service Fund.

6. Closing entries were made and the Term Bond Debt Service Fund was terminated.

Required (a) Prepare the journal entries required to record the 19Y9 transactions and events in the General Ledger accounts of the Burns County Term Bond Debt Service Fund. Use appropriately titled accounts to distinguish appropriations and related expenditures by purpose—for example, Appropriations—Interest and Expenditures—Interest.

(b) Prepare a Statement of Revenues, Expenditures, and Changes in Fund Balance for the Burns County Term Bond Debt Service Fund for the year ended December 31, 19Y9.

P 8-11 (Term DSF Worksheet, Statement) This problem requires an alternate solution to Problem 8-10.

Required (a) Based on the information in Problem 8-10, prepare a General Ledger worksheet to record the 19Y9 transactions and events affecting the Burns County Term Bond Debt Service Fund. Use appropriately titled accounts to distinguish appropriations and related expenditures—for example: Appropriations—Interest and Expenditures—Interest. Your worksheet should be headed as follows:

Columns	Headings
1–2	Trial Balance, 12/31/19Y8
3–4	19Y9 Budgetary and Transaction Entries
5–6	Preclosing Trial Balance, 12/31/19Y9
7–8	Closing Entries, 12/31/19Y9

(b) Prepare a Statement of Revenues, Expenditures, and Changes in Fund Balance for the Burns County Term Bond Debt Service Fund for the year ended December 31, 19Y9.

GENERAL FIXED ASSETS; GENERAL LONG-TERM DEBT: Introduction to Interfund-Account Group Accounting

The governmental funds for which accounting principles have been presented thus far are separate, self-balancing entities that may have seemed unrelated to one another. Fixed assets purchased through these governmental funds have been recorded as fund "expenditures," rather than as fund assets; and fixed asset sale proceeds have been recorded as fund "revenues" or "other financing sources." Likewise, the proceeds of general long-term debt issues have been recorded as "other financing sources" in governmental funds (e.g., Capital Projects Funds), and the retirement of such debt has been accounted for as "expenditures" in these funds (e.g., Debt Service Funds). Thus, both the "general government" fixed assets acquired through governmental funds and the "general government" long-term debt may seem to have "mysteriously disappeared" from the accounts.

These "mysteries" were dealt with briefly in Chapter 2 and are explained in depth in this chapter. The *first* part deals with the accounting procedures for **General Fixed Assets** and explains the relationship between them and the funds from which they are financed. The *second* part is concerned with the accounting procedures for a government's general obligation long-term debt—its **General Long-Term Debt**—and points out the relationship of that indebtedness to the General Fund, the Capital Projects Funds, and the Debt Service Funds. The *third* part provides a formal introduction to accounting for interfund and interfund-account group transactions and relationships, or **interfund-account group accounting.**

GENERAL FIXED ASSETS

Governments use many assets of a durable, long-term nature in their operations. Examples are land, buildings, and equipment. They possess physical substance and are expected to provide service for periods that extend beyond the year of acquisition. They are not physically consumed by their use, though their economic usefulness declines over their lifetimes. Their proper recording and control are necessary for efficient management and for financial reporting.

"General" Fixed Assets Defined

A clear-cut distinction is maintained between the accounting for **"general"** fixed assets in the General Fixed Assets Account Group (GFAAG) and that for fixed assets in specific fund entities. The GASB Codification defines *general fixed assets* as *all* fixed assets *other than* those accounted for in proprietary or Trust Funds.[1] In some Trust Funds and in Internal Service and Enterprise Funds, fixed asset increases and decreases are accounted for in the same manner as in profit-seeking enterprises.

The governmental funds, discussed in preceding chapters, are the vehicles used to account for the sources and uses of expendable, general government, financial resources. Recall that the governmental funds are essentially working capital entities. Therefore, acquisition of fixed assets is a *use* of governmental fund financial resources because the fixed assets are not expendable financial resources and belong to the organization as a whole, not to any specific fund. (The assets may or may not be used by agencies financed by the acquiring fund.) Thus, capital assets are not recorded as governmental fund assets. Rather, in all of the funds discussed in preceding chapters, acquisition of fixed assets has been recorded as an *expenditure* of governmental fund resources because the assets are considered *general* fixed assets to be capitalized in the General Fixed Assets Account Group.

Acquisition and Initial Valuation

A government may purchase or construct general fixed assets, or may acquire them by capital lease, gift, or escheat. Most GFA are recorded at cost.

Cost

General fixed assets should be recorded at cost. The cost principle used in fund accounting is essentially the same as that included in generally accepted accounting principles (GAAP) for business enterprises. Cost is generally defined as the value of consideration given or consideration received, whichever is more clearly determinable. Cost includes all normal and necessary outlays incurred to bring the asset into a state of readiness for its intended use.

The GASB Codification specifically states that general fixed assets include those acquired, in substance, through noncancellable leases.[2] Further, it contains extensive guidance for accounting and reporting SLG capital leases.

Estimated Cost

In the past, many governments failed to maintain adequate records of fixed assets. As they became concerned about not complying with GAAP and missing other benefits of proper accounting, most SLGs began accumulating cost data and recording them. Even today original records are not available in some cases and reconstruction of records is impossible or prohibitively expensive. In such cases the GASB Codification permits recording **estimated original cost** on the basis of available information. Specifically, the GASB Codification states that:

> **Initial costs** of fixed assets **usually** are **readily ascertainable** from contracts, purchase vouchers, and other transaction documents at the time of acquisition or construction. **However,** governmental units are **sometimes faced with the task of**

[1] GASB Codification, sec. 1400.106.
[2] Ibid., sec. 1400.108.

establishing appropriate fixed asset accounting records and valuations after many years of operation **without such records.** In such situations, the **original purchase documents may not be available, or an inordinate expenditure of resources may be required to establish original asset costs precisely.** It **may** therefore be necessary to **estimate** the **original cost** of such assets on the basis of such documentary evidence as may be available, including price levels at the time of acquisition, **and** to **record** these **estimated costs** in the appropriate **fixed asset accounts.**[3]

Although these estimates are less objective than the information usually available for recording cost, errors are gradually eliminated as the older assets are retired. The basis of fixed asset valuation, whether actual or estimated cost, should be clearly disclosed in the financial statements.

Gifts, Foreclosures, Eminent Domain, and Escheat

Governments may acquire fixed assets by **gift** as well as by purchase, construction, or capital lease. Fixed assets acquired by gift are recorded at their *fair market value when received,* which is the value of the "consideration received" under the cost principle discussed earlier.

     In addition, governments acquire assets by three methods not customary for business enterprises. In cases of **foreclosure,** the valuation should normally be the **lower of** (1) the **amount due** for taxes or special assessments, related penalties and interest, and applicable foreclosure costs, **or** (2) the appraised **fair market value** of the property. Both amounts should be included in the fixed asset records. **Eminent domain** is the power of government to seize private property for public use, compensation to the owner normally being determined through the courts. Property thus acquired is accounted for in the same manner as that acquired in a negotiated purchase. Acquisition by **escheat** occurs when title to property is vested in or reverts to the government because the rightful owner does not come forward to claim it or dies without known heirs. Fixed assets obtained in this manner are accounted for in the same manner as gifts; that is, they are capitalized in the General Fixed Assets accounts at estimated fair market value at acquisition.

Classification

Classification of general fixed assets involves classifying both (1) the general fixed assets and (2) the sources by which the GFA were financed.

Fixed Assets

The GASB has not specified a standard (uniform) classification of general fixed assets accounts. However, many SLGs follow or adapt the recommendation of the Government Finance Officers Association (GFOA) that fixed assets be classified as (1) Land, (2) Buildings, (3) "Infrastructure" or Improvements Other Than Buildings, (4) Machinery and Equipment, or (5) Construction in Progress.

1. ***Land.*** The cost of land includes the amount paid for the land itself, costs incidental to the acquisition of land, and expenditures incurred in preparing the land for use.

2. ***Buildings or Buildings and Improvements.*** The "buildings" or "buildings and improvements" classification includes (1) relatively permanent structures used to house persons or property, and (2) fixtures that are permanently

---

[3] Ibid., sec. 1400.112. (Emphasis added.)

attached to and made a part of buildings and that cannot be removed without cutting into walls, ceilings, or floors or without in some way damaging the building.

3. *"Infrastructure" or Improvements Other Than Buildings.* Long-lived improvements (other than buildings) that add value (including use value) to land. Examples of items in this category are bridges, sidewalks, streets, dams, tunnels, and fences. (Capitalization of GFA "infrastructure" assets is **optional,** as discussed momentarily.)

4. *Machinery and Equipment.* Examples are trucks, automobiles, pumps, desks, typewriters, computers, and bookcases. Since much machinery and equipment is movable, it must be accounted for with particular care.

5. *Construction in Progress.* The cost of construction work undertaken but incomplete at a balance sheet date. These costs are appropriately reclassified upon project completion.

These general fixed asset classifications are not all inclusive. For example, a county public school system might report **Library Books,** and a city museum might include **Museum Collections.**

GFA Financing Sources

In order to record and report the manner in which fixed assets were acquired, both currently and cumulatively, the GASB Codification recommends that the credit side of the General Fixed Assets Account Group be classified according to the **sources by which such assets were financed.** This information indicates, to some degree, the extent to which the government is financing its fixed asset acquisitions from its current taxes, gifts, borrowings, and so on. It also provides insight into how dependent the government is on other governments to finance its capital program.

In previous chapters, we have observed that General Fixed Asset acquisition may be financed through three major fund types:

- **Capital Projects Funds:** major facilities acquired through long-term borrowing, special assessments, intergovernmental grants-in-aid, interfund transfers, or some combination of sources.

- **General Fund or Special Revenue Funds:** various general fixed assets, particularly equipment, acquired from general or special revenues.

It is *not* sufficient merely to classify fixed asset sources by fund or fund type. This is because identifying the financing fund or fund type does not always definitively identify the underlying GFA financing source. Furthermore (1) general or special revenues may be transferred to Capital Projects Funds, (2) Capital Projects Funds may have several sources of financing, (3) some fixed assets are acquired by gift or in other nonpurchase manners, and (4) other governments often assist in fixed asset acquisition. Rather, they should be classified by the **original funding source** —such as (1) general obligation bonds, (2) federal grants, (3) state grants, (4) general (or unrestricted) revenues, (5) special (or restricted) revenues, (6) special assessments, and (7) gifts—**or in summary classifications**—such as (1) federal grants and entitlements, (2) state grants and entitlements, and (3) local taxes and other revenues. Therefore, **a single acquisition may require credits to several Investment in General Fixed Assets (source) accounts.** Figure 9-1 presents an overview of the accounting equation applicable to General Fixed Assets accounting.

Figure 9-1

GENERAL FIXED ASSETS ACCOUNTING

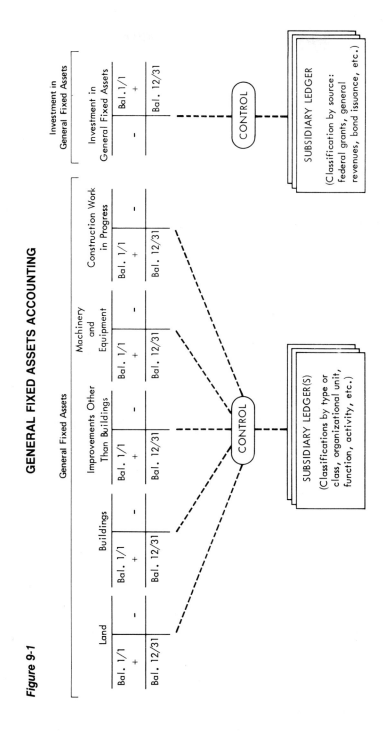

While some question the usefulness of the GFA "financing sources" data from a cost-benefit perspective, GAAP requires these data. GFA "financing sources" data also are required by statute or regulation in many states. Further, the terms of many federal grants, in particular—for example, those that require that proceeds of the sale of federally financed fixed assets be returned to the federal government—virtually require that federally financed fixed assets be readily identifiable in the fixed asset and/or GFA financing sources accounts.

"Infrastructure" GFA

The GASB Codification states that:

> Reporting public domain or **"infrastructure" fixed assets—roads, bridges, curbs and gutters, streets and sidewalks, drainage systems, lighting systems, and similar assets that are immovable and of value only to the governmental unit—is optional.** The accounting policy in this respect should be consistently applied and should be disclosed in the Summary of Significant Accounting Policies. **Appropriate legal and descriptive records** (for example, deeds, maps, and listings) **should be maintained for all fixed assets, however,** for both management and accountability purposes.[4]

This option, like the permission to use estimated costs where necessary, resulted from a standards-setting judgment that the costs involved in establishing and maintaining **cost and financing source** records on **infrastructure GFA** might well exceed the benefits of such data.

Determining either actual or estimated costs and financing sources of infrastructure GFA can be very difficult, and it may be equally difficult to classify infrastructure expenditures between capitalizable "capital outlay" expenditures and "maintenance and repair" expenditures. Thus, many SLGs have excellent accounting records on all GFA **except** infrastructure fixed assets, and to require them to establish and maintain **cost and financing source** records on infrastructure GFA to comply with GAAP was not deemed appropriate from a SLG cost-benefit perspective.

The effect of the GFA infrastructure option is that (1) those SLGs that **want** to maintain complete accounting records of infrastructure GFA, including cost and financing source data—and many do—**may** do so and may include infrastructure cost data in their GFA-related statements and schedules and in the SLG balance sheet; and (2) those SLGs that do **not** want to establish and maintain complete cost and financing source records on infrastructure GFA **need not** do so, but should be able to identify—and **should keep** relevant legal and descriptive records such as **deeds, maps, and listings** for—all GFA, **including infrastructure** GFA. In either event, the SLG's infrastructure GFA accounting (or nonaccounting) policy should be consistently applied and disclosed in the notes to the SLG's financial statements.

Capitalization Policy

Before establishing GFA property records, most SLGs establish a GFA **capitalization policy.** One aspect of a SLG's GFA capitalization policy obviously will be its decision on whether or not to capitalize infrastructure GFA, the primary GFA accounting option under present GAAP. Further, its capitalization policy must meet legal requirements and control needs. Thus, since GAAP applies only to items that

---

[4] Ibid., sec. 1400.109. (Emphasis added.)

are material and significant in the circumstances, the SLG may establish additional GFA accounting policies based on legal compliance, materiality, and control considerations.

Legal Compliance

Some state and local ordinances require every fixed asset costing a certain amount —say $500 or even $100—or more to be capitalized in the accounts. While the wisdom of such laws may be questioned from materiality and cost-benefit perspectives—particularly when assets such as highways, right-of-ways, buildings, and building improvements are involved—the SLG must comply with the laws. However, certain capitalization policies may be permissible even under such laws —for example, which expenditures are considered "capital outlay," and thus are capitalized if equal to or greater than the specified amount, and which are considered "maintenance" or "repairs." Also, it may be acceptable to capitalize certain fixed assets in groups (e.g., 100 folding chairs in an auditorium) rather than individually, and it may be acceptable to apply the capitalization policy to each item in a lot or group (say, to each chair) rather than to the total. If in doubt in such respects, practitioners should seek appropriate legal advice—for example, from the SLG attorney, the state attorney general, or perhaps the state auditor.

Materiality and Control Considerations

In accounting and auditing, an item is considered **"material"** if *either* (1) its **dollar magnitude** is **significant** to the financial statements, **or** (2) its **nature** is such that proper accounting is required regardless of its dollar magnitude. Thus, both the relative dollar amount and its nature must be considered in determining its materiality.

Materiality is important in GAAP accounting and reporting because, while items that **are** material must be accounted for and reported strictly in accordance with GAAP, those that are **not** material need not be. Thus, **within the confines of legal constraints, SLGs can set GFA accounting policies in a materiality context.**

GFA capitalization materiality judgments thus may be made in terms of the various classifications of GFA—Land, Buildings and Improvements, Infrastructure (if capitalized), Machinery and Equipment, and Construction in Progress—and **different capitalization policies** may be established for **each** GFA **classification.** But, again, the nature of the items, as well as their dollar magnitude, should be considered in establishing GFA capitalization policies.

Control considerations may dictate capitalization of certain types of GFA even if their cost is less than the legal or other materiality thresholds. This often occurs in the case of movable machinery and equipment—such as personal computers, guns, and communication devices (e.g., two-way radios, pagers)—that may readily be converted to personal use, pawned, or sold.

GFA Property Records

After the GFA capitalization policies have been established and the cost or other valuation of a fixed asset to be capitalized has been determined, it is recorded in an individual GFA property record. The Government Finance Officers Association (GFOA) recommends recording the following information relative to each unit of property:

1. Class code
2. Sequence or payment voucher number

3. Date of acquisition
4. Name and address of vendor
5. Abbreviated description
6. Department, division, or unit charged with custody
7. Location
8. Cost
9. Fund and account from which purchased
10. Method of acquisition
11. Estimated life
12. Date, method, and authorization of disposition

A separate record is established for each "unit" of property. (A unit of property is any item that can be readily identified and accounted for separately, but may be a group of similar items, such as folding chairs.) These records of individual assets or groups of similar minor assets constitute the subsidiary accounts that support the General Fixed Assets accounts in the general ledger.

These subsidiary records must provide for classification in a number of ways:

- **General Ledger-Subsidiary Ledger Control.** They should permit a reconciliation with the amounts in the Land, Buildings, and other control accounts in the general ledger.

- **Organizational Accountability.** The assets in use by the several organizational units of a government are the responsibility of the agencies, bureaus, departments, and so on; and the system should permit identification of such assets for custodial control and accountability purposes and for any cost finding that is carried out.

- **Availability.** Assets not in use should be easily identifiable so that requests for assets may be filled from assets on hand and unnecessary purchases can be avoided.

- **Location.** Assets should be classifiable by location so that custodial control by physical inventory will be feasible.

Inventory of Fixed Assets

Land, buildings, infrastructure, and other **immovable** GFA need **not** be inventoried annually—though their records should be reviewed regularly for accuracy and completeness. However, a physical inventory of machinery, equipment, and other **movable** GFA **should** be taken on a regular basis for internal control, accounting, and accountability purposes. The physical count can then be compared with recorded descriptions and quantities. All differences between counts and records should be investigated. Missing assets must be removed from the accounts, and significant shortages should be disclosed in the statements or notes. Management should correct the weaknesses in internal control or accounting systems revealed by the shortages and related investigations.

Inventories of machinery, equipment, and other movable GFA, may be taken annually or on a cycle approach throughout the year. GFA property records classified by organization unit responsible and location are essential to such an inventory. The usual procedure is for the SLG finance officer to send a list of the machinery and equipment for which each department is responsible to that department, asking that the inventory be made and any discrepancies noted. After the department has conducted the inventory—which may be observed or reviewed by the SLG's internal auditors and/or external auditors—the department head and finance officer (or their representatives) determine if any adjustments and corrective actions are necessary. Thereafter, the department head takes any needed corrective actions and the finance officer adjusts the GFA records as necessary.

Additions, Betterments, and Renewals

The costs of additions, betterments, and renewals are **additional** costs of general fixed assets. The costs may be incurred in one of the governmental funds, where the distinction between expenditures to be capitalized and those to be treated as repair or maintenance costs must be made. Since expenditures for both purposes must be authorized by appropriations, the distinction should first be made in the budget.

As noted earlier, the distinction between "capital outlay" and "repair and maintenance" expenditures is often difficult in practice. Moreover, it is common to find in practice that (1) amounts that do not meet the GFA capitalization criteria are recorded as "capital outlay" expenditures in governmental funds, but (2) amounts that should be recorded as "capital outlay" expenditures in governmental funds and capitalized in the GFAAG are misclassified—usually unintentionally—as "repair and maintenance" or as other operating expenditures (e.g., capital leases recorded as rentals) in the governmental funds. The first situation presents no problems—the GFAAG accountant need only select those "capital outlay" expenditures to be capitalized and perhaps prepare a reconciliation of the governmental fund "capital outlay" expenditures and those capitalized in the GFAAG. But the second situation may require extensive analysis and evaluation of the governmental fund operating expenditure accounts to determine additional amounts that should be capitalized in the GFAAG accounts.

Additions to fixed assets are not classified according to whether they are buildings, other improvements, or equipment until they are completed. As noted earlier, costs incurred are accumulated in the Construction Work in Progress account during the construction period and are reclassified by asset type following completion of the project.

Depreciation/Accumulated Depreciation

A major distinction between the accounting for governmental funds and that for proprietary funds and for profit-seeking enterprises results from GASB Principle 7a:

> Depreciation [expense] of general fixed assets should not be recorded in the accounts of governmental funds. Depreciation [expense] of general fixed assets may be recorded in cost accounting systems or calculated for cost finding analyses, and accumulated depreciation **may** be recorded in the General Fixed Assets Account Group.[5]

If accumulated depreciation **is** recorded in the General Fixed Assets Account Group—which is **not** common in practice—it should be reported with the asset type for which it is being recorded. The corresponding debit would reduce the related Investment in General Fixed Assets financing source account(s).

The **GFAAG is not a fund, but an account group**—a management control and accountability listing of a government's general fixed assets balanced by ac-

---

[5] Ibid., sec. 1100.107. (Emphasis added.)

counts indicating the sources by which the GFA were financed.[6] And, as discussed and illustrated later in this chapter, **the GFAAG accounts are reported only in the SLG balance sheet—and no "operating" statement is prepared for the GFAAG.** Thus, depreciation expense is **not** recorded in the GFAAG accounts, though accumulated depreciation may be recorded in the GFAAG accounts and reported in the SLG's balance sheet.

Figure 9-2 summarizes the key financial reporting provisions discussed to this point. The next section illustrates the accounting for fixed asset acquisitions of various types.

Recording Fixed Asset Acquisitions

Practice varies considerably as to both (1) the updating of the General Fixed Assets Account Group, and (2) the extent of subsidiary account use.

Computerized systems may be programmed to generate GFAAG entries continually, periodically, or at year end. In systems that are not fully automated (1) some accountants prefer to update the GFA ledger whenever a relevant transaction occurs—which typically is assumed in Uniform CPA Exam questions and problems; (2) others maintain a GFA journal that is posted to the GFA ledger periodically during the year or at year end; and (3) still others update the GFA ledger only at year end, perhaps based on worksheet analyses of fund capital outlay expenditures. Regardless of individual preference, there should be an established, workable system for updating General Fixed Assets subsidiary records and ***the account group at least annually prior to statement preparation.***

Similarly, the extent to which subsidiary ledgers are employed is a matter of accounting system design, individual preference, and the detailed information desired or required. Frequently, the Land, Buildings, Improvements Other Than Buildings (Infrastructure), Machinery and Equipment, Construction in Progress, and Investment in General Fixed Assets accounts are ***controlling*** accounts and details of assets owned and the sources by which they were financed are maintained in subsidiary ledgers.

Figure 9-1 illustrates the accounting equation (see "Classification" earlier in this chapter) applicable to the General Fixed Assets Account Group and the subsidiary information necessary to support the principal accounts. The following trial balance further illustrates the account relationships:

General Fixed Assets Account Group
Trial Balance
(Date)

Land	700,000	
Buildings	2,500,000	
Improvements Other Than Buildings (Infrastructure)	1,100,000	
Machinery and Equipment	619,200	
Construction in Progress	480,800	
Investment in General Fixed Assets from:		
General Obligation Bonds		2,500,000
Federal Grants		1,500,000
General Revenues		1,150,000
Special Assessments		250,000
	5,400,000	5,400,000

The entries to record the capital expenditures in each governmental fund have already been given. In order to illustrate more clearly the relationship between

---

[6] Ibid., sec. 1400.110.

Figure 9-2   **GENERAL FIXED ASSETS REPORTING SUMMARY**

A. Valuation of GFA acquired via: Purchase Gift Eminent domain Escheat Foreclosure	 Cost Fair market value when received Cost established by court Fair market value when escheat occurs Lower of (1) government's claims against the property or (2) the property's fair market value at foreclosure
B. Use of estimated costs	Permitted when: (1) establishing initial GFA records and (2) actual costs are not practicably determinable
C. Capitalization of infrastructure fixed assets	Optional
D. Reporting of accumulated depreciation	Optional
E. Classification of Investment in GFA	By original sources of financing

Source: Freeman, Robert J. and Craig D. Shoulders, *Governmental Accounting Principles and Financial Reporting,* New York, AICPA, 1993.

these funds and the General Fixed Assets accounts, some of the fund general ledger entries will be repeated and the corresponding entry in the General Fixed Assets Account Group will be indicated.

Assets Financed from the General Fund or Special Revenue Funds

If the $29,100 of capital outlay expenditures in the General Fund illustrative example (entries 5b and 20, Chapter 4) had been made for equipment **purchases,** the entry in the **General Fund** would be:

Expenditures—Capital Outlay.	29,100	
Vouchers Payable		29,100

To record purchase of equipment.

Expenditures Ledger (Expenditures):

Capital Outlay.	29,100

A **companion entry** would be made in the **General Fixed Assets Account Group:**

Machinery and Equipment.	29,100	
Investment in General Fixed Assets.		29,100

To record cost of fixed assets financed from current revenues.

Investment in GFA Ledger:

General Revenues.	29,100

General Fixed Assets acquired by **capital lease** are recorded similarly. Recall that the **governmental fund** general ledger entry (Chapter 6, page 214) upon the **inception** of a capital lease was:

Expenditures—Capital Outlay.	900,000	
Other Financing Sources—Capital Lease		900,000

To record capital lease expenditure and related other financing source.

The companion entry in the **General Fixed Assets Account Group**—assuming the lease was for land and a building—would be:

Land—Under Capital Lease	100,000	
Building—Under Capital Lease	800,000	
Investment in General Fixed Assets		900,000

To record land and building acquired by capital lease.

Investment in GFA Ledger:

Capital Leases (or General Revenues)	900,000

Note that the fixed assets are identified as "under capital lease" during the term of the lease. Then, if the government takes title to the fixed assets, they are reclassified to the usual accounts (e.g., Land and Buildings). The usual financing source description is "Capital Leases"—since capital leasing is often an alternative to bond issue financing—though some governments classify capital lease transactions according to the source of the capital lease payments (e.g., General Revenues).

Assets Financed through Capital Projects Funds and Special Assessments

Regardless of whether construction expenditures accounts are closed at the end of each year or only when the bridge construction is completed, this **Capital Projects Fund** general ledger entry (Chapter 7) is made—in the accounts or in the year-end worksheets—at the end of the first year:

Appropriations—Defliese & Co. Contract	1,000,000	
Appropriations—Labor	140,000	
Appropriations—Machine Time	81,000	
Appropriations—Fuel and Materials	49,000	
Expenditures—Defliese & Co. Contract		1,000,000
Expenditures—Labor		140,000
Expenditures—Machine Time		81,000
Expenditures—Fuel and Materials		49,000

To close the expenditures to date (project incomplete).

The following entry is required in the **General Fixed Assets Account Group:**

Construction in Progress	1,270,000	
Investment in General Fixed Assets		1,270,000

To record construction in progress financed through Capital Projects Fund.

Investment in GFA Ledger:

General Revenues [10%]	127,000
State Grants [20%]	254,000
Federal Grants [40%]	508,000
General Obligation Bonds [30%]	381,000
	1,270,000

The distribution of sources among general revenues (10%), state grants (20%), federal grants (40%), and issuance of general obligation bonds (30%) would be made in proportion to the **expected** total contribution of each to the project. Note also that **encumbered** amounts, whether or not closed out at year end, are **not** capitalized; only **expended** amounts are capitalized.

When the **project is completed,** during the second year in our example, the general ledger expenditures closing entry in the **Capital Projects Fund**—assuming the accounts are closed annually—is:

Appropriations—Defliese & Co. Contract	1,400,000	
Appropriations—Labor	160,000	
Appropriations—Machine Time	119,000	
Appropriations—Fuel and Materials	51,000	
Expenditures—Defliese & Co. Contract		1,410,000
Expenditures—Labor		129,000
Expenditures—Machine Time.		108,000
Expenditures—Fuel and Materials.		43,000
Unreserved Fund Balance		40,000

To close the accounts (project completed).

In the **General Fixed Assets Account Group** the entry is:

Improvements Other Than Buildings.	2,960,000	
Construction in Progress		1,270,000
Investment in General Fixed Assets.		1,690,000

To record the cost of completed bridge project financed through Capital Projects Fund and to close the Construction in Progress account.

Investment in GFA Ledger:

General Revenues.	203,000
State Grants	346,000
Federal Grants	660,000
General Obligation Bonds	481,000
	1,690,000

The **subsidiary entry** pertaining to **financing sources** was determined (see Figure 7-5 by the following **calculation:**

	Total	General Revenues	State Grant	Federal Grant	Bond Issue
Final project revenues and other financing sources	$3,007,000	$330,000	$600,000	$1,168,000	$909,000
Less: Fund balance transferred to Debt Service Fund.	(47,000)				(47,000)
Final Project cost/sources	$2,960,000	$330,000	$600,000	$1,168,000	$862,000
Less: Amounts credited to sources in previous Construction in Progress entry(ies)	(1,270,000)	(127,000)	(254,000)	(508,000)	(381,000)
Balance to be credited to Investment in General Fixed Assets subsidiary ledger source accounts	$1,690,000	$203,000	$346,000	$ 660,000	$481,000

As noted in Chapter 7, most special assessment projects are accounted for in Capital Projects Funds. In any event, the procedure for recording general fixed assets acquired through special assessments parallels that illustrated for Capital Projects Funds. However, the financing source may be reported as special assessments instead of general long-term debt proceeds when special assessments are the underlying source of financing for a project—even if debt is issued initially.

Assets Acquired through Foreclosure

We noted earlier that fixed assets acquired through foreclosure should be recorded at the **lower** of (1) fair market value, or (2) the amount of taxes or assessments, penalties and interest due on the property, and costs of foreclosure and sale. To illustrate, assume that land with an estimated value of $2,000 was acquired through foreclosure. At the time of foreclosure, the following were due a **Special Revenue Fund:**

Taxes	$ 900
Penalties	100
Interest	75
Costs of foreclosure and sale	25
	$1,100

Further assuming that these receivables had been reclassified as Tax Liens Receivable prior to the decision to return the property for the government's use, the following entry should be made in the **Special Revenue Fund:**

Expenditures	1,100	
Tax Liens Receivable		1,100

To record acquisition of land through foreclosure; estimated fair market value, $2,000.

<u>Expenditures Ledger (Expenditures):</u>

Capital Outlay	1,100

The accompanying entry in the **General Fixed Assets Account Group** would be:

Land	1,100	
Investment in General Fixed Assets		1,100

To record acquisition of land through foreclosure of tax lien.

<u>Investment in GFA Ledger:</u>

Special Revenues	1,100

Note that the Investment in General Fixed Assets subsidiary ledger credit is to "Special Revenues," rather than to Foreclosures (or some similar account). Note also that had the fair market value of the property been less than charges against it, say $800, the Special Revenue Fund expenditure would be recorded at $800 and $300 would be charged against the allowance for uncollectible taxes and interest (or tax liens) receivable.

Most of the examples cited thus far have provided a clear-cut indication within a fund ledger that a fixed asset has been acquired and should be capitalized, that is, there has been a charge to the Expenditures account of some fund. Laws or custom in some jurisdictions do not permit charging fixed asset acquisitions through foreclosure to the Expenditures account, however. Rather, for these or other reasons the uncollectible amount may have been *improperly* charged as a bad debt, and the following **non-GAAP** entry would appear in the governmental fund ledger, for example, a **Special Revenue Fund:**

Allowance for Uncollectible Tax Liens	1,100	
Tax Liens Receivable		1,100

To record write-off of uncollectible account and the acquisition of property through foreclosure, estimated fair market value, $2,000.

Such non-GAAP "bad debt" entries must be examined, since they may call for a **General Fixed Assets entry:**

Land	1,100	
Investment in General Fixed Assets		1,100
To record land acquired by tax lien foreclosure.		
<u>Investment in GFA Ledger:</u>		
Special Revenues		<u>1,100</u>

Likewise, the Special Revenue Fund accounts and GAAP statements would need to be corrected to record properly the Expenditures (and Allowance for Uncollectible Tax Liens) in conformity with GAAP.

Assets Acquired through Gifts

No governmental fund assets are relinquished in acquiring property donated to the government. Thus, "general government" fixed assets acquired by gift are recorded **only** in the General Fixed Assets Account Group. Donated property should be recorded in the GFA accounts at **estimated fair market value** at the time of donation:

Land	1,500	
Investment in General Fixed Assets		1,500
To record land received by gift at estimated fair market value.		
<u>Investment in GFA Ledger:</u>		
Private Gifts		<u>1,500</u>

Sale, Retirement, or Replacement

General fixed assets may be disposed of in sale, retirement, or replacement transactions with other governments, nongovernment organizations, and individuals. If accumulated depreciation of General Fixed Assets is *not* recorded, as is the usual case, an asset's carrying value in the accounts remains at original cost plus the cost of any additions and betterments made throughout the period of its use. Removal of the asset's carrying value upon its disposal requires the **reverse** of the usual acquisition entry. The **accounting procedure upon disposal** is, in sum:

1. **General Fixed Assets Account Group.** Remove the asset carrying value by debiting the Investment in General Fixed Assets account(s) and crediting the asset account(s) in the general and subsidiary ledgers. If a replacement asset is acquired, record it properly in the GFAAG.
2. **Fund receiving proceeds of sale.** Record any salvage value, insurance proceeds, or other receipts as Revenues (or as Other Financing Sources) in the accounts of the recipient governmental fund.

If a government has adopted the policy of recording accumulated depreciation on assets of the General Fixed Assets Account Group, the entries to record removal of an asset from the group, for whatever reason, would include removal of the accumulated depreciation related to the asset being removed.

     The preceding GFAAG illustrative entries assumed that an Investment in GFA subsidiary ledger was used to account for the GFA financing sources. The GFAAG entries that follow illustrate how a series of general ledger Investment in General Fixed Assets accounts may be used instead of a subsidiary ledger. They also illustrate the use of several Revenues and Expenditures accounts in governmental funds rather than Revenues and Expenditures control accounts and a Revenues Ledger and Expenditures Ledger.

Sale

If a fire truck with a book value of $100,000 is sold for $20,000, the following entries are made:

General Fund:

Cash	20,000	
Revenues—Sales of Equipment		20,000
To record sale of fire truck.		

General Fixed Assets Account Group:

Investment in General Fixed Assets—General Revenues	100,000	
Machinery and Equipment		100,000
To record sale of fire truck with book value of $100,000.		

Retirement

The entries to record retirements may be more complicated than other fixed asset sales because the cost of retirement, as well as the proceeds received from the sale of salvage, must be taken into account. For example, assume that the book value of a fire station that was torn down was $150,000, that the cost of tearing it down was $10,000, and that $15,000 was realized from the sale of salvage. The entries to record these transactions are:

General Fixed Assets Account Group:

Investment in General Fixed Assets—Bond Issues	150,000	
Buildings		150,000
To record retirement of fire station.		

General Fund:

Expenditures—Other	10,000	
Cash		10,000
To record cost of dismantling building, such cost to be reimbursed from sale of salvage.		

Cash	15,000	
Expenditures—Other		10,000
Revenues—Salvage Proceeds		5,000
To record sale of salvage.		

Note that while the salvage costs are temporarily recorded as Expenditures, those costs are netted against the gross salvage proceeds and the net amount is reported as Revenues—Salvage Proceeds.

Replacement (Trade-In)

If the fire truck is traded in on a new one costing $120,000 (fair market value), and an allowance of $30,000 is made for the old truck, the transaction is recorded as:

General Fund:

Expenditures—Capital Outlay	90,000	
Cash		90,000
To record purchase of fire truck costing $120,000, net of trade-in allowance of $30,000.		

General Fixed Assets Account Group:

Investment in General Fixed Assets—General Revenues	100,000	
Machinery and Equipment		100,000
To record *disposal* (trade-in) of old fire truck with book value of $100,000.		

Machinery and Equipment	120,000	
Investment in General Fixed Assets—General Revenues		120,000

To record **purchase** of fire truck at a cost of $120,000 less
  $30,000 trade-in allowance on old fire truck.

Note that the book value of the old fire truck traded in should be removed from the GFAAG accounts, as in a sale, and the new fire truck should be recorded at its **fair market value** in the GFAAG accounts. (One of the most common GFA accounting errors in practice is that the new fixed asset may erroneously be capitalized at the amount of the "boot" given in an exchange—the amount of the governmental fund expenditure—rather than at its fair market value.)

Intragovernmental Sale, Transfer, and Reclassification

Thus far we have assumed that the assets were sold or traded to private non-SLG organizations or persons. Sometimes property accounted for in a proprietary or similar Trust Fund is sold to a department financed through a governmental fund. Fixed assets may also be transferred among agencies of the government.

Intragovernmental Sale

Assume that an enterprise sells equipment at book value to the public works department, which is financed from the General Fund, in a quasi-external transaction. The following entries would be made:

Enterprise Fund:

Due from General Fund	15,000	
Accumulated Depreciation—Equipment	1,000	
Equipment		16,000

To record sale of equipment to department of public works at net
  book value.

General Fund:

Expenditures—Capital Outlay	15,000	
Due to Enterprise Fund		15,000

To record purchase of equipment from Enterprise Fund for
  department of public works and liability to that fund.

General Fixed Assets Account Group:

Machinery and Equipment	15,000	
Investment in General Fixed Assets—General Revenues		15,000

To record purchase of equipment for public works department.

If the sale were for more or less than book value, a gain or loss would be recognized in the Enterprise Fund, **assuming** the transaction was indeed a true **quasi-external transaction.**

     Interagency sales of fixed assets in quasi-external transactions appear to occur most often in state governments and in large local governments with rather autonomous departments and agencies. Fixed assets may also be transferred and reclassified (rather than sold) between agencies.

Intragovernmental Transfer

Fixed assets may be transferred both (1) between "general government" departments, financed by governmental funds, and (2) between "general government" departments and **proprietary** fund departments or agencies. The accounting procedures differ for each type of transfer and reclassification.

"General Government" Transfer. When fixed assets are transferred from one "general government" department or agency to another—both financed by a governmental fund(s)—or even from one location to another, a written authorization for the transfer should be issued by the proper authority. The authorization will be the basis for changes in the GFA **subsidiary records—reclassifications** of departmental responsibility and/or location—to permit continuing control. The GFA general ledger accounts will **not** be affected.

Note that such GFA "transfers" are **not** interfund transfers. Rather, while they may be referred to informally as "transfers," they are simply **reclassifications** within the GFAAG accounts.

Proprietary Fund-"General Government" Transfer. Transfers of assets between agencies financed by governmental funds and agencies financed by proprietary funds affect **both** the general ledger and the subsidiary property records of **both** the GFAAG and the proprietary fund. For example, if equipment was "transferred" from the Water Fund to the Fire, Police, and Public Works Departments—which are "general government" departments financed from governmental funds—the entries to record this transaction are as follows:

Water (Enterprise) Fund:

Retained Earnings (or Governmental Unit's Contribution)......	10,000	
Accumulated Depreciation—Equipment	20,000	
Equipment		30,000

To record transfer of equipment to other departments as follows:

Department	Cost of Equipment	Accumulated Depreciation	Net Book Value
Police.........................	$ 5,000	$ 3,000	$ 2,000
Fire	10,000	6,500	3,500
Public Works.	15,000	10,500	4,500
	$30,000	$20,000	$10,000

General Fixed Assets Account Group:

Machinery and Equipment	10,000	
Investment in General Fixed Assets—Enterprise Fund		
Contributions		10,000

To record receipt of equipment.

Observe that this transfer is recorded in the **Enterprise Fund** (1) at book value—**no gain or loss usually is recognized** since such transfers are **not** considered to be quasi-external transactions, and (2) as a **direct deduction from Retained Earnings or contributed capital**—depending on whether it is viewed as a "dividend" or as a return of contributed capital—and **not** as an Operating Transfer or Residual Equity Transfer. Although the substance of the transaction may be identical to that of an Operating Transfer or a Residual Equity Transfer, a fixed asset transfer is **not** an **"interfund" transfer** but a **"fund-account group" transfer** or **"reclassification."** Further, "operating" statements are **not** represented for the account groups in the GPFS. So if a "transfer out" were reported in the proprietary fund, no corresponding "transfer in" would be reported—and the "transfers out" reported would not agree with the "transfers in." In any event, such direct deductions from and additions to proprietary fund equity accounts are reported similarly to interfund transfers—and are illustrated in later chapters.

Note also that the fixed assets are recorded in the GFAAG accounts at the net book value at which they were carried in the Enterprise Fund. A separate GFA property record is established for each unit of equipment in each department, of course. No entry is made in the General Fund accounts, however, since (1) no appropriable General Fund assets were either provided or used as a result of the transfer, and (2) this is a **"proprietary fund-GFAAG" transfer** rather than an "interfund transfer."

"General Government"-Proprietary Fund Transfer. Fixed assets may also be transferred from the "general government" departments to proprietary fund departments or agencies. The GFAAG accounting required is to remove the fixed asset accounts as in any fixed asset disposal. The fixed assets are then recorded in the proprietary fund at the *lower* of their **depreciated cost**—as if they had been originally acquired for proprietary fund use—**or** their **use value** to the proprietary fund activity. Further, that amount is credited directly to proprietary fund ***contributed capital,*** rather than being reported as an interfund transfer.

Property Damaged or Destroyed

Expenditures for repairs necessary to restore damaged property to its former condition are reported as current operating expenditures in the fund from which the cost of repairs is financed. Insurance proceeds are reported as revenues. To illustrate, assume that the total book value of a police station is $300,000, that the station is destroyed by fire, and that the governmental unit collects insurance of $200,000. The following entries would be made in the General Fixed Assets Account Group and in the General Fund, respectively, to record these transactions.

General Fixed Assets Account Group:

Investment in General Fixed Assets—Bond Issue............	300,000	
Buildings..		300,000

To record destruction of police station by fire.

General Fund:

Cash...	200,000	
Revenues—Insurance Proceeds.....................		200,000

To record receipt of proceeds of insurance policy on police station.

If the government intends to use some or all of the proceeds for replacement purposes, a "Reserve for New Police Station" could be created in the General Fund. **Repair** expenditures are classified as "current operating"; only **betterment** expenditures are reported as "capital outlay."

The GASB Codification does not mention write-downs of General Fixed Assets because of damage, obsolescence, or abandonment. It would seem reasonable to write down an asset (say, a 1926 fire engine) to a much lower figure if it is now used for a purpose for which it was not purchased (say, a display in a park). Similarly, assets that are to be sold for scrap probably should be carried at salvage value.

General Fixed Assets Statements and Schedules

The purpose of financial statements and schedules for the General Fixed Assets Account Group is to provide reports on what the GASB Codification calls "a management control and accountability listing." The statements and schedules discussed in the following paragraphs are usually prepared.

Figure 9-3

STATEMENT (OR SCHEDULE) OF CHANGES IN GENERAL FIXED ASSETS

A Governmental Unit

Statement (or Schedule) of Changes in General Fixed Assets

For the Fiscal Year Ended (Date)

	Beginning Balance	Additions	Deductions	Ending Balance
Land	$ 700,000	$ 9,600		$ 709,600
Buildings	2,500,000	37,200	$ 50,000	2,487,200
Improvements other than buildings	1,100,000	878,200		1,978,200
Machinery and equipment	619,200	59,100	35,200	643,100
Construction work in process	480,800	100,000	280,800	300,000
	$5,400,000	$1,084,100	$366,000	$6,118,100

Statement (or Schedule) of General Fixed Assets

The GASB Codification requires that (1) the General Fixed Assets be presented in the Combined Balance Sheet, and (2) **if necessary** to present fairly the financial position of the account group, a more detailed Statement (or Schedule) of General Fixed Assets also must be presented.

Some governments present detailed General Fixed Assets data—such as those in the GFAAG trial balance presented earlier—in the Combined Balance Sheet, so do not need to present a separate Statement (or Schedule) of General Fixed Assets. But larger governments, in particular, often report a single amount for "General Fixed Assets" and "Investment in General Fixed Assets" in their Combined Balance Sheet—to keep that statement as brief as practicable—and include a more detailed Schedule of General Fixed Assets and of the sources of Investment in General Fixed Assets in the **notes** to the financial statements.

The Statement (or Schedule) of General Fixed Assets presents a summary of the assets by major category and source. Most SLGs also present a Schedule of General Fixed Assets—By Functions and Activities—as supplemental information. To be more useful to management, this schedule may be prepared on the basis of organizational units rather than by function and activity. It then indicates departmental use of and responsibility for assets.

Statement (or Schedule) of Changes in General Fixed Assets

The GASB Codification also requires that either a statement or a schedule (in the notes) of **changes** in General Fixed Assets be presented in the annual financial statements. Such a statement (or schedule) is not illustrated in the GASB Codification.

Most SLGs present a highly summarized schedule of changes in General Fixed Assets—such as that in Figure 9-3—in the notes to the financial statements. Some also present a more detailed statement or schedule of changes in GFA—such as that presented in Figure 9-4—usually as supplemental information. Further, some SLGs present a supplemental statement or schedule of changes in GFA by functions and activities—or by organization units—primarily for managerial accountability purposes.

Figure 9-4

DETAILED STATEMENT (OR SCHEDULE) OF CHANGES IN GENERAL FIXED ASSETS

A Governmental Unit

Detailed Statement (or Schedule) of Changes in General Fixed Assets—By Sources

For the Fiscal Year Ended (Date)

	Total	Land	Buildings	Improvements Other Than Buildings	Machinery & Equipment	Construction Work in Progress
General fixed assets (beginning of year)	$5,400,000	$700,000	$2,500,000	$1,100,000	$619,200	$480,800
Additions from:						
General obligation bonds	168,200			93,200		75,000
Federal grants	225,000			200,000		25,000
County grants	50,000			50,000		
Special assessments	400,000			400,000		
General revenues*	238,300	7,000	37,200	135,000	59,100	
Special revenues*	1,100	1,100				
Private gifts	1,500	1,500				
	1,084,100	9,600	37,200	878,200	59,100	100,000
Total balance and additions	6,484,100	709,600	2,537,200	1,978,200	678,300	580,800
Deductions:						
Cost of assets sold or traded	32,800				32,800	
Cost of assets lost by fire	50,000		50,000			
Cost of assets worn out and written off	2,400				2,400	
Cost of construction work in progress of prior year completed†	280,800					280,800
	366,000		50,000		35,200	280,800
General fixed assets (end of year)	$6,118,100	$709,600	$2,487,200	$1,978,200	$643,100	$300,000

*Includes amounts transferred to and expended through Capital Projects Funds.

†Included in costs capitalized to Land, Buildings, Improvements Other Than Buildings, and Machinery and Equipment.

General long-term debt of a government is defined in the GASB Codification as *all* of its *unmatured* long-term debt *except* that of proprietary funds or Trust Funds.[7] **General long-term debt (GLTD)** thus includes the **unmatured principal** of bonds, warrants, notes, capital leases, certificates of participation, underfunded pension plan contributions, claims and judgments, compensated absences, and other forms of **"general government"** debt that is not a primary obligation of any fund. Special assessment debt is included in GLTD *if* the government is obligated in *any* manner on the debt and it is not being serviced through a specific Enterprise Fund, as noted in Chapter 8.

Matured general obligation debt that has been recorded in and will be paid from a Debt Service Fund is *excluded* from the GLTD definition, as are debts to be paid by proprietary funds or Trust Funds. The excluded debt is not recorded in the General Long-Term Debt Account Group (GLTDAG), but the government's contingent liability should be disclosed if non-GLTD debt is guaranteed by the government.

Thus, the same type of clear-cut distinction maintained between fixed assets of specific funds and general fixed assets is maintained between (1) long-term debt that is the primary responsibility of specific funds and (2) general long-term debt. The liability for unmatured *general* long-term debt is recorded in the General Long-Term Debt Account Group, not in the fund in which the proceeds from its issuance were accounted for (e.g., the Capital Projects Fund) or the fund from which it will eventually be paid (e.g., the Debt Service Fund).

Overview of General Long-Term Debt Accounting

Accounting for General Long-Term Debt may be divided into three phases:

1. *When debt is incurred.* The **principal** of the debt owed is credited to an appropriate liability account; the corresponding debit is to an **"Amount to Be Provided for Payment of Debt Principal"** or similar account, indicating the extent to which future revenues are committed to the retirement of debt principal.

2. *While unmatured debt is outstanding.* As resources for the retirement of General Long-Term Debt **principal** are accumulated, usually in Debt Service Funds, the **"Amount to be Provided . . ."** account is *reduced* and an **"Amount Available . . ."** *account established or increased* to reflect their availability.

3. *When debt matures.* The matured debt is established as a liability of the fund through which it is to be paid—usually a Debt Service Fund—and the **liability and related "Amount Available . . ." and/or "Amount to Be Provided . . ."** **accounts** are *reversed* from the General Long-Term Debt Account Group.

The accounting process for General Long-Term Debt is summarized in Figure 9-5.

Practice varies somewhat as to the timing of the entries in the General Long-Term Debt Account Group. As a general rule (1) entries to record incurrence of debt are made immediately upon its incurrence, (2) entries to record accumulation of debt retirement resources are made in the course of the year-end adjustment process (but should be made immediately on the CPA exam), and (3) entries to record debt maturity are prepared at the date the debt is due. Further, unless

---

[7] Ibid., sec. 1500.103.

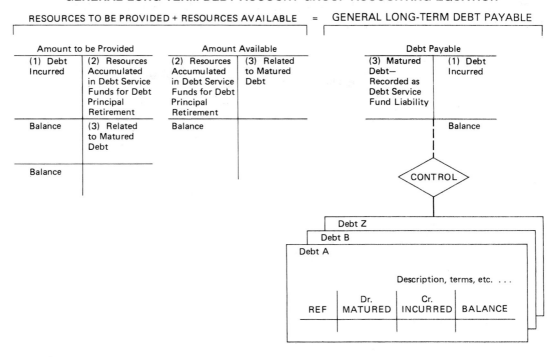

Figure 9-5 **GENERAL LONG-TERM DEBT ACCOUNT GROUP ACCOUNTING EQUATION**

some of the Debt Service Fund resources are restricted for interest payments—or otherwise must be used for interest payments—the entire fund balance typically is considered to be "available" for debt principal retirement.

Relationship to Debt Service and Capital Projects Funds

In order to illustrate the relationship among the Capital Projects and Debt Service Funds and the General Long-Term Debt Account Group, recall the Flores Park Bonds example in Chapter 8. Upon issuance of the debt instruments in 19X1 at par, entries would have been made as follows:

Capital Projects Fund

Cash	1,000,000	
Other Financing Sources—Bond Issue Proceeds		1,000,000
To record receipt of bond issue proceeds		

General Long-Term Debt Account Group

Amount to Be Provided for Payment of Serial Bonds	1,000,000	
Serial Bonds Payable		1,000,000
To record issuance of serial bonds.		

The liability is recorded at **par or maturity value** in the GLTD accounts, even if the debt is issued at a premium or discount. The proceeds are expended through the Capital Projects Fund and the fixed assets acquired are capitalized in the General Fixed Assets Account Group.

Recall, however, that a Flores Park Serial Bonds Debt Service Fund was established to service this debt. When the 19X1 principal ($100,000) and interest

($50,000) payment on the Flores Park bonds became due along with $10,000 of fiscal agent fees, the following entries were required:

Debt Service Fund

Expenditures	160,000	
Matured Bonds Payable.		100,000
Matured Interest Payable.		50,000
Fiscal Agent Fees Payable.		10,000

To record maturity of bonds and interest along with fiscal
agent fees.

General Long-Term Debt Account Group

Serial Bonds Payable.	100,000	
Amount to Be Provided for Payment of Serial Bonds		100,000

To record serial bonds maturing and being recorded as a DSF
liability.

At the end of 19X1 there was a balance of $87,000 in the Flores Park Serial Bond DSF—which was accumulated to protect bondholders—requiring the following adjustment to be made at year end in the **GLTD accounts:**

General Long-Term Debt Account Group

Amount Available in Debt Service Funds—Serial Bonds	87,000	
Amount to Be Provided for Payment of Serial Bonds		87,000

To record amount available for retirement of serial bonds.

When the 19X2 principal ($100,000) and interest ($45,000) payment on the Flores Park bonds became due along with $10,000 of fiscal agent fees, the following entries were required:

Debt Service Fund

Expenditures.	155,000	
Matured Bonds Payable		100,000
Matured Interest Payable		45,000
Fiscal Agent Fees Payable		10,000

To record maturity of bonds and interest along with fiscal agent
fees.

General Long-Term Debt Account Group

Serial Bonds Payable	100,000	
Amount to Be Provided for Payment of Serial Bonds		100,000

To record serial bonds maturing and being recorded as a DSF
liability.

Similarly, if at the end of 19X2 the Flores Park Serial Bonds Debt Service Fund had net assets (Fund Balance) of $150,000, the following **GLTD adjustment** would be required for the amount of the *increase:*

General Long-Term Debt Account Group

Amount Available in Debt Service Funds—Serial Bonds	63,000	
Amount to Be Provided for Payment of Serial Bonds		63,000

To record increase in the amount available for retirement of
serial bonds from $87,000 to $150,000.

Similar entries would be made at least annually throughout the life of the Debt Service Fund and the debt issue.

Relation to Serial Debt

Some serial Debt Service Funds closely parallel the Flores Park Serial Bonds Debt Service Fund example from Chapter 8 that was used in the previous section. Others are essentially "flow-through" vehicles through which current period principal and interest requirements and payments are accounted for. Many such funds have minimal (or zero) balances at year end and do not normally require entries in the General Long-Term Debt Account Group except upon debt principal maturities. For example, capital leases and long-term notes payable usually do not have "funded reserve" or other requirements that amounts in excess of the annual debt service requirements be accumulated in a related Debt Service Fund. Further, any related Debt Service Funds often are financed by interfund transfers in the amount of the annual debt service requirements. Hence, no excess resources are accumulated in the DSF in such cases, and no amount is reported as "Amount Available in DSF . . ." in the General Long-Term Debt Account Group. The appropriate GLTD entry upon maturity of debt principal in such situations is simply the reverse of the entry made to record debt incurrence.

In the case of regular serial bonds with *"funded reserve"* requirements—like the Flores Park Serial Bonds—an amount at least equal to the requirement(s) should be accumulated in the related Debt Service Fund, of course. Those resources typically are available for either principal or interest payments upon the occurrence of some contingency—such as a fiscal emergency—and, in any event, may be used to make the final debt service payments on the issue. Thus, they are reported as "Amount Available in DSF . . ." in the GLTDAG and should be reversed from the GLTDAG accounts when they are used for either purpose or, if not needed, are transferred to another fund after the related issue has been retired.

Where debt principal maturities are staggered over a period of years, the government may equalize its annual debt service provisions, thereby accumulating resources in "low requirement" years for use during "high requirement" years. Where a significant excess of serial Debt Service Fund assets over current year principal and interest requirements exists, the serial bond Debt Service Fund becomes similar to a term bond Debt Service Fund and should be accounted for similarly. The required annual adjustment to the GLTD accounts in such cases is simply a matter of reclassifying from the "Amount to Be Provided . . ." account to the "Amount Available . . ." account—or vice versa—an amount sufficient to bring the latter into agreement with the fund balance account of the serial bond Debt Service Fund that is available for debt principal retirement. Again, unless some of the DSF fund balance has been restricted for interest payments—or otherwise must be used for interest payments—the total fund balance of the DSF typically is considered to be available for debt principal retirement.

Relation to Special Assessment Debt

Recall from Chapter 8 that the GASB Codification (sec. S40) requires a government to report unmatured special assessment bonds, notes, or other debt in its GLTDAG **if** the government is even remotely *contingently* obligated in **any** manner on the debt. Thus, whereas other contingent liabilities are disclosed in the notes to the financial statements—rather than reported as liabilities in the financial statements—this GASB standard requires a unique exception with respect to special assessment indebtedness.

Recognizing the unusual nature of this requirement, the Board also specified that the special assessment liability be distinguished from other GLTD by being reported as **"Special Assessment Debt with Governmental Commitment."** Thus, issuance of $900,000 of special assessment bonds that are expected to be serviced by related special assessments—but on which a government *is obligated* in *some* manner—would be recorded in the **General Long-Term Debt Account Group** as follows:

Amount to be Provided by Special Assessments   900,000
    Special Assessment Bonds [or Debt] with Governmental
      Commitment   900,000
To record issuance of special assessment debt on which the
    government is obligated in some manner.

Thereafter, as debt service resources are accumulated in—and the debt is serviced through—a Debt Service Fund, the GLTDAG entries parallel those discussed earlier.

Relation to Other "General Government" Liabilities

Recall that the GASB Codification definition of the modified accrual basis of governmental (and similar trust) fund accounting states that a *fund expenditure* is recognized when a *fund liability* is incurred. Recall also that the Codification provides that all unmatured indebtedness except specific fund indebtedness is GLTD; and that GLTD "is not limited to liabilities arising from debt issuances *per se,* but may also include . . . other commitments that are not current liabilities properly recorded in governmental [or similar trust] funds."[8]

Further, the Codification states—with regard to claims and judgments, compensated absences, and unfunded actuarially required pension plan contributions—that "in governmental (and similar trust) funds, liabilities usually are **not** considered **current** until they are **normally expected to be liquidated with expendable available financial resources.**"[9] It then provides direction for determining the **liability** for "general government" **underfunded** pension contributions, claims and judgments, and compensated absences liabilities—and changes therein—and directs that (1) the amount of the liability that would normally be expected to be liquidated with available expendable financial resources be recorded as a governmental (or similar trust) fund expenditure and liability, and (2) the excess be recorded in the GLTD accounts.

Thus, the GLTDAG may account for numerous types of unmatured "general government" liabilities—such as for claims and judgments; accumulated vacation, sick leave, and other compensated absences; and underfunded pension contributions—as well as unmatured bonds, notes, and capital leases payable. "Amounts available" for such other liabilities typically are not accumulated in related Debt Service Funds. However, any resources accumulated in DSFs for such other liabilities would be accounted for and reported as discussed and illustrated previously.

To illustrate, recall the claims and judgments expenditures example from Chapter 6 (pages 221 to 223). This example assumed the following key information:

Year	Transaction/Information Summary	Amount
19X1	Claims and judgments paid during year	$300,000
19X1	Total accruable, unrecorded CJ liabilities outstanding at year end	200,000
19X1	Portion of CJ liabilities considered current at year end	50,000
19X2	Claims and judgments paid during year	450,000
19X2	Total accruable, unrecorded CJ liabilities outstanding at year end	325,000
19X2	Portion of CJ liabilities considered current at year end	75,000

[8] Ibid.
[9] Ibid., secs. C50.112, C60.109, and P20.112.

The entries required to record the preceding information in the General Fund and in the General Long-Term Debt Account Group are:

19X1 Entries

General Fund

Expenditures—Claims and Judgments	300,000	
Cash		300,000

To record payment of CJ expenditures.

General Fund

Expenditures—Claims and Judgments	50,000	
Accrued CJ Liabilities		50,000

To record additional expenditures for "current" CJ liabilities expected to be paid from existing fund assets.

General Long-Term Debt Account Group

Amount to Be Provided for Payment of CJ Liabilities	150,000	
Accrued CJ Liabilities		150,000

To record the increase in the "long-term" portion of CJ liabilities.

19X2 Entries

General Fund

Expenditures	400,000	
Accrued CJ Liabilities	50,000	
Cash		450,000

To record payment of CJ expenditures and accrued fund liabilities from 19X1.

General Fund

Expenditures	75,000	
Accrued CJ Liabilities		75,000

To record additional expenditures for "current" CJ liabilities expected to be paid from existing fund assets.

General Long-Term Debt Account Group

Amount to Be Provided for Payment of CJ Liabilities	100,000	
Accrued CJ Liabilities		100,000

To record the increase in the "long-term" portion of CJ liabilities.

Defaulted Bonds

The GASB Codification does **not** provide specific guidance for reporting if a government defaults on its **general** long-term debt, but does provide guidance where **proprietary fund** or **trust fund** long-term debt on which the unit is *contingently* liable is in (or near) default:

> In the event that **fund** liabilities for which the unit is **contingently liable** are in default—**or** where for other reasons it appears probable that they will not be paid on a timely basis from the resources of these funds and **default is imminent**—these liabilities should be **reported separately** from other liabilities in the **fund** balance sheet [rather than in the GLTDAG] in accordance with [Codification] Section C50 [on Claims and Judgments].[10]

Further, all significant facts concerning the government's contingent liability on the **proprietary fund or trust fund debt** in default, or which will soon be in default, should be disclosed in the notes to the financial statements.

Two accounting and reporting approaches to accounting for and reporting defaulted **general obligation** debt—which occurs rarely—have been suggested:

1. **Leave the defaulted debt in the GLTDAG**—but disclose the default in a note to the financial statements and/or in the Statement of General Long-Term Debt

---

[10] GASB Codification, sec. 1500.110. (Emphasis added.)

Figure 9-6 **STATEMENT OF GENERAL LONG-TERM DEBT**

Broward County, Florida
September 30, 19X1
(In Thousands)

	Total
Amount Available and to Be Provided for the Payment of	
General Long-Term Debt:	
Amount Available	$ 34,295
Amount to Be Provided:	
Tourist Tax Revenue Bonds	28,817
Gas Tax Revenue Bonds	66,316
General Obligation Bonds	388,947
Special Obligation Bonds	46,273
Loans Payable and Capital Lease Obligations	104,276
Compensated Absences	25,811
Total Available and to Be Provided	**$694,735**
General Long-Term Debt Payable:	
Tourist Tax Revenue Bonds	$ 35,156
Gas Tax Revenue Bonds	74,845
General Obligation Bonds	390,130
Special Obligation Bonds	51,070
Loans Payable and Capital Lease Obligations	115,177
Compensated Absences	25,811
Liability for Arbitrage	2,546
Total General Long-Term Debt Payable	**$694,735**

(Figure 9-6), and separately report the debt in the body of the statement as, say, **"Bonds Payable—In Default."**

2. **Record the maturity in a DSF**—and remove the debt from the GLTDAG, on the grounds that (a) GLTD is, by definition, the **"unmatured"** principal of "general government" long-term debt, and (b) thus, **matured** debt should be removed from the GLTDAG and recorded as a DSF expenditure—whether or not the related liability can be paid.

Reporting a deficit and **"Defaulted Bonds Payable"** in the DSF would draw attention to the default, as would its disclosure in a note to the financial statements and/or in the Statement of General Long-Term Debt. However, given the **"unmatured principal"** definition of "general long-term debt" and the lack of specific GASB guidance, the authors believe the second approach—record the maturity in a DSF and remove the debt from the GLTDAG—is the preferable alternative under current GAAP.

In-Substance Defeasance

As discussed in Chapter 8, governments may set aside resources in an irrevocable trust to provide for future debt service requirements for a particular debt issue. Where certain conditions are met as outlined in Chapter 8, the debt is deemed to be defeased in substance. General long-term debt (GLTD) that has been defeased in substance should be removed from a government's general long-term debt accounts as if it had been retired. This treatment is followed regardless of whether the defeasance was achieved using advance refunding bond proceeds or previously accumulated government resources. If long-term advance refunding bonds were issued, the liability would be recorded in the GLTD Account Group.

Sometimes governments fail to meet all the technical requirements for defeasance in substance of general long-term debt that the government desires to defease. If the in-substance defeasance criteria are ***not*** met, the "old" debt cannot be removed from the account group. The assets placed in trust would be accounted for as investments of the DSF servicing the "old" debt, resulting in a need to increase the "Amount Available . . ." account in the General Long-Term Debt Account Group. Any "new" advance refunding debt issued in such situations also would be recorded and reported in the GLTDAG.

GLTD Records

A file should be established for each debt issue at any early date, preferably while it is in the planning stage. The file should contain copies of, or references to, all pertinent correspondence, ordinances or resolutions, advertisements for the authorization referendum, advertisements or calls for bids, bond indentures or other agreements, debt service schedules, and the like.

Subsidiary records should be established and maintained for each liability in the account group. The exact nature of each record will vary with the pertinent details of the debt, but typical information would include title and amount of the issue; nature of the debt; dates of issue, required interest payments, and maturity; denominations; nominal and effective interest rates; and premium or discount. Further, if the issue is registered, provision must be made to record owners' names and addresses. The subsidiary record will support the liabilities recorded in the account group, as well as the related debt service payments.

The debt instruments should be prenumbered and carefully controlled at all stages of their life cycle. Most government bonds issued before the mid-1980s are "bearer" instruments with interest coupons attached, which makes strict control essential.

As debt principal and interest are paid, whether by the government or through a fiscal agent, paid coupons and bonds should be marked "Paid" or "Canceled," reconciled with reports of payments, and retained at least until the records have been audited. Paid bonds and coupons are typically destroyed periodically, usually by cremation, to conserve storage space and avoid even the slightest possibility of reissue or double payment. The number of each bond or coupon destroyed should be recorded, attested to by two or more responsible officials who have verified the accuracy of the list and witnessed the bond and coupon destruction, and filed for reference. Bonds and interest coupons may be destroyed by the fiscal agent. In this case, the certified statement of items destroyed (provided by the fiscal agent) should be recorded and filed for reference. As an extra safeguard, some governments microfilm canceled bonds and interest coupons before destroying them.

GLTD Statements, Schedules, and Statistical Tables

A **Statement (or Schedule) of General Long-Term Debt** (Figure 9-6) is prepared at each statement date in accordance with GASB standards. It is essentially a balance sheet of the GLTD Account Group, and may be presented in the Combined Balance Sheet. Like the GFAAG data, the GLTDAG data presented in the Combined Balance Sheet may be more summarized than that in Figure 9-6, with the details presented in a separate Statement of General Long-Term Debt or in a schedule in the notes to the financial statements. Footnotes should disclose any obligations that, although primarily the responsibilities of some specific fund, are also full faith and credit responsibilities of the government as a whole.

Figure 9-7 **SCHEDULE OF CHANGES IN GENERAL LONG-TERM DEBT**

Shelby County, Tennessee
Notes to Financial Statements
June 30, 19X1

Note (4)—General Obligation Debt

Changes in general long-term debt during the year were:

	Original Amounts	Balance July 1, 19X0	Debt Issues	Debt Retirements	Increase in Accrued Sick and Annual Leave	Balance June 30, 19X1
General Obligation Bonds	$471,631,318	$413,906,086	$48,998,682	$18,080,000	$ —	$444,824,768
Capitalized Lease Obligations	836,633	226,570	836,633	254,834		808,369
Sick and Annual Leave	21,166,862	21,166,862	—	—	147,533	21,314,395
Total	$493,634,813	$435,299,518	$49,835,315	$18,334,834	$147,533	$466,947,532

Source: A recent annual financial report of Shelby County, Tennessee.

Figure 9-8 **SCHEDULE OF DEBT SERVICE REQUIREMENTS TO MATURITY**

Shelby County, Tennessee
Notes to Financial Statements
June 30, 19X1

Note (4)—General Debt
The County is indebted for serial bonds with interest rates varying from 4.25% to 8.75%, variable rate bonds, and notes. The County has no legal debt limit. Debt service requirements for principal and interest in future years, using the actual rate on fixed rate bonds and notes and 8.4% for the variable rate issue, are as follows:

Years Ending June 30	Principal	Interest	Total
19X2	$ 23,155,000	$ 28,294,819	$ 51,449,819
19X3	25,905,000	26,940,566	52,845,566
19X4	27,605,000	25,176,331	52,781,331
19X5	29,405,000	23,371,704	52,776,704
19X6	30,895,000	21,405,220	52,300,220
19X7	32,750,000	19,318,796	52,068,796
19X8	33,775,000	17,095,697	50,870,697
19X9	36,200,000	14,697,179	50,897,179
20Y0	25,565,000	12,469,599	38,034,599
20Y1	24,455,000	10,647,588	35,102,588
20Y2	19,035,000	9,045,054	28,080,054
20Y3	19,075,000	7,705,550	26,780,550
20Y4	22,304,138	8,654,349	30,958,487
20Y5	17,157,040	13,967,329	31,124,369
20Y6	17,730,033	13,458,506	31,188,539
20Y7	15,391,684	7,077,053	22,468,737
20Y8	16,333,709	6,174,878	22,508,587
20Y9	13,173,163	5,347,700	18,520,863
20Z0	10,970,000	734,778	11,704,778
20Z1	3,945,000	256,426	4,201,426
	$444,824,767	$271,839,122	$716,663,889

These obligations are backed by the full faith and credit of the County and represent borrowings for the following:

General Government	$332,575,103
Education	112,094,664
Utility Bonds	155,000
	$444,824,767

Source: A recent annual financial report of Shelby County, Tennessee.

The GASB Codification also requires presentation of a **Statement of Changes in General Long-Term Debt** unless sufficiently disclosed in a **Schedule of Changes in General Long-Term Debt** (Figure 9-7) in the notes to the financial statements. This statement or schedule, by accounting for increases and decreases, forms a connecting link between Statements (or Schedules) of General Long-Term Debt at successive statement dates.

In order to present the resources requirements of the existing debt structure, for each future year and in total, the GASB Codification requires that a summary of **debt service requirements to maturity** be presented in the notes to the financial statements (the usual practice) or as a separate schedule to the general purpose financial statements. Figure 9-8 is a typical summary schedule, though some governments present detailed data for only five to ten years and summarize the data for later years. A detailed schedule of the requirements of each issue of general obligation long-term debt is recommended for inclusion in the statistical tables of the CAFR.

In addition to these GLTD financial statements or schedules, the comprehensive annual financial report ordinarily includes a number of detailed schedules that are designed to provide additional (usually unaudited) financial data. Several examples are presented in Chapter 14, "Financial Reporting."

INTRODUCTION TO INTERFUND-ACCOUNT GROUP ACCOUNTING

Thus far in this chapter we have indicated how the transactions in the various governmental funds affect the General Fixed Assets and General Long-Term Debt Account Groups. The following entries illustrate interfund-account group accounting when transactions in one fund affect another fund or account group:

1. A $500,000 serial bond issue to finance capital improvements was issued at a $5,000 premium.

Capital Projects Fund:

Cash	505,000	
Bond Proceeds		505,000

To record bond issue at a $5,000 premium.

General Long-Term Debt Account Group:

Amount to be Provided for Retirement of Serial Bonds	500,000	
Serial Bonds Payable		500,000

To record liability for serial bond issue.

2. The bond premium was transferred to the Debt Service Fund for either principal or interest payments on the serial bonds.

Capital Projects Fund:

Operating Transfer to Debt Service Fund	5,000	
Cash		5,000

To record transfer of cash representing premium on bonds to the Debt Service Fund.

Debt Service Fund:

Cash	5,000	
Operating Transfer from Capital Projects Fund		5,000

To record receipt of cash representing premium on bonds.

General Long-Term Debt Account Group:

Amount Available for Retirement of Serial Bonds	5,000	
Amount to be Provided for Retirement of Serial Bonds . .		5,000

To record additional amount available in Debt Service Fund.

3. An $80,000 contribution was made from the General Fund
to the Debt Service Fund: $30,000 for interest payments
and $50,000 for serial bond principal payments.

General Fund:

Operating Transfer to Debt Service Fund	80,000	
Cash		80,000

To record payment of contribution to Debt Service Fund.

Debt Service Fund:

Cash	80,000	
Operating Transfer from General Fund		80,000

To record receipt of contribution from General Fund.

General Long-Term Debt Account Group:

Amount Available for Retirement of Serial Bonds	50,000	
Amount to Be Provided for Retirement of Serial Bonds . .		50,000

To decrease amount to be provided and to increase the
amount available for the retirement of serial bonds.

4. Bond-financed Capital Projects Fund capital outlay
expenditures were made, $496,000, for improvements.

Capital Projects Fund:

Expenditures	496,000	
Vouchers Payable		496,000

To record capital improvement expenditures.

General Fixed Assets Account Group:

Improvements Other Than Buildings	496,000	
Investments in General Fixed Assets—Bond Issues		496,000

To record capital improvements made.

5. The $4,000 remaining balance of a Capital Projects Fund
was transferred to the Debt Service Fund for use as
needed.

Capital Projects Fund:

Residual Equity Transfer to Debt Service Fund	4,000	
Cash		4,000

To record transfer of balance of Capital Projects Fund to
Debt Service Fund.

Debt Service Fund:

Cash	4,000	
Residual Equity Transfer from Capital Projects Fund		4,000

To record receipts of Capital Projects Fund balance.

General Long-Term Debt Account Group:

Amount Available for Retirement of (Type of) Bonds.	4,000	
Amount to be Provided for Retirement of (Type of) Bonds		4,000

To record receipt of Capital Projects Fund Balance by Debt
Service Fund and corresponding increase in amount
available for retirement of bonds.

6. Maturing serial bonds ($50,000) and interest ($30,000)
were paid from the Debt Service Fund.

Debt Service Fund:

Expenditures—Bond Principal	50,000	
Expenditures—Interest on Bonds	30,000	
Cash.		80,000

To record payment of serial bond debt service.

General Long-Term Debt Account Group:

Serial Bonds Payable.	50,000	
Amount Available for Retirement of Serial Bonds		50,000

To record retirement of serial bonds.

7. A General Fund department entered into a capital lease of
equipment with a capitalizable cost of $250,000. A $25,000
down payment was made at the inception of the lease.

General Fund:

Expenditures—Capital Outlay	250,000	
Other Financing Sources—Increase in Capital Lease		
Liability.		225,000
Cash.		25,000

To record the inception of a capital lease and the initial
down payment.

General Long-Term Debt Account Group:

Amount to Be Provided for Retirement of Capital Lease		
Liabilities	225,000	
Capital Lease Liabilities		225,000

To record capital lease liabilities.

General Fixed Assets Account Group:

Assets Under Capital Lease	250,000	
Investment in General Fixed Assets—Capital Leases		250,000

To record leased assets.

8. Lease payments of $50,000, including $20,000 interest, were
paid.

General Fund:

Expenditures—Principal Retirement.	30,000	
Expenditures—Interest	20,000	
Cash.		50,000

To record periodic lease payments.

General Long-Term Debt Account Group:

Capital Lease Liabilities	30,000	
Amount to Be Provided for Retirement of Capital Lease		
Liabilities.		30,000

To record retirement of a portion of the capital lease
liabilities.

9. The government unit accrued its liability to pay part of
the cost of special assessment improvements being
accounted for in a Capital Projects Fund from the
General Fund.

General Fund:

Operating Transfer to Capital Projects Fund.	100,000	
Due to Capital Projects Fund		100,000

To record governmental unit's liability for contribution
toward construction of special assessment
improvements.

Capital Projects Fund:

Due from General Fund.	100,000	
Operating Transfer from General Fund		100,000

To record amount due from General Fund for governmental
unit's share of cost of project.

10. Special assessments of $100,000 became current and
$20,000 interest on special assessments was accrued. The
full amount of the current assessments and interest is
expected to be collected by the end of the current fiscal
year and is to be used to service general government
special assessment bonds that the government
guarantees.

Debt Service Fund:

Special Assessments Receivable—Current	100,000	
Interest Receivable on Assessments	20,000	
Special Assessments Receivable—Deferred		100,000
Revenues—Interest		20,000

To reclassify deferred receivables as current and accrue
interest.

Deferred Revenues—Assessments	100,000	
Revenues—Assessments.		100,000

To recognize current assessments revenues.

General Long-Term Debt Account Group:

Amount Available for Retirement of Special Assessment Bonds.	120,000	
Amount to Be Provided for Retirement of Special Assessment Bonds		120,000

To reflect increase in Special Assessment Debt Service Fund fund balance available for retirement of special assessment debt.

11. Inspection services were performed (**quasi-external transaction**) by a department financed through the General Fund for a capital project.

General Fund:

Due from Capital Projects Fund	8,000	
Revenues		8,000

To record revenues for inspection services rendered on capital projects.

Capital Projects Fund:

Expenditures.	8,000	
Due to General Fund.		8,000

To record cost of inspection services performed by a department financed through the General Fund.

12. Services were rendered by workers paid from a Capital Projects Fund for a department financed through the General Fund (**reimbursement**).

Capital Projects Fund:

Due from General Fund.	5,000	
Expenditures.		5,000

To record reduction of construction expenditures by cost of services rendered Department X.

General Fund:

Expenditures.	5,000	
Due to Capital Projects Fund		5,000

To record amount due to Capital Projects Fund on account of services rendered Department X.

13. A short-term (e.g., 90-day) loan was made from the General Fund to the Debt Service Fund.

General Fund:

Due from Debt Service Fund	40,000	
Cash.		40,000

To record short-term loan to Debt Service Fund.

Debt Service Fund:

Cash.	40,000	
Due to General Fund.		40,000

To record short-term loan from General Fund.

14. A noncurrent loan (e.g., two-year advance) was made from the General Fund to a Capital Projects Fund.

General Fund:

Advance to Capital Projects Fund	75,000	
Unreserved Fund Balance.	75,000	
Cash.		75,000
Reserve for Interfund Advance.		75,000

To record two-year advance to Capital Projects Fund.

Capital Projects Fund:

Cash.	75,000	
Advance from General Fund.		75,000

To record two-year advance from General Fund.

15. Cash payments for vacation and sick leave totaled $400,000. The payable for current vacation and sick leave increased $20,000 to $45,000. The noncurrent portion of the payable decreased by $67,000.

General Fund:

Expenditures—Vacation and Sick Leave.	375,000	
Current Liability for Vacation and Sick Leave	25,000	
Cash.		400,000

To record payments of vacation and sick leave.

Expenditures—Vacation and Sick Leave	45,000	
Current Liability for Vacation and Sick Leave		45,000

To accrue current liability for vacation and sick leave.

General Long-Term Debt Account Group:

Noncurrent Liability for Vacation and Sick Leave	67,000	
Amount to Be Provided for Retirement of Liability for Vacation and Sick Leave.		67,000

To record the decrease in the noncurrent portion of the vacation and sick leave liability.

CONCLUDING COMMENTS

These discussions and illustrations of General Fixed Assets, General Long-Term Debt, and Interfund-Account Group accounting and reporting conclude the several "general government" accounting and reporting chapters of this text. This **"general government accounting model"**—the governmental funds and account groups—clearly constitutes the most distinctive aspect of state and local accounting and reporting.

The remaining parts of the **governmental accounting model**—the fiduciary funds and proprietary funds—are discussed and illustrated in the following three chapters. As these additional funds are presented, typical interfund transactions and relationships of each type of fund with other funds are illustrated. Finally, a comprehensive summary of interfund and interfund-account group accounting is presented in Chapter 13.

QUESTIONS

9-1 Distinguish between *interfund transactions* and *interfund relationships.*

9-2 Distinguish between a *fund* and an *account group.*

9-3 What criteria must be met for an asset to be classified as a *fixed* asset? A *general* fixed asset?

9-4 Generally speaking, what is meant by the term *cost* when determining what costs should be assigned to a fixed asset?

9-5 A governmental unit acquired land, buildings, other improvements, and certain equipment for a single lump-sum purchase price. How should the portion of the total cost attributable to the various assets acquired be determined?

9-6 Fixed assets may be acquired through exercise of a government's power of *eminent domain* and by *escheat.* Distinguish between these terms.

9-7 A municipality was granted certain land for use as a playground. The property was appraised at $400,000 at the time of the grant. Subsequently, all land in the neighborhood rose in value by 30 percent. Should the increase be reflected in the GFA accounts?

9-8 A municipality owns a fire station and is required to pay assessments of $10,000 as an owner of property in the benefited area. As a result of the improvements, the property in the benefited area has risen in value by 15 percent. Should the asset be written up, and, if so, by how much?

9-9 Why does the GASB Codification not require the capitalization and reporting of **"infrastructure"** general fixed assets?

9-10 What liabilities are accounted for through the General Long-Term Debt Account Group? Which items of long-term debt are excluded?

9-11 In earlier years, general fixed assets and general long-term debt were both accounted for in a single "Capital Fund." Why do you suppose general fixed assets and general long-term debt are *not* now accounted for and reported in the same account group?

9-12 An asset originally financed out of a Special Revenue Fund and accounted for in the General Fixed Assets Account Group was sold. To which fund would you credit the proceeds? Why?

9-13 Assume that the asset referred to in the preceding question was financed from a Special Assessment Capital Projects Fund. To which fund should the proceeds from the sale of this asset be credited? Explain.

9-14 On June 1, 19W3, $300,000 par value of 20-year term general obligation sinking fund bonds were issued by a governmental unit. Only $50,000 had been accumulated in the Debt Service (Sinking) Fund by May 30, 19Y4, the end of the unit's fiscal year, and there was no possibility of retiring the bonds from resources of other funds during that year. Should the matured bonds be shown in the General Fund or in the Debt Service Fund, or should they continue to be carried in the General Long-Term Debt Account Group? Why?

9-15 What effect might "funded reserve" requirements of serial bond covenants have on the General Long-Term Debt Account Group?

9-16 **Unmatured** "general government" **liabilities** are recorded in the General Long-Term Debt Account Group. Neither (1) special assessment debt that is expected to be serviced by special assessments, but on which the government is "obligated in some manner," nor (2) underfunded pension contributions seem to fit this definition—yet both are recorded in the GLTDAG. Why do you suppose this is so?

9-17 Records of fixed assets owned by Lucas County have never been maintained in a systematic manner, and the auditor has recommended that an inventory be taken and that a General Fixed Assets Account Group be established and maintained. The governing board agrees that it needs better fixed asset control, but has tentatively concluded that no action will be taken in this regard because the appraisal fee estimates provided by reputable appraisal firms far exceed the amount of resources available for such an undertaking. What suggestions or comments, if any, would you offer upon your advice being sought by members of the board?

9-18 Near the end of 19X5, a city purchased an automobile at a cost of $12,000. The vehicle was wrecked during 19X6 and sold for salvage for $1,000. Assuming that the automobile was purchased from General Fund resources and the salvage proceeds were also recorded there, what entries would be made in 19X5 and 19X6 to reflect these facts? Might misleading inferences be drawn from the General Fund statements for 19X6?

9-19 Why is there no "operating" statement equivalent to that for governmental funds for either the General Fixed Assets Account Group or the General Long-Term Debt Account Group?

9-20 It has been proposed that (1) all General Fixed Assets, including "infrastructure" assets, be recorded, (2) only fixed asset-related noncurrent debt be considered General Long-Term Debt—and all other "general government" liabilities be considered "fund liabilities"—and (3) the redefined General Fixed Assets and General Long-Term Debt be accounted for and reported in a single "Capital Fund." What do you consider the advantages and disadvantages of this proposal to be?

PROBLEMS

P 9-1 (Multiple Choice)

1. Ariel Village issued the following bonds during the year ended June 30, 19X1:

Revenue bonds to be repaid from admission fees collected by the Ariel Zoo enterprise fund $200,000
General obligation bonds issued for the Ariel water and sewer enterprise fund which will service the debt . . .   300,000

How much of these bonds should be accounted for in Ariel's General Long-Term Debt Account Group?

a. $500,000	c. $300,000
b. $200,000	d. $0

2. The following assets are among those owned by the City of Foster:

Apartment building (part of the principal of a Nonexpendable Trust Fund)	$ 200,000
City Hall	800,000
Three fire stations	1,000,000
City streets and sidewalks	5,000,000

How much should be included in Foster's General Fixed Assets Account Group?

a. $2,000,000 or $7,000,000

b. $1,800,000 or $6,800,000

c. $6,800,000, without election of $1,800,000

d. $7,000,000, without election of $2,000,000

3. The Amount Available in Debt Service Funds is an account of a governmental unit that would be included in the

a. Liability section of the Debt Service Fund

b. Liability section of the General Long-Term Debt Account Group

c. Asset section of the Debt Service Fund

d. Asset section of the General Long-Term Debt Account Group

4. Which of the following will increase the fund balance of a governmental unit at the end of the fiscal year?

a. Appropriations are less than expenditures and reserve for encumbrances

b. Appropriations are less than expenditures and encumbrances

c. Appropriations are more than expenditures and encumbrances

d. Appropriations are less than estimated revenues

5. Fred Bosin donated a building to Palma City in 19X3. Bosin's original cost of the property was $100,000. Accumulated depreciation at the date of the gift amounted to $60,000. Fair market value at the date of the gift was $300,000. In the General Fixed Assets Account Group, at what amount should Palma record this donated fixed asset?

a. $300,000   c. $40,000

b. $100,000   d. $0

6. Ariel Village issued the following bonds during the year ended June 30, 19X3:

For installation of general government street lights, to be assessed against properties benefited	$300,000
For construction of public swimming pool; bonds to be paid from pledged fees collected from pool users	400,000

How much should be accounted for through Debt Service Funds for payments of principal over the life of the bonds?

a. $0   c. $400,000

b. $300,000   d. $700,000

7. The following items were among Payne Township's General Fund expenditures during the year ended July 31, 19X3:

Minicomputer for tax collector's office	$44,000
Equipment for Township Hall	80,000

How much should be classified as fixed assets in Payne's General Fund balance sheet at July 31, 19X3:

a. $124,000   c. $44,000

b. $ 80,000   d. $0

8. Proceeds of General Obligation Bonds is an account of a governmental unit that would be included in the

a. Enterprise Fund   d. Debt Service Fund

b. Internal Service Fund   e. General Long-Term Debt

c. Capital Projects Fund   Account Group

9. The following balances are included in the subsidiary records of Burwood Village's Parks and Recreation Department at March 31, 19X2:

Appropriations—supplies $7,500
Expenditures—supplies   4,500
Encumbrances—supply orders   750

How much does the department have available for additional purchases of supplies?

a. $0   c. $3,000

b. $2,250   d. $6,750

10. When fixed assets purchased from General Fund revenues were received, the appropriate journal entry was made in the General Fixed Assets Account Group. What account, if any, should have been debited in the General Fund?

a. No journal entry should have been made in the General Fund

b. Fixed Assets

c. Expenditures

d. Due from General Fixed Assets Account Group
    (AICPA, adapted)

P 9-2 (GFA Account Group Entries) Prepare general journal entries to record the effects on the General Fixed Assets Account Group of the following transactions. The transactions are independent of each other unless otherwise noted. Assume straight line depreciation is used when depreciation is required and that no depreciation is recorded or reported unless required.

1. A government leased computers with a capitalizable cost of $150,000, including $30,000 paid at the inception of the lease agreement. The lease is properly classified as a capital lease, and the computers are for the use of the government's finance and accounting division.

2. A government foreclosed on land against which it had tax liens amounting to $20,000. The estimated salable value of the land is $18,500. The government decided to use the land as the site for a new baseball park.

3. Construction costs billed during the year on a new addition to city hall totaled $8 million. $7,600,000 was paid to the contractors. Encumbrances of $10 million were outstanding at year end related to the project. $3 million of general revenues were transferred to the City Hall Addition Capital Projects Fund; the remainder of the construction costs are being financed from bond proceeds.

4. In the next year, the city hall addition in 3 was completed at an additional cost of $9,800,000. The building was inspected and approved, but $2,000,000 of the construction costs still have not been paid.

5. General government fixed assets with an original cost of $300,000 were sold three fourths of the way through their useful lives for $65,000. The assets were originally financed half from general revenues and half from bond proceeds.

6. An uninsured storage building used by general government departments was destroyed by a tornado. Its original cost was $92,000. Its useful life was only half over, and it is estimated that it will cost $250,000 to replace the building.

7. A dump truck originally purchased for and used by a city Enterprise Fund has been transferred to the Streets and Roads Department—a general government department. The truck originally cost $80,000 and is halfway through its estimated useful life. Its residual value is $18,000.

8. Computers with an original cost of $40,000 and estimated residual value of $5,000 were transferred out of General Fund departments to the municipal golf course, which is accounted for in an Enterprise Fund. The transfer occurred at the end of the estimated useful life of the computers.

P 9-3 (GLTD Account Group Entries) Prepare general journal entries to record the effects on the General Long-Term Debt Account Group of the following transactions. The transactions are independent of each other unless otherwise noted.

1. The fund balance of the Municipal Arts Center Debt Service Fund increased by $90,000 during the year. The entire fund balance is available for retirement of the Municipal Arts Center General Obligation Bonds.

2. Special assessment bonds guaranteed by the government matured and were paid during the year. $50,000 principal and $30,000 interest were paid. The beginning fund balance of the Special Assessment Debt Service Fund was $48,000—all of which was deemed available for principal retirement. The ending fund balance of that fund was $45,000.

3. Principal and interest on the County Courthouse Serial Bonds matured during the year. There was no beginning fund balance in the related Debt Service Fund. The maturing interest ($200,000) was paid but the maturing principal ($75,000) had not been by year end. General Fund revenues were transferred to cover the interest payments.

4. General Fund expenditures accounts included a Rent Expenditures account with a balance of $200,000. Further investigation of the account indicated that the balance resulted from the payment of $40,000 on operating leases and $160,000 of lease payments on a capital lease (of which $90,000 was for imputed interest).

5. The total general government underfunded pension liability at the beginning of the fiscal year was $14,000,000. Of this, $1,500,000 was considered "current." The total general government underfunded pension liability at the end of the fiscal year was $14,500,000. Of this, $2,500,000 was considered "current."

6. Advance refunding bonds ($10 million par) were issued. The proceeds of the refunding and $2 million of previously accumulated Debt Service Fund resources were set aside in an irrevocable trust to defease $11.5 million of School Bonds in substance.

7. Assume the same information as in 6, except that the School Bonds are not defeased in substance as a result of the transaction described.

8. Bond anticipation notes that meet the criteria for noncurrent treatment were issued to provide financing for a general government capital project. The notes, which have a par value of $5 million, are issued at 101.

P 9-4 **Part I.** (SA Project Entries) The City Council of Johnson City authorized special assessment project #13 during 19X1 to improve neighborhood storm drainage systems. The project is expected to cost $2,000,000, to be financed by a city contribution and by assessments. Johnson City uses private contractors on special assessment contracts and does not use budgetary accounts (except Encumbrances) in its special assessment accounting.

The following transactions and events relate to the Johnson City special assessment project during 19X1 and 19X2.

19X1 Transactions and Events

1. Awarded construction contracts to ABC Company, $1,200,000, and XYZ, Inc., $800,000.
2. Received the city's contribution, $200,000.
3. The improvements were completed and bills were received and approved for payment, less a 6% retainage pending final inspection, from ABC Company ($1,200,000) and XYZ, Inc. ($850,000). The increase in the XYZ, Inc. billing was caused by change orders approved during the course of construction.
4. Borrowed $1,900,000 on a five-year, 6% installment note at the Johnson City National Bank. (The note is guaranteed by Johnson City.)
5. Paid the contractor billings, net of the retained percentage.
6. Levied assessments of $1,900,000, based on appraisals of property value increments. The assessments are due in five equal annual installments, with 6% interest, beginning in 19X2.
7. Some property owners paid their entire assessments immediately, $100,000.

8. Paid interest to date on the note, $70,000.

9. The accounts were closed at the end of 19X1.

19X2 Transactions and Events

10. The project improvements passed final inspection and the contractors were paid the re-tainages.

11. The City Council ordered that the net assets remaining at the end of the construction phase of the project be dedicated to project debt service.

12. Billings were mailed to property owners for the assessments due in 19X2 and the related annual interest to date.

13. Collections from property owners were:

Assessments	$350,000
Interest on Assessments	107,400

14. The annual note debt service payment was made.

15. The accounts were closed at the end of 19X2.

Required   Prepare the journal entries necessary to record the preceding transactions and events in the general ledger accounts of the appropriate governmental funds of Johnson City in conformity with GAAP.

P 9-4   **Part II.** (SA Project Statements) Based on your solution to Part I, prepare a Statement of Revenues, Expenditures, and Changes in Fund Balance for each of the governmental funds in which the Johnson City special assessment project #13 transactions and events were recorded. The statements should be for the 19X1 and 19X2 fiscal years and should include a 19X1–19X2 total column.

P 9-5   (Interfund-Account Group Entries) Prepare all journal entries required in all funds and/or account groups to record the following transactions and events.

1. A state issued $50 million of 4% term bonds at 105 to provide financing for construction of a new state legislative office building. The premium, which is to be used for debt service, was transferred to the appropriate fund.

2. The state signed contracts for $55 million for construction of the building. Costs incurred for construction of the office building during Year 1 amounted to $18 million, all but 10% of which was paid.

3. Interest of $2 million was paid on the bonds in Year 1.

4. General Fund resources, $5 million, were transferred to the Legislative Office Building Capital Projects Fund for use on the project during Year 2.

5. The project was completed. Expenditures in Year 2 totaled $36.5 million, and all fund liabilities were paid. The remaining resources, to be used for debt service, were paid to the appropriate fund.

6. $3.3 million was transferred from the General Fund to provide for servicing the bonds in Year 2.

7. Interest of $2 million was paid in Year 2.

8. The bonds were paid in Year 20. $46 million had been accumulated in the Debt Service Fund to retire the bonds; the remainder needed to retire the bonds and make the last $2 million interest payment was transferred from the General Fund.

P 9-6   (Interfund-Account Group Entries) Prepare all journal entries required in all funds and/or account groups to record the following transactions and events.

1. The county sold old equipment, original cost $800,000, for $127,000. The equipment was included in the General Fixed Assets Account Group.

2. The county leased equipment for use by departments financed through the General Fund under a capital lease. The capitalizable cost is $780,000; an initial payment of $100,000 was made.

3. The county ordered new patrol cars estimated to cost $100,000.

4. The county received the patrol cars along with an invoice for $101,200.

5. Land with a fair market value of $90,000 was donated to the county. The donor had paid $37,000 for the land when he acquired it four years ago.

6. Bonds of $2,000,000 were issued at par for Enterprise Fund purposes. The bonds are to be repaid from the revenues of the Enterprise Fund. However, they are backed by the full faith and credit of the county; if the bonds cannot be repaid from the Enterprise Fund, general revenues must be used to repay them.

P 9-7 (Interfund-Account Group Entries) The following transactions and events (among others) affected the State of Texva during 19X3. (The State updates the account group accounts throughout the year.)

1. It was discovered that in 19X2 $440,000 of expenditures properly chargeable to Highway Patrol—Salaries and Wages in the General Fund had been inadvertently charged to the Highway Department—Salaries and Wages account in Special Revenue Fund #4. The amount was repaid during 19X3.

2. The Health Department, which is financed from Special Revenue Fund #2, entered a capital lease for equipment that could have been purchased outright for $600,000. (The capital lease has a 6% effective interest rate.)

3. Special Revenue Fund #4 was reimbursed for $700,000 of 19X3 salaries and wages for Highway Department employees working on a bridge construction project, which is financed by serial bonds and accounted for in Capital Projects Fund #7.

4. The first annual $100,000 payment on the Health Department equipment capital lease (transaction 2) was made.

5. A three-year advance was made from the General Fund to Debt Service Fund #12, $500,000.

6. Serial bonds, $4,000,000, were issued at 96 to finance a construction project being financed from Capital Projects Fund #7.

7. After its accounts were closed for 19X3, the $375,000 net assets (cash) of term bond Debt Service Fund #1 were transferred to establish Debt Service Fund #14 to service the serial bonds issued at transaction 6, and Debt Service Fund #1 was abolished.

8. Health Department land and buildings—originally purchased through Special Revenue Fund #2 for $50,000 and $450,000, respectively—were sold for $12,000,000, and the proceeds were recorded in Special Revenue Fund #2.

9. Although the actuarially required payment from the General Fund to the State pension plan was $15,000,000, only $6,000,000 was paid during 19X3. The 19X4 appropriation bill enacted recently provides for another $2,000,000 payment on the 19X3 contribution—which normally would have been paid from assets on hand at the end of 19X3. The $2,000,000 payment was provided for by continuing the 19X3 appropriations for that purpose, but it is uncertain when (if ever) the remaining 19X3 contributions will be made.

Required Prepare the journal entries to record these transactions and events in the general ledgers of the various governmental funds and account groups of the State of Texva. Assume that an appropriate series of Revenues, Expenditures, and Investment in General Fixed Assets accounts was used in each general ledger.

P 9-8 (Interfund-Account Group Entries) The following selected transactions and events (among others) affected the Vatexona Independent School District during the 19X8 and 19X9 fiscal years. (The Vatexona ISD updates the General Long-Term Debt Account Group accounts throughout the year, but updates the General Fixed Assets Account Group accounts only at year end.)

19X8 Transactions and Events

1. A $1,000,000 serial bond issue was issued at 102 during 19X8 to partially finance a new elementary school building that is expected to cost, and be financed, as follows:

Bond issue	$1,000,000
State grant	400,000
General Fund transfer.	200,000
	$1,600,000

(Assume that project appropriations and estimated financing sources were authorized previously, but budgetary accounts other than Encumbrances are not recorded in the CPF accounts.)

2. The bond premium was immediately transferred to the Debt Service Fund for the bond issue, and was ordered to be "fully reserved" for debt principal retirement.

3. Capital outlay expenditures incurred for the new elementary school building during 19X8 of $1,000,000, as encumbered, were vouchered for payment net of a 5% retained percentage.

4. The state grantor agency was billed for its share of the 19X8 elementary school building expenditures (25%) on the expenditure-driven reimbursement grant. (The billing is expected to be collected in 30–45 days.)

5. Transfers were made from the General Fund during 19X8 as follows:

Debt Service Fund

For bond principal retirement	$ 50,000
For interest and fiscal charges	65,000
	115,000

Capital Projects Fund

For elementary school building (only $80,000 paid during 19X8)	200,000
	$315,000

6. Debt Service Fund expenditures paid during 19X8 on the elementary school building bonds were:

Bond principal.	$ 50,000
Interest and fiscal agent charges	64,000
	$114,000

7. The Capital Projects Fund accounts were closed at the end of 19X8.

19X9 Transactions and Events

8. The elementary school building was completed during 19X9. The remaining state grant was billed and received; the contractor was paid in full, as was the General Fund transfer; and all other preclosing transactions and events were recorded. After all of these transactions and events were properly recorded (do **not** record them), the preclosing balances of the Capital Projects Fund at the end of 19X9 included Cash, Unreserved Fund Balance, and these "operating" amounts:

Revenues—State Grant	145,000
Expenditures—Capital Outlay	580,000

The remaining Capital Projects Fund balance was transferred to the Debt Service Fund and the CPF accounts were closed.

9. The Vatexona ISD estimates that it had these unrecorded estimated liabilities at the end of 19X9:

	Total	*"Current"* Portion
Claims and judgments	$300,000	$50,000
Vacation and sick leave	450,000	80,000

None of these amounts related to prior years, during which related amounts had been properly recorded. The "current" portion will be paid from the General Fund.

Required Prepare the entries required to record these transactions and events in the general ledger accounts of the affected funds and account groups of Vatexona Independent School District. Assume that an appropriate series of Revenues, Expenditures, and Investment in General Fixed Assets accounts is used in the general ledgers of the funds and account groups.

P 9-9 (Interfund-Account Group Entries) The following transactions of the Village of Lakeside are not related unless the transactions are given under the same numeral or unless the connection is specifically stated; not all of the village's transactions are given. You are to make all of the journal entries to which each transaction gives rise. Use general journal form; no explanation is required. Use the date columns to indicate the fund or account group in which each entry is made, using these abbreviations:

Fund or Account Group	Abbreviation
General	GF
Special Revenue	SR
Capital Projects	CP
Debt Service	DS
General Fixed Assets	GFA
General Long-Term Debt	GLTD

Separate the journal entries from each other by putting the transaction number and letter on the line above each entry.

1. An issue of serial bonds matured, $50,000, and was paid with interest of $3,000.

2. a. General obligation, 20-year, 6% term bonds were authorized, $5,000,000, for fixed asset acquisition, and the corresponding appropriation was recorded in the accounts.

   b. The bonds were issued at a discount of $40,000 and the project authorization was reduced accordingly.

   c. The sole purpose of the bond issue was to acquire land and a building. (The land was worth $500,000.) The property was purchased for $4,900,000 and the fund was closed, the balance being transferred to the sinking fund.

3. Ben E. Factor gave the Village 90 acres of land to be used as a park. The parcel had cost Mr. Factor $20,000 in 1945; its present market value is $800,000.

4. A fire truck, bought through the General Fund in 1948 at a cost of $40,000, was sold for $500; the proceeds were placed in the General Fund.

5. a. A special assessment paving project was approved in the amount of $750,000. (A budgetary entry was *not* made.)

   b. The village borrowed $600,000 at 6% interest—to be repaid with special assessment collections, but guaranteed by the Village—over five years to finance special assessment construction.

   c. The Village's share of the project cost was paid, $150,000.

   d. A contract for $740,000 was awarded to the ABC Company.

   e. The village engineer certified that the project was completed, and the contractor was paid.

   f. The property owners were assessed for $600,000—to be repaid in five equal installments, plus 6% interest, beginning late next year.

   g. The remaining net assets of the special assessment construction fund were ordered to be used for special assessment debt service and the fund was terminated.

6. a. The schedule of accumulation for the term bond sinking fund (see 2) showed an annual contribution requirement of $143,550 and estimated earnings of $9,850 for the current year in addition to the annual interest payment.

   b. The contribution—from unrestricted "general government" resources—was received and was invested.

c. Actual earnings totaled $9,600, of which $1,500 had not been collected by year end.

d. Annual interest on the bonds was paid.

e. The term bond sinking fund accounts were closed at year end.

P 9-10 (Interfund-Account Group GL Error Correction Entries) You have been engaged by the Town of Rego to examine its June 30, 19X8 balance sheet. You are the first CPA to be engaged by the town and find that acceptable methods of municipal accounting have not been employed. The town clerk stated that the books had not been closed and presented the following preclosing trial balance of the General Fund as of June 30, 19X8:

	Debit	Credit
Cash	$150,000	
Taxes Receivable—Current	59,200	
Allowance for Uncollectible Current Taxes		$ 18,000
Taxes Receivable—Delinquent	8,000	
Allowance for Uncollectible Delinquent Taxes		10,200
Estimated Revenues	310,000	
Appropriations		348,000
Donated Land	27,000	
Building Addition	50,000	
Serial Bonds Paid	16,000	
Expenditures	280,000	
Special Assessment Bonds Payable		100,000
Revenues		354,000
Accounts Payable		26,000
Fund Balance		44,000
	$900,200	$900,200

Additional Information:

(1) The estimated losses of $18,000 for current taxes receivable were determined to be a reasonable estimate. Current taxes become delinquent on June 30 of each year.

(2) Included in the Revenues account is a credit of $27,000 representing the value of land donated by the state as a grant-in-aid for construction of a municipal park.

(3) The Building Addition account balance is the cost of an addition to the town hall building. This addition was constructed and completed in June 19X8. The payment was recorded in the General Fund as authorized.

(4) The Serial Bonds Paid account reflects the annual retirement of general obligation bonds issued to finance the construction of the town hall. Interest payments of $7,000 for this bond issue are included in Expenditures.

(5) Operating supplies ordered in the prior fiscal year ($8,800) were received, recorded, and consumed in July 19X7. (Encumbered appropriations lapse one year after the end of the fiscal year for which they are made.)

(6) Outstanding purchase orders at June 30, 19X8 for operating supplies totaled $2,100. These purchase orders were not recorded in the accounts.

(7) The special assessment bonds are guaranteed by the Town of Rego and were sold in June 19X8 to finance a street-paving project. No contracts have been signed for this project and no expenditures have been made.

(8) The balance in the Revenues account includes credits for $20,000 for a note issued to a bank to obtain cash in anticipation of tax collections. The note was still outstanding at June 30, 19X8.

Required (a) Prepare the formal adjusting and closing journal entries for the General Fund for the fiscal year ended June 30, 19X8.

(b) The foregoing information disclosed by your examination was recorded only in the General Fund even though other funds or account groups were involved. Prepare the formal adjusting journal entries for any other funds or account groups involved.
(AICPA, adapted)

MEASUREMENT FOCUS AND BASIS OF ACCOUNTING (MFBA)— GOVERNMENTAL FUNDS

To this point in the text we have focused primarily on *one* way by which governmental fund accounting can be accomplished and governmental fund financial statements can be presented in accordance with current GAAP. Accordingly, we have *assumed* that the annual governmental fund budget was legally enacted on the modified accrual basis—and thus the "actual" data in the "budgetary comparison" statement were the same as those in the GAAP "operating" statement. Further, we have *assumed* that the governmental fund accounts were maintained essentially on the GAAP basis during the year—so that only a few year end entries were needed to adjust the accounts to the modified accrual basis and prepare the annual financial statements for each governmental fund in conformity with GAAP.

We have introduced some accounting and reporting alternatives—such as the purchases and consumption methods of inventory accounting, the "when due" and accrual methods of recording GLTD debt service expenditures, and two alternative governmental fund "operating" statement formats. But we introduced alternatives in earlier chapters only when we thought it was logical or essential to do so—since introducing too many alternatives too soon might have proved more confusing than enlightening.

While the previous chapters have focused on currently effective GAAP for governmental funds and account groups, a unique situation exists in governmental accounting and financial reporting at this time. In May 1990, the GASB issued GASB Statement 11, "Measurement Focus and Basis of Accounting—Governmental Fund Operating Statements," which changed the basic recognition and measurement guidance for governmental and expendable trust fund operating statement elements. Indeed, other significant changes are incorporated or implied in that statement. However, because (1) numerous issues that ideally would have been resolved in Statement 11 were not resolved and (2) several related GASB agenda projects needed to be completed to avoid piecemeal implementation of the GASBS 11 measurement focus and basis of accounting, the effective date of GASBS 11 was established at a date several years into the future. The effective date is for fiscal years ending on or after June 15, 1995. Further, the GASB **prohibits early application** of GASBS 11 "because of the need for simultaneous implementation with GASB pronouncements on financial reporting, capital reporting, pension accounting, risk financing and insurance, and the types of nonrecurring projects and activities that have long-term economic benefit and for which debt meets the definition of general long-term capital debt."[1] Finally, in December 1992 the **GASB** issued an **exposure draft** that **would delay** the **effective date** of GASBS 11 **indefinitely.**

One purpose of this chapter is to explain and illustrate the measurement focus and basis of accounting—called the "flow of financial resources" measurement focus—established in GASBS 11 so that readers will be aware of these significant, upcoming changes in GAAP. A second key goal of the chapter is to discuss and illustrate the use of a non-GAAP basis of accounting during the year to satisfy budgetary or other legal or contractual requirements and the conversion from the non-GAAP basis to the GAAP basis.

MEASUREMENT FOCUS AND BASIS OF ACCOUNTING—GASBS 11

As noted before, GASBS 11 provides new guidance for recognition and measurement of governmental and expendable trust fund operating statement elements—particularly revenues and expenditures—for all state and local governments. However, to appreciate the full impact of GASBS 11 and the unresolved issues associated with it, several other features of GASBS 11 also must be discussed. Therefore, before discussing the operating statement elements recognition and measurement criteria set forth in GASBS 11, we discuss the following topics:

- GASBS 11 scope limitations
- "Capital debt" versus "operating debt" classification

Too, the ultimate treatment required for operating debt will be significant. One alternative approach being considered by the GASB would report long-term, general government operating debt as fund debt. This treatment would change the basic governmental fund model and is being considered in a current GASB agenda project on implementation of GASBS 11. This project is described in Chapter 15, "Contemporary Issues."

GASBS 11 Scope Limitations

Although the basic purpose of GASBS 11 is to establish recognition and measurement criteria for governmental fund and expendable trust fund operating statement elements, the Statement specifically excludes most expenditure transactions that would result in differing amounts of expenditures being reported in governmental and expendable trust funds under the broad GASBS 11 expenditure guidance than are recognized under current GAAP. Some revenue transactions are excluded from the scope of GASBS 11 as well. Specifically, GASBS 11 does ***not*** provide *specific* operating statement *recognition and measurement criteria for:*

- pension expenditures
- other postemployment benefits (OPEB)
- special termination benefits
- claims and judgments (CJ) and related insurance transactions
- capital improvement special assessment transactions
- intergovernmental grants, entitlements, and shared revenues
- operating expenditures resulting from nonexchange transactions
- debt service fund expenditures on general long-term *capital* debt

---

[1] GASB, Statement No. 11, "Measurement Focus and Basis of Accounting—Governmental Fund Operating Statements," para. 100.

381

Chapter 10
MEASUREMENT
FOCUS (MFBA)—
GOVERNMENTAL
FUNDS

GASBS 11 *provides "basic guidance"* applicable to these issues in that it *presumes* that *later guidance* will be consistent with its "flow of financial resources" measurement focus.

Distinction Between Capital Debt and Operating Debt

One key feature of GASBS 11 is the classification of general government long-term debt into two categories—which it implies will be reported differently. GASBS 11 distinguishes long-term operating debt from general long-term capital debt. These two classifications of debt are defined[2] as follows:

1. *"Capital debt"*—debt issued to acquire *capital assets or* to finance certain [undefined] *nonrecurring projects or activities* that have *long-term economic benefit, and*

2. *"Operating debt"*—debt issued to finance *operations* or in anticipation of revenues.

Although GASBS 11 implies that capital debt and operating debt will be reported differently, it is not definitive in this regard. Too, the detailed discussion of capital debt in GASBS 11 seems somewhat arbitrary and subject to possible manipulation. Therefore, only the general operating statement guidance in GASBS 11 with respect to debt will be discussed here. More detail on the possible alternative approaches that could be used is presented in Chapter 15.

Flow of Financial Resources Measurement Focus

GASBS 11 states that financial reporting for governmental and expendable trust funds should focus on demonstrating "interperiod equity"—"whether current-year revenues were sufficient to pay for current-year services."[3] The flow of financial resources measurement focus established in GASBS 11 is supposed to accomplish this objective. Indeed, the statement describes the flow of financial resources measurement focus (FFR MF) as one that measures the extent to which financial resources obtained during a period are sufficient to cover claims incurred during that period against financial resources.

The FFR MF reflects increases and decreases only in financial resources (which are defined to include materials and supplies inventories and prepaid items) and uses an accrual basis of accounting. The FFR MF is not intended to measure "cost of services." Indeed, it includes the effects on financial resources of capital asset acquisitions and dispositions and capital debt issuances and repayments. Further, it does not include a periodic operating charge for capital asset use (such as depreciation).

Revenue and Other Inflows Recognition Under GASBS 11

GASBS 11 refers to three types of inflows of financial resources—revenues, other financing sources, and residual equity transfers. Little change from current GAAP is made regarding other financing sources and residual equity transfers. The focus of this part of the statement clearly is on revenue recognition.

[2] Ibid., paras. 86 and 94.
[3] Ibid., para. 8.

The general concept underlying revenue recognition under the FFR MF is that revenues (reduced by any estimated uncollectible amount) should be recognized when **both** (1) the underlying event generating the revenue has occurred **and** (2) they are due, whether or not they are collected in that period. The primary exceptions to this general rule are discussed in detail that is beyond the scope of this text. However, they typically result from the GASB's concern about the ability of governments to reliably measure the ultimate amounts of revenue to be recognized in certain circumstances.

GASBS 11 discusses revenue recognition in terms of three broad types of revenues:

1. Taxes
2. Other nonexchange revenues
3. Exchange revenues

For the major types of taxes, the related underlying events are:

Type of Taxes	Underlying Event
Property tax	Period for which levied
Income tax	Taxpayer earns taxable income
Sales Tax	Taxable sale is made

A government is deemed to have **"demanded"** the taxes if it has established a due date for the taxes that is no later than the end of the period (or two months thereafter if "administrative lead time"—for tax return filings—is needed for taxpayer assessed taxes, such as sales or income taxes).

Nonexchange revenues such as fines, licenses and permits, and donations generally are recognized in the period that the underlying event generating the revenue occurs and the government has an enforceable legal claim to the amounts involved. Revenues from exchange transactions—e.g., charges for services, investments, and operating leases—should be recognized when earned.

To illustrate the effect of the GASBS 11 revenue recognition guidance relative to current GAAP, consider the following example relating to property taxes. A government levies and collects the following property taxes during 19X1 and 19X2 fiscal years:

19X1 Property Tax Levy (Due January 1, 19X1).	$8,000,000
Estimated uncollectible 19X1 property taxes	160,000
Net estimated collectible amount	7,840,000
19X0 taxes collected in January and February, 19X1	380,000
19X1 taxes collected in 19X1	7,200,000
19X0 taxes collected during 19X1 after February, 19X1	200,000
19X2 Property Tax Levy (Due January 1, 19X2)	8,200,000
Estimated uncollectible 19X2 property taxes	164,000
Net estimated collectible amount	8,036,000
19X0 and 19X1 taxes collected during January and February, 19X2	400,000
19X2 taxes collected in 19X2	7,380,000
19X0 and 19X1 taxes collected during 19X2 after February, 19X2	205,000
19X1 and 19X2 taxes collected during January and February, 19X3	410,000
19X1 and 19X2 taxes collected after February, 19X3	300,000

Under the **GASBS 11** guidance the property tax **revenues** recognized each year **would** simply **be** the **net estimated collectible amount of** the **taxes levied** for that year—$7,840,000 in 19X1 and $8,036,000 in 19X2. Delinquent property

383

Chapter 10
MEASUREMENT
FOCUS (MFBA)—
GOVERNMENTAL
FUNDS

taxes receivable would not be offset by deferred revenues as is generally the case under current GAAP.

Under current GAAP, property tax revenues of $7,800,000 ($7,200,000 + $200,000 + $400,000) in 19X1 and $7,995,000 ($7,380,000 + $205,000 + $410,000) in 19X2 would be recognized. Since the legal availability criterion is met for each year's tax levy, the timing of the cash collections drives the revenue recognition in this example under current GAAP. Note that when the taxes are collected will have no impact on the timing of property tax revenue recognition when GASBS 11 becomes effective.

Other Financing Sources and Residual Equity Transfers

GASBS 11 does not explicitly change the recognition and measurement criteria for nonrevenue increases in net financial resources of governmental funds except that it requires "proceeds from the sale of fixed assets" to be reported as an other financing source. Under current GAAP, proceeds from fixed asset sales are reported as revenues in governmental funds.

Expenditures and Other Outflows Recognition Under GASBS 11

GASBS 11 also discusses three types of financial resource outflows—which also parallel current practice. Of these three types of financial resource outflows—expenditures, other financing uses, and residual equity transfers—the changes made in the area of expenditure measurement and recognition are the most significant.

Expenditure Recognition

Expenditures are discussed under three broad categories in Statement 11—operating, capital outlay, and debt service. According to Statement 11, "Unless otherwise specified, expenditures should be recognized when transactions or events that result in claims against financial resources take place, regardless of when cash is paid."[4] Current guidance requires expenditure recognition "when a fund liability is incurred." In most situations, capital outlay expenditures will be reported the same under GASBS 11 as they are currently.

GASB Statement 11 is silent regarding debt service accounting for **capital** debt, though it requires accrual of interest on **operating** debt at year end. Should the GASB decide to continue the "when due" (and "due early next year") capital debt service accounting approach, both current GAAP and GASBS 11 would make identical exceptions with respect to debt service expenditure recognition associated with capital debt. If so, the capital debt service expenditures recognized in a period would be identical under both the current and GASBS 11 requirements in the vast majority of circumstances. On the other hand, the GASB might change current GAAP significantly.

Hence, the key expenditure recognition differences may relate to operating expenditures. Further, since operating expenditures that result in short-term liabilities would meet the recognition criteria under both sets of requirements, it is those operating expenditures that result in the creation of long-term operating debt that result in significantly different amounts of expenditures being reported in a period under the two approaches.

Interestingly, these types of operating expenditures—e.g., claims and judgments and pension expenditures—were among the transactions excluded from the scope of GASBS 11. Recall, however, that the guidance eventually provided on these issues is to be consistent with the requirements of GASBS 11. Another less significant difference is that the purchases method cannot be used to

---

[4] *Ibid.*, para. 73.

account for materials and supplies expenditures or prepaid items because all of these are considered financial resources. Thus there is no use of financial resources—and thus no expenditures are recognized—until materials, supplies, or prepaid items are consumed.

Expenditure Recognition—GASBS 11 vs. Current Guidance

To visualize the impact of the preceding discussion, recognize that the salaries and wages expenditures, rental and professional services expenditures, utilities expenditures, capital outlay expenditures, and so on that were recorded in prior chapters typically would not be impacted by the implementation of GASBS 11. They are the same under both the current and the GASBS 11 requirements. However, recall the compensated absences expenditures example in Chapter 6. That example assumed the following information:

Accruable vacation and sick leave at the end of 19X0	$ 0
Vacation and sick leave paid or vouchered in 19X1	300,000
Accruable vacation and sick leave at the end of 19X1	200,000
Current portion of the accruable vacation and sick leave at the end of 19X1 . .	50,000
Vacation and sick leave paid or vouchered in 19X2	450,000
Accruable vacation and sick leave at the end of 19X2	325,000
Current portion of the accruable vacation and sick leave at the end of 19X2 . .	75,000

Under current GAAP, as illustrated in Chapter 6, compensated absences expenditures would have been $350,000 and $475,000 in 19X1 and 19X2, respectively. This results from only the current portion of the accruable vacation and sick leave liability being considered a fund liability and requiring expenditure recognition.

Under GASBS 11, the 19X1 compensated absences expenditures would have been $500,000—which includes the entire compensated absences liability incurred during 19X1. The 19X2 compensated absences liability would have been $575,000—the $450,000 paid or vouchered plus the $125,000 increase in the total accruable vacation and sick leave liability. Similar differences result from applying the GASBS 11 guidance to pension expenditures and claims and judgments expenditures under the current guidance and under GASBS 11.

Other Financing Uses and Residual Equity Transfers

GASBS 11 does not change the measurement or reporting of other financing uses or residual equity transfers from current requirements except that discounts resulting from the issuance of general long-term capital debt will be reported as an other financing use rather than being reflected in the net amount of bond issue proceeds reported as an other financing source as required currently. No changes in measurement and recognition of residual equity transfers out are made. The other differences relate to reporting the results of the issuance of, retirement of, and interest on general government long-term indebtedness.

Debt Issuance, Retirement, and Interest

The net operating statement effect of the issuance of general long-term **capital** debt under Statement 11 and under current GAAP are identical. However, whereas the net proceeds from issuing capital debt are currently reflected as a single amount—"bond issue proceeds"—GASBS 11 requires separate reporting of the face value of the capital debt, the effect of any issuance premium or discount, and bond issue costs incurred. The face amount of bonds issued and any bond premium must be separately identified among a government's other financing sources; any bond issuance discount must be reported as an other financing use;

385

Chapter 10
MEASUREMENT
FOCUS (MFBA)—
GOVERNMENTAL
FUNDS

and bond issue costs are to be reported as expenditures. Statement 11 does not change principal and interest expenditure recognition with respect to general long-term capital debt.

With respect to *operating debt,* Statement 11 states that *issuance* (incurrence) of such debt *should have no operating statement effect. Interest expenditure* on operating debt is to be measured *using* the *effective interest method* under GASBS 11 *and* recognized as it *accrues.* Operating debt *principal* retirements are *not* to be reported as *expenditures*—and presumably not as other financing uses.

Summary

The key revenue and expenditure impacts of GASBS 11 are highlighted in the comparison with current guidance in Figure 10-1.

Figure 10-1   **REVENUE AND EXPENDITURE RECOGNITION SUMMARY— GASBS 11 VS. CURRENT GAAP**

Revenues	*Current GAAP*	*GASBS 11*
Property taxes	Recognize in period for which levied *if* collected not more than 60 days thereafter	Recognize net realizable value in period for which levied *if* demanded
Income taxes	Recognize in period income is earned *if* collected not more than 60 days after the end of the period	Recognize in period income is earned *if* payment is due within two months thereafter
Sales taxes	Recognize in period of sale if collected (even if by another government) and paid to the SLG not more than 60 days thereafter	Recognize in period of sale *if* payment is due within two months thereafter
Other nonexchange revenues	Generally recognize on a cash basis	Generally recognize when establish an enforceable claim
Exchange revenues	Recognize in period earned *if* collected not more than 60 days thereafter	Recognize in period earned

Expenditures	*Current GAAP*	*GASBS 11*
General rule	Recognize in period that fund liability is incurred (purchases or consumption basis for materials, supplies, and prepaid items)	Recognize in period that transaction or event occurs that results in claims against government financial resources
Materials and supplies	Purchases or consumption basis	Consumption basis only
Prepaid items	Purchases or consumption basis	Consumption basis only
Salaries and wages	Recognize when fund liability incurred	Recognize when government liability incurred
Expenditures resulting in long-term accrued liabilities (e.g., pensions, claims and judgments, compensated absences)	Recognize when payable from available expendable financial resources	Recognize when government liability incurred
Debt service expenditures on GLTD	Recognize when legally payable ("when due" or "when due early next year")	1) GASBS 11 does not provide guidance on debt service on capital debt 2) Recognize interest accrued on operating debt—effective interest method
Capital outlay expenditures	Recognize when incurred	Recognize when incurred

Statement 11 will have a pervasive impact on state and local government financial reporting when it is implemented. It may be noted that the potential significance of this impact is greater with respect to expenditure recognition for most governments than it is for revenue recognition. One gets a sense of the relative potential impact of Statement 11 by considering the amounts of deferred revenue typically reported by SLGs versus the amounts of accrued long-term operating debt reported in their General Long-Term Debt Account Groups. Most of the amounts reported as deferred revenues by local governments would have already been included in revenues under Statement 11. Likewise, most of the amounts reflected in long-term operating debt would have already been reported as expenditures under Statement 11—but have not been under current GAAP. A review of a reasonable sample of SLG reports will demonstrate that these accrued operating debts (and hence deferred expenditures) typically far outweigh the deferred revenues.

NON-GAAP ACCOUNTING BASIS USED DURING THE YEAR

Rather than maintaining the governmental fund accounts on a GAAP basis during the year, some state and local governments (SLGs) make entries *during the year* on (1) the cash basis, or even the cash receipts and disbursements basis; (2) a non-GAAP basis prescribed by state or local law, for example, or by the terms of an intergovernmental grant agreement; or (3) a non-GAAP budgetary basis. Each of these non-GAAP bases of accounting is discussed and illustrated in this section.

Non-GAAP Accounting Basis Not Necessarily "Bad"

Maintaining the accounts on a non-GAAP basis **during the year** does *not* necessarily indicate improper or "bad" accounting systems or practices. Indeed, although mandatory where required by law or contract, using non-GAAP accounting procedures during the year also may be:

- **Necessary** to ensure adequate **budgetary control** during the year **and** proper **budgetary accountability** at year end.
- **Useful** in **facilitating** the **preparation of special purpose** non-GAAP financial **statements, schedules, and reports** during the year and at year end.
- **Efficient and effective** in **minimizing** the number and types of **accounting entries made—and** thus the **accounting costs incurred and errors made**—during the year.

Accordingly, most SLG accounting systems are maintained on (or essentially on) a non-GAAP basis during the year. This practice may well become even more common after GASBS 11 becomes effective. Even though the GASB states that one of its objectives in mandating the FFR MF was to require a MF that reflects the "intent" of budgetary laws, it is arguable whether that objective was accomplished. Few governments are likely to budget on the FFR basis. Since SLGs should maintain their accounts on the budgetary basis during the year to assure budgetary control, as discussed in Chapter 2, even more SLGs probably will maintain their accounts on a non-GAAP budgetary basis in the future. At year end, governments that maintain their accounts on a non-GAAP basis must **first** adjust the data in the accounts to the budgetary, grant, or other non-GAAP basis required to prepare annual *special purpose* statements, schedules, and reports on the non-GAAP basis. **Then** the data in the accounts are adjusted again to convert them from the non-GAAP basis to the GAAP basis in order to prepare the GAAP basis financial statements, schedules, and reports. This second adjustment process is often referred to as the **"conversion to GAAP."**

This two-phase adjustment process for preparing both non-GAAP special purpose (or supplemental) and GAAP basis financial statements and schedules re-

387

Chapter 10
MEASUREMENT
FOCUS (MFBA)—
GOVERNMENTAL
FUNDS

quires more analyses and adjusting entries, of course, than when the accounts are maintained on (or near) the GAAP basis during the year, as in earlier chapters. However, these more complex analyses usually are done only once a year—at year end—and typically are done by the government's most skilled accountants, its auditors, or both. Too, many of the adjusting (and "readjusting" or "conversion") entries are similar—both to each other and at each year end; only a few may require complex analyses or difficult calculations. Further, many SLG accountants and auditors make both sets of adjusting entries on year end worksheets—often computer spreadsheets—and only journalize and post to the accounts those adjusting entries that would not be reversed at the beginning of the next year.

The Two-Phase Adjustment Process

The **approach** to the **two-phase year-end adjustment process** is essentially the same regardless of the governmental fund accounting methods used during the year or the non-GAAP basis statements to be prepared at year end before preparing the GAAP basis financial statements for the year. **The steps are:**

1. **Analyze the Unadjusted Preclosing Year End Trial Balance.** Be certain you understand the accounts used during the year—including their classification and the nature and basis (e.g., cash, modified accrual, or other basis) of their unadjusted preclosing balances at year end.

2. **Determine the Non-GAAP Basis "Rules" and How They Differ from the Unadjusted Preclosing Balances.** (a) Study the legal and/or contractual non-GAAP financial reporting requirements—for example, provisions of relevant laws, grant agreements or regulations, the annual budget, bond indentures—to ensure that you understand the nature, account classification, basis, and presentation "rules" of the special purpose non-GAAP financial statements, schedules, or reports that must be prepared; and (b) Identify the differences between the non-GAAP basis—including account classifications—and the balances of the accounts in the unadjusted year end preclosing trial balance.

3. **Prepare the "Phase 1" Adjusting Entries and the Required Non-GAAP Financial Statements.** Based on your analyses and comparisons in steps 1 and 2, (a) determine the "phase 1" adjusting entries needed to adjust the account balances in the unadjusted preclosing trial balance (step 1) to the non-GAAP basis required (step 2); (b) prepare the "phase 1" adjusting entries and post them to a worksheet and/or to the accounts, as appropriate; and (c) prepare a "phase 1 adjusted" preclosing trial balance and the legally or contractually required non-GAAP statements, schedules, and reports.

4. **Identify and Evaluate the Differences Between the Non-GAAP Basis and the GAAP Basis.** Compare the account classifications and basis of the non-GAAP basis data in the accounts at this point—after step 3—with the account classifications and modified accrual basis data required to prepare financial statements that conform with GAAP.

5. **Prepare the "Phase 2" or "Conversion to GAAP" Adjusting Entries and the GAAP Basis Financial Statements.** Based on your analyses and comparisons in step 4, (a) determine the "phase 2" adjusting entries needed to convert the non-GAAP basis "phase 1 adjusted" account balances in the preclosing trial balance prepared at step 3 to the GAAP basis; (b) prepare the "phase 2" ("conversion to GAAP") adjusting entries and post them to a worksheet and/or to the accounts, as appropriate; and (c) prepare an adjusted ("phase 2") GAAP basis preclosing trial balance and the GAAP basis financial statements.

The two-phase adjustment process analytical approach and method is summarized in Figure 10-2, which also illustrates the type of year end worksheet that is often used to facilitate the two-phase adjustment process and preparation of both the non-GAAP and GAAP financial statements. **Note the logic and method illustrated in Figure 10-2 carefully** because, as noted earlier, the analytical approach and related adjustment processes are essentially the same regardless of the basis—cash basis, budgetary basis, or other non-GAAP basis—on which the accounts are maintained during the year.

Some of the major considerations in applying this two-phase adjustment process approach are discussed in the remainder of this section. These considerations are discussed in the context of the governmental fund accounts being maintained during the year on (1) the cash basis, (2) a legally prescribed or contractually agreed non-GAAP basis, and (3) a non-GAAP budgetary basis.

Cash Basis

Governments that maintain their governmental fund accounts on the cash basis during the year usually have fund asset, liability, fund balance, revenue, and expenditure accounts like those illustrated in earlier chapters. However, *they record revenues only when received in cash and they recognize expenditures only when cash is paid.* Likewise, they typically record cash investments made, but not accrued interest receivable, and record liabilities only when notes payable are issued or retired. Thus, many accruals and deferrals may be required to adjust cash basis data to a non-GAAP basis and/or the GAAP basis at year end.

To simplify our discussion of the cash basis, we assume for the moment that we do **not** have any **non-GAAP** reporting requirements and thus are concerned **only with adjusting the cash basis data to the GAAP basis.** No harm will be done by this momentary assumption since the non-GAAP basis discussions later in this section may readily be related to this section.

Revenues

Assuming that the proper amounts of cash receipts have been credited to each Revenues account during the period, adjusting those accounts to amounts properly reported as revenues on the modified accrual basis requires determining the amounts that were:

- **accrued** at the end of last year and are accrued at the end of this year, and
- **deferred** revenues at the end of last year and are deferred revenues at the end of this year,

as well as any related **allowances for uncollectible receivables.**

Revenues Adjustments: Example 1. To illustrate, observe this calculation to determine a revenue's amount—assuming the revenues are "available" and no allowance for uncollectibles adjustment is needed—for the current year:

Revenues Example 1: Adjusting from Cash Basis to GAAP (Modified Accrual) Basis

Revenues **(Cash Basis)**		$320,000
Accrued Revenues (Receivable):		
End of this year	$ 25,000	
End of last year	(15,000)	10,000
Deferred Revenues:		
End of this year	(22,000)	
End of last year	16,000	(6,000)
Revenues (GAAP Basis)		$324,000

Figure 10-2

ANALYTICAL APPROACH AND WORKSHEET
TWO-PHASE ADJUSTMENT PROCESS

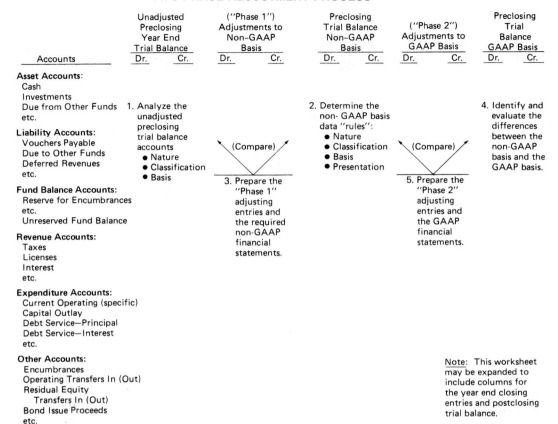

Accounts	Unadjusted Preclosing Year End Trial Balance Dr.	Cr.	("Phase 1") Adjustments to Non–GAAP Basis Dr.	Cr.	Preclosing Trial Balance Non–GAAP Basis Dr.	Cr.	("Phase 2") Adjustments to GAAP Basis Dr.	Cr.	Preclosing Trial Balance GAAP Basis Dr.	Cr.

Asset Accounts:
Cash
Investments
Due from Other Funds
etc.

Liability Accounts:
Vouchers Payable
Due to Other Funds
Deferred Revenues
etc.

Fund Balance Accounts:
Reserve for Encumbrances
etc.
Unreserved Fund Balance

Revenue Accounts:
Taxes
Licenses
Interest
etc.

Expenditure Accounts:
Current Operating (specific)
Capital Outlay
Debt Service—Principal
Debt Service—Interest
etc.

Other Accounts:
Encumbrances
Operating Transfers In (Out)
Residual Equity
    Transfers In (Out)
Bond Issue Proceeds
etc.

1. Analyze the unadjusted preclosing trial balance accounts
   ● Nature
   ● Classification
   ● Basis

(Compare)

3. Prepare the "Phase 1" adjusting entries and the required non-GAAP financial statements.

2. Determine the non- GAAP basis data "rules":
   ● Nature
   ● Classification
   ● Basis
   ● Presentation

(Compare)

5. Prepare the "Phase 2" adjusting entries and the GAAP financial statements.

4. Identify and evaluate the differences between the non-GAAP basis and the GAAP basis.

Note: This worksheet may be expanded to include columns for the year end closing entries and postclosing trial balance.

Thus, although $320,000 was received in cash this year, $15,000 accrued at the end of last year should have been recognized as revenues last year; but the $25,000 accrued at the end of this year should be recognized as revenues currently even though not collected. Further, the $16,000 of deferred revenues at the end of last year should be recognized as current year revenues, but the $22,000 of deferred revenues at the end of the current year should not be recognized as revenues until next year. Thus, the adjustment process is not difficult conceptually, though determining the accrued revenues and deferred revenues at the beginning and end of the year is sometimes difficult in practice.

The general ledger **adjusting entry** required in this example—assuming the amounts accrued and deferred at the end of the prior year (19X0) were posted to the accounts, were **not reversed,** and thus *are* in the accounts at the end of the current year (19X1)—is:

Accrued Receivables (specify)	10,000	
Deferred Revenues		6,000
Revenues		4,000

Revenues Adjustments: Example 2. Property taxes levied and other **receivables** often are not recorded by SLGs accounting on the cash basis during the year. Indeed, any adjusting entry made at the end of the previous year may have been posted only to a worksheet; and, if posted to the accounts, it may have been reversed at the beginning of the current year. The adjustment process in this case would be like our preceding example, but would also involve consideration of the

389

need for an **allowance for uncollectible accounts.** Thus, if the allowance for un-collectible taxes was $4,000 at the end of last year (19X0) and should be $5,000 at the end of the current year (19X1), the net Revenues adjustment required would be $3,000:

Revenues Example 2: Adjusting from Cash Basis to GAAP (Modified Accrual Basis)

Revenues (**Cash Basis**)		$320,000
Accrued Revenues (Receivable):		
End of this year	$ 25,000	
End of last year	(15,000)	10,000
Deferred Revenues:		
End of this year	(22,000)	
End of last year	16,000	(6,000)
Allowance for Uncollectible Receivables:		
End of this year	(5,000)	
End of last year	4,000	(1,000)
Revenues (**GAAP Basis**)		$323,000

The **adjusting entry**—assuming the property taxes are delinquent, reversing entries are not made, and the proper account balances from 19X0 *are* in the accounts—would be:

Property Taxes Receivable—Delinquent	10,000	
Deferred Revenues		6,000
Allowance for Uncollectible Delinquent Taxes		1,000
Revenues—Property Taxes		3,000
To adjust the property tax accounts at year end (19X1).		

Expenditures

Similarly, assuming that the proper amounts of cash disbursements have been debited to each Expenditures account during the period, adjusting those accounts to amounts properly reported as expenditures on the modified accrual basis is not difficult conceptually, though in practice it may be difficult to determine the related accruals and other amounts. Indeed, since the "available" criterion applies only to revenues, adjusting expenditures is often simpler than adjusting revenues.

Expenditures Adjustments: Example 1. **Accruals** at the end of both the prior year and the current year are the primary factor in the adjustment of most cash basis Expenditures account balances to the modified accrual basis. Indeed, accruals are often the only adjustment factor. To illustrate:

Expenditures Example 1: Adjusting from Cash Basis to GAAP (Modified Accrual) Basis

Expenditures (**Cash Basis**)		$300,000
Accrued Expenditures (Payable):		
End of this year	$ 28,000	
End of last year	(31,000)	(3,000)
Expenditures (**GAAP Basis**)		$297,000

Thus, while $300,000 was disbursed in cash for this type of expenditure during the current year, (1) $28,000 of expenditures were incurred during the year that will not be paid until next year, and (2) $31,000 was paid this year on last year's expenditures.

The expenditures adjusting entry at the end of 19X1—assuming the 19X0 adjusting entry was made and was **not** reversed—would be:

Accrued Expenditures Payable	3,000	
Expenditures		3,000
To adjust the expenditures at the end of 19X1.		

391

Chapter 10
MEASUREMENT
FOCUS (MFBA)—
GOVERNMENTAL
FUNDS

Expenditures Adjustments: Example 2. If **inventory or prepayments** accounted for on the **consumption method** are involved, the expenditure adjustment process is more complex:

Expenditures Example 2:
Adjusting from Cash Basis to GAAP (Modified Accrual) Basis
Inventories and Prepayments—Consumption Method

Expenditures (**Cash Basis**)		$300,000
Accrued Expenditures (Payable):		
End of this year	$ 28,000	
End of last year	(31,000)	(3,000)
Inventories or Prepayments:		
End of this year	(10,000)	
End of last year	18,000	8,000
Expenditures (**GAAP Basis**)		$305,000

Thus, while the current year expenditures would have been properly reported at $297,000 in the absence of a change in the levels of inventories or prepayments, the changes in those amounts during the current year must be considered in the adjustment process. Here the $8,000 net decrease indicates that amounts paid for last year were used during this year. Had the inventory or prepayment level increased during the current year, that amount would have been deducted in determining current year expenditures under the consumption method.

The year end 19X1 adjusting entry—assuming the 19X0 adjusting entry was properly made and **not** reversed—would be:

Accrued Expenditures Payable	3,000	
Expenditures	5,000	
Inventories or Prepayments		8,000
To record year end 19X1 expenditures adjustments.		

Other Accounts

The revenues and expenditures adjusting entries also adjust many of the related asset and liability account balances. However, any other asset accounts—such as the Investments account and related liability accounts—should be reviewed and adjusted as needed. Also, the encumbrances account should be reviewed as discussed in Chapter 6 and any necessary adjusting entries should be made.

Worksheet

A worksheet similar to that presented in Figure 10-2 is essential to organizing, accomplishing, and documenting most cash basis-to-GAAP basis conversions. If only GAAP basis statements are to be presented only three pairs of worksheet columns would be needed—since the "Phase 1" and "Phase 2" (or "Conversion to GAAP") adjustments could be made in the same columns.

Reconciliation

If the cash basis governmental fund statements are issued—for either external or internal use—the cash basis on which they are prepared should be described and it should be made clear that they do **not** purport to present fairly in conformity with GAAP. Further, a brief **reconciliation** of the cash basis and GAAP basis amounts should be prepared by summarizing the **cash basis-to-GAAP basis adjustments:**

1. To ensure adequate disclosure in the notes to the financial statements;

2. As part of the SLG accountant's year end adjustment-closing-statement preparation routine and/or as one of the audit procedures; or

3. To facilitate the explanation of the differences between the cash basis amounts —with which nonaccountant managers and governing body members are apt to be more familiar, particularly when monthly or other interim reports are prepared on the cash basis—and the modified accrual basis amounts presented in the GAAP basis financial statements.

Such **cash basis-to-GAAP basis reconciliations** typically are **brief summaries** of the **differences** between key statement amounts—usually ending fund balance or the excess of revenues and other financing sources over (under) expenditures and other financing uses—on each basis. They are prepared by summarizing the effects of the several (often many) adjusting entries into a few "**net effect**" categories, then adding and deducting these net effects to and from the key amount calculated using the cash basis to summarize the derivation of that amount on the GAAP basis, thus reconciling the differences.

Reconciliation Illustrations. To illustrate cash basis-to-GAAP basis reconciliation, assume for illustrative purposes that (1) the amounts in the revenues and expenditures adjustment examples earlier in this section are the SLG's **total** revenues and expenditures for the current year, (2) the data in the "Revenues Example 1" adjustment are "paired" with the "Expenditures Example 1" adjustment data, as are the "Revenues Example 2" and "Expenditures Example 2" adjustment data; (3) there were no "other" financing sources and uses, RETs, or fund balance restatements during the year; (4) the beginning fund balance amounts were as indicated below; and (5) the SLG accountant had properly calculated the following amounts.

| | **Revenues and Expenditures Adjustment Examples** | | | |
| | *Example No. 1* | | *Example No. 2* | |
	Cash Basis	*GAAP Basis*	*Cash Basis*	*GAAP Basis*
Revenues	$320,000	$324,000	$320,000	$323,000
Expenditures	300,000	297,000	300,000	305,000
Excess of Revenues over Expenditures	20,000	27,000	20,000	18,000
Fund Balance—Beginning of Year	60,000	90,000	60,000	68,000
Fund Balance—End of Year . . .	$ 80,000	$117,000	$ 80,000	$ 86,000

Note that every key amount will differ between "operating" statements presented on the cash basis and on the GAAP (modified accrual) basis under the assumptions of either set of illustrative revenues and expenditures adjusting entries. Obviously, this might confuse many nonaccountants (and some accountants) unless the differences are adequately explained and reconciled.

Using this information and that from the illustrative revenues and expenditures adjusting entry calculations earlier in this section, we can prepare ***summary*** reconciliations of the differences between the cash basis and GAAP (modified accrual) basis amounts that reconcile either (1) the excess of revenues over expenditures amounts or (2) the ending fund balance amounts. These two reconciliation approaches are often referred to as the "**excess**" approach and the "**fund balance**" approach, respectively,

The "**excess**" approach reconciliations under both sets of adjusting entry assumptions are presented (as Example 1 and Example 2) in Figure 10-3. The

Figure 10-3
"EXCESS" RECONCILIATION APPROACH

Cash Basis-to-GAAP (Modified Accrual) Basis Reconciliation

	Example No. 1		Example No. 2	
Excess of Revenues over Expenditures (**Cash Basis**)		$20,000		$20,000
Revenues:				
Increase in accrued revenues (receivable)	$10,000		$10,000	
Increase in deferred revenues	(6,000)		(6,000)	
Increase in allowance for uncollectible receivables	—	4,000	(1,000)	3,000
Expenditures:				
Decrease in accrued expenditures (payable)	3,000		3,000	
Decrease in inventory or prepayal	—	3,000	(8,000)	(5,000)
Excess of Revenues over Expenditures (**GAAP Basis**)		$27,000		$18,000

Note: Example No. 1 is based on the **first** revenues and expenditures adjustment to GAAP examples in the text; Example No. 2 is based on the **second** text examples of adjusting revenues and expenditures data from the cash basis to the GAAP basis.

"fund balance" approach reconciliations are presented in Figure 10-4. Only **one** reconciliation would be presented in practice, of course. That reconciliation would *summarize* the numerous cash basis-to-GAAP (modified accrual) basis conversion adjustments made—which may have involved hundreds of adjusting entries—in a few categories that reconcile the differences reported in **either** the "excess" or the ending fund balance amounts under the two bases.

"Excess" Reconciliation Approach.   Note that the "excess" reconciliation approach illustrated in Figure 10-3:

1. **Begins** with the "Excess of Revenues over Expenditures (**Cash Basis**)" amount—clearly indicating that this is a cash basis amount; then
2. **Summarizes** the **categories of adjustments** made **and** their **effects** in the cash basis-to-GAAP basis conversion; and
3. **Ends** with the "Excess of Revenues over Expenditures (**GAAP Basis**)"—again clearly indicating that this is a GAAP (modified accrual) basis amount.

Note also that the accountant should describe the reconciling items—to the extent practicable—in a manner that is understandable to the **nonaccountant** manager, governing body member, newspaper reporter, or other statement reader or public meeting participant.

Also observe in the reconciliations presented in Figure 10-3 that the revenues adjustments are added or deducted as in the related calculations. But the expenditures adjustments are added or deducted *oppositely,* since expenditures are deducted in determining the "excess" being reconciled.

The "excess" reconciliation approach is widely used in practice. This type reconciliation typically (1) is accompanied by an explanation of the differences between the cash and GAAP bases, and (2) is presented in the notes to the financial statements or in narrative explanations of the cash basis statements or sched-

Figure 10-4

"FUND BALANCE" RECONCILIATION APPROACH

Cash Basis-to-GAAP (Modified Accrual) Basis Reconciliation

	Example No. 1		Example No. 2	
Revenues: (**Cash Basis**—Detailed) . . .		$320,000		$320,000
Expenditures (**Cash Basis**—Detailed) .		300,000		300,000
Excess of Revenues over Expenditures (**Cash Basis**)		20,000		20,000
Fund Balance—Beginning of Year (**Cash Basis**)		60,000		60,000
Fund Balance—End of Year (Cash Basis)		80,000		80,000
Reconciliation to GAAP Basis:				
Revenues:				
Increase in accrued revenues (receivable)	$10,000		$10,000	
Increase in deferred revenues	(6,000)		(6,000)	
Increase in allowance for uncollectible receivables	—	4,000	(1,000)	3,000
Expenditures:				
Decrease in accrued expenditures (payable)	3,000		3,000	
Decrease in inventory or prepayal	—	3,000	(8,000)	(5,000)
Fund Balance—Beginning of Year:				
GAAP Basis	90,000		68,000	
Cash Basis	60,000	30,000	60,000	8,000
Fund Balance—End of Year (GAAP Basis)		$117,000		$ 86,000

ules included in the CAFR, though it may also be presented in a note at the bottom of the cash basis "operating" statement.

"Fund Balance" Reconciliation Approach. Whereas the "excess" approach reconciliation typically is presented in the notes to the financial statements or in the narrative explanations of supplemental statements and schedules, the **"fund balance"** approach **reconciliation** usually is presented as the **concluding section** of the **cash basis "operating" statement.** Thus, the "fund balance" reconciliation approach illustrated in Figure 10-4 contains two distinct sections: (1) a cash basis statement of Revenues, Expenditures, and Changes in Fund Balance—in standard format but with all amounts determined on the **cash basis**—and (2) the "Reconciliation to GAAP Basis" that concludes with "Fund Balance—End of Year" (**GAAP Basis**).

Note that most of the reconciling items are identical to those illustrated in Figure 10-3. However, one additional reconciling item—the **difference** between the cash basis and GAAP basis **beginning** fund balances amounts—usually must be included. This is because the other reconciling items explain the differences between the cash basis and GAAP basis amounts **during** the year, but do not consider any **accumulated** differences arising in **prior** years as of the **beginning** of the **current year.**

The "fund balance" reconciliation approach is widely used where both the GAAP basis and cash basis "operating" statements are presented in the same financial report—as when the budget is enacted on the cash basis. This is because in the "excess" approach the GAAP and budgetary (e.g., cash) basis "operating" statements not only contain different revenues and expenditures amounts, but

395

Chapter 10
MEASUREMENT
FOCUS (MFBA)—
GOVERNMENTAL
FUNDS

also conclude with different "Fund Balance—End of Year" amounts. This may confuse readers, who typically must turn to the notes to the financial statements to find the "excess" approach reconciliation—then turn back and forth between the "operating" statements and the notes to understand the reconciliation.

On the other hand, the "fund balance" approach reconciliation (Figure 10-4) is presented as an integral part of the budgetary (e.g., cash basis) "operating" statement, which typically is presented immediately after the similar GAAP basis statement. Further, while the revenues, expenditures, and other amounts differ from those in the GAAP basis statement, both the budgetary basis and GAAP basis "operating" statements conclude with the same amount—"Fund Balance—End of Year" (**GAAP Basis**)—which facilitates reader acceptance and understanding of both statements.

Legally Prescribed or Contractually Agreed Non-GAAP Basis

From Chapter 1 on—particularly in discussing the first GASB principle (Chapter 2) and the importance of budgetary accounting and reporting (Chapter 3)—we have often noted that non-GAAP accounting and reporting requirements may be imposed on, or agreed to by, state and local governments. Further, we observed the analogy between (1) the dual income tax basis and GAAP basis accounting and reporting requirements applicable to businesses, and (2) the dual (at least) budgetary basis—and perhaps other non-GAAP basis—accounting and reporting requirements and the GAAP reporting requirements applicable to SLGs. But until this chapter we have deferred discussion of non-GAAP accounting and reporting —focusing instead on GAAP basis accounting and reporting.

Non-GAAP basis budgetary accounting and reporting—including budgetary basis-to-GAAP basis explanations and reconciliations—**are so important that they are discussed and illustrated separately in the next section of this chapter rather than here. Other types of legally prescribed and contractually agreed non-GAAP accounting and reporting requirements are considered briefly in this section.**

Legally Prescribed Non-GAAP Basis

Some states prescribe uniform fund and account group structures, charts of accounts, and financial statements for their counties, cities, towns, and townships, school districts, and/or other special districts. Most of the states with such uniform accounting and reporting requirements intend for the requirements to be consistent with GAAP; and most issue detailed instruction manuals, which are updated regularly, to facilitate compliance. But a few states have uniform accounting requirements that are not consistent with GAAP.

These state-mandated non-GAAP uniform accounting and reporting requirements may intentionally differ from GAAP—as when non-GAAP fund types, account classifications, or revenue and expenditure recognition rules are specified to achieve some state purpose. But often the differences are unintentional—arising from a lack of understanding of GAAP applicable to SLGs by those who wrote the requirements or the failure to revise requirements that once were consistent with GAAP to reflect changed GASB requirements.

The analyses and procedures necessary to account and report on a state-mandated non-GAAP basis and also report on the GAAP basis are similar to those discussed and illustrated earlier in this chapter (see Figure 10-2). The most difficult steps often are understanding the legally prescribed non-GAAP accounting and reporting requirements—which may be unique to that jurisdiction—so the accounts can be maintained on and/or adjusted to the prescribed non-GAAP basis.

Contractually Agreed Non-GAAP Basis

We have noted at several points that federal and state grantor and contracting agencies, in particular, may include non-GAAP accounting and reporting requirements in the contractual provisions of intergovernmental grants, entitlements, and research and other contracts. The SLG must agree to abide by such non-GAAP accounting and specific purpose reporting requirements as a condition of accepting such grants, entitlements, and research or other contracts.

Such contractually agreed accounting and reporting provisions often require that specified accounts be maintained—perhaps on the encumbrances basis but with expenditures and encumbrances distinguished—and that special purpose financial statements be issued in prescribed formats, perhaps for periods other than the SLG's fiscal year. Further, both the accounts specified and the financial statements required may focus in detail on the distinction between **"allowable"** or "reimbursable" grant or contract expenditures and other costs—as defined contractually or in related regulations—and **"unallowable"** or "nonreimbursable" expenditures and costs.

Here again the analyses and procedures necessary to account for and report on a contractually agreed non-GAAP basis and also report on the GAAP basis are similar to those discussed and illustrated earlier in this chapter (see Figure 10-2). And, as noted at "Legally Prescribed Non-GAAP Basis," the most difficult steps often are understanding the contractually agreed non-GAAP accounting and reporting requirements—which may change as related regulations are issued during the course of the grant or contract—so the accounts can be maintained on and/or adjusted to the agreed non-GAAP basis.

Non-GAAP Budgetary Basis

We have discussed the legal and managerial significance of the SLG governmental funds annual budget(s) at numerous points earlier in the text. Indeed, the annual governmental funds budget(s) is so important in the SLG environment—from both legal compliance and accountability standpoints and managerial and oversight body planning, control, and evaluation perspectives—that four of the twelve basic GASB principles establish **budgetary** accounting and reporting standards as an integral part of the GASB's **GAAP** reporting standards. Further, the GASB standards require that a **budgetary comparison statement** for *all annually budgeted governmental funds* be presented—on the **budgetary basis**—as one of the five **primary** financial statements in general purpose financial statements (GPFS) presented in conformity with GAAP. Thus, assuming the annual governmental fund budget(s) is enacted on a **non-GAAP** basis, the budgetary comparison statement is the **only** non-GAAP basis statement that must be presented as a primary financial statement—together with the four required GAAP basis financial statements—in GPFS presented in conformity with GAAP.

Reasons for Non-GAAP Basis Budgets

Many SLGs prepare their annual governmental fund budget(s) on the **GAAP basis** because, for example:

1. They are **legally required** to do so by state law or local ordinance;
2. Their **managers and oversight bodies want to** do so for budgetary planning, control, and evaluation purposes and/or for budgetary oversight and accountability purposes; and
3. Their **managers and/or oversight bodies prefer to present all of the GPFS on the GAAP basis.** Or perhaps they prefer **not** to present the budgetary com-

397

Chapter 10
MEASUREMENT
FOCUS (MFBA)—
GOVERNMENTAL
FUNDS

parison statement on a non-GAAP basis—with amounts that differ from those in the GAAP basis "operating" statement, possibly confusing some statement users—which also requires that the budgetary basis-GAAP basis differences be explained and reconciled.

On the other hand, **most** SLGs budget on a **non-GAAP basis** because, for example:

1. They are **legally required** to do so by state law or local ordinance;
2. Their **managers and/or oversight bodies want to budget**—and establish budgetary control, evaluation, and accountability functions and responsibilities—**on a non-GAAP basis.** They may want **encumbrances** to be treated essentially like expenditures for budgetary control, evaluation, and accountability purposes, for example, and may not want revenues to be recognized for budgetary purposes until the cash is received (and thus can be spent).
3. Their **managers and/or oversight bodies may prefer a non-GAAP budgetary approach** such as just previously described **because they understand the non-GAAP budgetary basis better than the GAAP basis,** as do most nonaccountant department heads and financial statement users. Indeed, they may consider the interim and annual budgetary comparison statements to be more useful than the annual GAAP basis "operating" statement.

Non-GAAP Budgetary Bases

Unless a specified budgetary basis is legally required by a higher level government, a SLG may budget in any manner that its customs and the preferences of its leadership may call for. Thus, several different non-GAAP budgetary bases may be encountered in practice.

Most *non-GAAP budgetary bases* in common use are either:

- Cash basis
- Cash basis + Encumbrances
- Modified accrual basis + Encumbrances

Others are quite close to one of these bases. However, determining the budgetary basis in use is extremely difficult occasionally; and a "mixed" budgetary basis—where some revenues and expenditures are budgeted on one basis and others are budgeted on another basis—may also be encountered.

The Cash Basis section at the beginning of this chapter discusses and illustrates cash basis accounting, adjustments to both the cash basis and the GAAP basis, and both cash basis and GAAP basis reporting—including reconciliation of the cash basis and GAAP basis statements. Those methods and procedures are employed also when the budget is enacted on the cash basis—which is a major reason why those discussions and illustrations are quite thorough—so cash basis budgeting need not be considered further here. Accordingly, the remainder of this section of the chapter focuses on (1) the "cash basis + encumbrances" and "modified accrual + encumbrances" bases, both referred to as *"encumbrances bases,"* and (2) some illustrations of non-GAAP reporting and disclosure, including budgetary basis-GAAP basis reconciliations.

Encumbrances Bases

That encumbrances—the estimated cost of goods and services on order—are considered substantially equivalent to expenditures by many SLG budget officers, managers, governing body members, and others has been noted at several points earlier in the text. We have also noted that—regardless of the ultimate treatment accorded them—encumbrances are recorded as reductions of available expenditure authority in the Expenditure Subsidiary Ledger accounts and, assuming they will be honored in the next year, as reservations of fund balance at year end. Thus, data on encumbrances are required for both budgetary and GAAP reporting purposes.

But while GAAP standards are based on the legal definitions of expenditures and liabilities—and thus encumbrances are **not** reported with expenditures in GAAP "operating" statements or with liabilities in GAAP balance sheets—**encumbrances may be reported with (or even as) expenditures and liabilities in budgetary basis financial statements.** Thus, encumbrances often constitute another budgetary basis-GAAP basis difference that requires budgetary basis-to-GAAP basis adjusting entries, causes differences between the budgetary basis and GAAP basis "operating" statements, and must be explained and reconciled in the financial statements and/or in the notes to the financial statements.

The two common **variations** of the **"encumbrances" basis** are:

- **Cash basis + encumbrances**—in which the SLG accounts on the cash basis, as described earlier in this chapter, but also treats encumbrances as expenditures for budgetary purposes.

- **Modified accrual basis + encumbrances**—in which the SLG accounts on the modified accrual basis, as discussed and illustrated in earlier chapters, but also treats encumbrances as expenditures for budgetary purposes.

It is important to identify which "encumbrances" basis is in use, of course, to ensure that (1) the proper amounts are in the "Preclosing Trial Balance—Non-GAAP Basis" columns of the year end worksheet (Figure 10-2) after the "phase 1" adjustments are recorded, and (2) the "phase 2" adjustments made lead to a proper "Preclosing Trial Balance—GAAP Basis." Further, one must recognize and adjust for the fact that encumbrances outstanding at year end "overlap" two accounting periods—either the prior year and current year or the current year and following year.

Assuming the proper amounts of encumbrances are recorded in the accounts and in the "Preclosing Trial Balance—Non-GAAP Basis" (or "Budgetary Basis" or "Encumbrances Basis") columns of a worksheet like that in Figure 10-2, the differences between the budgetary and GAAP treatments of encumbrances must be understood to complete the "phase 2" or "conversion to GAAP" adjustments. To this end, consider the following expenditures and encumbrances amounts—assuming that the expenditures resulting from the encumbrances in the next year were equal to the encumbrances recorded in the previous year:

		Expenditures + Encumbrances ($540,000)	
Budgetary Basis	Encumbrances End of 19X0 ($60,000)	Expenditures During 19X1 ($500,000)	Encumbrances End of 19X1 ($40,000)
	19X0	19X1	19X2
GAAP Basis		Expenditures during 19X1 ($560,000)	

The 19X1 GAAP basis expenditures were properly computed as follows: $540,000 19X1 budgetary basis Expenditures − $40,000 19X1 year end Encumbrances (not GAAP basis expenditures) + $60,000 19X0 Encumbrances (included in 19X0 budg-

399

Chapter 10
MEASUREMENT
FOCUS (MFBA)—
GOVERNMENTAL
FUNDS

etary basis expenditures but in 19X1 GAAP basis expenditures) = $560,000 19X1 GAAP basis Expenditures. Or, more briefly:

19X1 Budgetary Basis	
Expenditures + Encumbrances	$540,000
Less: 19X1 Encumbrances	(40,000)
Add: 19X0 Encumbrances	60,000
19X1 GAAP Basis Expenditures	$560,000

But what if the actual 19X1 expenditures are more or less than the amounts encumbered at the end of 19X0? Normally any excess is charged against a similar appropriation in the 19X1 budgetary basis expenditure accounts, and any difference from a less-than-encumbered expenditure is credited to a similar or "miscellaneous" expenditure account in the 19X1 budgetary basis expenditure accounts. Thus, the calculation approach illustrated previously will work unless another disposition is made of the difference—such as improperly crediting the less-than-encumbered difference to Revenues in the budgetary basis accounts. In any event, such differences usually are immaterial to the governmental fund financial statements, though material differences are encountered occasionally.

In sum, the related 19X1 worksheet columns (Figure 10-2) and **non-GAAP-to-GAAP basis adjusting entries** might appear as:

	Preclosing Trial Balance Non-GAAP (Budgetary) Basis		Adjustments to GAAP Basis		Preclosing Trial Balance GAAP Basis	
	Dr.	Cr.	Dr.	Cr.	Dr.	Cr.
Expenditures and Encumbrances . . .	540,000			540,000 (1)	—	
Accounts and Vouchers Payable .		140,000	40,000 (3)			100,000
Expenditures			540,000 (1)		560,000	
			20,000 (3)			
Encumbrances			40,000 (2)		40,000	
Reserve for Encumbrances . . .				40,000 (2)		40,000
Unreserved Fund Balance		50,000		60,000 (3)		110,000

The initial Accounts and Vouchers Payable ($140,000) non-GAAP balance assumes that the 19X1 encumbrances were recorded as liabilities, whereas they should be excluded from the GAAP basis liabilities ($100,000) reported. Similarly, the Unreserved Fund Balance ($50,000) amount was assumed to demonstrate how the **change** in Reserve for Encumbrances ($60,000 − $40,000 = $20,000) may be recorded net in the worksheet in deriving expenditures. The adjusting entries may be made under other logical approaches and in other sequences, of course—and may be compounded—so long as the proper amounts are extended to the "Preclosing Trial Balance—GAAP Basis" columns.

Non-GAAP Budgetary Basis-to-GAAP Basis Reconciliations

Non-GAAP budgetary basis-to-GAAP basis reconciliations are similar to the cash basis-to-GAAP basis reconciliations discussed earlier and illustrated in Figures 10-3 and 10-4. Both may be presented in either the "excess" or "fund balance" approach, and may be presented either in the body of the statements and schedules or in the notes to the financial statements.

Non-GAAP budgetary basis-to-GAAP basis reconciliations vary more than cash basis-to-GAAP basis reconciliations, however, primarily because budgetary bases vary among governments. The only difference between the budgetary and GAAP bases in some SLGs is that encumbrances are considered tantamount to expenditures in the budgetary basis. In other SLGs there also are revenue accrual and other expenditure accrual differences between the budgetary and GAAP bases; and often some of the governmental funds are not budgeted annually.

The approach to preparing the reconciliation is the same in all cases, however. The "phase 2" adjustments from the non-GAAP budgetary basis to the GAAP basis (see Figure 10-2) are summarized by category—such as revenue accruals, expenditure accruals, encumbrances—and presented in a condensed manner that **explains the differences between** (reconciles) the budgetary basis and GAAP basis "excess" or "fund balance" amounts.

Reconciliation presentations vary widely both because of budgetary-GAAP basis differences and because of differing professional judgments of how reconciliations are best presented. Some governments reconcile from the budgetary basis to the GAAP basis, for example, and others reconcile from the GAAP basis to the budgetary basis. Any reasonable approach that is effective in communicating the differences between the budgetary basis and GAAP basis amounts seems acceptable under GAAP.

Brief budgetary basis-to-GAAP basis reconciliation examples extracted from recent annual financial reports of state and local governments are presented in Figures 10-5 and 10-6 to illustrate varying reconciliation presentations:

- **"Excess" Approach Budgetary Basis-to-GAAP Basis Reconciliation Examples (Figure 10-5)**
  Part I—City of Tulsa—illustrates a simple "excess" presentation reconciling differences in encumbrances, revenue accruals, and nonbudgeted funds in the notes to the financial statements.
  Part II—Hamilton County, Tennessee—demonstrates a simple "excess" presentation in the body of the budgetary operating statement—which concludes with the same GAAP basis fund balance amount as the GAAP operating statement—where the only budgetary-GAAP basis difference is the treatment of encumbrances.
- **"Fund Balance" Approach Budgetary Basis-to-GAAP Basis Reconciliation Examples (Figure 10-6)**
  Part I—State of Missouri—reconciles differences involving inventory accounting and deferred revenues as well as nonbudgeted funds, encumbrances, revenue accruals, and expenditure accruals.
  Part II—County of Los Angeles—illustrates a reconciliation involving differences in accounting for claims and judgments, compensated absences, and interfund payables and receivables as well as encumbrances and revenue accruals.

Again, these examples were selected to illustrate the variety of ways—**not** the **only** ways—that budgetary basis-to-GAAP basis reconciliations may be presented in the financial statements and schedules and/or in the notes to the financial statements. No two governments are apt to present identical reconciliations, of course, but most use presentation approaches similar to those illustrated here.

Figure 10-5

"EXCESS" APPROACH
BUDGETARY BASIS-TO-GAAP BASIS RECONCILIATION EXAMPLES

Part I—City of Tulsa
Budget Reconciliations

[Notes to the Financial Statements]

Items required to adjust actual revenues, expenditures, and encumbrances reported on the budgetary basis to those reported on the Combined Statement of Revenues, Expenditures and Changes in Fund Balance—All Governmental Fund Types and Expendable Trust Funds (GAAP basis) are as follows:

	Revenues	Expenditures	Other Financing Sources (Uses)
General Fund			
Budgetary basis	$126,084	($118,404)	($10,997)
To adjust for revenue accruals	2,314		(414)
To adjust for encumbrances		2,910	15
GAAP basis	$128,398	($115,494)	($11,396)
Special Revenue Funds			
Budgetary basis	$ 7,179	($ 24,721)	$14,101
To adjust for revenue differences	(1,350)		1,358
Nonbudgeted funds	17,667	(14,221)	(1,019)
To adjust for encumbrances		1,820	
GAAP basis	$23,496	($ 37,122)	$14,440

Part II—Hamilton County, Tennessee
Combined Statement of Revenues, Expenditures and Changes in Fund Balances—Budget and Actual
General, Special Revenue and Debt Service Fund Types
Hamilton County, Tennessee
Year Ended June 30, 1991

	General Fund		
	Budget	Actual (Non-GAAP Basis)	Variance- Favorable (Unfavorable)
Revenues:			
Taxes	$38,033,185	$38,191,551	$ 158,366
Excess (deficiency) of revenues and other financing sources over (under) **budgetary** expenditures and other financing uses	(3,250,481)	208,168	3,458,649
Fund balance allocation	3,250,481	—	(3,250,481)
	—	208,168	$ 208,168
Add encumbrances at end of year		812,952	
Less encumbrances at beginning of year		(753,805)	
Excess of revenues and other financing sources over expenditures and other financing uses—**(GAAP)**		267,315	
Fund balances at beginning of year—**(GAAP)**		17,444,806	
Fund balances at end of year—**(GAAP)**		$17,712,121	

Source: Adapted from recent annual financial reports of the City of Tulsa, Oklahoma, and Hamilton County, Tennessee.

Figure 10-6
"FUND BALANCE" APPROACH
BUDGETARY BASIS-TO-GAAP BASIS RECONCILIATION EXAMPLES

Part I—State of Missouri

Notes to the Financial Statements

The following is a reconciliation of the differences between the budgetary basis and the GAAP basis.

Budgetary Basis vs. GAAP (in thousands of dollars)

	General	Special Revenue	Debt Service	Capital Projects
Fund Balance **(Budgetary Basis)** June 30, 19X1	$ 216,968	$287,201	$84,675	$ 37,873
Add (Deduct):				
Accrued Revenues	230,081	63,533	633	50,980
Deferred Revenues	(4,767)	(1,889)	—	—
Accrued Expenditures	(275,404)	12,434	—	(3,027)
Inventory Balance	9,085	4,115	—	33,022
Fund Balances of Funds Not Budgeted (GAAP Basis)	38,718	(35,761)	—	51,183
Fund Balance **(GAAP Basis)** June 30, 19X1	$ 214,681	$329,633	$85,308	$170,031

Part II—County of Los Angeles

Notes to the Financial Statements

The following schedule is a reconciliation of the budgetary and GAAP fund balances (in thousands):

	General Fund	Special Revenue Funds	Debt Service Funds
Fund balance—**budgetary basis**	$342,357	$308,298	$ 21,850
Encumbrances outstanding at year end .	115,571	79,195	
Subtotal	457,928	387,493	21,850
Adjustments:			
Accrual of workers' compensation liability	(64,604)	(6,610)	
Accrual of estimated liability for litigation and self-insurance claims .	(15,350)	(9,712)	
Accrual of vacation and sick leave benefits	(237)	(1,691)	
Accrual of amounts due from and due to other funds	(3,748)		
Change in advances to and from other funds	11,200	(8,800)	
Change in revenue accruals	(8,573)	(4,813)	526
Subtotal	376,616	355,867	22,376
Fund balance—nonbudgeted funds		54,408	218,702
Fund balance—**GAAP basis**	$376,616	$410,275	$241,078

Source: Adapted from recent annual financial reports of the State of Missouri and the County of Los Angeles, California.

The Budgetary Fund Balance Account

One final, minor variation in budgetary accounting that was not discussed in previous chapters is the use of the "Budgetary Fund Balance" account. Some prescribed governmental fund accounting systems require—and some SLG account-

403

Chapter 10
MEASUREMENT
FOCUS (MFBA)—
GOVERNMENTAL
FUNDS

ants prefer—that the **budgeted increase or decrease in fund balance** for the year be recorded in a **Budgetary Fund Balance** (or similarly titled) general ledger account rather than in the Unreserved Fund Balance account. Use of the Budgetary Fund Balance account is an acceptable practice. Indeed, it probably should be used in some circumstances.

To illustrate the use of the Budgetary Fund Balance account, the general ledger **budgetary entry** in Chapter 4 (entry 1) using the Budgetary Fund Balance account would be:

(1) Estimated Revenues.............................	431,000	
Appropriations		426,000
Budgetary Fund Balance		5,000
To record appropriations and revenue estimates (the annual budget).		

The **closing entry** under the "Reverse the Budget—Close the Actual" approach would be:

(C1) Appropriations	426,000	
Budgetary Fund Balance	5,000	
Estimated Revenues		431,000
To close the budgetary accounts.		

Use of the Budgetary Fund Balance account does **not** affect the GPFS since (1) the general ledger budgetary entry is **reversed** in the closing entry process, so the budgeted change in fund balance does not affect the (actual) year-end balance of the Unreserved Fund Balance reported in the GPFS; and (2) the budgetary comparison statement will **not** be changed by the use of either the "traditional" budgetary entry or the Budgetary Fund Balance account budgetary entry.

The primary reason some SLG accountants prefer the Budgetary Fund Balance account approach is that some annual SLG budgets are extremely optimistic. That is, they are based on unrealistic or extremely uncertain projections of high revenue levels and/or low levels of expenditures. Similarly, some annual budgets are hurried "guesstimates" that are not based on proper budgetary analyses and estimates by qualified personnel or consultants; and others may be purposefully biased optimistically for political reasons. In cases such as these, the SLG accountant may properly balk at reporting an inflated estimate of the year end Unreserved Fund Balance and insist on using a Budgetary Fund Balance account to segregate the **"actual beginning balance"** and **"planned change"** components in the accounts and **interim** budgetary (and other) financial statements.

In an environment like any of those noted previously as giving rise to the Budgetary Fund Balance approach, that approach probably should be used. But otherwise the advantages of the traditional Unreserved Fund Balance budgetary entry approach should be weighed carefully before making the decision. The primary advantage of the Unreserved Fund Balance budgetary entry approach—given a sound budget—is that it focuses the attention of the governing body and managers on **"where they plan to be by year end"** rather than on "where they were at the beginning of the year." Thus, the Unreserved Fund Balance account balance is a **"target"** year-end balance—assuming no further budget revisions—and indicates to what extent additional appropriations may be made and financed by year end. Further, if the budget is regularly and properly revised, the Unreserved Fund Balance account automatically **"signals"** an impending deficit projected by year end—whether caused by decreased revenue estimates, increased appropriations, or other reasons—so that further budget revisions may be made on a timely basis and an actual deficit at year end may be avoided. Such "targets" and "signals" are not as readily apparent under the Budgetary Fund Balance budgetary entry approach.

CONCLUDING COMMENTS

Whereas prior chapters focus primarily on current GAAP for governmental funds and assume GAAP basis budgeting, this chapter focuses on *other* governmental fund budgeting, accounting, and reporting methods. One key basis of accounting discussed is the flow of financial resources measurement focus and basis of accounting set forth in GASBS 11. Each of the other methods discussed is used often in practice and may appear on the Uniform CPA Examination.

Earlier chapters assumed for illustrative (and CPA exam) purposes that the governmental fund budget was prepared—and the accounts were maintained during the year—on the GAAP basis. But many SLGs budget on a non-GAAP budgetary basis; and most SLGs use non-GAAP accounting methods *during* the year for various budgetary, legal or contractual, and accounting simplification reasons. At *year end,* these SLGs (1) adjust the data in the accounts to the budgetary or other required non-GAAP basis in order to prepare budgetary statements and/or special purpose reports on another non-GAAP basis, then (2) adjust the non-GAAP basis data to the GAAP basis in order to prepare the GAAP basis financial statements. The adjusting entries made in this two-phase adjustment process may be posted to the accounts or may be posted only to the year-end worksheets.

This chapter concludes the series of chapters on governmental fund and account group accounting and financial reporting. The next three chapters deal with fiduciary fund and proprietary fund accounting and reporting. Then, governmental fund accounting and reporting are again reviewed briefly in the contexts of the entire SLG accounting "model" and of SLG annual financial reporting. Finally, some of the important issues of government accounting and reporting are discussed (or discussed further) in Chapter 15, "Contemporary Issues."

QUESTIONS

10-1 Identify and explain (briefly) the various types of non-GAAP accounting methods and reporting requirements that may be encountered in SLG accounting, reporting, and auditing.

10-2 Why might a SLG properly prefer to maintain its governmental fund accounts on a non-GAAP basis during the year?

10-3 Why is it essential that the SLG accountant and auditor understand the SLG's non-GAAP special purpose reporting requirements and the basis on which its accounts are maintained *during* the year?

10-4 Briefly explain the two-phase adjustment process typically required for SLGs that have non-GAAP special purpose reporting requirements and also present financial statements in conformity with GAAP.

10-5 Distinguish between the cash basis of revenue and expenditure accounting and the cash receipts and disbursements basis.

10-6 Why might a SLG prepare and enact its governmental fund annual budget(s) on a non-GAAP budgetary basis?

10-7 A SLG may properly consider encumbrances to be essentially equivalent to expenditures in budgetary operating statements, but may not do so in GAAP operating statements. Explain this apparent inconsistency.

10-8 What is meant by "reconciling" or presenting a "reconciliation of" non-GAAP basis and GAAP basis financial statements?

10-9 (a) Distinguish between the "excess" and "fund balance" reconciliation approaches. (b) What are the *advantages* of each approach?

10-10 Why might a SLG governmental fund accountant properly prefer to use a "Budgetary Fund Balance" account?

P 10-1 (Multiple Choice) Choose the best answer to each of the following assuming (a) current GAAP is in effect and (b) GASBS 11 is in effect.

1. Which of the following is not to be reported as governmental fund revenue?
   a. Taxes
   b. Fines and forfeitures
   c. Special assessments
   d. Proceeds from the sale of general fixed assets
   e. Payments in lieu of taxes
   f. All of the above are reported as governmental fund revenues

2. Generally, sales tax revenues should be recognized by a local government in the period
   a. In which the local government receives the cash.
   b. That the underlying sale occurs, whether or not the local government receives the cash in that period.
   c. In which the state—which collects all sales taxes in the state—receives the cash from the collecting merchants.
   d. In which the state—which collects all sales taxes in the state—receives the cash from the collecting merchants if the local government collects the taxes from the state in that period or soon enough in the next period to be used as a resource for payment of liabilities incurred in the first period.

3. On June 1, 19X4 a school district levies the property taxes for its fiscal year that will end on June 30, 19X5. The total amount of the levy is $1,000,000 and it is expected that 1% will prove uncollectible. $250,000 of the levy is collected in June 19X4 and another $500,000 is collected in July and August 19X4. What amount of property tax revenue associated with the June 1, 19X4 levy should be reported as revenue in the fiscal year ending June 30, 19X4?
   a. $0
   b. $250,000
   c. $750,000
   d. $990,000

4. A city levied $2,000,000 of property taxes for its current fiscal year. The city collected $1,700,000 cash on its taxes receivable during the year and granted $72,000 in discounts to taxpayers who paid within the legally established discount period. It is expected that the city will collect another $88,000 cash on these taxes receivable during the first two months of the next fiscal year. One percent of the tax levy is expected to be uncollectible. What amount of property tax revenues should the city report for the current fiscal year?
   a. $1,788,000
   b. $1,860,000
   c. $1,980,000
   d. $2,000,000

5. What would the answer to 4 be if the city also collected $100,000 on prior year taxes during the first two months of the current fiscal year and another $53,000 of prior year taxes during the remainder of the current year?
   a. $1,788,000
   b. $1,860,000
   c. $1,941,000
   d. $1,980,000
   e. None of the above. The correct answer is $_____

6. A state acquired $80,000 of equipment through the enforcement of escheat laws. The General Fund statement of revenues, expenditures, and changes in fund balance should report
   a. Revenues from escheat of $80,000
   b. An other financing source of $80,000
   c. Both expenditures—capital outlay and revenues from escheat of $80,000
   d. Nothing, since the General Fund is not affected if the state plans to retain the equipment for its use because no financial resources were involved.

7. A county entered into a capital lease on June 30, 19X8 for equipment to be used by General Fund departments. The capitalizable cost of the leased asset was $200,000. An ini-

tial payment of $20,000 was made at the inception of the lease. The first annual lease payment of $35,000 is due on July 1, 19X9. Assuming a 10% implicit rate of interest on the lease, the county should report General Fund expenditures in the fiscal year ended December 31, 19X8 as follows:

a. Capital outlay expenditures of $20,000

b. Capital outlay expenditures of $200,000

c. Capital outlay expenditures of $20,000 and interest expenditures of $9,000

d. Capital outlay expenditures of $200,000 and interest expenditures of $9,000

e. Rent expenditures of $20,000 and no capital outlay or debt service expenditures

8. The county in 7 paid its first $35,000 lease payment as scheduled on July 1, 19X9. The county should report General Fund expenditures for the fiscal year ended December 31, 19X9 as follows:

a. Rent expenditures of $35,000

b. Interest expenditures of $35,000

c. Principal retirement expenditures of $35,000

d. Interest expenditures of $9,000 and principal retirement expenditures of $17,000

e. Interest expenditures of $18,000 and principal retirement expenditures of $17,000

f. Interest expenditures of $17,150 and principal retirement expenditures of $17,000

9. A city paid General Fund claims and judgments incurred during 19X1 of $20,000. Additional General Fund claims were incurred during 19X1 that are deemed probable to result in judgments against the city totaling $180,000. It is likely that these claims will not result in required payments for at least two years, however. The city General Fund expenditures reported for claims and judgments in 19X1 should be:

a. $20,000

b. $200,000

c. $20,000 with $180,000 of other financing uses reported

d. $200,000 with $180,000 of other financing sources reported

10. A school district Special Revenue Fund trial balance reported beginning materials inventory of $100,000; its ending materials inventory was $120,000. Materials costing $400,000 were purchased for the fund during the year. Accounts payable for the fund's materials were $17,000 at the beginning of the year and $7,000 at year end. The school district should report expenditures for materials in its Special Revenue Fund of

	If the School District Uses	
	Purchases Method	*Consumption Method*
a.	$400,000	$400,000
b.	$400,000	$380,000
c.	$410,000	$380,000
d.	$400,000	$420,000
e.	$410,000	$420,000
f.	Not permitted	$380,000

11. A state pays salaries and wages of $118 million to General Fund employees during a year. Unpaid, accrued salaries were $3 million at the beginning of the year and $6 million at year end. General Fund salary expenditures should be reported for the year in the amount of:

a. $115 million

b. $118 million

c. $121 million

d. $124 million

P 10-2 (Property Tax Entries—Current GAAP vs. GASBS 11) Prepare the general journal entries to record the following transactions in the general ledger accounts of a General or Special Revenue Fund of a city assuming (a) current GAAP standards are effective, and (b) GASB Statement 11 has become effective.

407

Chapter 10
MEASUREMENT
FOCUS (MFBA)—
GOVERNMENTAL
FUNDS

1. The city levied current year property taxes of $1,000,000, of which 5% is estimated to be uncollectible. Also, 70% of the taxes collected are normally collected within the 2% discount period; and 90% of all collectible taxes are expected to be collected during the year, or within two months after year end.

2. Current property taxes billed at $600,000 (gross) were collected within the recently expired discount period.

3. Assume current property taxes billed at $700,000 (instead of $600,000 in item 2) were collected before the discount period expired.

4. After item 3, $100,000 of current taxes (not collected in item 3) were collected after the discount period and the balance of current property taxes became delinquent. Interest and penalties of $5,000—one-quarter of which is estimated to be uncollectible—were assessed on delinquent taxes. Delinquent property taxes and interest now are not expected to be collected until late next year at the earliest.

5. A taxpayer is protesting a delinquent property tax billing of $2,000, on which $50 of interest and penalties were assessed in item 4. While the city expects to collect the taxes, interest, and penalties, the protest process will probably delay the collection until late in the following year.

P 10-3 (GL Entries—Leases, Pensions, CJ) The following transactions and events relate to the General Fund of Bean Township for the 19X8 fiscal year.

1. The Township entered into a capital lease for computer equipment with a fair market value (and net present value) of $500,000.

2. A capital lease payment on the computer equipment, $60,000 (including $40,000 interest), was vouchered for payment.

3. At year end it was determined that the Township had estimated liabilities (including legal and related costs and net of insurance recoveries) for unsettled claims and judgments of $700,000, of which $160,000 is considered a current liability. This is the first year the Township has recorded such liabilities—they had not been considered reasonably estimable in prior years.

4. Bean Township paid only $150,000 to the trustee of its defined benefit pension plan during 19X8, even though the actuarially required contribution for 19X8 was $400,000. The governing board agreed to pay another $75,000 early in 19X9, but it is uncertain when the remaining pension plan underfunded contribution will be paid.

Required Compute the amount of expenditures that should be reported in 19X8 as a result of the preceding transactions under (a) current GAAP and (b) GASBS 11.

P 10-4 (Cash Basis and Conversion to GAAP Entries)

1. The cash receipts of the Robintown General Fund for January 19X1 included the following:

$ 800,000	Collection of current taxes receivable
150,000	Collection of delinquent taxes receivable
5,000	Collection of interest and penalties not previously accrued
6,000	Collection of previously recorded interfund charges to departments financed by other funds for services rendered by departments financed by the General Fund—⅔ was for services rendered in 19X0, ⅓ for those in 19X1
20,000	Payment in lieu of taxes from the city water and sewer department
200,000	Proceeds of a grant from the state to be matched equally by the city and expended for street improvements
1,000	Fines and forfeitures
$1,182,000	

2. The cash disbursements of the Robintown General Fund for the month included:

$ 600,000	Payroll
200,000	Payments on accounts outstanding at 12/31/X0
50,000	To a Capital Projects Fund (City's contribution to project—not previously accrued)
75,000	To establish a fund to operate a new central print shop to serve town departments
80,000	For street improvements made from grant funds and matching funds; related liabilities of $32,000 remain outstanding at the end of the month
20,000	Purchase of police cars
120,000	To the Enterprise Fund to be repaid in 19X5
10,000	For supplies ordered in December 19X0 and reappropriated for and received in 19X1
$1,155,000	

Required Prepare general journal entries to record the Robintown General Fund cash receipts and disbursements for January 19X1 on the cash basis in the General Ledger. December 31 is the fiscal year end. Then prepare any other General Fund general journal "conversion to GAAP" entries required to prepare GAAP basis financial statements.

P 10-5 (Budgetary-to-GAAP Basis Adjustments and Reconciliation) The auditor has determined that the 19X8 budgetary basis operating statement of a Special Revenue Fund of Yarborough County is correct.

Yarborough County
Special Revenue Fund
Budgetary Basis Operating Statement
For 19X8 Fiscal Year

Revenues:	
Property taxes	$ 700,000
Sales taxes	600,000
Federal grants	500,000
Other	200,000
	2,000,000
Expenditures:	
Highways	1,150,000
Law enforcement	400,000
Administration	250,000
Other	150,000
	1,950,000
Excess of Revenues Over Expenditures	50,000
Fund Balance—Beginning of 19X8	300,000
Fund Balance—End of 19X8	$ 350,000

The following additional information was determined that may be relevant in the process of deriving the adjustments needed to convert the budgetary basis budgetary operating statement data to the GAAP basis.

1. The Yarborough County governmental fund annual operating budgets are prepared—and the governmental fund accounts are maintained—using its budgetary basis under which (a) revenues are recognized only when collected, and (b) expenditures are recorded when encumbrances are incurred or when payments are made for unencumbered expenditures.

2. The GAAP basis statements at the beginning of 19X8 indicate that total fund balance then was $275,000.

409

Chapter 10
MEASUREMENT
FOCUS (MFBA)—
GOVERNMENTAL
FUNDS

3. Accrued revenues receivable were:

	Beginning of 19X8	End of 19X8
Property taxes (2/3 "available")	$120,000	$150,000
Sales taxes	100,000	45,000
Federal grants	60,000	20,000
Other	—	10,000

4. Accrued expenditures payable were:

	Beginning of 19X8	End of 19X8
Highways	$ 30,000	$ 40,000
Law enforcement	50,000	—
Administration	15,000	5,000
Other	20,000	25,000

5. Encumbrances outstanding were:

	Beginning of 19X8	End of 19X8
Highways	$100,000	$150,000
Law enforcement	175,000	50,000
Administration	60,000	30,000
Other	—	20,000

6. There were no interfund transfers to or from this Special Revenue Fund during 19X8, nor were there any restatements of beginning fund balance.

Required

(1) Prepare a GAAP basis Statement of Revenues, Expenditures, and Changes in [Total] Fund Balance for the Yarborough County Special Revenue Fund for the 19X8 fiscal year. (A worksheet in statement format may be substituted for a formal statement.)

(2) Prepare an "excess" approach budgetary basis-to-GAAP basis reconciliation to be presented in the notes to the financial statements.

(3) Prepare a "fund balance" approach budgetary basis-to-GAAP basis reconciliation to be added to the budgetary basis operating statement presented previously. (You need not present the entire statement.)

P 10-6 (Budgetary-to-GAAP Basis Adjustments and Reconciliation) Unadjusted budgetary basis balances of the "operating" accounts of the General Fund of Tuscahassee Independent School District at the end of 19X3 were:

Revenues and Other Financing Sources

Property Taxes	$ 700,000
State Operating Grant	500,000
Interest	60,000
Other	40,000
Transfer from Special Revenue Fund	70,000
Transfer from Capital Projects Fund	100,000
	$1,470,000

Expenditures and Other Financing Uses

Educational Programs	$ 800,000
Transportation	200,000
Administration	150,000
Other	50,000
Transfer to Debt Service Fund	160,000
	$1,360,000

During the course of the 19X3 audit it was determined that:

1. The District's budgetary basis recognizes revenues and expenditures only as cash is received and disbursed, respectively, but considers encumbrances equivalent to expenditures.

2. The unadjusted budgetary basis accounts should be adjusted, as appropriate, in view of the following information:

   a. A $7,000 "other" revenue was inadvertently credited to "other" expenditures during 19X3.

   b. In addition to the recorded encumbrances ($25,000 Educational Programs and $15,000 Administration), there were unrecorded encumbrances outstanding at year end: $40,000 Educational Programs and $35,000 Transportation.

3. The following information should be considered in deriving the budgetary basis-to-GAAP basis adjustments:

	Beginning of Year	End of Year
a. *Accrued Revenues/Receivables*		
(1) Property taxes receivable	$120,000	$170,000
(2) State operating grant receivable	90,000	75,000
(3) Interest receivable	10,000	15,000
(All receivables were "available.")		

	Beginning of Year	End of Year
b. *Accrued Expenditures/Payables*		
(1) Education programs	$ 18,000	$ 44,000
(2) Transportation	—	12,000
(3) Other	17,000	—

	Beginning of Year	End of Year
c. *Reserve for Encumbrances*		
(1) Educational Programs	$ 20,000	$ 65,000
(2) Transportation	15,000	35,000
(3) Administration	35,000	15,000

	Beginning of Year	End of Year
d. *Other Accrued Liabilities*		
(1) Claims and judgments (other)		
–current liability	$ 25,000	$ 15,000
–noncurrent liability	200,000	240,000
(2) Compensated absences		
–current liability	40,000	70,000
–noncurrent liability	310,000	290,000
(Chargeable 7:2:1 to Educational Programs, Transportation, and Administration.)		

e. The beginning of 19X3 fund balance reported in the district's GAAP basis financial statements was:

Reserve for Encumbrances	$ 70,000
Unreserved	130,000
	$200,000

f. There were no accumulated differences from prior years between the budgetary basis and GAAP basis total fund balances at the beginning of 19X3.

g. The Special Revenue Fund and Debt Service Fund transfers were routine annual transfers; the Capital Projects Fund transfer was upon termination of the CPF.

Required (1) Prepare a simplified partial two-phase worksheet to derive the information needed to prepare both a budgetary basis and a GAAP basis Statement of Revenues, Expenditures, and Changes in [Total] Fund Balance. Your worksheet should (a) list the accounts and subtotals through the Excess of Revenues and Other Financing Sources Over (Under) Expenditures and Other Financing Uses, and (b) have these columns:

(1) Unadjusted Budgetary Basis

(2) Adjustments to Budgetary Basis

(3) Budgetary Basis

(4) Adjustments to GAAP Basis

(5) GAAP Basis

Your adjustments should be keyed to the problem.

(2) Prepare a detailed "fund balance" approach budgetary basis-to-GAAP basis reconciliation.

(3) Prepare a summarized "excess" approach budgetary basis-to-GAAP basis reconciliation.

TRUST AND AGENCY (FIDUCIARY) FUNDS

A ***Trust*** Fund is established to account for assets received and held by a government acting in the capacity of trustee or custodian. An ***Agency*** Fund is established to account for assets received by a government in its capacity as an agent for individuals, businesses, or other governments.

In all trust or agency relationships the government acts in a **fiduciary** capacity. In other words, the government is managing assets that either belong to another agency or individual or must be handled in conformity with another agency's or individual's directions. The difference between trust and agency relationships is often one of degree. Trust Funds, for example, may be subject to complex administrative and financial provisions set forth in trust agreements, may be in existence for long periods of time, and may involve investment or other management of trust assets. Thus, Trust Fund management and accounting may be very complex. Agency Funds, on the other hand, are primarily clearance devices for cash collected for others, held briefly, and then disbursed to authorized recipients. The essential equation for Agency Funds is that assets equal liabilities.

The similarity of the relationships and of the duties imposed by them justify considering Trust and Agency Funds as one "fiduciary funds" category of funds. Enterprise trust and agency relationships (such as customer deposits) are accounted for in Enterprise Funds (Chapter 13) following the "funds within a fund" approach. Separate Trust or Agency Funds need **not** be established in such cases; all that is required is that the restricted asset and related liability accounts be distinctively titled as trust- or agency-related. Too, minor agency relationships of general government activities may be handled in the governmental funds, if desired, as long as appropriate accountability is maintained.

THE ACCOUNTABILITY FOCUS

The accountability focus in General Fund and Special Revenue Fund accounting is primarily on operating budget compliance during a specified fiscal year. In Capital Projects Fund accounting, attention is generally focused mainly on the project, rather than a specific year, and on the capital program or capital budget. The accountability focus in Trust and Agency Fund accounting, on the other hand, is on the manner in which the government fulfilled its fiduciary responsibilities during a specified period of time and on those unfilled responsibilities remaining at the end of the period.

The aim in Trust Fund accounting is therefore to ensure that the money or other resources are handled in accordance with the terms of the trust agreement and/or applicable trust laws. The accounting procedure for Agency Funds must ensure that collections are properly handled and are turned over promptly to those for whom they are collected. The net amount of resources in a Trust Fund is usually indicated in a Fund Balance account, though in some cases (see the Pension Trust Fund discussions following) different account titles may be used. The accounts of this type measure the *accountability* of the governmental unit as trustee for the use and disposition of the resources in its care. In the case of the Agency Fund the accountability concept is the liability concept, and even in the Trust Fund there is an obligation for the government to use Fund resources to discharge the assigned function. Failure to comply with trust terms would ordinarily be grounds for the forfeiture of Fund resources.

TRUST FUNDS

The GASB classifies Trust Funds as *expendable, nonexpendable,* and *pension.* In general they may also be classified as (1) proprietary or governmental, (2) internal or external, and (3) public or private.

Expendable Trust Funds are of a **governmental** nature. They are oriented to the inflow, outflow, and balances of resources much as are the General and Special Revenue Funds. In fact, Expendable Trust Funds operate very much like Special Revenue Funds. An example would be a trust fund established to account for the use of income from endowments for purposes specified by a donor.

Nonexpendable Trust Funds require preservation of fund principal and the determination of net income or a similar figure. They are operated and accounted for in essentially the same manner as commercial counterparts in the private sector of the economy and hence are **proprietary** in nature. An endowment fund whose principal must be kept intact (while its earnings may be available to support a specified governmental activity and thus be accounted for in an expendable fund) is a good example of a proprietary or nonexpendable fund, as is a loan fund whose principal and earnings must be kept intact.

Pension Trust Funds are established (1) to accept payments made by the government, its employees, or others to finance pensions; (2) to invest fund resources; and (3) to calculate and pay pensions to beneficiaries. In its investment activities the pension fund is similar to the nonexpendable fund, but in its pension payment activities it is like the expendable fund.

Some Trust Funds are established *internally* for administrative expediency, whereas others are set up pursuant to formal agreements (e.g., trust indentures) with *external* persons or groups.

Trust Funds may also be classified as *public* and *private.* A public Trust Fund is one whose principal, earnings, or both must be used for a public purpose. An example is a fund established to account for resources received by bequest that are to be used to provide health care for the indigent. A private Trust Fund is one that will ordinarily revert to private individuals or will be used for private purposes. A guaranty deposits fund is an example of a private Trust Fund. The **accounting** procedure is not **determined by** whether the Fund is public or private, however, but by **whether** it is **expendable or nonexpendable.**

An exhaustive treatment of trust law and accounting is beyond the scope of this text. Rather, the more usual types of Trust Funds found in state and local governments are briefly considered here and the fundamental accounting and reporting procedures applicable in typical situations are illustrated. Determination of appropriate systems and procedures in specific cases may require a search of the more technical accounting, legal, and insurance literature or the assistance of specialists within one or more of these fields.

The authoritative literature provides little specific guidance for Trust and Agency Funds (other than Pension Trust Funds) except to specify certain instances in which they should be used. This lack of specific guidance is probably because (1) Agency Funds have no "operations" and (2) Trust Funds other than Pension Trust Funds are essentially accounted for either (a) like governmental funds (Expendable Trust Funds) or (b) like proprietary funds (Nonexpendable Trust Funds).

Budgetary Considerations

Because of the differences in complexity and purpose of Trust Funds, some should be formally budgeted and controlled by budgetary control accounts and some should not. In many cases the government manages or transmits fund resources in accordance with specific instructions or customary trust practices and does not need a formal budget. If the operations of a nonexpendable (proprietary) fund are complex, a flexible (business-type) budget may be used. Further, since most expendable (governmental) funds are in essence Special Revenue Funds, their resources may properly be budgeted as part of the government's operating budget and be subjected to formal budgetary control. No major budgetary problems are posed by Trust Funds; therefore, their budgetary accounting is not illustrated.

Expendable Trust Funds

The most frequently encountered type of Expendable Trust Fund results from the government's agreement to accept resources and to spend them in ways specified by the donor. For example, assets may be donated to support the operations of a library or to provide food, shelter, or health care to the needy. These assets should be recorded in a separate fund, a budget for the fund should be approved (frequently as a part of the government's operating budget), and expenditures should be controlled and recorded. The operation of such a fund is **like** that of a **Special Revenue Fund,** and is illustrated briefly in the section on Endowment Funds.

Nonexpendable Trust Funds

There are **two types** of Nonexpendable Trust Funds: those in which neither the principal nor the earnings of the fund may be expended, and those in which earnings may be expended but principal must be kept intact. A loan fund is an example of the former type; examples of the latter type are some common forms of endowment funds. Where ***both*** expendable and nonexpendable aspects are involved (1) a careful distinction between trust principal (corpus) and income must be maintained, and (2) income determination procedures may be uniquely defined by the trust instrument or applicable laws. The same principles and distinctions apply as in trust accounting generally; that is, the creator or donor has the right to specify which items of revenue, expense, gain, or loss are to affect trust principal and which are deemed to relate to trust earnings. ***Where both expendable and nonexpendable trust aspects are involved, separate Expendable and Nonexpendable Trust Funds*** usually are ***established.***

Loan Funds

The following transactions and entries illustrate the operation of a loan fund.

Transactions and Entries

1. A cash donation of $100,000 was received for the purpose of establishing a loan fund.

   (1) Cash 100,000
         Fund Balance—Nonexpendable 100,000
       To record receipt of cash and establishment of loan
       fund.

2. Loans amounting to $60,000 were made.

   (2) Loans Receivable 60,000
         Cash 60,000
       To record loans made.

3. A loan of $1,000 was collected with interest of $20.

   (3) Cash 1,020
         Loans Receivable 1,000
         Interest Revenues 20
       To record collection of loan with interest.

4. Interest receivable was accrued at year end.

   (4) Interest Receivable 2,300
         Interest Revenues 2,300
       To record interest receivable accrued at year end.

5. Several loans and the related interest receivable were written off as uncollectible.

   (5) Uncollectible Accounts Expense 2,100
         Loans Receivable 1,800
         Interest Receivable 300
       To record write-off of uncollectible loans and interest
       receivable.

6. Earnings were closed.

   (6) Interest Revenues 2,320
         Uncollectible Accounts Expense 2,100
         Fund Balance—Nonexpendable 220
       To close interest revenues.

A Loan Fund balance sheet prepared after the preceding transactions had been posted would show cash and loans receivable as assets and contain a loan fund balance of $100,220. Only one fund balance amount would appear; there is no need to distinguish between the original capital and the $220 increase during the period because earnings increase the amount of Fund capital available for loans.

A question arises as to what would happen if the costs of administration were payable out of the Fund. In that case it would technically cease to be a nonexpendable fund, since administration expenses would reduce its balance. Provision is sometimes made, however, for meeting administration expenses out of earnings; and, in that case, administrative expenses might be deemed deductible in determining *net* earnings. Note also that though theoretically the loan fund illustrated previously is nonexpendable, in actual practice the fund balance may be reduced through uncollectible loans.

Endowment Funds

Some trusts are most easily accounted for by **establishing both** an **Expendable** (governmental type) Trust Fund and a **Nonexpendable** (proprietary type) Trust Fund. For example, an individual may donate money or other property with the stipulation that the income earned on those assets be used to finance certain activities. Since the donor intended the principal to be held intact and only the income expended, two funds may be established: (1) a **Nonexpendable** Trust Fund to account for the *principal* and (2) an *Expendable* Trust Fund to account for the *earnings*.[1]

A trust agreement of the type just described imposes problems that are the same as, and require the use of the same principles as, those of accounting for a trust that provides for payment of trust income to a life beneficiary with the principal payable to a remainderman at death of the beneficiary. As noted earlier, a discussion of the principles of trust accounting is beyond the scope of this book. Selected principles are illustrated in the following transactions and entries for an endowment fund.

Transactions and Entries

1. Cash of $210,000 was received to establish a fund whose income is to be used to grant scholarships.

    (1) Endowment Principal Fund

Cash	210,000	
Fund Balance—Nonexpendable		210,000

    To record receipt of cash for establishment of endowment fund.

2. Investments, par value $200,000, were purchased at a premium of $3,000 plus accrued interest of $400.

    (2) Endowment Principal Fund

Investments	200,000	
Unamortized Premiums on Investments	3,000	
Accrued Interest on Investments Purchased	400	
Cash		203,400

    To record purchase of investments.

3. A check for $3,000 was received in payment of interest on the investments, and premiums of $125 were amortized.

---

[1] Alternatively, a single Trust Fund having separate Fund Balance—Principal and Fund Balance—Earnings accounts may be established. In this case, the gains, losses, revenues, and expenses attributed to principal (corpus) are closed to the Fund Balance—Principal account; those entering into the determination of trust income and expenditures of earnings for their designated uses, are closed to Fund Balance—Earnings. Even under this accounting approach, however, the trust should be reported as if it were accounted for in two separate funds.

(3) **Endowment Principal Fund**

Cash	3,000	
Accrued Interest on Investments Purchased		400
Unamortized Premiums on Investments		125
Interest Revenues		2,475

To record collection of interest and amortization of
premiums on investments.

Note that, if desired, investment premiums and discounts may be amortized
only in the year-end adjustment process (or upon sale of the investments during the year) rather than at each interest due date.

4. Securities, par value of $3,000, to which unamortized premiums of $42 were
applicable, were sold for $3,055 plus accrued (previously unrecorded) interest
of $35.

(4) **Endowment Principal Fund**

Cash	3,090	
Investments		3,000
Unamortized Premiums on Investments		42
Interest Revenues		35
Gain on Sale of Investments		13

To record sale of investments at a gain of $13; also to
record interest income of $35.

5. Interest receivable, $2,600, was recorded and premiums of $120 were amortized.

(5) **Endowment Principal Fund**

Interest Receivable on Investments	2,600	
Interest Revenues		2,480
Unamortized Premiums on Investments		120

To record interest accrued on investments and related
premium amortization.

6. The total interest earnings to date were recorded as a liability of the Endowment Principal Fund to the Endowment Earnings Fund.

(6) **(a) Endowment Principal Fund**

Operating Transfer to Endowment Earnings Fund	4,990	
Due to Endowment Earnings Fund		4,990

To record transfer of endowment earnings to date.

(6) **(b) Endowment Earnings Fund**

Due from Endowment Principal Fund	4,990	
Operating Transfer from Endowment Principal		
Fund		4,990

To record amount due from endowment principal fund
for earnings to date.

7. A $2,500 payment was made from the Endowment Principal Fund to the En-
dowment Earnings Fund.

(7) **(a) Endowment Principal Fund**

Due to Endowment Earnings Fund	2,500	
Cash		2,500

To record payment of part of total amount due to
endowment earnings fund.

(7) (b) Endowment Earnings Fund
Cash   2,500
    Due from Endowment Principal Fund   2,500
To record receipt of part of total amount due from
    endowment principal fund.

8. A $2,000 scholarship grant was made from the Endowment Earnings Fund. (Note: This is an outright grant, not a loan.)

(8) Endowment Earnings Fund
Expenditures—Scholarship Grant   2,000
    Cash   2,000
To record payment of scholarship.

9. Closing entries were prepared for both Funds.

(9) (a) Endowment Principal Fund
Interest Revenues   4,990
Gain on Sale of Investments   13
    Operating Transfer to Endowment Earnings Fund . .   4,990
    Fund Balance—Nonexpendable   13
To close accounts.

The Gain on Sale of Investments is added to the fund balance of the Endowment Principal Fund either because it resulted from sale of investments of the original corpus of the trust or because the trust agreement specifies that gains and losses affect the trust principal and are not expendable. If the trust agreement or applicable laws specify that gains and losses are part of the expendable income from a trust, the net gains or losses affect the amount transferred to the Expendable Trust Fund instead of affecting the fund balance of the Nonexpendable (Principal) Trust Fund.

(9) (b) Endowment Earnings Fund
Operating Transfer from Endowment Principal Fund . .   4,990
    Expenditures—Scholarship Grant   2,000
    Unreserved Fund Balance   2,990
To close accounts.

After the preceding entries are posted to the accounts, the Endowment Fund Balance Sheets in Figures 11-1 and 11-2 may be prepared. Additionally, (1) a statement of revenues, **expenditures,** and changes in fund balance should be prepared for the Endowment Earnings Fund and (2) both a statement of revenues, **expenses,** and changes in fund balance and a statement of cash flows should be prepared for the Endowment Principal Fund.

If endowments are in the form of fixed assets, these constitute the principal fund and the net income therefrom is transferred to an expendable fund. Both the revenues and the expenses of administering the property—for example, depreciation, rents, repairs, decorating expenses, and janitor's wages—would be accounted for in the principal fund. The net earnings would be transferred to the earnings fund and expended for the purpose designated—for example, granting scholarships.

It is important, in such cases, to account carefully for the revenues and expenses of the principal fund so that the income may be properly computed. Too, **whether income before or after depreciation is expendable will depend** on the provisions of the trust document or the implied intent of the donor. If the grant

Figure 11-1

NONEXPENDABLE TRUST FUND BALANCE SHEET

A Governmental Unit
Endowment Principal Trust Fund
Balance Sheet
At End of Fiscal Year

Assets

Cash		$ 10,190
Investments	$197,000	
Unamortized premiums on investments	2,713	199,713
Interest receivable on investments		2,600
		$212,503

Liabilities and Fund Balance

Due to Endowment Earnings Fund	$ 2,490
Fund balance—Nonexpendable	210,013
	$212,503

Figure 11-2

EXPENDABLE TRUST FUND BALANCE SHEET

A Governmental Unit
Endowment Earnings Trust Fund
Balance Sheet
At End of Fiscal Year

Assets

Cash	$ 500
Due from Endowment Principal Fund	2,490
	$2,990

Fund Balance

Unreserved fund balance	$2,990

contemplates the replacement of worn-out property, only income after depreciation should be expended in order to preserve the principal intact. On the other hand, if the property is not to be replaced, depreciation might not be deducted in determining the amount of trust income that is expendable. If the trust instrument is silent as to depreciation of fixed assets held in trust, and the donor's intent in this regard is unclear, state statutes control. If there are no relevant state statutes, the **general rule** is that depreciation or amortization of those assets comprising the *original* trust *principal* is charged against (closed to) trust *principal*—as are gains and losses on sales of investments present when the trust was established—and does not reduce the expendable income. On the other hand, the depreciation or amortization related to assets acquired by the trustee with other trust assets is charged to *earnings,* and thus reduces the amount of expendable income. Some authorities feel that this question has not been conclusively settled, however, and that the trend now appears to be toward charging depreciation in determining trust earnings. Obviously, accounting for such items as depreciation and investment gains and losses should be covered in the trust instrument. Competent legal advice should be sought whenever such questions are not explicitly treated in that document.

Agency Funds are conduit or clearinghouse funds established to account for assets (usually cash) received for and paid to other funds, individuals, or organizations. The assets thus received are usually held only briefly; investment or other fiscal management complexities are rarely involved, except in situations such as that of the Tax Agency and Special Assessment Agency Funds illustrated later in this chapter.

The GASB Codification requires an Agency Fund to be used to account for and report the assets of certain deferred compensation plans (GASB Codification, sec. D25). Too, as noted in Chapter 8, "Debt Service Funds," the Codification requires use of an Agency Fund to account for and report the debt service transactions for projects financed with special assessment debt for which the government is **not** obligated in any manner (GASB Codification, sec. S40).

However, not all agency relationships arising in the conduct of a government's business require an Agency Fund to be established. For example, payroll deductions for such items as insurance premiums and income tax withholdings create agency responsibilities that may often be accounted for (as liabilities) in the fund through which the payroll is paid. On the other hand, where payrolls are paid from several funds it may be more convenient to pay withheld amounts to an Agency Fund in order that a single check and remittance report may be forwarded to the recipient. **As a general rule,** Agency Funds should be used whenever (1) the volume of agency transactions, the magnitude of the sums involved, and/or the management and accounting capabilities of government personnel make it either unwieldy or unwise to account for agency responsibilities through other funds, or (2) financial management or accounting for interfund transactions or relationships is expedited through their use.

Simpler Agency Funds

Though agency relationships are commonly viewed as arising between the government and individuals or organizations external to it, recall that each fund of the government is a distinct fiscal and accounting entity. **Intragovernmental Agency Funds** may prove useful in (1) alleviating some of the awkwardness occasioned by the use of numerous fund accounting entities in governments, and (2) establishing clear-cut audit trails where a single transaction affects several funds. Thus, though a special imprest[2] bank account will often suffice, some governments establish an Agency Fund where (1) receipts must be allocated among several funds or (2) a single expenditure is financed through several funds. In the former case, a single check may be deposited in an Agency Fund and separate checks payable to the various funds drawn against it; in the latter, checks drawn against several funds are placed in an Agency Fund and a single check drawn against it in payment for the total expenditure. Judgment should be exercised in deciding whether an Agency Fund is useful in such cases; a special **imprest checking account** may serve the government's needs adequately without necessitating the additional record keeping occasioned by the establishment of an Agency Fund.

---

[2] An imprest bank account is one to which deposits are made periodically in an amount equal to the sum of the checks written thereon: when all checks written have cleared, the bank account balance will equal a predetermined amount, often zero. Imprest bank accounts are often used to enhance cash control and/or to facilitate bank-book reconciliations.

The GASB Codification notes three other situations where Agency Funds may be employed:

1. Where a government receives **"pass-through" grants**—grants that the recipient government must transfer to, or spend on behalf of, **another** governmental unit—it should *record the receipt and disbursement of the "pass-through" grant in an Agency Fund rather than as revenues and expenditures.*

2. Where a government receives a *grant, entitlement, or shared revenue that may be used, at its discretion, for programs or projects financed through more than one fund,* the resources should initially be accounted for in an Agency Fund. When decisions have been made as to which programs or projects —financed by which governmental and/or proprietary funds—the resources will be allocated to, the resources are removed from the Agency Fund and recorded in the governmental and/or proprietary fund(s). There they will be accounted for as revenues and as expenditures or expenses at the appropriate time.

3. When a *grant, entitlement, or shared revenue must be accounted for in a prescribed way that differs from GAAP for purposes of reporting to the grantor* government, the resources may be initially accounted for in an Agency Fund. The transactions are accounted for in the Agency Fund using *"memoranda" accounts* that accumulate data for the prescribed special purpose reports but are *not reported in the GAAP financial statements,* then are accounted for in the fund(s) financed as revenues or contributed capital and as expenditures or expenses, as appropriate, in conformity with GAAP.[3]

Whether the agency relationship is external or internal, the accounting in situations discussed thus far is not complicated. All that is required is that **Agency Fund** entries such as the following be prepared upon receipt and disbursement of cash or other assets:

Cash (or other assets)	100,000	
Due to Individual (or fund or organization)		100,000
To record receipt of assets.		
Due to Individual (or fund or organization).	100,000	
Cash (or other assets)		100,000
To record payment of assets.		

Note that *all Agency Fund assets are owed* to some person, fund, or organization. The *government has no equity* in the Agency Fund's assets.

Deferred Compensation Agency Funds

As mentioned earlier, governments must report certain deferred compensation plans in Agency Funds. The GASB Codification requires this treatment for plans that meet the requirements of Internal Revenue Code (IRC) Section 457. This code section permits state and local government employees to defer federal income taxes on a portion of their salaries by contributing to a deferred compensation plan. For contributions to a deferred compensation plan to qualify for this tax deferral, the assets of the plan must, from a strict legal perspective, remain **solely the property** and rights **of the** state or local **government** and the plan participants' claims to the plan assets are the same as the state's general creditors. This condition applies to all assets of the plan, whether from contributions, earnings, or any other sources. Under this section, (1) the assets of the plan **cannot** be restricted for the payment of plan benefits, but must be legally available to the government

---

[3] GASB Codification, sec. G60.106–108.

for unrestricted use, and (2) the employees participating in the plan have no greater security interest in the plan assets than any other general creditor of the government (which means that amounts contributed to the plan by employees could be used to satisfy claims of the government's creditors).[4]

While the assets of an IRC Section 457 plan legally belong to the governmental unit, the government has a fiduciary responsibility to the employees because, as the GASB points out, the employees have earned the amounts contributed to the plan and the governmental unit is contractually obligated to pay them. Thus, accounting and reporting for IRC Section 457 plans should recognize that in substance the government does have an obligation to the plan participants. Indeed, the **plan assets** are, **in substance,** the **employees' assets.** In the typical deferred compensation plan, the government's liability is limited to the market value of the plan assets, however, and the employees, not the government, assume the risk of loss resulting from decreases in the market value of the plan assets. Further, the reporting depends on whether (1) the plan is funded or unfunded, (2) the employer (salary-paying) fund is a governmental fund or a proprietary fund, and (3) plan assets have been used for nonplan purposes, that is, for purposes other than paying plan benefits. In all cases the **gross** salaries should be recorded as expenditures or expenses, as appropriate, in the salary-paying fund and any unfunded amounts should be recorded as liabilities of that fund.

Funded Plans

In **funded** plans—which are the most common type—the withholdings from employee's salaries are contributed to a plan for management and investment purposes. In such plans, the benefits to be paid often depend on the contributions made by an employee and the related plan earnings—that is, no specified benefit or interest rate is guaranteed. Whether the government itself or some other governmental or non-governmental entity administers the plan does not impact the government's reporting. Thus, the fact that governments often participate in multijurisdictional plans administered by a state Public Employee Retirement System or by nongovernmental entities, such as banks and insurance companies, does not affect the accounting and reporting (except for the governmental unit administering a multiemployer plan). The most significant factor affecting reporting is whether the employer funds are governmental or proprietary funds.

Employers Using Governmental Fund Accounting. IRC Section 457 plans that are **funded** should be reported in **Agency Funds** if they apply to **governmental fund** employees **or** to **both governmental fund and proprietary fund employees.** The government should report:

1. The assets to which it has legal access (i.e., the sum of its employees' claims to plan assets) as Agency Funds assets; and
2. A corresponding Agency Fund liability to employees for deferred compensation and related earnings.

If no specified benefit is guaranteed under the plan, the assets and the corresponding liability should be reported at the **market value** of the plan assets. If a certain benefit is specified or some other method is used to determine the benefits payable under the plan, that method should be used to value the plan assets and liability, assuming the plan is fully funded.

---

[4] GASB Codification, sec. D25.102.

Since deferred compensation plans often are administered by others, accounting for funded plans is typically uninvolved. Assume, for instance, that withholdings from employees that are paid to a statewide deferred compensation plan totaled $1,000,000 and that the fair value of the plan assets to which the government has legal access was $18,300,000 at the beginning of the year and $19,800,000 at the end of the year. The $1,000,000 would have been recorded as expenditures or expenses, as appropriate, in the salary-paying fund(s). Thus, the only entry needed in the Deferred Compensation Agency Fund during the year would be to adjust the **Agency Fund** assets and liabilities to their year end market value as follows:

Equity in State Deferred Compensation Plan Assets	1,500,000	
Liability to Employees for Deferred Compensation and Related Earnings		1,500,000

To adjust assets and liabilities to market value (or obligation determined per other method if appropriate) at year end.

If a government administers its own plan, it must account for contributions to the plan and payments from the plan and also maintain appropriate subsidiary records to account for amounts payable to individual employees.

If a **plan** is **partially funded,** (1) a liability for the unfunded amount should be reported in the employer fund, and (2) a corresponding receivable from the employer fund should be reported in the Deferred Compensation Agency Fund. If this liability results from nonpayment of required employer fund contributions to the plan—rather than from nonpayment of employee withholdings—expenditures (or expenses if a proprietary fund) should be recognized as well.

Employers Using Proprietary Fund Accounting. If employees of proprietary funds participate in the same funded IRC Section 457 plan as do governmental fund employees, the assets and related liabilities should be accounted for in an Agency Fund as described previously. However, if a government's proprietary fund employees have a **separate** plan, the assets and the corresponding liability (as described earlier) should be reported in the **proprietary fund balance sheet, not in an Agency Fund.**

Unfunded Plans

Unfunded plans are plans where the withholdings for the plan are retained in the employer fund (and probably used for its purposes) rather than being contributed to a separate plan entity, such as a bank or an insurance company trust. The GASB notes that such unfunded plans typically require specific amounts of benefits to be paid in the future—for example, the deferred amount of salary plus interest accrued at a specified rate. Agency Funds should **not** be used to account for such plans. Rather, **a liability for unfunded deferred compensation plans should be reported in the employer fund(s).** No portion of the liability is reported as general long-term debt.

Other Matters

Several other GASB requirements with respect to IRC Section 457 plans should be noted:

- A government that administers **multijurisdictional plans** should report all assets of the plan in an Agency Fund, but disclose the portion to which it has legal access.

- The **notes** should **disclose** any **nonplan use** of plan assets.

- The government also should **disclose** its responsibilities under the plan and the legal and contractual features of the plan agreement, including the conditions required by IRC Section 457 and a statement of its fiduciary responsibilities under the plan.

- A government's employees may participate in other deferred compensation plans that do not meet the IRC Section 457 conditions. This guidance does **not** apply to those entities since the assets of those plans are not considered solely the property of the government.

Tax Agency Funds

The Agency Funds cited in the preceding examples require little management action or expertise except where a government administers its own deferred compensation plan. Other Agency Funds, such as the Tax Agency Fund illustrated later, may involve significant management responsibilities and more complex accounting procedures.

In order to avoid duplication of assessment and collection effort and to enforce tax laws as equitably and economically as possible, all taxes levied upon properties within a state, county, or other geographic area may be billed and collected by one of the governments. That unit therefore becomes an agent for the other taxing units and establishes an Agency Fund such as the Tax Agency Fund described later. In the usual case, the several taxing bodies (e.g., the state, county, school districts) certify the amounts or rates at which taxes are to be levied for them by the designated government. The latter then levies the total tax, including its own, against specific properties and proceeds to collect the tax. In addition, it normally makes pro rata payments of collections to the various taxing bodies during the year, often quarterly, and charges a collection or service fee to the other units.

The following example illustrates the general approach to Tax Agency Fund accounting. Though not illustrated here, detailed records of levies and collections relative to each property taxed, by year of levy, are required.[5] **Collections** pertaining to each year's levy are **distributed** among the taxing bodies **in the ratio of each unit's levy to** the **total levy** of **that year.**

To illustrate Tax Agency Fund accounting, assume that **City A** serves as the **property tax collecting agent** for several governmental units. The city charges the other units a collection fee equal to 2 percent of the taxes collected for those units. City A's levies and those certified by the other units for 19X2 and 19X3 are as follows:

	19X3		19X2	
	Amount Levied	Percentage of Total	Amount Levied	Percentage of Total
City A*	$100,000	25.0	$ 91,200	24.0
School District B	200,000	50.0	188,100	49.5
Park District X	50,000	12.5	49,400	13.0
Sanitary District Y	50,000	12.5	51,300	13.5
	$400,000	100.0	$380,000	100.0

* Although these taxes are the taxes of the collecting governmental unit, they are treated in the same manner as if they were being collected for it by another unit.

[5] These records are discussed and illustrated in Chapter 5.

The Tax Agency Fund trial balance at December 31, 19X2 consists of $75,000 of Taxes Receivable for Taxing Units and Due to Taxing Units, $75,000. These amounts arose entirely from the 19X2 levy. Transactions and entries illustrated for the General Fund of City A are similar to those of the other recipient governmental units.

Transactions and Entries

1. The 19X3 levies are placed on the tax roll and recorded on the books.

(1)(a) Tax Agency Fund

Taxes Receivable for Taxing Units	400,000	
Due to Taxing Units		400,000

To record 19X3 taxes placed on the tax roll.

Due to Taxing Units Ledger **(Uncollected)**:

City of A	100,000
School District B	200,000
Park District X	50,000
Sanitary District Y	50,000
	400,000

(1)(b) General Fund

Taxes Receivable—Current	100,000	
Allowance for Uncollectible Current Taxes		1,000
Revenues		99,000

To record the 19X3 tax levy.

Revenues Ledger (Revenues):

Taxes	99,000

Taxes Receivable for Taxing Units may be classified into two accounts, Current and Delinquent, if desired. The distinction would be apparent in the subsidiary records, however, since (1) taxes are levied by year, and (2) a separate ledger account or column would be provided for each year's levy against each property. Appropriate subsidiary records for Taxes Receivable for Taxing Units by taxpayer would be maintained.

2. Collections of interest and penalties (not previously accrued in the Agency Fund) of $15,000 and taxes of $300,000 are received. Collections should be identified by type, year, and governmental unit so that distributions may be made in accordance with the original levies. (This detail is not provided here, so **assume the following amounts are correct.**)

(2) Tax Agency Fund

Cash	315,000	
Taxes Receivable for Taxing Units		300,000
Due to Taxing Units		15,000

To record collections of taxes and interest and penalties.

Due to Taxing Units Ledger (Uncollected):

City of A	74,250
School District B	149,625
Park District X	37,875
Sanitary District Y	38,250
	300,000

Due to Taxing Units Ledger **(Tax Collections)**:

City of A	77,850
School District B	157,050
Park District X	39,825
Sanitary District Y	40,275
	315,000

Note that the balances in the **"Tax Collections"** subsidiary ledger accounts are currently payable to the taxing units, whereas the **"Uncollected"** balances reflect amounts not yet payable to the taxing units since these amounts have not been collected.

3. The collections (transaction 2) are paid from the Tax Agency Fund to the respective governmental units, except for a 2% collection charge levied upon the *other* governments.

(3) Tax Agency Fund

Due to Taxing Units	315,000	
Cash		310,257
Due to General Fund		4,743

To record payment of amounts collected, with the retention of a 2% collection charge for taxes collected for *other* governmental units.

Due to Taxing Units Ledger (Tax Collections):

City of A.	77,850
School District B	157,050
Park District X	39,825
Sanitary District Y	40,275
	315,000

(3)(a) General Fund

Cash	77,850	
Taxes Receivable—Current.		56,250
Taxes Receivable—Delinquent		18,000
Interest and Penalties Receivable on Taxes		3,600

To record receipt of collections of taxes and interest and penalties from Tax Agency Fund.

Note that revenues for interest and penalties would be recognized in this entry if not previously accrued.

(3)(b) General Fund

Due from Tax Agency Fund	4,743	
Revenues		4,743

To record revenues charged for tax services rendered to other governmental units.

Revenues Ledger (Revenues):

Tax Collection Fees	4,743

The collection fee and the amounts paid to the other governments were calculated as follows:

	Collections	*2% Collection Fee*	*Net*
City of A	$ 77,850	—	$ 77,850
School District B	157,050	$3,141	153,909
Park District X	39,825	796	39,029
Sanitary District Y	40,275	806	39,469
	$315,000	$4,743	$310,257

The preparation of the tax roll, the accounting for taxes, and handling the collections involve considerable costs, and the collecting unit usually charges for these services. The charges are legitimate financial expenditures of the various

Figure 11-3

AGENCY FUND BALANCE SHEET

City A
Tax Agency Fund
Balance Sheet
December 31, 19X3

Assets

Cash	$ 4,743
Taxes receivable for taxing units	175,000
	$179,743

Liabilities

Due to General Fund	$ 4,743
Due to taxing units (for uncollected taxes)	175,000
	$179,743

units for which taxes are collected and are provided for in their budgets. The usual practice, illustrated earlier, is for the collecting unit to retain a portion of the taxes and interest and penalties collected rather than to go through the process of billing the charges to the several governmental units. To illustrate the procedure further, the journal entry which **School District B** would make to record receipt of cash from the Tax Agency Fund **(preceding transaction 3)** follows:

(3) School District B—General Fund

Cash	153,909	
Expenditures	3,141	
Taxes Receivable—Current		112,500
Taxes Receivable—Delinquent		37,125
Interest and Penalties Receivable on Taxes		7,425

To record receipt of amounts collected by City A less collection
  charge of 2 percent.

Expenditures Ledger (Expenditures):

Tax Collection Fees	3,141

Note again that revenues from interest and penalties would be recognized in this entry if they had not been accrued previously.

The Balance Sheet of the Tax Agency Fund of City A after the preceding transactions have been recorded is presented in Figure 11-3.

A Statement of Changes in Assets and Liabilities for the Tax Agency Fund is presented in Figure 11-4. Note that this statement does not report "operating results"—since Agency Funds have no "operations"—but simply reports, in summary form, the changes in each of the Fund's assets and liabilities.

Special Assessment Debt Service Agency Funds

As discussed in Chapters 7 and 8, most special assessment projects—and any related debt and debt service—are accounted for and reported in a manner similar to other capital projects, long-term debt, and related debt service. A significant exception to this occurs when a special assessment capital improvement is financed by issuing special assessment debt for which the ***government is* <u>not</u> *obligated in* <u>any</u> *manner.* In such situations, the GASB concluded that the **debt** should **not** be

Figure 11-4   **AGENCY FUND STATEMENT OF CHANGES IN ASSETS AND LIABILITIES**

City A
Tax Agency Fund
Statement of Changes in Assets and Liabilities
For the Year Ended December 31, 19X3

	Balances, January 1, 19X3	Additions	Deductions	Balances, December 31, 19X3
Assets				
Cash		$315,000	$310,257	$ 4,743
Taxes receivable for taxing units	$75,000	400,000	300,000	175,000
Total assets	$75,000	$715,000	$610,257	$179,743
Liabilities				
Due to General Fund		$ 4,743		$ 4,743
Due to taxing units for uncollected taxes	$75,000	415,000	$315,000	175,000
Total liabilities	$75,000	$419,743	$315,000	$179,743

reported in the government's financial statements since the government is merely acting as an **agent** for the property owners and would not honor the debt if default occurred.

Recall that in these cases the construction or acquisition of the fixed assets is **reported in** a **Capital Projects Fund** (or Enterprise Fund, if appropriate) since the government is acquiring a fixed asset. Further, the proceeds from the special assessment debt should be distinguished from "bond proceeds" since the government is not incurring debt. (The GASB suggests a title such as "Contributions from Property Owners.") Likewise, the **fixed assets** constructed or acquired will be **reported in** the **General Fixed Assets Account Group** (**or an Enterprise Fund** if for Enterprise Fund use).

Although the debt for which the government is **not** obligated in any manner is **not** reported as government debt, the government usually acts as a debt service **agent** for the special assessment district, and, in this capacity, (1) **collects** the special assessments levied for the project, and (2) **pays** the debt service costs **for the property owners** with collections of these receivables (and perhaps, any remaining construction phase assets). The government has a fiduciary responsibility to collect the special assessments and to remit the collections to the bondholders when debt service payments come due. Again, however, if collections are insufficient to cover required debt service payments, the government is **not** obligated to pay the difference and does not intend to do so. Thus, the government is acting purely in an **agency capacity** with respect to the debt service transactions, and the GASB requires these transactions to be accounted for in an Agency Fund.

To illustrate a **Special Assessment Agency Fund,** assume that Norwood Village approves a project in 19X1 to construct sidewalks in a subdivision. The project will be financed by issuing—upon completion of the project—ten-year, 6% notes for $1,000,000. The government is **not** obligated in any manner for payment of the debt or related interest, both of which are to be repaid from special assessments to be levied against the properties upon completion of construction and the related interest of 6% annually on unpaid balances. One tenth of the notes are payable at the end of each year, beginning one year after issuance.

1. Expenditures incurred to complete the sidewalks during the year totaled $1,000,000.

   (1) (a) Capital Projects Fund:
   Expenditures—Capital Outlay 1,000,000
      Vouchers Payable   1,000,000
   To record expenditures for sidewalk construction.

   (1) (b) General Fixed Assets Account Group:
   Improvements Other Than Buildings. 1,000,000
      Investment in General Fixed Assets—Special
        Assessments.   1,000,000
   To record cost of sidewalks constructed.

2. The notes were issued at par at the end of 19X1.

   (2) Capital Projects Fund:
   Cash. 1,000,000
      Other Financing Sources—Contributions from
        Property Owners   1,000,000
   To record issuance of special assessment debt for which
     the government is **not** obligated in any manner.

   Note that (1) the **note proceeds** are **not** recorded as debt proceeds but as Contributions from Property Owners, and (2) the **debt is not recorded** by the governmental unit.

3. Special assessments of $1,000,000 are levied at the end of 19X1. One tenth of the principal plus 6% interest on the uncollected assessments are due each year, one month before the notes are due. Collections are invested at 6% interest.

   (3) Agency Fund:
   Assessments Receivable—Current 100,000
   Assessments Receivable—Deferred 900,000
      Due to Special Assessment Note Creditors   1,000,000
   To record levy of special assessments.

4. The accounts are closed at the end of 19X1.

   (4) Capital Projects Fund:
   Other Financing Sources—Contributions from Property
      Owners. 1,000,000
      Expenditures—Capital Outlay   1,000,000
   To close the accounts.

5. Special assessment collections during 19X2 totaled $160,000, of which $60,000 was for interest.

   (5) Agency Fund:
   Cash 160,000
      Assessments Receivable—Current.   100,000
      Due to Special Assessment Note Creditors   60,000
   To record collections of current assessments and interest.

6. The first installment of the note was paid at the end of 19X2.

   (6) Agency Fund:
   Due to Special Assessment Note Creditors 160,000
      Cash   160,000
   To record payment of scheduled debt service on special
     assessment note.

7. The appropriate portion of assessments receivable was reclassified as current at the end of 19X2.

(7) Agency Fund:
Assessments Receivable—Current.   100,000
    Assessments Receivable—Deferred   100,000
To reclassify deferred assessments as current.

The 19X2 Balance Sheet for this Special Assessment Agency Fund would report the assessments receivable as assets and the (equal) liability for amounts due to the project creditors.

   In the preceding example, Norwood Village paid for the sidewalk construction from one of its Capital Projects Funds, which was reimbursed when the notes were issued. Alternatively, the notes might have been issued at the start of the project and all cash receipts and disbursements might have been recorded in the Special Assessment Agency Fund. Note that only the first two preceding entries would differ in this case:

1. The notes were issued at par at the beginning of 19X1.

(1) Special Assessment Agency Fund
Cash.   1,000,000
    Due to Special Assessment Note Creditors   1,000,000
To record issuance of notes for cash to finance sidewalk
    special assessment project construction.

2. Expenditures of $1,000,000 for sidewalk construction were paid.

(2) (a) Special Assessment Agency Fund
Due to Special Assessment Note Creditors   1,000,000
    Cash.   1,000,000
To record payment of SA project expenditures.

(2) (b) Capital Projects Fund (or General Fund)
Expenditures—Capital Outlay.   1,000,000
    Other Financing Sources—Contributions from
        Property Owners.   1,000,000
To record expenditure for general fixed assets financed
    by special assessments.

Note: This records the **substance** of the events—as if the Village had levied the assessments and constructed the sidewalks.

(2) (c) General Fixed Assets Account Group
Improvements Other than Buildings   1,000,000
    Investment in General Fixed Assets—Special
        Assessments.   1,000,000
To record cost of sidewalks constructed.

   Entries 3–7 are the same as those illustrated previously.

PENSION TRUST FUNDS

Public employee retirement systems (PERS) provide examples of more complex Pension Trust Funds (PTFs) common to governments. These funds are likely to be the largest Trust Funds of many governments. They are growing rapidly, the cost to the government of contributions to them is significant, and their ability to pay pensions on schedule is of vital importance to individual retirees and to the morale of the work force.

Many types of retirement plans are in existence in governments. Local governments often have retirement systems, though in some states employees of all governmental units of a certain type (e.g., municipalities) or all employees within certain functional fields (e.g., teachers, police, fire fighters) are included in a statewide retirement system. In some cases these plans are integrated with federal social security benefits: in others, employees are not covered under that program. The administrative mechanisms established also differ widely. In some instances the retirement system is managed and accounted for by the finance department or some other executive agency of the government. In other cases an independent board, or even a separate corporation, is charged with retirement system management and accountability.

PERS can also be classified according to whether they are for (1) the employees of only one unit of government, **single-employer PERS,** or (2) the employees of more than one employer government, **multiple-employer PERS.** The GASB further categorizes **multiple-employer PERS** in terms of the extent to which the interests and risks of the various employer governments are integrated:

> Some multiple-employer PERS are aggregations of single-employer PERS, with pooled administrative and investment functions; that is, the PERS acts as a common investment and administrative *agent* for each employer. These PERS are referred to as **agent PERS.** . . . **Each entity participating** in an **agent** PERS receives a **separate actuarial valuation** to determine its required periodic contribution. . . .
>
> Other multiple-employer PERS are essentially one large pension plan with *cost-sharing arrangements;* that is, **all risks and costs,** including benefits costs, are **shared proportionately** by the participating entities. **One actuarial valuation** is performed for the PERS as a whole, and the same contribution rate applies to each participating entity. These PERS are referred to as **"cost-sharing"** PERS. . . .[6]

Of far more consequence to sound public finance policy and to the public interest generally is the disparate array of financial management practices relating to retirement systems. PERS are not subject to the Federal ERISA (Employee Retirement Income Security Act) regulations on vesting, funding, and the like, though various PERISA (Public Employee Retirement Income Security Act) and similar bills have been proposed in Congress in recent years. Some governments are on a *pay-as-you-go* basis—pension payments are paid from current revenues. In such cases pensioners are dependent on the flow of revenues and other demands for appropriations and thus on the uncertainties of the budget process. At the other extreme are those governments whose retirement systems are **fully funded** and **actuarially sound.** Most governments fall between these extremes. Perhaps the system is properly designed from an actuarial point of view but the government has fallen behind in payments. Or perhaps benefits have been raised as a result of increased salary levels or for other reasons.

In considering accounting and reporting for PERS and PTFs, it is useful to **distinguish between** accounting and reporting (1) for the *PERS* or **Pension Trust Fund and** (2) for the pension costs and liabilities of *employer* funds and the account groups of the employer government(s). It is also useful to distinguish between (1) **reporting** in the financial statements, per se, **and** (2) **disclosures** required in the notes to the financial statements or as supplementary information. All of these areas are under study by the GASB; therefore, new guidance is expected to be forthcoming over the next few years. Accounting and reporting for PERS are the primary focus of the discussion of pensions in this chapter, though

---

[6] GASB Codification, sec. Pe6.109–110. (Emphasis added.)

accounting and reporting requirements for the employer governments are outlined briefly. Too, the discussion here assumes that the pension plans are **defined benefit plans,** in which the amounts of benefits to be paid under the plan are specified, rather than **defined contribution plans,** which specify a level of contributions to be made but do not guarantee a specific level of benefits.

Accounting Standards

Prior to the formation of the GASB, three alternative approaches to accounting, reporting, and disclosures for **defined benefit PERS** of state and local governments had gained some level of authoritative support. The traditional approach to accounting and reporting for PERS was set forth in GAAFR (68); and National Council on Governmental Accounting (NCGA) *Statement 1,* though it classified **Pension Trust Funds** as proprietary rather than governmental in nature, permitted the traditional approach to be used. The most significant change was that charges reported as expenditures under GAAFR (68) were reported as expenses under NCGA *Statement 1.* Also, fixed assets used in administering a plan could be recorded in the Pension Trust Fund and depreciated.

A second approach was set forth in FASB *Statement No. 35,* "Accounting and Reporting by Defined Benefit Plans,"[7] which included plans of state and local governments.[8] But the NCGA did not agree with all of the provisions of FASB *Statement No. 35,* as applied to governments, and developed a third approach which it set forth in NCGA *Statement 6,* "Pension Accounting and Financial Reporting: Public Employee Retirement Systems and State and Local Government Employer Entities."[9] Since significant conflicts existed between the FASB *Statement No. 35* requirements and those in NCGA *Statement 6,* the NCGA and FASB **mutually deferred** the effective dates of their pension pronouncements for state and local governments **indefinitely** in November 1983.[10] Thus, the issue was left for the GASB to settle.

As noted earlier, the GASB is in the process of developing new guidance on reporting pension plans. The GASB Codification recognizes the NCGA *Statement 6,* FASB *Statement No. 35,* and NCGA *Statement 1* approaches as acceptable alternatives for PERS accounting and reporting until the Board completes its study of the issue.[11] The Board divided its pension project into two parts: one to consider pension ***disclosure*** requirements and another more extensive project to consider pension ***accounting and reporting,*** including recognition, measurement, and display.

The **pension disclosure** project was completed in 1986 with the issuance of GASB *Statement No. 5,* "Disclosure of Pension Information by Public Employee Retirement Systems and State and Local Government Employers."[12] This statement does ***not*** affect the **accounting** for pension plans **or the reporting** of those plans in the financial statements. Rather, it requires extensive footnote disclosures for PERS and employer governments as well as ten-year trend data presentations for PERS. The GASB *Statement No. 5* disclosures are required—**in lieu of**

---

[7] FASB, *Statement of Financial Accounting Standards No. 35,* "Accounting and Reporting by Defined Benefit Plans" (Stamford, Conn.: FASB, 1980).

[8] Ibid., p. 2.

[9] GASB Codification, sec. Pe5.

[10] FASB, *Statement of Financial Accounting Standards No. 75,* "Deferral of the Effective Date of Certain Accounting Requirements for Pension Plans of State and Local Governmental Units: An Amendment of FASB Statement No. 35" (Stamford, Conn.: FASB, November 1983), and NCGA, *Interpretation 8,* "Certain Pension Matters" (Chicago, NCGA, November 1983).

[11] GASB Codification, sec. Pe5.102.

[12] Ibid., sec. Pe6.

other disclosures—when a PERS is reported under the NCGA *Statement 1* or *Statement 6* approach. However, the GASB *Statement No. 5* disclosures are required **in addition to** the FASB *Statement No. 35* disclosures when the FASB *Statement No. 35* approach is used; and the differences between the data reported in the GASB *Statement No. 5* and FASB *Statement No. 35* disclosures must be explained.

The Traditional (NCGA S*tatement* 1) Approach

Regardless of the external **reporting** approach eventually required by the GASB, most PERS will continue to **account** for their assets and transactions under some variation of the traditional PERS accounting approach. This is because Pension Trust Funds are—first and foremost—trust accounting entities. Thus, they must continually account for (1) the inflows, outflows, and balances of fund financial resources and (2) the claims against such balances—both by category of participants and by individual.

The NCGA determined in *Statement 1* that Pension Trust Funds should be classified as proprietary rather than governmental (this despite the payments that such funds make to deceased, resigned, and retired employees and to their survivors). The accrual basis is used in accounting for their revenues and expenses, and net income is computed. Further, Pension Trust Funds and Nonexpendable Trust Funds are grouped in combining and combined statements.

Under this **traditional approach**—the NCGA *Statement 1* approach permitted by the GASB Codification—the **actuarial present value of benefits payable** under the plan is **presented only in summary fashion** in the accounts. The **excess** of the actuarial present value of plan benefits over the net assets of the plan is reported as a **fund balance deficit** in the balance sheet. The actuarial present value of plan benefits can be computed under any of several actuarial cost methods under NCGA *Statement 1.*

Except for recording the actuarial deficiency, the traditional approach focuses on (1) **accountability** for the financial resources contributed to the plan, along with related earnings, and (2) appropriately *associating* the *net financial resources with specific employee groups* and, in the subsidiary ledgers, with specific employees. This is illustrated in the following example.

Retirement Fund Example—Traditional Approach

To illustrate the traditional approach to accounting for a PERS—whether it is a single-employer, agent, or cost-sharing PERS—let us assume that a fund is already in operation and its beginning trial balance appears as in Figure 11-5. Assume also that (1) the plan is financed by employer contributions, employee contributions, and investment earnings; (2) the equities of employees resigning or dying prior to retirement are returned to them or to their estates, but employer contributions on their behalf remain in the fund; (3) employer contributions and earnings thereon vest[13] to the benefit of the employee only upon retirement; (4) earnings of the fund are apportioned according to a predetermined formula among employee equity, employer equity, and retiree equity in the fund; and (5) actuarial requirements are recorded by year end adjusting entries.

The nature and purposes of most of the accounts in the beginning trial balance will become evident in the course of the illustration. However, understanding

---

[13] Employer contributions or pension benefits "vest" when they are irrevocably owed to the employee or the employee's estate. The trend is toward employer contributions being vested immediately or within a relatively short period (five to ten years), rather than only upon retirement, but this trend is less evident in government than in business.

Figure 11-5

**PENSION TRUST FUND TRIAL BALANCE
TRADITIONAL APPROACH**

A Governmental Unit
Pension Trust Fund
Trial Balance
At Beginning of Fiscal Year (Date)

	Debit	Credit
Cash	56,000	
Due from General Fund	8,000	
Interest Receivable	3,000	
Investments	980,000	
Unamortized Premiums on Investments	5,000	
Due to Resigned Employees		3,000
Annuities Payable		2,800
Reserve for Employee Contributions		470,200
Reserve for Employer Contributions		260,100
Actuarial Deficiency—Reserve for Employer Contributions		300,000
Reserve for Retiree Annuities		315,900
Unreserved Fund Balance	300,000	
	1,352,000	1,352,000

the nature and use of the various reserve accounts is critical to understanding Pension Trust Fund accounting under the traditional approach. Thus, note that:

1. The purpose of the various reserve accounts is to maintain **accountability** for the *claims of various employee groups* against the net assets of the fund. (The *claims* of *individual employees* are accounted for *in subsidiary ledgers* controlled by the reserve accounts);

2. The **Reserve for Employee Contributions** and the **Reserve for Employer Contributions** accounts represent (a) accumulated amounts paid into the fund by, or on behalf of, current employees, and (b) interest earned on those contributions;

3. The **Reserve for Retiree Annuities** is **increased** when employees retire— since the balances of the Reserve for Employee Contributions and the Reserve for Employer Contributions accounts associated with retiring employees are reclassified as Reserve for Retiree Annuities when employees retire—and **decreased** when benefit payments are accrued;

4. The **Actuarial Deficiency—Reserve for Employer Contributions** and **Unreserved Fund Balance** accounts have *equal but offsetting balances* since these accounts have traditionally been used to "insert" the actuarial deficiency of underfunded plans into the PTF balance sheet. Note that without these accounts there would be no indication under the traditional approach that the illustrative PTF has an actuarial deficiency. Indeed, the **total** beginning fund balance reported is the sum of the three reserves discussed previously ($1,046,200); and

5. *Additional reserves* such as a Reserve for Undistributed Investment Earnings will be needed if investment earnings are distributed to the various reserves listed here at a set rate and the plan earnings exceed that rate.

The following transactions or events occurred during the year and would be recorded in the **Pension Trust Fund** as indicated.

Transactions and Entries

1. Employer and employee contributions were accrued in the General Fund (a quasi-external transaction).

   (1) Due from General Fund   175,000
         Revenues—Employee Contributions   125,000
         Revenues—Employer Contributions   50,000
      To record employee and employer contributions due
      from the General Fund.

   Although the employer contribution would be budgeted in the fund through which payrolls are paid, the PERS in this example is not under formal budgetary accounting control. The levels of its activity are determined by factors such as levels of employment in the government and the changes in status of participants in the system.

2. A check for $170,000 was received from the General Fund.

   (2) Cash   170,000
         Due from General Fund   170,000
      To record receipt of contributions from the General
      Fund.

3. Accrued interest of $45,000 and premium amortization of $200 on investments were recorded.

   (3) Interest Receivable   45,000
         Unamortized Premiums on Investments   200
         Revenues—Interest   44,800
      To record accrued interest receivable and
      amortization of premiums on investments.

   Investment premiums and discounts are amortized as a part of the accrual basis calculation of investment earnings.

4. Interest receivable of $40,000 was collected.

   (4) Cash   40,000
         Interest Receivable   40,000
      To record receipt of interest receivable.

5. An employee retired, employer contributions in his behalf of $5,000 vested, and his retirement benefit formula was determined. His accumulated contributions and related interest were $10,000.

   (5) Reserve for Employee Contributions   10,000
      Reserve for Employer Contributions   5,000
         Reserve for Retiree Annuities   15,000
      To record reclassification of equities upon an
      employee's retirement and vesting of the
      government's contributions in his behalf.

   Note that the amount reclassified as Reserve for Retiree Annuities is traditionally based on the amounts in the Reserve for Employee Contributions and Reserve for Employer Contributions accounts associated with the retiring employees—that is, it is **not** actuarially based.

6. Three employees resigned and one died prior to retirement. The accumulated balances of their contributions totaled $16,000 and $9,000, respectively.

(6)	Expenses—Payments to Deceased Employees' Estates.................................	9,000	
	Expenses—Payments to Resigned Employees	16,000	
	Due to Deceased Employees' Estates		9,000
	Due to Resigned Employees................		16,000

To record amounts due upon employee resignations and the death of one employee prior to retirement.

7. Checks were mailed to two of the resigned employees ($13,000) and to the estate of the deceased employee ($9,000).

(7)	Due to Deceased Employees' Estates	9,000	
	Due to Resigned Employees..................	13,000	
	Cash...................................		22,000

To record payments to former employees and to the estate of a deceased employee.

8. Annuities payable of $24,000 were accrued.

| (8) | Expenses—Annuity Payments .... | 24,000 | |
| | Annuities Payable........................ | | 24,000 |

To record accrual of liability for annuities payable.

9. Annuities payable were paid, except for that owed to one retiree who is out of the country.

| (9) | Annuities Payable.......................... | 23,000 | |
| | Cash................................... | | 23,000 |

To record payment of annuities.

10. Additional investments were made for $150,000 less a discount of $7,000.

(10)	Investments.............................	150,000	
	Unamortized Discounts on Investments		7,000
	Cash...................................		143,000

To record investments.

11. At year end the following adjusting and closing entries were made. The actuary indicated that the actuarial deficiency had increased by $20,000 during the year and additional contributions would need to be made if the fund were to be actuarially sound.

| (11) | Unreserved Fund Balance .... | 20,000 | |
| | Actuarial Deficiency—Reserve for Employer Contributions .... | | 20,000 |

To record the change in the actuarial deficiency of the fund.

The latter account title is often phrased "Reserve for Employer Contributions —Actuarial Deficiency."

Since the PERS Unreserved Fund Balance account is used solely to reflect any actuarial deficiency, all PTF revenues and expenses ultimately affect one of

Figure 11-6   **EFFECT OF PTF TRANSACTIONS ON PTF EQUITY ACCOUNTS**

				Ultimate Impact on:	
	Reserve For			Actuarial Deficiency—Reserve for Employer Contributions	Fund Balance
Transaction or Event	Employee Contributions	Employer Contributions	Retiree Annuities		
1. Employee contributions	+				
2. Employer contributions		+			
3. Retirement of employees	−	−	+		
4. Investment earnings	+	+	+		
5. Payments to employees who withdraw from plan or die without vesting	−				
6. Accrual of annuities currently payable			−		
7. Increase in actuarial deficiency				+	−
8. Decrease in actuarial deficiency				−	+

the various reserve account balances in the closing process. This is because each revenue or expense has either increased or decreased the claims of particular plan participants to the net financial resources of the plan. The ultimate impact of various PTF transactions on the various reserves is reflected in Figure 11-6.

The Unreserved Fund Balance account could be used as a "clearinghouse" account in the closing process where (a) the revenue and expense accounts are closed to Unreserved Fund Balance and then (b) the reserve accounts are adjusted for the amounts of revenues and expenses that ultimately affect them. This will have a **zero net effect** on the Unreserved Fund Balance account since—as noted earlier and illustrated in Figure 11-6—each revenue and expense necessitates a corresponding change in a reserve account. Alternatively, the revenues and expenses could be **closed directly** to the **reserve accounts** as done here.

Closing Entries

(C1)	Revenues—Employee Contributions	125,000	
	Revenues—Employer Contributions	50,000	
	Reserve for Employee Contributions		125,000
	Reserve for Employer Contributions		50,000
	To close employee and employer contributions to related reserve accounts.		
(C2)	Reserve for Employee Contributions	25,000	
	Expenses—Payments to Deceased Employees' Estates.		9,000
	Expenses—Payments to Resigned Employees . . .		16,000
	To close expenses to related reserve accounts.		
(C3)	Reserve for Retiree Annuities.	24,000	
	Expenses—Annuity Payments		24,000
	To close annuity expense to related reserve.		
(C4)	Revenues—Interest	44,800	
	Reserve for Employee Contributions		18,300
	Reserve for Employer Contributions		15,700
	Reserve for Retiree Annuities		10,800
	To allocate interest to the reserve accounts.		

Under the traditional approach the Pension Trust Fund financial statements include a Balance Sheet and a Statement of Revenues, Expenses, and Changes in Fund Balance. Cash flow statements are permitted, but not required, for PTFs. Note that these statements are essentially "fiduciary-basis" statements. These statements are presented, using data from the illustrated retirement fund, in Figures 11-7 and 11-8.

The NCGA *Statement* 6 Approach

NCGA *Statement 6* generally reaffirms the traditional accounting and reporting approach of NCGA *Statement 1* but adds several additional accounting and reporting requirements. The primary accounting and reporting requirements of NCGA *Statement 6* are:

- *Equity security investments* and *fixed income security investments* are accounted for at *cost and amortized cost,* respectively—subject to write-down to market for apparently permanent declines in market value.
- *Fixed assets* are accounted for at *depreciated cost.*
- *Liabilities* recognized usually are *short-term* liabilities such as vouchers payable, accrued operating expense liabilities, and liabilities for benefits due but unpaid. ("**Actuarial obligations**" are *not* recorded as PERS/PTF liabilities, but are reported in the fund balance section of the PERS/PTF balance sheet.)
- Employer and employee contributions to the PERS/PTF and investment earnings are the **main** PERS/PTF **revenues** recognized.
- Benefit payments, refunds to resigned employees and estates of deceased employees, and administrative expenses are the primary PERS/PTF **expenses** recognized.
- *Investment gains and losses* are recognized when investments are sold or exchanged—*except* the "deferral and amortization" method *may* be used if a *fixed income* investment security transaction meets specified *"swap"* criteria.[14]
- "**Unit Credit Method**" Reporting. The *fund balance* section of the PERS/PTF *balance sheet* is to be presented in *two subsections:* (1) the **actuarial present value of credited projected benefits** section, computed using the *unit credit actuarial method,* and (2) the **unfunded (or overfunded) actuarial present value of credited projected benefits**—which is the *difference* between "net assets available for benefits" (assets less current liabilities) and the total actuarial present value of credited projected benefits.

Except for the "Unit Credit Method" reporting requirement, there is little difference between the traditional approach and the NCGA *Statement 6* approach. Thus, the illustrative entries are not repeated for the *Statement 6* approach since:

1. Most would be identical to those used under the traditional approach;
2. Most PERS will use the traditional "fiduciary-basis" accounting approach

---

[14] GASB Codification, sec. Pe5.118. A fixed income security "swap" is *defined* as the sale of one fixed income security (bond) and the purchase of another fixed income security (bond) *if:* (a) *both* the sale and the purchase are *planned simultaneously*—that is, each transaction is undertaken in contemplation of the other and its execution is conditioned upon execution of the other; (b) *both* the sale and the purchase *occur* on the *same day;* (c) the sale and purchase result in an *increase* in *net yield to maturity and/or* investment *quality* of the *portfolio;* and (d) the *bond purchased* is *"investment graded"* better than, equal to, or *no more than one grade below* the *bond sold.*

Figure 11-7

PENSION TRUST FUND BALANCE SHEET
TRADITIONAL APPROACH

A Governmental Unit
Pension Trust Fund
Balance Sheet
At Close of Fiscal Year (Date)

Assets

Cash.	$ 78,000
Due from General Fund.	13,000
Interest receivable	8,000
Investments (at amortized cost; fair market value, $xx).	1,127,800
	$1,226,800

Liabilities and Fund Balance

Liabilities:		
Due to resigned employees.		$ 6,000
Annuities Payable		3,800
Total liabilities		9,800
Fund balance:		
Reserve for employee contributions	$578,500	
Reserve for employer contributions.	320,800	
Actuarial deficiency—Reserve for employer contributions	320,000	
Reserve for retiree annuities	317,700	
Unreserved fund balance (deficit).	(320,000)	
Total fund balance		1,217,000
		$1,226,800

Figure 11-8

PENSION TRUST FUND OPERATING STATEMENT
TRADITIONAL APPROACH

A Governmental Unit
Pension Trust Fund
**Statement of Revenues, Expenses, and Changes
in (Total) Fund Balance**
For the Fiscal Year Ended (Date)

Revenues:		
Contributions		$ 175,000
Interest		44,800
Total		219,800
Expenses:		
Benefit payments		$ 24,000
Refunds		25,000
Total		49,000
Excess of revenues over expenses		170,800
Fund balance, beginning of year (date)		1,046,200
Fund balance, end of year (date)		$1,217,000

Note: *NCGA Statement 1 asserts that "Pension Trust Funds are similar to proprietary funds (accrual basis) and should be reported as [are] proprietary funds" (p. 21).*

even if the NCGA *Statement 6* or FASB *Statement No. 35* reporting approach is used; and

3. The most significant potential difference in the entries is that the accounts conceivably might be closed to accounts for the various components of actuarial present value of projected benefits payable to be reported in the fund balance section under the NCGA *Statement 6* approach. This is both unnecessary and highly unlikely, however, since (1) the information to be reported there must come from an actuarial study, and (2) the PERS fund balance accounts usually are *control accounts* over the individual employee subsidiary ledger accounts (particularly prior to employee retirement or termination).

Not surprisingly, the Statement of Revenues, Expenses, and Changes in **Total** Fund Balance is virtually identical under the traditional (NCGA *Statement 1*) and the NCGA *Statement 6* approaches. Hence, this statement is not repeated. The NCGA *Statement 6* balance sheet is markedly different, however, in that it reports fund balance in terms of the actuarial present value of credited projected benefits payable under the plan.

The *Statement 6* **balance sheet** is presented in Figure 11-9. To prepare that statement, the illustrative government needs the following information from the actuarial study performed for the PERS at the end of the fiscal year. Assume that the actuary computed the following using the unit credit actuarial cost method as required by NCGA *Statement 6* for reporting purposes:

- Actuarial present value of projected benefits payable to current retirees
  and beneficiaries . . . . $ 438,500
- Actuarial present value of projected benefits payable to terminated
  vested participants who have not reached the eligibility age for
  receiving benefits . . . . -0-
- Actuarial present value of credited projected benefits payable to active
  participants, financed by:
    Accumulated member contributions 578,500
    Employer 520,000
- Total actuarial present value of credited projected benefits $1,537,000

Note in studying the NCGA *Statement 6* approach balance sheet:

1. The presentation of **"Net Assets Available for Benefits"**—the difference between total assets and total liabilities.

2. The segregation of fund balance into the **actuarial present value of projected benefits payable** to different categories of plan participants as specified by *Statement 6.*

3. The actuarial present value of projected benefits payable to terminated, vested participants is zero for this illustration because vesting occurs only at retirement. Nonetheless, the category is presented to illustrate the *Statement 6* requirements more fully.

4. The **actuarial deficiency** reported is the difference between the "Total Actuarial Present Value of Credited Projected Benefits" and the "Net Assets Available for Benefits."

5. The actuarial amounts reported in the balance sheet (and in the disclosures required by GASB *Statement No. 5*) must be computed using the **unit credit** actuarial cost method ***regardless*** of the method, if any, used to determine the

Figure 11-9

**PENSION TRUST FUND BALANCE SHEET
NCGA STATEMENT 6 APPROACH**

A Governmental Unit
Pension Trust Fund
Balance Sheet
At End of Fiscal Year (Date)

Assets:

Cash	$ 78,000
Due from General Fund	13,000
Interest receivable	8,000
Investments (at amortized cost;	
fair market value, $xx)	1,127,800
Total Assets	1,226,800

Liabilities:

Due to resigned employees	6,000
Annuities payable	3,800
Total Liabilities	9,800
Net Assets Available for Benefits	$1,217,000

Fund Balance:

Actuarial present value of projected benefits payable to		
current retirees and beneficiaries		$ 438,500
Actuarial present value of projected benefits payable to		
terminated vested participants		—*
Actuarial present value of credited projected benefits for		
active employees:		
Member contributions.	$578,500	
Employer financed portion	520,000	1,098,500
Total Actuarial Present Value of Credited Projected		
Benefits.		1,537,000
Unfunded actuarial present value of credited projected		
benefits		(320,000)
Total Fund Balance		$1,217,000

This amount is zero in this illustration because vesting occurs only at retirement. The category is presented to illustrate the Statement 6 requirements more fully.

amount of **funding** to be received by the PERS from the employer government(s).

The FASB *Statement* No. 35 Approach

As noted earlier, "Accounting and Reporting by Defined Benefit Pension Plans" was intended by the FASB to be applicable to plans that provide pensions for employees of state and local governments as well as to those that provide pensions for employees of businesses and other organizations. FASB 35 approach financial statements provide quite different information from that in the preceding statements for the other approaches. This nontraditional approach has not been widely accepted by SLGs and is not illustrated here.

FASB *Statement No. 35* would **change** the traditional Pension Trust Fund accounting and reporting by requiring SLG Pension Trust Funds to (1) publish **different** types of financial **statements;** (2) value long-term security **investments** at *market* value—whereas such investments typically are accounted for at amortized cost (debt securities) or lower of cost or market (equity securities) by SLG Pension Trust Funds; (3) consider *only* pension *benefits earned to date* at *current salary rates*—and *not* consider *future* service or salary levels—in *actuarial* computations; and (4) make several *additional footnote disclosures* not required by the GASB Codification as discussed in the next section.

Neither the discussion of FASB *Statement No. 35* nor the discussion of the other approaches presented here is intended to be exhaustive. Rather, the intent is to indicate the unsettled state of accounting for PERS and PTFs and some of the variations of accounting thought and treatment that presently exist and are under consideration for the future.

EMPLOYER GOVERNMENT ACCOUNTING AND REPORTING

Like the accounting and reporting for PERS, the issues of **employer fund/employer government** accounting and reporting are being studied by the GASB. Indeed, the GASB issued an exposure draft, "Accounting for Pensions by State and Local Governmental Employers," in 1990. Further deliberations on this issue are being deferred until certain key issues on accounting and reporting for pension plans can be resolved, however.

The primary current guidance found in the GASB Codification comes from NCGA *Statement 6.* As discussed in Chapter 6, the GASB Codification requires that:

1. **Governmental Fund employers** must report as expenditures the portion of the actuarially required contributions that have been or will be funded with expendable available financial resources of the fund.
2. If a portion of the actuarially required contribution of governmental fund employers is not payable from expendable available financial resources, that **unfunded portion** is to be **reported** as an unfunded pension liability **in the General Long-Term Debt** Account Group.
3. In addition to reporting the pension expenditures in the employer governmental fund operating statement, the government must also **disclose**—either parenthetically or in the notes—
   a. The actuarially required contribution, and
   b. The increase or decrease in the unfunded pension liability reported in the General Long-Term Debt Account Group resulting from funding (paying or accruing) less than or more than the actuarially required contribution.

Any one of several actuarial cost methods may be used to compute the actuarially required **contribution** for the employer fund(s); the unit credit method is **not** required to be used.

For **proprietary and nonexpendable trust fund employers,** the Codification requires that pension expense equal either (a) the actuarially required contribution, as discussed above, or (b) an amount computed in accordance with Accounting Principles Board *Opinion No. 8,* "Accounting for the Cost of Pension Plans," Pending resolution by the GASB of employer government accounting for pension costs. Pending resolution by the GASB of employer government accounting for pension costs, the GASB has **prohibited** governments from **applying *FASB Statement No. 87,*** "Employers' Accounting for Pensions."

FOOTNOTE AND SUPPLEMENTARY INFORMATION DISCLOSURES

To this point our discussion has focused on accounting and reporting for PERS or for the pension costs of employer funds in the financial statements. However, pension **disclosures** in the notes to the financial statements of PERS and of employer governments also have been subject to much study and controversy. Different disclosures were required by NCGA *Statement 1,* NCGA *Statement 6,* and FASB *Statement No. 35.* The **required disclosures** for **both PERS and employer governments** set forth in GASB *Statement No. 5,* "Disclosure of Pension Information by Public Employee Retirement Systems and State and Local Governmental Employers," **supersede all previous pension disclosure guidance.** *Statement No. 5* requires two broad classes of disclosures—(1) disclosures **in the notes** to the financial statements and (2) ten-year historical trend information which is **required supplementary information.** Detailed discussion of the many specific disclosures required is beyond the scope of this chapter. Indeed, since different disclosures are required in different circumstances, it is essential to refer to GASB *Statement No. 5* for guidance to specific disclosure requirements in each situation.

COMBINING TRUST AND AGENCY FUND FINANCIAL STATEMENTS

In the Comprehensive Annual Financial Report (CAFR) of a SLG, the fiduciary funds should be reported in the combined financial statements as explained in Chapter 14. In addition, assuming there is more than one each of the various types of trust funds, several combining financial statements are required for these funds as well. They include:

Expendable Trust Funds	*Nonexpendable and Pension Trust Funds*
Combining Balance Sheet	Combining Balance Sheet
Combining Statement of Revenues, Expenditures, and Changes in Fund Balances	Combining Statement of Revenues, Expenses, and Changes in Fund Balances
	Combining Statement of Cash Flows (Nonexpendable trust funds only)

Since the combining Expendable Trust Fund statements are like those illustrated for various governmental fund types in previous chapters, and the combining Nonexpendable Trust and Pension Trust Fund statements are like those illustrated for proprietary funds in Chapter 12, they are not illustrated or discussed here.

A Combining Statement of Changes in Assets and Liabilities—All Agency Funds should be presented if a SLG has more than one Agency Fund. A Combining Statement of Changes in Assets and Liabilities—All Agency Funds is illustrated in Figure 11-10. This illustration is from the CAFR of Pima County, Arizona. Note that the statement is **not** an operating statement because, as discussed earlier, Agency Funds do not have operations per se. Rather, this statement simply discloses the changes in the unit's custodial responsibilities. Note also that this statement is not a required statement in the General Purpose Financial Statements (GPFS). It usually is presented in the notes to the GPFS and may be presented in the Combining and Individual Fund statements section of the CAFR.

Figure 11-10   COMBINING STATEMENT OF CHANGES IN ASSETS AND LIABILITIES—AGENCY FUNDS

Pima County

For the Year Ended June 30, 19X1
(in thousands)

	Balance 06/30/90	Additions	Deductions	Balance 06/30/X1
Deferred Compensation				
Assets				
Deposits with fiscal agents	$ 13,963	$ 3,505	$ 967	$ 16,501
Liabilities				
Employee compensation	$ 13,963	$ 3,505	$ 967	$ 16,501
Payroll Clearing				
Assets				
Cash and cash equivalents	$ 1,414	$ 163,664	$ 163,235	$ 1,843
Liabilities				
Deposits and rebates	$ 1,414	$ 163,664	$ 163,235	$ 1,843
Treasurer's Clearing				
Assets				
Cash and cash equivalents	$ 345	$ 586,759	$ 585,783	$ 1,321
Liabilities				
Due to other governments	2	412,128	412,107	23
Deposits and rebates	343	174,631	173,676	1,298
Total liabilities	$ 345	$ 586,759	$ 585,783	$ 1,321
School Districts				
Assets				
Cash and cash equivalents	$ 127,335	$ 8,915,764	$ 8,844,747	$ 198,352
Deposits with fiscal agents	12,793	29,011	7,880	33,924
Total assets	$ 140,128	$ 8,944,775	$ 8,852,627	$ 232,276
Liabilities				
Due to other governments	$ 140,128	$ 8,944,775	$ 8,852,627	$ 232,276
Other				
Assets				
Cash and cash equivalents	$ 17,842	$ 264,308	$ 262,418	$ 19,732
Liabilities				
Due to other governments	$ 4,646	$ 155,314	$ 151,474	$ 8,486
Deposits and rebates	13,196	108,994	110,944	11,246
Total liabilities	$ 17,842	$ 264,308	$ 262,418	$ 19,732
Totals – All Agency Funds				
Assets				
Cash and cash equivalents	$ 146,936	$ 9,930,495	$ 9,856,183	$ 221,248
Deposits with fiscal agents	26,756	32,516	8,847	50,425
Total assets	$ 173,692	$ 9,963,011	$ 9,865,030	$ 271,673
Liabilities				
Employee compensation	$ 13,963	$ 3,505	$ 967	$ 16,501
Due to other governments	144,776	9,512,217	9,416,208	240,785
Deposits and rebates	14,953	447,289	447,855	14,387
Total liabilities	$ 173,692	$ 9,963,011	$ 9,865,030	$ 271,673

Source: A recent comprehensive annual financial report of Pima County, Arizona.

CONCLUDING COMMENTS

Trust and Agency Funds are used to account for the fiduciary responsibilities of state and local governments. Although there is relatively little specific guidance regarding accounting and reporting for this fund type (other than Pension Trust Funds), most are similar in nature to and, thus, are accounted for much like either governmental funds or proprietary funds.

Expendable Trust Funds are similar in nature to governmental funds, and governmental fund accounting and reporting principles apply to those funds. The Nonexpendable Trust Funds are similar to proprietary funds in that these funds are to be "self-sustaining." Thus, for the most part, proprietary fund accounting and reporting principles apply to these funds. Agency Funds differ from proprietary funds and from governmental funds in that Agency Funds have no equity and, thus, no "operating results." Each increase in Agency Fund total assets is accompanied by a corresponding increase in its liabilities. Recent standards require certain SLG assets that are to be used for special assessment debt service and certain SLG deferred compensation plans to be accounted for in Agency Funds. Additionally, many other agency relationships typically are accounted for in such funds.

Three different reporting approaches are permitted for Pension Trust Funds currently, but this is a major issue being studied by the GASB. The traditional approach to **accounting** for Pension Trust Funds is likely to continue to be used regardless of the **reporting** guidance eventually adopted by the GASB. This is because the traditional approach focuses on maintaining accountability for the SLG's fiduciary responsibilities under the pension plan. The GASB has addressed the disclosure issue for Pension Trust Funds and requires extensive footnote disclosures and ten-year historical trend supplementary information as discussed in the chapter.

Note that while earlier chapters focus on governmental fund accounting and reporting, this chapter includes both governmental fund and proprietary fund accounting and reporting—as noted earlier—because of the differences in the nature of the various types of Trust and Agency Funds. The next two chapters discuss accounting and reporting principles and concepts for proprietary funds—Internal Service Funds and Enterprise Funds, respectively. These chapters complete the coverage of the current SLG accounting and reporting model; then Chapter 14 discusses and illustrates SLG financial reporting concepts and the Comprehensive Annual Financial Report.

QUESTIONS

11-1 Trust Funds and Agency Funds, though separate fund types, are treated in the same chapter in this text and are often spoken of collectively as "Trust and Agency" Funds. In what ways are they similar and how do they differ?

11-2 Compare the primary forms of accountability as among (1) the General and Special Revenue Funds, (2) Capital Projects Funds, and (3) Trust and Agency Funds.

11-3 A single trust agreement often gives rise to two separate Trust Funds. When is this so, and may a single trust agreement result in the establishment of three, four, or more separate funds?

11-4 In certain situations an Expendable (governmental) Trust Fund may be virtually identical to a Special Revenue Fund and should be budgeted and accounted for as though it were a Special Revenue Fund. Explain.

11-5 What is the difference between a Nonexpendable (proprietary) Trust Fund and an Agency Fund?

11-6 Accounting for separate Trust and Agency Funds on a "funds within a fund" approach was not illustrated in this chapter. Is it possible and/or permissible to account for more than one type of trust or agency relationship within a single Trust or Agency Fund?

11-7 Classify the following as to whether they are Expendable Trust Funds, Nonexpendable Trust Funds, or Agency Funds:

a. A fund established to handle tax collections by a governmental unit for other governments

b. A loan fund

c. A fund whose principal and income are both to be used in granting scholarships

d. A fund whose principal is to be held intact but whose income must be expended for bravery awards

e. A fund established to handle bidder deposits received by a county

f. A fund established to handle that part of the proceeds from the sale of property for taxes which is to be refunded to the property owner

11-8 Although Fund Balance and Reserve accounts may be used in Trust Funds, they may actually be *liability* accounts. Explain.

11-9 Why might the Balance Sheet prepared for a Pension Trust Fund report an Unreserved Fund Balance *deficit* when it also reports assets far in excess of its liabilities?

11-10 When should an Agency Fund be used to account for special assessments? Why?

11-11 How should the assets and liabilities of a Deferred Compensation Agency Fund be measured? Are all deferred compensation plans accounted for in Agency Funds?

11-12 Describe how the fund balance of a PERS is to be reported under the NCGA *Statement 6* approach.

11-13 How might *internal* (interfund or intragovernmental) Agency Funds be used to facilitate a governmental unit's financial management and accounting processes?

11-14 In accounting for a Tax Agency Fund, why is it necessary to maintain records of taxes levied and collected for each taxing authority involved by year of levy?

11-15 According to the terms of A's will, the city is to become the owner of an apartment building. The net income from the building is to be added to the Policemen's Pension Fund. (a) Is this new fund an Expendable or a Nonexpendable Trust Fund? (b) Suppose that net income before depreciation is to be added to the Pension Fund. Is the fund expendable or nonexpendable?

11-16 The earnings of a proprietary (nonexpendable as to corpus) Trust Fund are used to support the operation of a municipal museum, art gallery, and park complex. Should these activities be accounted for through the General Fund, a Special Revenue Fund, or a Trust Fund?

11-17 Should the financial statements of the PERS and PTFs be included in the combined statements issued as the GPFS of the governmental unit?

11-18 A trust indenture states that the principal (corpus) of the trust is to be maintained intact in perpetuity. Yet, although the governmental trustee did not violate the terms of the trust agreement—and it was not subsequently revised—the principal (corpus) had decreased to less than half its original amount five years after the trust was created. Why or how might this have happened?

11-19 What financial statements should be presented for (a) an Expendable Trust Fund, (b) a Nonexpendable Trust Fund, (c) an Agency Fund, and (d) a Pension Trust Fund?

PROBLEMS

P 11-1 (Multiple Choice)

1. Which of the following statements is required to be prepared for Agency Funds?

   a. Statement of Revenues, Expenses, and Changes in Fund Equity

   b. Statement of Revenues, Expenditures, and Changes in Fund Balances

   c. Balance Sheet

   d. Statement of Changes in Agency Fund Assets and Liabilities

   e. Both c and d

2. Which of the following items should be accounted for in an Agency Fund when a special assessment project is financed by issuing special assessment debt for which the government is not obligated in any manner?

a. The bond proceeds and construction costs

b. The debt service transactions

c. The long-term debt issued

d. The fixed asset constructed or acquired

e. None of the above

f. All of the above

3. The long-term debt issued in a situation like that described in item 2 should be reported by the government in

a. an Agency Fund

b. a Capital Projects Fund

c. a Debt Service Fund

d. the General Long-Term Debt Account Group

e. none of the above

4. Epperly County's employees participate in an IRC Section 457 deferred compensation plan. The assets to which the county has legal access and a corresponding liability should be reported in a County Agency Fund if the plan is administered by

a. the county

b. a statewide PERS

c. a private vendor of deferred compensation plans

d. none of the above

e. all of the above

5. Assume that Epperly County's deferred compensation plan is reported in an Agency Fund. The assets and liabilities of the plan at January 1, 19X1 amounted to $3,000,000. $850,000 was withheld from employee checks during 19X1 for contributions to the plan, and $180,000 of plan benefits were paid. If the market value of the plan assets at year end was $3,600,000, the reported value of the assets at December 31, 19X1 should be

a. $3,420,000　　　　　　d. $4,000,000

b. $3,600,000　　　　　　e. $4,270,000

c. $3,670,000

6. The GASB *Statement No. 5* pension disclosures for employer governments and for PERS apply when

a. the NCGA *Statement 1* reporting approach is used

b. the NCGA *Statement 6* reporting approach is used

c. the FASB *Statement No. 35* reporting approach is used

d. both a and b

e. none of the above

f. all of the above

7. In general, governmental fund accounting principles apply to

a. trusts of which the corpus and earnings are expendable

b. trusts of which the corpus and earnings are nonexpendable

c. trusts of which the corpus is nonexpendable and the earnings are expendable

d. none of the above

e. more than one of the above (explain)

8. Which of the following statements is not required to be presented for a Nonexpendable Trust Fund?

a. Balance sheet

b. Statement of revenues, expenses, and changes in fund balance

c. Statement of cash flows

d. All of the above are required.

9. Which of the following statements is not required to be presented for a Pension Trust Fund?

a. Balance sheet

b. Statement of revenues, expenses, and changes in fund balance

c. Statement of cash flows

d. All of the above are required.

P 11-2 (Nonexpendable and Expendable Trust Funds) The following is a trial balance of the Child Welfare Principal Trust Fund of the City of Slusher's Ridge as of January 1, 19X3:

Cash.	$ 98,000	
Land.	70,000	
Buildings	162,000	
Accumulated Depreciation.		$65,000
Accrued Wages Payable		150
Accrued Taxes Payable.		1,800
Due to Child Welfare Earnings Trust Fund.		15,000
Fund Balance—Trust Principal		248,050
	$330,000	$330,000

The endowment was in the form of an apartment building. Endowment principal is to be kept intact, and the net earnings are to be used in financing child welfare activities.

The following transactions took place during the year:

1. Expenses and accrued liabilities paid in cash were as follows:

Heat, light, and power	$5,200
Janitor's wages (including $150 previously accrued). .	3,000
Painting and decorating	3,750
Repairs	1,500
Taxes (including $1,800 previously accrued)	3,750
Management fees	4,500
Miscellaneous expenses	1,500
	$23,200

2. A special assessment of $2,000 levied by the municipality against the property (for a capital improvement) was paid.

3. Rents for 19X3 (all collected) amounted to $45,000.

4. The amount due to the Child Welfare Earnings Trust Fund at January 1, 19X3 was paid.

5. Expenditures of $13,500 were paid from the Child Welfare Earnings Trust Fund to finance 19X3 summer camp activities.

6. The following adjustments were made at the close of the year:

Depreciation	$ 6,000
Accrued Taxes	1,900
Accrued Wages	170

Required (a) Prepare a Balance Sheet as of December 31, 19X3 and a Statement of Revenues, Expenses, and Changes in Fund Balance for the fiscal year ended December 31, 19X3 for the Child Welfare Principal Trust Fund. (Support these statements with a worksheet, T-account, or other analysis.)

(b) Prepare a Balance Sheet as of December 31, 19X3 for the Child Welfare Earnings Trust Fund and a Statement of Revenues, Expenditures, and Changes in Fund Balance for the year then ended. (Assume that the Child Welfare Earnings Trust Fund had no activities or balances other than those indicated in the problem.)

P 11-3 (Tax Agency Fund) Prepare the general journal entries required to record the following transactions in the general ledgers of the State, the County General Fund, and the County Tax Agency Fund. You may omit formal entry explanations, but should key the entries to the numbered items in this problem.

1. The County Tax Agency Fund has been established to account for the county's duties of collecting the county and state property taxes. The levies for the year 19X0 were $600,000 for the County General Fund and $480,000 for the state. It is expected that uncollectible taxes will be $10,000 for the state and $15,000 for the county.

2. Collections were $300,000 for the county and $240,000 for the state.

3. The county is entitled to a fee of 1% of taxes collected for other governments. The amounts due to the state and to the County General Fund are paid except for the collection fee due to the County General Fund.

4. The fee is transmitted from the Tax Agency Fund to the County General Fund.

5. Uncollectible taxes in the account of $5,000 for the state and $6,000 for the county are written off.

P 11-4 (Tax Agency Fund) The following is a trial balance of the Tax Agency Fund of Cranor City as of June 30, 19X0:

Cash	$ 90,000	
Taxes Receivable for Teekell County.	22,500	
Taxes Receivable for Cranor City General Fund	48,000	
Taxes Receivable for Bonham School District	69,000	
Due to Teekell County		$ 37,500
Due to General Fund		78,000
Due to Bonham School District		114,000
	$229,500	$229,500

The following transactions took place:

1. Cash, $89,600, was paid over as follows:

Unit	Amount Due	Collection Fee	Amount Paid Over
Teekell County	$15,000	$100	$14,900
Cranor City General Fund	30,000	—	30,000
Bonham School District	45,000	300	44,700

2. The collection fees were paid over to the General Fund.

3. Taxes were levied as follows:

Unit	Amount Levied
Teekell County	$ 50,000
Cranor City	100,000
Bonham School District	150,000

Required
(a) Prepare journal entries.
(b) Post to T-accounts.
(c) Prepare a Balance Sheet as of June 30, 19X1.
(d) Or *in lieu of (a)–(c)* prepare a worksheet from which requirement (c) might easily be fulfilled.

P 11-5 (Special Assessment Project—Government Not Obligated)

1. The City of Robinsburg approved a $750,000 special assessment project in 19X5.

2. A $740,000 contract was let to M & M Murphy Company for construction of the project.

3. The project was completed and approved in 19X5, and the contractor billed the city accordingly for $740,000.

4. The city issued $740,000 of 7%, ten-year special assessment bonds at par and used the proceeds to pay the contractor. The debt is secured solely by the assessment liens against the benefited properties and the **government will not repay** the bonds in the case of default. One tenth of the bonds mature each year.

5. Assessments of $740,000 were levied in 19X5 upon completion of the project. Interest of 7% is charged on the balance of unpaid assessments. One tenth of the assessments is due each year.

6. Assessments collected during 19X6 totaled $74,000. Related interest collected was $51,800.

7. The first debt service payment on the special assessment bonds was made in 19X6.

Required

(a) Prepare all the general ledger entries required in all of the funds and account groups of the City of Robinsburg to record the preceding transactions.

(b) Repeat the entries assuming that Robinsburg is obligated in some manner on the debt.

P 11-6 (Pension Trust Fund Journal Entries) The following is a trial balance of the Policemen's Retirement Fund of the City of Cherrydale at January 1, 19X0:

Cash	$ 6,000	
Interest Receivable	450	
Investments	52,000	
Pensions Payable		$ 150
Reserve for Employee Contributions		20,100
Reserve for Employer Contributions		22,200
Actuarial Deficiency—Reserve for Employer Contributions		15,000
Reserve for Retiree Pensions		16,000
Fund Balance	15,000	
	$73,450	$73,450

The following transactions took place during the year:

1. Contributions became due from the General Fund, $38,000, and a Special Revenue Fund, $6,000. One-half of these amounts represents the employees' share of contributions.

2. Payments were received from the General Fund, $30,000, and the Special Revenue Fund, $4,000.

3. Securities were acquired for cash as follows:

a. First Purchase:		
	Par Value	$20,000
	Premiums	300
	Interest accrued at purchase	200
b. Second Purchase:		
	Par Value	15,000
	Discounts	150

4. Interest received on investments amounted to $3,000, including interest receivable on January 1, 19X0, and the accrued interest purchased.

5. Premiums and discounts in the amounts of $50 and $30, respectively, were amortized.

6. An employee retired whose contributions and interest earnings since employment were $500. Employer contributions accumulated in his behalf also amounted to $500. His retirement annuity formula was determined to have a present value of $1,500.

7. An employee resigned prior to retirement and was paid $300, which is the amount of her contributions and interest thereon. Employer contributions do not vest until retirement.

8. Retirement payments of $600 were made; pensions payable of $200 remained at year end.

9. An actuary indicated that the actuarial deficiency at year end was $19,000.

10. The Plan states that all earnings of the fund must be allocated proportionately among the three funded reserve accounts according to the beginning balances in the accounts.

Required Prepare journal entries—including closing entries—to record the transactions in the general ledger of the Policemen's Retirement Fund.

P 11-7 (Pension Trust Fund Entries and Statements) The following is a trial balance of the McCarthy County Public Employees Retirement Fund, a multiple-employer PERS in which the cities of Mooresville and Sutherland's Gap participate as well as the county.

Cash	$ 76,000	
Due from Sutherland's Gap	12,000	
Interest Receivable	14,200	
Investments	1,450,000	
Unamortized Premiums on Investments	6,000	
Due to Resigned Employees		$ 14,500
Due to Estates of Deceased Employees		3,000
Annuities Payable		1,700
Reserve for Employee Contributions		840,000
Reserve for Employer Contributions		360,000
Actuarial Deficiency—Reserve for Employer Contributions		480,000
Reserve for Retirement Annuities		339,000
Fund Balance	480,000	
	$2,038,200	$2,038,200

The employees' contributions are returned to them or to their estates upon resignation or death, respectively; vesting of employers' **matching** contributions occurs only at retirement. Interest revenue is prorated among the funded reserve accounts based on their beginning balances.

During 19X4 the following transactions occurred:

1. Employee contributions for the year were as follows:

Employees Of:	Contributions
McCarthy County	$60,000
Mooresville	35,000
Sutherland's Gap	25,000

2. All amounts due the McCarthy County PERS were collected except $20,000 each still due from the cities.

3. Interest accrued in the amount of $169,000; $1,000 of premiums were amortized.

4. Interest receivable of $168,400 was collected.

5. Three employees retired; their contributions were determined to have been $45,000.

6. Five employees resigned; their contributions were determined to have been $24,000. Two employees died prior to retirement; their contributions were determined to have been $36,000.

7. Checks mailed to resigned employees during the year amounted to $34,500. Checks mailed to the estates of deceased employees totaled $33,000.

8. Annuities were accrued in the amount of $63,000; annuities in the amount of $62,700 were paid.

9. Additional investments were made as follows:

Bonds (at par)	$160,000
Accrued interest	30,000
Discounts	(8,000)
	$182,000

10. An actuary's report showed that the actuarial deficiency at year end was $520,000.

Required (a) Prepare a worksheet (or journal entries and T-accounts) showing transactions, adjustments, and closing entries for the Retirement Fund for 19X4.

(b) Prepare a Balance Sheet as of December 31, 19X4; and a Statement of Revenues, Expenses, and Changes in Fund Balance and a statement analyzing changes in reserve accounts for the year ended December 31, 19X4.

P 11-8 (NCGA *Statement 1* Approach Balance Sheet) Following is the trial balance for the City of Vaughandale Pension Trust Fund at December 31, 19X9.

City of Vaughandale

Pension Trust Fund

Trial Balance

December 31, 19X9

Cash	$ 24,000	
Temporary Investments	230,000	
Due from General Fund	116,000	
Due from Enterprise Funds	32,000	
Accrued Interest Receivable	18,000	
Investments—Debt Securities	1,400,000	
Unamortized Premiums—Debt Securities	44,000	
Unamortized Discounts—Debt Securities		$ 37,000
Investments—Equity Securities	690,000	
Due to Resigned Employees		9,000
Due to Deceased Employee Estates		36,000
Annuities Payable		24,000
Accounts Payable		12,000
Reserve for Employee Contributions		711,000
Reserve for Employer Contributions		883,660
Reserve for Retiree Annuities		841,340
Actuarial Deficiency—Reserve for Employer Contributions		600,000
Fund Balance	600,000	
Total	$3,154,000	$3,154,000

Required Prepare the December 31, 19X9 Balance Sheet for the City of Vaughandale Pension Trust Fund under the NCGA *Statement 1* approach.

P 11-9 (NCGA *Statement 6* Approach Balance Sheet) Using the data from Problem 11-8 and the following actuarial data, prepare the December 31, 19X9 Balance Sheet for the City of Vaughandale Pension Trust Fund under the NCGA *Statement 6* approach. The actuarial study of the City of Vaughandale Pension Trust Fund, performed in late December 19X9, indicated the following:

Actuarial present value of projected benefits payable to current retirees and beneficiaries	$ 900,000
Actuarial present value of projected benefits payable to terminated vested participants	100,000
Actuarial present value of credited projected benefits for active employees	2,036,000
Total actuarial present value of credited projected benefits	$3,036,000

P 11-10 **Part I.** (Trust Fund Worksheet) Nancy Township had not been operating a public library prior to October 1, 19X1. On October 1, 19X1, James Jones died, having made a valid will that provided for the gift of his residence and various securities to the town for the establishment and operation of a free public library. The gift was accepted, and the library funds and operations were placed under the control of trustees. The terms of the gift provided that not more than $5,000 of the principal of the fund could be used for the purchase of equipment, building rearrangement, and purchase of such "standard" library reference books as, in the opinion of the trustees, were needed for starting the library. Except for this

$5,000, the principal of the fund is to be invested and the income therefrom used to operate the library in accordance with appropriations made by the trustees. The property received from the estate by the trustees included:

Description	Face or Par	Appraised Value
Residence of James Jones:		
Land		$ 2,500
Building (25-year estimated life)		20,000
Bonds:		
Wirt Company	$34,000	32,000
Bromley Company	10,000	11,200
Covey Company	20,000	20,000
Stocks:		
Eames Company, 6% preferred	12,000	12,600
Elliott Company, 5% preferred	10,000	9,600
Thurman Company, common (300 shares)	No par	12,900
Wright Company (200 shares)	4,000	14,500

The following events occurred in connection with the library operations up to June 30, 19X2:

1. 100 shares of Wright Company stock were sold on November 17, 19X1 for $6,875.

2. Cash payments were made for (a) alteration of the house—$1,310, (b) general reference books—$725, (c) equipment having an estimated life of ten years—$2,180. The trustees state that these amounts are to be charged to principal under the applicable provision of the gift.

3. The library started operation on January 1, 19X2. The trustees adopted the following budget for the year ended December 31, 19X2:

Estimated income from Trust Principal Fund earnings transfers	$5,000
Estimated income from fines, etc.	200
Appropriation for salaries	3,600
Appropriation for subscriptions	300
Appropriation for purchase of books	800
Appropriation for utilities, supplies, etc.	400

4. The following cash receipts were reported during the six months to June 30, 19X2:

a. Sale of Bromley Company bonds, including accrued interest of $80	$11,550
b. Interest and dividends	3,100
c. Fines	20
d. Gift for purchase of books	200
Total	$14,870

5. The following cash payments were made during the six months to June 30, 19X2:

a. Purchase of 100 shares of no-par common stock of Daniels Company, including commission and tax cost of $50	$ 9,655
b. Payment of salaries	1,500
c. Payment of property taxes applicable to the year ended December 31, 19X1 based on an assessment of June 30, 19X1	200
d. Purchase of books	900
e. Magazine subscriptions	230
f. Supplies and other expenses	260
Total	$12,745

6. On June 30, 19X2, there were miscellaneous library expenses unpaid, but accrued, amounting to $90. Also there were outstanding purchase orders for books in the amount of $70.

Required   Assuming that the township records budgetary accounts with respect to library operations, prepare in detail the worksheet(s) necessary to show the results of operations to June 30, 19X2, and the financial position of the Trust Fund(s) related to the library as of June 30, 19X2. Where alternative treatments of an item are acceptable, explain the alternative treatments and state the justification for your treatment. In designing your worksheet(s), you should observe the requirements of Part II of this problem in order that those requirements may be fulfilled readily from the worksheet(s) prepared here.

P 11-10   **Part II.** (Trust Fund Financial Statements) From the worksheet(s) prepared in Part I, construct the following formal statements relative to Nancy Township's library endowment and library operations:

(a) A Balance Sheet(s) for the Trust Fund(s) at June 30, 19X2.

(b) A Statement of Revenues, Expenditures, and Changes in Fund Balance—Budget and Actual—for the Library Endowment Earnings Trust Fund for the six months ended June 30, 19X2.

INTERNAL SERVICE FUNDS

Internal Service (IS) Funds are established in order to finance, administer, and account for the provision of goods and services by one department of a government **to** its **other departments** (or to other governments) on a **cost-reimbursement** basis. (The break-even objective has caused such funds to be referred to as "working capital" or "revolving" funds in many jurisdictions.) This type of fund serves internal users primarily and should be distinguished from Enterprise Funds—the other proprietary fund type. Enterprise Funds are used to account for and finance the provision of goods or services for compensation to the general public rather than to other departments of a government or to other governments.

IS Funds are internal **intermediary** fiscal and accounting entities through which some of the expenditures of other departments are made. They are used (1) to attain greater economy, efficiency, and effectiveness in the acquisition and distribution of common goods or services utilized by several or all departments within the organization; and (2) to facilitate an equitable sharing of costs among the various departments served and, hence, among the funds of the organization. They also may be used to provide interim financing for capital projects.

Activities accounted for through IS Funds vary widely in practice both as to type and complexity of operation. Among the simpler types are those used (1) to distribute common or joint costs—such as the cost of telephone, two-way radio, or other communication facilities—among departments; (2) to acquire, distribute, and allocate costs of selected items of inventory, such as office supplies or gasoline; or (3) to provide temporary loans to other funds in deficit situations or prior to the receipt of debt issue or grant proceeds. Activities of a more complex nature accounted for through IS Funds include motor pools; data processing activities; duplicating and printing facilities; repair shops and garages; cement and asphalt plants; purchasing, warehousing, and distribution services; and insurance and other risk management services.

OVERVIEW OF ACCOUNTING PRINCIPLES

IS Funds are **proprietary** (nonexpendable) funds and their accounting is essentially the same as that for a profit-seeking enterprise in the same business. Accordingly, the accrual basis of accounting is used; and both the related fixed assets—which normally are replaced from IS Fund resources—and any long-term debt to be serviced through the Fund are recorded as "fund" assets and liabilities in the IS Fund. Depreciation expense is recorded and net income or loss is computed. Leases and claims, judgments, and compensated absences are accounted for and reported just as for business enterprises. (Pension costs and liabilities are not accounted for in the same manner as for businesses, however, because FASB *Statement No. 87* is not applied by governments—as discussed in Chapter 11.) In sum, the capital maintenance measurement focus of proprietary funds is used.

The application of generally accepted business accounting principles facilitates achievement of the Funds' typical objectives. First, the usual policy requires break-even pricing and the maintenance of the invested capital. (As mentioned earlier, IS Funds sometimes are referred to as "revolving" funds because the Fund resources are used to provide goods or services and are subsequently replenished by charges to other funds. Then those resources are used to provide goods and services, and so on.) Information on revenues and expenses is essential to fulfilling this policy. Second, it is desirable to use full costing both to provide appropriate information on incremental costs for "make or buy" decisions and so the departments that use the services of the IS Fund may be charged on an equitable basis.

Creation of the IS Fund

Ordinarily an IS Fund will be created by constitutional, charter, or legislative action, though the chief executive may be empowered to do so. Capital to finance IS Fund activities may come from appropriations from the General Fund, the issue of general obligation bonds or other debt instruments, transfers from other funds, or advances from another government. Capital may also be provided by contributing all, or excessive, inventories of materials and supplies that a Fund's future "clients" (a governmental unit's departments) may have on hand at a specified time, as well as by reclassifying general fixed assets to be used in IS Fund operations as IS Fund fixed assets. The sources of capital used to finance a specific IS Fund depend to some extent on whether the IS Fund is being established to account for a new activity or for an activity previously accounted for in other funds.

If the General Fund provides **permanent capital** for the IS Fund, the following entries will be made:

General Fund
Residual Equity Transfer to IS Fund	50,000	
Cash		50,000

To record capital provided to IS Fund.

IS Fund
Cash	50,000	
Residual Equity Transfer from General Fund		50,000

To record receipt of capital from General Fund.

Residual equity transfers from other funds should be closed to an IS Fund contributed capital account such as "Contributed Capital—Governmental Unit."

Capital contributions must be distinguished from **loans and advances.** If the General Fund is ultimately to be repaid from the IS Fund, the following entries would be made rather than the preceding entries:

General Fund
Advance to IS Fund	50,000	
Cash		50,000

To record advance to IS Fund.

Unreserved Fund Balance. 50,000
    Reserve for Advance to IS Fund. 50,000
To record reservation of fund balance because of advance to IS
    Fund.

IS Fund
Cash 50,000
    Advance from General Fund 50,000
To record advance from General Fund.

The terms "advance to" and "advance from" are used earlier rather than "due to" and "due from" to indicate intermediate- and long-term receivables and payables, whereas "due to" and "due from" connote short-term relationships. A reserve was established in the General Fund to indicate that the asset "Advance to IS Fund" does not represent currently appropriable resources.

If general obligation **bonds** intended **to be repaid from the IS Fund** are issued to finance an IS Fund, the following entry will be made:

IS Fund
Cash 100,000
    Bonds Payable. 100,000
To record bond issue.

In this case the contingent "general government" liability for the bonds need only be disclosed in the notes to the financial statements. If the bonds were **not** intended to be repaid from the IS Fund and receipt of the bond proceeds were recorded in the General Fund, the following entries would be made:

General Fund
Cash 100,000
    Bond Issue Proceeds 100,000
To record issuance of bonds.
Residual Equity Transfer to IS Fund 100,000
    Due to IS Fund 100,000
To record transfer of bond proceeds to IS Fund.
General Long-Term Debt Account Group
Amount to be Provided for Retirement of Bonds 100,000
    Bonds Payable. 100,000
To record issuance of bonds to finance IS Fund but to be repaid
    from general revenues.
IS Fund
Due from General Fund 100,000
    Residual Equity Transfer from General Fund 100,000
To record residual equity transfer from General Fund.

If the IS Fund is being established to account for an activity previously financed and accounted for through the governmental funds, inventories or general fixed assets may be contributed to the IS Fund. If equipment with a five-year estimated useful life and acquired for $30,000 two years prior to creation of an IS Fund is contributed to the IS Fund when it is created, the following entries will be made:

General Fixed Assets Account Group
Investment in General Fixed Assets—General Revenues 30,000
    Equipment 30,000
To record reclassification of equipment to IS Fund.

IS Fund

Equipment	30,000	
Accumulated Depreciation—Equipment		12,000
Contributed Capital—Governmental Unit		18,000

To record fixed assets reclassified from General Fixed Assets
   Account Group.

Note that (1) the asset was recorded at its original cost less the accumulated depreciation that would have been recorded to date if the asset had been accounted for in the IS Fund all along (as discussed in Chapter 9), and (2) **no entry** is required **in** the **General Fund** since no General Fund resources are involved in the transaction. Recall also that if the asset's net utility value were less than the "book value" recorded in this entry, the asset would be written down further to its net "utility value." Finally, note that this contributed capital increase will be reported in the same manner as residual equity transfers in.

Pricing Policies

The preceding discussions relative to pricing assumed that the prices charged by the IS Fund would be based on (historical) **cost,** which most authorities assume is the proper pricing basis. Where IS Fund activities are very modest in scope and do not use full-time personnel or incur significant other costs, charges to user funds may be based on direct costs. This might be the case, for example, where (1) very limited group purchasing and warehousing is done only occasionally or as a small part of the overall purchasing operation, or (2) where the IS Fund is essentially a "flow-through" or clearance device for common costs, such as two-way radio facility rentals. In the more usual case, however, the activity involves substantial amounts of personnel, space, materials, and other overhead costs that are recovered through billing user departments for more than the direct cost of the goods or services provided.

    The IS Fund usually has a captive clientele, since in most governments the departments may not use another source of supply if a service or material is available through the IS Fund. The economy, efficiency, and effectiveness of IS Fund activities should be monitored closely under such circumstances since the lack of outside competition tends to lead to inefficiencies. Without such precautions, the convenience of having an "in-house" supplier may result in significantly higher costs than otherwise necessary.

    Being the sole source of a particular good or service also permits IS Fund prices to be set at levels that will produce profit or loss. In some cases IS Fund capital has been built up by means of substantial annual profits. The increase in capital was paid for, of course, by the funds that financed the expenditures used to buy IS Fund services or supplies. There have even been instances in which the retained earnings of an IS Fund provided the basis for a cash "dividend" that was transferred as "revenue" to the General Fund. To the extent that IS Fund revenues were derived from departments financed by the General Fund, the profit thus transferred merely had the effect of offsetting excessive charges to it previously; but if departments or activities financed through other funds patronized the IS Fund, the effect of overcharging was to transfer resources from these other funds to the General Fund.

    Use of IS Fund charges to divert restricted resources to other purposes cannot be condoned. Such a practice erodes confidence in the organization's administrators and in the accounting system, constitutes indirect fraud at best, and at worst results in illegal use of intergovernmental grant, trust, or other restricted resources. Where governments make such excessive charges for IS Fund goods or services to federally (or state) financed programs, the costs are properly disallowed for reimbursement and the government risks being penalized by having to repay the grantor government and not receiving such financial assistance in the future.

Pricing Methods

The pricing method used by an IS Fund is usually based on estimates of total costs and total consumption of goods or services. From these two estimates a rate is developed that is applied to each purchase. If the cost of materials to be issued by a Stores Fund during the coming year was expected to be $300,000 and other costs of fund operation were estimated at $12,000, goods would be priced to departments at $1.04 for every $1.00 of direct cost of materials issued. Similarly, rental rates for automotive equipment may be based on time or mileage, or both. If a truck was expected to be driven 12,000 miles during the year at a total cost of $2,400, the departments would be charged $0.20 per mile.

The alternative to using predetermined rates is to charge the departments on the basis of actual costs determined at the end of each month, quarter, or year. Though this method is often used for uncomplicated IS Funds, a predetermined charge rate is generally used for more complex operations because (1) some IS Fund expenses may not be determinable until the end of the month (or later), whereas it may be desirable to bill departments promptly so that they know how much expense or expenditure is charged to their jobs and activities at any time, and (2) charges based on actual monthly costs are likely to spread the burden unequally among departments. For example, assume that the costs of extensive equipment repairs made in June are included in the charges to the departments using the equipment during that month. In this situation, those departments that used the equipment in June would be billed for costs more properly allocated to several months or years, while the departments that used the equipment in previous or succeeding months would not bear their "fair share" of these costs. Furthermore, even if one department used the equipment throughout the year, charges based on actual monthly costs often would result in an unequitable distribution of costs among jobs and activities carried on by the department (as between June and other months in this example).

IS Fund expenses, including overhead, should be recorded in appropriately titled expense accounts. IS Fund charges for the goods or services provided are credited to a revenue account such as Billings to Departments and corresponding receivables from (Due From) other funds or other governments are recorded.

Relation to the Budget

The level of activity of an IS Fund will be determined by the demand of the user departments for its services. **IS Fund appropriations usually** are **not made,** and **formal budgetary control** is **seldom employed** in IS Fund accounts, because (1) the IS activity must be able to respond to service demands, not constrained by inflexible appropriation levels, and (2) the appropriations to the various user departments constitute an indirect budgetary ceiling on the IS activities.

Sound management requires that *flexible* budgetary techniques be employed in the planning and conduct of major IS Fund activities. Although the budget so developed may be formally approved, the expense element is not considered to have been appropriated. Budgetary control is exercised as in a business —the expenses incurred are compared with estimated expenses at the level of activity actually achieved.

Laws or custom in some cases prohibit the incurrence of obligations against or disbursement of cash from IS Funds without appropriation authority. Where this is the case, it is necessary to record not only those transactions that affect the actual position and operations of the fund (i.e., those transactions that affect the actual revenues, expenses, assets, liabilities, and capital) but also those relating to appropriations, expenditures, and encumbrances. Since this is the unusual case, rather than the usual one, the examples that follow illustrate the accounting for proprietary accounts only. Budgetary accounting for proprietary funds typically is accomplished using self-balancing budgetary accounts in which the budgetary effects of transactions are recorded. Accounting for the proprietary accounts is not affected by the budgetary accounting entries under this approach.

Financial Statements

The required IS Fund financial statements parallel those for businesses. The same financial statements are required for Enterprise Funds and Nonexpendable Trust Funds. The three required financial statements for these fund types are the:

- Balance sheet
- Statement of revenues, expenses, and changes in fund equity (or retained earnings)
- Statement of cash flows.

Balance Sheet

The balance sheet of a proprietary fund is like that of a similar business entity. Fixed assets, intangible assets, and similar accounts that are not included in governmental fund balance sheets are reported in proprietary fund balance sheets. This is consistent with the application of the business accounting model to proprietary funds as discussed in Chapter 2. Likewise, long-term liabilities payable from the resources of a proprietary fund are reported in the balance sheet of that proprietary fund. An IS Fund balance sheet is illustrated later in this chapter.

Statement of Revenues, Expenses, and Changes in Fund Equity (Retained Earnings)

As discussed in Chapter 2, the proprietary fund basic operating statement—the statement of revenues, expenses, and changes in fund equity (retained earnings)—closely resembles a business income statement. A simple example of this statement is provided later in this chapter. A more in-depth discussion of the statement of revenues, expenses, and changes in fund equity (retained earnings) is presented in Chapter 13.

Statement of Cash Flows

The statement of cash flows for proprietary funds serves essentially the same purposes as the business statement of cash flows. However, cash flows resulting from similar or identical transactions and events are often required to be classified differently in proprietary fund cash flow statements than in business cash flow statements. Instead of the three classifications of cash flows used in business cash flow statements (operating, financing, and investing), the GASB requires cash flows to be classified into the four following categories:

- Cash flows from **operating** activities
- Cash flows from **capital and related financing** activities

- Cash flows from **noncapital related financing** activities
- Cash flows from **investing** activities

The proprietary fund cash flows from **operating activities** classification differs from the business cash flows from operating activities primarily in that it generally incorporates only the cash effects of transactions and events that enter into operating income rather than net income. The consequence of this difference is that the cash effects associated with nonoperating revenues and expenses such as interest revenue and interest expense are not included in cash flows from operating activities. The GASB Codification states that:

> Operating activities generally result from providing services and producing and delivering goods, and include all transactions and other events that are not defined as capital and related financing, noncapital financing, or investing activities. . . .[1]

The Codification further states that the **direct method** of presenting cash flows from operating activities is **preferred,** but does permit use of the indirect (reconciliation) method. If the direct method is used, a reconciliation of operating income and cash flows from operating activities—that is, the indirect method presentation of cash flows from operating activities—is to be presented either at the bottom of the cash flow statement or as a separate schedule.

Noncapital financing activities and **capital and related financing activities** are distinguished by whether the cash flow is clearly attributable to the financing of capital asset acquisition, construction, or improvement. For example, cash received from issuing bonds that are clearly issued for the explicit purpose of financing construction of a fixed asset are reported as cash flows from capital and related financing activities as would be cash payments of interest or principal on those bonds. The cash effects of issuing or servicing all other debt issuances would be noncapital financing activities.

One striking difference from the business cash flow statement classifications is that cash payments to acquire fixed assets are reported as capital and related financing activities, not as investing activities. Likewise, cash received from the sale or disposal of fixed assets is reported as capital and related financing activities.

Investing activities include (a) making and collecting most loans, (b) making or disposing of investments in debt or equity instruments, and (c) the related interest and dividends received. As noted earlier, acquisition and disposition of capital assets are not reported as investing activities in government cash flow statements. The government cash flow classifications appear to center more on distinguishing capital asset-related cash flows from noncapital asset-related cash flows, whereas the business cash flow classifications focus on distinguishing financing cash flows and investing cash flows.

As in business cash flow statements, the GASB requires disclosure of information about significant noncash financing and investing activities. This information is to be presented in a schedule either on the face of the statement or separately.

Figure 12-1 summarizes the common classifications of the typical cash flows of proprietary funds. As indicated in the figure, some of the transactions resulting in these cash flows are discussed in the next chapter. A simple cash flow

---

[1] GASB Codification, sec 2450.113.

Figure 12-1

CASH FLOW CLASSIFICATIONS SUMMARY

Cash Flows from Operating Activities
- Cash received from sales of goods or services
- Cash paid for materials used in providing services or manufacturing goods for resale
- Cash paid to suppliers for other goods or services
- Cash paid to employees for services
- Cash received or paid resulting from quasi-external transactions
- Cash received from other funds for reimbursement of operating transactions
- Cash payments for taxes
- Cash received or paid from grants for specific activities that are part of grantor governments operating activities
- Other cash flows that are not properly reported in the other classifications

Cash Flows from Noncapital Financing Activities
- Cash received from issuing or paid to repay borrowings not clearly attributable to capital assets
- Cash paid for interest on those borrowings
- Cash received from operating grants (discussed in Chapter 13) not included in operating activities
- Cash paid for grants or subsidies to other governments that are not included in operating activities
- Cash paid for operating or residual equity transfers out and for interfund reimbursements
- Cash received from operating and residual equity transfers not clearly made for capital asset purposes

Cash Flows from Capital and Related Financing Activities
- Cash received from issuing or paid to repay borrowings clearly attributable to capital assets
- Cash paid for interest on those borrowings
- Cash received from capital grants (discussed in Chapter 13)
- Cash paid or received from acquisition or disposal of capital assets
- Cash received from operating or residual equity transfers from other funds for the specific purpose of financing capital assets
- Cash received from special assessments or taxes levied to finance capital assets

Cash Flows from Investing Activities
- Cash paid or received for the acquisition or disposal of investments in debt or equity securities
- Cash paid or received from loans made to others
- Cash received from interest and dividends

Note: This figure is not intended to be comprehensive. Many transactions and situations are beyond the scope of this text.

---

statement is presented in this chapter, while a more complex statement of cash flows is illustrated in Chapter 13.

IS FUND ACCOUNTING ILLUSTRATED

Three illustrations of IS Fund activities, accounting, and reporting make up this section of this chapter. The Fund activities illustrated are a central automotive equipment operation, a Stores Fund, and a Self-Insurance Fund. Only general ledger entries are illustrated in the examples. Subsidiary ledgers and cost accounting systems are maintained for IS Funds, but are not illustrated since they should be identical to those for similar business operations.

A Central Automotive Equipment Unit

Assume that a Central Automotive Equipment Fund has been created and that some of the assets needed have been acquired. The IS Fund balance sheet prior to beginning operations is presented in Figure 12-2. Fund resources will be used to buy automobiles, trucks, tractors, and the like. The use of each machine and the cost of operation on a per mile or per hour basis will be estimated and records of actual cost will be kept so that they may be compared with estimates and may be used in making estimates for coming years. Such records also are useful in evaluating the efficiency of management and economy of operation of various types and brands of equipment.

The following transactions and entries illustrate how a typical IS Fund equipment bureau operates.

Transactions and Entries

1. Purchased equipment by paying $25,000 cash and issuing a two-year, 6% note for $15,000 on October 1.

    (1) Machinery and Equipment 40,000
       Notes Payable 15,000
       Cash. 25,000
       To record purchase of equipment.

2. Materials and supplies purchased on credit, $10,000.

    (2) Inventory of Materials and Supplies 10,000
       Vouchers Payable 10,000
       To record purchase of materials and supplies.

3. Salaries and wages paid, $19,000, distributed as follows:

    Mechanics' Wages $9,000
    Indirect Labor 3,000
    Superintendent's Salary 3,500
    Office Salaries 3,500
                                      19,000

    (3) Expenses—Mechanics' Wages 9,000
       Expenses—Indirect Labor 3,000
       Expenses—Superintendent's Salary 3,500
       Expenses—Office Salaries 3,500
       Cash. 19,000
       To record salaries and wages expenses.

4. Heat, light, and power paid, $2,000.

    (4) Expenses—Heat, Light and Power 2,000
       Cash. 2,000
       To record heat, light, and power expenses.

5. Depreciation:

    Buildings $2,400
    Machinery and Equipment 9,200

    (5) Expenses—Depreciation—Buildings 2,400
       Expenses—Depreciation—Machinery and Equipment . . 9,200
       Accumulated Depreciation—Buildings. 2,400
       Accumulated Depreciation—Machinery and
          Equipment 9,200
       To record depreciation expense.

Figure 12-2

BEGINNING BALANCE SHEET

A Governmental Unit
Central Automotive Equipment (IS) Fund
Balance Sheet
(Date)

Assets

Current assets:		
Cash		$ 75,000
Fixed assets:		
Land	$10,000	
Buildings	40,000	
Machinery and equipment	10,000	60,000
		$135,000

Contributed Capital

Contributed capital—governmental	
unit	$135,000

6. Total billings to departments for services rendered, $42,800, of which $30,000 is payable from the General Fund and $12,800 is payable from the Enterprise Fund.

(6)	Due from General Fund	30,000	
	Due from Enterprise Fund	12,800	
	Revenues—Billings to Departments		42,800
	To record billings to departments.		

Expenditures will be charged in the General Fund, while an expense account will be charged in the Enterprise Fund. In both cases, the credit will be to Due to Central Automotive Equipment (Internal Service) Fund.

The "Billings to Departments" revenues account often is used by governments for IS Fund charges to user departments because (1) some consider the term to be more descriptive and (2) others consider terms such as "Sales" to connote the inclusion of a "profit" element in the charges, which should not be true with IS Fund charges. Alternatively, Sales, or Revenues from Sales, could be credited in this entry.

7. Vouchers payable of $7,500 were paid.

(7)	Vouchers Payable	7,500	
	Cash		7,500
	To record payment of vouchers payable.		

8. Cash collected from the General Fund, $29,000 and from the Enterprise Fund, $10,000.

(8)	Cash	39,000	
	Due from General Fund		29,000
	Due from Enterprise Fund		10,000
	To record collections on interfund receivables.		

9. Office maintenance expenses paid, $200.

(9)	Expenses—Office Maintenance	200	
	Cash		200
	To record miscellaneous office expenses.		

10. Materials and supplies issued during the period, $7,000.

(10) Expenses—Cost of Materials and Supplies Used	7,000	
Inventory of Materials and Supplies		7,000

To record cost of materials and supplies used.

11. Accrued salaries and wages, $1,000, distributed as follows:

Mechanics' Wages	$500
Indirect Labor	150
Superintendent's Salary	175
Office Salaries	175

Also, interest was accrued on notes payable, $400.

(11) Expenses—Interest	400	
Expenses—Mechanics' Wages	500	
Expenses—Indirect Labor	150	
Expenses—Superintendent's Salary	175	
Expenses—Office Salaries and Wages	175	
Accrued Interest Payable.		400
Accrued Salaries and Wages Payables		1,000

To record accrued salaries, wages, and interest.

After these entries have been posted the **trial balance** of the accounts of the IS Fund will appear as follows:

A Governmental Unit

Central Automotive Equipment (IS) Fund
Preclosing Trial Balance

(Date)

Cash	60,300	
Due from General Fund	1,000	
Due from Enterprise Fund	2,800	
Inventory of Materials and Supplies.	3,000	
Land	10,000	
Buildings	40,000	
Accumulated Depreciation—Buildings		2,400
Machinery and Equipment	50,000	
Accumulated Depreciation—Machinery and Equipment		9,200
Vouchers Payable		2,500
Accrued Salaries and Wages Payable		1,000
Accrued Interest Payable		400
Notes Payable.		15,000
Contributed Capital—Governmental Unit		135,000
Revenues—Billings to Departments.		42,800
Expenses—Cost of Materials and Supplies Used	7,000	
Expenses—Mechanics' Wages.	9,500	
Expenses—Indirect Labor	3,150	
Expenses—Superintendent's Salary.	3,675	
Expenses—Depreciation—Buildings	2,400	
Expenses—Depreciation—Machinery and Equipment	9,200	
Expenses—Heat, Light, and Power.	2,000	
Expenses—Office Salaries	3,675	
Expenses—Office Maintenance	200	
Expenses—Interest	400	
	208,300	208,300

Closing entries may be made in a variety of methods. Some accountants prefer to make one compound entry closing all revenue and expense accounts directly to Retained Earnings. Any reasonable closing entry or combination of entries will suffice that (1) updates the Retained Earnings account to its period end balance and (2) brings the temporary proprietary accounts to a zero balance so that they are ready for use during the succeeding period.

(C1)	Revenues—Billings to Departments	42,800	
	Expenses—Cost of Materials and Supplies Used		7,000
	Expenses—Mechanics' Wages.		9,500
	Expenses—Indirect Labor		3,150
	Expenses—Superintendent's Salary.		3,675
	Expenses—Depreciation—Buildings		2,400
	Expenses—Depreciation—Machinery and Equipment		9,200
	Expenses—Heat, Light, and Power.		2,000
	Expenses—Office Salaries		3,675
	Expenses—Office Maintenance.		200
	Expenses—Interest.		400
	Excess of Net Billings to Departments over Costs		1,600
	To close revenue and expense accounts and determine the excess of net charges over costs of services for the period.		
(C2)	Excess of Net Billings to Departments over Costs	1,600	
	Retained Earnings.		1,600
	To close net income for the period to Retained Earnings.		

Figures 12-3, 12-4, and 12-5 present the Balance Sheet; the Statement of Revenues, Expenses, and Changes in Fund Equity; and the Statement of Cash Flows for the Central Automotive Equipment Fund based on the illustrative transactions. Note that the fixed assets of the Fund and the related accumulated depreciation accounts appear in the balance sheet. Since departments are billed for overhead charges, including depreciation, part of the money received from departments represents depreciation charges. The money representing depreciation charges may be debited to a restricted cash account (set up in a separate "fund") to ensure its availability to replace assets; or it may be included in the Fund's general cash and used for various purposes pending the replacement of the assets. In the present case, it is assumed that no segregation is made, nor is a retained earnings reserve established.

Long-term debt incurred for IS Fund purposes is reported in the Fund balance sheet if the resources of the Fund are to be used to service and retire the debt. Certain types of long-term debt such as capital lease obligations and the long-term portion of the liability for compensated absences typically will be repaid from IS Fund resources. Others may be intended to be paid out of general taxation or other sources, such as enterprise earnings in the case of IS Funds furnishing services to a utility department. In such cases the debt should be reported in the General Long-Term Debt Account Group or in an Enterprise Fund, whichever is appropriate in the circumstances.

A Central Stores Fund

Many departments and agencies of a government often use similar or identical materials and supplies. In some governments each department or agency is responsible for acquiring and maintaining a sufficient inventory of the needed materials and supplies. However, many governments centralize their purchasing and ware-

Figure 12-3

ENDING BALANCE SHEET

A Governmental Unit

Central Automotive Equipment (IS) Fund
Balance Sheet

At Close of Fiscal Year (Date)

Assets

Current Assets:

Cash	$60,300	
Due from General Fund	1,000	
Due from Enterprise Fund.	2,800	
Inventory of materials and supplies	3,000	$ 67,100

Fixed Assets:

Land		10,000	
Buildings	$40,000		
Less: Accumulated depreciation	2,400	37,600	
Machinery and equipment	50,000		
Less: Accumulated depreciation	9,200	40,800	88,400
Total Assets			$155,500

Liabilities and Fund Equity

Current Liabilities:

Vouchers payable	$ 2,500	
Accrued salaries and wages payable	1,000	
Accrued interest payable	400	$ 3,900

Long-Term Liabilities:

Notes payable.		15,000
Total Liabilities		18,900

Fund Equity:

Contributed capital—governmental unit		135,000
Retained earnings		1,600
Total Fund Equity		136,600
Total Liabilities and Fund Equity		$155,500

housing operations and operate them as an IS Fund activity to enhance economy, efficiency, and control in these activities. In these latter governments the materials and supplies are purchased and stored by the personnel in the central stores operation and are eventually distributed to user departments when requisitioned by those departments. Departmental billings are usually based on direct inventory cost plus an overhead factor. To simplify the discussion it is again assumed that appropriations are not required for Fund expenditures.

Inventory Acquisition

The first step in the accounting process occurs here when an invoice for supplies of inventory items is approved for payment. At that time, an entry is made to record the purchase and to set up the liability. The entry is as follows:

Inventory of Materials and Supplies	20,000	
Vouchers Payable.		20,000

To record the purchase of materials and supplies.

Note that the debit is not made to a Purchases account but directly to an Inventory of Materials and Supplies account. The reason is that perpetual inventory records should be kept where a central storeroom is in operation.

Figure 12-4

OPERATING STATEMENT

A Governmental Unit

Central Automotive Equipment (IS) Fund

**Statement of Revenues, Expenses, and
Changes in Fund Equity**

For (Period)

Operating Revenues:		
Billings to departments.		$42,800
Operating Expenses:		
Cost of materials and supplies used	$ 7,000	
Other operating costs:		
Mechanics' wages	9,500	
Indirect labor	3,150	
Superintendent's salary	3,675	
Depreciation—building.	2,400	
Depreciation—machinery and equipment	9,200	
Heat, light, and power	2,000	
Office salaries	3,675	
Office maintenance.	200	
Total other operating costs	33,800	
Total Operating Expenses		40,800
Operating Income		2,000
Nonoperating Expenses:		
Interest expense		(400)
Net income		1,600
Fund equity, beginning of the period		135,000
Fund equity, end of the period.		$136,600

Perpetual Inventory Procedures

Materials or supplies purchased for central storerooms are not charged against departmental appropriations until the materials or supplies are withdrawn from the storeroom. One procedure in withdrawing materials and charging appropriations is as follows: When a department needs materials, a stores requisition is prepared. This requisition is made out in duplicate (at least) and is presented to the storekeeper. The storekeeper issues the items called for on the requisition and has the employee receiving them sign one copy of the requisition. This copy is retained by the storekeeper as evidence that the materials have been withdrawn; it is also the basis for posting the individual stock records to reduce the amount shown to be on hand. Subsequently, individual items on the requisition are priced and the total cost of materials withdrawn on the particular requisition is computed. Sometimes requisitions are priced before they are filled, in order to ensure that the cost of materials requisitioned does not exceed a department's unencumbered appropriation, but this procedure is not always practicable.

Billing Rates

In the perpetual inventory record, the unit cost should include the purchase price plus transportation expenses. If the IS Fund capital is to be kept intact, it is necessary also to recover **overhead** costs, such as the salary of the purchasing agent, wages of storekeepers, and amounts expended for heat, light, and power. As noted earlier, these expenses usually are allocated to each requisition based on a predetermined percentage of the cost of the materials withdrawn. The percentage is de-

Figure 12-5

STATEMENT OF CASH FLOWS

A Governmental Unit
Central Automotive Equipment (IS) Fund
Statement of Cash Flows
For (Period)

Cash Flows from Operating Activities:		
Cash received from user departments	$39,000	
Cash paid to suppliers for goods and services	(9,700)	
Cash paid to employees.	(19,000)	
Net cash provided by operating activities.		$10,300
Cash Flows from Capital and Related Financing Activities:		
Acquisition of equipment		(25,000)
Net decrease in cash		(14,700)
Cash and cash equivalents at beginning of year		75,000
Cash and cash equivalents at end of year		$60,300
Reconciliation of Operating Income to Net Cash Provided by Operating Activities:		
Operating income.		$ 2,000
Adjustments to reconcile operating income to net cash provided by operating activities:		
Depreciation	$11,600	
Increase in vouchers payable.	2,500	
Increase in accrued salaries and wages payable	1,000	
Increase in billings receivable	(3,800)	
Increase in inventories	(3,000)	
Total adjustments		8,300
Net cash provided by operating activities.		$10,300

* A schedule describing the Fund's noncash financing and investing activities would also be presented in the government's financial report.

termined by dividing the estimated total stores overhead expenses for the year by the total estimated costs of materials to be issued. Assuming that total stores overhead expenses for the forthcoming year are estimated to be $20,000 and that the cost of the materials to be withdrawn during the period is estimated at $500,000, the overhead rate applicable to materials issued is 4% ($20,000 ÷ $500,000). The amount of overhead to be charged upon the issue of materials that cost the Stores Fund $2,585 is $103.40 (4% of $2,585).

Inventory Issued

As soon as the requisition is priced, information is available for the purpose of billing the department withdrawing the materials. The entry to record the issue and billing is as follows:

Due from General Fund	2,688.40	
Cost of Materials and Supplies Issued	2,585.00	
Billings to Departments.		2,688.40
Inventory of Materials and Supplies		2,585.00

To record the billing and cost of materials issued to
Department of Public Works on Requisition 1405.

Note that the General Fund is billed for both the cost of the materials and a portion of the estimated overhead expenses ($2,585.00 + $103.40).

Overhead Expenses

Entries to record actual overhead expenses in the IS Fund are made at the time the expenses are incurred, not at the time materials are issued. For example, at the time that storekeepers' salaries are approved for payment, the following entry is made:

Salaries and Wages Expenses   1,000
    Vouchers Payable   1,000
To record storekeepers' salaries.

Physical Inventory

Under the system of accounting for materials described here, the inventory of materials and supplies on hand can be ascertained from the records at any time. To ensure that the materials and supplies shown by the records are actually on hand, a physical inventory should be taken at least annually. Usually the actual amount on hand will be smaller than the amount shown by the records. The variation may be due to such factors as shrinkage, breakage, theft, or improper recording. In any event, the records must be adjusted to correspond with the actual physical count by making entries on each perpetual inventory record affected. The Inventory of Materials and Supplies account in the general ledger must also be adjusted, of course. If the amounts according to physical count are less than the amounts shown on the records, the entry is as follows:

Inventory Losses   2,000
    Inventory of Materials and Supplies   2,000
To record inventory losses as revealed by actual physical
    count.

Inventory losses must be recovered if the capital of the IS Fund is to be kept intact, and should be taken into account in estimating the overhead expenses of the central storeroom and establishing the overhead rate to be applied to requisitions.

Closing Entries

Closing entries for the Stores Fund would parallel those illustrated earlier for the Central Automotive Equipment Fund. Similarly, a Balance Sheet; Statement of Revenues, Expenses, and Changes in Fund Equity; and Statement of Cash Flows like those illustrated in Figures 12-3 to 12-5 should be prepared at least annually.

Entries in Other Funds

Thus far we have discussed the entries to be made in the IS Fund. Corresponding entries are, of course, made for the departments receiving the particular materials. In the case of a public works department, whose activities are financed from the General Fund, the entry is as follows:

General Fund
Expenditures—Materials 2,688.40
    Due to IS Fund 2,688.40
To record receipt of materials by the Department of Public
    Works and liability to IS Fund.

A Self-Insurance Fund

The insurance crisis of recent years has made it more difficult for state and local governments to acquire needed amounts of insurance coverage at reasonable costs, if at all. One result of this crisis is that some governments are **"self-insuring"** a part or all of their properties, potential liabilities for claims and judgments, and other risks. To centralize its risk financing activities and **self-insure** a portion or all of its risks, a government must establish a program designed to provide for potential losses—other than those covered by outside insurers—from its own resources. The amount of resources that should be set aside must be actuarially determined to help ensure that it will be sufficient to cover losses actually incurred. Also, if the government is partially insured by third party insurers, insurance premiums will have to be paid to outside insurers for such coverage.

Some governments are centralizing their risk financing activities and others are not. Governments that do not centralize their risk financing activities account for claims and judgments associated with general government activities in the various governmental fund(s) and account groups affected in accordance with the guidance illustrated in Chapter 6. Governments that centralize their risk financing activities should use either the General Fund or an Internal Service Fund to account for those activities. If the General Fund is used, all covered claims and judgments are recorded as General Fund expenditures and any amounts charged to other (user) funds are reported as reductions of General Fund expenditures (as reimbursements—not as revenues). Use of Self-Insurance IS Funds is illustrated next.

Use of Self-Insurance IS Funds

In practice, self-insurance plans are often established by charging the various departments and agencies of the government for their share of the cost of the "self-insurance" coverage. Sometimes this cost is actuarially determined or is the amount that an insurance policy would have cost. In other instances the amount of the cost is based on other techniques that do not ensure as appropriate an allocation of self-insurance costs either over time or among departments as do actuarially based costing methods.

Current authoritative guidance now in effect does not address accounting and reporting for self-insurance Internal Service Funds definitively. GASB Statement 10, "Accounting and Financial Reporting for Risk Financing and Related Insurance Issues," has no effective date since its effective date is to be coordinated with the implementation of GASB Statement 11, "Measurement Focus and Basis of Accounting—Governmental Fund Operating Statements." GASBS 10 can be implemented early, however, within the context of the current reporting model. Under GASBS 10, if a government centralizes its risk financing and accounting in an Internal Service Fund, it should:

- Recognize all claims and judgments liabilities and expenses in the ISF.
- Charge the other funds amounts that are reasonable and equitable—preferably actuarially based—such that Self-Insurance IS Fund revenues and expenses are approximately equal. In addition charges may include a reasonable provision for expected future catastrophe losses.
- Reserve or designate any retained earnings resulting from incremental charges made to provide for expected future catastrophe losses.

- Determine whether payments to the Self-Insurance Fund that are more or less than the required amounts are in-substance interfund transfers or loans.

Accounting for Self-Insurance IS Funds

Accounting for Self-Insurance Funds entails primarily (1) accounting for the revenues from billings to departments for the actuarially determined contributions or "premiums" to be paid to the fund, (2) accounting for investment of the fund resources provided to establish the reserve for contingent losses, and (3) accounting for the recognition and settlement of claims and judgments against the fund for "self-insured" losses.

Revenues. **Amounts** paid to or accrued by Self-Insurance IS Funds **based on actuarial** or other acceptable **estimates** should be reported as **Revenues.** Amounts paid to the Self-Insurance IS Funds that differ from these charges should be evaluated carefully to determine the substance of the transaction or event. For instance, overpayments in one year may be in substance prepayals of subsequent years' "premiums"—if the intent is to reduce or eliminate the need for a particular department or agency to contribute to the fund in the next year. In such cases these overpayments should be treated as IS Fund **deferred revenues** and as prepayments in the payer fund(s).

In other cases overpayments are made to the Self-Insurance Fund from one or more other funds with no intention of payments being reduced or avoided in subsequent years. Rather, these payments might be interfund loans or advances or might be made to provide contributed capital from which losses in excess of those provided for through departmental billings can be financed temporarily until made up through increased charges to "insured" departments or agencies in subsequent years. In the latter case **residual equity transfers** should be recorded for the overpayment received. If routine, recurring overpayments are made to subsidize IS Fund losses, the overpayments should be reported as **operating transfers.**

Expenses. Claims and judgments for covered losses should be recorded as expenses in the **Self-Insurance IS Fund**—not in the insured funds—when **both** of the following conditions set forth in the GASB Codification for recognizing contingent losses are met:

1. Information prior to the issuance of the financial statements indicates that it is **probable** that an asset was impaired or a liability incurred at the date of the financial statements; and
2. The **amount** of the loss can be **reasonably estimated.**

Illustrative Transactions and Entries

These principles are illustrated in the following transactions and entries for a newly established Self-Insurance IS Fund of a Governmental Unit.

Transactions and Entries

1. General Fund resources of $500,000 were transferred to establish a Self-Insurance IS Fund, which is both (a) to acquire insurance from third party insurers, where available at reasonable cost and (b) to "self-insure" other risks.

General Fund
(1a) Residual Equity Transfer to IS Fund.   500,000
    Cash   500,000
    To record contribution of resources to establish a
    self-insurance fund.

Internal Service Fund
(1b) Cash   500,000
    Residual Equity Transfer from General Fund.   500,000
    To record contribution from General Fund.

(Note that the residual equity transfer will be closed to Contributed Capital—Governmental Unit at the end of the year.)

2. The actuarially determined payments required from "insured funds" were $80,000 from the General Fund and $20,000 from the Enterprise Fund.

General Fund
(2a) Expenditures   80,000
    Due to Self-Insurance IS Fund.   80,000
    To record billings for insurance coverage and
    self-insurance for departments financed from the
    General Fund.

Enterprise Fund
(2b) Expenses.   20,000
    Due to Self-Insurance IS Fund.   20,000
    To record billings for insurance coverage and
    self-insurance for the enterprise activity.

Internal Service Fund
(2c) Due from General Fund   80,000
    Due from Enterprise Fund   20,000
    Revenues—Billings to Departments (or Premiums)   100,000
    To record revenues from billings to departments
    "insured" through the IS Fund.

3. Three-fourths of the amounts due from the other funds were collected.

General Fund
(3a) Due to Self-Insurance IS Fund.   60,000
    Cash   60,000
    To record payment of interfund payable.

Enterprise Fund
(3b) Due to Self-Insurance IS Fund.   15,000
    Cash   15,000
    To record payment of interfund payable.

Internal Service Fund
(3c) Cash   75,000
    Due from General Fund   60,000
    Due from Enterprise Fund   15,000
    To record collection of interfund receivables.

Note again that if more than the actuarially determined amount had been paid to the IS Fund, only the actuarially required payments should be recorded as expenditures or expenses in the "insured" funds and as revenues in the Self-Insurance IS Fund. Any additional payments should be treated as discussed previously. Underpayments should be recorded as interfund payables/receivables, as in this example—if they are to be settled in some definite time frame—or, if not, as interfund transfers out of the IS Fund.

4. Investments with a par value of $460,000 were purchased at a discount of $10,000.

Internal Service Fund

(4)	Investments.	460,000	
	Unamortized Discounts on Investments.		10,000
	Cash.		450,000

To record purchase of investments.

5. Premiums paid to third party insurers were $8,000, of which $500 was for coverage for the next fiscal year.

Internal Service Fund

(5)	Expenses—Insurance Premiums.	7,500	
	Prepaid Insurance	500	
	Cash.		8,000

To record payment of insurance premiums.

6. Payments in settlement of claims and judgments incurred during the year amounted to $22,000, net of insurance recovery.

Internal Service Fund

(6)	Losses—Claims and Judgments	22,000	
	Cash.		22,000

To record settlement of claims and judgments during the year.

7. The accrued liability for probable losses for claims and judgments is estimated to total $70,000 at year end, net of expected insurance recovery (the accrued liability was zero at the beginning of the year). Administrative expenses paid totaled $3,800. Half of the liabilities for claims and judgments are expected to be settled in the next fiscal year and the remainder in subsequent periods.

Internal Service Fund

(7)	Losses—Claims and Judgments	70,000	
	Expenses—Administrative.	3,800	
	Liability for Claims and Judgments—Current		35,000
	Liability for Claims and Judgments—Long-Term. . .		35,000
	Cash.		3,800

To adjust the accrued liabilities for claims and judgments to their appropriate year end balances and record administrative expenses incurred.

8. Interest of $27,600 was accrued on investments at year end and discount amortization of $1,200 was recorded.

Internal Service Fund

(8)	Accrued Interest Receivable.	27,600	
	Unamortized Discounts on Investments.	1,200	
	Revenues—Interest		28,800

To record accrual of interest and discount amortization at year end.

9. The Self-Insurance Fund accounts were closed and the actuarially required balance was recorded in a reserve for losses.

Internal Service Fund

(9) (a)	Revenues—Billings to Departments	100,000	
	Revenues—Interest	28,800	
	Losses—Claims and Judgments		92,000
	Expenses—Administrative		3,800
	Unreserved Retained Earnings		33,000
	To close the accounts.		
(b)	Unreserved Retained Earnings	26,000	
	Retained Earnings Reserved for Losses		26,000
	To adjust the reserve for losses to its actuarially determined required balance.		

The financial statements required for the Self-Insurance IS Fund are a Balance Sheet, a Statement of Revenues, Expenses, and Changes in Fund Equity (or Retained Earnings), and a Statement of Cash Flows. Since these statements would be similar to those illustrated in Figures 12-3 to 12-5 for the Central Automotive Repair IS Fund, they are not presented here.

DISPOSITION OF PROFIT OR LOSS

The necessity of basing charges to departments on estimates means that in the usual case an IS Fund, even one that is intended to break even, has a profit or loss at the end of a year. The profit or loss may be disposed of in one of the following ways:

1. It may be charged or credited to the billed departments in accordance with their usage. If the intent is for the fund to break even, this procedure is theoretically the correct one.

2. The amount may be closed to Retained Earnings with the intent of adjusting the following year's billings to eliminate the balance. This procedure is a practical substitute for the first.

3. The amount may be closed to and left in Retained Earnings without subsequent adjustment of billing rates—on the theory that the Fund will break even over a period of several years.

In the absence of specific instructions, the profit or loss should be closed to Retained Earnings. No refunds, supplemental billings, or transfers should be made in the absence of specific authorization or instructions in this regard.

RETAINED EARNINGS

The cost-reimbursement focus of IS Funds would seem to indicate that significant retained earnings should **not** exist over the long term in IS Funds. Indeed, the AICPA audit guide, *Audits of State and Local Governmental Units,* states,

> . . . rates should not be established at confiscatory levels that siphon off assets earmarked for other purposes. Likewise, rates should not be set so low that significant losses are incurred that result in retained earnings deficits . . . Because the intent of these funds is to facilitate cost allocation, accumulation of resources or deficits over a long-term is considered inappropriate.[2]

[2] AICPA, *Audits of State and Local Governmental Units,* Exposure Draft, 1993, par. 13.29.

While the intent of an IS Fund implies that significant retained earnings should not exist in IS Funds except for Self-Insurance IS Funds where provisions for future catastrophe losses have been made, other exceptions do appear to exist. In practice many governments have significant retained earnings balances in various traditional IS Funds. Such balances may have resulted from "overcharging" user funds for goods or services provided in order to permit replacement of Fund fixed assets at higher replacement costs. As mentioned earlier, such excessive charges are not considered proper—particularly if the charges are passed on to federally- or state-financed programs, where they may not be allowable and may be illegal. On the other hand, the balance could result from routine operating transfers from the General Fund or other funds to provide additional financing needed to replace Fund fixed assets or gradually expand operations—which would be entirely appropriate even given the cost allocation focus of IS Funds.

DISSOLUTION OF AN IS FUND

When the services provided by an ISF are no longer needed, or when some preferable method of providing them is found, the Fund is dissolved. The net current assets of a dissolved fund are usually transferred to the funds from which the capital was originally secured. However, if capital was secured by incurring general obligation long-term debt, the net current assets usually are transferred to the Debt Service Fund that will retire the debt.

Fixed assets are usually transferred to departments financed from the funds that contributed the capital or to the departments that can best use them. Unless they are transferred to one of the governmental unit's proprietary funds, the assets are recorded in the General Fixed Assets Account Group accounts. If transferred to an enterprise, they are recorded in the Enterprise Fund.

COMBINING IS FUND FINANCIAL STATEMENTS

As with other fund types, combining financial statements must be prepared for IS Funds by governments having more than one IS Fund. Typically, individual fund statements for individual IS Funds are not necessary since sufficient individual fund detail is usually provided in the individual fund columns of the combining statements and any schedules accompanying those statements. The total columns of the combining statements are included in the combined financial statements—which make up the general purpose financial statements (GPFS) of a government as discussed and illustrated in Chapter 14.

The combining Internal Service Fund statements included in a recent Comprehensive Annual Financial Report for Arlington County, Virginia are presented in Figures 12-6, 12-7, and 12-8.

CONCLUDING COMMENTS

Internal Service Funds are used to account for departments or agencies of a state or local government that provide goods or services to its other departments or agencies or to other governments on a cost-reimbursement basis. Since such ac-

Figure 12-6

ARLINGTON COUNTY, VIRGINIA
INTERNAL SERVICE FUNDS
COMBINING BALANCE SHEET
JUNE 30, 19X1
(With Comparative Totals for 19X0)

	Automotive Equipment	Technology and Information Systems	Printing	Totals June 30 19X1	Totals June 30 19X0
ASSETS					
CURRENT ASSETS:					
Equity in pooled cash and investments	$2,951,429	$499,608	$243,445	$3,694,482	$2,593,931
Accounts receivable	321,723	86,575	7,696	415,994	111,272
Inventories	506,565	-	93,029	599,594	448,743
Total Current Assets	3,779,717	586,183	344,170	4,710,070	3,153,946
FIXED ASSETS, at cost:					
Equipment and other fixed assets	19,277,463	13,054,379	607,067	32,938,909	30,989,310
Less-allowance for depreciation	(9,077,055)	(7,822,290)	(380,510)	(17,279,855)	(15,489,727)
Net Fixed Assets	10,200,408	5,232,089	226,557	15,659,054	15,499,583
Total Assets	$13,980,125	$5,818,272	$570,727	$20,369,124	$18,653,529
LIABILITIES AND EQUITY					
CURRENT LIABILITIES:					
Accrued salaries payable	$ -	$ -	$ -	$ -	$208,276
Vouchers payable	572,087	443,156	38,274	1,053,517	424,662
Current portion-capital leases	-	963,048	-	963,048	182,913
Compensated absences	207,016	459,542	60,825	727,383	631,488
Due to other funds	11,500	3,113,361	-	3,124,861	-
Total Current Liabilities	790,603	4,979,107	99,099	5,868,809	1,447,339
LONG-TERM LIABILITIES-capital leases	-	353,659	-	353,659	2,733,540
Total Liabilities	790,603	5,332,766	99,099	6,222,468	4,180,879
EQUITY:					
Contributed capital	3,015,288	129,702	169,908	3,314,898	3,314,898
Retained earnings	10,174,234	355,804	301,720	10,831,758	11,157,752
Total Equity	13,189,522	485,506	471,628	14,146,656	14,472,650
Total Liabilities and Equity	$13,980,125	$5,818,272	$570,727	$20,369,124	$18,653,529

See accompanying notes to financial statements.

Source: Adapted from a recent comprehensive annual financial report of Arlington County, Virginia.

tivities are intended to be self-sustaining, net income determination and capital maintenance are important aspects of accounting and financial reporting for such funds. Thus, the accounting and reporting principles that apply are typically identical to those for similar business operations and the same financial statements are prepared.

Activities commonly managed and accounted for through IS Funds include communications, data processing, printing and duplication, motor pools and maintenance services, central purchasing and stores operations, and self-insur-

Figure 12-7

ARLINGTON COUNTY, VIRGINIA
INTERNAL SERVICE FUNDS
COMBINING STATEMENT OF REVENUES, EXPENSES AND CHANGES IN EQUITY
FOR THE YEAR ENDED JUNE 30, 19X1,
(With Comparative Totals for 19X0)

	Automotive Equipment	Technology and Information Systems	Printing	Totals June 30 19X1	Totals June 30 19X0
OPERATING REVENUES:					
Charges for services	$8,805,367	$7,823,083	$1,798,434	$18,426,884	$17,459,934
OPERATING EXPENSES:					
Cost of store issuances	1,622,097	-	725,042	2,347,139	1,627,593
Personnel services	1,877,466	2,457,921	406,441	4,741,828	4,248,106
Fringe benefits	542,105	620,431	116,882	1,279,418	1,120,821
Material and supplies	2,509,316	195,485	255,512	2,960,313	2,104,952
Utilities	88,792	1,229,493	9,882	1,328,167	1,540,549
Outside services	107,851	1,273,603	74,998	1,456,452	1,080,810
Depreciation	1,872,123	1,781,481	82,249	3,735,853	3,748,206
Insurance and other	399,830	1,181,073	145,844	1,726,747	1,421,147
Total Operating Expenses	9,019,580	8,739,487	1,816,850	19,575,917	16,892,184
Operating Income (Loss)	(214,213)	(916,404)	(18,416)	(1,149,033)	567,750
NON-OPERATING REVENUES (EXPENSES):					
Interest income	-	-	-	-	10,205
Interest expense	-	(169,970)	(102)	(170,072)	(307,447)
Gain (Loss) on disposal of assets	189,622	(11,543)	-	178,079	(289,398)
Total Non-operating Revenues (Expenses)	189,622	(181,513)	(102)	8,007	(586,640)
Income Before Operating Transfers	(24,591)	(1,097,917)	(18,518)	(1,141,026)	(18,890)
OPERATING TRANSFERS IN (OUT):					
Operating transfers in	234,222	610,774	100,036	945,032	1,242,912
Operating transfers out	(130,000)	-	-	(130,000)	(130,000)
Total Operating Transfers	104,222	610,774	100,036	815,032	1,112,912
Net Income (Loss)	79,631	(487,143)	81,518	(325,994)	1,094,022
EQUITY:					
Retained earnings, beginning of year	10,094,603	842,947	220,202	11,157,752	10,063,730
Retained earnings, end of year	10,174,234	355,804	301,720	10,831,758	11,157,752
Contributed capital	3,015,288	129,702	169,908	3,314,898	3,314,898
Total Equity	$13,189,522	$485,506	$471,628	$14,146,656	$14,472,650

See accompanying notes to financial statements.

Source: A recent comprehensive annual financial report of Arlington County, Virginia.

ance programs. Such activities often involve millions of dollars of government resources, as indicated in the Arlington County, Virginia financial statements presented in Figures 12-6 through 12-8.

Appropriately classifying activities that should be reported in Internal Service Funds rather than in the governmental funds and account groups is essential since significantly different accounting and reporting principles apply and different financial statements are prepared under the two treatments. Indeed, the assets, liabilities, and equities of an Internal Service Fund activity would be accounted for in several different funds and account groups if classified as a general government rather than as a proprietary fund operation.

Figure 12-8

ARLINGTON COUNTY, VIRGINIA
INTERNAL SERVICE FUNDS
COMBINING STATEMENT OF CASH FLOWS
FOR THE YEAR ENDED JUNE 30, 19X1
(With Comparative Totals for 19X0)

	Automotive Equipment	Technology and Information Systems	Printing	Totals June 30 19X1	June 30 19X0
CASH FLOWS FROM OPERATIONS:					
Cash received from customers	$8,523,225	$7,804,143	$1,794,795	$18,122,163	$17,767,322
Cash paid to suppliers	(4,439,775)	(3,609,471)	(1,291,570)	(9,340,816)	(7,776,288)
Cash paid to employees	(2,485,233)	(3,100,389)	(548,003)	(6,133,625)	(5,261,809)
Net cash flows from operations	1,598,217	1,094,283	(44,778)	2,647,722	4,729,225
CASH FLOWS FROM INVESTING ACTIVITIES:					
Interest received	-	-	-	-	11,931
Net cash flows from investing activities	-	-	-	-	11,931
CASH FLOWS FROM NON-CAPITAL FINANCING ACTIVITIES:					
Cash received (paid) to other funds	11,500	3,113,361	-	3,124,861	1,043,010
Operating transfers	104,222	610,774	100,036	815,032	1,112,912
Net cash flows from non-capital financing activities	115,722	3,724,135	100,036	3,939,893	2,155,922
CASH FLOWS FROM CAPITAL AND RELATED FINANCING ACTIVITIES:					
Principal payments under capital leases	-	(1,592,802)	(6,944)	(1,599,746)	(1,702,287)
Contributions from other sources	-	-	-	-	83,600
Purchases of equipment and other fixed assets	(2,240,965)	(1,884,145)	(13,757)	(4,138,867)	(4,633,869)
Proceeds from sale of equipment	279,832	141,790	-	421,622	98,326
Interest paid	-	(169,970)	(102)	(170,072)	(307,447)
Net cash flows from capital and related financing activities	(1,961,133)	(3,505,127)	(20,803)	(5,487,063)	(6,461,677)
Net increase (decrease) in cash and cash equivalents	(247,194)	1,313,291	34,455	1,100,552	435,401
Cash and cash equivalents at beginning of year	3,198,623	(813,682)	208,990	2,593,931	2,158,530
Cash and cash equivalents at end of period	$2,951,429	$499,609	$243,445	$3,694,483	$2,593,931
Reconciliation of operating income to net cash flows from operations:					
Operating income	($214,213)	($916,404)	($18,416)	($1,149,033)	$567,750
Adjustments to reconcile operating income to net cash provided by operating activities:					
Depreciation	1,872,123	1,781,481	82,249	3,735,853	3,748,206
(Increase)Decrease in accounts receivable	(282,142)	(18,940)	(3,639)	(304,721)	307,392
(Increase)Decrease in inventories	(97,472)	-	(53,380)	(150,852)	85,347
Increase(Decrease) in accrued salaries	(87,311)	(101,560)	(19,404)	(208,275)	26,236
Increase(Decrease) in vouchers payable	385,583	270,183	(26,912)	628,854	(86,588)
Increase(Decrease) in compensated absences	21,649	79,523	(5,276)	95,896	80,882
Net cash flows from operations	$1,598,217	$1,094,283	($44,778)	$2,647,722	$4,729,225

See accompanying notes to financial statements.

Source: A recent comprehensive annual financial report of Arlington County, Virginia.

479

QUESTIONS

12-1 Why might IS Funds be thought of as "revolving" or "working capital" funds?

12-2 IS Funds are proprietary (nonexpendable) funds. How does this cause IS Fund accounting to differ from that for governmental (expendable) funds?

12-3 Many governments use terms such as "Billings to Departments" and "Excess of Net Billings to Departments Over Costs" in IS Fund accounting and reporting rather than more familiar terms such as "Sales" and "Net Income." Why?

12-4 Why is an IS Fund typically not subject to fixed budgetary control?

12-5 Accounting for an IS Fund that is controlled by a fixed budget may be referred to as "double accounting." Why?

12-6 In what ways might the original capital required to establish an IS Fund be acquired?

12-7 What advantages might a governmental unit expect from the use of an IS Fund to account for the acquisition, storage, and provision of supplies for the various departments?

12-8 What major benefits should accrue from accurate cost data being maintained for activities accounted for through the IS Fund?

12-9 Under what circumstances would the *direct* cost of the goods or services provided (with no additions to acquisition cost for items such as depreciation or overhead) be the appropriate basis for IS Fund reimbursement? Explain.

12-10 Why are predetermined price schedules or overhead rates commonly used in IS Fund billings to user departments?

12-11 An IS Fund established by a county is intended to operate on a break-even basis. How might profits or losses (or a retained earnings balance remaining at year end) be disposed of?

12-12 A city operates a motor pool as an IS Fund. List and evaluate the ways that over- or underabsorbed overhead may be treated.

12-13 An IS Fund was established ten years ago through the sale of 20-year bonds. What disposition should be made of the assets of the fund if it is dissolved?

12-14 In a certain state a question has arisen as to whether the maintenance of one of the state office buildings should be financed by a single appropriation for maintenance or whether maintenance expenses should be financed through an IS Fund. If an IS Fund were established, the departments would be charged rent based on the amount of space occupied and an appropriation would be made to each department for this purpose. Which of the two methods would you recommend? Why?

12-15 The mayor wants to increase the size of an IS Fund by setting a higher than cost rate of reimbursement. What response would you make to his suggestion?

12-16 How should overtime premiums incurred in the conduct of IS Fund activities be charged to user departments where IS Fund charges are based on direct cost plus overhead?

(AICPA, adapted)

12-17 What are the major classifications of cash flows required to be presented for a proprietary or nonexpendable trust fund? Distinguish between them.

12-18 What are the key differences between the cash flow statement requirements for IS Funds and those for business enterprises?

PROBLEMS

P 12-1 (Multiple Choice)

1. Which of the following liabilities are not accounted for and reported in the same manner by an Internal Service Fund and a business enterprise?
   a. Capital leases
   b. Compensated absences
   c. Contingent liabilities
   d. Pension liabilities
   e. both c and d.

2. Initial financing for Internal Service Fund activities may be obtained from
   a. advances from another fund

    b. profits from the provision of goods or services to departments within the government

    c. appropriation of related materials held by governmental departments

    d. both a and c

    e. all of the above

3. The Yourtown Motor Pool Fund estimates that the cost of operating and maintaining its fleet of 20 vehicles during 19X8 will be $150,000. On the basis of past experience, each vehicle can be expected to be used 150 days during the year and can be expected to be driven 3,000 miles during the year. The other costs of operating the Fund are estimated at $15,000 for the year. The price that the Motor Pool fund should charge other Yourtown government departments for use of a motor pool vehicle is

    a. $50 per day   d. $2.75 per mile

    b. $55 per day   e. a or c

    c. $2.50 per mile   f. b or d

4. Residual equity transfers are always reported in an IS Fund operating statement if it reports revenues, expenses and changes in

    a. unreserved retained earnings   d. all of the above

    b. total retained earnings   e. none of the above

    c. total fund equity

5. If a computer previously recorded in the General Fixed Assets Account Group is contributed to a department accounted for in an IS Fund, the computer will be recorded in the IS Fund accounts

    a. at the historical cost recorded in the GFAAG accounts

    b. at the historical cost, less the amount of depreciation that would have been recorded if it had originally been purchased for the Internal Service Fund.

    c. at the computer's fair market value on the contribution date

    d. at the computer's replacement value on the contribution date

    e. either a or b

6. The "price" charged by an Internal Service Fund department to other departments for a service should include

    a. the direct cost to the fund of providing the service

    b. the direct cost to the fund of providing the service, plus a proportionate share of the fund's variable overhead costs

    c. the direct cost to the fund of providing the service, plus a proportionate share of the fund's total overhead costs

    d. the direct cost to the fund of providing the service, plus a proportionate share of the fund's variable overhead costs, plus a reasonable cushion for contingencies and capital growth

    e. the direct cost to the fund of providing the service, plus a proportionate share of the fund's total overhead costs, plus a reasonable cushion for contingencies and capital growth

7. The activity level of an Internal Service Fund is normally controlled by

    a. the appropriations made by its controlling legislative body

    b. the flexible budget enacted by its controlling legislative body

    c. the formal budget enacted by its controlling legislative body

    d. the needs of the various governmental departments using its services

8. The actuarially required contribution from the General Fund to a Self-Insurance IS Fund should be reported in the IS Fund as

    a. Operating transfers

    b. Revenues

    c. Residual equity transfers

d. Deferred revenues until claims and judgments are incurred

e. Revenues only if the required payment is made

P 12-2 (Cash Flow Statement Classifications) Use the letter beside the appropriate cash flow statement classification to indicate the section of the cash flow statement in which each of the following transactions of an IS Fund should be reported.

a. Cash flows from operating activities

b. Cash flows from noncapital financing activities

c. Cash flows from capital and related financing activities

d. Cash flows from investing activities

e. None of the above. Explain.

1. Cash purchase of equipment

2. Operating transfer received from the General Fund which represents an annual operating subsidy

3. Payment of accounts payable created by the acquisition of supplies on credit

4. A cash contribution by the General Fund for the purpose of financing half the cost of new equipment

5. Payment of capital lease payments

6. Cash received from the collection of billings to other departments

7. Cash paid for investments in bonds of other governments

8. Interest accrued on the investments in 7

9. Cash received from borrowing on a short-term basis to resolve a temporary cash shortage

10. Cash borrowed from other funds on a short-term basis to finance an equipment purchase

P 12-3 (Self-Insurance Fund Entries)

1. Sorensen County established a self-insurance program in 19X8 by transferring $2,000,000 of General Fund resources to an Internal Service Fund that is to be used to account for the county's self-insurance program.

2. An actuarial study indicated that to provide the appropriate loss reserve for the county's self-insurance program for risks self-insured for various departments, $75,000 should be charged to the General Fund for the year and $15,000 to the various Enterprise Funds of the county. The $75,000 General Fund payment was made to the Self-Insurance Fund, and $30,500 was paid from the Enterprise Funds to cover the estimated cost chargeable to those funds for the next fiscal year as well as the current year's cost.

3. Administrative expenses payable from the IS Fund totaled $3,600.

4. Claims filed against the county during the year were settled for $42,000 (paid).

5. The county attorney estimated that it is probable that the county will incur additional losses from current year incidents giving rise to claims and judgments of $36,000. Of those claims, $22,000 probably will be settled and paid within 30–60 days after the end of the year; the remainder most likely will not be finally settled for at least two to three years. In addition, it is reasonably likely that other claims for events occurring during 19X8 will result in additional losses of $4,200.

Required (a) Prepare the journal entries required in 19X8 for the Sorensen County Self-Insurance Fund.

(b) Prepare the IS Fund journal entries that would have been required in transactions 4 and 5 if (1) there were no Self-Insurance IS Fund—and thus transactions 1, 2, and 3 had not occurred, and (2) all of the claims relate to the Central Printing ISF.

P 12-4 (Worksheet) The trial balance for the Metro School District Repair Shop at January 1, 19X6 was as follows:

Cash	$ 30,000	
Due from Other Funds	40,000	
Inventory.	10,000	
Building	35,000	
Equipment	100,000	
Accumulated Depreciation—Building		$ 12,000
Accumulated Depreciation—Equipment.		30,000
Vouchers Payable.		35,000
Contributed Capital.		136,000
Retained Earnings.		2,000
	$215,000	$215,000

The Repair Shop Fund had the following transactions during 19X6:

1. Materials purchased on account, $20,000.

2. Materials used, $7,000.

3. Payroll paid, $12,000.

4. Utilities paid, $3,500.

5. Billings to departments for repair services, $29,500.

6. Collections from departments, $27,900.

7. Equipment acquired under a capital lease; capitalizable cost, $8,000, and initial payment, $300.

8. Subsequent lease payments, $1,000, including $100 interest.

9. Depreciation on:

Buildings	$2,000
Equipment	4,000
	$6,000

10. Payments on vouchers payable, $30,000.

Required Prepare a worksheet for the Metro School District Repair Shop Fund for 19X6 with columns for the beginning trial balance, transactions and adjustments, adjusted trial balance, closing entries (operating statement), and year-end balance sheet.

P 12-5 (Entries and Trial Balance) The City of Morristown operates a printing shop through an Internal Service Fund to provide printing services for all departments. The Central Printing Fund was established by a contribution of $30,000 from the General Fund on January 1, 19X5, at which time the equipment was purchased. The postclosing trial balance on June 30, 19X8 was as follows:

	Debits	*Credits*
Cash.	$35,000	
Due from General Fund.	2,000	
Accounts Receivable	1,500	
Supplies Inventory.	3,000	
Equipment	25,000	
Accumulated Depreciation—Equipment		$ 8,750
Accounts Payable		4,750
Advance from General Fund		20,000
Contributed Capital—City		30,000
Retained Earnings		3,000
	$66,500	$66,500

The following transactions occurred during fiscal year 19X9:

1. The Publicity Bureau, financed by the General Fund, ordered 30,000 multicolor travel brochures printed at a cost of $1.20 each. The brochures were delivered.

2. Supplies were purchased on account for $13,000.

3. Employee salaries were $30,000. One-sixth of this amount was withheld for taxes and is to be paid to the City's Tax Fund; the employees were paid.

4. Taxes withheld were remitted to the Tax Fund.

5. Utility charges for the year, billed by the Enterprise Fund, were $2,200.

6. Supplies used during the year cost $10,050.

7. Other billings during the period were: Electric Enterprise Fund, $300; Special Revenue Fund, $4,750.

8. The inventory of supplies at year end was $5,900.

9. Unpaid receivable balances at June 30, 19X9 were: General Fund, $3,000; Special Revenue Fund, $750.

10. Printing press number 3 was repaired by the central repair shop, operated from the Maintenance Fund. A statement for $75 was received but has not been paid.

11. The Accounts Receivable at June 30, 19X8 were collected in full.

12. Accounts Payable as of June 30, 19X9 totaled $2,800.

13. Depreciation expense was recorded, $2,500.

Required   (a) Journalize all transactions and adjustments required in the Central Printing Fund accounts.

(b) Prepare closing entries for the Central Printing Fund accounts as of June 30, 19X9.

(c) Prepare a postclosing trial balance for the Central Printing Fund as of June 30, 19X9.

P 12-6   (Worksheet) From the information in Problem 12-5, prepare a columnar worksheet to reflect the beginning balances, transactions and adjustments, closing entries (results of operations), and ending balances of the Central Printing Fund of the City of Morristown for the year ended June 30, 19X9.

P 12-7   (Worksheet and Financial Statements) The following is a trial balance of an Internal Service Fund established to finance the operations of a central garage of the City of Zeffler at January 1, 19X5:

Land	$ 35,000	
Buildings	70,000	
Accumulated Depreciation—Buildings		$ 10,000
Equipment	180,000	
Accumulated Depreciation—Equipment		60,000
Cash	45,000	
Inventory:		
Gasoline	4,000	
Oil and Grease	2,000	
Tires	6,500	
Parts	13,500	
Due from General Fund	20,000	
Vouchers Payable		75,000
Contributed Capital		228,000
Retained Earnings		3,000
	$376,000	$376,000

1. Wages and salaries (all chargeable to 19X5) were as follows:

Salary of superintendent	$10,000
Mechanics' wages	39,000
Garage office salaries	6,500

2. Purchases (on account) were as follows:

Gasoline	$20,000
Oil and grease	2,000
Tires	16,000
Parts	30,000

3. Departments are charged at a predetermined rate based on mileage. During the year 19X5, billings to departments amounted to $140,000, all of which was payable from the General Fund. At December 31, 19X5, $25,000 was owed the Internal Service Fund from the General Fund.

4. Other expenses were as follows:
Heat, light, and power, $10,000, which is due to the Enterprise Fund
Depreciation—
    Buildings, 5 percent of original cost
    Equipment, 10 percent of original cost

5. Vouchers payable paid, $35,000.

6. Closing inventories were as follows:

Gasoline	$ 7,000
Oil and grease	1,500
Tires	11,500
Parts	15,000

7. Accrued salaries and wages were as follows:

Salary of superintendent	$ 250
Mechanics' wages	830
Garage office salaries	180

Required   (a) Prepare a worksheet showing the beginning balances, transactions and adjustments, operations, and ending balances of the Internal Service Fund of the City of Zeffler for 19X5.

(b) Prepare a Balance Sheet as of December 31, 19X5, and Statements of Cash Flows and of Revenues, Expenses, and Changes in Fund Equity for the year ended December 31, 19X5 for the Internal Service Fund of the City of Zeffler.

P 12-8   (Transaction and Closing Entries) The City of Merlot operates a central garage through an Internal Service Fund to provide garage space and repairs for all city-owned and operated vehicles. The Central Garage Fund was established by a contribution of $500,000 from the General Fund on July 1, 19X7, at which time the building was acquired. The postclosing trial balance at June 30, 19X9 was as follows:

	Debit	Credit
Cash	$150,000	
Due from General Fund	20,000	
Inventory of Materials and Supplies	80,000	
Land	60,000	
Building	200,000	
Accumulated Depreciation—Building		$ 10,000
Machinery and Equipment	56,000	
Accumulated Depreciation—Machinery and Equipment		12,000
Vouchers Payable		38,000
Contribution from General Fund		500,000
Retained Earnings		6,000
	$566,000	$566,000

The following information applies to the fiscal year ended June 30, 19Y0:

1. Materials and supplies were purchased on account for $74,000.
2. The inventory of materials and supplies at June 30, 19Y0 was $58,000, which agreed with the physical count taken.
3. Salaries and wages paid to employees totaled $230,000, including related costs.
4. A billing from the Enterprise Fund for utility charges totaling $30,000 was received and paid.
5. Depreciation of the building was recorded in the amount of $5,000. Depreciation of the machinery and equipment amounted to $8,000.
6. Billings to other departments for services rendered to them were as follows:

General Fund	$262,000
Water and Sewer Fund	84,000
Special Revenue Fund	32,000

7. Unpaid interfund receivable balances at June 30, 19Y0 were as follows:

General Fund	$ 6,000
Special Revenue Fund	16,000

8. Vouchers payable at June 30, 19Y0 were $14,000.

Required   (a) For the period July 1, 19X9 through June 30, 19Y0, prepare journal entries to record all of the transactions in the Central Garage Fund accounts.

(b) Prepare closing entries for the Central Garage Fund at June 30, 19Y0.
(AICPA, adapted)

P 12-9   (Transaction and Adjusting Entries)

1. Fredrick County established a Central Data Processing Internal Service Fund in 19X7. Data processing services had previously been financed via General Fund appropriations. To establish the fund, $750,000 (original cost) of computers and peripheral equipment were provided to the IS Fund from general fixed assets. The equipment, on average, had two-thirds of its six-year useful life remaining (estimated residual value, $90,000). Also, computer paper and other supplies costing $32,000 were transferred to the IS Fund from the General Fund. General Fund inventories are accounted for on the consumption basis. In addition, $65,000 of General Fund cash was contributed to the Central Data Processing Fund to provide needed working capital.
2. Electric bills of $17,000 and payrolls of $41,000 were paid.
3. Insurance premiums of $6,400 were paid for a policy covering both the current and the next fiscal years.
4. Supplies purchased on account cost $65,000.
5. Cost of supplies used was $72,000.
6. Billings to departments for data processing services were $260,000.
7. Vouchers payable of $57,000 were paid.
8. Depreciation on equipment was recorded, $100,000.
9. Collections of amounts due from other funds for billings were $235,000.
10. Other information:
   a. Salaries and wages payable at year end were $1,100.
   b. Inventory of supplies on hand at year end was $24,700.

Required   Prepare the general journal entries required to record all transactions and adjustments for the Central Data Processing Fund for 19X7.

P 12-10   (Worksheet) From the information in Problem 12-9, prepare a worksheet to reflect the transactions and adjustments, results of operations, and year-end balance sheet for the Fredrick County Central Data Processing Fund.

ENTERPRISE FUNDS: Summary of Interfund- Account Group Accounting

Enterprise Funds are established to account for activities of a government that provide goods or services primarily to the public at large on a consumer charge basis. They should be distinguished from Internal Service Funds, which account for activities that provide goods or services to other departments of the governmental unit, and from activities of the general government that provide incidental services to the public for compensation, such as libraries, highway departments, and police departments.

The GASB states that Enterprise Funds should be used:

> to account for operations **(a)** that are **financed and operated** in a manner **similar to private business enterprises**—where the intent of the governing body is that the **costs** (expenses, including depreciation) of providing goods or services to the general public on a continuing basis be *financed or recovered primarily through user charges;* **or (b)** where the **governing body has decided** that periodic determination of revenues earned, expenses incurred, and/or net income is appropriate for capital maintenance, public policy, management control, accountability, or other purposes.[1]

This definition provides much flexibility. The first part (a) may be described as **"mandatory,"** since meeting this criterion **requires** the use of Enterprise Funds. Part (b), on the other hand, may be described as **"permissive."** It provides wide discretion to the governing body in determining the circumstances under which the Enterprise Fund approach will be used. The "permissive" part (b) of the Enterprise Fund definition was included because some types of activities, such as mass transit systems, meet the part (a) criterion (supported primarily by user charges) in some years and do not meet it in others. By using the part (b) "permissive" part of the definition a government can account for its mass transit system consistently through the years as an Enterprise Fund. Further, some types of activities, such as city markets or convention centers, may never be supported primarily by user charges, yet city officials may want them operated as Enterprise Funds in order to know their operating results on that basis as well as their expen-

[1] GASB Codification, sec. 1300.104b(1). (Emphasis added.)

dable resource flows and balances. This flexibility results in lack of uniformity among governments, of course.

State and local governments engage in a seemingly unlimited variety of businesses. Among the many types of activities of governments financed through Enterprise Funds are electric generation and/or distribution systems, water systems, natural gas distribution systems, sewer systems, public docks and wharves, hospitals, nursing homes, and other health care facilities, off-street parking lots and garages, toll highways and bridges, public housing, airports, garbage and other solid waste collection and disposal services, public transportation systems, lotteries, liquor wholesaling and retailing operations, swimming pools, and golf courses.

A discussion of Enterprise Fund accounting and reporting principles and procedures comprises the principal topic of this chapter. The chapter is concluded by a summary review of interfund (or multifund) and account group accounting concepts that is designed to assist the reader (1) review the material covered thus far, (2) integrate his or her knowledge of appropriate accounting principles and procedures for the various types of funds and account groups commonly employed by state and local governments, and (3) gain conceptual dexterity in the application of appropriate accounting principles and procedures in the multiple entity accounting environment of governments.

ENTERPRISE FUND ACCOUNTING

Enterprise activities may be administered through a department of a general purpose government, a separate board or commission under the jurisdiction of the government, or an independent special district not under the general purpose government's jurisdiction. Regardless of organizational location or the type of activity involved, certain characteristics, principles, and procedures are common to all Enterprise Fund accounting.

Characteristics of Enterprise Fund Accounting

For purposes of discussion, the major **distinguishing characteristics** of Enterprise Fund accounting may be categorized conveniently under the following headings: (1) accounting principles, (2) restricted asset accounts, and (3) budgeting and appropriations. Other features of certain enterprise situations, such as payments in lieu of taxes, are discussed later in the chapter.

Accounting Principles

Enterprise Funds, like Internal Service Funds, are **proprietary (nonexpendable) funds.** Thus, it is essential to distinguish between capital contributions and revenues and to account for revenues and expenses on an accrual basis so that periodic net income or loss can be determined. Fixed assets and long-term debt related to enterprise activities are accounted for in the Enterprise Fund, as are depreciation and amortization.

More specifically, the pertinent **accounting principles** or standards **are those used** in accounting **for privately owned enterprises** of **similar** types and sizes. Indeed, many municipally owned utilities are required by supervisory commissions to follow the same accounting as that prescribed for privately owned utilities of the same class. For external financial reporting purposes the pronouncements of the Financial Accounting Standards Board (and its predecessors) are to be followed, where applicable, unless GASB pronouncements indicate otherwise. Too, legal or contractual reporting requirements that differ from GAAP must be met in supplemental schedules presented in the Comprehensive Annual Financial Report or by issuing special purpose reports.

Most transactions between the enterprise and other governmental departments should be accounted for in the same manner as "outsider" transactions; that is, as **quasi-external transactions.** Therefore, goods or services provided by an Enterprise Fund department or activity to departments of the government financed from other funds should be billed at regular, predetermined rates; and all goods or services provided the enterprise by other governmental departments should be billed to it on the same basis that other users are charged. If this is not done, operating and position statements of all funds may be distorted.

A **separate fund** usually should be established **for each** government **enterprise,** and all transactions or events relating to a specific enterprise should be recorded in the appropriate Enterprise Fund records. The major exception to this general rule occurs in the case of related activities, such as water and sewer utilities, which may be merged because of their complementary nature or because joint revenue bonds often are used in financing such operations.

Restricted Asset Accounts

Enterprise activities may involve transactions or relationships that, if encountered in a general government situation, would require the use of several separate and distinct fund entities. Thus, utilities may require customers to post deposits (Trust or Agency), may acquire or construct major capital facilities (Capital Projects), or may have funded reserves or other debt-related resources (Debt Service). In some cases, certain enterprise-related **intrafund "funds"** are required to be established under terms of bond indentures or similar agreements.

In keeping with its recommendation that governmental enterprises follow appropriate commercial accounting principles, the GASB recommends that the term **"funds"** be interpreted in this instance in the usual commercial accounting connotation of **restricted assets.** Thus, Enterprise Funds may contain several **"funds within a fund,"** since the use of distinctively titled intrafund restricted asset accounts (accompanied by related liability and, if desired, by equity reserve accounts) is deemed preferable to the use of a series of separate fund entities in Enterprise Fund accounting. Application of the "funds within a fund" approach is demonstrated in the illustrative example in this chapter.

Budgeting and Appropriations

As in the case of Internal Service Funds, careful planning and realistic budgeting should be considered prerequisites to sound Enterprise Fund management. If flexible budgets are adopted, it is clear that, as in business enterprises, they are guides to action and means of managerial control, not fixed limitations as are the budgets of governmental funds. If fixed budgets are adopted because of legal requirements or executive or legislative body desire to control some (e.g., capital outlay) or all expenditures, the Enterprise Fund accounts may be maintained on the budgetary basis during the year, then converted to GAAP at year end. Alternatively, the budget may be incorporated into the chart of accounts as discussed in Chapter 12.

Enterprise Fund Accounting Illustrated

Services of the type generally referred to as **"public utilities"** are among the most common enterprise activities undertaken by local governments. Such activities invariably involve significant amounts of assets, liabilities, revenues, and expenses and are seldom considered in contemporary undergraduate accounting courses.

For these reasons, we have chosen an **electric utility example** to illustrate Enterprise Fund accounting procedures. The illustrative utility is assumed to be non-regulated. Regulated utilities are subject to special accounting and reporting requirements not discussed here. The illustrative example is presented in several phases.

Establishment of Fund and Acquisition of Plant

The acquisition of a utility may be financed wholly or partially by the sale of bonds to be retired from utility earnings, by contributions or grants from the governmental unit, by intergovernmental grants, by intergovernmental or intragovernmental loans, and by contributions from subdivision developers and prospective customers. Assuming that the acquisition of the illustrative utility plant is financed through a General Fund contribution, the entry to record the **receipt of the contribution and the establishment of the Fund** at the end of 19X1 is:

(1) Cash 400,000
          Residual Equity Transfer from General Fund   400,000
      To record governmental unit's contribution for acquisition
        of utility.

Next, assume that the net assets of an existing private electricity generation and distribution plant are acquired by the government at the end of 19X1. The government is to pay $280,000, which is the fair value of the assets acquired less the fair value of the liabilities assumed. The entry to record the **acquisition of the plant and the assumption of the liabilities** is:

(2) Land   50,000
     Buildings   90,000
     Improvements Other Than Buildings 480,000
     Machinery and Equipment 110,000
     Accounts Receivable   62,000
     Inventory of Materials and Supplies   10,000
          Allowance for Uncollectible Accounts   12,000
          Bonds Payable   500,000
          Vouchers Payable   10,000
          Due to ABC Electric Company   280,000
      To record the acquisition of the assets and liabilities of
        the ABC Electric Company.

Payment of the amount due to ABC Electric Company is recorded as follows:

(3) Due to ABC Electric Company 280,000
          Cash   280,000
      To record payment to ABC Electric Company.

At the **end of 19X1,** the **residual equity transfer account** would be **closed** with the following entry:

(4) Residual Equity Transfer from General Fund 400,000
          Contributed Capital—Governmental Unit   400,000
      To close residual equity transfer from General Fund.

Accounting for Routine Operating Transactions

The following transactions and entries illustrate the operation of an Enterprise Fund for a utility. These transactions occur in 19X2, the first year of operations. The accounting procedures for (1) the receipt and expenditure of bond proceeds,

(2) utility debt service and related "funds," and (3) customers' deposits require use of intrafund restricted asset accounts and are discussed in a subsequent phase of the example.

To simplify the discussion, all revenues, with the exception of interest and other nonoperating revenues, are assumed to be credited to an **Operating Revenues control account;** and all expenses are assumed to be charged to either an **Operating Expenses** or a **Nonoperating Expenses control account.** A detailed operating expense statement is illustrated in Figure 13-5.

Transactions and Entries—During 19X2

5.   Materials costing $59,000 were received.

(5)	Inventory of Materials and Supplies	59,000	
	Vouchers Payable		59,000
	To record purchase of materials.		

6.   Revenues billed during the year totaled $300,000.

(6)	Accounts Receivable	300,000	
	Operating Revenues		300,000
	To record operating revenue.		

7.   Equipment costing $50,500 was purchased on account.

(7)	Machinery and Equipment	50,500	
	Vouchers Payable		50,500
	To record purchase of equipment.		

8.   Rental due on equipment rented to the State Public Works Department totaled $7,000.

(8)	Due from State Public Works Department	7,000	
	Nonoperating Revenues—Equipment Rental		7,000
	To record rental of equipment to State Public Works Department.		

9.   Collections on accounts receivable were $290,000, and interest received totaled $1,000.

(9)	Cash	291,000	
	Accounts Receivable		290,000
	Nonoperating Revenues—Interest		1,000
	To record collection of accounts receivable and interest revenues.		

10.   A bill was received from an Internal Service Fund for services rendered, $12,800.

(10)	Operating Expenses	12,800	
	Due to Internal Service Fund		12,800
	To record cost of services rendered by Internal Service Fund.		

11. Cash payments were made during the year for:

Salaries and wages	$127,200
Telephone and telegraph services	500
Fire insurance premiums (two-year policy) . .	1,000
Bond principal retirement	50,000
Interest on bonds	20,000
Utilities	10,500
Vouchers payable (including $30,000 on the equipment from Transaction 7)	70,000
	$279,200

(11)	Operating Expenses	139,200	
	Bonds Payable	50,000	
	Nonoperating Expenses—Interest	20,000	
	Vouchers Payable	70,000	
	Cash		279,200

To record payments of various expenses and liabilities.

(Prepaid insurance, $600, is recorded in an adjusting entry later in the example.)

12. $10,000 was paid from the Enterprise Fund to the General Fund to subsidize General Fund operations.

(12)	Operating Transfer to General Fund	10,000	
	Cash		10,000

To record payment of operating transfer to General Fund.

13. A subdivision electricity system, valued at $30,000 was donated to the utility by the subdivision developer.

(13)	Improvements Other than Buildings	30,000	
	Contributed Capital—Contributions from Subdividers . .		30,000

To record dedication of subdivision distribution lines to the utility.

(Hookup, tapping, or tap fees and similar charges paid by customers also should be credited to a contributed capital account, such as Contributed Capital—Contributions from Customers, to the extent they exceed recovery of hookup costs.)

Note that (1) **contributed capital** changes are carefully **distinguished from revenues, expenses, gains, and losses** and (2) **operating and nonoperating** revenues and expenses are carefully **distinguished** in the illustrative entries. In Enterprise Fund (as in IS Fund) accounting and reporting the distinction between contributed capital and retained earnings is significant since proprietary-type activities typically are intended to be self-sustaining. The extent to which the activity is self-sustaining is reflected by its Retained Earnings account if increases and decreases in equity have been distinguished appropriately over time.

Likewise, the distinction between operating and nonoperating revenues and expenses is significant. If significant nonoperating revenues are needed to cover operating expenses, the full cost of services provided is not being charged to users of Enterprise Fund services. This implies that the activity may not be able to sustain itself in the future without rate increases if (1) the nonoperating revenue is reduced significantly or (2) the demand for the department's (underpriced) services increases significantly.

Finally, note and review the other key differences between governmental fund and proprietary fund accounting. These include the required use of the consumption method of inventory accounting (entry 5) and the gross revenue approach (entry 6) in proprietary funds, reporting fixed assets and noncurrent liabilities in proprietary funds (entries 2 and 7), and accounting for expenses (rather than expenditures) in proprietary funds.

Adjusting Entries—End of 19X2

14. Necessary adjusting entries at the end of 19X2 were based on the following data.

a.	Accrued salaries and wages payable	$ 6,000
	Accrued interest payable	2,000
	Accrued utilities payable	7,500
b.	Prepaid insurance	600
c.	Ending inventory of materials and supplies	30,000
d.	Estimated losses on accounts receivable . .	1,500
e.	Depreciation:	
	Buildings	5,000
	Improvements Other Than buildings . .	15,000
	Machinery and equipment	16,000
f.	Unbilled receivables	21,000
	Accrued interest receivable	200

(14)	(a)	Operating Expenses		13,500	
		Nonoperating Expenses—Interest		2,000	
		Accrued Salaries and Wages Payable			6,000
		Accrued Interest Payable			2,000
		Accrued Utilities Payable			7,500
		To record accrued expenses.			
	(b)	Prepaid Insurance		600	
		Operating Expenses			600
		To record unexpired insurance.			
	(c)	Operating Expenses		39,000	
		Inventory of Materials and Supplies			39,000
		To record operating expenses for materials used during year.			
	(d)	Operating Expenses		1,500	
		Allowance for Uncollectible Accounts			1,500
		To record estimated losses on accounts receivable.			
	(e)	Operating Expenses		36,000	
		Accumulated Depreciation—Buildings			5,000
		Accumulated Depreciation—Improvements Other than Buildings			15,000
		Accumulated Depreciation—Machinery and Equipment			16,000
		To record depreciation for fiscal year.			
	(f)	Unbilled Accounts Receivable		21,000	
		Accrued Interest Receivable		200	
		Operating Revenues			21,000
		Nonoperating Revenues—Interest			200
		To record unbilled receivables and revenues and accrued interest receivable at year end.			

Accounting for Restricted Asset Accounts

As indicated earlier, an enterprise's restricted assets are accounted for in the Enterprise Fund accounts rather than through separate fund entities. This is accomplished through use of **distinctively titled restricted asset, liability, and, if desired, equity reserve accounts**—by establishing **"funds" within the Enterprise Fund**—so that a single fund serves the purpose of several separate fund entities. Before studying the procedures that follow, note how the Trial Balance (Figure 13-2) and the Balance Sheet (Figure 13-3) presented at the conclusion of this example are designed to separate those **intrafund "funds"** from the unrestricted assets and other liabilities and equities.

The types of restricted asset situations that may be encountered in practice vary widely, from simple customer deposits "funds" to complex series of "funds" required under terms of bond indentures, through legislative decree, or for administrative purposes. Several of the more common restricted asset situations are presented here to illustrate the use of **intrafund restricted asset accounts,** sometimes referred to as **"secondary account groups,"** in Enterprise Fund accounting.

In the following illustrations we use distinctively titled asset and liability accounts for each "fund" and adjust the appropriate reserve accounts by inspection at period end. (The reserve accounts are commonly used, but are not required by GAAP.) **"Fund" revenues and expenses** are recorded in the Electricity (Enterprise) Fund **revenue and expense control** accounts under the assumption that any "fund" detail needed is provided in subsidiary records. Alternatively, we might have used detailed "fund" revenue and expense accounts and closed them at period end either (1) directly to the appropriate reserve account, or (2) to the Retained Earnings account, followed by an entry adjusting the appropriate reserve account. If needed, special purpose reports may be issued for these restricted subfunds to satisfy legal or contractual reporting requirements.

Customer Deposits "Trust or Agency Subfund." A utility usually requires its customers to post deposits, on which it normally pays interest, as a partial protection against bad debt losses. The following transactions and entries illustrate the procedures for recording the deposits, earnings thereon, interest paid to depositors, forfeited deposits, and the return of deposits upon termination of service:

Transactions and Entries—During 19X2

15. Deposits of $11,000 were received.

(15)	**Customer Deposits—Cash**	11,000	
	Customer Deposits—Deposits Payable		11,000
	To record receipt of customer deposits.		

16. Deposits of $10,000 were invested (assume that no premiums, discounts, or accrued interest were involved).

(16)	**Customer Deposits—Investments**	10,000	
	Customer Deposits—Cash		10,000
	To record investment of customer deposits.		

17. Interest accrued on investments but not received totaled $200.

(17)	**Customer Deposits—Accrued Interest Receivable**	200	
	Nonoperating Revenues—Interest		200
	To record interest revenues.		

Note that not all accounts affected by these transactions are "subfund" accounts. The "subfund" accounts are in boldface type to emphasize the effects of the transactions on the subfund.

18. Interest accrued on deposits at year end, $150.

(18)	Nonoperating Expenses—Interest	150	
	Customer Deposits—Accrued Interest Payable		150
	To record interest expense.		

19. A customer's deposit was declared forfeited for nonpayment of his account.

(19)	(a)	**Customer Deposits—Deposits Payable**	12	
		Customer Deposits—Accrued Interest Payable . . .	2	
		Allowance for Uncollectible Accounts	8	
		Accounts Receivable		22
		To record forfeiture of customer's deposit, offset against overdue receivable, and write-off of the uncollectible balance.		
	(b)	Cash	14	
		Customer Deposits—Cash		14
		To reclassify forfeited customer deposit cash to unrestricted cash.		

Note that entry 18(b) is made to reclassify the forfeited customer deposits as unrestricted cash. The customer no longer has a valid claim against the assets—as reflected in entry 18(a); therefore, use of the assets is no longer restricted.

20. A customer moving to another town requested that her service be disconnected. Her final bill was offset against her deposit, and the balance was remitted to her.

(20)	(a)	**Customer Deposits—Deposits Payable**	15	
		Customer Deposits—Accrued Interest Payable . . .	3	
		Accounts Receivable		10
		Customer Deposits—Cash		8
		To record offsetting of customer's final bill against her deposit account and remittance of the balance due her.		
	(b)	Cash	10	
		Customer Deposits—Cash		10
		To reclassify customer deposit cash applied to final bill as unrestricted cash.		

Adjusting Entry—End of 19X2

21. The appropriate reserve account was adjusted at period end to equal the net assets of the "fund."

(21)	Retained Earnings	50	
	Reserve for Earnings on Customer Deposits		50
	To reserve Retained Earnings to indicate that net assets of the Customer Deposits Subfund are available only for customer deposit interest requirements.		

This entry is based on the assumption that subfund revenues are **restricted** for paying interest on deposits. Under these conditions some accountants prefer to use distinctively titled "subfund" revenue and expense accounts to facilitate preparation of this entry. **If** the revenues from the restricted assets are **unrestricted,** no reserve would be established and the Customer Deposits subfund would be an Agency subfund rather than a Trust subfund.

Construction Financed by Bond Issue ("CPF Subfund"). Accounting for Enterprise Fund construction financed through the sale of bonds is not unlike that for private construction. Both the authorization of the bond issue and appropriations, if any, are normally recorded in memorandum form rather than formally within the accounts. However, Enterprise Fund bond indentures may **require** Capital Projects Funds and/or Debt Service Funds to be used to account for proceeds of the bond issue or resources required to be set aside for debt service, respectively. The **"funds within a fund"** approach illustrated here usually **satisfies** these **legal or contractual requirements.**

The following transactions and entries illustrate appropriate procedures in the typical case.

Transactions and Entries—During 19X2

22. Bonds of $200,000 (par) were sold at a premium of $2,000 to provide financing for expansion and modernization of the utility's distribution system. The premium cash was restricted for debt service.

(22)			
	Construction—Cash	200,000	
	Debt Service—Cash	2,000	
	Unamortized Premiums on Bonds		2,000
	Bonds Payable		200,000

To record sale of bonds at a premium.

23. A contract was entered into with Smith & Company for the construction of part of the project at a cost of $100,000.

(23) No entry is necessary to record entering into a contract; a narrative memorandum entry may be made.

24. Materials costing $41,000 were purchased by the utility and delivered to the construction site.

(24)			
	Construction Work in Progress	41,000	
	Construction—Vouchers Payable		41,000

To record cost of construction materials.

25. A bill for $30,000 was received from Smith & Company.

(25)			
	Construction Work in Progress	30,000	
	Construction—Contracts Payable		30,000

To record receipt of bill from Smith & Company for part of cost of contract.

26. The amount due Smith & Company was paid, as was the bill for materials purchased.

(26)			
	Construction—Vouchers Payable	41,000	
	Construction—Contracts Payable	30,000	
	Construction—Cash		71,000

To record payment of amount now due on contract and of bill for materials.

27. Construction labor and supervisory expenses of $56,000 were paid.

(27)			
	Construction Work in Progress	56,000	
	Construction—Cash		56,000

To record cost of labor and supervisory expenses.

28. Smith & Company completed its part of the construction project and submitted its bill for $70,000. The completed project was found to be satisfactory.

(28) (a) Construction Work in Progress   70,000

                  Construction—Contracts Payable   70,000

            To record receipt of bill from Smith & Company to
cover remaining cost of contract.

      (b) Improvements Other Than Buildings   197,000

                  Construction Work in Progress   197,000

            To close Construction Work in Progress account and
to record the cost of completed improvements.

29.   Smith & Company was paid in full, and the remaining bond cash was transferred to the Enterprise debt service "fund."

(29) **Construction—Contracts Payable**   70,000

      Debt Service—Cash   3,000

          Construction—Cash   73,000

      To record final payment to contractor and transfer of
unused bond proceeds to Debt Service Fund.

This entry assumes that the bond indenture requires unused bond proceeds to be used for debt service on the bonds.

Debt Service and Related Accounts.   A variety of intrafund "funds" related to bond issues may be required (in addition to a construction or Capital Projects "fund") under terms found in contemporary bond indentures. Among the most usual of these are:

1.   ***Term Bond Principal Sinking Fund.*** Often referred to merely as a "sinking" fund, its purpose is to accumulate specified amounts of assets, and earnings thereon, for the eventual retirement of **term** bond principal. These usually are for older issues, since most recent issues are serial bonds rather than term bonds.

2.   ***Serial Bond Debt Service Fund.*** This type of intrafund "fund," commonly referred to as an "Interest and Redemption," "Interest and Sinking," or "Bond and Interest" fund, is often required to assure timely payment of **serial** bond interest and principal. A common indenture provision is that one-sixth of the next semiannual interest payment, plus one-twelfth of the next annual principal payment, be deposited monthly in a "fund" of this type.

3.   ***Principal and Interest Reserve Fund.*** Often referred to simply as a "Reserve" fund, intrafund "funds" of this type are often required to provide bondholders an additional "cushion" or safety margin. "Funds" of this sort are usually required to be accumulated to a specific sum immediately or within the first 60 months after bonds are issued and are to be used (1) to pay matured bonds and interest if the resources in the Debt Service "fund" prove inadequate, or (2) if not required earlier to cover deficiencies, to retire the final bond principal and interest maturities.

4.   ***Contingencies Fund.*** This intrafund "fund," sometimes referred to as the "Emergency Repair" or "Operating Reserve" fund, is intended to afford bondholders even more security by providing in advance for emergency expenditures or for operating asset renewal or replacement. Thus, the bondholder receives additional assurance that (1) the operating facilities will not be permitted to deteriorate in order that bond principal and interest requirements be met and (2) the utility will not be forced into receivership because of such unforeseen expenditure requirements. Like the Principal and Interest Reserve "fund," the Contingencies "fund" is usually required to be accumulated in a specific amount early in the life of the bond issue.

In order to illustrate the operation and accounting for debt service-related "funds" within an Enterprise Fund, let us assume that Debt Service, Principal and Interest Reserve, and Contingencies "funds," as described in the preceding items 2, 3, and 4, are required under terms of an enterprise bond indenture. A total of $5,000 has already been classified as Debt Service—Cash (Construction "fund" transactions 22 and 29) as a result of a bond issue premium ($2,000) and unused bond issue proceeds ($3,000). The following transactions illustrate typical activities related to these restricted asset accounts:

Transactions and Entries—During 19X2

30. The Debt Service "fund" was increased by $25,000; and $10,000 each was added to the Principal and Interest Reserve "fund" and to the Contingencies "fund."

(30) **Debt Service—Cash**	25,000	
Principal and Interest Reserve—Cash	10,000	
Contingencies—Cash	10,000	
Cash		45,000
To record amounts restricted and set aside for these "funds."		

31. Interest on bonds, $15,000, was paid.

(31) Nonoperating Expenses—Interest	15,000	
Debt Service—Cash		15,000
To record payment of bond interest.		

32. A $7,000 unforeseen emergency repair was incurred and is to be paid from the Contingencies "fund."

(32) Operating Expenses	7,000	
Contingencies—Vouchers Payable		7,000
To record liability for emergency repair expense.		

33. Principal and Interest Reserve "fund" cash, $9,000, was invested.

(33) **Principal and Interest Reserve—Investments**	9,000	
Principal and Interest Reserve—Cash		9,000
To record investment of "fund" cash.		

34. Interest was earned on the investments, $450, of which $300 was received in cash.

(34) **Principal and Interest Reserve—Cash**	300	
Principal and Interest Reserve—Accrued Interest		
Receivable	150	
Nonoperating Revenues—Interest		450
To record interest earned and received.		

35. Bond interest payable had accrued at year end, $6,000; premium of $300 was amortized.

(35) Nonoperating Expenses—Interest	5,700	
Unamortized Premiums on Bonds	300	
Debt Service—Accrued Bond Interest Payable		6,000
To record bond interest accrued and amortization of bond premium.		

36. The appropriate reserve accounts were adjusted at year end to equal the net assets of the "funds."

(36)	Retained Earnings	22,450	
	Reserve for Bond Debt Service		9,000
	Reserve for Bond Principal and Interest Payments		
	Guarantee		10,450
	Reserve for Contingencies		3,000

To adjust reserve accounts at year end.

Retained Earnings reserves need to be adjusted to equal "fund" net assets only prior to statement preparation. Continuous adjustment merely constitutes "busy work," though such practice is technically correct and may occasionally be found in practice and on the Uniform CPA Exam. The purpose of these reserves is to indicate that restricted intrafund "fund" net assets are not available for "dividends" to the General Fund or for other purposes. The reserves also constitute the balancing accounts of the self-balancing "funds within a fund." Finally, as noted earlier, GAAP does **not** require that the reserves be maintained unless they are legally or contractually required. However, maintaining the reserves makes the "funds" self-balancing.

Special Assessment Improvements Affecting Enterprise Funds

Though special assessments projects most commonly relate to general government capital projects or services, special assessments also are sometimes a source of financing for Enterprise Fund services or capital assets. **Service-type** special assessments for Enterprise Fund services should be treated like Enterprise Fund user fees. Accounting for **capital-type** special assessment projects that result in Enterprise Fund capital assets being acquired or constructed depends upon whether the project is administered by the enterprise activity.

SA Project Administered Separately.

Special assessment projects that result in construction or acquisition of **Enterprise Fund fixed assets** may be accounted for in Capital Projects and Debt Service Funds, respectively. In such cases, the long-term debt, except for any portion that is to be repaid from Enterprise Fund resources, is included in the General Long-Term Debt Account Group. However, the fixed assets constructed or acquired are recorded in the Enterprise Fund as is any related debt, and the **net** amount is accounted for as **contributed capital.** For example, if improvements costing $900,000 were constructed in a special assessment project for Enterprise Fund use, and $100,000 of related notes payable are to be repaid from the Enterprise Fund, the entry in the **Enterprise Fund** would be:

Improvements Other Than Buildings	900,000	
Notes Payable		100,000
Contributed Capital—Contributions from Property Owners . .		800,000

To record construction of improvements via special assessment
projects, including Enterprise Fund share of project liabilities.

SA Project Administered by Enterprise Activity.

Special assessment projects that result in Enterprise Fund fixed assets may be **administered by** the **Enterprise Fund department** or activity. In such cases, **all** of the **assets, liabilities,** and **transactions** for the special assessment project **may be accounted for in** the **Enterprise Fund** using proprietary fund accounting principles. Hence, issuance of the debt would be reflected by recording the payable in the Enterprise Fund. Costs incurred on the construction of the project would be recorded as Enterprise Fund fixed assets. Segregation of special assessment project cash, investments, receivables, payables, and so on according to the purposes for which they are to be used would be accomplished by using restricted asset accounting as illustrated in this chapter. For instance, the bond proceeds to be used for construction would be accounted for in a Special Assessment Construction "fund" **within** the Enterprise Fund like the construction fund illustrated earlier.

Deferred Compensation Plans

As discussed in Chapter 11, IRC Section 457 deferred compensation plans covering **only** proprietary fund employees are to be reported in the specific proprietary fund(s). The assets of the plan to which the government has legal access (typically measured at fair market value as indicated in Chapter 11) are reported as **unrestricted assets of the proprietary fund(s) as is an equal liability to employees for benefit payments.** (The assets may be reported as "designated" for plan participants, but **not** as "restricted," according to the GASB Codification. Recall that if proprietary fund employees participate in plans that also cover governmental fund employees, **all** of the plan assets and liabilities to which the government has legal access should be reported in an Agency Fund. None will be reported in the proprietary funds in such cases.

Adjusting Entries

For ease of illustration, we have included most of the required adjusting entries in the various phases of our example. Most of the adjusting entries required are similar to those common in commercial accounting; and, as in commercial accounting, those of an accrual nature typically would be reversed at the beginning of the subsequent period. The adjusting entry for **unbilled receivables** may be less familiar to the reader, so is discussed further here. Also, the interest capitalization requirements for qualifying fixed assets financed with tax-exempt debt differ from the interest capitalization requirements for assets financed with taxable debt—as is typical for business entities. Since tax-exempt financing is far more common for business-type activities of government, those differences are discussed briefly.

Unbilled Receivables.   Accurate determination of the revenue earned during a year requires that significant amounts of **unbilled receivables** be accrued at year end, particularly if the amount of such receivables varies materially from year to year. This is not to say that a cutoff point in the billing cycle cannot be used, or that other expediency methods that do not distort reported net income or financial position cannot be employed. Such methods should be used only after careful consideration of their possible distortions or biases, however, and should be applied consistently each year.

Interest Capitalization.   State and local governments may issue both **taxable** and **tax-exempt** bonds and other debt securities to finance Enterprise Fund fixed assets. Capitalization of **material** amounts of **taxable debt** interest cost incurred during construction of assets to be used in operations (and certain other assets) is required by FASB *Statement No. 34,* "Capitalization of Interest Cost." The interest capitalized is determined by **multiplying** the **weighted average accumulated expenditures** for an asset **by** the weighted average **interest rate** on specific new borrowings associated with the asset (or by the weighted average rate on other borrowings if no specific borrowing is associated with the asset or if the average accumulated expenditures exceed the proceeds from the associated specific borrowings). However, the **interest capitalized** during a period **cannot exceed** the **actual interest** cost incurred **during the period. If** the **interest** on the **debt** is **tax-**

able, FASB *Statement No. 34* does **not permit offsetting** investment **earnings** on temporary investment of debt proceeds **against** the **interest expense** in determining the capitalizable interest.

When construction of a qualifying asset is financed with **taxable debt, capitalization begins** when three conditions are met:

- Expenditures for the asset have been made.
- Activities that are necessary to get the asset ready for its intended use are in progress.
- Interest cost is being incurred.[2]

Interest capitalization **ends** when the asset is substantially complete and ready for its intended use.

Since the Tax Reform Act of 1986 restricted the amounts of federally tax-exempt debt that state and local governments can issue and added various arbitrage provisions, **SLGs** are **likely** to **issue substantial** amounts of **taxable debt in** the **future.** Nonetheless, when feasible, SLGs will finance their major construction activities with **tax-exempt debt** and/or **grants** that are **restricted for construction** of a capital facility (or debt service on related debt).

FASB *Statement No. 62,* "Capitalization of Interest Cost in Situations Involving Certain Tax-Exempt Borrowings and Certain Gifts and Grants," *modifies* the FASB *Statement No. 34* **guidance if** the **proceeds of tax-exempt debt** or gifts and grants are **restricted** for construction of an asset that qualifies for interest capitalization. FASB *Statement No. 62* has three key provisions:

1. The **interest capitalization period** shall **begin when** tax-exempt **debt** restricted for construction of a qualifying asset is **issued.**
2. The **interest cost capitalized** for a period will be **all interest cost** of the borrowing during the capitalization period, **less** any **investment earnings** on temporary investment of the bond proceeds during that period—**when** qualifying assets are financed with tax-exempt debt **restricted for construction of the assets.**[3]
3. **No interest** cost should be **capitalized** on **assets financed by** gifts or **grants.**[4]

Since governments issue **both taxable and tax-exempt debt,** it is important to understand the guidance related to both situations. To help focus attention on other unique aspects of Internal Service Fund and Enterprise Fund accounting and reporting, interest capitalization has not been incorporated in the illustrative entries and statements. To highlight the differences in interest capitalization when qualifying assets are financed with taxable debt and when the assets are financed with tax-exempt debt, a brief illustration follows, assuming:

- $1,000,000 of 7%, ten-year bonds were issued at 100 on January 1, 19X6. Interest is payable each December 31.
- Proceeds of the bonds are restricted to use for constructing a clubhouse for the municipal golf course, which is operated as an Enterprise Fund activity.
- Weighted average accumulated expenditures on the building for 19X6 were $400,000.

[2] FASB *Statement No. 34,* "Capitalization of Interest Cost" (Stamford, Conn.: FASB, 1979), par. 17.

[3] This could result in negative interest capitalization, that is, in reducing the asset's cost. However, this is likely to be rare because current arbitrage regulations under the Tax Reform Act of 1986 require SLGs to rebate investment earnings on the proceeds of tax-exempt debt that exceed the interest cost of the debt.

[4] FASB *Statement No. 62,* "Capitalization of Interest Cost in Situations Involving Certain Tax-Exempt Borrowings and Certain Gifts and Grants" (Stamford, Conn.: FASB, 1982), paras. 3–4.

Figure 13-1

INTEREST CAPITALIZATION—TAXABLE VS. TAX-EXEMPT DEBT
ILLUSTRATIVE ENTRIES

Transaction/Event	Accounts	Taxable Debt		Tax-Exempt, Restricted Debt	
		Dr.	Cr.	Dr.	Cr.
Interest payment	Interest Expenses	70,000		70,000	
	Cash		70,000		70,000
Collection or accrual of interest earnings	Cash (Interest Receivable)	60,000		60,000	
	Interest Revenues		60,000		60,000
Adjusting entry to capitalize interest	Buildings	28,000		10,000	
	Interest Revenues			60,000	
	Interest Expenses		28,000		70,000
		($400,000 × .07)			
Closing entry	Interest Revenues	60,000			
	Interest Expenses		42,000		
	Retained Earnings		18,000		

- Investment earnings from temporary investment of the bond proceeds during 19X6 amounted to $60,000.
- The building was completed immediately before year end.

The entries pertaining to interest expenses, interest revenues, and capitalization of interest cost for the Golf Course Fund are illustrated in Figure 13-1, **both** (1) assuming that the debt is **taxable debt** (or tax-exempt debt that is not restricted to use for constructing the building) and (2) assuming that the debt is **tax-exempt** debt that is **restricted for** use in **constructing** the **building.**

Note that when the debt is assumed to be **taxable debt,** only that portion of interest expense equal to the weighted average accumulated expenditures for the year ($400,000) times the interest rate on the debt (7%) is capitalized as part of the cost of the building. The balance of the interest expense on the debt will be charged against earnings for the year and closed to Retained Earnings. Also, note that the **interest revenues** from temporary investment of the taxable debt proceeds **do not affect** the amount of **interest capitalized.** The entire amount of interest revenues will be included in the current year's income.

On the other hand, when the debt is assumed to be **tax-exempt debt restricted** for construction of the building, the **entire amount** of **interest expenses and** the full amount of **interest revenues** from temporary investment of the bond proceeds are **offset against one another,** and the **difference** is **capitalized** as part of the building cost. No portion of the interest expenses or the interest revenues is included in earnings for the year because the debt was outstanding the entire year and construction was not completed until year end.

Preclosing Trial Balance

An **adjusted, preclosing trial balance** for the Electric (Enterprise) Fund, **based on the numbered illustrative journal entries** in this chapter, appears as Figure 13-2. In order to illustrate the "funds within a fund" approach common to Enterprise Fund accounting, this trial balance has been **modified** from the usual trial balance format in that (1) it is divided into two major sections, entitled **"General Accounts"** and **"Restricted Accounts,"** respectively, and (2) **subtotals** have been included to indicate the self-balancing nature of many Enterprise Fund intrafund "funds."

Figure 13-2

PRECLOSING TRIAL BALANCE

A Governmental Unit
Electric (Enterprise) Fund
Preclosing (Adjusted) Trial Balance
(Date)

General Accounts:

Cash	76,824	
Accounts Receivable	71,968	
Allowance for Uncollectible Accounts		13,492
Unbilled Accounts Receivable	21,000	
Accrued Interest Receivable	200	
Due from State Public Works Department	7,000	
Inventory of Materials and Supplies	30,000	
Prepaid Insurance	600	
Land	50,000	
Buildings	90,000	
Accumulated Depreciation—Buildings		5,000
Improvements Other Than Buildings	707,000	
Accumulated Depreciation—Improvements Other Than Buildings		15,000
Machinery and Equipment	160,500	
Accumulated Depreciation—Machinery and Equipment		16,000
Vouchers Payable		49,500
Due to Internal Service Fund		12,800
Accrued Salaries and Wages Payable		6,000
Accrued Interest Payable		2,000
Accrued Taxes Payable		7,500
Bonds Payable		650,000
Unamortized Premiums on Bonds		1,700
Contributed Capital—Governmental Unit		400,000
Contributed Capital—Contributions from Subdividers		30,000
Retained Earnings	22,500	
Operating Revenues		321,000
Operating Expenses	248,400	
Nonoperating Revenues—Equipment Rental		7,000
Nonoperating Revenues—Interest		1,850
Nonoperating Expenses—Interest	42,850	
Operating Transfer to General Fund	10,000	
Subtotal	1,538,842	1,538,842

Restricted or Secondary Accounts:

Customer Deposits "Fund"	Customer Deposits—Cash	968	
	Customer Deposits—Investments	10,000	
	Customer Deposits—Accrued Interest Receivable	200	
	Customer Deposits—Deposits Payable		10,973
	Customer Deposits—Interest Payable		145
	Reserve for Earnings on Customer Deposits		50
	Subtotal	11,168	11,168
Debt Service "Fund"	Debt Service—Cash	15,000	
	Debt Service—Accrued Interest Payable		6,000
	Reserve for Bond Debt Service		9,000
	Subtotal	15,000	15,000
Principal and Interest "Fund"	Principal and Interest Reserve—Cash	1,300	
	Principal and Interest Reserve—Investments	9,000	
	Principal and Interest Reserve—Accrued Interest Receivable	150	
	Reserve for Bond Principal and Interest Payments Guarantee		10,450
	Subtotal	10,450	10,450
Contingencies "Fund"	Contingencies—Cash	10,000	
	Contingencies—Vouchers Payable		7,000
	Reserve for Contingencies		3,000
	Subtotal	10,000	10,000
	Total	1,585,460	1,585,460

This is **not** to say that all intrafund restricted account groups are self-balancing, for they need **not** be. Thus, had we not assumed in our example that the net assets of the Customer Deposits "fund" were restricted to guarantee future interest liabilities to customers (1) there would have been no need to establish a Reserve for Earnings on Customer Deposits, and (2) this "fund" would not be self-balancing.

Closing Entries

As observed earlier, any reasonable closing entry combination that brings the temporary proprietorship accounts to a zero balance and updates the Contributed Capital and Retained Earnings accounts is acceptable. Inasmuch as a multiple-step closing approach was illustrated in Chapter 12, the **compound closing entry** approach is demonstrated here:

(37)	Operating Revenues	321,000	
	Nonoperating Revenues—Equipment Rental	7,000	
	Nonoperating Revenues—Interest	1,850	
	Operating Expenses		248,400
	Nonoperating Expenses—Interest		42,850
	Operating Transfer to General Fund		10,000
	Retained Earnings		28,600

To close the temporary proprietorship accounts and
update Retained Earnings.

Financial Statements

As with Internal Service Funds, three primary statements are required for Enterprise Funds: the balance sheet; statement of revenues, expenses, and changes in total fund equity (or retained earnings); and statement of cash flows. These often include prior year data columns, which have been omitted here in order to emphasize the essential aspects of these financial statements.

Supplemental schedules may be prepared showing the details of any segments of the principal statements that need additional explanation. Typical schedules of this type are for "operating expenses—budgeted and actual" and for fixed assets and depreciation, including changes therein. Schedules describing aspects of intrafund restricted account groups may also be desirable or required. For example, contractual requirements may dictate a statement of assets restricted for bond debt service. Schedules detailing changes in the cash and investment accounts of other intrafund restricted asset account groups may be useful as well. Also, schedules demonstrating compliance with any pertinent legal requirements may be needed.

Balance Sheet. A Balance Sheet for the Electric (Enterprise) Fund is illustrated in Figure 13-3. Note that the balance sheet exhibited is similar to that of a profit-seeking public utility. Like the balance sheet of a business enterprise, or that of many Nonexpendable Trust and Internal Service Funds, this statement contains both fixed assets and long-term liabilities of the government enterprise.

Notice the asset categorization as among current assets, restricted assets, and plant and equipment in the Balance Sheet in Figure 13-3 and the parallel division of liabilities into current liabilities payable from current assets, liabilities payable from restricted assets, and long-term liabilities. Such **intrastatement categorization** permits ready "across the balance sheet" comparisons and analyses. The use of distinctively titled restricted asset and liability accounts and related retained earnings reserves distinguishes the restricted subfund assets, liabilities, and equity from unrestricted amounts. Use of these subfunds does not impact rev-

Figure 13-3

BALANCE SHEET

A Governmental Unit
Electric (Enterprise) Fund
Balance Sheet
December 31, 19X2

ASSETS			*LIABILITIES AND FUND EQUITY*		
Current Assets:			**Current Liabilities (Payable from Current Assets):**		
Cash	$	76,824	Vouchers payable	$	49,500
Accounts receivable (less allowance for doubtful accounts of $13,492)		58,476	Due to Internal Service Fund		12,800
Unbilled accounts receivable		21,000	Accrued salaries and wages payable		6,000
Accrued interest receivable		200	Accrued interest payable		2,000
Due from State Public Works Department		7,000	Accrued utilities payable		7,500
Inventory of materials and supplies		30,000	Total Current Liabilities (Payable from Current Assets)		77,800
Prepaid insurance		600	**Liabilities Payable from Restricted Assets:**		
Total Current Assets		194,100	*Customer deposits:*		
			Deposits payable		10,973
Restricted Assets:			Interest payable		145
Customer deposits:					11,118
Cash		968	*Debt service:*		
Investments		10,000	Accrued bond interest payable		6,000
Accrued interest receivable		200	*Contingencies:*		
		11,168	Vouchers payable		7,000
Debt service:			Total Liabilities Payable from Restricted Assets		24,118
Cash		15,000	**Long-Term Liabilities:**		
Principal and interest reserve:			Bonds payable		650,000
Cash		1,300	Unamortized premium on bonds		1,700
Investments		9,000	Total Long-Term Liabilities		651,700
Accrued interest receivable		150	Total Liabilities		753,618
		10,450	**Fund Equity:**		
Contingencies:			**Retained Earnings:**		
Cash		10,000	Reserved:		
Total Restricted Assets		46,618	Reserve for earnings on customer deposits		50
			Reserve for bond debt service		9,000
			Reserve for bond principal and interest guarantee		10,450
			Reserve for contingencies		3,000
Property, Plant, and Equipment:			Total reserved		22,500
Land		50,000	Unreserved		6,100
Buildings (less accumulated depreciation of $5,000)		85,000	Total Retained Earnings		28,600
Improvements other than buildings (less accumulated depreciation of $15,000)		692,000	**Contributed Capital:**		
			Contributed capital— governmental unit		400,000
Machinery and equipment (less accumulated depreciation of $16,000)		144,500	Contributions from subdividers		30,000
Total Property, Plant, and Equipment		971,500	Total Contributed Capital		430,000
			Total Fund Equity		458,600
Total Assets		$1,212,218	Total Liabilities and Fund Equity		$1,212,218

enues, expenses, net income, or total fund equity. Rather, it simply communicates the restrictions on the use of a portion of the Enterprise Fund's net assets.

The Contributed Capital—Governmental Unit account shows the amount of capital invested in the utility by the governmental unit. As indicated earlier, this

Figure 13-4

OPERATING STATEMENT

A Governmental Unit
Electric (Enterprise) Fund
Statement of Revenues, Expenses, and Changes in Fund Equity
For the Year Ended December 31, 19X2

Operating Revenues:
Residential sales	$155,200
Commercial sales	91,300
Industrial sales	62,500
Public street lighting	12,000
Total Operating Revenues	321,000

Operating Expenses:
Production	144,400
Distribution	49,200
Accounting and collection	15,300
Sales promotion	1,000
Administrative and general	38,500
Total Operating Expenses	248,400

Operating Income	72,600

Nonoperating Revenues (Expenses):
Equipment rental	7,000
Interest revenues	1,850
Interest expenses	(42,850)
Net Nonoperating Revenues (Expenses)	(34,000)

Income before Operating Transfers
Operating transfer to General Fund	(10,000)

Net Income	28,600
Fund equity, January 1	400,000
Contributions from subdividers	30,000
Fund Equity, December 31	$458,600

account is credited for the amount expended by the governmental unit in acquiring the utility. Similarly, the account is credited for subsequent capital contributions made by the governmental unit to the utility, such as those to increase its capital. The GASB position is that the Contributed Capital—Governmental Unit account should **not** be reduced by amounts routinely transferred each year from the Enterprise Fund to the General Fund, such as routine transfers of all or a portion of utility profits to the General Fund each year. Such transfers typically are considered to be operating transfers that first reduce Retained Earnings, since they usually are distributions of earnings rather than disinvestments of capital. Only when Retained Earnings has been reduced to zero are such routine "dividend-type" transfers deemed to reduce the governmental unit's capital contribution. However, major disinvestments of capital are residual equity transfers that reduce Contributed Capital—Governmental Unit.

Statement of Revenues, Expenses, and Changes in Fund Equity. A Statement of Revenues, Expenses, and Changes in Fund Equity (or Retained Earnings) should be prepared annually and as necessary on an interim basis. The statement for the Electric Fund shown in Figure 13-4 is prepared in the format specified in the GASB Codification. **Operating** revenues and expenses and **nonoperating** revenues and expenses are distinguished in the statement. In this example operating revenues are presented in detail in the statement since there are relatively few revenue sources. However, operating expenses are reported in summary form and supported by a Detailed Statement of Operating Expenses (Figure 13-5). Had there

Figure 13-5

DETAILED OPERATING EXPENSES STATEMENT

A Governmental Unit
Electric (Enterprise) Fund
Detailed Statement* of Operating Expenses
For the Fiscal Year Ended (Date)

Production Expenses:

Electric generating:

Supervision	$ 8,000	
Station labor	15,000	
Fuel	54,000	
Water	4,000	
Depreciation	20,000	
Supplies and other	8,400	$109,400

Maintenance of plant and equipment:

Supervision	4,000	
Maintenance of structures and improvements	8,000	
Maintenance of boiler plant equipment	10,000	
Maintenance of generating and electric plant equipment	10,000	
Depreciation	1,000	33,000
Power purchased		2,000
Total production expenses		144,400

Distribution Expenses:

Supervision	2,500	
Services on consumers' premises	4,500	
Street lighting and signal system	4,000	
Overhead system	18,200	
Depreciation	13,000	
Maintenance and servicing of mobile equipment	3,000	
Utility storeroom expenses	4,000	
Total distribution expenses		49,200

Accounting and Collection Expenses:

Customers' contracts and orders	2,500	
Meter reading	3,500	
Collecting offices	1,000	
Delinquent accounts—collection expense	2,000	
Customers' billing and accounting	4,000	
Provision for doubtful accounts	1,800	
Depreciation	500	
Total accounting and collection expenses		15,300

Sales Promotion Expenses		1,000

Administrative and General Expenses:

Salaries of executives	8,000	
Other general office salaries	3,500	
General office supplies and expenses	400	
Insurance	2,000	
Employees' welfare expenses	1,500	
Pension fund contributions	2,800	
Utilities	18,000	
Depreciation	1,500	
Miscellaneous general expenses	800	
Total administrative and general expenses		38,500
Total operating expenses		$248,400

The detailed amounts in this statement cannot be derived from the example in the chapter. They have been hypothesized for illustrative purposes only. Note: This statement would be prepared in comparative form when data for the prior year are available.

Figure 13-6

STATEMENT OF CASH FLOWS

A Governmental Unit
Electric (Enterprise) Fund
Statement of Cash Flows
For the Year Ended December 31, 19X2

Cash Flows from Operating Activities:	
Cash received from customers	$301,000
Cash paid to suppliers of goods and services	(41,500)
Cash paid to employees.	(127,200)
Cash paid for utilities	(10,500)
Cash deposits refunded to customers	(5)
Net cash provided by operating activities	121,795
Cash Flows from Noncapital Financing Activities:	
Cash paid for operating transfers	(10,000)
Cash paid for interest on customer deposits.	(3)
Net cash flows from noncapital financing activities	(10,003)
Cash Flows from Capital and Related Financing Activities:	
Cash received from issuing bonds.	202,000
Cash paid for retirement of bonds.	(50,000)
Cash paid for interest	(35,000)
Cash paid for property, plant, and equipment.	(30,000)
Cash paid for construction of fixed assets	(197,000)
Net cash flows from capital and related financing activities	(110,000)
Cash Flows from Investing Activities:	
Cash paid for investments	(19,000)
Cash received from interest	1,300
Net cash flows from investing activities	17,700
Net increase (decrease) in cash	(15,908)
Cash at beginning of year*	120,000
Cash at end of year*	104,092
Reconciliation of operating income to net cash flows from operating activities:	
Operating income.	$ 72,600
Adjustments to reconcile operating income to cash flows from operating activities:	
Depreciation.	36,000
Increase in vouchers payable (associated with operating activities) . . .	26,000
Increase in interfund payable	12,800
Increase in salaries and wages payable.	6,000
Increase in utilities payable	7,500
Increase in customer deposits payable	10,973
Increase in accounts receivable (adjusted for noncash decrease from offset against customer deposits interest payable—transaction no. 19)	(29,478)
Increase in inventories.	(20,000)
Increase in prepaid insurance	(600)
Net adjustments	49,195
Net cash provided by operating activities.	$121,795
Noncash Financing and Investing Activities:	
Subdivision electricity system donation [Transaction 13]	$ 30,000

* Includes both unrestricted and restricted cash

been many significant types of operating revenues, these too might have been reported in summary and supported by a detailed schedule.

Note that the statement explains changes in **total fund equity.** The authors prefer this approach because **all** changes in fund equity are presented, including all Enterprise Fund residual equity transfers in or out. **Contributed**

Capital changes, such as those resulting from capital grants and residual equity transfers, are **not** reported in the statement **if it explains only changes in** total **retained earnings** (or in unreserved retained earnings). Thus, the interfund residual equity transfers in and out reported in the government's financial statements will not balance when there are Enterprise Fund residual equity transfers if the statement explains only changes in Retained Earnings, and the statement will not be comprehensive in nature. The retained earnings approaches are permitted by the GASB, however.

The principal causes of changes in the Retained Earnings account are, as in commercial accounting, (1) net income or loss, (2) "dividends" (operating transfers) paid to the governmental unit, (3) increases or decreases in reserved retained earnings accounts (when using the unreserved retained earnings approach), and (4) corrections of prior year errors. When the statement explains changes in retained earnings, the changes in contributed capital would be disclosed by footnote or in a separate statement of changes in contributed capital.

Statement of Cash Flows. The third primary statement required for Enterprise Funds is the Statement of Cash Flows. This statement was discussed in Chapter 12. A Statement of Cash Flows is presented in Figure 13-6.

COMBINING ENTERPRISE FUND FINANCIAL STATEMENTS

If a government has more than one Enterprise Fund, combining Enterprise Fund financial statements are required in its Comprehensive Annual Financial Report. Individual fund statements may also be presented if additional detail, individual fund comparative data, or other additional information is deemed appropriate.

The total columns of the combining statements are included in the appropriate combined financial statements. Too, **"segment information"** on individual Enterprise Funds is typically required in the notes to the combined statements, as discussed in Chapter 14.

The combining Enterprise Fund financial statements in a recent City of Des Moines, Iowa annual financial report were preceded by these narrative explanations:

The following funds included in this fund type and their purposes are as follows:

Airport—to account for the operation and maintenance of the City's airport facility, including airport parking.

Convention Center—to account for the construction, operation, and maintenance of the City's convention center facility.

Golf Courses—to account for the operation and maintenance of the City's three golf courses—Waveland, Grandview, and A. H. Blank.

Parking Facilities System—to account for the operation and maintenance of all the City's "on" and "off" street public parking facilities, except for those facilities operated by the Airport.

Sewer System—to account for the operation and maintenance of the City's sanitary sewer system.

Solid Waste System—to account for the operation and maintenance of the City's solid waste collection system.

Veterans' Memorial Auditorium—to account for the operation and maintenance of Veterans' Memorial Auditorium.

Figure 13-7

COMBINING BALANCE SHEET
City of Des Moines, Iowa

**All Enterprise Funds
Combining Balance Sheet**
June 30, 19X1

	Airport	Convention Center	Golf Courses
ASSETS			
Current Assets:			
Cash and pooled cash investments.	$ 2,398,174	$ 4,106	$ 147,715
Accounts receivable.	487,806	32,038	37,507
Due from other governmental units	302,895	—	—
Inventory, at cost	22,725	—	—
Total Current Assets.	3,211,600	36,144	185,222
Restricted Assets:			
Cash and pooled cash investments.	37,940	52,539	608,156
Investments	—	—	—
Accrued interest receivable.	—	—	—
Total Restricted Assets.	37,940	52,539	608,156
Land.	6,835,164	—	106,829
Buildings.	12,294,058	13,727,650	213,114
Improvements other than buildings.	59,485,132	516,903	1,682,667
Machinery and equipment	4,271,231	815,341	572,723
Accumulated depreciation	(38,145,625)	(1,960,316)	(460,001)
Construction in progress	731,746	—	819,811
Investment in joint venture	—	—	—
Due from other governmental units.	—	—	—
Total Assets	**$48,721,246**	**$13,188,261**	**$3,728,521**
LIABILITIES AND FUND EQUITY			
Current Liabilities:			
Warrants payable.	$ 64,308	$ 4,106	$ 1,988
Accrued wages payable	37,764	9,054	15,774
Accrued employee benefits	28,230	6,125	11,860
Accounts payable	95,936	30,943	6,599
Accrued interest payable	66,198	—	—
Due to other funds.	29,737	301	8,459
Due to other governmental units	—	—	—
Advance from other funds.	—	—	16,115
Notes payable.	110,598	—	—
Revenue bonds payable	—	—	—
General obligation bonds payable	735,000	—	—
Total Current Liabilities	1,167,771	50,529	60,795
Liabilities Payable from Restricted Assets:			
Warrants payable.	6,677	—	1,707
Construction contracts.	31,263	—	283,060
Revenue bonds payable	—	—	75,995
Accrued interest	—	—	8,856
Total Liabilities Payable from Restricted Assets	37,940	—	369,618
Long-Term Liabilities:			
Accrued employee benefits.	207,018	44,919	86,971
Revenue bonds payable	—	—	1,319,115
General obligation bonds payable	9,969,450	—	—
Advance from other funds.	—	—	463,042
Deferred revenue.	—	—	—
Total Liabilities	11,382,179	95,448	2,299,541
Fund Equity:			
Contributed capital	45,237,247	14,792,155	540,358
Retained earnings (deficit):			
Reserved for:			
Revenue bond retirement	—	—	103,434
Unreserved	(7,898,180)	(1,699,342)	785,188
Total Fund Equity	37,339,067	13,092,813	1,428,980
Total Liabilities and Fund Equity.	$48,721,246	$13,188,261	$3,728,521

The notes to the financial statements are an integral part of this statement.

Source: A recent comprehensive annual financial report of the City of Des Moines, Iowa.

Figure 13-8

**COMBINING STATEMENT OF REVENUES, EXPENSES,
AND CHANGES IN FUND EQUITY**
City of Des Moines, Iowa

**All Enterprise Funds
Combining Statement of Revenues,
Expenses, and Changes in Fund Equity**
For the Fiscal Year Ended June 30, 19X1

	Airport	Convention Center	Golf Courses
Operating Revenues:			
Charges for services	$ 7,514,212	$ 633,243	$ 926,061
Operating Expenses:			
Personal services	1,895,144	586,434	381,276
Contractual services	2,479,168	478,531	228,831
Supplies	414,201	28,294	121,362
Depreciation	2,914,632	335,734	86,303
Total Operating Expenses	7,703,145	1,428,993	817,772
Operating Income (Loss)	(188,933)	(795,750)	108,289
Nonoperating Revenues (Expenses):			
Loss on joint venture	—	—	—
Interest revenue	269,805	—	519
Interest expense and fiscal charges	(906,821)	—	(70,725)
Gain on sale of fixed assets	—	—	—
Total Nonoperating Revenues (Expenses)	(637,016)	—	(70,206)
Income (Loss) Before Operating Transfers and Extraordinary Items	(825,949)	(795,750)	38,083
Operating transfers in	—	484,469	—
Operating transfers out	—	—	—
Income (Loss) Before Extraordinary Items	(825,949)	(311,281)	38,083
Extraordinary loss on advance refunding	—	—	—
Net Income (Loss)	(825,949)	(311,281)	38,083
Retained Earnings (deficit) at beginning of year (as restated)	(7,072,231)	(1,388,061)	850,539
Retained earnings (Deficit) at end of year	(7,898,180)	(1,699,342)	888,622
Contributed capital at beginning of year	44,820,578	14,792,155	471,431
Contributions from other governmental units	217,140	—	10,887
Contributions from other sources	199,529	—	58,040
Contributed capital at end of year	45,237,247	14,792,155	540,358
Total Fund Equity	$37,339,067	$13,092,813	$1,428,980

The notes to the financial statements are an integral part of this statement.

Source: A recent comprehensive annual financial report of the City of Des Moines, Iowa.

The City of Des Moines combining Enterprise Fund financial statements are reproduced in part (Airport, Convention Center, and Golf Courses columns) as follows:

- Figure 13-7, Combining Balance Sheet
- Figure 13-8, Combining Statement of Revenues, Expenses, and Changes in Fund Equity
- Figure 13-9, Combining Statement of Cash Flows

Figure 13-9

COMBINING STATEMENT OF CASH FLOWS
City of Des Moines, Iowa

All Enterprise Funds
Combining Statement of Cash Flows
For the Fiscal Year Ended June 30, 19X1

	Airport	Convention Center	Golf Courses
Cash Flows from Operating Activities:			
Cash received from customers	$ 7,619,745	$ 630,082	$ 889,162
Cash paid to suppliers.	(3,177,178)	(501,953)	(570,672)
Cash paid to employees.	(1,878,620)	(581,021)	(360,292)
Net cash provided (used) by operating activities	2,563,947	(452,892)	(41,802)
Cash Flows from Noncapital Financing Activities:			
Operating transfers.	—	484,469	—
Net cash provided (used) by noncapital financing activities	—	484,469	—
Cash Flows from Capital and Related Financing Activities:			
Contributed capital.	611,465	—	68,927
Advance from other funds	—	—	(13,821)
Interest paid	(899,374)	—	(61,869)
Notes payable (issued)	110,598	—	—
Acquisition and construction of capital assets	(3,833,533)	(23,928)	(761,311)
Principal paid on revenue bond maturities.	—	—	(29,890)
Proceeds from sale of revenue bonds	—	—	1,425,000
Proceeds from other city revenue bonds	—	—	—
Principal paid on general obligation bond maturities.	(693,000)	—	—
Proceeds from sale of general obligation bonds	2,004,250	—	—
Proceeds from other city general obligation bonds	—	—	—
Net cash provided (used) by capital and related financing activities	(2,699,594)	(23,928)	627,036
Cash Flows from Investing Activities:			
Interest on investments.	269,805	—	519
Investment in joint venture	—	—	—
Restricted asset investment maturities/sales	—	—	—
Restricted asset investment purchases	—	—	—
Net cash provided (used) by investing activities.	269,805	—	519
Net change in cash and cash equivalents	134,158	7,649	585,753
Cash and cash equivalents, beginning of year	2,301,956	48,996	170,118
Cash and cash equivalents, end of year.	2,436,114	56,645	755,871
Reconciliation of Operating Income (Loss) to Net Cash Provided (Used) **by Operating Activities:**			
Operating income (loss)	(188,933)	(795,750)	108,289
Adjustments to reconcile operating income (loss) to net cash provided (used) by operating activities:			
Depreciation.	2,914,632	335,734	86,303
Change in assets and liabilities:			
Change in accounts receivable	105,532	(3,161)	(36,899)
Change in inventory	(11,153)	—	—
Change in warrants payable.	4,061	(569)	(1,747)
Change in wages payable.	4,035	(600)	6,255
Change in accrued employee benefits	10,409	2,523	5,131
Change in accounts payable.	(296,116)	5,599	2,944
Change in long-term benefits payable	2,080	3,490	9,598
Change in amount owed other funds.	19,400	(158)	(221,676)
Change in deferred revenue.	—	—	—
Total adjustments	2,752,880	342,858	(150,091)
Net cash provided (used) by operating activities.	$2,563,947	$(452,892)	$ (41,802)

The notes to the financial statements are an integral part of this statement.

Source: Adapted from a recent comprehensive annual financial report of the City of Des Moines, Iowa.

The GASB Codification provides general guidelines for reporting for **all** proprietary funds with respect to grants, entitlements, and shared revenues. If receipts occur before the usual criteria for revenue recognition have been met, they should be reported as **deferred revenues,** a liability. When recognition criteria have been met, they are reported as **nonoperating revenues** unless they are **externally restricted** to **capital** acquisitions, as are **capital grants.** In the latter case they should be reported as **contributed capital** in an appropriately descriptive caption, such as "Contributed Capital—Capital Grants."[5]

Assets acquired via **intergovernmental capital grants**—which increase contributed capital—are subject to depreciation just as other fixed assets are, and depreciation of all depreciable assets is a part of operating expenses. The GASB *permits in this limited instance*—but **does not require**[6]—the **depreciation of assets acquired with intergovernmental grant resources externally restricted to capital acquisition** to be closed to the related **contributed capital** account, thus effectively reclassifying a portion of contributed capital as retained earnings. When the assets are fully depreciated, the related contributed capital would be eliminated.

There is no similar reclassification process available for similarly acquired nondepreciable fixed assets, nor for depreciable fixed assets acquired with other resources, and since the using up of depreciable assets has no bearing on the fact of the contribution, there seems to be no theoretical justification for the process. But many Enterprise Funds were heavily capital grant financed and had both large contributed capital balances and large retained earnings deficits. Officials with such funds argued that (1) they would not have acquired the depreciable fixed assets, and thereby incurred the related depreciation expenses, if such capital grants had not been available, and (2) they would not replace the fixed assets unless additional capital grants were available. The special capital grant accounting procedures for proprietary funds are permitted because of these arguments.

To illustrate the effects of the alternative process on the financial statements, assume the following for a proprietary fund of a government:

Gross amount of contributed capital from capital grants as
    of the beginning of the year . . . . $ 810,000
Contributed capital from governmental unit at beginning of
    the year.   1,085,000
Retained earnings, beginning of year   200,000
Operating revenues   4,000,000
Operating expenses   3,159,500
    (Includes $1,000,000 of depreciation expense, of which
        $175,000 is on fixed assets acquired with restricted
        capital grants)

The proprietary fund operating statement is presented in Figure 13-10 and the equity section of its balance sheet is presented in Figure 13-11.

Note in Figure 13-10 that depreciation on all of a proprietary fund's fixed assets is deducted in arriving at net income. However, the depreciation on fixed assets acquired with restricted capital grants is added back to net income to arrive at the change in Retained Earnings since under the optional treatment this portion of depreciation expense reduces Contributed Capital—Capital Grants, not Re-

---

[5] GASB Codification, sec. G60.114.
[6] Ibid., sec. G60.116.

Figure 13-10

PROPRIETARY FUND OPERATING STATEMENT—WITH OPTIONAL TREATMENT OF DEPRECIATION ON ASSETS ACQUIRED WITH INTERGOVERNMENTAL CAPITAL GRANTS

A Governmental Unit
A Proprietary Fund
Statement of Revenues, Expenses, and Changes in Retained Earnings
For the Fiscal Year Ended (Date)

Operating Revenues:	
(Detailed)	$ 4,000,000
Operating Expenses:	
(Detailed—includes depreciation on ***all*** depreciable fixed assets).	(3,159,500)
Operating Income (Loss)	840,500
Nonoperating Revenues (Expenses):	
(Detailed—nonoperating revenues include intergovernmental grants, entitlements, and shared revenues received for operations and/or such resources that may be used for either operations or capital outlay at the discretion of the recipient).	—
Income (Loss) before Operating Transfers	840,500
Operating Transfers:	
(Detailed)	—
Net Income (Loss)	840,500
Add depreciation on fixed assets acquired by intergovernmental grants, entitlements, and shared revenues externally restricted for capital acquisitions and construction that reduces contributed capital [Optional].	175,000
Increase (Decrease) in Retained Earnings.	1,015,500
Retained Earnings—Beginning of Period	200,000
Retained Earnings—End of Period	$ 1,215,500

Figure 13-11

PROPRIETARY FUND BALANCE SHEET EQUITY SECTION—WITH OPTIONAL TREATMENT OF DEPRECIATION ON ASSETS ACQUIRED WITH INTERGOVERNMENTAL CAPITAL GRANTS

Fund Equity:			
Contributed capital:			
Intergovernmental capital grants	$810,000		
Less: amortization [Optional]	175,000	$ 635,000	
Governmental unit.		1,085,000	$1,720,000
Retained earnings.			1,215,500
Total Fund Equity			$2,935,500

tained Earnings. Also, note in Figure 13-11 that the Contributed Capital—Capital Grants is reported **net** of accumulated depreciation on the assets acquired with the capital grants when the optional treatment of depreciation is used.

One approach to recording this equity reclassification in the accounts is to (a) close all revenue, expense, and other appropriate accounts balances to retained earnings as if not applying the option, then (b) reclassify the contributed capital affected by applying the option in a separate entry. The reclassification entry required in this example is:

Contributed Capital—Capital Grants.	175,000	
Retained Earnings		175,000
To charge depreciation on intergovernmental grant-financed fixed assets to contributed capital.		

At this point all the types of funds and nonfund account groups commonly employed in state and local government accounting have been presented and discussed. Additionally, recording and reporting of representative types of transactions have been illustrated for each individual fund type and account group. Recall that at the end of Chapter 9, accounting for representative transactions that affect more than one governmental fund and/or account group was illustrated to crystallize the reader's understanding of the various interrelationships between and among the governmental funds and account groups. This section extends the Chapter 9 illustration by presenting entries for additional interfund-account group transactions—those that involve at least one proprietary or fiduciary fund.

1. Seventy percent of the actuarially required contributions from the General Fund and an Enterprise Fund were paid to the government's Pension Trust Fund. The actuarially required contribution was $800,000 for each fund. The balance of the required contributions has not been scheduled for payment in the near future.

Pension Trust Fund

Cash	1,120,000	
Revenues—Employer Contributions		1,120,000
To record receipt of employer fund contributions.		

Enterprise Fund

Expenses—Pensions	800,000	
Cash		560,000
Unfunded Pension Liability		240,000
To record the pension expense for the year.		

General Fund

Expenditures—Pensions	560,000	
Cash		560,000
To record payment of budgeted pension fund contribution.		

General Long-Term Debt Account Group

Amount to Be Provided for Retirement of Pension Liabilities	240,000	
Unfunded Pension Liabilities		240,000
To record the long-term portion of underfunding of General Fund actuarially required pension contribution.		

2. A "payment in lieu of tax" of $900,000 was made from an Enterprise Fund to the General Fund. If the Enterprise Fund had been a private entity, its taxes would have been approximately $600,000.

General Fund

Cash	900,000	
Revenues—Payment in Lieu of Taxes		600,000
Operating Transfer from Enterprise Fund		300,000
To record receipt of payment in lieu of taxes and operating transfer from Enterprise Fund.		

Enterprise Fund

Expenses—Payment in lieu of taxes	600,000	
Operating Transfer to General Fund	300,000	
Cash		900,000
To record payment in lieu of taxes and operating transfer to General Fund.		

3. Water Enterprise Fund billings to other funds for services was as follows:

General Fund	$300,000
Special Revenue Fund	20,000
Internal Service Fund	50,000
Total	$370,000

Water Enterprise Fund
Due from Other Funds.................... 370,000
    Revenues—Charges for Services..............   370,000
To record interfund billings for services.

General Fund
Expenditures—Utilities..................... 300,000
    Due to Enterprise Fund.....................   300,000
To record billing for water used.

Special Revenue Fund
Expenditures—Utilities..................... 20,000
    Due to Enterprise Fund.....................   20,000
To record billings for water used.

Internal Service Fund
Expenses—Utilities....................... 50,000
    Due to Enterprise Fund.....................   50,000
To record billings for water used.

4. A $500,000 two-year advance was made from an Internal Service Fund to a Capital Projects Fund.

Internal Service Fund
Advance to Capital Projects Fund.............. 500,000
    Cash.....................................   500,000
To record advance to Capital Projects Fund.

Capital Projects Fund
Cash..................................... 500,000
    Advance from Internal Service Fund............   500,000
To record advance received from Internal Service Fund.

5. Because of insufficient Enterprise Fund revenues, debt service payments on long-term Enterprise Fund notes payable have been regularly paid from general government resources. A government determines that the Enterprise Fund will never be able to finance the debt service on the notes ($2,000,000 of bonds) and reclassifies the notes payable to the General Long-Term Debt Account Group to be serviced from general revenues.

Enterprise Fund
Notes Payable............................. 2,000,000
    Contributed Capital—Governmental Unit.........   2,000,000
To record reclassification of Enterprise Fund notes.

General Long-Term Debt Account Group
Amount to Be Provided for Retirement of Notes...... 2,000,000
    Notes Payable.............................   2,000,000
To record reclassification of notes liability from
  Enterprise Fund.

6. $2,500,000 was transferred from the General Fund to provide initial financing for an Internal Service Fund.

General Fund

Residual Equity to Internal Service Fund	2,500,000	
Cash		2,500,000

To record residual equity transfer to Internal Service
Fund.

Internal Service Fund

Cash	2,500,000	
Residual Equity Transfer from General Fund.		2,500,000

To record receipt of residual equity transfer from
General Fund.

7. Equipment with an original cost of $20,000 (fair market value, $12,000) was transferred from a General Fund department to an Enterprise Fund department halfway through its useful life.

General Fixed Assets Account Group

Investment in General Fixed Assets.	20,000	
Equipment.		20,000

To record reclassification of equipment as Enterprise
Fund asset.

Enterprise Fund

Equipment.	20,000	
Accumulated depreciation		10,000
Contributed Capital—Governmental Unit		10,000

To record general government contribution of fixed
asset.

8. General obligation bonds were issued several years ago to provide the contributed capital of an Enterprise Fund. The bonds have been serviced from general government taxes and other revenues. However, the Enterprise Fund activity has been sufficiently profitable that the governing body has decided to transfer money as a "dividend" each six months from the Enterprise Fund to the Debt Service Fund to pay the semi-annual debt service on the bonds. The first "dividend" was paid, $70,000.

Enterprise Fund

Operating Transfer to Debt Service Fund	70,000	
Cash		70,000

To record payment of "dividend" transfer to Debt
Service Fund.

Debt Service Fund

Cash	70,000	
Operating Transfer from Enterprise Fund.		70,000

To record receipt of "dividend" transfer from
Enterprise Fund.

9. Assume the same facts as in 8 except that the transfers are viewed as a return of contributed capital from the Enterprise Fund to the general government.

Enterprise Fund

Residual Equity Transfer to Debt Service Fund	70,000	
Cash		70,000

To record "return of Contributed Capital" transfer to
the Debt Service Fund.

Debt Service Fund

Cash	70,000	
Residual Equity Transfer from Enterprise Fund.		70,000

To record "return of contributed capital" transfer from
Enterprise Fund.

10. Additional claims and judgment liabilities were recognized, of which 10% are considered current liabilities:

Enterprise Fund	80,000	
General government (70% General Fund, 30% Capital Projects Fund #3)	80,000	100,000

Enterprise Fund

Expenses—Claims and Judgments.	80,000	
Current Liabilities—Claim and Judgments		8,000
Noncurrent Liabilities—Claims and Judgments		72,000

To record additional estimated claims and judgments liabilities.

General Fund

Expenditures (.1×.7×$100,000).	7,000	
Current Liabilities—Claims and Judgments		7,000

To record additional estimated current liabilities for claims and judgments.

Capital Projects Fund #3

Expenditures (.1×.3×$100,000).	3,000	
Current Liabilities—Claims and Judgments		3,000

To record additional estimated current liabilities for claims and judgments.

General Long-Term Debt Account Group

Amount to be Provided for Claims and Judgments.	90,000	
Noncurrent Liabilities—Claims and Judgments		90,000

To record additional estimated noncurrent liabilities for general government claims and judgments.

11. A four-year interest-free loan was made from the General Fund to an Enterprise Fund, $160,000.

General Fund

Advance to Enterprise Fund.	160,000	
Unreserved Fund Balance	160,000	
Cash.		160,000
Reserve for Interfund Advance		160,000

To record four-year loan to Enterprise Fund and related reserve for nonavailable financial asset.

Enterprise Fund

Cash.	160,000	
Advance from General Fund.		160,000

To record four-year loan from General Fund.

12. During the following year, $40,000 of the loan in transaction 11 was repaid.

Enterprise Fund

Advance from General Fund.	40,000	
Cash.		40,000

To record partial repayment of loan from the General Fund.

General Fund

Cash.	40,000	
Reserve for Interfund Advance	40,000	
Advance to Enterprise Fund.		40,000
Unreserved Fund Balance		40,000

To record partial repayment of interfund loan and reduction of related reserves.

13. During the next year (after transaction 12), it became apparent that the Enterprise Fund was undercapitalized, and the governing body ordered the interfund advance from the General Fund to the Enterprise Fund to be forgiven.

Enterprise Fund

Advance from General Fund	120,000	
Residual Equity Transfer from General Fund		120,000
To record forgiveness of loan to provide additional capitalization to this fund.		

General Fund

Residual Equity Transfer to Enterprise Fund	120,000	
Reserve for Interfund Advance	120,000	
Advance to Enterprise Fund		120,000
Unreserved Fund Balance		120,000
To record forgiveness of loan to provide additional capital to Enterprise Fund		

14. Analyses of the current year Operating Expenses account indicated that $19,000 charged to the Enterprise Fund should be charged to a Special Revenue Fund ($8,000) and an Internal Service Fund ($11,000).

Enterprise Fund

Due from Special Revenue Fund	8,000	
Due from Internal Service Fund	11,000	
Operating Expenses		19,000
To record reimbursements as indicated.		

Special Revenue Fund

Expenditures	8,000	
Due to Enterprise Fund		8,000
To record reimbursement due to Enterprise Fund.		

Internal Service Fund

Expenses	11,000	
Due to Enterprise Fund		11,000
To record reimbursement due to Enterprise Fund.		

15. The Inspection Department (financed from the General Fund) charged the Electric Department (financed from an Enterprise Fund) $7,000 for inspecting construction projects in process and $3,000 for routine semi-annual inspections of electricity generation equipment.

General Fund

Due from Enterprise Fund	10,000	
Revenues		10,000
To record billings for inspection fees.		

Enterprise Fund

Construction in Process	7,000	
Operating Expenses	3,000	
Due to General Fund		10,000
To record inspection charges owed to General Fund.		

CONCLUDING COMMENTS

Enterprise Funds are used to account for goods or services that a government provides to the public for a fee that is intended to cover the cost of providing the goods or services, including depreciation. The accounting equation for Enterprise Funds is the same as that for business enterprises, and accounting and reporting for Enterprise Funds parallels, in most respects, that of similar businesses.

Some unique aspects of Enterprise Fund accounting were discussed and illustrated. Most notable was the extensive use of restricted asset accounting, using a **"funds within a fund"** approach, found in many SLG enterprise activities.

This chapter concludes our discussion of specific SLG fund types and account groups. The next chapter concerns financial reporting for all the fund types and account groups of a government. The structure, content, and logic of a government's Comprehensive Annual Financial Report are explained in that chapter. Then Chapter 15 addresses numerous current issues facing the governmental accounting profession.

QUESTIONS

13-1 How should one determine whether a particular activity should be accounted for through an Enterprise Fund?

13-2 The garbage collection and disposal services of a local government might be accounted for through the General Fund, a Special Revenue Fund, or an Enterprise Fund. Indicate the circumstances in which each of these fund types might be the appropriate accounting vehicle for such an activity.

13-3 How does one distinguish between an Internal Service Fund and an Enterprise Fund?

13-4 Contrast and explain the accounting distinction between revenues and capital investments (or disinvestments) in a nonexpendable (proprietary) fund such as an Enterprise Fund with that made in an expendable (governmental) fund.

13-5 What is the purpose of reserves in Enterprise Fund accounting?

13-6 An asset costing $10,000 was reclassified from the General Fixed Assets Account Group of a governmental unit to the governmental unit's enterprise. What effect would this reclassification have on the General Fund and the Enterprise Fund, respectively?

13-7 Township City is located adjacent to a freeway leading to a nearby metropolitan area and has grown rapidly from a small village to a city of 75,000. Its population is expected to continue to double every ten years in the foreseeable future. The city has owned and operated the local electricity generation and distribution system since its inception many years ago and has never charged itself for electricity consumption. The newly employed comptroller of Township City seeks your advice in this regard. What is your response?

13-8 It is sometimes claimed that to include depreciation among the expenses and to provide money out of earnings to retire bonds that were used to finance the acquisition of the assets being depreciated is to overcharge the current generation of customers. Through retiring the debt, the customers are paying for the old plant, and through depreciation charges they are paying for a new plant. Is this claim correct? Explain.

13-9 Why is it not necessary to reserve Enterprise Fund Retained Earnings to the extent that assets are set aside in an equipment replacement intrafund "fund"? (Note particularly that this procedure is contrary to the practice followed in the case of a sinking "fund," where an amount corresponding to the addition made to the sinking fund is added to the appropriate reserve account.)

13-10 Having been told repeatedly during his many years of service that depreciation was charged "in order to provide for the replacement of fixed assets," a member of a government's electric utility (Enterprise Fund) board of directors was visibly upset upon being advised by the controller that it would be necessary for the utility to go deeply in debt "in order to replace some of our fixed assets." "How can it be true," he asks, "that we have operated profitably each year, have an $850,000 Retained Earnings balance and total Accumulated Depreciation account balances of $6,000,000, have never made transfers to the General Fund, and yet have Cash and Investments totaling only $100,000?"

13-11 It is sometimes suggested that the amount contributed to a municipally owned enterprise by the municipality or donated to it by others should be amortized to Retained Earnings as the property thereby acquired is depreciated in the accounts. Proponents of the amortization procedure believe that, in its absence, the Retained Earnings account is understated. Do you agree with the procedure proposed? Why?

13-12 Why does the GASB recommend the modified accrual basis of accounting for some funds and the accrual basis for others? Is this not inconsistent?

13-13 A city controller has expressed his desire to convert the city's fund and nonfund account group records, now maintained in separate ledgers, to a system in which all accounts would be maintained within a single general ledger. Is this permissible? Explain.

13-14 In what funds may "Buildings" properly appear as an account title? For which types of funds are profit and loss (income determination) accounting procedures employed?

13-15 Contrast and explain the differences in the accounting for bond premiums or discounts related to general obligation construction bonds and to enterprise revenue bonds.

PROBLEMS

P 13-1 (Multiple Choice)

1. Which of the following activities would be **least** likely to be operated as and accounted for in an Enterprise Fund?

   a. subway
   b. sports stadium
   c. parking garage
   d. low-income public housing

2. The City of Philaburg arranged for a ten-year, $40 million loan to finance construction of a toll bridge over the Tradewater River. Assuming that the toll bridge is accounted for as an Enterprise Fund activity and that a certain portion of the tolls collected are required to be set aside in a sinking fund to provide for payment of the principal on the loan, this sinking fund should be accounted for in

   a. a Debt Service Fund
   b. the General Fund
   c. the Toll Bridge Enterprise Fund
   d. a Capital Projects Fund
   e. none of the above

3. The City of Silerville operates a water authority that sells water to city residents. Each new customer is required to pay a $75 deposit at the time of hookup. The deposit is returnable with interest if the customer maintains a satisfactory payment record during the first two years of service. The City should record these deposits

   a. in an Expendable Trust Fund
   b. as restricted cash and a liability payable from restricted assets in a Water Fund subfund
   c. as unrestricted cash and a long-term liability in the Water Fund
   d. as restricted cash and a liability payable from restricted assets in the General Fund
   e. none of the above

   Use the following facts for Questions 4 and 5.

   On January 2, 19X7, the City of San Angeles issued $100 million of 10% bonds at par. The proceeds of these bonds were restricted for the construction of a new municipal water purification plant. The City invested the bond proceeds until needed and earned $8 million in interest during 19X7, $5.2 million of which was earned before construction began. The City made progress payments to the project contractor, beginning in April 19X7. The weighted average accumulated expenditures on the project for the year were $60 million. Interest was paid to the bondholders on December 31, 19X7.

4. Assuming that the San Angeles bonds are *tax-exempt*, the amount of interest that the City should capitalize on the water plant project during 19X7 is

   a. 0
   b. $2 million
   c. $3.2 million
   d. $4.7 million
   e. $6 million
   f. $10 million

5. Assuming that the San Angeles bonds are *taxable*, the amount of interest that the City should capitalize on the water plant project during 19X7 is

   a. 0
   b. $2 million
   c. $3.2 million
   d. $4.7 million
   e. $6 million
   f. $10 million

6. All Enterprise Fund residual equity transfers are reported in an Enterprise Fund's operating statement when it reports changes in
   a. Total Fund Equity
   b. Total Contributed Capital
   c. Total Retained Earnings
   d. Unreserved Retained Earnings
   e. none of the above

7. Enterprise Fund operating transfers are reported in an Enterprise Fund's operating statement
   a. after net income but before the beginning fund equity
   b. after net income and after beginning fund equity, but before residual equity transfers
   c. as part of operating income
   d. in a separate section following operating income and nonoperating revenues and expenses, and included in net income
   e. as part of nonoperating income and expenses

8. Depreciation expense on all of an Enterprise Fund's fixed assets must be reported as expenses in the Fund's operating statement. However, in computing the net change in Retained Earnings for the year, depreciation *may* be added back to the extent that it is on fixed assets
   a. financed from restricted donations
   b. financed from residual equity transfers
   c. financed from intergovernmental capital grants
   d. constructed by subdividers or financed with special assessments
   e. all of the above
   f. none of the above

9. Enterprise Fund resources, $3,000,000, are paid yearly to the Hogan County General Fund. Assuming that these payments are payments in lieu of taxes they shoud be recorded in the Enterprise Fund as
   a. expenses
   b. expenditures
   c. operating transfers out
   d. reductions of revenues
   e. residual equity transfers out

10. Assuming that the payments in item 9 are not payments in lieu of taxes, they should be recorded in the Enterprise Fund as
   a. expenses
   b. expenditures
   c. operating transfers out
   d. reductions of revenues
   e. residual equity transfers out

P 13-2 (Worksheet and Statements) The City of Lenn operates its municipal airport. The trial balance of the Airport Fund as of January 1, 19X0 was as follows:

Cash	$ 37,000	
Accounts Receivable	50,000	
Allowance for Uncollectible Accounts		$ 2,000
Land	200,000	
Structures and Improvements	700,000	
Accumulated Depreciation—Structures and Improvements		50,000
Equipment	250,000	
Accumulated Depreciation—Equipment		90,000
Vouchers Payable		48,000
Bonds Payable		800,000
Contributed Capital—Governmental Unit		200,000
Retained Earnings		47,000
	$1,237,000	$1,237,000

The following transactions took place during the year:

1. Revenues collected in cash: aviation revenues, $340,500; concession revenues, $90,000; revenues from airport management, $30,000; revenues from sales of petroleum products (net revenue, after deducting all costs relating to the sales), $10,500.

2. Expenses, all paid in cash with the exception of $24,000, which remained unpaid at December 31, were operating, $222,000; maintenance, $75,000; general and administrative, $73,000.

3. Bad debts written off during the year, $1,900.

4. The vouchers payable outstanding on January 1, 19X0 were paid.

5. Bonds paid during the year, $50,000, together with interest of $40,000.

6. The remaining accounts receivable outstanding on January 1, 19X0 were collected.

7. Accounts receivable on December 31, 19X0 amounted to $30,000, all applicable to aviation revenues, of which $1,400 is estimated to be uncollectible.

8. Accrued interest payable at the end of the year, $3,000.

9. Depreciation charges:

Structures and Improvements	$14,000
Equipment	21,000

Required   (a) Prepare a worksheet to reflect the beginning trial balance, the transactions and adjustments during 19X0, the revenues and expenses of the year (or closing entries), and the ending balance sheet data.

(b) Prepare a Balance Sheet for the Airport Fund as of December 31, 19X0.

(c) Prepare a Statement of Revenues, Expenses, and Changes in Fund Equity for the Airport Fund for the fiscal year ended December 31, 19X0.

P 13-3   (Cash Flow Statement) The following information was derived from the accounts, financial statements, and related data for the Heston County Electric Services Enterprise Fund for 19X2:

Sales of services to public	$800,000
Cost of electricity purchases paid	500,000
Sales of services to other county departments	100,000
Salaries and wages paid	150,000
Purchases of supplies	35,000
Payment in lieu of taxes paid to county General Fund	17,000
Annual transfer from General Fund received	70,000
Residual equity transfer paid to help establish a Central Equipment Fund, the sole purpose of which is to finance fixed asset purchases	212,000
Proceeds from sale of fixed assets	37,000
Investment purchases	25,000
Interest received from investments	10,000
Interest paid on bonds issued to finance plant construction	33,000
Retirement of six-month note issued to relieve cash shortfall:	
Principal	75,000
Interest	3,750
Decrease in receivables from customers	150,000
January 1 unrestricted cash balance	200,000
January 1 restricted cash balance	7,200

Required   Prepare the 19X2 statement of cash flows for the Heston County Electric Service Enterprise Fund. (Exclude accompanying schedules for which you do not have sufficient information.)

Problem 13-4   (Worksheet and Statements) The City of Clifton provides electric energy for its citizens through an operating department. All transactions of the Electric Department are recorded in a self-sustaining fund supported by revenue from the sales of energy. Plant expansion is financed by the issuance of bonds that are repaid out of revenues. All cash of the Electric Department is held by the city treasurer. Receipts from customers and others are deposited in the treasurer's account. Disbursements are made by drawing warrants on the treasurer.

The following is the postclosing trial balance of the department as of June 30, 19X7:

Cash and Investments with City Treasurer.	$ 2,250,000	
Due from Customers	2,120,000	
Other Current Assets	130,000	
Construction in Progress	500,000	
Land.	5,000,000	
Electric Plant.	50,000,000*	
Accumulated Depreciation—Electric Plant		$10,000,000
Accounts Payable and Accrued Liabilities		3,270,000
5% Electric Revenue Bonds Payable		20,000,000
Contributed Capital—Governmental Unit		5,000,000
Retained Earnings		21,730,000
	$60,000,000	$60,000,000

The plant is being depreciated on the basis of a 50-year composite life.

During the year ended June 30, 19X8, the department had the following transactions:

1. Sales of electric energy, $10,700,000.
2. Purchases of fuel and operating supplies, $2,950,000.
3. Construction expenditures relating to miscellaneous system improvements in progress (financed from operations), $750,000.
4. Fuel consumed, $2,790,000.
5. Miscellaneous plant additions and improvements constructed and placed in service at midyear, $1,000,000.
6. Wages and salaries paid, $4,280,000.
7. Sale at par on December 31, 19X7 of 20-year, 5% Electric Revenue bonds, dated January 1, 19X8, with interest payable semiannually, $5,000,000.
8. Expenditures out of bond proceeds for construction of Clifton Steam Plant Unit No. 1, $2,800,000.
9. Operating materials and supplies consumed, $150,000.
10. Payments received from customers, $10,500,000.
11. Expenditures out of bond proceeds for construction of Clifton Steam Plant Unit No. 2, $2,200,000.
12. Warrants drawn on City Treasurer in settlement of accounts payable, $3,045,000.
13. The Clifton Steam Plant was placed in service June 30, 19X8.
14. Interest on bonds paid during the year, $500,000.

Required   (a) Prepare a worksheet for the Electric Department Fund showing:

   (1) The balance sheet amounts at June 30, 19X7.
   (2) The transactions for the year and closing entries. (Note: Formal journal entries are not required and interest capitalization may be ignored.)
   (3) The balance sheet amounts at June 30, 19X8.

(b) Prepare a Statement of Cash Flows of the Electric Department Fund during the year ended June 30, 19X8.

P 13-5   (Various Entries)

1. On April 30, 19X2 the Pickens County Transit Authority leased ten buses under a six-year, noncancellable capital lease. The capitalizable cost of the buses was $680,000 and an $80,000 down payment was made. The county does not receive title to the leased buses at the end of the lease term.
2. Lease payments made during the fiscal year ended April 30, 19X3 totaled $130,262, including interest of $37,932.

3. The County estimates its probable losses from claims and judgments against the Transit Authority for events occurring in 19X2–19X3 at $227,000. However, only $85,000 of this can reasonably be expected to be payable from expendable, available financial resources of the fund.

Required Prepare all the general journal entries, including adjusting entries, that Pickens County must make in 19X1–19X2 and 19X2–19X3 to record these transactions and events—assuming that

(a) The Transit Authority is accounted for in an Enterprise Fund.

(b) The Transit Authority is accounted for as a general government activity.

P 13-6 (Interest Capitalization)

1. On January 1, 19X8, the City of Sunshine Park issued $8,000,000 of 6%, 15-year Water Fund revenue bonds at par to finance construction of new water treatment facilities.

2. The bond proceeds were invested in securities that bear interest at 7%.

3. Construction costs incurred and paid from February 1 to September 1 totaled $7,900,000. The costs were incurred evenly over that period, and the facilities were completed on September 1. Investments were sold as necessary to provide resources to pay the construction costs. December 31 is the fiscal year end.

Required Prepare the general journal entries necessary to record the preceding transactions, including interest capitalization in the accounts of the City of Sunshine Park assuming:

(a) The bonds issued are tax-exempt.

(b) The bonds issued are taxable.

P 13-7 (Restricted Asset Accounting) McKenzie's Point issued $1,200,000 of 6%, ten-year serial bonds at par on July 1, 19X4. Interest is due semiannually on January 1 and July 1 each year, and one tenth of the principal is due each July 1. The bond indenture requires that the proceeds be accounted for in a separate fund and used to construct an addition to the maintenance building for the municipal airport, which is accounted for in an Enterprise Fund. Further, the bond agreement requires McKenzie's Point to set aside airport revenues of $20,000 per month plus one-sixth of the next interest payment each month in a separate fund for debt service from which debt service payments are to be made. The following also occurred during 19X4:

July 2—The City signed a contract with Keith Construction for construction of the addition, $1,200,000.

July 31—The city set aside the required amount to provide for debt service.

August 29—The City received a bill from Keith Construction for $1,200,000 upon completion of the addition. After inspection and approval, the bill was paid.

August 31, September 30, October 31, November 30, and December 31—On each of these dates the city set aside the required amounts to provide for debt service.

Required Assuming August 31 is the end of the fiscal year of McKenzie's Point, prepare the general journal entries, including adjusting and closing entries, for the preceding transactions. Ignore interest capitalization.

P 13-8 (Special Assessments/Restricted Assets) The Wood Village Water Department is accounted for in an Enterprise Fund. The village's water lines are being extended throughout recently annexed properties. Half of the $3,000,000 cost of the project is being paid by the city, and the remaining cost is being financed by special assessments against the properties in the annexed area. The project is to be administered by the Water Department, which will collect assessments against the properties monthly by adding the assessment to the property owners' water bills. The law requires special funds to be maintained to account for special assessment resources and the special assessment bond indenture requires the bond proceeds to be accounted for in a special fund to be used for construction or for repayment of principal and interest on the debt. Any earnings on temporary investment of debt proceeds must also be used for debt service.

1. The village's contribution to the project, $1,500,000, was paid from the General Fund.

2. A contract was signed with Clayton-Travis Construction Co. for extension of the water lines, $3,000,000.

3. The village was billed $1,200,000 for work to date on the contract. The billing, less a 5% retained percentage, was paid.

4. At the end of Year 1 general obligation bonds were issued at par, $1,500,000, to finance the remaining construction costs. The 5% bonds are to be repaid from the special assessments levied on the benefited properties. Interest to date and $150,000 principal are due at the end of each fiscal year. Assessments of $1,500,000, bearing interest at 6% were levied; $150,000 is due each year end.

5. Construction was completed in Year 2. Construction expenditures in Year 2 were $1,800,000. This was paid except for a 5% retained percentage.

6. The project was inspected and approved, and the balance due on the contract was paid.

7. Collections of special assessments in Year 2 totaled $235,000, including $85,500 of interest.

8. The first installment of the bonds and interest was paid at the end of Year 2.

Required   Prepare the general journal entries to record the preceding transactions in the accounts of Wood Village.

P 13-9   (Worksheet and Balance Sheet with Restricted Assets) The following is a list of the accounts of the Electric Utility Fund of the City of Ditten as of June 1, 19X7:

Cash	$100,600	
Construction Fund—Cash	30,000	
Deposits Fund—Cash	2,000	
Construction Fund—Expenditures	100,000	
Construction Fund—Vouchers Payable		$ 40,000
Bonds Authorized—Unissued	50,000	
Accounts Receivable	77,000	
Deposits Fund—Interest Payable		350
Deposits Fund—Interest Receivable	400	
Deposits Fund—Investments	10,000	
Deposits Fund—Surplus		2,050
Deposits Payable		9,000
Sinking Fund—Cash	20,000	
Sinking Fund—Investments	50,000	
Sinking Fund—Retained Earnings		5,000
Retained Earnings		139,000
Vouchers Payable		5,000
Inventory of Materials	10,000	
Allowance for Uncollectible Accounts		4,600
Appropriations		180,000
Reserve for Retirement of Sinking Fund Bonds		65,000
(Actuarial Requirement).	450,000	450,000

You are given the following additional information:

The electric utility was formerly accounted for in the same manner as any other department. Beginning June 1, 19X7, the utility is to be accounted for as a self-supporting enterprise, no formal records are to be kept of appropriations or other authorizations, and proper account terminology is to be employed.

Fixed assets of the utility consist of the following:

Assets	Cost	Accumulated Depreciation
Land	$150,000	—
Structures and Improvements	320,000	$60,000
Equipment	105,000	30,000
	$575,000	$90,000

The utility began operations many years ago upon receiving a $360,000 cash contribution from the General Fund; the contribution was credited to Retained Earnings. Construction Fund expenditures were for construction work in progress. (Ignore interest capitalization.) Bonds outstanding amount to $300,000 at June 1, 19X7.

Required (a) Prepare a worksheet from which to prepare a corrected Balance Sheet for the Electric Utility Fund of the City of Ditten at June 1, 19X7. Your worksheet columns should be headed as follows:

Columns	Headings
1–2	Ledger Balances, June 1, 19X7—Dr./Cr.
3–4	Adjustments and Corrections—Dr./Cr.
5–6	Balance Sheet, June 1, 19X7—Dr./Cr.
7–10	Balance Sheet: Detail—Dr. (Cr.)

Operations	Construction Fund	Sinking Fund	Deposits Fund

(b) Prepare a Balance Sheet for the Electric Utility Fund of the City of Ditten as of June 1, 19X7 in proper and customary form.

P 13-10 (Worksheet and Financial Statements) The following information pertains to the operation of the Water Fund of the City of Marion. Included in the operations of this Fund are those of a special Replacement Fund for the Water Department, the accounts of which are a part of the accounts of the Water Fund.

The balances in the accounts of this fund on January 1, 19X5 were as follows:

Cash	$ 6,126
Accounts Receivable (net of $1,200 estimated to be uncollectible)	7,645
Stores	13,826
Investments—Replacement Fund	21,700
Property, Plant, and Equipment	212,604
Accumulated Depreciation	50,400
Vouchers Payable	4,324
Customer Deposits*	1,500
Replacement Fund Reserve	21,700
Retained Earnings	21,977
Bonds Payable	60,000
Contributed Capital	102,000

No restrictions are placed on deposits received or investment income thereon; interest is not paid on deposits.

The following items represent all transactions of the fund for the year ended December 31, 19X5:

1. Services billed	$146,867
2. Accounts collected	147,842
3. Uncollectible accounts of prior years written off; current provision made, $750	1,097
4. Invoices and payrolls approved and vouchered for current expense	69,826
5. Invoices approved and vouchered for water department stores purchased	31,424
6. Stores issued for use in operation	32,615
7. Supplies secured from General Fund stores and used in operations (cash paid to General Fund)	7,197
8. Vouchers approved for payment of annual serial bonds maturity, including interest of $3,000	23,000

9. Depreciation (replacement reserve and assets adjusted also "to fully reserve and fund" the accumulated depreciation)   10,600

10. Deposits received   400

    Deposits refunded.   240

11. Invoices approved and vouchered for replacement of fully depreciated equipment which had cost $6,200   7,800

12. Invoices approved and vouchered for additions to plant   12,460

13. Interest received on investments; none is accrued at year end   1,102

14. Purchased securities as necessary to fully invest the Replacement Fund to the nearest whole $100 . . . .   compute

15. Approved vouchers paid (general)   133,316

16. Stores inventory per physical count at December 31, 19X5 (any shortages or overages are assumed to be related to operating expenses)   11,820

Required

(a) A worksheet analysis of the beginning trial balance, transactions and adjustments during 19X5, revenues and expenses, and postclosing trial balance at December 31, 19X5 of the Water Fund of the City of Marion.

(b) A Balance Sheet of the Water Fund as of December 31, 19X5.

(c) A Statement of Revenues, Expenses, and Changes in Fund Equity for the Water Fund for the year ended December 31, 19X5.

(AICPA, adapted)

P 13-11 (Review Problem) The Village of Dexter was recently incorporated and began financial operations on July 1, 19X8, the beginning of its fiscal year. The following transactions occurred during this first fiscal year, July 1, 19X8 to June 30, 19X9:

1. The village council adopted a budget for general operations during the fiscal year ending June 30, 19X9. Revenues were estimated at $400,000. Legal authorizations for budgeted expenditures were $394,000.

2. Property taxes of $390,000 were levied; it was estimated that 2% of this amount would prove to be uncollectible. These taxes are available as of the date of levy to finance current expenditures.

3. During the year a resident of the village donated marketable securities valued at $50,000 to the village under the terms of a trust agreement. The terms of the trust agreement stipulated that the principal amount is to be kept intact; use of revenue generated by the securities is restricted to financing college scholarships for needy students. Revenue earned and received on these marketable securities amounted to $5,500 through June 30, 19X9.

4. A General Fund transfer of $5,000 was made to establish an Internal Service Fund to provide for a permanent investment in inventory.

5. The village decided to install lighting in the village park and a "general government" special assessment project was authorized to install the lighting at a cost of $75,000.

6. The assessments were levied for $72,000, with the village contributing $3,000 out of the General Fund. All assessments were collected during the year, including the village's contribution.

7. A contract for $75,000 was let for the installation of the lighting. At June 30, 19X9, the contract was completed but not approved. The contractor was paid all but 5%, which was retained to ensure compliance with the terms of the contract. Encumbrances and other budgetary accounts are maintained.

8. During the year Internal Service Fund supplies were purchased on account, $1,900.

9. Cash collections recorded in the General Fund during the year were as follows:

Property taxes.	$386,000
Licenses and permits	7,000

10. The village council decided to build a village hall at an estimated cost of $500,000 to replace space occupied in rented facilities. It was decided that general obligation bonds

bearing interest at 6% would be issued. On June 30, 19X9, the bonds were issued at their face value of $500,000, payable June 30, 19Z9. No contracts have been signed for this project and no expenditures have been made.

11. A fire truck was purchased for $15,000 and the voucher approved was paid from the General Fund. This expenditure was previously encumbered for $15,000.

Required   Prepare journal entries to properly record each of the preceding transactions in the appropriate fund(s) or account group(s) of Dexter Village for the fiscal year ended June 30, 19X9. Each journal entry should be numbered to correspond with the transactions described earlier. Do not prepare closing entries for any fund. Your answer sheet should be organized as follows:

Trans- action Number	Fund or Account Group	Account Titles and Explanations	Amounts	
			Debit	Credit

(AICPA, adapted)

P 13-12   (Review Problem) The following transactions were among those affecting the City of Sterlington during 19X2:

1. The 19X2 budget was approved. It provided for $520,000 of General Fund revenues and $205,000 of School Fund revenues.

2. Appropriations were made for the General Fund, $516,000.

3. General taxes were levied, $490,000; approximately $10,000 will prove uncollectible or will be abated, and the balance is deemed "available."

4. Contractors were paid $200,000 for construction of an office building. The payment was from proceeds of a general bond issue of 19X0. (Ignore interest capitalization.)

5. General obligation bonds were issued at par, $60,000, to finance a capital project.

6. Orders were placed for uniforms for the Police Department at an estimated cost of $7,500.

7. Salaries of town officers were paid, $11,200 (disregard withholding considerations).

8. The uniforms ordered above (item 6) were received and vouchers approved for the invoice price of $7,480.

9. Fire equipment was purchased for $12,500 and a voucher approved in that (the encumbered) amount.

10. A payment of $5,000 was made from the General Fund to a fund for the redemption of general obligation bonds.

11. Of the taxes levied (item 3), $210,000 was collected during 19X2; the balance is now delinquent.

12. Supplies for general administrative use were requisitioned from the Stores Fund. A charge of $1,220 was made for the supplies; they cost the Stores Fund $1,150. (Supplies are accounted for on a perpetual basis in the Stores Fund; on a purchases basis in other funds.)

13. $30,000 cash was borrowed on a three-year note to provide working capital for a fund out of which payment will be made for a new sewage system installation. Eventual financing will be by means of charges to property owners on the basis of benefit received. These charges will be collected over the next three years.

14. Equipment used by the Public Works Department was sold for $7,000 cash. This sale was not included in the budget. The equipment had been acquired ten years earlier, at which time its useful life was estimated at 20 years.

15. Receipts from licenses and fees amounted to $16,000.

16. A payment of $10,000 was made from the General Fund to a fund for the operation of a new central printing service used by all departments of the municipal government. (This had not been budgeted and is not expected to be repaid.)

17. Taxes amounting to $1,240 written off as uncollectible in 19X0 were collected. No amount was budgeted for such collections.

18. A total of $1,000 of the payment made in item 16 was returned because it was not needed.

19. The city received a cash bequest of $75,000 for the establishment of a scholarship fund.

20. Previously approved and recorded vouchers for Police Department salaries of $6,200 and for the payment of $500 to the Police Pension Fund were paid.

Required

(a) Set up an answer sheet like the format shown below.

(b) Indicate for each transaction (by means of the appropriate numerals) the accounts debited and credited in the General Fund. If two entries in the General Fund are required, place such entries one above the other.

(c) If a transaction requires an entry(ies) in a fund(s) or nonfund account group(s) other than the General Fund, indicate those affected by printing the appropriate letter symbol(s) in the column headed "Other Funds or Account Groups Affected." If no entry is required for a transaction, state "None" (Example: Payment by the General Fund of a bill owed by the Special Revenue Fund).

Answer Sheet Format

Transaction Number	General Fund		Other Funds or Account Groups Affected	"13" Account Explanation
	Dr.	Cr.		
Example	3	2	SR	
1.				
20.				

Symbol	Fund or Account Group		Number	Account Title
CP	Capital Projects		1	Appropriations
GLD	General Long-Term Debt		2	Cash
G	General		3	Due from Other Funds
GFA	General Fixed Assets		4	Due to Other Funds
DS	Debt Service		5	Encumbrances
SR	Special Revenue		6	Estimated Revenues
TA	Trust or Agency		7	Expenditures
E	Enterprise		8	Fund Balance
IS	Internal Service		9	Reserve for Encumbrances
			10	Revenues
			11	Taxes Receivable—Current
			12	Vouchers Payable
			13	Other (explain)

FINANCIAL REPORTING

State and local government financial reporting is addressed by the twelfth principle set forth in the GASB Codification. That principle states, in part:

Interim and Annual Financial Reports

a. Appropriate interim financial statements and reports of financial position, operating results, and other pertinent information should be prepared to facilitate management control of financial operations, legislative oversight, and, where necessary or desired, for external reporting purposes.

b. A comprehensive annual financial report [CAFR] should be prepared and published, covering all funds and account groups of the primary government (including its blended component units) and providing an overview of all discretely presented component units of the reporting entity—including introductory section; appropriate combined, combining and individual fund statements; notes to the financial statements; required supplementary information; schedules; narrative explanations; and statistical tables. The reporting entity is the primary government (including its blended component units) and all discretely presented component units. . . .

c. General purpose financial statements [GPFS] of the reporting entity may be issued separately from the comprehensive annual financial report. Such statements should include the basic financial statements and notes to the financial statements that are essential to fair presentation of financial position and results of operations (and cash flows of those fund types and discretely presented component units that use proprietary fund accounting). Those statements may also be required to be accompanied by required supplementary information, essential to financial reporting of certain entities.[1]

This chapter considers interim reporting briefly, then focuses on annual reporting.

---

[1] GASB Codification, sec. 1900.100, as modified by GASB Statement No. 14. (Acronyms and emphasis added.)

INTERIM REPORTING

Very few governments publish interim financial statements for external use. Rather, interim statements of governments are prepared on the **budgetary basis** and are designed primarily to meet the needs of administrative personnel such as the chief executive, departmental supervisors, and budget examiners, though legislators may be interested in them. Interim statements thus help determine how well the executive branch is complying with budgetary and other finance-related legal requirements. In addition, interim statements are important to controlling current operations—they disclose variations from plans that may require altering the plans or improving operating performance—and assist in planning future operations.

Interim balance sheets for a General Fund are discussed in Chapter 4. Interim operating statements presented earlier include the Interim Budgetary Comparison Statement in Figure 3-9. Other interim statements commonly prepared include detailed budgetary statements and statements of cash receipts, disbursements, and balances for each fund.

The GASB recognizes the importance of good interim reporting both by including it in the Reporting Principle and in its discussion of that principle:

> **Interim financial reports** are comprised principally of statements that **reflect current financial position at the end of a month or quarter** and **compare actual financial results with budgetary estimates** and limitations for the month or quarter and/or for the year to date. Interim reports typically are prepared primarily for **internal use.** Thus, they **usually** are **prepared on** the **budgetary basis** and often do not include statements reporting general fixed assets or general long-term debt. Further, they may properly contain budgetary or cash flow **projections and other information** deemed pertinent to effective management control during the year.
>
> The **key criteria** by which internal interim reports are evaluated are their **relevance and usefulness** for purposes of management control, which include planning future operations as well as evaluating current financial status and results to date. . . . Because managerial styles and perceived information needs vary widely, however, **appropriate internal interim reporting is largely a matter of professional judgment** rather than one to be set forth in detail here.[2]

Interim reporting typically is for internal use, and individual managers and environments require different types of interim reports. Thus, **neither the GASB nor any other recognized body has set forth what might be considered generally accepted principles of interim reporting.**

ANNUAL REPORTING

Reporting is the last phase of the annual budget and accounting cycle for which the executive branch of the government is responsible. In the **ideal** annual financial **report** the executive branch (1) **demonstrates** its **compliance with finance-related legal and contractual requirements,** including fund and appropriation requirements, under which the government is operated, **and** (2) **presents audited financial statements that conform with generally accepted accounting princi-**

---

[2] GASB Codification, sec. 1900.107–.108. (Emphasis added.)

ples. The annual financial report is designed to inform the legislative body, creditors, investors, analysts, students of public finance, political scientists, and the general public.

The GASB is emphatic that:

> **Every governmental unit should prepare and publish,** as a matter of public record, a **comprehensive annual financial report (CAFR) that encompasses all funds and account groups.** The CAFR should **contain both** (a) the *general purpose financial statements* **(GPFS)** by fund type and account group [and required supplementary information] **and** (b) **combining** statements by fund type **and individual fund statements.** The CAFR is the **governmental unit's official annual report** and should also contain introductory information, schedules necessary to demonstrate compliance with finance-related legal and contractual provisions, and statistical data.[3]

Principle 12b, quoted at the beginning of the chapter, states that the reporting entity being reported upon in a CAFR (or in GPFS) includes the primary government (defined later) and discretely presented component units (defined later). Indeed, many governments have no discretely presented component units; rather they have a **simple entity structure** in which the primary government is the reporting entity. Our initial discussion of financial reporting assumes that "primary government" is simply a synonym for the legal entity being reported upon. The last major division of the chapter explains (1) how a government determines if entities other than the primary government legal entity must be included in its reporting entity, (2) how the data of other included units (component units) are incorporated in the CAFR and the GPFS, and (3) how other associated organizations that are not component units (such as joint ventures) impact a primary government's CAFR.

THE PYRAMID CONCEPT—SIMPLE ENTITY STRUCTURE

The financial statements and schedules section of the CAFR is based on a "pyramid" concept of reporting. In studying the **financial reporting pyramid** (Figure 14-1) note that:

1. The top of the pyramid represents highly aggregated, consolidated financial statements, while the bottom of the pyramid represents highly detailed, voluminous reports that would include the details of virtually every transaction or event of a governmental unit. The GASB requires reports and statements between these two extremes. Thus **neither "Condensed Summary Data" nor "Transaction Data" falls within** the bounds of reports and statements to be prepared under **generally accepted accounting principles.**

2. A **dual external reporting approach** is employed. The Comprehensive Annual Financial Report **(CAFR) is** the **primary report,** the **"official" annual report** of the governmental unit, whereas the General Purpose Financial Statements **(GPFS)** in the CAFR **may be issued separately** for inclusion in official statements for bond offerings and for general widespread distribution **to users apt to require less detail** than is contained in the CAFR, **provided** the **GPFS refer** the reader **to the CAFR** in case more detailed information is needed.

---

[3] Ibid., sec. 1900.109. (Emphasis added.) Supplementary information is required in the CAFR and/or GPFS of many governments by GASB *Statement Nos. 5 and 10* (Cod. sec, 1900.105).

Figure 14-1   THE FINANCIAL REPORTING "PYRAMID"

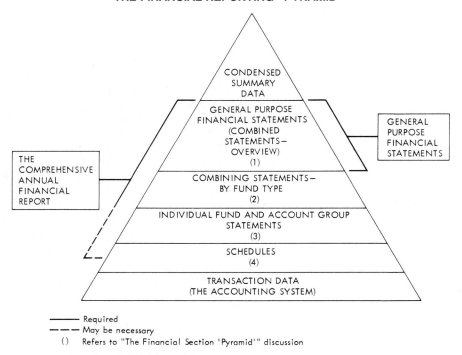

Required
— — — May be necessary
( )   Refers to "The Financial Section 'Pyramid'" discussion

Source: Adapted from GASB Codification, section 1900.117.

3. The contents of the **GPFS** are **limited to** several **combined** statements, whereas the CAFR includes the combined statements, combining statements, and, perhaps, individual fund and account group statements. The **dashed line** in Figure 14-1 **indicates** the area where professional **judgment** is **to be exercised in determining when adequate disclosure** has been **achieved** without overwhelming the user of the CAFR with excessive detail.

4. It is **essential** (a) to **distinguish** between and among **combined** statements, **combining** statements, and **individual fund and account group statements** and schedules and (b) to **realize** that the **data in combined** statements are **more summarized than** those in the **combining** statements, which are **more summarized than** those presented in the **individual fund** and account group **statements,** which are more summarized than those presented in most individual fund and account group **schedules.** Thus the **higher on** the **pyramid,** the **more summarized** the data presented; and the lower on the pyramid, the more detailed the data presented.

The relationships between the different levels of financial statements are illustrated in Figure 14-2. Note that the total columns of the various combining financial statements for each fund type are reported for that fund type in the corresponding combined statement (although probably in less detail). Thus, the **combined** financial statements **and combining** financial statements clearly **articulate.** Further, each individual fund financial statement presented will articulate with the corresponding column for that specific fund in the corresponding combining statement. Indeed, it will simply be a more detailed, or otherwise more informative, presentation of the same data.

The general outline and minimum contents of the CAFR include (1) the **Introductory** Section, (2) the **Financial** Section, and (3) the **Statistical** Section. These CAFR sections and their contents are illustrated in Figure 14-3, which should be studied now for an overview of the CAFR. It will be useful to refer to this figure and Figure 14-2 when studying specific components of the CAFR in order to visualize the relationships among the components.

The Introductory Section

The introductory section of the CAFR includes a table of contents, letter(s) of transmittal, and other material deemed appropriate by management—for example, organization chart, copy of current certificate of achievement for excellence in financial reporting awarded by the Government Finance Officers Association, roster of elected officials, and description of the government entity being reported on.

The transmittal letter from the chief finance officer is an extremely important part of the CAFR. Indeed, like the president's letter in private corporation reports, most readers direct their attention here initially for an overview of the financial position of the city at year end and the results of operations for the year. Readers also expect that the major significant events that occurred during the year, whether good or bad, will be highlighted here.

The Financial Section—Simple Entity Structure

As illustrated in Figure 14-3, the financial section for an SLG with a simple reporting entity structure has three subsections: (1) the auditor's report, (2) the General Purpose Financial Statements (GPFS)—the combined statements and notes to the financial statements (followed by any required supplementary information), and (3) the combining and individual fund statements and schedules.

The Auditor's Report

The auditor's report on the financial statements is the first item presented in the financial section of a government's CAFR. The auditor's report on the City of Orlando financial statements for a recent fiscal year appears in Figure 14-4. Note that this opinion is a **"dual opinion"** in that it **covers both** the combined statements in the **GPFS and** the **combining and individual fund** and account group **statements equally.** The report covers the financial and budgetary schedules only as "accompanying" (supplemental) data presented for purposes of additional analysis.

The Combined Statements (GPFS) and Notes

As shown in Figure 14-3, as few as five combined statements, accompanied by appropriate notes, may present fairly the financial position and results of operations of a state or local government (and the cash flows of its proprietary and nonexpendable trust funds) in accordance with GAAP. **Since** the data in **combined statements** are **aggregated by fund type,** not by individual fund, these statements have a **"fund type" entity focus.** This focus on fund types rather than on individual funds is reflected in Figure 14-2, which illustrates the overall structure of the various combined statements.

Figure 14-2
NATURE OF AND INTERRELATIONSHIPS BETWEEN DIFFERENT LEVELS OF FINANCIAL STATEMENTS—SIMPLE ENTITY STRUCTURE

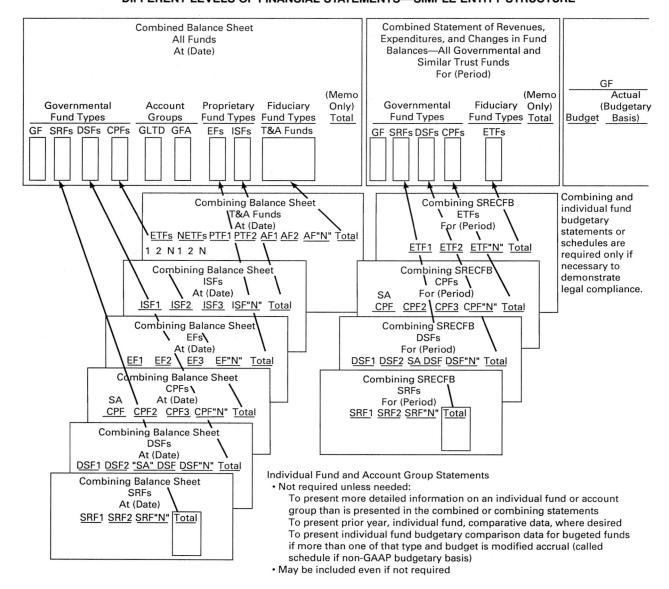

As shown in Figures 14-2 and 14-3, the combined statements in the GPFS are:

1. Combined Balance Sheet—**All Fund Types and Account Groups;**

2. Combined Statement of Revenues, Expenditures, and Changes in Fund Balances—**All Governmental Fund Types;**

3. Combined Statement of Revenues, Expenditures, and Changes in Fund Balances—Budget and Actual—**General and Special Revenue Fund Types** (and similar funds for which an annual budget is adopted);

4. Combined Statement of Revenues, Expenses, and Changes in Fund Equity (or Retained Earnings)—**All Proprietary Fund Types;** and

5. Combined Statement of Cash Flows—**All Proprietary Fund Types.**

536

Figure 14-2 (Continued)

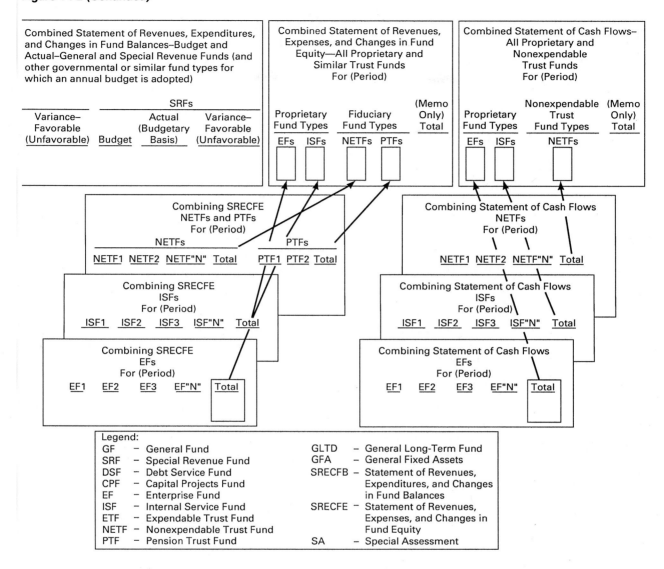

Legend:

GF	– General Fund	GLTD	– General Long-Term Fund	
SRF	– Special Revenue Fund	GFA	– General Fixed Assets	
DSF	– Debt Service Fund	SRECFB	– Statement of Revenues,	
CPF	– Capital Projects Fund		Expenditures, and Changes	
EF	– Enterprise Fund		in Fund Balances	
ISF	– Internal Service Fund	SRECFE	– Statement of Revenues,	
ETF	– Expendable Trust Fund		Expenses, and Changes in	
NETF	– Nonexpendable Trust Fund		Fund Equity	
PTF	– Pension Trust Fund	SA	– Special Assessment	

Note: All of the statements prepared for each level of financial statements are prepared on the GAAP basis, except for the budgetary comparison statements. The budgetary comparison statements (or schedules) are presented on the budgetary basis even if it differs from GAAP.

As indicated in Figure 14-2, the combined **balance sheet includes all fund types and account groups. Separate operating statements** are **required** for the governmental and the proprietary fund types, however, because governmental fund operations are measured on the expenditure basis while proprietary fund operations are measured on the expense basis. In the combined statements **Trust Fund operations** may be presented separately, but are more commonly **included in** the appropriate **governmental and/or proprietary fund** statements, as illustrated in the figure.

Combined Balance Sheet. A Combined Balance Sheet is presented in Figure 14-5. Note that the data in this statement are highly summarized since the purpose of the statement is to present an **overview.** The current year **total** and the prior year comparative total are labeled **"Memorandum Only"** to signal that these totals do **not** purport to show data **in conformity with GAAP,** as do the fund type columns in the statement.

Combined Statement of Revenues, Expenditures, and Changes in Fund Balances. Several aspects of this statement, illustrated in Figure 14-6, warrant attention: (1) it includes all of the governmental (expendable) funds and also the Expendable Trust Fund(s), as permitted by the GASB Codification; (2) the format of the statement is one of the acceptable alternatives set forth in the Codification—other financing sources and uses (in this case, operating transfers) are reported together after the excess of revenues over expenditures; (3) residual equity transfers are reported between beginning and ending fund balances; and (4) the statement presents changes in **total** fund balances, not unreserved fund balances, and thus has no "changes in reserves" section.

Combined Statement of Revenues, Expenditures, and Changes in Fund Balances—Budget and Actual. The **budget** for the City of Orlando is prepared and administered on the **modified accrual** basis **except** that **budgetary basis expenditures include encumbrances** outstanding at year end. Thus, the actual expenditures on the budgetary basis shown in the budgetary comparison statement in Figure 14-7 differ from those presented in the GAAP basis statement in Figure 14-6. The differences are reconciled in the budgetary statement (rather than in the notes as discussed and illustrated in Chapter 10) by reporting the **GAAP-basis expenditures** and **adding** the **encumbrances** outstanding at year end **to arrive at** the **budgetary basis expenditures** for the year.

Note also that Debt Service Funds are presented in the budgetary comparison statement—as are all other governmental fund types and Expendable Trust Funds—which indicates that they too are budgeted on an annual basis. Finally, note the fund balance allocation added to the budget of each fund type. This represents Orlando's budgeted use of a portion of beginning fund balance to cover the excess of budgeted expenditures over budgeted revenues and is presented only in the budgetary operating statement and only because it is a budgeted amount.

Combined Statement of Revenues, Expenses, and Changes in Retained Earnings/Fund Equity. This statement (Figure 14-8) resembles a combined income and retained earnings statement for a business concern, as it properly should under the GASB Codification. Note that (1) operating transfers are reported in a separate section *before* net income, and (2) Orlando chose to present its fiduciary fund statements with the governmental and proprietary fund statements, as appropriate, rather than separately.

Combined Statement of Cash Flows. GASB Statement No. 9 requires a Statement of Cash Flows to be presented for proprietary funds and nonexpendable trust funds. The direct method Orlando statement (Figure 14-9) is prepared in accordance with GASB Statement No. 9.

The Notes to the Financial Statements. The notes to the GPFS of a governmental unit are an integral part of the GPFS. The **notes provide information necessary for fair presentation** and appropriate understanding of the financial position and operating results of the various fund types of the government and of the financing

Figure 14-3

GENERAL OUTLINE AND CONTENT OF A CAFR—
SIMPLE ENTITY STRUCTURE

INTRODUCTORY SECTION

Components Required by the GASB	Other Items Commonly Included
1. Table of contents 2. Letter(s) of transmittal 3. Other material deemed appropriate by management	List of principal officials Organization chart GFOA certificate of achievement for excellence in financial reporting (if awarded)

FINANCIAL SECTION

Auditor's Report	General Purpose Financial Statements (Combined Statements—Overview)	Combining and Individual Fund and Account Group Statements and Schedules

	(1) *Combined Balance Sheet*—All Fund Types and Account Groups (Figure 14-5).
	
	(2) *Combined Statement of Revenues, Expenditures, and Changes in Fund Balances*—All Governmental Fund Types (Figure 14-6).
	
	(3) *Combined Statement of Revenues, Expenditures, and Changes in Fund Balances*—Budget and Actual—General and Special Revenue Fund Types (and similar governmental fund types for which annual budgets have been legally adopted) (Figure 14-7).
	
	(4) *Combined Statement of Revenues, Expenses, and Changes in Fund Equity or Retained Earnings*—All Proprietary Fund Types (Figure 14-8).
	
	(5) *Combined Statement of Cash Flows*—All Proprietary Fund Types (Figure 14-9).
	
	(6) *Notes to the financial statements* (Figure 14-10).
	
	[Trust Fund operations may be reported in (2), (3), (4), and (5) above, as appropriate, or separately.]
	
	(7) *Required supplementary information*—For example, certain ten-year historical trend information relating to pension plans must be presented after the notes by most governments with single-employer or agent multiple-employer PERS.
		(1) *Combining Statements*—by Fund Type—where a governmental unit has more than one fund of a given fund type (e.g., Figures 4-10, 4-11, 7-8, 8-5, 8-6 and 8-7).
		
		(2) *Individual fund and account group statements*—where a governmental unit has only one fund of a given type and for account groups and/or where necessary to present prior year and budgetary comparisons. (These statements are optional unless circumstances make them necessary for fair presentation of the financial statements.)
		
		(3) *Schedules*
		  (a) Schedules necessary **to demonstrate compliance** with finance-related legal and contractual provisions. (These schedules are required in some circumstances.)
		  (b) Schedules **to present information spread throughout the statements** that can be brought **together and** shown **in greater detail** (e.g., taxes receivable, including delinquent taxes; long-term debt; investments; and cash receipts, disbursements, and balances). (Optional schedules)
		  (c) Schedules **to present greater detail for information reported in the statements** (e.g., additional revenue sources detail and object of expenditure data by departments). (Optional schedules)
		
		(Narrative explanations useful in understanding combining and individual fund and account group statements and schedules that are not included in the notes to the financial statements should be presented on divider pages, directly on the statements and schedules, or in a separate section.)

STATISTICAL SECTION

Tables Covering Last Ten Fiscal Years		Other Tables
• General Government Expenditures by Function • General Revenues by Source • Property Tax Levies and Collections • Assessed and Estimated Actual Value of Taxable Property • Property Tax Rate—All Overlapping Governments	• Special Assessment Collections • Ratio of Net General Bonded Debt to Assessed Value and Net Bonded Debt per Capita • Ratio of Annual Debt Service for General Bonded Debt to Total General Expenditures • Revenue Bond Coverage • Property Value, Construction, and Bank Deposits	• Computation of Legal Debt Margin (If not presented in the GPFS) • Computation of Overlapping Debt (If not presented in the GPFS) • Demographic Statistics • Principal Taxpayers • Miscellaneous Statistics

---

and investing activities of its proprietary fund types, **but** which is **not** readily **apparent** from **or can not be included in** the **GPFS**. The notes in a typical report are quite extensive, often as long as 25–50 pages, and contain significant information.

The **GASB identifies** numerous **notes** that it considers **essential** to fair presentation of the GPFS for all governments, **and** many other **notes** that should be **presented when applicable**. Most of these are identified in Figure 14-10. The **distinctions** between the notes in each category are **not clear** since (1) some notes categorized as essential do not apply to all governments, and thus may not be presented, and (2) all pertinent notes presented should be essential to fair presentation at the GPFS level. Apparently, those notes listed as essential to fair presentation of the GPFS are those thought to be applicable for the overwhelming majority of governments.

Note in reviewing Figure 14-10 that a **number of** the **notes** listed **provide information** that should be **obvious from** the **combining and/or individual fund** financial **statements** included in the CAFR. Examples include notes regarding:

- Overexpenditure of appropriations in individual funds
- Deficit fund balance or retained earnings of individual funds
- Interfund receivables and payables
- Segment information for Enterprise Funds

This duplication occurs **because** the **GPFS and notes must** be sufficiently complete to **"stand alone,"** since they may be issued separately from the CAFR (but, if so, must indicate the availability of the CAFR for those wanting more detail).

The GASB also states that the list of notes in Figure 14-10 is **not** exhaustive and is **not** intended to replace professional judgment. Too, the Board emphasizes that the notes should not be "cluttered" with unnecessary disclosures.

Some of the notes typically presented by governments are very similar, if not identical, to notes presented in business financial statements. Others are unique to governments. Several of the unique notes that are discussed at different points in the book are illustrated or noted in the following sections.

Deposits and Investments. Governments have significant amounts of resources on deposit with financial institutions and invested in various types of securities. The degrees of risk associated with various deposits and investments often vary greatly among governments, among funds of the same government, or even within a single fund. Hence, the GASB requires several disclosures with respect to deposits and investments. The basic disclosure categories required are:

- Legal and contractual provisions regarding deposits and investments
- Segregation of deposits by three categories of credit risk
- Segregation of investments by three categories of credit risk
- Other specific disclosures

Repurchase agreements—in which a government buys securities and the seller agrees to buy them back later—are to be treated like other investments under this guidance, but unique disclosures are required for reverse repurchase agreements—in which a SLG sells securities it owns and agrees to buy them back at some future date. An example of a deposits and investments footnote is provided in Figure 14-11.

Segment Information for Enterprise Funds. The GASB also requires disclosure in the GPFS of certain specified information for certain Enterprise Funds. This segment (individual fund) information is required for each Enterprise Fund with bonds or other long-term debts outstanding, for each major nonhomogenous Enterprise Fund, and for any other Enterprise Fund that meets any one of five specified criteria that indicate that the fund may not be operating on a "break-even" basis, but instead may be charging users significantly less than or more than the cost of providing its services.

Figure 14-4   **REPORT OF INDEPENDENT ACCOUNTANTS**

Coopers
&Lybrand   certified public accountants

Report of Independent Accountants

Honorable Mayor and City Council
City of Orlando, Florida

We have audited the accompanying general purpose financial statements and the combining and individual fund and account group financial statements of the City of Orlando, Florida, as of September 30, 19X1, and for the year then ended, as listed in the Table of Contents on pages i to iii. These financial statements are the responsibility of the City of Orlando, Florida, management. Our responsibility is to express an opinion on these financial statements based on our audit.

We conducted our audit in accordance with generally accepted auditing standards and Government Auditing Standards, issued by the Comptroller General of the United States. Those standards require that we plan and perform the audit to obtain reasonable assurance about whether the financial statements are free of material misstatement. An audit includes examining, on a test basis, evidence supporting the amounts and disclosures in the financial statements. An audit also includes assessing the accounting principles used and significant estimates made by management, as well as evaluating the overall financial statement presentation. We believe that our audit provides a reasonable basis for our opinion.

In our opinion, the general purpose financial statements referred to above present fairly, in all material respects, the financial position of the City of Orlando, Florida, as of September 30, 19X1, and the results of its operations and cash flows of its proprietary and similar trust fund types for the year then ended in conformity with generally accepted accounting principles. Also, in our opinion, the combining and individual fund and account group financial statements referred to above present fairly, in all material respects, the financial position of each of the individual funds and account groups of the City of Orlando, Florida, as of September 30, 19X1, and the results of operations of such funds and the cash flows of individual proprietary and similar trust funds for the year then ended in conformity with generally accepted accounting principles.

Our audit was made for the purpose of forming an opinion on the general purpose financial statements taken as a whole and on the combining and individual fund and account group financial statements. The accompanying financial information listed as supplementary information on page iii in the Table of Contents is presented for purposes of additional analysis and is not a required part of the financial statements of the City of Orlando, Florida. Such information has been subjected to the auditing procedures applied in the audit of the general purpose, combining and individual fund and account group financial statements and, in our opinion, is fairly presented in all material respects in relation to the financial statement of each of the respective individual funds and accounting groups taken as a whole.

The information presented in the Statistical Section is presented for purposes of additional analysis and is not a required part of the basic financial statements. Such information has not been subjected to the auditing procedures applied in the audit of the financial statements and, accordingly, we express no opinion on it.

Coopers & Lybrand

[signature: Coopers & Lybrand]

Orlando, Florida
December 10, 19X1

Source: Adapted from a recent City of Orlando, Florida, annual report.

Enterprise Fund segment information disclosures can be accomplished in several ways. But, while the GASB permits two other approaches, it states that note disclosure is preferable. A segment information note is presented in Figure 14-12.

Figure 14-5

COMBINED BALANCE SHEET

All Fund Types and Account Groups
City of Orlando, Florida
September 30, 19X1

	Governmental Fund Types — General	Special Revenue	Debt Service	Capital Projects	Proprietary Fund Types — Enterprise	Internal Service	Fiduciary Fund Types — Trust and Agency	Account Groups — General Fixed Assets	General Long-Term Obligations	Totals (Memorandum Only) September 30, 19X1	19X0
Assets											
Current Assets											
Cash and Cash Equivalents	$33,699,977	$25,323,429	—	$10,735,667	$21,219,096	$6,504,088	—	—	—	$97,482,257	$80,246,571
Investments	—	—	—	16,699,787	—	—	—	—	—	16,699,787	26,058,091
Receivables (Net of Allowance for Uncollectibles):											
Accounts	1,894,861	53,525	—	71,432	4,244,159	48,329	—	—	—	6,312,306	7,173,825
Taxes	274,229	—	—	—	—	—	—	—	—	274,229	189,421
Special Assessments	1,442,272	—	—	—	—	—	—	—	—	1,442,272	1,484,937
Due from Other Funds	326,972	1,576,264	—	—	136,608	—	—	—	—	2,039,844	1,677,361
Due from Other Governments	2,899,385	759,455	—	12,000	1,391,869	4,006	—	—	—	5,066,715	4,640,990
Inventories	526,357	957,450	—	—	501,062	414,817	—	—	—	2,399,686	2,409,976
Prepaid Items	219,642	8,675	—	—	197,360	—	—	—	—	425,677	90,211
Advances to Other Funds	—	—	—	—	—	—	—	—	—	—	3,460,228
Total Current Assets	41,283,695	28,678,798	—	27,518,886	27,690,154	6,971,240	—	—	—	132,142,773	127,431,611
Restricted Assets											
Cash and Cash Equivalents	—	—	4,735,855	—	106,604,167	11,136,811	11,824,202	—	—	134,301,035	142,707,177
Investments	—	—	4,231,177	—	40,534,162	155,802,421	235,023,500	—	—	435,591,260	415,320,827
Accounts and Notes Receivable	—	—	—	—	486,205	1,004,292	4,210,027	—	—	5,700,524	5,226,463
Due from Other Governments	—	—	—	—	2,120,730	—	—	—	—	2,120,730	1,566,030
Due from Other Funds	—	—	—	—	—	—	—	—	—	—	22,885
Inventory	—	—	—	—	—	—	16,945	—	—	16,945	14,818
Equity in SSGF Commission	—	—	—	—	—	1,702,548	—	—	—	1,702,548	1,625,915
Loans to Other Funds	—	—	—	—	—	70,013,359	—	—	—	70,013,359	69,490,900
Other Assets	—	—	—	—	—	1,003,341	—	—	—	1,003,341	1,032,170
Total Restricted Assets	—	—	8,967,032	—	149,745,264	240,662,772	251,074,674	—	—	650,449,742	637,007,185
Property, Plant and Equipment											
Land	—	—	—	—	38,810,286	542,810	31,278	31,484,248	—	70,868,622	70,034,649
Buildings	—	—	—	—	258,723,129	296,985	1,466,325	56,658,516	—	317,144,955	302,002,202
Improvements Other Than Buildings	—	—	—	—	151,796,997	245,762	18,038	29,795,871	—	181,856,668	133,382,183
Equipment	—	—	—	—	96,237,808	1,203,032	8,683	18,522,373	—	115,971,896	106,254,444
Wastewater and Stormwater Lines and Pump Stations	—	—	—	—	191,106,484	—	—	—	—	191,106,484	178,795,168
Vehicles	—	—	—	—	—	27,442,424	—	—	—	27,442,424	24,743,353
Total	—	—	—	—	736,674,704	29,731,013	1,524,324	136,461,008	—	904,391,049	815,211,999
Less Accumulated Depreciation	—	—	—	—	(134,674,440)	(19,580,995)	(116,821)	—	—	(154,372,256)	(127,118,056)
Construction Work in Process	—	—	—	—	7,701,681	251,908	—	1,251,140	—	9,204,729	41,576,665
Net Property, Plant and Equipment	—	—	—	—	609,701,945	10,401,926	1,407,503	137,712,148	—	759,223,522	729,670,608
Long-Term Lease Receivable	—	—	—	—	1,102,262	—	—	—	—	1,102,262	1,102,262
Unamortized Bond Costs	—	—	—	—	3,531,466	—	—	—	—	3,531,466	3,787,228
Amount Available in Debt Service Funds	—	—	—	—	—	—	—	—	8,025,375	8,025,375	6,930,140
Amount to be Provided for Retirement of Long-Term Debt	—	—	—	—	—	—	—	—	80,326,479	80,326,479	68,892,127
Total Assets	$41,283,695	$28,678,798	$8,967,032	$27,518,886	$791,771,091	$258,035,938	$252,482,177	$137,712,148	$88,351,854	$1,634,801,619	$1,574,821,161
Liabilities and Fund Equity											
Current Liabilities (Payable from Current Assets)											
Accounts Payable	1,674,465	914,564	—	2,537,031	3,228,119	187,561	—	—	—	8,541,740	11,329,827
Accrued Liabilities	2,583,599	32,393	—	—	609,618	117,042	—	—	—	3,342,652	2,650,225
Current Portion of Capital Leases Payable	—	—	—	—	119,419	—	—	—	—	119,419	156,465
Compensated Absences	491,460	—	—	—	1,034,342	264,557	—	—	—	1,790,359	1,643,149
Advance Payments	1,390,715	199,343	—	647,577	1,678,402	—	—	—	—	3,916,037	3,744,753
Due to Other Funds	—	19,339	—	1,851,872	—	—	—	—	—	1,871,211	952,251
Other Current Liabilities	1,053	—	—	—	1,500	—	—	—	—	2,553	1,500
Deferred Revenue	1,441,135	476,716	—	—	—	—	—	—	—	1,917,851	1,380,884
Total Current Liabilities (Payable from Current Assets)	7,582,427	1,642,355	—	5,036,480	6,671,400	569,160	—	—	—	21,501,822	21,859,054

	Governmental Fund Types				Proprietary Fund Types		Fiduciary Fund Types	Account Groups		Totals (Memorandum Only)	
	General	Special Revenue	Debt Service	Capital Projects	Enterprise	Internal Service	Trust and Agency	General Fixed Assets	General Long-Term Obligations	September 30, 19X1	19X0
Current Liabilities (Payable from Restricted Assets)											
Accounts Payable	$	$	$ 22,299	$	$ 3,363,289	$ 105,117	$ 247,005	$	$	$ 3,737,710	$ 8,155,522
Accrued Liabilities						6,446,109	15,770			6,461,879	6,175,774
Compensated Absences						32,022	5,948			37,970	28,902
Claims Liabilities						6,022,593				6,022,593	6,342,270
Accrued Interest Payable			919,358		7,585,403		8,545			8,513,306	8,395,527
Due to Other Funds							168,633			168,633	747,995
Current Portion of Long-Term Debt					5,280,512	419,000	11,707		2,238,754	7,949,973	7,410,944
Obligations Under Reverse Repurchase Agreements					17,848,555		26,968			17,875,523	5,171,884
Advance Payments											18,495,064
Deferred Compensation Payable							14,484,932			14,484,932	11,831,558
Total Current Liabilities (Payable from Restricted Assets)			941,657		34,077,759	13,024,841	14,969,508		2,238,754	65,252,519	72,755,440
Long-Term Liabilities											
Bonds Payable After One Year					225,902,303	150,000,000			66,760,000	442,662,303	433,832,958
Advances from Orange County					3,959,000					3,959,000	3,759,000
Capital Leases Payable					3,451,139					3,451,139	3,464,377
Loans and Mortgages Due After One Year						69,752,141	1,277,148			71,029,289	71,446,321
Loans from Other Funds					54,006,233				13,677,860	67,684,093	67,152,969
Advances from Other Funds											3,460,228
Compensated Absences									5,675,240	5,675,240	4,957,540
Total Long-Term Liabilities					287,318,675	219,752,141	1,277,148		86,113,100	594,461,064	588,073,393
Total Liabilities	7,582,427	1,642,355	941,657	5,036,480	328,067,834	233,346,142	16,246,656		88,351,854	681,215,405	682,687,887
Fund Equity											
Investment in General Fixed Assets								137,712,148		137,712,148	120,822,953
Contributions					294,070,442	5,850,901	656,330			300,577,673	292,003,593
Retained Earnings											
Reserved for Debt Service					40,578,365	2,384,136				42,962,501	43,698,106
Reserved for Risk Management						5,628,368				5,628,368	3,680,388
Reserved for Vehicle Replacement						6,564,401				6,564,401	6,833,413
Reserved for Capital Projects					42,216,469					42,216,469	40,230,684
Reserved for Renewal and Replacement					12,468,088					12,468,088	10,262,512
Reserved for Contractual Obligation					7,302,927					7,302,927	6,470,635
Unreserved					67,066,966	4,261,990				71,328,956	65,823,800
Total Retained Earnings					169,632,815	18,838,895				188,471,710	176,999,538
Fund Balances											
Reserved for Debt Service			8,025,375							8,025,375	6,930,140
Reserved for Inventories	526,357	957,450					16,945			1,500,752	1,536,528
Reserved for Prepaid Items	219,642	8,675								228,317	31,668
Reserved for Encumbrances	340,388	2,340,210		5,522,707			1,498			8,204,803	24,465,348
Reserved for Advances to Other Funds											3,460,228
Reserved for Retirement Benefits							222,359,203			222,359,203	201,531,879
Reserved for Other Projects							3,186,829			3,186,829	2,872,032
Total Reserved Fund Balance	1,086,387	3,306,335	8,025,375	5,522,707			225,564,475			243,505,279	240,827,823
Designated for Working Capital	20,000,000									20,000,000	16,900,000
Designated for Project Appropriation	1,437,481									1,437,481	3,488,742
Designated for Capital Projects	7,000,000			16,959,699						23,959,699	6,052,058
Designated for Subsequent Year's Budget		23,730,108					9,979,977			33,710,085	31,760,170
Undesignated	4,177,400						34,739			4,212,139	3,278,397
Total Unreserved Fund Balance	32,614,881	23,730,108		16,959,699			10,014,716			83,319,404	61,479,367
Total Fund Balances	33,701,268	27,036,443	8,025,375	22,482,406			235,579,191			326,824,683	302,307,190
Total Fund Equity	33,701,268	27,036,443	8,025,375	22,482,406	463,703,257	24,689,796	236,235,521	137,712,148		953,586,214	892,133,274
Total Liabilities and Fund Equity	$41,283,695	$28,678,798	$8,967,032	$27,518,886	$791,771,091	$258,035,938	$252,482,177	$137,712,148	$88,351,854	$1,634,801,619	$1,574,821,161

Other Notes. Several other disclosure requirements have been discussed in previous chapters. These include disclosures concerning:

- Advance refundings (Chapter 8)
- Reconciliation of budgetary and GAAP-basis operating results or fund balances (Chapter 10, illustrated in Figures 10-5 and 10-6)
- Debt service requirements to maturity (Chapter 9, illustrated in Figure 9-8)
- Deferred compensation plans (Chapter 11)
- Pension plans and employer pension costs (Chapter 11)

Disclosures regarding the governmental reporting entity and joint ventures are discussed in the last major section of this chapter. Also, notes illustrating the disclosure and reconciliation of (1) individual fund interfund payables and receivables, and (2) operating transfers in and out and residual equity transfers in and out are illustrated in Figures 14-13 and 14-14, respectively. Careful study of these selected notes yields many "real-world" insights while illustrating some of the common disclosures listed in Figure 14-10.

The Combining and Individual Fund and Account Group Statements and Schedules. Combining and individual fund and account group statements and schedules have been presented in the preceding chapters both as integral parts of illustrative examples and as ancillary illustrations. The GASB Codification observes that:

> The **major differences between** the GPFS **and** the other statements in the **CAFR relate** to the **reporting entity focus** and the **reporting on finance-related legal** and contractual **provisions** that **differ from GAAP.** The CAFR includes (a) both individual fund and account group data and aggregate data by fund types, together with introductory, supplementary, and statistical information; and (b) schedules essential to demonstrate compliance with finance-related legal and contractual provisions. The **GPFS** present only aggregate data by the fund type and account group together with notes to the financial statements that are essential to fair presentation, including disclosures of material violations of finance-related legal and contractual provisions and other important matters that are not apparent from the face of the financial statements.[4]

The entity **focus** of the **combining and individual** fund and account group statements is on the **individual fund or account group**—and combining statements also present total data for a fund type—whereas the GPFS entity focus is on aggregated fund type data. In summarizing its intent with respect to financial reporting under the pyramid concept, the GASB observes:

> . . . The governmental unit need go only as far down the reporting pyramid—in terms of increasing levels of detail—as necessary to report the financial position and operating results of its individual funds and account groups, to demonstrate compliance with finance-related legal and contractual requirements, and to assure adequate disclosure at the individual fund [and account group] entity level.[5]

Thus, the purpose of the **combining** statements, individual fund and account group statements, and schedules is to "fill the gap," so to speak, between the GPFS that "present fairly" at the **fund type** entity level **and** the need in the CAFR also to "present fairly" under the **individual fund and account group** entity focus. Determining which financial statements and schedules must be presented in the CAFR

---

[4] Ibid., sec. 1900.111. (Emphasis added.)
[5] Ibid., sec. 1900.114.

City of Orlando, Florida
Combined Statement of Revenues, Expenditures, and Changes in Fund Balances
All Governmental Fund Types and Expendable Trust Funds
For the Year Ended September 30, 19X1

	Governmental Fund Types				Fiduciary Fund Types	Totals (Memorandum Only)	
						September 30,	
	General	Special Revenue	Debt Service	Capital Projects	Expendable Trust	19X1	19X0
Revenues							
Property Taxes.	$ 40,148,273	$ 1,009,125	$ —	$ —	$ —	$ 41,157,398	$ 37,694,369
Intergovernmental	41,421,468	16,450,361	—	1,260,807	—	59,132,636	52,554,394
Occupational Licenses and Franchise Fees	15,531,949	—	—	—	—	15,531,949	14,829,105
Utilities Services Tax	—	—	—	—	17,693,022	17,693,022	16,827,709
Other Licenses, Permits and Fees	11,279,725	3,091,624	—	—	—	14,371,349	14,809,173
Fines and Forfeitures	2,033,522	—	—	—	—	2,033,522	1,945,992
Other	7,328,707	3,016,137	120,574	2,610,385	1,459,811	14,535,614	15,225,501
Total Revenues	117,743,644	23,567,247	120,574	3,871,192	19,152,833	164,455,490	153,886,243
Expenditures							
Current Operating:							
General Administration . .	6,702,972	—	—	—	—	6,702,972	6,286,531
Planning and Development.	5,897,149	1,861,153	—	—	—	7,758,302	7,564,943
Finance	2,007,736	—	—	—	—	2,007,736	2,263,346
Public Works	16,936,114	4,884,877	—	—	—	21,820,991	18,829,678
Parks and Recreation. . . .	12,075,833	36,109	—	—	163,294	12,275,236	12,530,821
Centroplex.	494,213	—	—	—	—	494,213	561,169
Police	36,059,314	—	—	—	251,859	36,311,173	33,448,156
Information Systems	4,489,097	—	—	—	—	4,489,097	3,898,911
Human Resources	1,667,300	—	—	—	—	1,667,300	1,428,931
Fire.	19,582,447	—	—	—	—	19,582,447	18,272,490
Other Expenditures	11,539,050	—	—	—	6,412	11,545,462	10,913,236
Downtown Development Board.	—	1,295,730	—	—	—	1,295,730	1,195,039
Community Redevelopment Agency.	—	4,227,426	—	—	—	4,227,426	3,295,388
Capital Improvements.	—	—	—	35,225,552	—	35,225,552	24,177,219
Debt Service	—	—	4,030,121	—	—	4,030,121	2,357,509
Total Expenditures	117,451,225	12,305,295	4,030,121	35,225,552	421,565	169,433,758	147,023,367
Excess (Deficiency) of Revenues Over Expenditures.	292,419	11,261,952	(3,909,547)	(31,354,360)	18,731,268	(4,978,268)	6,862,876
Other Financing Sources and (Uses)							
Operating Transfers In	18,156,183	1,598,075	3,926,794	16,518,062	—	40,199,114	30,789,624
Operating Transfers (Out). .	(12,926,687)	(10,026,176)	(50,005)	(3,765,930)	(17,079,100)	(43,847,898)	(34,473,383)
Bond and Loan Proceeds . .	—	—	1,127,993	12,074,195	—	13,202,188	37,339,016
Bond Issuance Costs.	—	—	—	(100,808)	—	(100,808)	(246,442)
Total Other Financing Sources and (Uses) . . .	5,229,496	(8,428,101)	5,004,782	24,725,519	(17,079,100)	9,452,596	33,408,815
Excess (Deficiency) of Revenues and Other Sources Over Expenditures and Other (Uses).	5,521,915	2,833,851	1,095,235	(6,628,841)	1,652,168	4,474,328	40,271,691
Fund Balances at Beginning of Year	28,721,383	24,202,592	6,930,140	29,111,247	9,966,411	98,931,773	59,629,778
Residual Equity Transfers (Out)	(542,030)	—	—	—	(800,000)	(1,342,030)	(2,075,046)
Residual Equity Transfers In . .	—	—	—	—	—	—	1,105,350
Fund Balances at End of Year .	$ 33,701,268	$ 27,036,443	$ 8,025,375	$22,482,406	$10,818,579	$102,064,071	$ 98,931,773

The accompanying notes are an integral part of the financial statements.

Source: Adapted from a recent City of Orlando, Florida annual report.

Figure 14-7

**COMBINED GOVERNMENTAL FUND BUDGETARY BASIS
OPERATING STATEMENT**

City of Orlando, Florida

Combined Statement of Revenues and Expenditures—Actual and Budget

All Governmental Fund Types and Expendable Trust Funds

For the Year Ended September 30, 19X1

			General Fund		
	Actual	Encumbrances	Budgetary Basis	Budget	Variance Favorable (Unfavorable)
Revenues					
Property Taxes	$40,148,273	$ —	$40,148,273	$40,211,400	$ (63,127)
Intergovernmental	41,421,468	—	41,421,468	39,193,077	2,228,391
Occupational Licenses and Franchise Fees	15,531,949	—	15,531,949	14,889,142	642,807
Other Licenses, Permits, and Fees.	11,279,725	—	11,279,725	12,799,437	(1,519,712)
Fines and Forfeitures.	2,033,522	—	2,033,522	1,731,500	302,022
Other	7,328,707	—	7,328,707	5,987,105	1,341,602
Total Revenues	117,743,644	—	117,743,644	114,811,661	2,931,983
Expenditures					
Current Operating:					
General Administration	6,702,972	38,683	6,741,655	7,016,795	275,140
Planning and Development	5,897,149	31,397	5,928,546	6,273,100	344,554
Finance	2,007,736	26,884	2,034,620	2,068,390	33,770
Public Works.	16,936,114	101,700	17,037,814	17,592,031	554,217
Parks and Recreation	12,075,833	50,695	12,126,528	12,847,560	721,032
Centroplex	494,213	—	494,213	599,862	105,649
Police.	36,059,314	28,207	36,087,521	36,686,085	598,564
Information Systems	4,489,097	31,676	4,520,773	4,734,020	213,247
Human Resources	1,667,300	5,415	1,672,715	1,746,571	73,856
Fire	19,582,447	15,791	19,598,238	19,663,056	64,818
Other Expenditures	11,539,050	9,940	11,548,990	11,528,667	(20,323)
Downtown Development Board	—	—	—	—	—
Community Redevelopment Agency	—	—	—	—	—
Debt Service	—	—	—	—	—
Total Expenditures.	117,451,225	340,388	117,791,613	120,756,137	2,964,524
Excess (Deficiency) of Revenues Over Expenditures	292,419	(340,388)	(47,969)	(5,944,476)	5,896,507
Other Financing Sources and (Uses)					
Operating Transfers In	18,156,183	—	18,156,183	18,175,851	(19,668)
Operating Transfers (Out)	(12,926,687)	—	(12,926,687)	(14,223,702)	1,297,015
Bond Proceeds.	—	—	—	—	—
Loan Proceeds	—	—	—	—	—
Total Other Financing Sources and (Uses).	5,229,496	—	5,229,496	3,952,149	1,277,347
Excess (Deficiency) of Revenues and Other Sources Over Expenditures and Other (Uses)	5,521,915	(340,388)	5,181,527	(1,992,327)	7,173,854
Fund Balance Allocation	—	—	—	1,992,327	(1,992,327)
Excess (Deficiency) of Revenues and Other Sources Over Expenditures and Other (Uses)	$ 5,521,915	($340,388)	$ 5,181,527	$ -0-	$ 5,181,527

Figure 14-7 Continued

	Special Revenue Funds					Debt Service Funds		
Actual	Encumbrances	Budgetary Basis	Budget	Variance Favorable (Unfavorable)		Actual and Budgetary Basis	Budget	Variance Favorable (Unfavorable)
$ 1,009,125	$ —	$ 1,009,125	$ 955,958	$ 53,167		$ —	$ —	$ —
16,450,361	71,295	16,521,656	16,846,081	(324,425)		—	—	—
—	—	—	—	—		—	—	—
3,091,624	—	3,091,624	4,090,276	(998,652)		—	—	—
—	—	—	—	—				
3,016,137	—	3,016,137	4,296,659	(1,280,522)		120,574	—	120,574
23,567,247	71,295	23,638,542	26,188,974	(2,550,432)		120,574	—	120,574
—	—	—	—	—		—	—	—
1,861,153	71,295	1,932,448	3,509,762	1,577,314		—	—	—
—	—	—	—	—		—	—	—
4,884,877	2,340,210	7,225,087	18,522,788	11,297,701		—	—	—
36,109	—	36,109	138,606	102,497		—	—	—
—	—	—	—	—		—	—	—
—	—	—	—	—		—	—	—
—	—	—	—	—		—	—	—
—	—	—	—	—		—	—	—
—	—	—	—	—		—	—	—
1,295,730	—	1,295,730	1,455,352	159,622		—	—	—
4,227,426	—	4,227,426	6,144,700	1,917,274		—	—	—
—	—	—	—	—		4,030,121	6,555,413	2,525,292
12,305,295	2,411,505	14,716,800	29,771,208	15,054,408		4,030,121	6,555,413	2,525,292
11,261,952	(2,340,210)	8,921,742	(3,582,234)	12,503,976		(3,909,547)	(6,555,413)	2,645,866
1,598,075	—	1,598,075	1,777,867	(179,792)		3,926,794	4,985,145	(1,058,351)
(10,026,176)	—	(10,026,176)	(10,359,877)	333,701		(50,005)	—	(50,005)
—	—	—	—	—		1,127,993	1,127,993	—
—	—	—	—	—		—	—	—
(8,428,101)	—	(8,428,101)	(8,582,010)	153,909		5,004,782	6,113,138	(1,108,356)
2,833,851	(2,340,210)	493,641	(12,164,244)	12,657,885		1,095,235	(442,275)	1,537,510
—	—	—	12,164,244	(12,164,244)		—	442,275	(442,275)
$2,833,851	$ (2,340,210)	$ 493,641	$ -0-	$ 493,641		$ 1,095,235	$ -0-	$ 1,095,235

Source: A recent City of Orlando, Florida, annual report.

City of Orlando, Florida

Combined Statement of Operations and

Changes in Retained Earnings/Fund Balances

All Proprietary Fund Types and Similar Trust Funds

For the Year Ended September 30, 19X1

	Proprietary Fund Types		Nonexpendable Trust	Pension Trust	Totals (Memorandum Only) September 30,	
	Enterprise	Internal Service			19X1	19X0
Operating Revenues						
User Charges.	$ 51,574,359	$11,081,356	$ —	$ —	$ 62,655,715	$ 62,743,064
Fees.	12,965,839	8,831,430	—	—	21,797,269	20,970,723
Facility Rental	2,360,512	—	—	—	2,360,512	2,834,574
Parking Fines.	1,605,103	—	—	—	1,605,103	1,502,372
Contributions	—	—	—	13,925,950	13,925,950	11,818,798
Rent.	—	—	174,527	—	174,527	161,936
Other.	2,782,847	449,477	37,725	—	3,270,049	1,583,222
Total Operating Revenues	71,288,660	20,362,263	212,252	13,925,950	105,789,125	101,614,689
Operating Expenses						
Salaries, Wages, and Employee Benefits	19,315,367	5,129,788	107,290	—	24,552,445	22,672,617
Contractual Services, Materials and Supplies	29,661,518	4,995,446	76,051	279,189	35,012,204	33,656,272
Depreciation Expense.	25,691,732	3,616,348	40,235	—	29,348,315	26,908,206
Insurance and Other Expenses.	3,910,303	3,990,744	17,179	546,904	8,465,130	8,537,897
Retirement Benefits	—	—	—	7,975,922	7,975,922	7,179,048
Refunds of Employee Contributions	—	—	—	168,925	168,925	159,398
Total Operating Expenses.	78,578,920	17,732,326	240,755	8,970,940	105,522,941	99,113,438
Operating Income (Loss)	(7,290,260)	2,629,937	(28,503)	4,955,010	266,184	2,501,251
Nonoperating Revenues (Expenses)						
Income on Investments.	14,310,503	14,310,385	57,749	15,872,314	44,550,951	44,879,146
Impact Fees.	9,816,599	—	—	—	9,816,599	12,348,487
Interest Expense	(20,960,938)	(16,023,276)	(106,378)	—	(37,090,592)	(35,461,255)
Gain (Loss) on Sale of Fixed Assets	566,500	316,814	(2,973)	—	880,341	464,565
Total Nonoperating Revenues (Expenses)	3,732,664	(1,396,077)	(51,602)	15,872,314	18,157,299	22,230,943
Net Income (Loss) Before Operating Transfers	(3,557,596)	1,233,860	(80,105)	20,827,324	18,423,483	24,732,194
Operating Transfers						
Operating Transfers In	4,171,761	—	190,407	—	4,362,168	4,783,481
Operating Transfers (Out).	(420,557)	(272,617)	(20,210)	—	(713,384)	(1,097,672)
Total Operating Transfers.	3,751,204	(272,617)	170,197	—	3,648,784	3,685,809
Income Before Extraordinary Loss	193,608	961,243	90,092	20,827,324	22,072,267	28,418,003
Extraordinary Loss on Advance Refunding of Wastewater Revenue Bonds.	—	—	—	—	—	(509,771)
Net Income	193,608	961,243	90,092	20,827,324	22,072,267	27,908,232
Depreciation on Contributed Assets.	10,235,519	—	7,551	—	10,243,070	9,064,963
Net Increase in Retained Earnings/Fund Balances	10,429,127	961,243	97,643	20,827,324	32,315,337	36,973,195
Retained Earnings/Fund Balances at Beginning of Year	159,203,688	17,795,850	1,843,538	201,531,879	380,374,955	343,401,760
Residual Equity Transfers In*	—	81,802	460,228	—	542,030	
Retained Earnings/Fund Balances at End of Year.	$169,632,815	$18,838,895	$2,401,409	$222,359,203	$413,232,322	$380,374,955

* Terminated ISF had retained earnings deficit

The accompanying notes are an integral part of the financial statements.

Source: Adapted from a recent City of Orlando, Florida annual financial report.

beyond those of the GPFS requires careful consideration of the facts of each situation and professional judgment. When all three levels are presented, the **combining** statements "**link**" the **combined** statements **and** the **individual fund** statements presented in the CAFR.

The City of Orlando **Combining** Statement of Revenues, Expenditures, and Changes in Fund Balances for its Special Revenue Funds is presented in Figure 4-11. Compare the total column of this Combining Statement of Revenues, Expen-

Figure 14-9

City of Orlando, Florida

Combined Statement of Cash Flows

All Proprietary Fund Types and Nonexpendable Trust Funds

For the Year Ended September 30, 19X1

	Proprietary Fund Types			Totals (Memorandum Only)	
				September 30,	
	Enterprise	Internal Service	Nonexpendable Trust	19X1	19X0
Increase (Decrease) in Cash and Cash Equivalents:					
Cash Flows from Operations:					
Receipts from Customers	$ 71,794,405	$20,223,857	$ (118,723)	$ 91,899,539	$ 88,085,025
Repayment of Loans to Other Funds	—	7,924,426	—	7,924,426	1,499,066
Loans to Other Funds and Developers	—	(8,446,885)	—	(8,446,885)	(17,501,015)
Payments to Suppliers	(30,433,491)	(9,917,048)	(108,131)	(40,458,670)	(36,374,832)
Payments to Employees	(14,993,895)	(4,039,446)	(82,477)	(19,115,818)	(17,886,839)
Payments to Internal Service Funds and Administrative Fees	(6,386,572)	(972,941)	(522)	(7,360,035)	(7,021,885)
Net Cash Provided by (Used in) Operating Activities	19,980,447	4,771,963	(309,853)	24,442,557	10,799,520
Cash Flows from Noncapital Financing Activities:					
Operating Transfers In	4,171,761	—	190,407	4,362,168	4,783,481
Operating Transfers (Out)	(420,557)	(272,617)	(20,210)	(713,384)	(1,097,672)
(Increase) Decrease Advance to Other Funds	—	—	—	—	10,000,000
Increase (Decrease) Due to Other Funds	(815,554)	—	—	(815,554)	69,701
Increase (Decrease) Advance from Other Funds	—	—	(460,228)	(460,228)	95,508
Proceeds from Bonds and Loans	—	—	—	—	15,000,000
Principal Paid on Bonds and Loans	—	(392,000)	—	(392,000)	(366,000)
Interest Paid on Bonds and Loans	—	(15,581,954)	—	(15,581,954)	(16,851,431)
Bond Issuance Costs Paid	—	(8,297)	—	(8,297)	(21,364)
Increase (Decrease) Obligations Under Reverse Repurchase Agreements	(5,171,884)	—	—	(5,171,884)	(13,084,616)
Net Cash Flows from Noncapital Financing Activities	(2,236,234)	(16,254,868)	(290,031)	(18,781,133)	(1,472,393)
Cash Flows from Capital and Related Financing Activities:					
Proceeds from Bonds, Loans, and Advances	8,446,885	—	—	8,446,885	68,557,940
Additions to Property, Plant, and Equipment	(40,667,370)	(4,536,461)	(6,252)	(45,210,083)	(52,316,438)
Principal Paid on Bonds, Interfund Loans, Loans, and Leases	(13,621,597)	—	(11,527)	(13,633,124)	(25,461,410)
Payment for Advance Refunding of Bonds	—	—	—	—	(50,400,000)
Interest Paid on Bonds, Interfund Loans, Loans, and Leases	(21,170,699)	(152,452)	(106,185)	(21,429,336)	(24,878,284)
Proceeds from Sale of Property, Plant, and Equipment	1,800,433	337,692	—	2,138,125	919,343
Capital Contributions from Other Governments, Developers, and Funds	14,871,877	805,639	773,970	16,451,486	46,989,049
Impact Fees Received	9,141,972	—	—	9,141,972	9,808,049
Construction of Leased Asset	—	—	—	—	(1,102,262)
Original Issue Discount and Bond Issuance Costs	—	—	—	—	(505,293)
Net Cash Flows from Capital and Related Financing Activities	(41,198,499)	(3,545,582)	650,006	(44,094,075)	(28,389,306)
Cash Flows from Investing Activities:					
Purchases of Investments	(215,261,685)	—	—	(215,261,685)	(175,780,873)
Proceeds from Sales and Maturities of Investments	219,410,380	—	—	219,410,380	180,955,740
Interest on Investments	13,594,090	14,054,904	57,749	27,706,743	27,282,880
Net Cash Flows from Investing Activities	17,742,785	14,054,904	57,749	31,855,438	32,457,747
Net Increase (Decrease) In Cash and Cash Equivalents	(5,711,501)	(973,583)	107,871	(6,577,213)	13,395,568
Cash and Cash Equivalents at Beginning of Year	133,534,764	18,614,482	337,373	152,486,619	139,091,051
Cash and Cash Equivalents at End of Year	$127,823,263	$17,640,899	$ 445,244	$145,909,406	$152,486,619
Classified As:					
Current Assets	$ 21,219,096	$ 6,504,088	$ —	$ 27,723,184	$ 24,509,752
Restricted Assets	106,604,167	11,136,811	445,244	118,186,222	127,976,867
Total	$127,823,263	$17,640,899	$ 445,244	$145,909,406	$152,486,619
Reconciliation of Operating Income (Loss) to Net Cash Provided by (Used In) Operating Activities:					
Operating Income (Loss)	$ (7,290,260)	$ 2,629,937	$ (28,503)	$ (4,688,826)	$ (820,621)
Adjustments Not Affecting Cash:					
Depreciation	25,691,732	3,616,348	40,235	29,348,315	26,908,206
Amortization	255,762	37,126	—	292,888	284,973
Change in Assets and Liabilities:					
(Increase) Decrease in Accounts Receivable	282,928	(125,757)	(331,075)	(173,904)	(1,708,763)
(Increase) Decrease in Due from Other Funds	—	—	—	—	68,859
(Increase) Decrease in Due from Other Governments	(5,011)	(4,006)	—	(9,017)	(73,478)
(Increase) Decrease in Inventory	(71,459)	43,846	—	(27,613)	(56,701)
(Increase) Decrease in Prepaid Items	(138,817)	—	—	(138,817)	107,427
(Increase) Decrease in Loans to Other Funds	—	(522,459)	—	(522,459)	(15,905,047)
Increase (Decrease) in Due to Other Funds	—	(45,769)	—	(45,769)	45,769
Increase (Decrease) in Accounts Payable	753,295	(558,294)	5,209	200,210	564,251
Increase (Decrease) in Accrued Liabilities	167,763	7,228	3,072	178,063	39,342
Increase (Decrease) in Compensated Absences	80,372	13,440	1,109	94,921	140,002
Increase (Decrease) in Advance Payments	254,142	—	100	254,242	(212,857)
Increase (Decrease) in Claims Payable	—	(319,677)	—	(319,677)	1,418,158
Total Adjustments	27,270,707	2,142,026	(281,350)	29,131,383	11,620,141
Net Cash Provided by (Used In) Operating Activities	$ 19,980,447	$ 4,771,963	$ (309,853)	$ 24,442,557	$ 10,799,520
Noncash Investing, Capital, and Financing Activities:					
Contributed Property, Plant, and Equipment	$ 1,019,057	$ —	$ —	$ 1,019,057	$ 25,232,692
New Lease Obligations	115,373	—	—	115,373	133,735
Equity in Earnings of SSGFC	—	76,633	—	76,633	41,353
Reclassification of Assets	—	—	35,255	35,255	—
Total Noncash Investing, Capital, and Financing Activities	$ 1,134,430	$ 76,633	$ 35,255	$ 1,246,318	$ 25,407,780

The accompanying notes are an integral part of the financial statements.

Source: Adapted from a recent City of Orlando, Florida annual financial report.

ditures, and Changes in Fund Balances with the Special Revenue Fund column in its **Combined** Statement of Revenues, Expenditures, and Changes in Fund Balances (Figure 14-6) and note how the two statements articulate.

Combining statements are always **required** where a government has **more than one fund of a fund type.** Combining statements also may be presented in more detail than is possible in combined statements, often in sufficient detail to "present fairly" and thus avoid the need for several individual fund statements.

Individual fund statements are **required only if** sufficient detail is not presented in combining statements or, in the case of the General Fund and the account groups, in the combined statements. They may also be needed to present budgetary comparisons in sufficient detail and/or to present prior year comparative data.

Schedules are used primarily to (1) demonstrate finance-related legal and contractual compliance, such as when the budgetary basis differs from the GAAP basis, the budget is adopted in more detail than is presented in the financial statements, or bond indentures require certain data to be presented in the CAFR; (2) present more detailed data than that appearing in the combined, combining, and individual fund and account group statements, such as detailed schedules of revenues and of expenditures; and (3) present other data management may wish to present such as cash receipts and disbursements schedules for one, some, or all funds. **Schedules** are **not** considered to be **required** for fair presentation in conformity with GAAP **unless** they are **referenced in** a **statement or footnote.** However, the **notes** to the financial statements (Figure 14-10) **often include** several **schedules** that are deemed essential to reporting in conformity with GAAP, and schedules demonstrating legal (particularly budgetary) compliance are often required for fair presentation.

Narrative explanations are in essence additional **notes to** the **combining and individual fund statements and schedules.** They are not called notes under the GASB's dual reporting approach so that they will not be confused with the notes to the GPFS, which are referred to as the "Notes to the Financial Statements" in the GASB Codification. The Codification summarizes the nature and role of the narrative explanations in the CAFR as follows:

> **Narrative explanations** of combining, individual fund, and account group statements and schedules, should provide information *not* included in the financial statements, notes to the financial statements, and schedules that is necessary: (a) to **assure** an **understanding** of the combining and individual fund and account group statements and schedules, and (b) to **demonstrate compliance** with finance-related legal and contractual provisions. (In extreme cases, it may be necessary to prepare a separate legal-basis special report. . . .) The narrative explanations, including a description of the nature and purpose of the various funds, should be presented on divider pages, directly on the statements and schedules, or in a separate section.[6]

Additional Observations on Financial Reporting—Simple Entity Structure. The GASB offers several other guidelines to financial reporting. At one point the Codification states that "financial statements should present data summarized appropriately to their pyramid level."[7] This is an important point because, consistent with the pyramid concept, it emphasizes that **combined** statements are the **most summarized; combining** statements should **articulate with, but** be in **more detail than,** the

---

[6] Ibid., sec. 2200.122. (Emphasis added.)
[7] Ibid., sec. 2200.107.

Figure 14-10

COMMON NOTE DISCLOSURES

Notes *Essential* to Fair Presentation of GPFS

1. Summary of significant accounting policies, including
   - Reporting entity criteria and component units
   - Revenue recognition policies
   - Encumbrance accounting and reporting methods
   - Policies as to reporting infrastructure GFA
   - Policies with regard to capitalization of interest on fixed assets
   - Cash and cash equivalents definition for cash flow statements
2. Cash deposits with financial institutions (related legal and contractual provisions and categories of risk)
3. Investments—including repurchase agreements (related legal and contractual provisions and categories of risk)
4. Significant contingent liabilities
5. Encumbrances outstanding
6. Significant effects of subsequent events
7. Pension plan obligations
8. Material violations of finance-related legal and contractual provisions
9. Schedule of debt service requirements to maturity
10. Commitments under noncapitalized (operating) leases
11. Construction and other significant commitments
12. Schedule of changes in general fixed assets (unless reported by including a Statement of Changes in General Fixed Assets in the GPFS)
13. Schedule of changes in general long-term debt (unless reported by including a Statement of Changes in General Long-Term Debt in the GPFS)
14. Any excess of expenditures over appropriations in individual funds
15. Deficit fund balance or retained earnings of individual funds
16. Interfund receivables and payables

Additional Note Disclosures, if Applicable, including

1. Reporting Entity [associated agencies]
2. Property taxes
3. Budgetary basis of accounting—including an explanation of the differences between the budgetary and GAAP bases
4. Segment information for Enterprise Funds
5. Claims and judgments; litigation
6. Deferred compensation plans
7. Short-term debt instruments and liquidity
8. Related party transactions
9. Capital leases
10. Joint ventures
11. Special termination benefits, claims and judgments, compensated absences, and so on
12. Debt extinguishment, including advance refundings
13. Nature of total column(s) in combined statements
14. Methods of estimation of fixed asset costs
15. Fund balance designations
16. Contingencies
17. Reverse repurchase and dollar reverse repurchase agreements
18. Special assessment debt and related activities
19. Grants, entitlements, and shared revenues
20. Pension plans—in both separately issued plan financial statements and employer statements.
21. Risk management activities
22. Condensed financial statements of discretely presented component units (Complex Entity Structure only)
23. Nature of accountability for related organizations
24. Joint ventures and jointly governed organizations
25. Other, as appropriate in the circumstances.

Source: Adapted from GASB Codification, sec. 2300.104—.105.

Cash and Investments

The City's investments policies are governed by State statute and city ordinances. Permissible investments include direct obligations of the U.S. government and agency securities, certificates of deposit, and savings accounts or savings certificates of savings and loan associations, repurchase agreements, and bank investment contracts. Collateral is required for demand deposits, certificates of deposits and repurchase agreements at 102% of all amounts not covered by federal deposit insurance. Obligations that may be pledged as collateral are obligations of the United States and its agencies and obligations of the state and its subdivisions. The City's deposits and investments are categorized as follows to indicate the level of risk assumed by the City at June 30, 19X1.

- **Investment Categories of Credit Risk**
  (1) Insured or registered or securities held by the entity or its agent in the entity's name.
  (2) Uninsured and unregistered, with securities held by the counterparty's trust department or agent in the entity's name.
  (3) Uninsured and unregistered, with securities held by the counterparty or by its trust department or agent but not in the entity's name.

- **Deposit Categories of Credit Risk**
  (A) Insured or collateralized with securities held by the entity or by its agent in the entity's name.
  (B) Collateralized with securities held by the pledging financial institution's trust department or agent in the entity's name.
  (C) Uncollateralized

- **Pooled Cash and Investments**
  The City's pooled cash and investments consist of deposits with financial institutions, certificates of deposits, U.S. government and agency securities, and repurchase agreements. These investments have varying maturies ranging from 30 days to 12 years. A minimum of two thirds of pooled funds shall be invested for terms less than one year except Government National Mortgage Association Securities (limited to 10% of the portfolio) and monies accumulated for bond or building funds. The following is a schedule of the City's pooled cash and investments at June 30, 1991 categorized by risk:

Deposits	Category A	B	C	Bank Balance	Carrying Amount
Cash and Certificates of deposit	$ 6,114	$	$	$ 6,114	$ 6,488

Investments	Category 1	2	3	Carrying Amount	Market Value
U.S. Government Obligations	$156,172			$156,172	$162,404
Certificates of Deposit	1,875			1,875	1,875
Repurchase Agreement	8,500			8,500	8,500
U.S. Instrumentality Securities	25,549			25,549	26,334
	$192,096			$192,096	$199,113

- **Nonpooled Cash and Investments**
  Deposits: Deposits are carried at cost. The bank balances are categorized to give an indication at the level of risk assumed by the entity at year end as follows:

Deposits	Category A	B	C	Bank Balance	Carrying Amount
Cash and Certificates of deposit	$ 12,109	$ 1,990	$ 159	$ 14,258	$ 12,446

Investments	Category 1	2	3	Carrying Amount	Market Value
U.S. government obligations	$ 66,078	$ 17,235		$ 83,313	$ 84,612
Corporate bonds (donated)	35	10,394		10,429	10,517
Repurchase agreements	6,879			6,879	6,879
Commercial paper	10,191			10,191	10,191
Municipal investments		430		430	448
U.S. agency securities	1,936	20,164		22,100	22,928
Common stock		17,382		17,382	21,051
Other		2,454		2,454	2,460
	$ 85,119	$ 68,059		$153,178	$159,086
Mutual Fund, including funds invested in U.S. instrumentality securities				62,999	62,999
Bank Investment Contract				109,181	109,152
TOTAL NONPOOLED INVESTMENTS				$325,358	$331,237

SUMMARY OF CASH AND INVESTMENTS

	Carrying Amount Deposits	Investments	Total
Pooled	$ 6,488	$192,096	$198,584
Nonpooled	12,446	325,358	337,804
	$ 18,934	$517,454	$536,388

Balance Sheet Accounts:
Unrestricted:

Cash and cash equivalents	$138,715		
Investments	109,542		

Restricted:

Cash and cash equivalents	213,913		
Investments	74,218		
Total Cash and Investments	$536,388		

Source: A recent annual report of the City of Tulsa, Oklahoma.

Segment Information—Enterprise Funds

The City maintains six enterprise funds: (1) the Water and Sewer Facilities Fund, which provides water and sewer services to the City and outlying areas; (2) the Parking Facilities Fund, which operates certain city-owned parking garages, lots, and meters; (3) the Food Service Fund, which operates the restaurant located in Sidney Park; (4) the Columbia Neighborhood Redevelopment Commission which promotes the development and redevelopment of affordable housing and commercial properties outside of the Congree Vista but within the city; (5) the Columbia Development Corporation, which promotes and assists the economic development and growth of the City; and (6) the Columbia Housing Development Corporation which stimulates the development of better housing within the City.

Following is certain segment information for these funds:

	Water and Sewer Facilities Fund	Parking Facilities Fund	Food Service Fund	Columbia Neighborhood Redevelopment Commission	Columbia Development Corporation	Columbia Housing Development Corporation	Total
Operating Revenue	$ 38,497,585	$ 3,933,255	$3,072	$46,154	$ 365,382	$ 311,109	$ 43,156,557
Depreciation and Amortization	6,832,741	297,281	—	—	18,909	58	7,148,989
Operating Income (Loss)	14,875,989	2,820,562	1,563	42,783	129,883	224,772	18,095,522
Operating Transfers In (Out)	(1,000,000)	(2,000,000)	—	—	—	—	(3,000,000)
Net Income (Loss)	3,025,740	232,409	1,563	43,001	90,076	261,581	3,654,370
Capital Contributions	3,224,384	—	—	—	—	—	3,224,384
Property, Plant, and Equipment:							
Additions	22,578,792	421,324	—	40,615	270,451	471,020	23,782,202
Deletions	374,416	—	—	—	—	254,664	629,080
Net Working Capital (Deficit)	76,496,571	3,344,092	1,563	3,386	(281,965)	1,775	79,565,422
Total Assets	336,953,710	20,208,481	1,563	46,029	1,167,067	1,637,589	360,014,439
Bonds and Other Long-Term Liabilities:							
Payable From Operating Revenues	144,643,098	8,735,000	—	—	444,851	107,096	153,930,045
Payable From Other Sources	—	3,070,000	—	—	—	—	3,070,000
Total Equity	$184,502,300	$ 8,248,371	$1,563	$43,001	$ 356,954	$1,526,636	$194,678,825

Source: A recent annual report of the City of Columbia, South Carolina.

combined statements; and **individual** fund and account group statements should be **in more detail than combining or combined** statements.

Additionally, **we recommend** that:

1. Combined statements should be in **no more** detail **than** can be presented on **two pages.** Some reduction is acceptable, but the published statements should be **readable.**

2. **If** a combining statement involves **so many** different **funds** that, after reduction, the statement would not be readily readable, a **two-tier approach** should be **used.** Under this approach the **major funds** of the type are **presented** and an **"Other" column summarizes** all of the **other funds,** which are **presented in** a **second combining** statement or schedule supporting the main combining statement.

3. Statements that would **exceed two** pages because of reporting **detailed subclassifications** of accounts should be **restructured to present more summarized** data, **with the detail presented in** the next **lower-level** statement or in a schedule(s).

The GASB Codification also notes that **combined statements** may have **total columns,** but they must be labeled **"Memorandum Only."** Also, combined or combining statements **may** have an *"interfund and similar eliminations"* col-

Interfund Receivables and Payables

Interfund receivables and payables at June 30, 19X1 were as follows:

Amount	Due To	Due From
$ 124	General Fund	Tulsa Airport Authority
9	General Fund	Psychological Services
56	Convention Fund	Economic Development Fund
231	1981–1985 Sales Tax	Stormwater Management Fund
62	1986–1991 Sales Tax	Stormwater Management Fund
195	TMUA-Water Enterprise Fund	TMUA-Sewer Enterprise Fund
84	Tulsa Public Facilities Authority	Tulsa Authority for Recovery of Energy
249	Tulsa Public Facilities Authority	Emergency Medical Services Authority
145	Tulsa Public Facilities Authority	TMUA-Water Enterprise Fund
306	Computer Service Fund	General Fund
6	Computer Service Fund	Stormwater Management Fund
61	Computer Service Fund	TMUA-Water Enterprise Fund
1	Computer Service Fund	Equipment Management Service Fund
11	Computer Service Fund	Tulsa Authority for Recovery of Energy
346	Equipment Management Service Fund	General Fund
26	Equipment Management Service Fund	Park Fund
1	Equipment Management Service Fund	Job Training Partnership Act Grant
1	Equipment Management Service Fund	Community Development Block Grant
40	Equipment Management Service Fund	Stormwater Management Fund
89	Equipment Management Service Fund	TMUA-Water Enterprise Fund
51	Equipment Management Service Fund	TMUA-Sewer Enterprise Fund
34	Equipment Management Service Fund	Tulsa Authority for Recovery of Energy
47	Agency Funds	TMUA-Water Enterprise Fund
$ 2,175		

Amount	Advance From	Advance To
$ 300	General Fund	Equipment Management Service Fund
1,848	General Fund	E 911 Construction Fund
405	General Fund	Job Training Partnership Act Grant
381	General Fund	Other Grants
539	General Fund	Metropolitan Tulsa Transit Authority
1,194	1981–1985 Sales Tax	Tulsa Development Authority
6,010	1986–1991 Sales Tax	Tulsa Public Facilities Authority
2,168	Tulsa Public Facilities Authority	1991–1996 Sales Tax
9,568	Tulsa Public Facilities Authority	Tulsa Authority for Recovery of Energy
4,108	Tulsa Public Facilities Authority	Emergency Medical Services Authority
17,552	Tulsa Public Facilities Authority	Capital Cost Recovery Fund
6,113	Tulsa Public Facilities Authority	TMUA-Water Enterprise Fund
127	Tulsa Airports Funds	General Fund
$50,313		

The interfund receivables and payables at June 30, 1991 are reflected in the financial statements as follows:

Due from other funds	$ 1,697
Due from other funds—Restricted assets	478
Due to other funds	1,905
Due to other funds—Restricted liabilities	270
Advances to other funds	10,677
Advances to other funds—Restricted assets	39,636
Advances from other funds	50,313

Source: A recent annual report of the City of Tulsa, Oklahoma.

NOTE 11. OPERATING AND RESIDUAL EQUITY TRANSFERS

Operating transfers among funds occur when a fund receiving revenues transfers resources to a fund where the resources are to be expended. The transfers occur only after being legally authorized by the legislature through statute or an *"Appropriation Act."* The schedule includes $2,075,000 operating transfer out of the General Fund into the Enterprise Fund for the Comprehensive Health Insurance Fund. The Fund began operations in 19X1 and will have a December 31 fiscal year end. The Fund will not be reported in the Enterprise Funds of the State until fiscal year 19X2. For the fiscal year ended June 30, 19X1, the operating transfers by fund are as follows:

Operating Transfers
(Expressed in Thousands)

	General Fund	Special Revenue Funds — Uniform School Fund	Trans-portation Fund	Capital Projects Fund	Debt Service Fund	Enter-prise Funds	Internal Service Funds	Trust and Agency Funds	College and University Funds*	Total Transfers Out
Transfers Out:										
General Fund	$ —	$7,260	$29,325	$16,806	$61,067	$2,075	$ 107	$2,924	$306,311	$425,875
Special Revenue Funds:										
Uniform School Fund	12,676	—	—	—	—	80	—	—	—	12,756
Transportation Fund	23,220	—	—	—	—	—	—	—	—	23,220
Sports Authority Fund	—	—	—	2,933	—	—	—	—	—	2,933
Capital Projects Fund	336	—	—	—	—	—	—	—	—	336
Enterprise Funds	17,571	—	—	—	—	—	43	—	—	17,614
Internal Service Funds	1,549	—	—	—	—	—	—	—	—	1,549
Trust and Agency Funds	12,735	—	—	—	—	—	—	—	—	12,735
Total Transfers In	$68,087	$7,260	$29,325	$19,739	$61,067	$2,155	$ 150	$2,924	$306,311	$497,018

Residual Equity transfers occur when nonroutine transfers are made from one fund to another. These transfers are usually made to provide funds for working capital. In addition to fund equity transfers, fixed assets with an original cost of $2,746,000 and estimated accumulated depreciation of $2,116,000 were transferred from the Internal Service Funds to the General Fixed Assets Account Group. Additionally, the discontinued Internal Service Fund long-term liabilities for compensated absences of $182,000 were transferred to the General Long-Term Obligation Account Group. Contributed capital of $662,000, plus the reduced liability for compensated absences of $182,000, plus net cash transfers of $325,000 from other funds were transferred to retained earnings to cover deficit retained earnings in the discontinued portion of the Internal Service Funds. This resulted in a contributed capital decrease of $1,292,000. For the fiscal year ended June 30, 19X1, the residual equity transfers by fund are as follows:

Residual Equity Transfers
(Expressed in Thousands)

	General Fund	Enterprise Funds	Internal Service Funds	Total Transfers Out
Transfers Out:				
General Fund	$ —	$ 2,629	$ 756	$ 3,385
Uniform School	—	—	326	326
Enterprise Funds	582	—	—	582
Internal Service Funds	139	—	—	139
Total Transfers in	$ 721	$ 2,629	$ 1,082	$ 4,432

* This is an example of "discrete presentation" of component unit data, discussed later in this chapter.

Source: Adapted from a recent annual report of the State of Utah.

umn; or the total may be based on such eliminations even if an eliminations column does not appear in the statement. Interfund and similar eliminations are a **permissible option** but, if made, **must be apparent** from the headings of the statement **or disclosed** in the notes and narrative explanations, as appropriate.

Figure 14-15

STATISTICAL TABLE—TEN-YEAR DATA

County of Los Angeles
General Governmental Expenditures by Function
Last Ten Fiscal Years (in $ thousands)

Function	19W1–19W2	19W2–19W3*	19W3–19W4	19W4–19W5	19W5–19W6	19W6–19W7	19W7–19W8	19W8–19W9	19W9–19X0	19X0–19X1	Function
General government	$ 413,591	421,309	413,216	467,254	536,137	$ 560,636	477,189	491,518	577,216	536,766	General government
Public protection	822,122	1,095,054	1,136,048	1,228,331	1,353,044	1,533,311	1,629,994	1,905,283	2,133,042	2,370,265	Public protection
Public ways and facilities	96,256	137,739	141,355	133,295	153,909	197,272	187,812	166,506	154,819	151,694	Public ways and facilities
Health and sanitation	337,749	404,132	409,219	421,168	474,744	515,070	549,646	611,299	683,661	743,398	Health and sanitation
Public assistance	547,988	1,604,257	1,760,123	1,910,958	2,102,990	2,257,504	2,307,896	2,486,169	2,737,791	3,084,846	Public assistance
Education	27,003	29,414	31,134	36,689	37,526	38,655	41,742	49,084	56,410	60,970	Education
Recreation and cultural services	67,854	66,778	71,846	75,072	78,841	80,446	85,412	105,757	112,807	128,445	Recreation and cultural services
Debt service	81,028	161,390	163,990	410,661	328,750	196,243	240,891	283,575	275,393	314,011	Debt service
Capital outlay	963	29,226	53,314	35,260	40,699	96,606	219,659	186,602	160,517	157,556	Capital outlay
Total	$2,394,554	3,949,299	4,180,245	4,718,688	5,106,640	$5,475,743	5,740,241	6,285,793	6,891,656	7,547,951	Total

Source: Annual Report of the Board of Supervisors and Comprehensive Annual Financial Report, includes General, Special Revenue, Debt Service, and Capital Projects Funds.

Notes:

* Fiscal years prior to 19W2–W3 have not been retroactively adjusted to reflect inclusion of certain organizations, functions, and activities included in 19W1–W3 pursuant to National Council on Governmental Accounting Statement 3, *Defining the Governmental Reporting Entity* as adopted by GASB. Accordingly, fiscal years prior to 19W2–W3 exclude the operations of Fire Protection, Flood Control, Street Lighting, Garbage Disposal and Sewer Maintenance Special Districts, Transit and Paratransit Operations Funds, the Community Development Commission (including the Housing Authority of the County of Los Angeles), and various Nonprofit Corporations and Joint Powers Authorities.

Figure 14-16   STATISTICAL TABLE—SINGLE-YEAR DATA

City of Louisville
Computation of Direct and Overlapping Bonded Debt
General Obligation Bonds
June 30, 19X1

Governmental Unit	Net General Obligation Bonded Debt Outstanding	Percentage Applicable to City of Louisville	Amount Applicable to City of Louisville
Direct debt—City of Louisville Serial Bonds	$ 12,361,000	100.00%	$ 12,361,000
Overlapping debt:			
Louisville and Jefferson County Board of Education	149,468,114	32.86%	49,115,222
Jefferson County	146,925,000	32.86%	48,279,555
Total direct and overlapping debt	$308,754,114		$109,755,777

Source: A recent City of Louisville, Kentucky, annual report.

Finally, recall from prior chapters that there are several acceptable options for formats of statements of revenues, expenditures, and changes in fund balances prepared for governmental funds and similar trust funds. The GASB Codification illustrates one format, which is the basis for the illustrative example statement in Chapter 4 and is used by the City of Orlando, as shown in Figure 14-6. Another acceptable approach is illustrated in Chapter 7.

Statistical Tables

The final section of the CAFR contains several types of **statistical presentations. Some** of the data are **extracted from** present and past **financial statements,** such as the table of General Government Expenditures by Function—**Last Ten Years** (Figure 14-15), to give the reader a historical and trend perspective of the government. **Other** data **relate** only **to one year**—such as the computation of legal debt margin and the computation of overlapping debt (Figure 14-16)—to demonstrate compliance with laws on the amount of debt that can be incurred, to indicate approximately how much more debt could be issued before reaching the legal debt ceiling, or to provide a perspective of the total local government tax load on the citizens in the government's jurisdiction. **Other types of economic and demographic data** are also presented here to give the reader a perspective on such matters as employment and unemployment, the major employers and taxpayers, and the general condition of the local economy.

The GASB Codification specifies that certain statistical tables be included in the CAFR unless clearly inapplicable in the circumstances. These tables are listed in Figure 14-3. The GASB Codification also urges preparers to devise new types of statistical statements as needed.

Although space precludes illustrating all 15 of these statistical tables, one example of each of the broad types—that is, those presenting (1) ten-year data, (2) single-year data, and (3) other economic and demographic data—are included in Figures 14-15, 14-16, and 14-17, respectively.

Figure 14-17   **STATISTICAL TABLE—ECONOMIC AND DEMOGRAPHIC DATA**

County of Los Angeles
Principal Taxpayers
June 30, 19X1

Taxpayers	Total Tax Levy Fiscal Year 19X0–19X1	Percentage of Total*	Percentage of Total Tax Levy Fiscal Year 19X0–19X1
Pacific Bell	$ 48,434,114	22.09	1.05
Southern California Edison Company . .	40,814,286	18.61	.88
GTE California, Inc.	33,068,576	15.08	.71
Southern California Gas Company	20,416,080	9.31	.44
Hughes Aircraft Company	17,079,508	7.79	.37
Northrop Corporation	13,916,348	6.35	.30
Chevron USA Inc.	13,013,864	5.93	.28
Shuwa Investments Corporation	11,824,517	5.39	.26
McDonnell Douglas Corp.	10,757,062	4.91	.23
Atlantic Richfield	9,959,110	4.54	.21
Total	$219,283,465	100.00	4.73

*Detail may not add to total due to rounding. *Source:* Los Angeles County Treasurer-Tax Collector.

Source: A recent County of Los Angeles, California, annual report.

SUPPLEMENTAL AND SPECIAL PURPOSE REPORTING

A variety of **special reports** has emerged in recent years. **Some** are necessary **because** a government prepares its CAFR in accordance with GAAP but **must** also **submit** a **non-GAAP report** (possibly of cash receipts, disbursements, and balances) to a state agency. This type of situation is contemplated and discussed in the GASB Codification.

Another type of report that has emerged may be called **"condensed summary (or "popular") reports"** that are directed at the top of the financial reporting pyramid. These vary from highly condensed (even consolidated) financial statements, perhaps presented in short booklets or brochures highlighting the key aspects of a government's operating results and status, to misleading presentations of selected data of only a few of a government's funds and account groups. In other words, some appear to be sincere efforts to communicate vital data at a more condensed level than that of the GPFS, whereas others appear to hide more than they disclose.

Presentations of data **more aggregated than** the **GPFS** are **not** considered **GAAP.** At the same time, the GASB Codification recognizes that GAAP continually evolve and notes:

Some governmental units have for many years published highly *condensed summary* financial data, usually as **"popular"** reports directed primarily to citizens. Often the data in such reports are presented **in charts or graphs** rather than in financial statements. More recently, several professional association committees and individuals have undertaken research and experimentation directed toward the design of highly condensed summary financial statements for governmental units. Such research and **experimentation is encouraged, but** at the present time **such statements** should **supplement, rather than supplant, the CAFR** and the separately issued **GPFS.** Further, the data in such highly condensed summary statements should be reconcilable with the combined, combining, and individual fund and account group statements, and the reader of such statements should be referred to the CAFR and/or the separately issued GPFS of the governmental unit.[8]

Indeed, the GASB recently sponsored a popular reporting research project and published the results of the research.[9]

Finally, the GASB Codification recognizes that the standards established by the Board and its predecessors are **minimum standards** of financial reporting, **not maximum** standards. Accordingly, the finance officer should assume responsibility for preparing other information needed for management, policy, and other decisions. The GASB also notes that supplementary information may be as valuable as GAAP information in meeting some information needs.

FINANCIAL REPORTING—COMPLEX ENTITY STRUCTURE

To this point we have illustrated and discussed financial reporting in the context of a simple entity structure—that is, the legal entity is the entire reporting entity. While this assumption is valid for most governments, many state governments and local **units of general government**—such as counties, parishes, cities, towns and townships, and villages—**have varying degrees of authority over** and/or responsibilities for **other** legally separate governmental, quasi-governmental, or other entities or **units**—such as school districts, housing authorities, building authorities, fire districts, water districts, airport authorities, and transit authorities. This is illustrated in Figure 14-18.

As a result of these relationships between units of general government (such as the City of Lubburg) and other associated, but legally separate, organizations (like those shown in Figure 14-18), a government must **determine** (1) **whether** its **reporting entity** should be **limited to** its own **legal entity** (referred to by the GASB as the **primary government) or** (2) **whether** one or more of the **associated organizations** (referred to as **potential component units**) are also **part of** the government's **reporting entity.**

The GASB requires certain associated organizations to be included as component units of the government's reporting entity. A government's financial report thus does not fairly present financial position or results of operations if it erroneously includes or excludes a potential component unit from its reporting entity.

Reporting Entity Definition

According to the GASB Codification, each general purpose unit of government—that is, states, counties, cities, and so on—is a **primary government.** Any organization that is legally dependent on a primary government is defined as part of that primary government. Special purpose units of governments such as school districts also are primary governments if they meet certain criteria. Too, the Codification says that any government organization that is not a primary government should define its reporting entity and incorporate its component units into its CAFR as if it were a primary government.

---

[8] Ibid., sec. 2700.104. (Emphasis added.)
[9] Frances H. Carpenter and Florence C. Sharp, *Popular Reporting: Local Government Financial Reports to the Citizenry* (Norwalk, CT: GASB, 1992).

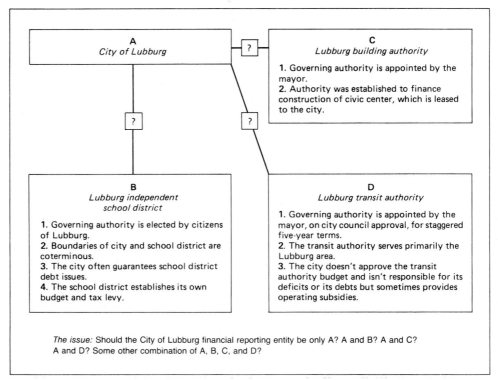

A
City of Lubburg

?

C
Lubburg building authority

1. Governing authority is appointed by the mayor.
2. Authority was established to finance construction of civic center, which is leased to the city.

?

?

B
Lubburg independent school district

1. Governing authority is elected by citizens of Lubburg.
2. Boundaries of city and school district are coterminous.
3. The city often guarantees school district debt issues.
4. The school district establishes its own budget and tax levy.

D
Lubburg transit authority

1. Governing authority is appointed by the mayor, on city council approval, for staggered five-year terms.
2. The transit authority serves primarily the Lubburg area.
3. The city doesn't approve the transit authority budget and isn't responsible for its deficits or its debts but sometimes provides operating subsidies.

The issue: Should the City of Lubburg financial reporting entity be only A? A and B? A and C? A and D? Some other combination of A, B, C, and D?

Source: Robert J. Freeman and Craig D. Shoulders, "Defining the Governmental Reporting Entity," *Journal of Accountancy* (October 1982), p. 52.

Whether or not a potential component unit is to be included in a primary government's reporting entity typically depends on whether the primary government is deemed "financially accountable" for the potential component unit. A primary government is **financially accountable** for a potential component unit if the organization is *fiscally dependent* on the primary government. Likewise, a primary government is **financially accountable** for another organization if *both* of the following conditions are met:

1. The primary government *either* **appoints** (or has ex officio representation constituting) a **voting majority of** the potential component unit's **governing body** *or* it **can** unilaterally **abolish** the other organization, *and*
2. The primary government *either* (a) has the **ability to impose** its **will** on the potential component unit **or** (b) has the **potential** to receive **specific financial benefits** from **or** be subject to specific financial **burdens** because of the organization.

The conditions that must be met for the "fiscal dependence," "ability to impose will," and "financial benefit or burden" criteria to be met are summarized in Figure 14-19.

An associated organization is a component unit of a primary government's reporting entity if the primary government is financially accountable for the organization. Likewise, an organization is a component unit of a primary government if it is a for-profit corporation in which the primary government holds majority ownership for the purpose of directly facilitating provision of government services. Too, a government's reporting entity should include any other potential com-

Figure 14-19   **GASB REPORTING ENTITY DEFINITION CRITERIA**

- **FISCAL DEPENDENCE exists if the primary government's substantive approval is required for a potential component unit to:**
  - Establish its budget, **or**
  - Levy taxes or set other rates or charges, **or**
  - Issue bonded debt

- **ABILITY OF A PRIMARY GOVERNMENT TO IMPOSE ITS WILL on a potential component unit exists if the primary government has the substantive authority to:**
  - Remove appointed governing board members at will, **or**
  - Approve or require modification of the organization's budget, **or**
  - Approve or require modification of rate or fee changes affecting the organization's revenues, **or**
  - Veto, overrule, or otherwise modify other governing body decisions, **or**
  - Appoint, hire, reassign, or dismiss the organization's management, **or**
  - Take other actions that indicate its ability to impose its will on the organization

- **A FINANCIAL BENEFIT OR BURDEN RELATIONSHIP exists if the primary government:**
  - Has the ability to access the resources of the entity without dissolution of the entity, **or**
  - Is legally or otherwise obligated to finance the deficits of, or provide financial support to the organization, **or**
  - Is "obligated in some manner for the debt" of the organization

ponent unit necessary to keep the reporting entity financial statements from being misleading or incomplete.

The GASB established two modifying rules with respect to the reporting entity definition that impact some governments. First, the Codification prohibits an organization being included as a component unit of two different primary governments, even if the conditions for inclusion are met for both. (However, the guidance provided does not indicate how to determine which primary government reporting entity should exclude the potential component unit based on its inclusion in the other primary government's reporting entity.) Second, the Codification requires "bottom-up" application of the reporting entity criteria. Hence, if Organization A is a component unit of Organization B and Organization B is a component unit of Organization C, then Organization A is a component unit of Organization C because it is a component unit of one of Organization A's component units. Note that Organization A is a component unit of Organization C even if it would not otherwise meet the criteria for inclusion in Organization C's reporting entity.

Reporting Entity Disclosures

Extensive reporting entity **disclosures**—including (1) the **component units** of a government's reporting entity, (2) the **criteria used** to determine which potential component units to include, and (3) other related information—are **required in** the **notes** to the financial statements. Specifically, the following disclosures are required:

1. The ***component units*** included in the reporting entity
2. The ***criteria used*** in determining the scope of the reporting entity, ***including*** the ***"key" decision criteria***
3. ***How*** the component units were reported
4. How to obtain the separate financial statements of individual component units

Two different approaches to incorporating component unit data into a primary government's CAFR are required by the GASB. The approach used for each component unit depends upon whether the component unit is in substance part of the primary government. To be considered part of the substantive primary government, a component unit must:

- Have substantively the same governing body as the primary government's governing body. [The GASB defines "substantively the same" as "sufficient representation of the primary government's **entire** governing body on the component unit's governing body to allow complete control of the component unit's activities"[10]], **or**
- Provide services only to the primary government (meaning to the government itself, not to its constituency), **or**
- Benefit the primary government exclusively even though it does not provide services directly to the primary government.

Note that, by definition, the overwhelming majority of component units will **not** meet either of the last two criteria for being part of the substantive primary government. Only certain types of organizations—such as building authorities—have the potential to meet these latter criteria. Organizations such as school districts, airport authorities, civic center commissions, transit authorities, and so on can be part of the substantive primary government only if the "substantively the same governing body" criterion is met.

Financial data of component units that are defined as **part of** the **primary government in substance** are to be **"blended"** with the financial data of the primary government legal entity (as are all entities that are legally part of the primary government). **All other** component units—those that are not part of the substantive primary government—are **discretely presented.** Both "blending" and "discrete presentation" are described in the following sections.

Blending

The **basic purpose of blending** is to incorporate the data of the blended component units into a report that **treats** the **primary government** legal entity and **all** of the blended **component units as a single entity.** Accordingly, after obtaining the data of the various component units to be blended and, if necessary, converting those data so that they conform with GASB standards, the data are combined with those of the appropriate fund types and account groups of the primary government legal entity. **Some blended component units** may be **accounted for in a single fund. Other blended component units** may be reported in **several funds** and account groups. **In general,** blended component unit funds and account groups (classified per the GASB fund types) are **reported as** the **same types of funds** and account groups in the statements **of the primary government legal entity.** The single exception is that the **General Fund** of a **blended component unit** is **treated as** a **Special Revenue Fund** of the substantive primary government. This is because those resources are to be used only for the purposes of that component unit. Hence, the General Fund of the legal entity is the General Fund of the primary government of the reporting entity. Each blended component unit fund should be presented in a separate column in the pertinent combining financial statements of the

---

[10] GASB, *Statement No. 14 of the Governmental Accounting Standards Board,* "The Financial Reporting Entity," (Norwalk, Conn.: GASB, June 1991) footnote 7—footnote to para. 53a.

Figure 14-20

CLASSIFICATION OF COMPONENT UNIT FUNDS AND ACCOUNT GROUPS INTO REPORTING ENTITY FUND TYPES AND ACCOUNT GROUPS

Reporting Entity Funds and Account Groups

	GF	SRFs	CPFs	DSFs	EFs	ISFs	T&A	GFAAG	GLTDAG
Blended Component Units' Funds and AGs / Primary Government Legal Entity Funds and AGs	X	X	X	X	X	X	X	X	X
Transit Authority: (Enterprise Fund)					X				
Pension Board: (Trust Fund)							X		
School District:									
General Fund		X							
Special Revenue Funds		X							
Capital Projects Fund			X						
Debt Service Fund				X					
Internal Service Fund						X			
Trust Funds							X		
General Fixed Assets Account Group								X	
General Long-Term Debt Account Group									X

reporting entity. Figure 14-20 illustrates the classification of funds for several component units of an illustrative government assuming that they are to be blended.

The GASB states that the data of the blended entity, that is, the substantive primary government, is the focal point of interest for users of a government's financial reports. For many (if not most) governments, this entity will be comprised solely of the legal entity; that is, there will be no blended component units.

Discrete Presentation

The philosophy behind discrete presentation—the reporting approach required for most component units—reflects the notions that the discretely presented component units are of secondary interest to financial statement users and, therefore, that a broad "overview" of their financial position and operating results will provide sufficient information for fair presentation within the reporting entity context. Hence, the purpose of discrete presentation is to present component unit data with, but separate from, primary government data.

The GASB requires that the data of discretely presented component units be reported in a manner that clearly reflects that the discretely presented component units are not part of the primary government in substance. At the GPFS level, this is accomplished in each combined financial statement by labeling the several columns necessary to present the primary government fund type and account group data as "Primary Government" and including the "Component Units" data in one or more appropriately headed additional columns to the right of the primary government columns. (An exception is that budgetary comparisons are not required for these component units.) A combined balance sheet with three discretely presented component units is illustrated in Figure 14-21. In this illustration all three discretely presented component units are aggregated in a single column. This approach is permitted on each combined financial statement. At the other ex-

Figure 14-21

REPORTING ENTITY COMBINED BALANCE SHEET
(WITH SINGLE COMPONENT UNIT COLUMN)

Our City (Reporting Entity)
Balance Sheet
September 30, 19X1

	GENERAL	SPECIAL REVENUE	DEBT SERVICE	CAPITAL PROJECTS	ENTERPRISE	INTERNAL SERVICE	FIDUCIARY FUNDS
ASSETS:							
Cash	$1,500,000	$1,000,000	$100,000	$300,000	$ 685,000	$ 50,000	$330,000
Investments	475,000	200,000	75,000	100,000	160,000	100,000	350,000
Receivables, Net	150,000			100,000	500	300,000	
Due from Federal Government							
Due from Other Funds . . .							
Due from Component Units	30,000						
Inventory.							
Fixed Assets.					3,190,000	250,000	220,000
Amount Available in Debt Service Funds							
Amount to Be Provided For Retirement of General Long-Term Debt.							
TOTAL ASSETS	2,155,000	1,200,000	175,000	500,000	4,035,500	700,000	900,000
LIABILITIES AND FUND BALANCES/EQUITY							
LIABILITIES:							
Accounts Payable	500,000	400,000		300,000	54,000	50,000	100,000
Wages Payable	300,000	400,000		100,000	100,000	50,000	5,000
Notes Payable.	200,000				31,500		
Interest Payable							
Contracts Payable							
Due to Other Funds							
Due to Primary Government							
Deferred Revenues	125,000	100,000					145,000
Bonds Payable					700,000	200,000	
TOTAL LIABILITIES . . .	1,125,000	900,000		400,000	885,500	300,000	250,000
INVESTMENT IN GENERAL FIXED ASSETS							
CONTRIBUTED CAPITAL. . .					2,100,000	200,000	100,000
RETAINED EARNINGS.					1,050,000	200,000	450,000
FUND BALANCES.	1,030,000	300,000	175,000	100,000			100,000
TOTAL LIABILITIES AND FUND BALANCES/FUND EQUITY.	$2,155,000	$1,200,000	$175,000	$500,000	$4,035,500	$700,000	$900,000

Source: Adapted from James Walter Rhea, Judith Ann Runyon, and Aristarchos Hadjieftychiou, "Case Illustration for Applying GASB Statement No. 14, 'The Financial Reporting Entity' " (A working paper).

treme, each discretely presented component unit may be reported in a separate column. Various degrees of aggregation of component units are possible and permissible between these two extremes.

Any component unit column in a combined statement that aggregates two or more component units must be supported in the GPFS by a corresponding combining component unit financial statement that articulates with and supports it (Figure 14-22). This relationship parallels that between combining fund type financial statements and the columns for each fund type in the combined financial statements. In other words, a combining component unit financial statement consists of adjacent columns presenting data on individual component units and a

Figure 14-21 Continued

GENERAL FIXED ASSETS	GENERAL LONG-TERM DEBT	Primary Government (Memorandum Only Totals)		COMPONENT UNITS	Reporting Entity (Memorandum Only Totals)		
		19X1	19X0		19X1	19X0	
							ASSETS:
$	$	$ 3,965,000		$2,686,000	$ 6,651,000		Cash
		1,460,000		990,000	2,450,000		Investments
		550,500		169,000	719,500		Receivables, Net
				500,000	500,000		Due from Federal Government
				11,000	11,000		Due from Other Funds
		30,000			30,000		Due from Component Units
				53,000	53,000		Inventory
700,000		4,360,000		4,110,000	8,470,000		Fixed Assets
	200,000	200,000		190,000	390,000		Amount Available in Debt Service Funds
	200,000	200,000		710,000	910,000		Amount to Be Provided For Retirement of General Long-Term Debt
700,000	400,000	10,765,500		9,419,000	20,184,500		TOTAL ASSETS
							LIABILITIES AND FUND BALANCES/ EQUITY
							LIABILITIES:
		1,404,000		940,000	2,344,000		Accounts Payable
		955,000		400,000	1,355,000		Wages Payable
		231,500		1,557,000	1,788,500		Notes Payable
				6,000	6,000		Interest Payable
				50,000	50,000		Contract Payable
				11,000	11,000		Due To Other Funds
				30,000	30,000		Due To Primary Government
		370,000		307,000	677,000		Deferred Revenues
	400,000	1,300,000		1,700,000	3,000,000		Bonds Payable
	400,000	4,260,500		5,001,000	9,261,500		TOTAL LIABILITIES
700,000		700,000		1,500,000	2,200,000		INVESTMENT IN GENERAL FIXED ASSETS
		2,400,000		955,000	3,355,000		CONTRIBUTED CAPITAL
		1,700,000		514,000	2,214,000		RETAINED EARNINGS
		1,705,000		1,449,000	3,154,000		FUND BALANCES
$700,000	$400,000	$10,765,500		$9,419,000	$20,184,500		TOTAL LIABILITIES AND FUND BALANCES/ EQUITY

total column in which the individual component unit data have been summed. This total column—perhaps in different account classification detail—is what is reported in the combined financial statement discretely presented components unit column to which it relates.

The combining component unit balance sheet for the discretely presented component units in Figure 14-21 is presented in Figure 14-22. Note that the data reported for the Parks and Recreation Commission and the School District in the combining component unit statements are from the "Memorandum Only" (optional) total columns from the combined financial statements in their separately issued financial reports. These data are not considered GAAP presentations in the separately issued financial statements of the individual component units, but the GASB states that they are GAAP presentations (not memorandum only) in the re-

Figure 14-22 COMBINING COMPONENT UNIT
BALANCE SHEET

Our City
Component Units
Combining Balance Sheet
September 30, 19X1

	Parks and Recreation Commission	School District	Airport Authority	Totals
Assets:				
Cash	$2,050,000	$ 585,000	$ 51,000	$2,686,000
Investments	350,000	490,000	150,000	990,000
Receivables, Net	100,000	64,000	5,000	169,000
Due from Federal Government . .		500,000		500,000
Due from Other Funds		11,000		11,000
Inventory		53,000		53,000
Fixed Assets	1,500,000	1,900,000	710,000	4,110,000
Amount Available in Debt Service Fund	100,000	90,000		190,000
Amount To Be Provided for General Long-Term Debt Retirement	400,000	310,000		710,000
Total Assets	4,500,000	4,003,000	916,000	9,419,000
Liabilities and Fund Balances/ Equity				
Liabilities:				
Accounts Payable	670,000	230,000	40,000	940,000
Wages Payable	400,000			400,000
Notes Payable	525,000	1,025,000	7,000	1,557,000
Interest Payable		6,000		6,000
Contracts Payable		50,000		50,000
Due to Other Funds		11,000		11,000
Due to Primary Government	30,000			30,000
Deferred Revenues	300,000	7,000		307,000
Bonds Payable	1,300,000	400,000		1,700,000
Total Liabilities	3,225,000	1,729,000	47,000	5,001,000
Fund Balances/Equity				
Investment in Fixed Assets	600,000	900,000		1,500,000
Contributed Capital	150,000	250,000	555,000	955,000
Retained Earnings	150,000	50,000	314,000	514,000
Fund Balance	375,000	1,074,000		1,449,000
Total Liabilities and Fund Balances/ Equity	$4,500,000	$4,003,000	$916,000	$9,419,000

porting entity financial report. Further, the totals of the data of these various component units—which are presented as the component unit column in the combined statements (as in Figure 14-21) also are deemed GAAP presentations and are not labeled "Memorandum Only."

Discretely presented component units may be aggregated into a column even when the component units use different reporting models—for example, governmental fund accounting and proprietary fund accounting. When such component units are aggregated, the component unit fund equity data can be presented in the combined balance sheet using the same classifications as for the primary government. Alternatively, discretely presented component units' equity may be aggregated into other classifications such as "Fund balance—governmental fund component units," "Contributed capital—proprietary fund component units," or "Equity—component units."

Similarly, operations data for component units such as school districts that have both governmental and proprietary funds may be disaggregated and included in the component unit column(s) of the applicable combined operating statement. In this approach the component unit governmental fund operations data would be included in the combined statement of revenues, expenditures, and changes in fund balances and the component unit proprietary fund operations data would be reflected in the combined statement of revenues, expenses, and changes in fund equity (retained earnings). Alternatively, the aggregated operations data of all of a discretely presented component unit's fund types may be presented in the component unit column(s) of either the combined governmental fund or proprietary fund operating statement, as deemed most appropriate in the circumstances. Under this approach, the operating results of the component unit fund types that use the other method of accounting would be summarized as a single line item such as "Net income from proprietary operations" or "Excess of revenues and other financing sources over expenditures and other financing uses of governmental fund activities."

Finally, if the combining component unit financial statements are not included in the GPFS, the notes to the GPFS must include condensed financial statements for each "major" discretely presented component unit that has been aggregated with other component units in the combined financial statements. The minimum detail to be disclosed in such condensed financial statements is outlined in Figure 14-23.

Other Issues

Several other issues must be addressed in combining the data of several component units into a single reporting entity report. These issues include:

- The budget basis **budgetary comparison statement** in the reporting entity GPFS should report the **aggregation** of **all** of the **legally approved** budgets, **as amended,** of the primary government (including blended component units) compared to related actuals. Budgetary comparison data for discretely presented component units are not required to be included.

- **Any receivables and payables** between blended component units or between a blended component unit and the primary government should be reclassified and reported as amounts due to and due from (or advances to and advances from) other funds. Receivables and payables between discretely presented component units or between a discretely presented component unit and the primary government should also be reclassified. They should be reported as amounts due to/from or advances to/from the primary government or discretely presented component units to distinguish them from interfund payables and receivables between entities that are part of the in-substance primary government, as illustrated in Figure 14-21.

- **Transactions between the various component units**—which typically are accounted for as revenues and expenditures or expenses by the various legally separate units during the year—must be evaluated from the perspective of being **interfund transactions.** Only those that qualify as quasi-external transactions should be reported as revenues, expenditures, or expenses. Other transactions should be reclassified and reported as operating or residual equity transfers, as appropriate. Once again operating and residual equity transfers within the in-substance primary government and those involving one or more discretely presented component units are distinguished in the financial statements by labeling those involving discretely presented component units as

Figure 14-23   CONDENSED FINANCIAL STATEMENTS

Major Discretely Presented Component Units
Minimum Disclosures

- **CONDENSED BALANCE SHEET**
  - Current assets (intraentity receivables separately identified)
  - Property, plant, and equipment
  - Amounts to be provided (available) for the retirement of GLTD
  - Current liabilities (intraentity payables separately identified)
  - Bonds and other long-term debts outstanding (intraentity payables separately identified)

- **CONDENSED STATEMENT OF REVENUES, EXPENSES, AND CHANGES IN EQUITY (PROPRIETARY-TYPE FUNDS)**
  - Operating revenues (intraentity sales separately identified)
  - Operating expenses
  - Operating income or loss
  - Operating grants, entitlements, and shared revenues
  - Transfers to/from the primary government and other component units
  - Tax revenues
  - Net income or loss
  - Current capital contributions

- **CONDENSED STATEMENT OF REVENUES, EXPENDITURES, AND CHANGES IN FUND BALANCES (GOVERNMENTAL-TYPE FUNDS)**
  - Revenues
  - Current expenditures
  - Capital outlay expenditures
  - Debt service expenditures
  - Transfers to/from the primary government and other component units
  - Excess (Deficiency) of revenues and expenditures

"Operating (or Residual equity) transfers to/from discretely presented component units (or the primary government)."

- The combined statements of a reporting entity may include a **memorandum only total column** for the primary government fund types and account groups to the left of the discretely presented component unit column(s)—as illustrated in Figure 14-21. If a primary government memorandum only total column is presented, a second memorandum only total column—aggregating the data in the primary government total column with that in the component unit column(s) may be presented as well—as is also illustrated in Figure 14-21. This reporting entity memorandum only total column cannot be presented unless the primary government total column is also presented. Recall that the component unit columns are considered GAAP presentations and thus are not labeled "Memorandum Only."

Transactions with **potential** component units that are **not** ultimately **included** in the reporting entity are **not affected** by this guidance.

Finally, the GASB Codification provides guidance if the oversight unit and one or more component units have **differing fiscal years.** The most desirable solution from a reporting simplicity standpoint is to have component units **adopt a common fiscal year.** This is **not always practicable** or desirable for other reasons, however. When component units have differing fiscal years, the reporting entity financial statements are prepared for the **oversight unit's fiscal year** and include **component unit data** for the **other** component unit fiscal years ended **either** (1) **during** the oversight unit's fiscal year or (2) **within** the **first quarter after** the oversight unit's fiscal year end **if accurate** component unit **data** are **available** on a **timely** basis. If including component unit data for differing fiscal years results in material inconsistencies in amounts, such as in due to/from and transfer to/from amounts, the nature and amount of the transactions involved (and the inconsistencies) should be disclosed in the notes.

SEPARATE ISSUANCE OF PRIMARY GOVERNMENT FINANCIAL STATEMENTS

The GASB acknowledges that there may be instances in which a government may find it desirable to issue a financial report that covers its primary government but does not incorporate the data of discretely presented component units. However, the Board clearly states that such a financial report would **not** constitute reporting in conformity with **GAAP.**

RELATED ORGANIZATIONS, JOINT VENTURES, AND JOINTLY GOVERNED ORGANIZATIONS

A final reporting issue that should be addressed is accounting and reporting for potential component units in which an SLG participates. There are three broad categories discussed in the GASB Codification—related organizations, joint ventures, and jointly governed organizations. The three are distinguished as follows:

- **Related organizations** are potential component units that were excluded from the reporting entity because although the appointment authority criterion was met, the primary government is not financially accountable for the organization—that is, the primary government does not have the ability to impose its will over the potential component unit and does not have a financial benefit or burden relationship with it.
- **Joint ventures** and **jointly governed organizations** are potential component units which are subject to the joint control of two or more other entities. Joint control implies that the primary government does not appoint a voting majority of the potential component unit governing body. (Another participant in the joint venture or jointly governed organization may appoint a voting majority of the organization's governing body, however, and may treat it as a component unit.)
- **Joint ventures** are distinguished from jointly governed organizations by the presence in joint ventures of an "ongoing financial interest" or an "ongoing financial responsibility."
- An *ongoing financial interest* is evidenced by the primary government having an equity interest (an explicit and measurable right to joint venture net assets that is set forth in the joint venture agreement) or another arrangement under which the primary government can access the joint venture net resources.
- An *ongoing financial responsibility* exists if the primary government is obligated in some manner for the joint venture debts or if the joint venture cannot continue to exist without the continued financing of the primary government.

For related organizations and jointly governed organizations, a government must disclose required related party transactions information. Additionally, a government is to disclose the nature of its accountability for its related organizations.

A government is required to report its joint venture participation as follows:

- The explicit and measurable amount of any equity interest in a joint venture is reported as an asset.
- Proprietary fund joint venture investments are reported in the investing proprietary fund using the equity method.
- Governmental fund joint venture investments are reported:
  1. As governmental fund assets (or liabilities) only if they represent financial resources receivable or payable.
  2. As governmental fund revenues and expenditures only if the governmental fund revenue and expenditure recognition criteria are met.
  3. As assets in the General Fixed Assets Account Group to the extent that the equity interest of governmental fund joint venture investments exceeds the amount to be reported in the governmental funds.
- The notes to the financial statements should provide:
  1. A general description of each joint venture, including any ongoing financial interest in or responsibility for the joint venture and information on whether the joint venture is either accumulating significant financial resources or experiencing fiscal stress. (Such conditions may give rise to an additional financial benefit or burden in the future.)
  2. Any other required related party transactions information.

CONCLUDING COMMENTS

The "pyramid" reporting concept embraced in the GASB Codification represents a major change in annual financial reporting by state and local governments that was implemented during the 1980s. Previously the reporting focus had been almost completely on individual fund and account group statements, with four statements typically required for each fund. By requiring only two or three statements for each governmental, proprietary, and fiduciary fund, and with many separate funds reported in combining statements, the pyramid concept facilitates the streamlining of the CAFRs of many state and local governments to a fraction of their former size. Further, the CAFR is far more usable and understandable than before, since it permits users to begin with the combined overview statements—the General Purpose Financial Statements (GPFS)—and proceed to the more detailed combining and individual fund and account group statements in a logical manner.

Even more important, perhaps, is the dual "reporting entity" focus: (1) the GPFS, which include data aggregated by fund type and account group; and (2) the other financial statements in the CAFR, which include combining and individual fund and account group data as well as the GPFS. Together they provide both overview and more detailed financial information.

The reporting changes incorporated in current GAAP are more drastic than some wanted. On the other hand, others continue to urge the GASB to develop and promulgate standards for condensed summary or even consolidated financial statements for state and local governments. Too, some consider recent changes as improvements; others see them as faulty. For example, recent standards have changed the definition of the reporting entity and made discrete presentation the most common method of incorporating component unit data into a government's CAFR. While some hail these changes as significant improvements in government financial reporting, others believe that these changes have both added complexity to the CAFR and diminished the usefulness and completeness of the data reported for the primary government. Indeed, many argue that the primary government excludes organizations that should be reported (blended) as if they are in substance part of the primary government.

The GASB is studying virtually every aspect of government financial reporting—including the types, levels, and formats of statements to be presented; how to implement the flow of financial resources measurement focus and "an accrual" basis of accounting; and many other specific, topical issues. Thus, it is likely that other major changes will result during the next few years. Several of these current GASB projects are discussed briefly in Chapter 15.

QUESTIONS

14-1 What standard(s) are prescribed by the GASB for interim financial statements? Explain.

14-2 Distinguish between the content and purpose(s) of the general purpose financial statements (GPFS) and the comprehensive annual financial report (CAFR).

14-3 Explain the "pyramid" reporting concept utilized by the GASB.

14-4 Why is a good transmittal letter essential to the comprehensive annual financial report (CAFR)?

14-5 Distinguish between combined statements and combining statements.

14-6 Distinguish between combining component unit financial statements and combining financial statements.

14-7 (a) Why is the total column of the Comined Balance Sheet (e.g., Figure 14-5) labeled "Memorandum Only"? (b) Why is it not necessary to label the total(s) column(s) of combining statements "Memorandum Only"?

14-8 Are interfund eliminations proper under generally accepted accounting principles? Explain.

14-9 What is the purpose(s) of the notes to the financial statements? The narrative explanations?

14-10 Why do the notes to the GPFS contain much information that is also reported elsewhere in the CAFR? Give some examples of this duplication.

14-11 What is the purpose(s) of schedules, as contrasted with statements? Are schedules necessary for reporting in conformity with GAAP?

14-12 What is the purpose(s) of statistical tables as contrasted with that (those) of financial statements? What are the broad types and purposes of statistical tables?

14-13 Does the GASB approve consolidated financial statements and consider them within the bounds of generally accepted accounting principles? Explain.

14-14 Referring to the auditor's report in Figure 14-4, which data are (a) included fully in the auditor's scope and depth of examination, (b) included in the scope but reported on only in relationship to the data in (a), and (c) excluded from the auditor's scope?

14-15 How can one quickly determine, by observation, whether a statement of revenues, expenditures, and changes in fund balances explains the changes in *total* fund balances or *unreserved* fund balances?

14-16 A Lakesiditis resident became concerned when reviewing the City of Lakesiditis annual report because the amount of property taxes reported for the General Fund in the Combined Statement of Revenues, Expenditures, and Changes in Fund Balances —All Governmental Fund Types differs significantly from the amount of actual property taxes reported for that fund in the Combined Statement of Revenues, Expenditures, and Changes in Fund Balances—Budget and Actual—General and Special Revenue Funds. The resident is certain an error has occurred and calls it to the attention of the mayor, who immediately calls the chief accountant in to explain how such an error has occurred. Can such a discrepancy exist under generally accepted accounting principles applicable to governments? Explain.

14-17 (a) What is a joint venture? (b) Under what circumstances must a government apply the special joint venture accounting and disclosure requirements set forth in the GASB Codification? (c) What are those requirements?

14-18 The finance officer of the City of Beamstown is concerned about whether to include the City School District, the Beamstown Transit Authority, and the Beamstown-Thais

County Regional Airport in the city's reporting entity. Explain how the finance director should determine which, if any, of these related entities should be included in the city's reporting entity.

14-19 If the primary government memorandum only total columns in Figure 14-21 had been omitted, what other changes would be required? Why?

14-20 Assume that in addition to the component units indicated in Figures 14-21 and 14-22, there is a blended component unit which has both governmental and proprietary funds. In the combined budgetary comparison statement for the reporting entity, which component unit budgetary comparison data should be incorporated?

PROBLEMS

P 14-1 (Multiple Choice)

1. The proper ordering of the following statements (from highest degree of summarization to lowest degree of summarization) is
   a. combining statements, combined statements, individual fund and account group statements
   b. combined statements, individual fund and account group statements, combining statements
   c. combined statements, combining statements, individual fund and account group statements
   d. individual fund and account group statements, combined statements, combining statements
   e. individual fund and account group statements, combining statements, combined statements
   f. combining statements, individual fund and account group statements, combined statements.

2. Should the notes to the City of Weaver's General Purpose Financial Statements provide information concerning its interfund receivables and payables even if such information is contained in the combining and/or individual fund financial statements?
   a. No, because such information is not required to be included in the notes.
   b. No, because disclosure of the same information in two separate portions of the CAFR would be redundant.
   c. Yes, because the General Purpose Financial Statements and accompanying notes must be sufficiently complete to stand alone.
   d. Yes, because the GASB has ruled that interfund payable and receivable information must be presented in both portions of the CAFR Financial Section.

3. The principal purpose for the required footnote disclosures on government deposits and investments is
   a. to enable users to identify potential conflicts of interest
   b. to encourage governments to obtain the highest return possible on deposits and investments
   c. to enable users to assess the credit risk of a government's deposits and investments
   d. to enable users to better estimate a government's future cash flows
   e. none of the above

4. Narrative explanations differ from notes to financial statements in that
   a. narrative explanations relate to combining and individual fund statements, while the notes relate to the General Purpose Financial Statements
   b. narrative explanations need not conform with generally accepted accounting principles, while the notes must conform
   c. narrative explanations are essentially verbal in nature, while the notes are basically quantitative in nature
   d. there is no difference, since narrative explanations provide essentially the same information included in the notes

5. The statistical section of a Comprehensive Annual Financial Report (CAFR)
   a. is required for fair presentation of a government's financial position and operating results
   b. is required in the CAFR
   c. is composed solely of ten-year historical trend information
   d. is an optional section of the CAFR
   e. is required in the CAFR but, except for ten-year trend data on general government revenues and expenditures, its content is based solely on the judgment of the government's management
   f. none of the above

6. A combining statement differs from a combined statement in that:
   a. the combining statement contains less detailed information than a combined statement
   b. the combining statement may have "total" columns, while the combined statement may not
   c. the combining statement may have an "interfund and similar eliminations" column, while the combined statement may not
   d. the combined statement is required where the government has more than one fund of a specific fund type, while the combining statement need not be used if there is more than one fund of a specific fund type
   e. none of the above

7. In determining whether to include the Rio Lobo Airport Authority as part of the City of Rio Lobo reporting entity, which of the following facts is *least* relevant?
   a. The City of Rio Lobo is not responsible for any of the airport authority's debts
   b. The airport is located within the city limits
   c. The mayor of Rio Lobo is an *ex officio* member of the airport authority's board of directors
   d. The City Council of Rio Lobo does not have the power to approve or reject the airport authority's budget.

8. A government has four discretely presented component units reported in a single column in its appropriate combined financial statements. Condensed financial statements for the discretely presented component units
   a. Must be presented for each discretely presented component unit in the CAFR, but not necessarily in the GPFS.
   b. Must be included in the notes to the financial statements unless the combining component unit financial statements are presented in the CAFR.
   c. Must be included in the notes to the financial statements unless the combining component unit financial statements are presented in the GPFS.
   d. Must include a column for each individual component unit.
   e. Must include a column for each major individual component unit.
   f. More than one of the above statements is true. Indicate the letters for the true statements.

9. Individual fund and account group statements are required to be presented
   a. in both the GPFS and the CAFR
   b. in the GPFS, but not in the CAFR
   c. in the CAFR, but not in the GPFS
   d. only when there is just one fund of a particular type
   e. for the General Fund
   f. none of the above

10. Segment information for Enterprise Funds (EF) is
    a. required to be presented for each EF with long-term debt outstanding
    b. best presented in a footnote

c. information on specific individual EFs

d. required for each major nonhomogenous EF

e. all of the above

f. none of the above

P 14-2 (Discrete Presentation)

1. Modify Figures 14-21 and 14-22 in the manner that would be appropriate to present individual component unit data in the combined balance sheet. Begin with the primary government total columns in the combined balance sheet.

2. How would your answer to the preceding item differ if the government did not want to present the primary government total column?

P 14-3 (CAFR Preparation) The City of Duffy's Den has the following funds:

General Fund

Parks Special Revenue Fund

Community Development Fund

Intergovernmental Grant Fund

City Hall Debt Service Fund

Police Station Bond Debt Service Fund

Special Assessment Debt Service Fund

Park Improvement Capital Projects Fund

Street Improvements Capital Projects Fund

Duffy Memorial Bridge Capital Projects Fund

Firemen's Pension Trust Fund

Municipal Workers' Pension Trust Fund

Deferred Compensation Fund

Property Tax Fund

Central Electronic Data Processing Fund

Central Stores Fund

Self-Insurance Internal Service Fund

Duffy's Den Electric Service

Duffy's Den Municipal Golf Course Fund

Required (a) Prepare a detailed table of contents for the City of Duffy's Den CAFR. Assume that (1) only the General and Special Revenue Funds are budgeted annually and (2) the minimum permissible number of statements are to be presented.

(b) Prepare the headings, including each column heading, for each of the financial statements included in the City of Duffy's Den CAFR. Also indicate the source of the data that would be presented in each column—drawn directly from the accounts, taken from another statement(s), and so on. If the data are derived from another statement(s), specify the source(s).

P 14-4 (Incorporation of Component Units) Beets County officials have concluded that several legally separate entities must be included as component units of its reporting entity in its Comprehensive Annual Financial Report. Three of those entities and the funds used to account for them are:

Puryear Corner School District

    General Fund

    Gymnasium Construction Fund

    Educational Buildings Improvement Fund

    Gymnasium Debt Service Fund

    Payroll Withholding Fund

    Deferred Compensation Fund

    Food Services Enterprise Fund

Central Printing Services Fund

General Long-Term Debt Account Group

General Fixed Assets Account Group

Brown-Beets-Milton Tri-County Airport Authority (Enterprise Fund)

Beets County Public Employee Retirement System

The Beets County Board of Commissioners also serves as the governing board of the Beets County Public Employee Retirement System and the county appoints the voting majority of the boards of the Airport Authority. The School Board is elected.

Required   Indicate the reporting entity fund type or account group in which each of the funds and account groups listed previously for the component units of Beets County should be reported. Explain the reasons for your answer in detail.

P 14-5   (Review of Orlando Statements) Examine the City of Orlando General Purpose Financial Statements presented in the chapter and respond to each of the questions. Each question is taken directly from or adapted from the Government Finance Officers Association Certificate of Achievement for Excellence in Financial Reporting checklist.

Part I. Combined Balance Sheet

1. Is there a *Combined Balance Sheet—All Fund Types and Account Groups?* If so, (a) Is it referred to by that title? (b) Does it include a column for each generic fund type in use which presents combined data for all funds of that type? YES   a) YES   b) YES

2. Has the government improperly included more than one column for any generic fund type?   NO

3. Is there a separate column for the General Fixed Assets Account Group? The General Long-Term Debt Account Group?   YES / YES

4. Are columns captioned with generic fund type or account group titles and/or discrete presentation titles?   YES

5. Is there a total column captioned "memorandum only"?   YES

6. Has the government improperly reported nonasset "other debits" in fund type balance sheets? (They should be reported only in the General Long-Term Debt Account Group.)   NO

7. Are all nonasset "other debits" referred to as "amounts available" and/or "amounts to be provided," so that it is clear that they do not represent assets?   YES

8. Are fixed assets reported only in appropriate columns (Enterprise, Internal Service, and Trust Fund Types and the General Fixed Assets Account Group)?   YES

9. Do interfund receivables equal interfund payables?   YES

10. Are long-term liabilities reported only in appropriate columns (Enterprise, Internal Service, and Trust Fund Types and the General Long-Term Debt Account Group)? Specify any exception.   YES

11. Is the long-term liability portion of claims, judgments, compensated absences, capital leases, and employer pension contributions for governmental fund types recorded in the General Long-Term Debt Account Group?   YES

12. Has the government improperly reported interest payable in future years in the General Long-Term Debt Account Group?   NO

13. Is there a subtotal for total liabilities? Is it labeled as such?

14. Is there a subtotal for total equity? Is it labeled as such?

15. Has the government improperly reported amounts in a separate category between liabilities and fund equity?

16. Are amounts reported as "fund balance" only in appropriate columns (General, Special Revenue, Debt Service, Capital Projects, and Trust Fund Types)?

17. Are amounts reported as "retained earnings" only in appropriate columns (Enterprise and Internal Service Fund Types)?

18. Are separate amounts reported for contributed equity and retained earnings for proprietary fund types?

19. Is other proprietary fund equity section terminology appropriate? (For example, appropriated, unappropriated, restricted, and unrestricted are inappropriate terms.)

20. Are reserves reported on the Combined Balance Sheet—All Fund Types and Account Groups?

21. Has the government improperly used the term "reserve" on the asset side of the balance sheet?

22. Are all reported reserves appropriate? ("Reserved" fund balances should not be negative.)

23. Are the nature and purposes of all reported reserves sufficiently described either on the face of the Combined Balance Sheet—All Fund Types and Account Groups or in the notes to the financial statements?

24. If encumbrances are reported, are they presented in accordance with the following GASB Codification requirements?

   a. As "Reserved for Encumbrances" on the balance sheet?

   b. Within fund equity section of the balance sheet?

   c. Not treated as GAAP expenditures in current year?

25. Has the government improperly reported encumbrances for proprietary fund types?

Part II. Combined GAAP Operating Statement—Governmental Funds

1. Is there a *Combined Statement of Revenues, Expenditures, and Changes in Fund Balances —All Governmental Fund Types* (and similar trust funds)? If so, (a) Is it referred to by that title? (b) Does it include a column for each governmental fund type and similar trust fund in use which presents combined data for all funds of that type?

2. Has the government improperly included more than one column for any generic fund type?

3. Are columns captioned with generic fund type titles?

4. Are revenues classified by source?

5. Are proceeds of long-term debt issues reported separately from fund revenues and classified as "other financing sources"?

6. Are capital leases, which represent an acquisition or construction of a general fixed asset, reflected as an expenditure and an "other financing source"?

7. (a) Are expenditures classified by character (current, intergovernmental, capital outlay, and/or debt service)? (b) Are current expenditures further classified by function and/or program?

8. Are interfund operating transfers reported separately from fund revenues and expenditures and classified as "other financing sources (uses)"?

9. Are revenue and expenditure classifications sufficiently detailed to be meaningful?

10. Has the government refrained from using the term "expenses" in connection with governmental fund types?

Part III. Combined Budgetary Statement

1. Is there a *Combined Statement of Revenues, Expenditures, and Changes in Fund Balances —Budget and Actual—General and Special Revenue Fund Types* (and other governmental fund types for which annual budgets have been legally adopted)? If so, is it referred to by that title?

2. Does it include columns for all governmental fund types for which annual budgets have been legally adopted?

3. Are both budget and actual data presented on the budgetary basis?

Part IV. Combined Proprietary Fund Operating Statement

1. Is there a *Combined Statement of Revenues, Expenses, and Changes in Retained Earnings (or equity)—All Proprietary Fund Types* (and similar trust funds)? If so: (a) Is it referred to by that title? (b) Does it include a column for each proprietary fund type and trust fund type in use which presents combined data for all funds of that type?

2. Has the government improperly included more than one column (each) for Internal Service, Nonexpendable Trust, and Pension Trust Funds?

3. Are columns captioned with generic fund type titles?

4. Are operating grants reported as nonoperating revenues after the reported "operating income or loss"?

5. Are interfund operating transfers in or out reported in a separate classification after the reported "income or loss before operating transfers"?

6. If fixed assets are reported in the proprietary fund types columns of the balance sheet, is depreciation expense reported on the operating statements of:

   a. Enterprise Funds?

   b. Internal Service Funds?

7. Are revenue and expense classifications sufficiently detailed to be meaningful?

8. Are the "all-inclusive" operating statement formats used for all of the Combined Statements—Overview level operating statements rather than separate operating statements and statements of changes in fund equity?

9. Do operating and residual equity transfers reconcile on and/or between the operating statements?

10. Has the government improperly used the term "expenditures" in connection with proprietary fund types?

Part V. Combined Statement of Cash Flows

1. Is there a *Combined Statement of Cash Flows—All Proprietary Fund Types* (and similar trust funds)? (a) Is it referred to by that title? (b) Does it include a column for each proprietary fund type and for nonexpendable trust funds in use which presents combined data for all funds of that type?

City of Armstrong
General Fund
Schedule of Revenues and Expenditures
Budgeted and Actual
For the Year Ended December 31, 19X7
(in thousands)

	Budget (Revised)	Actual (Budgetary Basis)	Actual (Mod. Accrual Basis)
Revenues:			
Taxes.	$ 77,500	$ 75,300	$ 72,500
Licenses	2,680	3,320	3,320
Charges for services	9,340	8,400	8,200
Fines and forfeitures	23,500	20,100	20,000
Other	1,980	2,880	980
	$115,000	$110,000	$105,000
Expenditures:			
Current operating:			
Protection of people and property	$ 58,900	$ 55,740	$ 53,722
Community cultural and recreation	13,900	11,500	11,400
Community development and welfare . . .	11,700	10,900	9,400
Transportation and related services	23,200	19,280	17,900
Administration.	4,300	3,580	3,578
	112,000	101,000	96,000
Capital outlay	10,400	6,400	3,400
Debt Service.	6,600	6,600	6,600
	$129,000	$114,000	$106,000
Excess of revenues over (under) expenditures.	$(14,000)	$ (4,000)	$ (1,000)

2. Has the government improperly included more than one column (each) for Internal Service, Nonexpendable Trust, and Pension Trust Funds?

3. Are columns captioned with generic fund type titles?

P 14-6 (Budgetary Statement) The General Fund Schedule of Revenues and Expenditures—Budgeted and Actual—for the year ended December 31, 19X7 for the City of Armstrong has been competently prepared and you may assume it is accurate. The budgetary basis employed is (1) cash receipts for revenues and (2) cash disbursements plus encumbrances outstanding for expenditures.

Required (a) Analyze the statement presented carefully and respond to the following questions:

1. How might it be possible for a city to budget an excess of fund expenditures over revenues? Is that a bad practice? Is an excess of actual expenditures over revenues bad?

2. Why might the modified accrual and budgetary basis revenue data differ somewhat with respect to taxes, charges for services, and fines and forfeitures, yet be identical for licenses and permits?

3. Why might the modified accrual and budgetary basis expenditure amounts differ in most instances, yet agree on the debt service expenditure?

(b) After giving consideration to the following additional information, prepare a Statement of Revenues, Expenditures, and Changes in Fund Balance—Budget and Actual for the City of Armstrong General Fund for the year ended December 31, 19X7 in standard format. The following numbers are in thousands of dollars, as are the schedule and the statement you are to prepare.

1. The beginning of year fund balance was $4,000 (budgetary) and $3,000 (modified accrual).

Fullerton City
Statement of Revenues, Expenses and Changes in Fund Balance
December 31, 19X8

Revenues:

Property taxes	$ 600,000
Sales taxes	400,000
Licenses and permits	100,000
Federal grant	300,000
Traffic violations and court costs	50,000
Internal Service Fund	75,000
Capital Projects Fund	25,000
Other	60,000
	$1,610,000

Expenses:

Salaries and wages	$ 645,000
Contractual services	130,000
Rentals	90,000
Prior year	40,000
Debt service	120,000
Enterprise Fund	125,000
Special Revenue Fund	160,000
Property taxes	5,000
Depreciation of general fixed assets	100,000
Other	30,000
	$1,445,000
Profit for the year	$ 165,000
Fund Surplus, beginning of year	200,000
Surplus receipts	135,000
Increase in Reserve for Contingencies	(100,000)
Fund Surplus, end of year	$ 400,000

2. A budgeted operating transfer of $20,000 was made to the General Fund from a Special Revenue Fund.

(c) Whenever the basis of the budget differs from GAAP, the GASB Codification requires that the difference(s) between the budgetary basis and GAAP be explained in the notes to the financial statements. Draft an appropriate note for this purpose.

P 14-7 (Review Problem: Error Identification and Statement Correction) The following statement was prepared by the new accountant at Fullerton City:

Additional Information:

(1) The statement purports to present information for the General Fund of Fullerton City.

(2) The Property Taxes revenue figure represents (a) collections during 19X8 of 19X7 taxes that were properly recorded as revenues and receivables in 19X7, $80,000; (b) the gross property taxes levied for 19X8; and (c) a $3,000 payment on 19X9 taxes by a property owner who plans an extended vacation overseas. The expenditure figure is for 19X7 property taxes written off during 19X8; some $20,000 of the current year property tax levy is expected to prove uncollectible. An allowance for uncollectible taxes has not been used in the past.

(3) The Sales Taxes amount is the total of sales taxes collected during 19X8, $350,000; some $20,000 certified by the state as collected and due Fullerton City; and $30,000 estimated by the city controller to be due the city as a result of Christmas sales in November and December.

(4) The Licenses and Permits data include $85,000 of licenses and permits collected during 19X8 and $15,000 representing the final one-third payment of 19X8 business permit applications due January 15, 19X9.

(5) The Federal Grant amount is the total of a recently approved cost reimbursement grant to develop an improved water supply system for Fullerton City. Only $20,000 has been spent so far, as the project is still in the preliminary stages.

(6) Traffic Violations and Court Costs includes all fines and court costs collected during 19X8, $1,000 of which was on 19X7 offenses; and $6,000 of parking tickets issued during 19X8, of which $4,000 has been collected and $2,000 appears to be uncollectible.

(7) The Internal Service Fund amount results from the repayment of an interfund advance.

(8) The Capital Projects Fund figure represents the balance of a Capital Projects Fund returned to the General Fund at the end of the project so the Capital Projects Fund could be terminated.

(9) Other revenues includes (a) $15,000 arising upon reinventorying the warehouse at the beginning of 19X0; the inventory was $60,000 rather than the $45,000 reported initially; and (b) $2,000 paid the General Fund from a Special Revenue Fund in reimbursement of contractual services expenditures initially made from the former but attributable to the latter.

(10) Salaries and Wages includes the gross pay earned by employees during 19X8 and $25,000 of 19X7 gross wages that were not recorded as 19X7 expenditures.

(11) Contractual Services includes consultation fees paid to individuals and firms, including $8,000 attributable to an Enterprise Fund and $10,000 for services rendered in 19X7 but not recorded as 19X7 expenditures. Some $18,000 of 19X8 consulting services had been rendered, but not formally billed, at the end of 19X8.

(12) Rentals includes the aggregate rentals paid under a lease-purchase arrangement on city buildings used to house the city shop and warehouse. If this were a private business these capital lease payments would be reported as 75 percent interest and 25 percent principal reduction.

(13) Prior Year represents the amount paid during 19X8 on 19X7 bills that had been recognized as expenditures and liabilities in 19X7.

(14) Debt Service Fund indicates the amount paid from the General Fund to a Debt Service Fund as the annual contribution from the former to the latter.

(15) The Enterprise Fund amount is (a) the amount (not expected to be repaid) that was

transferred from the General Fund to acquire (with other borrowings) a local electric utility, and (b) the general government electric bills totaling $35,000.

(16) The Special Revenue Fund amount arose from a two-year loan from the General Fund to a Special Revenue Fund.

(17) Other expenditures includes $20,000 of encumbrances at the end of 19X8.

(18) Surplus Receipts is the amount realized from selling (during 19X8) a house the city owned.

(19) The beginning of the year Fund Surplus account was correct except for any errors noted in items 1 to 18.

Required   (a) Identify the errors in the General Fund Statement of Revenues, Expenditures, and Changes in Fund Balance prepared by the new accountant at Fullerton City and prepare a schedule showing the uncorrected amounts, corrections and reclassifications, and correct classifications and amounts.

(b) Prepare a correct Statement of Revenues, Expenditures, and Changes in Fund Balance for the General Fund of Fullerton City for the year ended December 31, 19X8 in acceptable form.

P 14-8   (Course Project) Obtain a copy of a recent Comprehensive Annual Financial Report of a state or local government. Evaluate the report using the Government Finance Officers Association reviewers' checklist for the Certificate of Achievement for Excellence in Financial Reporting. Cross-reference the checklist to the CAFR by indicating (1) in the CAFR the question number to which specific items pertain and (2) in the checklist the CAFR page number where you found the answer to the checklist question.

Prepare a one-page summary of the major strengths and weaknesses of the CAFR that you reviewed. Also, indicate any questions you have and any aspects of the report that differ from what you expected.

(*Instructor's note:* A copy of the GFOA checklist that has been modified for classroom use is provided in the Instructor's Manual.)

CONTEMPORARY ISSUES

The state and local government (SLG) accounting and reporting model has deep roots historically and is firmly entrenched in practice. Formalized and formally adopted in the United States by the National Committee on Municipal Accounting in the 1930s, the model has evolved in several stages during the past 60 years, most recently as the result of key pronouncements of the Governmental Accounting Standards Board (GASB). Further, the GASB's agenda includes projects that could have a pervasive and dramatic impact on the SLG accounting model.

How good is the SLG model? Opinions vary. At one extreme are its staunch advocates and defenders—who point to its heritage, note that it has proven practical and workable in practice, and cite the time-honored adage: "If it ain't broke, don't fix it." At the other extreme are its staunch critics, who say that such an "old" model cannot serve today's needs—that the complexities of modern governments and of their financial transactions cannot be adequately accommodated by the model from either an accounting or a reporting standpoint—and that an entirely new SLG accounting and reporting model should be developed. As is so often the case, "truth" probably lies somewhere between these extremes.

The Governmental Accounting Standards Board (GASB) has undertaken a **complete reexamination** of the **SLG financial reporting model.** Many broad and specific issues are under study—including issues such as the types of financial reports to be required for various user groups, the appropriate levels of data aggregation and disaggregation, the role of fund budgetary reporting and of more standardized accrual-based information, and the "pervasive" issues discussed next.

Some of the unresolved conceptual and practical issues are considered in this chapter. Most of these issues are currently on the GASB's agenda. Some of the issues are pervasive in nature and are likely to have a broad impact on most government financial reports. Other issues are topical in nature and only affect reporting for certain funds or specific assets, liabilities, or other reporting elements.

The more **pervasive** issues discussed in this chapter are **(1) implementation of GASB Statement 11 on measurement focus and basis of accounting, (2) reporting service efforts and accomplishments (SEA), (3) popular reporting, and (4) fund structure and classification-related issues.** These issues are discussed in that order. The **topical issues** discussed, in the order listed, include:

- Pension accounting
- Note disclosures

- Fixed assets/infrastructure
- Price level adjusted data
- Applicability of FASB pronouncements
- Deep discount debt

MEASUREMENT FOCUS AND BASIS OF ACCOUNTING

Perhaps the most pervasive and critical issue currently being addressed by the GASB is when and how to implement GASB Statement 11, "Measurement Focus and Basis of Accounting—Governmental Fund Operating Statements." As discussed in Chapter 10, in most circumstances Statement 11 requires accruing revenues, operating expenditures, and capital outlay expenditures without regard to when collection or payment is expected. Another key feature of Statement 11 is the distinction between capital debt and operating debt.

Statement 11 requires long-term **capital debt** to be reported essentially the same as does current GAAP. The debt is reported in the General Long-Term Debt Account Group, the proceeds from the issuance of such debt are reported as an "other financing source" in governmental fund operating statements, and the retirement of capital debt principal is reported as expenditures. However, Statement 11 does not indicate whether long-term **operating debt** is to be reported as general long-term debt or as fund liabilities. However, the Statement does prohibit reporting the incurrence of long-term operating debt as an "other financing source" and reporting the retirement of such debt as "expenditures." As a result, **the most significant underlying distinction between the two major proposals for implementing Statement 11 is whether long-term operating debt will be reported in the governmental funds or in the General Long-Term Debt Account Group.**

The two different approaches to implementing Statement 11 were explained and illustrated by the GASB in a "preliminary views" document entitled, "Implementation of GASB Statement No. 11—'Measurement Focus and Basis of Accounting—Governmental Fund Operating Statements.'" The preliminary view notes that two members of the Board (the "minority view") preferred to defer implementation of Statement 11 until certain projects—including reexamination of the SLG financial reporting model—were completed. However, the other three members (the "majority view") preferred to implement Statement 11 as originally scheduled. Thus, the "alternative view" of the minority is "if we must implement Statement 11 as scheduled, let's make only the essential reporting model changes."

To understand the underlying difference between the "majority" and "minority" approaches, recall that the basic accounting equation for a governmental fund under current GAAP is:

$$\text{Current Assets} - \text{Current Liabilities} = \text{Fund Balance}$$

A governmental fund is therefore essentially a working capital entity. Recognize that this accounting equation is complicated by a variety of transactions such as interfund advances (receivables are offset by fund balance reserves) and by application of current revenue and expenditure guidance. As a result, some receivables are offset by deferred revenues either because they are not legally available for expenditure or because they are not collected soon enough after the end of the fiscal year to be used to pay the current liabilities of the period. Long-term receivables of governmental funds therefore are offset by either deferred revenues accounts or fund balance reserves.

Majority View Approach to Implementing Statement 11

The implementation approach currently favored by the majority of the GASB would change the basic accounting equation to the following:

Current Assets $\quad+\quad$ **Noncurrent Financial Assets**
minus
Current Liabilities $\quad+\quad$ **Long-Term Operating Liabilities**
equals
Equity

"**Equity**" is defined as having two components—"fund balance" and "long-term equity." **Fund balance** is supposed to reflect essentially the same meaning that it does under current GAAP. In other words, fund balance reflects working capital under this approach. **Long-term equity** is equal to a fund's noncurrent assets minus its long-term operating debt.

Recognize that, with the exception of Debt Service Fund investments, the majority of governments have insignificant amounts of noncurrent assets in their governmental funds. Too, under this majority view approach to implementing Statement 11, all marketable Debt Service Fund investments are deemed to be current assets. Hence, should the majority view prevail, the primary effect of this model change for most governments would be the reporting of long-term operating debts in the General Fund and Special Revenue Funds rather than in the General Long-Term Debt Account Group.

A classified balance sheet is required under the majority view approach and the two distinct components of equity must be reported—but do not have to be totaled together. This approach is sometimes referred to as the "captioned" or "captioning" fund equity approach. It might also be understood better if thought of as a layered accounting entity approach. Under this approach, governmental funds could be thought of—and would need to be understood in terms of—two distinct pieces (or layers). The two layers are:

1. Current Assets − Current Liabilities = Fund Balance, and
2. Noncurrent Assets − Long-Term Operating Debt = Long-Term Equity

Some argue that the long-term equity amount is in essence like the amount to be provided and amount available accounts reported in the account groups.

Operations reporting under the majority view essentially explains changes in total fund equity. That is, it is based strictly on Statement 11 criteria—ignoring the traditional meaning of fund balance that is carefully maintained for balance sheet purposes. Thus, the majority view proposes a separate statement of revenues and other sources over (under) expenditures and other uses based on Statement 11. This new "operating statement" would emphasize the "**bottom line**"—the excess of revenues and other financing sources over (under) expenditures and other uses of financial resources.

A separate statement of changes in fund balances is proposed under the majority view to adjust the excess of revenues and other sources over (under) expenditures and other uses for differences between (1) the items and amounts reported on the preliminary view operating statement and (2) items and amounts reported under current GAAP in the statement of revenues, expenditures, and changes in fund balances. Thus, one might summarize the majority view "operations" reporting by saying that (1) Statement 11 determines the changes in total equity, (2) current GAAP determine the changes in fund balance, and (3) the change in long-term equity is simply the difference between the two.

Minority View Approach to Implementing Statement 11

The alternative (minority) view approach to implementing Statement 11 is to leave the basic accounting equation as it is under current GAAP. Some differences would result from the requirements of Statement 11, however. First, revenues that are currently deferred because of failure to meet the "collected within 60 days after the end of the fiscal year" criterion would typically be recognized—resulting in a larger total fund balance than is currently reported. (Some revenues deferred because of the legal availability criterion of current GAAP would have to be deferred under Statement 11 because they fail to meet the "underlying event" criterion of Statement 11 and would not affect fund balance.) The effect on unreserved fund balance is minimized because of the requirement that fund balance be reserved for financial assets related to accrued revenues to the extent that they are not available for appropriation and expenditure.

Operations reporting under the minority view is accomplished via the familiar all-inclusive statement of revenues, expenditures, and other changes in fund balances. Recognition of revenues, expenditures, and other financing sources and uses in this statement follows Statement 11 guidance. Hence, the same excess of revenues and other sources over (under) expenditures and other uses is reported as in the majority view approach. Note that, in substance, changes in total equity as defined in the majority view are being reported to this point.

The statement concludes with other changes in fund balance reported between beginning and ending fund balance. This section essentially reconciles the excess (which is consistent with the majority view accounting equation) with the changes in fund balance as defined under the minority view. In addition to residual equity transfers and similar fund balance changes, the reconciling items are for (1) increases in accrued long-term operating debt reported in the GLTDAG under the minority view, that is, amounts recognized as expenditures that do not decrease fund balance currently and (2) retirement of such long-term operating debt, that is, amounts that reduce fund balance but are not reported as expenditures or other financing uses.

Majority View–Minority View Compared

The key points regarding each approach to implementing Statement 11 are illustrated in the abbreviated financial statements in Figures 15-1 (Majority View) and 15-2 (Minority View). In the **Majority View** balance sheet, note that:

- Long-term capital debt is reported in the "Long-Term Capital Debt Account Group."
- Other long-term liabilities—such as for claims and judgments and compensated absences—are reported in the governmental funds.
- Both fund assets and fund liabilities are classified as current and long term.
- Governmental fund equity is reported in two components—fund balance and long-term equity.
- Total fund balance ($254,300 in the General Fund) is equal to Current Assets ($469,350 in the General Fund) less Current Liabilities ($215,050 in the General Fund).
- Long-term fund equity (negative $745,000 in the General Fund) is equal to long-term fund assets ($25,000 in the General Fund) less long-term fund liabilities ($770,000 in the General Fund).
- To determine the total long-term liabilities to be retired through general government resources ($3,595,000) requires summing the long-term liabilities reported in the various governmental funds ($940,000) and the long-term liabilities reported in the account group ($2,655,000).

Figure 15-1

MAJORITY VIEW STATEMENTS

Combined Balance Sheet

	Governmental Fund Types		Capital Account Groups		
	General	*Special Revenue*	*Fixed Assets*	*Long-Term Debt*	*Totals (Memo Only)*
Assets and Other Debits					
Current assets	$469,350	$196,860	—	—	$ 666,210
Long-term assets	25,000	28,000	$7,326,500	—	7,379,500
Other debits:					
Amount available for capital debt in debt service funds	—	—	—	$ 56,280	56,280
Amount to be provided for capital debt . .	—	—	—	2,598,720	2,598,720
Total assets and other debits	$494,350	$224,860	$7,326,500	$2,655,000	$10,700,710
Liabilities					
Current liabilities	$215,050	$ 56,150	—	—	$ 271,200
Long-term liabilities:					
Bonds payable	—	—	—	$2,655,000	2,655,000
Compensated absences	570,000	170,000	—	—	740,000
Claims and judgments	200,000	—	—	—	200,000
Total liabilities	985,050	226,150	—	2,655,000	3,866,200
Equity					
Fund balance:					
Reserved	85,200	23,690	—	—	108,890
Unreserved.	169,100	117,020	—	—	286,120
Total fund balance	254,300	140,710	—	—	395,010
Long-term fund equity.	(745,000)	(142,000)	—	—	(887,000)
Investment in general fixed assets.	—	—	$7,326,500	—	7,326,500
Total equity	(490,700)	(1,290)	7,326,500	—	6,834,510
Total liabilities and equity	$494,350	$224,860	$7,326,500	$2,655,000	$10,700,710

Combined Operating Statement

	Governmental Fund Types		
	General	*Special Revenue*	*Totals (Memo Only)*
Total revenues	$1,414,500	$1,171,125	$2,585,625
Total expenditures	1,687,700	1,153,450	2,841,150
Excess of revenues over (under) expenditures	(273,200)	17,675	(255,525)
Total other financing sources (uses)	(50,000)	—	(50,000)
Excess of revenues and other sources over (under) expenditures and other uses	$ (323,200)	$ 17,675	$ (305,525)

Combined Statement of Changes in Fund Balances

	Governmental Fund Types		
	General	*Special Revenue*	*Totals (Memo Only)*
Fund Balances			
Beginning of year	$ 302,500	$ 106,035	$ 408,535
Excess of revenues over (under) expenditures	(323,200)	17,675	(305,525)
Adjustments between fund balances and long-term fund equity:[a]			
Net increase in net liabilities to be financed in future periods[b]	275,000	17,000	292,000
End of year	$ 254,300	$ 140,710	$ 395,010

[a] *These adjustments affect both fund balance and long-term fund equity. If the only changes to long-term fund equity are those that are the reciprocal of changes in fund balance (as in this example), no additional reporting is required.*

[b] *This adjustment reports the effect of the net change in:*

	General	*Special Revenue*
Compensated absences	*$ 70,000*	*$20,000*
Claims and judgments	*200,000*	*—*
Long-term receivable	*5,000*	*(3,000)*
Net charge	*$275,000*	*$17,000*

Source: GASB *Action Report*, April 1992, pp. 4–5.

Figure 15-2

MINORITY VIEW STATEMENTS

Combined Balance Sheet

	Governmental Fund Types		Account Groups		
	General	Special Revenue	General Fixed Assets	General Long-Term Debt	Totals (Memo Only)
Assets					
Assets.	$494,350	$224,860	$7,326,500	—	$ 8,045,710
Amounts available in debt service funds	—	—	—	$ 56,280	56,280
Amounts to be provided:					
For capital debt.	—	—	—	2,598,720	2,598,720
For other liabilities	—	—	—	940,000	940,000
Total assets	$494,350	$224,860	$7,326,500	$3,595,000	$11,640,710
Liabilities					
Accounts payable	$215,050	$ 56,150	—	—	$ 271,200
Bonds payable	—	—	—	$2,655,000	2,655,000
Compensated absences	—	—	—	740,000	740,000
Claims and judgments	—	—	—	200,000	200,000
Total liabilities	215,050	56,150	—	3,595,000	3,866,200
Equity					
Investment in general fixed assets.	—	—	$7,326,500	—	7,326,500
Fund balance:					
Reserved:					
For encumbrances	85,200	23,690	—	—	108,890
For long-term receivables	25,000	28,000	—	—	53,000
Unreserved.	169,100	117,020	—	—	286,120
Total equity	279,300	168,710	7,326,500	—	7,774,510
Total liabilities and equity	$494,350	$224,860	$7,326,500	$3,595,000	$11,640,710

Combined Statement of Revenues, Expenditures, and Changes in Fund Balances

	Governmental Fund Types		
	General	Special Revenue	Totals (Memo Only)
Total revenues	$1,414,500	$1,171,125	$2,585,625
Total expenditures	1,687,700	1,153,450	2,841,150
Excess of revenues over (under) expenditures	(273,200)	17,675	(255,525)
Total other financing sources (uses)	50,000	—	(50,000)
Excess of revenues and other sources over (under) expenditures and other uses	(323,200)	17,675	(305,525)
Fund balances—beginning of year	332,500	131,035	463,535
Other changes in fund balances:			
Accrued expenditures to be financed in future periods, net[a].	270,000	20,000	290,000
Fund balances—end of year	$ 279,300	$ 168,710	$ 448,010

[a] This adjustment reports the effect of the net change in:

	General	Special Revenue
Compensated absences	$ 70,000	$20,000
Claims and judgments	200,000	—
Net change	$270,000	$20,000

Source: GASB *Action Report*, April 1992, pp. 6–7.

Note with respect to the **majority view** combined operating statement and combined statement of changes in fund balance in Figure 15-1:

- The emphasis placed on an operating statement having a "bottom line."
- The "adjustments between fund balances and long-term fund equity." This amount reflects the difference between the amount of revenues and other sources and expenditures and other uses recognized under (1) Statement 11 and (2) current GAAP. This permits the ending fund balance to be reported at the same amount it would be under current GAAP. In this example, the assumed differences in the General Fund resulted from a $5,000 increase in long-term receivables (which resulted in revenue being recognized under Statement 11 that is deferred under current GAAP) and increases of $70,000 and $200,000 in long-term liabilities for compensated absences and for claims and judgments, respectively. These increases are reflected in compensated absence and claims and judgments expenditures under Statement 11 but not under current GAAP.

In contrast, when reviewing the **minority view** balance sheet in Figure 15-2, note that:

- All general government long-term debt, whether capital or operating, is reported in the GLTDAG. (The total is the $3,595,000 computed earlier in the majority view discussion.)
- The governmental fund balance sheets closely resemble those under current GAAP. The key difference is that total fund balance is greater by the amount of fund balance reserved for long-term receivables which have been recognized as revenue under Statement 11. Current GAAP would require deferred revenues to be reported rather than revenues and this fund balance reserve.
- The unreserved fund balance is the same as under the majority view, but the total fund balance is greater by the amount of receivables that would be offset by deferred revenues under current GAAP.

Further, note that the **minority view** operating statement retains the **all-inclusive** presentation in a single statement that essentially stacks the majority view operating statement from Figure 15-1 on top of a modified change in fund balance statement. Note that the key difference between the amounts reported under the two approaches is that the change in long-term receivables does not affect fund balance under the minority view as it does under the majority view. This is because the change in equity associated with the amount of revenues related to long-term receivables impacts fund balance under the minority view and does not have to be backed out. Under the majority view, this change in equity affects long-term equity; therefore, the effect of the change on the excess of revenues over expenditures has to be reversed in the fund balance statement.

Also note that the minority view de-emphasizes the "operations subtotal" compared to the majority view "bottom-line" emphasis. This is perhaps even more significant in Debt Service Funds and particularly in Capital Projects Funds, where this operations subtotal is often expected to be negative even if no problems exist with the financing of the project.

Concerns About the Majority View

Concerns about the appropriateness of the majority view approach to implementing Statement 11 are numerous, but the most critical arise from the required change in the basic accounting equation and from Statement 11 requirements that are consistent with the proposed model change. For example, the majority view accounting equation could be stated as:

Working Capital — Net Long-Term Operating Debt = Fund Equity

This presumes that net long-term operating debt is equal to long-term fund operating liabilities less long-term fund assets. Recognizing that long-term fund receivables or other financial assets (not offset by deferred revenues) are small for most governments, this equation usually requires that working capital of the General Fund must exceed a significant portion of a government's long-term liabilities for governmental fund equity to be positive.

It is known that General Fund and other governmental fund equity will be negative for many governments under this model—even though many of these governments are not in financial difficulty. Hence, the majority view approach creates an accounting entity in which one of the two major components of equity (long-term equity) will almost always be negative and total equity will often be negative even if there is no financial difficulty. How are financial statement users to interpret such statements? Indeed, how should users interpret a positive fund equity balance caused by delinquent property taxes that cannot be collected for many years into the future?

Further, the majority view operating statement reports changes in total equity. If total equity can be negative when all is well, then the operations total reported in this statement must also be negative periodically even when no problem exists. Too, can it be positive when a negative situation exists? Again, how are users to interpret the statement?

Some argue that the underlying problem is flaws in the logic of Statement 11 that are drawn to a logical conclusion in the majority view accounting equation. Statement 11 was supported based on the notion of "demonstrating interperiod equity." Expenditures associated with long-term accrued liabilities such as pensions, claims and judgments, and compensated absences needed to be reflected because they indicate that current taxpayers are "borrowing" from future-year taxpayers to finance current-year services. Likewise, the majority view accounting equation reflects the notion that these borrowings from future-year taxpayers should be reflected in the appropriate governmental fund balance sheet, not "hidden" in the GLTDAG.

Opponents would argue, however, that the majority view and Statement 11 approaches reflect all these "borrowings" from future generations of taxpayers by current taxpayers but do not reflect significant contributions that current-year taxpayers make to future years. For example, when capital assets are purchased from current revenues, no asset is reported in the fund. Indeed, expenditures for the full cost of the assets are reported in the year of purchase even though they may be used to provide services to future taxpayers for years to come. Likewise, capital debt principal retirement typically occurs faster than the related capital asset is used up. Hence, part of most capital debt principal retirements actually contributes to covering the cost of future-year services. But these payments reduce fund equity rather than increase it.

As a result of these and similar problems, some believe that Statement 11 is flawed. And they feel strongly that, at a minimum, the majority view approach to implementing Statement 11 results in an illogical, unsound governmental fund accounting entity that does not achieve the objective of demonstrating interperiod equity.

Concerns About the Minority View

While the minority view to implementing Statement 11 avoids significantly changing the basic nature of a governmental fund (which is done under the majority view), operations reporting under the minority view is subject to most of the same criticisms and concerns as under the majority view. This is to be expected since the same basic operations reporting guidance of Statement 11 is applied in both approaches. The only possible advantages of the minority view over the majority view from an operations reporting standpoint are that (1) the excess of revenues and other sources over expenditures and other uses is de-emphasized, (2) fund balance has greater eminence, and (3) only one operations statement—a comprehensive all-inclusive statement—is required rather than two (or possibly three, since changes in long-term equity must be reported in the majority view if they are not strictly reciprocals of fund balance changes).

Should Statement 11 Be Deferred?

Many experts feel that Statement 11 needs modification and its implementation should be deferred. Others are pressing for deferral because related projects that the GASB said needed to be completed before implementation of Statement 11 have not been, and likely will not be, completed by the established effective date of Statement 11. Indeed, the stated position of the GASB members who supported the minority view approach is that Statement 11 should not be implemented at all at this time. (Thus, the minority view is designed to minimize the impact of implementing Statement 11 on the current model.)

The GFOA has taken a strong stand against implementing Statement 11, as have several other national professional organizations and public interest groups, as well as numerous government officials, public accountants, and other respondents. Moreover, over 75 percent of the respondents to the MFBA PV urged the GASB to defer the implementation of Statement 11. Thus, in December 1992 the GASB issued an Exposure Draft proposing to delay the implementation of Statement 11 indefinitely.

SERVICE EFFORTS AND ACCOMPLISHMENTS (SEA)

Another area receiving increasing attention from academe, governments, and the GASB is the reporting of service efforts and accomplishments (SEA) information. Traditional financial reporting—whether under current GAAP guidance or with the possible changes that the GASB will mandate over the next few years—is limited in what it can communicate. The growth in the scope, complexity, and size of governments in recent decades has drawn attention to these limitations and to the need of government officials to give an account of more than simply how they have raised and used financial resources.

The electorate is entitled to hold government officials responsible for the efficient use of resources in providing government services. Moreover, government officials are also accountable for whether government programs and activities are achieving the desired or planned results—and are doing so in a frugal and efficient manner. Further, the electorate even has the right to hold such officials accountable for whether or not the established goals and objectives of government programs are appropriate.

Traditional financial-statement-focused reporting does not provide the information needed by the electorate to assess government performance in terms of economy, efficiency, and effectiveness. Many persons and groups think that being able to evaluate whether governments are using resources efficiently and effectively is a higher level of accountability than is the accountability for flows and balances of resources per se. They feel strongly that making progress toward appropriate measurement and reporting of indicators of the efficiency and effectiveness of government programs is of paramount importance. SLG auditors, in particular, have urged the GASB to undertake SEA-related projects. The GASB has actively encouraged and supported research in this area and has issued a Preliminary Views document on a proposed Concepts Statement on concepts related to service efforts and accomplishments reporting.

Figure 15-3   TEN OUTCOME AREAS FOR HIGHER EDUCATION

1. **Student Knowledge and Skills Development**
   Information about student understanding, competencies, and attitudes relative to bodies of facts and principles and use of their intellectual and physical abilities.

2. **Student Educational Career Development**
   Information about student attitudes and success concerning certain academic pursuits (e.g., student educational degree aspirations and attainments).

3. **Student Educational Satisfaction**
   Information that indicates the satisfaction of students about the knowledge and skills they have acquired and their progress toward their educational and occupational career objectives.

4. **Student Occupational Career Development**
   Information about student attitudes and success concerning certain occupational goals and their job performance.

5. **Student Personal Development**
   Information about changes in students concerning the growth and maintenance of their personal life (e.g., their ability to adapt to new situations, their self-concept, etc.).

6. **Student Social/Cultural Development**
   Information about student abilities and attitudes in dealing with people and their interest in cultural activities.

7. **Community Educational Development**
   Information about the attitudes and success of nonmatriculating participants concerning their acquisition of knowledge and skills, personal and social development, and occupational career goals and performance.

8. **Community Service**
   Information about the impact of the opportunities and services provided by the institution and received by the community (e.g., agricultural extension services, cultural and recreational opportunities, etc.).

9. **Community Impact**
   Information about the impact of an institution's programs and its faculty, staff, and students (current and former) on the financial health, manpower supply, and attitudes of the community (local, state, or national).

10. **Development of New Knowledge and Art**
    Information about new knowledge and art forms created, applied, and reorganized as a result of an institution's programs and its faculty, staff, and students (current and former).

Source: The National Center for Higher Education Management Systems, *The Higher Education Outcome Measures Identification Study,* 1974, cited in Committee on Nonprofit Entities' Performance Measures, Government and Nonprofit Section, American Accounting Association, *Measuring the Performance of Nonprofit Organizations: The State of the Art,* 1988, pp. 88–89.

While the desirability of reporting indicators of service efforts and accomplishments is logically and intuitively appealing, such reporting is subject to many potential problems. These include possible poor association of reported performance measures with goals and desired effects, manipulation of reported performance by taking actions designed to improve reported performance that do not result in improved performance, lack of comparability where governments with apparently identical programs have notably different underlying goals for the programs, difficulty of accurate measurement of some possible performance indicators, and the potential for information overload because multiple measures are typically necessary to communicate performance from different perspectives or related to different goals for a single program. Indeed, many people believe that SEA is **not** within the proper purview of GAAP and the GASB.

Some of the hurdles and problems that must be addressed with respect to service efforts and accomplishments reporting may be highlighted in a familiar

Resources Approach
    Student Selectivity (admission scores, acceptance rate, and yield)
    Student Demand (pool of applicants, number of majors, enrollment trends)
    Student Composition (ethnicity, part-time/full-time students)
    Faculty Prestige
    Faculty Training (% doctorate)
    Faculty Composition (full-time/part-time faculty)
    Faculty Teaching Loads
    Size of Budget
    Library Holdings
    Condition and Adequacy of Equipment
    Size of Endowment

Reputational Approach
    Reputational Ranking of Programs
    Reputational Ranking of Students (for example, top ten institutions with the
        enrollment of National Merit Scholars)
    Reputational Ranking of Faculty's Scholarly Productivity
    Relative Ranking of Resources (for example, faculty compensation and size of
        endowment)
    Reputational Ranking of Institution's Prestige

Outcomes Approach
    Faculty Scholarly Productivity (publication counts, citation index count, perceived
        reputation)
    Faculty Awards and Honors
    Faculty Research Support
    Faculty Teaching Performance
    Student Academic Achievement
    Student Achievement Following Graduation
    Student Placement
    Alumni Satisfaction
    Student Retention Rate
    Student Transfer Rate to Senior Institutions
    Student Graduation Rates
    Student Rate of Advanced Graduate Study
    Student Job Placement Rate
    Employer Satisfaction
    Passing Rate of Professional Certification Exams

Value-added Approach
    Changes in Students' Cognitive Abilities (ACT-COMP)
    Student Personal Development
    Student Career Development
    Social Benefits

Source: Susy S. Chan, "Service Efforts and Accomplishments of Higher Education Institutions: Issues in Measurement and Reporting." Fifth Annual University of Illinois at Chicago Governmental Accounting Symposium, 1988.

context by considering the types of areas about which information on university student outputs was considered desirable by respondents to a National Center for Higher Education Management Systems survey. The areas are listed in Figure 15-3. Further, it may be useful to consider the different types of performance indicators that might be useful depending on the perspective from which a university's success is being viewed by a report user. The different perspectives and indicators in Figure 15-4 are numerous, yet are not exhaustive in scope.

Finally, the GASB research report, *Service Efforts and Accomplishments Reporting: Its Time Has Come—Elementary and Secondary Education,* recommends a set of SEA indicators for elementary and secondary schools to select from for SEA reporting purposes (see Figure 15-5). Different schools might report using different subsets of these indicators because of differing goals, objectives, and needs.

Figure 15-5   **ELEMENTARY AND SECONDARY EDUCATION SEA INDICATORS**

SEA Indicator	*Rationale for Selecting Indicator*
Inputs: Expenditures[a] (in millions) (may be also broken out by type of activity such as instructional and administrative)	
Current dollars / Constant dollars	To provide a measure of resources used to provide services
Total number of personnel	To provide a measure of the size of the organization
Outputs: Number of student-days (thousands)	To provide a general measure of workload
Number of students promoted/graduated	To provide a measure of students satisfactorily completing educational requirements
Carnegie units as percentage required[b] (with number of required units shown parenthetically—can be reported by major subject area)	To provide an indication of courses taken by students in certain critical subject areas
Absenteeism rate	To provide a measure of student participation in classes and an indication of their interest in learning
Dropout rate	To indicate the school's success in keeping students actively involved in the learning process
Outcomes: Test score results—*for each major subject area*	
Average percentile on standardized tests / Percentage of students above the 50th percentile[c] / Percentage of students reaching their grade level of proficiency or higher	To provide measures of student achievement in academic subjects and a comparison with expected achievement and established norms
Percentage of students receiving grade-level gain on achievement test[d] (may be presented for major subject areas as well as overall)	To provide a measure of student annual progress—the indicator is also used to develop a measure of cost-effectiveness
Percentage of students scoring higher than specified level of self-esteem / Percentage of students achieving specified physical fitness test standards	To provide an indication of the development of noncognitive skills and abilities generally considered as objectives of formal education
Percentage of graduates gainfully employed or continuing education two years after graduation	To provide an indication of the school system's results in preparing graduates for further education or to become members of the work force
Percentage of students rating as good, excellent, or improved—their own: Work and study skills / Self-discipline / Interpersonal skills / Knowledge gained	To provide measures of students' perceptions of their acquisition of knowledge and selected noncognitive skills and behavior
Percentage of parents rating their children good, excellent, or improved in: Work and study skills / Self-discipline / Interpersonal skills / Knowledge gained	To provide parents' perceptions of their child's acquisition of knowledge and important noncognitive skills and behavior; to allow comparison with student perceptions; to indicate the school system's contribution to the acquisition of these skills and behavior
Efficiency (input/output and input/outcome measures):	
Cost per output / Per student-day / Per student promoted/graduated	To provide an indication of the school system's "technical" efficiency of operation
Cost per outcome / Per student achieving grade-level score gain	To provide an indication of the school system's "true" efficiency in achieving student outcomes
Explanatory Data: Controllable / Average number of hours per student in oversized classes (per day)	
Not controllable / Average daily attendance / Percentage of minority students / Percentage of students participating in subsidized lunch or other public welfare program / Percentage of students needing special remedial programs / Student mobility rate / Percentage of students with English as second language / Student enrollments	To provide information on factors that are likely to have some effect on student achievement and that can be important in understanding performance on output, outcome, and efficiency indicators

[a] *A clear description of which expenditures are included or excluded should be provided.*

[b] *One Carnegie unit equals five hours per week of instructional class time on a subject for an entire school year.*

[c] *The 50th percentile is the point at which one-half of the students being scored are below the score of that student or group of students.*

[d] *A grade-level gain is the measure of a student's progress by school year, as assessed by a test score, for example, from the 6.1 grade level to the 7.1 grade level.*

SEA continues to be experimented with and debated. No doubt SEA information will continue to evolve for budgetary, managerial, and audit purposes—regardless of whether it becomes a part of GAAP applicable to SLG financial statements and reports.

POPULAR REPORTING

Like service efforts and accomplishments reporting, another reporting development that is motivated by the desire to meet needs of users that are not met effectively by current CAFRs is "popular reporting." Broadly speaking, popular reporting encompasses various attempts to communicate information about an entity in a form that is understood by a larger portion of the targeted users of government reports—especially citizens. Few citizens have ever seen a CAFR, and only a few would be able to understand its implications for their voting or other decisions. Therefore, standards-setters have for years encouraged experimentation with popular reporting.

Popular reporting takes various forms—from consolidated financial statements to financial statements limited to the total columns of the combined statements to other condensed summary financial statements to budgetary data presentations to narrative presentations supplemented with graphs and charts. Popular reporting is referred to on the financial reporting pyramid discussed in Chapter 14 as "condensed summary reporting." Many believe that to develop a report that will be useful to the citizenry means developing some type of condensed summary financial report. Indeed the "popular report" might include some service efforts and accomplishments (SEA) reporting, so these two developments may actually complement each other.

Moreover, the GASB has sponsored popular reporting research, the AICPA has developed guidance for auditor association with condensed summary statements, and the GFOA has developed an award program for innovative popular reports. Thus, considerable progress in popular reporting is expected in the next few years.

FUND STRUCTURE AND CLASSIFICATION ISSUES

Another pervasive issue that has various implications for government financial reporting is identifying the appropriate fund structure and fund classification criteria. The most significant change in fund structure in recent decades was the elimination of the Special Assessment Fund type in the mid-1980s. This change simply required the normal fund structure to be used for the special case of special assessment projects, for which a special fund had been required in the past. In essence, it eliminated an exception to the fund structure that had been required in the past.

Capital Account Group or Capital Fund

The GASB is considering fundamental changes to the fund structure in its current financial reporting projects, however. Among other issues, the GASB Discussion Memorandum, *Capital Reporting,* seeks input into whether the two account groups should be combined into a capital account group, whether the account groups and the capital projects funds should be combined to form a "capital fund," and whether the debt service and capital projects funds should be combined with the account groups to form a "capital fund"—with a somewhat different nature. Formation of a capital fund, in particular, would be a fundamental change in fund structure. It also seems to imply that there would be only one capital fund, whereas governments currently may have multiple capital projects and debt service funds.

Number of Funds

This latter observation raises a related fund structure issue. The current literature does not provide clear guidance as to when separate capital projects, debt service, or other funds are required. One city, for instance, has over 70 individual capital projects—several of which are financed by separate, major bond issues—but reports only one Capital Projects Fund. Other cities with similar circumstances report numerous Capital Projects Funds. Should this wide variation in practice—limited by little more than the preferences of individuals—be permitted? Or are there common guiding principles that should be established and followed with respect to how many individual funds of a particular type are appropriate in differing circumstances?

Proprietary or Governmental Fund?

Perhaps the most significant aspect of fund structure and classification that should be considered is **whether a given program, function, or activity should be accounted for in a proprietary fund or in a governmental fund** (and perhaps in the GFA and GLTD accounts). Specifically, this conceptual and practice issue may arise in two forms: (1) Enterprise Fund or governmental fund, and (2) Internal Service Fund or governmental fund. These are important issues since they will determine or impact such things as:

1. Whether the program, function, or activity is accounted for in a single proprietary fund entity or in several entities—governmental funds and account groups;
2. The measurement focus and basis of accounting used—that is, whether expenses or expenditures are measured;
3. In the case of Internal Service Funds, whether charges are borne centrally or are charged to the user agencies; and
4. Rates to be charged for goods and services.

Many of these issues are being considered in the GASB's "business-type activities" agenda project.

Enterprise or Governmental Fund?

The Enterprise Fund issue most often arises from the flexibility permitted in the two-part (mandatory and permissive) Enterprise Fund definition:

> **Enterprise Funds**—to account for operations (a) that are financed and operated in a manner similar to private business enterprises—where the intent of the governing body is that the costs (expenses, including depreciation) of providing goods or services to the general public on a continuing basis be financed or recovered primarily through user charges; **or** (b) where the governing body has decided that periodic determination of revenues earned, expenses incurred, and/or net income

is appropriate for capital maintenance, public policy, management control, accountability, or other purposes.[1]

Part (a) of this definition, the **mandatory** provision, is designed to include government-owned utilities and other profitable or break-even activities. Its most critical aspect is determining the intent of the governing body. That intent may or may not have been expressed in the minutes or in discussions with knowledgeable persons. But actions can also imply intent, and if a governing board has consistently operated a function as an enterprise, setting rates to recover full cost and in other ways acting like the activity is an enterprise, it probably is one under part (a) of the definition.

Changes in intent can occur when membership and attitudes of a governing board change, of course, but it clearly is not intended for an activity to be accounted for as an enterprise one year, a governmental activity the next, and so forth. When a new activity is the center of the Enterprise Fund or governmental fund issue, persuading the proper people to agree upon and document the intent of the governing board may be the best approach. On the other hand, a strong finance officer will often make such decisions, then have the council ratify them and record the ratification in the minutes.

The **"permissive"** part (b) of the Enterprise Fund definition is intended to cover governmental bus lines, city markets, and other activities apt to incur losses. This criterion requires positive action by a governing board—to state and document its intent that a given program, function, or activity that does not meet the usual Enterprise Fund definition is to be accounted for as an Enterprise Fund for one or more of the several possible reasons noted. In such cases the usual reason is to see how much is being lost on a "full cost" basis as well as to know the sources, uses, and balances of the working capital or cash devoted to the activity.

The disadvantage of this criterion is that it essentially provides governments with a **"free choice"**—total flexibility in deciding whether to report an activity as an Enterprise activity. Many feel that such a "free choice" criterion is no criterion at all, that it essentially says "report activities in whatever manner pleases you," and that it leads to noncomparability among governments since different governments may report identical activities in different fund types.

Internal Service or Governmental Fund

The Internal Service Fund or governmental fund question may arise in connection with a variety of functions or activities, for example, data processing, communications, purchasing, and materials storage and handling. There are two aspects of this decision, of which the first may be the easier: (1) Internal Service Fund or governmental fund, and (2) if Internal Service Fund, which costs are to be recovered through the fund and thus constitute "cost" in this situation?

Whether an activity is established as an Internal Service Fund—and thus its costs are allocated to those using its goods or services—is typically a policy decision. Often it begins with or is made by (with approval of superiors) the chief finance officer, who seeks to obtain better accountability for the function as well as better cost control and distribution of costs to user agencies.

While the Internal Service Fund definition does not appear at first glance to be as flexible as the Enterprise Fund definition, as it has been interpreted and applied in practice, it permits **total free choice** and thus is fraught with all the disadvantages of the permissive Enterprise Fund criterion as discussed previously.

---

[1] GASB Codification, sec. 1300.104b(1). (Emphasis added.)

Assuming that an activity will be accounted for as an Internal Service Fund, there should be a determination of precisely which costs are to be charged to user agencies and on what basis. This should be agreed to by all agencies affected and should be documented.

The Problems

Two significant problems arise from the proprietary fund versus governmental fund classification issue. First, the **reporting of the activity will be significantly different** under the two different classifications. Thus, it is important that the situations in which each reporting approach provides the most useful information be identified clearly. Current GAAP provide no such clear delineation. Indeed, the standards are weak with respect to the classification of activities as proprietary or governmental. As noted above, whether a government reports an activity as an Enterprise activity is a matter of its own "free choice" unless the mandatory criterion —part (a)—is met. Furthermore, whether to use an Internal Service Fund to account for provision of goods or services to other departments of the government is a matter of totally "free choice" since, as interpreted and applied in practice, the standards **permit** use of Internal Service Funds any time but **never require** use of Internal Service Funds.

Second is the issue of **comparability** among governments. Assume that two governments have precisely the same activities and circumstances. Under current standards one government might account for an activity in a proprietary fund and another account for the same (hypothetically equivalent) activity in its governmental funds and account groups. The reason is that "intent" is the fundamental thread that runs throughout the proprietary or governmental fund issue. And intent varies among governments and may vary within one government through time.

PENSIONS

Many state and local governments administer their own pension plans. As discussed in Chapter 11, SLGs have faced a unique problem for several years because three different approaches to accounting for SLG Pension Trust Funds are permissible under current GAAP. Likewise, different disclosures were required for pension plans under the FASB approach than under the NCGA approaches to reporting pensions. Finally, the amount of employer government pension expenditures and expenses can be determined in several different ways. The **disclosure** issues were resolved, for the most part, with the issuance of GASB *Statement 5* as discussed in Chapter 11, but the **measurement and recognition alternatives** are still **permitted.** Further, modifications in disclosures may well be needed once the other, more central reporting issues are resolved. The remaining issues center on the valuation of Pension Trust Fund investments, measurement of Pension Trust Fund liabilities, and measurement of employer fund expenditures/expenses and liabilities.

Investments

Pension Trust Fund investments currently are reported at cost or amortized cost. However, the FASB requires investments of businesses' defined benefit pension plans to be reported at market value rather than at cost. Others have suggested that some type of moving average market valuation should be used to value pension plan assets to reduce the volatility of that measurement and because pension plan investment objectives typically are long-term rather than short-term in nature.

Liabilities

The appropriate measurement of **Pension Trust Fund liabilities** is another area in which there has been considerable debate in recent years. Most governments recognize only the currently payable **current** liabilities of their pension plans as Pension Trust Fund liabilities, as can be seen in reviewing the NCGA *Statement 1* and *Statement 6* approaches to accounting and reporting for Pension Trust Funds presented in Chapter 11. The FASB requires the actuarial present value of accumulated plan benefits to be reported as plan **liabilities** in FASB *Statement No. 35,* but the NCGA *Statement 6* approach requires the actuarial present value of credited projected benefits to be reported as elements of **fund balance.** Hence, one issue is whether only currently payable benefits or some measure of the present value of future benefits should be reported as liabilities of a Pension Trust Fund.

If the present value of future benefits is to be reported as a liability in the Pension Trust Fund, a related issue is how that liability should be measured. Various actuarial cost methods result in different amounts of liabilities. The major issues here appear to be whether a single actuarial method should be prescribed or several methods permitted, whether salary progression should be taken into account in the actuarial cost method, and whether the interest rate applied should be short-term or long-term oriented.

Employer Fund Expenditures/Expenses

Several measures of the **employer** fund pension **expenditures/expenses** are allowed currently under governmental GAAP. Possible alternatives to be considered by the GASB include expenditure/expense recognition based on funding, computing pension expenditures or expenses using the same actuarial cost method and assumptions used to compute the liability for the Pension Trust Fund, adopting the FASB *Statement No. 87* approach prescribed for business plans by the FASB, and adopting a method similar to the Accounting Principles Board *Opinion No. 8* approach, which was superseded for businesses by FASB *Statement No. 87.* The GASB has tentatively decided, according to a 1990 Exposure Draft on accounting for employer pension costs, to require use of a method that limits the alternatives available to governments in choosing the actuarial methods, assumptions, and periods used to measure their pension costs.

The GASB continues to address these and other pension issues and has conducted extensive research on them. These pension accounting and reporting issues are expected to be resolved in the near future.

NOTES TO THE FINANCIAL STATEMENTS

Under the pyramid concept explained in Chapter 14, the primary financial statement reporting focus is on the fund type data reported in the combined general purpose financial statements (GPFS). Individual fund data are not a required part of the GPFS, but are to be reported in the official comprehensive annual financial report (CAFR) of the SLG unit.

The GASB Codification provides that the notes to the financial statements are those applicable to the GPFS; additional notes that might be necessary at the individual fund level are referred to as "narrative explanations." Certain types of notes to the GPFS, some of which are individual fund disclosures, are required. Too, any other disclosures necessary in the circumstances for fair presentation of the financial statements should also be included. The GASB Codification (sec. 2300) contains a checklist of note disclosures cross-referenced to the Codification section requiring each note. Relatively little guidance is provided as to the specific content of many of the notes, however, and practice appears to vary considerably with respect to the disclosures presented. Accounting and audit practitioners should use the GASB Codification checklist but also should review the notes to the financial statements in several good reports to help ensure that they do not fail to include important notes to the financial statements.

Another potential problem with respect to the notes to the financial statements—currently under consideration by the GASB—is that they tend to be quite extensive—often 25 to 45 pages or more. The GASB apparently has adopted the philosophy that many reporting problems can be handled better, at least temporarily, by disclosing information in the notes than by incorporating such information into the financial statements. This is evident in several recent GASB pronouncements. Some believe that while any one of the numerous notes typically found in government reports may be useful when taken by itself, it is not useful to have the extensive note disclosure currently found in most government reports. They believe that the volume of material and the number and significance of "adjustments" users interpreting the financial statements must make—as a result of the notes—tend to overwhelm or confuse many readers. Others consider the level of note disclosure found in most reports both appropriate and essential. Indeed, many emphasize that **full disclosure** is required in SLG reporting rather than the "adequate" disclosure of business reporting. It is difficult to say who is correct, but clearly note disclosures should be viewed from the context of their overall impact on clarity and fair presentation, not solely on their own merits.

GENERAL FIXED ASSETS REPORTING

Accounting and reporting for general fixed assets of governmental units has received relatively little attention in the governmental accounting authoritative literature. Significant amounts are invested in such assets, however, and the needs for expansion and replacement of general fixed assets and for maintenance of existing fixed assets are significant considerations in the budgetary process. Too, it seems logical that appropriate presentation of general fixed assets and related information is an important element in appropriately reporting government financial condition and operating results.

Many question the usefulness of the current accounting and reporting for general fixed assets discussed in Chapter 9. Particularly troublesome to some critics are such features as (1) the optional capitalization of infrastructure general fixed assets, (2) the prohibition against reporting depreciation expense on general fixed assets, and (3) the fact that the financial reports currently do not indicate when governments are delaying the maintenance of fixed assets—thereby shortening their useful lives and/or significantly increasing future maintenance costs—in order to provide additional services currently (to the detriment of future years' taxpayers).

Recognizing the significance of the capital assets owned by governments and their potential impact on a government's ability to continue to provide current types and quality of services in the future, the GASB issued a discussion memorandum, "Accounting and Financial Reporting for Capital Assets," in the fall of 1987. Among the issues being studied by the Board are:

- Whether reporting of infrastructure general fixed assets should be required rather than optional. (Or, perhaps, whether reporting such "assets" should be precluded.)

- Whether deferred maintenance costs should be reported as an operating cost in the financial statements, disclosed in the notes, or not reported.

- Whether general fixed assets should continue to be reported at historical cost, some other valuation is more appropriate, or other valuations should be disclosed in addition to the historical cost valuation.
- Whether recording accumulated depreciation should be required, optional, or prohibited.
- Whether some measure of asset expiration should be reported in the financial statements.
- Whether disclosure of capital projects plans should be required in the CAFR.
- Whether comparisons of budgeted and actual capital expenditures should be required.
- Whether disclosures of fixed asset aging, condition, capacity measures, or other information should be required.
- Whether general fixed assets, general long-term debt, debt service resources, and/or capital projects resources should be reported together in a plant fund (or capital fund) similar to that used by colleges and universities or by voluntary health and welfare organizations (as discussed in Chapters 18 and 19, respectively).

PRICE LEVEL ADJUSTED DATA

Whether governments should report data adjusted for changes in the general price level, for current replacement costs, or for other inflation or capital maintenance-related factors is **not** one of the most debated issues surrounding SLG accounting and financial reporting. Perhaps it should be. Indeed, the GASB must address some aspects of this issue(s) in its "capital assets" agenda project.

State and local governments are not to report general price level adjusted supplemental statements or replacement cost disclosures. Yet some are concerned with the effects of inflation and/or changing factor prices on the meaningfulness and propriety of SLG financial statements and statistical tables. At the least there needs to be some significant conceptual and applied research and experimentation in applying general price level adjustments, replacement cost data, and/or other inflation or capital maintenance data to SLG financial statements and statistical presentations. However, the authors are aware of no significant research and experimentation along these lines.

DEEP DISCOUNT DEBT

The issuance of deep discount debt is a relatively recent type of transaction of governments. **Deep discount debt** is long-term debt with no stated interest rate, or with a stated interest rate significantly lower than (less than 75% of has been suggested) the effective interest rate. Deep discount general long-term debt presents a problem because **discounts** (and premiums) on general long-term debt instruments such as bonds **traditionally** have been **ignored** in "general government" accounting. The face value of debt has been recorded as general long-term debt and the **stated** interest as interest expenditures (as the interest matures). Likewise, retirement of bonds has been recognized as debt principal expenditures. So long as debt discounts and premiums are not significant, this practice creates no major problems. However, when such discounts are major, the long-term debt is overstated by a portion (or all) of the effective interest costs to be incurred in future years. Too, it could be argued that interest costs and perhaps fund liabilities are understated both yearly and over the life of the debt.

Traditional Approach

To provide a framework for discussing alternative approaches of accounting for deep discount debt, assume that a government issued a $1,000,000 five-year, zero (0%) coupon bond on July 1, 19X2 to finance a capital project. The **net proceeds** from the bond sale were **$680,600,** and the **effective interest rate** on the transaction was **8%.** Under the **traditional approach** to recording bonds, the $1,000,000 face value of the bonds would be recorded as General Long-Term Debt. No interest expenditures would ever be recognized and no debt service expenditures would be recognized except in the fifth year, upon maturity of the bonds. In substance, this reporting approach records interest payable in future years as general long-term debt and defers recognition of all debt service expenditures until the bonds are due, thereby failing to provide any indication in previous years if the government has not been providing appropriately for the eventual maturity of the bonds.

Alternative (Present Value Oriented) Approaches

An **alternative** approach (which some consider preferable) is to record the bonds at their **present value** upon issuance by either (1) recording the discount on deep discount debt in the General Long-Term Debt Account Group as a contra account to the Bonds Payable account in which the face value of the bonds is recorded, or (2) recording the Bonds Payable account at the net amount, that is, the present value. In the ensuing discussion (1) the *present value* will be referred to as the **principal** of the debt, and (2) it will be assumed that the bonds are recorded at their *gross* amount (face value) and the discount is recorded in a separate account. Under the present value approach, debt service expenditures might be recognized in a manner consistent with viewing deep discount debt as either **term debt** or **serial debt.**

"Term Debt" Type Alternatives for Recognizing Debt Service Expenditures.

Under the **term** debt perspective, **debt service expenditures** might be recognized in any of several ways. One alternative is to postpone interest recognition until the due date (the end of year 5 in our example). This is consistent with current GAAP, which requires GLTD principal and interest expenditures to be recognized in the period that they mature—become due and payable. In this case, in year 5 our example city would recognize debt service expenditures for principal of $680,600 and for interest of $319,400. No debt service expenditures would be recognized in the first four years.

Another debt service recognition approach consistent with the "term debt" perspective is to recognize interest expenditures but not principal expenditures each year until maturity and to recognize principal expenditures only upon maturity. Either (1) an accrued interest liability could be reported in the Debt Service Fund (DSF) and the unamortized discount and Bonds Payable in the GLTDAG reduced by the effective interest each year or (2) Other Financing Sources equal to the interest expenditures could be reported in the DSF and the discount reduced in the GLTDAG.

"Serial Debt" Alternatives for Recognizing Debt Service Expenditures.

If the deep discount debt is viewed as **serial** debt, a government should not only recognize effective interest costs as expenditures, as discussed previously, but should also recognize a portion of the ultimate principal expenditures each year. This might be accomplished by amortizing the principal portion of the debt on a straight line basis. In our example $136,120 ($680,600 ÷ 5 years) of principal expenditures would be recognized in the Debt Service Fund each year and an equal amount of Bonds Payable and Amount to be Provided would be removed from the GLTDAG. Recall that the discount and an equal amount of Bonds Payable also is being removed from the account group as interest expenditures are recognized, so at the end of year 5 no Bonds Payable or related amounts remain in the GLTDAG. Rather the $1,000,000 liability is recorded wholly in the Debt Service Fund at this point and retirement is recorded there by debiting the liability and crediting Cash for $1,000,000. This approach results in reporting amounts that are roughly comparable to debt service expenditures that would be incurred for similar serial bond issues.

Another variation of this approach to reporting deep discount debt is supported by some accountants. Under this approach the amount of principal and interest expenditures recognized would depend on the funding provided for the debt. If it is systematic and rational, the funding pattern would supplant the effective interest amortization of interest and the straight line amortization of deep discount debt principal discussed earlier. The wisdom of basing expenditure recognition on funding is debatable, and even its proponents recommend that it be used only when a systematic, rational funding pattern is used.

OTHER ISSUES

The GASB is studying a number of other issues not discussed in this chapter, and other topics on the GASB agenda are worthy of note as well. Among these are:

- Other postemployment benefits (OPEB) measurement and reporting.
- Can interperiod equity (IPE) be measured? If so, how should IPE be reported?
- Should proprietary fund reporting continue to distinguish contributed capital from retained earnings? If so, should the distinction be clarified to assure more consistent application than in current practice?
- Fund vs. fund type vs. other financial statement entity focus—Should the primary focus of the financial statements be to report data on individual funds? On fund types? On the government reporting entity taken as a whole?
- Should a Statement of Cash Flows (SCF) be required for governmental funds? the "general government"? the government reporting entity?

CONCLUDING COMMENTS

Controversy and change frustrate some persons. Others view them as positive signs that the attention of the accounting profession—including SLG finance officers, professors, and independent public accountants—is increasingly being directed toward the improvement of state and local government accounting and financial reporting. The latter is our view, though it admittedly is frustrating to realize that some aspects of our text are apt to be outdated soon after its release and that, on some issues, we feel the "old" was better than the "new."

Accounting and reporting concepts and practices should and must evolve in all fields—business, nonprofit, and government. Through the combined efforts of the GASB and many persons and organizations, this evolution appears to be accelerating in the public sector.

SELECTED BIBLIOGRAPHY

Governmental Accounting Standards Board Publications

I. Research Reports

"The Needs of Users of Governmental Financial Reports," by Jones and Others (1985)

"Infrastructure Assets: An Assessment of User Needs and Recommendations for Financial Reporting," by Van Daniker and Kwiatkowski (1986)

"Financial Reporting Practices of Local Governments," by Ingram and Robbins (1987)

"An Empirical Study of Governmental Financial Reporting Entity Issues," by Patton (1987)

"A Study of the Usefulness of Disclosures Required by GASB Standards," by Hay (1988)

"Information Needs of College and University Financial Decision Makers," by Engstrom (1988)

"Other Postemployment Benefits in State and Local Governmental Units," by Bokemeier, Van Daniker, and Parrish (1990)

"Financial Reporting by State and Local Governments: A Survey of Preferences among Alternative Formats," by Wilson (1990)

"Popular Reporting: Local Government Financial Reports to the Citizenry," by Carpenter and Sharp (1992)

"The Relationships between Financial Reporting and the Measurement of Financial Condition," by Berne (1992)

II. Service Efforts and Accomplishments Reporting: Its Time Has Come

"Elementary and Secondary Education," by Hatry, Alexander, and Fountain (1989)

Executive Summary, "Elementary and Secondary Education" (1989)

"An Overview," by Hatry, Fountain, Sullivan, and Kremer, eds. (1990)

"Water and Wastewater Treatment," by Burnaby and Herhold (1990)

"Mass Transit," by Wallace (1991)

"Sanitation Collection and Disposal," by Rubin (1991)

"Fire Department Programs," by Parry, Sharp, Vreeland, and Wallace (1991)

"Public Health," by Carpenter, Ruchala, and Waller (1991)

"Police Department Programs," by Drebin and Brannon (1992)

"Road Maintenance," by Hyman, Alfelor, and Allen (1993)

QUESTIONS

15-1 Briefly explain the two major alternatives for implementing GASBS II in a manner understandable to a nonaccountant city council member. What are the advantages and disadvantages of each approach?

15-2 What problems do you foresee in applying the GASB's "Enterprise Fund" definition in practice?

15-3 The notes to the financial statements of a government are often quite extensive. What problems are associated with the use of note disclosures to communicate information essential to fair presentation of a government's financial position and operating results? What are the advantages of such disclosures?

15-4 How useful is the current approach for reporting general fixed assets, including infrastructure? What are the weaknesses of the current approach?

15-5 Why should state and local governments consider restating financial statements and statistical schedules for the effects of inflation?

15-6 What is "deep discount debt"? How would it be accounted for and reported if treated like other general long-term debt?

15-7 Explain, clearly but concisely, the alternative ways in which "deep discount" general long-term debt and related debt service expenditures might be reported.

PROBLEMS

P 15-1 (MF/BA Alternatives) Powley County entered into the following transactions over a period of several years:

1. Salaries and wages were $1,000,000 for 19X1, $1,100,000 for 19X2, and $1,200,000 for 19X3 for work performed in each of those years. Salaries and wages of $950,000 were paid in 19X1, $1,020,000 in 19X2, and $1,180,000 in 19X3.

2. At the end of 19X1, the County determined that it probably would have to pay a $5,000,000 general-government-related claim as a result of current litigation against the county. It was expected that the claim would not have to be paid until 19X3. (A judgment against the County for $5,000,000 was entered late in 19X2 and was paid in mid-19X3.)

3. The County purchased and paid for equipment costing $2,000,000 on January 1, 19X1. The equipment had a three-year useful life and an estimated salvage value of $500,000.

Required Indicate how each of these transactions would be reflected in 19X1, 19X2, and 19X3—by Powley County using:

(a) Current GAAP

(b) The Majority View for implementing GASB Statement II

(c) The Minority View for implementing GASB Statement II

P 15-2 (Research Problem) Obtain the Comprehensive Annual Financial Report (CAFR) or General Purpose Financial Statements (GPFS) of several governments. Analyze the notes to the financial statements for each government in terms of:

a. Whether the notes required are presented

b. Understandability of the notes

c. Consistency of notes presented by various governments and types of information presented in similar notes

d. The extent to which individual notes enhance your analysis and understanding of the financial statements

e. Whether the volume of notes diminishes their value significantly

f. Other strengths or weaknesses related to the notes

Prepare a 10 to 20 page report presenting your analyses and conclusions.

P 15-3 (Research Problem) Study the GASB's statement of objectives of accounting and reporting for governmental units and compare them with the reporting objectives for nonbusiness organizations set forth in FASB Statement of Financial Accounting Concepts (SFAC) No. 4. Prepare a 10 to 20 page report summarizing your research and analyses, with particular emphasis being given to the similarities and differences of the FASB and GASB approaches and conclusions. Also, **explain and justify your position** as to which GASB Statement II implementation alternative will best meet the financial reporting objectives adopted by the GASB.

P 15-4 (Research Problem) Study the GASB's statement of objectives of accounting and reporting for governmental units and compare them with the current principles and practices discussed in Chapters 2 to 15. Prepare a 10 to 20 page report analyzing the extent to which current GAAP fulfills the objectives.

P 15-5 (Research Problem) Select one of the current issues identified in the chapter to research in depth. Prepare a 10 to 20 page paper identifying the **advantages and disadvantages of alternative positions** on the issue.

P 15-6 (Research Problem) Select one of the current issues identified in the chapter to research in depth. Prepare a 10 to 20 page paper that **explains and justifies** the accounting and reporting **alternative** that you consider most appropriate.

P 15-7 (Research Problem) Obtain a copy of a current GASB Discussion Memorandum and research the issues involved in depth. Prepare a 10 to 20 page report that explains and justifies the accounting and reporting alternative that you consider most appropriate.

FEDERAL GOVERNMENT ACCOUNTING

The federal government of the United States is engaged in an unparalleled number and variety of functions, programs, and activities both here and abroad. It is by far the country's biggest employer and also its biggest consumer. Federal disbursements were $591 billion during 1980, up about twelvefold from 1950, and were estimated to exceed $1,475,000,000,000 ($1.4 trillion) in 1992.

Federal accounting, like that of state and local governments, is heavily influenced by law and regulation. It serves as a major tool of fund and appropriation control at both the central government and agency levels. But it is noticeably different in that (1) the **agency**[1] is generally considered the **primary accounting entity,** (2) agency accounting provides—via "dual-track" systems—for **both** budgetary and proprietary accounting and reporting, and (3) accounting is concerned with both budgetary and proprietary accountability for the federal government as a whole **and** of individual agencies.

Thus, the accounting system of the federal government must be, and is, composed of many sets of systems and subsystems. Complete financial data are to be maintained for each agency by its system; financial reports are to be prepared by the agency. Financial reports for the federal government as a whole are compiled by the Office of Management and Budget (OMB) and the Department of the Treasury from the central accounts and from agency reports.

THE FEDERAL FINANCIAL MANAGEMENT ENVIRONMENT

The importance of budgeting, accounting, and reporting to governmental financial management and accountability was recognized by those drafting the Constitution of the United States. Thus, they included a mandate (Article I, Section 9) that:

> No money shall be drawn from the treasury, but in consequence of appropriations made by law; and a regular statement and account of the receipts and expenditures of all public money shall be published from time to time.

---

[1] The term *agency* is used in this chapter to refer to departments, establishments, commissions, boards, or organizational entities thereof, such as a bureau.

From the outset, therefore, financial management was seen as a shared function of the legislative and executive branches of the federal government. Then, as now, the "power of the purse string" was vested in Congress, while the executive branch was charged with administering the activities of the federal government and reporting on its stewardship both to the Congress and to the public.

Accounting and Financial Reporting Roles and Responsibilities

Several federal organizations have significant influence on financial management directives, requirements, and trends. However, in the financial management component of accounting and financial reporting, responsibilities center primarily around three oversight agencies—the Department of the Treasury, the Office of Management and Budget, and the General Accounting Office (Comptroller General)—the newly created Federal Accounting Standards Advisory Board, and the individual agencies. Figure 16-1 contains a summary of these responsibilities which are discussed in the following sections.

Department of the Treasury

The Department of the Treasury, in the executive branch, is headed by the Secretary of the Treasury. The Treasury acts as both chief accountant and banker for the federal government. The Treasury's functions include:

- Central accounting and reporting for the federal government as a whole, including development of government-wide consolidated financial statements.
- Cash receipt and disbursement management—including supervision of the federal depository system and disbursing cash for virtually all civilian agencies.
- Management of the public debt—including the scheduling of borrowing to meet current needs, repayment of debt principal, and meeting interest requirements.
- Supervision of agency borrowing from the Treasury.
- Maintenance of the government-wide Standard General Ledger (SGL).

Numerous directives issued by the Secretary of the Treasury affect federal accounting and reporting, the most comprehensive being the *Treasury Financial Manual.* This manual includes agency proprietary reporting requirements as well as agency requirements to implement the SGL.

Office of Management and Budget (OMB)

An agency within the Executive Office of the President, the OMB has broad financial management powers as well as the responsibility of preparing the executive budget. Among the accounting and financial reporting duties assigned the OMB are:

- To apportion appropriations (enacted) among the agencies and establish "reserves" in anticipation of cost savings, contingencies, and so on.
- To set forth the requirements for accounting and reporting on budget execution.
- To prescribe the form and content of financial statements consistent with applicable accounting principles, standards, and requirements.
- To provide guidance on all matters related to budget preparation and execution.

Figure 16-1

**FEDERAL ACCOUNTING AND FINANCIAL REPORTING ROLES
AND RESPONSIBILITIES—A SUMMARY**

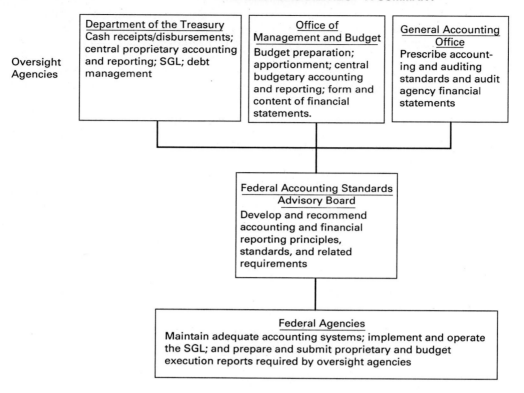

Oversight Agencies

Department of the Treasury
Cash receipts/disbursements; central proprietary accounting and reporting; SGL; debt management

Office of Management and Budget
Budget preparation; apportionment; central budgetary accounting and reporting; form and content of financial statements.

General Accounting Office
Prescribe accounting and auditing standards and audit agency financial statements

Federal Accounting Standards Advisory Board
Develop and recommend accounting and financial reporting principles, standards, and related requirements

Federal Agencies
Maintain adequate accounting systems; implement and operate the SGL; and prepare and submit proprietary and budget execution reports required by oversight agencies

Numerous bulletins, circulars, and other directives relating to federal budgeting, accounting, and reporting that are required to be followed by agencies have been issued by the OMB.

General Accounting Office (GAO)

A multitude of roles and responsibilities have been assigned to the GAO—headed by the Comptroller General of the United States—since its inception in 1921. The primary responsibilities of the GAO are assisting the Congress in the general oversight of the executive branch and serving as the independent legislative auditor of the federal government. The GAO's two primary responsibilities related to accounting and financial reporting are:

1. ***Prescribing principles and standards for federal agency accounting and financial reporting, internal control, accounting systems, and auditing.*** This is done largely through the *General Accounting Office Policy and Procedures Manual for Guidance of Federal Agencies,* published in loose-leaf form and updated periodically.

2. Auditing the financial statements of federal agencies. In recent years, the GAO has begun auditing agency financial statements for the purpose of rendering opinions on their fair presentation with the goal of being able to audit the consolidated financial statements of the overall federal government within the next few years.

Federal Accounting Standards Advisory Board (FASAB)

The Federal Accounting Standards Advisory Board (FASAB), created by a joint agreement between the Treasury, OMB, and GAO, began operations in early 1991. Its purpose is to develop and recommend accounting principles and standards to be followed by federal agencies. Upon approval by the heads of the Treasury, OMB, and GAO, OMB, and GAO issue these principles and standards.

The FASAB is a nine-member board with one representative each from the Treasury, OMB, GAO, the Congressional Budget Office, civil agencies, and defense and international agencies, and three representatives from outside the federal government. The chairperson is a nonfederal member. The FASAB has a staff director and full-time dedicated staff.

As of early 1993, the FASAB had issued two exposure drafts. One dealt with nine less controversial accounting subjects involving financial resources and funded liabilities. The other was on credit reform which covers accounting for loans and loan guarantees. Additional issues being considered by the FASAB are: (1) user needs and reporting objectives, (2) long-term liabilities and other commitments, (3) physical assets and revenue recognition, and (4) inventories.

Federal Agencies

The effectiveness of federal financial management depends upon the individual federal agencies. Similarly, federal budgeting, accounting, and reporting can be no better than that of the related agency systems and subsystems upon which the central systems depend. Among the many accounting-related functions and activities of agencies are these:

- To prepare agency budget requests for submission to the President through the OMB.
- To establish and maintain effective systems of accounting and financial reporting and internal control, in conformity with the principles and standards prescribed by the GAO.
- To implement and operate the SGL. The SGL Board, comprised of agency representatives, maintains account definitions, transactions, and crosswalks to reports.
- To prepare and submit proprietary reports and budget execution reports in accordance with the accounting and reporting requirements of the oversight agencies.

Most federal agencies have an **Inspector General** (IG) or similar internal audit and investigation officers who continually study and evaluate the agency's activities. Each IG must prepare a semiannual report on audit findings and forward it to appropriate congressional committees. Most Inspector Generals are involved in the audit of the financial statements of the agency.

Overview Summary

Responsibility for accounting and financial reporting principles, standards, and related requirements in the federal sector is not as simple or clear cut as those in the private or state and local government sectors. The Congress, through legislation, has established numerous guidelines for accounting and financial reporting. As discussed throughout this chapter, responsibility for developing, promulgating, and implementing accounting and financial reporting principles, standards, and requirements within the guidelines set forth in law, is shared within the federal government. The two major categories of principles, standards, and requirements are budgetary and proprietary.

Although budgetary accounting and financial reporting guidelines have not traditionally been labeled as principles and standards, there are significant requirements that direct its practices in the federal sector. Budgetary requirements are developed and promulgated by OMB. Implementation mandates are also set by OMB, but it is the agencies that must actually implement the mandates received from OMB. Also, Treasury sets forth several requirements to help implement fiscal reporting and management in the federal government and provide support for the SGL Board. Moreover, GAO also issues requirements consistent with OMB directives.

Proprietary principles, standards, and requirements are required by law to be promulgated by GAO. The current process, however, calls for the principles and standards to be developed by the FASAB; approved by the heads of OMB, Treasury, and GAO; and promulgated by OMB and GAO. GAO also develops and promulgates requirements such as those for accounting systems and internal controls. OMB is required by law to promulgate the requirements for the "form and content" of financial statements. In addition, Treasury implements the principles, standards, and requirements by directing agencies to provide it with financial statements (balance sheet, statement of operations, statements of cash flows, and statement of reconciliation between budget and proprietary amounts) periodically and annually. (Treasury is moving simply to require agencies to submit a trial balance which will provide the information needed to prepare the consolidated financial statements.)

THE BUDGETARY PROCESS

The budgetary process in the federal government along with the related budgetary accounting is far more complex than in a municipality. (Although the process involves many intricate steps and is multifaceted, only those major processes impacting accounting are covered here.) The following primary reasons highlight the differences and the complexity of the federal budget process:

- Agency authority to incur obligations for future disbursement is usually not directly based on estimates of revenues, either at the agency or overall federal level.
- Budget authority to incur obligations is granted by the Congress under three types—appropriations, contract authority, or borrowing authority. Still further, appropriations can be one-year, multiyear or no-year, or permanent authorizations. Contract and borrowing authority can also contain various year limitations. Additional authority may be derived from collections from performing services to other agencies and the public.
- The process of spending budget authority is divided into five clearly distinct steps, most of which are closely monitored for legal and regulatory compliance. The five steps are: apportionment, allotment, commitment, obligation, and expended appropriation.

The Budget Cycle

The federal budget cycle, like that of state and local governments, has four phases: (1) formulation, (2) approval, (3) execution, and (4) reporting. (Auditing is included in the fourth phase; however, discussions of it are omitted in this text.)

Formulation and Approval

Budget formulation begins in the executive branch and ends when the budget is formally presented to the Congress. Budget preparation and presentation of the budget to the Congress is a presidential responsibility. Preparation requires continuous exchange of information, proposals, evaluations, and policy determination among the President, central financial agencies, and operating agencies.

Budget approval is a congressional function. The Congressional Budget Act of 1974 created the present procedure by which the Congress determines the annual federal budget. At the beginning of consideration, by concurrent resolution, it establishes target levels for overall expenditures, budget authority, budget outlays, broad functional expenditure categories, revenues, the deficit, and the public debt.

An appropriation is contained in an act passed by the Congress that becomes a public law. There are about 13 major laws passed through the normal congressional budget process each year containing between 1,200 to 1,400 individual appropriations. Congressional appropriations are not based directly on expended appropriations (i.e., receipt of goods or services), but on authority to obligate the federal government ultimately to make disbursements.

Execution

When an appropriation bill becomes law, an appropriation warrant is drawn by the Treasury and forwarded to the agency. The agency sends a request for apportionment to OMB. The **OMB makes apportionments** to the agency, reserving appropriations for contingency, savings, timing, or policy reasons. The **agency** carries on its programs with the apportioned appropriations through **allotments** for programs and activities; committing, obligating, and expending money; and providing services. It reports to the OMB on its activities and uses of budgetary authority. The agencies prepare vouchers for expended appropriations and submit them to the Treasury or disbursement officers for payment.

An explanation of each aspect of budget execution with respect to basic operating appropriations follows.

Warrants.   A warrant is a document required by law as a means of verification of an appropriation amount contained in a public law. A warrant is signed by the Secretary of the Treasury (or by the Secretary's designee). The warrant contains the amount of the appropriation and is the primary source of recognition by an agency in its accounts for the budget resources awarded to it. Treasury or the disbursing agent maintains central control by limiting an agency to a line of credit for disbursements not to exceed the amount of the warrant.

Apportionment.   Apportionments are divisions, or portions, of appropriations granted agency heads by OMB. Apportionments are required by law to prevent obligation or use of an appropriation at a rate that might result in a deficiency or a supplemental appropriation. Apportionments divide appropriation amounts available for use by specific time periods, activities, projects, types of uses, or combinations thereof. The most common apportionments are divisions based on time periods, usually quarterly. An agency will record its entire appropriation in its accounts when it receives a warrant from the Treasury. However, it can only use the amount of the apportionment received from OMB. The total apportionments granted for each appropriation cannot exceed the amount of the appropriation. (Note that apportionments by time periods are the equivalent of allotments for SLGs, as discussed in Chapter 6.) Apportionment control is maintained centrally by OMB "after the fact"—it is monitored from the monthly budget execution reports submitted by agencies.

Allotment.   An allotment is budget authority in the form of apportionments delegated by the agency head to subordinate managers for use. Suballotments are further divisions of budget authority to lower management levels. The total allotments per apportionment cannot exceed the amount of the apportionment and the total suballotments cannot exceed the total of their related allotment amount. (Note that allotments in federal government terminology are like SLG allocations discussed in Chapter 6.)

Commitment.   A commitment is a preliminary, administrative reservation of budget authority (allotment or suballotment) for the order of goods and services or program purposes. It is a charge to an allotment account based on a **preliminary** estimate. A commitment is usually a **request within an agency** for the purchase of items, travel, or other related purposes. Commitment accounting is not required by law, regulation, or directive from oversight agencies. However, it is a useful planning tool that agencies employ to reserve appropriation authority prior to obligation. Indeed, commitments might be thought of as "pre-encumbrances."

Obligation.   An obligation is a formal reservation of budget authority. It is a formal charge to an allotment or related commitment with the **latest** estimate of the cost of goods or services being purchased. Obligations for the purchase of goods and services are required by regulations and directives from the oversight agencies. Obligations represent orders for the acquisition of goods and/or services for program purposes and compare to encumbrances in SLG budgetary accounting.

Expended Appropriations.   Expended appropriations represent the amount of goods and/or services received and accepted or program costs incurred. It is the formal use of budget authority in an **actual** amount and either (1) it releases the related prior obligation or (2) in cases where obligations are not required, for example, in payroll in some agencies, it is a charge to the related allotment. Expended appropriations are equivalent to expenditures in state and local government accounting.

Expired Authority.   Expired authority represents unexpended, unobligated (that is, unused) appropriation authority of prior years. Expended appropriations against prior year obligations that exceed the previously obligated amount are charged against this expired authority. Expired authority is cancelled at the end of the fifth year after the authority first became expired.

   One aspect of the preceding description bears repetition and emphasis: **only part of an agency's annual obligational authority is available** to it at any time—the **apportioned** part. The **agency head** (or designee), in turn, **allots** its apportioned obligation authority to subordinate managers to operate their programs and/or organizational subunits. **Only allotted apportionments may be obligated** by organizations within an agency.

Reporting

Budget execution is reported periodically and annually to OMB. For each category of appropriation or other budget authority, agencies report the amount of authority, the amount of expended appropriations, the amount of obligations, the amount of apportionments unobligated (unused budget authority), and the amounts of outlays (essentially disbursements) incurred. OMB reports centrally for the overall government on an obligations and outlay basis each year in the annual budget proposal submitted to the Congress by the President. The annual budget proposal contains the current year's projected amounts along with summary amounts of "actuals" (total obligations and total outlays) for preceding years. Although OMB reports amounts related to the budget, both proposed and prior years actuals, the Treasury reports periodic and annual amounts of actual disbursements.

611

Chapter 16
FEDERAL
GOVERNMENT
ACCOUNTING

Exceeding Budget Authority

Numerous laws and regulations highlight the impropriety of exceeding budget authority. Budget authority is considered exceeded when any of the four following events occur:

1. An apportionment exceeds an appropriation.
2. An allotment exceeds an appropriation or an apportionment.
3. An obligation exceeds an allotment, apportionment, or appropriation.
4. An expended appropriation exceeds an appropriation, an apportionment, or an allotment.

Note that commitments are not considered formal use of budget authority.

Laws and regulations provide for criminal penalties for those responsible (the agency head or the managers responsible for allotments and suballotments) when authority is exceeded. In addition, agency management is required to submit reports to the President and the Congress when budget authority is exceeded. The Congress makes the decision whether to provide for a deficiency appropriation to make up the amounts exceeded and the administrative and judicial process determines any punishment.

PROPRIETARY ACCOUNTING PRINCIPLES AND STANDARDS FOR FEDERAL AGENCIES

The accounting principles and standards for federal agencies prescribed by the Comptroller General are contained in Appendix I, "Accounting Principles and Standards," of Title 2—"Accounting," of the *GAO Policy and Procedures Manual for Guidance of Federal Agencies*. A portion of Title 2 is published separately as *Accounting Principles and Standards for Federal Agencies* (revised 1984). Title 2 sets forth primarily proprietary accounting principles and standards for agencies. Proprietary principles and standards cover assets, liabilities, equity, revenues, expenses, gains and losses, and other items. Agencies must disclose any departures from those standards.[2]

Framework of Accounting

Title 2 contains a framework of accounting which includes the objectives, definitions of elements, the federal entity, and reporting requirements. A summary of selected aspects of this framework follows.

The two primary objectives of proprietary accounting are to provide information useful in: (1) allocating resources and (2) assessing management's performance and stewardship. Agencies are required by law and Title 2 to maintain accounts on the full accrual basis. Consequently, Title 2 has defined the elements (assets, liabilities, equity, revenues, expenses, and gains and losses) similar to that of the FASB in the private sector. However, since budget authority does not exist in the private sector, the definition of equity has added features, which are explained in subsequent sections of this chapter. The entity is defined as a management unit, the manager being a political appointee (that is, the head of a department, agency, bureau, and/or other entity). Title 2 also calls for the elements to be reported in four basic year-end statements:

- Balance sheet
- Statement of operations

[2]The process for establishing and enforcing federal accounting principles is still evolving. One current proposal would eliminate the requirement to disclose departures from the Title 2 guidance. In substance, agencies would be permitted, but not required, to follow Title 2.

- Statement of cash flows
- Statement of reconciliation between budgetary and proprietary amounts.

Treasury implements these mandates by requiring agencies to submit to it these four basic financial statements.

The Federal Model

The federal model of accounting is different than the private or state and local government models. It contains what is referred to as a "dual-track" system. This dual-track system contains a complete set of self-balancing accounts for both budgetary and proprietary amounts. Each set of self-balancing accounts reflects an accounting equation.

The budgetary equation is: Budgetary Resources = Status of Authority. The components of each side of the equation are:

Budgetary Resources	=	**Status of Authority**
Appropriations		Unapportioned Appropriations (Authority)
+ Borrowing Authority		+ Apportionments
+ Contract Authority		+ Allotments
+ Reimbursable Authority (between agencies)		+ Commitments
		+ Obligations
+ Collections from other sources		+ Expended Appropriations (Authority)
		+ Expired Authority

The proprietary equation is the private sector equation of: Assets = Liabilities + Equity. However, because of the processes in the federal government and the need to account for appropriations, there are several additions to this equation that do not exist in the private sector. The three primary additions deal with the cash account and disbursements, equity accounts, and the potential use of either current or prior year appropriations to acquire long-lived assets or fund expenses.

Cash and Disbursements

Although agencies have small balances of cash for imprest funds and in rare cases significant balances, the predominant amount is represented by a line of credit with the Treasury (or in the case of the Department of Defense a disbursing agent) in the amount of the warrants it has received. This line of credit is referred to as Fund Balance with Treasury and is handled as cash in a bank account would be by a business. To use this line of credit, the normal process is for an agency to complete a request for payment to Treasury. When the request for payment is forwarded to Treasury, a liability account, Disbursements In Transit, is recognized. When the agency receives the completed request back from Treasury indicating that checks have been written and mailed (referred to as an "accomplished" request), the agency reduces the liability account Disbursements In Transit and the Fund Balance with Treasury for the same amount.

Equity[3]

The Equity of the U.S. Government represents the **residual equity of the federal government in the agency** and is equal to the difference between the assets and liabilities of the agency. The **Equity of the U.S. Government** is composed of *five* items:

1. Invested Capital
2. Cumulative Results of Operations

[3]At the time of this printing, a proposal that would change the term used from "Equity" to "Net Position" was being considered and is apt to be adopted.

3. Appropriated Capital

4. Trust Fund Balances

5. Donations and Other Items

The first three of these are illustrated in Figure 16-2 and discussed in the chapter.

Capital Investments. Capital Investments is the portion of an agency's equity representing (1) the book value of agency fixed assets, inventory, loans made, and other capitalized assets that were financed with appropriations or provided by other agencies without reimbursement, and (2) investments (contributed capital) in the agency's revolving funds and business-type activities made to provide initial financing for those operations or to finance expansion of the services offered. In a pure business-type operation, this will essentially be the equivalent of contributed capital.

Cumulative Results of Operations. The Cumulative Results of Operations is defined as "the net difference between (1) expenses[4] and losses from the inception of an agency or activity and (2) financing sources (i.e., appropriations and revenues) and gains from the inception of an agency or activity (whether financed from appropriations, revenues, reimbursements, or any combination) to the reporting date."[5] **For a revolving fund or business-type activity,** this portion of equity could be referred to as **retained earnings.** If an **agency is financed exclusively** or almost exclusively **with appropriations,** this **component** of equity will be **zero**— or very small—because appropriations are recognized in operations only when expenses financed by those appropriations are recognized (discussed in detail later). Thus, the expenses incurred each year are approximately offset by appropriations recognized in that year.

Appropriated Capital. Appropriated Capital—the ***budgetary fund balance*** of an agency—represents amounts of obligational authority (appropriations) that have neither been expended nor withdrawn as of the reporting date. To the extent that unused appropriations have not been withdrawn, this portion of the equity of the

Figure 16-2   **COMPONENTS OF EQUITY OF A FEDERAL AGENCY**

[4] Under currently proposed changes, only funded expenses and losses would affect cumulative results of operations. Unfunded expenses would result in a "contra-net-position" account called "Future Funding Requirements."

[5] U.S. General Accounting Office, *GAO Policy and Procedures Manual for Guidance of Federal Agencies,* "Title 2-Accounting" (Washington, D.C.: U.S. Government Printing Office, 1984), Appendix I, sec. E20.06.

Figure 16-3   CHANGES IN COMPONENTS OF EQUITY OF U.S. GOVERNMENT

Capital Investments	Cumulative Results of Operations	Appropriated Capital

-------------------------------- **Increases** -------------------------------- **Increases** --------------------------------

(1) Purchases of fixed assets, inventory, loans made, and other capitalizable assets financed by appropriations
(2) Initial investments made to begin operations or a new activity of a revolving fund or businesslike activities

(1) Financing sources:
   (a) Expended appropriations used to finance expenses of the period
   (b) Operating revenues from businesslike activities
   (c) Reimbursements from other agencies
(2) Gains

(1) Appropriation authority granted for the fiscal year

-------------------------------- **Decreases** -------------------------------- **Decreases** --------------------------------

(1) Fixed assets, inventory, or other assets are used, depreciated, sold, or exchanged.
(2) Amounts representing initial investments in revolving funds or businesslike activities are returned to investor agency or entity or otherwise transferred out.

(1) Expenses
(2) Losses

(1) Expended appropriations
(2) Withdrawal of unexpended and/or unobligated appropriation authority.

agency equals the sum of the unapportioned appropriations, unallotted apportionments, unobligated allotments, obligations at the reporting date and expired authority. If an **agency is operated solely** on a **business-type basis** and receives no appropriations, this **component** of equity will be **zero.**

Changes in Equity

The causes of changes in each of the three most common components of equity are illustrated in Figure 16-3. The most significant ones are discussed in the following sections. The changes in equity are recorded in separate temporary accounts as necessary for proper reporting.

Appropriations. Perhaps the most difficult to understand feature of federal agency accounting is the interrelationships among appropriations and the various components of equity. These interrelationships can be explained best in a simplified context. Therefore, assume that an agency is financed solely from appropriations. How would a $1,000,000 appropriation affect the equity components of the agency?

    First, when the **appropriation is made,** it will increase the Appropriated Capital component of Equity, as indicated in Figure 16-4. From the perspective of the agency, appropriations are increases in equity (although the equity of the consolidated federal government entity does not change). If a portion of this **appropriation** authority is withdrawn by the OMB or the Congress before it is used, the Appropriated Capital account will be reduced by that amount.

Expended Appropriations. When **expended appropriations** are **incurred,** the proprietary accounts are affected in several ways. First, the appropriated capital account is reduced reflecting the decrease in unused obligational authority. Second, either (1) the capital investment account or (2) a temporary account, appropriated capital used, is increased by the same amount. If the expended appropria-

Figure 16-4   **INTERRELATIONSHIP OF EQUITY OF U.S. GOVERNMENT COMPONENTS
(FOR AGENCY FINANCED SOLELY BY ANNUAL APPROPRIATIONS)**

Transaction	Capital Investments	Cumulative Results of Operations	Appropriated Capital
Appropriation granted			+
Expenditure incurred to finance operating expense		— Operating Expense + Report Appropriated Capital Used as financing source in Statement of Operations	—
Expenditure incurred to acquire fixed asset, inventory, etc.	+		—
Fixed asset depreciated or other assets expensed	—	— Depreciation (or other) expense + Report transfer of Capital Investments (Appropriated Capital Used) in Statement of Operations (amount equals expense)	
Unfunded expenses, e.g., employees annual leave		—	
Unobligated appropriations are withdrawn			—
Year end balance	Book value of nonmonetary assets	Equal to liability for unfunded expenses	Equals sum of obligations outstanding (undelivered orders) and expired authority

tion was for the acquisition of a long-lived asset or other items not currently expensed, the capital investment account is increased. If, however, the expended appropriation was for the acquisition of goods or services that were immediately expensed, a financing source (a temporary account called Appropriated Capital Used) is recorded. The Appropriated Capital Used account is reported in the statement of operations as a financing source. The Appropriated Capital Used offsets the expenses incurred which were funded from appropriations. Finally, either (a) fixed assets, inventory, or other assets are capitalized or (b) expenses are recorded in the amount of the expended appropriations.

Use of Assets. When long-lived assets, inventory, or other assets are used—as recognized through depreciation, amortization, depletion, or other expense—the Capital Investment account is reduced in the amount of the expense and the Appropriated Capital Used account is credited for the same amount. Thus, the net effect on the cumulative results of operations when recognizing expenses funded with appropriations is zero.

Unfunded Expenses. Not all expenses are funded, however. A few expenses are unfunded in the year the expenses are incurred, although they will be funded in future periods. Examples of unfunded expenses include: pension costs, contingent liabilities, and employees' annual leave earned but not taken. Most agencies incur at least one unfunded expense, that of the annual leave benefits earned by employees. In most agencies these expenses are immaterial to the total expenses, however, in smaller, service-oriented agencies, these can be material. Recognition of unfunded expenses is the same as in the private sector. The expense is debited and a liability is credited. The net effect of unfunded expenses on the cumulative results of operations is a debit balance, or a cumulative loss.

Figure 16-4 illustrates the interrelationships among the various components of equity discussed earlier. These relationships are illustrated further in accounting for an illustrative federal agency. Too, it may be useful to refer to Figure 16-15 at this point. That figure presents a "Capital Statement" for an agency.

Standard General Ledger

The Government Wide Standard General Ledger (SGL) was developed in 1986 and issued as a requirement to all agencies by the three oversight agencies in 1988. The SGL has perhaps been the most influential requirement inducing agencies to implement the dual-track federal model which was first required by the 1984 Title 2. Treasury oversees an SGL Board made up of members representing the major federal agencies. The Board which meets frequently maintains and updates the SGL.

The SGL contains approximately 200 separate accounts in its chart of accounts. The principal SGL accounts, account definitions, transactions, and crosswalks to reports are organized as follows:

1000s	Asset Accounts
2000s	Liability Accounts
3000s	Equity Accounts
4000s	Budgetary Accounts
5000s	Revenues and Other Credits in the Statement of Operations
6000s	Expenses
7000s	Gains and Losses

Since this chapter is a summary overview of federal accounting, we will use only 22 of the SGL accounts, 8 budgetary and 14 proprietary, and we will assume budgetary authority is granted only in the form of a one-year operating appropriation. The eight budgetary accounts are as follows.

Budgetary Resources (Normal Debit Balance):
  Other Appropriations Realized

Status of Authority (Normal Credit Balances):
  Authority Available for Apportionment
  Apportionment Available for Distribution
  Allotment Available for Commitment/Obligation
  Commitment Available for Obligation
  Undelivered Orders
  Expended Appropriations
  Expired Authority

Figure 16-5 shows the effect on the accounts when budgetary authority is granted, delegated, and used as well as the closing entries involved. Note that "Expended Appropriations" is closed to the Budgetary Resources account, "Other Appropriations Realized" and that "Undelivered Orders" (encumbered amounts) is not closed. The remaining "Status" accounts are closed into the "Expired Authority" account making its balance equal to the unobligated, unexpended appropriation authority that has not been cancelled.

Figure 16-6 contains a graphic illustration of the proprietary accounts used. As with the budgetary accounts, the account titles are those required in the SGL.

Integration of both budgetary and proprietary accounts is an important concept required when implementing the SGL. Integration occurs when entries are required in both budgetary and proprietary accounts as a result of the same transaction. For example, when an agency receives a warrant as a result of the passage of an appropriation bill into law, the agency recognizes one entry each in the budgetary and proprietary accounts, as follows:

Budgetary: Other Appropriations Realized XXX
                  Authority Available for Apportionment XXX
Proprietary: Fund Balance with Treasury XXX
                  Appropriated Capital. XXX

The case illustration at the end of this chapter will show other example entries required by both "tracks" as a result of the same transaction.

Funds and the Federal Entity

Fund structures employed in federal government accounting may be broadly classified as (1) funds derived from general taxing and revenue powers and from business operations, also known as "Federal" or "Government-owned" funds, and (2) funds held by the government in the capacity of custodian or trustee, sometimes referred to as "Not Government-owned" or "Trust and Agency" funds. Six types of funds are employed within these two broad categories.

Government-owned or "Federal" Funds	*Trust or Custodian Funds*
General Fund	Trust Funds
Special Funds	Deposit Funds
Revolving Funds	
Management Funds	

However, in the federal sector, the fund type or the specific fund does not influence accounting or financial reporting as it does in the state and local government sector. The federal entity instead is twofold. For budgetary purposes, the entity is each appropriation or other budget authority granted by the Congress. Budget execution reports are required for each appropriation. Thus, each appropriation for each specific year has a complete SGL. The proprietary entity is broader, although it can also be each appropriation. Treasury requires approximately between 650 and 750 complete sets of the four primary proprietary financial statements each year. These sets include many single-year appropriations as well as consolidated statements of agencies and departments. The SGL is designed to separately maintain two proprietary accounts, Fund Balance with Treasury and Appropriated Capital, on an appropriation basis by year in the subsidiary accounts.

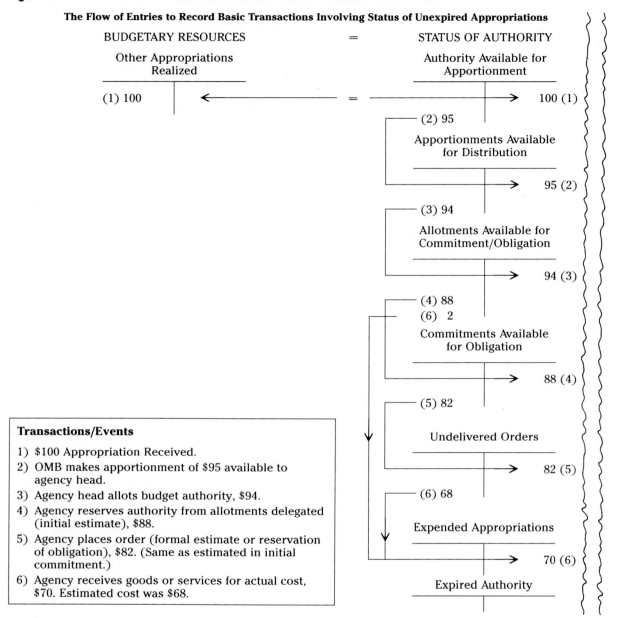

The Flow of Entries to Record Basic Transactions Involving Status of Unexpired Appropriations

Transactions/Events

1) $100 Appropriation Received.
2) OMB makes apportionment of $95 available to agency head.
3) Agency head allots budget authority, $94.
4) Agency reserves authority from allotments delegated (initial estimate), $88.
5) Agency places order (formal estimate or reservation of obligation), $82. (Same as estimated in initial commitment.)
6) Agency receives goods or services for actual cost, $70. Estimated cost was $68.

Financial Reporting

Federal financial reporting includes both agency-level and government-wide statements.

Agency Level

Although agency managers determine the internal reports needed, one basic budgetary statement and **four** basic proprietary **statements** are **required** at least

Figure 16-5 (continued)

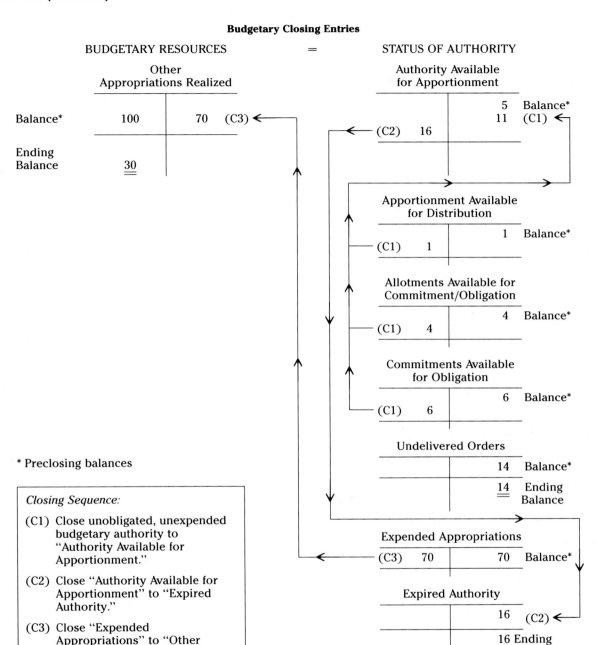

Budgetary Closing Entries

BUDGETARY RESOURCES $=$ STATUS OF AUTHORITY

Other
Appropriations Realized

Balance*	100	70	(C3)	
Ending Balance	30			

Authority Available
for Apportionment

		5	Balance*
(C2)	16	11	(C1)

Apportionment Available
for Distribution

(C1)	1	1	Balance*

Allotments Available for
Commitment/Obligation

(C1)	4	4	Balance*

Commitments Available
for Obligation

(C1)	6	6	Balance*

Undelivered Orders

	14	Balance*
	14	Ending Balance

Expended Appropriations

(C3)	70	70	Balance*

Expired Authority

	16	(C2)
	16	Ending Balance

* Preclosing balances

Closing Sequence:

(C1) Close unobligated, unexpended budgetary authority to "Authority Available for Apportionment."

(C2) Close "Authority Available for Apportionment" to "Expired Authority."

(C3) Close "Expended Appropriations" to "Other Appropriations Realized."

annually of all federal agencies. The budgetary statement is the Report on Budget Execution. The proprietary statements are:

1. Statement of Financial Position (Balance Sheet).
2. Statement of Operations.
3. Statement of Cash Flows.
4. Statement of Reconciliation to Budget Reports.

Figure 16-6   OVERVIEW OF THE FEDERAL GOVERNMENT PROPRIETARY ACCOUNTING EQUATION

ASSETS   =   LIABILITIES   + EQUITY OF THE UNITED STATES GOVERNMENT

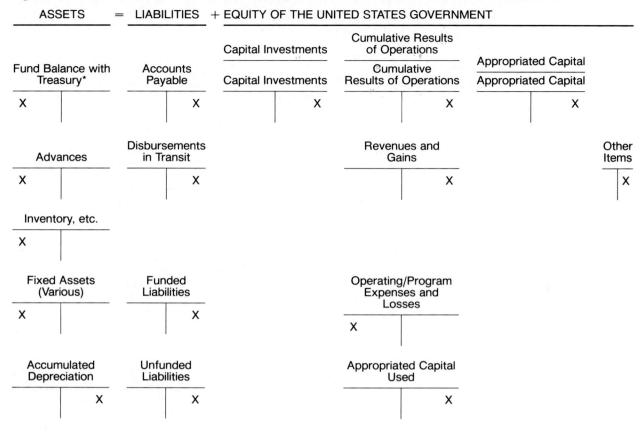

These and other statements are illustrated in the final section of this chapter. Other financial reports are required by the Congress, its committees, or the central oversight agencies.

Government-Wide Statements

The same four proprietary financial statements required for each agency also are required annually on a ***consolidated*** entity basis. The reporting entity for the consolidated statements of the U.S. government is required to include all of its departments, agencies, and other units. Title 2 further states:

> Also, in the interest of providing a **more complete and accurate presentation** of the government's financial position and results of operations, the consolidated financial statements **should also include** the **legislative and judicial branches** of the federal government, as well as the federally owned government corporations.[6]

In preparing the statements for the consolidated entity, all interdepartmental and interagency balances and transactions should be eliminated. Depreciation should be recorded for agency fixed assets on which depreciation is not reported by the agencies. Any other adjustments needed to report the consolidated entity's financial statements from the perspective of the U.S. government as a single entity must be made as well.

[6] Ibid., Appendix I, sec. C40.05. (Emphasis added.)

FEDERAL AGENCY ACCOUNTING AND REPORTING ILLUSTRATED

This section of the chapter contains (1) a case illustration of federal agency accounting and (2) illustrative agency financial statements. The case is designed to illustrate the major federal accounting principles and standards. Those interested in more in-depth and specific coverage of federal government accounting may wish to review the United States Standard General Ledger developed by the Treasury and the prescribed financial report formats established by the OMB.

In the case illustration, we initially demonstrate how the agency would maintain budgetary accountability in its accounting system. Next, the simultaneous maintenance of proprietary information is illustrated. Then various transactions of the agency are presented with both budgetary and proprietary entries being made as needed. The accounts are closed at year end in a manner that highlights the relationship between the budgetary accounts and the proprietary accounts. Finally, illustrative financial statements are presented for the agency.

Although specific methods of accounting vary among agencies, as do their functions and financing methods, the approach illustrated is typical and serves to highlight the major aspects of federal agency accounting and reporting.

A Case Illustration

In order to illustrate the principal aspects of federal agency accounting, assume that (1) an agency began the 19X0–X1 fiscal year with the trial balance in Figure 16-7; and (2) its activities are financed solely through a single-year appropriation. To simplify the illustration, we also (1) assume that general ledger control accounts similar to those in Figures 16-5 and 16-6 are employed, (2) limit our presentation to general ledger entries, and (3) in order to demonstrate the entire cycle, make summary entries where similar transactions typically recur throughout the year. The agency's functions primarily entail rendering services to the public.

Maintaining Agency Budgetary Control

Budgetary control is maintained on a fixed-dollar basis for operations of the federal government agencies, as is true with state and local governments. However, as indicated in Figure 16-8, the means for implementing budgetary control in the accounting system tends to be somewhat more complex than with SLGs.

Budgetary accounting and proprietary accounting are shown simultaneously in this illustration using the "dual-track" approach required for federal agencies.

Summary of Transactions and Events/Entries

1. Congress enacted appropriations that included $225,000 for XYZ Agency. The agency received an appropriation warrant in that amount from Treasury.

Proprietary Entry

(1a)	Fund Balance with Treasury—19X1	225,000	
	Appropriated Capital—19X1		225,000
	To record receipt of appropriation warrant.		

Figure 16-7

BEGINNING TRIAL BALANCE

XYZ Agency
Trial Balance
October 1, 19X0

Budgetary Accounts

Other Appropriations Realized	$ 13,000	$ —
Authority Available for Apportionment		—
Apportionment Available for Distribution		—
Allotments Available for Commitment/Obligation		—
Commitments Available for Obligation		—
Undelivered Orders		—
Expended Appropriations		—
Expired Authority		13,000
	$ 13,000	$ 13,000

Proprietary Accounts

Fund Balance With Treasury—19X0	$ 62,200	
Fund Balance With Treasury—19X1	—	
Advances to Others	800	
Inventory for Agency Operations	17,000	
Equipment	20,000	
Accumulated Depreciation on Equipment		$ 8,000
Disbursements in Transit		12,000
Accounts Payable		30,000
Accrued Funded Payroll and Benefits		8,000
Accrued Unfunded Annual Leave		50,000
Appropriated Capital—19X0		13,000
Appropriated Capital—19X1		—
Capital Investments		29,000
Cumulative Results of Operations	50,000	
	$150,000	$150,000

This proprietary entry establishes the agency's "line of credit" with the Treasury as an asset of the agency and the related equity increase. Recall that you may wish to think of the Fund Balance with Treasury as if it were a Cash account.

Budgetary Entry

(1b) Other Appropriations Realized	225,000	
Authority Available for Apportionment		225,000
To record receipt of budgetary authority.		

This budgetary-track entry establishes initial accountability for the agency's appropriation for the fiscal year.

The budgetary accounting and control mechanism appears more complex in the federal government in part because not all of the appropriations adopted by the Congress serve as valid expenditure authority for the various agencies. Instead, as mentioned earlier, the OMB apportions part of the appropriation authority to the agencies initially. Thus, it is necessary to distinguish between appropriations (Authority Available for Apportionment) and apportionments (Apportionments Available for Distribution) of the federal agency just as we distinguish between Unallotted Appropriations and Allotments in state and local governments (see Chapter 6). However, not all of the apportionments are typically available to agency field offices for any purpose because the agency head will normally make allotments of the apportionments. Therefore, a federal agency must also distinguish between **Apportionments Available for Distribution** and allotments. (The allotments account is called **Allotments Available for Commitment/ Obligation.**) Hence, only the balance in Allotments Available for Commitment/Ob-

Figure 16-8   **MAINTAINING BUDGETARY ACCOUNTABILITY FOR A FEDERAL AGENCY**

Event	Effect on Budgetary Accounts					
	Authority Available for Apportionment	*Apportionments Available for Distribution*	*Allotments Available for Commitment/ Obligation*	*Commitments Available for Obligation*	*Undelivered Orders*	*Expended Appropriations*
1. Congress enacts appropriations	+					
2. OMB apportions appropriation authority to agencies	–	+				
3. Agency directors allot apportionments to various purposes		–	+			
4. Goods/Services are requested for order			–	+		
5. Goods are ordered or contracts for services are signed				–	+	
6. Expenditures are incurred upon receipt of goods or services					–	+

ligation provides valid budgetary authority against which field offices can obligate the agency. The next two transactions and entries illustrate the reclassification of appropriations as apportionments and allotments are made.

2. The OMB apportioned $220,000 of the congressional appropriation, reserving $5,000 for possible cost savings and contingencies. The apportionments were distributed as follows:

First quarter	$ 68,000
Second quarter	58,000
Third quarter	44,000
Fourth quarter.	50,000
	$220,000

Proprietary Entry—None
Budgetary Entry
> (2a)   Authority Available for Apportionment.   68,000
>   Apportionment Available for Distribution   68,000
>   To record OMB apportionment of appropriation for
>   the first quarter.

Note that only the $68,000 balance in Apportionment Available for Distribution can be allotted, committed, or obligated during the first quarter. Similar entries would be made as additional apportionments are made:

Proprietary Entry—None
Budgetary Entry

(2b)	Authority Available for Apportionment.	152,000	
	Apportionment Available for Distribution		152,000
	To record OMB apportionments of appropriation for the remaining quarters.		

Entry 2b is a summary entry. In practice an entry would be made each quarter; the $122,000 is the total of the apportionments made during the last three quarters. Subsequent transactions will assume that the entire $220,000 has been apportioned.

3. Administrative allotments made by the agency head were distributed as follows:

Salaries and benefits	$135,000
Materials and supplies	40,000
Fixed assets	12,000
Travel	2,000
Other.	25,000
	$214,000

Proprietary Entry—None
Budgetary Entry

(3)	Apportionment Available for Distribution.	214,000	
	Allotments Available for Commitment/Obligation . . .		214,000
	To record allotments of apportioned appropriations.		

The subsequent accounting for obligations (encumbrances) and expended appropriations incurred by a federal agency against its allotments differs from the treatment illustrated in state and local government accounting. Separate encumbrance and expenditure accounts are used in state and local government accounting, and their total is subtracted from allotments to determine the unencumbered balance still available for encumbrance and expenditure for a particular purpose. In federal agency accounting, however, this *unencumbered balance* is maintained in a single account, the **Allotments Available for Commitment/Obligation** account, or in that account and a **Commitments Available for Obligation** account which may be used to formally capture purchase requests prior to orders being approved and placed. Too, the "encumbrances" of a federal agency are referred to as "obligations" and recorded in an account called **Undelivered Orders.** The recording of commitments, obligations, and expended appropriations of a federal agency is illustrated in the next three transactions.

4. Preliminary requests were made within the agency for the purchase of $37,000 of supplies and equipment expected to cost $11,000.

Proprietary Entry—None
Budgetary Entry

(4)	Allotments Available for Commitment/Obligation	48,000	
	Commitments Available for Obligation		48,000
	To record purchase requisitions being processed within the agency.		

Note that this entry reduces the Allotments Available for Commitment/Obligation by the estimated cost of the purchase request, leaving the unobligated (unencumbered), uncommitted balance of the allotments (or the unused expenditure authority) in the account.

5. Purchase orders were approved and placed for materials estimated to cost $37,000—all of which had been previously committed in that amount.

Proprietary Entry—None
Budgetary Entry

(5)	Commitments Available for Obligation	37,000	
	Undelivered Orders		37,000
	To record purchase orders outstanding.		

6. Materials estimated to cost $30,000 were received; the invoice was for $30,500.

Budgetary Entry

(6a)	Undelivered Orders	30,000	
	Allotments Available for Commitment/Obligation	500	
	Expended Appropriations		30,500
	To record expenditure of budgetary authority.		

Note that the actual cost of the materials purchased is reflected as Expended Appropriations, while the estimated cost is removed from the Undelivered Orders (encumbrances) account.

Maintaining Agency Accrual Accounting Information

The preceding entries demonstrate how budgetary control is maintained in the agency's accounting records. However, as stated earlier, the agencies are also required to account for and report their activities in proprietary accounts. Therefore, in addition to the budgetary accounting entries illustrated earlier, the agency must record the following entries:

Proprietary Entry

(6b)	Inventory of Materials and Supplies	30,500	
	Accounts Payable		30,500
	To record materials received.		
(6c)	Appropriated Capital—19X1	30,500	
	Capital Investment		30,500
	To reclassify appropriated capital as capital investment as a result of the increase in materials inventory.		

The first entry above records the materials purchased as inventory and the related payable. The second entry reclassifies Appropriated Capital as Capital Investments as discussed earlier. No financing source is recorded at this point because no expense has been incurred.

Subsequently, the cost of materials used is recorded as an expense of the agency. An equal financing source, Appropriated Capital Used, is recorded at that time as well. But no budgetary entry is necessary since the expended appropriations were already recorded.

7. Materials costing $25,000 were used by the agency.

Proprietary Entry

(7a)	Operating/Program Expenses—Materials and Supplies	25,000	
	Inventory of Materials and Supplies		25,000

To record cost of materials used.

(7b)	Capital Investments	25,000	
	Appropriated Capital Used		25,000

To record the reclassification of capital investment as a
financing source as a result of the use of materials.

Budgetary Entry—None

Other Miscellaneous Transactions and Entries During the Year

Various other transactions entered into by the agency are recorded in this section.
Notice that budgetary entries and proprietary entries often are required simultaneously.

8. Treasury notified the agency that the checks ordered but not issued in fiscal
year 19X0 (Disbursements in Transit in the beginning trial balance—$12,000)
were issued in 19X1.

Proprietary Entry

(8)	Disbursements in Transit	12,000	
	Fund Balance with Treasury—19X0		12,000

To record notification of issuance of checks requested in
19X0.

Budgetary Entry—None

9. Travel orders in the amount of $1,200 were issued.

Proprietary Entry—None
Budgetary Entry

(9)	Allotments Available for Commitment/Obligation	1,200	
	Undelivered Orders		1,200

To record approval of travel orders.

10. Checks for travel advances totaling $1,000 were requested from Treasury.

Proprietary Entry

(10)	Advances to Others	1,000	
	Disbursements in Transit		1,000

To record request to Treasury for payment of travel
advances.

Budgetary Entry—None

11. Travel vouchers for $1,050 were received, including $880 to which advances
were to be applied. Travel orders had not been issued (in transaction 9) for
$50 of the travel costs.

Proprietary Entry

(11a)	Operating/Program Expenses—Travel	1,050	
	Advances to Others		880
	Accounts Payable.		170

To record travel expenses incurred.

(11b) Appropriated Capital—19X1   1,050
     Appropriated Capital Used   1,050
To record financing source for appropriated capital used to
finance operating expenses.

Budgetary Entry

(11c) Allotments Available for Commitment/Obligation   50
     Undelivered Orders   1,000
       Expended Appropriations   1,050
To record expenditure of budgetary authority for travel
costs.

12. Checks to pay the travel claims were ordered from Treasury.

Proprietary Entry

(12) Accounts Payable   170
     Disbursements in Transit   170
To record order of checks from Treasury to settle accounts
payable.

Budgetary Entry—None

13. The Advances to Others related to the prior fiscal year were repaid by employees, $800.

Proprietary Entry

(13) Fund Balance with Treasury—19X0   800
     Advances to Others   800
To record collection of unused advances.

Budgetary Entry—None

14. Treasury notified the agency that the checks ordered to date, $1,170, were issued.

Proprietary Entry

(14) Disbursements in Transit   1,170
     Fund Balance with Treasury   1,170
To record issuance of checks by Treasury.

15. The agency incurred rental expenses, $13,000, utility costs, $8,200, and other miscellaneous expenses totaling $3,200 during the year. These items had not been obligated previously.

Proprietary Entry

(15a) Operating/Program Expenses—Rent   13,000
     Operating/Program Expenses—Utilities   8,200
     Operating/Program Expenses—Miscellaneous   3,500
       Accounts Payable.   24,700
To record various expenses incurred.

(15b) Appropriated Capital—19X1   24,700
     Appropriated Capital Used   24,700
To record financing source for appropriated capital used to
finance various operating expenses.

Budgetary Entry

(15c) Allotments Available for Commitment/Obligation   24,700
     Expended Appropriations   24,700
To record expenditure of budgetary authority for various
operating expenses.

16. Purchase orders were approved and placed for equipment estimated to cost $10,200—which had been previously committed at $10,500.

Proprietary Entry—None
Budgetary Entry

(16)	Commitments Available for Obligation	10,500	
	Allotments Available for Obligation/Commitment		300
	Undelivered Orders		10,200
	To record purchase orders outstanding.		

17. The equipment was received, together with an invoice for $10,000.

Proprietary Entry

(17a)	Equipment	10,000	
	Accounts Payable.		10,000
	To record acquisition of equipment.		
(17b)	Appropriated Capital—19X1	10,000	
	Capital Investment		10,000
	To reclassify appropriated capital as capital investment as a result of equipment purchases.		

Budgetary Entry

(17c)	Undelivered Orders	10,200	
	Allotments Available for Commitment/Obligation		200
	Expended Appropriations		10,000
	To record expenditure of budgetary authority.		

18. Salaries and wages totaling $134,000 were paid during the year, including the agency's share of related payroll expenses. $8,000 of this amount was accrued at the beginning of the year. (Withholding deductions and the use of the disbursements in transit account are omitted for purposes of this illustration.)

Proprietary Entry

(18a)	Accrued Funded Payroll and Benefits	8,000	
	Operating/Program Expenses—Salaries and Benefits	126,000	
	Fund Balance with Treasury—19X0		8,000
	Fund Balance with Treasury—19X1		126,000
	To record payment of payroll.		
(18b)	Appropriated Capital—19X1	126,000	
	Appropriated Capital Used		126,000
	To record financing source for appropriated capital used to finance payroll expenses.		

Budgetary Entry

(18c)	Allotments Available for Commitment/Obligation	126,000	
	Expended Appropriations		126,000
	To record expenditure of budgetary authority for payroll costs.		

19. Commitments were placed for contractual services estimated at $3,000.

Proprietary Entry—None
Budgetary Entry

(19)	Allotments Available for Commitment/Obligation	3,000	
	Commitments Available for Obligation		3,000
	To record commitment for contract request.		

20. A contract was approved for the services requested in transaction 19.

Proprietary Entry—None
Budgetary Entry

(20)	Commitments Available for Obligation	3,000	
	Undelivered Orders		3,000
	To record approval of contract for services.		

21. The contracted services were received, $3,000.

Proprietary Entry

(21a)	Operating/Program Expenses—Contractual Services	3,000	
	Accounts Payable.		3,000
	To record receipt of contractual services.		
(21b)	Appropriated Capital—19X1	3,000	
	Appropriated Capital Used		3,000
	To record financing source for appropriated capital used to finance contractual services expense.		

Budgetary Entry

(21c)	Undelivered Orders	3,000	
	Expended Appropriations		3,000
	To record expended appropriations for contractual services.		

22. Checks to pay all accounts payable except that for the contractual services were requested from Treasury, $95,200.

Proprietary Entry

(22)	Accounts Payable.	95,200	
	Disbursements in Transit		95,200
	To record request for Treasury to issue checks to settle accounts payable.		

Budgetary Entry—None

23. Treasury notified the agency that checks totaling $85,000 were issued, including $30,000 relating to accounts payable outstanding at the beginning of the fiscal year.

Proprietary Entry

(23)	Disbursements in Transit	85,000	
	Fund Balance with Treasury—19X0		30,000
	Fund Balance with Treasury—19X1		55,000
	To record issuance of checks by Treasury.		

24. Depreciation on agency equipment amounted to $2,500.

Proprietary Entry

(24a)	Operating/Program Expenses—Depreciation	2,500	
	Accumulated Depreciation		2,500
	To record depreciation of equipment.		

(24b) Capital Investment 2,500
        Appropriated Capital Used   2,500
      To record reclassification of capital investment as financing
        source resulting from the depreciation charge.

Budgetary Entry—None

25.   Salaries and benefits (other than annual leave) amounting to $7,000 were accrued at year end.

Proprietary Entry

(25a) Operating/Program Expenses—Salaries and Benefits 7,000
        Accrued Funded Payroll   7,000
      To accrue payroll at year end.

(25b) Appropriated Capital—19X1 7,000
        Appropriated Capital Used   7,000
      To accrue financing source for appropriated capital used to
        finance accrual of payroll expenses.

Budgetary Entry

(25c) Allotments Available for Commitment/Obligation 7,000
        Expended Appropriations   7,000
      To record accrual of expended appropriations against
        budgetary authority for payroll.

26.   The liability for accrued annual leave increased $10,000 during the year.

Proprietary Entry

(26) Operating/Program Expenses—Salaries and Benefits 10,000
        Accrued Unfunded Annual Leave Liability   10,000
      To accrue annual leave earned in excess of leave used.

Budgetary Entry—**None**

Closing Entries

The closing process for a federal agency entails closing both budgetary and proprietary accounts. The closing entries for the budgetary accounts and for the proprietary accounts for the illustrative agency are illustrated in the following separate sections.

Budgetary Accounts

Unexpended appropriation authority is retained by law by the agency until cancelled. The purpose of this retention is for:

1. Expended appropriations resulting from prior year obligations to be charged against the "Undelivered Orders" balance established in the prior year.

2. Any excess of actual over estimated cost of expended appropriations from prior year obligations to be charged against expired appropriation authority from the prior year.

Hence, note that the unobligated, unexpended appropriations are closed to an account called Expired Authority. Also, note that Expended Appropriations are closed to Other Appropriations Realized—leaving the unexpended balance of Appropriations in that Budgetary Resources account.

(27a)	Apportionment Available for Distribution	6,000*	
	Allotments Available for Commitment/Obligation	4,050	
	Commitments Available for Obligation	500	
	Authority Available for Apportionment.		10,550

To close apportionments, allotments, and commitments.

(27b)	Authority Available for Apportionment.	15,550	
	Expired Authority		15,550

To close expired appropriation authority.
*(Note that a balance was left in "Authority Available for
Apportionment" for illustrative purposes. The OMB
normally must apportion the full amount of an agency's
appropriations.)

(27c)	Expended Appropriations	202,250	
	Other Appropriations Realized		202,250

To close expended appropriations.

Proprietary Accounts

Expended Appropriations and the budgetary accounts were closed separately to emphasize better the complete separation of budgetary and proprietary accounting. The proprietary accounts must also be closed.

28. The proprietary accounts are closed with the following entries:

(28a)	Appropriated Capital Used	189,250	
	Net Results of Operations	10,000	
	Operating/Program Expenses—Salaries and Benefits . .		143,000
	Operating/Program Expenses—Materials and Supplies.		25,000
	Operating/Program Expenses—Rent		13,000
	Operating/Program Expenses—Utilities		8,200
	Operating/Program Expenses—Depreciation		2,500
	Operating/Program Expenses—Travel		1,050
	Operating/Program Expenses—Contractual Services . .		3,000
	Operating/Program Expenses—Miscellaneous.		3,500

To close proprietary accounts to net results of
operations.

(28b)	Net Results of Operations	10,000	
	Cumulative Results of Operations		10,000

To close the net operating loss.

Reporting

As noted earlier, the principal financial statements prepared for federal agencies include the following:

1. Balance Sheet (Figure 16-10)
2. Statement of Operations (Figure 16-11)
3. Statement of Cash Flows (Figure 16-12)
4. Statement Reconciling Expended Appropriations with Operating/Program Expenses (Figure 16-13)
5. Report on Budget Execution (Figure 16-14)
6. Capital Statement (Figure 16-15)

As noted earlier, the **first five statements** just listed are **required of all agencies.** To facilitate your transition from the journal entries to the financial statements presented for our illustrative agency, the agency's September 30, 19X1 preclosing trial balance is presented in Figure 16-9.

Figure 16-9

PRECLOSING TRIAL BALANCE

XYZ Agency
Preclosing Trial Balance
September 30, 19X1

Budgetary Accounts

Other Appropriations Realized	$238,000	
Authority Available for Apportionment		$ 5,000
Apportionment Available for Distribution		6,000
Allotments Available for Commitment/Obligation		4,050
Commitments Available for Obligation		500
Undelivered Orders		7,200
Expended Appropriations		202,250
Expired Authority		13,000
	$238,000	$238,000

Proprietary Accounts

Fund Balance with Treasury—19X0	$ 13,000	
Fund Balance with Treasury—19X1	42,830	
Advances to Others	120	
Inventory for Agency Operations	22,500	
Equipment	30,000	
Accumulated Depreciation on Equipment		$ 10,500
Disbursements in Transit		10,200
Accounts Payable		3,000
Accrued Funded Payroll and Benefits		7,000
Accrued Unfunded Annual Leave		60,000
Appropriated Capital—19X0		13,000
Appropriated Capital—19X1		22,750
Capital Investments		42,000
Cumulative Results of Operations	50,000	
Net Results of Operations		—
Appropriated Capital Used		189,250
Operating/Program Expenses—Salaries and Benefits	143,000	
Operating/Program Expenses—Materials and Supplies	25,000	
Operating/Program Expenses—Rent	13,000	
Operating/Program Expenses—Utilities	8,200	
Operating/Program Expenses—Depreciation	2,500	
Operating/Program Expenses—Travel	1,050	
Operating/Program Expenses—Contractual Services	3,000	
Operating/Program Expenses—Miscellaneous	3,500	
	$357,700	$357,700

CONCLUDING COMMENTS

The federal government is the largest, most complex entity in the United States. Accordingly, the accounting and reporting systems of the various agencies must meet the many multifaceted needs of both internal and external persons and groups. The discussion of the financial management structure of the federal government in the first part of this chapter indicates the many agencies involved in helping meet those needs.

Federal agency accounting and reporting are the focus of the latter part of this chapter. These agencies are significant reporting entities; further, the reports for the government as a whole must be derived from the accounts and reports of the various agencies. Each agency's accounting and reporting systems must provide both information needed by the agency's management and that needed to ensure and demonstrate compliance with budgetary and other legal requirements.

Figure 16-10

FEDERAL AGENCY BALANCE SHEET

XYZ Agency
Comparative Balance Sheet
September 30 of Fiscal Years 19X1 and 19X0

		September 30 of Fiscal Year 19X1		September 30 of Fiscal Year 19X0
Assets				
Fund Balance with Treasury—19X0.		$13,000		$ 62,200
Fund Balance with Treasury—19X1.		42,830		—
Advance to Others		120		800
Inventory for Agency Operation		22,500		17,000
Equipment	$30,000		$20,000	
Less Accumulated Depreciation	(10,500)	19,500	(8,000)	12,000
Total Assets		$97,950		$ 92,000
Liabilities and Government Equity				
Liabilities				
Disbursements in Transit	$10,200		$12,000	
Accounts Payable.	3,000		30,000	
Accrued Funded Payroll and Benefits	7,000		8,000	
Accrued Unfunded Annual Leave	60,000		50,000	
Total Liabilities.		$80,200		$100,000
Equity of the U.S. Government				
Appropriated Capital—19X0	13,000		13,000	
Appropriated Capital—19X1	22,750		—	
Capital Investments	42,000		29,000	
Cumulative Results of Operations*	(60,000)		(50,000)	
Total Equity of the U.S. Government		17,750		(8,000)
Total Liabilities and Government Equity		$97,950		$ 92,000

*Under proposed changes, this would be reported as "Future Funding Requirements."

Figure 16-11

FEDERAL AGENCY OPERATING STATEMENT

XYZ Agency
Operating Statement
For Year Ended September 30 of Fiscal Year 19X1

Appropriated Capital Used		$189,250
Operating/Program Expenses		
Depreciation on Equipment	$ 2,500	
Payroll and Benefits	143,000	
Contractual Services	3,000	
Materials and Supplies Used.	25,000	
Travel Expense	1,050	
Rent Expense	13,000	
Utilities Expense.	8,200	
Miscellaneous Expense	3,500	
Total Operating/Program Expenses		$199,250
Excess of Expenses Over Financing Sources		($ 10,000)

Federal government accounting integrates accrual basis accounting and budgetary accounting in a unique manner. Some aspects of federal agency accounting are unique to the federal government, others are somewhat similar to state and local government accounting; other aspects are similar to business accounting. This chapter discusses and illustrates the basic principles and concepts required by the GAO in Title 2 and by the OMB and Treasury in the SGL.

Figure 16-12

FEDERAL AGENCY STATEMENT OF CASH FLOWS

XYZ Agency
Cash Flow Statement
For Year Ended September 30 of Fiscal Year 19X1

Cash Provided by Operations

Excess of Expenses over Financing Sources.		($10,000)	
Add: Increase in Unfunded Annual Leave Liability.	$ 10,000		
Depreciation Expense.	2,500		
Supplies Used	25,000		
Decrease in Advances to Others	680		
Deduct: Appropriated Capital Used	(189,250)		
Acquisition of Inventory	(30,500)		
Decrease in Accrued Funded Payroll and Benefits.	(1,000)		
Decrease in Disbursements in Transit	(1,800)		
Decrease in Accounts Payable	(27,000)	(211,370)	
Cash Used in Operating Activities			($221,370)

Cash Used by Investing

Acquisition of Equipment	(10,000)

Cash Provided by Financing

Appropriation Received	$225,000
Decrease in Cash.	(6,370)
Beginning Cash, October 1, 19X0	62,200
Ending Cash, September 30, 19X1	$ 55,830

Figure 16-13

FEDERAL AGENCY RECONCILIATION OF EXPENDED APPROPRIATIONS WITH EXPENSES

XYZ Agency
Statement Reconciling Expended Appropriations With Operating/Program Expenses
For Year Ended September 30 of Fiscal Year 19X1

Expended Appropriations

Fiscal Year 19X0	$ —	
Fiscal Year 19X1	202,250	
Total Expended Appropriations		$202,250

Operating/Program Expenses

Total Operating Expenses.	$199,250	
[a] Add: Acquisition of Inventory.	30,500	
Acquisition of Fixed Assets	10,000	
Deduct: Unfunded Annual Leave Expense.	(10,000)	
Depreciation Expense	(2,500)	
Expense for Supplies Used	(25,000)	
Total Expended Appropriations		$202,250

[a] Note that the key reconciling items are to incorporate the effects of (1) assets purchased but not expensed in the current year, (2) expensing of assets purchased in prior fiscal years, and (3) unfunded expenses.

Figure 16-14

FEDERAL AGENCY REPORT ON BUDGET EXECUTION

XYZ Agency
Report on Budget Execution
Fiscal Year End 19X1

Part I: **Budgetary Resources**

Appropriations realized..............................	$225,000
Plus other authority	—0—
Less withdrawals	—0—
Total Budgetary Authority.........................	$225,000

Part II: **Status of Authority**

Obligations incurred................................	$209,450[a]
Plus unobligated balances available	—0—
Less unobligated balances not available	15,550[b]
Total Budgetary Authority.........................	$225,000

Part III: **Relationship of Obligations to Outlays to Expended Appropriations**

Obligations incurred................................	$209,450
Less obligations not yet disbursed	(27,280)[c]
Outlays	182,170[d]
Plus changes in funded liabilities	20,080[c]
Expended Appropriations...........................	$202,250

[a] *Expended appropriations plus undelivered orders.*

[b] *Increase in Expired Authority.*

[c] *Computations:*

Disbursements in Transit	*$10,200*
Accounts Payable	*3,000*
Accrued Funded Payroll and Benefits	*7,000*
Undelivered Orders	*7,500*
	27,400
Less: Advances	*(120)*
Obligations not yet disbursed	*27,280*
Less: Undelivered Orders	*(7,200)*
Change in Funded Liabilities	*$20,080*

[d] *Proposed changes would conclude this report at this point.*

Figure 16-15

FEDERAL AGENCY CAPITAL STATEMENT

XYZ Agency
Capital Statement
For Year Ended September 30 of Fiscal Year 19X1

	Appropriated Capital	Invested Capital	Cumulative Results of Operations[b]
Balance October 1	$ 13,000	$29,000	($50,000)
Appropriation Received...............	225,000		
Acquisition of Inventory	(30,500)	30,500	
Acquisition of Fixed Assets	(10,000)	10,000	
Financing Sources Provided[a]	(161,750)	(27,500)	
Excess of Expenses over Financing Sources			(10,000)
Balance September 30	$ 35,750	$42,000	($60,000)

[a] *Total Appropriated Capital Used in the Statement of Operations coming from:*
(1) Capital Investments: Depreciation and Inventory Usage, $27,500
(2) Appropriated Capital $189,250 less $27,500

[b] *Under proposed changes this column would be headed "Future Funding Requirements."*

QUESTIONS

16-1   Explain the meaning of the following terms in federal accounting:

    a. Apportionment   e. Expended Appropriations

    b. Allotment   f. Obligations Incurred

    c. Obligation   g. Fund Balance with Treasury

    d. Commitment

16-2   List the types of financial statements required to be issued annually by federal agencies.

16-3   Describe the components of the Equity of the United States Government.

16-4   Compare the manner in which budgetary accounting is accomplished in a federal agency with that of a municipality.

16-5   Why is Appropriated Capital Used reported as financing sources in an agency's Statement of Operations only when appropriation authority is used to finance operating expenses rather than asset acquisitions?

16-6   What are the principal duties of the Federal Accounting Standards Advisory Board?

16-7   Describe the function of a federal agency's Inspector General. To whom and in what manner does the agency Inspector General report?

16-8   What are the key functions and responsibilities of the General Accounting Office?

16-9   When a federal agency purchases a fixed asset, what are the impacts on the components of equity? On the statement of operations?

16-10   What is expired authority? What is its primary purpose?

PROBLEMS

P 16-1   (Multiple Choice)

1. Formal notification that Congress has enacted an appropriation for an agency requires recognition by the agency in

    a. budgetary accounts only

    b. proprietary accounts only

    c. both budgetary and proprietary accounts

    d. neither budgetary or proprietary accounts (No entry is required until apportionments are made.)

2. Primary responsibility with respect to accounting for agency resources and expended appropriations rests with

    a. each individual agency

    b. the Department of the Treasury

    c. the General Accounting Office

    d. the Office of Management and Budget

    e. the Federal Accounting Standards Advisory Board

3. A federal agency's accounting system does *not* need to include information pertaining to

    a. expended appropriations

    b. fixed assets

    c. obligations

    d. expenses

    e. all of the above must be included

4. In 19X5, the U.S. Weather Service purchased a parcel of land near Carmel, California, with $850,000 of appropriated funds with the intention of constructing a facility thereon. The effect of this transaction on Capital Investments is

    a. no change

    b. increase it by $850,000

    c. no change, but Appropriated Capital would be decreased by $850,000

    d. no change, but a financing source of $850,000 should be reported

    e. none of the above

5. An appropriation that has expired

    a. is reported by a federal agency as authority available for apportionment

    b. is reported by a federal agency as unexpended appropriations

    c. is reported by a federal agency as appropriated capital

    d. is reported by a federal agency as unobligated allotments

    e. is not reported by a federal agency in any of its equity accounts

6. Direct labor costs incurred by a federal agency during a period will be reflected in the agency's budgetary accounts as follows:

    a. debit to Expended Appropriations and credit to Cash

    b. debit to Expended Appropriations and credit to Cumulative Results of Operations

    c. debit to Allotments Available for Obligation and credit to Expended Appropriations

    d. debit to Undelivered Orders and credit to Expended Appropriations

7. On June 1, 19X7, the Department of Labor ordered $10,000 worth of stationery and office supplies from an authorized contractor. At the time of the purchase order, this transaction should be recorded by the agency as

    a. a $10,000 debit to current assets and a $10,000 credit to liabilities

    b. a $10,000 debit to Allotments Available for Obligation and a $10,000 credit to Undelivered Orders

    c. a $10,000 debit to Expended Appropriations and a $10,000 credit to Cumulative Results of Operations

    d. a $10,000 debit to Allotments Available for Obligation and a $10,000 credit to Expended Appropriations

    e. a $10,000 debit to Authority Available for Apportionment and a $10,000 credit to Expended Appropriations

8. Authority Available for Apportionment is reclassified as Apportionments Available for Distribution when

    a. the Office of Management and Budget releases enacted appropriations to the federal agency

    b. the appropriate agency officials assign appropriations to various departments within the agency

    c. purchase orders are approved and sent to suppliers of goods

    d. suppliers are paid for goods furnished to an agency

    e. assets are returned by a federal agency to the Treasury

9. Four proprietary financial statements are required by Title 2, as indicated in the chapter. Title 2 requires that these statements be prepared and presented for

    a. each federal agency, but not for the federal government as a whole

    b. for the government as a whole, but not for each agency

    c. the statements are actually optional, since Title 2 does not require that financial statements be prepared, but only requires that when prepared the four statements referred to above must be included

    d. each federal agency and for the federal government as a whole

    e. None of the above

P 16-2 (Budgetary Accounting) Prepare the general journal entries required to record each of the following transactions.

1. The Interstate Fur Trading Commission received a warrant from Treasury for a $2,000,000 appropriation from the Congress for the fiscal year beginning October 1, 19X7.

2. The OMB apportioned the commission $500,000 of its appropriation.

3. The Commission head allotted $400,000 to specific purposes.

4. Salaries incurred and paid for the quarter totaled $120,000.

5. Purchase orders for equipment estimated to cost $50,000 were requested.

6. Equipment estimated to cost $33,000 was ordered.

7. The equipment was received along with an invoice for its cost, $32,890.

P 16-3 (Expended Appropriations and Transfers to Equity) Prepare the general journal entries to adjust and close the Environmental Enhancement Agency's accounts at year end assuming the agency is financed solely from appropriations.

Appropriations expended for operating costs . .	$3,700,000
Appropriations expended for inventory	400,000
Appropriations expended for property, plant, and equipment	1,200,000
Depreciation expense	250,000
Cost of inventory used during the period	420,000
Expired authority for the year.	212,000
Undelivered Orders at year end	185,000

P 16-4 (Various Transactions) Record the following transactions and events of Able Agency, which occurred during the month of October 19X6:

1. Able Agency received a warrant for its fiscal 19X7 appropriation of $2,500,000.

2. The Office of Management and Budget apportioned $600,000 to Able Agency for the first quarter of the 19X7 fiscal year.

3. Able Agency's chief executive allotted $500,000 of the first quarter appropriation apportionment.

4. Obligations incurred during the month for equipment, materials, and program costs amounted to $128,000.

5. Goods and services ordered during the prior year—and to be charged to obligations carried over from the 19X6 fiscal year—were received:

	Obligated For	Actual Cost
Materials	$ 20,000	$ 21,000
Program A costs	7,000	6,200
Program B costs	3,000	2,500
	$ 30,000	$ 29,700

6. Goods and services ordered during October 19X6 were received and vouchered:

	Obligated For	Actual Cost
Materials	$ 6,000	$ 5,000
Equipment	10,000	10,000
Program A costs.	30,000	32,000
Program B costs.	80,000	81,000
	$126,000	$128,000

7. Depreciation for the month of October was estimated at $200, chargeable to Overhead.

8. Materials issued from inventory during October were for: Program A, $18,000; Program B, $7,000; and general (Overhead), $3,000.

9. Liabilities placed in line for payment by the U.S. Treasurer totaled $145,000.

10. Other accrued expenses at October 31, 19X6, not previously recorded, were: Program A, $1,000; Program B, $6,000; and general (Overhead), $1,500.

P 17-5 Following is the September 30, 19X8 trial balance for ABC Agency.

ABC Agency
POST-CLOSING TRIAL BALANCE

September 30 of Fiscal Year 19X8
(Amounts in thousands of dollars)

Budgetary Accounts:

Other Appropriations Realized	$ 18	
Expired Authority		$ 18
	$ 18	$ 18

Proprietary Accounts:

Fund Balance with Treasury—19X8	$168	
Advances to Others	15	
Inventory for Agency Operations	75	
Equipment	300	
Accumulated Depreciation on Equipment		$135
Disbursements in Transit		30
Accounts Payable		60
Accrued Funded Payroll and Benefits		75
Accrued Unfunded Annual Leave		210
Appropriated Capital—19X8		18
Capital Investments		240
Cumulative Results of Operations	210	
	$768	$768

The agency applies the following accounting policies:

- Commitment accounting is used only for fixed assets, inventories for agency operations, and services.
- Salaries and benefits do not have undelivered orders placed in advance of expending the appropriation for them.
- All disbursements except for salaries, benefits, and advances to others must have accounts payable established first.

Following are transactions during Fiscal Year 19X9. All are in thousands of dollars.

1. The agency received an appropriation warrant from Treasury in the amount of $30,000, notifying it that its appropriation had been enacted in that amount. The enabling legislation specified that $9,000 was for salaries and benefits, $6,000 was for travel, and $15,000 was for fixed assets, materials, and services.

2. OMB apportioned the entire appropriation during the year.

3. The agency head allotted $8,700 for salaries and benefits, $6,000 for travel, and $14,450 for fixed assets, inventory, and supplies.

4. Treasury notified the agency that the checks ordered but not issued in Fiscal Year 19X8 were issued.

5. a. Travel orders in the amount of $5,400 were issued.

   b. Checks for travel advances totaling $3,000 were requested from Treasury.

   c. Travel vouchers in the amount of $5,700 were received, including $5,250 related to $5,325 of the travel for which orders had been issued. Advances of $2,970 were to be applied.

   d. Checks to pay the travel claims were ordered from Treasury.

   e. The advances related to Fiscal Year 19X8 were repaid by employees.

   f. Treasury notified the agency that checks ordered in (b) and (d) were issued.

6. a. The agency head allotted the remaining payroll budget.

   b. Payroll paid during the year, including the agency's share of expenses, amounted to $9,015. Ignore withholding deductions and omit going through the disbursements in transit account. Remember that $75 was included in Year 19X8 Expended Appropriations and is accrued.

7. a. Commitments were placed for $14,450 of fixed assets, inventory, and services.

   b. The agency head allotted an additional $300 for fixed assets, inventory, and services.

   c. Orders were placed for $14,700 of fixed assets, inventory, and services. Of those, $14,250 had previously been committed in the amount of $14,400. Due to failure to follow procedures, the remaining $450 had not been previously committed.

   d. Orders in (c) were received and approved, as follows:

	Estimate	Actual
Equipment	$ 3,000	$ 3,300
Inventory	600	540
Services Used . . .	10,875	10,800
	$14,475	$14,640

   e. Checks for accounts payable of $14,100 were requested from Treasury during the year, including those related to Fiscal Year 19X8. Treasury notified the agency that checks amounting to $13,980 were issued during Fiscal Year 19X9, including those relating to Fiscal Year 19X8 accounts payable.

8. The following year-end information was compiled.

   a. Depreciation on equipment amounted to $45.

   b. Salaries and benefits other than annual leave to be accrued amounted to $60.

   c. According to a report from the Payroll Department, the annual leave liability at fiscal year end was $219.

   d. A physical count of inventory indicated that $164 of inventory had been used.

Requirements (a) Prepare the general journal entries required for ABC Agency for Fiscal Year 19X9.

(b) Post the entries to T-accounts.

(c) Prepare a preclosing trial balance for September 30, 19X9.

(d) Close the accounts.

P 16-6 Using the information from Problem 16-5, prepare the six financial statements illustrated in the chapter for federal agencies:

a. Balance sheet

b. Statement of operations

c. Cash flow statement

d. Statement reconciling expended appropriations with operating/program expenses

e. Report on budget execution

f. Capital statement

ACCOUNTING
FOR HEALTH CARE
ORGANIZATIONS

The scope and complexity of the health care environment have undergone swift and dramatic changes in recent years. Correspondingly, health care financial management and accounting practices have evolved rapidly and significantly to keep abreast of environmental changes such as:

1. Increases in the volume of services to meet demand, followed by excess capacity due to increased emphasis on outpatient care
2. Increases in the range of services offered, based on:
   a. Continuing improvements in health care techniques and equipment
   b. Broadened expectations of hospital clientele
3. Increased diversity in health care delivery mechanisms:
   a. Hospitals
   b. Home health care organizations
   c. Continuing care retirement communities
4. Increases in health care costs:
   a. Increases in the number of personnel and in the level, complexity, and costliness of training
   b. Introduction of new technology
   c. Increases in malpractice insurance costs and malpractice claims and judgments against hospitals and other providers
   d. Inflationary pressures on all cost components
5. Decrease in the percentage of support from local governments and philanthropists for expansion of facilities and for services
6. Increase in the proportion (today, approximately 90%) of charges paid by third-party payers, accompanied by changes in the basis used by some major third-party payers to determine amounts to be paid
7. Increases in alternative payment systems and competitive pressures, such as health maintenance organizations and preferred provider organizations, as well as increased competitive pressures both with other providers and from third-party payers.

Because it is more difficult the 1 in the past to generate cash by operations —and since government grants and gifts from philanthropists for construction have decreased, and for other reasons as well—health care entities have found it necessary to turn to the capital markets for loans for expansion. Audited financial statements are highly desirable, if not mandatory, to support borrowing activities; and auditors have therefore increasingly influenced the reporting practices of health care entities. The AICPA's audit guide, *Audits of Providers of Health Care Services,*[1] is now recognized to constitute, together with applicable GASB and FASB pronouncements, *generally accepted accounting principles for health care providers.* Since the same accounting and reporting principles apply to the various types of health care providers, those principles will be discussed and illustrated in the context of hospitals—the most familiar and most prominent health care provider organization. These principles, with slight variations for unique circumstances and transactions, apply to nursing homes, continuing care retirement communities, home health care agencies, and so on.

Two industry professional associations—the American Hospital Association (AHA) and the Healthcare Financial Management Association (HFMA)—have been dominant forces in the development and improvement of healthcare financial management, accounting, and reporting. Accounting and statistical manuals, data processing services, symposiums and workshops, advisory services, and recognized journals are provided for the industry on a regular basis through these associations.[2] These organizations encourage their members to follow generally accepted accounting principles in reporting and to have annual audits. Additionally, HFMA's Principles and Practices Board issues Statements of Principles and Practices providing guidance on certain health care accounting and financial reporting issues.

Accounting for hospitals is very **similar** to accounting for a specialized industry in **business accounting.** In fact, in the absence of resources whose use is restricted by donors or grantors, the only significant differences between hospital accounting and business accounting are certain revenue recognition practices of hospitals and the absence, in government and nonprofit hospitals, of the distinction between contributed capital and retained earnings. But when donor- or grantor-restricted assets are held, separate funds may be used to account for those resources.

Hospitals may be categorized as governmental, voluntary not-for-profit, and for-profit. The accounting and reporting guidance for all three types is largely the same. However, governmental hospitals are under the primary standards-setting authority of the GASB and other hospitals are under the authority of the FASB. A further complication results from the fact that there is currently no generally accepted basis for distinguishing government hospitals from nongovernment hospitals. Differing guidance has been provided by the two standards boards on such topics as reporting cash flows and measuring pension expense. This chapter illustrates the accounting and reporting for governmental hospitals—but presents the cash flow statement in accordance with both GASB and FASB requirements. To date, the differences in FASB and GASB guidance for hospitals have been limited to specific topical areas such as those mentioned previously.

---

[1] Health Care Committee and Health Care Audit and Accounting Guide Task Force, American Institute of Certified Public Accountants, *Audits of Providers of Health Care Services* (New York: AICPA, 1990). (Including Statements of Position issued by the Auditing Standards Division and the Accounting Standards Division). (Hereafter referred to as the Health Care Audit Guide.)
[2] *Hospitals* is the official journal of the American Hospital Association; *Healthcare Financial Management* is that of the Healthcare Financial Management Association (formerly the Hospital Financial Management Association).

The AICPA Health Care Audit Guide recognizes only two major classes of funds: **general** and **donor restricted.** Assets *restricted* to use for specific purposes *by donors or grantors* must be accounted for in one of the Donor-Restricted Funds. All other assets—including assets whose use is limited by bond indenture, governing board, or other nondonor or nongrantor restrictions—should be accounted for in the General Fund.

General Fund

Four types of resources are accounted for in the General Fund: (1) **"current"** (sometimes called "operating"), (2) **"assets whose use is limited,"** (3) **"plant,"** and (4) assets held in an agency capacity. **Assets whose use is limited** include (a) board-designated resources and (b) resources required to be used for a specific purpose as a result of bond indentures, trust agreements, third-party (Blue Cross, Medicare, Medicaid, and so on) reimbursement agreements, or other similar arrangements. Resources whose use is **restricted by donors** or grantors are **not included** in this category of assets or in the General Fund (except as noted later). The logic for including assets whose use is limited (by other than donor or grantor restrictions) in the General Fund appears to be that the agreements creating the limitations on the use of these resources are entered into at the discretion of the hospital governing board.

The limitations on the use of **board-designated** resources clearly are created at the board's discretion. These are **unrestricted** resources that the board has designated **(not restricted)** to be used for a specific purpose. Board designations might be established, for example, for expansion of the physical plant, to retire debt, or even to serve as an endowment for the hospital. Board designation of assets for specified purposes **does not change** the **unrestricted status** of the assets and does *not* create *separate funds.* In essence, it creates a segregation of the General Fund fund balance similar to appropriations of retained earnings of businesses or designations of fund balances of municipal governmental funds. Nonetheless, from the point of view of the hospital management, the designation creates restrictions as valid as those of donors. Hospital management may use the resources only for those purposes specified by the board. *But,* since the board has the power to remove its designation, the resources are not contractually or legally restricted and should be accounted for in the General Fund.

Unlike board-designated resources, *other* assets whose use is limited by bond indentures, third-party reimbursement arrangements, and so on, *are legally restricted*—just as donor-restricted assets are legally restricted. The AICPA Committee distinction between these assets and donor- or grantor-restricted resources is that the bond agreements and third-party reimbursement agreements were entered into voluntarily at the discretion of the governing board of the hospital. Also, the Committee notes that such transactions are prevalent throughout American industry and are normal, recurring activities related to the general business operations of a hospital. Thus, Donor-Restricted Funds are used *only* to account for *donor- or grantor-restricted* resources.

All fixed assets are recorded in the General Fund unless they are (1) endowment-related or (2) donated fixed assets not yet placed in service. The theory is that the board can use its discretion in deciding how these assets are to be used and that readers of the financial statements should be presented with a total of all assets subject to discretionary use. Likewise, a hospital should account for **all liabilities** that are incurred for the hospital's benefit in the General Fund—unless endowment-related—if the hospital is responsible for their repayment. Thus, the basic accounting equation for a hospital General Fund is:

$$\begin{array}{ccccccc} \text{Current} \\ \text{Assets} \end{array} + \begin{array}{c} \text{Noncurrent} \\ \text{Assets} \end{array} - \begin{array}{c} \text{Current} \\ \text{Liabilities} \end{array} - \begin{array}{c} \text{Long-Term} \\ \text{Liabilities} \end{array} = \begin{array}{c} \text{Fund} \\ \text{Balance} \end{array}$$

This equation varies from the business accounting equation only with respect to the presentation of equity in government or nonprofit hospitals. As noted earlier, hospital accounting differs relatively little from basic business accounting.

Donor-Restricted Funds

The term "restricted" is reserved for resources that are **restricted** as to use by **donors or grantors.** Examples of purposes for which resources may be restricted are (1) specific operating purposes, (2) addition to fixed assets, (3) endowment, (4) loan, (5) annuity, and (6) life income. Many restrictions are temporary and are removed either (1) by meeting a specific condition—as with restrictions for specific purposes—or (2) by passage of time—as with term endowments. "Pure" endowments—in which the endowment principal can never be expended—create permanent restrictions on those net assets.

Specific Purpose Funds

Funds **restricted** by **donors or grantors** to **specific operating purposes** should be accounted for as restricted fund balance in the General Fund or placed in a Specific Purpose Fund until appropriate expenditures are incurred. When the expenditures are incurred and recorded in the General Fund, a corresponding amount of revenues also is recognized in that fund. When a Specific Purpose Fund is used—as is assumed in this chapter—restricted resources should be transferred to the General Fund as *"other revenues"* to offset the expenditures incurred—which are also recorded as assets or expenses, as appropriate, in the General Fund. Exactly when an expenditure satisfies the terms set by the donor (and agreed to by the hospital board) is a matter for careful interpretation.

Plant Replacement and Expansion Funds

Financial resources and other investments that are given to the hospital by **donors or grantors** to be used only **for additions to fixed assets** increase the hospital's permanent capital and should be credited to fund balance in a Plant Replacement and Expansion Fund. When expenditures that satisfy the donor's terms are made, the **fixed assets acquired** and the related **fund balance** amount should be recorded in the General Fund by debiting the asset account and crediting the Fund Balance. At the same time, both the assets and the fund balance of the Plant Replacement and Expansion Fund are reduced. Likewise, fixed assets donated to a hospital are recorded in the Plant Replacement and Expansion Fund until they are placed into service. When placed into service, they also are recorded in the General Fund along with the related fund balance amount and are removed from the Plant Replacement and Expansion Fund.

Endowment Funds

Endowment Funds, including income therefrom, should be accounted for in accordance with the terms of the donor. Income may be unrestricted, in which case it goes to the General Fund—typically as "nonoperating gains." The principal of "pure" endowments must be maintained in perpetuity. The principal of term endowments may become available to the board for either unrestricted or restricted use when the term expires. The financial statements should disclose the essential terms of the endowment—length; uses of resources; restrictions, if any, on the use of income; and the like.

INCOME DETERMINATION AND ASSET VALUATION FEATURES

Although hospital accounting may be fund-based, the **excess of revenues over expenses** of the **hospital as a whole** is calculated and reported. As noted earlier, this does not mean that all hospitals are profit-seeking organizations. Rather, it reflects the predominant view that (1) hospitals are "going concerns," even if nonprofit or "not-for-profit," and (2) revenues and gains must cover all **expenses** and losses if the hospital's capital is to be maintained. Generally accepted accounting principles applicable to hospitals are a blend of the principles of financial accounting for businesses and of fund accounting. Some hospital transactions are more like those of nonprofit organizations than those of business enterprises, and hospital accounting involves several unique income determination and asset valuation features. Many of these are highlighted in Figure 17-1 which summarizes hospital revenue recognition and fund structure.

Distinguishing Revenues and Expenses from Gains and Losses

According to FASB Concepts Statement No. 6, *Elements of Financial Statements,* revenues and expenses arise from an entity's ongoing, major, or central operations. The Health Care Audit Guide applies this definition—and the related Concepts Statement No. 6 definition of gains and losses—to health care entities. Hence, the audit guide states that revenues and expenses arise from "activities associated with the provision of health care services"—which constitute "the ongoing, major, or central operations of providers of health care services."[3] Further, the guide states:

> Gains and losses . . . result from a provider's peripheral or incidental transactions and from other events stemming from the environment that may be largely beyond the control of the provider and its management.[4]

As opposed to revenues and expenses, gains and losses occur casually or incidentally in relation to the provider's ongoing activities. The classification of items as revenue or gain and expense or loss therefore depends on the individual health care provider. The same transaction may result in reporting revenues for one health care provider and gains for another.

Gains and losses can be further classified as either *operating* or *nonoperating* depending on their relation to a provider's major ongoing or central operations. Many gains and losses are classified as nonoperating because of their peripheral or incidental nature. However, a gain or loss closely related to a provider's ongoing operations may be classified as operating.

Several observations should be made relative to the guidance provided by the guide:

1. The distinction between revenues and expenses and gains and losses depends upon the activities deemed to be part of the ongoing, major, or central operations of the hospital.

---

[3] Health Care Audit Guide, para. 12.2.

[4] Ibid.

Figure 17-1

HOSPITAL REVENUE AND GAIN RECOGNITION

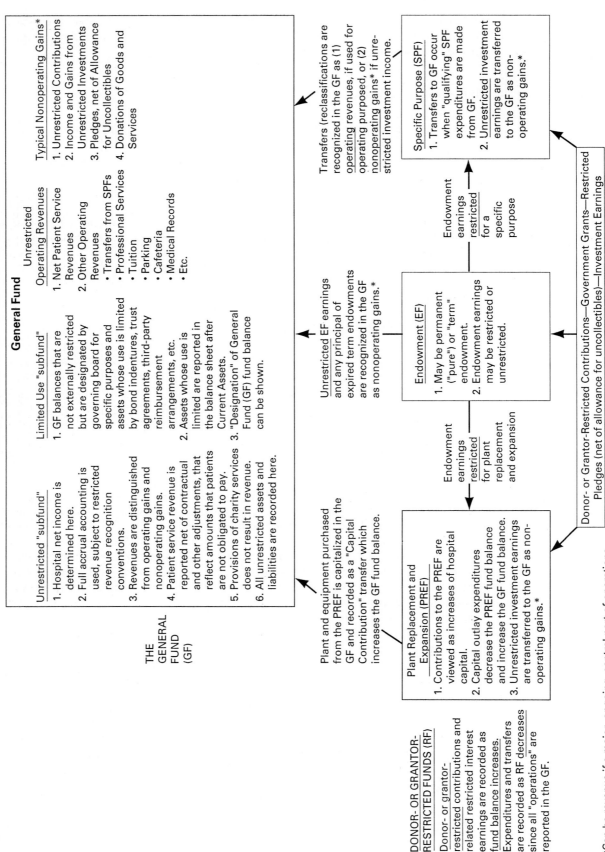

General Fund

THE GENERAL FUND (GF)

Unrestricted "subfund"

1. Hospital net income is determined here.
2. Full accrual accounting is used, subject to restricted revenue recognition conventions.
3. Revenues are distinguished from operating gains and nonoperating gains.
4. Patient service revenue is reported net of contractual and other adjustments, that reflect amounts that patients are not obligated to pay.
5. Provisions of charity services does not result in revenue.
6. All unrestricted assets and liabilities are recorded here.

Limited Use "subfund"

1. GF balances that are not externally restricted but are designated by governing board for specific purposes and assets whose use is limited by bond indentures, trust agreements, third-party reimbursement arrangements, etc.
2. Assets whose use is limited are reported in the balance sheet after Current Assets.
3. "Designation" of General Fund (GF) fund balance can be shown.

Unrestricted Operating Revenues

1. Net Patient Service Revenues
2. Other Operating Revenues
   - Transfers from SPFs
   - Professional Services
   - Tuition
   - Parking
   - Cafeteria
   - Medical Records
   - Etc.

Typical Nonoperating Gains*

1. Unrestricted Contributions
2. Income and Gains from Unrestricted Investments
3. Pledges, net of Allowance for Uncollectibles
4. Donations of Goods and Services

Transfers (reclassifications are recognized in the GF as (1) operating revenues, if used for operating purposed, or (2) nonoperating gains* if unrestricted investment income.

Specific Purpose (SPF)

1. Transfers to GF occur when "qualifying" SPF expenditures are made from GF.
2. Unrestricted investment earnings are transferred to the GF as nonoperating gains.*

Endowment earnings restricted for a specific purpose

Unrestricted EF earnings and any principal of expired term endowments are recognized in the GF as nonoperating gains.*

Endowment (EF)

1. May be permanent ("pure") or "term" endowment.
2. Endowment earnings may be restricted or unrestricted.

Endowment earnings restricted for plant replacement and expansion

Plant and equipment purchased from the PREF is capitalized in the GF and recorded as a "Capital Contribution" transfer which increases the GF fund balance.

Plant Replacement and Expansion (PREF)

1. Contributions to the PREF are viewed as increases of hospital capital.
2. Capital outlay expenditures decrease the PREF fund balance and increase the GF fund balance.
3. Unrestricted investment earnings are transferred to the GF as nonoperating gains.*

DONOR- OR GRANTOR-RESTRICTED FUNDS (RF)

Donor- or grantor-restricted contributions and related restricted interest earnings are recorded as fund balance increases. Expenditures and transfers are recorded as RF decreases since all "operations" are reported in the GF.

Donor- or Grantor-Restricted Contributions—Government Grants—Restricted Pledges (net of allowance for uncollectibles)—Investment Earnings

*Can be revenue if a major, ongoing, central part of operations.

2. The distinction between operating and nonoperating items is essentially the same as that for revenue/expense versus gain/loss.

3. Hence, all revenues and expenses are operating items—they are not classified as operating versus nonoperating.

4. Similarly, virtually all gains and losses are nonoperating. The possible exception appears to be gains or losses that result "from other events stemming from the environment that may be largely beyond the control of the provider and its management,"[5] but which are closely related to its major ongoing operations. The guide gives little guidance as to what specific types of transactions are contemplated as "operating gains or losses." This classification is apt to be rare.

5. Certain transactions such as contributions may be revenue or expense for some hospitals but gain or loss for others. For example, donors' contributions are revenues for hospitals for which fund raising is a major, ongoing activity through which resources are raised to finance the basic functions of the hospital. Hospitals that receive only occasional contributions and have no ongoing, active fund-raising function would report donations as gains.

Classes of Revenues

Hospital revenues are classified broadly into two major categories:

1. ***Patient Service Revenues*** are earned in the several revenue-producing centers through rendering inpatient and outpatient services. Patient service revenues include revenues generated from (1) daily patient services such as room, board, and general nursing services; (2) other nursing services such as operating room, recovery room, and labor and delivery room nursing services; and (3) other professional services such as laboratories, radiology, anesthesiology, and physical therapy.

2. ***Other Revenues*** are those revenues that are derived from ongoing activities ***other than*** patient care and service. Major sources are (1) student tuition and fees derived from schools that a hospital operates; (2) revenues recognized when donor- or grantor-restricted resources are used for the specified operating purposes—such as research or education—that fulfill the donor or grantor restrictions; (3) revenues from gifts, grants, or endowment income restricted by donors to finance charity care, and (4) miscellaneous sources such as rentals of hospital plant, sales of scrap, cafeteria sales, sales of supplies to physicians and employees, and fees charged for copies of documents.

Patient service is the major source of revenues for most hospitals. Only the amount of patient service revenues that someone has a responsibility to pay are reported in the hospital statement of revenues and expenses. Patient service revenues are reported net of charity services, contractual adjustments arising from third-party payer agreements or regulations, policy discounts extended to patients who are members of the medical profession, clergy or others, administrative adjustments, and any similar amounts that neither patients nor third-party

---

[5] Ibid.

payers are deemed obligated to pay. **Revenues are not reduced for estimated uncollectible accounts.**

Typical types of deductions from revenues include (1) *charity services* for patients who do not pay the established rates because they are indigent, (2) *policy discounts* for members of groups (doctors, clergymen, employees, or employees' dependents) who receive allowances in accordance with hospital policy, and (3) *contractual adjustments* for patients' bills that are paid to the hospital by third-party payers at lower than established rates in accordance with contracts between the hospital and third-party payers. A hospital must have established criteria to distinguish charity services from bad debts. Only services rendered under circumstances that meet the pre-established criteria for charity services should be treated as charity services. Other uncollectible amounts are reported as bad debt expense. The distinction is significant both in terms of financial reporting and funding under certain federal and state programs.

When third-party payers (usually Medicare, Medicaid, and Blue Cross) contract with hospitals to pay patients' bills, agreed reimbursement rates are likely to be based on cost or some national or regional "average charge" for similar hospital services. Established (standard) hospital rates are not necessarily based on cost; indeed, they are not likely to represent cost. Hence, whereas gross revenues for services rendered to Medicare and other third-party payer patients are initially recorded at standard established rates, a contractual allowance is needed to reduce gross revenues to amounts actually receivable. This internal accounting approach provides information useful for management analyses of revenue patterns and certain note disclosures—for example, the amount of charity services rendered.

To illustrate, assume that a hospital's standard gross charges for services rendered in a year total $1,000,000, but the amount it ultimately expects to collect is only $850,000. The hospital rendered $40,000 of charity services and had estimated contractual adjustments of $60,000 and estimated bad debts of $50,000. The required entries are:

General Fund

Accounts and Notes Receivable.	1,000,000	
Patient Service Charges		1,000,000

To record gross billings for services at established rates.

Contractual Adjustments	60,000	
Charity Services	40,000	
Allowance for Uncollectible Receivables and Third-Party		
Contractuals		60,000
Accounts and Notes Receivable		40,000

To record deductions from gross revenues, and the related allowance.

Expenses—Provision for Bad Debts	50,000	
Allowance for Uncollectible Receivables and Third-Party		
Contractuals		50,000

To record estimated bad debts.

Note that when specific receivables are identified as not being collectible, the receivables should be written off against the allowance. The **appropriate reporting** of this information is:

Balance Sheet—General Fund

Accounts and Notes Receivable	$960,000	
less: Allowance for Uncollectible Receivables and Third-Party		
Contractuals	110,000	$850,000

Statement of Revenues and Expenses

Net Patient Service Revenues $900,000
    ($1,000,000 − $40,000 − $60,000)

Bad Debt Expense. . . . . $ 50,000

Gains

As noted earlier, gains arise from (1) activities that are not part of a hospital's major, ongoing, or central operations or (2) events resulting from the environment and largely beyond the control of management. Too, whereas revenues are reported prior to deducting related costs, gains often will be reported net of such costs, for example, gains on sales of investments in securities or fixed assets. Typical gains of hospitals result from

> Sales of investments in securities
>
> Sale of fixed assets
>
> Gifts or donations (which are revenue for some hospitals)
>
> Investment income (which is revenue for some hospitals)

Whether items such as contributions and investment income are revenues or gains depends upon the definition of the mission of individual hospitals. The treatment is determined by whether fund-raising (for contributions) or investment income are intended to be major ongoing sources of financing for the hospital. If so, the related amounts are revenue; otherwise they are gains.

Donations

Hospitals receive several kinds of donations. **Unrestricted** gifts, grants, and bequests are typically recorded as nonoperating gains of the General Fund. Hospitals also may receive donations in the form of *professional services.* For example, retired physicians or pharmacists may voluntarily work part time in their professional capacities. Or priests and nuns who are physicians, pharmacists, or nurses, may work full time for no pay. For the fair market value of such services to be recorded as other revenues or as gains, they must be significant services that would be performed by salaried personnel if not for the volunteers, there must be an employer-employee relationship, and the value of the services must be objectively determinable. (See transaction 19 on page 656.) Gifts of *supplies and commodities* are recorded as other revenues or as gains.

Resources that donors require to be used for a specific operating purpose are ordinarily recorded as temporarily restricted net assets (fund balance) in the General Fund or as additions to fund balance in a Specific Purpose Fund, as assumed here. When the terms of the gift (or grant) have been satisfied by appropriate expenditures, the operating revenues should be recognized in the General Fund. Donations or grants made to the hospital for the *care of charity patients* should be reported as revenues as well.

When a donor specifies that resources are to be used for the *acquisition of fixed assets,* such gifts increase the permanent capital, and the resources are recorded as an increase in the fund balance of the Plant Replacement and Expansion Fund. Upon appropriate expenditure of the resources, a transfer of fund balances from the Plant Replacement and Expansion Fund to the General Fund is reported. If the donation consists of fixed assets, they are recorded directly in the General Fund with a credit to **Fund Balance** unless the assets are not placed in service immediately. Donated fixed assets not placed in service immediately are initially recorded in the Plant Replacement and Expansion Fund. They are transferred to the General Fund—increasing General Fund fund balance when placed in service. The rationale for not recognizing revenue or gain is that a restricted "capital" gift has been made. A more practical reason might be to avoid the distortion of reported revenues and gains that would result from reporting the gift of a major asset as revenues or gains.

Timing of Revenue and Gain Recognition

As we have seen, a significant feature of hospital accounting is that revenue or gain is recognized in the period in which the related assets become available for **unrestricted** use by the governing board **or** are **expended** for the donor-specified restricted purposes. Unrestricted revenues and gains are recognized on the accrual basis. Assets restricted to expenditure for specified purposes, such as research grants, are considered realized in the period of expenditure.

Two reasons underlie the delay of recognition of revenue or gain for donor-restricted assets. First, it permits recognition of revenues or gains in the same period that the related expenses are incurred. Second, it can be said that externally restricted resources are not truly "earned" until they are used for their designated purpose.

Expense Classification

The measurement and recognition criteria for expenses and losses are generally identical to those for business entities. A key exception is that the pension expense measurement for government hospitals differs since government entities cannot apply SFAS 87, "Employers' Accounting for Pensions." Hospital expenses are typically classified by such major functions as:

1. Nursing services
2. Other professional services
3. General services
4. Fiscal services
5. Administrative services
6. Other services

Each of these major expense classifications may be subclassified further according to organizational unit and object classification, thus creating a multiple classification scheme not unlike the multiple classification of expenditures used in state and local government accounting.

Nursing services expenses includes the nursing services provided in the various patient care facilities of a hospital—for example, medical and surgical, pediatrics, intensive care, operating rooms—as well as nursing administrative, educational, and various other related costs. *Other professional services expenses* is used to classify expenses incurred in providing other medical care to patients—such as laboratories, blood bank, radiology, pharmacy, anesthesiology, and social service—as well as expenses incurred for research, education, and administration in these areas. Care of the physical plant, dietary services, and other nonmedical services that are part of the ongoing physical operations of a hospital are classified as *general services expenses.* Expenses incurred for accounting, admitting, data processing, storerooms, and similar activities are grouped as *fiscal services expenses;* and expenses incurred by the executive office, personnel, purchasing, public relations, and the like are classified as *administrative services expenses.* Depreciation, bad debts, employee benefits, interest, taxes, insurance, and similar costs may be reported under the above functional classifications or may be reported as separate line items in a hospital Statement of Revenues and Expenses.

Property, Plant, and Equipment

Hospital fixed assets should be recorded at historical cost in the General Fund and depreciated. If appropriate records have not been maintained, the assets should be inventoried, appraised on the basis of historical cost, and recorded. The basis of fixed asset valuation should be disclosed, of course, as should the depreciation policy.

Assets used by the hospital may be owned outright, leased from or made available by independent or related organizations, or provided by a governmental agency or hospital district. The nature of such relationships must be disclosed in the financial statements, and they should be accounted for and reported in conformity with GAAP. Specifically, the provisions of FASB *Statement No. 13*, "Accounting for Leases," as amended, should be followed in accounting for leases.

Marketable Equity Securities

The Health Care Audit Guide applies FASB *Statement No. 12*, "Accounting for Certain Marketable Securities," to all profit-seeking hospitals. Additionally, the audit guide specifies how that statement is to be applied in hospital accounting and reporting.

Statement No. 12 provides for a distinction between short-term and long-term investments in marketable equity securities. In general, hospitals hold long-term securities for income and appreciation.

To apply FASB Statement No 12, a hospital must classify the marketable equity security investments of its General Fund into separate current and noncurrent portfolios. In addition, a hospital must group the marketable equity securities included in the various restricted funds into separate portfolios according to types of funds. Additionally, the audit guide requires that marketable debt securities be reported at amortized cost if they are intended to be held until maturity and at lower of cost or market if not.

Pooling of Investments

There are substantial advantages, in terms of total investment return, to placing all the investments of all hospital funds in a single pool. Where hospitals have several funds with investments, and where investments and disinvestment transactions occur frequently, it is essential that the accounting for the pool be on a *market value* basis. The pool and its operation and accounting closely resemble a mutual fund (open-end investment trust), which should record all transactions on a market value basis. This position does **not** alter the application of GAAP to marketable securities in the accounts of the several funds and in the financial statements.

ILLUSTRATIVE TRANSACTIONS AND ENTRIES

Accounting for the varied, complex, and voluminous transactions of a hospital requires many subsidiary ledgers and other similar records. In this illustrative case we deal only with the general ledger accounts.

The case example presented here relates to Alzona Hospital, a medium size, government-owned, general short-term health care facility financed from patient services fees, donations, and investment earnings. The Balance Sheet of Alzona Hospital at October 1, 19A, the beginning of the fiscal year to which the example relates, is presented as Figure 17-2.

Figure 17-2

BEGINNING BALANCE SHEET

Alzona Hospital
Balance Sheet
October 1, 19A

General Fund

Assets

Current:		
Cash		$ 175,000
Accounts and notes receivable	$ 700,000	
Less: Estimated uncollectibles and allowances	85,000	615,000
Due from Specific Purpose Fund		145,000
Inventories		165,000
Total current assets		1,100,000
Noncurrent:		
Investments		100,000
Property, plant, and equipment:		
Land	130,000	
Land improvements	80,000	
Buildings	5,000,000	
Fixed equipment	600,000	
Major movable equipment	90,000	
Total property, plant, and equipment	5,900,000	
Less: Accumulated depreciation	2,450,000	
Net property, plant, and equipment		3,450,000
Total Assets		$4,650,000

Liabilities and Fund Balances

Current Liabilities:		
Notes payable		$ 150,000
Accounts payable		175,000
Total current liabilities		325,000
Long-term debt:		
Mortgage payable		100,000
Total		425,000
Fund balance		4,225,000
Total Liabilities and Fund Balance		$4,650,000

Donor-Restricted Funds*

Specific Purpose Fund:

Cash	$ 20,000
Investments	360,000
Due from Endowment Fund	20,000
Total	$ 400,000

Specific Purpose Fund:

Due to General Fund	$ 145,000
Fund balance	255,000
Total	$ 400,000

Endowment Fund:

Cash	$ 25,000
Investments	475,000
Total	$ 500,000

Endowment Fund:

Due to Specific Purpose Fund	$ 20,000
Fund balance	480,000
Total	$ 500,000

Plant Replacement and Expansion Fund:

Cash	$ 25,000
Investments	300,000
Total	$ 325,000

Plant Replacement and Expansion Fund:

Fund balance	$ 325,000
Total	$ 325,000

* Note that each Donor-Restricted Fund may have resources restricted for various purposes. Thus, the components of fund balance—by purpose—should be presented for each Donor-Restricted Fund either on the face of the Balance Sheet or in the notes, as assumed here.

Summary of Transactions and Events

General Fund:

1. Gross charges to patients at standard established rates were $4,400,000.

(1) Accounts and Notes Receivable. 4,400,000
      Patient Service Charges   4,400,000
    To record gross billings for services at established
    rates.

2. $85,000 of receivables were written off against the prior year allowance balance—$70,000 for uncollectible accounts and $15,000 for contractual adjustments.

(2) **Allowance for Uncollectible Receivables and**
      Third-Party Contractuals 85,000
      Accounts and Notes Receivable.   85,000
    To record write-off of receivables.

3. The hospital wrote off $265,000 of receivables established in 19B (entry 1) due to contractual adjustments.

(3) Contractual Adjustments 265,000
      Accounts and Notes Receivable.   265,000
    To record contractual adjustments.

4. The hospital determined that $125,000 of the services it provided were to patients who met the hospital criteria for charity services.

(4) Charity Services 125,000
      Accounts and Notes Receivable.   125,000
    To record charity services.

Recall that charity services do not result in patient service revenues—gross or net—under the audit guide since there is no expectation of payment. If a hospital discloses the composition of its net patient service revenues in its notes, charity services are not part of that disclosure. Disclosure of the level of charity service is required—but may be in terms of revenue, cost, units, or other statistics.

5. Collections of accounts receivable totaled $3,800,000.

(5) Cash 3,800,000
      Accounts and Notes Receivable.   3,800,000
    To record collections of accounts receivable.

6. Additional accounts receivable written off as uncollectible during the year totaled $55,000.

(6) Allowance for Uncollectible Receivables and Third-Party
      Contractuals 55,000
      Accounts and Notes Receivable   55,000
    To record write-off of accounts deemed uncollectible.

General Fund (continued)

7. The estimated bad debts for the year totaled $120,000. Also, additional contractual adjustments related to 19B of $25,000 are expected to result from final settlements with third-party payers of their clients' accounts.

(7)	**Expenses—Bad Debts**.	120,000	
	Contractual Adjustments.	25,000	
	Allowance for Uncollectible Receivables and Third-Party Contractuals		145,000

To adjust bad debt expense, deductions from gross revenues, and the allowance accounts to appropriate year-end balances.

8. Materials and supplies, including food, purchased on account during the year totaled $600,000. A perpetual inventory system is in use.

(8)	Inventories.	600,000	
	Accounts Payable		600,000

To record inventory purchases on account.

9. Materials and supplies were used by major functions as follows:

Nursing services	$170,000
Other professional services.	50,000
General services	319,000
Fiscal services.	8,000
Administrative services	3,000
	$550,000

(9)	**Expenses—Nursing Services**	170,000	
	Expenses—Other Professional Services	50,000	
	Expenses—General Services	319,000	
	Expenses—Fiscal Services.	8,000	
	Expenses—Administrative Services	3,000	
	Inventories.		550,000

To record inventory usage.

10. Accounts payable paid during the year were $725,000.

(10)	Accounts Payable.	725,000	
	Cash		725,000

To record payment of accounts payable.

11. Salaries and wages paid during the year were for the following:

Nursing services	$1,316,000
Other professional services	828,000
General services	389,000
Fiscal services	102,000
Administrative services	65,000
	$2,700,000

(11)	Expenses—Nursing Services	1,316,000	
	Expenses—Other Professional Services	828,000	
	Expenses—General Services	389,000	
	Expenses—Fiscal Services	102,000	
	Expenses—Administrative Services	65,000	
	Cash		2,700,000

To record salaries and wages paid.

General Fund (continued)

12. Expenses, other than for salaries and materials and supplies, paid during the year were chargeable as follows:

Nursing services	$ 86,000
Other professional services	79,000
General services	221,000
Fiscal services	44,000
Administrative services	327,000
	$757,000

(12) Expenses—Nursing Services	86,000	
Expenses—Other Professional Services	79,000	
Expenses—General Services	221,000	
Expenses—Fiscal Services	44,000	
Expenses—Administrative Services	327,000	
Cash		757,000

To record expense payments.

13. Salaries and wages accrued at year end were for the following:

Nursing services	$35,000
Other professional services	21,000
General services	19,000
Fiscal services	6,000
Administrative services	2,000
	$83,000

(13) Expenses—Nursing Services	35,000	
Expenses—Other Professional Services	21,000	
Expenses—General Services	19,000	
Expenses—Fiscal Services	6,000	
Expenses—Administrative Services	2,000	
Accrued Salaries and Wages Payable		83,000

To record accrued expenses at year end.

14. Interest expense on notes payable was $8,000, of which $1,000 was accrued at year end; the principal was reduced by $20,000.

(14) Notes Payable	20,000	
Expenses—Interest	8,000	
Accrued Interest Payable		1,000
Cash		27,000

To record interest payment and accrual, and reduction of principal of notes payable.

15. Interest earned during the year on General Fund investments was $5,000, of which $2,000 was accrued at year end.

(15) Cash.	3,000	
Accrued Interest Receivable	2,000	
Nonoperating Gains—General Fund Investment Income		5,000

To record interest earned on General Fund investments.

16. **Unrestricted** earnings on Specific Purpose Fund investments, $24,000, were received and accounted for directly in the General Fund.

General Fund (continued)

(16)	Cash	24,000	
	Nonoperating Gains—Unrestricted Investment Income from Specific Purpose Fund		24,000

To record unrestricted interest earnings on Specific
Purpose Fund investments deposited directly in the
General Fund.

17. Money collected as an agent for special nurses for private duty services rendered by them amounted to $48,000.

(17)	Cash	48,000	
	Due to Special Duty Nurses		48,000

To record fees collected as agent for special nurses.

18. Of the total collected for special nurses, $45,000 was paid to them; the balance has not yet been claimed.

(18)	Due to Special Duty Nurses	45,000	
	Cash		45,000

To record payment of fees collected in an agency
capacity to special nurses.

19. Professional services donated to the hospital were objectively valued and charged as follows:

Nursing services	$17,000
Other professional services	3,000
	$20,000

(19)	Expenses—Nursing Services	17,000	
	Expenses—Other Professional Services	3,000	
	Nonoperating Gain—Donated Services		20,000

To record the value of donated services received.

20. Other revenues collected during the year were from the following:

Cafeteria sales.	$45,000
Television rentals	30,000
Medical record transcript fees.	15,000
Vending machine commissions	5,000
	$95,000

(20)	Cash	95,000	
	Revenues—Cafeteria Sales		45,000
	Revenues—Television Rentals		30,000
	Revenues—Medical Record Transcript Fees		15,000
	Revenues—Vending Machine Commissions		5,000

To record receipt of miscellaneous revenues.

21. General contributions received in cash, $100,000.

(21)	Cash	100,000	
	Nonoperating Gains—General Contributions		100,000

To record receipt of unrestricted contributions.

General Fund (continued)

22. Bonds were issued at par, $3,000,000, to be used to pay for a new building wing and to retire the mortgage payable.

(22)	**Cash—Construction**	2,900,000	
	Cash—Debt Service	100,000	
	Bonds Payable.		3,000,000

To record sale of bonds at par.

23. The mortgage notes (Figure 17-2) were paid and the contractor billed Alzona $2,500,000 for work completed on the new wing to date. All but a 5% retained percentage was paid.

(23)	Construction in Process	2,500,000	
	Mortgage Payable	100,000	
	Contracts Payable—Retained Percentage—		
	Construction		125,000
	Cash—Construction		2,375,000
	Cash—Debt Service		100,000

To record payment of mortgage payable and the progress billings on the building, less percentage of contract retained pending final inspection of new wing.

24. Equipment costing $100,000, on which there was accumulated depreciation of $60,000, was sold for $30,000.

(24)	Cash.	30,000	
	Accumulated Depreciation	60,000	
	Nonoperating Losses—Disposal of Fixed Assets.	10,000	
	Fixed Equipment		100,000

To record the sale of fixed equipment at a loss.

25. The board of directors designated $100,000 for future plant replacement and expansion. Although this action is binding on hospital management, it does not remove resources from the General Fund.

(25)	(a)	**Investments—Designated for Plant**		
		Replacement	100,000	
		Investments.		100,000

To reclassify investments per Board designation.

(25)	(b)	**Fund Balance**	100,000	
		Fund Balance Designated for Plant		
		Replacement and Expansion		100,000

To record the board's designation for plant replacement and expansion.

26. The charges to General Services Expenses were found to include $5,000 for major movable equipment. (No depreciation need be recorded for the current year.)

(26)	Major Movable Equipment	5,000	
	Expenses—General Services		5,000

To capitalize equipment previously charged to expense.

General Fund (continued)

27. Depreciation expense for the year was $300,000.

(27)	Expenses—Depreciation	300,000	
	Accumulated Depreciation		300,000
	To record depreciation expense.		

28. Accrued interest on bonds payable at year end (see transaction 22) was $30,000.

(28)	Expenses—Interest	30,000	
	Accrued Interest Payable		30,000
	To record interest accrued at year end on bonds outstanding.		

Specific Purpose Fund (Transactions and entries 29 to 32 affect only the Specific Purpose Fund.)

29. A $400,000 grant to defray specific operating costs was received.

(29)	Cash	400,000	
	Fund Balance		400,000
	To record receipt of a grant to be used to pay certain operating costs.		

Note that different gifts or grants may be required to be used for different operating purposes. Thus, several fund balance accounts must be maintained for the Specific Purpose Fund. We assume that the detail in this example is maintained in a fund balance subsidiary ledger—which is not illustrated in the example—rather than in separate general ledger fund balance accounts. The latter approach is illustrated in the college and university Restricted Current Funds example in Chapter 18.

30. Investments made during the period were $300,000.

(30)	Investments	300,000	
	Cash		300,000
	To record investments during the period.		

31. Investments maturing during the period, $150,000, had been originally purchased at par.

(31)	Cash......................................	150,000	
	Investments		150,000
	To record the maturity of investments originally purchased at par.		

32. Earnings on investments, **restricted to specific purposes,** were $15,000. (Compare this transaction with transaction 16.)

(32)	Cash	15,000	
	Fund Balance		15,000
	To record receipt of investment income that is restricted to specific purposes.		

Endowment Fund (Transactions and entries 33 to 36 affect only the Endowment Fund)

33. A benefactor gave rental properties valued at $300,000, and subject to a $100,000 mortgage, to the hospital. The corpus is to be maintained intact; earnings may be used for general operating purposes.

Endowment Fund (continued)

(33)	Rental Properties	300,000	
	Mortgage Payable		100,000
	Fund Balance		200,000

To record a gift of properties, subject to mortgage
assumed. The corpus is to be maintained intact;
earnings are not restricted as to use.

34. Rentals received in cash were $45,000.

| (34) | Cash | 45,000 | |
| | Rental Revenues | | 45,000 |

To record receipt of rentals.

35. Depreciation of rental property was $6,000.

| (35) | Expenses—Depreciation | 6,000 | |
| | Accumulated Depreciation | | 6,000 |

To record depreciation.

36. Other expenses related to rental property, paid in cash, were $9,000.

| (36) | Expenses—Other | 9,000 | |
| | Cash | | 9,000 |

To record payment of rental expenses.

Plant Replacement and Expansion Fund (Transaction and entry 37 affects only the Plant Replacement and Expansion Fund.)

37. Earnings on Plant Replacement and Expansion Fund investments, $16,000, are **restricted** to plant expansion.

| (37) | Cash | 16,000 | |
| | **Fund Balance** | | 16,000 |

To record earnings on plant fund investments; these
earnings are restricted to use for plant expansion.

Interfund (The remaining transactions and entries impact more than one fund, as indicated.)

38. Specific Purpose Fund investments costing $165,000 were sold for $170,000; proceeds from gains on these investments are available for unrestricted use.

Specific Purpose Fund:

(38)	Cash	170,000	
	Investments		165,000
	Due to General Fund		5,000

To record sale of investments at a gain and the
resulting liability to the General Fund.

General Fund:

| (38) | Due from Specific Purpose Fund | 5,000 | |
| | **Nonoperating Gains—Unrestricted Income from Specific Purpose Fund** | | 5,000 |

To record gain on sale of Specific Purpose Fund
investments and a receivable therefor.

(Had the proceeds of the sale in excess of cost not been available for unrestricted use, the $5,000 would have been credited to Specific Purpose Fund Fund Balance; no entry would have been made in the General Fund and no gain would have been recognized at this time.)

Interfund (continued)

39. Cash was "transferred" as necessary to settle the beginning of year interfund receivables and payables.

General Fund:

(39)	Cash	145,000	
	Due from Specific Purpose Fund		145,000

To record settlement of beginning interfund balances.

Specific Purpose Fund:

(39)	Due to General Fund	145,000	
	Due from Endowment Fund		20,000
	Cash		125,000

To record settlement of beginning interfund balances.

Endowment Fund:

(39)	Due to Specific Purpose Fund	20,000	
	Cash		20,000

To record settlement of beginning interfund balances

40. A $300,000 transfer from the Specific Purpose Fund was authorized to reimburse the General Fund for specified expenses incurred; $200,000 of this amount was paid by the Specific Purpose Fund.

General Fund:

(40)	Cash	200,000	
	Due from Specific Purpose Fund	100,000	
	Revenues—Transfers from Specific Purpose Fund		300,000

To record revenue transfer.

Specific Purpose Fund:

(40)	**Fund Balance**	300,000	
	Due to General Fund		100,000
	Cash		200,000

To record transfer to General Fund.

41. Endowment rental property earnings were established as a liability to the General Fund.

Endowment Fund:

(41)	Rental Revenues	45,000	
	Expenses—Depreciation		6,000
	Expenses—Other		9,000
	Due to General Fund		30,000

To close operating accounts and record liability to General Fund for earnings.

General Fund:

(41)	Due from Endowment Fund	30,000	
	Nonoperating Gains—Unrestricted Income from Endowment Fund		30,000

To record net rental income due from Endowment Fund.

42. Major movable equipment was purchased for $18,000 from the General Fund, which was reimbursed by the Plant Replacement and Expansion Fund.

General Fund:

(42)	(a)	Major Movable Equipment	18,000	
		Cash		18,000

To record purchase of equipment.

Interfund (continued)

(42) (b) Cash.. 18,000
                  Fund Balance   18,000
                  To record reimbursement for purchase of
                  equipment.

Plant Replacement and Expansion Fund:

(42) **Fund Balance**............................. 18,000
        Cash   18,000
        To record reimbursement of the General Fund for
        purchase of equipment.

43.   Restricted earnings received on Endowment Fund investments, $25,000, were recorded as a liability to the Specific Purpose Fund.

Endowment Fund:

(43) Cash 25,000
        Due to Specific Purpose Fund   25,000
        To record restricted earnings due to the Specific
        Purpose Fund.

Specific Purpose Fund:

(43) Due from Endowment Fund................... 25,000
        Fund Balance   25,000
        To record restricted purpose earnings due from the
        Endowment Fund.

Closing:

44.   Closing entries were made at your end:

General Fund:

(44) (a) Patient Service Charges................... 4,400,000
          Revenues—Cafeteria Sales................. 45,000
          Revenues—Television Rentals 30,000
          Revenues—Medical Record Transcript Fees..... 15,000
          Revenues—Vending Machine Commissions 5,000
          Revenues—Transfers from Specific Purpose Fund. 300,000
          Nonoperating Gain—Unrestricted Income from
             Endowment Fund 30,000
          Nonoperating Gains—General Fund Investment
             Income 5,000
           Nonoperating Gains—Unrestricted Investment
             Income from Specific Purpose Fund 29,000
          Nonoperating Gains—Donated Services........ 20,000
          Nonoperating Gains—General Contributions 100,000
          Excess of Expenses and Losses over Revenues
             and Gains........................... 9,000
             Expenses—Bad Debts   120,000
             Contractual Adjustments   290,000
             Charity Services.......................   125,000
             Expenses—Nursing Services   1,624,000
             Expenses—Other Professional Services......   981,000
             Expenses—General Services   943,000
             Expenses—Fiscal Services...............   160,000
             Expenses—Administrative Services.........   397,000
             Expenses—Interest....................   38,000
             Expenses—Depreciation   300,000
             Nonoperating Losses—Disposal of Fixed
              Assets   10,000
          To close accounts at year end.

Closing (continued)

(44) (b) Fund Balance   9,000
            Excess of Expenses and Losses over Revenues
                and Gains   9,000
         To close the net loss to Fund Balance.

Revenues and expenses of the other funds have been closed in preceding entries or carried directly to fund balance. Thus no closing entries are required for the Specific Purpose, Endowment, or Plant Replacement and Expansion Funds.

FINANCIAL STATEMENTS

The financial statements that a hospital should prepare for external use include a Balance Sheet, a Statement of Revenues and Expenses, a Statement of Changes in Fund Balances, and a Statement of Cash Flows. Statements should be comparative in form to provide maximum information to readers.

Balance Sheets

Figures 17-2 and 17-3 provide Balance Sheets of the Alzona Hospital at the beginning and end of the year that has been used as the example for hospital operations. Since Figure 17-2 does not contain comparative data, Figure 17-3 should be considered the better example. *Note* the *"Assets whose use is limited" section* of the year-end Balance Sheet (Figure 17-3). These are essentially special subfunds —cash and investments designated or restricted for specific purposes—but exclude donor- or grantor-restricted assets since such amounts are reported in the Donor-Restricted Funds. The portion of assets whose use is limited that is required to meet current liabilities payable from those assets ($125,000) is (1) reported as current assets and (2) then deducted from total assets whose use is limited in the noncurrent assets section in deriving net noncurrent assets whose use is limited.

The style of the two statements is often referred to as "pancake," since data for the several funds are provided in self-balancing layers. Major divisions of the layered balance sheets are labeled **"General Fund"** and **"Donor-Restricted Funds."** All the funds in the latter group are externally restricted as to use by donors or grantors—the governing board can only administer the funds in accordance with the terms established by a donor or grantor. On the other hand, most of the resources in the "General" category may be used by the board as it sees fit. This includes resources that are "board-restricted" to a specific purpose, since, from the point of view of a third party, the board is accountable for the proper administration of all assets subject to its control. Other resources in the "General Fund" category are subject to external restrictions as to use, resulting from bond indentures, third-party reimbursement arrangements, and other arrangements entered into at the board's discretion.

Statement of Revenues and Expenses

Alzona Hospital's Statement of Revenues and Expenses, Figure 17-4, is based on the **operations of** the **General Fund.** Increases and decreases in other funds are considered "changes in fund balance" rather than revenues and expenses. Only when these amounts affect the General Fund are they reported as revenues and expenses. (Note that amounts restricted by donors or grantors to plant expansion and replacement are **never** recorded as revenues. When they are expended for the designated purpose, the assets acquired are recorded in the General Fund with a corresponding increase in fund balance.)

This statement illustrates some of the points made earlier. Notice that patient service revenues are reported at the net amount that patients or third-party payees are obligated to pay—that is, net of deductions from revenues. Too, bad debts are reported as expenses. Also, note (1) the distinction between patient service revenues, other revenues, and nonoperating gains, (2) the sources of revenues and gains, and (3) the distinction between expenses and losses. Finally, observe the strong similarity of this statement and a typical business organization's income statement.

Statement of Changes in Fund Balances

The Statement of Changes in Fund Balances covers all of the funds of a hospital and is usually shown in conventional pancake form (Figure 17-5). Note the reporting of the aggregate changes in the General Fund fund balance resulting from the excess of revenues over (under) expenses. This "summary" reporting of these changes is employed because the detail is presented in the Statement of Revenues and Expenses. Also, notice that the **other** changes in General Fund fund balance reported in the Statement of Changes in Fund Balances are **not** reported in the Statement of Revenues and Expenses. For example, transfers to the General Fund from the Plant Replacement and Expansion Fund are treated as direct additions to General Fund fund balance and thus are not reported as revenues. Finally, observe that investment income restricted for a specific operating purpose by donors and grantors is reported as a direct increase in fund balance of the appropriate Donor-Restricted Funds. However, unrestricted investment income of the Donor-Restricted Funds is reported as nonoperating gains in the Statement of Revenues and Expenses (Figure 17-4).

Statement of Cash Flows

The Statement of Cash Flows, Figure 17-6, is conventional for enterprise-type organizations. Note that it reports all cash flows for the hospital—whether affecting the General Fund cash balance, the cash included in assets whose use is limited, or cash of donor-restricted funds. The cash balances reported in the cash flow statement are the beginning and ending balances of the sum of the cash reflected in those three different classifications.

The cash flow statement for Alzona Hospital is presented in Figure 17-7 under the assumption that the hospital is a nongovernmental, nonprofit entity— and thus not subject to GASB pronouncements. FASB Statement No. 95, "Statement of Cash Flows," excludes nonprofit organizations from its scope. However, the Health Care Audit Guide requires a statement of cash flows to be presented for nonprofit hospitals as well as for investor-owned hospitals so that the same information is presented for each type. Note that there are significant differences in the cash flow statement for a nongovernment, nonprofit hospital (Figure 17-7) compared to the cash flow statement of a government-owned hospital (Figure 17-6). In addition to the differences in the classification of specific types of cash flows discussed in Chapter 11, there are two major differences. First, the nonprofit hospital cash flow statement reports only General Fund cash flows. Therefore, such items as cash contributions to Specific Purpose Funds are not reported. These contributions are reported as cash flows only when transferred to the General Fund. Too,

Figure 17-3

YEAR-END BALANCE SHEET

Alzona Hospital
Balance Sheet
September 30, 19B
With Comparative Figures for September 30, 19A

General Fund

Assets	September 30 19B	September 30 19A
Current:		
Cash	$ 366,000	$ 175,000
Assets whose use is limited—required for current liabilities	125,000	
Receivables	770,000	700,000
Less: Estimated uncollectibles and allowances	90,000	85,000
	680,000	615,000
Accrued interest receivable	2,000	
Due from Endowment Fund	30,000	
Due from Specific Purpose Fund	105,000	145,000
Inventories	215,000	165,000
Total current assets	1,523,000	1,100,000
Noncurrent:		
Investments		100,000
Assets whose use is limited:*		
By board for plant expansion and replacement	100,000	
Under bond indenture agreement—for plant expansion	525,000	
Total assets whose use is limited	625,000	
Less assets whose use is limited and that are required for current liabilities	125,000	
Noncurrent assets whose use is limited	500,000	

Liabilities and Fund Balances	September 30 19B	September 30 19A
Current Liabilities:		
Notes payable	$ 130,000	$ 150,000
Accounts payable	50,000	175,000
Accrued interest payable	31,000	
Accrued salaries and wages payable	83,000	
Due to special duty nurses	3,000	
Contracts payable, retained percentage	125,000	
Total current liabilities	422,000	325,000
Long-term debt:		
Mortgage payable		100,000
Bonds payable	3,000,000	
Total liabilities	3,422,000	425,000
Fund balance	4,234,000	4,225,000

Property, plant and equipment:

Land	130,000	130,000
Land improvements	80,000	80,000
Buildings	5,000,000	5,000,000
Fixed equipment	500,000	600,000
Major movable equipment	113,000	90,000
Construction in process	2,500,000	
Total property, plant, and equipment	8,323,000	5,900,000
Less: Accumulated depreciation	2,690,000	2,450,000
Net property, plant, and equipment	5,633,000	3,450,000
Total noncurrent assets	6,133,000	3,550,000
Total assets	$7,656,000	$4,650,000
Total liabilities and fund balance	$7,656,000	$4,650,000

Donor-Restricted Funds

Specific Purpose Fund:

Cash	$ 130,000	$ 20,000
Investments	345,000	360,000
Due from Endowment Fund	25,000	20,000
Total assets	$ 500,000	$ 400,000

Specific Purpose Fund:

Due to General Fund	$ 105,000	$ 145,000
Fund balance	395,000	255,000
Total liabilities and fund balance	$ 500,000	$ 400,000

Permanent Endowment Fund:

Cash	$ 66,000	$ 25,000
Investments	475,000	475,000
Rental properties	300,000	
Less: Accumulated depreciation	6,000	
Net rental properties	294,000	
Total assets	$ 835,000	$ 500,000

Permanent Endowment Fund:

Due to Specific Purpose Fund	$ 25,000	$ 20,000
Due to General Fund	30,000	
Mortgage Payable	100,000	
Total liabilities	155,000	20,000
Fund balance	680,000	480,000
Total liabilities and fund balance	$ 835,000	$ 500,000

Plant Replacement and Expansion Fund:

Cash	$ 23,000	$ 25,000
Investments	300,000	300,000
Total assets	$ 323,000	$ 325,000

Plant Replacement and Expansion Fund:

Fund balance	$ 323,000	$ 325,000
Total liabilities and fund balance	$ 323,000	$ 325,000

* The composition of "Assets whose use is limited" is disclosed in the notes. In this illustration it includes $525,000 of cash and $100,000 of investments.

Figure 17-4

STATEMENT OF REVENUES AND EXPENSES

Alzona Hospital

Statement of Revenues and Expenses

For the Year Ended September 30, 19B*

Net Patient Service Revenues	$3,985,000**
Other operating revenues:	
Cafeteria sales	45,000
Television rentals	30,000
Medical record transcript fees	15,000
Vending machine commissions	5,000
Transfers from Specific Purpose Fund	300,000
Total Other Operating Revenues	395,000
Total Operating Revenues	4,380,000
Operating expenses:	
Nursing services	1,624,000
Other professional services	981,000
General services	943,000
Fiscal services	160,000
Administrative services	397,000
Depreciation	300,000
Bad debts	120,000
Interest expense	38,000
Total Operating Expenses	4,563,000
Loss from Operations	(183,000)
Nonoperating Gains and (Losses):	
Unrestricted income from Endowment Fund	30,000
General Fund investment income	5,000
Unrestricted income from Specific Purpose Fund	29,000
Donated services	20,000
General contributions	100,000
Loss on disposal of assets	(10,000)
Total Nonoperating Gains (Losses)	174,000
Excess of Expenses over Revenues	$ 9,000

* *Although the hospital operated in fiscal 19A, the figures for that year's activities were not needed for the example in the chapter.*
** *Calculation: Patient service charges ($4,400,000) less charity services ($125,000) and contractual adjustments ($290,000)*

the nonprofit hospital cash flow statement reconciles the beginning and ending balances of the cash account reported in the General Fund balance sheet—excluding cash reported as assets whose use is limited. Thus, the nonprofit cash flow statement includes the "Increase in cash invested in assets whose use is limited" as a "Cash flow from investing activities."

AGGREGATED BALANCE SHEETS

The Health Care Audit Guide permits health care organizations to report their financial position in an aggregated balance sheet instead of in the fund-based, layered balance sheet used in this illustration. Use of an aggregated balance sheet entails three key differences from the layered balance sheets presented earlier:

- Donor- or grantor-restricted assets are reported in the General Fund as assets whose use is limited and related liabilities are included in General Fund liabilities.

Figure 17-5

STATEMENT OF CHANGES IN FUND BALANCES

Alzona Hospital
Statement of Changes in Fund Balances
For the Year Ended September 30, 19B

General Fund:

Balance, beginning of year	$4,225,000
Transferred from Plant Replacement and Expansion Fund to finance expenditures for property, plant, and equipment	18,000
Excess of expenses over revenues	(9,000)
Balance, end of year	$4,234,000

Donor-Restricted Funds:

Specific Purpose Fund:

Balance, beginning of year	$ 255,000
Specific purpose grant	400,000
Investment income of Specific Purpose Fund—Restricted	15,000
Investment income from Endowment Fund—restricted to a specific purpose	25,000
Transferred to General Fund as other operating revenue	(300,000)
Balance, end of year	$ 395,000

Endowment Fund:

Balance, beginning of year	$ 480,000
Endowment received, net of mortgage assumed	200,000
Balance, end of year	$ 680,000

Plant Replacement and Expansion Fund:

Balance, beginning of year	$ 325,000
Investment income—restricted to plant expansion	16,000
Transferred to General Fund to finance expenditures for property, plant, and equipment	(18,000)
Balance, end of year	$ 323,000

- Interfund payables and receivables are eliminated.

- Fund balance is distinguished between that associated with unrestricted net assets, temporarily restricted net assets, and permanently restricted net assets. Permanent endowment fund net assets are the only permanently restricted net assets. All other restricted net assets are temporarily restricted.

The Alzona Hospital balance sheet is presented in aggregated form in Figure 17-8.

RELATED ORGANIZATIONS

Hospitals have a variety of contacts with foundations, auxiliaries, and guilds. They have in some cases created legally separate organizations such as foundations and financing authorities to raise or borrow and hold certain assets for them. In at least some cases the purpose of the foundations is to segregate resources so that their availability will not cause external forces (governmental programs and controls) to require their use to subsidize services other than those the hospital board would select.

Such organizations are **"related"** if the hospital controls the separate organization's operations *or* if the hospital is the organization's sole beneficiary. Nongovernmental hospitals must apply the same criteria as business enterprises to determine whether related organizations should be treated as part of the hospital reporting entity. Governmental hospitals should consider the reporting entity

Figure 17-6

STATEMENT OF CASH FLOWS

Alzona Hospital
Statement of Cash Flows
For the Year Ended September 30, 19B

Cash flows from operating activities:		
Cash received from patients.	$ 3,800,000	
Cash received from other revenues.	95,000	
Cash paid to suppliers of goods and services	(1,477,000)	
Cash paid to employees.	(2,700,000)	
Cash received from specific purpose gifts	400,000	
Cash collected as agent for nurses	48,000	
Cash paid to special duty nurses	(45,000)	
Net cash flows from operating activities		$ 121,000
Cash flows from noncapital financing activities:		
Cash paid to retire note.	(20,000)	
Cash paid for interest	(7,000)	
Cash received from unrestricted contributions.	100,000	
Net cash flows from noncapital financing activities		73,000
Cash flows from capital and related financing activities:		
Cash received from issuing bonds	$ 3,000,000	
Cash paid to retire mortgage	(100,000)	
Cash paid to purchase fixed assets	(2,398,000)	
Cash received from sale of equipment.	30,000	
Net cash flows from capital and related financing activities. . . .		532,000
Cash flows from investing activities:		
Cash paid for investments	(300,000)	
Cash received from sale of investments.	320,000	
Cash received from investment earnings	83,000	
Cash received from rent of Endowment Fund properties	45,000	
Cash paid for Endowment Fund expenses	(9,000)	
Net cash flows from investing activities		139,000
Net increase in cash.		865,000
Cash, October 1, 19A		245,000*
Cash, September 30, 19B.		$1,110,000*
Reconciliation of Net Cash Flows from Operating Activities to Loss from Operations:		
Loss from operations.	$ (183,000)	
Adjustments to reconcile net cash flows from operating activities and operating loss:		
Depreciation	300,000	
Interest expense.	38,000	
Value of donated services expensed	20,000	
Increase in inventory	(50,000)	
Increase in accounts receivable	(65,000)	
Increase in salaries payable.	83,000	
Increase in due to special duty nurses	3,000	
Decrease in accounts payable	(125,000)	
Excess of specific purpose fund cash contributions over revenue transfers recognized	100,000	
Net cash flows from operating activities	$ 121,000	
Significant noncash financing and investing activities:		
Equity in property donated for endowment	$ 200,000	

The cash balance is comprised of:

	October 1, 19A	September 30, 19B
General Fund cash account balance	$175,000	$ 366,000
Cash in assets whose use is limited	—	525,000
Specific Purpose Fund cash.	20,000	130,000
Endowment Fund cash.	25,000	66,000
Plant Replacement and Expansion Fund cash.	25,000	23,000
Total	$245,000	$1,110,000

Figure 17-7 **STATEMENT OF CASH FLOWS FOR NONGOVERNMENT HOSPITAL**

Alzona Hospital
General Fund
Statement of Cash Flows
For the Year Ended September 30, 19B

Net Cash Flow from Operating Activities:	
Excess of expenses over revenues	$ (9,000)
Adjustments to reconcile net income to cash provided from operating activities:	
Depreciation	300,000
Loss on sale of fixed assets	10,000
Net increase in receivables, inventory, and payables	(177,000)
Net decrease in interfund receivables	10,000
Increase in interest accrued but not paid	31,000
Increase in interest earned but not received	(2,000)
Net increase in deposits held for special nurses	3,000
Net Cash Flow from Operating Activities	166,000
Cash Flows from Investing Activities:	
Cash paid for property, plant, and equipment	(2,398,000)
Net increase in cash invested in assets whose use is limited	(525,000)
Proceeds from sale of equipment	30,000
Net Cash Used in Investing Activities	(2,893,000)
Cash Flows from Financing Activities:	
Issuance of long-term debt	3,000,000
Transfer from Plant Replacement and Expansion Fund	18,000
Retirement of mortgages payable	(100,000)
Net Cash Flow from Financing Activities	2,918,000
Net Increase in Cash	191,000
Cash balance, October 1, 19A	175,000
Cash balance, September 30, 19B	$ 366,000

criteria in the GASB *Codification* in making the reporting entity decision. The Health Care Audit Guide contains disclosure requirements for related organizations that are not consolidated or combined with the hospital.

CONCLUDING COMMENTS

Health care accounting and reporting has evolved over the past 50 years to adapt to the ever-changing health care environment. Today, health care accounting and reporting is very similar to accounting and reporting for business enterprises. However, because of the many unique features of the health care environment, health care financial management and accounting practices have several unique features.

The most significant unique features of health care accounting, compared to business accounting, are (1) the use of funds, (2) various unique income determination features, and (3) the inclusion of the Statement of Changes in Fund Balances in the basic statements required for health care entities. Many of these same unique features characterize accounting and reporting for colleges and universities, discussed in Chapter 18. Note the many similarities and also the very significant differences between health care accounting and college and university accounting when studying that chapter in order to enhance your understanding of both.

Figure 17-8

YEAR-END BALANCE SHEET—AGGREGATED FORM

Alzona Hospital
Balance Sheet
September 30, 19B
With Comparative Figures for September 30, 19A

Assets

	September 30 19B	September 30 19A
Current:		
Cash	$ 501,000	$ 195,000
Assets whose use is limited—required for current liabilities	125,000	
Receivables	770,000	700,000
Less: Estimated uncollectibles and allowances	90,000	85,000
	680,000	615,000
Accrued interest receivable	2,000	
Inventories	215,000	165,000
Total current assets	1,523,000	975,000
Noncurrent:		
Investments		225,000
Assets whose use is limited:		
By board for plant expansion and replacement	100,000	
By bond indenture agreement—for plant expansion	525,000	255,000
By donors for specific operating purposes	395,000	325,000
By donors for plant replacement and expansion	323,000	
By donors for permanent endowments	780,000	480,000
Total assets whose use is limited	2,123,000	1,060,000
Less assets whose use is limited and that are required for current liabilities	125,000	
Noncurrent assets whose use is limited	1,998,000	1,060,000
Property, plant, and equipment:		
Land	130,000	130,000
Land improvements	80,000	80,000
Buildings	5,000,000	5,000,000
Fixed equipment	500,000	600,000
Major movable equipment	113,000	90,000
Construction in process	2,500,000	
Total property, plant, and equipment	8,323,000	5,900,000
Less: Accumulated depreciation	2,690,000	2,450,000
Net property, plant, and equipment	5,633,000	3,450,000
Total noncurrent assets	7,631,000	4,735,000
Total assets	$9,154,000	$5,710,000

Liabilities and Fund Balances

	September 30 19B	September 30 19A
Current Liabilities:		
Notes payable	$ 130,000	$ 150,000
Accounts payable	50,000	175,000
Accrued interest payable	31,000	
Accrued salaries and wages payable	83,000	
Due to special duty nurses	3,000	
Contracts payable, retained percentage	125,000	
Total current liabilities	422,000	325,000
Long-term debt:		
Mortgage payable	100,000	100,000
Bonds payable	3,000,000	
Total liabilities	3,522,000	425,000
Net assets:		
Unrestricted	4,234,000	4,225,000
Temporarily restricted by donors or grantors	718,000	580,000
Permanently restricted by donors	680,000	480,000
Total net assets	$5,632,000	$5,285,000
Total liabilities and fund balance	$9,154,000	$5,710,000

QUESTIONS

17-1 Prepare a list of the funds recommended for use by a hospital. Opposite the funds indicate the fund(s) or account group(s) recommended for municipalities that is most nearly comparable in nature.

17-2 What General Fund treatment is accorded transfers from funds restricted to use for specific operating purposes? From funds restricted to use for fixed asset additions? Explain the difference.

17-3 What is the difference between funds designated by hospital boards for specific purposes and those designated by outside donors for specific purposes? What are the differing accounting effects?

17-4 A county hospital derives its revenues solely from a special tax levy made for this purpose. Would the accounting procedures outlined throughout this chapter apply to such a hospital? If not, indicate the fund or funds in which the financial transactions of the hospital should be recorded.

17-5 Why is it important to distinguish between "unrestricted" assets, assets whose use is limited, and "donor-restricted" assets in hospital accounting? (Define these terms in your answer.)

17-6 Explain the increase of the influence of the AICPA over hospital accounting.

17-7 List the principal classifications of hospital revenues.

17-8 Why should hospitals report only the net amount of patient service revenue in their statements of revenues and expenses? Why are bad debts treated differently than deductions from revenues such as contractual adjustments?

17-9 Identify the required financial statements for a government hospital and the fund or funds included in each statement.

17-10 Diagnostic and analysis equipment developed by the federal government at a cost of $1,000,000 per unit was donated to Peoples' Hospital for medical and research use. Similar equipment is available from a commercial supplier at a cost of $600,000 new or for $400,000 if used and of about the same age as that received. The hospital will use the equipment extensively, but the administrator doubts that it will be replaced when it is worn out or obsolete due to its high cost. (a) Should the contribution be accounted for as either revenue or gain or contributed capital by the hospital? Explain. (b) Should depreciation be recorded and, if so, on what "cost" basis?

17-11 (a) Should depreciation be charged on the fixed assets of a hospital if these assets have been financed from contributions but are intended to be replaced from hospital revenues? (b) Assume that the replacement of the fixed assets is intended to be financed from contributions. Should depreciation be charged on such fixed assets?

17-12 A hospital's assets include:
  a. $2,000,000 set aside by the hospital board as an endowment to support research for curing the common cold;
  b. $25,000,000 donated by various individuals and organizations to finance construction and equipping of a cancer treatment and research center;
  c. $3,500,000 from a bond issue to finance expansion of the maternity wing; and
  d. $1,000,000 received from Blue Cross–Blue Shield (BCBS) as part of the hospital's reimbursement for services rendered to BCBS insurees. The reimbursement agreement with BCBS requires that this portion of the reimbursement be used for plant replacement and expansion.
  In which fund should each of the preceding assets be reported?

17-13 Identify the key differences between health care accounting and commercial accounting.

17-14 (a) What is a term endowment? (b) How should a hospital account for the receipt of a term endowment? (c) How should a hospital account for the resources of a term endowment when the term of the endowment expires?

17-15 Under what circumstances are financial resources that are required to be used to acquire or construct a fixed asset accounted for in the Plant Replacement and Expansion Fund? Under what circumstances are hospital fixed assets and/or the related long-term debt accounted for in the Plant Replacement and Expansion Fund?

17-16 Following are various types of revenues, gains, and other amounts that may be received or accrued by a hospital. For each type of revenue or gain, indicate whether it should typically be classified as:

1. Patient Service Revenue (P)
2. Other Operating Revenue (O)
3. Nonoperating Gain (N)
4. Operating Gain (G)
5. None of the above (X)

———— a. Unrestricted income from Endowment Funds
———— b. Operating room charges
———— c. Gains from sale of land owned by the hospital
———— d. General nursing service charges
———— e. Harrimon Foundation grant received by hospital in recognition of outstanding past service to community
———— f. Room and board charges
———— g. Cafeteria sales
———— h. Professional services donated to the hospital
———— i. Sales of scrap materials
———— j. Tuition and fees from an affiliated nursing school
———— k. Contractual Medicare allowances
———— l. Physical therapy fees
———— m. Interest on General Fund investments
———— n. Nursing salaries
———— o. Rockefeller Foundation grant received by hospital for medical research

PROBLEMS

P 17-1 (Multiple Choice)

1. Depreciation should be recognized in the financial statements of
   a. proprietary (for-profit) hospitals only
   b. proprietary (for-profit), governmental, and not-for-profit hospitals
   c. (1) proprietary (for-profit) and (2) governmental and not-for-profit hospitals when they are affiliated with a college or university
   d. all hospitals, as a memorandum entry not affecting the statement of revenues and expenses

2. A gift to a voluntary not-for-profit hospital that is not restricted by the donor normally should be credited directly to
   a. Fund balance   c. Operating revenue
   b. Deferred revenue   d. Nonoperating gain

3. Donated medicines that normally would be purchased by a hospital should be recorded at fair market value and should be credited directly to
   a. Other operating revenue   c. Fund balance
   b. Nonoperating gain   d. Deferred revenue or gain

4. On July 1, 19X1, Lilydale Hospital's Board of Trustees designated $200,000 for expansion of outpatient facilities. The $200,000 is expected to be expended in the fiscal year ending June 30, 19X4. In Lilydale's balance sheet at June 30, 19X2, this cash should be classified as a $200,000
   a. restricted current asset
   b. restricted noncurrent asset
   c. unrestricted current asset
   d. unrestricted noncurrent asset

5. During the year ended December 31, 19X1, Melford Hospital received the following donations stated at their respective fair values:

Employee services from members of a
religious group. . . . . $ 100,000

Medical supplies from an association of
physicians. These supplies were restricted
for indigent care, and were used for such
purpose in 19X1   30,000

How much revenue or gain from donations should Melford report in its 19X1
statement of revenues and expenses?

a. $0

b. $30,000

c. $100,000

d. $130,000

6. Glenmore Hospital's property, plant, and equipment (net of depreciation) consists of
the following:

Land	$ 500,000
Buildings	10,000,000
Movable Equipment.	2,000,000

What amount should be included in the restricted funds?

a. $0

b. $2,000,000

c. $10,500,000

d. $12,500,000

7. An unrestricted pledge from an annual contributor to a voluntary not-for-profit hospital
made in December 19X1 and paid in cash in March 19X2 would generally be credited to

a. Nonoperating gain in 19X1

b. Nonoperating gain in 19X2

c. Operating revenue in 19X1

d. Operating revenue in 19X2

8. Which of the following would normally be included in Other Operating Revenues of a
voluntary not-for-profit hospital?

a. unrestricted interest income from an endowment fund

b. an unrestricted gift

c. donated services

d. tuition received from an educational program

9. Which of the following would be included in the General Funds of a not-for-profit hospital?

a. permanent endowments

b. term endowments

c. board-designated funds originating from previously accumulated income

d. plant expansion and replacement funds

10. On May 1, 19X4, Lila Lee established a $50,000 endowment fund, the income from which
is to be paid to Waller Hospital for general operating purposes. Waller does not control
the fund's principal. Anders National Bank was appointed by Lee as trustee of this fund.
What journal entry is required on Waller's books?

	Debit	Credit
a. Memorandum entry only	—	—
b. Nonexpendable endowment fund	$50,000	
Endowment fund balance		$50,000
c. Cash	50,000	
Endowment fund balance		50,000
d. Cash	50,000	
Nonexpendable endowment fund balance		50,000

Items 11 and 12 are based on the following data:

Under Abbey Hospital's established rate structure, the hospital would have earned patient service revenue of $6,000,000 for the year ended December 31, 19X3. However,

Abbey did not expect to collect this amount because of charity allowances of $1,000,000 and discounts of $500,000 to third-party payers. In May 19X3, Abbey purchased bandages from Lee Supply Co. at a cost of $1,000. However, Lee notified Abbey that the invoice was being canceled and that the bandages were being donated to Abbey.

11. For the year ended December 31, 19X3, how much should Abbey record as patient service revenue in its statement of revenues and expenses?

   a. $6,000,000 c. $5,000,000
   b. $5,500,000 d. $4,500,000

12. For the year ended December 31, 19X3, Abbey should record the donation of bandages as

   a. a $1,000 reduction in operating expenses
   b. nonoperating gain of $1,000
   c. other operating revenue of $1,000
   d. a memorandum entry only

   (AICPA adapted)

P 17-2 (Multiple Choice)

1. Assets designated by a hospital's governing board for use in financing the expansion of its physical plant should be accounted for in the hospital's
   a. Plant Replacement and Expansion Fund
   b. Restricted Fund
   c. General Fund
   d. Specific Purpose Fund
   e. Endowment Fund

2. Simon Philanthropist has given $15 million to the Whitesburg General Hospital, subject to a written provision that the money be used solely for the construction of a new Phillip P. Philanthropist Memorial Wing. This $15 million should be initially reported in the hospital's
   a. Plant Replacement and Expansion Fund
   b. Specific Purpose Fund
   c. Endowment Fund
   d. General Fund
   e. Capital Projects Fund

3. A hospital's restricted funds include assets that are legally restricted by
   a. bond indentures
   b. donors and grantors
   c. third-party reimbursement arrangements
   d. the hospital's governing board
   e. all of the above
   f. a, b, and c

4. On December 15, 19X3, Bonham Hospital was awarded a $500,000 grant from the Travis Foundation to conduct a detailed survey of 200 former lung cancer patients. Half of the grant money was received by the hospital on August 15, 19X4 and the remaining $250,000 was received on May 10, 19X6 upon delivery of the final survey report. The grant money was expended as follows:

   9/X4–12/X4: $50,000 on planning and design of the survey

   1/X5–12/X5: $350,000 on the active conduct and analysis of the survey

   1/X6–5/X6: $100,000 on the preparation and publication of the survey report in a form satisfactory to the Travis Foundation.

   Bonham Hospital must recognize revenue from the Travis Foundation grant as follows:
   a. the entire $500,000 in 19X3
   b. $250,000 in 19X4 and $250,000 in 19X6

c. $50,000 in 19X4, $350,000 in 19X5, and $100,000 in 19X6

d. the entire $500,000 in 19X6

5. Fixed assets used in hospital operations are accounted for

a. solely in the Specific Purpose Fund

b. solely in the General Fund

c. solely in the Plant Replacement and Expansion Fund

d. partially in the General Fund and partially in the Plant Replacement and Expansion Fund

e. partially in the General Fund and partially in the Specific Purpose Fund

6. Theodore Cleaver has given the Edward Haskell Hospital $10.2 million, subject to the provision that the money be used solely for the operation of its Alcohol Treatment Center. At the time of their receipt, these resources

a. must be accounted for as deferred revenues in the General Fund

b. must be accounted for as an increase in the fund balance of the Specific Purpose Fund

c. must be accounted for as an increase in the fund balance of the Endowment Fund

d. may be accounted for as an increase in the fund balance of the General Fund or as an increase in the fund balance of the Specific Purpose Fund

7. The financial statements a nonprofit hospital should prepare for public use include

a. statement of changes in fund balance

b. statement of cash flows

c. statement of changes in retained earnings

d. balance sheet

e. all of the above

f. a, c, and d

g. a, b, and d

8. Grants received by a hospital for specific research should be recognized as revenue

a. in the period in which the grant is awarded

b. in the period or periods in which the grant funds are received

c. in the period or periods in which the grant funds are expended in connection with the research

d. in the period in which the research is completed

P 17-3 (Funds-Statements Relationships) Using the following answer sheet format, place an X in the column for each type of fund reported on in each of the following hospital financial statements.

Statement	General Fund	Specific Purpose Fund	Endowment Fund	Plant Replacement and Expansion Fund
a. Balance sheet				
b. Statement of revenues and expenses				
c. Statement of changes in fund balances				
d. Statement of cash flows—government hospital				
e. Statement of cash flows—not-for-profit hospital				

Hospital Financial Reporting Classifications

Balance Sheet		Statement of Revenues and Expenses	
CA	Current Assets	PSR	Patient Service Revenues
AWUL	Assets Whose Use Is Limited	OOR	Other Operating Revenues
PPE	Property, Plant, and Equipment	NG	Nonoperating Gains
IA	Intangible Assets	NSE	Nursing Services Expenses
OA	Other Assets	OPE	Other Professional Services Expenses
CL	Current Liabilities	GSE	General Services Expenses
LTL	Long-Term Liabilities	FSE	Fiscal Services Expenses
FB	Fund Balance	ASE	Administrative Services Expenses
		OE	Other Expenses

Using the preceding abbreviations, indicate how each of the following items should be reported in these hospital financial statements. If none of the preceding items is appropriate, explain how the item should be reported.

1. Anesthesiology expenses
2. Qualifying expenses under a restricted grant
3. Provision for bad debts
4. Fixed asset purchased from donor-restricted resources
5. Expiration of term endowments—restricted to use for plant expansion
6. Gain on sale of equipment
7. Admitting office expenses
8. Donated services
9. Bond sinking fund
10. Cash and investments set aside by board to finance cancer research
11. Emergency services expenses
12. Unrestricted contributions
13. Bonds payable (issued to finance construction underway)
14. Provision for depreciation
15. Gift restricted for operations
16. Intensive care expenses
17. Power plant expenses
18. Income and gain from board-designated funds
19. Dietary service expenses
20. Interest expense

P 17-5   **Part I.** (Fixed Asset-Related Entries) Rocky Memorial Hospital entered into the following transactions in 19X8:

April 1—Purchased incubators for the nursery for $47,300. (Assume straight line depreciation on all hospital fixed assets.)

July 1—Issued $10,000,000 of 10%, 20-year bonds at par to finance construction of a major hospital addition. Construction is to begin early in 19X9, but bond market conditions are expected to become much less desirable over the next few months. The proceeds are invested in securities that also yield 10% interest.

October 31—Sold a kidney dialysis machine for $19,000 halfway through its useful life. The machine originally cost $25,000 and was expected to have a $10,000 salvage value.

December 31—(a) The incubators have a five-year useful life. (b) The first semiannual interest payment on the bonds is made.

Required   Prepare all entries required on the preceding dates for these transactions. (Assume straight line depreciation.)

P 17-5 **Part II.** (Selected Revenue-Related Entries)

1. Svoboda County Regional Medical Center's gross charges for services rendered to patients in 19X7 were $82,000,000. Of this, $2,500,000 was for services rendered to individuals who were certified by the county as having no means to pay. Also, contractual adjustments granted on services rendered to insured patients and Medicare patients during 19X8 totaled $4,800,000 by December 31, 19X8, and it was estimated that another $350,000 of contractual adjustments would be made associated with those services. In addition, the hospital estimated that it will incur bad debt losses of approximately $3,200,000 associated with the services rendered in 19X8.

2. Svoboda County Regional Medical Center received $875,000 of donations in 19X8 to be used to cover the cost of charity services provided to patients who do not have sufficient means to pay for the needed medical care.

Required (a) Prepare the general journal entries that Svoboda County Regional Medical Center should make to record these transactions.

(b) Prepare the portion(s) of the Svoboda County Regional Medical Center's Statement of Revenues and Expenses that report these transactions.

P 17-6 (Donation-Related Entries) Miss Jenny Russ donated $3,000,000 to Broadus Memorial Hospital on June 17, 19X8.

1. Assume that no restrictions are placed on the use of the donated resources.
   a. Prepare the required June 17, 19X8 entry.
   b. Prepare any entries necessary in 19X9 if $400,000 of the gift is used to finance hospital operating expenses.

2. Assume that the donation was restricted to leukemia research.
   a. Prepare the required June 17, 19X8 entry.
   b. Prepare any entries required in 19X9 as a result of spending $400,000 for leukemia research during 19X9.

3. Assume that the donation was restricted for use in adding a pediatrics intensive care unit to the hospital.
   a. Prepare the required June 17, 19X8 entry.
   b. Prepare any entries required in 19X9 if $400,000 of the gift is used to begin constructing the intensive care unit.

4. Explain or illustrate how each of the three situations described previously would be reported in Broadus Memorial Hospital's financial statements in 19X8 and in 19X9.

P 17-7 (Various Entries) The following transactions and events relate to the operation of a hospital. Prepare journal entries to record the effects of these transactions and events in the general ledger accounts of the appropriate fund(s). Explanations of entries may be omitted, but indicate the fund in which each is made.

1. Total billings for patient services rendered, $85,000; it was estimated that bad debt losses on these billings would be $1,000 and that contractual adjustments would amount to $6,000.

2. A transfer from the Heart Research Fund to the General Fund was authorized, $15,000, to defray such expenses previously recorded in the General Fund. The cash will be transferred later in the year.

3. An item of fixed equipment (cost, $8,000; accumulated depreciation, $5,000) was sold for $1,000.

4. Depreciation expense on buildings was recognized, $18,000.

5. Earnings of the Endowment Fund are restricted to use for intern education. The net income of the Endowment Fund (revenues, $18,000; expenses, $4,000) was established as a liability to the appropriate fund.

6. Unrestricted income on Endowment Fund investments, $3,500, was received and recorded directly in the General Fund.

7. An $11,000 designation of the General Fund fund balance was authorized to partially "fund" depreciation expense.

8. Of the billings for patient services rendered (see item 1), $1,000 was written off, $600 of which was related to charity cases.

P 17-8 (Worksheet—Fund Classification) The Community Hospital began operations in early January 19X0 in facilities financed largely by donations from the James family. No capital expenditures were made during 19X0 and no fixed assets were retired. By action of the board of trustees, the administrator is responsible for funding depreciation unless excused by action of the board. No such action has been taken.

The Edna May James Fund has been established for the special purpose of making loans to X-ray students. The Julian James Fund has been established to buy additional X-ray equipment, $10,500 in cash and $12,000 in securities were donated to form the Julian James Fund and these assets were combined with other cash and securities restricted for plant building use.

The books were closed on December 31, 19X0. No financial statements have ever been prepared, but the list of accounts shown is in balance.

Required From the information available to you, prepare a worksheet that provides balance sheet information for each of the necessary funds. (A formal balance sheet is not required.) Include in the worksheet columns for the December 31, 19X0, trial balance, adjustments, and adjusted balances for the necessary funds.

Schedule of Account Balances

Accounts payable.	7,000
Accounts receivable	70,000
Accrued interest payable	20,000
Accrued salaries and wages payable.	10,000
Accrued taxes payable.	500
Accumulated depreciation—buildings.	30,000
Accumulated depreciation—equipment. . . .	37,000
Allowance for doubtful accounts	7,800
Allowance for uncollectible pledges	20,000
Buildings.	1,500,000
Building drive pledges receivable	115,000
Capital	2,660,400
Cash—Building drive fund	73,000
Cash—Edna May James	700
Cash—Operating fund.	41,500
Cash—Payroll account	2,500
Equipment.	600,000
Inventory.	20,000
Investments—Building drive fund	840,000
Investments—Edna May James.	2,000
Land	25,000
Mortgage payable.	500,000
Petty cash	500
Prepaid expenses	2,500

(FHFMA, adapted)

P 17-9 (Operating Statement) The following selected information was taken from the books and records of Glendora Hospital (a voluntary hospital) as of and for the year ended June 30, 19X2:

■ Patient service revenues totaled $16,000,000, with associated allowances for contractual adjustments ($2,400,000) and uncollectible accounts ($1,000,000). Other operating revenues aggregated $346,000, and included $160,000 from Specific Purpose Funds. Revenue of $6,000,000 recognized under cost reimbursement agreements is subject to audit and retroactive adjustments by third-party payers. Estimated retroactive adjustments under these agreements have been included in allowances.

- Unrestricted gifts and bequests of $410,000 were received.

- Unrestricted income from endowment funds totaled $160,000.

- Income from board-designated funds aggregated $82,000.

- Operating expenses totaled $13,270,000, and included $500,000 for depreciation computed on the straight-line basis. However, accelerated depreciation is used to determine reimbursable costs under certain third-party reimbursement agreements. Net cost reimbursement revenue amounting to $220,000, resulting from the difference in depreciation methods, was deferred to future years.

- Fixed assets acquisitions during the year totaled $1,300,000.

- Endowment earnings restricted to artificial heart implant research were $250,000.

- Also included in operating expenses are pension costs of $100,000, in connection with a noncontributory pension plan covering substantially all of Glendora's employees.

Required   Prepare a formal statement of revenues and expenses for Glendora Hospital for the year ended June 30, 19X2.
(AICPA, adapted)

P 17-10   (Worksheet with Correcting Entries) Following is Esperanza Hospital's postclosing trial balance at December 31, 19X6.

Esperanza Hospital

Trial Balance

December 31, 19X6

	Debit	Credit
Cash	60,000	
Investment in U.S. Treasury Bills	400,000	
Investment in Corporate Bonds.	500,000	
Interest Receivable	10,000	
Accounts Receivable	50,000	
Inventory.	30,000	
Land	100,000	
Building	800,000	
Equipment	170,000	
Allowance for Depreciation		410,000
Accounts Payable.		20,000
Notes Payable		70,000
Endowment Fund Balance		520,000
Other Fund Balances		1,100,000

Esperanza, which is a nonprofit hospital, did **not** maintain its books in conformity with the principles of hospital fund accounting. Effective January 1, 19X7, Esperanza's board of trustees voted to adjust the December 31, 19X6 general ledger balances, and to establish separate funds for the general (unrestricted) funds, the endowment fund, and the plant replacement and expansion fund.

Additional account information:

- *Investment in corporate bonds* pertains to the amount required to be accumulated under a board policy to invest cash equal to accumulated depreciation until it is needed for asset replacement. The $500,000 balance at December 31, 19X6, is less than the full amount required because of errors in computation of building depreciation for past years. Included in the allowance for depreciation is a correctly computed amount of $90,000 applicable to equipment.

- *Endowment fund balance* has been credited with the following:

Donor's bequest of cash	$300,000
Gains on sales of securities.	100,000
Interest and dividends earned in 19X4, 19X5, and 19X6.	120,000
Total	$520,000

The terms of the bequest specify that the principal, plus all gains on sales of investments, are to remain fully invested in U.S. government or corporate securities. At December, 31, 19X6, $400,000 was invested in U.S. Treasury bills. The bequest further specifies that interest and dividends earned on investments are to be used for payment of current operating expenses.

■ *Land* comprises the following:

Donation of land in 19W0, at appraised value	$ 40,000
Appreciation in fair value of land as determined by independent appraiser ten years later in 19X0	60,000
Total	$100,000

■ *Building* comprises the following:

Hospital building completed 40 years ago (as of the beginning of 19X7), when operations were started (estimated useful life 50 years), at cost . . .	$720,000
Installation of elevator 20 years ago (as of the beginning of 19X7) (estimated useful life 20 years), at cost	80,000
Total	$800,000

Required   Using a worksheet with the following column headings, enter the adjustments necessary to restate the general ledger account balances properly. Distribute the adjusted balances to establish the separate fund accounts, and complete the worksheet. Formal journal entries are not required, but supporting computations should be referenced to the worksheet adjustments.

Column Headings	*Column Numbers*
Trial balance—December 31, 19X6	1–2
Adjustments	3–4
General Fund	5–6
Endowment Fund	7–8
Plant Replacement and Expansion Fund	9–10

(AICPA, adapted)

ACCOUNTING
FOR COLLEGES
AND UNIVERSITIES

The development of accounting and reporting principles for colleges and universities followed a pattern almost identical to that of municipalities. A few publications on the subject appeared during the 1910–1935 era; the first attempt at standardization, undertaken cooperatively by the various regional associations of college and university business officers, was published in 1935. This was followed by a series of interpretive and advisory studies by the American Council on Education (ACE) during the 1935–1942 period.

A National Committee on the Preparation of a Manual on College and University Business Administration prepared *College and University Business Administration.* This two-volume work, published by the ACE in 1952 and 1955, respectively, was the first authoritative publication covering all areas of higher education business administration. A one-volume 1968 revised edition of *College and University Business Administration*[1] *(CUBA)* found widespread acceptance in practice and in textbooks on college and university accounting.

The AICPA Committee on College and University Accounting and Auditing prepared *Audits of Colleges and Universities,*[2] an industry audit guide issued in 1973. The audit guide basically endorsed *CUBA* as a primary authoritative source of generally accepted accounting principles but took exception to several practices suggested or permitted in *CUBA.* Thus, a Joint Accounting Group (JAG) was

---

[1] *College and University Business Administration,* rev. ed. (Washington, D.C.: American Council on Education, 1968). Specifically, see Part 2, "Principles of Accounting and Reporting"; Appendix A, "The Chart of Accounts"; and Appendix B, "Illustrative Forms."
[2] Committee on College and University Accounting and Auditing, American Institute of Certified Public Accountants, *Audits of Colleges and Universities* (New York: AICPA, 1973).

formed to achieve consensus on numerous matters related to higher education accounting and reporting and, in 1974:

1. NACUBO[3] issued the third edition of *College & University Business Administration*[4] *(CUBA),* the fifth part of which deals with "Financial Accounting and Reporting,"
2. the *Report of the Joint Accounting Group*[5] was published, and
3. the AICPA issued *Statement of Position 74-8*,[6] which amended the audit guide to complete the reconciliation of differences between the 1974 edition of *CUBA* and the audit guide.

In 1979, the FASB assumed responsibility for all nonbusiness organization (except government) accounting and reporting standards and designated those in the audit guide "preferable" standards pending any FASB statements on college and university accounting and reporting.[7] Pending possible FASB pronouncements related to colleges and universities, the fourth edition of *CUBA,* issued in 1982, did not include a comprehensive revision of college and university financial accounting and reporting principles.[8] NACUBO replaced the CUBA accounting and reporting guidance in 1990 with its *Financial Accounting and Reporting Manual for Higher Education* (FARM) loose-leaf manual.[9]

In 1984 the FASB-GASB jurisdiction agreement granted the GASB authority for establishing standards for colleges and universities that are part of state and local governments. As noted in Chapter 1, this presents the *possibility* of different standards for government-supported and private colleges and universities.

From 1984–1992, FASB standards were presumed to apply to state and local government (SLG) entities unless the GASB issued a "negative" standard to the contrary. One of the four GASB negative statements issued during the 1984–1992 period was directed specifically to SLG colleges and universities. FASB *Statement No. 93,* "Recognition of Depreciation by Not-for-Profit Organizations," requires nongovernmental colleges and universities to report depreciation. However, the GASB stated that **government** colleges and universities should **not** change their accounting practices as a result of FASB *Statement No. 93.*[10] Similarly,

---

[3] The various regional associations formed the National Federation of College and University Business Officers Associations in 1950, which in 1960 became the National Association of College and University Business Officers (NACUBO). NACUBO and the American Council on Education (ACE) have been instrumental in the continuing development and improvement of college and university financial management, accounting, and reporting.

[4] National Association of College and University Business Officers, *College & University Business Administration,* 3rd ed. (Washington, D.C.: NACUBO, 1974). Specifically, see Part 5, "Financial Accounting and Reporting."

[5] Report of the Joint Accounting Group (Boulder, Colo.: Western Interstate Commission for Higher Education, March 1974).

[6] Accounting Standards Division, American Institute of Certified Public Accountants, *Statement of Position 74-8,* "Financial Accounting and Reporting by Colleges and Universities" (New York: AICPA, August 31, 1974).

[7] Financial Accounting Standards Board, *Statement of Financial Accounting Standards No. 32,* "Specialized Accounting and Reporting Principles and Practices in AICPA Statements of Position and Guides on Accounting and Auditing Matters" (Stamford, Conn.: FASB, September 1979) (Rescinded by SFAS No. 111 in 1992).

[8] National Association of College and University Business Officers, *College and University Business Administration,* 4th ed. (Washington, D.C.: NACUBO, 1982). Hereafter cited as *CUBA.*

[9] National Association of College and University Business Officers, *Financial Accounting and Reporting Manual for Higher Education* (Washington, D.C.: NACUBO, 1990) Hereafter cited as *FARM.*

[10] Governmental Accounting Standards Board, *Statement No. 8,* "Applicability of FASB *Statement No. 93,* 'Recognition of Depreciation by Not-for-Profit Organizations,' to Certain State and Local Governmental Entities" (Stamford, Conn.: GASB, January 1988).

the GASB prohibited SLG entities from applying FASB Statement No. 87, "Employers' Accounting for Pensions," pending completion of the GASB's pension-related projects; and the GASB does not require SLGs to record OPEB (other postemployment benefits) pending completion[11] of its OPEB project.

The new AICPA GAAP hierarchy that became effective in 1992 eliminates the need for GASB to issue negative standards on college and university accounting and reporting standards. However, it also left the status of the related NACUBO and AICPA guidance in doubt. But GASB Statement 15, "Governmental College and University Accounting and Financial Reporting Models,"[12] gives the guidance in the AICPA audit and accounting guide—which is based on the NACUBO literature—the highest (Rule 203) status under the new GAAP hierarchy. Thus, subject to any related GASB and FASB pronouncements, the NACUBO *Financial Accounting and Reporting Manual for Higher Education (FARM)* and the AICPA audit [and accounting] guide, as amended, are the most authoritative sources of college and university accounting and reporting principles. Accordingly, this chapter is based on those recommendations.

OVERVIEW

College and university accounting and reporting may be visualized as a **composite** of selected aspects of municipal and hospital accounting and reporting. Among the features shared with both municipalities and hospitals is the fund principle.

Fund Groups

Both *FARM* and the AICPA Committee endorse the use of the following fund groups by colleges and universities:

Fund Group	Major Subdivisions
1. Current Funds	Current Funds—Unrestricted
	Current Funds—Restricted
2. Plant Funds	Unexpended Plant Funds
	Funds for Renewals and Replacements
	Funds for Retirement of Indebtedness
	Investment in Plant
3. Loan Funds	
4. Endowment and Similar Funds	Endowment Funds ("pure" or "true")
	Term Endowment Funds
	Quasi-Endowment Funds (Funds Functioning as Endowment)
5. Annuity and Life Income Funds	Annuity Funds
	Life Income Funds
6. Agency Funds	

Since the last four fund groups are all "fiduciary" fund groups, college and university funds may be discussed and illustrated in three broad categories—**Current Funds, Plant Funds, and Trust and Agency Funds.**

[11] Governmental Accounting Standards Board, *Statement No. 4,* "Applicability of FASB Statement No. 87, "Employers' Accounting for Pensions," to State and Local Government Employers (Stamford, Conn.: GASB, September 1986) and *Statement No. 12,* "Disclosure of Information on Postemployment Benefits Other Than Pension Benefits by State and Local Governmental Employers" (Norwalk, Conn.: GASB, May 1990).

[12] Governmental Accounting Standards Board, *Statement No. 15,* "Governmental College and University Accounting and Financial Reporting Models" (Norwalk, Conn.: GASB, October 1991).

These fund groups are based on the restrictions on and the purposes of the funds. A college or university may (1) establish *several* separate fund entities of each group, as needed, but prepare its financial reports on a fund group basis, *or* (2) maintain *only one* fund accounting entity for each fund group and account for the subfunds on an intrafund "funds within a fund" basis. Either approach is acceptable; however, within each of the fund groups each fund must, as a minimum, have separate accounts to show the balance of the fund and the results of its operations. These fund groups are discussed and illustrated more fully following a brief comparison of the major features of college and university accounting and reporting with those of municipalities and hospitals.

Comparison with State and Local Government Accounting and with Hospital Accounting

Many of the features of college and university accounting are similar to their counterparts in either governmental or hospital accounting. Recognizing these similarities facilitates understanding college and university accounting.

Fund Structure

As Figure 18-1 illustrates, there are many similarities between the fund structure of colleges and universities and those of state and local governments (SLGs) and hospitals. Note the parallels between the three fund structures; then, throughout the remainder of this chapter, observe the similarities and differences in usage of each college and university fund compared to each SLG and hospital fund.

Measurement Focus

As with accounting for governmental funds of SLGs, college and university accounting and reporting is **concerned primarily with measuring and reporting revenues and expenditures—funds flows and balances—rather than determining net income of the organization.** Thus, depreciation expense is **not** recorded in the Current Funds of colleges and universities (nor in governmental funds of SLGs). However, *accumulated* depreciation **may** be recorded in a university's Investment in Plant accounts in the same manner as is *permitted* for general fixed assets of a SLG in the General Fixed Assets Account Group. Finally, accounting and reporting for interfund transfers of colleges and universities is similar to that for SLGs; and accounting for restricted contributions and restricted investment earnings is similar to that for restricted grants in governments and revenues restricted for operations of a hospital.

Financial Statements

In reporting for colleges and universities, as in hospitals and in SLG governmental funds:

1. Combined balance sheets and operating statements are presented.
2. Statements analyzing changes in fund balances are a major operating statement for most fund groups.

Additionally, college and university operating revenues and expenditures are reported in a "Current Funds" Statement of Revenues, Expenditures, and Other Changes for the Current Funds group, just as hospital revenues and expenses are reported only for the General Fund in the Statement of Revenues and Expenses.

Figure 18-1

SUMMARY COMPARISON OF FUND STRUCTURES

Colleges and Universities with Municipalities and Hospitals

Primary Purpose of Funds and Account Groups	State and Local Governments	Colleges and Universities	Hospitals
Finance current operations	General Special Revenue (and Expendable Trust)	Unrestricted Current Restricted Current*	General Specific Purpose

Fiduciary responsibilities	Nonexpendable Trust	Loan
		Endowment and
		  Similar:
		    Endowment (true)
		    Term Endowment
		    Quasi-Endowment
		
		Annuity and Life
		  Income:
		    Annuity
		    Life Income
			
			Endowment
			
			"Board-Designated"
			(General)

Acquisition of and accountability for major fixed assets and related long-term debt	Agency
	Capital Projects‡
	
	Debt Service
	
	General Fixed Assets/General Long-Term Debt
		Agency†
		Plant:
		  Unexpended
		  For Renewals and
		    Replacements
		  For Retirement of
		    Indebtedness
		  Investment in Plant
			Plant Replacement and Expansion§

* Restricted Current Funds revenue is considered realized, and hence is recognized as revenue, only to the extent that it has been expended for the specified purpose. Thus, the realization rule here is similar to that of a hospital Specific Purpose Fund: (1) restricted earnings or contributions are credited to fund balance, then (2) in the period of expenditure, fund balance is debited and an appropriate revenue account is credited.

† Hospitals usually account for agency relationships in the General Fund rather than by setting up separate Agency Funds.

‡ Financial resources for renewals and replacements of SLG fixed assets may be accounted for in the General Fund or in Capital Projects, Expendable Trust, or Special Revenue Funds, as appropriate to the restrictions on or purpose of these resources and their materiality.

§ Hospital fixed assets and long-term debt and unused proceeds of long-term debt are accounted for in the General Fund.

Budgetary Accounts and Subsidiary Ledgers

The current period expenditures of both colleges and universities and governments are typically controlled by budgets or appropriations. Thus, budgetary accounts often are established in governmental funds of governments. Both account for and report encumbrances, and university statements setting forth detailed revenues and expenditures for the year may include budgetary comparisons as in SLG reporting.

Likewise, as in accounting for governmental funds of state and local governments, both Revenues Subsidiary Ledgers and Expenditures Subsidiary Ledgers are employed in college and university accounting. However, this chapter focuses on *general ledger* accounting for transactions and events. Therefore, subsidiary ledger entries are not illustrated.

Chapter Overview

Many of the main aspects of college and university accounting and reporting may be observed from the presentations in Figure 18-1 (discussed earlier) and Figure 18-2. Figure 18-2 provides an overview of college and university fund structure, revenue and expenditure recognition, and interfund relationships. Study this figure now for an overview of college and university accounting and reporting. Also, refer to it in studying the remainder of the chapter to reinforce your understanding of the principles and concepts in the chapter; and use it as a basis for reviewing the chapter.

Each of the fund groups commonly found in college and university accounting is discussed more fully in the following pages. These discussions are illustrated by means of a **continuing case example.** For simplicity of illustration we assume that "A University" is in its first full year of operation, though some of the physical plant was acquired in the preceding year.

CURRENT FUNDS

Current Funds financial resources available for current operations may be either restricted or unrestricted. Typically they may be used either for general educational purposes or for auxiliary enterprises. A careful distinction should be maintained between **_Unrestricted_** Current Funds and **_Restricted_** Current Funds, as the accounting and reporting procedures are quite different for these two subgroups of Current Funds.

Unrestricted Current Funds

The **_Unrestricted_** Current Funds subgroup includes those **financial resources** of the institution that have **_not_** been **_restricted externally_** (by grantors, donors, and so on) for specific purposes and are **expendable** for **_any_** legal and reasonable purpose agreed upon by the governing board in carrying out the primary purposes of the institution (e.g., instruction, research, public service). Thus, the Unrestricted Current Funds are similar to the General Fund of a government. Resources restricted by donors, grantors, or outside agencies for specific current operating purposes are accounted for in the **_Restricted_** Current Funds.

Unrestricted Current Funds resources that are **designated** by the governing board to serve as loan or quasi-endowment funds, or to be expended for plant purposes, are transferred to the Loan, Endowment, and Plant Funds, respectively. Such unrestricted amounts are distinguished from the restricted portions of those funds by using Fund Balance—Unrestricted and Fund Balance—Restricted accounts. Unrestricted Current Funds resources that are **_designated_** by the governing board for specific **current operating** purposes should be accounted for in the **_Unrestricted_** Current Funds, either as formal appropriations or as allocations, designations, or reservations of the fund balance, as appropriate.

Restricted Current Funds

The **Restricted** Current Funds subgroup is used to account for resources that are **expendable** but are **_restricted_** by donors, grantors, or other outside agencies to expenditure for specific **_operating_** purposes. They are similar to Specific Purpose Funds of hospitals, and similar revenue recognition conventions apply to both. **_Earnings_** of **_or contributions_** to **_Restricted_** Current Funds are **_not recognized as revenue until expended for their intended purpose._** Amounts received or accrued are credited initially to a Fund Balance account. Prior to preparation of financial statements, an amount equal to that expended for the restricted purpose is deducted from the appropriate Fund Balance account and added to the appropriate Revenues account. Thus *Restricted* Current Funds *revenues and expenditures* are typically *equal.*

The more common additions to **Restricted** Current Funds include (1) restricted gifts for specific operating purposes; (2) restricted endowment income; and (3) grants received from private organizations or governments for research, public service, or other specific purposes. Reductions of *Restricted* Current Funds fund balances result from (1) expenditures charged to the funds, when corresponding amounts are recognized as revenues to "match" the revenues and expenditures; (2) refunds to donors and grantors; and (3) transfers to the Unrestricted Current Funds for indirect cost recoveries on sponsored programs—when the resources are initially accounted for in the *Restricted* Current Funds. (Any *unrestricted* resources received as indirect cost recoveries *may* be recorded directly in the *Unrestricted* Current Funds.)

The Fund Balance accounts are titled according to restricted use or source, such as:

> Fund Balances:
> > Restricted Income from Endowment Funds
> > Gifts Restricted for Operating Purposes
> > Federal Government Grants for Research
> > Auxiliary Enterprises

The Fund Balance accounts may be separately titled in the general ledger, the subsidiary ledger, or in both ledgers. Further, the governing board may designate portions of these balances for specific purposes or projects permissible under the restrictions placed on them, which may require that more detailed Fund Balance accounts be established.

Current Funds Revenues and Expenditures

Current Funds **revenues** are accounted for essentially on the accrual basis and are classified by source. Typical revenue sources include:

1. Tuition and fees,
2. Appropriations from various levels of government,
3. Government grants and contracts,
4. Private gifts, grants, and contracts,
5. Endowment income, and
6. Sales and services of educational activities.

Expenditures result from using resources of the Current Funds group to finance the current operations of a college or university. Current Funds expenditures are recognized when liabilities to be paid from the Current Funds are incurred. Current Funds expenditures are reported by function, and *educational and general* expenditures are reported separately from *auxiliary enterprise* and *hospital* expenditures. Functional classifications of educational and general expenditures include:

1. Instruction,
2. Research,

Figure 18-2

COLLEGE AND UNIVERSITY ACCOUNTING OVERVIEW

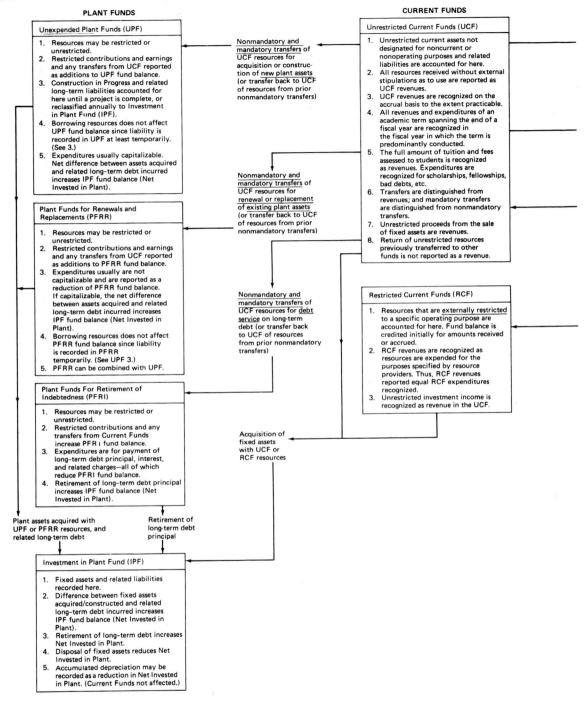

3. Public service,
4. Academic support,
5. Student services,
6. Institutional support,
7. Operation and maintenance of plant, and
8. Scholarships and fellowships.

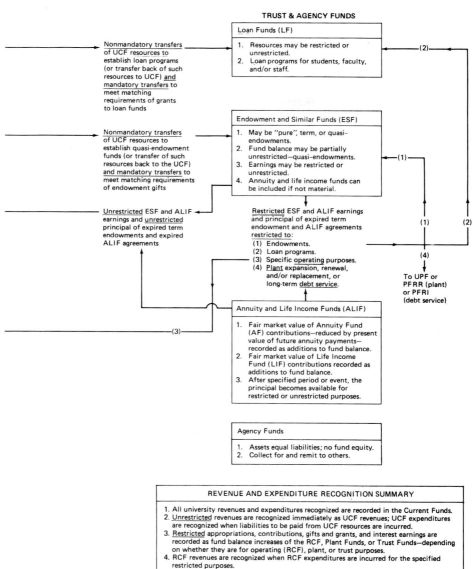

Figure 18-2
(continued)

TRUST & AGENCY FUNDS

Loan Funds (LF)

1. Resources may be restricted or unrestricted.
2. Loan programs for students, faculty, and/or staff.

Nonmandatory transfers of UCF resources to establish loan programs (or transfer back of such resources to UCF) and mandatory transfers to meet matching requirements of grants to loan funds

Nonmandatory transfers of UCF resources to establish quasi-endowment funds (or transfer of such resources back to the UCF) and mandatory transfers to meet matching requirements of endowment gifts

Endowment and Similar Funds (ESF)

1. May be "pure", term, or quasi-endowments.
2. Fund balance may be partially unrestricted—quasi-endowments.
3. Earnings may be restricted or unrestricted.
4. Annuity and life income funds can be included if not material.

Unrestricted ESF and ALIF earnings and unrestricted principal of expired term endowments and expired ALIF agreements

Restricted ESF and ALIF earnings and principal of expired term endowment and ALIF agreements restricted to:
(1) Endowments.
(2) Loan programs.
(3) Specific operating purposes.
(4) Plant expansion, renewal, and/or replacement, or long-term debt service.

To UPF or PFRR (plant) or PFRI (debt service)

Annuity and Life Income Funds (ALIF)

1. Fair market value of Annuity Fund (AF) contributions—reduced by present value of future annuity payments—recorded as additions to fund balance.
2. Fair market value of Life Income Fund (LIF) contributions recorded as additions to fund balance.
3. After specified period or event, the principal becomes available for restricted or unrestricted purposes.

Agency Funds

1. Assets equal liabilities; no fund equity.
2. Collect for and remit to others.

REVENUE AND EXPENDITURE RECOGNITION SUMMARY

1. All university revenues and expenditures recognized are recorded in the Current Funds.
2. Unrestricted revenues are recognized immediately as UCF revenues; UCF expenditures are recognized when liabilities to be paid from UCF resources are incurred.
3. Restricted appropriations, contributions, gifts and grants, and interest earnings are recorded as fund balance increases of the RCF, Plant Funds, or Trust Funds—depending on whether they are for operating (RCF), plant, or trust purposes.
4. RCF revenues are recognized when RCF expenditures are incurred for the specified restricted purposes.
5. Plant and Trust Funds revenues and expenditures or expenses are not recognized as university revenues or expenditures. However, unrestricted earnings and the unrestricted principal of expired term endowments and ALIF agreements are recognized as UCF revenues.

The major Revenues, Expenditures, and Transfers accounts recommended in FARM are presented in Figure 18-3. More detailed accounts would be established in practice, of course—in the general ledger, the subsidiary ledger(s), or in both ledgers. For ease of illustration, we use only general ledger control accounts in the illustrative entries in this chapter.

Transfers

Transfers of resources to or from other funds may result in nonrevenue and nonexpenditure changes in the fund balances of Current Funds. Transfers are ***nonloan movements of financial resources*** from one fund group to another in order for the resources to be used for the objectives of the recipient fund group. Transfers

Figure 18-3

**CLASSIFICATION OF CURRENT FUNDS
REVENUES, EXPENDITURES, AND TRANSFERS**

Revenues	*Expenditures and Transfers*
Tuition and Fees	Educational and General
Appropriations	Instruction
Federal	Research
State	Public Service
Local	Academic Support, e.g.,
Grants and Contracts	Computing Services
Federal	Libraries
State	Student Services, e.g.,
Local	Counseling and Career Guidance
Private Gifts, Grants, and Contracts	Dean of Students
Endowment Income	Financial Aid Administration
Sales and Services of Educational	Intramural Athletics
Activities, e.g.,	Institutional Support, e.g.,
Film Rentals	Legal Counsel
Testing Services	Alumni Office
Sales and Services of Auxiliary	Purchasing
Enterprises, e.g.,	Operation and Maintenance of Plant
Residence Halls	Scholarships and Fellowships
Food Services	Mandatory Transfers
College Union	Nonmandatory Transfers
Athletic Programs	Auxiliary Enterprises, Hospitals,
Sales and Services of Hospitals	and Other
Other Sources	Auxiliary Enterprises
Independent Operations	Hospitals
	Independent Operations

Source: National Association of College and University Business Officers, *Financial Accounting and Reporting Manual for Higher Education* (Washington, D.C.: NACUBO, 1990).

may involve either Unrestricted Current Funds or Restricted Current Funds, but transfers involving Unrestricted Current Funds are far more common. Whereas governments distinguish "operating" and "residual equity" transfers, colleges and universities distinguish **"mandatory transfers"** and **"nonmandatory transfers."**

If the **board,** at its discretion, **directs** that a portion of the Current Funds resources be set aside for a noncurrent or nonoperating purpose, a **nonmandatory** (discretionary) **transfer** to other funds—not an expenditure—is reported as a Current Funds fund balance decrease. Likewise, if the board directs that previously transferred resources be returned to the Current Funds, a nonmandatory transfer from other funds is reported in the Current Funds—not revenues. **Mandatory transfers,** on the other hand, are legally or contractually **required** transfers of Current Funds resources to other funds—such as required transfers to the Plant Funds for Retirement of Indebtedness to provide for debt service and transfers to Loan Funds required by federal grants. No "Mandatory" transfers to the Current Funds are reported. Rather, required transfers of resources from other funds, such as the transfer of unrestricted Endowment Funds earnings—initially recorded in the Endowment Funds—to the Current Funds are recorded and reported by source of resources (e.g., endowment income).

The terms "mandatory transfer" and "nonmandatory transfer" are unique to college and university accounting. *FARM* further defines and explains them as follows:

> **Mandatory transfers.** Transfers from the Current Funds group to other fund groups arising out of (1) binding legal agreements related to the financing of educational plant, such as amounts for debt retirement, interest, and required provi-

sions for renewals and replacements of plant, not financed from other sources; and (2) grant agreements with agencies of the federal government, donors, and other organizations to match gifts and grants to loan and other funds. Mandatory transfers may be required to be made from either unrestricted or restricted current funds.

Nonmandatory transfers. Transfers from the Current Funds group to other fund groups made at the discretion of the governing board to serve a variety of objectives, such as additions to loan funds, additions to quasi-endowment funds, general or specific plant additions, voluntary renewals and replacements of plant, and prepayments on debt principal.[13]

Nonmandatory transfers also may include the retransfer of resources back to the Current Funds. Both mandatory transfers and nonmandatory transfers are reported separate from revenues and expenditures in university operating statements.

Revenue and Expenditure Recognition Conventions—Unrestricted Current Funds

Several revenue and expenditure recognition conventions of **Unrestricted** Current Funds accounting should be noted. These relate to (1) tuition and fee waivers and uncollectible accounts, (2) legally restricted fees, (3) academic terms that span two fiscal years, (4) auxiliary enterprises and hospitals, (5) expired endowments and other trusts, and (6) other special considerations.

Tuition and Fee Waivers and Uncollectible Accounts

Accounting for tuition and fees has several unique features. One is that in college and university accounting , the full amount of the **standard** tuition and fees is **recognized as revenues.** *Scholarships, fellowships, bad debts,* and similar items are accounted for as **expenditures.**

For example, assume that Higgins College has gross tuition and fee charges for 19A of $20,000,000. Higgins College grants full or partial tuition waivers totaling $600,000 for the year, and estimates that $100,000 of the 19A tuition and fees will be uncollectible. The entries in the Unrestricted Current Funds accounts are:

Unrestricted Current Funds

Accounts Receivable	20,000,000	
Revenues—Educational and General		20,000,000
To record tuition and fees earned.		
Expenditures—Educational and General—Tuition		
Waivers	600,000	
Expenditures—Educational and General—Bad Debts . . .	100,000	
Accounts Receivable		600,000
Allowance for Uncollectible Accounts		100,000
To record expenditures for tuition waivers and estimated uncollectible accounts.		

Legally Restricted Fees

Another unique feature of college and university accounting is the reporting of *specific fees and other revenue sources* that are legally or contractually pledged (externally *restricted*) to *nonoperating* purposes (such as debt service or plant

---

[13] *FARM,* ¶340-341.

construction or renovation). Where the *full amount* of such fees or other revenue sources is externally **restricted** to *non*operating purposes, the revenues are not reported in the Unrestricted Current Funds. Rather, they are *recorded as additions to* the *fund balance of* the *appropriate other fund*—for example, the Plant Funds in the examples cited above. On the other hand, if **only part** of the specific fees or other revenue sources is legally or contractually pledged for *non*operating purposes, (1) the **full amount** of the fees or other revenue sources is reported as *revenues in* the *Unrestricted* Current Funds and (2) the **restricted amount** is reported as a *mandatory transfer* to the appropriate other fund—for example, the Plant Funds in the example cited earlier.

To illustrate the latter situation, assume that a college charges student fees totaling $1,000,000. Also, assume that 20% of the fees are restricted to payment of debt service on bonds issued to finance modernization and expansion of the college's student activity center. The **entries** required in the Unrestricted Current Funds are:

Unrestricted Current Funds

Cash	1,000,000	
Revenues—Tuition and Fees		1,000,000

To record student fee revenues.

Mandatory Transfers to Plant Funds	200,000	
Due to Plant Funds		200,000

To record required transfer of student fees restricted for
  debt service to the Plant Funds.

Even if **none of the fees** were **pledged** to a specific purpose, the *governing board* might allocate part of these resources for debt service, or plant construction or renovation, or some other specific purpose. The accounting treatment would differ from the above example only in that the transfer of resources to the appropriate other fund group would be a **nonmandatory** (not mandatory) transfer. Likewise, the return of **unrestricted** resources that had been transferred previously to a Quasi-Endowment Fund or to the Plant Funds, for example, should be reported as a **nonmandatory** transfer, not as revenues, in the Statement of Current Funds Revenues, Expenditures, and Other Changes.

Term Spanning Two Fiscal Years

A final practice related to tuition and fees concerns tuition and fees assessed for a term of instruction that spans two fiscal years. All tuition and fees assessed for that term of instruction are reported as revenues of the fiscal year in which the term is *predominantly* conducted, as are all expenditures incurred to finance that term.

For instance, if Forrest College's six-week summer term begins July 15 and its fiscal year ends July 31, the term is predominantly conducted in the next fiscal year. Thus, the $1,000,000 of tuition and fees charged and collected as of July 31 and the related expenditures of $250,000 should be recorded as follows:

Unrestricted Current Funds

Cash	1,000,000	
Deferred Revenues		1,000,000

To record deferred revenues for the summer term.

Deferred Expenditures	250,000	
Cash/Inventory/Payables		250,000

To record deferred expenditures for the summer term.

These deferred revenues and expenditures should be recognized as revenues and expenditures of the next fiscal year.

Auxiliary Enterprises and Hospitals

Auxiliary enterprises are **self-sustaining** activities of a university—such as *residence halls, food services, and bookstores*—that provide goods or services to students, faculty, or staff and charge fees, often related to costs, for the goods or services. Auxiliary enterprises may be accounted for in a separate subfund, but their operating accounts are reported as part of the Current Funds. The fixed assets and long-term debts related to auxiliary enterprises are accounted for in the Plant Funds.

Auxiliary enterprises are *not* accounted for on a revenues and expenses basis as are proprietary funds of governments, but on a revenues, expenditures, and fund balances basis like that of SLG governmental funds. Thus, the "auxiliary enterprises" revenue category is used to account for all revenues generated through the *operations* of auxiliary enterprises. Likewise, all auxiliary enterprise expenditures are reported as such in the Current Funds operating statement.

University **hospitals** are similar to auxiliary enterprises. Some apply hospital GAAP (Chapter 17), but our examples assume they apply *FARM* guidelines. Thus, hospital patient service revenues (net of deductions from revenues for discounts and allowances) and hospital revenues arising from other hospital services are reported in this revenue source category in the **Unrestricted** Current Funds. But *restricted* gifts, grants, or endowment income to be used for auxiliary enterprise or hospital operations are *not* immediately recognized as revenues. Rather, they are initially accounted for as **Restricted** Current Funds fund balance increases, then are reported as Restricted Current Funds revenues upon expenditure of the restricted resources for the specified operating purpose.

Expired Endowments and Other Trusts

The **principal** of some endowment gifts received by a college or university is **not expendable** (nonexpendable trust) for a specified term (e.g., 20 years). In addition to these term endowments, colleges and universities sometimes receive gifts with the stipulation that a fixed payment **(annuity gifts)** or the income earned on the donated assets **(life income gifts)** be paid to a specified beneficiary for some period of time. Upon expiration of the term or conditions of these gift agreements, the principal of the gifts may be expended for either restricted or unrestricted university purposes.

If the **principal** of a term endowment or of an annuity or life income agreement becomes available for *unrestricted* use by the university when its term expires, the principal of the expired gift agreement is recognized as Unrestricted Current Funds **revenues** upon its expiration. But if the principal for the expired endowment, annuity, or life income agreement is **restricted** to a specific use, it will **not** be reported as **revenues**. Rather, it will be added to the fund balance of the appropriate "restricted use" fund: Restricted Current Funds (for operations), Endowment Funds (held in trust), or Plant Funds (for capital outlay or debt service). **Earnings** on investments of restricted assets are accounted for similarly.

Other Special Considerations

Several other accounting practices related to operations of colleges and universities should be noted. Significant amounts of **inventory** should be reported in the year end balance sheet, and Expenditures should be increased or reduced, as appropriate, by the amount of the inventory change during the year. (This compares with the **"consumption"** or "use" method of inventory accounting by state and local governments.) Similarly, if significant amounts of service costs benefit subsequent periods, such **prepayals** should be recorded as deferred charges and the Expenditures account reduced.

Also, the account **"Deductions from Fund Balances"** may be encountered in higher education accounting and reporting. Refunds to donors and grantors, the return of unencumbered or unexpended balances of lapsed appropriations to the state, and similar transactions are recorded and reported as deductions from fund balances rather than as expenditures.

Budgetary Accounts

As in state and local governments, colleges and universities typically use fixed-dollar budgeting. Thus, it usually is necessary to maintain budgetary control accounts for a college or university in much the same manner as for a government.

Budgetary accounts may be incorporated in the ledger of either Unrestricted or Restricted Current Funds in a manner similar to that used in the General Fund of a municipality. Slightly different account titles are commonly used by colleges or universities, as compared with municipalities. Further, the difference between estimated revenues and estimated expenditures is usually carried in an "Unassigned Budget Balance" or "Unallocated Budget Balance" account—similar to the Budgetary Fund Balance account used by some governments—during the period rather than in the Fund Balances account. The **budgetary entry** for a college or university Current Fund would appear as follows:

Estimated Revenues (or Unrealized Revenues)	1,000,000	
Expenditures and Other Changes Allocations (or Budget Allocations for Expenditures and Other Changes)		990,000
Unallocated Budget Balance (or Unassigned Budget Balance)		10,000

To record the college or university budget.

These amounts would be reversed from the accounts at year end when their purpose has been served. Budgetary accounting for colleges and universities closely parallels that of a municipal General Fund, so is not illustrated further in this chapter.

Transactions and Entries—Unrestricted Current Funds

Assume for purposes of illustration that two Current Fund accounting entities—an Unrestricted Current Fund and a Restricted Current Fund—are in use and that most auxiliary enterprises are accounted for as part of the Unrestricted Current Fund. The following are some typical Unrestricted Current Fund transactions and the entries to record them. Transactions 10, 11, and 12 require entries not only in the Unrestricted Current Fund but also in the Plant Funds; entry 13 requires an entry in the Endowment and Similar Funds; and entry 15 corresponds with entry 3 in the Restricted Current Fund illustration.

Note that while Figure 18-3 contains an excellent classification of Current Funds Revenues, Expenditures, and Transfers accounts, our illustrative examples use an even simpler approach for ease of illustration. Both revenues and expenditures are classified simply as either (1) educational and general or (2) auxiliary enterprises. Further, Revenues Subsidiary Ledger and Expenditures Subsidiary Ledger entries are **not** illustrated since they would be similar to those illustrated for SLG General and Special Revenue Funds; only general ledger entries are presented in the example.

Unrestricted Current Funds (continued)

Transactions and Entries

1. Educational and general revenues earned during the year amounted to $2,600,000, of which $2,538,000 has been collected.

(1)	Cash	2,538,000	
	Accounts Receivable	62,000	
	Revenues—Educational and General		2,600,000
	To record educational revenues earned.		

Note that the *gross* amount of tuition and fees is recorded as revenues without regard to the ultimate collectibility of the amounts.

2. It is estimated that $2,000 of this year's accounts receivables will never be collected, and $12,000 of tuition scholarships were granted.

(2)	**Expenditures—Educational and General**	14,000	
	Accounts Receivable		12,000
	Allowance for Uncollectible Accounts		2,000
	To record provision for uncollectible accounts and scholarships.		

3. Other revenues of $700,000 were collected through auxiliary enterprises.

(3)	Cash	700,000	
	Revenues—Auxiliary Enterprises		700,000
	To record revenues of auxiliary enterprises.		

4. Total purchases of materials and supplies for the year amounted to $600,000, of which $560,000 has been paid.

(4)	**Inventory of Materials and Supplies**	600,000	
	Cash		560,000
	Accounts Payable		40,000
	To record purchases of materials and supplies.		

5. Materials and supplies used during the year amounted to $550,000, of which $250,000 is chargeable to educational and general activities and $300,000 to auxiliary enterprises.

(5)	Expenditures—Educational and General	250,000	
	Expenditures—Auxiliary Enterprises	300,000	
	Inventory of Materials and Supplies		550,000
	To record cost of materials and supplies used.		

6. Salaries and wages paid amounted to $2,200,000, of which $1,920,000 is chargeable to educational and general activities and $280,000 to auxiliary enterprises.

(6)	Expenditures—Educational and General	1,920,000	
	Expenditures—Auxiliary Enterprises	280,000	
	Cash		2,200,000
	To record salaries and wages paid.		

Unrestricted Current Funds (continued)

7. Legal fees, insurance, interest on money borrowed temporarily for operating purposes, and telephone and telegraph expenditures, all chargeable to educational and general activities, amounted to $100,000; all had been paid by the end of the year.

   (7) Expenditures—Educational and General   100,000
          Cash   100,000
        To record legal and insurance expenditures, interest on
          money borrowed for operating purposes, and
          telephone and telegraph expenditures.

8. Other expenditures chargeable to auxiliary enterprises and paid for totaled $10,000.

   (8) Expenditures—Auxiliary Enterprises   10,000
          Cash   10,000
        To record expenditures of auxiliary enterprises other
          than those for materials and supplies or for salaries.

9. Student aid cash grants totaled $8,000.

   (9) Expenditures—Educational and General   8,000
          Cash   8,000
        To record student aid granted.

10. Unrestricted Current Funds cash, $25,000, was transferred to the Funds for Retirement of Indebtedness—as required by the terms of the loan agreement—to pay a scheduled installment of the mortgage note carried as a liability in the Investment in Plant accounts. (See entry 1, Funds for Retirement of Indebtedness.)

  (10) **Mandatory Transfers to Plant Funds**   25,000
          Cash   25,000
        To record transfer to Plant Funds to provide for
          payment of mortgage note carried as a liability in the
          Plant Funds.

11. A $30,000 nonmandatory transfer was made from the Unrestricted Current Fund to the Unexpended Plant Fund for the purpose of financing additions to the plant. (See entry 2, Unexpended Plant Funds.)

  (11) **Nonmandatory Transfers to Plant Funds**   30,000
          Cash   30,000
        To record transfers to Plant Funds for purposes of
          making additions to plant.

12. Unrestricted Current Funds cash, $10,000, was spent for equipment. (See entry 1, Investment in Plant Fund.)

  (12) Expenditures—Educational and General   10,000
          Cash   10,000
        To record cost of plant additions financed from the
          Unrestricted Current Fund.

Unrestricted Current Funds (continued)

Purchases of equipment and similar items are often financed directly from Current Funds resources as assumed here. The proper handling of other more significant plant additions is (1) to transfer financial resources to the Plant Funds and (2) to record the acquisition of the asset in that fund group. If that had been done for this example, Nonmandatory Transfers to Plant Funds would have been debited instead of Expenditures.

13. In accordance with a resolution of the board of trustees of the university, $100,000 was transferred from the Unrestricted Current Fund to the Endowment and Similar Funds group for the purpose of establishing a fund that is to function as an endowment. (See entry 10, Endowment and Similar Funds.)

| (13) | Nonmandatory Transfers to Endowment and Similar Funds | 100,000 | |
| | Cash | | 100,000 |

To record transfer of cash to Endowment and Similar Funds group for the purpose of establishing a fund which is to function as an endowment.

14. The board of trustees voted to reserve $75,000 of the Unrestricted Current Fund resources for a computer use survey during the subsequent year.

| (14) | **Fund Balances—Unallocated** | 75,000 | |
| | **Fund Balances—Allocated** | | 75,000 |

To establish a fund balance reserve for the estimated cost of a computer use survey to be made during the subsequent period.

15. Indirect overhead recovery on sponsored research, $8,000, was paid from the Restricted Current Fund to the Unrestricted Current Fund. (See entry 3, Restricted Current Fund.)

| (15) | Cash | 8,000 | |
| | Revenues—Educational and General | | 8,000 |

To record receipt of indirect cost recovery on sponsored research from the Restricted Current Fund.

Recall that if the reimbursement for the indirect cost recoveries is initially identified or received separately from the restricted portion of the research grant, it may be recorded directly in the Unrestricted Current Funds as revenues—rather than being recorded in the Restricted Current Funds and later reclassified.

16. The university borrowed $6,000 for current operations.

| (16) | Cash | 6,000 | |
| | **Notes Payable** | | 6,000 |

To record issuance of note for current operations.

17. Accrued interest on the note at year end was $100.

| (17) | Expenditures—Educational and General | 100 | |
| | Accrued Interest Payable | | 100 |

To accrue interest on note.

Unrestricted Current Funds (continued)

18. Revenue, expenditure, and transfer accounts were closed at year end.

(18)			
Revenues—Educational and General	2,608,000	
Revenues—Auxiliary Enterprises	700,000	
Expenditures—Educational and General		2,302,100
Expenditures—Auxiliary Enterprises		590,000
Mandatory Transfers to Plant Funds		25,000
Nonmandatory Transfers to Plant Funds		30,000
Nonmandatory Transfers to Endowment and Similar		
Funds		100,000
Fund Balances—Unallocated		260,900

To close revenues, expenditures, and transfers
accounts at year end.

Transactions and Entries—Restricted Current Funds

The following are typical transactions of the Restricted Current Funds and the entries made to record them.

Transactions and Entries

1. Cash receipts during the year were as follows:

Federally Sponsored Research (grant)	$100,000
Gifts—Library Operations	200,000
Endowment Income—Supplemental Salary Payments* . .	62,400
Endowment Income—Student Aid*	15,600
Endowment Income—Auxiliary Enterprise*	9,700
	$387,700

See also Endowment and Similar Funds, transaction 5.

(1)	Cash	387,700	
	Fund Balances—Grants—Federally Sponsored		
	Research		100,000
	Fund Balances—Gifts—Library Operations		200,000
	Fund Balances—Endowment Income—		
	Supplemental Salary Payments		62,400
	Fund Balances—Endowment Income—		
	Student Aid		15,600
	Fund Balances—Endowment Income—		
	Auxiliary Enterprises		9,700

To record resources received.

(Fund Balances **subsidiary** ledger accounts usually show the sources and purposes of the resources received or accrued. Alternatively, a series of Fund Balances **general** ledger accounts may be used, as is done here for clarity of illustration.)

2. Expenditures were incurred as follows, of which $7,000 remained unpaid at year end:

Sponsored Research	$ 40,000
Library Operations	130,000
Instruction and Departmental Research	
(Supplemental Salary Payments)	50,000
Student Aid	12,000
Auxiliary Enterprises	2,000
	$234,000

Restricted Current Funds (continued)

(2) Expenditures—Educational and General   232,000
    Expenditures—Auxiliary Enterprises   2,000
       Accounts Payable   7,000
       Cash   227,000
    To record expenditures incurred.

3. Recovery of indirect costs of $8,000, associated with the $40,000 of sponsored research expenditures, was transferred to the Unrestricted Current Fund. (See also Unrestricted Current Fund, transaction 15.)

(3) **Fund Balances—Grants—Federally Sponsored
     Research**   8,000
     Cash   8,000
    To record payment to Unrestricted Current Fund of **indirect cost recovery** under provisions of research grant.

(The indirect cost recovery revenue is recognized in the Unrestricted Current Fund in entry 15. Recall that in some instances indirect cost recoveries may be recorded directly in the Unrestricted Current Fund rather than being recorded initially in the Restricted Current Fund.)

4. Income due from the Endowment and Similar Funds group at year end was as follows:

For Supplemental Salary Payments $25,000
For Student Aid   5,000
                                  $30,000

(See also Endowment and Similar Funds, transaction 9.)

(4) Due from Endowment and Similar Funds   30,000
    **Fund Balances—Endowment Income—
     Supplemental Salary Payments**   25,000
    **Fund Balances—Endowment Income—
     Student Aid**   5,000
    To record resources due from endowment earnings.

5. Revenue for the period was recognized and fund balances were adjusted accordingly at year end.

(5) **Fund Balances—Grants—Federally Sponsored
     Research**   40,000
    Fund Balances—Gifts—Library Operations   130,000
    **Fund Balances—Endowment Income—Supplemental
     Salary Payments**   50,000
    **Fund Balances—Endowment Income—
     Student Aid**   12,000
    **Fund Balances—Endowment Income—
     Auxiliary Enterprises**   2,000
       Revenues—Educational and General   232,000
       Revenues—Auxiliary Enterprises   2,000
    To recognize revenues to the extent that restricted resources were expended during the period.

(Compare this entry to entry 2. Note again that revenues are recognized only to the extent that the restricted resources are expended for the purposes or functions designated by donors, grantors, or outside agencies.)

Restricted Current Funds (continued)

6. Closing entries were made.

(6)			
Revenues—Educational and General	232,000	
Revenues—Auxiliary Enterprises	2,000	
Expenditures—Educational and General		232,000
Expenditures—Auxiliary Enterprises		2,000

To close the revenues and expenditures accounts at
year end.

(Obviously, the entries to close the Revenues and Expenditures accounts
must be in corresponding amounts in the case of Restricted Current Funds,
because revenue is realized only upon expenditure of the restricted resources.)

In each preceding case, less resources were expended (and recognized as
revenue) than were received or accrued. Had fund balances been brought forward
from prior years, the opposite might have been true. Again, as in the case of Specific Purpose Funds of hospitals, the logic of the realization (revenue recognition)
convention employed in Restricted Current Funds accounting—as recommended
in *FARM* and as done in most colleges and universities—is that the resources have
not been earned until they have been expended for their restricted purposes.

Operating Statement—Current Funds

A **Statement of Current Funds Revenues, Expenditures, and Other Changes,**
based on the journal entries for the two Current Funds subgroups, is presented in
Figure 18-4. It shows the total revenues from each source and the total expenditures for each major activity, both classified as to whether they pertain to Unrestricted or Restricted Current Funds.

Since detailed revenue and expenditure accounts are not used in the journal entries in this chapter, the most common accounts (see Figure 18-3) are listed
in Figure 18-4. The amounts presented in the Restricted Current Funds columns
are properly classified, as are the mandatory and nonmandatory transfers and
auxiliary enterprises revenues and expenditures. The other amounts in the Unrestricted Current Funds columns have been **allocated (arbitrarily)** among the
more common revenue and expenditure accounts solely for **illustrative** purposes.
Also, some accounts with zero balances are included for illustrative purposes.
Schedules of the details of the current revenues and expenditures, and of the
transfers, should be prepared for internal uses. For example, details of the operations of each department should be shown, and a separate statement of revenues
and expenditures should be prepared for each of the auxiliary activities.

BALANCE SHEET—FOR THE UNIVERSITY

A **Balance Sheet** for the university at the close of the fiscal year is presented in
Figure 18-5. Data from the transactions already presented for the Unrestricted
Current and Restricted Current Funds are the bases of the balance sheet for the
Current Funds group. The year end balance sheets of the other funds or fund
groups (after the transactions discussed later) are added to the Balance Sheets of
the two types of funds already discussed.

Figure 18-4

STATEMENT OF CURRENT FUNDS REVENUES, EXPENDITURES, AND OTHER CHANGES

A University

Statement of Current Funds Revenues, Expenditures, and Other Changes

For the Year Ended October 31, 19A

	Total	Unrestricted	Restricted
Revenues:			
Tuition and fees	$1,358,000	$1,358,000	$ —
State appropriations	1,000,000	1,000,000	—
Federal grants and contracts	40,000	—	40,000
State grants and contracts	—	—	—
Local gifts, grants, and contracts	132,000	130,000	2,000
Private gifts, grants, and contracts	130,000	—	130,000
Endowment income	62,000	—	62,000
Sales and services of educational activities	70,000	70,000	—
Sales and services of auxiliary enterprises	700,000	700,000	—
Expired term endowment	—	—	—
Other sources (if any)	50,000	50,000	—
Total Revenues	3,542,000	3,308,000	234,000
Expenditures and mandatory transfers:			
Educational and general:			
Instruction	932,000	882,000	50,000
Research	140,000	100,000	40,000
Public service	50,000	50,000	—
Academic support	330,000	200,000	130,000
Student services	150,000	150,000	—
Institutional support	400,100	400,100	—
Operation and maintenance of plant	500,000	500,000	—
Scholarships and fellowships	32,000	20,000	12,000
Total Educational and General Expenditures	2,534,100	2,302,100	232,000
Mandatory transfers for:			
Principal and interest	25,000	25,000	—
Renewals and replacements	—	—	—
Loan fund matching grant	—	—	—
Total Educational and General	2,559,100	2,327,100	232,000
Auxiliary enterprises:			
Expenditures:	592,000	590,000	2,000
Mandatory transfers for:			
Principal and interest	—	—	—
Renewals and replacements	—	—	—
Total Auxiliary Enterprises	592,000	590,000	2,000
Total Expenditures and Mandatory Transfers	3,151,100	2,917,100	234,000
Other transfers and additions (deductions):			
Excess of restricted receipts over transfers to revenues	175,700	—	175,700
Nonmandatory transfer to plant funds	(30,000)	(30,000)	
Nonmandatory transfer to Endowment and Similar Funds	(100,000)	(100,000)	—
Net Increase in Fund Balance	$ 436,600	$ 260,900	$175,700

This "pancake" form of the university-wide balance sheet seems to be the preferred form, though college and university balance sheets are often presented in columnar form. Even though like balances of the several fund groups are placed on the same line using a columnar format, no total column is usually provided. This recognizes that assets and liabilities of the fund groups are in most cases subject to legal or donor restrictions, and other obligations that may make it misleading to show totals for the university as a whole.

Figure 18-5

YEAR-END BALANCE SHEET—ALL FUNDS

A University
Balance Sheet
October 31, 19A

Assets

Current Funds:
Unrestricted:

Cash		$ 209,000
Accounts receivable, less allowance for uncollectible accounts of $2,000		48,000
Inventory of materials and supplies		50,000
Total unrestricted		307,000

Restricted:

Cash		152,700
Due from endowment and similar funds		30,000
Total restricted		182,700
Total Current Funds		$ 489,700

Loan Funds:

Cash		$ 25,400
Loans receivable		49,500
Investments		25,000
Total Loan Funds		$ 99,900

Endowment and Similar Funds:
Assets other than fixed assets:

Cash		$ 205,800
Investments:		
Preferred stocks, at cost (market value $625,000)	$ 500,000	
Common stocks, at cost (market value, $1,215,000)	1,065,000	
Bonds, at cost (market value, $465,000)	454,700	
Held in trust by others (cost, $200,000; market value, $234,000)	—	
	2,019,700	
	2,225,500	

Liabilities and Fund Balances

Current Funds:
Unrestricted:

Accounts Payable		$ 40,000
Notes payable		6,000
Interest payable		100
Fund balances		260,900
Total unrestricted		307,000

Restricted:

Accounts payable		7,000
Fund balances		175,700
Total restricted		182,700
Total Current Funds		$ 489,700

Loan Funds:

Fund balances*		$ 99,900
Total Loan Funds		$ 99,900

Endowment and Similar Funds:

Due to restricted current funds		$ 30,000
Fund balances:*		
Endowment	$2,925,500	
Quasi-Endowment	100,000	
	3,025,500	

Fixed assets:

Land		100,000
Buildings, less accumulated depreciation of $6,000		594,000
Equipment, less accumulated depreciation of $14,000		136,000
		830,000
Total Endowment and Similar Funds		**$3,055,500**

Annuity and Life Income Funds:

Cash	$ 10,000	
Investments, at cost (market value, $22,100)	176,000	
Total Annuity and Life Income Funds		$ 186,000

Plant Funds:

Unexpended:

Cash	$ 318,000	
Investments, at cost (market value $22,100)	20,000	
Construction in progress	240,000	
Total unexpended		$ 578,000

For retirement of indebtedness:

Investments	$ 25,000	
Sinking fund—bank trustee	200,000	
Total for retirement of indebtedness		$ 225,000

Investment in plant:

Land	$ 300,000	
Buildings, less accumulated depreciation of $4,159,000**	3,841,000	
Improvements other than building, less accumulated depreciation of $600**	11,400	
Equipment, less accumulated depreciation of $1,080,400**	728,600	
Library books	200,000	
Total investment in plant		$5,081,000
Total Plant Funds		**$5,884,000**

Total Endowment and Similar Funds		**$3,055,500**

Annuity and Life Income Funds:

Annuities payable	$ 162,881	
Fund balances—Annuities*	23,119	
Total Annuity and Life Income Funds		$ 186,000

Plant Funds:

Unexpended:

Accounts payable	$ 40,000	
Notes payable	500,000	
Fund balances—Unrestricted*	18,000	
Fund balances—Restricted	20,000	
Total unexpended		$ 578,000

For retirement of indebtedness:

Fund balances—Restricted*		$ 225,000
Total for retirement of indebtedness		$ 225,000

Investment in plant:

Mortgage payable	$ 370,000	
Net invested in plant*	4,711,000	
Total investment in plant		$5,081,000
Total Plant Funds		**$5,884,000**

* Statements analyzing changes in the balances of each fund group should be presented in the financial report.

** State and local government colleges and universities are **not** required to report accumulated depreciation on Plant Funds assets, but may elect to do so.

As noted earlier, college and university fixed assets and long-term debt are **not** accounted for in the Current Funds group. Instead, the fixed assets and long-term liabilities are accounted for in the **Plant Funds** group. Any financial resources that are internally designated or externally restricted either to plant expansion, renewal, or replacement or to servicing long-term debt also are accounted for in the Plant Funds.

The Plant Funds consist of four **fund subgroups:**

1. *Unexpended Plant Funds:* to account for resources to be used for the acquisition of institutional fixed assets.
2. *Funds for Renewals and Replacements:* to account for resources to be used for the remodeling, renovation, or replacement of existing fixed assets.
3. *Funds for Retirement of Indebtedness:* to account for resources to be used to service the debt incurred in relation to the physical plant.
4. *Investment in Plant:* to account for the institution's fixed assets, related indebtedness, and net investment in plant.

The Unexpended Plant Funds and the Funds for Renewals and Replacements are similar to Capital Projects Funds of municipalities; the Funds for Retirement of Indebtedness compare to Debt Service Funds of municipalities; and the Investment in Plant subgroup is like a combination of the General Fixed Assets and General Long-Term Debt Account Groups of a municipality.

All but the Investment in Plant subgroup are used to account for financial resources (cash, investments, and so on). Sometimes these financial resources are recorded directly in the Plant Funds, as when (1) resources are dedicated by donors for plant purposes, and (2) specific student fees are assessed under binding external agreements for plant improvement or related debt service purposes. Other restricted financial resources may come from the Endowment and Similar Funds; and unrestricted resources may be transferred to the Plant Funds from the Unrestricted Current Funds. The distinction between unrestricted and restricted (externally) resources should be maintained in the accounts and reports (1) to ensure that the restricted resources are used for the proper purposes, and (2) because the governing board can transfer unrestricted resources back to the Unrestricted Current Funds or to the Endowment and Similar Funds.

For external reporting purposes all Plant Funds subgroups may be reported either separately or combined, as long as the separate fund balances are reported. Any encumbrances outstanding should be disclosed by a Reserve for Encumbrances or in the notes to the financial statements. The results of the transactions and entries of each Plant Funds subgroup are shown in the Balance Sheet presented in Figure 18-5 and the Statement of Changes in Fund Balances presented at the end of this Chapter.

Unexpended Plant Funds

The purpose of the Unexpended Plant Funds is to account for the inflows, uses, and balances of financial resources (and any related liabilities) obtained from various sources to finance the acquisition of **new** long-lived plant assets. Most expenditures from this fund will ultimately be capitalized in the Investment in Plant accounts.

If **debt** is issued to finance a project, the debt is **initially** accounted for in the Unexpended Plant Funds. **Expenditures** are debited to **Construction in Prog-**

ress unless they are noncapitalizable, in which case they are debited to Fund Balance.

The *construction in progress* and any *related liabilities,* should be *reclassified* from the Unexpended Plant Funds to the Investment in Plant accounts either (1) at each year end, or (2) at the conclusion of the project. When this is done at the end of each year, equal amounts of Construction in Progress and liabilities are moved to the Investment in Plant accounts until all liabilities have been reclassified; thereafter, Unexpended Plant Funds Fund Balance is reduced. In our example we assume that the reclassification occurs at the conclusion of the project.

Some typical Unexpended Plant Funds transactions and the related entries are given below. Transaction and entry 3 also affect the Investment in Plant accounts.

Transactions and Entries

1. An individual donated preferred stock valued at $20,000 to finance additions to the plant.

(1) Investments   20,000
　　　Fund Balances—Restricted   20,000
　　To record investments donated for the purpose of
　　financing additions to plant. (The Fund Balances
　　account controls accounts for separate funds or
　　subfunds in this subgroup.)

2. Cash ($30,000) was transferred from the Unrestricted Current Fund to this subgroup to finance additions to the plant. (See transaction 11, Unrestricted Current Fund.)

(2) Cash   30,000
　　　Fund Balances—Unrestricted   30,000
　　To record receipt of cash from the Unrestricted Current
　　Fund for the purpose of financing additions to plant.

3. A small house trailer costing $12,000 was purchased for cash. (See transaction 2, Investment in Plant.)

(3) **Fund Balances—Unrestricted**   12,000
　　　Cash   12,000
　　To record purchase of a house trailer.

4. A $500,000 loan was secured to finance a building addition.

(4) Cash   500,000
　　　Notes Payable   500,000
　　To record borrowing to finance a building addition.

5. By year end $240,000 of capitalizable building addition expenditures had been incurred, of which $200,000 had been paid.

(5) **Construction in Progress**   240,000
　　　Cash   200,000
　　　Accounts Payable   40,000
　　To record capitalizable construction expenditures and the
　　related payments.

Unexpended Plant Funds (continued)

Since this illustration assumes that the construction costs and the note will be left in the Unexpended Plant Funds until the project is completed, no reclassification entry is required at year end in the Plant Funds. However, **if** the university **reclassified** its fixed assets acquired with the proceeds of long-term debt to the Investment in Plant accounts **annually,** the following *reclassification entry* would be required in the Unexpended Plant Funds:

Notes Payable	240,000	
Construction in Progress		240,000

To reclassify Construction in Progress and Notes Payable to the
    Investment in Plant accounts.

A corresponding entry would be made in the Investment in Plant accounts to record the Construction in Progress and Notes Payable in that subgroup.

Also, note that these costs are recorded as **Construction in Progress** because they are *capitalizable. Noncapitalizable* costs would have been recorded as **reductions in the fund balance** of the Unexpended Plant Funds.

Funds for Renewals and Replacements

The Funds for Renewals and Replacements are accounted for in the same way as the Unexpended Plant Funds. The only difference is that the expenditures of this fund are for *renewals and replacements* of plant assets, most of which are charged to Fund Balance rather than being capitalized. In practice it is often difficult to distinguish betterments and improvements, which are capitalized, and expenditures for renewals and replacements, which are not capitalized. In any event, some of the expenditures of the Funds for Renewals and Replacements may properly be capitalized in the Investment in Plant accounts.

Again, the accounting and reporting for Funds for Renewals and Replacements are identical to that for the Unexpended Plant Funds. Indeed, this plant fund subgroup may be combined with the Unexpended Plant Funds. Thus, we assume that A University does not have such a fund and do not illustrate any transactions or entries for the Funds for Renewals and Replacements subgroup.

Funds for Retirement of Indebtedness

The purpose of the Funds for Retirement of Indebtedness subgroup is to account for the accumulation and expenditure of financial resources to **service the institution's plant-related indebtedness.** Payments of debt principal, interest, and fiscal agent fees are made from this fund. These payments reduce the Fund Balance of the Funds for Retirement of Indebtedness. (When debt principal payments are made from the Funds for Retirement of Indebtedness, the additional net investment of the university in fixed assets is recognized in the Net Invested in Plant account in the Investment in Plant subgroup.) Assets of the Funds for Retirement of Indebtedness are also sometimes required to be paid into debt service sinking funds. Such payments do not reduce the Fund Balance of the Funds for Retirement of Indebtedness; rather, they are treated as investments of this subgroup.

The following are some typical transactions of this Fund and the related entries. Transactions 2 and 4 affect not only this Fund but also the Investment in Plant accounts.

Funds for Retirement of Indebtedness (continued)

Transactions and Entries

1. A mandatory transfer of $25,000 was received from the Unrestricted Current Fund. (See entry 10, Unrestricted Current Fund.)

(1) Cash 25,000
         Fund Balances—Restricted 25,000
         To record receipt of mandatory transfer from Unrestricted
         Current Fund.

2. The $25,000 received from the Unrestricted Current Fund was used to pay an installment of the mortgage note, including $5,000 interest. (See entry 3, Investment in Plant.)

(2) Fund Balances—Restricted 25,000
         Cash 25,000
         To record payment on mortgage note, including $5,000
         interest.

3. A donation of $15,000 was received for the purpose of paying a $10,000 mortgage installment falling due during the current year, plus $5,000 interest.

(3) Cash 15,000
         Fund Balances—Restricted 15,000
         To record receipt of money to pay mortgage installment
         falling due during the current year.

4. The money was used for this purpose. (See transaction 4, Investment in Plant.)

(4) Fund Balances—Restricted 15,000
         Cash 15,000
         To record payment of mortgage installment: $5,000 interest
         and $10,000 principal.

5. A donation of $25,000 was received for the purpose of paying a mortgage installment falling due next year.

(5) Cash 25,000
         Fund Balances—Restricted 25,000
         To record receipt of money to pay part of mortgage
         installment falling due during the following year.

6. The cash received in transaction 5 was invested.

(6) Investments 25,000
         Cash 25,000
         To record investing the donated cash.

7. A $200,000 gift was received with the stipulation that the funds be managed as a debt service sinking fund by the Last National Bank. The donor is attempting to get others to match his gesture so a major building program may be begun.

Funds for Retirement of Indebtedness (continued)

(7) (a) Cash 200,000
                Fund Balances—Restricted 200,000
                To record gift to be used to set up sinking fund at the
                Last National Bank.

    (b) Sinking Fund—Last National Bank 200,000
                Cash 200,000
                To record payment to the Last National Bank to
                establish a debt service sinking fund.

Investment in Plant

The asset accounts in the Investment in Plant subgroup contain the book values of the institutional plant properties except for any that are accounted for in Endowment and Similar Funds. **Nongovernmental** colleges and universities **must** report *accumulated* depreciation on these assets in the Investment in Plant balance sheet and the periodic depreciation provision **must** be reported in the statement of changes in fund balances for the Investment in Plant subgroup. But **state and local government** colleges and universities have the **option** of reporting these amounts and, historically, have not done so. (We include accumulated depreciation and periodic provision for depreciation in our examples for illustrative purposes.)

    The liabilities incurred in the acquisition or construction of plant, including those arising from capital leases, also are accounted for here—with increments of construction in progress and related liabilities being added each year, or with the total liability and asset cost being added here at the conclusion of the project. The net equity in fixed assets is maintained in the Net Invested in Plant account, which may be kept in such detail as seems necessary. For example, separate categories might be maintained for net investment from gifts; appropriations; federal, state, and local grants; Current Funds; and other funds.

    The balances in the Investment in Plant accounts at the beginning of the period were as follows:

	Debit	Credit
Land	$ 300,000	
Buildings	8,000,000	
Accumulated Depreciation*		$ 4,000,000
Equipment	1,800,000	
Accumulated Depreciation*		1,010,000
Library Books	200,000	
Mortgage Payable		400,000
Net Invested in Plant		4,890,000
	$10,300,000	$10,300,000

** Government colleges and universities are **not** required to report accumulated depreciation on Plant Funds assets.*

Transactions and Entries

For transactions originating in:

1. Unrestricted Current Fund (See transaction 12 in that Fund): Equipment was purchased for $10,000.

Investment in Plant (continued)

(1) Equipment 10,000
      Net Invested in Plant 10,000
    To record purchase of equipment with Unrestricted Current
    Fund Cash.

2. Unexpended Plant Funds (See transaction 3 in that fund): A house trailer costing $12,000 was purchased for cash.

(2) Improvements Other Than Buildings 12,000
      Net Invested in Plant 12,000
    To record purchase of house trailer out of the Unexpended
    Plant Funds.

3. Funds for Retirement of Indebtedness (See transaction 2 in that Fund): Mortgage notes carried as a liability of the Investment in Plant subgroup $20,000, were paid from Funds for Retirement of Indebtedness. (Recall that $5,000 interest was paid also, but only the principal payment affects the Investment in Plant accounts.)

(3) **Mortgage Payable** 20,000
      Net Invested in Plant 20,000
    To record payment of mortgage principal from the Funds
    for Retirement of Indebtedness.

4. Funds for Retirement of Indebtedness (See transaction 4 in that Fund): An installment of the mortgage note in the amount of $10,000 was retired.

(4) Mortgage Payable 10,000
      Net Invested in Plant 10,000
    To record payment of part of mortgage payable from the
    Retirement of Indebtedness Fund.

5. Investment in Plant Accounts: New, uninsured equipment financed from current revenues and costing $1,000 was destroyed by fire.

(5) Net Invested in Plant 1,000
      Equipment 1,000
    To remove the original cost of equipment destroyed.

6. Investment in Plant Accounts: The provision for depreciation of the university's plant assets totaled $240,000.

(6) Net Invested in Plant 230,000
      Accumulated Depreciation 230,000
    To record the provision for depreciation for the year.

Recall that recording and reporting depreciation and accumulated depreciation of Plant Funds assets is **optional** for **government** colleges and universities.

TRUST AND AGENCY TYPE FUND GROUPS

All university resources being ***used in operations*** are accounted for in the Current Funds and Plant Funds. In addition, colleges and universities often have significant amounts of resources that are accounted for in ***fiduciary fund groups that*** *are in essence trust and agency type funds.* These fund groups include Loan Funds, Endowment and Similar Funds, Annuity and Life Income Funds, and Agency Funds.

Most of the assets accounted for in these fiduciary type funds are *restricted* by donors. However, *unrestricted* resources *designated* by the governing board for loan or endowment purposes are accounted for in the Loan Funds and the Endowment and Similar Funds along with resources externally restricted for those purposes. While accounting for these trust and agency type funds is similar to that for similar types of funds of governments and hospitals, there are sufficient differences to warrant brief explanations and illustrations of each of these fund groups.

LOAN FUNDS

Loan Funds are used to account for resources that may be loaned to students and, in some cases, to faculty and staff. If only the fund's income may be loaned, the principal is included in the Endowment and Similar Funds group and only the income is included with the Loan Funds. The fund balances of Loan Funds should be classified in appropriate ways, such as by sources of resources, purposes for which loans may be made, and restricted versus unrestricted. For example, some may come from appropriations, others from private donors, and still others from Unrestricted Current Funds set aside for this purpose by the college or university governing board. Some may be refundable to donors under specified conditions.

Loan funds have become major activities requiring professional management at many higher education institutions. Some have raised large sums for loan purposes through gifts, and many participate in federal and state government loan programs. Both federal and state programs must be administered in accordance with many regulations, and typically require the college or university to contribute a percentage of the total loan fund balance.

Covering such programs, which are subject to change, is beyond the scope of this text. Rather, since loan funds of governments were covered earlier, accounting for loan losses in colleges and universities is discussed briefly and a simplified example of a college or university Loan Fund is presented.

Loan losses may be accounted for in one of two ways. Under one method, an Allowance for Loan Losses is deducted from both the total loans and the Loan Funds Fund Balance in the year end balance sheet. It is reversed at the start of the new year and loan losses are charged against specific Loan Fund Fund Balance accounts. Under the second method, an allowance method, estimated losses are deducted from the Loan Funds Fund Balance accounts to which they are expected to relate and an Allowance for Loan Losses is established. Loan losses incurred are charged against the allowance account.

In reviewing the following transactions assume that a Loan Fund was established to make interest-free loans and that (1) income on Fund investments is to be added to the principal of the Fund, and (2) the total assets of the Fund, both the original principal and that from earnings, may be loaned.

Transactions and Entries

1. A donation of $100,000 was received for the purpose of making loans to students.

(1)	Cash	100,000	
	Fund Balance—Restricted		100,000

To record donation received for the purpose of setting up Loan Fund.

Loan Funds (continued)

2. Loans of $50,000 were made.

(2)	Loans Receivable	50,000	
	Cash		50,000
	To record loans made.		

3. $25,000 was invested in bonds. The bonds were purchased at par plus accrued interest of $100.

(3)	Investments	25,000	
	Accrued Interest on Investments Purchased	100	
	Cash		25,100
	To record investments and accrued interest purchased.		

4. A $500 check in payment of bond interest was received.

(4)	Cash	500	
	Accrued Interest on Investments Purchased		100
	Fund Balance—Restricted		400
	To record receipt of interest payment.		

5. A student died and it was decided to write off his loan of $500 as uncollectible.

(5)	Fund Balance—Restricted	500	
	Loans Receivable		500
	To write off loan as uncollectible.		

ENDOWMENT AND SIMILAR FUNDS

Endowment and Similar Funds are used to account for assets that, at least at the moment, cannot be expended, although usually the income from them may be. Assets donated by outsiders fall into two categories: (1) those that have been given in perpetuity, which are accounted for in **Endowment Funds,** sometimes referred to as "true" or "pure" Endowment Funds; and (2) those that the donor has specified may be expended after a particular date or event, which are accounted for in **"Term Endowment Funds."**

The appropriate policy-making body of an institution may also set aside (designate) available resources for the same purposes as those donated as endowments. These are accounted for in "Quasi-Endowment Funds" or "Funds Functioning as Endowments," and, of course, are subject to reassignment by the authority that created them.

Donors may choose to make the income from endowment-type funds available to a university but to leave the principal in the possession and control of a *trustee other than the university.* Such funds usually are **not** included among the Endowment and Similar Funds of the university, but should be disclosed in the financial statements by an appropriate note. *Unrestricted* income from such funds is reported as revenue in the Unrestricted Current Funds. *If restricted* to specific, *operating* purposes, the income is recorded as an addition to the Restricted Current Funds fund balance. When expended, it is reported there as Endowment Income if the trust is irrevocable or as Gifts if it is a revocable trust. If the income is restricted to plant or debt service uses, it is recorded in the appropriate Plant Funds.

Determining and Reporting Income

One of the most debated issues in Endowment Fund accounting is: What is Endowment Fund income? The key issue is: What portion, if any, of *net appreciation* of Endowment Fund investments should be treated as additions to endowment income rather than as part of the endowment principal?

Several views have found their way into practice. The alternatives range from the **classical trust or fiduciary principle** that includes no net appreciation of Endowment Fund assets (realized or unrealized) in income (or yield) to the various "total return" approaches. Under the **total return approaches** a "prudent portion" of the net appreciation is considered income and spent along with the dividends, rents, royalties, interest, and other realized revenues that constitute the yield under the classical trust principle.

While some universities use a portion of the net appreciation of Endowment Fund assets as if it were income—where permitted by donor provisions and state law—neither *FARM* nor the AICPA college and university audit guide permits accounting for Endowment Fund income using the total return concept. Instead, the principles of the classical trust or fiduciary method are applied. Under this approach gains and losses are **not** considered in calculating endowment income.[14] Moreover, any amounts of unrealized appreciation that are considered "total return incomes" and are expended or transferred must be reported as nonmandatory transfers.

Thus, both *FARM* and the AICPA audit guide require reporting Endowment Fund income as follows:

1. Income **required** to be used for specified purposes is added to the appropriate Fund Balance accounts in the Restricted Current Funds, Loan Funds, Endowment and Similar Funds, or Plant Funds, as specified in the gift agreement.
2. If the income is **unrestricted,** it is recognized as Unrestricted Current Funds revenues.
3. Any amounts representing realized or unrealized **appreciation expended or transferred** to another fund should be reported as **transfers.** Amounts that are transferred to the Current Funds should not be included in revenues.

Transactions and Entries—Endowment Funds

The following transactions and entries illustrate the operation of Endowment and Similar Funds, which are similar to SLG Nonexpendable Trust Funds.

Transactions and Entries

1. Cash was donated by a family during the year to establish three separate endowments, as follows:

Endowment A (for Supplemental Salary Payments). . .	$1,000,000
Endowment B (for Supplemental Salary Payments). . .	600,000
Endowment C (for Student Aid)	400,000
	$2,000,000

    These endowments included a provision that any *earnings in excess of $78,000* be dedicated to the athletic program, an auxiliary enterprise of the university.

---

[14] *FARM,* ¶613.3, and Committee on College and University Accounting and Auditing, pp. 37–40.

Endowment Funds (continued)

(1) Cash   2,000,000
      Fund Balance—Endowment A   1,000,000
      Fund Balance—Endowment B   600,000
      Fund Balance—Endowment C   400,000
To record receipt of money for the purpose of
establishing three endowments.

2. It was decided to invest this money in securities that were to be pooled. The following securities were acquired at the prices indicated:

Preferred stocks	$ 500,000
Common stocks	1,000,000
Bonds:	
Par value	200,000
Premiums	10,000
Bonds:	
Par value	250,000
Discounts	5,000
Accrued interest on investments	
purchased	1,000

(2) Investments in Preferred Stocks   500,000
    Investments in Common Stocks   1,000,000
    Investments in Bonds   450,000
    Accrued Interest on Investments Purchased   1,000
    Unamortized Premiums on Investments   10,000
        Unamortized Discounts on Investments   5,000
        Cash   1,956,000
To record purchase of pooled investments.

3. Cash received on these investments for the year was as follows:

Dividends on preferred stocks	$20,000
Dividends on common stocks	60,000
Interest	9,000

No material amounts of investment income were accrued at year end.

(3) Cash   89,000
    Income on Pooled Investments   88,000
    Accrued Interest on Investments Purchased   1,000
To record investment income received.

4. Premiums on investments in the amount of $500 and discounts in the amount of $200 were amortized at the end of the year.

(4) Unamortized Discounts on Investments   200
    Income on Pooled Investments   300
        Unamortized Premiums on Investments   500
To record amortization of premiums and discounts.

5. The earnings on Endowments A, B, and C exceeded $78,000. Thus, $78,000 was paid to the Restricted Current Funds for the primary purposes of these

Endowment Funds (continued)

endowments and the remainder of the net income from pooled investments was paid to the Restricted Current Funds for auxiliary enterprise purposes. (See transaction 1 and also transaction 1, Restricted Current Funds.)

(5) Income on Pooled Investments   87,700
    Cash   87,700
To record payment of endowment income to the
Restricted Current Funds as follows:

Fund	Fund Balance*	Percentage of Total	Income Apportioned
A	$1,000,000	50%	$39,000
B	600,000	30	23,400
C	400,000	20	15,600
	$2,000,000	100%	$78,000
Earnings			87,700
Balance—for auxiliary enterprises			$ 9,700

It is assumed that market values and book values of the several funds are in this case identical.[15]

6. Common stock with a book value of $10,000 was sold for $10,500.

(6) Cash   10,500
    Investments in Common Stock   10,000
    Fund Balance—Endowment A   250
    Fund Balance—Endowment B   150
    Fund Balance—Endowment C   100
To record sale of common stock at a gain of $500 and
the addition of its share of the gain to the balance
of each Endowment Fund.

7. An individual donated common stock that had cost $65,000 (hereafter referred to as Endowment Fund D). At the time of the donation the stock had a market value of $75,000. The *income* from these securities is *unrestricted* and may be used for any university purposes.

(7) Common Stock   75,000
    Fund Balance—Endowment D   75,000
To record donation of common stock with a market
value of $75,000; the net income of Endowment D is
unrestricted.

8. Another individual had a small apartment complex constructed and equipped and then turned it over to the university with the specification that the net income therefrom was to be used for student aid and for supplemen-

---

[15] Both the NACUBO *FARM* and the AICPA audit guide permit colleges and universities to account for their investments at either cost or at market value. However, both recognize that investment pools must be operated using a market value method for allocating shares in the pool and investment income. Book value methods do not result in appropriate allocation of the income and appreciation of the investment pool.

Endowment Funds (continued)

tal salary payments (hereafter referred to as Endowment Fund E). The total cost was $850,000, divided as follows:

Land	$100,000
Building	600,000
Equipment	150,000

(8)	Land	100,000	
	Building	600,000	
	Equipment	150,000	
	Fund Balance—Principal—Endowment E		850,000

To record gift of an apartment complex as an endowment, the net income of which is restricted to certain purposes.

9. Gross income from the apartments (Endowment Fund E) for the current year was $170,000; and total expenses were $120,000, exclusive of depreciation of $20,000 (building, $6,000; equipment, $14,000). No receivables or payables were outstanding at year end and the net income of Endowment Fund E was established as a liability to the Restricted Current Fund. (See transaction 4, Restricted Current Funds.)

(9a)	Cash	170,000	
	Fund Balance—Earnings—Endowment E		170,000

To record **revenues** from the apartments.

(9b)	**Fund Balance—Earnings—Endowment E**	120,000	
	Cash		120,000

To record rental **expenses,** other than depreciation, incurred in operating the apartments.

(9c)	**Fund Balance—Earnings—Endowment E**	50,000	
	Accumulated Depreciation—Building		6,000
	Accumulated Depreciation—Equipment		14,000
	Due to Restricted Current Funds		30,000

To record depreciation expenses for Endowment E and the liability to the Restricted Current Funds for the net income of Endowment E.

10. $100,000 was received from the Unrestricted Current Fund for the purpose of establishing a fund functioning as an endowment (Quasi-Endowment Fund) in accordance with a resolution adopted by the university's Board of Trustees. (See transaction 13, Unrestricted Current Funds.)

(10)	Cash	100,000	
	Fund Balance—Quasi-Endowment		100,000

To record receipt of money from Unrestricted Current Fund for purpose of setting up a fund to function as an Endowment Fund in accordance with resolution adopted by the university's Board of Trustees.

11. An individual set up a trust (to be administered by the Village National Bank) in the amount of $200,000, the income from which is to go to the university.

(11) No entry, or memorandum entry. The trust would be **disclosed** in the notes to the financial statements.

Annuity and Life Income Funds are used to account for assets given to the institution with the stipulation that the institution make certain payments to a designated recipient(s). **Annuity Funds** are used if the gift agreement requires a *fixed-dollar* payment *regardless* of the income of the fund. **Life Income Funds** are used if the amount of the *payment* to the beneficiary *varies* according to the earnings of the fund. Typically, *annuity* agreements also specify a certain number of years during which the beneficiary is to receive the annuity, but the period need not be fixed. Indeed, the period could be specified as the lifetime of the beneficiary. Similarly, a *life income* agreement usually requires payment of the income of the fund—or some portion of the income of the fund—until the death of the beneficiary or the donor. However, a life income agreement could specify that the earnings, or some portion of the earnings, be paid to the designated beneficiary for a specified number of years. After the specified payment period, the principal is transferred to the fund group specified by the donor or, if unrestricted, to the Unrestricted Current Funds.

Accounting for Annuity and Life Income Funds is similar to that for Endowment and Similar Funds. Indeed, if these funds are small, they may be reported with the Endowment and Similar Funds.

Annuity Funds

The Internal Revenue Code and regulations state the conditions under which an annuity trust may be accepted and must be administered from an income tax standpoint, and several states also regulate annuity trusts. Too, since the institution accepts some risk by guaranteeing the beneficiary a fixed amount for a specified period, perhaps for life or even for the lifetime of two or more persons, the governing board will want assurances (1) that the assets donated should generate sufficient income to pay the specified amounts, or (2) if some of the payments must come from principal, that a significant residual balance should be available to the institution at the end of the annuity period.

When the Annuity Fund is established the assets should be recorded at their fair market value, together with any liabilities against the assets assumed by the institution. The *liability* for the annuity payments is recorded at its *present value,* based on the expected earnings rate and, if appropriate, life expectancy tables. Any *difference* between the assets and liabilities should be debited or credited, as appropriate, to an Annuity Fund Fund Balance account.

To illustrate Annuity Funds accounting, assume that an individual donated $20,000 cash and investments worth $180,000 to A University on January 2, 19X3 with the stipulation that she be paid $25,000 each December 31 for the next ten years. Any remaining net assets should then be used to remodel the business and public administration building. The university finance officer expects to earn at least 7 percent on the fund's assets during each of the next ten years. The entry to record creation of this Annuity Fund would be:

Cash	20,000	
Investments	180,000	
Annuities Payable		175,589
Fund Balance—Annuity		24,411

To record *establishment* of Annuity Fund. Calculation of annuity
payable: $25,000 × 7.023582, the present value of an ordinary
annuity of $1 for 10 periods at 7 percent, is $175,589.

Investment earnings and gains are credited, and annuity payments and losses are debited, to **Annuities Payable.** Assuming that various investment transactions have been recorded during the year and that the annuity payments are due each December 31, the following entries would be made on December 31, 19X3, the end of the university's fiscal year:

Annuities Payable	25,000	
Cash (or Annuities Currently Payable)		25,000
To record the annual ***annuity payment.***		

Investment Earnings	13,000	
Investment Gains	3,000	
Investment Losses		5,000
Annuities Payable		11,000
To ***close*** the (amounts assumed) investment earnings, gains, and losses accounts at year end.		

Since the **Annuities Payable** account should always be carried at the ***present value*** of the ***future series of required payments,*** the Annuities Payable account must be ***adjusted annually*** to its present value. If actuarial assumptions such as yield estimates or life expectancies are revised, the adjustment to Annuities Payable should reflect those changes. The adjustments to Annuities Payable will cause a change in the Annuity Funds Fund Balance to be reported in the Statement of Changes in Fund Balances (Figure 18.6). In this example the Annuities Payable balance at year end should be equal to the present value of the nine remaining annuity payments ($25,000 \times 6.515232$), or $162,881. The required adjustment to Fund Balance is the difference between the Annuities Payable balance after the preceding entries ($161,589) and the present value of the nine remaining payments. This adjustment of $1,292 is recorded as follows:

Fund Balance—Annuity	1,292	
Annuities Payable		1,292
To ***adjust annuities payable*** to present value at year end.		

The preceding approach to accounting for Annuity Funds earnings and the fund balance adjustment is consistent with the audit guide description of accounting for Annuity Funds. This approach results in reporting—in the Statement of Changes in Fund Balances—only the **net** adjustment to Fund Balance that results from investment earnings, interest expenses, and changes in actuarial assumptions, such as changes in the appropriate interest rate for discounting the remaining annuity payments.

However, some colleges and universities use a different **accounting** approach in which the income of the Annuity Funds is closed to Fund Balance. This approach would result in the ***last two entries*** in this example being as follows:

Investment Earnings	13,000	
Investment Gains	3,000	
Investment Losses		5,000
Fund Balance—Annuity		11,000
To ***close*** the investment earnings, gains, and losses accounts at year end.		
Fund Balance—Annuity	12,292	
Annuities Payable		12,292
To ***adjust annuities payable*** to its present value at year end.		

Figure 18-6

STATEMENT OF CHANGES IN FUND BALANCES

A University
Statement of Changes in Fund Balances
For the Year Ended October 31, 19A

	Current Funds		Loan Funds	Endowment and Similar Funds	Annuity and Life Income Funds	Plant Funds			
	Unrestricted	Restricted				Unexpended	Renewal and Replacement	Retirement of Indebtedness	Investment in Plant
Revenues and other additions:									
Unrestricted current fund revenues	$3,308,000								
Expired term endowment—restricted		xxx							
State appropriations—restricted		xxx				xxx	xxx		
Federal grants and contracts—restricted		**100,000**	xxx						
State grants and contracts		xxx				xxx			
Local government grants and contracts		xxx							
Private gifts, grants, and contracts— restricted		**200,000**	**100,000**	**2,925,000**	xxx	**20,000**	xxx	**240,000**	
Endowment income—restricted		117,700	400				xxx		
Investment income—restricted		xxx	xxx	xxx		xxx	xxx	xxx	
Realized gains on investments—restricted		xxx	xxx	500		xxx	xxx	xxx	
Interest on loans receivable			xxx				xxx		
Proceeds from disposal of plant facilities									
Expended for plant facilities (including $10,000 charged to current funds expenditures)									22,000
Retirement of long-term debt principal									30,000
Matured annuity and life income funds— restricted to endowment				xxx					
Gift in excess of actuarial liability for annuity payable					24,411				
Total revenues and other additions	3,308,000	417,700	100,400	2,925,500	24,411	20,000		240,000	52,000

Statement of changes in fund balances (continued):

Expenditures and other deductions:									
Educational and general expenditures	2,302,100	232,000							
Auxiliary enterprises expenditures	590,000	2,000							
Indirect costs recovered		8,000							
Refunded to grantors		xxx							
Loan cancellations and write-offs			500						
Administrative and collection costs			xxx						
Adjustment of actuarial liability for annuities payable				1,292					
Expended for plant facilities (including noncapitalized expenditures of $xxx)						12,000			xxx
Retirement of long-term debt principal								30,000	xxx
Interest on indebtedness								10,000	
Disposal of plant facilities									1,000
Provision for depreciation*									230,000
Expired term endowments ($xxx unrestricted, $xxx restricted to accounting program and plant)					xxx				
Matured annuity and life income funds restricted to endowment				xxx					
Total expenditures and other deductions	2,892,100	242,000	500	1,292	xxx	12,000		40,000	231,000
Transfers among funds—additions/(deductions):									
Mandatory:									
Principal and Interest	(25,000)							25,000	
Renewals and replacements	(xxx)						xxx		
Loan fund matching grant	(xxx)		xxx						
Nonmandatory:									
Additions to plant	(30,000)					30,000			
Quasi-endowment	(100,000)				100,000				
Total transfers	(155,000)		xxx		100,000	30,000	xxx	25,000	
Net increase/(decrease) for the year	260,000	175,700	99,900	23,119		38,000		225,000	(179,000)
Fund balance at beginning of year					3,025,500				4,890,000
Fund balance at end of year	$ 260,900	$ 175,700	$ 99,900	$23,119	$3,025,500	$38,000		$225,000	$4,711,000

* State and local government colleges and universities are **not** required to report a provision for depreciation of Plant Funds assets, but may elect to do so.

A college or university using this accounting approach still could report only the **net adjustment** of Fund Balance, the decrease of $1,292, in its Statement of Changes in Fund Balances. At the end of the annuity period any remaining balance should be transferred to the Plant Funds since the donor specified that it should be used to remodel the business and public administration building.

Life Income Funds

Life Income Funds are subject to Internal Revenue Code and regulation provisions, as are Annuity Funds, and may be subject to state regulations. Since only the earnings inure to the beneficiary(ies) of Life Income Funds, and no fixed payment is guaranteed, the college or university does **not** have an earnings risk as in the case of Annuity Funds.

The accounting for Life Income Funds is not as complex as that for Annuity Funds. All that is involved is:

1. **at its inception**—record the assets at fair market value and record any liabilities assumed; the difference is credited to Life Income Fund Balance;
2. **during the term** of the fund—record fund revenues, expenses, gains, and losses—following donor instructions or, in the absence of instructions, applicable law in determining whether gains or losses affect income or the principal—and distribute the earnings to the beneficiary(ies); and
3. **at the end of the benefit period or upon the death of the beneficiary(ies)**—distribute the net assets of the fund as specified by the donor or, in the absence of such instructions, to the Unrestricted Current Funds.

AGENCY FUNDS

A university usually serves as a **depository and fiscal agent** for a number of student, faculty, and staff organizations. It holds money and other assets belonging to others in these cases; and only the usual asset and liability accounts of Agency Funds need be maintained, since there is no Agency Fund fund balance.

FINANCIAL REPORTING

The three basic financial statements recommended in the NACUBO *FARM* and in the AICPA audit guide for colleges and universities are:

1. Balance Sheet
2. Statement of Changes in Fund Balances
3. Statement of Current Funds Revenues, Expenditures, and Other Changes

Both a Balance Sheet (Figure 18-5) and a Statement of Current Funds Revenues, Expenditures, and Other Changes (Figure 18-4) have been presented for the A University example. Figure 18-6 presents a **Statement of Changes in Fund Balances** for the A University example. The **boldface type** in this statement indicates accounts and amounts that are presented based on the data in the A University example. The other accounts are items commonly found in more complex situations. The funds that these items typically affect are indicated by "xxx."

In reviewing the Statement of Current Funds Revenues, Expenditures, and Other Changes (Figure 18-4), note particularly the additions to Restricted Current Funds balances—such as through gifts and investment earnings—that would be reported as revenue immediately were it not for the convention of recognizing revenue only to the extent that restricted resources are expended. Note also, in the Statement of Changes in Fund Balances (Figure 18-6), that **additions** to the Restricted Current Funds, **not revenues,** are reported. Both statements report a net Fund Balance increase of $175,700 for the Restricted Current Funds, because the difference between restricted receipts and restricted revenues recognized during a year is reported in the Statement of Current Funds Revenues, Expenditures, and Other Changes. Similarly, in studying the Statement of Changes in Fund Balances (Figure 18-6) note the additions to the Endowment and Similar Funds that will not be recognized as revenue until such time, if ever, that the investment earnings are expended for operating purposes.

The primary statements should be accompanied by detailed supporting schedules and footnotes appropriate to ensure full disclosure and fair presentation of the operations and balances of the various fund groups and subgroups. The NACUBO *FARM* suggests numerous supplemental schedules for consideration.

CONCLUDING COMMENTS

Accounting and reporting for colleges and universities has evolved rapidly in recent years, and may be expected to evolve still further in the future. The efforts of the AICPA, NACUBO, and other committees, which ultimately led to the Joint Accounting Group (JAG) Report, were extensive. Numerous major improvements in college and university accounting and reporting resulted from these joint efforts by preparers, auditors, and users of higher education financial reports.

Some contend that further changes are needed in college and university accounting and reporting. For example, some believe that the Current Funds should be combined, and the restricted fund balances reported as deferred revenues in the one Current Fund; others question the propriety of deferring revenue recognition in Restricted Current Funds until resources are expended; and some contend that all unrestricted funds, including those in Quasi-Endowment and Plant Funds, should be reported as part of the Current Funds.

The future of college and university accounting standards now rests with the GASB and FASB. It will be interesting to see what conceptual and procedural changes in college and university accounting and reporting are prescribed by those Boards, and how they reconcile differences of opinions that they may have regarding reporting for colleges and universities.

QUESTIONS

18-1 Prepare a list of the funds recommended for use by a college or university. Opposite the funds indicate the funds or account groups recommended for SLGs that are most nearly comparable in nature.

18-2 Depreciation expense must be recorded on all fixed assets of hospitals, whereas NACUBO recommends that no depreciation expense be recorded in the Current Funds on the fixed assets of colleges, though accumulated depreciation may be recorded in the Investment in Plant subgroup. Do you think there is a better reason for recording depreciation on the fixed assets of hospitals than on the fixed assets of colleges?

18-3 What is the purpose of recording depreciation expense on the fixed assets of an Endowment Fund? Explain.

18-4 Under what circumstances are resources expendable for operating purposes accounted for in Restricted Current Funds? At what point should contributions to Restricted Current Funds be recognized as revenue?

18-5 Name three differences between the accounting procedures of colleges and those of hospitals.

18-6 Why is it necessary to distinguish "restricted" and "unrestricted" balances in the Endowment and Similar Funds, Loan Funds, and Plant Funds?

18-7 Student tuition, fees, and other assessments may be restricted, in whole or in part, to debt service or plant acquisition, renewal, or replacement. How should these amounts be accounted for by a college or university?

18-8 Distinguish between mandatory and nonmandatory transfers and how they are reported in higher education financial statements.

18-9 What is an auxiliary enterprise? How are they accounted for and reported on by colleges and universities?

18-10 When are earnings of Endowment and Similar Funds reported as revenue? Might the principal of such funds also be reported as revenue? Explain.

18-11 Distinguish between the key accounting aspects of Annuity Funds and of Life Income Funds.

18-12 Should plant-related long-term debt and construction in progress be accounted for in the Unexpended Plant Funds or the Plant Funds for Renewal and Replacement until completion of the project, or should appropriate amounts be reclassified to the Investment in Plant accounts at the end of each year?

18-13 Distinguish between expenditures and transfers.

18-14 How should college and university revenues and expenditures be classified for external financial reporting purposes?

18-15 Identify the required financial statements for colleges and universities and the fund groups covered by each statement.

Note: Problems 18-6 to 18-8 relate to X University. These problems with Problem 18-10, together comprise a comprehensive review problem.

PROBLEMS

P 18-1 **Part I.** (Multiple Choice)

1. The current funds group of a not-for-profit private university includes which of the following?

	Annuity funds	Loan funds
a.	Yes	Yes
b.	Yes	No
c.	No	No
d.	No	Yes

2. For the spring semester of 19X4, Lane University assessed its students $3,400,000 (net of refunds), covering tuition and fees for educational and general purposes. However, only $3,000,000 was expected to be realized because scholarships totaling $300,000 were granted to students, and tuition remissions of $100,000 were allowed to faculty members' children attending Lane. How much should Lane include in educational and general current funds revenues from student tuition and fees?

   a. $3,400,000   c. $3,100,000

   b. $3,300,000   d. $3,000,000

3. The following funds were among those on Key University's books at April 30, 19X4:

Funds to be used for acquisition of additional properties for University purposes (unexpended at 4/30/X4)	$3,000,000
Funds set aside for debt service charges and for retirement of indebtedness on University properties	5,000,000

How much of the previously mentioned funds should be included in plant funds?

a. $0

c. $5,000,000

b. $3,000,000

d. $8,000,000

4. During the years ended June 30, 19X0 and 19X1, Sonata University conducted a cancer research project financed by a $2,000,000 gift from an alumnus. This entire amount was pledged by the donor on July 10, 19W9, although he paid only $500,000 at that date. The gift was restricted to the financing of this particular research project. During the two-year research period Sonata's related gift receipts and research expenditures were as follows:

	Year Ended June 30	
	19X0	19X1
Gift receipts	$1,200,000	$ 800,000
Cancer research expenditures	900,000	1,100,000

How much gift revenue should Sonata report in the restricted column of its statement of current funds revenues, expenditures, and other changes for the year ended June 30, 19X1?

a. $0

c. $1,100,000

b. $800,000

d. $2,000,000

5. On January 2, 19X2, John Reynolds established a $500,000 trust, the income from which is to be paid to Mansfield University for general operating purposes. The Wyndham National Bank was appointed by Reynolds as trustee of the fund. What journal entry is required on Mansfield's books?

		Dr.	Cr.
a.	Memorandum entry only		
b.	Cash	$500,000	
	Endowment fund balance		$500,000
c.	Nonexpendable endowment fund	$500,000	
	Endowment fund balance		$500,000
d.	Expendable funds	$500,000	
	Endowment fund balance		$500,000

(AICPA, adapted)

P 18-1   **Part II.** (Multiple Choice)

1. The fiscal year of Redfern University ends on June 30 of each year. In 19X6, the school's summer session started on June 20 and ended on July 30. Tuition and fees for the 19X6 summer session should be recognized as revenue

   a. entirely in the July 1, 19X5–June 30, 19X6 fiscal year

   b. entirely in the July 1, 19X6–June 30, 19X7 fiscal year

   c. 25% in the July 1, 19X5–June 30, 19X6 fiscal year and 75% in the July 1, 19X6–June 30, 19X7 fiscal year

   d. in the fiscal year that payment is actually received

   e. none of the above

2. Loan Funds are used to account for assets that

   a. are received as loans from banks and other financial institutions for restricted uses

   b. are received as loans from federal and state government agencies for restricted uses

   c. are received as loans from banks and other financial institutions for general (unrestricted) uses

d. are received from private donors to be used to make loans to students or staff

e. are to be used to pay principal and interest on university long-term debt

3. The carrying value of the Annuities Payable account in a college's Annuity Fund

   a. should be adjusted to reflect changes in actuarial assumptions such as life expectancies or yield estimates

   b. should be adjusted only for benefit payments made and investment income earned

   c. must be adjusted annually to the present value of the required payments

   d. a and b

   e. a and c

4. Boris Badinoff gave 250,000 shares of Natasha, Inc., stock to Bullwinkle University to endow two scholarships for outstanding students in the school's Cartoon Department. Dividend income received on these shares should be included in the school's

   a. Loan Fund   d. Endowment Funds

   b. Unrestricted Current Funds   e. Quasi-Endowment Funds

   c. Restricted Current Funds

5. Wildcat University charges each student an annual student activity fee, which is pledged, via a written contract, for payment of debt service on the Massimino Student Center. The student activity fees, when received, should be recorded

   a. as revenues in the Restricted Current Funds

   b. as revenues in the Unrestricted Current Funds and as mandatory transfers to the Plant Funds

   c. as additions to the Plant Funds

   d. as revenues in the Unrestricted Current Funds and as nonmandatory transfers to the Plant Funds

   e. as revenues in the Restricted Current Funds and as mandatory transfers to the Plant Funds

6. The governing board of Slippery Stone University has decided that 10 percent of tuition for the 19X6 academic year will be set aside for construction of a new physical science building. The designated portion of the tuition should be recorded initially in the

   a. Unrestricted Current Funds   d. Unexpended Plant Funds

   b. Restricted Current Funds   e. Quasi-Endowment Funds

   c. Investment in Plant accounts

P 18-2 (Fund Group Identification) Abbreviations such as the following are often used to identify the college and university fund groups and subgroups:

UCF—Unrestricted Current Funds   UPF—Unexpended Plant Funds
RCF—Restricted Current Funds   PFRR—Plant Funds for Renewals and
ESF—Endowment and Similar Funds   Replacement
LF—Loan Funds   PRFI—Plant Funds for Retirement of
AF—Annuity Funds   Indebtedness
LIF—Life Income Funds   IPF—Investment in Plant subgroup

Using these abbreviations, indicate the fund group or subgroup to be used to account for each of the following items.

1. Unrestricted resources set aside to provide travel loans to students to cover reimbursable expenses incurred on job interviews

2. Fixed assets used in operation

3. Resources set aside by board to establish a Presidential Honor Scholarship Fund

4. Short-term debt incurred to provide temporary financing for operations

5. Long-term debt related to plant assets in use

6. Fixed assets of a bookstore that is an auxiliary enterprise

7. Bond debt service sinking fund

8. Resources donated to the university with the stipulation that the donor—an active university supporter—receive $80,000 per year for the remainder of his life.

9. The resources in 8 after the donor's death, assuming

   a. There are no restrictions on use of the resources

   b. The resources are to be used to finance a fine arts center

10. Tuition and fees—a portion of which is required to be used for expanding the student activity center and the library

11. Construction in progress

12. Unrestricted earnings of a term endowment

13. Resources externally restricted by donors for plant additions

14. Earnings of an endowment required to be used to finance scholarships

15. Resources from a grant received to finance cancer research

16. Unrestricted resources set aside by the board of trustees of the university for plant expansion

17. Unrestricted resources set aside by the governing board to finance development of specialized governmental and nonprofit accounting courses

18. Principal of a term endowment upon expiration of the term of the endowment, assuming no restrictions on the use of the resources

P 18-3   (Unrestricted Current Funds Entries) Prepare the necessary journal entries to record each of the following transactions in the Unrestricted Current Funds of Dewey College.

1. Tuition and fees charged for the Fall 19X8 semester totaled $3,700,000. $100,000 of this amount was waived as a result of scholarships and fee waivers, and $12,000 more is expected to be uncollectible.

2. For the Winter 19X9 semester Dewey College levied a general student fee that resulted in $18,000 of revenues. The full amount of this fee is restricted for the purchase of computer equipment and software needed to establish computer labs at the college.

3. What would the entries for 2 be if half of the revenue from the student fees was unrestricted as to use?

4. What would the entries for 2 be if there were no external restrictions on the use of the resources, but the board requires the fees to bet aside for purchase of computer equipment and software?

5. What would the entries for 2 be if the fees were to supplement the income of a specific auxiliary enterprise of the college?

P 18-4   **Part I.** (Grant-Related Entries)

January 10, 19X8—Buchanan College received a $100,000 grant to be used to finance a study of the effects of the Tax Reform Act of 19X6 on the economy.

During 19X8—Expenditures of $72,000 were incurred and paid on the research project.

Required   (a) Record these transactions in the accounts of the appropriate fund groups of Buchanan College and explain how the effects of the transactions should be reported in the college's financial statements.

   (b) Repeat requirement a under the assumption that the grant was to finance plant expansion.

P 18-4   **Part II.** (Endowment Entries) Mr. Harvey Robinson donated $2,000,000 to the University of Aggiemania with the stipulation that earnings of the first ten years be used to endow professorships in each of the university's colleges. At the end of the ten-year period the principal of the gift will become available for unrestricted use.

Required   (a) Prepare the entry(ies) needed in the various fund groups to record the gift.

   (b) Prepare the entry(ies) needed in the various fund groups to record the expiration of the term of the endowment.

P 18-5   (Plant Funds Entries)
Hitech University issued $14,000,000 of bonds to finance construction of a new computer facility on March 25, 19X8.

The contractor billed Hitech University $3,200,000 for work completed during 19X8. The university paid all but a 5% retained percentage.

In 19X9 the contractor completed the facility and billed Hitech for $10,800,000. The university has paid all but a 5% retained percentage as of year end.

Required

(a) Prepare the necessary journal entries for 19X8 and 19X9 to account for the preceding transactions assuming that Hitech reclassifies its Construction in Progress from the Unexpended Plant Funds at the end of each year.

(b) Prepare the necessary journal entries for the preceding transactions assuming that the university carries the construction costs in the Unexpended Plant Funds until construction is complete.

(c) What is the effect on the fund balances of the various Plant Fund subgroups under these two alternatives?

P 18-6 **Part I.** (Unrestricted Current Funds Entries) The trial balance of the Unrestricted Current Funds of X University on September 1, 19X0, was as follows:

Cash	$155,000	
Accounts Receivable	30,000	
Allowance for Uncollectible Accounts		$ 2,000
Inventory of Materials and Supplies	25,000	
Vouchers Payable		23,000
Fund Balance		185,000
	$210,000	$210,000

X University's dormitory and food service facilities are operated as auxiliary enterprises. The following transactions took place during the current fiscal year:

1. Collections amounted to $2,270,000, distributed as follows: tuition and fees, $1,930,000; unrestricted gifts, $170,000; sales and services of educational activities, $115,000; other sources, $25,000; accounts receivable, $30,000.

2. Receivables at end of the year were $29,000, consisting entirely of tuition and fees revenues.

3. It is estimated that tuition receivable of $3,000 will never be collected.

4. Revenues from auxiliary enterprises were $300,000, all collected in cash.

5. Materials purchased during the year for cash, $500,000; on account, $50,000.

6. Materials used amounted to $510,000, distributed as follows:

Educational and general:		
Institutional support	$ 30,000	
Research	5,000	
Instruction	305,000	
Academic support	7,000	
Other	53,000	$400,000
Auxiliary enterprises		110,000
		$510,000

7. Salaries and wages paid:

Educational and general:		
Institutional support	$170,000	
Research	63,000	
Instruction	1,212,000	
Academic support	80,000	
Other	85,000	$1,610,000
Auxiliary enterprises		90,000
		$1,700,000

8. Other expenditures paid:

Educational and general:		
Institutional support	$10,000	
Research	2,000	
Instruction	53,000	
Academic support.	3,000	
Other	7,000	$75,000
Auxiliary enterprises		20,000
		$95,000

9. Interest expenditures chargeable to Institutional Support, $3,000, were paid.

10. Vouchers payable paid, $40,000.

11. A transfer of $20,000 was made to the Fund for Retirement of Indebtedness, as required by the bond indenture.

12. The board of trustees of the university passed a resolution ordering the transfer of $150,000 to a fund that is to function as an endowment, and the transfer was made.

13. $30,000 was transferred from the Unrestricted Current Fund, one-half for additions to the plant and one-half for plant renewals and replacements.

Required   Prepare journal entries for the Unrestricted Current Funds for the 19X0–19X1 fiscal year.

18-6   **Part II.** (Restricted Current Funds Entries) The trial balance of the Restricted Current Funds of X University on September 1, 19X0 was as follows:

Cash	$32,000	
Vouchers Payable		$ 2,000
Fund Balance*		30,000
	$32,000	$32,000

The Fund Balance was from private gifts to be used only for academic support.

The following transactions took place during the current fiscal year:

1. Cash was received as follows for the purposes noted:

Educational and general:		
Endowments—Institutional support and		
research	$ 75,000	
Private gifts—Research	40,000	
Federal grants—Instruction	150,000	
State grant—Student services	20,000	
	$285,000	
Auxiliary enterprises.	130,000	
	$415,000	

2. Expenditures paid in cash:

Educational and general:		
Institutional support	$ 40,000	
Research	30,000	
Instruction	125,000	
Student services.	20,000	$215,000
Auxiliary enterprises		90,000
		$305,000

3. Investments of $100,000 were made.

Required Prepare journal entries for the Restricted Current Funds for the 19X0–19X1 fiscal year.

P 18-7 (Endowment Funds Entries) X University had no Endowment Funds prior to September 1, 19X0. The following transactions took place in the Endowment Funds of X University during the fiscal year ended August 31, 19X1:

1. At the beginning of the year, a cash donation of $900,000 was received to establish Endowment Fund X, and another donation of $600,000, also in cash, was received for the purpose of establishing Endowment Fund Y. The income from these funds is restricted for specific purposes. It was decided to invest this money immediately; to pool the investments of both funds; and to share earnings, including any gains or losses on sales of investments, at the end of the year based on the ratio of the original contributions of each fund.

2. Securities with a par value of $1,000,000 were purchased at a premium of $10,000.

3. Securities with a par value of $191,500 were acquired at a discount of $2,000; accrued interest at date of purchase amounted to $500.

4. The university trustees voted to pool the investments of a new endowment, Endowment Fund Z, with the investments of Endowment Funds X and Y under the same conditions as applied to the latter two Funds. The investments of Endowment Fund Z at the date it joined the pool at midyear amounted to $290,000 at book value and $300,000 at market value. (Hereafter, the investment pool earnings are to be shared 9:6:3.)

5. Cash dividends received from the pooled investments during the year amounted to $70,000, and interest receipts amounted to $5,500.

6. Premiums of $500 and discounts of $100 were amortized.

7. Securities carried at $30,000 were sold at a gain of $2,400.

8. Each fund was credited with its share of the investment earnings for the year (see transactions 1 and 4).

9. A provision of Endowment Fund Y is that a minimum of $75,000 each year, whether from earnings or principal or both, is to be paid to the Restricted Current Funds to support specified institutional services and research projects. The payment was made.

10. An apartment complex comprised of land, buildings, and equipment valued at $800,000 was donated to the university, distributed as follows: land, $80,000; buildings, $500,000; equipment, $220,000. The donor stipulated that an endowment fund (designated as Endowment Fund N) should be established and that the income therefrom should be used for a restricted operating purpose.

11. $150,000 was received from Unrestricted Current Funds as a quasi-endowment (or fund functioning as an endowment) and was designated Fund O.

12. A trust fund in the amount of $350,000 (cash) was set up by a donor with the stipulation that the income was to go to the university to be used for general purposes. This fund was designated Endowment Fund P.

Required Prepare journal entries for the Endowment and Similar Funds Group for 19X0–19X1.

P 18-8 (Annuity and Life Income Funds Entries) The following transactions affected the Annuity and Life Income Funds and the Loan Funds of X University during the fiscal year ended August 31, 19X1:

Annuity and Life Income Funds

1. A gift of $500,000 cash, from the Lobo family, was received by X University on September 3, 19X0. According to the terms of the bequest, the University must pay the donor, or her estate should she die, $50,000 on each August 31 for 20 years, beginning in 19X1. The balance remaining at the end of the 20-year period is to be used to supplement the income of outstanding professors at X University. The chief finance officer expects to earn an average of at least 9% on investments over the next 20 years.

2. Another gift, from the Mann family, was received, composed of:

Assets	Donor's Cost	Fair Market Value
Land.	$ 50,000	$ 70,000
Building.	300,000	400,000
Equipment	80,000	40,000
Common Stock.	100,000	90,000
	$530,000	$600,000

The University is to pay the income (as conventionally determined) from these assets to the donor or his spouse as long as either lives. Their combined life expectancy is 15 years according to recognized life expectancy tables.

3. The $500,000 cash received from the Lobo family was invested.

4. The Lobo investments earned $55,000 during the year, all received in cash.

5. The Mann investment earnings were (a) office complex: revenues, $900,000; expenses of $700,000, including $30,000 depreciation on the building and $4,000 depreciation on the equipment; an amount equal to net income before depreciation was received by X University; (b) common stock: dividends of $75,000, all received in cash.

6. The appropriate payments were made to the Lobo and Mann families and appropriate adjusting and closing entries, if any, were made.

Loan Funds

1. A donation of $150,000 was received in cash for the purpose of making loans to students.

2. Cash in the amount of $50,000 was invested in bonds acquired at par.

3. Loans of $60,000 were made to students.

4. Interest on investments, $300, was received in cash.

5. Student loans of $1,000 were written off as uncollectible.

Required   Prepare journal entries for the appropriate funds for 19X0–19X1.

P 18-9   (Plant Funds Entries) The trial balance of the Investment in Plant subgroup of X University as of September 1, 19X0, was as follows:

Land	$ 200,000	
Buildings	3,300,000	
Accumulated Depreciation—Buildings		$ 900,000
Equipment	1,200,000	
Accumulated Depreciation—Equipment		300,000
Mortgage Payable		250,000
Net Invested in Plant—Federal Grants		625,000
Net Invested in Plant—Unrestricted Funds		525,000
Net Invested in Plant—Gifts		2,100,000
	$4,700,000	$4,700,000

X University is a state university, but has **elected** to record accumulated depreciation of its Plant Funds fixed assets.

The following transactions took place during the year:

1. A cash donation of $40,000 was received from an individual for the purpose of financing new additions to the business and public administration building.

2. The money was invested in securities acquired at par.

3. Cash was received from the Unrestricted Current Fund as follows:

For retiring indebtedness	$20,000
For plant improvements and renovations	15,000
For plant additions	15,000
	$50,000

4. Of the money received from the Unrestricted Current Fund, $10,000 was used to finance the acquisition of additional equipment.

5. A $1,000,000 addition to the business and public administration building was begun. Expenditures of $600,000 were incurred (and paid) by August 31, 19X1, financed by a loan (note) in that amount from the Last National Bank pending the receipt of more donations. X University's accounting policy is to account for construction in progress and related debt in the Investment in Plant accounts.

6. $13,000 was spent in remodeling an art building classroom.

7. A cash donation of $75,000 was received for the purpose of paying part of the mortgage.

8. A mortgage installment of $35,000 ($10,000 principal and $25,000 interest) which became due during the year was paid from the above donation.

9. An uninsured piece of equipment costing $5,000 and financed from the Unrestricted Current Fund was destroyed. Related accumulated depreciation was $2,000.

10. The provision for depreciation for the year was $270,000 for buildings and $120,000 for equipment.

Required Prepare journal entries for the several types of Plant Funds, as needed, for 19X0–19X1.

P 18-10 (Statements) Analysis of the accounts of Jonimatt State College for the fiscal year ended June 30, 19X7 provided the following information:

	Unrestricted	Restricted
Current Funds Revenues from:		
Tuition and fees	$7,300,000	
State appropriations	5,920,000	$ 413,000
Federal grants and contracts		2,000,000
Private gifts, grants, and contracts	2,950,000	1,112,000
Sales and services of auxiliary enterprises	3,000,000	
Sales and services of educational activities	500,000	
Current Funds Expenditures for:		
Instruction	5,830,000	760,000
Research	1,200,000	610,000
Public service	300,000	2,000,000
Academic support	2,000,000	
Student services	925,000	
Institutional support	2,500,000	
Operation and maintenance of plant	3,125,000	
Scholarships and fellowships	200,000	155,000
Auxiliary enterprises	2,660,000	

Jonimatt State College has **elected** to report accumulated depreciation of Plant Funds assets.

Additional Information:

1. Earnings of the endowment funds included the following:

Unrestricted	$100,000
Restricted for:	
Scholarships and fellowships	45,000
Plant expansion	75,000
Total	$220,000

2. Contributions received during fiscal year 19X7 were for these purposes:

a.	Unrestricted	$2,950,000
b.	Scholarships and fellowships	320,000
c.	Specific academic programs	1,800,000
d.	Endowment	4,300,000
e.	Plant expansion	850,000
f.	Debt service	40,000
g.	Life income trust	160,000

3. Restricted investment income was earned for:

a.	Scholarships and fellowships	$195,000
b.	Specific academic programs	250,000
c.	Plant expansion	78,000
d.	Debt service	30,000

4. Federal grants and contracts received during the year of $2,230,000 were restricted for specific operating purposes. State appropriations of $340,000 restricted to specific academic programs and $500,000 restricted to expansion of the business building also were received.

5. Jonimatt State College accounts for its investments at cost. Realized gains on restricted endowment funds investments amounted to $50,000 during the year.

6. Proceeds of equipment sales during the year, $27,000, are unrestricted. The cost of the assets sold was $140,000, and the related accumulated depreciation was $104,000.

7. Depreciation of plant facilities for the fiscal year was $800,000.

8. $1,300,000 of plant assets were acquired during fiscal year 19X7, including $280,000 acquired with proceeds of long-term debt issued during the year and $600,000 recorded as current funds expenditures (included in previous information). The remainder of the plant assets was acquired with Unexpended Plant Fund resources. Also, the university issued $4,000,000 of bonds at par to finance construction of a new chemistry building, but construction had not begun at June 30, 19X7.

9. $300,000 of long-term debt and $340,000 of interest matured and were paid in fiscal year 19X7.

10. A $1,000,000 annuity gift was received during the year. The present value of the annuity payments was $480,144 when the gift was received. Investment income for the year was $100,000 and a $90,000 annuity payment was made as stipulated in the gift agreement. The present value of the remaining annuity payments at June 30, 19X7 was $438,158.

11. The principal of a life income fund became available for endowment purposes, $500,000. In addition, two term endowments expired during 19X7. One became available for unrestricted purposes, $350,000; the other is to be used for environmental engineering research, $190,000.

12. $30,000 of a grant restricted for operating purposes which expired during the year was refunded to the federal government.

13. Transfers during fiscal year 19X7 included:

$600,000 to cover scheduled debt service payments

$300,000 to match restricted contributions for plant additions

$100,000 which the board voted to use for plant expansion

$200,000 to establish an endowment for a professorship to honor the university's first president

14. Fund balances of the various funds at the beginning of the year were:

Unrestricted Current Funds	$ 2,012,000
Restricted Current Funds	978,000
Endowment and Similar Funds	1,022,000
Annuity and Life Income Funds	702,000
Unexpended Plant Funds	320,000
Retirement of Indebtedness Fund . . .	450,000
Investment in Plant subgroup	22,717,000

Required (a) Prepare a Statement of Current Funds Revenues, Expenditures, and Other Changes for Jonimatt State College for the fiscal year ended June 30, 19X7.

(b) Prepare a Statement of Changes in Fund Balances for Jonimatt State College for the fiscal year ended June 30, 19X7.

ACCOUNTING
FOR VOLUNTARY HEALTH
AND WELFARE AND OTHER
NONPROFIT ORGANIZATIONS

The authoritative pronouncements of the accounting and reporting standards-setting bodies for businesses, state and local governments, hospitals, and colleges and universities have been recognized in preceding chapters. Voluntary health and welfare organizations and certain other nonprofit organizations were not addressed by universally recognized accounting and reporting standards until 1979.

In 1964 the National Health Council and its member agencies and the National Assembly for Social Policy and Development issued the first definitive guidance for financial reporting by voluntary health and welfare organizations in a handbook entitled *Standards of Accounting and Financial Reporting for Voluntary Health and Welfare Organizations.*[1] An American Institute of Certified Public Accountants (AICPA) committee issued an audit guide, *Audits of Voluntary Health and Welfare Organizations,* in 1966 and issued a revised audit guide in 1974.[2] Recently, the National Health Council, the National Assembly for National Voluntary Health and Social Welfare Organizations, and the United Way of America revised *Standards of Accounting and Financial Reporting for Voluntary Health and Welfare Organizations*[3] to make it consistent with the audit guide and subsequent developments.

The Accounting Standards Division of the AICPA issued *Statement of Position (SOP) 78-10,* "Accounting Principles and Reporting Practices for Certain Nonprofit Organizations,"[4] in 1978. SOP 78-10 was issued without an effective date since the Financial Accounting Standards Board (FASB) had a project on "nonbusiness" accounting and reporting on its agenda.

In 1979 the FASB assumed responsibility for setting accounting and report-

---

[1] National Health Council and National Assembly for Social Policy and Development, *Standards of Accounting and Financial Reporting for Voluntary Health and Welfare Organizations* (Washington, D.C., 1964).

[2] Committee on Voluntary Health and Welfare Organizations, American Institute of Certified Public Accountants, *Audits of Voluntary Health and Welfare Organizations* (New York: AICPA, 1974). Hereafter cited as VHWO audit guide.

[3] National Health Council, National Assembly for National Voluntary Health and Social Welfare Organizations, and United Way of America, *Standards of Accounting and Financial Reporting for Voluntary Health and Welfare Organizations,* 3rd ed. (Washington, D.C., 1988).

[4] Accounting Standards Division, American Institute of Certified Public Accountants, *Statement of Position 78-10,* "Accounting Principles and Reporting Practices for Certain Nonprofit Organizations" (New York: AICPA, December 31, 1978). Hereafter cited as SOP 78-10.

ing standards for all nonbusiness organizations except governments. The Board accepted responsibility for the specialized accounting and reporting principles and practices in the AICPA SOPs, audit guides, and accounting guides in FASB *Statement No. 32.*[5] The FASB did not fully endorse all such AICPA publications as constituting generally accepted accounting principles, but (1) announced its intention to study them and, after due process, issue guidance as FASB standards; and (2) stated that, in the interim, the principles and practices in the audit guides, accounting guides, and SOPs listed in FASB *Statement No. 32* are **"preferable"** for purposes of justifying a change in accounting principles under *Accounting Principles Board Opinion 20,* "Accounting Changes."

Both *Audits of Voluntary Health and Welfare Organizations* and AICPA SOP 78-10, "Accounting Principles and Reporting Practices for Certain Nonprofit Organizations," are covered by FASB *Statement No. 32.* These are the most authoritative pronouncements on accounting and reporting for these types of organizations. Both were widely accepted in practice prior to FASB *Statement No. 32* and have become more accepted since its issuance. Accordingly, this chapter is based on the guidance and illustrations in the VHWO audit guide and in SOP 78-10.

This chapter distinguishes voluntary health and welfare organizations (VHWOs) from other nonprofit organizations (ONPOs) because of the differences in the accounting and reporting principles of the two types of organizations. VHWOs are discussed and illustrated initially. ONPOs are discussed in the closing sections of the chapter.

Illustrative entries and financial statements are presented for a **VHWO** that **uses** fund accounting. Next, the primary differences in accounting and reporting for the two types of organizations are highlighted. Then, the differences in the entries and the financial statements are illustrated, assuming that the illustrative entity is an **ONPO** that **uses** fund accounting. Finally, since **fund accounting is optional** for both types of organizations, differences in the entries and the financial statements that would result if the illustrative ONPO did **not** use fund accounting are explained.

CLASSIFICATION OF ORGANIZATIONS

Properly classifying nonprofit organizations is important because of the differences in the accounting and financial reporting principles that apply to them. Hospitals and colleges and universities typically are clearly distinguishable from VHWOs and ONPOs. But it is sometimes difficult to distinguish VHWOs from ONPOs. The focus in this decision typically is on **whether** the organization is a **VHWO,** since **ONPOs** are defined as **all** nonprofit organizations **other than** hospitals (and similar health care institutions), colleges and universities, and VHWOs. As with hospitals and colleges and universities, it is also important to distinguish VHWOs and ONPOs that are "governmental" organizations from those that are not. This distinction determines whether the GASB or the FASB is the pertinent standards-setting body. Indeed, this classification may soon become more critical since FASB issuance of significant pronouncements affecting nongovernmental VHWOs and ONPOs appears imminent.

---

[5] Financial Accounting Standards Board, *Statement of Financial Accounting Standards No. 32,* "Specialized Accounting and Reporting Principles and Practices in AICPA Statements of Position and Guides on Accounting and Auditing Matters" (Stamford, Conn.: FASB, September 1979). The FASB rescinded SFAS No. 32 in November 1992 (*Statement of Financial Accounting Standards No. 111,* "Rescission of FASB Statement No. 32 and Technical Corrections"). The FASB considered SFAS No. 32 unnecessary under the new GAAP hierarchy (discussed in Chapter 1) adopted by the AICPA in *Statement on Auditing Standards No. 69.*

Voluntary Health and Welfare Organizations

Voluntary health and welfare organizations are formed to provide various kinds of health, welfare, and community services voluntarily (for no fee or a low fee) to various segments of society. VHWOs are tax exempt, organized for the public benefit, supported largely by public contributions, and operated on a not-for-profit basis. Thus, the **features that distinguish VHWOs from ONPOs** are:

1. Their purpose—to meet a community health, welfare, or other social service need;
2. Their voluntary nature—no fee is charged, or only a very small fee in proportion to the services provided is charged; and
3. Providers of resources are not the primary recipients of services or benefits of a VHWO.

Some ONPOs may provide services similar to those provided by certain VHWOs. But, **ONPOs** finance the services with **user charges or membership fees charged** to the **primary recipients** of the services.

The United Way—or another federated community contribution solicitation and allocation organization—is active in most cities and is perhaps the most widely recognized type of VHWO in the United States. Numerous other VHWOs exist in most cities, however, such as the Boy Scouts and Girl Scouts, the American Heart Association, the YMCA, the YWCA, and various mental health associations. Many of these organizations are financed wholly or partly by allocations from the United Way or equivalent organizations. Among the many types of services provided through VHWOs are child care for working mothers, family counseling, nutritious meals and recreation for the elderly, family planning assistance, care and treatment of mentally and/or physically handicapped persons, protection of children from parental or other abuse, halfway houses for criminal or drug offenders, and sheltered workshops for physically and/or mentally handicapped citizens. Most VHWOs charge modest fees to those who can afford to pay them, using a sliding fee schedule based on family size and income.

Other Nonprofit Organizations

The **other** nonprofit organizations addressed by SOP 78-10 include **all** nonprofit organizations **except** (1) hospitals, colleges and universities, state and local governments, and voluntary health and welfare organizations, and (2) those nonprofit organizations that operate essentially as business enterprises for the direct economic benefit of their members or stockholders. Thus, whereas SOP 78-10 does *not* apply to employee benefit and pension plans, mutual insurance companies or banks, agricultural cooperatives, or similar **member benefit organizations,** it *does* apply to the following types of organizations and to other truly nonprofit organizations:

- Cemetery organizations
- Civic organizations
- Fraternal organizations
- Libraries
- Museums
- Other cultural institutions
- Performing arts organizations

- Political parties
- Private and community foundations
- Private elementary and secondary schools
- Professional associations
- Religious organizations
- Research and scientific organizations
- Social and country clubs
- Trade associations
- Zoological and botanical societies

Member benefit organizations should be accounted for like their private sector counterparts.

PURPOSES OF FINANCIAL STATEMENTS

The VHWO audit guide and SOP 78-10 indicate similar purposes for financial statements of the organizations covered by the respective documents. Financial statements of these organizations are designed primarily for those who are interested in the organizations as "outsiders," not members of management. Presumably the latter group can access whatever data it may want. But the organization's contributors, beneficiaries of services, employees, creditors and potential creditors, related organizations, and even the trustees or directors need information that comes in a complete package ready for their appropriate uses. The same can be said of representatives of governments that may have jurisdiction over these organizations.

The financial statements should provide information that describes and discloses the following:[6]

1. The nature and amount of available resources
2. The degree of control exercised by donors and the amount of freedom management has in determining which resources will be used and how they will be used.
3. The uses made of resources, including identification of the nature and costs of the principal programs
4. The net changes in fund balances during the reporting period
5. A basis for evaluating management's performance
6. A basis for evaluating the likelihood that management can carry out its prescribed or announced programs with available resources

BASIS OF FINANCIAL REPORTING

Because of the emphasis on providing cost of services data, the financial statements should be prepared on the ***accrual*** basis of accounting—that is, accounting for revenues and **expenses.** It is acceptable to keep the accounts on some other basis, such as the cash basis, and make period-end adjustments to convert them to GAAP.

---

[6] Adapted from SOP 78-10, par. 9.

The accrual basis may not be necessary for some organizations where statements prepared on the cash basis do **not differ materially** from those that would be prepared on the accrual basis. (These statements can be said to be in conformity with GAAP.) But cash basis statements for more complex operations are special reports, and are **not** in conformity with GAAP.

FUND ACCOUNTING—VHWOs

Neither the VHWO audit guide *nor* SOP 78-10 *requires* fund accounting to be used. However, most VHWOs receive grants and contributions restricted for specific purposes and use fund accounting to facilitate observing and demonstrating accountability for such restrictions. Many ONPOs also receive significant amounts of restricted resources. The more significant the amount of restricted resources held by an ONPO, the more useful fund accounting is in enhancing fiscal control and the fairness of presentation of the organization's financial statements.

Some ONPOs use fund accounting even though normally they do not have significant amounts of restricted resources. Fund accounting is typically used by such organizations as private schools and religious organizations, for instance, because it is a well-established practice in those "industries." Other ONPOs may use fund accounting because (1) they have material amounts of property, plant, and equipment, and/or (2) depreciation is not provided for in budgeting but capital additions are budgeted. Using fund accounting when an organization has material amounts of property, plant, and equipment and a significant portion of its total equity results from its net investment in those assets may permit clearer presentation of the resources available to finance ongoing services in the financial statements.

No specific fund structure is required by the VHWO audit guide or by SOP 78–10 for organizations that use fund accounting. However, the VHWO audit guide notes that the **most commonly used funds** for VHWOs are:

1. **Current Unrestricted Fund:** to account for all **unrestricted** resources that the governing body may use as it sees fit, consistent with the organization's charter and bylaws, except for unrestricted amounts invested in land, buildings, and equipment that are accounted for in the Land, Buildings, and Equipment (or Plant) Fund.

2. **Current Restricted Fund(s):** to account for **restricted** resources that are expendable, and are available for use, but may be expended only for **operating** purposes specified by the donor or grantor.

3. **Endowment Fund(s):** to account for the principal of gifts and bequests accepted with donor stipulations that (a) the principal is to be maintained intact in perpetuity, for a specific period, or until a specified event occurs, and (b) only the income on the fund's investments may be expended for general purposes or for purposes specified by the donor.

4. **Custodian Fund(s):** to account for assets received that are to be held for, or disbursed only on instructions from, the person or organization from whom they were received.

5. **Loan and Annuity Fund(s):** to account for assets held for purposes of making loans or paying annuities to recipients, typically with the provision that the VHWO is the "remainderman" of the annuity trust.

6. **Land, Buildings, and Equipment (or Plant) Fund:** to account for (a) **restricted** resources to be used to acquire or replace land, buildings, or equipment for use in operating the organization; (b) land, buildings, and equipment

used in operating the organization; (c) mortgages or other liabilities relating to the land, buildings, and equipment used in operations; and (d) the net investment in land, buildings, and equipment (or plant).

Note that this **fund structure** is **virtually identical** to the **college and university fund structure** (Chapter 18). However, there are two critical **accounting differences:**

1. Except for fixed assets only **externally restricted** resources and related liabilities are accounted for in the VHWO restricted funds.
2. The **accrual (revenue and expense) basis** is used in accounting for VHWO funds, not the revenue and expenditure basis used for colleges and universities.

Note in studying the fund structure that—except for the land, buildings, and equipment—all of the resources accounted for in funds other than the Current Unrestricted Funds are **externally restricted** either explicitly or implicitly (as by requesting donations for a specific purpose). All **unrestricted** resources other than fixed assets, even if designated by the board for a specific use, are accounted for in the Current Unrestricted Fund. Thus, VHWOs account for **board-designated** resources in the same fund as other unrestricted assets.

VHWO FINANCIAL STATEMENTS

The financial statements required for **VHWOs** are the (1) Balance Sheet(s); (2) **Statement of Support, Revenue, and Expenses and Changes in Fund Balances;** and (3) **Statement of Functional Expenses.** Each of these statements reports on **all** of the funds of the VHWO. A statement of cash flows is ***not*** required by the VHWO audit guide since the information normally presented in a statement of cash flows "will, in most cases, be readily apparent from [the] other financial statements."[7] Further, the statements illustrated are viewed as guidelines rather than mandates, and the VHWO audit guide states: "Modifications to the financial statements illustrated should be made to fit the facts and circumstances of each specific organization."[8] The illustrative VHWO financial statements presented on pages 754–756 should be studied briefly now and referred to throughout the discussion of VHWOs.

Each of the basic financial statements is discussed and illustrated and the underlying principles are explained in the following sections. Each of the statements can be presented in either the "pancake" or layered format illustrated by the college and university balance sheet or in the columnar format typically used for state and local governments. The columnar format facilitates presentation of totals for all funds in the financial statements. This practice is permitted for VHWOs and SOP 78-10 states that it is preferred, but not required, for ONPOs that use fund accounting.

Balance Sheet

Although no specific VHWO balance sheet format is prescribed, numerous asset, liability, and fund balance accounting and reporting guidelines, many of which also affect the statement of activity, are specified.

[7] VHWO audit guide, p. 33.
[8] Ibid.

Restricted vs. Unrestricted

The balance sheet should clearly distinguish ***externally restricted*** assets, related liabilities, and fund balances from ***unrestricted*** assets, related liabilities, and fund balances available to the organization. This may be done by presentation of fund data, as on pages 745 and 754, or by use of **restricted-unrestricted** balance sheet classifications.

Current vs. Noncurrent

VHWOs having only unrestricted assets, liabilities, and fund balances should classify the assets and liabilities as either "current" or "noncurrent" (or "fixed," "long-term," and so on). Organizations with both restricted and unrestricted assets, related liabilities, and fund balances also should classify the assets and liabilities as "current" or "noncurrent" unless the fund structure adequately indicates the current or noncurrent status of the assets and liabilities.

Investments

Investments of VHWOs are recorded initially at cost, except that donated securities are recorded at their fair market value at the date of the gift. (Interfund exchanges or transfers of investments are accounted for at market, which is treated as the new "cost" to the fund receiving the investments.) Thereafter, investments of **VHWOs** may be accounted for at cost (or lower of cost or market) or at market value. All investments of a VHWO should be accounted for on the same basis.

Finally, VHWOs may establish investment pools. Such pools should be accounted for on a fair market value basis—to ensure equitable allocations of pooled investment income or loss—though the investments, including the investment in the pools, may be accounted for on a cost or market basis in the several funds. But, the investments of all funds of a VHWO (excluding the investment pool) must be accounted for on the same basis, either cost or market.

Pledges

VHWOs should recognize pledges receivable in the accounts and establish an appropriate allowance for uncollectible pledges. If **VHWOs** charge uncollectible pledges to an expense account, the gross amount pledged is reported as public support. Typically, however, the uncollectible amount is deducted from the gross pledges rather than being reported as expenses, and **only the net expected pledge collections** are recognized as public **support.** Pledges or contributions **required to be used for future periods** should be recorded as **deferred support.**

Fixed Assets

Fixed assets of VHWOs are recorded at cost or, if donated, at fair market value at donation. If historical cost or fair market value data are not available, fixed asset costs may be estimated. In such cases the valuation method(s) used should be disclosed in the notes to the financial statements.

When fund accounting is used, fixed assets used in current operations are recorded in the Land, Buildings, and Equipment (or Plant) Fund. Sales of these fixed assets are also recorded there, together with losses and gains on sales. Sales proceeds may remain in the fund or, if unrestricted, may be transferred to the Current Unrestricted Fund.

Donated fixed assets may not be immediately usable or salable because of donor restrictions or conditions. These fixed assets are reported as contributions to the Current Restricted Fund or another restricted fund. When the donor restrictions expire, or donor conditions have been met, the fixed assets are transferred to the Land, Buildings, and Equipment Fund if they are to be used in VHWO operations. If they are to be sold or held to produce income, the fixed assets are recorded in the Current Unrestricted Fund, if the income and/or sale proceeds are unrestricted, or in the Current Restricted Fund if the income and/or sale proceeds are restricted as to use. Sales of such fixed assets, together with the gain or loss upon sale, are recorded in the fund in which the fixed asset is recorded.

Depreciation expense and accumulated depreciation are recorded for exhaustible fixed assets in operating use or held to produce income. Depreciation is not recorded on fixed assets held for sale.

Liabilities

When fund accounting is used, all VHWO liabilities are reported in the fund to which they relate, if that is apparent, or in the Current Unrestricted Fund. Long-term debt usually relates to the Land, Buildings, and Equipment Fund or to the Endowment Fund. However, liabilities related to fixed assets held for income or sale are reported with the assets in the Current Restricted Fund or the Current Unrestricted Fund, as appropriate.

Deferred Support and Revenue.   Assets that are otherwise unrestricted but (1) are intended by donors to finance operations of future years or (2) result from prepayments of service charges or other revenues should be reported as deferred support or revenue, as appropriate. **VHWO** resources that are ***restricted*** for specified purposes—whether operating, capital additions, or endowment purposes—are recognized as revenue or support when the receivable is recordable or the cash gift is received unless they are to finance future period activities or are prepayments.

Future Interests.   Future interests should be appropriately reported in the balance sheet. The most common types of future interests given VHWOs are annuity and life income gifts. The same factors discussed previously for other gifts determine whether support would be recognized or deferred for annuity and life income gifts. Accounting and reporting for annuity and life income funds are illustrated for colleges and universities (Chapter 18), so are not discussed or illustrated further in this chapter.

Fund Balance

The **fund balances** of the Current Unrestricted Fund and the Current Restricted Fund of a VHWO may be "designated" by the governing board for specific purposes and projects or for investment. Such ***designations*** do ***not*** constitute, and should not be confused with, donor ***restrictions.*** The board can change or reverse its designation action at will, and designations report only tentative plans that may be changed.

Fund Balances of the Current Restricted Fund are identified according to the ***purposes*** for which they may be used. Endowment Fund balances may also be reported according to purpose, donor, or otherwise. Finally, the Fund Balance of the VHWO Land, Buildings, and Equipment (or Plant) Fund should be separated between its ***expended and unexpended*** components, and the unexpended balance should be further classified as to whether it is restricted or unrestricted, when possible.

Other Balance Sheet Guidance

Other matters relating to VHWO balance sheets include:

- **Interfund borrowings** should be disclosed when restricted funds have been loaned or when the liquidity of either fund is in question. Also, any unauthorized or illegal interfund loans should be disclosed, and interfund loans should be reported as transfers when it is evident that repayment is unlikely.
- **Funds held in trust by others** that are in neither the possession nor the control of the VHWO are **not reported in** the **balance sheet** but are disclosed, either parenthetically in the Endowment Fund balance sheet or in the notes to the financial statements.

Operating Statements

The major **VHWO** operating statement is the **Statement of Support, Revenue, Expenses and Other Changes in Fund Balances.** Figure 19-1 summarizes the format of the VHWO operating statement. Note "Support and Revenue" are reported by source. Expenses, classified as between program services and supporting services, are reported by function. As Figure 19-1 shows, VHWOs present all "other changes in fund balances" in a section immediately before beginning and ending fund balances.

When fund accounting is used, the public support, revenue, expenses, and other changes in fund balances must be classified by fund as well as by source or function. Presentation of prior year data is suggested but not required.

Public Support and Revenue

The term **"public support"** indicates **resources provided** by donors in **nonreciprocal transactions.** Current contributions to fund-raising drives, special fund-raising events, legacies and bequests, and contributions from federated (e.g., United Way) and other fund-raising campaigns are typical major support sources of VHWOs. Note that **only** the **net** contributions—gross contributions less direct costs incurred—of **special fund-raising events** are **reported** as **"Public Support."**

"Revenues" include such items as membership dues (often really "public support" in VHWOs), investment income, gains and losses on disposal of fixed

Figure 19-1	**VHWO OPERATING STATEMENT FORMAT**

(Public) Support and Revenue
    Public Support (listed by source) X
    Revenue (listed by source). . . . . <u>X</u>
        Total Support and Revenue . . . . <u>X</u>

Expenses
    Program Services (listed by function). X
    Supporting Services
        Management and General X
        Fund Raising . . . . <u>X</u>
          Total Expenses . . . . <u>X</u>
Excess (Deficiency) of Support and Revenue Over (Under) Expenses X
Other Changes in Fund Balances (e.g., Transfers) X

Fund Balances, Beginning of Year . . . . <u>X</u>
Fund Balances, End of Year . . . . <u>X</u>

assets or investments, and fees for services rendered. Investment income may be reported on either the cost or market value approach, as noted earlier, and the gains and losses reported should be consistent with the investment accounting method employed.

The deferral of revenue and support items by VHWOs when not available for use in the current period was discussed in the preceding sections. **Support and revenue** recognized in the **VHWO** operating statement includes:

1. **Unrestricted and restricted** contributions, gifts, bequests, service fees, investment income, and the excess of annuity gifts of the period over the present value of related liabilities. (Recall that if restricted to use in future periods, rather than as to purpose, support and revenue recognition is deferred to the future period.)

2. Support and revenue classified as **deferred in prior periods that apply to the current period.**

Pledges, Membership Dues, and Other Fees

VHWOs report the **net** pledges expected to be collectible as public support once any conditions associated with the pledges are met. Membership dues or subscription fees that relate to several periods usually should be recognized as revenues of those periods. However, fees from life memberships may be recognized currently, unless significant future costs are involved, as may dues, assessments, and similar items that are in-substance contributions.

Investment Income and Gains/Losses

Investment income reported and gains and losses recognized on investment transactions are determined partly by the investment valuation method(s) used. Where the market value method of investment accounting is used, the changes in market value, as well as interest and dividends, are reported as investment income. In either event (1) interfund sales, exchanges, or transfers of investments should be reported at fair value, with gain or loss recognized in the transferor fund, and (2) the notes to the financial statements should contain a summary of the total realized and unrealized investment gains, losses, and income of all funds except life income and custodial funds (since the investment earnings, gains, and losses of such funds do not inure to the organization).

Donated Materials, Facilities, and Services

The fair market value of significant amounts of **materials** donated to VHWOs should be reported as **support** when the materials are received and **expenses** when the materials are used **if** (1) their omission would cause the statement of support, revenue, expenses, and other changes in fund balances to be misleading; and (2) the organization has an objective, unbiased basis of estimating their fair market value. The same is true for donated (free) **use of facilities and other assets.**

Donated services should also be reported both as public support and expense in some instances. VHWOs should report donated services as support and expense **if** the following conditions are met:

1. The services performed are a normal part of the program or supporting services and would otherwise be performed by salaried personnel.

2. The organization exercises control over the employment and duties of the donors of the services.

3.   The organization has a clearly measurable basis for the amount.[9]

These criteria are rather restrictive, and preclude recording most volunteer services, for example, in fund raising or in assisting VHWO staff work with agency clients.

Expenses

Expenses of VHWOs that receive significant support from the general public should be appropriately categorized between (1) **"program expenses,"** which relate directly to the primary missions of the organization, and (2) **"supporting services,"** which do not relate directly to the primary missions and include such costs as general administration, membership development, and fund raising. Further, the expenses are to be reported by major programs or functions within these two categories.

Accounting for expenses (and expenditures) during the year may center on departmental responsibility and type (object) of expense or expenditure incurred rather than on functions. Further, some personnel may work in more than one function and some expenses may involve several functions. In such cases it is necessary to maintain time and activity records by function, and other records where appropriate, so that all expenses can be assigned, directly or by allocation, to the functions of the organization. If such records are not maintained during the year, it may be difficult and costly—if not impossible—to classify expenses properly by function at year end as required by the VHWO audit guide.

Program Services

Program services expenses are those that relate *directly* to the *primary missions* of the organization. Such expenses should be classified by *functions* using terms that best convey the primary thrust of programs of the organization. Program service expenses include both *direct expenses* that are clearly identifiable with the program or function and rational *and* systematic *allocations of indirect costs.*

Some VHWOs remit a portion of their receipts to an affiliated state or national organization. **If** an organization is **in essence** serving as a **collecting agency** for the state or national affiliate—for example, one that must remit a percentage of all collections to the affiliate—it should report such payments as **deductions from total support and revenue. Otherwise,** organizations should **report** dues and other remittances to affiliates as **program expenses.**

Some VHWOs make grants to other organizations. **Grants** should be recorded as expenses and liabilities at the time the recipient is entitled to them. However, if the grantor reserves the right to revoke the grant, only the amounts that the grantee is clearly entitled to should be recorded as expenses and liabilities. Grants subject to periodic renewal are recorded as expenses and liabilities upon renewal and the remaining commitment is disclosed in the notes to the financial statements.

Supporting Services

Supporting services expenses do not relate directly to the primary missions of the organization and include *management and general, fund raising, and other costs* not associated directly with rendering program services. Analysts and regulators of VHWOs pay close attention to the relationship of supporting services ex-

---

[9] VHWO audit guide, pp. 20–21.

penses to program services expenses and total expenses. In particular, fund-raising costs are often compared among organizations and for individual organizations through time.

Management and General Costs.   Management and general costs are not identifiable with a specific program or fund-raising activity but are necessary to the organization's existence and effectiveness. They include such costs as board meetings, business management, record keeping, budgeting, accounting, and overall direction and leadership. To the extent that some of these costs are directly related to the primary programs, they should be allocated to those program costs in a systematic and rational manner.

Fund-Raising and Other Supporting Services.   Fund-raising costs are incurred to induce contributions of money, securities, real estate or other properties, materials, or time to the organization. Fund-raising efforts and costs vary widely among the many types of VHWOs, but fund-raising costs such as the following are often incurred: mailing lists, printing, mailing, personnel, occupancy, newspaper and other media advertising, and costs of unsolicited merchandise sent to encourage contributions. Some organizations combine fund-raising efforts with educational materials or program services. In such cases, the combined costs incurred must be allocated appropriately among fund-raising and the various program functions so that each is reflected appropriately in the organization's operating statement.[10]

Fund-raising costs paid directly by a contributor should be recorded by the organization as **both** a contribution and a fund-raising expense. When fund-raising banquets, dinner parties, theater parties, merchandise auctions or drawings, and similar events are held, only the **net** (after related direct costs) proceeds of such functions should be **reported as support.** However, costs of the fund-raising merchandise, meals, or other direct benefits to donors should be disclosed in the notes to the financial statements. Where several fund-raising efforts are undertaken with mixed success, it may be appropriate to summarize the results of each fund-raising activity in the Statement of Activity or in the notes to the financial statements.

Fund-raising costs usually are expensed each year. However, if pledges or restricted contributions received in a fund drive are appropriately recorded as deferred support, directly related fund-raising costs may be deferred if the donor(s) is aware that the contribution could be used to cover fund-raising costs. Similarly, costs of literature, materials, and so on incurred in one year to be used in fund raising the next year should be deferred and recognized as fund-raising costs of that year.

Costs of soliciting grants from foundations or government agencies should be reported as separate categories of fund-raising expenses. Similarly, the costs of membership development efforts should be reported as a separate item of "supporting services."

Transfers and Other Changes in Fund Balances

Other changes in fund balances include direct and indirect interfund transfers, as well as certain external transactions. An external transaction that might be reported in this section is the refund of resources to donors.

Transfers are shifts of fund balances from one fund to another, usually as a result of an intended change in the use of the assets. Transfers include (1) **direct**

---

[10] Not-for-Profit Organization Committee, American Institute of Certified Public Accountants, *Statement of Position 87-2,* "Accounting for Joint Costs of Informational Materials and Activities of Not-for-Profit Organizations that Included a Fund-Raising Appeal" (New York: AICPA, 1987).

transfers of money or other assets from one fund to another, as occurs when realized Endowment Fund appreciation is transferred to some other fund, and (2) **indirect transfers,** such as capitalization of fixed assets acquired with Current Unrestricted Fund resources in the Land, Buildings, and Equipment (or Plant) Fund. Since transfers are neither revenues, support, nor expenses, they are reported separate from those items under "Other Changes in Fund Balances." Transfers required under contractual arrangements and those required upon expiration of a term endowment fund should be separately disclosed.

Note that the Statement of Support, Revenue, Expenses, and Changes in Fund Balances presented on page 755 explains the changes in *total* fund balances. The VHWO audit guide does not provide for "reserves" or for "reserved" and "unreserved" fund balances, and designations are not the equivalent of reserves. Hence, the emphasis on total fund balance seems proper, although an explanation of changes in designations during the year might be necessary (or at least useful) in many situations.

Statement of Functional Expenses

The VHWO Statement of Functional Expenses (illustrated later) presents a detailed analysis of the "Expenses" section of the Statement of Support, Revenue, Expenses, and Changes in Fund Balances by object class or type of expense. Note that (1) the headings correspond to the "Program Services" and "Supporting Services" expense categories of the Statement of Support, Revenue, Expenses, and Changes in Fund Balances, and that (2) a "Total expenses before depreciation" subtotal is presented, followed by "Depreciation of buildings, improvements, and equipment" and "Total expenses." The detailed statement of functional expenses is considered a **supplemental schedule,** rather than a basic statement, when presented by **ONPOs.**

VHWO ACCOUNTING AND REPORTING ILLUSTRATED

VHWO accounting and reporting principles are illustrated in *this section* through the transactions, entries, and financial statements of an illustrative VHWO. The balance sheet of the **Illustrative VHWO** at December 31, 19X0 is presented in Figure 19-2. Note that it is prepared in the "pancake" or "layered" format illustrated for colleges and universities and hospitals. Also note:

1. The **Deferred Support—Contributions,** which are for cash gifts or pledges donated for use in 19X1;
2. The **segregation of fund balances** by management designations in the Current Unrestricted Fund, by restricted purpose in the Current Restricted Fund, and according to whether it is expended or unexpended in the Land, Buildings, and Equipment Fund.

Summary of Transactions and VHWO Entries

Transactions and entries for each of the major VHWO fund types are illustrated in this section. First, several entries that affect only the Current Unrestricted Fund are presented. These entries are followed in turn by transactions and entries that affect the Current Restricted Fund, the Endowment Fund, and the Land, Buildings, and Equipment Fund. Then the entries for several interfund transactions are presented.

Figure 19-2

VHWO BEGINNING BALANCE SHEET

Illustrative Voluntary Health and Welfare Organization
Balance Sheet
December 31, 19X0

Assets		Liabilities and Fund Balances	

Current Unrestricted Funds

Cash	$ 75,000	Vouchers payable	$ 17,000
Pledges receivable (less allowance for		Deferred support—contributions.	22,000
uncollectibles of $4,000)	46,000	Total Liabilities and Deferred Support	39,000
Accrued interest receivable.	2,000	Fund Balances:	
Inventory of materials	3,000	Designated by the governing board for	
Investments (market, $105,000)	90,000	capital additions	100,000
		Undesignated.	77,000
		Total Fund Balance	177,000
Total	$216,000	Total	$216,000

Current Restricted Funds

Cash	$ 50,000	Vouchers payable	$ 11,000
		Deferred support—contributions.	5,000
		Total Liabilities and Deferred Support	16,000
		Fund Balances:	
		Education	24,000
		Research.	10,000
		Total Fund Balance	34,000
Total	$ 50,000	Total	$ 50,000

Land, Buildings, and Equipment Fund

Cash	$150,000	Mortgages payable	$205,000
Investments	120,000	Fund Balances:	
Land	50,000	Expended	240,000
Buildings and improvements (net of		Unexpended	270,000
accumulated depreciation of $140,000)	280,000	Total Fund Balance	510,000
Equipment (net of accumulated			
depreciation of $85,000)	115,000		
Total	$715,000	Total	$715,000

Endowment Funds

Cash	$132,000		
Investments	313,000	Fund Balance	$445,000
Total	$445,000	Total	$445,000

Current Unrestricted Fund

1. Unrestricted gifts and pledges of prior years that donors designated for 19X1 were recognized as support.

(1)	Deferred Support—Contributions	22,000	
	Support—Contributions		22,000

To recognize prior year contributions designated for 19X1.

2. Unrestricted cash gifts of $5,000 available for use in 19X1 and $10,000 designated by donors to be used to finance operations in 19X2 were received.

Current Unrestricted Fund (continued)

(2)	Cash.	15,000	
	Support—Contributions.		5,000
	Deferred Support—Contributions.		10,000
	To record cash gifts received in 19X1 for 19X1 and 19X2.		

3. Unrestricted pledges of $250,000 were received in 19X1, of which $50,000 is designated by donors for use during 19X2. Ten percent of the pledges are expected to be uncollectible.

(3)	**Pledges Receivable**	250,000	
	Allowance for Uncollectible Pledges		25,000
	Support—Contributions		180,000
	Deferred Support—Contributions.		45,000
	To record pledges received in 19X1 for 19X1 and 19X2 and the estimated uncollectibles.		

4. Pledges receivable of $205,000 were collected in 19X1 and pledges of $18,000 were written off as uncollectible.

(4)	Cash.	205,000	
	Allowance for Uncollectible Pledges	18,000	
	Pledges Receivable.		223,000
	To record collection and write-off of pledges receivable.		

5. Land and a building were donated to the organization in 19X1 and held for resale. The fair value of the land and building when donated was $150,000. There are no restrictions on the donated property.

(5)	**Land and Buildings Held for Resale**	150,000	
	Support—Contributions		150,000
	To record donated land and building held for resale.		

6. The donated land and building were sold for $150,000.

(6)	Cash.	150,000	
	Land and Building Held for Resale		150,000
	To record sale of land and building held for resale.		

7. Investment income of $20,000 on Current Unrestricted Fund investments and $14,000 of unrestricted investment income from endowments were received. Interest accrued at the end of 19X0 was also received, $2,000.

(7)	Cash.	36,000	
	Accrued Interest Receivable.		2,000
	Revenue—Investment Income.		34,000
	To record investment income available for unrestricted purposes.		

8. A fund-raising banquet was held. Proceeds were $75,000 and related direct costs of $25,000 were incurred and paid.

(8)	(a) Cash	75,000	
	Support—Special Events		75,000
	To record support from fund-raising dinner.		

Current Unrestricted Fund (continued)

(b) **Support—Special Events** 25,000
    Cash 25,000
    To record direct costs incurred for fund-raising
    dinner.

Recall that support from special fund-raising events is reported **net** of direct costs of the events.

9. Donated materials and contributed use of facilities that are recordable in 19X1 were:

    a. Materials, $10,000 (40% in inventory at year end; 60% used on fund-raising projects)

    b. Facilities, $8,000 (60% used for research offices; 40% for record keeping)

(9) (a) Inventory of Materials 4,000
       Expenses—Fund Raising 6,000
         Support—Donated Materials 10,000
       To record donated materials.
(9) (b) Expenses—Research 4,800
       Expenses—Management and General 3,200
         Support—Donated Facilities 8,000
       To record donated facilities.

10. Donated services that are recordable include the time of:

    a. A CPA, who audited the agency at no cost, $6,000;

    b. An attorney, who did necessary legal work at no cost, $1,000; and

    c. A physician, who assisted in a research project, $3,000.

(10) Expenses—Management and General 7,000
     Expenses—Research 3,000
      Support—Donated Services 10,000
    To record donated services.

11. Membership dues of $17,300 were collected for 19X1.

(11) Cash 17,300
      Revenues—Membership Dues 17,300
    To record collection of dues.

12. Salaries and wages paid during 19X1 totaled $85,000 and $3,000 was accrued at year end, allocated as follows:

Management and General	$30,000
Fund Raising	15,000
Education	27,000
Research	16,000
Total	$88,000

(12) Expenses—Management and General 30,000
     Expenses—Fund Raising 15,000
     Expenses—Education 27,000
     Expenses—Research 16,000
      Cash 85,000
      Accrued Salaries Payable 3,000
    To record salaries and wages for 19X1.

Current Unrestricted Fund (continued)

13. Other 19X1 expenses, payments, and vouchers were:

	Expenses Incurred	Amounts Paid	Unpaid at Year End
Vouchers Payable, January 1, 19X1		$ 17,000	
Management and General Expenses.	$98,000	98,000	
Fund Raising Expenses	67,000	60,000	$ 7,000
Education Expenses	85,000	80,000	5,000
Research Expenses	50,000	48,000	2,000
Materials Purchased		800	
Total	$300,000	$303,800	$14,000

(13)	Vouchers Payable	17,000	
	Inventory of Materials.	800	
	Expenses—Management and General	98,000	
	Expenses—Fund Raising	67,000	
	Expenses—Education	85,000	
	Expenses—Research.	50,000	
	Cash.		303,800
	Vouchers Payable		14,000

To record various expenses incurred during 19X1 and
payments of vouchers payable.

14. The board of directors designated $50,000 of investments to be used as an
endowment, the earnings of which will be used to finance research.

(14)	Fund Balance—Undesignated	50,000	
	Fund Balance—Designated for Endowment		50,000

To record board designation of fund balance.

Current Restricted Fund

15. Restricted gifts and pledges of prior years designated by donors for use in
19X1 were recognized as support.

(15)	Deferred Support—Contributions	5,000	
	Support—Contributions.		5,000

To recognize prior year contributions designated for 19X1.

16. Cash gifts of $30,000 and pledges of $100,000, both restricted to use for education, were received. Ten percent of the pledges are estimated to be uncollectible.

(16)	Cash.	30,000	
	Pledges Receivable.	100,000	
	Allowance for Uncollectible Pledges		10,000
	Support—Contributions.		120,000

To record gifts and pledges restricted to education.

17. Pledges of $80,000 for restricted purposes were collected and $7,000 of restricted pledges were written off as uncollectible.

(17)	Cash.	80,000	
	Allowance for Uncollectible Pledges	7,000	
	Pledges Receivable.		87,000

To record collection and write-off of pledges receivable.

18. Investment income of $10,000 on the Current Restricted Fund investments

Current Restricted Fund (continued)

(restricted for education use) and $10,500 on Endowment Fund investments (restricted to research) were received.

```
(18)  Cash...........................................  20,500
          Revenue—Investment Income ..................         20,500
      To record investment earnings restricted for operating
      uses.
```

Note that the distinction between investment income restricted for education and that restricted for research is assumed to be maintained in subsidiary ledger accounts in this illustration.

19. Education expenses of $70,000 were incurred and paid, as were $18,000 of research expenses.

```
(19)  Expenses—Education ...........................  70,000
      Expenses—Research............................  18,000
          Cash......................................         88,000
      To record expenses for education and research.
```

Endowment Funds

20. Cash gifts of $55,000 were received to endow one of the education programs provided by the organization.

```
(20)  Cash...........................................  55,000
          Support—Contributions.......................         55,000
      To record gifts received for endowment purposes.
```

21. Endowment Fund investment earnings that are restricted to increasing the endowment base were received, $10,500.

```
(21)  Cash...........................................  10,500
          Revenue—Investment Income ..................         10,500
      To record investment income restricted to endowment.
```

22. Endowment Fund investments that cost $13,000 were sold for $14,400. Realized gains and losses on this endowment must be added to or deducted from endowment principal.

```
(22)  Cash...........................................  14,400
          Investments................................         13,000
          Gain on Sale of Investments.................          1,400
      To record sale of investments.
```

Again, recall that the various restrictions on the use of resources assumedly are being accounted for in subsidiary ledger accounts.

Land, Buildings, and Equipment (Plant) Funds

23. Cash gifts of $100,000 restricted for acquisition of fixed assets were received in 19X1.

```
(23)  Cash...........................................  100,000
          Support—Contributions.......................          100,000
      To record restricted contributions for capital additions.
```

24. Equipment costing $140,000 was acquired using donated resources restricted for that purpose.

Land, Buildings, and Equipment (Plant) Funds (continued)

(24)	Equipment....................................	140,000	
	Cash		140,000
	To record purchase of equipment with restricted resources.		

25. Depreciation expense for 19X1 on plant assets was $30,000, allocated as follows:

Management and General............	$13,000
Research........................	12,000
Education	2,000
Fund Raising	3,000

(25)	Depreciation Expense—Management and General.......	13,000	
	Depreciation Expense—Fund Raising	3,000	
	Depreciation Expense—Education	2,000	
	Depreciation Expense—Research	12,000	
	Accumulated Depreciation—Building		14,000
	Accumulated Depreciation—Equipment............		16,000
	To record depreciation of plant assets.		

The depreciation expense recorded here is on fixed assets accounted for in the Land, Buildings, and Equipment Fund. Recall from the discussion of fixed assets that (1) Endowment Fund fixed assets are accounted for in the Endowment Fund and (2) other fixed assets held to produce income—rather than for use in providing services—are accounted for in the Current Unrestricted Fund or Current Restricted Fund, as appropriate.

26. Investment income of $15,000 was earned, of which $12,000 was received, on Land, Buildings, and Equipment Fund investments.

(26)	Cash.......................................	12,000	
	Interest Receivable............................	3,000	
	Revenue—Investment Income		15,000
	To record investment earnings.		

27. Mortgage payments of $60,000, of which $20,000 was for interest, matured and were paid from resources restricted for that purpose.

(27)	Mortgage Payable............................	40,000	
	Expenses—Interest............................	20,000	
	Cash.......................................		60,000
	To record mortgage payments.		

If Current Unrestricted Fund resources (instead of Land, Buildings, and Equipment Fund resources) had been used to make the mortgage payment, the following entries would have been made:

Current Unrestricted Fund

Transfer to Land, Buildings, and Equipment Fund	40,000	
Expenses—Interest............................	20,000	
Cash		60,000
To record payment of mortgage principal and interest with unrestricted resources.		

Land, Buildings, and Equipment Fund

Mortgage Payable............................	40,000	
Transfer from Current Unrestricted Fund		40,000
To record reduction of mortgage principal as a result of mortgage payment from Current Unrestricted Fund resources.		

Interfund Transactions

28. A $200,000 building addition was completed and paid for using $100,000 of contributions received previously for that purpose and $100,000 of Current Unrestricted Fund resources.

Current Unrestricted Fund

(28) (a) **Transfer to Land, Buildings, and Equipment Fund** . 100,000
Cash 100,000
To record payment of $100,000 of construction costs.

(28) (b) Fund Balance—Designated for Capital Additions 100,000
Fund Balance—Undesignated 100,000
To remove designation of fund balance as resources
are used for designated purpose.

Land, Buildings, and Equipment Fund

(28) Buildings and Improvements 200,000
Cash 100,000
Transfer from Current Unrestricted Fund 100,000
To record building addition.

29. Equipment that had been used in operations was sold for $40,000. The cost of the equipment was $75,000, and related accumulated depreciation at the date of sale was $45,000. The proceeds from the sales are *not* restricted.

Land, Buildings, and Equipment Fund

(29) (a) Cash 40,000
Accumulated Depreciation—Equipment 45,000
Equipment 75,000
Gain on Sale of Equipment 10,000
To record sale of equipment.

(29) (b) Transfer to Current Unrestricted Fund 40,000
Cash 40,000
To record transfer of unrestricted proceeds from
equipment sale to Current Unrestricted Fund.

Current Unrestricted Fund

(29) Cash 40,000
Transfer from Land, Buildings, and Equipment Fund . . . 40,000
To record transfer of unrestricted proceeds of equipment
sale.

30. A ten-year term endowment with a balance of $100,000 expired; $65,000 of the expired term endowment must be used for capital outlay; but the remainder is unrestricted.

Endowment Fund

(30) Transfer to Land, Buildings, and Equipment Fund 65,000
Transfer to Current Unrestricted Fund 35,000
Cash 100,000
To record transfer of assets of expired term endowment.

Land, Buildings, and Equipment Fund

(30) Cash 65,000
Transfer from Endowment Fund 65,000
To record receipt of assets of expired term endowment
that are restricted to capital outlay.

Interfund Transactions (continued)

Current Unrestricted Fund

(30) Cash.	35,000	
Transfer from Endowment Fund		35,000
To record transfer of unrestricted portion of expired term endowment.		

31. The accounts of the various funds were closed at year end.

Current Unrestricted Fund

(31) Support—Contributions.	357,000	
Support—Donated Materials	10,000	
Support—Donated Facilities.	8,000	
Support—Donated Services	10,000	
Support—Special Events	50,000	
Revenue—Membership Dues	17,300	
Revenue—Investment Income	34,000	
Transfer from Land, Buildings, and Equipment Fund	40,000	
Transfer from Endowment Funds	35,000	
Expenses—Education		112,000
Expenses—Research.		73,800
Expenses—Management and General		138,200
Expenses—Fund Raising		88,000
Transfer to Land, Buildings, and Equipment Fund		100,000
Fund Balance—Undesignated		49,300
To close revenue, support, expenses, and transfer accounts.		

Current Restricted Fund

(31) Support—Contributions.	125,000	
Revenue—Investment Income	20,500	
Expenses—Research.		18,000
Expenses—Education		70,000
Fund Balance—Research		2,500
Fund Balance—Education		55,000
To close revenue, support, and expense accounts.		

Endowment Funds

(31) Support—Contributions.	55,000	
Revenue—Investment Income	10,500	
Gain on Sale of Investments	1,400	
Fund Balance	33,100	
Transfer to Land, Buildings, and Equipment Fund		65,000
Transfer to Current Unrestricted Fund.		35,000
To close revenue, support, and transfer accounts.		

Land, Buildings, and Equipment Fund

(31) (a) Support—Contributions	100,000	
Revenue—Investment Income.	15,000	
Gain on Sale of Equipment	10,000	
Transfer from Current Unrestricted Fund	100,000	
Transfer from Endowment Funds.	65,000	
Interest Expense		20,000
Depreciation Expense—Education		2,000
Depreciation Expense—Research		12,000
Depreciation Expense—Management and General		13,000
Depreciation Expense—Fund Raising.		3,000
Transfer to Current Unrestricted Fund		40,000
Fund Balance—Unexpended		200,000
To close revenue, support, expense, and transfer accounts.		

Interfund Transactions (continued)

(31)	(b)	**Fund Balance—Unexpended**	320,000	
		Fund Balance—Expended		320,000

To adjust Fund Balance—Expended to reflect the increase in the net amount invested in plant assets.

Illustrative VHWO Financial Statements

The financial statements for 19X1 for the illustrative VHWO include the Balance Sheet, the Statement of Support, Revenue, Expenses, and Other Changes in Fund Balances, and the Statement of Functional Expenses. Note that:

- **Balance Sheet.** The balance sheet in Figure 19-3 is a better balance sheet example than Figure 19-2 because the year end balance sheet includes comparative prior year amounts, whereas none are presented in Figure 19-2.

- **Operating Statement.** The operating statement in Figure 19-4—the Statement of Support, Revenue, Expenses, and Changes in Fund Balances—follows the format illustrated for VHWOs in Figure 19-1.

- **Statement of Functional Expenses.** The Statement of Functional Expenses in Figure 19-5 is a basic, required financial statement for VHWOs and presents the expenses incurred for each program or function in detail by object class. Again, this statement is considered *a supplemental schedule for ONPOs*.

No statement of cash flows is required for the VHWO. Cash flows statements are permitted but are not illustrated here.

ACCOUNTING AND REPORTING DIFFERENCEs—ONPOS VERSUS VHWOs

As noted at the beginning of the chapter, the similarities between VHWO and ONPO reporting requirements are extensive. However, there are several noteworthy differences as well. Those differences are summarized and illustrated in the remainder of the chapter. The primary differences are:

1. Different fund names (but for funds that are identical in substance),
2. Different criteria for recording pledges receivable,
3. Noncapitalization of certain fixed assets,
4. Different (but similar) criteria for recognizing donated services,
5. The ONPO classification distinction between "public support and revenue" and "capital additions" (which are not classified separately by VHWOs),
6. Different recognition criteria for restricted public support, capital additions, and revenues, and
7. Differences in financial statements.

Fund Names

While SOP 78-10 does not specify a fund structure to be used by nonprofit organizations using fund accounting, certain funds appear frequently in the illustrative financial statements in the SOP. These funds are virtually identical to those noted in the VHWO audit guide, but the names are somewhat different. A comparison of the VHWO and ONPO fund structures is presented in Figure 19-6.

Figure 19-3

VHWO ENDING BALANCE SHEET

Illustrative Voluntary Health and Welfare Organization
Balance Sheet
December 31, 19X1 and 19X0

Assets	19X1	19X0	Liabilities and Fund Balances	19X1	19X0
Current Unrestricted Funds					
Cash	$134,500	$ 75,000	Vouchers payable	$ 14,000	$ 17,000
Pledges receivable (less allowance for uncollectibles of $11,000 in 19X1 and $4,000 in 19X0)	66,000	46,000	Deferred support—contributions	55,000	22,000
			Accrued salaries payable	3,000	
Accrued interest receivable		2,000	Total Liabilities and Deferred Support	72,000	39,000
Inventory of materials	7,800	3,000	Fund Balances:		
Investments (market, $105,000)	90,000	90,000	Designated by the governing board for:		
			Capital additions		100,000
			Endowment	50,000	
			Undesignated	176,300	77,000
			Total Fund Balance	226,300	177,000
Total	$298,300	$216,000	Total	$298,300	$216,000
Current Restricted Funds					
Cash	$ 92,500	$ 50,000	Vouchers payable	$ 11,000	$ 11,000
Pledges receivable (less allowance for uncollectible pledges of $3,000)	10,000		Deferred support—contributions		5,000
			Total Liabilities and Deferred Support	11,000	16,000
			Fund Balances:		
			Education	79,000	24,000
			Research	12,500	10,000
			Total Fund Balance	91,500	34,000
Total	$102,500	$ 50,000	Total	$102,500	$ 50,000
Land, Buildings, and Equipment Fund					
Cash	$ 27,000	$150,000	Mortgages payable	$165,000	$205,000
Accrued interest receivable	3,000		Fund Balances:		
Investments	120,000	120,000	Expended	560,000	240,000
Land	50,000	50,000	Unexpended	150,000	270,000
Buildings and improvements (net of accumulated depreciation of $154,000 and $140,000)	466,000	280,000	Total Fund Balance	710,000	510,000
Equipment (net of accumulated depreciation of $56,000 and $85,000)	209,000	115,000			
Total	$875,000	$715,000	Total	$875,000	$715,000
Endowment Funds					
Cash	$111,900	$132,000	Fund balance	$411,900	$445,000
Investments	300,000	313,000			
Total	$411,900	$445,000	Total	$411,900	$445,000

Figure 19-4

VHWO OPERATING STATEMENT

Illustrative Voluntary Health and Welfare Organization

Statement of Support, Revenue, Expenses, and Changes in Fund Balance

For the Year Ended December 31, 19X1

	Current Funds		Land, Buildings, and Equipment Fund	Endowment Funds	Total All Funds
	Unrestricted	Restricted			
Public Support and Revenue:					
Public Support					
Contributions (net of estimated uncollectible pledges of $25,000)	$ 357,000	$125,000		$ 55,000	$ 537,000
Contributions to building fund. . . .			$100,000		100,000
Special events (net of direct costs of $25,000).	50,000				50,000
Donated facilities.	8,000				8,000
Donated materials	10,000				10,000
Donated services	10,000				10,000
Total Public Support	435,000	125,000	100,000	55,000	715,000
Revenue:					
Membership dues	17,300				17,300
Investment income	34,000	20,500	15,000	10,500	80,000
Realized gains on investment transactions.				1,400	1,400
Gain on sale of equipment			10,000		10,000
Total Revenue	51,300	20,500	25,000	11,900	108,700
Total Support and Revenue	486,300	145,500	125,000	66,900	823,700
Expenses:					
Program Services:					
Research	73,800	18,000	12,000		103,800
Education.	112,000	70,000	2,000		184,000
Total Program Services	185,800	88,000	14,000		287,800
Supporting Services:					
Management and general	138,200		33,000		171,200
Fund raising	88,000		3,000		91,000
Total Supporting Services	226,200		36,000		262,200
Total Expenses	412,000	88,000	50,000		550,000
Excess (Deficiency) of Public Support and Revenue over Expenses.	74,300	57,500	75,000	66,900	$ 273,700
Other Changes in Fund Balance:					
Property and equipment acquisitions from unrestricted funds	(100,000)		100,000		
Transfer of expired term endowment.	35,000		65,000	(100,000)	
Transfer of proceeds of equipment sale	40,000		(40,000)		
Fund Balances, beginning of year. . . .	177,000	34,000	510,000	445,000	1,166,000
Fund Balances, end of year	$ 226,300	$ 91,500	$710,000	$ 411,900	$1,439,700

Pledges

While VHWOs recognize pledges receivable in the accounts and establish an appropriate allowance for uncollectible pledges, reporting of pledges receivable is not common for most **ONPOs. SOP 78-10 only permits recognition of legally enforceable pledges that the ONPO intends to enforce.** For pledges to be legally enforceable, usually (1) they must be in writing, (2) the ONPO must have made commitments as a result of its reliance on the pledges, and (3) the donor must have the apparent capacity to make the gift as pledged.

Figure 19-5

STATEMENT OF FUNCTIONAL EXPENSES

Illustrative Voluntary Health and Welfare Organization

Statement of Functional Expenses

For the Year Ended December 31, 19X1

	Program Services			Supporting Services			
	Research	Education	Total	Management and General	Fund Raising	Total	Total Expenses
Salaries	$ 16,000	$ 27,000	$ 43,000	$ 30,000	$15,000	$ 45,000	$ 88,000
Employee health and retirement benefits	1,289	3,340	4,629	4,648	1,284	5,932	10,561
Payroll taxes, etc.	644	1,670	2,314	2,324	642	2,966	5,280
Total Salaries and Related Expenses	17,933	32,010	49,943	36,972	16,926	53,898	103,841
Professional fees and contract service payments	34,996	90,710	125,706	13,428	2,283	15,711	141,417
Supplies	4,852		4,852	9,296	6,000	15,296	20,148
Telephone and telegraph	1,245	1,670	2,915	7,747	5,965	13,712	16,627
Postage and shipping	1,192	1,670	2,862	6,714	8,015	14,729	17,591
Occupancy	10,000		10,000	15,494	7,707	23,201	33,201
Rental of equipment	322	835	1,157	1,549	4,567	6,116	7,273
Local transportation	966	2,505	3,471	11,879	8,563	20,442	23,913
Conferences, conventions, meetings	2,577	6,680	9,257	19,626	3,711	23,337	32,594
Printing and publications	1,289	3,340	4,629	7,231	18,268	25,499	30,128
Awards and grants	16,106	41,747	57,853				57,853
Interest				20,000		20,000	20,000
Miscellaneous	322	833	1,155	8,264	5,995	14,259	15,414
Total Expenses before Depreciation	91,800	182,000	273,800	158,200	88,000	246,200	520,000
Depreciation of buildings, improvements, and equipment	12,000	2,000	14,000	13,000	3,000	16,000	30,000
Total Expenses	$103,800	$184,000	$287,800	$171,200	$91,000	$262,200	$550,000

Noncapitalization of Certain Fixed Assets

ONPO and VHWO fixed asset accounting and reporting are largely identical. However, *inexhaustible collections* owned by museums, art galleries, botanical gardens, or other ONPOs are **not required** to be valued or **capitalized,** but they should be cataloged and controlled. If inexhaustible collections are not recorded in the accounts they should be listed on the balance sheet, with no valuation indicated, with a reference to a note to the financial statements that describes the collections. Also, **depreciation expense** and accumulated depreciation **need not be recorded on an ONPOs' "individual works of art or historical treasures whose** economic benefit or service potential is used up so slowly that their **estimated useful lives are extraordinarily long."**[11] Although capitalization of inexhaustible collections is not required by SOP 78-10, it is encouraged—at any reasonable estimate of cost,

---

[11] Financial Accounting Standards Board, Statement of Financial Accounting Standards No. 93, "Recognition of Depreciation by Not-for-Profit Organizations" (Stamford, Conn.: FASB, August 1987), par. 6. (Emphasis added.)

Figure 19-6   **COMPARISON OF VHWO AND ONPO FUND STRUCTURES**

Voluntary Health and Welfare Organization Funds	Corresponding Other Nonprofit Organization Funds
Current Unrestricted Funds	Operating Funds—Unrestricted
Current Restricted Funds	Operating Funds—Restricted
Endowment Funds	Endowment Funds
Loan and Annuity Funds	Annuity and Life Income Funds Deposit and Loan Funds
Land, Buildings, and Equipment Funds (sometimes called Plant Funds)	Plant Funds
Custodian Funds (Agency Funds)	

fair market value, or other valuation. Further, **exhaustible** collections, such as some exhibits, should be capitalized and depreciated.

Donated Services

Another difference between VHWO and ONPO reporting guidance relates to donated services. While both types of entities account for donated materials and facilities essentially the same, ONPOs must meet one condition to record donated services that VHWOs do not have to meet. SOP 78-10 requires that services be significant and that the services of the ONPO not be primarily for the benefit of its members. This requirement generally precludes religious organizations, professional and trade associations, labor unions, political parties, fraternal organizations, social and country clubs, and other "member benefit" ONPOs from recording donated services. In any event, the notes to the financial statements should disclose (1) the method used by the ONPO in valuing, recording, and reporting donated or contributed services and (2) the donated or contributed services for which values have and have not been recorded.

Distinction of Capital Additions from Public Support and Revenue

One of the more significant and prominent differences between reporting for ONPOs and VHWOs is that items that VHWOs would report as public support must be separated into two classifications—public support and capital additions—by ONPOs. Too, some restricted investment income must be reported as capital additions by ONPOs. Capital additions were defined earlier for **ONPOs** to include:

- Nonexpendable gifts, grants, and bequests restricted, either permanently or for an extended period of time, to endowment, plant, or loan funds.
- Legally restricted income, gains, and losses on investments held by such funds that must be added to fund principal.

ONPOs report all other contributions and revenues as public support or revenues, as appropriate.

Recognition Criteria for Public Support, Capital Additions, and Revenues

Probably the most significant difference between VHWO and ONPO accounting is the difference in the recognition criteria for restricted gifts, grants, and revenues. Such items are recognized in the period pledged, received, or accrued by VHWOs —unless restricted to use in future periods. However, **ONPO resources that are restricted for specified operating purposes should not be reported as support or revenue, as appropriate, until the restrictions are met.** Deferred support or deferred revenue should be reported until then. **Restrictions are considered to have been met to the extent that expenses have been incurred during the year for the purposes specified by the donor or grantor.**

      ONPOs report capital additions separate from public support, as noted earlier. Capital additions of Endowment, Loan, and similar funds are recognized in the year that the gift or grant is received or the restricted income is earned. Capital additions for acquiring plant assets are recognized when expended for that purpose. Until then they are reported as **deferred capital additions.**

Financial Statements

The basic financial statements prescribed for **ONPOs** by SOP 78-10 are very similar to the VHWO statements. SOP 78-10 requires:

- Balance Sheet
- ***Statement of Activity (including changes in fund balances)***
- ***Statement of Cash Flows***[12]

As with VHWOs, titles and formats for these statements are not prescribed in the SOP. Each organization should develop the statement formats most appropriate to its situation and needs in conformity with the principles discussed in the SOP.

      The balance sheets of VHWOs and ONPOs are identical except for differences resulting from differing valuations of assets and liabilities, differing revenue and expense recognition concepts, and differing fund names. The ONPO operating statement is essentially the same as the VHWO operating statement. Indeed, another permissible title for a Statement of Activity of an ONPO is a Statement of Support, Revenues, Expenses, Capital Additions, and Other Changes in Fund Balances. The major differences, are that (1) **ONPOs** are required to prepare a Statement of Cash Flows; (2) the Statement of Functional Expenses is viewed as a supplemental schedule by ONPOs, not as a basic financial statement; (3) ONPOs distinguish between public support (and revenues) and capital additions; and (4) ONPOs recognize ***restricted*** revenues, support, and capital additions using different criteria than VHWOs (discussed earlier).

ILLUSTRATIVE ONPO ENTRIES AND FINANCIAL STATEMENTS

The entries and financial statements presented for our illustrative organization assumed that the organization is a VHWO. **Now assume that the organization is an ONPO** that had the same beginning balances and transactions during the year as the illustrative VHWO. The following sections explain the **differences** in **ONPO** accounting and reporting.

---

[12] SOP 78-10 requires a statement of changes in financial position—of which the statement of cash flows is the recommended form.

Beginning Balance Sheet

Several differences would be apparent in the balance sheet (Figure 19-3) if our illustrative organization were an ONPO. First, the fund titles would likely differ. As illustrated in Figure 19-6, the Current Unrestricted Fund and the Current Restricted Fund would likely be called the "Operating Funds—Unrestricted" and the "Operating Funds—Restricted." Likewise, the Land, Buildings, and Equipment Fund probably would be called simply the "Plant Fund" (as it might be for a VHWO as well).

The beginning balance sheet for the illustrative VHWO's Current Unrestricted Fund would be the same for an ONPO, except for the change in the fund name, assuming that (1) the pledges receivable are legally enforceable, (2) the investments are carried on the same basis, and (3) the somewhat different ONPO criteria for recognizing donated materials, facilities, or services are met. Recall that VHWOs report all pledges receivable, whereas ONPOs report only legally enforceable pledges.

The beginning **Current Restricted Fund balance sheet** would **differ** if the organization were an ONPO. Since ONPOs recognize restricted operating gifts and grants only as the organization incurs qualifying expenditures, whereas VHWOs recognize them when pledged or received (if cash gifts), an ONPO would have reported **Deferred Support of $39,000** for this fund. The VHWO reported Deferred Support of $5,000 and Fund Balance of $34,000.

Likewise, the **Land, Buildings, and Equipment Fund** beginning **balance sheet** would have included liabilities for **deferred capital additions of $270,000** rather than Fund Balance—Unexpended of $270,000. Too, the Fund Balance—Expended might have been called "Net Investment in Plant," but it would still be reported as equity. The ONPO beginning balance sheet for the **Endowment Funds would be identical** to the VHWO balance sheet.

Transactions and Entries

The **entries** to record *most* of the *transactions* in the illustration are **identical** *for VHWOs and ONPOs if* (1) pledges are legally enforceable, (2) the same basis for reporting investments is used, and (3) the conditions of both types of organizations for recording donated materials, facilities, and services are met. **Differences** result from:

1. *Differing recognition criteria* for restricted contributions, restricted interest earnings, and other restricted sources of support and revenue; and
2. The *ONPO distinction of capital additions from public support and revenue.*

Figure 19-7 identifies the transactions requiring different entries for ONPOs than for VHWOs and presents the entries required. Note that—given the assumptions stated earlier—**all Current Unrestricted/Operating Fund entries are identical** for the two types of organizations. All of the differences are related to recognition of public support, revenue, and/or capital additions.

Ending Balance Sheet

The differences between the ending VHWO and ONPO balance sheets for the illustrative entity parallel the beginning balance sheet differences. Thus, they are not discussed here.

Figure 19-7

TRANSACTIONS REQUIRING DIFFERENT ENTRIES FOR ONPOS THAN FOR VHWOS*

Transaction Entry No.	Description	Funds/Accounts	VHWO Entry Dr.	VHWO Entry Cr.	ONPO Entry Dr.	ONPO Entry Cr.
15	Recognition of support for prior year contributions designated for current year	**Current Restricted Fund:** *Deferred Support—Contributions* *Support—Contributions*	*5,000*	*5,000*	**No entry**— Recognize support as qualifying expenditures are incurred.	
16	Restricted gifts and pledges	**Current Restricted Fund:** Cash Pledges Receivable Allowance for Uncollectible Pledges *Support—Contributions* **Deferred Support—Contributions**	30,000 100,000	 10,000 *120,000*	30,000 100,000	 10,000 **120,000**
18	Investment earnings restricted for operations	**Current Restricted Fund:** Cash *Revenue—Investment Income* **Deferred Revenue—Investment Income**	20,500	*20,500*	20,500	 **20,500**
19	Expenses incurred for restricted purposes	**Current Restricted Fund:** (a) Expenses—Education Expenses—Research Cash	70,000 18,000	 88,000	70,000 18,000 (same)	 88,000
		(b) **Deferred Support—Contributions** **Deferred Revenue—Investment Income** **Support—Contributions** **Revenue—Investment Income**			**80,000** **8,000**	 **80,000** **8,000**
20	Cash gifts for endowment	**Endowment Fund:** Cash *Support—Contributions* **Capital Additions—Contributions**	55,000	*55,000*	55,000	 **55,000**
21	Endowment fund earnings restricted for endowment	**Endowment Fund:** Cash *Revenue—Investment Income* **Capital Additions—Investment Income**	10,500	*10,500*	10,500	 **10,500**
22	Sale of endowment fund investments (gain added to endowment principal)	**Endowment Fund:** Cash Investments *Gain on Sale of Investments* **Capital Additions—Gain on Sale of Investments**	14,400	 13,000 *1,400*	14,400	 13,000 **1,400**
23	Cash gifts restricted for capital additions	**Land, Buildings, and Equipment Fund:** Cash *Support—Contributions* **Deferred Capital Additions—Contributions**	100,000	*100,000*	100,000	 **100,000**
24	Purchase of equipment with donor-restricted resources	**Land, Buildings, and Equipment Fund:** (a) Equipment Cash (b) **Deferred Capital Additions—Contributions** **Capital Additions—Contributions**	140,000	 140,000	140,000 (same) **140,000**	 140,000 **140,000**

* Italics and boldface are used to highlight differences in entries.

Figure 19-7
(continued)

Entry No.	Description	Funds/Accounts	VHWO Entry Dr.	VHWO Entry Cr.	ONPO Entry Dr.	ONPO Entry Cr.
26	Investment earnings restricted for capital additions	**Land, Buildings, and Equipment Fund:** Cash	12,000		12,000	
		Interest Receivable	3,000		3,000	
		Revenue—Investment Income		15,000		
		Deferred Revenue—Investment Income				15,000
27	Mortgage payments made from resources restricted for that purpose	**Land, Buildings, and Equipment Fund:** (a) Mortgage Payable	40,000		40,000	
		Interest Expense	20,000		20,000	
		Cash		60,000		60,000
		(b) **Deferred Capital Additions— Contributions**			60,000	
		Capital Additions— Contributions				60,000
28	Building addition financed partially from unrestricted and partially from restricted resources	**Current Unrestricted Fund:** (a) Transfer to Land, Buildings, and Equipment Fund	100,000		100,000	
		Cash		100,000		100,000 (same)
		(b) Fund Balance—Designated for Capital Additions— Fund Balance	100,000	100,000	100,000	100,000 (same)
		Land, Buildings, and Equipment Fund: (a) Buildings and Improvements	200,000		200,000	
		Cash		100,000		100,000
		Transfer from Current Unrestricted Fund		100,000		100,000 (same)
		(b) **Deferred Capital Additions— Contributions**			100,000	
		Capital Additions— Contributions				100,000
Closing entries		The closing entry differences would simply reflect the differences in the above entries and therefore are not illustrated.				

Statement of Activity

The ONPO Statement of Activity is quite similar to the VHWO operating statement. However, in addition to some format differences, ONPOs (1) distinguish **capital additions** from public support and (2) recognize **restricted** support, revenues, and capital additions using different recognition criteria than VHWOs. A Statement of Activity for the illustrative entity is presented in Figure 19-8 under the assumption that it is an ONPO.

Statement of Cash Flows

No statement of cash flows was presented for the illustrative VHWO since it is not required for VHWOs. ONPOs must present a statement of cash flows when reporting both financial position and operating results. Figure 19-9 is the Statement of Cash Flows for the Illustrative ONPO, assuming that it is a **non-government** entity. Note that it reports cash flows for all funds. Also, the cash flows from operations section of the statement begins with the "Excess (Deficiency) of Support and Revenue over Expenses **before** Capital Additions." Capital additions are reported next, followed by support, revenue, and expenses not affecting cash.

Figure 19-8

ONPO OPERATING STATEMENT

Illustrative Other Nonprofit Organization
Statement of Activity
For the Year Ended December 31, 19X1

	Operating Funds		Plant Fund	Endowment Fund	Total All Funds
	Unrestricted	Restricted			
Support and Revenue:					
Support:					
Contributions (net of estimated uncollectible pledges of $25,000)	$357,000	$80,000			$437,000
Special events (net of direct costs of $25,000)	50,000				50,000
Donated facilities	8,000				8,000
Donated materials	10,000				10,000
Donated services	10,000				10,000
Total Support	435,000	80,000			515,000
Revenue:					
Membership dues	17,300				17,300
Investment income (including realized gains)	34,000	8,000			42,000
Gain on sale of equipment			$ 10,000		10,000
Total Revenue	51,300	8,000	10,000		69,300
Total Support and Revenue	486,300	88,000	10,000		584,300
Expenses:					
Program Services:					
Research	73,800	18,000	12,000		103,800
Education	112,000	70,000	2,000		184,000
Total Program Services	185,800	88,000	14,000		287,800
Supporting Services:					
Management and general	138,200		33,000		171,200
Fund raising	88,000		3,000		91,000
Total Supporting Services	226,200		36,000		262,200
Total Expenses	412,000	88,000	50,000		550,000
Excess (Deficiency) of Support and Revenue over Expenses before Capital Additions . . .	74,300		(40,000)		34,300
Capital Additions:					
Contributions			300,000	$55,000	355,000
Investment income (including net realized gains)				11,900	11,900
Total Capital Additions			300,000	66,900	366,900
Excess (Deficiency) of Support and Revenue over Expenses after Capital Additions	74,300		260,000	66,900	401,200
Fund Balances, beginning of year . . .	177,000		240,000	445,000	862,000
Property and equipment acquisitions from unrestricted funds	(100,000)		100,000		
Transfer of expired term endowment	35,000		65,000	(100,000)	
Transfer of gain on equipment sale . .	40,000		(40,000)		
Fund Balances, end of year	$226,300		$625,000	$411,900	$1,263,200

Figure 19-9

ONPO STATEMENT OF CASH FLOWS

Illustrative Other Nonprofit Organization (Nongovernmental)
Statement of Cash Flows
For the Year Ended December 31, 19X1

	Operating Funds			Endowment Funds	Total All Funds
	Unrestricted	Restricted	Plant Funds		
Net Cash Flow from Operating Activities:					
Excess (Deficiency) of support and revenue over expenses before capital additions	$ 74,300		$ (40,000)		$ 34,300
Capital additions			300,000	$ 66,900	366,900
Adjustments to reconcile excess of support and revenue over expenses after capital additions with net cash flow from operating activities:					
Depreciation			30,000		30,000
Excess of investment income received over investment income	2,000				2,000
Net increase (decrease) in deferred support and capital additions	33,000	$ 52,500	(185,000)		(99,500)
Net increase in receivables, inventory, and payables	(24,800)	(10,000)	(3,000)		(37,800)
Gain on sale of assets			(10,000)	(1,400)	(11,400)
Net Cash Flows from Operating Activities	**84,500**	**42,500**	**92,000**	**65,500**	**284,500**
Cash Flow from Investing Activities:					
Proceeds from sale of investments				14,400	14,400
Proceeds from sale of equipment	40,000				40,000
Acquisition of buildings and equipment.	(100,000)		(240,000)		(340,000)
Net Cash (Outflows) Inflows from Investing Activities.	**(60,000)**		**(240,000)**	**14,400**	**(285,600)**
Cash Flows from Financing Activities:					
Transfer of expired term endowment	35,000		65,000	(100,000)	
Retirement of mortgages payable			(40,000)		(40,000)
Net Cash (Outflows) Inflows from Financing Activities	**35,000**		**25,000**	**(100,000)**	**(40,000)**
Net Increase (Decrease) in Cash	**$ 59,500**	**$ 42,500**	**$(123,000)**	**(20,100)**	**(41,100)**

ONPOs Not Using Fund Accounting

Accounting for an ONPO when fund accounting is **not** used is the *same* as when the ONPO uses fund accounting *except* (1) interfund transaction entries such as entries 28 (a and c), 29 (b and c), and 30 (a–c) are not needed; (2) restricted asset and liability accounts may have to be used to maintain accountability for restricted assets; and (3) fund balance will need to be segregated according to the various restrictions on net assets since this will no longer be evident via the fund classifications.

ONPO reporting differs when fund accounting is *not* used in that:

1. A single balance sheet presenting all assets and liabilities will be presented.
2. The Statement of Activity and Statement of Cash Flows will report only the data in the total columns of Figure 19-8 and Figure 19-9. Too, interfund transfers will not exist and thus will not be reported.

Both the VHWO audit guide and SOP 78-10 discuss circumstances in which associated organizations should be included in the reporting entity of a VHWO or an ONPO, respectively. For VHWOs the guidance focuses on the functions performed by associated organizations and the degree of independence of associated organizations from the VHWO being reported upon. The ONPO guidance centers on the existence of control by the ONPO over the associated organizations and whether an organization's purpose is "compatible" with that of the ONPO being reported upon. (Also, note that if the VHWO or ONPO is a government entity, the GASB reporting entity guidance must be applied.)

VHWO Reporting Entity Guidance

Various types of organizations may be associated with a VHWO. For instance, national organizations may have state and local chapters and local organizations may have auxiliaries. These associated organizations may perform various functions ranging from program functions to purely fund-raising activities. In discussing whether associated organizations should be combined with a VHWO when reporting on the VHWO, the VHWO audit guide generally does not require combining if the associated organization is "independent" of the reporting entity. The guide lists several indicators of independence that should be considered when deciding whether to combine an associated organization with a VHWO.[13]

ONPO Reporting Entity Guidance

When a group of organizations is financially interrelated, the entity assumption indicates that a single set of financial statements for the group should be made available to the public. Nonprofit organizations have many kinds of relationships, ranging from outright control to association only in terms of a similarity of purpose. The SOP poses two tests for determining the desirability of combined statements:

1. Control, which means "the direct or indirect ability to determine the direction of management and policies through ownership, by contract, or otherwise."[14]
2. Compatible purpose (which was left undefined).

Both tests must be affirmative for combined statements to be required.

More specifically, if any of the following relationships exist in combination with control as defined previously, combined statements should be presented:

a. Separate entities solicit funds in the name of and with the expressed or implicit approval of the reporting organization, and substantially all of the funds solicited are intended by the contributor or are otherwise required to be transferred to the reporting organization or used at its discretion or direction.
b. A reporting organization transfers some of its resources to another separate entity whose resources are held for the benefit of the reporting organization.
c. A reporting organization assigns functions to a controlled entity whose financing is primarily derived from sources other than public contributions.[15]

---

[13] VHWO audit guide, pp. 34–35.
[14] SOP 78-10, par. 42.
[15] Ibid., par. 44

Financial statements of included entities may be presented in addition to combined statements.

Certain national and international organizations have local chapters and affiliates that may or may not meet the tests for statement combination. Examples of characteristics of relationships that would not require combination are local determination of programs, financial independence, and control of assets. Even when combined statements are not required, the notes should disclose the existence of affiliates, the nature of their relationships with the reporting entity, and other related party information.

CONCLUDING COMMENTS

VHWOs and ONPOs encompass a myriad of diverse types of not-for-profit organizations. Yet, despite some differences, their accounting and reporting—a unique blending of the accrual basis and the traditional expendable-nonexpendable, restricted-unrestricted fund structure—are markedly similar.

Whereas separate AICPA committees largely determined what now constitutes GAAP in the VHWO/ONPO environment, the GASB and FASB have now assumed this responsibility. Both have projects in process that will impact these entities.

QUESTIONS

19-1 Compare the fund accounting structure of voluntary health and welfare organizations (VHWOs) with that for other nonprofit organizations (ONPOs).

19-2 Compare the basic financial statements required for VHWOs with those required for ONPOs. Explain how and why they differ.

19-3 Although most VHWOs and ONPOs use fund accounting, both use the accrual basis of accounting rather than the modified accrual basis. Why do you suppose this is so?

19-4 Neither VHWOs or ONPOs are **required** to use fund accounting. The accountants for a newly established ONPO have asked your advice in establishing its accounting system. Specifically, they ask you: "What is fund accounting and how do we know if we should use it?" Respond.

19-5 Distinguish between the terms "support" and "revenue" as they are used in VHWO and ONPO accounting and reporting.

19-6 VHWOs and ONPOs may receive unrestricted contributions and service fees, yet properly account for them as deferred support and deferred revenue rather than as support and revenue. Explain.

19-7 All fixed assets of VHWOs and ONPOs may not be recorded in the Plant (or equivalent) Fund and depreciated. (a) In which other VHWO and ONPO funds might fixed assets properly be carried? (b) In which circumstances would it be proper not to recognize depreciation and accumulated depreciation of fixed assets?

19-8 Inexhaustible collections of ONPOs are not required to be capitalized, much less depreciated. Why is this so, and what accounting and reporting recognition, if any, is given such inexhaustible collections?

19-9 Gifts, contributions, and bequests to VHWOs and ONPOs may be restricted to use for specified operating or capital outlay purposes. Explain how restricted gift contributions, and so on, are accounted for (a) at receipt, and (b) upon expenditure, by VHWOs and by ONPOs.

19-10 Distinguish between fund balance "reserves" and "designations."

19-11 When VHWOs and ONPOs hold fund-raising banquets, auctions, bazaars, and similar events only the net amount raised, after deducting related direct costs, is accounted for as "support." Why is this so?

19-12 Donated materials, facilities, and services are sometimes given accounting recognition—and at other times are not given accounting recognition—in the accounts and statements of VHWOs and ONPOs. Explain why some are given accounting recognition and others are not. (Do not list the criteria.)

19-13 Some VHWOs and ONPOs remit portions of their support and revenue to affiliated state or national VHWOs and ONPOs. How should they account for and report such remittances?

19-14 (a) What is meant by "capital additions" as that term is used in accounting and reporting for ONPOs? (b) How are "capital additions" accounted for and reported by ONPOs?

19-15 (a) What is meant by "other changes in fund balances" as that term is used in accounting and reporting for VHWOs? (b) How are "other changes in fund balances" reported by VHWOs?

19-16 Some VHWOs and ONPOs combine educational and program brochures with their fund-raising mailings and charge part or all of the cost of the mailings to program services. Why? Also, is this permitted by GAAP?

PROBLEMS

P 19-1 (Multiple Choice)

1. Why do voluntary health and welfare organizations, unlike some not-for-profit organizations, recognize depreciation of fixed assets?

   a. Fixed assets are more likely to be material in amount in a voluntary health and welfare organization than in other not-for-profit organizations.

   b. Voluntary health and welfare organizations purchase their fixed assets, and therefore have a historical cost basis from which to determine amounts to be depreciated.

   c. A fixed asset used by a voluntary health and welfare organization has alternative uses in private industry and this opportunity cost should be reflected in the organization's financial statements.

   d. Contributors look for the most efficient use of assets; and since depreciation represents a cost of employing fixed assets, it is appropriate that a voluntary health and welfare organization reflect it as a cost of providing services.

2. Which of the following funds of a voluntary health and welfare organization does not have a counterpart fund in governmental accounting?

   a. Current Unrestricted Fund

   b. Land, Buildings, and Equipment Fund

   c. Custodian Fund

   d. Endowment Fund

3. A reason for a voluntary health and welfare organization to adopt fund accounting is that

   a. restrictions have been placed on certain of its assets by donors

   b. it provides more than one type of program service

   c. fixed assets are significant

   d. donated services are significant

4. Securities donated to a voluntary health and welfare organization should be recorded at the

   a. donor's recorded amount

   b. fair market value at the date of the gift

   c. fair market value at the date of the gift, or the donor's book value, whichever is lower

   d. fair market value at the date of the gift, or the donor's book value, whichever is higher

Items 5 and 6 are based on the following data:

The Eames Community Service Center is a voluntary health and welfare organization financed by contributions from the general public. During 19X3, unrestricted pledges of $900,000 were received, half of which were payable in 19X3, with the other half payable in 19X4 for use in 19X4. It was estimated that 10% of these pledges would be uncollectible. In addition, Louease Jones, a social worker on the Center's permanent staff, contributed an additional 800 hours of her time to the Center at no charge. Jones' annual salary is $20,000 based on a workload of 2,000 hours.

5. How much should the Center report as net support and revenue for 19X3 from the pledges?

   a. $0
   c. $810,000

   b. $405,000
   d. $413,000

6. How much should the Center record in 19X3 for contributed service expense?

   a. $8,000
   c. $800

   b. $4,000
   d. $0

7. Cura Foundation, a voluntary health and welfare organization supported by contributions from the general public, included the following costs in its statement of functional expenses for the year ended December 31, 19X3:

Fund Raising	$500,000
Administrative (including	
data processing)	300,000
Research.	100,000

   Cura's functional expenses for 19X3 program services were

   a. $900,000
   c. $300,000

   b. $500,000
   d. $100,000

8. The operating funds of an ONPO include which of the following subgroups?

	Term Endowment Funds	Life Income Funds
a.	No	No
b.	No	Yes
c.	Yes	Yes
d.	Yes	No

9. During the years ended June 30, 19X0 and 19X1, an ONPO conducted a cancer research project financed by a $2,000,000 restricted gift. This entire amount was pledged by the donor on July 10, 19W9, although he paid only $500,000 at that date. During the two-year research period the ONPO-related gift receipts and research expenses were as follows:

	Year Ended June 30	
	19X0	19X1
Gift receipts	$1,200,000	$ 800,000
Cancer research expenses	900,000	1,100,000

   How much support should the ONPO report in its statement of activity for the year ended June 30, 19X1?

   a. $0
   c. $1,100,000

   b. $800,000
   d. $2,000,000

10. A voluntary health and welfare organization received a pledge in 19X0 from a donor specifying that the amount pledged be used in 19X2. The donor paid the pledge in cash in 19X1. The pledge should be accounted for as

    a. deferred support in the balance sheet at the end of 19X0, and as support in 19X1

    b. deferred support in the balance sheet at the end of 19X0 and 19X1, and as support in 19X2

    c. support in 19X0

    d. support in 19X1, and no deferred support in the balance sheet at the end of 19X0
       (AICPA, adapted)

P 19-2 (Multiple Choice)

1. Financial statements of voluntary health and welfare organizations must be prepared under what basis of accounting?
   a. Cash
   b. Accrual
   c. Modified Accrual
   d. Cost
   e. Modified Cash

2. The primary financial statement(s) required to be prepared by voluntary health and welfare organizations do **not** include
   a. Balance Sheet
   b. Statement of Cash Flows
   c. Statement of Functional Expenses
   d. Statement of Support, Revenue, Expenses, and Changes in Fund Balances
   e. b and c

3. On December 31, 19X7, the Greater Otumnwa (Iowa) United Fund had $150,000 in pledges receivable, all of which were receivable during 19X8. During the past five years, the agency has collected an average of 90% of all pledges. With respect to the agency's 19X7 financial statements, what amount of support should be recognized for the pledges?
   a. $0
   b. $135,000
   c. $150,000
   d. none of the above

4. Which of the following statements is **not** true concerning the Statement of Activity of an ONPO?
   a. It will report restricted contributions that have been expended in the current period for their specified purpose.
   b. It will report interfund transfers of investments at fair market value, with any gain or loss recognized by the transferor fund.
   c. It will report donated services as support and as expense if they are not primarily for the benefit of the organization's members.
   d. It distinguishes between program expenses and supporting services.
   e. It reports accounting expenses as management and general costs.
   f. None of the above.

5. Financial statements for an ONPO must be prepared on
   a. the accrual basis
   b. the modified accrual basis
   c. the cash basis
   d. the modified cash basis

6. Donations restricted for equipment purchases should be recognized by
   a. ONPOs when received
   b. ONPOs when expended for equipment
   c. VHWOs when expended for equipment
   d. Both ONPOs and VHWOs when received
   e. Both ONPOs and VHWOs when expended for equipment

7. In its Statement of Cash Flows, an ONPO must report capital additions
   a. as part of cash flows from operating activities
   b. as part of cash flows from financing activities
   c. as part of cash flows from investing activities
   d. none of the above

8. The fund structure and usage of colleges and universities and VHWOs
   a. are identical
   b. are quite similar, but only externally restricted assets and fixed assets can be accounted for in college and university funds other than the Unrestricted Current Funds
   c. are quite similar, but only externally restricted resources and fixed assets can be accounted for in VHWO funds other than the Current Unrestricted Fund

    d. are quite similar, but college and university funds are reported on a revenue and expenditure basis rather than the revenue and expense basis of VHWOs

    e. More than one of the above is true. (Specify) _____

9. The principal operating statement of a voluntary health and welfare organization is its

    a. Statement of Current Funds Revenues, Expenditures, and Other Changes

    b. Income Statement

    c. Statement of Support, Revenue, Expenses, and Changes in Fund Balances

    d. Statement of Functional Expenses

    e. Statement of Changes in Financial Position

10. Which of the following would **not** be reported by an ONPO in its Statement of Activity?

    a. Depreciation expense

    b. Restricted contributions expended for the restricted purpose in the current year but received in cash in a prior year

    c. Gain on the sale of investments

    d. Purchase of fixed assets from Current Unrestricted Fund resources

    e. None of the above

P 19-3 (Fund Group Identification) Abbreviations such as the ones below are often used to identify certain funds of VHWOs or ONPOs:

CUF—Current Unrestricted Fund

CRF—Current Restricted Fund

EF—Endowment Fund

LBEF—Land, Buildings, and Equipment Fund

Required Using these abbreviations, indicate the fund group or subgroup to be used to account for each of the following items.

    (1) Fixed assets used in operations

    (2) Resources set aside by the board to endow scholarships

    (3) Short-term debt incurred to provide temporary financing for operations

    (4) Long-term debt related to plant assets

    (5) Bond debt service sinking fund (restricted externally)

    (6) Contributions required to be used for a specific program

    (7) Construction in progress

    (8) Unrestricted earnings of a term endowment

    (9) Resources restricted by donors for plant additions

    (10) Earnings of an endowment required to be used to finance scholarships

    (11) Resources from a grant received to finance cancer research

    (12) Unrestricted resources set aside by the board of trustees for plant expansion

    (13) Principal of a term endowment upon expiration of the term of the endowment, assuming no restrictions on the use of the resources

P 19-4 (Donation-Related Entries) Mr. Larry Leininger donated $3,000,000 to a VHWO on June 17, 19X8.

Part A.

1. Assume that no restrictions are placed on the use of the donated resources.

    a. Prepare the required June 17, 19X8 entry.

    b. Prepare any entries necessary in 19X9 if $400,000 of the gift is used to finance VHWO operating expenses.

2. Assume that the donation was restricted to research.

    a. Prepare the required June 17, 19X8 entry.

    b. Prepare any entries required in 19X9 as a result of spending $400,000 for research during 19X9.

3. Assume that the donation was restricted for capital additions.

   a. Prepare the required June 17, 19X8 entry.

   b. Prepare any entries required in 19X9 if $400,000 of the gift is used to begin constructing a new building.

4. Explain or illustrate how each of the three preceding situations would be reported in the VHWO's financial statements in 19X8 and in 19X9.

Part B. Repeat Part A assuming that the organization is an ONPO. Prepare *only* those entries that *differ* from the VHWO entries.

P 19-5 **Part I** (Fixed Asset-Related Entries) The Perfater Society entered into the following transactions in 19X8:

April 1—Purchased equipment for $47,300. The equipment has a five-year useful life.

July 1—Issued $10,000,000 of 10%, 20-year bonds at par to finance construction of a major building addition.

During 19X8—$800,000 of contributions to be used to service the bonds were received. Interest and five percent of the principal is due each June 30.

October 31—Sold machinery for $19,000 halfway through its useful life. The machine originally cost $25,000 and was expected to have a $10,000 salvage value. (Assume straight line depreciation.)

December 31—The first semiannual interest payment on the bonds was made.

Required (a) Prepare all entries required on the preceding dates to record these transactions, assuming that the Perfater Society is a VHWO and that December 31 is the end of the fiscal year.

(b) Repeat requirement a, assuming that the Perfater Society is an ONPO.

P 19-5 **Part II** (Endowment Entries) P. S. Callahan, a noted philanthropist, donated $2,000,000 to the Neuland Community Center with the stipulation that the first ten years of earnings be used to endow specific programs of the organization. At the end of the ten-year period, half of the principal of the gift will become available for unrestricted use and half for capital additions.

Required (a) Assume that the Neuland Center is a VHWO.

(1) Prepare the entry(ies) needed in the various fund groups to record the gift.

(2) Prepare the entry(ies) needed in the various fund groups to record the expiration of the term of the endowment.

(b) Repeat requirement a, assuming that the Neuland Center is an ONPO.

P 19-6 (VHWO and ONPO Operating Statements) The Neece Health Association (a VHWO) Current Unrestricted Fund preclosing trial balance at the end of 19X4 included the following accounts, listed in alphabetical order:

	Dr. (Cr.)
Community Services	670,000
Contributions	(2,800,000)
Fund Balance	(1,900,000)
Fund Raising.	400,000
Gains on Investments	(200,000)
General and Administrative	580,000
Investment Income	(100,000)
Legacies and Bequests.	(150,000)
Public Education	700,000
Rehabilitation Services.	1,050,000
Research.	400,000
Special Events.	(250,000)
Transfer to Plant Fund.	300,000
Transfer from Endowment Fund	(50,000)
United Way Allocation	(450,000)
Total—Net Balance.	(1,800,000)

(a) Prepare in good form a statement of support, revenue, expenses, and changes in fund balance for the Neece Health Association Current Unrestricted Fund for 19X4.

(b) If the Neece Health Association were an ONPO, how would the Statement of Activity prepared for its Current Unrestricted Fund differ from the statement prepared at requirement (a)?

P 19-7 (ONPO Balance Sheet) The bookkeeper of the West Texas Zoological and Botanical Society, an ONPO, prepared the following balance sheet:

West Texas Zoological and Botanical Society

Balance Sheet
December 31, 19X5

Assets

Cash	$ 350,000
Accounts receivable	120,000
Allowance for doubtful accounts	(20,000)
Pledges receivable	700,000
Allowance for doubtful pledges.	(100,000)
Inventories.	300,000
Investments	15,000,000
Land	1,000,000
Buildings and improvements	35,000,000
Equipment.	2,000,000
Accumulated depreciation.	(10,000,000)
Other assets	150,000
	$ 44,500,000

Liabilities and Fund Balance

Accounts payable.	$ 525,000
Accrued expenses payable	100,000
Deferred revenue—unrestricted	75,000
Deferred support—restricted.	4,500,000
Deferred capital additions	1,200,000
Long-term debt	6,000,000
	$12,400,000
Fund Balance:	
Invested in plant	$22,000,000
Endowment	2,850,000
Restricted—specific programs	1,000,000
Unrestricted	6,250,000
	$32,100,000
	$44,500,000

Additional information:

(1) The Endowment Fund consists solely of investments, except for $50,000 of cash, and has no liabilities.

(2) The Plant Fund has $10,000 cash and some investments. No receivables or other assets besides fixed assets relate to the Plant Fund, which has no current liabilities.

(3) The Operating Fund—Restricted has $115,000 cash, the pledges receivable, and $25,000 of accounts payable, in addition to investments.

Required Prepare in good form a corrected balance sheet for the West Texas Zoological and Botanical Society at December 31, 19X5. Use a columnar format.

P 19-8 (Various VHWO Entries) Prepare the general journal entries needed to record the following transactions and events in the general ledger accounts of the appropriate funds of the Cecil Helping Hand Institute, a VHWO. The Institute has the following funds: Current Unrestricted, Current Restricted, Plant, and Endowment.

1. Contributions were received as follows:

   a. Cash:

$	700,000	for general operations
	600,000	for building addition
	200,000	for aid to the elderly
	500,000	as an endowment, the income to be
$2,000,000		used for assisting handicapped persons

   b. Pledges:

$	750,000	for aid to the handicapped
	950,000	for building additions
	150,000	for general operations in future years
$1,850,000		

   Experience indicates that 10% will prove uncollectible.

2. A building addition was completed at a cost of $1,500,000. The $600,000 received in item 1 was paid the contractor, and the balance is owed on a five-year, 12 percent note.

3. Expenditures, all paid, were made as follows:

From:	For:	Amount
Current Unrestricted	Fund Raising.	$100,000
	General and Administrative . .	80,000
	Aid to Children (Program A) .	320,000
		$500,000
Current Restricted	Aid to Elderly (Program B).	$200,000
	Aid to Handicapped (Program C).	400,000
		$600,000
Plant	1/10 of the note principal . . .	$ 90,000
	and six months' interest . .	54,000
		144,000
Endowment	Investments	$450,000

4. Equipment costing $300,000 was purchased through the Current Unrestricted Fund.

5. An older piece of equipment, original cost $100,000, accumulated depreciation $65,000, was sold for $40,000. The cash received was unrestricted.

6. A lot and building, estimated fair market value $700,000, were donated to the Institute on the condition that they be sold and the proceeds used for Program D, which serves physically and mentally handicapped babies and children.

7. The lot and building (6) sold immediately for $850,000.

8. Investment earnings were accrued and received as follows:

Current Unrestricted Fund	$ 40,000	accrued
Current Restricted Fund	60,000	accrued
Endowment Fund [Restricted: see 1 above]	65,000	cash
Plant Fund [Restricted for capital outlay purposes]	35,000	cash
	$200,000	

9. A fund-raising bazaar, tasting bee, and banquet were held. Receipts were:

$100,000	Unrestricted
170,000	Restricted for Program D
30,000	Restricted for Program A
$300,000	

Costs incurred—including food, gifts, kitchen help, and waiters—totaled $60,000. They would have been higher but the hotel waived its normal charge ($10,000) and a local supermarket donated food and other merchandise valued at $7,500.

10. To ensure that the babies, young children, and elderly clients are receiving proper medical attention, a local doctor gives each a thorough physical examination annually. He has a young child in one of the VHWO programs and refuses to accept payment for his services, conservatively valued at $30,000. Similarly, a clinical psychologist, who also has a child in the program, ensures that each child is properly tested (e.g., intelligence, aptitudes, progress) on a timely basis. His time would be conservatively valued at $15,000. Both the doctor and the psychologist have assigned duties, keep regular hours, maintain case records on each child, and call to the attention of Institute staff persons each child's status, potential, and psychological or medical needs. Both of their time is spent approximately 30% on Program A, 20% on Program B, and 50% on Program C clients.

11. The family that donated the lot and building (in item 7) also donated land and a small building adjacent to the Institute offices for use as an infant nursery and playground. The land and building are conservatively appraised at:

Land	$100,000
Building	250,000
	$350,000

However, there is a 6%, $50,000 mortgage note payable on the building, which the Institute assumed.

P 19-9 (ONPO Operating Statement and Correcting Entries) The Kenley Museum, which has been in operation for many years, presented the following "operating" statement for its Operating Fund for the year ended September 30, 19X3:

Kenley Museum, Inc.
Operating Statement
September 30, 19X3

Income

Auxiliary activities	$ 510,000
Admissions.	135,000
Investment Income	300,000
Investment Gains on Sales	120,000
Gifts.	550,000
Grants for Equipment.	440,000
Membership Dues	60,000
City Contribution	125,000
Life Memberships	30,000
Transfer from Endowment Fund	200,000
	2,470,000

Expenses

Curatorial and Conservation.	625,000
Accession of Art Collection	300,000
Management and General	70,000
Fund Raising.	400,000
Exhibits.	110,000
Education	145,000
Fellowships.	75,000
Public Information	30,000
Membership Development	25,000
Nonmandatory Transfer to Plant Fund . . .	120,000
Mandatory Transfer to Plant Fund	100,000
	2,000,000
Net Income	470,000
Fund surplus, beginning of year	1,130,000
Fund surplus, end of year	$1,600,000

Additional information:

(1) The equipment grant was received in 19X3.

(2) The mandatory transfer to the Plant Fund is for debt service and is required by a mortgage loan agreement.

(3) The nonmandatory transfer to the Plant Fund is to reimburse it for expenditures for equipment covered by the grant.

(4) Kenley Museum elects not to capitalize art collection expenditures.

(5) Membership dues and life memberships are in-substance "support."

(6) Of the gifts, $150,000 was given for library book purchases.

(7) Half of the investment income is restricted to developing a new artifacts collection.

Required
(a) Prepare a statement of activity, in proper form, for the Kenley Museum, Inc., Operating Fund—Unrestricted for the year ended September 30, 19X3.

(b) Prepare the general journal entries necessary to correct the general ledger accounts of the various funds for any errors noted in completing requirement (a) assuming that (1) the accounts for 19X3 have not been closed, and (2) the accounts for 19X3 have been closed.

P 19-10 (VHWO Operating Statement and Balance Sheet) Following are the adjusted current funds trial balances of Community Association for Handicapped Children, a voluntary health and welfare organization, at June 30, 19X4:

Community Association For Handicapped Children

Adjusted Current Funds Trial Balances
June 30, 19X4

	Unrestricted		Restricted	
	Dr.	Cr.	Dr.	Cr.
Cash	$ 40,000		$ 9,000	
Bequest receivable.			5,000	
Pledges receivable	12,000			
Accrued interest receivable	1,000			
Investments (at cost, which approximates market)	100,000			
Accounts payable and accrued expenses		$ 50,000		$ 1,000
Deferred revenue.		2,000		
Allowance for uncollectible pledges.		3,000		
Fund balances, July 1, 19X3:				
Designated		12,000		
Undesignated		26,000		
Restricted				3,000
Transfers of endowment fund income		20,000		
Contributions.		300,000		15,000
Membership dues		25,000		
Program service fees		30,000		
Investment income		10,000		
Deaf children's program	120,000			
Blind children's program	150,000			
Management and general services. .	45,000		4,000	
Fund-raising services	8,000		1,000	
Provision for uncollectible pledges .	2,000			
	$478,000	$478,000	$19,000	$19,000

Required
(a) Prepare a statement of support, revenue, expenses, and changes in fund balances, separately presenting each current fund, for the year ended June 30, 19X4.

(b) Prepare a balance sheet separately presenting each current fund as of June 30, 19X4.
(AICPA, adapted)

AUDITING

Auditing is the process of *collecting and evaluating* **evidence** to formulate an independent, professional opinion or other judgment *about assertions* made by management. The auditing **process** should be conducted in accordance with standards adopted to assure audit quality; and the auditor's **opinion or other judgment** relates to the degree of correspondence with established criteria, such as generally accepted accounting principles, laws and regulations, or contractual agreements.

The typical readers of financial statements or operational reports issued by management have no opportunity to review the operations or balances in question or to assess the credibility of management's representations, and few could do a good job given the opportunity. The **auditor's examination** *provides* an *expert's independent, professional judgment* on the matters covered in the audit report. The purpose of the auditor's **opinion** is to *add credibility to* those *representations properly made* by management and to *reduce* the *credibility of those* that the auditor does *not* consider *appropriate.* These **representations** may take the form of **financial statements, other reports** on the activities of organizations in conducting programs assigned by legislative action or financed by intergovernmental grants, *or implied representations* regarding the carrying out of basic managerial responsibilities. For example, *management* is *responsible* for *compliance with legal requirements,* for maintaining adequate *internal controls,* and for conducting programs *economically and efficiently.* The auditor may be asked to give an opinion or to present other findings on such matters even when management's representation is an implied one.

OVERVIEW

This chapter is intended to familiarize the reader with the major unique aspects of government auditing. An **overview** of the nature, purpose, and scope of government auditing is presented first. This overview is followed by a **summary** of generally accepted governmental auditing standards **(GAGAS)** established by the U.S. General Accounting Office (GAO). Finally, the concept and framework of a **"single audit"** are explained.

What Is an Audit?

Although there are several specific types of audits, most audits can be visualized generally as illustrated in Figure 20-1:

1. An **"auditee"** is considered accountable for certain events, activities, and transactions—and makes assertions, either directly or indirectly, regarding such accountability.
2. The **"auditor"** compares the auditee's assertions against established criteria —following an appropriate audit process and standards—and reports an opinion or other judgment based on the result of the audit.
3. The audit report **"users"** are provided information by both the auditee (assertions) and the auditor (opinion or other judgment) to use in making their evaluations and decisions regarding the auditee's accountability.

Classifications of Audits

The term *preaudit* refers to the work done to control the accuracy of the collecting and recording of revenues and the incurring and recording of expenditures and disbursements. Preaudit work is part of the accounting and control processes and therefore is *not included in* the definition of **auditing as** that term is *used here.* **Postaudits,** examinations conducted *after* transactions and events have occurred, *are* the *principal focus of this chapter.*

Audits may be classified as *internal* or *external* on the basis of the relationship of the auditor to the agency being examined. Management customarily uses **internal auditors**—who are employees of the agency being audited—to *review* the **operations of** the **agency,** including employee compliance with managerial policies, and to *report to management* on these matters. Although the internal auditor's responsibility is ordinarily of the postaudit type (that is, the internal auditor is not directly involved in the accounting processes), he or she is employed by and reports to top management of the agency.

External auditors are *independent of* the **auditee agency** and are *responsible to* the **legislative body,** the **public,** and *other* governmental units. **External auditors** typically express an opinion—primarily for the benefit of third parties—concerning the fairness of financial statements. However, their audit scope may extend beyond financial statements.

GAGAS (the GAO audit standards) further subdivide postaudits into four categories:

Financial Audits

a. **Financial statement audits—determine** (a) **whether** the **financial statements** of an audited entity **present fairly** the financial position, the results of operations, and cash flows or changes in financial position in accordance with generally accepted accounting principles, **and** (b) **whether** the entity has **complied with laws** and regulations **for those transactions and events** that may have a **material effect on** the **financial statements.**
b. **Financial related audits—include determining** (1) **whether** the financial **reports and related items,** such as **elements, accounts, or funds** are fairly stated, (2) **whether** financial **information** is presented in accordance with **established or stated criteria,** and (3) **whether** the entity has **adhered** to specific **financial compliance requirements.** More specifically, **financial related audits** may include audits of segments of financial statements, budget requests, contracts, internal control systems and structure, computer-based systems, payroll systems, and other finance-related matters.

Figure 20-1

THE AUDIT PROCESS

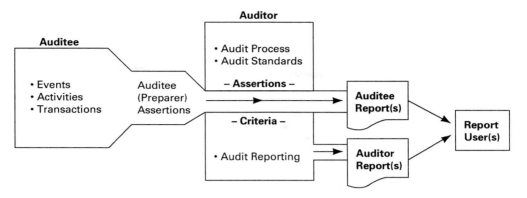

Performance Audits

a. **Economy and efficiency audits**—include **determining** (a) **whether** the entity is managing and **utilizing** its **resources** (such as personnel, property, space) **economically and efficiently,** (b) the **causes of inefficiencies** or uneconomical practices, and (c) **whether** the entity has **complied with laws and regulations concerning** matters of **economy and efficiency.**

b. **Program audits**—includes (a) **determining** the **extent** to which the **desired results** or benefits established by the legislature or other authorizing body **are being achieved,** (b) **assessing** the **effectiveness** of the organization, program, activity, or function, and (c) **determining compliance with specific requirements of program laws and regulations.**[1]

The purposes of each type of audit identified by the GAO have to do with an evaluation of the responsibility and accountability of public officials. **Financial audits**—financial statement audits and financial related audits—deal with compliance with fiscal requirements. **Performance audits**—economy and efficiency audits and program audits—emphasize managerial effectiveness. An audit intended to fulfill all these purposes or objectives is referred to as a **"comprehensive" audit.** The scope of a comprehensive audit, and the components to which a given audit may be limited, are summarized in Figure 20-2.

Few (if any) audits of governments today are intended to include all aspects of the comprehensive audit in depth. Rather, audits are increasingly being designed to meet the specific needs of agency managers, other governments, investors, and the public in a given situation. Thus, while some attention may be given to all areas of the comprehensive audit, one aspect may receive the principal thrust of the audit effort while the others receive secondary attention. The **primary thrust of most** contemporary **general audits** of governments is on the "financial statements"—**the financial and compliance (fiscal) aspects.** Indeed, most state and local governments are subject to the requirements of the Single Audit Act of 1984, which focuses on the financial statement audit with specific additional requirements with respect to internal control over—and compliance with the provisions of—federal financial assistance programs. However, **special audits** are often directed toward the efficiency and economy or program results (effectiveness) aspects. These various audit aspects (or "thrusts") are not mutually exclusive, but overlap significantly. The alternative thrusts of public sector auditing

---

[1] Comptroller General of the United States, *Government Auditing Standards* (Washington, D.C.: U.S. General Accounting Office, 1988), pp. 2-1–2-3. (Emphasis added.) Hereafter cited as the GAO Audit Standards.

Figure 20-2

POTENTIAL SCOPE OF A GOVERNMENTAL AUDIT

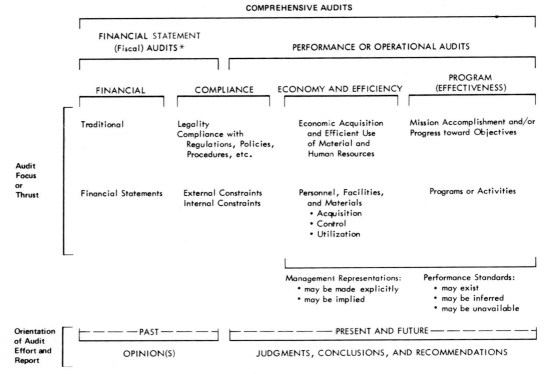

Audits also may entail an evaluation of financial-related items that are more limited in scope than a financial statement audit. Audits of specific funds only, of internal control systems, and of other components of financial accounting and reporting and management control systems are examples of financial-related audits.

and the overlapping nature of these alternative audit thrusts are illustrated in Figure 20-3.

    Financial audits are performed by independent public accountants and auditors or by state auditors, whereas ***performance audits*** typically are performed by internal audit divisions of a government or by a subunit of a state audit organization. Relatively little performance auditing is conducted by independent public accounting firms. The U.S. General Accounting Office (GAO) has also developed auditing standards for performance audits (summarized later in the chapter) and has published guidelines for conducting performance audit (or review) engagements. The ***primary focus of this chapter,*** however, is on ***external auditing —particularly "single audits";*** in-depth discussion of performance auditing is beyond the scope of the chapter.[2]

Management's Representations

In forming an opinion on the fairness of financial statements, the auditor is dealing with **representations** specifically made **by management.** Assuming that the representations made are proper, the purpose of an opinion on these statements is

---

[2] U.S. General Accounting Office, *Guidelines for Economy and Efficiency Audits of Federally Assisted Programs and Comprehensive Approach for Planning and Conducting a Program Results Review* (Washington, D.C.: U.S. Government Printing Office, 1981). See also American Institute of Certified Public Accountants, *Guidelines for CPA Participation in Government Audit Engagements to Evaluate Economy, Efficiency, and Program Results,* Management Advisory Services Guideline Series Number 6 (New York: AICPA, 1977).

Figure 20-3   ALTERNATIVE THRUSTS OF PUBLIC SECTOR AUDITING

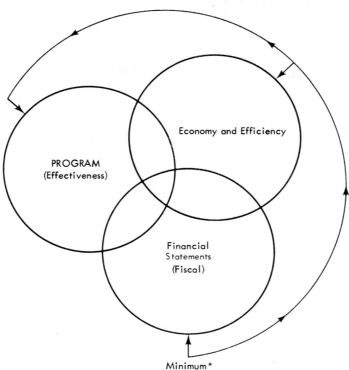

PROGRAM
(Effectiveness)

Economy and Efficiency

Financial
Statements
(Fiscal)

Minimum*

* Most authorities believe that the *minimum* acceptable scope of contemporary public sector audits should include in-depth consideration of the financial and compliance (fiscal) aspects plus review and comment upon significant aspects relative to the economy and efficiency and program results (effectiveness) aspects that come to the auditor's attention during the course of the fiscal audit work. Most state and local government audits now require significant internal control and compliance testing because they are subject to the requirements of the Single Audit Act, discussed later. Others believe that certain economy and efficiency and program results aspects should be included in the *minimum* acceptable scope (and procedural steps) of public sector audits.

clearly to add credibility to these representations. However, the same thing may be said of the other objectives. If it does not publicly address itself to the other matters, **management implicitly asserts** that it has **complied with** the **law,** has **achieved** agency and program **objectives** or made reasonable progress toward them, and has **operated economically and efficiently.** Although these representations may not be as specific as those regarding finances, they may still be evaluated and the auditor's opinion may be as useful as if specific representations had been made.

Classification of External Auditors

External audits are performed by persons who are independent of the administrative organization of the unit audited. There are **three groups of independent auditors:** (1) those who are **officials** of the governmental **unit** being **examined,** (2) those who are **officials** of a **government other than** the **one** being **examined,** and (3) **independent public accountants** and auditors.

　　Most states and a few municipalities have an **independent** auditor either **elected** by the people **or appointed by** the **legislative body.** In such cases the auditor is responsible directly to the legislative body or to the people, *not to the chief executive* or anyone else in the executive branch of the government. **Elec-**

tion of the independent auditor works well in some jurisdictions; but in others only minimal qualifications are needed to seek the office and the auditor may be elected "on the coattails of" the governor. The elected auditor's independence and effectiveness are impaired significantly in the latter situation.

The term "auditor" is **sometimes applied to the principal accounting officer** of a state. In such cases the auditor is **not,** of course, an independent external auditor. In other cases the external auditor is vested with some of the preaudit responsibilities such as ruling on the legality of proposed expenditures requested by the operating agencies. Such a provision is unsound. The accounting processes are a part of the executive function; assigning accounting functions to an auditor who is not responsible to the chief executive represents a division of the authority and, hence, the responsibility of the chief executive. In addition, the provision results in the auditor reviewing his or her own work when performing the audit function.

State audit agencies in some states are responsible for auditing local governmental units, either at or without the request of the units. Such audit agencies do not necessarily audit any of the state agencies, though some do. Most local governmental audits are done by independent certified public accountants, however, and state agencies increasingly are concerning themselves with (1) setting standards for the scope and minimum procedures of local government audits in their jurisdiction, (2) reviewing reports prepared by independent auditors to ensure compliance with the standards, (3) performing "spot check" or test audit procedures where audit coverage appears to be insufficient, and (4) accumulating reliable and useful statewide statistics on local government finance.

The Audit Contract

To ensure that there is no misunderstanding as to the nature, scope, or other aspects of the independent auditor's engagement, the contract should be in **written** form. Frequently, correspondence is simply exchanged, though formal contracts are generally considered preferable. Among the matters to be covered in the **contract** are (1) the type and purpose of the audit—including a clear specification of the audit scope, any limitation of the scope, and the parties at interest; (2) the exact departments, funds, agencies, and the like to be audited; (3) the period the audit is to cover; (4) approximate beginning and completion dates and the date of delivery of the report; (5) the number of copies of the report; (6) the information and assistance that the auditee will provide for the auditor; (7) the means of handling unexpected problems, such as the discovery of fraud, which require a more extensive audit than was agreed upon, and the manner by which—and to whom—the auditor is to report any fraud, malfeasance, and so on, discovered; (8) the terms of compensation and reimbursement of the auditor's expenses; and (9) the place at which the audit work will be done.

Preliminary steps in the audit of an organization that uses fund accounting include familiarization with the nature of the organization, investigation of its system of internal control, and familiarization with the appropriate principles of accounting and financial reporting. The auditor must also become knowledgeable of the legal and contractual provisions that govern the agency's fiscal and reporting activities. These include the restrictions governing its revenues and expenditures and those controlling its funds and budget practices. An understanding of the requirements of the Single Audit Act of 1984 and related implementation guidance is essential as well if the audit is to be a "single audit." *Some* of these *preliminary steps,* or portions of them, often *must be taken before the auditor can determine whether to accept the engagement or before the terms of the engagement may be intelligently agreed upon.*

Audit procedures must be distinguished from audit standards. **Standards are guidelines that *deal with* overall audit *quality,* while procedures** are the *actual work* that is *performed.* Standards govern the auditor's judgment in deciding which procedures will be used, the way they will be used, when they will be used, and the extent to which they will be used. No listing of audit procedures is attempted here. Many of the procedures for a government audit are essentially the same as those for the examination of a profit-seeking organization; however, the procedures used must be tailored to the characteristics of the organization, which include legal requirements and restrictions, generally accepted accounting principles, and the objectives of the audit.

In conducting audits of governments, auditors must comply with **both** generally accepted auditing standards **(GAAS)** established by the AICPA **and** generally accepted **government** auditing standards **(GAGAS)**—the GAO audit standards established by the Comptroller General. **GAGAS incorporate but go beyond GAAS.** This section provides an *overview* of GAAS and GAGAS.

AICPA Auditing Standards—GAAS

The general membership of the American Institute of Certified Public Accountants (AICPA) has approved a set of standards of quality for the performance of an audit. These ten standards, reaffirmed most recently in 1988, which apply to **all** audits, whether private sector or public sector, are:

■ **General Standards**

1. The audit is to be performed by a person or persons having **adequate technical training and proficiency** as an auditor.
2. In all matters relating to the assignment an **independence in mental attitude** is to be maintained by the auditor or auditors.
3. **Due professional care** is to be exercised in the performance of the examination and the preparation of the report.

■ **Standards of Field Work**

1. The work is to be **adequately planned and assistants,** if any, are to be properly **supervised.**
2. A **sufficient understanding** of the **internal control structure** is to be obtained to plan the audit and to determine the nature, timing, and extent of the tests to be performed.
3. **Sufficient competent evidential matter** is to be obtained through inspection, observation, inquiries, and confirmations **to afford a reasonable basis for an opinion** regarding the financial statements under examination.

■ **Standards of Reporting**

1. The report shall **state whether** the financial statements are presented in accordance with **generally accepted accounting principles.**
2. The report shall **identify** those **circumstances** in which such **principles** have **not** been **consistently observed** in the current period in relation to the preceding period.
3. Informative **disclosures** in the financial statements are to be regarded as reasonably adequate unless otherwise stated in the report.
4. The report shall either contain an expression of **opinion** regarding the financial statements, taken as a whole, **or an assertion** to the effect **that an opinion cannot be expressed.** When an overall opinion cannot be expressed, the reasons therefore should be stated. In all cases where an auditor's name is associated

with financial statements the report should contain a **clear-cut indication of the character of the auditor's examination, if any, and the degree of responsibility he is taking.**[3]

In addition to these 10 broad standards, auditors are provided more detailed guidance in *Statements on Auditing Standards* (SASs) issued by the AICPA Auditing Standards Board (ASB). For some special types of audits, including governmental audits, specific recommended procedures are set forth in AICPA Audit Guides and Statements of Position (SOPs). In the remainder of this chapter, reference to GAAS includes all of these sources and levels of audit standards.

The AICPA standards—GAAS—are applicable to examinations of financial statements of organizations that use fund accounting, but some interpretation seems desirable. For example, an auditor may have adequate technical training and proficiency to audit a profit-seeking enterprise but lack the knowledge of governmental accounting or of the laws of a specific government necessary for an adequate audit of a government. If so, the auditor should acquire the necessary knowledge or refuse the engagement. Additional guidance and interpretation are provided by the governmental auditing standards set forth by the Comptroller General of the United States, known as the GAO audit standards or GAGAS.

Government (GAO) Auditing Standards—GAGAS Overview

Though there are many similarities between auditing profit-seeking and governmental organizations, there are also many differences. Further, there was no comprehensive statement of generally accepted government auditing standards prior to issuance of *Standards for Audit of Governmental Organizations, Programs, Activities & Functions*[4] by the Comptroller General of the United States in 1972. Those standards were designed because:

> Public officials, legislators, and the general public want to know whether governmental funds are handled properly and **in compliance with** existing **laws** and whether governmental programs are being conducted **efficiently, effectively, and economically.** They also want to have this information provided, or at least **concurred in, by someone who is** not an advocate of the program but is **independent and objective.**
>
> This demand for information has widened the scope of governmental auditing so that such auditing no longer is a function concerned primarily with financial operations. Instead, **governmental auditing** now is **also concerned** with **whether** governmental **organizations** are *achieving* the **purposes** for which programs are authorized and funds are made available, are **doing so economically and efficiently,** and are **complying with** applicable **laws and regulations.** The standards contained in this statement were developed to apply to audits of this wider scope.[5]

The GAO audit **standards** are **intended** to be applied **in audits of all governmental organizations,** programs, activities, and functions—**whether** they are **performed by auditors employed by** federal, state, or local **governments; independent public accountants; or others qualified** to perform parts of the audit work contemplated under the standards. Similarly, they are intended to **apply to both internal audits and audits of contractors, grantees, and other external organizations** performed by or for a governmental agency. Too, federal legislation

---

[3] American Institute of Certified Public Accountants, *Codification of Statements on Auditing Standards* (New York: AICPA, 1992), par. 150.02.

[4] Comptroller General of the United States, *Standards for Audit of Governmental Organizations, Programs, Activities & Functions* (Washington, D.C.: U.S. General Accounting Office, 1972).

[5] Ibid., p. i. (Emphasis added.)

requires that (1) the federal Inspectors General comply with the GAO audit standards in audits of federal agencies and (2) the GAO audit standards be followed by those conducting audits of state and local governments under the Single Audit Act of 1984 (discussed later in this chapter). Several state and local government audit agencies have adopted these standards, and the AICPA has issued guidance to its members, discussed later in this chapter, concerning the GAO audit standards.

The GAO auditing standards set forth by the Comptroller General **recognize and incorporate** the **standards** of the **AICPA.** The **AICPA standards** are recognized as being necessary and **appropriate to financial statement** audits, but **insufficient for** the **broader scope** of governmental auditing. Thus, as noted earlier, the **GAO audit standards (GAGAS) incorporate the AICPA audit standards and add additional auditing standards that are unique to public sector auditing.**

The governmental auditing standards are built around the four categories of postaudits discussed earlier, which include the three elements of a comprehensive audit illustrated in Figures 20-2 and 20-3. Again, these four categories are: (1) Financial statement audits, (2) Financial related audits, (3) Economy and efficiency audits, and (4) Program audits. Provision for such a broad audit scope as the comprehensive audit is **not** intended to imply that all audits are or should be of such an extensive scope. Indeed, the introduction to the original *Standards* publication notes that:

> Auditors may **perform audits that are** a **combination** of the above **or** audits **that include only some aspects** of one of the above. It is not intended, or even feasible or desirable, that every audit include all of the above.
>
> The above expansion of governmental auditing **highlights** the **importance of** a **clear understanding of** the **audit scope** by all interested parties. This takes on added importance **when contracting and/or arranging for audits.** The engagement agreement should specify the scope of the work to be performed to avoid misunderstandings.[6]

Since the standards are structured so that any one of the four categories of audits can be performed separately, if desired, it is *essential* (1) that *audit contracts* or letters of engagement specifically identify the *scope* of the audit and (2) that the *auditor's report* clearly indicate the *scope* of the audit as well. Obviously, *in the governmental environment "an audit" is not necessarily synonymous with "an audit"*—as the *scope* of audit engagements *varies* considerably.

GAO Auditing Standards (GAGAS) Summary

The GAO audit standards (GAGAS), as stated in the 1988 revision,[7] are summarized in Figure 20-4.

Among the particularly significant aspects of the GAO government auditing standards, or GAGAS, are that:

1. The AICPA auditing standards, or **GAAS,** are **adopted and incorporated into GAGAS.**
2. GAGAS include additional **supplemental standards** for government audits.
3. The GAGAS supplemental **field work and reporting standards** for **financial audits** require that

---

[6] GAO Audit Standards, p. 1-6. (Emphasis added.)

[7] Comptroller General of the United States, *Government Auditing Standards* (Washington, D.C.: U.S. General Accounting Office, 1988).

Figure 20-4   GOVERNMENT (GAO) AUDITING STANDARDS—GAGAS

SCOPE OF AUDIT WORK	
■ **Financial Audits** —Financial Statement Audits —Finance-related Audits	■ **Performance Audits** —Economy and Efficiency Audits —Program Audits

GENERAL STANDARDS	
■ Qualifications ■ Independence	■ Due Professional Care ■ Quality Control

FIELD WORK AND REPORTING STANDARDS	
FINANCIAL AUDITS	**PERFORMANCE AUDITS**
■ **Field Work Standards** —Planning —Evidence —Internal control	■ **Field Work Standards** —Planning —Supervision —Legal and Regulatory Requirements —Internal Control —Evidence
■ **Reporting Standards** —Statement on Auditing Standards —Report on Compliance —Report on Internal Control —Reporting on Finance Related Audits —Privileged and Confidential Information —Report Distribution	■ **Reporting Standards** —Form —Timeliness —Report Contents —Report Presentation —Report Distribution

Source: Comptroller General of the United States, *Government Auditing Standards* (Washington, D.C.: U.S. General Accounting Office, 1988).

- audit **planning** must consider the requirements of **all levels** of governments.
- the auditor's report must include a **statement** that the audit was made **in accordance with** generally accepted **government** auditing standards (GAGAS).
- the auditor must make **written reports** on the auditor's
    —tests of **compliance with applicable laws and regulations,** and
    —understanding of the entity's **internal control structure and** the assessment of control risk made as part of a financial audit.

4. GAGAS also requires specified types of **continuing professional education** by auditors of state and local government.

AUDITING PROCEDURES

Whereas audit **standards** provide guidelines for what an audit should accomplish, audit **procedures** are specific tests and other activities performed to accomplish those objectives. An authoritative coverage of government auditing procedures is contained in *Audits of State and Local Governmental Units* (ASLGU),[8] an AICPA industry audit and accounting guide. The auditor should be thoroughly familiar with this guide. In addition, several states and state CPA societies prescribe or recommend minimum audit programs or procedures. Audit guides are also available for

[8] State and Local Government Accounting Committee, American Institute of Certified Public Accountants, *Audits of State and Local Governmental Units* (New York: AICPA, 1986). An exposure draft of an updated audit guide is scheduled for release in 1993.

some federal programs. These should be studied carefully by the auditor in formulating an audit program. Finally, guidelines are available for those performing financial and compliance audits, economy and efficiency audits, and program audits. Several of these are cited in the following sections.

THE FINANCIAL STATEMENT (FISCAL) AUDIT

The usual purpose of a financial statement audit is to determine whether the financial statements of the government being audited fairly present the financial position and operating results of the funds and account groups of a government (and the changes in financial position of its proprietary funds) in accordance with GAAP. In making this determination, the auditor must, among other things, ascertain whether the entity has complied with laws and regulations applicable to transactions and events **for which noncompliance** might have a **material effect** on the entity's **financial statements.** Legal compliance is considered an integral part both of managerial responsibility and accountability and of the fiscal audit of governments. The financial statement audit must be concerned with the possibility that noncompliance might create contingent or actual liabilities or invalidate receivables that are material to the entity's financial statements. The legal constraints under which governments operate and control orientation of governmental accounting systems have been commented upon at numerous points throughout this book. Obviously, the accountability process is incomplete if the audit of the financial statements does not include the legal compliance aspects within its scope or these are not included in the auditor's report.

Auditing Standards

The AICPA standards are designed for the financial aspects of the financial statement audit and, as noted earlier, are incorporated in the GAO audit standards. The laws, regulations, and other legal constraints under which the government operates establish the standards against which legal compliance is measured.

Audit Procedures

The procedures commonly employed in financial statement auditing are covered adequately in the several standard auditing textbooks available. But they usually must be adapted to the G&NP environment.

Specific guidance for audits of governments, hospitals, colleges and universities, voluntary health and welfare organizations, and other nonprofit organizations is available in the several AICPA audit guides for these types of organizations, cited at various points in this text. The most detailed guidance to the procedural aspects of fiscal audits generally is contained in ASLGU. This guide covers topics such as audit standards to be applied, audit procedures to be followed, audit reports to be prepared, planning the audit, audit workpapers, compliance with legal and regulatory requirements, study of internal control, and tests of account balances.

The procedures involved in auditing legal compliance will vary with the circumstances. The auditor must determine the legal provisions of laws, ordinances, bond indentures, grants, and so on, that are applicable in the situation. The auditor then determines the extent to which they have been complied with and the adequacy of the disclosure in the financial statements in this regard. The auditor must also ensure that the auditee has not incurred significant unrecorded liabilities through failure to comply with, or through violation of, pertinent laws and regulations.

The Audit Report

The auditor's report on a financial statement audit of a government is similar to an auditor's report on an examination of business financial statements, as is seen in Figure 14-4, the auditor's report on the City of Orlando, Florida, financial statements. The **key differences** in an auditor's report on the examination of government financial statements result from (1) the need to **follow generally accepted governmental auditing standards** (GAGAS) as well as GAAS and (2) the **different levels of financial statements**—combined, combining, and individual fund and account group statements—as discussed in Chapter 14. *Since an auditor can assume differing levels of responsibility for differing levels of financial statements, the audit report must clearly indicate the responsibility assumed* for the different levels of financial statements as well as for any accompanying information. The **GASB position** on the degree of responsibility that auditors should accept for different levels of financial statements is that:

> The GPFS . . . are designed to present fairly the financial position of the fund types and account groups, the results of operations by fund type, and the changes in financial position of the proprietary funds in conformity with generally accepted accounting principles. Thus, the **GPFS** comprise the **minimum** acceptable scope of annual audits.
>
> It is **recommended** that the **scope** of the annual audit **also encompass** the **combining and individual financial statements of the funds and account groups.**[9]

Thus the GASB clearly would approve of audit reports like that in Figure 14-4 in which the auditor accepts full responsibility for all levels of statements presented, as recommended by the GFOA.

As noted earlier, GAGAS also require the auditor to issue written reports regarding auditee internal control and compliance with applicable laws and regulations. While these are **not** "opinion" reports, they can be very important to grantors and others who attempt to evaluate the auditee entity's management style and abilities.

Finally, while the independent auditor is engaged primarily to render an opinion on the financial statements, one of the auditor's most valuable services can be to provide analyses and recommendations on related matters learned of during the process of the examination. This additional information typically is presented in a letter to responsible officials known as the **"management letter."** In the management letter the auditor provides discussions, analyses, and recommendations on operational matters such as accounting systems and procedures, including internal accounting and administrative controls; protection, utilization, and disposition of assets; number of funds; cash management; organizational arrangements; and insurance and bonding practices.

THE SINGLE AUDIT

The $100+ billion of federal grants to and contracts with state and local governments, universities, hospitals, and other not-for-profit organizations each year led to greater scrutiny of the use of federal financial assistance and the method of auditing entities for compliance with grant provisions and other federal requirements. These factors resulted in the development of the concept known as the

---

[9] GASB Codification, Appendix B., par. 103–104. (Emphasis added.)

"**single audit.**" Several states also require the auditor to include state financial aid programs in the scope of single audits.

To illustrate the single audit concept, consider Figure 20-5, which presents one way that a state or local government might be viewed from a financial standpoint. The rectangle represents a government entity—for which the basic financial statements are prepared by fund type and account group. Its top part is assumed to be **nonfederal resources** used to finance the government's expenditures; the **bottom** portion of the diagram represents resources provided to the SLG by the federal government, that is, **federal financial assistance. Each circle** in this section of the diagram is assumed to be resources received from a **separate** federal financial assistance **program.** Most governments receive resources from various programs. Smaller circles for individual grants or contracts might also be drawn within each "program" circle. Governments may have literally hundreds of **individual grants and contracts,** several of which **may be provided under** the **same** federal financial assistance **program.**

Grant by Grant Audits

Before the single audit concept was developed, federal agencies responsible for the various federal financial assistance programs typically required recipients of program grants or contracts to have an audit conducted of each grant or contract. Each of these numerous special audits was designed to ensure that resources provided to the recipient under **a specific grant or contract** had been used only for purposes allowable under that grant or contract and that the recipient had complied with any other legal requirements and agency regulations related to the program.

As a result of this grant by grant, contract by contract, or program by program approach to auditing federal financial assistance programs, state and local governments (and other organizations that received federal assistance) were subjected to numerous different audits by various federal and state audit agencies and independent public accountants. Most of the audits were limited in scope to different facets of the organization's operations, such as a research grant, the food

Figure 20-5   **A STATE OR LOCAL GOVERNMENT
FEDERAL VS. NONFEDERAL RESOURCES**

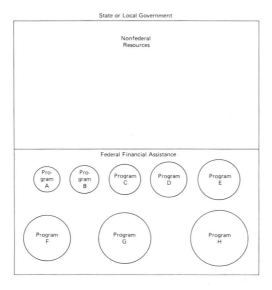

stamp program, or a day care center. In other words, such audits typically covered only one of the many grants or programs (circles) in the bottom portion of Figure 20-5. Often **no** one **audit** was **sufficient** in scope **to provide** a basis for establishing an **opinion** on the **fairness of presentation** of the financial statements of the recipient **governmental entity as a whole** and its compliance with federal requirements.

The **basic notion** of the "**single audit**" is that **one audit (a "single" audit) can provide both** (1) a **basis for** an **opinion on** the recipient **entity's financial statements and** (2) a basis **for determining whether** federal financial assistance **program resources** are being **used appropriately** and **in accordance with legal and contractual requirements.**

One *disadvantage* of the *single audit approach* from the perspective of some grantor agencies, however, is that the grantor agencies do not receive as much information about the programs administered by them as they do when grant by grant audits are performed. As a result, some grantor agencies require work to be done that goes beyond the single audit requirements. Grantor agencies have the right to require such **additional** work when necessary to fulfill their oversight responsibilities as long as they pay the additional audit costs. Thus, while most federal financial assistance is audited using the single audit concept discussed below, *some grant-by-grant and program-by-program audits are still performed* either in addition to the single audit or instead of a single audit under some of the options and exceptions permitted by the Single Audit Act of 1984 as discussed below. Too, some state audit agencies perform grant by grant audits on selected state assistance programs.

Purposes of a Single Audit

Congress stated that the purposes of the Single Audit Act of 1984 (the Act) are to:

- Improve the financial management and accountability of state and local governments with respect to federal financial assistance programs;
- Establish uniform requirements for audits of federal financial assistance provided to state and local governments;
- Promote the efficient and effective use of audit resources; and
- Ensure that federal departments and agencies rely upon and use audit work done pursuant to the Act to the maximum extent practicable.

Under the Act, a **single audit** is to achieve several **audit objectives:**

- **Related to the Entity as a Whole**—both parts of the box representing the SLG in Figure 20-5—The audit should be designed to determine **whether** the **basic financial statements fairly present** the financial position and results of operations **in accordance with GAAP** (or the non-GAAP basis indicated). This also **includes:**
  - Determining **whether** the government has **complied with laws and regulations** with which **noncompliance** may **have** a **material** effect **on** the **financial statements** of the entity
  - **Study and evaluation of internal controls** of the **entity to determine** the nature, extent, and timing of the auditing **procedures necessary to express** an **opinion on the entity's** financial **statements.**
- **Related to All Federal Financial Assistance Programs**—The audit should determine **whether** the **supplementary schedule of federal financial assistance is fairly stated** in all **material respects** in **relation to** the basic financial **statements taken as a whole.** (This schedule is required by the Act, but no format

has been specified. An example of a schedule of federal financial assistance is presented in Figure 20-9).

- **Related to All Federal Financial Assistance Programs**—The audit should determine **whether** the government has **established** internal control systems, including both **accounting and administrative controls,** to **provide "reasonable assurance"** that **federal monies** are **managed in compliance with** applicable **laws.**
- **Related to Each Major Federal Assistance Program**—The audit should be designed to determine **whether** the **SLG** has **complied with** the **laws and regulations** that may have a **material effect** on **each "major federal assistance program."**

Single Audit Overview

The single audit incorporates both GAAS and GAGAS—and also requires additional audit procedures and reports with respect to federal financial assistance (FFA) programs. Three illustrations have proven helpful in overviewing the single audit before studying its details:

Figure 20-6: GAAS-GAGAS-Single Audit Relationships

Figure 20-7: Levels of Reporting in Governmental Single Audits

Figure 20-8: GAAS, Governmental Audit Standards, and Single Audit—SAS 68

Figure 20-6 illustrates how GAGAS incorporates but adds requirements beyond GAAS, and how single audit incorporates GAGAS (including GAAS) and adds requirements beyond GAGAS.

Figure 20-7 indicates from an audit reporting perspective how the single audit encompasses and goes beyond the requirements of GAAS and GAGAS. (The bottom of the pyramid diagram indicates the additional single audit reports required.) Figure 20-8 provides a more detailed overview of the single audit proc-

Figure 20-6   **GAAS—GAGAS—SINGLE AUDIT RELATIONSHIPS**

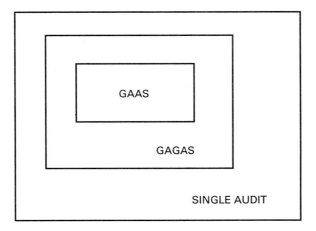

■ GAGAS incorporates GAAS–and includes
 additional requirements

■ SINGLE AUDIT incorporates GAGAS–and
 includes additional requirements

Figure 20-7   **LEVELS OF REPORTING IN GOVERNMENTAL SINGLE AUDITS**

GAAS Audit vs. Government Auditing Standards Audit vs. Single Audit

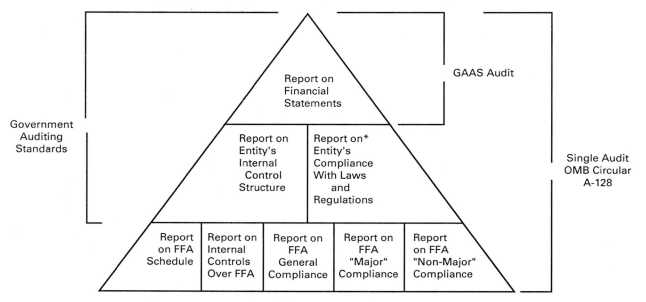

*A report on illegal acts which may also be required.

Source: American Institute of Certified Public Accountants, Statement of Position 92-7, "Audits of State and Local Governmental Entities Receiving Federal Financial Assistance" (New York: AICPA, 1992).

esses and reports. Too, **Figure 20-8 is designed to be referred to often as the "single audit" section of this chapter is studied and reviewed.**

Applicability of the Single Audit Act

The Single Audit Act—as implemented by OMB Circular A-128—generally requires **SLGs** that receive, in a fiscal year, **"federal financial assistance"** of:

1. **$100,000 or more** to **have** a **"Single Audit"** for **that** fiscal **year**
2. **$25,000 but less than $100,000** to have **either** a **"Single Audit"** or a **series** of **separate grant program audits** (i.e., audits pertaining to the circles in the bottom portion of Figure 20-5) for that fiscal year

Some *exceptions* to these requirements are permitted under the Act. Specifically, a series of audits of a SLG's individual departments, agencies, and establishments for the same fiscal year satisfies the audit requirements of the Act—providing all of the SLG's operations are included. In addition, government hospitals, colleges, and universities may be audited under unique requirements set forth in OMB Circular A-110, "Uniform Administrative Requirements for Grants and Other Agreements with Institutions of Higher Education, Hospitals, and Other Nonprofit Organizations."

Finally, SLGs that receive **less than $25,000** in federal financial assistance in any fiscal year are **exempt** from the single audit requirements—as well as other federal audit requirements—**for that year.** However, such governments must **keep adequate** accounting **records** and make them **available** for inspection and audit **upon request.**

790

Figure 20-8   GAAS, GOVERNMENTAL AUDIT STANDARDS, AND SINGLE AUDIT—SAS 68

AUDITOR REPORTS

I. For the Entity

1. Financial Statements *
2. Internal Accounting Control
   [overall—based on financial statement audit: SAS 55, 60, and GAGAS]
3. Compliance ***
   [overall—based on financial statement audit: SASs 53 & 54]

II. For the Federal Programs

4. Schedule of Federal Financial Assistance / Awards (FFA) **
5. Internal Accounting and Administrative Controls [applicable to FFA programs—based on SOP 90-9]
6. Compliance ***
   [with FFA program rules and regulations—including a Schedule of [any] Findings and Questioned Costs]
7. Fraud, irregularities, etc. [if any noted]

a) M/nm — General Requirements *** [Limited Procedures]
b) nm — Positive / Negative Assurance ***
c) M — Specific Requirements *

---

*   Auditor Opinion (or Disclaimer)

**   Auditor "Supplemental Information" Opinion

***   Positive Assurance / Negative Assurance

M = Major FFA program

nm = Nonmajor FFA Program

G = Grant

Notes: Auditor reports 2 and 5 may be combined, as may report 3 and certain 6 reports.
Auditor reports 6a, 6b, and 6c may be combined into one or two reports.

Basic Financial Statements

FINANCIAL AUDIT

Accts	GF	SRFs	CPFs	EFs	...	Total (Memo Only)

Included in the above are:

G1 nm		G3	G5 M	G6 nm
	G2 nm	M		G4

Internal Control Structure

"Preliminary Review" Understanding			"Detailed Study" Test Controls (50% Rule)		
nm	nm	nm	M	M	M
Certain Tests			Audits		
Compliance					

Schedule of Federal Financial Assistance / Awards

SINGLE AUDIT

	1/1	Rev	Expend	12/31
Agency 1				
Program A				
Grant 1	x	xx	xx	xx
Grant n	x	xx	xx	xx
	x	xx	xx	xx
Program B				
≈≈≈≈≈	≈≈≈≈≈	≈≈≈≈≈	≈≈≈≈≈	≈≈≈≈≈
Agency n				
Program A				
≈≈≈≈≈	≈≈≈≈≈	≈≈≈≈≈	≈≈≈≈≈	≈≈≈≈≈
Total	x	xx	xx	xx

I. For the Entity

2. Internal Accounting Control—report only "material weaknesses" and "reportable conditions."
3. Compliance—report only "material" noncompliance.

II. For the Federal Programs

5. Internal Accounting and Administrative Controls—"materiality" based on FFA programs.
6. Compliance—report any [all] noncompliance noted, regardless of materiality.

Auditor Reports Required

■ GAAS—1

■ Government Audit Standards—1,2,3, (7) [GAGAS]

■ Single Audit—1,2,3,4,5,6, (7)

OMB Circular A-133 contains similar requirements with respect to **"federal financial awards"** received by **non**-SLG **nonprofit** organizations. References to single audit, the Single Audit Act, and OMB Circular A-128 in the remainder of this chapter also include OMB Circular A-133 requirements for NPOs except where OMB Circular A-133 differences are noted.

Federal Financial Assistance/Awards Defined

"Federal financial assistance" is defined in the Act as "assistance provided by a federal agency in the form of grants, contracts, cooperative agreements, loans, loan guarantees, property, interest subsidies, insurance, or direct appropriations"[10]—including both direct federal awards received and those received indirectly ("pass through") from other SLGs. However, direct cash assistance to individuals is not considered federal financial assistance under the Act. In sum, federal financial assistance is defined to include all assistance provided by federal agencies to state or local governments, even if that aid is subsequently passed on to other governments, organizations, or individuals. **"Federal financial awards"** is defined by OMB Circular A-133 as including **both** federal financial assistance **and** cost-reimbursement type contracts. (See Figure 20-9.)

"Received" is not defined in the Act or in the Office of Management and Budget (OMB) Circular (A-128) dealing with implementation of the Act. It appears preferable to define "received" based upon the **basis** of accounting **used** by the auditee government in its **basic financial statements.** Thus, if a government's financial statements are prepared on the cash basis, "received' means when the cash is received from the federal government. However, a government that presents GAAP basis financial statements would define "received" as meaning when recognized as revenues or as capital contributions—which typically depends on when expenditures are incurred for the purposes for which a grant was awarded.

Auditing Standards, Guidance, and Relationships

Several sources of guidance are available to those conducting a single audit. First, the Single Audit Act requires generally accepted governmental auditing standards (GAGAS) to be applied in conducting audits under the Act. The Act defines GAGAS as "the standards for audit of governmental organizations, programs, activities, and functions, issued by the Comptroller General."[11] These standards are in *Standards for Audit of Governmental Organizations, Programs, Activities, and Functions*—commonly referred to as the "GAO Audit Standards," or simply as the "Yellow Book"—that are summarized earlier in this chapter.

As noted earlier, the **requirements** of the **Single Audit Act** go **beyond** those of **GAAS and GAGAS.** For example, the level of compliance auditing and internal control study and evaluation is much more extensive than that required by GAGAS for a financial statement audit. Thus, auditors who conduct single audits must be familiar with the Act and related implementation guidance provided in OMB Circulars A-128 and A-133 as well as with GAGAS and the OMB A-128 and A-133 Compliance Supplements—which summarize relevant Federal rules and regulations and include suggested compliance auditing procedures. Too, the AICPA state and local government audit guide (ASLGU) and related statements of position (SOPs) and the OMB A-128 "questions and answers" publication provide extensive implementation guidance based upon the Act, OMB Circular A-128, and

---

[10] Single Audit Act of 1984, sec. 7501(4).
[11] Ibid., sec. 7501(7).

extensive consultations with representatives of the OMB, the GAO, and the Inspectors General. Similar guidance is available for A-133 single audits.

Two other sources of implementation guidance are the **President's Council on Integrity and Efficiency** (PCIE) and the auditee's **cognizant agency.** The **PCIE** is composed of the federal Inspectors General and is responsible for overseeing implementation of the single audit. The PCIE issues Statements of Position on issues related to the single audit as questions and problems arise.

Federal cognizant agencies are federal agencies assigned by the OMB to oversee implementation of the single audit. Cognizant agencies are assigned for states and larger local governments and for the subdivisions of each. (Smaller local governments have no cognizant agency, but are under the general oversight of the federal agency or department from which they receive the most assistance in a particular year.) OMB Circular A-128 places the following *responsibilities* on *cognizant agencies:*

1. **Ensure** that **audits** are **made** and reports are received in a **timely** manner and **in accordance with** the **requirements** of this Circular [A-128].
2. Provide **technical advice and liaison** to State and local governments and independent auditors.
3. **Obtain or make quality control reviews** of selected audits made by non-Federal audit organizations, and provide the results, when appropriate, to other interested organizations.
4. Promptly **inform other** affected Federal **agencies** and appropriate Federal law enforcement officials **of any reported illegal acts** or irregularities. They should also inform State or local law enforcement and prosecuting authorities, if not advised by the recipient, of any violation of law within their jurisdiction.
5. Advise the **recipient [government being audited] of audits** that have been found **not** to have **met** the **requirements** set forth in this Circular. In such instances, the recipient will be expected to work with the auditor to take corrective action. If corrective action is not taken, the cognizant agency shall notify the recipient and Federal awarding agencies of the facts and make recommendations for follow-up action. Major inadequacies or repetitive substandard performance of independent auditors shall be referred to appropriate professional bodies for disciplinary action.
6. **Coordinate,** to the extent practicable, **audits made by** or for **Federal agencies** that are **in addition** to the [single] audits made pursuant to this Circular, so that the additional audits build upon such single audits.
7. **Oversee** the **resolution of** audit **findings** that **affect** the programs of **more than one agency.**[12]

OMB Circular A-133 provides similar cognizant agency assignments and oversight agency arrangements for nonprofit organization single audits.

In view of the oversight and quality control responsibilities of cognizant agencies, as well as their responsibility to provide technical assistance with regard to single audits of governments for which they are responsible, *auditors often seek the advice or concurrence of the cognizant agency when planning and conducting a single audit.* In addition to the federal cognizant agencies, some states assign cognizant agencies to local governments in the state—particularly to those that have no federal cognizant agency.

Major Federal Financial Assistance Program (MFAP)

The Single Audit Act does not modify the auditing procedures designed to determine whether the entity's financial statements fairly present its financial position and operating results. However, it **requires that extensive work** be performed **to**

---

[12] Office of Management and Budget (OMB), Circular No. A-128, "Audits of State and Local Governments," April 12, 1985, pp. 7–8. (Emphasis added.)

Figure 20-9

SCHEDULE OF FEDERAL FINANCIAL ASSISTANCE

City of Greensboro, North Carolina
Federal Programs

Schedule of Federal Financial Assistance

For the Year Ended June 30, 1991

Federal Grantor/Pass—Through Grantor/Program Title	Federal CFDA Number	Grant Award Number	Program or Award Amount	Accrued (Deferred) Revenue (1) July 1, 1990	Receipts	Expenditures	Accrued (Deferred) Revenue (1) June 30, 1991
DEPARTMENT OF THE INTERIOR							
Passed Through State Department of Cultural Resources:							
Historical Survey and Planning 1989–90	15.909		$ 15,000	$	$ 5,350	$ 5,350	$
National Register Nomination 1990–91	15.914		10,000		3,000	3,000	
Total Department of Interior			25,000		8,350	8,350	
DEPARTMENT OF LABOR							
Passed Through State Department Human Resources:							
Jobs Training Partnership Act:							
* Title IIA 87-3504	17.250	7-3504-09		(3,666)		3,666	
* Title IIA 88-3504 Carry Over	17.250	8-3504-09	216,195		3,145	3,145	
* Title IIA 89-3504	17.250	9-3504-09	806,659	(110,808)	108,113	191,713	(27,208)
JTPA Dislocation 88-3506	17.246	8-3506-09	6,660				
JTPA Dislocation 89-3519	17.246	9-3519-09	37,280	983	3,380	2,397	
JTPA Adjustment 88-3521	17.246	8-3521-09	6,768		6,768	6,768	
JTPA Technical Assistance 88-3508	17.246	8-3508-09	62,377		2,000	2,000	
JTPA Technical Assistance 89-3508	17.246	9-3508-09	16,500		16,500	16,500	
* Title IIB 88-3505 Carry Over	17.250	8-3505-09	158,844	(85,353)		85,353	
* Title IIB 89-3505	17.250	9-3505-09	351,049	61,316	315,944	271,950	17,322
* Title IIB 90-3505	17.250	0-3505-09	388,642		75,000	6,534	(68,466)
* Title IIA 90-3504	17.250	0-3504-09	787,605		560,422	533,298	(27,124)
JTPA Dislocation 90-3519	17.246	0-3519-09	59,432		47,125	54,742	7,617
JTPA Worker's Trust 90-3590	17.246	0-3590-09	49,499		49,499	49,499	
JTPA Technical Assistance 90-3508	17.246	0-3508-09	15,335			1,076	1,076
JTPA Older Workers 90-3501	17.246	0-3501-09	26,585		16,835	18,625	1,790
Program Income				(5,444)	756		(6,200)
Total Department of Labor			2,989,430	(142,972)	1,205,487	1,247,266	(101,193)
DEPARTMENT OF JUSTICE							
Passed Through State Department of Crime Control and Public Safety:							
Victim Assistance—1989-90	16.575	41-289-K3-V053	71,177		19,130	19,130	
Victim Assistance—1990-91	16.575	41-190-K3-V046	40,000		29,713	29,713	
Victim Assistance—1991-92	16.575	41-290-K3-V0118	40,000				
Child Victim Advocate—1990-91	16.575	41-190-K1-H001	31,273				
Neighborhood Resource Center—1989-90	16.579	41-189-E6-0061	155,000		120,000	120,000	
Total Department of Justice			337,450		168,843	168,843	
FEDERAL EMERGENCY MANAGEMENT AGENCY							
Passed Through State Department of Crime Control and Public Safety:							
Emergency Management Assistance	83.503	EM-PA88-107-038	27,890		22,190	22,190	
ENVIRONMENTAL PROTECTION AGENCY							
Solid Waste Volume Reduction	66.504	D004-837-90-0	89,600		25,000	25,610	610
TOTAL FEDERAL FINANCIAL ASSISTANCE			$17,442,618	$ (14,089)	$4,357,513	$4,346,690	$ (24,912)

Federal Grantor/Pass-Through Grantor/Program Title	Federal CFDA Number	Grant Award Number	Program or Award Amount	Accrued (Deferred) Revenue (1) July 1, 1990	Receipts	Expenditures	Accrued (Deferred) Revenue (1) June 30, 1991
DEPARTMENT OF HOUSING AND URBAN DEVELOPMENT			$ 2,334,000	$	$	$ 31,393	$
* Community Development	14.218	B-86-MC-37-0007	2,334,000			31,393	
* Community Development	14.218	B-87-MC-37-0007	2,240,000			166,758	
* Community Development	14.218	B-88-MC-37-0007	2,075,765		266,979	15,704	
* Community Development	14.218	B-89-MC-37-0007	2,407,965		1,473,157	566,170	
* Community Development	14.218	B-90-MC-37-0007	2,107,000			1,389,964	
* Community Development	14.218		334,000		12,967	17,053	
Rental Rehabilitation 88 Funds	14.230	R-88-MC-37-0205	130,000		3,911	(175)	
Rental Rehabilitation 89 Funds	14.230	R-89-MC-37-0205	111,000			3,029	
Rental Rehabilitation 90 Funds	14.230	R-90-MC-37-0205	57,000		(722)		
Rental Rehabilitation Program Income—90			27,000		42,000	32,758	
Emergency Shelter	14.231		42,000		6,357	6,357	
Emergency Shelter	14.231		42,000		19,311	24,899	
Emergency Shelter	14.231		25,000				
Special Projects	14.232	B-90-SP-37-16221	300,000				
Special Projects	14.232	B-88-SP-37-0007	30,000		21,144	21,144	
Fair Housing Assistance	14.401	FF-204K-89-4028	35,000		26,250	12,395	(13,855)
Fair Housing Assistance	14.401	FF-204K-90-4028			90,114		(134,233)
Rental Rehabilitation Program Income					465,192		
Community Development Program Income					8,877		
UDAG Program Income							
Total Department of Housing And Urban Development			12,297,730		2,435,537	2,287,449	(148,088)
DEPARTMENT OF TRANSPORTATION							
Direct Programs:							
Urban Mass Transit Administration:							
Technical Studies—1990-91	20.505	91-08-007	35,000		10,049	35,000	24,951
* Section 9 Planning—1988-89	20.507	NC-90-X076	148,800	18,685	33,044	14,359	113,270
* Section 9 Planning—1989-90	20.507	NC-90-X096	256,000	29,276	128,000	211,994	
* Section 9 Planning—1990-91	20.507	NC-90-XIII	265,452		50,805	58,467	7,662
* Section 9 GATA Planning—1989-90	20.507	NC-90-XIII	73,442				
Total Urban Mass Transit Administration			778,694	47,961	221,898	319,820	145,883
Passed Through City of High Point:							
Urban Mass Transit Administration:							
* Ridesharing/Greensboro/High Point—1989-90	20.507	90-R-02	82,384		15,787	15,787	
Passed Through State Dept. of Transportation:							
Federal Highway Administration:							
Transportation Planning—1988-89	20.205		48,770	13,775	13,775	(1,097)	
Transportation Planning—1989-90	20.205		48,770	48,770	47,673	40,473	40,473
Transportation Planning—1990-91	20.205		48,103				
Transportation Planning—1990-91	20.600		107,000	18,377	18,377		
Governors Highway Safety Program—1988-89	20.600	89-02-C308-06	324,658		65,846	65,846	8,715
Governors Highway Safety Program—1989-90	20.600	90-02-C308-01	64,276		30,419	39,134	28,688
Speed Enforcement—1990-91	20.600	PT-91-04-BH-08	172,863		78,331	107,019	
Traffic Safety Program—1990-91	20.600	CP-91-02-01					
Total Federal Highway Administration			814,440	80,922	254,421	251,375	77,876
Total Department of Transportation			1,675,518	128,883	492,106	586,982	223,759

* Major federal financial assistance program.

determine (1) **whether laws** that might have a **material effect on major federal financial assistance programs** have been **complied with and** (2) whether **internal control systems** have been **established over** federal financial **assistance programs** to **ensure** that the **resources** are **expended in accordance with** applicable **laws and grant provisions.** Moreover, the **amount of work required** with respect to compliance and internal controls for specific programs is **much more extensive if** the program is a **major** federal assistance **program** than if it is a nonmajor program. Hence, it is important to understand the Act's definition of a **major** federal assistance program **(MFAP)**—and to recall that OMB Circular A-133 expands the federal financial assistance definition to include cost-type contracts in defining federal financial **awards** subject to single audit.

A **MFAP** is **defined by** the amount of **expenditures** (not receipts) **incurred for** a federal assistance **program during** the fiscal **year.** For governments with **federal expenditures in excess of $100,000 but less than $100 million,** a **MFAP** is defined as **one with expenditures** equal to or greater than the **larger** of $300,000 or 3% of the SLG's total federal assistance expenditures. For governments with federal expenditures in excess of $100 million, a sliding scale is provided in the Act to define a MFAP. Thus, a program

- Is a MFAP for SLGs with up to $10 million of federal financial assistance expenditures in a year if the program expenditures are $300,000 or more in that year.
- Is a MFAP for SLGs with $10 million to $100 million of federal financial assistance expenditures in a year if expenditures for the program equal or exceed 3% of the SLG's total federal financial assistance expenditures for that year.
- Is a MFAP for SLGs with federal expenditures over $100 million if program expenditures exceed the amount specified in the Act.

Major federal financial **awards** are defined similarly under OMB Circular A-133, but can be as small as $100,000 (rather than $300,000). **All other** programs are **nonmajor** programs. Note that under these criteria a program may be a MFAP of one government or nonprofit organization but not of another, and may be a MFAP of a government or nonprofit organization in one year but not in the next.

The $300,000 MFAP "threshold" (1) relieves smaller SLGs and their auditors of MFAP identification and audit concerns, yet (2) ensures that larger SLGs—that expend 75% to 80% of all federal assistance—are audited under the MFAP approach. Also, note again that these **definitions** are **based on programs,** not on grants. (The same is true for the $100,000 NPO MFAP threshold.) As noted earlier, a SLG **may have several grants from** the **same program,** such as several Community Development Block Grants, operative in one fiscal year that represent **one program** for purposes of this definition. The *Catalog of Federal Domestic Assistance* (CFDA) published by the U.S. Government Printing Office is the most useful reference for identifying programs.

Internal (Accounting and Administrative) Control Review

The Single Audit Act requires the independent auditor to determine and report on whether the organization has **internal (accounting and administrative) control systems** that provide "reasonable assurance" that it is managing federal assistance programs **in compliance** with applicable laws and regulations. Too, both the Act and OMB Circular A-128 (and A-133) define internal controls as the plan of organization and methods and procedures adopted by management to ensure that

1. Resource use is consistent with laws, regulations, and policies;
2. Resources are safeguarded against waste, loss, and misuse; and

a government is required to follow **are the criteria or standards upon which the audit is based,** just as GAAP provide the criteria or standards for financial statement audits.

Non-MFAP Testing

For **non-MFAPs,** however, only those transactions selected for testing in the examination of the financial statements and the evaluations of internal controls must be tested for compliance with specific laws and regulations that apply to such transactions. (Certain general compliance requirements typically are tested overall rather than with respect to individual programs.)

Schedule of Findings and Questioned Costs

The auditor's report on compliance is accompanied by a **schedule of findings and questioned costs.** ASLGU (1986) notes in this regard that:

> Standards for Audit issued by the GAO identifies as special terms audit **findings** and **questioned costs.** It describes a finding as the "result of information development; a logical pulling together of information . . . about an organization, program, activity, function, condition, or other matter which was analyzed or evaluated and considered to be of interest, concern, or use to the entity." It also states that factual data supporting all findings should be presented accurately and fairly in the auditor's report and that those findings should be adequately supported by sufficient evidence in the working papers.[19]

While compliance testing is required only to be **designed to test** for **material** noncompliance, Circular A-128 requires that the auditor's **report** on compliance summarize **all findings of noncompliance and** identify the total **amounts questioned,** if any, for **each** federal financial assistance **award,** as a result of noncompliance. For example, **even though** a finding related to a small, unauthorized expenditure or the late filing of quarterly financial status reports might **not** have a **material** effect on the entity's financial statements or the specific federal financial assistance programs, the finding **should be reported.**

ASLGU (1986) states with respect to questioned costs that:

> Though the term **questioned costs** is not defined by the GAO, such costs are often considered **those that,** in the opinion of the auditor, **may not comply with or may not be consistent with** the requirements set forth in contracts, statutes, or regulations governing the allocability, allowability, or reasonableness of costs charged to awards and programs, and thus **may not be reimbursable.**[20]

More specifically, ASLGU (1986) states that:

> **Findings** of **noncompliance** are generally **listed** in a **schedule that** also **identifies** the **dollar amount** of **questioned costs.** Those costs are amounts expended not in compliance with the terms and conditions of the assistance agreements and regulations. In reporting noncompliance, auditors should **place** their **findings in proper perspective.** The extent of noncompliance should be related to the number of cases examined and the dollar amount questioned in order to give the reader a basis for judging the prevalence of noncompliance. The **auditor's report** on compliance should **contain** a **summary of all** instances **(findings)** of noncompliance **and** should identify **total amounts questioned,** if any, for **each** federal financial assistance **award** (grant).[21]

---

[19] Ibid., par. 21.24. (Emphasis added.)
[20] Ibid., par. 21.26. (Emphasis added.)
[21] Ibid., par. 23.16. (Emphasis added.)

Illegal Acts

In addition to the internal control evaluation and compliance testing required in a single audit, the auditor is required to report any illegal acts discovered during the audit. The auditor is not required to test for illegal acts. But if the auditor becomes aware of situations or transactions that could be indicative of fraud, abuse, or illegal expenditures, additional audit steps and procedures should be applied to determine whether such irregularities have occurred. Both ASLGU and the GAO audit standards contain specific guidance as to the steps to be taken if such situations or transactions are discovered, which is relatively rare.

Subrecipients

SLGs that receive federal financial assistance and provide $25,000 or more of it in a fiscal year to a subrecipient must:

- **Audit.** Determine whether SLG subrecipients have met the audit requirements of OMB Circular A-128, A-133, or A-110, as appropriate.
- **Compliance.** Determine whether the subrecipient spent federal assistance funds provided in accordance with applicable laws and regulations (1) by reviewing an audit of the subrecipient made in accordance with Circular A-128 or A-110, as appropriate, or (2) if the subrecipient has not yet had such an audit, through other means (e.g., program reviews).
- **Corrective Action.** Ensure that appropriate corrective action is taken within six months after receipt of the audit report in instances of noncompliance with federal laws and regulations.
- **Adjust Recipient's Records.** Consider whether subrecipient audits necessitate adjustment of the recipient's records.
- **Access.** Require each subrecipient to permit independent auditors to have access to the records and financial statements as necessary to comply with OMB Circular A-128.

ASLGU (1986) observes that:

> Those [primary recipient] responsibilities may be discharged by [1] relying on independent audits performed of the subrecipients, [2] relying on appropriate procedures performed by the primary recipient's internal audit or program management personnel, [3] expanding the scope of the independent financial and compliance audit of the primary recipient to encompass testing of subrecipients' charges, or [4] a combination of those procedures. The **primary recipient is responsible for reviewing** audit and other **reports** submitted by subrecipients and **identifying questioned costs and other findings** pertaining to the federal financial assistance passed through to the subrecipients, **and** properly **accounting for and pursuing resolution of** questioned costs **and ensuring** that prompt and appropriate **corrective action** is taken on instances of material noncompliance with laws and regulations.[22]

Additionally, ASLGU notes that subrecipient noncompliance can result in questioned costs for the primary recipient. Thus, the primary recipient controls established to monitor subrecipient compliance should be studied and evaluated.

Specific instances of subrecipient noncompliance need not be included in the primary recipient's audit report. However, the auditor should consider

[22] Ibid., par. 21.34–35. (Emphasis added.)

whether reported subrecipient exceptions, or events, or indications of material weaknesses in the primary recipient's monitoring system could materially affect each major federal financial assistance program of the primary recipient.

Auditor Reports—Single Audit Act

Audit reports prepared at the completion of the audit should meet these requirements of the Single Audit Act:

- **Statement of Auditor Compliance.** The audit report must state that the audit was made in accordance with GAAS, GAGAS, and the provisions of the Single Audit Act and OMB Circular A-128 or OMB Circular A-133.
- **Content.** The audit report(s) must include (Figure 20-7) at least:
  1. **Financial.** The auditor's opinion on the financial statements and on a schedule of federal financial assistance awards, the financial statements, and a schedule of federal assistance awards showing the total expenditures for each federal assistance award program as identified in the *Catalog of Federal Domestic Assistance.* (Federal programs or grants that have not been assigned a catalog number should be identified under the caption "other federal assistance.")
  2. **Internal Control.** The auditor's report on the study and evaluation of internal control systems must identify:
     - the organization's **significant** internal **accounting controls;**
     - **those** controls **designed to provide reasonable assurance that federal programs** are being **managed in compliance** with laws and regulations; and
     - the **controls** that were **evaluated** and how they were evaluated (e.g., by cycle), the **controls** that were **not evaluated,** and the **material weaknesses identified** as a result of the evaluation.
  3. **Compliance.** The auditor's report on **specific program compliance** should contain:
     - a statement of *positive assurance* with respect to those items *tested* for compliance—including compliance with laws and regulations pertaining to financial reports and claims for advances and reimbursements;
     - *negative assurance* on those items *not tested;*
     - a *summary* of *all* instances of *noncompliance;* and
     - an identification of total **amounts questioned**—for *each* federal assistance award—as a result of noncompliance.

In addition, the auditor must make a report of the results of certain procedures with respect to auditee compliance with certain **general requirements** (e.g., nondiscrimination, Davis-Bacon Act, drug-free workplace).

Note that the Act and OMB Circular A-128 distinguish **"materiality"** as between:

1. **Testing.** The auditor's *tests* are to be designed and implemented in terms of *"material"* noncompliance, and
2. **Reporting.** The auditor must report a summary of *all* noncompliance found and *all* questioned costs—**regardless of materiality.**

Recall that OMB Circular A-133 provides that only "material" noncompliance be reported in the auditor's report. "Immaterial" noncompliance is to be reported by

Figure 20-11   **SINGLE AUDIT REPORTS**

For the Organization or Other Entity:	For Its Federal Financial Assistance Programs:
■ A report on an examination of the general purpose or **basic financial statements** of the **entity as a whole,** or the department, agency, or establishment covered by the audit. Includes **opinion** on fairness of presentation of financial statements. **(GAAS)**	■ A report on a **supplementary schedule** of the entity's **federal financial assistance** award programs, showing total expenditures for each federal assistance award program. Includes **opinion** on whether fairly stated relative to the GPFS taken as a whole.
■ A report on **Internal accounting control based solely on a study and evaluation** made **as a part of the audit** of the general purpose or **basic** financial **statements. (GAGAS)**	■ A report on **internal controls (accounting and administrative)** used in administering **federal** financial assistance award **programs.**
■ A report on **compliance** with laws and regulations **that may have a material effect on** the **financial statements. (GAGAS)**	■ A report on **compliance** with **specific program requirements,** including related **federal** laws and regulations, including **identifying all findings of** noncompliance **and questioned costs.** Includes **opinion** on whether **MFAPs** were administered in compliance with those **specific program** laws and regulations for which noncompliance could have a material effect on the allowability of program expenditures. (Positive and negative assurance provided for nonmajor programs.)
	■ A report on **compliance** with certain **general requirements** to all federal financial assistance/ award programs.
A report on **illegal acts, or indications** of such acts, when **discovered** (a written report is required). Normally, such reports are issued separately and only if such irregularities are discovered.	

letter to the **recipient/auditee,** who must forward it to the cognizant agent and grantor.

The **single audit report** is required to include several components that can either be bound into a single report or presented together as separate documents. The **required components,** as well as any report needed on illegal acts, are summarized in Figure 20-11 and categorized in terms of whether they relate to the entity as a whole or only to its federal financial assistance programs. The types of procedures performed and reports issued are summarized by audit type in Figure 20-12. Finally, note that **three of the reports**—those on the examination of the financial statements, the schedule of federal financial assistance, and compliance for MFAPs—**require** expression of an **opinion** by the auditor. The others do not.

SLG Audit Report Responsibilities

Governments must provide copies of the single audit reports to **each** federal department or agency from which they received financial assistance, including the cognizant agency. In addition, governments that receive **more than $100,000** in federal financial assistance in a year **also** must submit one copy of the report to the Bureau of the Census, which serves as a central clearinghouse for the reports. (Governments that are subrecipients must provide the reports to the primary recipients that provided them federal assistance.) The reports must be submitted within 30 days after completion of the audit and not more than one year after the end of the audit period (unless the cognizant agency agrees to a longer period). Copies of the single audit reports also must be made available for **public inspec-**

Figure 20-12 AUDIT AND REPORTING REQUIREMENTS UNDER THE SINGLE AUDIT ACT AND OMB CIRCULAR A-128, OR UNDER OMB CIRCULAR A-133

Type of Audit	Procedures Performed	Report Issued
GAAS (only)	1. Audit of the financial statements in accordance with **generally accepted auditing standards**	■ Opinion on the financial statements ■ Report on supplementary schedule of federal financial assistance
GAGAS (includes GAAS)	2. Audit of the financial statements in accordance with **Government Auditing Standards**	■ Report on compliance with laws and regulations that may have a material effect on the financial statements ■ Report on internal control structure-related matters based solely on an assessment of control risk performed as part of the audit of the financial statements
Single Audit (includes GAAS and GAGAS)	3. Obtain an understanding of the internal control structure over federal financial assistance, assess control risk, and perform tests of controls	■ Report on internal controls over federal financial assistance
	4. Testing of compliance with **general requirements** applicable to federal financial assistance programs **and** audit of compliance with **specific requirements** applicable to major federal financial assistance programs as defined by the Single Audit Act or OMB Circular A-133	■ Report on compliance with general requirements applicable to federal financial assistance programs ■ Opinion on compliance with specific requirements applicable to *each* major federal financial assistance program ■ Schedule of findings and questioned costs
	5. Testing of compliance with laws and regulations applicable to nonmajor federal financial assistance program transactions selected for testing in connection with procedure 1 or 3	■ Report on compliance with laws and regulations applicable to nonmajor federal financial assistance program transactions tested ■ Schedule of findings and questioned costs

Source: Adapted from Auditing Standards Board, American Institute of Certified Public Accountants, *Statement on Auditing Standards 68,* "Compliance Auditing Applicable to Governmental Entities and Other Recipients of Governmental Financial Assistance" (New York: AICPA, 1991).

tion within 30 days after completion of the audit and kept on file by the SLG for three years after issuance.

In addition to the single audit reports, the government must respond to findings and recommendations in the reports. This response is to include a **"corrective action plan"** explaining the steps that the government has taken or will take to correct problems identified in the report and to implement the auditor's recommendations. **If** corrective action is **not** necessary, a statement describing why it is not necessary should accompany the report. In addition, the SLG's response must contain comments on the **status of corrective action** taken **on prior findings.**

Other Matters

This discussion explains the general requirements and framework of a single audit under the Single Audit Act. More detailed guidance is included in the Act, OMB Circulars A-128 and A-133, the GAO audit standards and other GAO publications, ASLGU, AICPA Statements of Position (SOPs) on A-128 and A-133 single audits, OMB and PCIE "question and answer" (Q&A) publications, and the literature of certain federal agencies other than the OMB and GAO. Practitioners continue to raise numerous questions regarding implementation as they conduct single audits. In response to these questions and concerns, the AICPA, OMB, GAO, and the President's Council on Integrity and Efficiency continue to study, discuss, and interpret the Act and the related guidance and to provide additional guidance on implementing the specific requirements of the Act and regulations.

CONCLUDING COMMENTS

Both the theory and the practice of governmental auditing are evolving rapidly. The Single Audit Act was the most important development in governmental auditing in the 1980s. This act and OMB Circular A-133 require that governmental and nonprofit audits go significantly beyond the traditional fiscal audit in evaluating legal compliance and internal controls for federal financial assistance award programs.

The Single Audit Act has had a significant impact on the audit profession— including internal, external, and governmental auditors. The Act covers all 50 states, over 80,000 local governmental units, and many other organizations that receive federal financial assistance. Indeed, whereas public accountants perform fewer than 5,000 audits of publicly held corporations each year, they perform over 20,000 single audits.

The single audit concept and guidance continue to evolve as new issues and concerns are raised. This evolution is critical to the long-term success of the single audit concept for, while the concept is sound, some are not satisfied with the single audit as it exists today. Some federal agencies are concerned that the single audit does not provide sufficient information for them to fulfill their oversight roles appropriately. Also, some cognizant agents are concerned that not enough compliance testing is being done under the single audit concept. These and other concerns must be addressed as the single audit concept. Ideally, those involved will be able to meld the best features of the single audit and grant by grant audits in the coming years.

QUESTIONS

20-1 Compare the responsibilities of a municipality's officers and its independent auditor for the financial report.

20-2 In the course of auditing an independent school district, you find that the financial statements, when prepared on the basis required by law, do not reflect the true financial condition or financial operations of the municipality. What would be your procedure?

20-3 What are the responsibilities of the government being audited with respect to the single audit report?

20-4 A municipality requires auditors to submit bids as to how much they would charge for the annual audit. The audit contract is awarded to the lowest bidder. What might be wrong with this method of engaging auditors?

20-5 Upon completion of your audit and presentation of the report to a city council, one of the council members takes exception to the phrase "in our opinion" which appears in your audit. He states that you were engaged to make a sufficiently complete and detailed examination to determine all pertinent facts about the city; that if you have not completed all the work necessary to that end, you should continue your investigation as long as necessary, but that he wants a certificate consisting of positive statements of fact, without any questions of "opinion." Discuss the logic of the council member's remarks and the position that you would take. (AICPA, adapted).

20-6 The comptroller of D City is responsible for approval of all city receipts and disbursements. The city council takes the position that, since the comptroller is auditing both receipts and disbursements for accuracy and legality, no additional audit by independent accountants is necessary. What position would you, a new council member, take?

20-7 The state auditor has for years been responsible for examinations of the financial operations of all state agencies. A bill is under consideration to make the state auditor the chief accounting officer of the state as well. You are testifying before a legislative committee that is considering the bill. What is the tenor of your testimony?

20-8 Auditing has been defined as the process of collecting and evaluating evidence in order to formulate an opinion about assertions made by management. What assertions does the external auditor address in an opinion as the result of a fiscal audit? What assertions does the external auditor address in giving an opinion as the result of a performance audit? What assertions does the external auditor address in giving an opinion as the result of a compliance audit of a MFAP?

20-9 Describe the nature of a single audit of a state or local government.

20-10 When is a state or local government required to have a single audit performed?

20-11 Distinguish between **major** federal financial assistance award programs and **non-major** federal financial assistance award programs. Why is this distinction important?

20-12 What reports are required to be presented as a result of a single audit?

20-13 What is a cognizant agency? What are its responsibilities? What federal agency would be the cognizant agency for smaller governments such as the City of Providence, Kentucky, which has a population of approximately 5,000?

20-14 What is an OMB Compliance Supplement? What is its purpose?

20-15 Distinguish between the internal control evaluation required for MFAPs and for non-MFAPs. What level of internal control evaluation is required if a government has **no** MFAPs?

20-16 Distinguish the compliance audit requirements for MFAPs from those for non-MFAPs. What requirements apply if there are **no** MFAPs?

20-17 How do single audits performed under OMB Circular A-133 differ from single audits performed under the Single Audit Act of 1984 and OMB Circular A-128?

PROBLEMS

20-1 (Multiple Choice)

1. A performance audit is concerned with which of the following issues?
   a. The minimization of expenditures for agency programs
   b. The extent to which agency programs met their objectives
   c. The extent to which agency programs produced benefits greater than or equal to their cost
   d. All of the above
   e. a and c

2. Generally accepted governmental auditing standards are issued by the
   a. Office of Management and Budget
   b. General Accounting Office
   c. Governmental Accounting Standards Board
   d. Auditing Standards Board
   e. Department of Treasury

3. In performing audits under the Single Audit act, auditors must comply with
   a. generally accepted auditing standards (GAAS)
   b. generally accepted governmental auditing standards (GAGAS)
   c. both GAAS and GAGAS
   d. neither GAAS nor GAGAS, since the provisions of the Act override both

4. Which of the following would **not** be an element of a "single audit"?
   a. Determination of whether the government's financial statements are fairly and consistently presented

b. Determination of whether the government has established adequate internal control systems

c. Determination of whether the government has complied with laws and regulations relating to major federal financial assistance programs

d. Determination of whether the government has accurately listed the federal financial assistance it has received during the period in its schedule of federal financial assistance

e. None of the above.

5. During the 19X9 fiscal year, the City of Metropolis Human Services Department received a $20,000 federal grant. The only other Metropolis department or agency that received a federal grant during the fiscal year was its Police Department, which received a $15,000 federal grant. The City of Metropolis

a. is exempt from all auditing requirements for the 19X9 fiscal year

b. is exempt from audit requirements for the 19X9 fiscal year, but is required to keep adequate accounting records and to make them available for inspection and audit upon request

c. must either have a single audit or separate grant or program audits for the 19X9 fiscal year

d. must have a single audit for the 19X9 fiscal year

e. none of the above

6. The City of Tampando learned in December 19X6 that it was being awarded a $90,000 grant from the U.S. Department of Transportation to lengthen the main runway at the Tampando International Airport. The City paid $90,000 for the construction on November 15, 19X7 and received the $90,000 from the Department of Transportation on January 2, 19X8. Tampando's fiscal year runs from January 1 to December 31, and its financial statements are prepared according to generally accepted accounting principles. For the purpose of the Single Audit Act, the City would recognize the grant as receipts in

a. 19X6

b. 19X7

c. 19X8

d. either of the three is acceptable

7. The State of Oklabraska received a total of $125,000 in federal financial assistance during its 19X8 fiscal year. It passed on $30,000 of these grants to the City of Lineman to help finance a pilot police training program. The City of Lineman also received $80,000 in financial assistance directly from federal government agencies during fiscal 19X8. Which government(s) would be **required** to have a single audit for the 19X8 fiscal year?

a. the State of Oklabraska only

b. the City of Lineman only

c. both the State of Oklabraska and the City of Lineman

d. neither the State of Oklabraska nor the City of Lineman

8. The City of Celtics received $7,000,000 in federal financial assistance and incurred $6,000,000 in federal financial assistance program expenditures during fiscal 19X8. The City of Lakers received $12,000,000 in federal financial assistance and made $11,500,000 in federal financial assistance program expenditures during fiscal 19X8. During the fiscal year, each city received $310,000 for, and expended $290,000 on, a Driver Safety Education Program financed by the U.S. Department of Transportation. This program would constitute a **major** federal assistance program.

a. for Celtics, but not for Lakers

b. for Lakers, but not for Celtics

c. for both Celtics and Lakers

d. for neither Celtics nor Lakers

9. Cognizant agencies are assigned to

a. state governments only

b. large local governments only

c. small governments only

d. both a and b

e. both b and c

f. all governments.

10. The City of Lukeville has three major federal assistance programs with the following expenditures in 19X7:

Program	Expenditures
A	$2,000,000
B	1,000,000
C	500,000

If the City has total federal assistance expenditures for 19X7 of $5,500,000, Lukeville's single audit should include a study and evaluation of internal controls of the type conducted when intending to rely upon those controls to reduce substantive testing for which programs?

a. program A

b. program B

c. program C

d. both A and B

e. all three programs

20-2. (Single Audit) The City of Greensboro Schedule of Federal Financial Assistance is presented in Figure 20-9. What level of internal control and compliance auditing work should be performed for each of the City's programs? Justify your response.

20-3. (Single Audit) Presented below are the expenditures incurred in 19X2 and 19X3 by Thompson Parish under each of its federal assistance programs.

Federal Program	Grant	19X2 Expenditures	19X3 Expenditures
A	1	$ 180,000	$ 40,000
	2	75,000	120,000
	3	60,000	100,000
B		271,000	250,000
C		3,000,000	220,000
D		500,000	—
E	1	80,000	80,000
	2	130,000	110,000
Total		$4,296,000	$920,000

Required

(1) Which of Thompson Parish's federal financial assistance programs are "major" federal assistance programs in 19X2? In 19X3?

(2) What level of internal control study and evaluation must be performed for each program in 19X2 under the single audit requirements? In 19X3?

(3) What level of compliance auditing is required for each program in 19X2 under the single audit requirements? In 19X3?

20-4 How would your responses to requirements 1–3 of Problem 20-3 differ if the expenditures data were for a nonprofit organization subject to OMB Circular A-133?

20-5 (Research Project—Single Audit) Obtain a copy of a recent single audit report and evaluate it in terms of the requirements for single audit reports discussed in this chapter and summarized in Figures 20-7, 20-8, 20-11, and 20-12. Prepare a brief report (3–8 pages) summarizing your analyses, findings, and conclusions, and attach a photocopy of any unusual or otherwise noteworthy examples.

Index